Television

TELEVISION

The Critical View

Sixth Edition

Edited by

HORACE NEWCOMB

New York   Oxford
OXFORD UNIVERSITY PRESS
2000

Oxford University Press

Oxford   New York
Athens   Auckland   Bangkok   Bagotá   Buenos Aires   Calcutta
Cape Town   Chennai   Dar es Salaam   Delhi   Florence   Hong Kong
Istanbul   Karachi   Kuala Lumpur   Madrid   Melbourne
Mexico City   Mumbai   Nairobi   Paris   São Paulo   Singapore   Taipei
Tokyo   Toronto   Warsaw

and associated companies in
Berlin   Ibadan

Published by Oxford University Press, Inc.,
198 Madison Avenue, New York, New York, 10016
http://www.oup-usa.org

Oxford is a registered trademark of Oxford University Press

Library of Congress Cataloging-in-Publication Data

Television : the critical view / edited by Horace Newcomb. — 6th ed.
    p.   cm.
Includes bibliographical references.
ISBN 0-19-511927-4 (pbk. : alk. paper)
1. Television broadcasting—United States.   I. Newcomb, Horace.
PN1992.3.U5T42   1999
791.45'0973—dc21
                                                          99-26151
                                                              CIP

Printing (last digit): 9 8 7 6 5 4 3 2 1
Printed in the United States of America on acid-free paper

For all the students who use this book—
and who will continue to live with television

Contents

Preface to the Sixth Edition

This edition of *Television: The Critical View* provides ample evidence that television criticism must now be concerned with "television," that is, with television within quotation marks. Moreover, the meaning of even that "television" continues to shift and change. What once seemed so familiar, so solid, regularized, routinized, so "common" and commonly shared, has in many ways disappeared.

Fundamentally, then, the essays collected here point to the end of "the network era." It is true that critics, television professionals, and scholars have variously marked the conclusion of that phase of television from as early as the mid-1980s. But the implications of shifts and developments within and among technologies, industrial configurations, policies, and the organization and allocation of economic resources continue. And perhaps only now are those implications sufficiently clear to be studied, analyzed, and applied to our understanding of television.

This is particularly true when the focus of concern is, as it has always been with this collection, the cultural implications of television and the factors that go into its making, distribution, and reception, into the forms it takes and the appeals and threats it presents to potential viewers and users. Where the collection once focused on "prime-time television fiction," it now explores a far wider range of forms and schedules. Where it once dealt primarily with "American TV," it now includes explorations of international programming and formats.

Some of the essays address these shifts directly. David Marc's "What Was Broadcasting?" is perhaps the most pointed exploration of the cultural implications of changes in television. But Charlotte Brunsdon's "What is the 'Television' of Television Studies?" raises equally pertinent issues, and John Thornton Caldwell's "Excessive Style: The Crisis of Network Television" addresses television's responses to the new media environment fostered by technologies such as cable and satellites, VCRs, and remote-control devices.

Even those essays focused on the television of the network era, essays confident of their perspectives at the time of writing, are now repositioned. The questions they frame, the answers they offer must be seen as perhaps appropriate for only one type of television, and the careful student must now consider whether or not these approaches hold for newer forms of the medium.

Despite all these variations and alterations, however, the fact remains that television, no matter how defined, remains central to social and cultural life. Indeed, if anything, its significance, its pervasive nature, has only been extended by the new formations. If, as many suggest, television is now approaching forms of convergence with home computers, its reach into our lived experience may become even deeper and stronger.

The implications are clear. Now, as much as ever, a critical perspective is essential. If the demands made upon critics are greater, our preparation must be equally increased. This collection of essays is offered with the assumption that it can continue to contribute to that process.

Austin, Texas   H.N.

Preface to the First Edition

The essays in this collection were selected because they view television in broad rather than narrow perspectives. Newspaper columns have not been included. This is not to say that newspaper criticism is excluded by definition from a breadth of vision, but simply that the pieces included here all develop their point of view in the single essay rather than over a period of time, as is the case with the columnist.

The essays in the first section all deal with specific program types. They serve as excellent models for practical television criticism because they show us that there is a great deal of difference between watching television and "seeing" it. They are, of course, involved with critical interpretation and assertion. Other analyses of the same programs may be offered by other critics, and the audience, as critic, must learn to make its own decisions. These essays will help in that learning process.

The second section is comprised of essays that attempt to go beyond the specific meanings of specific programs or program types. They suggest that television has meaning in the culture because it is not an isolated, unique entity. These writers want to know what television means, for its producers, its audiences, its culture.

The essays in the final section are concerned with what television is. They seek to define television in terms of itself, to determine how it is like and how it is different from other media.

All the essays are seeking connections, trying to place television in its own proper, enlarged critical climate. Consequently, many of them use similar examples, ask similar questions, and rest on shared assumptions. Some of the connections are obvious. Others will occur to the reader using the book. In this way the reader too becomes a critic and the printed comments may serve to stimulate a new beginning, a new and richer viewpoint regarding television.

I would like to express my thanks to John Wright of Oxford University Press for his initial interest and continued support for this book. His suggestions have strengthened it throughout. A special note of thanks must go to all my friends and colleagues who have made suggestions about the book and who, in some cases, have offered their own fine work for inclusion. Thanks, too, goes to my family for the supportive world in which I work.

Baltimore
November 1975   H. N.

Television and the Present Climate of Criticism

HORACE NEWCOMB

The purpose of this collection has always been the same, to contribute to what Moses Hadas many years ago referred to as the "climate of criticism." In defining that concept, he admonished "all who take education seriously in its larger sense" to "talk and write about television as they do about books." Earlier editions of the collection struggled with the fact that this was hardly the case, with the realization that television was rarely considered a prominent, significant, or special contributor to culture and society. It was seen as neither conduit for nor commentator on the aesthetic, political, or moral lives of citizens—except in the most negative manner. When television was "seriously" thought of by anyone who would take education seriously in its large sense, it was most often figured as intruder, as complicator, as rogue or polluter. Many of these attempts to understand the medium must now be seen as incomplete, partial, narrow definitions supporting one limited perspective or another.

This is not to say that television should have been warmly and naively welcomed into society and home. Many aspects of the medium (less than fifty years old in its basic forms) were and are troublesome, threatening, oppressive, repressive, and obnoxious. So, too, are many books. The issue—the problem for criticism, in this collection and others, for teachers and students—has been the development of vocabularies sufficient to consider all these matters.

A second purpose of this anthology has been to explore the development of that vocabulary from the perspective of the "humanities" as broadly defined. That is to say, because television was early on considered as a social problem, many approaches and considerable terminology had already been developed to deal with the medium by the time scholars, critics, and thinkers who had traditionally focused their attention on books turned to this newer medium. Those first approaches, terms, and analytical paradigms were drawn largely from the realms of social psychology and sociology and had little use for strategies that would look closely at television as an expressive form.

This aspect of the "climate" of television criticism is the one that has altered most perceptibly in recent years, years encompassing previous editions of *Television: The Critical View* and now affording work for the present volume. And while this feature has changed, many others implied in Hadas's comments have remained essentially the same. This introduction focuses on the differences and similarities that can be marked in the present critical climate.

The most prominent change in our understanding and approach to television has occurred within academic settings. Television Studies is now an established area of study in many universities. Although the concept, the term, and the designation are constantly under discussion and revision, it is clear that, from this academic perspective, Hadas's admonition is taken quite seriously. Interestingly enough, however, the development of Television Studies has modified our basic notions of what the medium is, what "humanities approaches" consist of, and what "academic" discourse surrounding television (or any other subject) has to do with "education in its larger sense."

Television Studies as an academic enterprise developed from four major backgrounds. In the United States, the first of these was literary studies that redirected critical analysis toward the study of popular entertainment forms: novels, material culture, magazines, radio programs, and so on. The study of popular films was also important in this enterprise, but developed through a somewhat different route, to be discussed below. The choice to examine these "inferior" or "unappreciated" forms was motivated by a number of concerns. Philosophically, scholars in this movement often felt the works they wished to examine were more indicative of larger cultural preferences, expressive of a more "democratic" relationship between works and audiences than the "elite" works selected, archived, and taught as the traditional canon of humanistically valued forms of expression.

Politically, these same impulses suggested that it was important to study these works precisely because their exclusion from canonical systems also excluded their audiences, devalued large numbers of citizens, or saddled them with inferior intellectual or aesthetic judgment. It is not coincidental that the study of popular entertainment developed momentum at the end of the 1960s, when many cultural categories were under question and when these questions made their way into educational institutions as questions concerning curricula, canonical content, and the value of "traditions."

For the most part, although these early studies were politically motivated and presented as part of far larger political movements and actions, they did not offer systematic ideological analyses of the works they examined. Their agenda was broadly cultural, examining popular forms for their contribution to ongoing discussions about various "meanings" within expressive culture. They did, however, open questions of how we might study nontraditional forms of cultural expression: games, events, designs, fashion. And it is necessary to remember that many of these analyses were carried out prior to the intense concern with theories of how meanings might be systematically imposed through cultural codes, social strategies, industrial organization, or other more embedded and socially grounded influences on expression. These early studies of popular culture were, rather, one of the final applications of critical analysis rooted in what is referred to in traditional literary studies as the New Criticism. And in this linkage, they represent the extension of New Critical questions to "profane" culture, thus contributing, in my view, to a radical modification and appropriation of that form of analysis. What remains of New Critical approaches, an immensely valuable contribution, is the close attention to textual detail, even when this "close analysis" is exercised in the examination of social constructs, cultural patterns, behaviors, and artifacts that far exceed earlier notions of "texts."

The second major influence on Television Studies emerged in Europe, its primary sources for American students coming from Great Britain. Cultural Studies, developing from the work of Raymond Williams, Richard Hoggart, and Stuart Hall, had already begun to examine similar artifacts, television among them, as American popular culture scholars, but had done so within a far more formidable analytical tradition. Where American approaches had acknowledged something about "politics" in their work, the British scholars systematically explored "ideology."

This work was profoundly influenced by continental Marxism and structural anthropology, two varying but in their early stages almost equally powerful forms of "structuralism." While Marxist theory analyzed structures grounded in the economic determination of social categories, structural anthropology searched (for and presumably in) "mental structures" that crossed specific social, geographic, and cultural boundaries. The argument that much of human experience, from "texts" to forms of social organization and action, was informed, ordered, and directed by "deeper" structures was immensely powerful. It allowed scholars and critics to bundle vast amounts of discreet artifacts and events into significant and manageable "patterns." The patterns, the formulas, the genres, the classes—of citizens or of texts—were the item to be analyzed. Complexities of contemporary life were thus more easily handled, described, and written about.

Work done at the Centre for Contemporary Cultural Studies at the University of Birmingham struggled with these varied and mixed approaches, sorted through theories and methods, and offered a number of powerful models for research on a number of topics. One of the primary syntheses accomplished centered on the work of Antonio Gramsci and the application of notions of hegemony to the study of contemporary culture. Mass media generally and television specifically occupied central positions of inquiry in these efforts.

When these approaches reached American universities, they reached into work already primed for more systematic analysis, and Television Studies, among other topics, eagerly appropriated some of the models, techniques, and styles of analysis. These American appropriations also distorted, in the view of some scholars and critics, the critical analysis of ideology that undergirded British work.

They did mesh well, however, with a third influence on the developing field of Television Studies. This work maintained the ideological focus and drew on the tradition of critical sociology associated with the Frankfurt School of sociological analysis. In the United States, analysis of television carried out in departments of sociology and philosophy was most involved with these sources. Academic critics working from this tradition were able to critique what they perceived to be a central weakness in the earlier "popular culture" approach, its reliance on a naive notion of "liberal pluralism" central to many expressive forms. The arrival of "British Cultural Studies" required and enabled some scholars working within that earlier tradition to sharpen their own critiques, to recognize weaknesses and gaps in their work, and to move to a more complex perspective on television and other aspects of popular expressive culture. Generally, the arrival and conflicted acceptance of Cultural Studies approaches in the United States overlaps heavily with the development of Television Studies, and ongoing debates have developed around the varying emphases on and definitions of ideology.

A fourth influence on Television Studies emerged from the growing body of film studies in the United States and abroad. Unlike television, film had been accepted, in some quarters since its earliest days, as a "fine art." In popular, general discussion, many of the same issues and concerns that would occupy critics of television—crass commercialism, "debased" moral attitudes, direct influence on viewer behavior, ideological agendas—were central to discussions of movies. Still, some early popular, and much academic, discussion of film took on a far more appreciative tone. And at times film occupied a decidedly noble position within public discourse. Put another way, the "climate of criticism" for film has, throughout its history, been more favorable than that surrounding television. In its most recent stages, film criticism, both for the general reader and for the academic community, developed sophisticated and complex forms and styles of analysis widely accepted as legitimate.

Even in these discussions, however, much of the work focused historically on its own canonical topics: films produced in Europe or other parts of the world, experimental or lyrical personal films created by individual artists in all countries, and early popular film that had taken on a valued status because of the announced "declines" (formal, social, aesthetic) that followed. Categories of analysis were initially quite close to those used for formal analysis of literary works by New Critics, but moved quickly to the appropriation and development of various forms of structuralism. And perhaps even more significantly, film studies explored an extraordinary range of applications of psychoanalytic theory to its objects.

The study of popular American film, the "Hollywood film," came later and with considerable opposition. But much of the recognition of the particular value of these works came from European critics and filmmakers who saw in Hollywood a form of personal and cultural expression with its own powerful creative techniques, its own intrinsic values. Gradually, the study of popular American film was accepted in the United States as a legitimate enterprise. At times this work was related to the broader study of popular culture, but because of the history of film studies, it remained, for the most part, separate.

When these approaches were infused by the same European theories of structuralism, Marxism, and Cultural Studies, another wave of work emerged; first slowly then more swiftly, film scholars turned their attention to television. In some cases this involved the straightforward application of film theory to the newer medium. And in many instances it also involved the modification or rejection of those theories because of the many significant differences between the two media.

Operating throughout this history, crossing all these influences, and so widespread as to be an influence on almost every field of study in the humanities and elsewhere, was and is feminist theory. I list it as a separate force because it is more far-reaching than Television Studies even while it is now central to that topic.

The recognition of gendered distinctions has been central to Television Studies in two ways. First, as in many other fields, it has called into question the theoretical base of many approaches from considerations of form to the organization of labor in the creation of television texts.

Second, and more problematic, television itself has been defined at times as a "feminine" medium. This designation rises on the one hand from the economic-social fact of television's "address" to women through its base in advertiser-supported, consumer-targeted content. On the other hand, it emerges from arguments that the form of television (again in advertiser-supported commercial systems such as American television), with its demand for open, unending narrative strategies, relates somehow to feminine experience. Discussion of such questions continues. Within either formulation, feminist theorists have been among the most active and perceptive in the study of television and all theoretical positions must take note of these approaches to the medium.

None of these influences, however, should be taken as fully definitive, fully encompassing the study of television. For one thing, their application to television was merely part of larger discussions of their usefulness in studying an array of cultural artifacts: literary, cinematic, pictorial, social. And they were applied to "high" as well as "low," or "popular," forms and behaviors.

Moreover, no sooner than one influence was fully absorbed, others were layered upon it. Much of the discussion in what might be termed the "theory wars" in the academic life of the seventies and eighties had to do with ways in which varying methods and systematic approaches might be applied in varying contexts or might be combined for more powerful forms of analysis.

These ongoing intellectual discussions and struggles are not conducted merely over the utility of methods and theories. They are also directed by more profound questions of epistemology, of how we know what we know. And they are legitimate attempts to come to terms with the role of expressive forms in the social and political lives of citizens as individuals and members of social groups. They are attempts to contribute to social and cultural improvement, to understand the role of expressive media in constructing or altering forms of inequality and oppression. Despite attempts to present these ongoing discussions as mere tempests in small teapots, or as the corrupt agenda of "radicals" in universities, these sometimes fierce exchanges, these often arcane presentations of ideas, have most often been good faith attempts to recognize and understand how social life, now dependent on mass media, on popular forms of expression and entertainment, on the far-reaching lines of information afforded by new technologies, can best be taught and understood, learned and used by all citizens.

Thus it is that various forms of structuralism have been challenged by what have now been defined as "poststructuralist" assumptions. From these perspectives the very notions of "unified" or "coherent" patterns of meaning, of social organization, or of individual psychology are called into question. How can invariant meanings be established by individuals who are themselves constructed of multiple and conflicting psychological, social, and cultural influences? How can mass audiences "receive" coherent meanings from ambiguous and conflicted texts, be they television programs, canonically approved "high culture," films, or rock 'n' roll? And if these varying, conflicting, multiple, unstable artifacts and users are constantly engaged in the process of "constructing" their own social meanings and behaviors, how can any coherent ideological effects be determined?

Added to poststructuralist problems are those suggested by a related category, "postmodernism." Here the issues of instability and potential incoherence are taken in still other directions, in some cases to still greater levels of challenge.

For some critics, commentators, and scholars, the notion of postmodernism means simply that all citizens are now both creator and critic, making up their own individual or group culture from the massive resources of our "cultural archives." In this view, the mixing of style and fashion, image and ideology, meaning and significance are evidence of a new, liberated consciousness.

For others, however, the consequences of postmodernism are far more significant, more dire. The very possibility of meaningful discourse—about politics and ideology, about categories of thought and social organization, about any sense of "shared culture"—seems either impossible or now requires new forms of analysis, argument, and expression. This is especially the case if, as some arguments would have it, there is no longer any way to establish the "real" in human experience if all has dissolved into "representation."

Most important for our concerns here, television has often been seen as both cause and effect, source and symptom, agent and evidence of these newer social and cultural developments. This is especially the case when "television" is defined as or by "American commercial television." And because the form of American commercial television is shared throughout the world, either through the export of programming or through the collapse of various forms of public service broadcasting in the face of an advancing privatization of investment, "television" in any context often means "American TV."

American TV is defined most fundamentally in these discussions by its commercialism. And commercialism results in, indeed demands, continuous programming flow, organized programming strategies matched to other forms of social organization, and the constant attempts to enforce existing power relationships. Thus, television secures conventional and dominant formations of race, class, gender, age, ethnicity, region, and style. So long as the fundamental purpose of the medium can be defined as the delivery of audiences to advertisers, or perhaps more significantly as uniting the world within an equation of television, consumerism, and "reality," using all possible strategies to accomplish this end, civilization itself must be thought of as sliding into the postmodern condition exemplified by television. This concern, fear, pessimistic conclusion has been heightened in recent years by vast changes in the technological and economic contexts of television. As we have moved, in American and world television, from a few central network presentations to the vast proliferation of televisual options, the postmodern model has taken on ever increasing power.

Again, however, our very notion of a "climate of criticism" should alert us to the fact that climates are changeable, always unstable, never the same in two places at once. The field of Television Studies is neither closely bounded or fixed. Questions implied by this brief survey of the winds that have crossed the field in the past ten years remain unsettled, unanswered. In many cases they are in constant states of reconsideration. Keeping this background in mind, then, I will now suggest some of the most pressing categories of questions that define the field at the present moment. These are, in some cases, the questions that have directed the reorganization of this collection, changing its format from that of previous editions. It is necessary in examining these questions to remember that none of the issues discussed above has gone away. Rather, new problems, new issues, are woven into others. Some of them are refined and some approaches are made stronger. Others are seen as less helpful and partially discarded. Still others are applied under new conditions, in response to changes in television itself. In all cases, criticism works with both the wisdom and the burden of its own pasts carried into the present. Moreover, it is equally important to remember that while questions may be grouped in patterns, answers remain more diverse. Even when several essays are presented here as focused on similar questions their approaches and techniques for understanding and answering those questions may differ widely.

Early television criticism focused on definitions of the television "text," its forms and conventions, and the meanings of these patterns. Often the analysis was conducted as a form of genre study, and the question of meanings circulated between individual instances of a genre—programs or series—and the larger group to which the instance belonged. Meaning was discovered in both the generic pattern and at the level of plot or story.

Another wave of critical discussion focused on issues of ideology, and here meaning, significance, and effect were discovered at the level of structure and organization. Clearly, genre remains central in such inquiry, but the primary shift was from meaning residing *in* genre and individual instance to the ways in which these patterns reorganized and reinforced existing social meanings.

This critical discussion of television and ideology continues to offer some of the most prominent questions for Television Studies, questions that inform many of the essays in this collection and are directly or indirectly addressed by all of them. In one sense this merely indicates that television criticism is part of a much larger critical enterprise, for the centrality of ideological issues is now common to almost all humanistic discourse. The remaining problem is, what are the unique features of television that demand critical explication?

Early explorations of television from this perspective often viewed television as little more than an "ideology machine," churning out replications of the most oppressive and repressive aspects of contemporary American society. Some of this work was grounded in film study and could not escape more widespread notions that television is merely a degenerate cinematic form. Other versions were far more sophisticated and sought to define television's specific economic, social, aesthetic, and cultural characteristics in order to show that it contributed to, rather than replaced, other forms of ideological discourse.

These views of television as ideologically monolithic, however, were quickly displaced by some of these same attempts. As the medium was analyzed and described more precisely and from different perspectives, the question shifted. Instead of asking how television performs this monolithic ideological function, questions came to center on whether or not television was so unified in its forms and effects. One way to formulate the problem at this moment is to grant that the medium (like all others) is varied and conflicted, but to ask whether or not it is more "open" or "closed," more rigid or flexible as a form of ideological expression. Even more precisely, we must seek to determine the circumstances in which either condition will define the case. Clearly, this means that all the questions of form, genre, content—broadly defined as the aesthetic questions—must still come into play. Many of the questions focused on these topics are addressed by essays in Part II of this collection, essays that focus on specific programs or program types. As some of these essays indicate, the questions must be examined in far richer contexts than in many early studies.

Defining contexts is the problem at the center of the second major focus of contemporary television criticism, and various attempts to establish these contexts now occupy a far more prominent place in Television Studies than before. Again, these developments lead to the reorganization of this collection.

Major contributions to this area of concern came from the introduction of Cultural Studies approaches to our critical repertoire for the reinsertion of expressive forms into social context lies at the heart of this enterprise. The two most significant contextual categories in contemporary Television Studies are broadly defined as the context of "production" and the context of "reception." Part I of the current collection focuses on various forms of production studies. The essays variously examine historical contexts of television production both social and industrial, broad applications of technique and design within television program types, and case studies of the production of specific television programs.

Essays in Part III focus on the reception context. Here the studies are also informed by serious disagreements over the limits of audiences' interpretive power. Are meanings constructed in the process of "receiving" television? If so, are audiences able to "subvert" those meanings that interpretive critics might find repressive or regressive? In what instances is such power exercised? What other social factors might direct or limit this process of meaning making? These questions have become central to the current discussions of this medium and others.

The final section of the collection offers essays that attempt larger overviews of the entire medium of television. Some focus on aesthetic concerns, some on social. Many see the necessity of avoiding such easy dichotomies and seek various forms of synthesis. It is in this section that a clearer distinction between earlier approaches and later ones emerges. Overviews developed to explain television in "the network era" have a historical tone to them. Newer essays, more focused on television's social and technological proliferation, and informed by notions of poststructuralism and postmodernism, ask decidedly different questions. But the newer questions could not have been formulated without the older ones, and the resonances among these explanations are telling.

As stated above, almost all these developments in the burgeoning field of Television Studies have taken place within academic settings. There it is now commonplace for television to be taken as seriously as books by scholars and critics in various fields. This has not been the case, however, in writing offered to more general audiences. There the best writing about television remains essentially personal, individualized, subjective. While occasionally interesting, the commentary is most often repetitive, familiar, unwilling to consider the possibility that television presents itself in terms distinctive and definable. Questions remain much the same as over the past decades.

Answers to those questions that might be available from academic television criticism are overlooked or ignored. In worst cases, writers for general readers look on in bemused and thinly veiled contempt at the academic critics. The implication is that no one should take television *this* seriously.

There remains, then, another step, another stage in the history of television criticism. In that stage the serious histories, the detailed analyses, the studies of television reception that now remain, in every sense of the word, "academic" approaches to television, will be shared more widely with all audiences. This book is an attempt to assist in taking that next step. And it must be stated here that there are problems with presenting some academic criticism to general audiences. Academic critics and scholars bear responsibility for making their work clear, powerful, accessible, usable.

But an equal responsibility is borne by editors and writers for more generally distributed publication. One part of that responsibility rests in taking the academic criticism more seriously, learning from its insights, its hard historical work, its detailed case studies. Another part of the responsibility is grounded in the very lack of opportunity for anyone to write seriously about television for the public. Too many newspapers relegate television criticism to small columns on back pages. Too few magazines print television commentary of any sort other than the contemptuous or satirical.

There is no doubt that we are closer now to Hadas's preferred state of television commentary. For one thing, more and more students have the opportunity to make Television Studies a part of their general education. These opportunities do not replace their experiences with books, as some might fear. Rather, with books as their tutors, they learn to see television more clearly, more critically. And perhaps these students will come to demand more powerfully and precisely informed commentary about television in their wider experience as citizens.

More to the point, perhaps some of these students, the present users of this collection, will come to write the sort of criticism, the informed, precise, exploratory, and explanatory criticism that has been missing from our shared experiences of this medium in other times. Hadas's concern, finally, was with the making of critics, not merely with the making of criticism. That, too, is the primary purpose of this collection.

Nowhere are we made more aware of these matters than in Eric Michaels's astonishing essay, "For a Cultural Future." A portion of that essay closes this anthology. His case study of the making of television in an Australian Aboriginal community encompasses and capsulizes every issue touched on in this collection, for there all the issues are faced anew. More than in any other succinct single presentation, Michaels faces and analyzes the aesthetic and ideological, the cultural and social, the context of home and the context of nation, the application of practical politics and the analysis of ideology, apparently overwhelming issues of technological power and the recognition of personal resilience. As often stated throughout the essays that follow, it is television that gathers and focuses all these questions.

The intrusion—welcomed, feared, protested, and embraced—of this medium into collective human social experience is refigured in Yuendumu. Moreover, it is refigured in a world already altered by that intrusion in the worlds surrounding Yuendumu. It is the subtlety of these interactions that Michaels captures. We are constantly reminded that while we might generalize some of the comparisons of this encounter to the overall history of television, the significance of his analysis lies precisely in its individual case and context.

And the outcome of his analysis suggests that we must consider television as subtly as he does whenever we seek to discuss this medium in any form. For out of subtlety comes the extraordinary power of his conclusions. The political and moral authority with which Michaels speaks is a reminder that too often we waste words on trivial matters. Sometimes, as critics, we can justify our trivialities by arguing that from such minutia we build larger intellectual edifices. But such claims are often as much rationalization as justification.

This is not to argue that Michaels is correct, or true in every aspect of his argument, whether social, cultural, aesthetic, or political. Indeed, his work in Australia, closely tied to matters of actual practice and policy, remains much contested. Even for those of us removed from the actual locus of those debates, removed from all the complexities and details, however, the force of the arguments rings true. If we wish to disagree here we will have to do so in a manner equal to the arguments we confront. Michaels's work demands of us a higher level of critical exchange and discourse, and his too early loss from that exchange remains tragic in its implications.

But the work remains, powerfully present, distinctive in its voice, committed, engaged. It serves as a model for our attempts to come to terms with television both old and new. It reminds us of the power of the medium. But it reminds us, too, of the power of criticism. Those of us who have turned to the study of this medium have often done so because we experienced or sensed the kinds of links to lived experience limned by Michaels in his essay. Other essays throughout this collection are strong attempts to frame perspectives grounded in those connections. It remains now for users of the essays to do the same.

Part I

THE PRODUCTION
CONTEXTS
OF TELEVISION

This section brings together essays that are both historical and practical. The purpose of the section is to provide contexts for understanding how the material we "see" on television comes to be there. Several influences underlie the development of more detailed and precise analysis of these various contexts. The end of the network era in the United States, for example, has led many scholars to more precise and detailed accounts of how the television industry developed, how it changed, and how it produced certain types of content. But changes in television have also exposed the multiple mechanisms and practices that go into the making and distributing of television in any historical moment, and one result of this exposure is the discussion of television-making as a complex process of cultural, industrial, economic, aesthetic, and individual encounters.

Christopher Anderson's essay on the development of "Disneyland"—television program and theme park—illustrates the breadth and depth of these interactions. He traces the deeply held interests of Walt Disney and the executives at the fledgling American Broadcasting Company's television network. But he does so in the context of post–World War II American culture, the rise of consumerism, leisure, and tourism. One need only consider the perhaps ironic turn of events that culminated in Disney's development of internationally located theme parks and its purchase of ABC to grasp the full implication of Anderson's conclusion.

> Television made possible Disney's vision of "total merchandising" because it gave him the ability to integrate apparently isolated segments of the national commercial culture that developed after the war. . . . Disney pro-

vided the impulse for the major studios to enter television and a blueprint
for the future development of the media industries.

That blueprint, as Mark Alvey shows in his discussion of independent production companies was quickly followed. In this first close look at the range
of organized, industrialized Hollywood television, Alvey argues against the
grain of received history. Rather than the "wasteland" so often cited in
accounts of 1960s television, Alvey asserts that development of independent
production companies assured that the "terrain of 1960s television would
not be a sterile expanse of banality, but rather a diverse field for cultural
expression, marked by both imitation and invention, convention and creativity." Such an argument forces us to reconsider the role of the "Golden
Age" of New York productions. It also suggests that we make use of new
videotape resources to actually reexamine the programming so frequently
dismissed in conventional accounts.

That reexamination and reconsideration are made possible largely
because of the development of telefilm, and the use of telefilm for economic
reasons in the development of the infamous "rerun." Often used as the ultimate example of television's inferior cultural and social status (who would
care—or could bear—to see a television program more than once), the rerun
is carefully presented by Phil Williams as a logical industrial strategy.
Williams's account of the slow recognition of the utility and the viability of
rerunning the same program is the first to explore this entity in detail. Moreover, he goes on to show how reruns evolve into a complex cultural phenomenon. His discussion of the Nickelodeon cable network's use of these
cultural factors in creating the successful "Nick at Nite" programming strategy was published before Nickelodeon went on to create a second cable network, TV Land. But the essay makes clear why such an enterprise would be
both reasonable and successful in the context of contemporary television. As
the network era disappears it becomes a valuable commodity. But in becoming a (rerun) commodity, it is also reframed and resold as nostalgic artifact,
television as the "history" of a childhood or adolescence now all but lost.

The next three essays are presented as a small unit focused on the contexts surrounding the production of "women's television." Lynn Spigel's
"Women's Work" is an outstanding example of the social history of television. What emerges most clearly here is that by placing television squarely
within the domestic sphere early TV broadcasters in many ways equated
television with home, family, and woman. In some ways, then, women's
television in the early periods was everybody's television. Programming distinctions regarding dayparts, genre, and the practices that defined viewing
were constructed in the context of a world in which a particular conception
of "woman" was central. Thus, even "male genres" would have to be delineated in terms of their relations to television's "ideal viewer."

Julie D'Acci's discussion of the struggle to bring *Cagney and Lacey* to
network television demonstrates how complicated these same questions had
become in two short decades. But her essay, the first chapter of a book

examining the case in far greater detail, also demonstrates that while some concepts of "woman," the "feminine," had not changed, the contradictions and tensions masked by those terms were now exposed. The tangled relations among gender and genre, the battles between independent producers and networks, the participation of public activists and individual viewers are all part of this story. And one major contribution of D'Acci's work is to remind us that similar stories lie hidden behind many television programs and to provide a model of how research and criticism can probe more than the surface text.

Jackie Byars and Eileen Meehan also explore more complex relationships, this time among programming and the newer, technologically defined "cable television." To the degree that cable television seeks to distinguish itself by providing "specialized programming," it must define its audiences more precisely. *Narrowcasting* is the term most often used to describe strategies for reaching "target audiences." The case of the Lifetime cable network is instructive in showing just how deeply these strategies are woven into fundamental cultural assumptions. As with Spigel's essay on early television's appropriation of "the domestic" and D'Acci's study of a single program, so this examination of a network explores industrial and narrative strategies grounded in complicated notions of "the feminine" and "woman." In their study of Lifetime's remake of the Alfred Hitchcock film *Notorious*, Byars and Meehan, like the other authors, demonstrate the multiple assumptions buried in the decision-making process. Their model can be used for exploring other cable networks and other specialized broadcasting entities. Indeed, as U.S. network television has responded to the competition from cable television, and as cable, satellite, and the proliferation of broadcast channels in other parts of the world are forced to battle for audience attention, the specific strategies used can become the focus of careful critical analysis.

Still, within this welter of change and alteration, many of the specific production strategies of television remain much the same. David Barker's essay on specific visual strategies of various types of television continues to describe much of what appears on television. Visual experimentation is far more rare than other attention-getting strategies. And even in cases where technical variation occurs (as described in some essays in other sections), the techniques outlined by Barker remain the baseline, standard, economical production methods. One need only look at the situation comedies that dominate ratings lists to note the accuracy of his descriptions.

Some of the most vital experimentation, however, occurs in the production of television commercials. Hal Himmelstein's analysis of Kodak's "America" commercials appeared in a previous edition as a genre study. It is that, of course, but the details he presents are also a superb account of how a commercial is made and it is fitting that the essay be used here as part of the discussion of production contexts. While few students will have access to the "inside" information Himmelstein managed to secure, it is possible to use his other sources, the trade magazines, to find source material helpful in performing this type of study. Moreover, this essay also demonstrates the deeply embedded cultural assumptions that undergird attempts to sell products. Thus, as textual analysis, the essay is a model for the analysis of any commercial.

Similarly, John Corner's overview of the assumptions, techniques, and narrative strategies of documentary production can be applied to programs as diverse as local news stories and high-budget network documentaries. This essay is particularly important in a time when more and more programming draws on documentary traditions. Because news "magazine" programs are far less expensive to produce than original fiction programs, it should come as no surprise that more and more such programs find their way into transmission. But many of these new programs appear to have little of the civic responsibility called for by the inventors of cinematic documentary. When sensationalism and suggestion replace document and the search for fact, critical viewers need to be especially aware of the techniques used and modified. Central to this critical awareness is Corner's reminder that while documentary in other contexts addressed viewers as citizens, members of a public, it now often addresses them as consumers, made available to commercial appeals. Examining documentary with such distinctions in mind can remain an act of public criticism.

Each of these essays addresses a specific topic, but taken together they serve as a map of the factors that surround the production of any television program. The fact that they also demonstrate the constantly shifting relations among those factors provides an additional perspective. Careful historical study—of industrial relations, technological developments, and programs themselves—is becoming more possible as more records are made available and more careful examination of trade and professional journals continues. Videotape makes available the programs themselves, and provides opportunities for very close analysis of production techniques. Work on the history and practice of the multiple "televisions" we have known provides excellent topics for further research and analysis.

Disneyland

CHRISTOPHER ANDERSON

The month of October 1954 marked a watershed for television production in Hollywood. Alongside those marginal movie industry figures who had labored to wring profits from television production during the late 1940s and early 1950s, there appeared a new breed of established producers attracted by television's explosive growth following the end of the FCC's station application freeze in 1952.[1] Early in the month, Columbia Pictures became the first major studio to produce episodic TV series when its TV subsidiary, Screen Gems, debuted *Father Knows Best* on CBS and *The Adventures of Rin Tin Tin* on ABC. Within three days in late October, two of the film industry's top independent producers, David O. Selznick and Walt Disney, joined the migration to prime time. Selznick, producer of *Gone With the Wind* (1939), made Hollywood's most auspicious debut with a program broadcast simultaneously on all four existing networks, a two-hour spectacular titled *Light's Diamond Jubilee*. Selznick was soon joined by fellow independent producer Walt Disney, whose premiere television series, *Disneyland*, entered ABC's regular Wednesday-night schedule on the twenty-seventh of October. Disney had forged a reputation as the cinema's maestro of family entertainment; now his *Disneyland* series promised to deliver what *Time* described as "the true touch of enchantment" to American homes.[2] Unlike their predecessors in television, these were established members of the movie industry who diversified into TV production without leav-

---

ing movies behind. The first to link production for the two media, these producers sparked the full-scale integration of movie and TV production in Hollywood during the second half of the 1950s.

As the recipient of nearly two dozen Academy Awards for his studio's cartoon animation, Walt Disney was one of Hollywood's most acclaimed independent producers and certainly, along with Selznick, the most celebrated Hollywood producer to enter television by 1954. Disney possessed the independent producer's belief in television as an alternative to the movie industry's restrictive studio system, but his conception of television's role in a new Hollywood was more sweeping than that of colleagues who saw the electronic medium as nothing more than a new market for traditional film production. Unlike virtually every other telefilm producer in Hollywood, Disney harbored no illusions about dominating TV production; his modest production plans initially encompassed only the *Disneyland* series. Still, Disney was the first Hollywood executive during the 1950s to envision a future built on television's technical achievements—the scope of its signal, the access it provided to the American home. For Disney network television arrived as an invitation to reinvent the movie business, to explore horizons beyond the realm of filmmaking.

Disney later admitted that he was "never much interested" in radio, but television, with its ability to display the visual appeal of Disney products, was another matter entirely. The studio aired its first television program on NBC during December 1950. Sponsored by Coca-Cola, "One Hour in Wonderland" was set in a Disney Christmas party and featured excerpts promoting the studio's upcoming theatrical release, *Alice in Wonderland* (1951). In 1951 Disney produced its second hour-long program for NBC, a special sponsored by Johnson and Johnson. Disney's subsequent plans for a television series started with a seemingly outlandish demand: To obtain the first Disney TV series, a network would have to purchase the series and agree to invest at least $500,000 for a one-third share in the studio's most ambitious project, the Disneyland amusement park planned for construction in suburban Los Angeles. NBC and CBS balked at these terms, but ABC, mired in third place, decided to accept.[3] In uniting the TV program and the amusement park under a single name, Disney made one of the most influential commercial decisions in post-war American culture. Expanding upon the lucrative character merchandising market that the studio had joined in the early 1930s, Disney now planned to create an all-encompassing consumer environment that he described as "total merchandising." Products aimed at baby boom families and stamped with the Disney imprint—movies, amusement park rides, books, comic books, clothing, toys, TV programs, and more—would weave a vast, commercial web, a tangle of advertising and entertainment in which each Disney product—from the movie *Snow White* to a ride on Disneyland's Matterhorn—promoted all Disney products. And television was the beacon that would draw the American public to the domain of Disney. "We wanted to start off running," Walt later recalled. "The investment was going to be too big to wait for a slow buildup. We needed terrific initial impact and television seemed the answer."[4]

Television served a crucial role in Disney's plans for creating an economic and cultural phenomenon that exceeded the boundaries of any single communications medium. By raising capital through the ABC investment and raising consciousness through its depiction of the park's construction, television's figurative representation of Disneyland actually called the amusement park into existence, making it possible for the first time to unite the disparate realms of the Disney empire. With the home as its primary site of exhibition, television gave Disney unparalleled access to a family audience that he already had cultivated more effectively than any Hollywood producer in the studio era. As a result of the post-war baby boom, Disney's target audience of children between the ages of five and fourteen grew from 22 million in 1940 to 35 million in 1960.[5] Television provided the surest route to this lucrative market.

As a text, the *Disneyland* television program also marked a rite of passage for the Disney studio. Its broadcast signaled the studio's transition from the pre-war culture of motion pictures to a post-war culture in which Disney's movies were subsumed into an increasingly integrated leisure market that also included television, recorded music, theme parks, tourism, and consumer merchandise. By depicting the new amusement park as another of Walt's fantasies brought to life by the skilled craftsmen at the Disney studio, the *Disneyland* TV program gave a recognizable symbolic form to Disney's elaborate economic transformation, mediating it for the American public by defining it as another of the Disney studio's marvels. It is only a slight exaggeration, therefore, to claim that Disney mounted an entertainment empire on the cornerstone of this first television series.

Unlike many who groped for a response to the dramatic changes that swept the movie industry following World War II, Walt Disney and his brother Roy answered uncertainty with a calculated plan for diversification. Biographer Richard Schickel has suggested that the Disneys addressed the unstable post-war conditions more aggressively than other Hollywood leaders because their company had suffered misfortunes during the early 1940s, when virtually everyone else in Hollywood had prospered. During the late 1930s, Disney had stood for a moment at the pinnacle of the movie industry. Although an independent producer who worked outside the security of the major studios, Disney took extraordinary financial risks that ultimately paid off in the critical and financial success of *Snow White* (1937), which trailed only Selznick's *Gone With the Wind* as one of the two most profitable Hollywood movies of the 1930s.[6] But Disney's good fortunes lasted only briefly. Following *Snow White*, Disney nearly buried his studio beneath ambitious plans for expansion. With box-office disappointments like the costly animated feature *Fantasia* (1940), the closing of foreign markets due to the war, and over-investment in new studio facilities, Disney faced burdensome corporate debts that weighed even more heavily once banks shut off credit to the studio in 1940. Disney raised funds reluctantly by offering stock to the public, but only government contracts to produce educational cartoons kept the studio active during the war. "The only good thing about the situation," according to Schickel, "was that the problems that were later to plague the rest of the industry had been met by Disney at a time when the government could help out and when the general buoyancy of the industry could at least keep him afloat. The result, of course, was a head start in gathering know-how to meet the crisis that was coming—a head start in planning for diversification first of the company's motion picture products, then of its overall activities."[7]

Plagued by adversity during the 1940s, Walt and Roy Disney entered the 1950s with a plan to transform the Disney studio from an independent producer of feature films and cartoon short-subjects into a diversified leisure and entertainment corporation. Instead of retrenching, as others had, the Disneys fortified their company through a careful process of diversification. Beginning in 1953, the company implemented a series of changes designed to redefine its role in Hollywood. Disney established its own theatrical distribution subsidiary, Buena Vista, in order to end its reliance on major studio distribution. The studio also ceased production on its by-then unprofitable cartoon short subjects, cut back on expensive animated features, and began to concentrate on nature documentaries and live-action movies following the success of *Treasure Island* (1950) and *Robin Hood* (1952).[8] Blueprints for Disneyland and ideas about television production took shape during this period of corporate transition.

As Disney's schemes for expansion pointed toward television, the ABC-TV network eagerly cultivated ties with the motion picture industry.[9] Hollywood-produced television series became the cornerstone in ABC's plans for differentiating itself from NBC and CBS. As the third-place network, ABC elected to build its audience in direct opposition to the established networks. While the other networks touted their established stars or experimented with expensive spectaculars and the possibility of attracting viewers with unique video events, ABC remained committed to the traditional strategy of programming familiar weekly series that defined television viewing as a consistent feature in the family's domestic routine. Robert Weitman, the network's vice-president in charge of programming, emphasized the importance of habitual viewing in ABC's programming strategies. "The answer seems to be in established patterns of viewing," he explained. "People are annoyed when their favorite show is pre-empted, even for a super-special spectacular." Leonard Goldenson, who had spent decades in the business of movie distribution and exhibition, recognized the similarities between television viewing and the experience of moviegoing during the studio era. "The real strength and vitality of television," he claimed, "is in your regular week-in and week-out programs. The strength of motion pictures was always the habit of going to motion pictures on a regular basis, and that habit was, in part, taken away from motion pictures by television."[10] ABC's programming strategy was built on the belief that television's fundamental appeal was less its ability to deliver exotic events, than its promise of a familiar cultural experience.

As a result, ABC's regularly scheduled series would serve as the basis for network counter-programming, the principal tactic in the network's assault on CBS and NBC. Rather than compete against an established series or live event with a program of similar appeal, ABC hoped to offer alternative programming in order to attract segments of the audience not being served by the other networks. The network would construct and project a specific identity by treating its schedule as the expression of a unique relation to the broadcast audience. "Whatever the audience is not watching at any given time makes for new possibilities," Goldenson noted. "We are not trying to take away audiences from CBS and NBC. . . . We are trying to carve our own network character, to create new audiences."[11] This tactic was based on a related aspect of ABC's programming philosophy—its attention to audience demographics. Governed by the belief that "a network can't be all things to all people," ABC chose to target "the youthful families" with children, a section of the audience whose numbers had increased rapidly since World War II. "We're after a specific audience," claimed Goldenson, "the young housewife—one cut above the teenager—with two to four kids, who has to buy the clothing, the food, the soaps, the home remedies." As this statement implies, ABC chose to align itself with small-ticket advertisers, those selling the type of products that young families might be more likely to need and afford. Goldenson justified ABC's entire programming strategy when he remarked, "We're in the Woolworth's business, not in Tiffany's. Last year Tiffany made only $30,000."[12]

Anxious to acquire Hollywood programming that appealed to a family audience, ABC gambled on Disney by committing $2 million for a fifty-two-week series (with a seven-year renewal option) and by purchasing a 35 percent share in the park for $500,000. Without even a prospective format to present to advertisers, ABC invoked the Disney reputation alone to sell the program under a joint-sponsorship package to American Motors, the American Dairy Association, and Derby Food. Sponsorship of the season's twenty original episodes was sold at $65,000 per episode, and the network time was billed to advertisers at $70,000 per hour. During the late 1950s, when ABC's ratings and advertising revenue finally approached the levels of NBC and CBS, Leonard Goldenson consistently referred to the Disney deal as the network's "turning point." Indeed, *Disneyland* attracted nearly half of ABC's advertising billings during 1954, the final year during which the network operated at a loss.[13]

Although Walt Disney repeatedly assured the press that the *Disneyland* TV series would stand on its own terms as entertainment, the program served mainly to publicize Disney products. *Disneyland*'s identification of the amusement park and the TV series was confirmed during the first episode when Walt informed viewers that "Disneyland the place and Disneyland the show are all the same." Both the series and the park were divided into four familiar movie industry genres: Fantasyland (animated cartoons), Adventureland (exotic action-adventure), Frontierland (Westerns), and Tomorrowland (science-fiction). Introduced by Walt himself, each week's episode represented one of the park's imaginary lands through a compilation of sequences drawn from the studio's cartoon short-subjects, nature documentaries, animated and live-action features, or short films produced as outright promotions for Disney movies about to enter theatrical release. *Disneyland's* format and pervasive self-promotion were unprecedented for television, but it had roots in the popular radio programs broadcast from Hollywood during the 1930s and 1940s. Hosted by actors, directors, or celebrity journalists, programs like *Hollywood Hotel* and *Lux Radio Theatre* offered musical performances or dramatizations of studio feature films, but their strongest lure was the glimpse they provided into the culture of Hollywood. Through informal chats with performers and other members of the industry, these radio programs perpetuated an image of Hollywood glamour while promoting recent studio releases.[14] Disney simply adapted this format for television. As the master of ceremonies, he turned himself into a media celebrity, much as director Cecil B. DeMille earlier had ridden *Lux Radio Theatre* to national fame.[15]

The actual production of *Disneyland* required a minimal financial investment by the Disney studio. At a time when the typical network series featured thirty-nine new episodes each season, Disney's contract with ABC called for only twenty original episodes, with each of them repeated once, and twelve broadcast a third time during the summer. Instead of producing twenty episodes of new television programming each season, Disney viewed the deal as an opportunity to capitalize on the studio's library of films dating back to the debut of Mickey Mouse in the late 1920s. The wisdom of this format, as Richard Schickel has noted, "was that it allowed the studio to participate in TV without surrendering control of its precious film library."[16] Long after many of the major studios had sold the TV rights to their films, the Disneys boasted that they still owned every film they ever made. Although it is not generally remembered, during the first three years of *Disneyland,* the studio produced only one narrative film made expressly for the series—the three-part "Davy Crockett" serial that took the nation by storm during that first season.[17] More typically, the *Disneyland* TV series introduced a new generation of children to the studio's storehouse of cartoons.

Even with a program that consisted largely of recycled material, the studio admitted that it would not turn a profit from its first year in television. There were production costs in preparing the theatrical product for broadcast (editing compilation episodes or filming Walt's introductory appearances) and in producing its limited amount of original programming. But these costs generally were defrayed throughout the studio's various operations. The three hour-long episodes of the "Davy Crockett" series, for instance, cost $600,000—more than three times the industry standard for telefilm production—and yet, during that year alone, the cost was spread over two separate network broadcasts and a theatrical release. By employing up to 80 percent of the studio's production staff, the television operation also enabled the Disney studio to meet the expense of remaining at full productivity. In addition, all costs not covered by the network's payments were charged to the studio's promotion budget—another indication of the program's primary purpose.[18]

Nearly one-third of each *Disneyland* episode was devoted directly to studio promotion, but the entire series blurred any distinction between publicity and entertainment. Indeed, *Disneyland* capitalized on the unspoken recognition that commercial broadcasting had made it virtually impossible to distinguish between entertainment and advertising. One episode, "Operation Undersea," provided a behind-the-scenes glimpse at the making of *20,000 Leagues Under the Sea* (1954) just one week before Disney released the film to theaters.[19] This episode was later followed by "Monsters of the Deep," a nature documentary that provided another opportunity to plug the studio's most recent theatrical release. An episode titled "A Story of Dogs" preceded the release of *Lady and the Tramp* (1955), Disney's second major feature distributed to theaters during the initial TV season.

Viewers didn't mind that *Disneyland* was simply a new form of Hollywood ballyhoo, because Disney framed the program within an educational discourse, reassuring viewers that they inhabited a position of privileged knowledge that was available only through television. Amidst paternalistic fears over the pernicious influence of television, comic books, and other forms of mass culture, Disney's middle-brow didacticism was disarming. In each episode, *Disneyland* rewarded its viewers with an encyclopedic array of general information borrowed loosely from the fields of history, science, and anthropology, while also sharing more specialized knowledge about the history of the Disney studio and its filmmaking procedures. Through this specialized knowledge about the Disney studio, the *Disneyland* TV series defined a particular relationship between television and movies, one in which television served an inchoate critical function by providing commentary on Disney movies. Though produced by the studio itself, *Disneyland* nevertheless contained elements of a critical discourse on the cinema. It educated viewers to perceive continuities among Disney films, to analyze certain aspects of the production process, and to recognize the studio's body of work as a unified product of Walt's authorial vision.

Disneyland's most obvious strategy for educating viewers was its use of behind-the-scenes footage from the Disney studio. The first episode introduced the Disney studio through images of Kirk Douglas playing with his sons on the studio lot, James Mason fighting a man-made hurricane on the stage of *20,000 Leagues Under the Sea,* animators sketching models, and musicians recording the score for a cartoon. By representing the studio as an active, self-contained creative community bustling with activity, these scenes evoke impressions of studio-era Hollywood while masking the fact that historical conditions had rendered those very images obsolete. Disney also used behind-the-scenes footage to demonstrate the elaborate process of filmmaking, particularly the intricacies of animation. Although one might think that a filmmaker like Disney would be afraid of ruining the mystery of animation by revealing how its effects are achieved, Richard Schickel has observed that "Disney always enjoyed showing people around his studio and explaining to them exactly how the exotic process of creating an animated film proceeded." In fact, Disney originally planned for the amusement park to be located at the studio, with demonstrations of the filmmaking process as one of its major attractions.[20] In one feature film, *The Reluctant Dragon* (1941), Disney displayed the animation process by allowing Robert Benchley to lead moviegoers on a tour of the Disney studio. But this was a one-shot experiment that couldn't be repeated in other movies without becoming a distracting gimmick. Following in the tradition of the earlier Hollywood radio shows, therefore, Disney defined television as a companion medium to the cinema, an informational medium that could be used to reveal the process of filmmaking—since that impulse could not be indulged in the movies themselves. While Disney movies were presented as seamless narratives, television gave Disney the license to expose their seams.

Disney's willingness to display the process of filmmaking suggests that reflexivity in itself is not a radical impulse. More a disciple of Barnum than Brecht, Disney had no intention of distancing his audience from the illusion in his movies. Instead, he appealed to the audience's fascination with cinematic trickery. Disney exhibited what historian Neil Harris describes as an "American vernacular tradition" perhaps best exemplified by P. T. Barnum. Barnum's showmanship depended on his recognition that the public delights both in being fooled by a hoax and in discovering the mechanisms that make the hoax successful. Through his fanciful exhibitions, Barnum encouraged "an aesthetic of the operational, a delight in observing process and examining for literal truth."[21] Far from being hoodwinked by Barnum's artifice, the audiences that witnessed his exhibitions took pleasure in uncovering the process by which these hoaxes were perpetrated.

Inheriting Barnum's sense of showmanship, Disney developed his own "operational aesthetic" through television, enhancing his audience's pleasure—and anticipation—by offering precious glimpses of the filmmaking process. Of course, Disney's depiction of the production process was selective; it ignored the economics of filmmaking in favor of focusing on the studio's technical accomplishments. *Disneyland* never explored such issues as labor relations at the Disney studio or the economics of merchandising that sent the largest share of profits into Walt's pockets. Instead, in what has become a cliche of "behind-the-scenes" reporting on filmmaking, *Disneyland* treated each movie as a problem to be solved by the ingenuity of Disney craftsmen. This created a secondary narrative that accompanied the movie into theaters, a story of craftsmen overcoming obstacles to produce a masterful illusion. With this strategy, viewers were given an incentive to see the completed movie, because the movie itself provided the resolution to the story of the filmmaking process as depicted on *Disneyland*.

The program also educated viewers through its attention to Disney studio history. The determination to recycle the Disney library shaped the series during its early seasons, making *Disneyland* an electronic museum devoted to the studio's artistic achievements. Before the arrival of television, Hollywood's history was virtually inaccessible to the general public, available only sporadically through the unpredictable re-release of studio features and short subjects. Movies themselves may have been preserved in studio vaults, but for moviegoers accustomed to an ever-changing program at local theaters, the Hollywood cinema during the studio era was much like live television— an ephemeral cultural experience in which each text inevitably dissolved into memory, swept away in the endless flow of serial production. Although much of television in the mid-1950s traded on the immediacy of live broadcast, the sale of motion pictures to broadcasters meant that television also became the unofficial archive of the American cinema, in which Hollywood's past surfaced in bits and pieces, like fragments of a dream. One of the pleasures of *Disneyland* was the chance it offered to halt the flow of mass culture by remembering relics from the Disney vaults.

Although *Disneyland* may have struck a nostalgic chord for older viewers, the program's presentation of studio history was less sentimental than reverential. Cartoons nearly forgotten were resurrected with a solemnity normally reserved for the most venerable works of art. This attitude is apparent from the first episode when Walt announces that the end of each episode will be reserved for Mickey Mouse. After leading the viewer through an elaborate description of the proposed amusement park and other studio activities, Disney stands behind a lectern and turns the pages of a massive bound volume, an illustrated chronicle of Mickey's adventures. In spite of the flurry of changes at the studio, he explains, one should not lose sight of an eternal truth: "It all started with Mickey. . . . The story of Mickey is the story of Disneyland." As he continues, the scene segues into Mickey's first appearance in the cartoon "Plane Crazy," and then dissolves to one of his most famous appearances, as the Sorcerer's Apprentice in *Fantasia*. The tone of the scene—Disney's scholarly disposition, the sight of Mickey's history contained in a stately book—implies that the Disney studio's products are not the disposable commodities of pop culture, but artifacts worthy of remembrance. Walt's role as narrator is to reactivate forgotten cartoons in the public's cultural memory by demonstrating their canonical status within the artistic history of the Disney studio. As an electronic museum, *Disneyland* invoked the cultural memory of its audience mainly to publicize new Disney products. In spite of its commercial motives, however, the series also made it possible to conceive of Hollywood as having a history worthy of consideration.

"Monsters of the Deep," a typical episode from the first season of *Disneyland*, demonstrates the strategies for situating new Disney movies in the context of the studio's history and production practices. The episode introduces Walt in his studio's research department. Wearing a dark tweed jacket and surrounded by books and charts, he appears professorial. Inspired by knowledge, yet free from scholastic pretension, he is television's image of an intellectual, kindly and inviting. Speaking directly to the camera, he leads the viewer through a discussion of dinosaurs, using illustrations from enormous books to punctuate his presentation. This lecture seems motivated only by Disney's inquisitive character until the Disney sales pitch gradually seeps in. "We told the story of dinosaurs large and small in *Fantasia*," Disney reminds viewers as the screen dissolves to images from the animated feature. As Disney explains the habitat, feeding patterns, and behavior of dinosaurs, the footage from *Fantasia* becomes recontextualized, as though it were a segment from a nature documentary, a reminder that even Disney's most fantastic films have educational value. Disney segues into a report on sea monsters, asking whether giant squids have existed among the mysteries of the ocean, tracing the enigma through debates over the veracity of historical accounts. This query provides a transition to a discussion of the problems involved in creating a plausible giant squid for the Disney feature, *20,000 Leagues Under the Sea*. From the research department, the scene dissolves to a studio soundstage where star Kirk Douglas performs a song from the movie and then guides the television viewer through a behind-the-scenes glimpse of the special effects used to stage the movie's spectacular battle sequence featuring a giant squid. Afterwards, Disney draws a line of continuity through the studio's present and past accomplishments by introducing viewers to an extended sequence from the studio's most famous scene of undersea adventure, Pinocchio's escape from the whale, Monstro, in the 1940 feature, *Pinocchio*. Even the last two sequences, so clearly intended to advertise Disney products, carry the promise of edification as they define a limited and specialized knowledge—the Disney canon, the production of Disney movies—that is directed toward enhancing the experience of *20,000 Leagues Under the Sea*.

Because the *Disneyland* TV series delivered viewers like no program in ABC history, even the program's advertisers didn't mind subsidizing Disney's opportunity for self-promotion. *Disneyland* concluded the season as the first ABC program ever to appear among the year's ten highest-rated series. It was viewed weekly in nearly 40 percent of the nation's 26 million TV households.[22] The trade magazine, *Sponsor*, applauded Disney's skill at blending entertainment and salesmanship, quoting an unnamed ABC executive who quipped, "Never before have so many people made so little objection to so much selling."[23] Through its Emmy awards, the television industry affirmed its approval of Disney's venture, nominating Walt as TV's "Most Outstanding New Personality" and honoring "Operation Underseas"—an episode about the making of *20,000 Leagues Under the Sea*—as TV's Best Documentary.[24]

For the movie industry, the most telling detail in the entire Disney phenomenon was the surprising performance of the studio's feature films. By releasing its features through its own distribution company, Buena Vista, and by timing the release dates to coincide with simultaneous promotion on the television program, Disney emerged as the top-grossing independent production company of 1955. Undoubtedly aided by its exposure on the TV series, *20,000 Leagues Under the Sea* grossed $8 million when it finally played in movie theaters—the largest sum ever reached by a Disney movie on its initial release. It finished the year as Hollywood's fourth highest-grossing movie and became the first Disney movie ever to crack the list of twenty all-time top-grossing films. In addition, Disney's new animated feature, *Lady and the Tramp*, pulled in $6.5 million—the highest figure for any of Disney's animated films since *Snow White*. Even its first feature-length True-Life Adventure, *The Vanishing Prairie* (1955), grossed a respectable $1.8 million.[25]

The most startling evidence of TV's marketing potential came from the studio's experience with Davy Crockett. Disney edited together the "Davy Crockett" episodes that already had aired twice on TV and released them as a feature film during the summer of 1955. *Davy Crockett: King of the Wild Frontier* may have been a typical "program oater," as *Variety* claimed, but it earned another $2 million at the box office because it had been transformed by television into a national phenomenon.[26] The accompanying Crockett merchandising craze gathered steam throughout the year, ultimately surpassing the Hopalong Cassidy boom of the early 1950s. By mid-1955, as "The Ballad of Davy Crockett" climbed the pop music charts, Crockett products—including jeans, pistols, powder horns, lunch boxes, the ubiquitous coonskin caps, and much more—accounted for nearly 10 percent of all consumer purchases for children, with sales figures for Crockett merchandise estimated to exceed $100 million by the end of the year.[27] Disney's apparent golden touch during 1954 and 1955 demonstrated to Hollywood that the studio had tapped into a rich promotional vein by integrating its various activities around television and the family audience.

The *Disneyland* TV program's most significant accomplishment, however, was the fanatical interest it generated in the Disneyland amusement park. Without the growth of national network television and the access it provided to the American family, Disney would not have gambled on the park. "I saw that if I was ever going to have my park," he explained, "here, at last, was a way to tell millions of people about it—with TV."[28] Disney needed television not simply to publicize the park, but to position it properly as a new type of suburban amusement, a bourgeois park designed to provide edifying adventures for baby-boom families instead of cheap thrills for the urban masses. To distinguish his park from such decaying relics as Luna Park at Coney Island, Disney assured the public that any amusement experienced in his park would be tempered by middle-class educational values. Disneyland wouldn't be another park trading in the temporal gratifications of the flesh, but a popular monument to human knowledge, a "permanent world's fair" built around familiar Disney characters and a number of unifying social goals, including educating the public about history and science.[29] The park was inextricably linked to television, because TV enabled Disney to redefine the traditional amusement park as a "theme park." With the assistance of the *Disneyland* TV series, Disney brought discipline to the unruly pleasures of the amusement park, organizing them around the unifying theme of Disney's authorial vision. By invoking cultural memories of Disney films, the TV series encouraged an impulse to re-experience texts that became one of the theme park's central attractions.

Just as it hooked American television viewers with the serialized story of Davy Crockett, the *Disneyland* TV series also bound up its audience in the ongoing story of what came to be mythologized as "Walt's dream." The seriality of *Disneyland*—and its direct relationship to the creation and continued development of the park—was crucial to the program's success. Before Disney, prime-time series were episodic; narrative conflicts were introduced and resolved in the course of a single episode. Open-ended serials were confined to daytime's soap opera genre. Disney certainly wasn't concerned about issues of TV narrative, but the *Disneyland* series demonstrated an incipient understanding of the appeal of serial narrative for network television. The success of the three-part "Davy Crockett" serial was attributable at least in part to its ability to engage viewers in an ongoing narrative. Similarly, with Walt as on-screen narrator, the *Disneyland* series, in effect, narrated the construction of Disney's amusement park, making the project a matter of continued concern for the show's viewers by creating a story out of the construction process and certifying it as the crowning achievement of an American entrepreneurial genius in a league with Thomas Edison and Henry Ford.

No less than three entire episodes, and portions of others, were devoted to the process of conceiving, building, and inaugurating the park. As the climax of the construction process, viewers witnessed the park's opening ceremonies on July 17, 1955, in a live, two-hour broadcast hosted by Art Linkletter, Robert Cummings, and Ronald Reagan. It was only appropriate that the first amusement park created by television should be introduced in a ceremony designed explicitly for television as a media event.[30] The first season of *Disneyland* was a unique type of television text, an open-ended series in which the episodes built toward a final resolution, staged as a television spectacular. By constructing a story around the events of the park's development, and by creating an analogy between the TV program and the park, the Disney organization provided a narrative framework for the experience of Disneyland.

The series represented the transition from the movie studio to the theme park by treating the park as the studio's most ambitious production. In the first episode, "The Disneyland Story," Walt introduces viewers to the park as an idea, shifting constantly between a huge map of the park, a scale-model replica, and stock footage that invokes each of the park's imaginary lands. The first season of *Disneyland,* he explains, will enable viewers "to see and share with us the experience of building this dream into a reality." The second construction episode, "A Progress Report," initiates the journey from the studio to the park as Walt takes a helicopter flight from his office to the new location. This episode also begins the process of identifying Disneyland with the culture of the automobile and the superhighway. Although the transition to the construction site could be managed by a straight cut or a dissolve, the helicopter flight instead laboriously tracks the highway that a typical traveler would follow to reach the park. With Walt providing commentary, the flight depicts both a literal and figurative passage from Hollywood to Disneyland, tracing a path from the Disney studio in Burbank, over the heart of Hollywood, down the Hollywood Freeway, connecting to the Santa Ana Freeway, and finally reaching the Disneyland exit in Anaheim—"a spot chosen by traffic experts as the most accessible spot in Southern California." Once at the construction site, the labor of construction is depicted through fast-motion photography. Accompanied by ragtime music, the scurrying workers driving bulldozers, digging ditches, and planting trees seem like animated figures; their labor takes on a cartoonish quality. In keeping with the tradition of the program's behind-the-scenes footage, Walt pauses to demonstrate how the technical feat of time-lapse photography works, but never addresses the actual labor of the workers whose activities are represented.

The third episode picks up the construction after the park's major structures have been built, as the various rides and special effects are being installed. Again, the series demonstrates how these devices, such as authentic-looking mechanical crocodiles, were designed and created at the Disney studio. This episode establishes a continuity between motion picture production and the creation of the park, demonstrating studio activities that have been reoriented to service the park. The underwater monorail employed to move the submarine in *20,000 Leagues Under the Sea* has become the basis for the Disneyland monorail train; the stage where Davy Crockett recently fought the battle of the Alamo is now the site of construction for the park's authentic Mississippi River steamboat; the sculptors and technicians who created the squid in *20,000 Leagues Under the Sea* are now making a mechanical zoo for the park. Once these devices are loaded onto trucks, they are transported to the park. As voice-over commentary reviews the route, viewers again follow the highway from the studio to the park, making the journey at ground level this time.

Television made the entire Disney operation more enticing by fashioning it as a narrative experience which the family TV audience could enhance—and actually perform—by visiting the park. Here again Disney shrewdly perceived television's ability to link diverse cultural practices that intersected in the domestic sphere of the home. In effect, Walt identified the program with the park in order to create an inhabitable text, one that would never be complete for a television-viewing family until they had taken full advantage of the postwar boom in automobile travel and tourism to make a pilgrimage to the park itself. A trip to Disneyland—using the conceptual map provided by the program—offered the family viewer a chance to perform in the Disneyland narrative, to provide unity and closure through personal experience, to witness the "aura" to which television's reproductive apparatus only could allude.

In a sense, Disney succeeded by exploiting the quest for authentic experience that has become central to the culture of modernity. In fact, tourism, as Dean MacCannell suggests, is based on the modern quest for authenticity, the belief that authentic experience exists somewhere outside the realm of daily experience in industrial society.[31] While Walter Benjamin predicted that mass reproduction would diminish the aura surrounding works of art, Disney seems to have recognized that the mass media instead only intensify the desire for authenticity by invoking a sublime, unmediated experience that is forever absent, just beyond the grasp of a hand reaching for the television dial. As a tourist attraction, Disneyland became the destination of an exotic journey anchored firmly by the family home, which served not only as the origin and terminus of the journey, but also as the site of the television set that would confirm the social meaning of the vacation experience. A father visiting the park expressed something of this sentiment. "Disneyland may be just another damned amusement park," he explained, "but to my kids it's the Taj Mahal, Niagara Falls, Sherwood Forest, and Davy Crockett all rolled into one. After years of sitting in front of the television set, the youngsters are sure it's a fairyland before they ever get there."[32] Television defined Disneyland as a national amusement park, not a park of local or regional interest like previous amusement parks, but a destination for a nation of television viewers. In the first six months alone, one million paying customers passed through the gates at Disneyland; 43 percent arrived from out of state. After the first full year of operation the park had grossed $10 million, one-third of the company's revenue for the year, and more than any Disney feature had ever grossed during its initial release.[33]

Disney's integration of television into the studio's expansive marketing schemes identified television as a worthy investment for Hollywood's major studios. Events leading up to Disney's debut may have suggested to executives of the major studios that they reconsider television production, but only Columbia, through its Screen Gems subsidiary, had acted decisively before Disney's triumph during the 1954–55 TV season. Disney's video success made it apparent that television had become the dominant national advertising medium by the mid-1950s. Providing a channel to an ever-expanding family audience, television could become the most effective marketing tool ever imagined by the movie industry. By following Disney's example and forming alliances with television networks, rather than with advertisers, the studios could ensure their access to the medium without surrendering autonomy to television's traditionally powerful sponsors.

Disney expanded his role in television during Fall 1955 with the premiere of *The Mickey Mouse Club* in ABC's weekday afternoon schedule. With this new program and the ongoing *Disneyland* series, Disney continued to use television mainly as an opportunity for studio publicity. Besides producing a sequel to "Davy Crockett," for instance, Disney created no original programming for *Disneyland* until the 1957–58 season. Disney's concept of "total merchandising" continued to shape the type of text that his company produced for television. Whereas traditional notions of textuality assume that a text is singular, unified, and autonomous, with a structure that draws the viewer inward, Disney's television texts were, from the outset, fragmented, propelled by a centrifugal force that guided the viewer away from the immediate textual experience toward a more pervasive sense of textuality, one that encouraged the consumption of further Disney texts, further Disney products, further Disney experiences. *Disneyland* drew the attention of viewers to the TV text only to disperse it outward, toward Disney products.[34]

Television made possible Disney's vision of "total merchandising" because it gave him the ability to integrate apparently isolated segments of the national commercial culture that developed after the war. In this sense, the entire Disneyland phenomenon may have been the first harbinger of Max Horkheimer and Theodor Adorno's prediction for the apotheosis of the television age, the moment when "the thinly veiled identity of all industrial culture products can come triumphantly out into the open, derisively fulfilling the Wagnerian dream of the *Gesamtkunstwerk*—the fusion of all the arts in one work."[35] By offering the first glimpse of a new Hollywood—in which television profitably obscured conventional distinctions among the media—Disney provided the impulse for the major studios to enter television and a blueprint for the future development of the media industries.

Notes

1. For an account of the post-1952 boom in new television stations, television advertising revenue, and television set ownership, see J. Fred MacDonald, *One Nation Under Television: The Rise and Decline of Network TV* (New York: Pantheon, 1990), 59–62.

2. "This Week in Review," *Time*, 8 November 1954, 95.

3. Katherine and Richard Greene, *The Man Behind the Magic: The Story of Walt Disney* (New York: Viking, 1991), 119; Frank Orme, "Disney: 'How Old Is a Child?'" *Television* (December 1954): 37; "Disney 'Not Yet Ready' for TV," *Variety* (23 May 1951): 5; "Disney's 7-Year ABC-TV Deal," *Variety* (21 February 1954): 41.

4. "The Wide World of Walt Disney," *Newsweek* (31 December 1962): 49–51; "The Mouse That Turned to Gold," *Business Week* (9 July 1955): 74. The origins of Disney's character merchandising are described in "The Mighty Mouse," *Time* (25 October 1948): 96–98. For a more detailed discussion of the Disney corporation's use of character merchandising in relation to other TV producers of the early 1950s, see "He'll Double as a Top-Notch Salesman," *Business Week* (21 March 1953): 43–44.

5. John McDonald, "Now the Bankers Come to Disney," *Fortune* (May 1966): 141.

6. During its initial release, *Snow White* grossed $8 million and became the first movie to exceed $5 million at the box-office. *Gone With the Wind* grossed over $20 million in its first year of release. Richard Schickel, *The Disney Version* (New York: Simon and Schuster, 1968), 229; Ronald Haver, *David O. Selznick's Hollywood* (New York: Bonanza Books, 1980), 309.

7. Schickel, *The Disney Version*, 28.

8. McDonald, "Now the Bankers Come to Disney," 141, 224; Schickel, *The Disney Version*, 308–16; "Disney's Live-Action Profits," *Business Week* (24 July 1965): 78.

9. For a more detailed description of the history of ABC-TV's relations with the motion picture industry during this period, see Christopher Anderson, *Hollywood TV* (Austin: University of Texas Press, 1994).

10. "The Spectaculars: An Interim Report," *Sponsor* (15 November 1954): 31; "Twenty-Five Years Wiser About Show Business, Goldenson Finds TV the Biggest Star," *Broadcasting* (14 July 1958): 84.

11. Herman Land, "ABC: An Evaluation," *Television Magazine* (December 1957): 94.

12. Ibid., 93; "The abc of ABC," 17; "The TV Fan Who Runs a Network," *Sponsor* (15 June 1957): 45. It should be noted that ABC did not possess demographic ratings that would have enabled the network to determine the success of its programming strategy.

13. "Peaches and Cream at ABC-TV," *Variety*, 16 June 1954, 25; "The abc of ABC," 17; Klan, "ABC-Paramount Moves In," 242; Albert R. Kroeger, "Miracle Worker of West 66th Street," *Television* (February 1961): 66; "Corporate Health, Gains in Radio-TV Theme of AB-UPT Stockholders Meeting," *Broadcasting-Telecasting* (21 May 1956): 64; Frank Orme, "TV's Most Important Show," *Television* (June 1955): 32.

14. See Michele Hilmes, *Hollywood and Broadcasting: From Radio to Cable* (Champaign: University of Illinois Press, 1990), pp. 63–72; 78–112.

15. Walt also recognized that the Disney empire needed an identifiable author to crystallize the company's identity for the public, to "personify the product," as *Business Week* once noted. The naming of an author became an issue within the company as far back as the 1920s, when Walt convinced Roy to change the name of the company they had co-founded from Disney Brothers Productions to Walt Disney Productions. Consequently, as the studio expanded in 1953, Walt began to assume a more public persona, hosting the TV program and identifying himself with all things Disney, while diminishing Roy's identity. In 1953—against Roy's opposition—Walt formed Retlaw Enterprises (Walter spelled backwards), a private company which completely controlled merchandising rights to the name Walt Disney. In return for licensing the name to Walt Disney Productions, Retlaw received 5 percent of the income from all corporate merchandise. Since the Disney name was imprinted on everything associated with the company, Retlaw immediately generated enormous wealth for Walt. See John Taylor, *Storming the Magic Kingdom: Wall Street, the Raiders, and the Battle for Disney* (New York: Alfred A. Knopf, 1987), 7, 10.

16. Schickel, *The Disney Version*, 20.

17. "Disneyland Repeats Getting Bigger Audiences Than First Time Around," *Variety* (20 April 1955): 32. A complete filmography of Disney television programs through 1967 appears in Leonard Maltin, *The Disney Films*, second edition (New York: Crown Publishers, 1984), 321–26. For an examination of the Disneyland-inspired Davy Crockett phenomenon that swept through American culture beginning in 1954, see Margaret Jane King, *The Davy Crockett Craze: A Case Study in Popular Culture* (Unpublished Ph.D. Dissertation, University of Hawaii, 1976).

18. Orme, "How Old Is a Child?" 37, 72.

19. Critics within both the movie and television industries sarcastically referred to this episode as "The Long, Long Trailer," after the Lucille Ball-Desi Arnaz film of the same title. See "A Wonderful World: Growing Impact of the Disney Art," *Newsweek* (18 April 1955): 62–63.

20. Schickel, *Disney Version*, 152; "Tinker Bell, Mary Poppins, Cold Cash," *Newsweek* (12 July 1965): 74.

21. Neil Harris, *Humbug: The Art of P. T. Barnum* (Chicago: University of Chicago Press, 1973), 79.

22. Tim Brooks and Earle Marsh, *The Complete Directory to Prime Time Network TV Shows*, Third Edition (New York: Ballantine Books, 1985), 1031. *Disneyland* remained among the top fifteen programs through 1957, and then fell from the top twenty until it shifted to NBC—and color broadcasts—in 1961.

23. Charles Sinclair, "Should Hollywood get it for free?" *Sponsor* (8 August 1955): 102.

24. Maltin, *The Disney Films*, 315.

25. "Disney Parlays Romp Home," *Variety* (30 November 1955): 3; "All-Time Top Grossing Films," *Variety* (4 January 1956): 84. At the time, *20,000 Leagues Under the Sea* was the nineteenth highest-grossing film of all time.

26. Ibid.

27. "The Wild Frontier," *Time* (23 May 1955): 92. Unfortunately for Disney, the studio could not control licensing of Crockett products, because it did not possess exclusive rights to the name or character of Davy Crockett. Since the mid-nineteenth century companies had used the Crockett name on products from chewing tobacco to whiskey. The Disney studio never again made this mistake. See also "U.S. Again Subdued by Davy," *Life* (25 April 1955): 27; "Mr. Crockett is a Dead Shot As a Salesman," *New York Times*, 1 June 1955, 38.

28. Schickel, *The Disney Version*, 313.

29. "Father Goose," *Time* (27 December 1954): 42; "Tinker Bell, Mary Poppins, Cold Cash," 74.

30. For an account of the opening ceremonies, see Bob Chandler, "Disneyland As 2-Headed Child of TV & Hollywood Shoots for $18 Mil B.O.," *Variety* (20 July 1955): 2. Chandler observes that the inauguration of Disneyland marked the "integration and interdependence of all phases of show biz."

31. Dean MacCannell, *The Tourist: A New Theory of the Leisure Class* (New York: Schocken Books, 1976), 159.

32. "How To Make a Buck," *Time* (29 July 1957): 76.

33. Ibid., Schickel, *The Disney Version*, 316.

34. Michele Hilmes describes the use of this strategy in the Hollywood-produced radio program, *Lux Radio Theater*. See Hilmes, *Hollywood and Broadcasting*, 108–10.

35. Max Horkheimer and Theodor W. Adorno, *Dialectic of Enlightenment* (New York: Continuum, 1987), 124.

The Independents

Rethinking the Television Studio System

MARK ALVEY

By 1960 American television was, by and large, Hollywood television. The three networks had solidified their control over prime-time programming during the previous decade, in the process delegating the bulk of production matters to motion picture makers. By the mid-1950s most of the major movie studios were involved in producing series for the small screen, and when the 1960 prime-time schedule was unveiled, over 80 percent of it was generated in Hollywood.[1] With the network-Hollywood alliance cemented, telefilm production established as an integral part of the American film industry, and the filmed series set as the fundamental form of television, the late 1950s has been seen as a period of stabilization, setting the stage for the stasis—both industrial and creative—of the 1960s. As one historian put it, "The economic and programming trends within the TV industry climaxed at the end of the 1950s, giving American television a relatively stable set of commercial structures and prime-time program forms."[2]

Yet the dawn of the 1960s did not mark a point of closure and inertia for commercial television, but rather a transition into another stage of the medium's development, a stage characterized by continuing transformation and redefinition. Indeed, the new decade arrived on the heels of quiz show scandals, a perceived programming crisis, and mounting criticism from both inside and outside the television community. It was virtually inevitable that the industry would enter the new decade in a flurry of conscious and explicit change.[3] This atmosphere of crisis and criticism intensified the creative and commercial stakes in an already competitive arena, and played into the industry's inherent quest for apparent novelty and regulated difference.

Certainly the 1960s witnessed further consolidation of the networks' control over programming—but against a backdrop of shifting Hollywood power relations, marked by the growing status of independent producers, the rise and fall of various major program suppliers, and ongoing struggles for survival among telefilm majors and independents alike. The central role played by the independents has been largely overlooked in the standard scenario of the telefilm's development as essentially a continuation of the Hollywood factory system. Tino Balio, for example, writes that "after the majors entered telefilm production the market underwent consolidation as independent producers either went out of business or merged with larger firms."[4] In fact, independent producers dominated television production during the 1960s. It was in the interests of the networks and indeed the major studios themselves to subcontract production duties, delegating the nuts and bolts of program creation to independent producers, while retaining the considerable financial benefits of distribution—a logical expectation, since the Hollywood majors had shifted to precisely the same model for features. Such a process of "vertical disintegration," as one critic has put it, is a function of "both the externalization of risk and the attempt to exploit a maximum variety of creative resources."[5] By drawing on a range of independent suppliers, the American television industry could re-invigorate programming while minimizing risk and exploiting the established rewards of distribution. The creative tensions of the telefilm era and the competitive dynamics of Hollywood TV, informed by the enterprising efforts of independent producers, ordained that the terrain of 1960s television would be not a sterile expanse of banality, but rather a diverse field for cultural expression, marked by both imitation and invention, convention and creativity.

The Network-Hollywood Axis

Television's shift from a predominantly "live from New York" operation to a largely filmic medium, and the associated rise of Hollywood as the center for television production, has been well-documented over the past decade. A rich body of scholarship has demonstrated the symbiosis between Hollywood and television, and clarified the impact that the small screen had on the movie business. In 1959, *Broadcasting* magazine claimed: "To the movie capital, the dreaded destroyer that they thought TV would be has turned out instead to be the good provider."[6] The reasons for telefilm's rise to dominance are many, but the most important can be summed up in one word: residuals. Where live production was generally a one-shot event, forever lost in the ether, the filmed series was a durable product—with a durable profit potential via syndication. This revenue potential was significant for the networks as well as producers, and proved to be a pivotal factor in the development of the telefilm.

In addition to the promise of residuals, the rise of the Hollywood film industry as the dominant source of television product was also a function of increasing network control over prime-time programming. Throughout the 1950s the networks had gradually been consolidating their hegemony over program scheduling and selection, and the telefilm series offered the networks a greater opportunity for program control, since it could be brokered by networks to sponsors, rather than the reverse (the dominant practice for live shows). By ordering programming from outside producers, networks left the cost and complications of production to an industry already equipped with the infrastructure and resources to produce a polished entertainment product.[7] Both NBC and CBS increased their reliance on filmed series during the late 1950s, cutting back on in-house programming. ABC had already embraced the telefilm, achieving its earliest successes with filmed programming from Disney and especially Warner Bros., which produced a steady diet of westerns and detective series exclusively for that network (e.g., *Cheyenne, Maverick, 77 Sunset Strip, Hawaiian Eye*). NBC went on to establish a similar relationship with MCA's Revue studios, leading to the oft-cited tale of one NBC executive's instructions to a Revue studios vice president: "Here are the empty spots, you fill them."[8] The quiz scandals of 1958 and 1959, coming on the heels of a widely-lamented "crisis" in programming quality, afforded the networks an occasion to further tighten their grip with much rhetoric of "cleaning up" and "taking charge."[9] By dumping the largely New York-based quiz shows, the networks further increased Hollywood's stake in prime time, helping it reach the 80 percent-plus mark noted above.

Once masters of their own time slots, and sometimes producers of their own shows, advertisers were effectively squeezed out of program production and ownership in favor of "participation sponsorship." There can be little doubt of the networks' calculation in this regard, yet there is also no doubt that the economics of the industry played into their hands. Program costs were ever increasing, especially as hour-long shows became more widespread, and the higher costs helped to strengthen the practice of multiple sponsorship. With the price of an hour-long show at $100,000 or more by 1960, few sponsors could afford "a week-in, week-out ride on a 60-min. show," as *Variety* put it. Even those that could came to embrace the wisdom of spreading advertising dollars across several shows. While this strategy sacrificed traditional single-sponsor identification, it minimized risk by increasing the odds of being attached to a hit, and promised a potentially greater audience "reach."[10]

Whatever its ostensible benefit to advertisers, of course, the move to multiple sponsorship further tightened the networks' grip on programming. A few sponsors retained some control over programming in the early 1960s, but shows owned by advertisers were a disappearing breed, *The Andy Griffith Show* and *The Rifleman* being among the last surviving examples. There is no question that sponsors still meddled in production matters and asserted some influence over time slots and content well into the decade, even in shows they did not own.[11] Nevertheless, this influence was relative, and it was quite clear by this time that the networks held ultimate power in programming—not only in terms of scheduling, but, increasingly, in program production matters as well.

As they solidified their control over the schedules, the networks increasingly demanded ownership interests in the series they aired. Typically, they would underwrite pilot and/or series production in return for shares of both first-run and syndication profits. As early as the fall 1960 season, the networks had ownership positions in 62 percent of their prime-time offerings, and the practice became more and more common as the decade progressed.[12] Here again one could argue—as the networks unfailingly did during FCC inquiries into program procurement—that network involvement worked to the benefit of producers and sponsors by reducing their financial risk in pilot production, and that the networks' profit participation was justified by their shouldering of the risk in program development.[13] Of course, their "risk" was relative. If a network-financed pilot was not picked up as a series, the network's investment could be written off; its interests in the rest of the prime-time line-up would offset the expenditures on unsold pilots (and the network's risk was further minimized in those cases in which it chose not to commission a pilot at all).[14] As for the benefits of such arrangements, the payoffs in domestic and foreign syndication, as well as possible merchandising tie-ins, ultimately proved quite lucrative. Clearly, the network position in all such arrangements was reasonably safe and highly profitable.

The networks' reliance on outside program packagers continued during 1960s, and their insistence on profit participations increased, although the network-producer relationships shifted as each of the three "webs" pursued its own strategy of dealing with its suppliers. For the 1964 season *Variety* observed that CBS was casting its "non-patronage plague" on the studios in favor of independent producers, contrasted with ABC's "reliance on the same giant production companies" it had always favored. NBC, on the other hand, was striking a relative balance between independents and "Hollywood factory" deals.[15]

Although by this time the distinction between independents and "majors" in some cases was ambiguous or academic, it is important to recognize that independent producers maintained a significant role in telefilm production in the 1960s. While Hollywood's move into the telefilm business is often reductively glossed as a perpetuation of the old massproduction studio system, or an extension of "B" movie production, the production systems and financial arrangements of the telefilm industry beyond the mid-1950s replicated the new realities of the motion picture business. The telefilm was inextricably bound to the Hollywood system, but it reflected the package-oriented structure of the contemporary film industry more than the studio system of old.

From Minor-Leaguers to "TV Majors": The Independents

Independent production had long been a component of the Hollywood system, but the "Paramount decrees," which forced the major studios to abandon the exhibition side of the film business after 1948, led to its solidification. As a result of divestiture, the "factory" system of film production was replaced by a decentralized model wherein each film was created as an autonomous project. As Thomas Schatz has written, "the studios became primarily *distribution companies,* financing independently produced films . . . shot on sound stages and lots rented from the studio by the independent producer."[16] The same held true for the telefilm. By 1960 the telefilm business was dominated by various forms of independent production and the "packaging" of series on a project-by-project basis, with the major studios serving more often as financiers and distributors than as strict producer-owners.

In feature production an independent was traditionally defined as a firm that was neither owned by a distribution company, nor owned a distribution arm.[17] In television production, the term generally was used to designate firms devoted solely to TV production, or sometimes more narrowly defined as companies that owned no studio facility.[18] Independent television production in the 1960s was characterized by two main systems, primarily distinguished by their respective financing and distribution arrangements: the self-contained firm, and the coproduction deal with an established studio (which might involve one or multiple projects). While the term "independent" does bear some qualification in terms of the power relationships that obtained during this period, in the context of the 1960s telefilm it served to distinguish a new breed of independent operator from the old Hollywood majors.

The earliest of telefilm pioneers were independents in the truest sense of the term—small, entrepreneurial, and unaffiliated with the big studios. During the late 1940s and early 1950s, while the major studios were investigating co-optation strategies such as theater TV and subscription TV, enterprising producers from the margins of the movie industry and related entertainment fields moved into telefilm production, establishing a niche in network and syndicated programming with half-hour anthologies or genre-based series. Most of the self-contained independents shot in rented studio space, financed their own projects (sometimes with network assistance), and distributed their own product under their own logos.[19] Many independents established a solid foothold in production before the motion picture majors entered the field in 1955.

While not all of the pioneering independents survived (e.g., Jerry Fairbanks Productions folded, Ziv Television was absorbed by United Artists), many thrived. Desilu, for example, went from shooting the *I Love Lucy* pilot on a rented soundstage in 1951 to purchasing the entire RKO studio facility in 1957, becoming one of the medium's top suppliers by the early 1960s with shows such as *The Untouchables, The Lucy Show, The Greatest Show on Earth,* and *The Lineup.* Four Star was dubbed a "TV major" by the trades in 1962, with six shows in prime time (down from a peak of twelve in 1960); its output included *The Rifleman, Burke's Law, Honey West, The Rogues,* and *The Big Valley.*[20] Many other early independents also retained a solid presence as telefilm manufacturers well into the 1960s and beyond, in some cases launching distinctive program dynasties, e.g.: Bing Crosby Productions (*Ben Casey, Breaking Point, Hogan's Heroes*); Danny Thomas/Sheldon Leonard's T and L Productions (*The Danny Thomas Show, The Dick Van Dyke Show, The Andy Griffith Show, I Spy*), and Filmways (*Beverly Hillbillies, Mr. Ed, Petticoat Junction, Green Acres, The Addams Family*). Smaller companies with smaller inventories also continued to operate in the shadow of the major film studios during the decade, among them Rod Serling's Cayuga Productions (*The Twilight Zone*), Herbert Brodkin's Plautus Productions (*The Defenders, The Nurses*), Jack Chertock Productions (*My Favorite Martian, My Living Doll*), Don Fedderson Productions (*My Three Sons, Family Affair*), and Jack Webb's Mark VII (*Dragnet '67, Adam-12*). The fortunes of such unaffiliated operators shifted during the decade, but they maintained a steady and important role in the industry, holding their own with the majors to account for a significant share of prime-time product.

As such self-contained independents flourished, others found success through coproduction with established Hollywood powers. Many of the majors opened their doors to independent partnerships in the mid-1950s, mirroring the increasingly dominant practice in feature production, a practice that bloomed in the 1960s. In such cases the studio provided financing, studio and office space, postproduction facilities, and distribution services, while the outside producer supplied the concept, hired the talent, and coordinated the production. Columbia's TV division, Screen Gems, first adopted this practice in 1954, about the same time as the leading TV major, Revue; MGM and United Artists followed around 1960, as did 20th Century-Fox in 1964. Of the Hollywood movie studios active in television production, only Warner Bros. remained closed to independent deals until the mid-1960s. It should be stressed that Screen Gems, MGM, Fox, and Revue continued to produce and distribute wholly owned projects as well, while United Artists confined its television output exclusively to coproductions (as it did with its features). In-house independents during the 1960s included Herbert Leonard, whose *Route 66* and *Naked City* were distributed by Screen Gems; Norman Felton's MGM-based Arena Productions (*Dr. Kildare, The Lieutenant, The Man from U.N.C.L.E., The Eleventh Hour*); Irwin Allen's science fiction factory (*Lost in Space, Voyage to the Bottom of the Sea, Land of the Giants*), associated with 20th Century-Fox; Leslie Stevens's Daystar, distributing through United Artists (*The Outer Limits, Stoney Burke*); and of course Alfred Hitchcock, whose Shamley Productions (*Alfred Hitchcock Presents, Suspicion*) was headquartered at Revue. The prolific Quinn Martin (QM Productions) was more explicitly "independent," striking three co-production deals with three different studios for 1965: *The Fugitive* with UA-TV, *Twelve O'Clock High* with 20th Century-Fox, and *The F.B.I.* with Warners; likewise, David Susskind's Talent Associates teamed up with various partners during the 1960s, including UA (*East Side, West Side*), Paramount (*Get Smart*), and CBS (*He and She*).

To further qualify the relative independence of these producers, one could distinguish between those that used talent agencies to handle the selling of their products (e.g., Talent Associates, Arena, Daystar) and those that didn't (e.g., Leonard, Martin). While talent agents had been involved in the packaging of series from television's earliest days, they became key players in the 1960s, as they were hired with increasing frequency as packagers and/or selling agents for self-contained firms and writer-producers. After 1960 it became increasingly common for independent producers to retain talent agencies to broker their network deals, and/or put together entire series projects—another byproduct of divestiture and "the package system." In the feature film arena, the agency "came to perform the same function as the studio of old," writes Schatz, as mass production gave way to individual packages, with writers, directors, and actors no longer bound to studio contracts.[21] Although the agencies did not consolidate their power in features until the mid-1960s, agency packaging of television series was well in place by the beginning of the decade as unaffiliated producers and small independents struggled to maintain a stake in the industry. Moving beyond mere talent representation, agents now brought together producers, writers, and performers in series packages, or in some instances represented existing packages to networks, in return for a ten percent commission on the entire package price (around $100,000 per episode for a one-hour show in 1960).

Although they were less visible to the public, the agencies became as powerful in the telefilm business as the Hollywood majors. As the parent company of Revue Productions since 1952, MCA was the largest de facto agency-packager in the business (and remained so until a 1962 consent decree forced the firm to divest its talent arm). And as early as 1957, William Morris and General Artists together represented over fifteen hours on the air. In some cases, talent agencies even brokered coproduction projects for producers in league with established Hollywood powers (e.g., Arena at MGM and Daystar at UA), especially when one or more of their clients were involved as above-the-line personnel.[22] The agencies also were recruited by some of television's key independent "majors": Four Star signed William Morris as selling agent for its entire product line in 1956, and four years later the venerable agency had twenty-five shows booked in prime time (nearly half of them Four Star entries). Similarly, General Artists was hired to represent Desilu's program sales beginning in 1961.[23] Ashley-Steiner, with an established reputation as a "literary" shop, concentrated on putting together prestige packages such as *The Twilight Zone, Dr. Kildare, Mr. Novak,* and *The Defenders,* going on to become one of television's leading packagers after MCA's 1962 breakup. By 1963 the talent agencies' television divisions were their biggest and most profitable components. The Morris agency estimated that it drew 60 percent of its commissions from its television projects (including talent and packaging), while Ashley-Steiner confirmed that its television division was the firm's largest, and its major source of income.[24]

By the early 1960s, television was dominated by independent production and "package deals," accounting for nearly 70 percent of prime-time fiction shows by 1963.[25] Admittedly, as small outfits like Desilu and Four Star became top suppliers of prime-time product, and as producers teamed up with old-line majors or powerful agents, the term "independent" became more and more ambiguous, and sometimes meaningless in any "alternative" sense. Likewise, the ostensible autonomy of any producer during the 1960s was further qualified by network financing and ownership interests in many shows, and strong relationships between particular suppliers and networks. Independent producer Lee Rich (Mirisch-Rich), for example, argued that independent firms like Filmways and Talent Associates were in fact "house companies" because of their close relationship with CBS.[26]

Still, neither a partnership with a major studio nor a network development deal guaranteed longevity in the television production game. Under network deficit-financing arrangements (whereby a producer sold a show below cost in anticipation of residual revenues), even "house companies" were gambling—and the syndication profits they hoped for, of course, were increasingly being divided with the networks. Independent suppliers operated at the whim of the market, and it was a market that had only three buyers. Producer-network relationships were notoriously tenuous and network buying patterns could be unpredictable. A self-contained firm was only as stable as its last hit, and one package sale did not guarantee another. Rod Serling's Cayuga Productions managed to mount only one post-*Twilight Zone* series project during the 1960s. Perhaps as a result of its long-standing refusal to cut the networks in on foreign and domestic syndication, Four Star went from being a "TV major" with twelve network shows in 1960, to a single prime-time slot in 1963, to receivership in 1967. Filmways found itself with no program base when CBS "purged" its rural-slanted programming in 1970, ending the studio's bucolic sitcom reign. (On the other hand, David Susskind of Talent Associates went from damning the networks in the 1950s when his programming was "out," to praising their vision in the mid-1960s when he had several shows in prime time. Within a year of forecasting oblivion for independent producers, Lee Rich himself had formed Lorimar Productions and went on to great success in the 1970s and 1980s with shows like *The Waltons* and *Dallas*.)[27] By the end of the 1960s, all of the powerful movie giants, as well as telefilmeries like Desilu and Revue, were involved in coproduction ventures with "in-house" independents.

The Open-Door Policy: The Majors

Although their fortunes fluctuated from year to year, the major studios not only survived but flourished in the 1960s; yet the fact that those familiar Hollywood logos continued to mark a significant share of television fare during the decade was due in large part to the fact that they opened their doors to independents. It had not always been so. During the mid-1950s the studios conceived of television as an adjunct to the feature film business, rather than a site for autonomous, differentiated texts. The earliest TV projects from the majors—for example, *MGM Parade, Warner Bros. Presents, 20th Century Fox Hour*—promoted the studios' new big-screen releases and/or offered small-screen remakes of old features. The film factories' blindness to the need for innovation is not surprising, perhaps, when we recognize that the studio era was just winding down, and the majors were just beginning to shed the residual practices of their mass production days.

The telefilm track record of these three Hollywood majors is revealing. MGM and Fox first tested the TV production waters in 1955, but their earliest efforts were short lived, and the two studios subsequently sold fewer than a half-dozen series combined by the end of the decade.[28] Significantly, both of these Hollywood powers opened their doors to coproductions as part of their retooling efforts, supporting both in-house projects and joint ventures. MGM geared up in 1961 under a new television production chief, making several network sales. Its single hit that season, Arena Production's *Dr. Kildare,* helped turn around the television division's fortunes, and by 1963 MGM ranked among TV's top suppliers. As for Fox, most of its remaining prime-time inventory was canceled in 1961; soon after, the entire studio underwent reorganization, and for the next two years the studio's role in television production was that of a rental space. But in 1964 the studio staged a comeback with a program line-up that included *Daniel Boone, Voyage to the Bottom of the Sea, Twelve O'Clock High,* and the seminal prime-time soap opera *Peyton Place.*[29]

Warner Bros., on the other hand, became the definitive example of the dangers of "assembly line" thinking, as it continued its factory system of production, maintaining its roster of contract players, writers, directors, and producers, eschewing outside deals until the late 1960s. Rigidly bound to its conception of television as a formula-genre medium, Warners stuck to its original telefilm path of westerns and private eyes until it was too late. Admittedly, much of the responsibility for the studio's rigid reliance on the same formulas was the conservatism of its network partner, ABC, which demanded almost literal carbon copies of previous hit shows. By 1963, after ABC had begun to broaden its programming menu, Warners had only two series in production (a western and a private eye yarn). The studio made an ill-fated attempt to diversify into the sitcom arena in 1965; its single success, the cavalry-and-Indians sitcom *F-Troop,* was canceled in 1967, the same year the studio was acquired by Seven-Arts, a television distributor. By the end of the decade the only program being distributed under the familiar Warner Bros. banner, *The F.B.I.,* was in fact a coproduction with independent Quinn Martin.[30] If nothing else, the Warner's example suggests that the assembly line approach to television production was outmoded, and that its closed system limited the studio's potential for innovation.

The telefilm fortunes of the other major film studios fluctuated during the 1960s, but most maintained a fairly successful output. Columbia-Screen Gems, the first of the Hollywood majors to embrace full-scale television production, maintained a steady spot in the upper ranks of telefilm producers throughout the decade. In contrast to Warners, the varied menu of programming offered by Screen Gems through its coproductions (*Father Knows Best, Rin-Tin-Tin, Naked City, The Donna Reed Show, Route 66, The Flintstones*) and its wholly-owned shows (*Bewitched, The Flying Nun, The Partridge Family*) suggests that inviting joint ventures offered more variety to a studio's output than maintaining a closed system of in-house production. MGM and Fox, after their initial struggles, solidified their positions among the top telefilm producer-distributors, with MGM going on to produce or coproduce hits like *Medical Center* and *Flipper* (as well as misses like *Please Don't Eat the Daisies* and *A Man Called Shenandoah*), and Fox turning out (solely or in partnership) such projects as *Julia, Room 222, Judd for the Defense,* and *The Ghost and Mrs. Muir.* Paramount, barely active as a telefilm supplier during the early 1960s, save as a partner in David Susskind's Talent Associates (and later, Herbert Brodkin's Plautus Productions) and as a rental studio (notably for NBC's *Bonanza*), did an about-face in 1967, when its new parent conglomerate, Gulf+Western, bought Desilu. Paramount very soon became a significant force, playing host to a mix of wholly-owned projects and joint ventures, including *Star Trek, Mission: Impossible* (both inherited from Desilu), *Mannix, Get Smart,* and *The Brady Bunch.*[31] By contrast, when United Artists merged with Transamerica Corp. the same year, it was already out of the telefilm business, having begun to phase out its television production activities after all of its proposed series were rejected by CBS in 1965.[32]

The one constant among the majors during the decade was the presence of MCA's Revue studios (known as Universal TV as of 1964) at or near the top of the hierarchy of powerful telefilm producers. An observation made by *Television* magazine in 1963 held throughout the decade: "In Hollywood the major film studio always has been known as the big one. Revue studios is the big one in Hollywood these days and it's getting bigger all the time."[33] The studio, which had pioneered hour-long shows in the 1950s, and the 90-minute format in the early 1960s (*Wagon Train, Arrest and Trial,* and *The Virginian*), also generated hit sitcoms (*McHale's Navy, The Munsters*), while remaining the industry's leading supplier of drama series throughout the decade with such programs as *The Name of the Game, It Takes a Thief, Ironside, Marcus Welby, M.D.,* and *The Bold Ones.* Universal initiated an even greater lock on prime-time hours in 1966 when it developed made-for-TV movies for NBC.[34]

Despite being "the big one," Universal's television division was far removed from the Hollywood factory system of old. It, like MGM, Fox, and Screen Gems, retained a vital role in the industry by embracing rather than eschewing coproduction, benefiting the studios with an infusion of ideas—as well as overhead—not possible under the factory system preserved by Warners. As Christopher Anderson has suggested, the other studios thrived because they diversified their programming, distribution methods, and financing and production arrangements, while Warners, with "an astonishingly narrow definition of the television business," continued to rely on one type of product, one customer (ABC), and one system of financing and production.[35] Acting as partner-distributors for a variety of independent producers, the old guard Hollywood studios as well as TV majors like Desilu and Four Star were able to reap the benefits of a more diverse product line in a highly competitive market.

Independents and Innovation

While imitation is a staple strategy in popular culture production—nowhere more obvious than in television—product differentiation is also essential to market strength and profitability, in television as in any industry. Media scholar Joseph Turow, drawing on organizational and "production of culture" sociology, has suggested that "a firm is much more likely to produce innovative products when it or its environment experiences tension-inducing changes"—in competition, technology, distributors' demands, and government policy.[36] No industry is fraught with more such tensions than the television industry, and no period in the medium's history is more apt an example of such an environment than the late 1950s and early 1960s. As *Variety* reported in late 1959, networks and producers were busily seeking alternatives that would free them from "the quiz-violence-western hook."[37] In the prevailing climate of the television industry as the 1960s began, the calls for innovation could not be ignored. This atmosphere of change and differentiation established a tenor that would characterize the evolution of programming throughout the decade. Reaction to the Warner/ABC-inspired western-crime formats sparked a shift from the action-adventure to "people drama," in the words of one trade reporter, as producers and networks embraced character study, social realism, and topical issues (*Naked City, Route 66, Bus Stop, The Defenders, Dr. Kildare, Slattery's People,* and *East Side, West Side*). Many producers were "presenting anthologies in the guise of more orthodox series" in an attempt to "circumvent" continuing-character conventions, according to *Television* magazine—a form dubbed the "semi-anthology" by *Variety*. The early 1960s even saw a "modest renaissance" in New York production, sparked by an easing of bureaucratic and union restrictions, improvements in studio facilities, and most of all, the success of *Naked City* and *The Defenders.*[38] The medium's more frivolous fare also changed, as the wholesome, well-scrubbed sitcom families of the late 1950s were replaced by a host of bizarre, supernatural, or surreal clans (*The Beverly Hillbillies, The Addams Family, Bewitched*), and the heroic marshalls and trailhands gave way to suave spies (*The Man from U.N.C.L.E., I Spy*) and caped crusaders (*Batman, The Green Hornet*). Granted, most of these innovations were incremental, and aside from controversial or "downbeat" social dramas like *The Defenders* and *East Side, West Side,* most were safely commercial. But they were innovative nonetheless.

Admittedly, the concrete strategies for upgrading and diversification of television fare were constrained by the conservatism inherent in the medium. While the industry condemned imitation, it also feared radical innovation.

Producers tended to place most of the blame for the imitation problem at the feet of networks and sponsors, who (the suppliers argued) tended to reject the new and different and stick with the tried and true. Yet at the same time producers understood sponsors' reticence to stray too far from established successes, given the large sums at stake.[39] The producers, on the other hand, had more to gain by gambling with innovation, to set themselves apart from the crowd of concepts and pilots being pitched each season.

It is evident that the entry of independent producers on the telefilm scene contributed a measure of innovation and diversity when compared to the rigidly controlled factory mode of production like that at Warners. Even early independent products like *I Love Lucy* and *Dragnet,* while hardly radical—both were, in fact, radio spinoffs—were nonetheless stylistically and formally groundbreaking for their time. Whether driven by creativity or desperation, independents—both in feature films and telefilms—were willing to take chances that the convention-minded and tradition-bound studios often were not.

This view was affirmed within the industry. Dick Dorso of United Artists, which was devoted exclusively to independent projects, cited diversity of product as a key benefit of the coproduction system. "The independent producers make it possible to attain a full dramatic spectrum of production, from comedy to documentaries to hour-long dramas," Dorso claimed. In addition, he argued, the independent coproduction arrangement appealed to "talented producers" because deals were made on the basis of specific projects, generally of their own conception, unlike the studio contract system "where producers are assigned to projects they may or may not have enthusiasm for."[40] With the studios acting primarily as distributors, the independent producers retained a degree of creative autonomy from the front office—sometimes total, often contractually guaranteed—promising at minimum the freedom from a conservative "house format" (à la Warners), and at best, the freedom to take chances.

CBS-TV president James Aubrey, who favored independent packages during his tenure (1959–1965), framed the independent producers' inducements for quality and creativity in more practical financial terms. "Independent producers are not more capable than major studios," he argued. "But individuals who are involved with the creation of a show tend to remain with that show. And if they have an ownership deal, they have an incentive to devote more time and energy to its success than if they were on the staff of a major studio." In Aubrey's view, "the factory process cannot work in creative areas."[41]

While we should be cautious in attaching to "independent" producers any mythic implications of rebellion or artistic commitment, it is important to interpret the independent label, as it was used in the 1960s, as a marker of distance and autonomy from the feature film majors. If nothing else the term signals a recognition of significant changes among the studios and the "outside" producers, and an acceptance of the new configuration of the industry in postwar Hollywood.[42] Further, there can be little doubt that much of the change and innovation that marked the industry during the 1960s was due in great part to the competitive efforts of independents.

Hollywood has always been adept at exploiting "conventional innovation." As David Bordwell has written, "Hollywood itself has stressed differentiation as a correlative to standardization."[43] In the context of 1960s television, innovative practices and strategies must be viewed primarily as attempts at product differentiation aimed at achieving competitive advantage in the program-selling marketplace. The independent producer had to differentiate to survive, had to distinguish his product from the competition. Granting that independent production is an avowedly commercial enterprise, concerned with producing popular texts for a large audience, the evidence suggests that the independents were testing the limits of convention and expanding the horizons of popular television entertainment, albeit within fairly circumscribed formal limits. At minimum, independent production can be said to have broadened the creative possibilities within the given narrative and ideological constraints of the industry at the time. Indeed, the "programming crisis" of the late 1950s was due in some measure to the entrenched ideologies and practices of the old studio system (e.g., Warner's western/action cycles), while the drive for differentiation was in large part a function of the "New Hollywood."

Fade-Out

As the 1960s drew to a close, majors and independents alike were competing in a business driven by the Nielsen ratings and programmers' whims. The market for series had actually been shrinking throughout the 1960s due to the increase in longer-form programs and the growing population of feature films and made-for-TV movies on network schedules. Five network "nights at the movies" by 1966 meant ten less hours of prime time for television producers to fill, and although some observers declared that the studios' feature packages were competing with their own series products, the profits from an extant feature film library obviously held many advantages by comparison to the uncertainty involved in developing new series projects.[44]

As available time slots shrank, network power grew. The major studios had a hand in generating much of what America watched on prime time during the 1960s, but even these titans of tinseltown had to pay their tribute to their de facto "partners," the networks. As the decade wore on, the networks not only tightened their hold on scheduling, but expanded their authority in program ownership and even production. By 1964, for example, CBS was not only insisting on profit positions in most of the programs it carried, but creative control as well. Network profit participation in prime time was nearing saturation. Whereas in 1960 the networks held profit participations in 62 percent of their prime-time line-ups, by mid-decade the figure had risen to 91 percent.[45] In 1965 the FCC issued a proposal, known in the industry as the "50–50 rule," that would have barred the networks from owning or controlling more than 50 percent of prime-time non-news programming, prohibited them from owning interests in independently produced shows, and severed their involvement in domestic syndication. The rule was debated by the commision, networks, producers, and advertisers throughout the latter half of the decade, ultimately taking shape in 1971 as a set of restrictions known as the Financial Interest and Syndication Rule.[46]

Even with the network's monopolistic grip on programming, and despite some pessimistic prognostications, the independents survived. By the fall of 1971, the bulk of prime-time series were still being generated under familiar Hollywood banners—Universal, 20th Century-Fox, Paramount, and Screen Gems—but all were in league with independents. Smaller firms continued to play a significant role in the new era, although many of the names had changed: Filmways, T & L, and Talent Associates had given way to the likes of Leonard Freeman (*Hawaii Five-0*), MTM Enterprises (*The Mary Tyler Moore Show*), Tandem/TAT (*All in the Family*), and James Komack (*Welcome Back, Kotter*).[47]

Television programming at the end of the 1960s looked very different from the way it had at the beginning, in some respects. The decade was, admittedly, a time of continued imitation and business-as-usual as well as innovation and change. Action-adventure flourished on ABC throughout the decade, western heroes still wandered the video frontier (albeit in smaller numbers), and *Dragnet* even returned in 1967. Lucy, Matt Dillon, and Ed Sullivan all survived well into the 1970s. Time, and television, bore out critic Gilbert Seldes' 1956 observation that "the seesaw between repetition and originality will probably be a permanent characteristic of television."[48]

Nonetheless, the 1960s was a period of flux for American television, both formally and industrially. The structural changes in the motion picture industry influenced the evolving systems and shifting fortunes of independent producers and established Hollywood majors as they struggled to maintain a viable presence in program production. The prevailing climate of crisis in which the decade had begun, fraught with perceived mediocrity and genre overload, and the industry's self-imposed sense of responsibility, resulted in explicit ongoing attempts at differentiation in the telefilm series. As it was in the 1950s, and as it is today, television's forms and the television industry were in transition.

Television, then as now, was a business of regulated innovation, and nowhere is this more clearly evidenced than in the evolution of television's storytelling strategies. The economic mechanisms that determine the life and form of popular TV narrative dictate that television must change in order to survive. Producers and networks are involved in a constant process of redefinition, attempting to strike the right balance of entertainment and ideas, familiarity and innovation, continuity and flexibility. The simple imperative of product differentiation, driven by a belief in the audience's desire for novelty, decreed that the telefilm circa 1960 had to diversify. Innovation in this environment was borne of industry pressures and desperation, a product of brainstorming, spitballing, recombination, imitation, theft, *bricolage*, and, on occasion, originality and creativity. And at the end of the decade television was still in flux, reinventing its dramatic forms as part of its ongoing efforts to navigate the creative and commercial imperatives of standardization and innovation. To say that the early 1960s was a period of differentiation is to isolate one moment in the ongoing process of differentiation that characterizes the entire history of television storytelling. To propose that the decade was dominated by the Hollywood telefilm demands the recognition that the telefilm itself was a varied textual phenomenon, and that it continued to evolve.

As yet there has been little in the literature to indicate that American television between the late 1950s and early 1970s was anything but homogeneous, formulaic, static, violent, and/or idiotic. Not so distant historically, and still so familiar via syndication, '60s TV is easy to take for granted. As we tend to accept received assumptions about program forms (e.g., 1960s as escapist wasteland), so do we affirm too easily stock accounts of television's development. Claims of the stability of the industry and its programming after 1959 give only the broadest outlines of the processes and practices at work during a remarkable period of change. Television was stable insofar as Hollywood largely dominated the telefilm, but still quite dynamic in terms of who dominated Hollywood. Obviously, this is complicated territory, which will be fully understood only cumulatively, one step—one case study—at a time. At this stage it may be enough to acknowledge the overarching hegemony of the networks while recognizing the significant role of independent producers and the shifting power relationships within the industry during the 1960s. The questions that emerge as we look more closely at the industry and its products suggest that there is still much to discover about what 1960s television—as industry and as artifact—really was.

Notes

1. Morris J. Gelman, "The Hollywood Story," *Television* (September 1963): 33.

2. William Boddy, *Fifties Television* (Urbana: University of Illinois Press, 1990): 2.

3. "Is There a Programming Crisis?," *Television* (February 1957): 50–52, ff.; "A Need for Innovation: Levy," *Variety* (30 September 1959): 23; "Aubrey of CBS: A New Era Ahead," *Television* (September 1959): 58 ff.; Murray Horowitz, "Vidfilmeries' Soul-Searching," *Variety* (29 November 1959): 31; Harold Hackett, "A Plea to Widen TV's Horizons for More Creativity," *Variety* (1 January 1960): 80.

4. Tino Balio, ed. *Hollywood in the Age of Television* (Boston: Unwin Hyman, 1990): 35

5. Kevin Robins, "Reimagined Communities? European Image Spaces, Beyond Fordism," *Cultural Studies* 3 (May 1989): 152. Also see Michael Curtin, "On Edge: Culture Industries in the Neo-Network Era," in Richard Ohmann, ed., *Making and Selling Culture* (Hanover, NH: Wesleyan University Press, 1996).

6. "Hollywood in a Television Boom," *Broadcasting* (26 October 1959): 88–90. Some important recent scholarship on Hollywood-TV symbiosis includes: Robert Vianello, "The Rise of the Telefilm and the Networks' Hegemony Over the Motion Picture Industry," *Quarterly Review of Film Studies* 9 (Summer 1984): 204–18; William Boddy, "The Studios Move into Prime Time: Hollywood and the

Television Industry in the 1950s," *Cinema Journal* 24 (Summer 1985): 23–37; Douglas Gomery, "Failed Opportunities: The Integration of the U.S. Motion Picture and Television Industries," *Quarterly Review of Film Studies* 9 (Summer 1984): 219–28; Michele Hilmes, *Hollywood and Broadcasting* (Urbana: Illinois, 1990); Tino Balio, ed. *Hollywood in the Age of Television* (Boston: Unwin Hyman, 1990); and Christopher Anderson, *Hollywood TV: The Studio System in the Fifties* (Austin: University of Texas Press, 1994).

7. As Vance Kepley has noted apropos of NBC, that company's emphasis on outside suppliers allowed it to minimize risk, cut overhead costs, and streamline its operations. Vance Kepley, "From Operation Frontal Lobes to the Bob and Bob Show," in Balio, ed., *Hollywood in the Age of Television*, 54. On the similar CBS strategy see William Boddy, "Building the World's Largest Advertising Medium: CBS and Television, 1940–1960," in the same volume, 78–80.

8. The "empty spots" story is repeated in Boddy, *Fifties*, 238; Hilmes, 66; Kepley, 55; Laurence Bergreen, *Look Now, Pay Later* (New York: New American Library, 1980), 229; James Baughman, *The Republic of Mass Culture* (Baltimore: Johns Hopkins, 1992): 88.

9. See, for example, "CBS Eye on 3 Areas," *Variety* (18 November 1959): 27.

10. "Plateau on Hour Film Shows," *Variety* (24 February 1960): 27. See also "King-Size 'Bread & Butter'," *Variety* (13 February 1957): 29, 71; Murray Horowitz, "Hour Vidpix Yen Still Hot," *Variety* (4 November 1959): 27; "Why the Rush to Hour-Long Shows?," *Broadcasting* (17 April 1961): 108–9.

11. George Rosen, "Kintner: We'll Take Charge," *Variety* (11 December 1963): 21. See also "Magazine Concept a Panacea for Program Evils? Hardly," *Variety* (25 November 1959): 32; "Who Controls What in TV Films," *Broadcasting* (17 October 1960): 29–36.

12. See also "Co-Financing on Pilots Continues to Pose Problems," *Variety* (18 November 1959): 30. On network control and ownership see "CBS: If We Play 'Em, We Own 'Em," *Variety* (30 March 1960): 25; "The Swing to Network Control," *Broadcasting* (16 May 1960): 92.

13. For the network line on their "risk" in program development see "Swing to Network Control," 93; "For TV Networks: A Long Day In Court," *Television* (March 1962): 72–102.

14. For the fall of 1964, CBS-TV president Aubrey ordered only eight pilots (compared to 20-plus at the other networks), and was considering most series on the basis of scripts or treatments. George Rosen, "A to Z: (Aubrey to Zanuck)," *Variety* (4 December 1963): 17. Richard Oulahan and William Lambert, "The Tyrant's Fall That Rocked the TV World," *Life* (10 September 1965): 96. According to Kepley, NBC eventually began ordering MCA product without pilots. With the right track record, a producer might sell a series without a pilot; see Deborah Haber, "In the Wings," *Television* (January 1964): 38–41, 68–70.

15. Rosen, "A to Z."

16. Thomas Schatz, *Old Hollywood/New Hollywood: Ritual, Art and Industry* (Ann Arbor: UMI Research Press, 1984): 172. For an essential examination of independent feature production before and after the decrees see Janet Staiger, "Individualism vs. Collectivism," *Screen* 24 (July–October 1983): 68–79. Also see Staiger's Chapter 24, "The Labor Force, Financing, and the Mode of Production," in David Bordwell, Janet Staiger, Kristin Thompson, *The Classical Hollywood Cinema* (New York: Columbia University Press, 1985): 317–19, and Chapter 26 on the Package Unit system, 330–337.

17. Staiger, "Individualism vs. Collectivism, " 68–69.

18. Thus the designation excluded the feature film "majors," but included producers partnered with the majors in financing and distribution deals. See Edwin H. James, "The Boss is His Brightest Star" *Television* (September 1962): 50; and "Six Studios Big in Network TV," *Broadcasting* (13 August 1962): 59.

19. Early independents included the likes of Hal Roach (Laurel and Hardy and *Our Gang* veteran), Frederick Ziv (radio syndicator), Jerry Fairbanks (Paramount short subjects producer), and General Television Enterprises (former movie executives). Performers-turned-producers also entered the field around 1951–52, with notable success: Desi Arnaz and Lucille Ball's Desilu, Jack Webb's Mark VII Productions, Bing Crosby Enterprises, Ozzie Nelson's Stage 5 Productions, and Four Star Television (formed by Dick Powell, David Niven, and Charles Boyer). On early independents see Hilmes, *Hollywood and Broadcasting;* Balio, ed. *Hollywood in the Age of Television;* Boddy, "The Studios Move into Prime Time"; Anderson, *Hollywood TV.* Trade sources on independent TV production, in addition to those cited above, are Gelman, "Hollywood Story"; *American Cinematographer,* especially "Television Filming Activities" and "Current Assignments" columns, 1949–1968; and Broadcasting magazine's "Detailed Look at Fall Schedules" columns, 1960–1965.

20. "Six Studios Big in Network TV," 59. For a useful account of Four Star's genesis, via a profile of Dick Powell, see James, "The Boss is His Brightest Star."

21. Schatz, *Old/New,* 172.

22. "Above-the-line" denotes the creative talent involved in a project: writers, directors, performers, producers. "Below-the-line" personnel are the craftspersons and technicians.

23. Background on the talent agencies' role as TV packagers is derived from "Who Controls What in TV Films," 29–36; "How the Big Talent Agencies Operate," *Broadcasting* (24 October 1960): 70–81; "Financial Outlook 'Good' for Film Production Companies," *Telefilm* (September 1961): 10; Albert Kroeger, "Veni, Vidi, Vici. [Closeup: Ted Ashley]," *Television* (April 1963): 67–80; Deborah Haber, "The Men From Morris: All the Talent Isn't on Stage," *Television* (September 1964): 2–7.

24. "The Men from Morris," 3; Kroeger, "Vini," 70.

25. "A Detailed Look at Fall TV Schedules," *Broadcasting* (27 June 1960): 34–5; "Who Controls What in TV Films;" Gelman, "Hollywood Story."

26. "TV Film Makers Headed For Oblivion?," *Broadcasting* (3 April 1967): 110.

27. On Four Star see James, "Boss is His Brightests Star," 62; "Four Star Goes to Syndicate," *Broadcasting* (21 August 1967): 58; on Cayuga see Joel Engel, *Rod Serling* (Chicago: Contemporary, 1989); on the CBS rural purge see Les Brown, *Television: The Business Behind the Box* (New York: Harcourt Brace Jovanovich, 1971); Susskind is interviewed in "Says the Critic," *Television* (April 1963): 58–9, 90–100.

28. In addition to *20th-Century Fox Hour,* Fox produced *My Friend Flicka* in 1955, followed by *Dobie Gillis, Adventures in Paradise,* and *Five Fingers* (all 1959); the 1960 and '61 Fox menu included *Hong Kong, Follow the Sun, Margie* and the widely excoriated *Bus Stop.* After *MGM Parade,* Metro sold two feature retreads, *The Thin Man* (1957), and *Northwest Passage* (1958), followed in 1960 by *National Velvet* and *The Islanders.* MGM's other 1961 offerings were the short-lived *Cain's Hundred, Father of the Bride,* and *The Asphalt Jungle* (Spring '61 only).

29. Deborah Haber, "The Studio That Came in From the Cold," *Television* (September 1965): 32; Gelman, "Hollywood Story"; *American Cinematographer* columns, 1949–1968; *Broadcasting* "Detailed Look" columns, 1960–1965.

30. "Who Controls What"; Gelman, "Hollywood Story." The whole Warners TV story is told in fascinating detail in Anderson, *Hollywood TV.*

31. "Desilu, Famous Players to G & W," *Broadcasting* (20 February 1967): 71.

32. Les Brown, ed., *Les Brown's Encyclopedia of Television* (New York: Zoetrope, 1982): 129.

33. Gelman, "Hollywood Story," 38.

34. Morris Gelman, "A $15-Million Gamble on Movies Made for TV," *Television* (December 1966): 42, 54–62.

35. *Hollywood TV,* 257.

36. Joseph Turow, "Unconventional Programs on Commercial Television," in *Individuals in Mass Media Organizations,* ed. James S. Ettema and D. Charles Whitney (Beverly Hills: Sage, 1982): 108.

37. "Situation Comedy Comeback," *Variety* (18 November 1959): 29.

38. On "people drama" and New York TV see Morris Gelman, "New York, New York," *Television* (December 1962): 39–45, ff. On the "semi-anthology" see Gelman, "The Hollywood Story," 51; George Rosen, "TV Debut: 'No Mischief' Season," *Variety* (5 September 1962): 1, 30; "TV Anthologies Hit Peak With 8 in 1963–64," *Variety* (26 June 1963): 27.

39. See, for example, Leon Morse, "The Hollywood Viewpoint," *Television* (May 1960): 77.

40. Gelman, "Hollywood Story," 53.

41. Albert R. Kroeger, "Iron Fist Less Velvet Glove," *Television* (March 1964): 52.

42. It should be stressed that "independent production" in this context refers to a form of production that is firmly implicated in the structures and practices of the Hollywood movie-making business—what might be termed mainstream independent production—rather than the current usage of low-budget, self-financed, alternative filmmaking, operating outside of and sometimes in opposition to mainstream business and formal practice. Mainstream independent production is an alternative to the studio system, but it is not an alternative to the Hollywood mode of production; rather it is a component and a version of it, and it operates within the conventional and qualitative norms of dominant commercial filmmaking. As Janet Staiger has pointed out, commercial independent production "has reproduced the dominant practices of Hollywood." "Individualism vs. Collectivism," 69.

43. *Classical Hollywood Cinema,* 70.

44. "Hollywood's Hot New Romance," *Broadcasting* (10 January 1966): 27–30; "$93 Million Week's Film Jackpot," *Broadcasting* (3 October 1966): 25–27.

45. "CBS Control: Not So Remote," *Variety* (19 February 1964): 27; "Aubrey's Show Business Credo," *Variety* (25 March 1964): 26; "Swing to Network Control," 92; "The 'Three Men' Theme," *Time* (12 March 1965): 81.

46. See: "'Three Men' Theme"; "In Defense of Network Programming," *Broadcasting* (7 March 1966): 31–33; "Another View on 50–50 Rule," *Broadcasting* (7 March 1966): 34–35; "50–50 Rule gets a Lashing," *Broadcasting* (2 May 1966): 36–38; "Coup d'etat for 50–50 Proposal?," *Broadcasting* (6 June 1966): 52–54; "50–50 Fades," *Broadcasting* (27 February 1967): 5. On the "fin-syn" rules see "FCC Ruling a Boon, But . . . ," *TV-Radio Age* (1 June 1970): 23; J. Fred MacDonald, *One Nation Under Television: The Rise and Decline of Network TV* (New York: Pantheon, 1990): 184–6.

47. Brown, *The Business Behind the Box,* 358.

48. *The Public Arts* (New York: Simon and Schuster, 1956): 181–82.

Feeding Off the Past

The Evolution of the Television Rerun

PHIL WILLIAMS

Up and down the dial, day and night, the television rerun glows as a rarely appreciated byproduct of mass culture. Within the television industry, however, the rerun is a product in and of itself. For more than four decades, the marketing and programming practices surrounding the rerun have evolved, first cautiously, then by aggressive leaps and bounds. The stories of the rerun's evolution form particularly revealing, and mostly unnoticed, chapters in the history of American television.

"No Sound Reason": Concept and Practice

As the new medium of television stood at the edge of exponential growth at mid-century, valuable precedents for repetition were provided by the film and radio industries. Hollywood, since Edison's day, had battled for profits along aggressive distribution and exhibition lines. This competition, waged among a handful of industry giants, was conducted on a weekly basis. Repeat audience attendance was desirable, but maintaining a constant flow of individual patrons week after week remained a greater priority.

From *Journal of Popular Film and Television*, vol. 21, no. 4, Winter 1994. Reprinted with permission of the Helen Dwight Reid Educational Foundation. Published by Heldref Publications, 1319 Eighteenth St., N.W., Washington, D.C. 20036-1802. Copyright © 1994.

Until World War II, reissues were infrequent. As the supply from the studios ebbed during the war years, however, a small syndication industry appeared on Hollywood's perimeter. These companies met the demand of theatres searching to round out double features and Southern movie-houses, where twin bills had never flourished to the extent that they had elsewhere. Consequently, these films could be promoted as first-run products (Pryor B3; "Film Classics" 15). After the war, anti-trust decrees pushed the uncertain majors increasingly toward reissues as a means to supplement the continued decline in first-run product. In 1947, the entire industry released 53 reissues, 105 in 1948, and 136 in 1949 ("Box Score" 6; "Reissues Ease" 7).

Wartime exigencies also unleashed the possibility of sustained broadcast repetition in the radio industry. Programmers had had 16-inch disk recordings at their disposal since the dawn of the industry in the 1920s. Yet these program recordings were expensive, frequently marred by cracks and scratches, and—due to FCC requirements that such shows be identified as a transcription—thought to be anathema to audiences. The effective development and application of tape in Armed Forces Radio broadcasts promised to solve these difficulties and, indeed, the networks turned to magnetic tape recorders after the war.

Still, the transition was not immediate. ABC and Mutual began recording their broadcasts in 1946. CBS and NBC, fearing dead air mishaps, waited until 1948. ABC and NBC, also in 1948, were the first networks to opt for the new taping systems. These delays were partially attributable to the cost of taping machinery, which, unlike the actual tapes, remained formidable. More important, audience acquiescence to taped programming remained in doubt. Not until 1950 was the public's acceptance of the technology conventional wisdom within the industry. By that time, the ascendancy of television had thrown the established radio industry into disarray. The veterans of radio programming who flocked to the new medium brought a developed appreciation of taped broadcasts. Whether the broadcasts could be re-aired remained in doubt (Baughman, *The Republic* 67; "Disks Catch On" 68–69; "Transcription Boom" 58–59; "Tape" 52).

The issue, in fact, had been addressed a decade earlier before conflict relegated the nascent television industry to a dormant state. These observers adopted the existing logic of Hollywood: Television would be dependent upon filmed programming—and such programming could not be rerun. In a 1939 *Public Opinion Quarterly* piece, Jack Western argued, "Rarely does a moviegoer see a film more than once. There is no reason to believe that the looker will consent to see a telecine transmission more frequently. Afterwards, the film must be relegated to the vaults." A year later, NBC President Lenox R. Lohr echoed these concerns: "It appears to be inadvisable to broadcast most programs more than once. On the second broadcast, the audience is likely to become hypercritical and to lose interest" (qtd. in Boddy 67).

Despite earlier predictions, the industry, led by the networks, did not adopt filmed programming during its first explosive years. This was both a measure of preference—film was viewed as having greater production costs—and necessity—the networks were not yet willing to strike deals with Hollywood. The result was the live programming, with each show airing 52 weeks of the year, that defined the medium's mischievous Golden Age.

It was also during this brief era that local stations enjoyed their most autonomous moments. The networks' daily schedules were limited, coaxial cables remained on the drawing board, and local advertisers proved eager sponsors of the new medium. One result of this relative freedom was the hours of cooking shows, talent showcases, and interview programs that were produced.

Another result—given the costs associated with the production of live programming—was a scramble by the stations for additional material. This product, the first influx of filmed programming into the medium, was supplied by the young television syndication industry. The role of Hollywood in the development of this industry—production units and aged stars flocking toward the networks as the film industry staved off Supreme Court rulings and witch hunts—has been well documented (Baughman, *The Republic* 77–90; Boddy 132–54). For the rerun's purpose, however, the resulting product and its applications deserve examination.

First, syndicators offered movie packages. Stations, as an analyst indicated in 1950, were particularly eager for Hollywood features: "The surest bet in television programming is sponsorship of Hollywood movies and westerns. No other category has consistently come up with such high ratings at such low cost" (Kugel 15). Until the mid-1950s, when lasting unions between the networks and Hollywood were struck, the flow of features consisted of badly dated efforts from lesser studios.

Battling to meet the expectations of hundreds of thousands of new TV sets, the quality of these films became something of a moot concern. Moreover, the supply was limited and, in bidding scrambles, a considerable strain was placed on even the healthiest station's budget. Almost immediately, local stations re-aired these features, pausing afterwards to provide justification. "Let's concede that television is in the fortunate position of finding itself the recipient of the products of an established medium and being able to adapt these for its own needs," stated Carol Levine, film supervisor of New York's powerful independent station WPIX in 1953. Levine's adaptive strategy was the station's First Show, an attractive movie aired Monday to Friday in the 7:30 to 9 P.M. time slot, with a fresh feature introduced each Wednesday. Ratings, she noted, had "shown a tendency not to suffer appreciably on reruns, and . . . the individual cost of each showing is considerably lower" (89).

In addition, syndicators marketed independently produced filmed series—the "westerns" that spellbound the 1950 insider—to the local stations. At this stage of the industry the syndication companies faced competition from the networks. As early as 1950, CBS had migrated "upstream" to produce series such as *Strange Adventure* and *The Gene Autry Show* for distribution (Kugel 16).

But the bulk of syndicated programs came from independent companies. Of these, Ziv Television Programs was the most successful. Ziv's success suggests that the burgeoning television syndication industry was as indebted to radio as it was to the film colony. Formed in 1937, Frederick W. Ziv Inc. boasted 24 programs on 850 radio stations, generating a gross of $10 million (a dollar amount questioned by competitors) when its founder decided to strike at television a decade later. Throughout the 1950s, Ziv rolled out one stock action half-hour program after another—*The Cisco Kid, Boston Blackie, Highway Patrol, Mr. District Attorney,* and *I Led Three Lives.* As an independent syndication company, Ziv needed a substantial capital outlay to begin operation, faced increasing production costs, and had to be aware of competition in pricing its products. As a result, the revenue generated by repeated showings quickly became necessary to earn a profit ("Transcription Boom" 58; "Millions" 44, 48–49; Moore).

Stations discovered—as they had with movies—that re-airing syndicated series did not necessarily equate with lost viewers and advertisers. *Television Magazine* answered its February 1954 article "Are Re-Runs a Good Buy?"

> There's no valid argument against the re-run concept, if the show is good and used properly. The record shows that it is possible for a return engagement program of almost any type to reach a sizable audience, comparable to that of high-rated network programming. (24)

The "record" received further support from the A. C. Nielsen Company. Surveying 254 repeat broadcasts from the 1953–1954 season, Nielsen concluded that the audience share dropped only 9 percent from the original broadcasts while the average minutes of viewing time fell 6 percent ("Nielsen" 30).

In assessing rating successes, industry insiders saw reruns as proof of the public's love affair with television. At times, especially from syndicators, the vision was an upbeat, if faintly sadistic one. Saul J. Turell, president of Sterling Television, stated in 1952, "We feel people not only can take an indefinite amount of film, but never tire of the same film, if it's good. One of ours, *Sandy,* has been shown in N.Y. alone 37 times, and the stations obviously are happy with it" ("Syndicated Film" 63). Others drew attention to the explosive demand for the medium. As early as 1950, distributor Robert D. Wolfe noted, "Running a film a year after its first run, the sponsor can reach millions who missed the first showing, or have bought their sets since then" ("Trend" 12). WPIX's Levine drew a comparison to a suddenly endangered Hollywood: "Reissues are money in the bank for movie production companies. There is no sound reason why the same principle cannot be applied to television" (93).

Network Summer: "Some People Just Have to Watch Television"

As regional programmers and their syndicated partners backed into programming repetition, the networks gravitated toward the economics of the summer rerun. Production costs, especially for the favored live productions, became increasingly difficult to bear over a 52-week run. Quickly, 39 weeks of original programming became the norm, and the summer lull was mostly populated with less costly variety shows.

In a spirited defense of local programming, WSB-TV assailed this phenomenon in an advertisement in the 25 June 1951 issue of Broadcasting. Under the heading "No Summer Doldrums in Atlanta," the station reminded the potential advertiser: "The primary interest of WSB-TV is still audience . . . and lots of it. Despite the normal difficulties of summer programming (hiatuses, replacements, and replacement for replacements), WSB-TV has resisted the take-it-easy convenience of network scheduling." WSB's clients, instead of substandard network fare, were treated to locally produced programming (*Broadcasting* 67).

The networks countered such budding heresy. CBS and NBC launched "Operation Summer" in 1951 to retain sponsors. Rates were cut and NBC provided a brochure reporting that, for sponsors who stayed with the network through the 1950 summer, "an idle summer became a summer idyll" as "virtually all piled up more TV homes during the summer months than they had during the April, May and June just preceding" ("'Operation Summer'" 62).

"Operation Summer," however, proved an ineffective campaign. *Broadcasting* reported in its 13 August 1951 issue that "June marked the first sign of a summer decline in TV network billings comparable to the traditional summer slump of radio broadcasting" as the combined gross sales for the four networks fell from the May total of $10,011,144 to $8,996,940 ("June" 72).

Such numbers, and the growing suspicion that alliances with independent production facilities—if not the major studios—would prove more cost effective than the growing inflexibilities and expenses associated with live programming, provided the impetus to finally accept filmed programs. The direction was sensed by one analyst in the 10 September 1951 issue of *Broadcasting*: "While the networks continue to talk up live TV shows, the fact remains that they are in the foreground of film production, either present or future" (Glickman 94). Led by such sitcoms as *I Love Lucy* and *The Adventures of Ozzie and Harriet,* the movement toward film steadily progressed. By the 1956–1957 season, 44 percent of all network primetime programming was on film ("Now—More" 54). Four years later, the total stood at 83 percent (MacDonald 118).

Filmed programs were adaptable for virtually any programming needs. And, by the time *TV Guide* editorialized on the subject in September 1956, filmed reruns had replaced live replacement shows: "Not too many years ago the networks were using the summer months as a try-out time for different kinds of programs. Now they save their 'different' shows for their regular winter season." However, repeats or not, viewers remained glued to the set: "Some people just have to watch television and if only reruns are on, they watch reruns" ("As We See It" 2).

Film was still a rather rare commodity in the first years of the summer repetition. Many reruns were remnants from previous seasons. Highlighting the resurrection of ABC's failed 1956 sitcom *Hey, Jeanie,* CBS's 1959 summer flop *Peck's Bad Girl,* and the drab 1957 NBC play *Wedding Present* for the 1960 summer, *Newsweek* struck an already familiar chord: "'April is the cruelest month,' wrote T. S. Eliot, but obviously he never reckoned with television in June, July, and August. This TV summer is shaping up as a wasteland of stupefying familiarity . . . and . . . neither quality nor popularity necessarily has anything to do with the choice of revivals" ("Thirsty" 92).

Lacking competition and facing increasing production costs—the $50,000 cost of the average half-hour and the $100,000 cost for the average hour in 1960 doubled by 1973—deeper cuts occurred in original programming (Davidson 8). In 1960, the networks began to offer only 26 weeks of original programming. When, a dozen years later, this number fell to 22 or 24 weeks, the summer rerun inched into March.

Only the emergence of competition from cable and the Fox network forced the established networks to consider fewer reruns.[1] John Severino, ABC president, told *Broadcasting* in 1983, "We can't kid ourselves. We can't think we can go into summer reruns and still retain the audience" ("New Network" 35). Seven years later, Warren Littlefield, an executive vice president at NBC Entertainment, confessed to an industry gathering, "We've put crap on the air in the summer. That's got to change" ("Networks Promise" 52).

The networks were good to their promises. During the 1991–1992 season, reruns accounted for 17 percent of NBC's programming, 16 percent of ABC's, and 9 percent of CBS's (significantly, the young Fox network had the highest total at 26 percent). Specials had chipped away at the rerun base. CBS's share of such programming had risen to 31 percent (a figure inflated by the 1992 Winter Olympics and a seven-game World Series that helped the network win the season's rating sweepstakes) while specials accounted for 11 percent of NBC's slate, 10 percent of ABC's, and 8 percent of Fox's. Furthermore, the networks increasingly aired reruns in non-sweep periods outside the summer. In December 1991, for example, reruns accounted for 27 percent of the total programming for the four networks. In December 1982, this figure stood at only 4 percent. The number of original program episodes had rarely increased but, relegated to non-sweep periods and often preempted by specials, reruns began to disappear from the warmer months (especially in the sweep periods of May and July). The summer rerun had, slowly but steadily, become an endangered species ("Study Blames" 36; Mandese 54).[2]

The Impact of the Off-Network Strip

The American television viewer also became familiar with another brand of rerun in the mid-1950s: off-network strips, the showing of a previously broadcast network program five times a week in a particular time slot. It appears that the first strip was *Amos 'n' Andy*, available to local stations in the fall of 1953 after concluding a two-year run on CBS (Ely 239–42; "Hot Market" 27). Another early off-network product was NBC's *My Little Margie*. After a three-year network run, Official Films began to market *Margie*'s 126 episodes in the fall of 1955. WPTZ, a Philadelphia independent looking to compete against CBS's strong daytime lineup, was one such buyer. The contract was for two-and-a-half years, allowing for five showings of each episode. Reporting on WPTZ's use of *Margie*, *Television Magazine* noted a "most satisfactory" initial return on the sponsors' investment and concluded, "The key to the economics of this daytime strip, as it is to the financing of all syndicated films, is the rerun. And as long as the rerun is delivering satisfactorily, the advertiser is getting a good buy" ("'Nighttime'" 77–78).

Strips took off. *Broadcasting*, surveying 60 markets, concluded that combined network and independent strips rose from 440.5 hours per week in 1956 to 800.5 hours per week in 1957 and to 1,070.5 hours per week in 1958 ("Syndicators Off" 162). Still, the real growth had not occurred. After only seven network programs totaling 423 half-hours were released for syndication in 1960, "the flood of 1961" brought 23 programs totaling 1,528 half-hours and 146 hours into the marketplace by July of that year ("Hot Market" 27). Before the pace finally slowed in 1964, 100 network programs hit the market in a five-year period ("Off-Network Scarcity" 52).

The impact was tremendous. The networks grabbed many of the most valuable commodities for their daytime programming, beginning a trend that introduced many of the best loved reruns. The most famous, *I Love Lucy*, first appeared in CBS's daytime schedule on 5 January 1957, where it ran for almost eight years before it was cast toward the open market (Simon 51).

For individual stations, especially the independents, the off-network strip was an even greater blessing. A network product, usually deemed a superior product, could grab a better time period, was more attractive as a proven product, and was more durable in reruns than a syndicated offering. More important, perhaps, the product existed. Unless a package contained approximately 100 half-hour episodes, the minimal optimal six-month run was impossible. Shorter, more frequent cycles, the stations had discovered, would usually exhaust both audience and advertiser ("Timebuying" 17).

For the syndicator of non-network programming, this was a considerable hurdle to pass. If fortunate enough to possess an adequate cache of episodes, the syndicator faced the equally difficult task of selling an increasingly unattractive product to a substantial number of markets to fully recoup production costs. Locked into this cycle, independent syndicators usually responded by cutting costs, falling further and further behind.

Therefore, as a 1961 Broadcasting survey indicated, a "virtual breakdown in new production for syndication" resulted ("Program Sources" 20). From a 1956 high of 29, the number of first-run series offered by independent syndicators plunged to six five years later with little indication that the trend would be halted ("Hot Market" 27). On the other hand, network programming, now mostly produced by powerful Hollywood studios, survived by largely defining the industry's economies of scale. This network/studio alliance, and the reruns that it left in its wake, virtually destroyed the independent syndicator.

In addition to the syndicated product, the well of theatrical films, even as the vaults spilled open, was also running dry. In August 1956, *Broadcasting* estimated that half of the 12,000 to 14,000 old features had been released. Because television's appetite for these films was still increasing, it was noted that the source might be exhausted by 1962 ("Films for Fall" 40).

The journal was only slightly more optimistic five years later, predicting that the backlog would be "substantially" exhausted by the end of 1964 and completely exhausted by 1967 ("Will First-Run Films" 27). The networks, by that time, began to produce their own "TV movies." For individual stations, however, it was, as Albert Kroeger observed in the April 1964 *Television Magazine*, "a seller's market and distributors tell balky station buyers, 'Haven't you heard? There aren't any more movies behind this batch.' And they're right" (96).

As the supply of non-network syndicated programs and the first-run movie backlog evaporated, it was becoming increasingly difficult for individual stations to produce their own programming. Again, the industry's economies of scale were the deciding factor. Bernard Smith perceptively argued in a 1962 *Harper's* piece that:

> It is a fallacy to think of TV as chiefly a medium for "local" talent and interests. . . . Good TV programming is just too expensive for the resources of a single station, and it is getting costlier all the time. Nor will the local advertiser foot the bill. A local Chicago program, for instance, can reach less than 5 percent of TV homes in America. For it an advertiser will not pay more than 5 percent of what he would pay for a national network show.[29]

Although never abundant, quality local programming became the exception to the rule.

In the decade following the debut of *My Little Margie* on WPTZ, therefore, a hierarchical programming structure took firm root. At the peak was network programming—increasingly filmed and limited to half- hour sitcoms and hour-long westerns or adventure series. The networks netted the best of this material after its original run for their own use during the daytime and, after these shows lost their luster, they were released to individual stations where they were aired yet again. But most off-network shows went straight to the WPTZs of the dial where the rerun was no longer the hesitant, almost humble, force of the early 1950s. On the local level, the abundance and popularity of strips were quickly driving, either by direct competition or indirect opportunities, other forms of programming—syndicated non-network shows, movies, and local productions—from the playing field.

"Freezing the Wasteland"

Few moments capture the essence of the New Frontier more convincingly than FCC Chairman Newton Minow flaunting the sins of television's "vast wasteland" at the podium of the 39th Annual Convention of the National Association of Broadcasters on 2 March 1961. For several years, a flow of indictments from disgruntled postwar liberals, an increasingly disenchanted viewing public, and those displaced by the industry's film wave had been targeted at the medium. [3] Minow's rallying call to arms led aspirations for a richer and more informative medium into uncharted areas of federal regulation. As the FCC moved forward on two fronts to improve first-run programming, the promises inherent in greater competition quickly cemented the hierarchical programming structure and the reruns that largely defined it for the next two decades.

A day before his speech to the NAB, Minow spoke to John Bartlow Martin of the *Saturday Evening Post:*

> We're only using twelve channels, Two through Thirteen. We could use thirty more, the ones in the ultrahigh frequency band. It's the only way to increase competition in television. If we used the ultrahigh frequencies, you might have ten or twelve stations in Chicago instead of four. (Martin 64)

The history of UHF television had taken a decisive turn when, during the closing months of World War II, the FCC froze the development of UHF channels until 1953. When the freeze was lifted, only a third of all televisions produced in the United States could receive UHF signals. Consequently, many of the stations that set up shop past channel 13 after the freeze hoping to lure audiences away from the network affiliates and established independents of the VHF spectrum faced an uphill battle for survival. Within two years 123 of these stations folded and the number of televisions that could tune in UHF fell to 15 percent ("Hopes Fade" 27). By the time the 1962 All-Channel Act requiring all domestic televisions to have UHF capabilities was passed, there were 85 UHF stations in operation and five million of the 55 million sets in the U.S. could receive such signals ("TV Trade" 40).

Two years after the "wasteland" speech, Minow, claiming that "the time has come for more than speeches," again addressed the NAB convention. While a UHF dial, under the terms of the All-Channel Act, would not be mandatory on sets produced in the United States until 30 April 1964, Minow saw a number of roles it could play. These included an educational network, a system of pay TV, and a base for a fourth network. He also envisioned a relationship between "first-run" VHF network affiliates and "second-run" affiliates on the UHF dial. The first-run stations would air original network programming; the UHF second-run stations would allow the public "a second chance to see the best the networks have to offer" and a scattering of foreign programming. Moreover, in such a system, advertisers unable to afford network fees could find a new source, program costs could be more effectively amortized, and producers could receive additional rerun fees ("Minow Proposes" 60).

Minow's salesmanship was effective. *Broadcasting* reported that the growth of UHF stations had been "the single brightest development in the syndication industry" in 1966, as their total sales had quadrupled since 1965 and grown to 10 percent of the total domestic syndicated market ("U's Newest" 31). There were 265 UHF stations by the end of the decade and 60 percent of all sets could tune them in ("UHF Band" 61). A number of these stations provided bilingual, public affairs, and quality foreign programming. Also, the UHF dial served as a friendly habitat for struggling educational channels. The majority of these new stations, however, veered toward the second-run path, using off-network reruns and syndicated film packages to fill most of their programming day. The base of the hierarchical programming structure had been widened considerably, creating more demand for the off-network product.

The discrepancy between Minow's original vision of UHF and the vaster wasteland that it largely led to illustrates the ineffectiveness of the FCC as a means to an end of better television in the early 1960s. One obstacle was the holdover commissioners from the Eisenhower years who represented a daunting majority. This bloc, Minow quickly discovered, would support rulings that forwarded increased competition as a solution to the industry's programming shortcomings but balked at any direct interventions by the federal government. Also, haunted by the agency's fumbling of the UHF question in the early 1950s, the entire commission was tentative and inconsistent in its efforts a decade later (Baughman, *Television's Guardians* 153–59).

But, in fact, Minow's FCC was largely unconcerned with reruns and, insofar as they prospered in the wake of the agency's actions, their growing role in American television. Nowhere in the "wasteland" address did the chairman allude to reruns. Rather, in an era of quiz show scandals, hordes of derivative westerns, and fewer and fewer "quality" efforts such as *See It Now* and *Omnibus,* Minow had captured the essence of existing criticism in damning the networks. Building tangible regulatory legislation from this base was not only unpalatable to the entrenched Eisenhower appointees but a policy of initiating showdowns with corporate America was unlikely to gain approval in Camelot. Consequently, Minow's vision of increased competition was one of promise: Prisoners to an unimaginative programming hierarchy in the short run, it was possible that, in the long run, the young UHF stations could gain firm financial footing and pose an alternative from below.

The FCC also began to struggle with the question of how much involvement the networks should have "downstream" in the syndication market. As early as 1957, the agency issued studies concerning the vertical reach of ABC, CBS, and NBC. When concrete proposals came in 1965, the networks promptly joined forces to counter the threat. First, they claimed that their share of the syndicated market amounted to only 12 percent of the total, down from 25 percent in 1958 ("In Defense" 33). Second, they launched a prolonged legal campaign to protect what *Broadcasting* called "an estimated $30 million-a-year bonanza" ("$30-Million Plum" 26). The networks staved off the threat until 1 June 1973. By then CBS, considerably more involved in the syndicated market than ABC or NBC, had created a corporate spin-off, Viacom, to handle the network's syndication and fledgling cable efforts.[4] In 1971, its first year, Viacom pulled in almost $21 million in revenue from these two sources, a figure that increased eightfold by 1980 ("Viacom" 32).

With the onset of the Reagan deregulatory revolution, the FCC, under the captaincy of Mark Fowler, moved to strike the syndication rulings from the books. Again, legal action and lobbying ground legislation to a halt. A break came in 1991 when a U.S. Court of Appeals ruled that the law was unconstitutional and, after yet several more delays, the networks were allowed, on 1 April 1993, to reenter the syndication market (Jessell 7, 10).

Convoluted even by FCC standards, the push to remove the networks from the syndication market had a great impact on the development of the rerun. Although they could, and did, pressure producers to grant them distribution rights, the networks' first priorities were ratings and advertising revenues.[5] Whether a program remained on the air long enough to prove attractive as a product for off-network stripping was, at best, a secondary concern.[6] In fact, a quickening of cancellations in the late 1970s and early 1980s in the face of competition from other programming sources contributed to a crucial drought in the off-network market.

For the producers who capitalized on the FCC's rulings against the networks, the length of a program's run on the networks was the greatest of concerns. The production of network programming was, and remains, a deficit-financed operation. Broadcast fees from the networks covered only part of production costs. Reruns brought a break-even point or, if the program enjoyed a lengthy network run, profits as stations would eagerly bid for a popular series with enough episodes to ensure successful stripping.[7] Large producers, such as Universal and Paramount, or independent syndication companies, if the producer lacked the resources to follow operations downstream, were left to scavenge fiercely as the networks weathered and then fell to the FCC's fire.

The insights of those who occupied the industry's trenches reveal what was at stake as the FCC began to fumble with the UHF and syndication dilemmas. Several months after Minow's indictment of the networks, *Broadcasting* surveyed industry leaders for their opinions of the crossroads where American television had arrived:

"If we have a wasteland in television programming now," said one station executive, "then what we're doing is freezing the wasteland for a long time to come." Another put the same thought in this way: "What we're doing is perpetuating the 'sameness' in television programming and stretching it out over a longer period of time. If a western is taken off the network and put into syndication and then is replaced on the network by a new western, what you have is summer reruns 40 times over." ("Program Sources" 20)

As the off-network programming chokehold continued, such prognoses became more pessimistic. In the aforementioned 1964 Kroeger piece, Jay Faragan, program director and film buyer for WFLA Tampa, reckoned that, of the rerun cycle, "The audience will get used to it and we'll get by with it—for a while, but without a doubt we're going to have to come up with something new." Samuel S. Carey, holding the same positions at WRVA Richmond, warned, "The end of the road is coming on rerunning reruns . . . shows like *My Little Margie,* run in local time for years, are wearing out. Once they could maintain most of the audience, but no more" (Kroeger 102–4).

"I'd Sell My Soul for a Half-Hour"

Audiences and stations were, however, increasingly locked into a rerun cycle as FCC actions led to the crystallization of the hierarchical programming structure. Network programming had not been improved and the syndication industry broke from the gate at a breakneck pace that has not diminished to this day. It is this competitive force that has defined the rerun's role in television over the last three decades.

Immediately after the flood of off-network programs glutted the market in the early 1960s, the flow slowed to a trickle. After 30 shows hit the market in 1963, only 19 became available in 1964 and 12 in 1965 ("Syndicators Confident" 68; "Off-Network Bonanza" 25). Although the number rose again in 1966—with 22 shows offered—variances of supply in this era were exacerbated by other factors ("Syndicators Have" 100). Residual payments increased as the Screen Actors Guild contracted concessions from the Association of Motion Picture and Television Producers during union/industry showdowns and as actors, writers, and directors with the greatest leverage independently struck even more costly payment schedules ("Those TV Reruns" 62; "Color Tones Up" 69). Also, starting in 1966, syndicators began to scramble for color off-network programs as the American viewer began to demand the fruits of this long-awaited breakthrough ("Color Tones Up" 69).

With quality color products a scarcity, contingency selling became the norm. Richard Wollen, vice president of programming of Metromedia Television, introduced this strategy in 1967. Seeking to purchase top-notch off-network products for the stations under the Metromedia umbrella, he grabbed *The Man From U.N.C.L.E.* and *Mission Impossible* while the shows were in the midst of their network run. The latter was an especially risky move because the show had only been on the air for 10 weeks. As Wollen told *Television Magazine* a year later: "If *Mission* had run only one season I would have had my neck out. . . . But my instincts told me it was too good to run only one season. I just figured this thing has got to be a barn burner and it's going to run at least two years and maybe four" ("What Stations Want" 63). Six years later, Wollen's gamble bore fruit and Metromedia's stations, rather than their competitors, possessed the program for stripping.

Contingency selling, however, threatened to dampen the appetite of stations. In waiting for a program to conclude a lengthy network run before picking up rerun rights, datedness might offset the show's popularity with viewers. An ingenious solution was not long in appearing. In 1973, Louis Friedland, chairman of MCA's syndication efforts, as *Forbes* told the story five years later, had a bright idea. Why not, he reasoned, take a series while it was going strong on the network and sell its reruns for a definite delivery date in the future? "Before, stations didn't get a shot at a show until it had been publicly executed," says Friedland. "They were prepared to pay much more for something that might still be punching it out when they got it." (Jaffee 98) Thus, *Happy Days, M*A*S*H, All in the Family,* and *Laverne & Shirley* led the way in what Forbes concluded had become "a true futures market in this most volatile of entertainment commodities" (Jaffee 98).

For individual stations, the risks, now dictated by the possibility of an early cancellation, increased accordingly. Production companies, seeking to offer a safer product and combat a new off-network drought in the early 1980s, responded in a twofold manner. First, in 1983, the production runs of two canceled network shows with only 63 episodes apiece, *Fame* and *Too Close for Comfort,* were continued. Revenues were quickly garnished from both selling the first-run property and by marketing a larger, and thus more attractive, package for stripping ("How Independents" 62). Second, larger companies, as Paramount did with *Family Ties* and *Cheers,* began to guarantee—for which they extracted a surcharge from stations—a certain number of episodes. If the networks canceled such programs, they would follow *Fame* and *Too Close for Comfort* into non-network production runs ("The World of TV" 55). Yet, no less than they had been in the early 1950s with an independent product, local stations were as resourceful as their syndicator partners in molding the off-network strip as a programming tool. On the networks, such programs had been primetime entities molded by the nobility of American mass culture—network executives and Hollywood producers—with the aggressive intent to grab the attention of advertisers by capturing the loyalties of the public. On their off-network run, the appeal of these programs to advertisers was far more powerful than the cartoons and unsophisticated syndicated programs they replaced ("Off-Network Bonanza" 26).

Therefore, in an ironic turn consistent with Minow's aspirations for the UHF dial, increased dependence on the off-network rerun provided an opening for independent stations to make a bid for the entire adult market. After solidifying the hierarchical programming structure, the rerun emerged as a threat to its health. Specifically, this threat was counterprogramming: the running of attractive off-network strips by independents in the early fringe period (5 to 7:30 P.M., 5 to 8 after 1971 when the FCC forced the networks to give the 7:30 to 8 slot back to their affiliates) to compete with the network news and other non-primetime programming of the affiliates.

An NBC study of the early 1980s traced the damage that counterprogramming inflicted upon its affiliates. From a 7.4 share in 1971, the average UHF independent's early fringe ratings rose to a 13.5 share in 1982 ("Independent TV" 26).[8] In 1981, Bud Hirsch, a vice president in NBC's sales division, told *New York* that, in the nation's largest market, "The independents, predominantly WNEW and WPIX, keep growing every season, and I'm worded. . . . They are mainly successful now in the 6-to-8 P.M. slot, when they can program reruns of *M*A*S*H* or *Laverne & Shirley* against local and network news. We just can't compete with independents in that period" (Nobile 26).

Advertising revenues followed the ratings. In 1972, for the first time, the average UHF channel turned a profit ("UHF" 35). All independents earned a combined $7 million in profits in 1973; by 1977 the amount leapt to $131 million (Jaffee 98). In 1984 there were 193 independents, twice the number of 1979 ("Happy Days" 74).

In this wildly competitive environment the price of the off-network product rocketed. When *I Love Lucy* first became available to local stations in 1967, WNEW paid just over $4,300 per episode (Jaffee 98).[9] WPIX, in 1976, paid $35,000 for each episode of *Happy Days* (Mariani 27). Two years later, 33-year-old Randy Reiss, a vice president for domestic syndication at Paramount, launched the *Laverne & Shirley* campaign. Labeled "one of those upwardly mobile types whose nervous stomach could no longer accommodate 16-ounce steaks at expensive Manhattan restaurants" by *TV Guide,* Reiss knew that the show would be especially desirable to stations seeking to take on competitors who had snatched up *Happy Days* (Mariani 27). The show was also powerful enough to become a station's "hooker spot," forcing advertisers to buy packages that included time for less-attractive spots in addition to the precious *Laverne & Shirley* presence. Reiss set the minimum bid at $50,000 for New York stations; other markets, as is the case with syndication sales, would bid after this benchmark had been set. WPIX outbid its New York rivals, purchasing the show for $54,000 per episode, while KTLA earned Los Angeles rights for $61,000 per half-hour (Mariani 30).

The ideal counterprogramming product is maneuverable and capable of appealing to a wide demographic viewer base. Sitcoms, at half the length of the hour-long drama and more easily digested by young adults, had long since been established as the staple of the syndication market by the time Reiss leapt to proto-Yuppie fame. Yet, led by the success of *Dallas* and *Hill Street Blues* and the demise of mainstay half-hour comedies, the networks swung toward hour-long dramas while producers and critics pronounced the sitcom to be dead as a network entity.

The effect on the off-network market was not difficult to gauge: Syndicators and local stations knew that only a single network sitcom would be available in both 1985 (*Gimme a Break*) and 1986 (*Facts of Life*). Putting canceled programs such as *Too Close for Comfort* and *It's a Living* on non-network syndication runs was, at best, a minimal response to the drought. The development of first-run syndicated material as an alternative to the entrenched rerun was an obvious solution, but the products that rolled off the assembly line were painfully weak. Of *Small Wonder*, a landmark pilot produced in 1984 by a consortium of five of the industry's largest station groups, one wag noted: "All those brains and they come up with a show about an 8-year-old girl who's a robot?" (Rosenthal 44). Thoroughly mediocre, by both aesthetic and ratings yardsticks, the scarce off-network sitcoms went for top dollar (*Gimme a Break* fetched a top price of $77,000). The mood of the industry was captured by a chief programmer from a major station group: "I'd sell my soul for a half-hour" ("Off Network Sitcoms" 34).

Then what *TV Guide* called the "most shamelessly arrogant exercise in hardball salesmanship the television industry had ever seen" was launched to sell *The Cosby Show* (Hill, "The Cosby Push" 3). The show was marketed as having a "halo" effect: so popular that programs in surrounding time periods would gain and retain *Cosby* viewers. It was also sold as having a "halo" effect: bids set so high that stations could only hope to offset the costs with heightened advertiser interest in the surrounding programs. A Machiavellian marketing campaign stressed that, whatever the costs, non-*Cosby* stations would be at the mercy of competitors who possessed the program. Furthermore, Viacom demanded a minute of the six-and-half minutes of advertising (during its network run, the program had four-and-half minutes of advertising space—editing more ad space into a rerun was an established practice) for its own use. Barter deals had been commonly struck for first-run independent programming; *Cosby*, however, represented the first application of this practice for an off-network product. When the feeding frenzy of bidding passed, barter time generated approximately $100 million of the $600 to $650 million of revenue from the Cosby sale ("Cosby" 76). New York's superstation WOR-TV submitted the top bid, $350,000 an episode ("The 'Cosby' Numbers" 58).

Dénouement and Rebirth

Cosby's ratings in syndication did not, in the eyes of industry analysts, justify its price. Nor did it have a significant "halo" effect ("Mixed Results" 38; Hill, "*Cosby* Reruns" 32). The boom market in independent stations, fueled by FCC rulings allowing more stations to be owned by individual companies and easier sales of stations within the industry, went belly up in 1987 as several dozen went into Chapter 11 or were incorporated into the Home Shopping Network (Grillo 64; Cray 44). If there was any room for hope for the independents in the post-*Cosby* era, it was, as Jean Bergantini Grillo scolded in a January 1988 *Channels* piece, that they "have studied the primer on how not to run a station that they helped write during their wild expansion and painful contraction over the past few years" (Grillo 64).

One of the chief lessons was to avoid deadly bidding wars for off-network programs. "*Cosby* told us how to say 'no,'" observed Rick Lowe, general manager of KOKI, Fox's Tulsa outpost (Heuton 37). Such discipline, and the fruits of the resurrected sitcom, drove prices down for syndicated material. For example, whereas *Cosby* went for $100,000 an episode in the Detroit market, *Perfect Strangers* was bought for less than $20,000 and *ALF* for less than $30,000 ("Sitcoms" 36).

Also, Lowe and other station managers could shed their independent status and align themselves with the Fox network. Although Fox shows eventually flowed down the programming hierarchy—witness *Married . . . With Children*—the network offered a source of first-run material that had proved so elusive during the previous three decades. First-run material also began to blossom in the form of dramas such as *Baywatch* and a new wave of talk shows. Furthermore, there was the appeal of products produced by individual stations. Greg Nathanson, general manager of KTLA, told *Broadcasting* in 1993: "I think our whole future is in local programming . . . when we run a movie or an off-network sitcom, even though we run a lot and we're very successful with it, every cable system, every USA Network or Nickelodeon can bring you rerun programming" ("To Live and Program" 74).

Nathanson's cable examples are especially relevant to the present and future state of the rerun. USA led the way in pulling recent off-network strips away from individual stations, adding *Riptide* to its schedule in 1986, *Miami Vice* in 1987, and—in the first case of a cable network acquiring a network ranked in the top 10—*Murder, She Wrote* in 1988 (Brown 26; "USA Network" 45; "'Murder, She Wrote'" 102). For syndicators this trend helped to salvage some of the costs associated with the largely unwanted off-network hour-long drama in an era of sitcom demand, but not always enough to put a show in the black. *Miami Vice*, for example, cost MCA Inc. a reported $1.3 million per episode to produce, of which $850,000 was covered by the license fee paid by NBC. The USA deal did not cover the $450,000 deficit. This, in turn, led MCA and other companies away from the production of hour-long dramas, especially those that were particularly topical and expensive ("USA Network" 46).

In 1985, Nickelodeon judged its evening slate of children's programming expendable, opted for a slate of network relics, and launched its Nick at Nite programming (Schneider B22). The decision coincided with the appearance of "evergreen" divisions within several nervous syndication companies scavenging for products in the midst of the drought of recent off-network strips. Individual stations and superstations have continued to snap up dated shows—often, given the cost of the most attractive strips and the need to flesh out a programming schedule, out of necessity ("New Life" 54–59). Nonetheless, Nick at Nite has arguably cornered the market of vintage reruns.

A long-standing relationship with the nostalgic consciousness of the American viewing public has carved a broad swath through the rerun's history. The recycling of movies in the 1950s—in particular B Westerns and the *Little Rascals* and *Three Stooges* series—attracted both younger audiences and the adults who had flocked to the theaters in the days before television.[10] In the mid-1970s, a wave of programs from the 1950s such as *The Mickey Mouse Club* and *You Bet Your Life* grabbed both ratings and the attention of the media (Doan 10; "Second Childhood" 48). *Leave It to Beaver* and *The Brady Bunch*, although perennial rerun success stories, enjoyed renaissances of sorts in, respectively, the early 1980s and early 1990s (Friedman 18–21; Stengal 76; Briller 13–20).

It is difficult to imagine, however, a friendlier habitat for the rerun than Nick at Nite. Through its clean-cut promotional jingles the rerun itself is exalted and the viewer's memories of dusty UHF dens and a family's summertime bewilderment with *TV Guide* listings are affectionately coddled. For example, before being dethroned by Dick Van Dyke, Dr. Will Miller served as Nick at Nite's chairman, providing soothing psychological insights into the viewer's relationship with programs being viewed for the umpteenth time. Gilligan's failed efforts to leave his island are attributable to his reluctance to leave the stranded community, no more than the viewer can abandon yet another escapade of coconuts and gorillas. Meanwhile, in-house giggles follow the bottom line: Reruns helped to boost Nickelodeon's advertising revenues to $78.5 million in 1991, an increase of 34 percent from the previous year (Winski S-2).

But the secret of Nick at Nite's success would seem to lie more in the atomization of American television in the age of cable than in the average viewer's sophisticated appreciation of postmodern camp. Traditionally, whimsical mid-life crises equated only partial rerun success. Unless younger viewers were also attracted, a rerun would wither on the dial. DLT Entertainment's recent marketing campaign for the "new" *Three's Company* illustrates this objective in no uncertain terms:

> So why do we call it new? Because every season *THREE'S COMPANY*'s audience completely re-generates itself! *THREE'S COMPANY* and *MASH* are the only two sitcoms to stay on the top 10 syndication sitcom list for 29 consecutive sweeps!

> That's why. . . . For 20 million teenagers, *THREE'S COMPANY* is this season's newest hit!
> For 68 million young adults, it's still their all time favorite program!
> For 36 million kids, every episode is first run!
> That's why we call it new! (*Channels* 67)

For Nickelodeon this concern is largely a secondary one. Aiming for a specific niche—movies, music videos, news, sporting events and summaries, cartoons and comedians, infomercials and shopping marketplaces—few cable channels bother to submit a full week's, or a full day's, worth of original programming. Instead, they seek a minimal hold on a targeted audience to attract enough local and national advertisers to offset this selected and cost-effective programming. Thus the feasibility of Nick at Nite.

And thus, the art form saluted by Nickelodeon is wildly embraced by its cable brethren. Constant, albeit increasingly specialized, repetition flows from the modern American TV set. Conspiring is the viewer, armed with remote control and a VCR, an independent programmer free to finicky repeat at will. Tom Shales, in labeling the 1980s "The Re Decade," provided a definitive encapsulation of a future that has come to pass:

> With so many more channels out there, we are more than ever before feeding off the work of the past. We are even more parasitical of the past, and the past is more easily accessed than ever. We're accessin' it like crazy, all the time; you can get a fix of yesterday at almost any hour of the day and night, whereas it's not quite so easy to get a fix on, or a fix of, Right Now, This Minute. (72)

In this expanding environment, delineations on the rerun continuum fade. Summer reruns dissipate across the calendar. Off-network strips seep from traditional UHF havens into one cable outpost after another. A fresh wave of repetition foams about these products of postwar mass culture as they gradually melt into the concept that they began to define some 40 years ago. The reverence shown to the rerun by Dr. Miller and his cohorts is wholly fitting. After an elusive trek through our television heritage, the rerun basks in its blinding, omnipresent triumph.

Acknowledgment

The author is indebted to Professor Randy Roberts of the Department of History at Purdue University for his assistance and encouragement with this study.

Notes

1. An ineffective flurry of presidential interest in summer reruns, however, emanated from the 1972 Nixon re-election campaign in its efforts to court Hollywood unions dissatisfied with residual payments for rebroadcasts. See "Don't Play It Again," *Newsweek* 25 Sept. 1972: 105; "The Rerun Syndrome," *Time* 2 Oct. 1972: 63; Peter Funt, "Are Viewers Getting the Old Rerun-Around?" *TV Guide* 1 Feb. 1975: 2–5.

2. In 1972, *Broadcasting* estimated that 44.8 percent of CBS's schedule consisted of reruns, 42.2 percent of NBC's, and 36 percent of ABC's ("The Realities of Reruns in Network TV," *Broadcasting* 2 Oct. 1972: 15). Although this study included reruns of theatrical films and the study two decades later ignored such repeats, choosing instead to include them in the "specials" category, the rerun share had clearly diminished.

3. For detailed analysis of this criticism, see Baughman's "The National Purpose and the Newest Medium: Liberal Critics of Television, 1958–60," *Mid-America* 64 (1982): 41–55.

4. ABC's spinoff, Worldvision, was in place by 1972, as was NBC's NTA.

5. For a discussion of the tactics and results of such network intrusions see A. Frank Reel, *The Networks: How They Stole the Show* (New York: Charles Scribner's

Sons, 1979): 125–27. For a rare insight into the hegemonic reach of the networks from an industry insider during the initial FCC/network clashes, see independent producer Don McGuire's "Another View on 50-50 Rule," *Broadcasting* 7 Mar. 1966: 34+.

6. A noted example: Todd Gitlin's description of Lou Grant's demise in *Inside Prime Time* (New York: Pantheon, 1985): 3–11.

7. Producers also depend upon foreign sales. This was especially true before the massive rise of off-network products and the increased production capabilities and programming protectionism of other nations in the late 1960s and early 1970s. See "World Laps Up U.S. TV Fare," *Business Week* 23 Apr. 1960: 129–131; Ross Drake, "From Daniel Boone to Mod Squad," *TV Guide* 29 Apr. 1972: 33–36.

8. The study also concluded that the late fringe strategy of placing local newscasts versus the final primetime hour also led to substantial ratings gains.

9. Until the 1980s, the terms of a rerun purchase allowed each episode to be aired six times within a given time period.

10. An interesting analysis of the beginnings of the Stooges' revival may be found in "Out of Vault, Into Limelight," *Broadcasting* 16 Feb. 1959: 62.

Works Cited

"A $30-Million Plum to Be Picked?" *Broadcasting* 3 May 1965: 26–28.
"Are Re-Runs a Good Buy?" *Television Magazine* Feb. 1954: 24–25.
"As We See It." *TV Guide,* 8 Sept. 1956: Inside front cover.
Baughman, James. "The National Purpose and the Newest Medium: Liberal Critics of Television, 1958–60." *Mid-America* 64 (1982): 41–55.
———. *The Republic of Mass Culture: Journalism, Filmmaking, and Broadcasting in America Since 1941.* Baltimore: Johns Hopkins UP, 1992.
———. *Television's Guardians: The FCC and the Politics of Programming, 1958–1967.* Knoxville: U of Tennessee P, 1985.
Boddy, William. *Fifties Television: The Industry and Its Critics.* Urbana: U of Illinois P, 1990.
"Box Score of 1947 Releases." Variety 31 Dec. 1947: 6.
Briller, Bert. "Will the Real Live Brady Bunch Stand Up?" *Television Quarterly* 26 (1992): 13–20.
Broadcasting 25 June 1951: 67.
Brown, Rich. "Off-Net Hours Find Good Home on Cable." *Broadcasting* 29 June 1992.
Channels Feb. 1990: 67.
"Color Tones Up Syndication Sales Picture." *Broadcasting* 21 Mar. 1966: 69–76.
"The 'Cosby' Numbers in Syndication." *Broadcasting* 27 Apr. 1987: 58–64.
"'Cosby': Off-Network's Biggest Deal Ever." *Broadcasting* 12 Sept. 1988: 76–78.
Cray, Ed. "The Toughest Year." *Channels* Feb. 1988: 44–46.
Davidson, Bill. "The Facts Behind Those Network Reruns." *TV Guide* 8 June 1973: 6–13.
"Disks Catch On." *Business Week* 21 June 1947: 68–69.
Doan, Richard K. "All Together, Now—M-I-C-K-E-Y. . . . " *TV Guide* 21 June 1975: 9–11.
"Don't Play It Again." *Newsweek* 25 Sept. 1972: 105.
Drake, Ross. "From *Daniel Boone* to *Mod Squad*." *TV Guide* 29 Apr. 1972: 33–36.
Ely, Melvin Patrick. *The Adventures of Amos 'n' Andy.* New York: Free Press, 1991.

"Film Classics Sticks with Reissues." *Variety* 16 Mar. 1946: 15.

"Films for Fall." *Broadcasting* 13 Aug. 1956:37–48+.

Friedman, Elise. "Never Say 'Bye.'" *TV Guide* 18 June 1983: 18–21.

Funt, Peter. "Are Viewers Getting the Old Rerun-Around?" *TV Guide* 1 Feb. 1975: 2–5.

Gitlin, Todd. *Inside Prime Time*. New York: Pantheon, 1985.

Glickman, Dave. "Film in the Future." *Broadcasting* 10 Sept. 1951: 79+.

Grillo, Jean Bergantini. "The Cautious Survivors." *Channels* Jan. 1988: 64–65.

"Happy Days for the 'Indies.'" *Newsweek* 5 Mar. 1984: 74.

Heuton, Cheryl. "An Enviable Situation." *Channels* 17 Dec. 1990: 36–38.

Hill, Doug. "The Cosby Push Wasn't Going for Laughs: 'We Gotta Confuse 'Em and Scare 'Em.'" *TV Guide* 7 May 1988:3–10.

———. "*Cosby* Reruns: Was the Big Bill Worth It?" *TV Guide* 29 July 1989: 32.

"Hopes Fade for UHF Television." *Business Week* 19 Nov. 1955: 27.

"The Hot Market in Used Shows." *Broadcasting* 17 July 1961: 27–29.

"How Independents See Their Fates." *Broadcasting* 20 Feb. 1984: 62.

"In Defense of Network Programs." *Broadcasting* 7 Mar. 1965: 31–33.

"Independent TV: It's Come a Long Way." *Broadcasting* 27 June 1983: 49–54.

Jaffee, Thomas. "The Great TV Hold-up." *Forbes* 18 Sept. 1978: 98–100.

Jessell, Harry A. "Networks Victorious in Fin-Syn Fight." *Broadcasting* 5 Apr. 1993: 7+.

"June Gross Lags." *Broadcasting* 13 Aug. 1951: 72.

Kroeger, Albert R. "Programming: Short Supply, Big Demand." *Television Magazine* Apr. 1964: 72+.

Kugel, Fred. "The State of Film." *Television Magazine* Aug. 1950: 15+.

Levine, Carol. "Film Re-Runs Can Pay Off." *Broadcasting* 10 Aug. 1953: 89+.

MacDonald, J. Fred. *One Nation Under Television: The Rise and Decline of Network TV*. New York: Pantheon Books, 1990.

Mandese, Joe. "More Reruns Creeping Into Regular Season." *Advertising Age* 4 May 1992: 54

Mariani, John. "Waiting For the Ring—and the 'Sale of the Century.'" *TV Guide* 12 May 1979: 26–30.

Martin, John Bartlow. "The Big Squeeze." *Saturday Evening Post* 11 Nov. 1961: 62–72.

McGuire, Don. "Another View on 50-50 Rule." *Broadcasting* 7 Mar. 1966: 34+.

Millions in TV Film. *Broadcasting* 4 June 1956: 44–52.

"Minow Proposes Second Run UHF Network." *Broadcasting* 8 Apr. 1963: 60.

"Mixed Results for Off-Network 'Cosby,'" *Broadcasting* 10 Oct. 1988: 38–39.

Moore, Barbara. "*The Cisco Kid* and Friends: The Syndication of Television Series from 1948 to 1952." *Journal of Popular Film and Television* 8 (1980): 26–34.

"'Murder, She Wrote' to Appear on Cable." *Broadcasting* 8 Feb. 1988: 102.

"Networks Promise Summer Punch." *Broadcasting* 19 Feb. 1990 52–56.

"New Life in Old TV Shows." *Broadcasting* 18 Mar. 1985: 54–59.

"A New Network Summer Song." *Broadcasting* 7 Feb. 1983: 35–36.

"Nielsen: Film Re-Runs Hold Audience." *Broadcasting* 24 Jan. 1955: 30.

"'Nighttime in the Daytime' with Film." *Television Magazine* Dec. 1955: 49+.

Nobile, Philip. "The Greening of Channels 5, 9, 11." *New York* 26 Oct. 1981: 26+.

"Now—More Innovations, More Film Than Ever." *Television Magazine* July 1956: 54–56.

"Off-Network Bonanza for Buyers." *Broadcasting* 2 May 1966: 25–27.

"Off-Network Program Scarcity Ahead?" *Broadcasting* 30 Sept. 1963: 52–55.

"Off Network Sitcoms Set for Syndication." *Broadcasting* 29 July 1985: 34–37.

"'Operation Summer.'" *Broadcasting* 9 Apr. 1951: 15+.

"Out of Vault, Into Limelight." *Broadcasting* 16 Feb. 1959: 62.

"Program Sources Drying Up?" *Broadcasting* 18 Sept. 1961: 19–21.

Pryor, Thomas M. "Boom Market for Yesteryear's Movies." *New York Times* 30 Jan. 1944: B3.

"The Realities of Reruns in Network TV." *Broadcasting* 2 Oct. 1972: 15–16.

Reel, A. Frank. *The Networks: How They Stole the Show.* New York: Charles Scribner's Sons, 1979.

"Reissues Ease Off as Quality Lags, Though Top Pix Continue Strong." *Variety* 16 Nov. 1949: 7+.

"The Rerun Syndrome." *Time* 2 Oct. 1972: 63.

Rosenthal, Sharon. "$77,000 for 30 Minutes? Gimme a Break!" *TV Guide* 8 Dec. 1984: 43–45.

Schneider, Steve. "Nickelodeon Branches Out." *New York Times* 30 June 1985: B22.

"Second Childhood." *Newsweek* 3 Mar. 1975: 48.

Shales, Tom. "The Re Decade." *Esquire* Mar. 1985: 67–72.

Simon, Ronald. "The Eternal Rerun: Oldies but Goodies." *Television Quarterly* 22 (1986): 51–58.

"Sitcoms: The (Lower?) Price of Success." *Broadcasting* 7 May 1990: 36–37.

Smith, Bernard B. "A New Weapon to Get Better TV." *Harper's* July 1962: 27–34.

Stengal, Richard. "When Eden Was in Suburbia." *Time* 9 Aug. 1982: 76.

Women's Work

LYNN SPIGEL

The Western-Holly Company in 1952 marketed a new design in domestic technology, the TV-stove. The oven included a window through which the housewife could watch her chicken roast. Above the oven window was a TV screen that presented an even more spectacular sight. With the aid of this machine the housewife would be able to prepare her meal, but at the same time she could watch TV. Although it was clearly an odd object, the TV-stove was not simply a historical fluke. Rather, its invention should remind us of the concrete social, economic, and ideological conditions that made this contraption possible. Indeed, the TV-stove was a response to the conflation of labor and leisure time at home. If we now find it strange, this has as much to do with the way in which our society has conceptualized work and leisure as it does with the machine's bizarre technological form.[1]

Since the nineteenth century, middle-class ideals of domesticity had been predicated on divisions of leisure time and work time. The doctrine of two spheres represented human activity in spatial terms: the public world came to be conceived of as a place of productive labor, while the home was seen as a site of rejuvenation and consumption. By the 1920s, the public world was still a sphere of work, but it was also opened up to a host of commercial pleasures such as movies and amusement parks that were incorporated

---

Reprinted from *Make Room for TV: Television and the Family Ideal in Postwar America,* pp. 73–78, 206–211, by Lynn Spigel, with permission of the publisher, University of Chicago Press, and the author.

into middle-class life styles. The ideal home, however, remained a place of revitalization and, with the expansion of convenience products that promised to reduce household chores, domesticity was even less associated with production.

As feminists have argued, this separation has justified the exploitation of the housewife whose work at home simply does not count. Along these lines, Nancy Folbre claims that classical economics considers women's work as voluntary labor and therefore outside the realm of exploitation. In addition, she argues, even Marxist critics neglect the issue of domestic exploitation since they assume that the labor theory of value can be applied only to efficiency-oriented production for the market and not to "inefficient" and "idiosyncratic" household chores.[2]

As feminist critics and historians have shown, however, the home is indeed a site of labor. Not only do women do physical chores, but also the basic relations of our economy and society are reproduced at home, including the literal reproduction of workers through childrearing labor. Once the home is considered a workplace, the divisions between public/work and domestic/leisure become less clear. The way in which work and leisure are connected, however, remains a complex question.

Henri Lefebvre's studies of everyday life offer ways to consider the general interrelations between work, leisure, and family life in modern society. In his foreword to the 1958 edition of *Critiquè de la Vie Quotidienne*, Lefebvre argues:

> Leisure . . . cannot be separated from work. It is the same man who, after work, rests or relaxes or does whatever he chooses. Every day, at the same time, the worker leaves the factory, and the employee, the office. Every week, Saturday and Sunday are spent on leisure activities, with the same regularity as that of the weekdays' work. Thus we must think in terms of the unity "work-leisure," because that unity exists, and everyone tries to program his own available time according to what his work is—and what it is not.[3]

While Lefebvre concentrated on the "working man," the case of the housewife presents an even more pronounced example of the integration of work and leisure in everyday life.

In recent years, media scholars have begun to demonstrate the impact that patterns of domestic leisure and labor have on television spectatorship. British ethnographic research has suggested that men and women tend to use television according to their specific position within the distribution of leisure and labor activities inside and outside the home.[4] In the American context, two of the most serious examinations come from Tania Modleski (1983) and Nick Browne (1984), who have both theorized the way TV watching fits into a general pattern of everyday life where work and leisure are intertwined. Modleski has suggested that the soap opera might be understood in terms of the "rhythms of reception," or the way women working at home relate to the text within a specific milieu of distraction—cleaning, cooking, childrearing, and so on.[5] Browne concentrates not on the individual text, but rather on the entire TV schedule, which he claims is ordered according to the logic of the workday of both men and women. "[T]he position of the programs in the television schedule reflects and is determined by the work-structured order of the real social world. The patterns of position and flow imply the question of who is home, and through complicated social relays and temporal mediations, link television to the modes, processes, and scheduling of production characteristic of the general population."[6]

The fluid interconnection between leisure and labor at home presents a context in which to understand representations of the female audience during the postwar years. Above all, women's leisure time was shown to be coterminous with their work time. Representations of television continually addressed women as housewives and presented them with a notion of spectatorship that was inextricably intertwined with their useful labor at home. Certainly, this model of female spectatorship was based on previous notions about radio listeners, and we can assume that women were able to adapt some of their listening habits to television viewing without much difficulty. However, the added impact of visual images ushered in new dilemmas that were the subject of profound concern, both within the broadcast industry and within the popular culture at large.

The Industry's Ideal Viewer

The idea that female spectators were also workers in the home was, by the postwar period, a truism for broadcasting and advertising executives. For some twenty years, radio programmers had grappled with ways to address a group of spectators whose attention wasn't focused primarily on the medium (as in the cinema), but instead moved constantly between radio entertainment and a host of daily chores. As William Boddy has argued, early broadcasters were particularly reluctant to feature daytime radio shows, fearing that women's household work would be fundamentally incompatible with the medium.[7] Overcoming its initial reluctance, the industry successfully developed daytime radio in the 1930s, and by the 1940s housewives constituted a faithful audience for soap operas and advice programs.

During the postwar years, advertisers and networks once more viewed the daytime market with skepticism, fearing that their loyal radio audiences would not be able to make the transition to television. The industry assumed that, unlike radio, television might require the housewife's complete attention and thus disrupt her work in the home.[8] Indeed, while network prime-time schedules were well worked out in 1948, networks and national advertisers were reluctant to feature regular daytime programs. Thus, in the earliest years, morning and afternoon hours were typically left to the discretion of local stations, which filled the time with low budget versions of familiar radio formats and old Hollywood films.

The first network to offer a regular daytime schedule was DuMont, which began operations on its owned and operated station WABD in New

York in November of 1948. As a newly formed network which had severe problems competing with CBS and NBC, DuMont entered the daytime market to offset its economic losses in prime time at a time when even the major networks were losing money on television.[9] Explaining the economic strategy behind the move into daytime, one DuMont executive claimed, "WABD is starting daytime programming because it is not economically feasible to do otherwise. Night time programming alone could not support radio, nor can it support television."[10] Increasingly in 1949, DuMont offered daytime programming to its affiliate stations. By December, it was transmitting the first commercially sponsored, daytime network show, *Okay, Mother,* to three affiliates and also airing a two-hour afternoon program on a full network basis. DuMont director Commander Mortimer W. Loewi reasoned that the move into daytime would attract small ticket advertisers who wanted to buy "small segments of time at a low, daytime rate."[11]

DuMont's venture into the daytime market was a thorn in the side of the other networks. While CBS, NBC, and ABC had experimented with individual daytime television programs on their flagship stations, they were reluctant to feature full daytime schedules. With huge investments in daytime radio, they weren't likely to find the prospects of daytime television appealing, especially since they were using their radio profits to offset initial losses in prime-time programming. As *Variety* reported when DuMont began its broadcasts on WABD, the major networks "must protect their AM [radio] investment at all costs—and the infiltration of daytime TV may conceivably cut into daytime radio advertising."[12] In this context, DuMont's competition in the daytime market posed a particularly grave threat to advertising revenues. In response, the other networks gradually began expanding the daytime lineups for their flagship stations.[13]

It was in 1951 that CBS, NBC, and, to a lesser extent, ABC first aggressively attempted to colonize the housewife's workday with regularly scheduled network programs. One of the central reasons for the networks' move into daytime that year was the fact that prime-time hours were fully booked by advertisers and that, by this point, there was more demand for TV advertising in general. As the advertising agency BBDO claimed in a report on daytime TV in the fall of 1950, "To all intents and purposes, the opportunity to purchase good night-time periods of TV is almost a thing of the past and the advertiser hoping to enter television now . . . better start looking at Daytime TV while it is still here to look at."[14] Daytime might have been more risky than prime time, but it had the advantage of being available—and at a cheaper network cost. Confident of its move into daytime, CBS claimed, "We aren't risking our reputation by predicting that daytime television will be a solid sell-out a year from today . . . and that once again there will be some sad advertisers who didn't read the tea leaves right."[15] ABC vice president Alexander Stronach Jr. was just as certain about the daytime market, and having just taken the plunge with the *Frances Langford-Don Ameche Show* (a variety program budgeted at the then steep $40,000 a week),

Stronach told *Newsweek*, "It's a good thing electric dishwashers and washing machines were invented. The housewives will need them."[16]

The networks' confidence carried through to advertisers who began to test the waters of the daytime schedule. In September of 1951, the trade journal *Televiser* reported that "forty-seven big advertisers have used daytime network television during the past season or are starting this Fall." Included were such well-known companies as American Home Products, Best Foods, Procter and Gamble, General Foods, Hazel Bishop Lipsticks, Minute Maid, Hotpoint, and the woman's magazine *Ladies' Home Journal*.[17]

Despite these inroads, the early daytime market remained highly unstable, and at least until 1955 the competition for sponsors was fierce.[18] Indeed, even while the aggregate size of the daytime audience rose in the early fifties, sponsors and broadcasters were uncertain about the extent to which housewives actually paid attention to the programs and advertisements. In response to such concerns, the industry aggressively tailored programs to fit the daily habits of the female audience. When it began operations in 1948, DuMont's WABD planned shows that could "be appreciated just as much from listening to them as from watching them."[19] Following this trend in 1950, Detroit's WXYX aired *Pat 'n' Johnny*, a program that solved the housework-TV conflict in less than subtle ways. At the beginning of the three-hour show, host Johnny Slagle instructed housewives, "Don't stop whatever you're doing. When we think we have something interesting I'll blow this whistle or Pat will ring her bell."[20]

The major networks were also intent upon designing programs to suit the content and organization of the housewife's day. The format that has received the most critical attention is the soap opera, which first came to network television in December of 1950. As Robert Allen has demonstrated, early soap opera producers like Irna Philips of *Guiding Light* were skeptical of moving their shows from radio to TV. However, by 1954 the Nielsen Company reported that soaps had a substantial following; *Search For Tomorrow* was the second most popular daytime show while *Guiding Light* was in fourth place. The early soaps, with their minimum of action and visual interest, allowed housewives to listen to dialogue while working in another room. Moreover, their segmented storylines (usually two a day), as well as their repetition and constant explanation of previous plots, allowed women to divide their attention between viewing and household work.[21]

Another popular solution to the daytime dilemma was the segmented variety show that allowed women to enter and exit the text according to its discrete narrative units. One of DuMont's first programs, for example, was a shopping show (alternatively called *At Your Service* and *Shoppers Matinee*) that consisted of twenty-one entertainment segments, all of which revolved around different types of "women's issues." For instance, the "Bite Shop" presented fashion tips while "Kitchen Fare" gave culinary advice. Interspersed with these segments were twelve one-minute "store bulletins" (news and service announcements) that could be replaced at individual stations by local commercials.[22] While DuMont's program was short-lived, the basic principles survived in the daytime shows at the major networks. Programs like *The Garry Moore Show* (CBS), *The Kate Smith Show* (NBC), and *The Arthur Godfrey Show* (CBS) catered to housewife audiences with their segmented variety of entertainment and advice.[23]

Indeed, the networks put enormous amounts of money and effort into variety shows when they first began to compose daytime program schedules. Daytime ratings continually confirmed the importance of the variety format, with hosts like Smith and Godfrey drawing big audiences. Since daytime stars were often taken from nighttime radio shows, the variety programs were immediately marked as being different from and more spectacular than daytime radio. *Variety* reported in October of 1951:

> The daytime television picture represents a radical departure from radio. The application of "nighttime thinking" into daytime TV in regards to big-league variety-slanted programs and projection of personalities becomes more and more important. If the housewife has a craving for visual soap operas, it is neither reflected in the present day Nielsens nor in the ambitious programming formulas being blueprinted by the video entrepreneurs. . . . The housewife with her multiple chores, it would seem, wants her TV distractions on a "catch as catch can" basis, and the single-minded concentration on sight-and-sound weepers doesn't jibe with her household schedule. . . . [Variety shows] are all geared to the "take it awhile leave it awhile" school of entertainment projection and practically all are reaping a bonanza for the networks.[24]

Television thus introduced itself to the housewife not only by repeating tried and true daytime radio formulas, but also by creating a distinct product tailored to what the industry assumed were the television audience's specific needs and desires.

Initially uncertain about the degree to which daytime programs from an audio medium would suit the housewife's routine, many television broadcasters turned their attention to the visual medium of the popular press. Variety shows often modeled themselves on print conventions, particularly borrowing narrative techniques from women's magazines and the women's pages. Much as housewives might flip through the pages of a magazine as they went about their daily chores, they could tune in and out of the magazine program without the kind of disorientation that they might experience when disrupted from a continuous drama. To ensure coherence, such programs included "women's editors" or "femcees" who provided a narrational thread for a series of "departments" on gardening, homemaking, fashion, and the like. These shows often went to extreme lengths to make the connection between print media and television programming foremost in the viewer's mind. *Women's Magazine of the Air,* a local program aired in Chicago on WGN, presented a "potpourri theme with magazine pages being turned to indicate new sections."[25] On its locally owned station, the *Seattle Post* presented *Women's Page,* starring *Post* book and music editor Suzanne Martin. The networks also used the popular press as a model for daytime programs. As early as 1948, CBS's New York station aired *Vanity Fair,* a segmented format that was tied together by "managing editor" Dorothy Dean, an experienced newspaper reporter. By the end of 1949, *Vanity Fair* was boasting a large list of sponsors, and in the fifties it continued to be part of the daytime schedule. Nevertheless, despite its success with *Vanity Fair,* CBS still tended to rely more heavily on well-known radio stars and formats, adapting these to the television medium. Instead, it was NBC that developed the print media model most aggressively in the early fifties.

Faced with daytime ratings that were consistently behind those of CBS and troubled by severe sponsorship problems, NBC saw the variety/magazine format as a particularly apt vehicle for small ticket advertisers who could purchase brief participation spots between program segments for relatively low cost.[26] Under the direction of programming vice president Sylvester "Pat" Weaver (who became NBC president in 1953), the network developed its "magazine concept" of advertising. Unlike the single sponsor series, which was usually produced through the advertising agency, the magazine concept allowed the network to retain control and ownership of programs. Although this form of multiple sponsor participation had become a common daytime practice by the early 1950s, Weaver's scheme differed from other participation plans because it allowed sponsors to purchase segments on a one-shot basis, with no ongoing commitment to the series. Even if this meant greater financial risks at the outset, in the long run a successful program based on spot sales would garner large amounts of revenue for the network.[27]

Weaver applied the magazine concept to two of the most highly successful daytime programs, *Today* and *Home.* Aired between 7:00 and 9:00 A.M., *Today* was NBC's self-proclaimed "television newspaper, covering not only the latest news, weather and time signals, but special features on everything from fashions to the hydrogen bomb."[28] On its premier episode in January 1952, *Today* made the print media connections firm in viewers' minds by showing telephoto machines grinding out pictures and front page facsimiles of the *San Francisco Chronicle.*[29] Aimed at a family audience, the program attempted to lure men, women, and children with discrete program segments that addressed their different interests and meshed with their separate schedules. One NBC confidential report stated that, on the one hand, men rushing off to take a train would not be likely to watch fashion segments. On the other hand, it suggested, "men might be willing to catch the next train" if they included an "almost sexy gal as part of the show." This, the report concluded, would be like "subtle, early morning sex."[30]

Although it was aimed at the entire family, the lion's share of the audience was female. (In 1954, for example, the network calculated that the audience was composed of 52 percent women, 26 percent men, and 22 percent children.)[31] *Today* appealed to housewives with "women's pages" news stories such as Hollywood gossip segments, fashion shows, and humanistic features. In August 1952, NBC's New York outlet inserted "Today's Woman" into the program, a special women's magazine feature that was produced in cooperation with *Look* and *Quick* magazines.[32] Enthused with *Today*'s success, NBC developed *Home* with similar premises in mind, but this time aimed the program specifically at women. First aired in 1954 during the 11:00 A.M. to noon time slot, *Home* borrowed its narrative techniques from women's magazines, featuring segments on topics like gardening, child psychology, food, fashion, health, and interior decor. As *Newsweek* wrote, "The program is planned to do for women on the screen what the women's magazines have long done in print."[33]

In fashioning daytime shows on familiar models of the popular press, television executives and advertisers were guided by the implicit assumption that the female audience had much in common with the typical magazine reader. When promoting *Today* and *Home,* NBC used magazines such as *Ladies' Home Journal, Good Housekeeping,* and *Collier's* (which also had a large female readership) as major venues. When *Home* first appeared it even offered women copies of its own monthly magazine, *How To Do it.*[34] Magazine publishers also must have seen the potential profits in the cross-over audience; the first sponsor for *Today* was Kiplinger's magazine *Changing Times,* and *Life* and Curtis magazines were soon to follow.[35]

The fluid transactions between magazine publishers and daytime producers were based on widely held notions about the demographic composition of the female audience. In 1954, the same year that *Home* premiered, NBC hired W. R. Simmons and Associates to conduct the first nationwide qualitative survey of daytime viewers. In a promotional report based on the survey, Dr. Tom Coffin, manager of NBC research, told advertisers and manufacturers, "In analyzing the findings, we have felt a growing sense of excitement at the qualitative picture emerging: an audience with the *size* of a mass medium but the *quality* of a class medium." When compared to nonviewers, daytime viewers were at the "age of acquisition," with many in the twenty-five- to thirty-four-year-old category; their families were larger with more children under eighteen; they had higher incomes; and they lived in larger and "better" market areas. In addition, Coffin characterized the average viewer as a "modern active woman" with a kitchen full of "labor-saving devices," an interest in her house, clothes, and "the way she looks." She is "the kind of woman most advertisers are most interested in; she's a good customer."[36] Coffin's focus on the "class versus mass" audience bears striking resemblance to the readership statistics of middle-class women's magazines. Like the magazine reader, "Mrs. Daytime Consumer" was an upscale, if only moderately affluent, housewife whose daily life consisted not only of chores, but also, and perhaps even more importantly, shopping for her family.

With this picture of the housewife in mind, the media producer had one primary job—teaching her how to buy products. Again, the magazine format was perfect for this because each discrete narrative segment could portray an integrated sales message. Hollywood gossip columns gave way to motion picture endorsements; cooking segments sold sleek new ranges; fashion shows promoted Macy's finest evening wear. By integrating sales messages with advice on housekeeping and luxury lifestyles, the magazine format skillfully suggested to housewives that their time spent viewing television was indeed part of their work time. In other words, the programs promised viewers not just entertainment, but also lessons on how to make consumer choices for their families. One production handbook claimed: "Women's daytime programs have tended toward the practical—providing shopping information, marketing tips, cooking, sewing, interior decoration, etc., with a dash of fashion and beauty hints. . . . The theory is that the housewife will be more likely to take time from her household duties if she feels that her television viewing will make her housekeeping more efficient and help her provide more gracious living for her family."[37] In the case of *Home,* this implicit integration of housework, consumerism, and TV entertainment materialized in the form of a circular stage that the network promoted as a "machine for selling."[38] The stage was equipped with a complete kitchen, a workshop area, and a small garden—all of which functioned as settings for different program segments and, of course, the different sponsor products that accompanied them. Thus, *Home*'s magazine format provided a unique arena for the presentation of a series of fragmented consumer fantasies that women might tune into and out of, according to the logic of their daily schedules.

Even if the structure of this narrative format was the ideal vehicle for "Mrs. Daytime Consumer," the content of the consumer fantasies still had to be carefully planned. Like the woman's magazine before it, the magazine show needed to maintain the subtle balance of its "class address." In order to appeal to the average middle-class housewife, it had to make its consumer fantasies fit with the more practical concerns of female viewers. The degree to which network executives attempted to strike this balance is well illustrated in the case of *Home.* After the program's first airing, NBC executive Charles Barry was particularly concerned about the amount of "polish" that it contained. Using "polish" as a euphemism for highbrow tastes, Barry went on to observe the problems with *Home*'s class address: "I hope you will keep in mind that the average gal looking at the show is either living in a small suburban house or in an apartment and is not very likely to have heard of Paul McCobb; she is more likely to be at a Macy's buying traditionally." After observing other episodes, Barry had similar complaints: the precocious stage children weren't "average" enough, the furniture segment featured impractical items, and the cooking segment showcased high-class foods such as vichyssoise and pot-de-crème. "Maybe you can improve tastes," Barry conceded, "but gosh would somebody please tell me how to cook corned beef and cabbage without any smell?"[39] The television producer could educate the housewife beyond her means, but only through mixing upperclass fantasy with tropes of averageness.

The figure of the female hostess was also fashioned to strike this delicate balance. In order to appeal to the typical housewife, the hostess would ideally speak on her level. As one producer argued, "Those who give an impression of superiority or 'talking down' to the audience, who treasure the manner of speaking over naturalness and meaningful communication . . . or who are overly formal in attire and manners, do not survive in the broadcasting industry. . . . The personality should fit right into your living room. The super-sophisticate or the squealing life of the party might be all right on occasion, but a daily association with this girl is apt to get a little tiresome."[40] In addition, the ideal hostess was decidedly not a glamour girl, but rather a pleasingly attractive, middle-aged woman—Hollywood's answer to the home economics teacher. When first planning *Home,* one NBC executive considered using the celebrity couple Van and Evie Johnson for hosts, claiming that Evie was "a sensible woman, not a glamor struck movie star's wife, but a wholesome girl from a wholesome background. . . . She works hard at being a housewife and Mother who runs a not elaborate household in Beverly Hills with *no swimming pool.*" Although Evie didn't get the part, her competitor, Arlene Francis, was clearly cut from the same cloth. In a 1957 fanzine, Francis highlighted her ordinariness when she admitted, "My nose is too long and I'm too skinny, but maybe that won't make any difference if I'm fun to be with."[41] Francis was also a calming mother figure who appealed to children. In a fan letter, one mother wrote that her little boy took a magazine to bed with him that had Arlene's picture on the cover.[42] Unlike the "almost sexy" fantasy woman on the *Today* show who was perfect for "morning sex," *Home's* femcee appealed to less erotic instincts. Francis and other daytime hostesses were designed to provide a role model for ordinary housewives, educating them on the "good life," while still appearing down to earth.

In assuming the role of "consumer educator," the networks went beyond just teaching housewives how to buy advertisers' products. Much more crucially in this early period, the networks attempted to teach women and their families how to consume television itself. Indeed, the whole system pivoted on the singular problem of how to make the daytime audience watch more programming. Since it adapted itself to the family's daily routine, the magazine show was particularly suited for this purpose. When describing the habits of *Today's* morning audience, Weaver acknowledged that the "show, of course, does not hold the same audience throughout the time period, but actually is a service fitting with the family's own habit pattern in the morning."[43] Importantly, however, NBC continually tried to channel the movements of the audience. Not merely content to fit its programming into the viewer's rhythms of reception, the network aggressively sought to change those rhythms by making the activity of television viewing into a new daily habit. One NBC report made this point quite explicit, suggesting that producers "establish definite show patterns at regular times; do everything you can to capitalize on the great habit of habit listening."[44] Proud of his accomplishments on this front, Weaver bragged about fan mail that demonstrated how *Today* changed viewers' daily routines. According to Weaver, one woman claimed, "My husband said I should put casters on the TV set so I can roll it around and see it from the kitchen." Another admitted, "I used to get all the dishes washed by 8:30—now I don't do a thing until 10 o'clock." Still another confessed, "My husband now dresses in the living room." Weaver boastfully promised, "We will change the habits of millions."[45]

The concept of habitual viewing also governed NBC's scheduling techniques. The network devised promotional strategies designed to maintain systems of flow, as each program ideally would form a "lead in" for the next, tailored to punctuate intervals of the family's daily routine. In 1954, for example, an NBC report on daytime stated that *Today* was perfect for the early morning time slot because it "has a family audience . . . and reaches them just before they go out to shop." With shopping done, mothers might return home to find *Ding Dong School,* "a nursery school on television" that allowed them to do housework while educator Frances Horwich helped raise the pre-schoolers. Daytime dramas were scheduled throughout the day, each lasting only fifteen minutes, probably because the network assumed that drama would require more of the housewife's attention than the segmented variety formats like *Home.* At 5 P.M., when mothers were likely to be preparing dinner, *The Pinky Lee Show* presented a mixed bag of musical acts, dance routines, parlor games, and talk aimed both at women and their children who were now home from school.[46]

NBC aggressively promoted this kind of routinized viewership, buying space in major market newspapers and national periodicals for advertisements that instructed women how to watch television while doing household chores. In 1955, *Ladies' Home Journal* and *Good Housekeeping* carried advertisements for NBC's daytime lineup that suggested that not only the programs, but also the scheduling of the programs, would suit the housewife's daily routine. The ads evoked a sense of fragmented leisure time and suggested that television viewing could be conducted in a state of distraction. This was not the kind of critical contemplative distraction that Walter Benjamin suggested in his seminal essay, "The Work of Art in the Age of Mechanical Reproduction."[47] Rather, the ads implied that the housewife could accomplish her chores in a state of "utopian forgetfulness" as she moved freely between her work and the act of watching television.

One advertisement, which is particularly striking in this regard, includes a sketch of a housewife and her little daughter at the top of the page. Below this, the graphic layout is divided into eight boxes composed of television screens, each representing a different program in NBC's daytime lineup. The caption functions as the housewife's testimony to her distracted state. She asks, "Where Did the Morning Go? The house is tidy . . . but it hasn't seemed like a terribly tiring morning. . . . I think I started ironing while I watched the *Sheila Graham Show*." The housewife goes on to register each detail of the programs, but she cannot with certainty account for her productive activities in the home. Furthermore, as the ad's layout suggests, the woman's daily activities are literally fragmented according to the pattern of the daytime television schedule, to the extent that her everyday experiences become imbricated in a kind of serial narrative. Significantly, her child pictured at the top of the advertisement appears within the contours of a television screen so that the labor of childrearing is itself made part of the narrative pleasures offered by the network's daytime lineup.[48]

Negotiating with the Industry's Ideal Viewer

The program types, schedules, and promotional materials devised at the networks were based upon ideal images of female viewers and, consequently, they were rooted in abstract conceptions about women's lives. These ideals weren't always commensurate with the heterogeneous experiences and situations of real women and, for this reason, industrial strategies didn't always form a perfect fit with the audience's needs and desires. Although it is impossible to reconstruct fully the actual activities of female viewers at home, we can better understand their concerns and practices by examining the ways in which their viewing experiences were explained to them at the time. Popular media, particularly women's magazines, presented women with opportunities to negotiate with the modes of spectatorship that the television industry tried to construct. It is in these texts that we see the gaps and inconsistencies—the unexpected twists and turns—that were not foreseen by networks and advertisers. Indeed, it is in the magazines, rather than in the highrise buildings of NBC, CBS, and ABC, where female audiences were given the chance to enter into a popular dialogue about their own relations to the medium.

While the networks were busy attempting to tailor daytime programming to the patterns of domestic labor, popular media often completely rejected the idea that television could be compatible with women's work and showed instead how it would threaten the efficient functioning of the household. The TV-addict housewife became a stock character during the period, particularly in texts aimed at a general audience where the mode of address was characterized by an implicit male narrator who clearly blamed women—not television—for the untidy house. In 1950, for example, *The New Yorker* ran a cartoon that showed a slovenly looking woman ironing a shirt while blankly staring at the television screen. Unfortunately, in her state of distraction, the woman burned a hole in the garment.[49] Women's magazines also deliberated upon television's thoroughly negative effect on household chores, but rather than poking fun at the housewife, they offered sympathetic advice, usually suggesting that a careful management of domestic space might solve the problem. In 1950, *House Beautiful* warned of television: "It delivers about five times as much wallop as radio and requires in return five times as much attention. . . . It's impossible to get anything accomplished in the same room while it's on." The magazine offered a spatial solution, telling women "to get the darn thing out of the living room," and into the TV room, cellar, library, "or as a last resort stick it in the dining room."[50]

In *The Honeymooners*, a working-class situation comedy, television's obstruction of household work was related to marital strife. The first episode of the series, "TV or Not TV" (1955), revolves around the purchase of a television set and begins with an establishing shot of the sparsely decorated Kramden kitchen where a clothes basket filled with wet wash sits on the table. Entering from the bedroom in her hausfrau garb, Alice Kramden approaches the kitchen sink and puts a plunger over the drain, apparently attempting to unclog it. As pictured in this opening scene, Alice is, to say the least, a victim of household drudgery. Not surprisingly, Alice begs Ralph for a television set, hoping that it will make her life more pleasant.

In a later scene, after the Kramdens purchase their TV set, this situation changes, but not for the better. Ralph returns home from work while Alice sits before her television set. Here is the exchange between the couple:

> *Ralph:* Would you mind telling me where my supper is?
> *Alice:* I didn't make it yet. . . . I sat down to watch the four o'clock movie
>   and I got so interested I . . . uh what time is it anyway?
> *Ralph:* I knew this would happen Alice. We've had that set three days now,
>   and I haven't had a hot meal since we got it.

Thus, television is the source of a dispute between the couple, a dispute that arises from the housewife's inability to perform her productive function while enjoying an afternoon program.

A 1955 ad for Drano provided a solution to television's obstruction of household chores. Here the housewife is shown watching her afternoon soap opera, but this unproductive activity is sanctioned only insofar as her servant does the housework. As the maid exclaims, "Shucks, I'll never know if she gets her man 'cause this is the day of the week I put Drano in all the drains!" The Drano Company thus attempted to sell its product by giving women a glamorous vision of themselves enjoying an afternoon of television. But it could do so only by splitting the functions of relaxation and work across two representational figures—the lady of leisure and the domestic servant.[51]

If the domestic servant was a fantasy solution to the conflict between work and television, the women's magazines suggested more practical ways to manage the problem. *Better Homes and Gardens* advised in 1949 that the television set should be placed in an area where it could be viewed, "while you're doing things up in the kitchen." Similarly in 1954, *American Home* told readers to put the TV set in the kitchen so that "Mama sees her pet programs. . . . " Via such spatial remedies, labor would not be affected by the leisure of viewing nor would viewing be denied by household chores.[52] In fact, household labor and television were continually condensed into one space designed to accommodate both activities. In a 1955 issue of *American Home,* this labor—leisure viewing condensation provided the terms of a joke. A cartoon showed a housewife tediously hanging her laundry on the outdoor clothesline. The drudgery of this work is miraculously solved as the housewife brings her laundry into her home and sits before her television set while letting the laundry dry on the television antenna.[53]

The spatial condensation of labor and viewing was part of a well entrenched functionalist discourse. The home had to provide rooms that would allow for a practical orchestration of "modern living activities" that now included watching television. Functionalism was particularly useful for advertisers, who used it to promote not just one household item but an entire product line. In 1952, for example, the Crane Company displayed its kitchen appliance ensemble, complete with ironing, laundering, and cooking facilities. Here the housewife could do multiple tasks at once because all the fixtures were "matched together as a complete chore unit." One particularly attractive component of this "chore unit" was a television set built into the wall above the washer/dryer.[54]

While spatial condensations of labor and leisure helped to soothe tensions about television's obstruction of household chores, other problems still existed. The magazines suggested that television would cause increasing work loads. Considering the cleanliness of the living room, *House Beautiful* told its readers in 1948: "Then the men move in for boxing, wrestling, basketball, hockey. They get excited. Ashes on the floor. Pretzel crumbs. Beer stains." The remedy was again spatial: "Lots of sets after a few months have been moved into dens and recreation rooms."[55] In a slight twist of terms, the activity of eating was said to be moving out of the dining area and into the television-sitting area. Food stains soiling upholstery, floors, and other surfaces meant extra work for women. Vinyl upholstery, linoleum floors, tiling, and other spill-proof surfaces were recommended. Advertisers for all kinds of cleaning products found television especially useful in their sales pitches. In 1953, the Bissell Carpet Sweeper Company asked housewives, "What do you do when the TV crowd leaves popcorn and crumbs on your rug? You could leave the mess till morning—or drag out the vacuum. But if you're on the beam, you slick it up with a handy Bissell Sweeper."[56] In addition to the mess generated by television, the set itself called for maintenance. In 1955, *House Beautiful* asked if a "misty haze dims your TV screen" and recommended the use of "wipe-on liquids and impregnated wiping cloths to remedy the problem." The Drackett Company, producer of Windex Spray, quickly saw the advantage that television held for its product; in 1948 it advertised the cleaner as a perfect solution for a dirty screen.[57]

Besides the extra cleaning, television also kept housewives busy in the kitchen. The magazines showed women how to be gracious hostesses, always prepared to serve family and friends special TV treats. These snacktime chores created a lucrative market for manufacturers. For example, in 1952 *American Home* presented a special china collection for "Early Tea and Late TV," while other companies promoted TV snack trays and TV tables.[58] The most exaggerated manifestation appeared in 1954. The TV dinner was the perfect remedy for the extra work entailed by television, and it also allowed children to eat their toss-away meals while watching *Hopalong Cassidy*.

While magazines presented readers with a host of television-related tasks, they also suggested ways for housewives to ration their labor. Time-motion studies, which were integral to the discourses of feminism and domestic science since the Progressive era, were rigorously applied to the problem of increasing work loads. All unnecessary human movement that the television set might demand had to be minimized. Again, this called for a careful management of space. The magazines suggested that chairs and sofas be placed so that they need not be moved for watching television. Alternatively, furniture could be made mobile. By placing wheels on a couch, it was possible to exert minimal energy while converting a sitting space into a viewing space. Similarly, casters and lazy Susans could be placed on television sets so that housewives might easily move the screen to face the direction of the viewers.[59] More radically, space between rooms could be made continuous. In 1952, *House Beautiful* suggested a "continuity" of living, dining, and television areas wherein "a curved sofa and a folding screen mark off [the] television corner from the living and dining room." Via this carefully managed spatial continuum, "it takes no more than an extra ten steps or so to serve the TV fans."[60]

Continuous space was also a response to the more general problem of television and family relationships. Women's household work presented a dilemma for the twin ideals of family unity and social divisions, since housewives were ideally meant to perform their distinctive productive functions but, at the same time, take part in the family's leisure-time pursuits. This conflict between female isolation from and integration into the family group was rooted in Victorian domestic ideology with its elaborate social and spatial hierarchies; it became even more pronounced as twentieth-century lifestyles and housing contexts changed in ways that could no longer contain the formalized spatial distinctions of the Victorian ideal.

The problems became particularly significant in the early decades of the century when middle-class women found themselves increasingly isolated in their kitchens due to a radical reduction in the number of domestic servants. As Gwendolyn Wright has observed, women were now cut off from the family group as they worked in kitchens designed to resemble scientific laboratories, far removed from the family activities in the central areas of the home. Architects did little to respond to the problem of isolation, but continued instead to build kitchens fully separated from communal living spaces, suggesting that labor-saving kitchen appliances would solve the servant shortage.[61] In the postwar era when the continuous spaces of ranch-style architecture became a cultural ideal, the small suburban home placed a greater emphasis on interaction between family members. The "open plan" eliminated some of the walls between dining room, living room, and kitchen. However, even in the continuous ranch-style homes, the woman's work area was "zoned off" from the activity area, and the woman's role as homemaker still worked to separate her from the leisure activities of her family.

Women's magazines suggested intricately balanced spatial arrangements that would mediate the tensions between female integration and isolation. Television viewing became a special topic of consideration. In 1951, *House Beautiful* placed a television set in its remodeled kitchen, which combined "such varied functions as cooking, storage, laundry, flower arranging, dining and TV viewing." In this case, as elsewhere, the call for functionalism was related to the woman's ability to work among a group engaged in leisure activities. A graphic showed a television placed in a "special area" devoted to "eating" and "relaxing" which was "not shut off by a partition." In continuous space, "the worker . . . is always part of the group, can share in the conversation and fun while work is in progress."[62]

While this example presents a harmonious solution, often the ideals of integration and isolation resulted in highly contradictory representations of domestic life. Typically, illustrations that depicted continuous spaces showed the housewife to be oddly disconnected from the general flow of activities. In 1951, for example, *American Home* showed a woman in a continuous dining-living area who supposedly is allowed to accomplish her housework among a group of television viewers. However, rather than being integrated into the group, the woman is actually isolated from the television crowd as she sets the dining room table. The TV viewers are depicted in the background while the housewife stands to the extreme front-right border of the composition, far away from her family and friends. In fact, she is literally positioned off-frame, straddling between the photograph and the negative (or unused) space of the layout.[63]

The family circle motif was also riddled with contradictions of this sort. In particular, Sentinel's advertising campaign showed women who were spatially distanced from their families. In 1952, one ad depicted a housewife holding a tray of beverages and standing off to the side of her family, who were clustered around the television set. The following year, another ad showed a housewife cradling her baby in her arms and standing at a window far away from the rest of her family, who were gathered around the Sentinel console.[64] In a 1948 ad for Magnavox Television, the housewife's chores separated her from her circle of friends. The ad was organized around a U-shaped sofa that provided a quite literal manifestation of the semicircle visual cliché. A group of adult couples sat on the sofa watching the new Magnavox set, but the hostess stood at the kitchen door, holding a tray of snacks. Spatially removed from the television viewers, the housewife appeared to be sneaking a look at the set as she went about her hostess chores.[65]

This problem of female spatial isolation gave way to what can be called a "corrective cycle of commodity purchases." A 1949 article in *American Home* about the joys of the electric dishwasher is typical here. A picture of a family gathered around the living room console included the caption, "No martyr banished to kitchen, she never misses television programs. Lunch, dinner dishes are in an electric dishwasher." In 1950, an advertisement for Hotpoint dishwashers used the same discursive strategy. The illustration showed a wall of dishes that separated a housewife in the kitchen from her family, who sat huddled around the television set in the living room. The caption read, "Please . . . Let Your Wife Come Out Into the Livingroom! Don't let dirty dishes make your wife a kitchen exile! She loses the most precious hours of her life shut off from pleasures of the family circle by the never-ending chore of old-fashioned dishwashing!"[66]

This ideal version of female integration in a unified family space was contested by the competing discourse on divided spaces. Distinctions between work and leisure space remained an important principle of household efficiency. Here, room dividers presented a perfect balance of integration and isolation. In 1952, *Better Homes and Gardens* displayed a room divider that separated a kitchen work area from its dining area. The cutoff point was a television set built into the wall just to the right of the room divider. Thus, the room divider separated the woman's work space from the television space, but as a partial wall that still allowed for continuous space, it reached the perfect compromise between the housewife's isolation from and integration into the family. It was in the sense of this compromise that *American Home*'s "discrete" room divider separated a wife's work space from her husband's television space in a house that, nevertheless, was designed for "family living." As the magazine reported in 1954, "Mr. Peterson . . . retired behind his newspaper in the TV end of the living kitchen. Mrs. P. quietly made a great stack of sandwiches for us behind the discrete screen of greens in the efficient kitchen end of the same room."[67]

This bifurcation of sexual roles, of male (leisure) and female (productive) activities, served as an occasion for a full consideration of power dynamics among men and women in the home. Typically, the magazines extended their categories of feminine and masculine viewing practices into representations of the body. For men, television viewing was most often represented in terms of a posture of repose. Men were usually shown to be sprawled out on easy chairs as they watched the set. Remote controls allowed the father to watch in undisturbed passive comfort. In many ways, this representation of the male body was based on Victorian notions of rejuvenation for the working man. Relaxation was condoned for men because it served a revitalizing function, preparing them for the struggles for the workaday world. For women, the passive calm of television viewing was never so simple. As we have seen, even when women were shown watching television, they often appeared as productive workers.

Sometimes, representations of married couples became excessively literal about the gendered patterns of television leisure. In 1954, when the Cleavelander Company advertised its new "T-Vue" chair, it told consumers, "Once you sink into the softness of Cleavelander's cloud-like contours, cares seem to float away." Thus, not only the body, but also the spirit would be revitalized by the TV chair. But while the chair allowed Father "to stretch out with his feet on the ottoman," Mother's TV leisure was nevertheless productive. As the caption states, "Mother likes to gently rock as she sews."[68] Similarly, a 1952 advertisement for Airfoam furniture cushions showed a husband dozing in his foam rubber cushioned chair as he sits before a television set. Meanwhile, his wife clears away his TV snack. The text reads, "Man's pleasure is the body coddling comfort" of the cushioned chair while "Woman's treasure is a home lovely to look at, easy to keep perfectly tidy and neat" with cushioning that "never needs fluffing."[69] In such cases, the man's pleasure in television is associated with passive relaxation. The woman's pleasure, however, is derived from the aesthetics of a well-kept home and labor-saving devices that promise to minimize the extra household work that television brings to domestic space. In addition, the Airfoam ad is typical as it depicts a female body that finds no viewing pleasures of its own but instead functions to assist with the viewing comforts of others.

As numerous feminist film theorists have demonstrated, spectatorship and the pleasures entailed by it are culturally organized according to categories of sexual difference. In her groundbreaking article on the subject of Hollywood film, Laura Mulvey showed how narrative cinema (her examples were Von Sternberg and Hitchcock) is organized around voyeuristic and fetishistic scenarios in which women are the "to-be-looked-at" object of male desire.[70] In such a scheme, it becomes difficult to pinpoint how women can have subjective experiences in a cinema that systematically objectifies them. In the case of television, it seems clear that women's visual pleasure was associated with interior decor and not with viewing programs. In 1948, *House Beautiful* made this explicit when it claimed, "Most men want only an adequate screen. But women alone with the thing in the house all day have to eye it as a piece of furniture."[71] In addition, while these discussions of television were addressed to female readers, the woman's spectatorial pleasure was less associated with her enjoyment of the medium than it was with her own objectification, her desire to be looked at by the gaze of another.

On one level here, television was depicted as a threat to the visual appeal of the female body in domestic space. Specifically, there was something visually unpleasurable about the sight of a woman operating the technology of the receiver. In 1955, Sparton Television proclaimed that "the sight of a woman tuning a TV set with dials near the floor" was "most unattractive." The Sparton TV, with its tuning knob located at the top of the set, promised to maintain the visual appeal of the woman.[72] Beyond this specific case, there was a distinct set of aesthetic conventions formed in these years for male and female viewing postures. A 1953 advertisement for CBS-Columbia Television illustrates this well. Three alternative viewing postures are taken up by family members. A little boy stretches out on the floor, a father slumps in his easy chair, and the lower portion of a mother's outstretched body is gracefully lifted in a sleek modern chair with a seat that tilts upward. Here as elsewhere, masculine viewing is characterized by slovenly body posture. Conversely, feminine viewing posture takes on a certain visual appeal even as the female body passively reclines.[73]

As this advertisement indicates, the graphic representation of the female body viewing television had to be carefully controlled. It had to be made appealing to the eye of the observer, for in a fundamental sense, there was something taboo about the sight of a woman watching television. In fact, the housewife was almost never shown watching television by herself. Instead, she typically lounged on a chair (perhaps reading a book) while the television set remained turned off in the room. In 1952, *Better Homes and Gardens* stated one quite practical reason for the taboo. The article gave suggestions for methods of covering windows that would keep neighbors from peering into the home. It related this interest in privacy to women's work and television: "You should be able to have big, big windows to let in light and view, windows that let you watch the stars on a summer night without feeling exposed and naked. In good conscience, you should be able to leave the dinner dishes on the table while you catch a favorite TV or radio program, without sensing derogatory comments on your housekeeping."[74] Thus, for the housewife, being caught in the act of enjoying a broadcast is ultimately degrading because it threatens to reveal the signs of her slovenly behavior to the observer. More generally, we might say that the magazines showed women that their subjective pleasure in watching television was at odds with their own status as efficient and visually attractive housewives.

Although these representations are compatible with traditional gender roles, subtle reversals of power ran through the magazines as a whole. Even if there was a certain degree of privilege attached to the man's position of total relaxation—his right to rule from the easy chair throne—his power was in no way absolute, nor was it stable. Although such representations held to the standard conception of women as visually pleasing spectacles—as passive objects of male desire—these representations also contradicted such notions by presenting women as active producers in control of domestic affairs. For this reason, it seems that the most striking thing about this gendered representation of the body is that it inverted—or at least complicated—normative conceptions of masculinity and femininity. Whereas Western society associates activity with maleness, representations of television often attributed this trait to the woman. Conversely, the notion of feminine passivity was typically transferred over to the man of the house.[75] It could well be concluded that the cultural ideals that demanded women be shown as productive workers in the home also had the peculiar side effect of "feminizing" the father.

Perhaps for this reason, popular media presented tongue-in-cheek versions of the situation, showing how television had turned men into passive homebodies. In the last scene of *The Honeymooners'* episode "TV or Not TV," for example, the marital dispute between Alice and Ralph is inverted, with Alice apparently the "woman on top."[76] After Ralph scolds Alice about her delinquent housekeeping, Alice's TV addiction is transferred over to her husband and his friend Ed Norton, who quickly become passive viewers. Ralph sits before the television set with a smorgasbord of snacks, which he deliberately places within his reach so that he needn't move a muscle while watching his program. Norton's regressive state becomes the center of the comedic situation as he is turned into a child viewer addicted to a sciencefiction serial. Wearing a club-member space helmet, Norton tunes into his favorite television host, Captain Video, and recites the space scout pledge. After arguing over program preferences, Ralph and Norton finally settle down for the *Late, Late, Late Show* and, exhausted, fall asleep in front of the set. Alice then enters the room and, with a look of motherly condescension, covers Ralph and Norton with a blanket, tucking them in for the night.

Men's magazines such as *Esquire* and *Popular Science* also presented wry commentary on male viewers. In 1951, for example, *Esquire* showed the stereotypical husband relaxing with his shoes off and a beer in his hand, smiling idiotically while seated before a television set. Two years later, the same magazine referred to television fans as "televidiots."[77] Nonetheless, while these magazines provided a humorous look at the man of leisure, they also presented men with alternatives. In very much the same way that Catharine Beecher attempted to elevate the woman by making her the center of domestic affairs, the men's magazines suggested that fathers could regain authority through increased participation in family life.

Indeed, the "masculine domesticity" that Margaret Marsh sees as central to Progressive era lifestyles also pervaded the popular advice disseminated to men in the 1950s. According to Marsh, masculine domesticity has historically provided men with a way to assert their dominion at home. Faced with their shrinking authority in the new corporate world of white-collar desk jobs, the middle-class men of the early 1900s turned inward to the home where their increased participation in and control over the family served to compensate for feelings of powerlessness in the public sphere. Moreover, Marsh argues that masculine domesticity actually undermined women's growing desire for equal rights because it contained that desire within the safe sphere of the home. In other words, while masculine domesticity presented a more "compassionate" model of marriage where men supposedly shared domestic responsibilities with women, it did nothing to encourage women's equal participation in the public sphere.[78]

Given such historical precedents, it is not surprising that the postwar advice to men on this account took on explicitly misogynistic tones. As early as 1940, Sydnie Greenbie called for the reinstitution of manhood in his book, *Leisure For Living*. Greenbie reasoned that the popular figure of the male "boob" could be counteracted if the father cultivated his mechanical skills. As he wrote, "At last man has found something more in keeping with his nature, the workshop, with its lathe and mechanical saws, something he has kept as yet his own against the predacious female. . . . And [it becomes] more natural . . . for the man to be a homemaker as well as the woman."[79]

After the war the reintegration of the father became a popular ideal. As *Esquire* told its male readers, "Your place, Mister, is in the home, too, and if you'll make a few thoughtful improvements to it, you'll build yourself a happier, more comfortable, less back breaking world. . . . "[80] From this perspective, the men's magazines suggested ways for fathers to take an active and productive attitude in relation to television. Even if men were passive spectators, when not watching they could learn to repair the set or else produce television carts, built-ins, and stylish cabinets.[81] Articles with step-by-step instructions circulated in *Popular Science,* and the *Home Craftsman* even had a special "TV: Improve Your Home Show" column featuring a husband and wife, Thelma and Vince, and their adventures in home repairs. *Popular Science* suggested hobbies through which men could use television in an active, productive way. The magazine ran several articles on a new fad—TV photography. Men were shown how to take still pictures off their television sets, and in 1950 the magazine even conducted a readership contest for prize winning photos that were published in the December issue.[82]

The gendered division of domestic labor and the complex relations of power entailed by it were thus shown to organize the experience of watching television. These popular representations begin to disclose the social construction of television as it was rooted in a mode of thought based on categories of sexual difference. Indeed, sexual difference, and the corresponding dynamics of domestic labor and leisure, framed television's introduction to the public in significant ways. The television industry struggled to produce programming forms that might appeal to what they assumed to be the typical housewife, and in so doing they drew an abstract portrait of "Mrs. Daytime Consumer." By tailoring programs to suit the content and organization of her day, the industry hoped to capture her divided attention. Through developing schedules that mimicked the pattern of her daily activities, network executives aspired to make television a routine habit. This "ideal" female spectator was thus the very foundation of the daytime programs the industry produced. But like all texts, these programs didn't simply turn viewers into ideal spectators; they didn't simply "affect" women. Instead, they were used and interpreted within the context of everyday life at home. It is this everyday context that women's magazines addressed, providing a cultural space through which housewives might negotiate their peculiar relationship to a new media form.

Women's magazines engaged their readers in a dialogue about the concrete problems that television posed for productive labor in the home. They depicted the subtle interplay between labor and leisure at home, and they offered women ways to deal with—or else resist—television in their daily lives. If our culture has systematically relegated domestic leisure to the realm of nonproduction, these discourses remind us of the tenuousness of such notions. Indeed, at least for the housewife, television was not represented as a passive activity; rather, it was incorporated into a pattern of everyday life where work is never done.

Notes

1. This stove was mentioned in *Sponsor*, 4 June 1951, p. 19. It was also illustrated and discussed in *Popular Science*, May 1952, p. 132. The *Popular Science* reference is interesting because this men's magazine did not discuss the TV component of the stove as a vehicle for leisure, but rather showed how "a housewife can follow telecast cooking instructions step-by-step on the TV set built into this electric oven." Perhaps in this way, the magazine allayed men's fears that their wives would use the new technology for diversion as opposed to useful labor.

2. Nancy Folbre, "Exploitation Comes Home: A Critique of the Marxist Theory of Family Labour," *Cambridge Journal of Economics* 6 (1982), pp. 317–29.

3. Henri Lefebvre, foreword, *Critique de la Vie Quotidienne* (Paris, L'Arche, 1958), reprinted in *Communication and Class Struggle*, ed. Armond Mattelart and Seth Siegelaub, trans. Mary C. Axtmann (New York: International General, 1979), p. 136.

4. See David Morley, *Family Television: Cultural Power and Domestic Leisure*

(London: Comedia, 1986); and Ann Gray, "Behind Closed Doors: Video Recorders in the Home," *Boxed In: Women and Television,* ed. H. Baehr and G. Dyer (New York: Pandora, 1987), pp. 38–54.

5. Tania Modleski, "The Rhythms of Reception: Daytime Television and Women's Work," *Regarding Television: Critical Approaches,* ed. E. Ann Kaplan (Frederick, Md.: University Publications of America, 1983), pp. 67–75. See also the fourth chapter in Modleski, *Loving With A Vengeance: Mass-Produced Fantasies for Women* (New York: Methuen, 1984).

6. Nick Browne, "The Political Economy of the Television (Super) Text," *Quarterly Review of Film Studies* 9 (3) (Summer 1984), p. 176.

7. William Boddy, "The Rhetoric and Economic Roots of the American Broadcasting Industry," *Cinetracts* 6 (2) (Spring 1979), pp. 37–54.

8. William Boddy, "The Shining Centre of the Home: Ontologies of Television in the 'Golden Age'," *Television in Transition,* ed. Phillip Drummond and Richard Paterson (London: British Film Institute, 1985), pp. 125–33.

9. For a detailed analysis of the rise and fall of the DuMont Network, see Gary Newton Hess, *An Historical Study of the DuMont Television Network* (New York: Arno Press, 1979).

10. Cited in "DuMont Expansion Continues," *Radio Daily,* 12 April 1949, p. 23. See also "DuMont Skeds 7 A.M. to 11 P.M.," *Variety,* 22 September 1948, p. 34; "Daytime Tele As Profit Maker," *Variety,* 27 October 1948, pp. 25, 33; "Round-Clock Schedule Here to Stay As DuMont Programming Makes Good," *Variety,* 10 November 1948, pp. 29, 38.

11. Cited in "Daytime Video: DuMont Plans Afternoon Programming," *Broadcasting-Telecasting,* 28 November 1949, p. 3. See also "WTTG Gives Washington Regular Daytime Video with New Program Setup," *Variety,* 19 January 1949, p. 30; "Video Schedule on Coax Time," *Variety,* 12 January 1949, p. 27; "DuMont's 'Mother' Goes Network in Daytime Spread," *Variety,* 27 November 1949, p. 27.

12. "ABC, CBS, NBC Cold to Full Daytime Schedule; DuMont to Go It Alone," *Variety,* 6 October 1948, p. 27.

13. "CBS All-Day TV Programming," *Variety,* 26 January 1949, p. 34; "Video Schedule on Co-Ax Time," *Variety,* 12 January 1949, p. 27; "WNBT, N.Y., Swinging into Line as Daytime Video Airing Gains Momentum," *Variety,* 19 January 1949, p. 24; Bob Stahl, "WNBT Daytime Preem Has Hausfrau Pull but Is Otherwise Below Par," *Variety,* 9 February 1949, p. 34; "Full CBS Airing Soon," *Variety,* 2 March 1949, p. 29; "Kathi Norris Switch to WNBT Cues Daytime Expansion for Flagship," *Variety,* 1 March 1950, p. 31.

14. Cited in "Daytime TV," *Broadcasting-Telecasting,* 11 December 1950, p. 74.

15. *Sponsor,* 4 June 1951, p. 19.

16. *Newsweek,* 24 September 1951, p. 56.

17. *Televiser,* September 1951, p. 20.

18. In the early 1950s, many of the shows were sustaining vehicles—that is, programs that were aired in order to attract and maintain audiences, but that had no sponsors.

19. "DuMont Skeds 7 A.M. to 11 P.M." *Variety,* 22 September 1948, p. 25.

20. "Pat 'N' Johnny," *Variety,* 1 March 1950, p. 35. This example bears interesting connections to Rick Altman's more general theoretical arguments about the aesthetics of sound on television. Altman argues that television uses sound to signal moments of interest, claiming that, "the sound track serves better than the image

itself the parts of the image that are sufficiently spectacular to merit closer attention on the part of the intermittent viewer." See Altman, "Television/Sound," *Studies in Entertainment: Critical Approaches to Mass Culture,* ed. Tania Modleski (Bloomington and Indianapolis: Indiana University Press, 1986), p. 47.

21. Robert C. Allen, *Speaking of Soap Operas* (Chapel Hill: University of North Carolina Press, 1985).

22. See "Daytime Video: DuMont Plans Afternoon Program" and "DuMont Daytime 'Shoppers' Series Starts," *Broadcasting-Telecasting,* 12 December 1949, p. 5.

23. Some variety programs included fifteen minute sitcoms and soap operas.

24. "TV's 'Stars in the Afternoon'," *Variety,* 3 October 1951, p. 29.

25. "Women's Magazine of the Air," *Variety,* 9 March 1949, p. 33; "Women's Page," *Variety,* 1 June 1949, p. 34.

26. NBC had particular problems securing sponsors and, especially during 1951 and 1952, many of its shows were sustaining programs. So critical had this problem become that in fall of 1952 NBC temporarily cut back its schedule, giving afternoon hours back to affiliates. Affiliates, however, complained that this put them at a competive disadvantage with CBS affiliates. See "NBC-TV's 'What's the Use?' Slant May Give Daytime Back to Affiliates," *Variety,* 3 September 1952, p. 20; "Daytime TV—No. 1 Dilemma," *Variety,* 24 September 1952, pp. 1, 56; "NBC-TV to Focus Prime Attention on Daytime Schedule," *Variety,* 24 December 1952, p. 22; "NBC-TV Affiliates in Flareup," *Variety,* 6 May 1953, p. 23.

27. Weaver's concept was adopted by CBS executives who in 1952 instituted the "12 plan" that gave sponsors a discount for buying twelve participations during the daytime schedule. "Day TV Impact," *Broadcasting,* 3 November 1952, p. 73; Bob Stahl, "CBS-TV's Answer to 'Today,'" *Variety,* 12 November 1952, pp. 23, 58.

28. John H. Porter, memo to TV network salesmen, 11 June 1954, NBC Records, Box 183: Folder 5, Wisconsin Center Historical Archives, State Historical Society, Madison.

29. George Rosen, "Garroway 'Today' Off to Boff Start As Revolutionary News Concept," *Variety,* 16 January 1952, p. 29.

30. Joe Meyers and Bob Graff, cited in William R. McAndrew, confidential memo to John K. Herbert, 23 March 1953, NBC Records, Box 370: Folder 22, Wisconsin Center Historical Archives, State Historical Society, Madison.

31. *Daytime Availabilities: Program Descriptions and Estimates,* 1 June 1954, NBC Records, Box 183: Folder 5, Wisconsin Center Historical Archives, State Historical Society, Madison.

32. "Early Morning Inserts Get WNBT Dress-Up," *Variety,* 13 August 1952, p. 26.

33. "For the Girls at Home," *Newsweek,* 15 March 1954, p. 92. NBC's advertising campaign for *Home* was unprecedented for daytime programming promotion, costing $976,029.00 in print, on-air promotion, outdoor advertising, and novelty gimmicks. See Jacob A. Evans, letter to Charles Barry, 28 January 1954, NBC Records, Box 369: Folder 5, Wisconsin Center Historical Archives, State Historical Society, Madison.

34. Jacob A. Evans, letter to Charles Barry, 28 January 1954, NBC Records, Box 369: Folder 5, Wisconsin Center Historical Archives, State Historical Society, Madison.

35. In a promotional report, NBC boasted that on *Today*'s first broadcast, Kiplinger received 20,000 requests for a free copy of the magazine. Matthew J. Cul-

ligan, sales letter, 27 January 1953, NBC Records, Box 378: Folder 9, Wisconsin Center Historical Archives, State Historical Society, Madison.

36. The report cited here was commentary for a slide presentation given by Coffin to about fifty researchers from ad agencies and manufacturing companies in the New York area. *Commentary for Television's Daytime Profile: Buying Habits and Characteristics of the Audience,* 10 June 1954, NBC Records, Box 183: Folder 5, Wisconsin Center Historical Archives, State Historical Society, Madison. For the actual survey, see W. R. Simmons and Associates Research, Inc., *Television's Daytime Profile: Buying Habits and Characteristics of the Audience,* 15 September 1954, NBC Records, Box 183: Folder 8, Wisconsin Center Historical Archives, State Historical Society, Madison. A short booklet reviewing the findings was sent to all prospective advertisers; *Television's Daytime Profile: An Intimate Portrait of the Ideal Market for Most Advertisers,* 1 September 1954, NBC Records, Box 183: Folder 5, Wisconsin Center Historical Archives, State Historical Society, Madison. For NBC's exploitation of the survey, see also Ed Vane, letter to Mr. Edward A. Antonili, 7 December 1954, NBC Records, Box 183: Folder 5, Wisconsin Center Historical Archives, State Historical Society, Madison; Hugh M. Bellville, Jr., letter to Robert Sarnoff, 27 July 1954, NBC Records, Box 183: Folder 5, Wisconsin Center Historical Archives, State Historical Society, Madison; Thomas Coffin, letter to H. M. Beville, Jr., 21 July 1954, NBC Records, Box 183: Folder 5, Wisconsin Center Historical Archives, State Historical Society, Madison. The survey also made headlines in numerous trade journals, newspapers, and magazines. For press coverage, see NBC's *clipping file,* NBC Records, Box 183: Folder 5, Wisconsin Center Historical Archives, State Historical Society, Madison.

37. Edward Stasheff, *The Television Program: Its Writing, Direction, and Production* (New York: A. A. Wyn, 1951), p. 47.

38. Consumer spectacles were further achieved through rear-screen projection, an "aerial" camera that captured action with a "telescoping arm," and mechanical devices such as a weather machine that adorned products in a mist of rain, fog, sleet, or hail. *Daytime Availabilities: Program Descriptions and Cost Estimates,* 1 June 1954, NBC Records, Box 183: Folder 5, Wisconsin Center Historical Archives, State Historical Society, Madison.

39. Charles C. Barry, memos to Richard Pinkham, 2 March 1954, 3 March 1954, and 4 March 1954, NBC Records, Box 369: Folder 5, Wisconsin Center Historical Archives, State Historical Society, Madison.

40. Franklin Sisson, *Thirty Television Talks* (New York, n.p., 1955), p. 144. Cited in Giraud Chester and Garnet R. Garrison, *Television and Radio* (New York: Appleton-Century-Crofts, Inc., 1956), p. 414.

41. Caroline Burke, memo to Ted Mills, 20 November 1953, NBC Records, Box 377: Folder 6, Wisconsin Center Historical Archives, State Historical Society, Madison; Arlene Francis, cited in Earl Wilson, *The NBC Book of Stars* (New York: Pocket Books, 1957), p. 92.

42. Cited in Wilson, *The NBC Book,* p. 94.

43. Sylvester L. Weaver, memo to Harry Bannister, 10 October 1952, NBC Records, Box 378: Folder 9, Wisconsin Center Historical Archives, State Historical Society, Madison.

44. Joe Meyers, cited in William R. McAndrew, confidential memo to John K. Herbert, 23 March 1953, NBC Records, Box 370: Folder 22, Wisconsin Center Historical Archives, State Historical Society, Madison.

45. A. A. Schechter, "'Today' As An Experiment Bodes Encouraging Mañana," *Variety,* 16 July 1952, p. 46. NBC also advertised *Today* by claiming that "people are actually changing their living habits to watch 'Today.'" See *Sponsor,* 25 February 1952, pp. 44–45.

46. *Daytime Availabilities: Program Descriptions and Cost Estimates,* 1 June 1954, NBC Records, Box 183: Folder 5, Wisconsin Center Historical Archives, State Historical Society, Madison.

47. Walter Benjamin, "The Work of Art in the Age of Mechanical Reproduction," in *Illuminations: Essays and Reflections,* ed. Hannah Arendt (New York: Schocken, 1969), pp. 217–51.

48. *Ladies' Home Journal,* April 1955, p. 130. See also *Ladies' Home Journal,* February 1955, p. 95; *Good Housekeeping,* July 1955, p. 135.

49. *The New Yorker,* 3 June 1950, p. 22.

50. Crosby, "What's Television Going to Do to Your Life?" *House Beautiful,* February 1950, p. 125.

51. *American Home,* October 1955, p. 14.

52. Walter Adams and E. A. Hungerford, Jr., "Television: Buying and Installing It Is Fun; These Ideas Will Help," *Better Homes and Gardens,* September 1949, p. 38; *American Home,* December 1954, p. 39.

53. *American Home,* May 1955, p. 138. The cartoon was part of an advertisement for the *Yellow Pages.*

54. *House Beautiful,* June 1952, p. 59.

55. W. W. Ward, "Is It Time To Buy Television?" *House Beautiful,* October 1948, p. 220.

56. *Ladies' Home Journal,* May 1953, p. 148.

57. "The Wonderful Anti-Statics," *House Beautiful,* January 1955, p. 89; *Ladies' Home Journal,* November 1948, p. 90.

58. Gertrude Brassard, "For Early Tea and Late TV," *American Home,* July 1952, p. 88.

59. In August 1949, for example, *House Beautiful* suggested that a swiveling cabinet would allow women to "move the screen, not the audience" (p. 69). Although portable sets were not heavily marketed in the early 1950s, they were sometimes presented as the ideal solution to the problem of moving the heavy console set.

60. *House Beautiful,* May 1952, p. 138.

61. Wright, *Building the Dream,* p. 172.

62. *House Beautiful,* June 1951, p. 121.

63. Vivian Grigsby Bender, "Please a Dining Room!" *American Home,* September 1951, p. 27.

64. *Better Homes and Gardens,* December 1952, p. 144; *Better Homes and Gardens,* February 1953, p. 169; see also *American Home,* September 1953, p. 102.

65. *House Beautiful,* November 1948, p. 5.

66. Edith Ramsay, "How to Stretch a Day," *American Home,* September 1949, p. 66; *House Beautiful,* December 1950, p. 77.

67. *American Home,* February 1954, p. 32.

68. *House Beautiful,* November 1954, p. 158. For additional examples, see *American Home,* November 1953, p. 60; *Better Homes and Gardens,* December 1951, p. 7; *TV Guide,* 18 December 1953, p. 18.

69. *Better Homes and Gardens,* October 1952, p. 177.

70. Laura Mulvey, "Visual Pleasure and Narrative Cinema," *Screen* 16 (3) (1975), pp. 6–18. Since the publication of Mulvey's article, numerous feminists— including Mulvey—have theorized ways that women might find subjective pleasures in classical cinema, and feminists have also challenged the idea that pleasure in the cinema is organized entirely around scenarios of "male" desire. For a bibliography on this literature and a forum on contemporary views on female spectatorship in the cinema, see *Camera Obscura* 20–21 (May–September 1989).

71. W. W. Ward, "Is It Time to Buy Television?" *House Beautiful,* October 1948, p. 172.

72. *House Beautiful,* May 1955, p. 131.

73. *Better Homes and Gardens,* October 1953, p. 151. There is one exception to this rule of male body posture, which I have found in the fashionable men's magazine *Esquire.* While *Esquire* depicted the slovenly male viewer, it also showed men how to watch television in fashion by wearing clothes tailored specifically for TV viewing. In these cases, the male body was relaxed, and the men still smoked and drank liquor, but they were posed in more aesthetically appealing ways. See "Town-Talk Tables and Television," *Esquire,* January 1951, pp. 92–93; and "Easy Does It Leisure Wear," *Esquire,* November 1953, p. 74. The figure of the fashionable male television viewer was taken up by at least one male clothing company, The Rose Brothers, who advertised their men's wear by showing well-dressed men watching television and by promising, "You Can Tele-Wise Man by His Surretwill Suit." See *Colliers,* 1 October 1949, p. 54.

74. Robert M. Jones, "Privacy Is Worth All That It Costs," *Better Homes and Gardens,* March 1952, p. 57.

75. This is not to say that television was the only domestic machine to disrupt representations of gender. Roland Marchand, for example, has argued that advertisements for radio sets and phonographs reversed traditional pictorial conventions for the depiction of men and women. Family-circle ads typically showed husbands seated while their wives were perched on the arm of the chair or sofa. In most of the ads for radios and phonographs in his sample, the opposite is true. Marchand argues that "in the presence of culturally uplifting music, the woman more often gained the right of reposed concentration while the (more technologically inclined) man stood prepared to change the records or adjust the radio dials." See *Advertising the American Dream,* pp. 252–53. When applied to television, Marchand's analysis of radio does not seem to adhere since men were often shown seated and blatantly unable to control the technology.

76. I am borrowing Natalie Zemon Davis's phrase with which she describes how women in preindustrial France were able to invert gender hierarchies during carnival festivities and even, at times, in everyday life. See "Women On Top," *Society and Culture in Early Modern France* (Stanford, Calif.: Stanford University Press, 1975), pp. 124–51.

77. *Popular Science,* May 1954, p. 177; *Esquire,* March 1951, p. 10; Jack O'Brien, "Offsides in Sports," *Esquire,* November 1953, p. 24.

78. Marsh, *Suburban Lives,* p. 82.

79. Greenbie, *Leisure for Living,* p. 210. Greenbie, in fact, presented a quite contradictory account of mechanization in the home, at times seeing it as the man's ally, at other times claiming that modern machines actually took away male authority.

80. "Home Is for Husbands Too," *Esquire,* June 1951, p. 88.

81. In addition, companies that produced home-improvement products and workshop tools continually used television sets in their illustrations of remodeled

rooms. Typically here, the Masonite Corporation promoted its do-it-yourself paneling in an advertisement that displayed a television set in a "male room" just for Dad. See *Better Homes and Gardens,* August 1951, p. 110. For similar ads, see *American Home,* June 1955, p. 3; *Better Homes and Gardens,* February 1953, p. 195; *American Home,* November 1952, p. 105. It should be noted that some of these ads also showed women doing the remodeling work.

82. "From Readers' Albums of Television Photos," *Popular Science,* December 1950, p. 166. See also "TV's Images Can Be Photographed," *Popular Science,* August 1950, pp. 184–85; R. P. Stevenson, "How You Can Photograph the Fights Via Television," *Popular Science,* February 1951, pp. 214–216.

Women Characters and "Real World" Femininity

JULIE D'ACCI

During *Cagney and Lacey's* creation and the whole of its network run, the key players involved in production and reception continuously battled over what women on television should and should not or could and could not be. These players included those we would expect to be part of any negotiation of television's meanings—the TV network, the production company and production team, the television audience, the press, and various interest and pressure groups.

All these groups, of course, supported definitions of *woman, women,* and *femininity* that suited their particular interests, whether those were political, economic, cultural, "personal," or some combination thereof. Many network executives, for instance, wanted the show to include topical and relevant representations of women while they simultaneously hoped to preserve the conventional ways of depicting female characters. Despite the examples set by a number of 1970s sitcoms (which I discuss below), these conventions still presented women as primarily young, white, middle class, stereotypically "attractive," and domesticated. They specifically portrayed women as wives, mothers, heterosexual sex objects, subsidiaries of men, and as "vulnerable" and "sympathetic" characters; in addition, women were traditionally cast as the protagonists of situation comedies rather than prime-time dramas.[1]

In contrast, *Cagney and Lacey's* independent production company, Orion Television (formerly Filmways), appeared at least somewhat committed to generating more innovative representations. Richard Rosenbloom, Orion Television's president, in fact had a reputation for producing the highest percentage of work written by women in Hollywood at the time. The series's production team (the creators, writers, producers, and main actresses), for its part, was powerfully influenced by the liberal women's movement and explicitly fashioned *Cagney and Lacey* (especially in its first few years) on early feminist terms. A significant segment of the women's audience for the series, as well as for other working women–targeted programs of the time, was looking for progressive, multidimensional, and "real" female depictions. The mainstream press, as can be imagined, demonstrated extremely varied interests: One sector, very much affected by feminism, agitated for a wider range of women characters on television and, specifically, for roles shaped by women's movement concerns. Other media factions called for a return to "tried and true" femininity.[2]

Similarly, a number of interest and pressure groups weighed in according to their own stakes in divergent meanings and portrayals: The National Gay Task Force, for example, vehemently protested the network's effort to shield the series from connotations of lesbianism by replacing one actress portraying Cagney with another "more feminine" one. The National Right to Life Committee fiercely opposed Cagney and Lacey's support of a woman character who chose to have an abortion, while Planned Parenthood and the National Abortion Rights Action League (NARAL) applauded the program's embrace of reproductive rights. And spokespeople for the U.S. liberal women's movement generally and consistently championed the series for depicting "independent" working women and emphasizing the women's friendship.

Because the women's movements were such fundamental forces in U.S. social history of the 1970s and 1980s, and in the controversies surrounding *Cagney and Lacey,* I need to say a few things about them here. The taxonomy of the different "camps" that I will draw upon has been well critiqued—among other problems, it tends to ignore the countless overlaps from camp to camp and to oversimplify a wide diversity of viewpoints. But because many feminists in the seventies and eighties defined themselves in relation to its terms, it warrants discussion. As I have already indicated, the camp that most influenced *Cagney and Lacey* is generally called the liberal women's movement. In America, this segment is associated with *Ms.* magazine, Gloria Steinem, and the National Organization for Women (NOW). Its primary emphasis, especially in the 1970s, was on equality under the law and in the labor force, with a focus on white, heterosexual, middle-class women; its programs for social change were oriented toward "reform" rather than a radical structural reorganization of American political and social life. In the late 1970s and the 1980s, due to the efforts of women of color and lesbians, the movement became more attentive to groups beyond the white middle class, and it also recognized the existence of structural reasons for women's oppression that required more than personal solutions. By and large, the movement has worked to train public attention on the social and cultural problems that women face involving wages, labor conditions, abortion and other reproductive rights, rape laws, women's safety, childcare issues, educational opportunities, female solidarity, and the importance of mass media in bringing about social change.

But feminism during the 1970s and 1980s was represented by other segments and theoretical approaches in addition to the liberal one. These various approaches have been profiled in other works, and I just want to flag four major positions—radical, cultural, socialist, and poststructuralist feminism. Many early radical feminists engaged in a sound critique of liberal feminism, made the oppression of women and the operations of patriarchy their central concerns, and favored the elimination of sex differences. But throughout the 1970s and into the 1980s, some radical feminists drifted toward a belief in a natural female essence. This approach, which came to be called cultural feminism, evolved into a celebration of, rather than a challenge to, "essential" sex differences. Associated with such groups as Women against Pornography, such feminism often valorized a biological femininity that was life- and nurturance-oriented and that was universally oppressed by a dominating and conquest-oriented patriarchy.

Socialist feminism, on the other hand, argued for the social construction of both femininity and masculinity and focused on such issues as the relationship between women's relegation to the domestic sphere and the maintenance of capitalism. Poststructuralist feminism argued for myriad differences within the seemingly coherent categories "woman" and "women" and for the notion that these concepts encompass a multitude of heterogeneous meanings produced in language rather than nature. Although liberal feminism plays the most active role in my case study of *Cagney and Lacey*, the other strands surface in some of the media and scholarly criticism I draw upon and discuss.[3]

The Representational Context

Cagney and Lacey's earliest period, from its conception in 1974 to its production as a made-for-TV movie in 1981, seethed with conflicts over definitions of women and their many negotiations. But it was not the only project so beset. Generally speaking, representations of women in motion pictures and television programs were highly contradictory throughout the 1970s. Films such as *Alice Doesn't Live Here Anymore, Julia, The Turning Point,* and *An Unmarried Woman* expressed tensions between the emerging interests of the women's movements and more traditional notions of femininity. On prime-time television, a number of industry and social conditions combined to spawn a collection of amazingly paradoxical depictions. As Eileen Meehan demonstrates, by 1970 the A. C. Nielsen Company (which measures the television audience and publishes series "ratings") had changed its fixed group of designated Nielsen "families" from a sample that dated back to its surveys of radio audiences, replacing it with younger and more urban households. Also, CBS discovered that, although its programming was bringing in more total viewers than the other networks, its five "owned and operated" stations in New York, Los Angeles, Chicago, Philadelphia, and St. Louis were doing badly in ratings and revenues. The implications of this discovery, along with the Nielsen Company's changeover to a younger, more urban ratings sample, helped to alter the face of prime-time television.[4]

It is important to understand that Federal Communication Commission regulations at the time allowed each network to own five VHF-TV stations.[5] Called the "O and O's" (for owned and operated), these stations were responsible for a large share of the networks' actual profits and were located in highly lucrative metropolitan markets. Some CBS executives realized in 1969 that their schedule was heavily weighted with country programs such as *Green Acres, The Beverly Hillbillies, Mayberry RFD, Hee Haw, Petticoat Junction,* and *Gunsmoke.* These programs, although extremely popular in the United States at large, were not popular (or, because of ratings, were presumed to be unpopular) with the urban audiences of the O and O's—or, more precisely, with the newly designated Nielsen households. In a bold and internally contested move, CBS canceled its winning country schedule and oriented its programming toward what Jane Feuer has called "socially conscious sit-coms," and Todd Gitlin, "relevant" programming. Some network executives thought that these series would appeal not only to the desired eighteen-to-forty-nine-year-old, upwardly mobile target audience, but also to the *urban,* eighteen-to-forty-nine-year-old, upwardly mobile audience.[6]

The new socially relevant sitcoms were produced primarily by Norman Lear's Tandem and TAT Productions, by Mary Tyler Moore's MTM Enterprises, and by Twentieth Century–Fox (*M*A*S*H*), and Warner Bros. (*Alice*). The civil rights movement, the Black Power movement, the antiwar movement, the women's movements, and the accelerated entry of women into the labor force were all tapped for subject material. The effort to simply keep its programming up to date had already led ABC (in the late 1960s) into the social ferment of the times with such programs as *Mod Squad* and *Judd for the Defense.* (To some degree, NBC's *Julia* [1968] may also be seen as part of this trend.) But the push to attract specific upscale urban audiences intensified CBS's mining of thematic material that it thought would appeal to young, educated city dwellers. The move had enormous repercussions for the ways women were represented; programs featuring working women, African American women, older women, divorced women, single mothers, and working-class women filled the 1970s home screen. *The Mary Tyler Moore Show, Rhoda, Good Times, The Jeffersons, Maude, One Day at a Time, Alice,* and *All in the Family* were prominent examples of the new fare. Controversial women's issues such as abortion, rape, equal employment opportunities, and racial and gender prejudice were featured subjects. At least in some prime-time programs, "woman," "women," and "femininity" were no longer conceived solely in terms of young, white, and middle-class characteristics. Because this new "urban and sophisticated" programming was such a success at CBS, the other networks followed suit with a number of clones.[7]

However, as Lauren Rabinovitz, Serafina Bathrick, and Bonnie Dow have pointed out, these programs often produced contradictory and troubling representations of femininity and "independent" women, and most of the social issues raised were domesticated—that is, they were represented as contained and resolvable at the level of the family. With regard to their treatment of African Americans, Donald Bogle argued that these comedies "take authentic issues in the black community and distort them." Esther Rolle, who played the character Florida on *Good Times*, quit the show because of differences with the producers over the portrayals, which she called "an outrage, an insult." And the National Black Feminist Organization charged that the representations of blacks and other "minorities" in these comedies were "slanted toward the ridiculous with no redeeming counter images" and that the programs gave the impression that black people did not perform effectively in professional positions. The issues raised by these series regarding both African Americans and women—problematic, delimited, racist, and sexist as they were—nevertheless became part of negotiated public discourse, introduced a measure of visible difference into television's repertoire, and challenged prime time's equation of women (since the 1953 disappearance of *Beulah* and *Amos 'n' Andy*) with white and upscale characteristics exclusively.[8]

Beginning in the mid-1970s and continuing into the next decade, different conditions in society and the television industry combined once again to generate even more paradoxical female characters. This time, pressure on the networks from groups such as the Parent-Teachers Association (PTA) to reduce incidents of televised violence led directly to the display of women's bodies as sexual attractions: "If you can't have Starsky pull a gun and fire it fifty times a day on promos," said Brandon Tartikoff (at the time vice-president of NBC's programming), "sex becomes your next best handle." Before this period, images of women on prime time had not been charged with the sexual display of motion picture imagery; instead, female TV characters were generally domesticated. However, from the mid-1970s to the early 1980s, female sex objects dominated the TV landscape in what is often called the "jiggle" era, or in the industry's noneuphemistic tag, the "T&A" ("tits and ass") period. It is, of course, no accident that these representations coincided with the ever-mounting backlash over the concerns and demands of the women's movements.[9]

One of the main paradoxes of this period is that, during it, women starred in more dramatic programs than at any other time in television history. Series like *Police Woman, Get Christie Love, Charlie's Angels*, and *Wonder Woman* are major offspring of that era. Each of these programs could be squarely classified under the jiggle category, and each promoted sensationalism by providing raw material for setting up the classic "woman in distress" situation. The women protagonists ultimately were either rescued by male colleagues or used superhuman capabilities to resolve their predicaments. Other jiggle examples include *Flying High* and *American Girls* (about stewardesses and reporters, respectively) and the women characters in *WKRP in Cincinnati* and *Three's Company.*[10]

Some television scholars have seen these programs as overt instances of the backlash against the women's movements, whereas others have read them as prime time's way of killing two birds with one stone and capturing both segments of a divided audience. As Todd Gitlin says of *Charlie's Angels,* the show "appealed at once to elements of the new feminism and its conservative opposition. The Angels are skilled working women and sex objects at the same time." The jiggle phenomenon, in the face of audience and interest-group protest, tapered off (at least in its most blatant form) by the early 1980s. But its complex and multidimensional legacy included the breaking of barriers to women—both black and white (*Get Christie Love* featured African American actress Teresa Graves)—as stars of TV dramas. It also introduced a "spectacle" aspect to the representation of female bodies—that is, a more explicit sexual dimension to the traditionally more domesticated woman, revealing her as sex and beauty object.[11]

Getting New Representations to the Screen

Cagney and Lacey came upon the scene in the midst of this history. Its first script, written in 1974, fell squarely within the conceptual terms of the liberal women's movement, in that it featured role reversals—women in a traditionally male profession and women in a standard, male, public-sphere genre. Historically and industrially speaking, its creators considered it an idea whose time had come. According to Barbara Avedon, Barbara Corday, and Barney Rosenzweig, *Cagney and Lacey* was specifically conceived as a response to an influential book from the early liberal women's movement, Molly Haskell's *From Reverence to Rape: The Treatment of Women in the Movies.* Avedon and Corday were engaged in the literature and politics of this movement, and both were in women's groups. Rosenzweig was "setting out to have his consciousness raised." They read Haskell's book and were intrigued by the fact that there had never been a Hollywood movie about two women "buddies" comparable to the men portrayed in *M*A*S*H* or *Butch Cassidy and the Sundance Kid.*[12] According to Rosenzweig, "The Hollywood establishment had totally refused women those friendships, the closest thing being perhaps Joan Crawford and Eve Arden in *Mildred Pierce,* the tough lady boss and her wise-cracking side-kick. So I went to my friend Ed Feldman, who was then head of Filmways [now Orion], and I said, 'I want to do a picture where we turn around a conventional genre piece like *Freebie and the Bean* with its traditional male situations and make it into the first real hit feminist film.'"[13]

Corday said, "Barney came to this conclusion not so much, at that time, as a feminist—because he was very new to all of those ideas then—but [he] came to the conclusion as a commercial producer, that it was *extraordinary* that there had never been a female buddy movie, and at that moment in history, it would probably be a great idea. He talked to me about it and I went to my partner, Barbara, and we talked about it. We conceived of it, all of us, as a feature, because that's what the buddy movies were, they were feature films."[14]

One of the main motivations behind *Cagney and Lacey* from its inception was the creators' notion that two women could, in fact, be represented as friends who worked and talked together, rather than as more conventional competitors. Both Avedon and Corday recalled that the relationship between the protagonists was modeled (if somewhat unconsciously) on their own eight-year relationship as writing partners and friends. As Corday said,

> We were women, we were partners, we were best friends. We were a lot of the things that we were writing about. . . . We spent a good deal of the eight years that we wrote together talking about our lives. . . . What we tried to get into the characters . . . was us. We didn't say we were doing it, or set out to do it, but there we were. . . . I'm more Mary Beth, Barbara's more Chris, but there are pieces of each of us in the other. . . . Barbara is very politically involved, very active in causes. I'm more conservative. . . . I finish her sentences for her. She's the one who races off as Chris does. I'm the one who says maybe we should talk about this for a minute.[15]

Ed Feldman at Filmways was, in fact, interested in the idea Rosenzweig had pitched to him, and he approved the "seed" money to hire Avedon and Corday as writers. Barbara Avedon recalled that, although Filmways was "excited" about the idea, its executives had difficulty understanding the view of women involved. They persisted in situating the characters in the film industry's context of women as spectacles and sex objects. According to Avedon, "They [Filmways] told us things like, when [Cagney or Lacey] rips her shirt back and shows her badge to the guys, they can all stare [at her breasts]. That was the level of consciousness, even though they were doing a women-buddy movie."[16]

Avedon and Corday prepared for writing the script by spending ten days with New York City policewomen. Avedon recalled, "The women cops we met were first and foremost cops. Unlike Angie Dickinson in *Police Woman,* who'd powder her nose before she went out to make a bust, these women took themselves seriously as police officers." Both Corday and Avedon were convinced that the only way for *Cagney and Lacey* to work was for them to cast "strong, mature" women with "senses of humor"; because the script was thought to be so controversial for the time, they did not, however, consider mixing the races of the protagonists. They envisioned Sally Kellerman as Cagney and Paula Prentiss as Lacey.[17]

The creators all agreed that because they were dealing with potentially incendiary "feminist" material, their film would have to be, first and foremost, "entertaining." The original script, entitled "Freeze," was a spoof in which Cagney and Lacey uncover the existence of the Godmother, the female intelligence behind a brothel where men are the prostitutes and women the patrons. The major narrative device was the early women's movement notion of role reversals. Not only did the Godmother replace the Godfather and the prostitutes and patrons reverse roles, but, with regard to the protagonists, as Avedon said, "We turned every cliché over, even the unpleasant ones. We had Cagney say to a guy 'I'll give you a call sometime,' and then turn around and walk out insensitively. I really didn't like her very much for doing it."[18]

After getting the script financed by Filmways, Rosenzweig needed a major motion picture studio to pick up the project and do the actual production. He took the original property to every studio in Hollywood and received predictable "Hollywood" responses for the time, along the lines of "these women aren't soft enough, aren't feminine enough." Rosenzweig himself saw such responses as products of the studio heads' own personal views about femininity: "In those days," he said, "all the studio heads were males, and they didn't like [the *Cagney and Lacey* script]. They didn't think it was funny, they didn't think the women were feminine. It wasn't a conspiracy. Just from their own subjective point of view, they didn't think it was what America wanted to see because it wasn't something they wanted to see."[19]

Finally, Sherry Lansing (who was later to become the first woman head of a major motion picture studio, Twentieth Century–Fox) persuaded her boss at MGM, Dan Melnik, to make the movie. MGM said it would, but only if the well-known "sex symbols" Raquel Welch and Ann-Margret starred. (Their versatility as actresses was not yet widely recognized at this point in Hollywood history.) The other condition was a $1.6 million budget that, in true catch-22 fashion, prohibited the hiring of such high-priced actresses. The property, therefore, lay dormant for the next five years.[20]

In 1980 Rosenzweig decided to try again. This time he pitched the idea to the television networks as a pilot for a weekly series. Corday and Avedon reconceived the script, updating it and making it less of a spoof and more of a "realistic" crime drama. Because Corday, by this time, had taken a job as vice-president of comedy development at ABC, Barbara Avedon wrote the actual script herself. Although CBS declined to pick up the series, it decided to make the script as a less costly, less risky, made-for-TV movie, and Norman Powell in the TV movie department put it into development. The network also suggested that the producer cast "two sexy young actresses" in the leading roles. According to Rosenzweig, he told CBS, "You don't understand, these policewomen must be mature women. One has a family and kids, the other is a committed career officer. What separates this project from *Charlie's Angels* is that Cagney and Lacey are women; they're not girls and they're *certainly* not objects."[21]

During this impasse CBS, which had an outstanding "pay-or-play" commitment to Loretta Swit of *M*A*S*H,* asked Rosenzweig to cast her as Cagney. Avedon and Corday, who had recently worked with Sharon Gless on the TV series *Turnabout,* wanted her for the part; Avedon even said she had actually considered Gless the model for Cagney while writing the new script. But because Gless could not be released from her contract to Universal, Rosenzweig cast Swit as Cagney even though her *M*A*S*H* contract would preclude her availability should *Cagney and Lacey* turn into a series. Tyne Daly was cast as Lacey. Richard Rosenbloom, then president of Filmways Television and a staff producer at Filmways, joined the project as the movie's line producer, and Ted Post, who was known primarily as an action director, was hired to direct. The movie was shot in Toronto with a budget of $1.85 million; it was scheduled for broadcast on 8 October 1981 and was publicized in various ways by the women's movement, the network, and the mainstream press.[22]

The preproduction publicity trumpeted *Cagney and Lacey*'s importance to the cause of feminism. Gloria Steinem at *Ms.* magazine had been sent a script by the creators and was so enthusiastic that she appeared with Loretta Swit on *Donahue* to plug the movie. According to one media critic, the two were so "reverential" that it "sounded as though they were promoting the first woman president."[23]

Steinem also featured Loretta Swit and Tyne Daly, in character in their police uniforms, on the cover of the October issue of *Ms.* The issue contained a feature article on *Cagney and Lacey* written by Marjorie Rosen, a well-known feminist film critic and author of *Popcorn Venus: Women, Movies, and the American Dream.* Rosen related the troubled history of the property, emphasized its importance for feminism, underscored the specific feminist characteristics she believed *Cagney and Lacey* brought into "distinctive focus," and ended with a pitch for a weekly series. The feminist characteristics especially applauded included the presentation of women as the subjects of narrative action and adventure in a traditionally male-dominated genre, as holders of traditionally male jobs, and as friends. Also emphasized were the movie's characterizations of women as autonomous, "individualistic," and "independent." Rosen concluded, "Watching *Cagney and Lacey*, it is virtually impossible *not* to think of its potential as a weekly series. For here's a rare TV movie that not only sports such surefire ingredients as crime, cops, and a pair of great buddies, but also maintains its distinctive focus on two highly individualistic, courageous, and thoroughly independent women—women we'd like to get to know better, and women who are worth visiting with again and again." At the bottom of the article appeared the message, "If you would like to see *Cagney and Lacey* expanded into a TV series, write to Richard Rosenbloom, Filmways, 2049 Century Park East, Los Angeles, California 90067."[24]

CBS's promotion department, having its own motivations and vested interests, publicized the movie according to a standard television practice called "exploitation advertising." This is a tactic, with precedents in the Hollywood film industry, in which a sensational—usually sexual or violent—aspect of a program is highlighted for the purposes of audience attraction. *Cagney and Lacey*'s *TV Guide* advertisement filled three-quarters of a page. A large close-up of Loretta Swit, with her long blond hair, dominated the left side of the composition, while her clasped, outstretched hands held a pointed revolver that dominated the right. A significantly smaller, medium shot of the lesser-known (at the time) Tyne Daly in police coat, shirt, and tie appeared below the Swit close-up. On the lower far left of the page, underneath and smaller than the Daly image, was another shot of Swit lying on her back (presumably naked) with a sheet draped over her. One bare shoulder and arm and one bare leg, bent at the knee, were exposed. A man (also naked), depicted only from his waist up, was leaning over her, his arm across her body. The copy read, "It's their first week as undercover cops! Cagney likes the excitement. Lacey cares about the people she protects. They're going to make it as detectives—or die trying!"[25]

Various conceptions of femininity were set into play here, and it seems evident that CBS, in dealing with a movie about women in nontraditional roles, was careful to invoke not only connotations regarding the "new woman," but also more traditional notions as well. Cagney was shown as a cop with an aimed revolver, but also as a conventionally beautiful woman with eye makeup, lipstick, and long blond hair. She was also shown as a conventional object rather than subject of sexual desire. Lacey was shown in traditionally male clothing but was described in the conventionally feminine terms of "caring about the people she protects." And although they were both trying to "make it" as detectives, they were also stereotypical "women in distress" who might "die trying." The emphasis on stereotyped feminine behaviors and predicaments in an ad for a movie about women in new roles fulfilled the formula for exploitation advertising by suggesting sexual and violent content to the audience, while also reassuring it about women's traditional roles and positions in relationship to social power. This initial industry ad illustrates the negotiation of differently oriented interests in one cultural artifact. It furthermore exemplifies the workings of what John Fiske calls a "secondary" or "second-level" text (any publicity, review, or "official" public discourse about the "first-level" text, or the program itself), which promotes, through the process of intertextuality, various readings or interpretations of the program. The ad thus demonstrates how the network fostered ambiguous or varied meanings of femininity both in a promotional "text" and in the potential audience.[26]

The *Cagney and Lacey* made-for-TV movie was also publicized in the mainstream press. In an article in the *New York Times*, published the day before the program aired, Barbara Basler interviewed three New York City policewomen who had seen a sneak preview. The article exemplifies both how the press joined in the struggle over meanings and the way in which "reality" got invoked in the process. Different participants in the history of *Cagney and Lacey* called upon "reality," "real life experience," or the experiences of "real policewomen" (and policewomen invoked their individual "real" experiences) as supports for their own particular notions of what the movie and the series meant for and about women. The title of Basler's article was "Real Women View the TV Variety," and the policewomen she interviewed basically praised the characters as "true-to-life," offering an "accurate portrayal of their jobs and problems." A few months later, however, Howard Rosenberg of the *Los Angeles Times* interviewed two Los Angeles policewomen who strongly challenged the "reality" of the representations ("it was two women trying to do exactly what men do") in favor of their own definitions of women and femininity. In relating the made-for-TV movie to women's lives on the police force, the Basler article generally demonstrated the ways that *Cagney and Lacey*, from the earliest moments of its history, generated discussion about the possibilities for women, not only in a television series, but also in the world beyond the TV frame.[27]

The movie aired at 8:00 P.M. on Thursday, 8 October 1981, and captured an astonishing 42 percent share of the television audience. (CBS had been getting a 28 or 29 share in that time period.) Within thirty-six hours, CBS was on the telephone to Barney Rosenzweig, asking him to start planning a weekly program. Gloria Steinem and the *Ms.* magazine staff had already lobbied members of the CBS board, urging them to make a series based on the movie.[28]

Controversial Representations of Women

In the second phase of *Cagney and Lacey*'s history, the television series starring Tyne Daly and Meg Foster (Swit's replacement as Cagney) aired from March 1982 to August 1982 (including summer reruns). These dates coincide with the period during which the network was most ardently courting and constructing a prime-time audience of working women. The huge ratings success of the *Cagney and Lacey* made-for-TV movie appeared to convince the network that women-oriented programming that drew on feminist discourses and subject matter was a winning bet. But such a hunch, in the midst of the Reagan years' opposition to the women's movements, only intensified the battlefield nature of the negotiations surrounding the production and reception of female television characters.

The series's first script was written by Avedon, Corday, and Rosenzweig and directed by Georg Stanford Brown. Filmways press releases for the premiere episode described the main characters as "two top-notch female cops who fight crime while proving themselves to male colleagues." This theme of women working in nontraditional jobs—in roles that called for rough action—and fighting sexism was, in fact, emphasized both in the publicity and in the episodes themselves. Keeping alive the link between the women's movement and the TV program, Gloria Steinem and *Ms.* magazine organized a reception for the creators and stars in early March.[29]

The very night and hour that *Cagney and Lacey* came to CBS, the series *9 to 5* (based on the hit movie of the same name that dealt with secretaries agitating for better working conditions) debuted on the rival ABC network. Gloria Steinem, speaking at a Hollywood Radio and Television Society luncheon a month earlier, had vigorously protested this scheduling, saying it might "split the audience and hurt each other's [the two programs'] chances." The head-to-head competition, without a doubt, proved costly for both series in terms of ratings.[30]

Of the thirty-five press reviews I read on *Cagney and Lacey*'s premiere, most were favorable or had some good things to say. Most mentioned the feminist elements in the script: the "chauvinism" of the male detectives, Mary Beth and Harvey's role reversals, and working women's "juggling" of both personal lives and careers. "Tyne Daly," said one article, "is Mary Beth Lacey, wife, mother and breadwinner who juggles a tough career along with her family responsibilities. . . . Meg Foster is Chris Cagney, a single, attractive and ambitious policewoman who takes 'dead aim' on criminals and department chauvinists alike." Several qualified their support with comments such as "the show's message of female discrimination is too obvious and heavy-handed" and "the not-too-subtle message here is that women have to be twice as good to look equal with a man—a topic which could be the Achilles' heel of the series if pounded home too strongly." Many also pointed out the difference between Cagney and Lacey and other female television characters. Phrases like "no racy 'Charlie's Angels' style glamour here," "mature women, not girls or sex objects," "not clothes horses à la Angie Dickinson," and "realistic crimebusting from the female perspective minus the giggle and jiggle," were common.[31]

Other pieces commented brazenly on the women's bodies, appraising them with regard to conventional television notions of glamour. "Ms. Daly," one of them claimed, "has a plain face, a schlumpy figure, a thick Eastern accent. She's not sexy on the outside. . . . Meg Foster is the better looking but far more of a tomboy than a sex symbol." Another noted, "While Foster and Daly are attractive, they look and act ordinary enough to be believable. . . . They are even occasionally permitted to look rumpled, discouraged, crabby." And another, "Past shows have had one token woman—with the exception of 'Charlie's Angels,' which featured a team of Wonder Women dressed and coifed from Rodeo Drive rather than DC Comics. Cagney and Lacey, on the other hand, are cops. They look like real people. They are cute rather than beautiful."[32]

For the next full year, such running commentary on the appearances of the two characters was standard in many press pieces. The practice demonstrates several things: First, the critics perceived a difference between Cagney and Lacey and other television depictions of women on the level of their bodies. This difference was, of course, produced through the televisual technique of mise-en-scène and related to the characters' sizes, shapes, hairstyles, makeup, clothing, gestures, and mannerisms.[33] However, the critical commentary also demonstrates a tendency to limit the perception of that difference to physical characteristics. By focusing on the actresses' bodies, the critics reproduced a traditional way of assessing the value of women, and this worked (in many instances despite the critics' apparent intentions) to contain the difference set into play by Cagney and Lacey. The phenomenon illustrates how difficult it is for females to escape being "pinned to" their biological difference or to get beyond the conventional equation of women with sex or sex object. It also demonstrates the presumed access to women's bodies, and the license to discuss and evaluate them, that television, film, and photographic images have helped to routinize.

Many reviews stressed the rapport between the two actresses and the friendship between two women characters. "It is the natural charisma which exists between Daly and Foster," read one, "which makes Cagney and Lacey a step above the norm. It is this caring for each other that allows the viewer to care for them." Another critic wrote, somewhat prophetically, "The two women are human beings, not just women, and as Simone de Beauvoir wrote, whenever women start acting like human beings they are accused of trying to be men."[34]

Despite the favorable press, and without much consideration for the fact that its program was pitted against *9 to 5*, which attracted the same audience, CBS wanted to cancel *Cagney and Lacey* after just two installments. The network did not, in fact, allocate any advertising money to promote the third episode in *TV Guide* (*9 to 5* had a half-page ad). There is no doubt that the first few episodes of *Cagney and Lacey* were a ratings disappointment to the network and failed to hold on to the large lead-in audience attracted by *Magnum, P.I.*, the program that immediately preceded it. But the high share garnered by the made-for-TV movie/pilot and the series's competition from *9 to 5* would normally have indicated a schedule change rather than cancellation as the networks' first strategy.[35]

The program's history suggests several reasons behind the push to cancel rather than to rearrange the series's position in the weekly lineup. The first involves the original ambivalence of executives in CBS's series development division. According to Rosenzweig, some were reluctant to support *Cagney and Lacey* as a weekly program from the beginning. "The thing you have to realize about *Cagney and Lacey*," he said, "is that it was not developed as a series, but as a movie for CBS. At CBS, there are series executives and there are movie executives. And not only do they not talk to each other in the hallways, they're in different buildings. Now remember that the series people had all turned it down the first time around—it was developed by the movie people. So there was a whole group of executives at CBS who didn't want *Cagney and Lacey* to succeed." However, in another interview Rosenzweig said, "There were also people [at series development] who believed in it for a series."[36]

The show would have halted abruptly had not Rosenzweig persuaded Harvey Shephard, vice-president in charge of programming for CBS, to give *Cagney and Lacey* a *Trapper John, M.D.* rerun spot on Sunday, 25 April, at 10:00 P.M. Rosenzweig argued that *Cagney and Lacey* was an adult program requiring a time slot later than 9:00 P.M. Shephard reluctantly agreed but once again voiced CBS's ambivalence by telling Rosenzweig to "save his money" when Rosenzweig revealed that Filmways planned to spend $25,000 on new publicity for the show.[37]

Filmways took the financial risk anyway, sending Foster and Daly on a cross-country tour. In a week-long campaign organized by the Brocato and

Kelman public relations company, Daly and Foster traveled to major urban areas and gave approximately fifty radio, television, and print interviews; included on the schedule was a Washington, D.C., television talk show interview with Tyne Daly and Betty Friedan "on the topic of women's rights."[38]

The 25 April episode of *Cagney and Lacey* pulled an impressive 34 share and ranked number seven in the overall ratings for that week. Despite that success, Harvey Shephard told Rosenzweig that many members of the CBS board (which was responsible for final renewal decisions) would consider the 34 share "a fluke." He said he would fight for the series's renewal only if Rosenzweig made a significant change in the program. The change was to replace Meg Foster as Cagney.[39]

At this point, other aspects of the network's dubiety began to surface. They were directly related to notions of femininity generated by the program and seem to be the most salient factors in CBS's hesitation. In a *Daily Variety* article dated 25 May 1982 and a *Hollywood Reporter* article from 28 May, Harvey Shephard spoke publicly about Foster's replacement. He was quoted in both articles as saying that "several mistakes were made with the show in that the stories were too gritty, the characterizations of both Cagney and Lacey were too tough and there was not enough contrast between these two partners." Several weeks after Shephard's statements appeared, an article in *TV Guide* revealed still other reasons for CBS's ambivalence and its decision to replace Foster. According to critic Frank Swertlow, *Cagney and Lacey* was to be "softened" because the network believed the main characters were "too tough, too hard and not feminine." The article quoted an unnamed CBS programmer who said the show was being revised to make the characters "less aggressive." "They were too harshly women's lib," he continued. "These women on 'Cagney and Lacey' seemed more intent on fighting the system than doing police work. We perceived them as dykes."[40]

There are undoubtedly many dimensions to this incident, but I will focus on only two here. The first is the presence, from the beginning of the series, of discourses that either associated Meg Foster with lesbianism or implied a lesbian overtone to the relationship between Cagney and Lacey. The second is CBS's claims that audience research indicated that viewers perceived the characters as "tough" and "masculine."

In the weeks surrounding the premiere of the series, there were straightforward references in the press to Meg Foster's earlier portrayal of a lesbian in the film *A Different Story*. Foster was, perhaps provocatively, quoted in an article in *US* magazine as saying, "I played a lesbian; it was my favorite role." Barbara Avedon recalled an event that occurred after Meg Foster's reading for the Chris Cagney part. According to Avedon, after a "brilliant" reading by Foster that "stood out head and shoulders above all the others," Avedon said to the assembled group, "She's my choice." An executive in casting, Avedon continued, "walked me out of the room with the other executives and said, 'She's trouble, she's a dyke, she can't carry a series.'" The executive, says Avedon, "was really a detractor from the beginning."[41]

In addition, Tyne Daly, in an article by Jane Ardmore, discussed what she called the "fear" that surrounded the concept of *Cagney and Lacey.* "We are," she said, "playing two women in what are customarily thought of as men's jobs; that's where the fear comes in." Ardmore continued, "Her [Tyne Daly's] first glimpse of fear occurred on the first episode of the series in which the two cops dressed up like hookers to go out on the street and apprehend solicitors. While they were dressing for the assignment, Chris Cagney came over and helped her partner with the clasp of her necklace. Somebody on the set said it looked 'seamy'. . . . She [Daly] and Meg were interviewed for *Entertainment Tonight.* . . . The first question was, 'What's all this stuff about a lesbian connection on the show?'" And finally, an article by Sal Manna in the *Los Angeles Herald Examiner,* written after the broadcast of the first three episodes, said, "Because nearly everyone is perplexed at the show's ratings failure, rumors have circulated that viewers were uncomfortable with the friendship of the two women, some even implying lesbianism."[42]

Whatever the connections among the above examples, it seems safe to say that homophobia, outright discrimination (at least on the part of the executive who maintained that the actress was a "dyke"), and associations of the series with lesbianism were operative from the outset. Apparently they gave CBS a way in which to voice its objections to the nonconventional and seemingly threatening depictions of women on the series. This would explain why the network rushed to cancel the program and then to demand Foster's removal as a condition of its reprieve. It would also explain why CBS gave more importance to comments it may have picked up in its audience research than to the conflicting comments from the press reviews quoted earlier.

New and expanded representations of women on TV could not, it seems, include even a hint of lesbianism. This taboo must, of course, be situated within the history of lesbianism's representation on prime time, but a few things are worth noting here. During the quest for "relevance" and socially "hip" subject matter during the 1970s, several programs aired episodes about lesbians, including *All in the Family* and *Medical Center.* Likewise, in the early 1980s, such prime-time programs as *Kate and Allie, Hotel, Hill Street Blues, St. Elsewhere,* and *The Golden Girls* included lesbianism as a single-episode story line, and the daytime serial *All My Children* featured an ongoing lesbian character for several weeks in 1983. In the late 1980s, *Heartbeat* included as a regular a lesbian character, whose presence was instrumental in the show's cancellation by ABC after protests from religious groups. The main point here is that each of these "liberal" representations of lesbianism, in varying degrees (*Heartbeat* and *All My Children* tried to downplay this facet), underscored the "social problem" aspect of lesbianism and played off the notion of lesbianism as an "aberration."[43] That viewers might interpret the relationship between Cagney and Lacey as having homosexual overtones, or that two strong, recurring women characters might be perceived as "dykes" without the accompanying suggestion that "dykeyness" was a deviation from the norm, was something that CBS (at least in the early 1980s, on its prime-time schedule) simply would not chance. Such a characterization stretched the limits of difference regarding the representation of women well beyond the boundaries of TV's permissible zone.

The network's official explanation of Meg Foster's removal was that audience research had revealed objections to the characters. According to Arnold Becker, chief of research for CBS, a sample of 160 audience members had yielded comments about the women protagonists like "inordinately abrasive, loud and lacking warmth" and "they should be given a measure of traditional female appeal, especially Chris." But Becker also included his own personal opinion about the characters: "Even in the first show," he said, "when they [Cagney and Lacey] dressed like hookers, they weren't sexy looking—they were sort of like burlesque. . . . There's certain amount of resistance to women being in male-oriented jobs. I think it's fair to say, in light of what has happened to ERA, that most people favor equal pay for equal work, but not women as truck drivers or ditch diggers or that sort of male work." He added that the allusion "to homosexuality" in *TV Guide* was "quite unfair." "Those tested," he said, "thought of Cagney and Lacey as masculine, not that they were lovers." It is also possible, of course, that the research survey inadvertently elicited particular responses from the viewers tested.[44]

The differential treatment given to the characters and the actresses during this incident underscores some of the specific dimensions of the network's anxiety. The *TV Guide* article said the married character played by Tyne Daly was being kept because CBS considered her "less threatening." The original Chris Cagney's nonglamorous, feminist, sexually active image and her working-class, single status manifested too many "non-feminine" markers, according to the network's definition of femininity. Cagney had no acceptable class, family, or marriage contexts that could contain, domesticate, or nullify those threatening differences.

The changes in the series and the firing of Meg Foster generated heated debates in the press and viewer letters over what constituted appropriate "femininity" (and "masculinity"). These debates referred to many aspects of the mise-en-scène: the characters' clothing, hairstyles, facial mannerisms, and the use of props such as cigarettes. They furthermore consistently referred to femininity and women's bodies as they appeared in the social world beyond the domain of the TV characters.

Howard Rosenberg of the *Los Angeles Times* began a satiric column on the issues raised by the incident with the questions, "What is feminine? What is masculine? What is CBS doing?" He then asked, "Are the old Cagney and Lacey too strident? Even too masculine? For the definitive answer," he continued, "I contacted Detective Helen Kidder and Detective Peggy York, partners in the Los Angeles Police Department." He quoted Kidder as saying, "'I watched the show once and I was so turned off. They looked rough and tough, and they weren't terribly feminine, just in the way they dressed and acted. They were so, you know, New York. . . . Peggy and I wear good suits, nylons and pretty shoes, silk blouses, the hair, everything. Not that

that keeps you from being a dyke.'" Rosenberg concluded with his own analysis of the characters:

> Although Cagney is the character to be softened, Lacey seemed to be far the toughest of the two. . . . Many of the symbols were conflicting, however. Cagney frequently spoke admiringly of men, which was good, but wore slacks more than Lacey did, which was suspicious. Yet, Cagney had pink bed sheets and longer and curlier hair than Lacey. . . . In Lacey's favor, there was a scene in which she sank amorously into bed with Hawvey [*sic*] and another in which she cooked breakfast for the family. Good signs. Yet she also dangled a cigarette from her mouth like Bogie. Cagney always drove, and Lacey didn't which could mean something. But Lacey talked without moving her mouth. Lacey convinced me, however, when she took off her skirt in one sequence, she was wearing a slip, not boxer shorts.[45]

Rosenberg's column was just one of many following the removal of Meg Foster, and numerous women reporters vented their outrage. Sharon Rosenthal of the *New York Daily News* wrote, "Not feminine enough? By whose standards? I wondered. Wasn't the whole point of the show to portray women on television in a new, more enlightened manner?" And Barbara Holsopple of the *Pittsburgh Press,* writing about what the network wanted for the series, quipped, "Not tough cops, mind you. Nice feminine, good ones. Those yo-yos at the network were second-guessing us again."[46]

As Howard Rosenberg's interview with the two Los Angeles policewomen indicates, it is plausible and even predictable that a segment of viewers would find Cagney and Lacey problematic, some for the specific reasons mentioned by the network. The dominant viewer reaction in the letters I have seen, however, was critical of CBS; *TV Guide* also printed a series of angry responses to Foster's dismissal.[47]

Letters to CBS, to Orion Television, and to Rosenzweig's office fervently defended Foster and the series. "The program *Cagney and Lacey,*" said one, "is being ruined. I have thoroughly enjoyed it: the actresses had good chemistry and I enjoyed seeing a tough female." Another read, "With Cagney and Lacey, Meg and Tyne, we at least have a program that shows two women doing a hard job, but we also see an honest and warm friendship. Their chemistry is just right. We can see they care for each other, there isn't much about a good friendship between women on TV. . . . It's nice to see two women enjoying this kind of relationship." And another, "I read in last week's *TV Guide* something about replacing Meg Foster for such reasons as she is too threatening? I don't understand where TV executives come up with such craziness. I get the feeling there's a card game at the Hillcrest Country Club called 'Let's go with the path of least resistance when it comes to women on TV.' There seems to be a NEED for all women TV stars to be a carbon copy of Cheryl Ladd. Where's the female Al Pacino? Where is the female Bobby de Niro?" Still another said, "Foster and Daly did a marvelous job of portraying strong, confident women living through some trying and testing circumstances. Too strong? Too aggressive? Come on! They are cops in the city. They aren't supposed to be fragile, delicate wimps." And a final one from England: "The excuse that Cagney and Lacey are too butch is pathetic. A policewoman in America let alone Britain not butch enough wouldn't last in the public streets."[48]

Two months after the removal of Foster, CBS may have, in the words of one reviewer, "shuddered a little" when a previously unaired Meg Foster/Tyne Daly episode, broadcast on 21 June, scored a 38 share and ranked number 2 in the week's overall ratings. However, the network continued to manifest its caution and discomfort with potentially controversial portrayals of women when it pulled the other new Foster/Daly episode (scheduled for 28 June) a few hours before air time. The network said it had received phone calls and letters protesting the episode, which was about a Phyllis Schlafly–type anti-ERA spokeswoman whom Cagney and Lacey were assigned to protect. Even though the attempt to add the Equal Rights Amendment to the Constitution had already failed, CBS decided to avoid controversy by yanking the episode and airing it later in August. The network, furthermore, had asked Rosenzweig not to invite Gloria Steinem to appear on the show, as he had originally intended. Steinem, due to an overcrowded schedule, had already declined. In the *TV Guide* advertisements for these summer episodes, a considerable "feminization" of the images of Daly and Foster was evident, especially when compared to previous *TV Guide* advertisements for the show; longer hair, earrings, makeup, and more "feminine" clothing were prominent for both characters.[49]

Bringing Women Back in Line

CBS's ultimate decision on *Cagney and Lacey* was that the series should be revised to "combine competency with an element of sensuality." Its solution was twofold: replace Meg Foster with someone more "feminine" and change Chris Cagney's socioeconomic background. Sharon Gless, whom one reviewer described as "blond, single, [and] gorgeous in the imposing manner of Linda Evans on *Dynasty*," was hired to replace Foster. The Gay Media Task Force, in light of allegations that the original characters were "too masculine," protested the replacement, saying that Gless's acting was "very kittenish and feminine."[50]

Instead of being from the working class, Cagney would now have been raised by a wealthy mother and grandmother in Westchester. Her father, a retired New York City policeman who had already been featured in the series, would be the divorced husband of that mother, and the marriage presented as a cross-class mistake. A new CBS press kit was issued to publicize the series in a different way. "Cagney and Lacey," it read, "are two cops who have earned the respect of their male counterparts and at no expense to their femininity." Furthermore, Cagney underwent a radical fashion change to accompany her class transformation. A network memo stated that "the new budget will include an additional $15,000 for wardrobe costs, the revised concept for character calls for Cagney to wear less middle class, classier clothes so that her upward mobility is evidenced." This revision must also be seen in relation to the history of television's skewed representation of class and to the advertising industry's decision, at this time, to target the upscale professional segment of the working women's market.[51]

The new Chris Cagney was more of a rugged individualist than a feminist and was actually conservative on many social issues. Lacey more often espoused feminist positions and liberal politics. A CBS promo for the 1982–83 season made these new differences between the characters explicit and also foregrounded Cagney's heterosexuality. The promo began:

> *Mary Beth:* Ya know Chris, there've been some great women in the twentieth century.
> *Chris:* Yeah! And some great men. (dreamily)
> *Mary Beth:* Susan B. Anthony!
> *Chris:* Jim Palmer!
> *Mary Beth:* Madame Curie.
> *Chris:* Joe Montana . . . ooo, can he make a pass!
> *Mary Beth:* (lightly annoyed with Chris) Amelia Airhart! [*sic*]
> *Chris:* The New York Yankees!
> *Mary Beth:* Chris, can't you think about anything else than men?[52]

A comparison of the opening credit sequences for the Foster/Daly and Gless/Daly series also underscores the changes. The original opening featured the protagonists, in police uniforms, running through streets, down dark alleys, and up and down stairways and culminated with them standing—weapons drawn and arms outstretched—in the "freeze, police" position. The soundtrack was a sardonic jazz vocal called "Ain't That the Way." The opening for the Gless/Daly series, by contrast, included whimsical scenes of Cagney and Lacey in plainclothes. They did chase a suspect down into the subway and apprehend him, but they also window-shopped and got "flashed" by a man in a trenchcoat. Cagney additionally jogged and bought a hot dog from a sidewalk vendor while Lacey, leaning up against the squad car, waited for her; they "toasted" each other with their coffee mugs and attempted to leave work for the day—Lacey in a bowling shirt and Cagney in a fur. The soundtrack was an upbeat, playful, instrumental melody.

The Struggle Over Femininity: The Press and the Viewers

The new and revised series starring Sharon Gless and Tyne Daly began its run in the fall of 1982 and generated a good deal of attention and enthusiasm in the press. The program's revisions make most sense when viewed in the context of the overall shifts in new television shows directed toward working women and drawing on feminism, and in the context of the general social and political backlash against the women's movements. During this period, many other burgeoning feminist-oriented programs also had their political edges completely blunted.

The mainstream press, in commenting on the Gless/Daly *Cagney and Lacey*, focused on the "changes" from the previous season. Many critics noted the general "softening" and "feminization" of the program. For example, one noticed that "the entire show this season appears less gritty than last year's style," and another remarked, "Some of the rougher, tougher edges are gone." Others discussed the diminution of the series's feminism: "The old CAGNEY AND LACEY coughed up a lot of feminist smoke, heavy-handedly pitting its two female heroines against their male detective counterparts in a way that blurred the dramatic focus. . . . The clubbing approach of last season is gone. . . . Tonight's good-looking production depends largely on nuance."[53]

But the *Los Angeles Herald Examiner*'s Frank Torrez, who thought that the last two episodes of the Foster/Daly series had already deviated significantly from the first shows, disagreed with these assessments of the "new" changes and challenged the whole practice of network interference. Among other things, his comments demonstrate the many variations in viewer interpretations and analyses:

> This episode has virtually no "feminist" dialogue in it, nor does it go out of its way to make the leads more feminine. . . . The whole idea of networks tampering with series after they're on the air rarely serves viewer interests. . . . "Cagney and Lacey" has gone from stereotyped cops and robbers to being one of the better series on television. But it made that transition well before CBS executives fiddled with it. Fortunately, it has been able to maintain its quality level and integrity despite the interference.[54]

A large number of articles responding to Foster's replacement by Gless read like a semiotic register of the word *feminine,* and they serve (not always intentionally) to problematize its various meanings. Many singled out specific elements such as clothing, hairstyles, makeup, personality traits and behaviors, vocal qualities, and body movements as evidence for the presence or absence of femininity, although some also wrote of the nonconventional, potentially problematic character of the femininity embodied by Gless's Cagney. According to Gail Williams of the *Hollywood Reporter,* "If the series' executives wanted a 'softer' single woman costar, Gless could be a disappointment. She may be ultrafeminine in appearance, but Gless doesn't stint when it comes to evincing the appropriate toughness her part of an effective detective demands."[55]

Carol Wyman of the *New Haven Register* said of Gless's Cagney, "She's one of those people who is very pretty, and at the same time a jock, the kind of person who ruins her good stockings to chase a crook, talks loud when she gets drunk and gets impatient with a woman witness who cries too much." And Sharon Rosenthal of the *New York Daily News* wrote that Gless was "at a loss to explain all the fuss about predecessor Meg Foster's alleged 'lack of femininity,' saying only that she certainly wasn't about to start 'wearing lace' in an effort to appease CBS executives. Her costume? Sure enough: mannish trousers, a bulky sweater and a short suede jacket left rakishly unzippered."[56]

Contradictory interpretations of the new Cagney's femininity were, however, plentiful. "Not only is Chris Cagney now blessed with thick eyelashes and soft blond hair," read one article. "She dresses in clingy sweaters and silky blouses. That's not to say that she overdoes the feminine thing. She's just a more attractive, feminine character. Cagney's personality has changed too. She's not as tough as she used to be. She even cried in the last episode." And in a piece entitled "CBS Softens Show to Toughen Ratings," Candy Justice wrote of the "softening" not only of Cagney but also of Lacey: "Aside from changes in Cagney, Lacey also has changed some over the summer. Tyne Daly last year talked with a thick Brooklyn accent, wore her hair *very* short and wore little makeup. This year her hair is a little longer, with some soft curls to feminize her looks. Earrings and a bit more makeup have been added, and the Brooklynese has been toned down considerably. Now we'll have to wait and see if the feminine 'Cagney and Lacey' does better in the Nielsen ratings than the tomboy version."[57]

An article in the *Bryan (Texas) Eagle,* based on a mistaken version of the events leading to Foster's replacement by Gless (or written with an extremely dry sense of humor), provides a strong example of how a viewer's interpretation may be influenced by information that guides her or him to emphasize particular items in a program and deemphasize others. In this instance it reveals how assessments of femininity were derived not only from conventional markers of the feminine, but also from what the viewer believed to be public consensus on one actress as "too feminine" and the other as the countermeasure to that excess. "Meg Foster," the piece read, "a green-eyed beauty with exotic looks, was tabbed for Cagney when the series entered the schedule for a limited run last spring. But the producers felt that Foster was 'too feminine' for the role. Out with Foster, in with . . . Sharon Gless. Gless's hoarse voice and strong walk make her a natural as an authority figure. In fact, she once played a man in a woman's body [in the series *Turnabout*]."[58]

Gless herself, in most press interviews at the time and later, attempted to move the discussion away from comparisons between her femininity and Meg Foster's and from the "feminization" of Cagney. In one interview, playing explicitly on the language involved, she said, "The press has come to me and asked, 'Are you going to make the show more feminine?' And my flat answer is, 'NO, the show is feminine—it's about two women.'"[59]

Some articles that commented on the "feminization" of the program also noted changes in the relationship between the characters and the innuendo of lesbianism: "Miss Daly's tomboy quality was balanced by the introduction of a partner with more feminine characteristics than her original co-star. . . . This second-season rematch [is] perhaps more compatible with the network's definition of a conventional female relationship . . . [but] who cares if a cop is gay or not as long as he or she shoots *straight*." And, "Cagney and Lacey suddenly became adversaries, instead of buddies. This could be construed as a tactic designed to squelch any gay implications CBS apparently is convinced viewers associate with scenarios in which women work seriously together."[60]

Judging from audience letters, viewers were at first reluctant to accept Gless, but within two months a large and avid fan following began to develop. Two letters from viewers who had been angered by Meg Foster's removal exemplify these feelings: "To be honest with you, when you fired Meg Foster I swore never to watch your show again—but Sharon Gless has proven herself and won back the admiration I had for the show." And, "I thought Meg Foster and Tyne Daly were a great combination, but apparently some 'genius' of the male persuasion, obviously, decided that Meg Foster wasn't 'feminine' enough. My Gawd, should cops wear aprons and be pregnant? Gimme a break! However, *Lady* Luck was with you when you found Sharon Gless. I must admit that you did something right by putting her in the Cagney role. . . . She's extremely feminine with just the right amount of 'butch' to strike a very appealing balance."[61]

An ironic note here—and another strong testament to the operation of multiple and contradictory viewer interpretations or readings—is that according to published articles and viewer letters, Sharon Gless had at the time of the series's first run, and later, a large lesbian audience.[62] And this audience invested the Cagney character with unique meanings by drawing on a variety of nonconventional and nonpredictable strategies for viewing and interpretation. Taken in conjunction with the audience letters protesting the removal of Meg Foster and the press's comments on the appeal of the friendship between Cagney and Lacey, this development demonstrates that the network's investments in particular notions of "femininity" and the investments of at least certain viewers were squarely at odds. The potentially homoerotic overtones in the representations of the two women that formed the basis for the network's discomfort were, in fact, the foundation of particular audience members' pleasure. There was, of course, a continuum of responses, ranging from fans who found pleasure in the fictional representation of a close friendship between two women to those whose viewing strategies purposely highlighted the homoerotic nuances in the relationship.

The initial burst of articles on the "feminization" of the characters and the series was followed by a wide array of feminist-oriented pieces in mainstream newspapers that highlighted the importance of *Cagney and Lacey* to women. These hailed the series as "pioneering the serious role of women on TV" and "helping to break new TV ground." Many of the articles emphasized the notion that Cagney and Lacey, unlike previous TV characters, represented "real women." Elaine Warren's piece in the *Los Angeles Herald Examiner* entitled "Where Are the Real Women on TV?" read, "The single bright promise for women on TV this season is 'Cagney and Lacey' . . . which appears as though it genuinely wants to portray the sensitivity and strength of two women cops—without a lot of airbrushed fantasy. The strains and rewards of two women working together give the show its definition." Judy Mann of the *Washington Post* wrote that the series was "a show of contemporary interest that portrays women as human beings . . . the heroines look and talk like real women and they have real working women's ambitions and problems." And Laura Daltry of the *Los Angeles Times* said that *Cagney and Lacey* portrayed an "encouraging partnership of sharp women . . . who hurl crooks up against walls, who keep each other on track, who sometimes disagree and don't speak to each other for days. The Gee-Whiz-women-in-men's-jobs! self-consciousness is delightfully absent. Rather, the series succeeds in something rare and wondrous: bringing a genuine women's sensibility to a rough job. They even shop for clothes on their lunch hour."[63]

Articles that stressed the difference between *Cagney and Lacey* and other TV representations of women and that continued the trend of commentary on the bodies of the characters/actresses and women's bodies in general were also prevalent during this period. Although not greatly different in kind from some of the earlier articles written about the Tyne Daly/Meg Foster series, this new crop was different in degree. They forcefully demonstrate a phenomenon in which cultural stereotypes, especially conventional television stereotypes, seem to work against women—certainly against the women who play the stereotypical roles, but also against women at large. References to "sit-com bozos," "clowns," "buffoons," "busty bimbos," women who "jiggle" and "bounce," "sexpots," "dumb blonds," and "bitches" appear frequently and are used in offhand ways, apparently to make a graphic or colorful comparison with conventional television depictions or to provide humor. The fact that these phrases are used by supporters of *Cagney and Lacey* in touting the series's perceived advances over other TV representations dramatically foregrounds how naturally and unconsciously we equate woman with the body and how common it is to evaluate women's bodies and the stock behaviors of particular women's roles with impunity.

Most of the press reviews and articles on the Gless/Daly *Cagney and Lacey* were favorable and supportive, but a few were critical. One in the *Evansville (Indiana) Press* exemplified the social ramifications of TV's stereotypical depictions and definitions of women and spoke from a solid investment in those definitions. Written by Larry Wood, a seventeen-year-old, it dealt overtly with some of the effects of television's combination of feminism and "jiggle," and it negotiated discourses of the women's movement, traditional conceptions of femininity, and mid-1970s definitions of women as TV sex objects: "It's tough, let me tell you," began Wood,

> to be seventeen in the new world of feminism. Not so much when opening doors or addressing letters. More when watching a blonde in a tight skirt get into a car. After watching "Cagney and Lacey," the new series about policewomen, I've come to two conclusions: Feminism's fine. But there's something nicer about pretty feminists. . . . In the several years television has been promoting working women it's always concentrated on attractive women—women who looked like models but played lawyers instead. Angie Dickinson, television's first policewoman, was sexy, even flaunted it. . . . My style of chauvinism is not pretty, but maybe it explains why as fine a show as "Cagney and Lacey" can leave one unfulfilled.[64]

Such reviews notwithstanding, the first Gless/Daly season was met with widespread accolades. But despite the positive press, the series did not do well in the overall ratings and did only marginally well with a women-only target audience. (Its competition during much of the season was female-oriented prime-time movies). Consequently, CBS put the series on its cancellation list.

In an effort to save it, Barney Rosenzweig coordinated a large letter-writing campaign in which the network and major newspapers throughout the country were deluged with thousands of viewer letters protesting the impending axe. The National Organization for Women and the Los Angeles chapter of NOW publicized the letter-writing campaign and urged their members to write. The Los Angeles chapter, according to state delegate Jerilyn Stapleton, had only two goals for the period: to get Ronald Reagan out of office and to keep *Cagney and Lacey* on the prime-time schedule.[65]

Virtually all the viewer letters from this outpouring mentioned the uniqueness of *Cagney and Lacey*'s women and the relationship between them. The writers repeatedly suggested that the protagonists were good role models for women and girls; that they were unique because they were "real" and "different" from all previous TV women; and that they were extremely important to the individual writer, the writer's friends and family, and the culture at large. Most fans related the series's depictions of women to their own everyday lives, often placing themselves in a particular social situation and at a particular point on the "feminism spectrum." Phrases such as "I'm a thirty-three-year-old nursing administrator," a "single working mother," a "married woman and mother who works inside the home," and "a feminist," or "not a women's libber—just a concerned woman," were common. Many of the letters echoed discourses of the liberal women's movement and demonstrated the workings of an "interpretive community" or a "community of heightened consciousness," as described in the work of such feminist scholars as Elizabeth Ellsworth and Jacqueline Bobo.[66] They also illustrated the many specific ways in which women fans were reconfiguring and redefining their notions of what it meant to be a woman.

Repeatedly, the writers said such things as, "It's good to see smart, functioning, strong women"; "It's a pleasure to see women in such active roles"; "It's one of the few programs that neither glamorizes nor degrades women"; and "At last women are being portrayed as three-dimensional human beings."[67] Long letters describing the particular significance of the series to the writers were plentiful. Wrote one viewer,

> It's the only show on television I feel I can relate to. While I'm not a police detective, I do work in a high-pressure, fast-paced, male-oriented field. I am a twenty-six year old single woman, and a broker for a major Wall Street firm. I have worked on an institutional trading floor for the past few years, and I feel I've experienced the same kind of camaraderie AND conflict that I see between the characters on "Cagney and Lacey." . . . I think it's extremely important that "Cagney and Lacey" be given every fair chance to really succeed. It's a new concept in television and it may take some time for the audience to adjust to it. I believe "Cagney and Lacey" holds an especially important message for our youth on the changing role of women in our society.

Another wrote:

> My office alone contains six technical editors, RABID fans of "Cagney and Lacey." We're all highly paid, well-educated women in our forties with very

different life-styles. Since we are "specialists" and work very closely with each other, each of us regards the others as "extended family," and we nurture and support each other in the best ways possible. We enjoy "Cagney and Lacey" because it contains so many moments that ring familiar in a woman's daily life. We see ourselves in it so often, even though OUR jobs are unbelievably unexciting. It's gotten so that Tuesday mornings are spent hashing over Monday night's episode. We're really addicted.

A letter that related TV's depictions of women to the possibilities for actual historical women read, "It's such an exciting show from a woman's point of view. Watching those two women makes one realize how much more attractive we are as women when we dare to be all our possible dimensions rather than the stereotypical images we have been taught to be and continually see on the screen. You have affected some of us profoundly."

The relationship between the two actresses and their characters and its effect on the viewers were discussed with equal enthusiasm. Tyne Daly and Sharon Gless were described as a "superb combination," a "winning team" who "together have great charisma" and "natural and genuine chemistry." "The vivid interaction of Chris and Mary Beth," wrote one viewer, "has actually made honest female relationships into major dramatic entertainment." Another claimed, "In the final analysis, it was the friendship between the two lead characters wherein lay the show's strongest appeal for me." One of the many male viewers who also protested the show's cancellation wrote, "I will miss watching the friendship between the title characters. Their arguments often evoked some in-depth soul-searching on my part. No other series has ever handled human relationships better."

Viewer delight in the series often stemmed from powerful identification with the characters. Said one fan, "People really do need their heroes and heroines." "To do away with Cagney and Lacey," continued another, "is an affront to our pleasure." Many writers spoke in detail of their strong connections to the protagonists: "I cannot remember EVER becoming so fond of continuing characters that I actually looked forward to being warmed by them week after week. In fact this show ruined all other viewing for me. It became my yardstick. Nothing else measures up. And I doubt that anything ever will."

The main factor in this sense of identification, for a great number of fans, appeared to be their perception that the characters were "down to earth," "normal," or more "real" than all previous TV depictions. One letter read, "An overdose of gloss and dazzle bores me as a viewer. It's as though I'm being forced to watch a party and knowing I wasn't invited, that I'm not a part of it. It's no fun to observe all the time. . . . Being able to see a little of myself in the women you portray is a nice thing for me— it's like having friends with whom there is empathy, and that's what I enjoy, that sense of involvement." Many others said such things as, "I feel like they are my friends, like they are people I know."

Tyne Daly's Mary Beth Lacey was often written of as the most "honest," "refreshing," "natural," "real," "believable," and "likable" woman character in television history. One viewer described her as "someone whose pain and frustration and warmth I feel and share." Lacey's relationship with her husband Harvey was described as the "best portrayal of a marriage I have ever seen."

Sharon Gless's Christine Cagney was repeatedly acknowledged as an unprecedented "role model." And her presentation as a single working woman—by choice and not by default—was specifically mentioned: "Chris," said one writer, "is a role model. She is single and fulfilled by that life style. Most single women in film and TV are seen as losers, incomplete, dependent or lacking somehow. 'Chris' is autonomous and knows where she is going." "Her character," said another, "is one of an assertive single woman who really enjoys her career. It's about time there was a television program which portrays women in this role."

Preteen and teenage girls, and a few boys also, wrote of their own identifications with the characters. Some girls described being completely caught up in the fiction: "My life is part of you. It's like I've known you for many years. You guys mean so much in my life. My hairdo I get done like Lacey's but the length of Cagney's. . . . My friend and I renovated part of my room into a detective's office—typewriter, maps, telephone, recorder etc. We went on strike. . . . We refused to eat supper unless my friend's mother called us Detectives Cagney and Lacey."

Despite the volume of viewer mail, and despite the fact that this mail came primarily from the desired target audience (upscale working women between the ages of eighteen and fifty-four), the program was canceled in the spring of 1983. After the cancellation, a widely syndicated column by Gary Deeb vitriolically attacked the series and its women on the very grounds for which most reviewers and fans had praised them, thereby touching off a letter-writing battle of its own. The program, according to Deeb, was a far cry from being "feminist" or important to women:

> Here's a terrific quote: "I fear for the future of quality work for women in TV." Now what noble and talented human being could possibly have made that thoughtful statement? Why, it's none other than Sharon Gless, the co-star of "Cagney and Lacey," the horrible CBS female cop series that finally got put to sleep this month. Gless actually believes that "Cagney and Lacey" was a first rate, realistic drama, and that its cancellation spells doom for women-oriented programming on all three networks. What a crock. "Cagney and Lacey" was a piece of filth that more often than not exploited females and featured thoroughly implausible stories. Furthermore, the stars, Gless and Tyne Daly, were two of the phoniest and most unappealing actresses on the tube. Good riddance to them and their program. And just as patriotism is the last refuge of a scoundrel, so is the embracing of the female flag the final argument to be used by a fraudulently feminist program that never could ingratiate itself into the consciousness of women viewers.[68]

In a fiery demonstration of the struggle over meanings, viewers responded to the newspapers in which "Deeb's Diatribe," as one paper called it, was printed.[69] One exemplary retort, lambasting Deeb's "feminism" and invoking that of the liberal women's movement, read:

> I feel strongly that the vituperative tone of Gary Deeb's critique of "Cagney and Lacey" was uncalled for and unjust. I deplore the implied obscenities in his overemotional response to Sharon Gless's comment about the future of women role models on TV. She offered her point of view and does not deserve to have her show called "filth" as a result, nor to have her feminism labeled fraudulent. Perhaps he ought to keep his fantasies of what feminists think to himself until he stops trying to excuse his behavior by his "ingratiating" consciousness. Contrary to Mr. Deeb's point of view, the national NOW newsletter has found "Cagney and Lacey's" presentation of real dilemmas a refreshing, down-to-earth contrast to the polished purposelessness of women in most other shows.[70]

The exact reasons why Deeb found the series "fraudulently feminist" are not totally clear. But the fury of Deeb's attack is somewhat perplexing and his own "feminist" position difficult to assess.

In the midst of this controversy and public debate, several factors caused CBS to reverse its decision and bring the series back to life. First, the audience letters continued to come in. Second, after cancellation *Cagney and Lacey* received four Emmy nominations, and Tyne Daly won an Emmy as best dramatic actress. Third, *Cagney and Lacey* scored number one in the ratings for the first week of summer reruns and remained in the top ten throughout the rest of the season. Nonetheless, CBS hedged its bets by reinstating the series with a very limited seven-episode trial run.

The Struggle Goes On: The Production Team, the Network, Interest Groups, TV News, and the Tabloid Press

Several important trends were evident in the period of *Cagney and Lacey's* history that began with the reinstated Gless/Daly series in the spring of 1984. First, television's portrayal of feminism, limited as it already was, underwent "mainstreaming." In other words, the strength of feminist views was severely diluted. This resulted in an increasing ambiguity about the meaning of feminism itself and programming that offered "something for everyone," depending on particular viewers' political positions and interpretations. Terry Louise Fisher (a producer/writer for *Cagney and Lacey* and cocreator of *L.A. Law*) described this as a shift from "political" issues to "entertainment value." During this period, some of the key players from the *Cagney and Lacey* production team, particularly Barney Rosenzweig, began to think more in conventional "network" terms and less in women's movement terms when it came to portraying the characters. This move sparked disputes among the production team over the women detectives' hairstyles, makeup, and clothing.[71]

Determined to assure the series's renewal beyond the limited seven episodes, Rosenzweig called for a general upgrading of the styles and "looks" of the two characters. He wanted a renovation of the Cagney look to include more "stylish, glamorous" outfits and a new hairstyle that would "move" and "bounce." Sharon Gless, reluctant to make her character "too frilly" and concerned about not being able to fix her own hair (she would have to arrive on the set a couple of hours early to have it done the new way), objected at first but finally conceded to the new coif. "You can have my hair for seven weeks," she told Rosenzweig, "but after that it's my own."[72]

For several months, Rosenzweig had wanted to change Lacey's overall appearance. Tyne Daly, who had designed the Mary Beth Lacey look by shopping with wardrobe designer Judy Sabel in the "sale" and "basement" sections of New York department stores, continually refused, however, to change the character's plain yet eccentric dress. Rosenzweig and Daly also disagreed over issues of makeup. These disagreements actually went back several months to an episode called "Burnout," in which Lacey has a breakdown and disappears for a day and a night. Because her character was supposed to have stayed up all night on the beach, Tyne Daly arrived on the set looking, according to Rosenzweig, "like death." He insisted that she go to makeup, she refused, and finally they compromised: she went to makeup but wore very little. "Burnout," interestingly enough, was the episode for which Tyne Daly won her first Emmy, and about which a woman journalist wrote, "Mary Beth was suffering from burnout and went AWOL. . . . She forgot to wear makeup. . . . She looked truly like a woman in trouble. A wife from *Dallas* would have perched on one of those sand dunes like someone in a Club Med travel poster."[73]

Battles over Lacey's hairdo were also frequent occurrences on the set. Rosenzweig would ask Daly's hairdresser to get to her between takes and tease and spray her hair. During one such incident, Daly shouted to the crew and staff, "Can anyone tell me why my producer wants me to look like Pat Nixon?" Furthermore, Rosenzweig and Daly had confrontations about Daly's weight, with Rosenzweig suggesting she be careful about putting on pounds and Daly incorporating whatever weight fluctuations she might have into her conception of the character.[74]

During this period, there were also negotiations and struggles at the level of script development. An episode involving Cagney's pregnancy scare (the last of the seven trial episodes, aired in May 1984) provides a powerful example. The script negotiations revolved around how to represent an unmarried woman's pregnancy, the whole issue of working women and childbearing, and the issues of contraception and abortion. A synopsis from my personal observations and notes gathered during February and March 1984 reveals some of the actual processes involved in the debates.

As conceived by Terry Louise Fisher, the story originally dealt with Cagney's discovery that she is pregnant. Fisher had struggled with how to resolve the pregnancy. Knowing that the network would never allow abortion as a possibility for Cagney, Fisher self-censored that consideration but was less than satisfied with resorting to the clichéd miscarriage route. After working on the script, however, she felt it opened up interesting possibilities. Then Tony Barr, an executive at CBS, rejected the script, saying that the network did not "want to shine the spotlight on pregnancy" and the problems of a pregnant unmarried woman.

Barney Rosenzweig, Barbara Corday (at the time, creative consultant for the series), Terry Louise Fisher (writer-producer), Peter Lefcourt (writer-producer), P. K. (Patricia) Knelman (at the time, coproducer), and Ralph Singleton (at the time, unit production manager) discussed various options at a meeting. CBS had suggested that they turn the episode into a "biological clock" story in which Cagney is faced with the decision of whether or not she will ever have children. Fisher felt that the biological clock angle was not dramatically sound because it would offer no "resolution" or "closure." She asked Rosenzweig if he would fight for the original story with the network. But Corday wondered if they wanted to fight at this point, thinking it would be better to hold off and do the episode the following season (if CBS were to renew the series)—in, for instance, the fifth show, so they could lead up to the situation by having Cagney become seriously involved with one person. Because the subplot of the script dealt with officers at the precinct preparing for the sergeant's exam, and because attaining the rank of sergeant was one of Cagney's immediate ambitions, Lefcourt suggested that the issue could be cast as a "my job or having a baby kind of choice." Fisher said she refused to do that to working women: "It sounds too much like waiting for Prince Charming to come." Lefcourt agreed, "You're right, the Cinderella story."

Finally, Rosenzweig suggested they leave the first act exactly as it was—Cagney *thinks* she's pregnant. In actuality, however, she is not. Because the network had seemed so adamant about not focusing on a pregnancy at all, Rosenzweig (in the midst of the meeting and in the presence of the participants) called Tony Barr with his compromise option. Barr agreed that Cagney could *think* she was pregnant, but only on the condition that Lacey accuse her of being totally irresponsible. A long discussion on how they would cast Cagney's irresponsibility then followed: "Should we say it was a night of passion?" "Cagney could say something like, 'I know it was my fault, I was acting like a teenager'; or, 'Well, it happens, I mean the diaphragm is not foolproof.'" Rosenzweig objected that "as the father of four daughters, I don't want to put down the diaphragm." The other four agreed that it was the only "safe method for women's bodies," and they did not want to portray Cagney as "being on the pill."

In the final episode, "Biological Clock," Cagney thinks she is pregnant but is not, and Lacey is only mildly accusatory. There is no mention of specific birth control technologies or how the "mistake" might have happened. There is no mention of what Cagney would do if she *were* pregnant, although Lacey strongly pushes marriage; Cagney seems to be developing a relationship with the "baby," and abortion is never mentioned as an option.

During this time, the producers and writers also were talking about where, in general, to go with the Cagney character. The discussions revolved around making Cagney more "sympathetic" and "committed," which would be accomplished by linking her romantically with one man. According to Terry Louise Fisher and Barbara Avedon, the word "sympathetic" is industry jargon used almost exclusively in connection with female characters, to describe female roles that evoke stereotypically "feminine" behaviors and situations. But the decision to make Cagney more sympathetic by showing her in a committed relationship with her boyfriend, Dory, was unpopular with viewers. During the "letters-from-viewers" segment on *60 Minutes,* one of the reporters actually read a letter that advocated the removal of Dory from the series.[75]

Cagney's single life and her sexuality were, however, continually troubling to the producers, writers, and network. According to a *New York Times Magazine* article, her "unmarried status does not hold appeal for CBS," which believed that "the only true states of grace for a woman are being married or actively looking for a spouse." Barbara Corday, in commenting on the problem, said, "We've been accused of Cagney being promiscuous, but she's barely what I consider to be a healthy active heterosexual female." And Tyne Daly, speaking about Cagney's and Lacey's sexuality and the network's investments in these issues, said that the CBS powers-that-be were nervous about the possibility that Chris "would be considered a sleepabout if she had a boyfriend every couple of weeks. . . . First they didn't want me [Lacey] to go to bed with my husband, and then when I begged and pleaded for us to have a little fun in the hay, they didn't want me to ever turn him down."[76]

In the spring of 1984, after the seven trial episodes, the series was renewed by CBS. During the 1984–85 season, Cagney was once again associated with some conventionally feminist actions. In one episode, in which she ends her relationship with Dory, she overtly rejects (in a long conversation with Lacey) the institution of marriage. In the same season, she files sexual harassment charges against a captain in the police department, urges Lacey to get a second opinion on a mastectomy treatment and consequently introduces the option of a lumpectomy, is the only one in her precinct to make the rank of sergeant, and continually emphasizes the importance of her career and her goal of becoming the first woman chief of detectives. In the face of critical and industry acclaim, a more secure place in the ratings (at least with target audience women), and the requisite changes in the characters' class and glamour, the network, it appears, became less skittish about the show's less-than-conventional representations of women.

The public struggles over *Cagney and Lacey* and definitions of femininity, however, showed no signs of abating during this period; many different voices in the political spectrum continued to comment on the program and its women. For example, the tabloid *National Examiner* printed a small color photo of Tyne Daly and Sharon Gless on its cover, captioned "Cagney and Lacey are shaming the men of America—say experts." The accompanying article cited the conclusions of two mental health "experts" and of Martin Kove, a supporting actor in the series. It overtly criticized *Cagney and Lacey*—and feminism in general—for belittling men and adapted feminist language ("female chauvinists") to make its point. Most strikingly, it related the well-being of the United States and its international reputation to conventional definitions of femininity. "Television cops Cagney and Lacey," the article embarked,

> are female chauvinists . . . and they're poised to destroy the manhood of America, according to top psychologists who warn that the show is, in fact, a dangerous trendsetter that could lower the esteem of men around the world. "It's really a feminist show that makes all the men look like wimps or stupid or just plain bad," protested Martin Kove. . . . "It's appalling how many times I've been emasculated on the show. . . . They've taken away my pants and given me a tutu. My gun is rusty and there's dust on the trigger." CAGNEY AND LACEY has been . . . twice reprieved, largely due to the protests of women's libbers who closely identify with the two characters on the show. . . . Said clinical psychologist Dr. Henry Fairclough, "CAGNEY AND LACEY probably satisfies aspirations in women but it does involve its stars in improbable heroics, and challenges the masculinity of the actors." . . . Psychotherapist Dr. Harland Toft warned, "If that impression becomes pervasive overseas it could alter the view the rest of the world has about the U.S."[77]

In this interpretation, the new women characters were seen as downright dangerous in their capacity to shift social perceptions not just about femininity but about masculinity, and the emasculating threat of powerful women was indeed hysterically rendered.

Bridget Smith, in the British feminist journal *Spare Rib,* criticized the whole series on feminist grounds. Her challenge came from a radical, perhaps cultural, feminist point of view, which saw the program as ultimately defining and portraying women as male-identified agents of status quo power relations:

> "Cagney and Lacey" is proving very popular with many feminists. So WHY? Cagney and Lacey themselves are portrayed as whole characters, they are defined by their relationship with one another (both professional and personal), and not in terms of their relationship to men. The issues covered tend to be much more controversial than the overworked and stereotypical storylines usually found in "Cop" shows. The programme has tackled prostitution, breast cancer etc. However, despite the fact that the series seems to be specifically relevant to women, "Cagney and Lacey" offers little to us. The BBC presenter introduces the programme as "Cagney and Lacey, fighting crime the feminine way." This sums up the inherent contradiction therein. The women are required to retain their femininity while brutally combating "crime." Their aggression is not part of their enlightened feminism but the result of their male defined training. Like any other police series "Cagney and Lacey" serves to glorify the police force. It may represent a different approach but the exercise remains the same.[78]

Smith's criticisms, as had Gary Deeb's before her, bring to the surface issues that contribute to the contradictory character of the series's texts and its femininity—"fighting crime the feminine way" and the "exploitation" of women. But Smith and Deeb each also seize upon a contradictory textual aspect and apparently see that as revealing and bespeaking the total "truth" of the text. All the meanings of the text, including its meanings of *women, woman,* and *femininity,* may never be tacked down and decided once and for all, no matter how impassioned the critic's interpretation or how clear the analysis.

The contradictory aspects of the texts and the women characters were exacerbated by a number of episodes between 1984 and 1988, particularly those dealing with wife-beating, abortion, breast cancer, sexual harassment, date rape, and alcoholism. These programs simultaneously treated issues of enormous social importance to women and raised questions about the use of "exploitation topics" in programs for and about females.[79] They both "cashed in on" and became part of intense public debates involving the institutional and social control over women's bodies and what women generally should and should not be. And they also brought several social interest groups and institutions into the overall discursive struggle over femininity and women TV characters.

A two-part program on breast cancer, from the 1984–85 season, and an episode on abortion, from 1985–86, offer interesting examples. Both episodes could be considered overt "exploitation" programs, and both were broadcast during ratings sweeps periods.[80] The breast cancer episodes, aired on 11 and 18 February 1985, centered on early detection, getting quick medical attention, and lumpectomy as an alternative to mastectomy. They remained well within the parameters of standard medical practice and did not critique the relationship between women and the medical institution, nor did they broach the topic of "disfigurement" in relation to the idealization and fetishization of women's bodies. *American Medical News,* a publication of the American Medical Association, in fact printed a highly respectful article on the programs. And Barney Rosenzweig said he put aside "some of my prejudices about the medical profession, specifically because we did not want to get mired down in controversy. . . . We wanted to be very careful—we wanted to simply get the information out. And we felt in order to do that and serve our viewers, it was imperative to be as straightforward and non-controversial as possible."[81] Tyne Daly, however, in a cover-story article on the episodes in *People,* was overtly critical of the medical institution's relationship with women. She said that after some hesitation, she decided to do the part because "I realized that as long as there are women being led astray by the medical establishment, women getting hacked up into pieces, it's important that I tell the story."[82]

The episode about abortion, broadcast 11 November 1985, played a central part in the ongoing public battles over one of the most inflammatory social issues of the decade, and it further testifies to CBS's increased tolerance (however cautious) regarding some aspects of representing women. Entitled "The Clinic," the program centers on the bombing of an abortion clinic and Cagney and Lacey's support (after considerable debate between them) of a poor Latina's choice to terminate her pregnancy. In her book on advocacy groups and entertainment television, Kathryn C. Montgomery chronicles the history of this episode, revealing that for several months the producers, writers, network executives, and the Program Practices Department (often called the network "censors") had debated the script. Program Practices wanted to ensure that the script had "balance," preferably by having Cagney and Lacey take different sides on the issue of abortion.[83]

In the episode as it actually aired, Cagney (a Catholic) is initially reluctant but ultimately supports the woman's right to choose, and the strongest antiabortion arguments are made by her father, Charlie. Program Practices and the network executives, after calling for numerous revisions, were ultimately satisfied that the final version represented the balance they had envisioned. But Rosenzweig, seeking publicity, managed to stir up a fair amount of controversy around the script. He rallied the National Organization for Women, which issued "Action Alert" reports to its members about potential trouble over the episode, and he circulated videotape copies of the program itself around the country for local grassroots screenings. CBS executives were, of course, aggravated that the executive producer of the series was instigating trouble after they had gone to such pains to avoid it, and they were especially concerned that Rosenzweig was publicizing the program as "pro-choice."

Led by its public relations director, Daniel Donehey, the National Right to Life Committee (a group heavily invested in traditional definitions of women and their bodies) took Rosenzweig's bait and launched a protest several days before air time. The *Los Angeles Times*'s Howard Rosenberg noted that Rosenzweig had spun "controversy from straw," but antiabortion groups were already appealing to CBS to pull the episode, which the NRLC called a "piece of pure political propaganda."[84] When CBS, saying that it found the program to be "a fair and well-balanced view," refused to pull the episode from the schedule, the NRLC asked CBS affiliates to black it out. If an affiliate did not want to do this, it was asked to offer the NRLC air time for a half-hour film of the latter's choosing (such as the antiabortion film *A Matter of Choice*) or a half-hour to "put some of our folks on to rebut this." If none of these measures worked, the NRLC's next plan was to "call for a nationwide black-out of CBS during the balance of the month of November which is their rating month."[85]

As a promotional effort, Tyne Daly and Barney Rosenzweig flew to Washington, D.C., for a luncheon cosponsored by the National Abortion Rights Action League and Orion Television to "counter opposition" to the episode. According to Daly, "We feel we've done something very balanced. . . . I don't think I know a woman who hasn't struggled or knows someone who hasn't struggled with this issue." Planned Parenthood also organized a press conference about the episode in New York. John Wilke, president of the NRLC, and Barney Rosenzweig debated the topic on the *MacNeil/Lehrer News Hour*. To Wilke's charges that "this program is the most unbalanced, most unfair program we've seen in a number of years. . . . We did not hear a single right-to-life answer properly given,"

Rosenzweig answered, "A year ago we had an episode in which Christine Cagney believed she was pregnant, and never once considered abortion as an alternative. I didn't hear from the National Organization for Women or the Voters for Choice then about banning the show or boycotting us. I just got some rather nice letters from the pro-life people."[86]

One CBS affiliate pulled the show, and one, WOWT-TV in Omaha, Nebraska, offered equal time to the NRLC. Even after the broadcast, the political struggle continued: an antiabortion spokesperson suggested that "any further violence at abortion clinics would be on CBS's conscience." But in the *Washington Post,* Judy Mann praised the episode and the actions of CBS, saying of television that "no other medium is as capable of dramatizing and educating the public about some of life's most difficult experiences."[87]

In a scholarly article about the episode, written several years after it aired and apparently informed by aspects of liberal, socialist, and poststructuralist feminism, Celeste Michelle Condit raised questions about "The Clinic" and its feminist politics. She described it as breaking "new ideological ground" and inserting "new political codes into the public culture," but she also labeled it as a progressive rather than a radical text and said that it "favored the interests of career women but only marginally supported other groups of women." She went on,

For women in poverty and women of color the program is more mixed. It explicitly affirmed the choices of a particular minority woman, but it did not deal with the ways in which poor women might fund abortion or contraception. It did not deal with the options provided by extended families or with the importance of motherhood in different cultures. It offered a sugary and unrealistic moral, "have an abortion so you can go to school and get off welfare," that may have appealed to latent racism in white audiences more than assisting poor women with real options. In the face of such silences, the Republican administration could continue its largely hidden work in pro-natalism by dismantling funding for family planning. From the perspective of these groups of viewers, this restricted presentation of abortion represents a serious political short-coming of this episode.[88]

That the program was among the first in a number of years to confront abortion, that CBS worked so hard to make it "balanced," and that conservative discourses were currently on the rise, all undoubtedly contributed to such mixed, contradictory, and problematic meanings.

In both the 1984–85 and the 1985–86 seasons, *Cagney and Lacey* won the Emmy Award for best dramatic program. Tyne Daly won for best actress in 1982–83, 1983–84, 1984–85, and 1987–88, and Sharon Gless in 1985–86 and 1986–87. The series also won many other awards, including the award for best program given by the National Committee on Working Women in 1985 and the Humanitas Award in 1986.[89] In 1985 the "early lives" of the protagonists were novelized in a Dell paperback by Serita Deborah Stevens, called simply *Cagney and Lacey.* In 1986 the magazine *Channels* included *Cagney and Lacey* among its "Class of '86 Honor Roll"— seven recipients who "set the highest standards in the media." And in January

1987, Sharon Gless and Tyne Daly were featured on the cover of *Ms.*, along with ten other women, as women of the year. (Gless and Daly appeared in the top two positions after international woman of the year Winnie Mandela.)[90]

As this chapter has made clear, the negotiation of meanings of *women*, *woman*, and *femininity* took place among a variety of vested interests and with considerable conflict. We have seen how a number of players in the overall television enterprise vied for the primacy of their own definitions. And I would argue that CBS executives, in interfering with *Cagney and Lacey's* scripts and representations, achieved a certain amount of "discursive authority" of their own by delimiting the dimensions of class, "femininity," and feminism. This delimitation, however, by no means *contained* the differences of the characters on any of these levels—in production as well as reception: Tyne Daly, for example, continued to contest the issues of makeup, hairstyle, and costume, and Sharon Gless resisted letting the new Cagney become "frilly." Furthermore, some elements of the original Cagney characterization not only continued but were expanded upon in the revised and recast series.

The production team also continued to battle with network executives over how women could actually be represented on 1980s prime-time television, especially with respect to a single woman's sex life and her decisions on pregnancy and abortion. Similarly, the mainstream press (including syndicated columnist Gary Deeb), the *National Examiner*, interest groups (including the women's movements, the Gay Media Task Force, the National Abortion Rights Action League, and the National Right to Life Committee), and viewers continued to generate many different and often contradictory interpretations of the characters and definitions of femininity. Viewers, for one thing, continued to find in Cagney and Lacey's relationship the erotic dimensions that CBS had sought to squelch; Gless's large lesbian following, in fact, indicates that homoerotic interpretations of the women's friendship actually flourished.

It is important to note that many of the network's interventions were especially aimed at containing those aspects of the characterizations that challenged not only conventional definitions of femininity but also institutionalized differences among women—the differences that structure U.S. society. In this chapter the particular institutionalized differences were those of class and sexual preference. (Differences of race had been delimited from the outset.) Other interventions also focused on differences that posed a threat to what one CBS programmer referred to as "the system"—that is, differences involving "women's lib" and general female bonding.

Notes

1. To refer to the stake individuals and institutions have in their own particular meanings, I use the term *investment*, as it has been elaborated by Teresa de Lau-

retis and Wendy Hollway. De Lauretis defines investment as "something between an emotional commitment and a vested interest, in the relative power (satisfaction, reward, payoff) which that position promises (but does not necessarily fulfill). . . . Power is what motivates (and not necessarily in a conscious or rational manner) individuals' investments" (*Technologies of Gender: Essays on Theory, Film, and Fiction* [Bloomington: Indiana University Press, 1987], p. 16). Her discussion draws on Wendy Hollway, "Gender Difference and the Production of Subjectivity," in Julian Henriques, Wendy Hollway, Cathy Urwin, Couze Venn, and Valerie Walkerdine, *Changing the Subject: Psychology, Social Regulation, and Subjectivity* (London: Methuen, 1984), pp. 228–52.

"Vulnerable" and "sympathetic" are the two terms used most often by the TV networks to describe what they want in women characters (from personal conversations with Terry Louise Fisher and Barbara Avedon, Feb. 1984, Los Angeles, Calif.).

2. Michael Leahy and Wallis Annenberg, "Discrimination in Hollywood: How Bad Is It?," *TV Guide,* 13–19 Oct. 1984, p. 14. According to Leahy and Annenberg, Orion TV hired women writers for 37 percent of its projects.

Articles in the mainstream press should be read with four things in mind. First, they provide examples of a particular critic's or journalist's own interpretation and thus figure as aspects of reception. Second, such articles often provide direct forums for program publicity. They may be "planted" by the public relations firm responsible for promoting a series, or they may offer program spokespeople (particularly producers and stars) free coverage in the form of interviews. Similarly, television reporters often reproduce the language of publicist-prepared press releases in their columns and stories about programs. Third, over the past forty years, particular ways of writing about television programs have become conventional, and TV critics often invoke Western culture's dominant strategy for evaluating popular fiction: reflection theory. They therefore tend to set a standard of "reality" for programs and characters whereby a program is "good" if it accurately reflects "reality" and if its characters are "real" or "true-to-life." And fourth, all press coverage, whether an unsolicited critical review or an industry plant, becomes what John Fiske refers to as "second-level" or "secondary" texts—part of the intertextual network that situates and influences future readings of the program itself (see note 26 below).

3. For more on poststructuralist feminism, see Introduction, note 13. For discussions and critiques of the taxonomy of feminisms employed here, see Alison M. Jaggar, *Feminist Politics and Human Nature* (Totowa, N.J.: Rowman and Allanheld, 1983); Katie King, "The Situation of Lesbianism as Feminism's Magical Sign: Contests for Meaning and the U.S. Women's Movement, 1968–1972," in *Communication* 9 (1987): 65–91.

4. Eileen Meehan, "Why We Don't Count: The Commodity Audience," in Patricia Mellencamp, ed., *Logics of Television: Essays in Cultural Criticism* (Bloomington: Indiana University Press, 1990), p. 129; Les Brown, *Television: The Business Behind the Box* (New York: Harcourt Brace Jovanovich, 1971), pp. 47–139; Todd Gitlin, *Inside Prime Time* (New York: Pantheon, 1983), pp. 203–20; Sally Bedell, *Up the Tube: Prime Time TV in the Silverman Years* (New York: Viking, 1981), pp. 31–104.

5. VHF means "very high frequency" and is distinguished from UHF, or "ultra high frequency." VHF stations produce stronger signals, which carry greater distances.

6. Jane Feuer, "Melodrama, Serial Form, and Television Today," *Screen* 25, no. 1 (1984): 15; Gitlin, *Inside Prime Time,* pp. 203–20. I am using the hybrid

phrase "socially relevant" to describe the programs. See also Brown, *Television;* and Gitlin, *Inside Prime Time.*

7. CBS had attempted "relevant" programming in the early 1960s with *The Defenders* (1961–65), *The Nurses* (1962–65), and *East Side/West Side* (1963–64). But for a whole series of reasons, the practice did not "catch on." See U.S. Commission on Civil Rights, *Window Dressing on the Set: An Update* (Washington, D.C.: Government Printing Office, 1979), p. 2.

8. Lauren Rabinovitz, "Sitcoms and Single Moms: Representations of Feminism on American TV," *Cinema Journal* 29, no. 1 (Fall 1989): 3–19; Serafina Bathrick, "*The Mary Tyler Moore Show:* Women at Home and at Work," in Jane Feuer, Paul Kerr, and Tise Vahimagi, eds., *MTM: "Quality Television"* (London: British Film Institute, 1984), pp. 99–131; Bonnie J. Dow, "Hegemony, Feminist Criticism, and *The Mary Tyler Moore Show,*" *Critical Studies in Mass Communication* 7 (Sept. 1990): 261–74; U.S. Commission on Civil Rights, *Window Dressing on the Set,* pp. 2, 3.

The overall history of television's representation of African American and other women of color is bleak. *Beulah* (1950–53), a situation comedy about a black maid in a white household, starred in succession two famous African American film actresses, Ethel Waters and Louise Beavers. (Hattie McDaniel had been slated to replace Waters but became ill.) When Beavers decided to leave and the show stopped production, the portrayal of black women on television virtually ceased until the late sixties, although Cicely Tyson played a secretary in *East Side/West Side* (1963–64). In 1968 *Julia,* influenced at least in part by the civil rights movement, starred Diahann Carroll as a widowed mother and a nurse. The depiction, although considered a "positive role" by the U.S. Commission on Civil Rights, was also criticized by black groups for "saccharine content and a distorted presentation of black family life" (see U.S. Commission on Civil Rights, *Window Dressing on the Set,* p. 1; Diana M. Meehan, *Ladies of the Evening: Women Characters of Prime-Time Television* [Metuchen, N.J.: Scarecrow Press, 1983], p. 157). *Star Trek* (1966–69) featured a black woman, Nichelle Nichols, in a supporting role as Lt. Uhura; and *Mannix* (1968–75) featured Gail Fisher as secretary Peggy Fair. In the 1970s, socially relevant sitcoms, primarily those of Norman Lear, reintroduced black characters to prime time.

After airing a number of comedies in the seventies that featured African American women (*The Jeffersons, Good Times, That's My Mama, What's Happening,* the short-lived *Baby, I'm Back,* and to some degree *Sanford and Son*), the networks decided to pull back on black programming, calling it financially too risky. They were reluctant to gamble that the majority-white audience would watch programs that starred black people (see Todd Gitlin, "Prime-Time Whitewash," *American Film* 9, no. 2 [Nov. 1983]: 36–38). *The Jeffersons,* featuring several black women, survived into the 1980s, and *Gimme a Break,* starring Nell Carter as a household manager/nanny for a white family, premiered in 1980. (*Benson,* about a black male household manager for a white governor, premiered in 1979. The other programs starring blacks were *Diff'rent Strokes* and *Webster,* both centering on young black boys adopted by white families.)

The runaway ratings success in 1984 of *The Cosby Show,* starring Bill Cosby, for a time put to rest the networks' fears about black programming and white audiences; Cosby's show also spawned a number of programs starring or featuring African American women. *Melba,* with Melba Moore, and *Charlie and Company,* which costarred Gladys Knight and featured Della Reese, are two examples of shows that did not make it past their first season. *227,* created by and starring Marla Gibbs (formerly of *The Jeffersons*), was one survivor of this burst of cloning; it not only featured a black woman as the main character but had several other black women as supporting characters and also represented the working class. *A Different World* joined the network schedule as a *Cosby* spinoff in 1987, and in the late eighties *Frank's Place, Family Matters, Fresh Prince of Bel Air, Sugar and Spice,* and *Baghdad Café* also appeared. The early 1990s saw the addition of several new shows featuring African Americans (especially on the FOX network), but they continued to fall within the tradition of situation comedies.

The very few representations of Latina women included those in *9 to 5, AKA Pablo,* and occasionally *Chico and the Man.* Native American women occasionally appeared on *How the West Was Won.* A Japanese woman was featured on *The Courtship of Eddie's Father,* and Vietnamese women have appeared on *Night Court* and *China Beach.* Even the representation of white women has been very much homogenized. Since *The Goldbergs* (1949–54), starring Gertrude Berg, for example, Jewish women virtually disappeared from television until the character Rhoda was introduced on *The Mary Tyler Moore Show* in 1970.

9. Artikoff is cited in Gitlin, *Inside Prime Time,* p. 72. Former Federal Communications Commissioner Nicholas Johnson corroborates Tartikoff's view and says that the "T & A" period was a direct response to pressures for the reduction of violence: The networks, impervious to the implications of sexism, replaced program violence with the displays of women's bodies (personal conversation, Madison, Wis., Feb. 1980).

10. *The Bionic Woman* is a program from this period in which a woman character, Jaime Sommers (played by Lindsay Wagner), is an active protagonist but is not cast in the extreme spectacle dimension of the other active women protagonists of the time.

11. Gitlin, *Inside Prime Time,* p. 73. See also Cathy Schwichtenberg, "*Charlie's Angels:* A Patriarchal Voice in Heaven," *Jump Cut,* no. 24/25 (1981): 13–16. In early 1950s television, women were sometimes showcased for their "spectacle" dimensions, such as dancers in variety programs.

Many women and women's groups protested the "spectacle" representations; the 18,000-member Association of Flight Attendants issued a statement about *Flying High* that said, "The script used every stereotype and cliché that has ever been used in a derogatory manner toward flight attendants. . . . We have worked so many years to dispel the mistaken image of flight attendants as sex goddesses and this program is a real setback in these efforts." In 1978 Kathleen Nolan, president of the Screen Actors' Guild, said, "Women . . . are desperately disheartened to be faced in 1978 with the disgraceful trash which is being transmitted in the guise that this is the American Woman" (U.S. Commission on Civil Rights, *Window Dressing on the Set,* pp. 5, 6).

12. Barbara Avedon, interview with author, Los Angeles, Calif., Feb. 1984; Barbara Corday, interview with author, Los Angeles, Calif., Feb. 1984; Barney Rosenzweig, interview with author, Los Angeles, Calif., Oct. 1983; Molly Haskell, *From Reverence to Rape: The Treatment of Women in the Movies* (New York: Holt, Rinehart and Winston, 1974).

13. Marjorie Rosen, "Cagney and Lacey," *Ms.,* Oct. 1981, pp. 47–50, 109.

14. Corday interview.

15. Ibid.

16. Rosen, "Cagney and Lacey," p. 49; Barbara Corday, "Dialogue on Film," *American Film* 10, no. 9 (July–Aug. 1985): 12; Avedon interview.

17. Rosen, "Cagney and Lacey," p. 49; Corday interview; Avedon interview.

18. Rosenzweig interview; Rosen, "Cagney and Lacey," p. 49; Avedon interview.

19. Rosen, "Cagney and Lacey," p. 49; Rosenzweig quoted in Lori Watson, "Women Get Buddy-Buddy in New Series," *Longmont Daily Times Call,* 3–4 Apr. 1982.

20. Rosen, "Cagney and Lacey," p. 49.

21. Ibid., p. 50; Corday, "Dialogue on Film," p. 2; Rosenzweig interview.

22. Rosenzweig interview; Avedon interview; Corday interview; Rosen, "Cagney and Lacey," p. 50. It is important, in examining the history of *Cagney and Lacey,* to consider the fact that Ted Post, an action director, was hired to direct the movie. As the series progressed, the "action" components of the scripts became almost totally subservient to the "interaction" components.

23. Sharon Rosenthal, "Cancellation of 'Cagney and Lacey' to Mean Loss of 'Rare' TV Series," *New York Daily News,* 3 June 1983.

24. Rosen, "Cagney and Lacey," p. 109. Some of the characteristics applauded by Rosen demonstrate the ways in which, at this particular point in the history of the American women's movement, advertising's definitions of women and those of the liberal women's movement could coexist without much trouble. Later in the 1980s it became harder to yoke together the discourses of the women's movement and advertising without encountering much conflict and contradiction. In the late 1970s and very early 1980s, the women's movement placed its greatest emphasis on equality in the labor force, primarily for white, heterosexual, middle-class women. But in the early 1980s, this emphasis began to shift to include women of color and lesbians.

25. *TV Guide,* 3–10 Oct. 1981, p. A-137.

26. V. N. Volosinov, quoted in Stuart Hall, "The Rediscovery of 'Ideology': Return of the Repressed in Media Studies," in Michael Gurevitch, Tony Bennett, James Curran, and Janet Woollacott, eds., *Culture, Society and the Media* (London: Methuen, 1982), p. 77; John Fiske, *Television Culture* (London: Methuen, 1987), pp. 84–85. See also Introduction, note 6. Fiske also describes a third-level or tertiary text, which is the discussion generated by viewers about the primary text or TV program itself.

Intertextuality refers to the "use of language that calls up a vast reserve of echoes from similar texts, similar phrasings, remarks, situations, characters" (Rosalind Coward and John Ellis, *Language and Materialism* [London: Routledge and Kegan Paul, 1977], p. 52). Intertextuality works to demonstrate both the multiplicity of meaning—its deferral onto and across many different texts—and also the ways that particular meanings, at particular historical moments, may "pile up" on one another and achieve a temporary discursive authority (Robert C. Allen, *Speaking of Soap Operas* [Chapel Hill: University of North Carolina Press, 1985], p. 61). See also Tony Bennett, "The Bond Phenomenon: Theorizing a Popular Hero," *Southern Review* 16, no. 2 (1983): 209, for a discussion of Pierre Machery's notion of "encrustation," which is also helpful here. See also Mimi White, "Television Genres: Intertextuality," *Journal of Film and Video* 38 (Summer 1985): 41–47, for a demonstration of the term as it applies to TV genres. Tony Bennett and Janet Woollacott use the term *inter-textuality* to refer to "the social organization of the relations between texts within specific conditions of reading" (*Bond and Beyond: The Political Career of a Popular Hero* [New York: Methuen, 1987], p. 45).

27. Barbara Basler, "Real Policewomen View the TV Variety," *New York Times,* 7 Oct. 1981; Howard Rosenberg, "'Cagney and (Uh) Lacey': A Question of a Pink Slip," *Los Angeles Times,* 23 June 1982, Calendar section.

28. Richard Turner, "The Curious Case of the Lady Cops and the Shots That Blew Them Away," *TV Guide*, 8–14 Oct. 1983, p. 52; "Gloria Gets Action," *Soho News*, 9 Mar. 1982.

29. "Meg Foster to Join Tyne Daly as CBS 'Cagney and Lacey' Duo," Filmways news release, 1982, Rosenzweig files; "Gloria Gets Action." Although Barbara Corday remained with the series as executive story consultant, Barbara Avedon left to pursue other writing projects.

30. Tom Bierbaum, "Steinem Takes Right Turn on TV Violence," *Daily Variety*, 2 Feb. 1982.

31. Bowden's Information Service, "Tyne Daly Returns to Detective Role," *The Leader Post*, 12 Mar. 1982; Barbara Holsopple, "Two New Series on Women: All Work, No Play," *Pittsburgh Press*, 25 Mar. 1982; Beverly Stephen, "Policewomen: TV Show on the Case," *Los Angeles Times*, 11 Apr. 1982; Bonnie Malleck, "Real Women at Last: Pinch-Hitter 'Cagney and Lacey' Is a Mid-Season Bonus," *Kitchner-Waterloo Record*, Apr. 1982.

32. Ed Bark, "Ratings May Kill Quality Cop Show," *Dallas Texas Morning News*, 1 Apr. 1982; Malleck, "Real Women at Last"; Bill Musselwhite, "No There's No Farm Raising Tiny Animals for Airlines," *Calgary Herald* (Alberta), 3 Apr. 1982.

33. The technique of mise-en-scène includes, among other things, the characters' body sizes, makeup, hairstyles, clothing, or costumes; character movement, gestures, and mannerisms; and use of props (see David Bordwell and Kristin Thompson, *Film Art: An Introduction*, 4th ed. [New York: McGraw-Hill, 1993], pp. 145–84).

34. Richard Hack, "TeleVisions," *The Hollywood Reporter*, 26 Mar. 1982; Musselwhite, "There's No Farm."

35. Turner, "Curious Case of the Lady Cops," p. 53; Rosenzweig interview; *TV Guide*, 3–10 Apr. 1982, pp. A-116–17. *Magnum, P.I.* was getting an average share of 38. When *Cagney and Lacey* aired, it pulled in a 25 share the first week and a 24 the second week. According to Rosenzweig, "At 9 o'clock all over America, 12 million people were getting up out of their seats *en masse* and walking away, or leaving the network."

36. Turner, "Curious Case of the Lady Cops," p. 54; Barbara Holsopple, "'Cagney and Lacey' Hanging by (Blond) Thread," *Pittsburgh Press*, 19 Nov. 1982, sec. B.

37. Turner, "Curious Case of the Lady Cops," p. 53. Harvey Shephard declined my requests for an interview.

38. "Itinerary for Tyne Daly and Meg Foster," public relations release from Brocato and Kelman, Inc., 27 Apr. 1982, Rosenzweig files.

39. Turner, "Curious Case of the Lady Cops," p. 54; Rosenzweig interview. After Meg Foster was released from her contract, she initially had difficulty getting other work. According to a United Feature syndicate article, before that time she "was an in-demand actress. But there was no official announcement of why she was fired, so people jumped to some pretty wild conclusions. . . . They want no part of a troublemaker." The article continues, "Later an official story came out and from then on Meg's offers picked up again" (Dick Kleiner, "TV Scout Sketch #1: Cagney and Lacey Situation, the Story behind Meg's Ouster," week of 23 Aug. 1982, Rosenzweig files). Rosenzweig says he tried to save Foster's job by suggesting to CBS that they dye her hair blond (as a way of achieving character contrast with the also-brunette Daly). He admits, however, to giving in to the network rather quickly and making Foster the "scapegoat" in order to save the series (Rosenzweig interview).

Foster later appeared as a district attorney on *The Trials of Rosie O'Neill,* starring Sharon Gless and produced by Barney Rosenzweig in the early 1990s.

40. Dave Kaufman, "CBS Ent Prez Grant Asks Crix for Fair Chance," *Daily Variety,* 25 May 1982; Richard Hack, "TeleVisions," *The Hollywood Reporter,* 28 May 1982, p. 6; Frank Swertlow, "CBS Alters 'Cagney,' Calling It 'Too Women's Lib,'" *TV Guide,* 12–18 June 1982, p. A-1.

41. Malleck, "Real Women at Last"; Alan W. Petrocelli, "Cagney and Lacey," *US,* 27 Apr. 1982, p. 46; Avedon interview. Meg Foster did not reply to my letters requesting an interview.

42. Jane Ardmore, "Who Is the Enemy?," draft of article for "Sunday Woman," 1982, Rosenzweig files; Sal Manna, "Cagney and Lacey on Trial," *Los Angeles Herald Examiner,* 22 Apr. 1982, sec. B.

43. My point here is that even though the programs presented "positive" portrayals of lesbians, the organizing principle of each story was that lesbianism is considered socially "deviant"—the point of the humor or drama.

44. Howard Rosenberg, "'Cagney and (Uh) Lacey.'"

45. Ibid., pp. 1, 7.

46. Rosenthal, "Cancellation of 'Cagney and Lacey'"; Holsopple, "'Cagney and Lacey' Hanging by (Blond) Thread."

47. Letters section, *TV Guide,* 10–16 June 1982, p. A-4.

48. Viewer letters, Rosenzweig files.

49. Frank Torrez, "TV Ratings," *Los Herald Examiner,* 2 July 1982; Sal Manna, "Sorry This Show Wasn't Seen," *Los Angeles Herald Examiner,* [1st week of July] 1982, sec. B.

50. Arnold Becker, quoted in Rosenberg, "'Cagney and (Uh) Lacey'"; John J. O'Connor, "'Cagney and Lacey'—Indisputably a Class Act," *The Patriot Ledger* (Quincy, Mass.), 5 July 1984; Tim Brooks and Earle Marsh, *The Complete Directory of Prime Time Network Television, 1946 to the Present,* 5th ed. (New York: Ballantine, 1992), p. 137. Although Corday and Avedon had wanted Sharon Gless for the part from the beginning, I found no evidence that Meg Foster was sacrificed in order to finally get Gless. Barbara Corday, however, contends that from the first time she saw Foster and Daly read a script together, she was sure they had made a mistake in casting. She recalls saying to Rosenzweig, "Oh, my God, this is a mistake." Corday believed that although Foster was a consummate actress, she played Cagney too much like Daly played Lacey. According to her, the Cagney part would have been played more upscale from the beginning of the series had not Foster inflected it with a more working-class interpretation (Corday interview).

51. Rick Du Brow, "Cagney and Lacey Hang Tough," *Los Angeles Herald Examiner,* 25 Jan. 1983, sec. C; "Analysis of Costs for CBS for 'Cagney and Lacey,'" prepared by *Cagney and Lacey* production offices, 1982, Rosenzweig files. Since the mid-1950s, advertisers had made it clear that they did not want their products associated with lower-class characters and settings (see Erik Barnouw, *The Image Empire: A History of Broadcasting in the United States from 1953* [New York: Oxford University Press, 1970], pp. 5–8).

52. "Advertising and Promotion," from CBS Entertainment Division, 1982, Rosenzweig files.

53. "Review," *Daily Variety,* 28 Oct. 1982; Marilyn Preston, "If 'Cagney and Lacey' Fails, Other TV Women May Suffer," *Chicago Tribune,* 8 Nov. 1982; Howard Rosenberg, "The New Season," *Los Angeles Times,* 25 Oct. 1982, Calendar section.

54. Frank Torrez, "'Cagney and Lacey' Has Integrity Intact," *Los Angeles Times*, 25 Oct. 1982, sec. D.

55. Gail Williams, "Review," *The Hollywood Reporter*, 1 Nov. 1982.

56. Carol Wyman, "'Cagney and Lacey' Has Grown," *New Haven Register*, 24 Feb. 1983; Sharon Rosenthal, "Second-hand Roles Brought Actress Double Trouble," *New York Daily News* to the *Jacksonville (Florida) Times-Union*, 4 Nov. 1982, sec. E.

57. Candy Justice, "CBS Softens Show to Toughen Ratings," *Memphis (Tennessee) Scimitar*, 15 Nov. 1982.

58. Jim Butler, "'Cagney and Lacey' Works Well," *Bryan (Texas) Eagle*, 7 Nov. 1982.

59. Michael Bandler, "Gless Is More," *American Way*, 22 Jan. 1985, p. 46.

60. Terrence O'Flaherty, "Women in the Line of Fire," *San Francisco Chronicle*, 11 Oct. 1983, sec. B; Gail Williams, "Review."

61. Viewer letters, Rosenzweig files.

62. Barbara Grizzuti Harrison, "I Didn't Think I Was Pretty: An Interview with Sharon Gless," *Parade Magazine*, 23 Feb. 1986, pp. 4–5. The word "readings" may be applied to film and televisual texts (programs) as well as to literary ones and emphasizes the particular ways in which individual viewers make sense of or interpret the text.

63. Caption for cover photo of Tyne Daly and Sharon Gless, *Los Angeles Herald Examiner*, 25 Jan. 1983; Du Brow, "Cagney and Lacey Hang Tough"; Elaine Warren, "Where Are the Real Women on TV?," *Los Angeles Herald Examiner*, 31 Oct. 1982, sec. E; Judy Mann, "Women on TV," *Washington Post*, 7 Jan. 1983; Laura Daltry, "Grandmother, What Big Role Models You Had!," *Los Angeles Times*, 28 Nov. 1982, Calendar section.

64. Larry Wood, "'Cagney and Lacey' Doesn't Fit Policewoman Image," *Evansville Press*, 17 Nov. 1982.

65. Jerilyn Stapleton, personal interview with author, Feb. 1984, Los Angeles, Calif. The letter-writing campaign will be described in more detail in Chapter 2.

66. Such communities or networks (often based on exposure to similar cultural products such as films, TV programs, newspapers, magazines, novels, and so forth) give "participants" the language and analyses for articulating everyday life experiences. See Elizabeth Ellsworth, "Illicit Pleasures: Feminist Spectators and *Personal Best*," in Leslie G. Roman and Linda K. Christian-Smith with Elizabeth Ellsworth, eds., *Becoming Feminine: The Politics of Popular Culture* (Philadelphia, Pa.: Farmer Press, 1988), pp. 102–19; Jacqueline Bobo, "*The Color Purple*: Black Women as Cultural Readers," in E. Deidre Pribram, ed., *Female Spectators: Looking at Film and Television* (London: Verso, 1988), pp. 90–109.

67. The viewer letters quoted below were selected from correspondence in Barney Rosenzweig's files. See Introduction, note 18.

68. Gary Deeb, "Tube Watch," *Syracuse Post Standard*, 30 May 1983.

69. The *Sacramento Bee* used this phrase in printing a letter from Archie Brown, who was outraged at Deeb's column (date unknown, from Rosenzweig files).

70. Irene Baros-Johnson, letter to the editor, *Syracuse Standard Post*, 14 June 1983.

71. Terry Louise Fisher, interview with author, Feb. 1984. In April 1984, Susan McHenry wrote an article for *Ms.* about the revived show that discusses some of the history I have presented here ("The Rise and Fall—and Rise of TV's 'Cagney and

Lacey,'" *Ms.*, Apr. 1984, pp. 23–25). See also Sue Reilly, "The Double Lives of Cagney and Lacey," *McCall's*, Apr. 1985, pp. 14, 20, 23; Mary Gordon, "Sharon Gless and Tyne Daly," *Ms.*, Jan. 1987, pp. 40, 41, 86–88.

72. Barney Rosenzweig, interview with author, Jan. 1984, Los Angeles, Calif.; Sharon Gless, interview with author, Mar. 1984, Los Angeles, Calif.

73. Judy Sabel, conversation with author, Feb. 1984, Los Angeles, Calif.; Rosenzweig interview, Oct. 1983; Joyce Sunila, "Are the Laceys Too Real for Television?," *Los Angeles Times*, Sunday Calendar section.

74. Personal observations, Feb. 1984; conversations with Eddie Barron, hairdresser for Tyne Daly, Feb. 1984, and with Tyne Daly, Mar. 1984, Los Angeles, Calif.

75. Personal observation, Feb. 1984; Avedon interview; Fisher interview; *60 Minutes*, CBS, Dec. 1984. According to Avedon, "sympathetic" means such things as showing women "in the kitchen"; to Terry Louise Fisher, it means showing them as "warm."

76. Karen Stabiner, "The Pregnant Detective," *New York Times Magazine*, 22 Sept. 1985, p. 104; Judith Michaelson, "Ironies in the Fired 'Cagney,' " *Los Angeles Times*, 14 Sept. 1983, Calendar section.

77. Mark Carlisle, "Cagney and Lacey Are Shaming the Men of America," *National Examiner*, 2 Apr. 1985, p. 21.

78. Bridget Smith, *"Cagney and Lacey,"* *Spare Rib*, no. 161 (Dec. 1985): 31. Another review, picking up from a different angle on some of the same contradictions as *Spare Rib*, described the representations as typically "Hollywood," emphasized the generally ludicrous character of police/crime genres, and saw Cagney and Lacey simply as female imports into the form. The protagonists, it said, were a "pair of female crime chasers who demonstrate that they can be just as dauntless, efficient, egotistical and generally silly as their male counterparts in Hollywood's Wonderful World of Crime" (O'Flaherty, "Women in the Line of Fire"). And a British reviewer said, "The hard-hittin', handbag-swinging New York police toughettes return to spit, bite and claw their way through TV's idea of the all-American criminal underworld" (Sarah Bond, "Tonight's Choice," 25 Sept. 1983, newspaper unknown, Rosenzweig files).

79. Exploitation topics use sensational—usually sexual or violent—subject material in order to attract an audience.

80. Sweep periods are times (usually one month, three times a year) during which the ratings companies survey all the television markets in the United States; this is when local stations get rated. Networks and affiliates usually engage in a practice called "hyping" during the sweeps: they promote shows heavily and tend to air high-budget miniseries and "exploitation" programming.

81. Carol Cancila, "Cop Show Focuses on Breast Cancer," *American Medical News*, 8 Feb. 1985, pp. 2, 47.

82. Michael Ryan, "A Method in the Madness," *People*, 11 Feb. 1985, p. 96.

83. Kathryn C. Montgomery, *Target Prime Time: Advocacy Groups and the Struggle over Entertainment Television* (Oxford: Oxford University Press, 1989), pp. 201–15. Most of the direct pressure on the series in the instances I have discussed came from CBS programming executives. The activities of the Program Practices Department (the network "censors," called Standards and Practices at other networks) were less overt and consisted mostly of regular letters to the producers following the evaluations of scripts and script revisions. These letters delineated areas of concern, including language, wardrobe and sexuality, police procedures, com-

mercial identification, and ethnic portrayals. Some of their aims were toning down obscenities; being sure, for example, that "Mary Beth's nightgown will not be unduly revealing"; certifying that most police actions were in accord with Los Angeles Police Department specifications; ensuring that the brand names of products were not identifiable; and preventing ethnic slurs. But at other times, as the example of "The Clinic" demonstrates, the Program Practices Department was a more active "censor" of the series (examples in letter from Christopher Davidson to Barney Rosenzweig, 12 Feb. 1982, Rosenzweig files).

84. Montgomery, *Target Prime Time*, p. 215; "An Episode of 'Cagney' under Fire on Abortion," Associated Press release, *New York Times,* 11 Nov. 1985.

85. CBS vice-president George Schweitzer, quoted in Nancy Hellmich, "Daly Defends 'Cagney' Show on Abortion," *USA Today,* 6 Nov. 1985, sec. D; NRLC president John Wilke, on *MacNeil/Lehrer News Hour,* PBS, 8 Nov. 1985.

86. Hellmich, "Daly Defends 'Cagney' Show on Abortion"; *MacNeil/Lehrer News Hour,* PBS, 8 Nov. 1985.

87. Judy Mann, "Cagney and Lacey, and Abortion," *Washington Post,* 15 Nov. 1985; Hellmich, "Daly Defends 'Cagney' Show on Abortion."

88. Celeste Michelle Condit, "The Rhetorical Limits of Polysemy," *Critical Studies in Mass Communication* 6, no. 2 (June 1989): 118.

89. Also, 12 April 1984 was declared Cagney and Lacey Day by Marion Barry, mayor of Washington, D.C., and by the Commission on Working Women.

90. Serita D. Stevens, *Cagney and Lacey* (New York: Dell, 1985); *Ms.,* Jan. 1987, cover; Gordon, "Sharon Gless and Tyne Daly," pp. 40, 41, 86–88. See also *Channels* 6, no. 6 (Oct. 1986): 39–59, esp. William A. Henry III, "*Cagney and Lacey:* No Copping Out," pp. 52–53.

Once in a Lifetime

Constructing "The Working Woman" through Cable Narrowcasting

JACKIE BYARS and EILEEN R. MEEHAN

We feared people would see us as "The Feminism Channel" or the "Betty Crocker Channel."

Marge Sandwick, Senior Vice President for Marketing and Communication (1989), Lifetime[1]

While denying that it is "feminist," Lifetime lays claim to the "feminine" side of television and in its advertising defines "feminine" television as strong-willed, smart, funny, compassionate, passionate—and only on cable. Such a claim raises a series of interesting questions and observations concerning gender, technology, and industry. Scholars of media and culture have long recognized the gendering of genres, narrative forms, iconography, and technologies by the culture industries and by consumers.[2] In film and television studies, we too have followed the industrial practice of sorting genres by genders, treating soap operas as women's television and horse operas as men's television. In this way, we recognize four social constructs: first, that culture industries target gendered audiences, aiming specific artifacts and particular genres at either men or women; second, that particular audiences, defined by gender, seem to have special relationships with particular genres; third, that stereotypical expectations about both social behavior and cultural taste are utilized profitably by media corporations and advertisers; and fourth, that media texts are widely believed to influence their consumers, leading to the conclusion that media representations of gendered categories at least in part define the categories themselves.

These recognitions about industrial practices, audiences, and consumerism lead to a number of questions, among them: What leads a single

From *Camera Obscura*, no. 33–34, 1995. Copyright ©1995 by Indiana University Press. Reprinted by permission of Duke University Press.

media entity, one cable channel—Lifetime—to call itself *the* feminine side of television? What exactly *is* feminine television? What is Lifetime's construction of "the feminine"? How does Lifetime's attempt at gendered narrowcasting actually affect its programming? Is its programming different from other cable channels and from broadcast networks? In exploring the implications of these questions, we outline the history of the category "women's television" and the development of a new and valuable commodity audience, "working women," that Lifetime explicitly targets; analyze Lifetime's policies regarding its programs; and examine the effect of its corporate philosophical assumptions on actual content, focusing primarily on that programming explicitly designed for "working women." Our analysis culminates in a comparison of Lifetime's remake of the film *Notorious* with its original version, illustrating the link between industry and text and making explicit just who that "woman" is that Lifetime seeks to construct.

What Was—and Is—"Women's Television"?

From the inception of commercial broadcasting, advertisers, networks, and the ratings monopolists[3] have had a strong interest in the "ladies of the house," as they once called women working in the home. Such women were perceived as comprising a daytime audience of domestic purchasing agents—agents who bought for the entire family.[4] Every standard history of broadcasting notes that the innovation of radio's daily domestic melodrama can be traced to the willingness of soap manufacturers to buy time from the networks and scripts from Irna Phillips (or her imitators) in order to mount an inexpensive but continuing story in which their products were frequently featured.[5] Such soap operas were structured around the rhythm of housework, with enough repetition to allow the stereotypical housewife to perform her noisy chores without missing anything important.[6] Although highly profitable, soaps were generally treated as second class entertainment by those in the broadcasting industry and in the news media. Of the few behavioral researchers to address soaps, Herta Hertzog found that women did indeed seem to have a special relationship with the genre, using soaps as sources of advice on personal problems and modes of polite behavior.[7] During the Golden Age of Radio, soaps remained an important form of radio entertainment targeted at women.

Less often noted in the standard histories is the phenomenon of daytime talk shows for women. As Michele Hilmes's research on the daytime host Mary Margaret McBride demonstrates, daytime radio also included talk shows organized around a host who often rose to celebrity status.[8] Talk programs ranged from local "breakfast" shows hosted by a married couple to home-and-family shows focused solely on domestic concerns to McBride's innovative blending of domestic topics with features and interviews exploring world events, national politics, and current issues. Long before Sylvester Weaver "invented" magazine programming and advertising, McBride and colleagues were hosting women's magazines on radio with each 15-minute segment sponsored by a different advertiser.

During radio's hegemony, then, broadcasting for women meant daytime serial dramas and talk shows. When evening fell, broadcasters assumed that the family, with father as its focus, gathered around the radio. Networks shifted genres to match this shift in audience, offering genres targeted to the entire family in the early evening (situation comedies, variety shows) and, as the evening wore on, moving to more adult genres that tended to be male identified (Westerns, cop shows, private detective shows, adventure programs, and so forth).[9]

The technological move by CBS and NBC from radio to television meant a similar move in genres and programs from radio to television. Although some programs were simulcast, the networks' decision to replace radio with television—and advertisers' acceptance of that decision—ultimately spelled the demise of radio as a distributor of generic programming. However, the types of programming that had filled the radio airwaves were simply rerouted to deliver the same genres and often the same programs over the very high frequencies in the electromagnetic spectrum. Women's radio, then, became women's television. Over time, women's television developed new twists and variations in both representational and industrial practices that would have an impact on Lifetime's subsequent definition of women's cable television.

Any review of soap operas on television must begin by noting the brief period in which sponsors were suspicious of television. Concerned by the higher production costs associated with TV, sponsors worked out deals for simultaneous broadcast of soaps on radio and television that brought costs within acceptable limits. By 1960, however, sponsors transferred their daytime melodramas entirely to the home screen and all three networks (CBS, NBC, and the fledgling ABC) discontinued radio broadcasts of soaps. Sponsors of the television melodramas—companies like Procter and Gamble, Lever Bros., and Colgate Palmolive Peet—retained control over the writing and production of their programming. Given ABC's inability to deliver as many viewers as CBS or NBC, soap manufacturers were reluctant to produce materials for the younger network. However, by the late 1960s, ABC took matters into its own hands and invested considerable resources in the production of original soap operas for itself. On CBS and NBC, soap opera programming remained the property of the soap manufacturers, despite the general trend in prime-time television for advertisers to give up ownership, replacing sponsorship of a single show with spot advertising on many.

While CBS and NBC enjoyed the benefits of sponsored soaps in the daytime with advertisers paying all production costs, the two networks were confined to running material that advertisers believed appropriate for the promotion of their products. In contrast, ABC's in-house soaps had more latitude. While those on CBS and NBC were rather staid and slow-moving, ABC revamped the genre, introducing more adult themes, sexually explicit representations, more action, outdoor shooting, and faster plots.[10] This set off a spiraling competition among networks to revitalize the form to make it appear more expensive, more relevant, and more racy. (This rivalry continues to the present day, and the soaps that have resulted apparently succeed in attracting the targeted 18–49 age group among women.[11])

The networks' continuing struggle for control of a female viewership, and thereby for dominance of daytime ratings and the lion's share of daytime profits, still relies on the serial melodramas that are nationally distributed from ABC, CBS, and NBC to their affiliates. Soap operas still dominate the networks' programming during the heart of the house worker's day, when the (presumably male) primary wage earner and older children are expected to be away from the house. Today's soaps follow the classic formula of the serial, domestic melodrama. All emphasize personal relations, familial ties, and emotional crises, which are generally worked out in domestic space or in a domesticated work place. The multiple story lines are woven together to generate the complex and fabulous plots that distinguish the form. Powerful matriarchs, scheming vixens, clever businesswomen, and sincere beauties still populate the soaps, along with their male counterparts—powerful patriarchs, scheming gigolos, clever businessmen, and sincere hunks. However, in the struggle to win ratings, current soaps also include more location shooting, physical action, fashionable costuming, elaborate sets, sexual play, and discussion of social issues than were previously incorporated in the genre. But if soaps are the jewels in the crown of network daytime television, those jewels are still surrounded by talk shows. Ranging from the networks' morning shows (NBC's *Today,* ABC's *Good Morning America,* CBS's *This Morning*) distributed nationally by the networks to the syndicated shows that plug the off-network holes in affiliates' schedules (such as *Oprah Winfrey, Donahue, Geraldo, Ricki Lake,* and *Sally Jessy Raphael*), the talk show remains a staple of women's television.[12] But even as soaps have changed, so too have talk shows. By sketching the development of the talk show from the 1950s to the 1990s, we sketch the process by which the daytime talk show has absorbed some of the melodramatic elements of the soap opera to produce a highly volatile hybrid that attracts large and loyal audiences of women.

In the 1950s, the quintessential daytime host was Art Linkletter, whose *Art Linkletter's House Party* featured folksy interviews with children, housewives, and celebrities before a large studio audience. The 1960s and 1970s replaced folksiness with celebrity patter as syndicated talk shows adopted the highly successful *Tonight Show* format. Actors, singers, authors, and others who could profit from promoting their wares enjoyed informal chats with such friendly hosts as Mike Douglas, Merv Griffin, John Bartholomew Tucker, or John Davidson.

In contrast with such innocuous personalities were the personae of Phil Donahue, Sally Jessy Raphael, Oprah Winfrey, and Geraldo Rivera, who reinvented the talk show in the late 1970s and early 1980s. The "big four" of talk shows cultivated reputations as socially concerned individuals and tough interviewers. These hosts replaced celebrities with real people who were willing to talk about social controversies in front of studio audiences and to submit themselves to the analysis of "expert" therapists. Further, audiences were encouraged to ask sharp questions and deliver strong judgments of the guests. Tensions often ran high, as when Rivera pitted John Metzger and his neo-nazi supporters against Roy Innes of the Congress on Racial Equality and his supporters. Metzger's race-baiting of Innes resulted in an on-camera melee in which a neo-nazi broke Rivera's nose. Although unusual in 1988, such melodramatic confrontations and physical reactions became standard fare on talk shows in the 1990s.

This emphasis on melodrama has meant a shift from social controversies to domestic controversies. Hosts like Ricki Lake, Richard Bey, Jenny Jones, and Jerry Springer have further revolutionized the talk show; they engage their guests and their audience in highly charged arguments about the guests' personal lives, focusing mainly on sexual relations, familial ties, and emotional crises. These newer talk shows have dispensed with professional therapists, allowing the audience this role as hosts arrange often melodramatic confrontations between would-be lovers, ex-lovers, adulterous spouses, birth mothers, lost siblings, absentee fathers, and so on.[13] Called "ambushes" in the trade, such confrontations trigger on-camera reactions ranging from embarrassment to fist fights. This focus on the melodramatic— on personal issues and personal confrontations—imports the essence of soap opera into the talk show format.

But where the soap opera is fiction, melodramatic talk shows are "reality television" in which the outcomes of confrontations between real people are always unpredictable. The success of this melding is suggested by the strong female audiences that view both the new talk shows and the old soap operas as well as by the proliferation of new melodramatic talk shows that increasingly dominate the syndication market. Although such melodramatic talk shows have triggered discussions of ethics, the mixed genre's success in the ratings has precluded any interest in abandoning melodrama to gain respectability. The recent murder of Scott Amedure by John Schmitz after an "ambush" arranged by the *Jenny Jones Show* seems unlikely to change that, unless the show is held to be legally liable.[14]

Where melodramatic talk shows have been profitable and unrespectable, soaps have retained their profitability and gained new respectability within the television industry. Selections from the Daytime Emmys are even broadcast on evening television. Melodrama, whether packaged as fiction or reality, clearly draws a strong female audience and remains the vital force in women's television. When packaged as fiction, daytime melodrama seems to enjoy a higher status in the 1990s than previously; packaged as reality, melodrama attracts large audiences of women, especially the 18–34 year old females that advertisers prize highly. This new respectability accorded to soaps matched with the new profitability of melodramatic talk shows suggests that the overall industrial status of women's television may be changing.

Traditionally treated as second-class television, women's television now figures in primetime. Networks commission series that interweave elements of the soap opera into traditionally male genres (*Hill Street Blues, NYPD Blue*). Affiliates move melodramatic talk shows and tabloid news shows (*A Current Affair, American Journal, Hard Copy*) into the time slots leading up to local news. And networks utilize "reality" series that intermix personal confrontation, threats to domesticity, and unpredictability (*Rescue 911, America's Most Wanted, Sightings*) to fill out their schedules. Overall, this embrace of melodrama suggests a rise in the industrial status of women's television and female audiences. But this rise is not a function of changes in television programming alone.

Television and the "Working Woman"

The new status is due, at least in part, to the economic impact of second wave feminism in the 1970s, multiple recessions starting in 1975, changes in the working life of middle-class women, changes in the television industry itself, and changes in technology. In this section, we explore these five forces, forces that combined not only to raise the status of women's television but also to make possible the creation of a cable channel targeted to women.

The histories of second wave feminism are many and we will only sketch some of the effects of that multifaceted, highly variegated movement. Suffice to say that the women's movement, rising out of the civil rights struggle and the anti-war movement of the 1960s, addressed the significant disparities in social, economic, political, sexual, and cultural power that existed between the genders and that still persist to the present day. In terms of employment, pay, and working conditions, the movement won considerable legal changes, including the publication of job advertisements by employers engaged in governmental contracts, gender desegregation of job advertisements, equal pay for equal work, and criminalization of sexual harassment.

All this might have been in vain had the movement not addressed sexist ideologies that linked women's self-worth to dependency, both economic and emotional, on males. The combination of consciousness raising and legal access to careers was an especially potent force for those women who turned college educations into a career. Spurning the chance to earn her "MRS" or to prepare for employment in traditional pink collar jobs, these "new women" sought careers as business executives, financial officers, lawyers, professors, research scientists, physicians, and so forth. The potential spending of such women attracted considerable attention from advertisers seeking to intertwine feminist notions with product consumption. Perhaps the best remembered slogan from the period was that used to promote Virginia Slims cigarettes. Noting that "you've come a long way, baby," the ad campaign humorously suggested that the right to smoke cigarettes in public was the ultimate goal of the women's movement. In retrospect, this equal right to addiction and lung disease holds little humor. At the time, however, it marked the recognition of a new market: females with considerable disposable income who maintained control over that income. With manufacturers targeting advertisements at these women, it is little wonder that, in 1976, the A.C. Nielsen Company added a new category to its demographic measurements of the television audience: working women. This category measured the viewing of women who worked outside the home for a minimum of 30 hours per week and then divided those working women into "upscale," meaning white collar, and "downscale," meaning blue collar. Advertisers expressed considerable interest in reaching those upscale working women.

But if the early 1970s presented college educated women with greater economic opportunities, that largesse came under pressure by mid-decade as the US economy began to suffer recurrent recessions that persist to this day. The early recessionary waves had the greatest impact on blue collar workers as corporations in the manufacturing sector downsized operations through massive lay-offs, plant closings, de-unionization campaigns, decreases in wages or benefits, and exportation of operations to Third World countries. By the 1980s, the cooperative relationship that had been forged among big business, big labor, and big government to counteract the "Communist threat" was thoroughly undermined.[15] This destabilization has worked against the interests of labor, regardless of "collar," resulting in periodic increases in unemployment and underemployment as well as declines in real wages, job benefits, and buying power. These problems were exacerbated by Reaganist economic policies fostering deregulation, financial speculation, militarization, privatization, and further de-industrialization. Such monetarist policies fostered the transfer of real wealth from the middle and working classes to the capitalist elite, resulting in a significant loss of income for most Americans.

For the middle class, this loss placed considerable pressure on the familial division of labor. Now many households required two incomes to achieve the spending power that one had previously insured. In order to help their families remain in the middle class, many homemakers joined the flood of women that deluged the paid labor force. Furthermore, marketing studies not only demonstrated that women in dual income households retained some control over their own wages, but also that they continued to fulfill the traditional female role as domestic purchasing agent for the household. The significance of this phenomenon was not lost on advertisers, on the media corporations that sell advertisers access to consumers, or on the companies that measure the quality and quantity of audiences drawn to the media.

For television's advertisers and networks, these economic shifts effectively narrowed the consumerist caste. That is, a smaller proportion of the population had sufficient disposable income to regularly purchase a broad array of goods and services according to brand rather than price, as well as to frequently purchase items on the basis of impulse. More people had less money to spend, and those who suffered the greatest cut in disposable incomes—now termed "downscale viewers"[16]—were the least attractive to advertisers regardless of gender. Advertisers responded to these economic changes by targeting their commercials to "upscale viewers" who comprised the consumerist caste. With advertisers exerting a demand for upscale view-ers, networks responded by targeting their programming to such viewers. With upscale working women specifically measured by the ratings, advertis-ers could and did demand access to this attractive target audience, and net-works began to program for both upscale men *and* women.

This provides one explanation for network experiments in so-called hybrid series. Such prime-time series blended elements of serial melodrama into traditionally males genres. An early example of a hybridized series is *Cagney and Lacey* (1981–1988) that introduced personal issues and con-tinuing stories into the buddy cop genre.[17] In later hybrids, characters were connected variously by professional status (*St. Elsewhere, L.A. Law*), work-place (*Hill Street Blues*), intergalactic missions (*Star Trek: The Next Gener-ation*), generational status (*thirtysomething*), and even geography (*Northern Exposure*). As *Northern Exposure* demonstrates, the generic hybrid can secure high ratings that the television industry interprets as wide acceptance by viewers. For the networks, trying to attract both upscale males and females, hybrid series may well be more cost efficient than series that stick to a spe-cific, gendered genre. This emerging practice falls nicely within the net-works' traditional formula for manufacturing broadcast series: every show is completely new and totally familiar; every show provides something for everybody. Increasingly, the "new" relies on a mix of generic elements while the "familiar" relies on the genres themselves. And "everybody" excludes downscale men and women but includes upscale women, with particular attention paid to upscale working women.

The impact of second wave feminism and economic recession gradually changed the way that television networks competed for advertisers' dollars. The competition for television viewers narrowed to a competition for upscale viewers as measured by the Nielsen ratings. But, since 1977, the Nielsen sam-ple was no longer limited to network television viewers or to "real time" view-ing. Nielsen's ratings increasingly sampled cable subscribers thereby expand-ing the overall competition in the marketplace. They also included those programs that were recorded on videocassette recorders (VCRs) for (pre-sumably) later viewing by both broadcast and cable audiences. In essence, the business of television became larger than the business of broadcasting.

As measured by the Nielsen ratings since the late 1970s, audiences for broadcast television were gradually being eroded by increased access to and use of cable television. The quantity of the audience for broadcast televi-sion was shrinking as the quantity of audience for cable expanded. But this was not the only bad news for networks: Nielsen also found that the audi-ence for broadcast television mixed together upscale and downscale view-ers, while cable television attracted more upscale viewers who watched sig-nificant amounts of television. Apparently, having paid the toll to get access to cable, subscribers organized much of their leisure time around the con-sumption of its channels. So, although these channels had relatively small audiences, those viewers were of high quality. Nielsen ratings, then, con-firmed the cable industry's promotional materials: cable's total audience was comprised by large numbers of the consumerist caste, of those upscale men and women targeted by advertisers. Further, marketing studies suggested that cable subscribers were high quality consumers: they bought more advertised products than users of other media. For advertisers and the Nielsen Company, this made cable subscribers a high quality audience, despite the fact that they were still a low quantity one compared to that for broadcast television.

Advertisers interpreted these indicators as signs that cable television was becoming viable as a commercial medium for national distribution of advertising. As the cable industry marched towards the magic goal of 50% penetration, a goal that was actually achieved by 1988, cable channels began earning revenues from car manufacturers, soda makers, candy companies, and other name brand advertisers that had long patronized the broadcast networks.[18]

Trade papers and financial analysts had widely argued that a 50% penetration rate, and its resulting subscription base, was essential for cable operators to earn profits and for cable channels to deliver an adequate quantity of high quality viewers to attract advertisers. Achieving that penetration rate meant achieving status as a mass medium. Yet, cable was not a mass medium in the same manner as broadcast television. Cable system operators separated communities into those that had sufficient profit potential for the firm to incur costs of installing the cable infrastructure and those deemed lacking in profit potential. Within those favored communities, cable's subscription fees separated households into subscribers and non-subscribers. In the current recessionary cycle, subscription has proven that a household is comprised by bona fide consumers who want to consume television, who can afford fees for such consumption, and who subsequently organize their domestic lives around TV viewing. This makes cable a particularly attractive buy: it can sift the consumerist wheat from the non-consumerist chaff.

One effect of Reaganist deregulation was the networks' invasion of the cable industry. Networks themselves started cable channels ranging from CBS's ambitious attempt to deliver very upscale audiences via its high culture Arts channel (an offer that advertisers easily refused) to channels started by ABC and NBC that targeted more traditional demographic groups. ABC's A&E targeted the PBS crowd, its ESPN targeted sports fans, and its Daytime targeted women. NBC's recent soft-news channel CNBC targets upscale men and women interested in news features and informational programming. Other cable channels have also proliferated. Some non-affiliated stations in large markets (KTVU in San Francisco-Oakland; WGN in Chicago; WTBS in Atlanta), which had successfully mixed local sports with movie packages and off-network reruns, used satellite-to-cable distribution to become the first "super-stations." Other cable channels targeted some slice of the consumerist caste with formats based on programming practices developed by networks to target demographic segments. For example, Nickelodeon targeted all children just as local after-school programming and networks' Saturday cartoons had; MTV turned *American Bandstand, Dance*

Party, and similar teen rock shows into a 24-hour format that replaced lip-synching live performers with videotaped performances, and so on.[19]

Perhaps the most notable characteristic of such "narrowly" targeted cable channels as NIK, MTV, ESPN, or Daytime was the sheer breadth of their potential appeal to what are actually large, undifferentiated groups of people: *all* children, rockers, sports fans, and women 18–49 hardly constitute narrow, highly differentiated, homogeneous blocs of the television audience. Yet much popular, trade, and academic discourse about such targeting focused on the potential divisiveness of this narrowcasting. Pundits editorialized over the loss of a cohesive television experience, suggesting that targeted channels functionally destroyed the unified American culture created by network television.[20] Less often discussed was cable's ability to divide the audience into people who can afford to pay a monthly fee and people who cannot. Cable subscription's ability to thus presort the audience into bona fide consumers and mere viewers was enhanced during Reaganist deregulation, as cable operators doubled and even tripled the cost of basic subscription while lowering the prices for extra services on pay channels. Such a division of the audience, in conjunction with economic downturns and Reaganism, piqued advertisers' interest in cable, perhaps especially in the new category of upscale working women.

That interest was not limited to programs such women watched in real time. VCRs allowed that audience to record programs for viewing at more convenient times or, depending on the technology of their cable system, to watch one program while recording another. By 1987, almost half of US households (48.7% or 43 million) reported owning a VCR; those numbers climbed to 77.1% and 72 million by 1993, making the VCR one of the most quickly adopted technologies to hit the consumer market.[21] This created a measurement problem for the Nielsen ratings: although the Nielsen meters could identify what channel was being taped, they could not subsequently determine if the taped program was ever played for viewing. Nielsen's decision that taping was the equivalent of viewing seems generous given research that suggests that shows taped may well be shows never viewed.[22] However, the impact of this decision was significant indeed, especially in light of the fact that many upscale working women taped their soaps. If such upscale women could be persuaded to master VCR technology in order to tape serial melodramas, perhaps they could be attracted to programs that incorporated elements of the soaps into the slicker, more expensive programs that filled primetime. Here we find another impetus to hybridize prime-time programs.

The road to women's cable television, then, was paved by social, economic, technological, and industrial changes. Upscale women gained the opportunity for economic independence through the feminist movement of the 1970s, only to find that long-term recessions required them to remain employed in order to secure their household's class position. Even upscale women who eschewed feminism reaped the benefits of feminism in terms of employment opportunities when the recessions hit. As upscale women left the house for daywork, their VCRs allowed them to record daytime programming and the Nielsen sample duly noted their time shifting. Attracting upscale audiences, and specifically upscale women, became increasingly important as advertisers reacted to the recessions' narrowing of the consumerist caste, as cable fees guaranteed that their subscribers were bona fide consumers, and as the Nielsen ratings increasingly reported cable subscribers as *the* television audience. Networks identified "female" programming as the key to securing gender integration of upscale audiences through the hybridization of male-identified genres ranging from buddy cop shows to news. Taken together, these events not only raised the industrial status of women's television but also made possible the creation of a cable channel targeted to women.

From Women's Television to Women's Cable Television

Changing conditions, then, opened a market niche into which Lifetime firmly settled in 1984. The result of a merger between Viacom's Cable Health Channel and Hearst/ABC's Daytime, Lifetime's original schedule combined exercise programs, cooking shows, talk shows based on Hearst's magazines for women, and medical in-service programming. This thematically confused line-up still managed to attract an upscale, female audience that Lifetime set about cultivating as it developed a more coherent mix of programming.[23]

Like Daytime, Lifetime consistently identified itself to affiliates and to advertisers as a channel that especially targeted women, but Lifetime did not "come out" to its viewers as "Television for Women" until February of 1995.[24] Lifetime had announced its audience orientation in the trades via campaigns in 1986 and 1988; in 1988, its print ads in the trades described the channel as a "unique environment designed to attract an elusive audience" comprised by "high spending women" who were "highly selective about the programming they watch and the ads they buy,"[25] thereby reiterating a consistent metaphor in capitalist cultures where ideas as well as products are bought. In fact, women's role as domestic purchasing agent matched with cable's ability to assemble an audience of bona fide consumers gave Lifetime tremendous commercial potential.

How, then, to attract those upscale, female homemakers? Lifetime's daytime programming drew from the programming models used by the networks and independent stations, mixing talk shows, game shows, old movies, and melodramatic series. Early morning series such as *Everyday Workout, Old MacDonald's Sing-Along Farm,* and *Your Baby & Child* addressed homemakers and their young children. Midday has variously been programmed with game shows (*Supermarket Sweep, Shop Til You Drop*), talk shows (*Barbara Walters Interviews of a Lifetime, Live from Queens*), syndicated "reality" shows (*Unsolved Mysteries*), programs on domestic arts (*Our Home, The Frugal Gourmet*), movies, or syndicated series (*Sisters, thirtysomething*). Late afternoon has also featured movies, syndicated shows, and game shows. This programming mix has been focused on concerns traditionally identified as feminine: exercise, food, decorating, children, family, celebrities, and melodrama.

But if daytime was women's time, primetime was for upscale men and women. Lifetime may conceptualize its working women as economically independent, but not as emotionally independent from men. The channel thus programmed its prime-time hours for upscale women *and* men who would spend their evening "cocooning" in front of the television set—hence the stress on Lifetime as feminine but never feminist. Such a practice has positioned the channel as a consistent buyer of hybrid programs after their network runs, including the series *Cagney and Lacey, Spenser for Hire, The Days and Nights of Molly Dodd, thirtysomething, China Beach,* and *L.A. Law.* Similarly, Lifetime acquired series that often placed strong female characters in traditionally male roles, including private detectives (*Partners in Crime*), physicians (*Kay O'Brien*), and police officers (*Lady Blue*). The channel continued this practice in its original series (*Confessions of Crime, The Hidden Room, Veronica Clare*) as well as in the movies that it purchased (*The Burning Bed, Runaway Father, Deadly Deception*), made (*Stop at Nothing, Stolen Babies, Shame*), or remade (*Notorious*). This move into originating series and movies allowed Lifetime to exercise considerable control over content, topics, and casting, and thereby to enact its own vision of women's television.

Made for Lifetime: Male-Friendly Women's Television

Lifetime's basic formula for its World Premiere Movies (made specifically for Lifetime) revolves around a strong, competent woman who overcomes adversity. Generally, the films involve a social issue believed to be of particular concern to women: domestic violence, sexual harassment, adoption, AIDS, or rape. Female protagonists generally work within the system to correct some injury, often in a professional capacity. Most of the actresses cast in these original movies are white and middle-aged. Actresses like Blair Brown, Stephanie Zimbalist, Christine Lahti, and Cathy Lee Crosby typify Lifetime's vision of female protagonists as fully adult women with weaknesses, soft edges, and strong emotions. This emphasis on emotions inflects Lifetime's productions with a distinctly melodramatic edge, regardless of genre. Lifetime consistently focuses on the personal and the familial, even when the setting is institutional. Systemic challenge is rare; solutions are generally personal, as the following sketch of some typical movies indicates.

In *Stolen Babies* (1992), Lea Thompson's social worker exposes Mary Tyler Moore's misuse of the courts to take babies from poor families and sell the infants to wealthy, childless couples.[26] In *The Good Fight* (1992), a lawyer (Christine Lahti) sues a giant tobacco company after one of her children's friends dies from cancer. The case reunites her with her estranged husband. In *Shame* (1992), another lawyer (Amanda Donohoe) obtains justice for a young girl raped in a small town. In *Wildflower* (1992), a girl with epilepsy (Patricia Arquette) is imprisoned in a shed by her brutish father. She is saved by a young girl who, with the aid of her brother, helps the girl with epilepsy find a better life. In *And Then There Was One* (1994), a comedy-writing couple discover, after the birth of a daughter, that the entire family is HIV positive. In *Other Women's Children* (1993), a pediatrician (Melanie Mayron) struggles to balance work and family. The pattern throughout emphasizes the personal as individuals right individual wrongs through individual actions. Even in one of the few Lifetime movies that suggests that a major institution can be flawed, *Stop at Nothing* (1991), solutions are ultimately personal: Veronica Hamel solves the problem of abusive ex-husbands having visitation rights or custody by helping their ex-wives hide their children.

Of course, not all Lifetime movies directly address social issues. But, given the channel's commitment to a strong female protagonist as an essential part of its formula, even the "pure entertainment" movies indirectly raise social concerns. For example, in the gothic thriller *Night Owl* (1993), a woman (Jennifer Beals) defeats the ghost that has endangered her husband. In the costume drama *Guinevere* (1994), Camelot's queen (Sheryl Lee) gives up Lancelot as well as her goddess to steer Arthur and England toward a glorious future under his masculine and male-dominated Christian religion. By transforming such male-identified characters as crusading lawyers, overworked physicians, and ghost chasers into women, Lifetime ruptures gender stereotypes. By emphasizing the emotional, personal, and domestic concerns of such characters, Lifetime sutures that rupture. The result is "male friendly" but feminine movies—movies that attract upscale working women without alienating either upscale homemakers or upscale men.

Remaking a Male-Oriented Film in Lifetime's Mold

Lifetime relied on this strategy when it decided to remake the suspense thriller *Notorious,* originally scripted by Ben Hecht and directed by Alfred Hitchcock (1946). Lifetime's former director of original movies, Bari Carrelli, felt bound to follow the original fairly closely, although it deviates from Lifetime's general formula. However, she found sufficient latitude within the original to inject enough of Lifetime's formula for the 1992 remake to be doable. Comparing the remake to the original, then, illustrates the impact of Lifetime's basic philosophy on program content, especially since the original version was based on a script written for a market in which male tastes were predominant and was directed by a man often described as misogynist.[27]

In adapting *Notorious,* executive producer Ilene Berg moved the setting from the end of World War II to the current day. The female protagonist, Alicia, was changed from the daughter of a convicted Nazi spy (Ingrid Bergman) to the daughter of a convicted Soviet spy (Jenny Robertson). In both films, Alicia reacted to her father's conviction by developing a reputation for notorious behavior through her wild parties, moonlight drives, and alcohol abuse. In both films, Alicia became involved with a US spy named

Devlin (Cary Grant; John Shea), was persuaded by him to spy on her father's associates, was betrayed by Devlin, married a man named Alex who was connected to enemies of the US, was almost poisoned by Alex's female relative, and was rescued by Devlin. The script's victimization of Alicia and its reliance on a "white knight" to save her presented serious departures from Lifetime's formula. However, within the constraints of the story, Lifetime's remake constructed Alicia as a more capable, more active, less victimized character. Dialogue identified Lifetime's Alicia as a Phi Beta Kappa who spoke numerous languages and the action was significantly—if subtly—altered.[28]

The first significant alteration occurred fairly early in the film. Both versions began with the courtroom sentencing of the father, followed by Alicia's exit from the courthouse.[29] Barraged by reporters, the Lifetime Alicia more aggressively repelled them. In both versions, one policeman ordered another to follow her. In both versions, the film then cut to a party at Alicia's house, where an attractive and uninvited stranger named Devlin flirted with Alicia. In the Lifetime version, she was more overtly sexually aggressive (not surprising, given the changes in what is permissible and acceptable across a nearly 50-year time span). In both versions, Alicia drank heavily and the stranger matched her drink for drink. While he remained perfectly sober, Alicia became drunk. After all the other guests had left or passed out, Alicia proposed a drive and Devlin accompanied her. Alicia drove her convertible sportscar erratically and fast. She was stopped by a police officer who left without giving her a ticket—after inspecting the identification Devlin passed over to him. Alicia realized that Devlin was a federal-level law enforcement officer. Devlin then insisted on driving, and Alicia refused. At this point, the two films diverged significantly.

In the Hitchcock version, Alicia ineffectively pummeled Devlin's chest and Devlin stopped her by grabbing her wrists. When he released her hands, she again tried to push him away. Devlin responded by firmly and forcefully punching Alicia in the face, rendering her unconscious. In contrast, the Lifetime version replaced violence against women with non-violence and humor. Although the drunken Alicia again struck Devlin and Devlin again grasped her wrists, Lifetime's Alicia exited the car and immediately dropped from sight, having passed out. Devlin's reaction—a sigh—was presented via a low angle shot from (had she been conscious) Alicia's point of view, indicating the significance of the female protagonist's perspective. The scene ended, having transformed an uncritical representation of violence against women into a humorous depiction of the alcohol's effects.[30]

The next few scenes revealed more depth to Alicia's character. In both versions, Devlin manipulated her by playing a recording of a supposedly private conversation between Alicia and her father in which she refused to be his accomplice and defended the US. Although secretly a patriot with a strong sense of honor, Alicia loved her father and resisted hurting him. But Devlin persuaded her to help the US government pursue her father's evil friends. They flew off to an exotic spot (Rio de Janeiro in the Hitchcock version, Paris in Lifetime's remake). On the plane, Devlin learned and then told Alicia that her father had committed suicide. In the Hitchcock version, Alicia's response suggested dependency and self-loathing:

> I don't know why I should feel so bad. When he told me, a few years ago, what he was, everything went to pot. I didn't care what happened to me. Now, I remember how nice he was, how nice we both were. Very nice. And it's a very curious feeling—as if something had happened to me and not to him. You see, I don't have to hate him anymore—or myself.

Not only had her father betrayed his country, but also his daughter, who was his most significant victim. In the Lifetime version, Alicia's response indicated a more active, more independent character with a healthier emotional life: "Well, at least I don't have to hate him anymore." Alicia then wept and Devlin comforted her. Where Hitchcock's Alicia was emotionally crippled by her father's life and released by his death, Lifetime's Alicia hated the spy who sold out his country, but loved her father all the same and mourned his death. This degree of emotional sophistication diminished Alicia's victimization, reformulating the character in Lifetime's terms as a survivor whose self-esteem was shaken, but not destroyed, by her father's betrayal.

In both versions, the scene shifted to the foreign city (Hitchcock, Rio; Lifetime, Paris) in which Alicia and Devlin began their mission. Lifetime's adaptation developed Alicia as an independent but domestic woman enrapt with her now-beloved Devlin. The couple spent a week making love and visiting the sights in romantic Paris. In contrast, Hitchcock's Alicia and Devlin had only a day together at an apartment in Rio where she cooked dinner for him. The older version implied a sexual relationship but without the standard visual references to romance. The degree of emotion attached to Devlin and Alicia's sexual encounter became important as, in both versions, Devlin's superior (Agent Prescott) intended to use Alicia to seduce the enemy. In the Hitchcock version, when this was made clear to Devlin, he visibly hardened but did not object. Lifetime's Devlin did object, asserting "I'm not sure she's that kind of woman." This objection, paired with the firmly established week-long romance, made Lifetime's Devlin more sympathetic than Hitchcock's. It also clarified Devlin's conflict: would he sacrifice his love for his country? Where the remake made this conflict explicit in Devlin's protest to Agent Prescott, the original depended on the subtlety of his body language. Hitchcock's Devlin may have been unhappy about Alicia's assignment, but he remained silent before his superiors. In both versions, Devlin communicated the sexual nature of Alicia's assignment to her, but he was unable to tell her directly and explicitly. While production codes did constrain Hitchcock's treatment of sexuality, no such codes precluded Lifetime from scripting an open discussion of sex and espionage. Such a discussion, however, would raise questions regarding larger issues ranging from the need for espionage to the morality of nationalism. As with other Lifetime movies, this film referenced social issues but was really about personal change. Espionage and the Cold War were merely backdrops; the real story in Lifetime's *Notorious* was how Alicia and Devlin met, fell in love, were separated, and were finally reunited.

As a spy, Alicia succeeded quite remarkably: she met and seduced Alexander Sebastian, a friend of her father's who had been fond of her in the past. In the Hitchcock version, Alex was an expatriate German Nazi determined to keep Nazism alive. Lifetime's remake presented him as a rogue Russian arms dealer, operating after the breakup of the Soviet Union, whose customers included Arabs. Devlin facilitated their meeting in an encounter that led Alex to suspect that Devlin and Alicia were romantically involved. Alicia denied the connection, and Alex invited her to a dinner at his home. During the dinner, Alicia picked up information that she subsequently reported to her superiors. The information proved useful and Alicia earned a commendation. Alex subsequently proposed marriage, triggering Agent Prescott's belief that Alicia would be a productive plant in her prospective husband's household. Although not keen on the prospect, Alicia still agreed to marry Alex, hoping all the while that Devlin would intervene. In the Hitchcock version, it was clear that Devlin had not only disappointed her but actually betrayed her for a political cause. Devlin simply compounded her victimization. In the Lifetime version, however, where Alicia was less a victim, Devlin's silence carried a sense of tragedy: their romance had been explicit and they were asked to sacrifice that love for the greater good. In this way, Lifetime had redeemed Devlin's silence and Alicia's sex-for-secrets marriage. Acceptably romantic *and* patriotic, Alicia and Devlin presumably raised no difficult issues for the upscale, heterosexual couples that Lifetime targeted.

Alicia was not the only person with doubts about the marriage. In both films, Alex had a female relative who was even more ruthless than he. Where Hitchcock assigned that role to Alex's mother, Madame Sebastian, Lifetime gave him an evil sister, Katerina. She objected to the marriage and suspected Alicia even before meeting her. Sebastian dismissed these suspicions as jealousy. The marriage occurred quickly—during a cut—and Alicia moved into Alex's luxurious home. She soon made an important discovery: only one person had a key to the wine cellar. When she reported this to Devlin, he plotted to search the cellar and proposed that she persuade Alex to host a party to which Devlin would be invited, ostensibly to prove to her husband that she was not in love with Devlin.

In both versions, Alicia was moderately resourceful. Before the party, she removed the crucial key from Alex's key ring. During the party, she and Devlin visited the wine cellar, accidentally discovering that a strange substance had replaced the wine in some bottles. The Hitchcock version showed Alicia drinking champagne and only refusing more to keep Alex out of the wine cellar. In the Lifetime version, Alicia drank mineral water, maintaining sobriety (and, thus, respectability) and a clear head. In both versions, Alex discovered that his key was missing and, when it reappeared on his key ring the next morning, he realized who had taken it. Panicking, he awakened his ruthless female relative and told her that he had married an American spy. She gloated, reminding him of her suspicions. In the Hitchcock version, Madame Sebastian lit a cigarette and assured her son that all was not lost; the enormity of his stupidity would help them keep this a secret from his associates. In the Lifetime version, Katerina smoked and paced, proposing that Alicia become ill.

In both versions, the duo began poisoning Alicia, resulting in the heroine's headaches and blurred vision. When she went to a scheduled meeting with Devlin, Agent Prescott showed up instead. He informed her that the substance discovered in the wine bottles was used in the production of weaponry and that Devlin had requested reassignment. Returning home, Alicia slowly became groggier and groggier, a condition Devlin mistook for a hangover when they next met. At that meeting, she gave Devlin the opportunity to tell her that he was leaving, but he did not. She again returned home, where she finally realized that she was being served poison in her coffee. Close-ups on the coffee cup, followed by unsteady and blurred subjective camerawork from Alicia's optical point of view made this clear. In the Hitchcock version, she stumbled from the room and tried to go upstairs to bed, but collapsed. In the Lifetime version, she headed for the outside door but collapsed before she could get there. This difference is particularly significant: Lifetime's Alicia tried to escape where Hitchcock's tried to hide in her bed. In both versions, however, Alicia was taken to her bedroom, and the telephone—her only means of communication—was removed.

When Alicia failed to appear at a prearranged meeting, Devlin went to Prescott. In the final scenes of both versions, Devlin redeemed himself. In the Hitchcock version, he convinced Prescott that Alicia was not on a binge but was ill, and Prescott agreed that Devlin should go to Alex's house. In the Lifetime version, Prescott dismissed Devlin's suggestion, insisting that Alicia would contact them if she needed help. This time Devlin did not stop at objections; he returned to his hotel, pulled a gun from under his mattress, and stuffed it in the waistband of his trousers, saying, "Sorry, Norman [Prescott], this one's for me." When contrasted, the two versions' treatment of this scene generated two very different readings of Devlin. In Hitchcock's movie, the hero won his case and his superior's approval through cold reason. In Lifetime's remake, Devlin defied his superior but only to the degree that Alicia's plight was a personal—not a professional—matter.

In both versions, Devlin went to the Sebastians' house, where he was told that Alex was unavailable (in a meeting with his evil associates) and that Alicia was ill. While supposedly waiting to see Alex, Devlin went upstairs to rescue Alicia and, finally, he declared his love. As Devlin helped Alicia down the stairs, they were discovered first by Alex and then by his evil female relative. They all understood that Alicia posed a threat to Alex if it were revealed to his associates that he was married to an American spy. Devlin coerced Alex into helping him move Alicia. As they carried her down the stairs, Alex's associates found them and began to inquire as to what was going on. Alex made excuses sufficient to get the trio out of the house. As they approached the car, Alex begged to go with them. At this crucial point, the Hitchcock and Lifetime versions again diverged. Hitchcock's Alicia remained weak and passive: Devlin put her in the car, reached across her to lock the door (to keep Alex out), and drove away. Alex was summoned back to the house and, presumably, to his death, the film ending as the doors shut behind him. In contrast, Lifetime's Alicia locked her own door, saying, "Sorry, Alex," as she left her husband to be killed by his associates. While she and Devlin drove away, Alex was summoned back into the house and the doors again closed behind him. But Lifetime's remake did not end on this somber note. Two brief scenes were added that produced a much happier ending. Devlin's car was shown driving through the Parisian night under a lighted Eiffel Tower, proving that the pair had made its escape. Then, in daylight and from a different angle, a shot of the Eiffel Tower pulled back to show Devlin looking towards it, with Alicia standing behind him, her arms holding him. The film ended with romance, not impending death, and it ended with Alicia in a position of relative power.

With these changes, Lifetime created an entirely different Alicia. The new heroine had it all: a notorious youth, an exciting career as a spy, and true romance. Presumably, this Alicia was more palatable to Lifetime's upscale working women, upscale homemakers, and their men than the victimized, passive, and weak Alicia of Hitchcock's *Notorious*. Similarly, the updated *Notorious* remained a story about personal concerns and the transition from Alicia's status as a wild youth to a woman in love and, by implication, to a married woman. Following the Lifetime formula, the remake ignores institutional questions such as the effects of the Cold War, the ethics of patriotism, or the exploitation of women as sex objects. Taken together, the restructuring of Alicia and the stress on romance transformed *Notorious* into an appropriate product for Lifetime—a cable channel committed to a unique mixture of innovation and convention in its portrayal of women.

The Lifetime Woman and Feminine Television

Our analyses of *Notorious,* Lifetime, narrowcasting, broadcasting, new technology, and their larger social, economic, and legal contexts lead us to pose some answers to our opening questions. Promoted as the feminine side of television, Lifetime shares some basic assumptions with network broadcasting about women as cultural consumers and about their preferred genres. Whether upscale or downscale, wage earners or homemakers, women have been assumed to prefer melodrama. This has been confirmed by the Nielsen ratings that report that homemakers have been joined by VCR-using working women to comprise large and loyal audiences for the soap operas and melodramatic talk shows aired on daytime television. Further, the more confrontational and uncontrolled of those melodramatic talk shows (*Ricki Lake, Jenny Jones*) not only attract large female audiences, they also attract that segment of the female audience most wanted by advertisers: younger, upscale working women who control their disposable income and who are committed to a consumerist lifestyle. Apparently a taste for melodrama spans differences of age, employment, race, and class among women.

Catering to this taste, then, meant building a female audience. From the 1920s to the 1960s, the broadcasting industry had cultivated that audience mainly in its daytime programming. This altered as advertisers responded to the social and economic changes wrought by second wave feminism in the 1970s. The women's movement repealed legal protections for gender discrimination in the workplace; opened white collar, professional jobs to women; and promulgated ideologies of independence and self-worth. The result was not only a deluge of upscale women into the workplace, but also an "empowerment" of women as "high quality" consumers. Responding to advertisers' demands for measures of this new audience, the A.C. Nielsen Company began reporting on working women, both upscale and downscale, in 1976.

The significance of that class differentiation became immediately clear in light of the recessionary waves that started in 1975. Corporate and governmental responses to these periodic setbacks supported falling incomes and rising unemployment among blue collar and pink collar workers, making downscale working men and women increasingly unattractive to advertisers. The general impact of the recessions meant that middle-class incomes also declined, sending many upscale home-makers into the work force in order to maintain their households' standard of living. This fueled advertisers' demand for bona fide consumers that sent networks scurrying to find or attract such viewers to their programs and sent Nielsen scurrying to include cable channels in its reports of viewing by men and women, both upscale and downscale. Cable's subscription fees acted as a "natural" obstacle, sorting bona fide consumers from mere viewers, and advertisers' demands for such upscale audiences placed cable channels in direct competition with broadcast networks.

While networks continued to command the masses of viewers, cable channels marketed themselves as narrowcasting that attracted upscale consumers according to their demographic characteristics. Most channels occupied marketing niches that presumed a male audience, but none promoted themselves as the men's channel or masculine television. As implied in our discussion of broadcast television, primetime television addressed, first, the entire family and, then, as the evening progressed, an increasingly adult audience. When middle-class women were employed principally in the home and therefore accessible through daytime television, advertisers had strong interests in using prime time to gain access to males who had presumably spent the day working at sites that lacked television sets. This encouraged networks to emphasize male genres in prime time. With the recessions of the 1970s, advertisers modified their targets during prime time, narrowing their focus on upscale, employed women and men as the most prized audiences. To attract that audience, networks experimented with "hybrid programs," mixing continuing melodrama with episodic action-adventure.

Similarly, advertisers had narrowed their definition of the most prized audience for daytime television from housewives to women under 50 years of age who controlled some disposable income, served as the household purchasing agent, and were committed to a consumerist lifestyle. Emphasizing serial melodramas and melodramatic talk shows, the networks' daytime schedule remained women's "special time" with television, and advertisers continued using daytime television to target women. Interestingly, the first cable service to target women was even called Daytime and was a joint operation of Hearst, a publisher with an extensive line of women's magazines, and ABC, which had innovated the "new" soaps. By merging Daytime with Viacom's Cable Health Channel, Hearst and ABC guaranteed that their joint venture would have extensive distribution, given Viacom's status as a major operator of cable systems. The new channel, Lifetime, took as its niche that audience that had already watched Daytime and Cable Health: upscale female audiences. The problem then became twofold: how to acquire and produce programming for that audience and how to expand that audience—specifically, how to include these women and their men in a prime-time audience.

Lifetime responded to those challenges by first applying industry wisdom: women watch genres that are specifically gendered as female. Lifetime's daytime schedule approximates network programming with its line-up of talk shows, game shows, and domestic arts programs. As a substitute for soap operas, Lifetime runs syndicated series and movies. The films are generally melodramatic examinations of personal lives. By stripping the series, that is, by running the shows every weekday in the same time slot, Lifetime heightens their similarity to the daily unfolding of the soap opera. This similarity is strengthened by the use of hybrid series that incorporate continuing plots that are explicitly melodramatic. In these practices, Lifetime agrees with the major networks that women prefer melodramas and hybrid shows heavily inflected with melodrama.

However, for Lifetime, there is more to feminine television than melodrama. In the major networks' hybrid series, the male genre generally dominates; melodrama is typically subordinated and functions as a way to develop the main characters by giving them lives beyond what is strictly necessary in terms of the dominant genre. The assumption seems to be that women presumably filter out any story elements that are supposed to appeal to men but not women. The three most obvious "masculine" story elements are the absence of strong, female protagonists; fairly explicit violence, often against women; and the objectification of women. At this writing, Lifetime has been reluctant to acquire rights to syndicated series and movies that simply overlay such story elements with a bit of domesticity. As its World Premier Movies suggest, Lifetime is committed to the notion that upscale audiences of working women, homemakers, and men will watch melodramas in which strong women overcome adversity, particularly if that triumphant struggle involves the love of a good man. In its remake of *Notorious,* Lifetime applied its formula to the Hitchcock film to produce a remake that was more sympathetic to both Alicia and Devlin. In the remake, Alicia was less victimized, less passive, and less dependent. She exerted her agency in an active struggle to make her life meaningful regardless of her father, Agent Prescott, or Alex. For Alicia, the center of that meaningful life was Devlin—a spy who was vulnerable, loving, and romantic. Thus *Notorious* was remolded in Lifetime's image and industrial practices, becoming an emotional tale of love found, briefly suspended for patriotism's sake, and then reconfirmed.

In Lifetime's enactment, feminine television offers viewers a complex, contradictory vision: women act in the public domain, work in the "real" world, and earn their independence—but ultimately rely on heterosexual relationships to round out their lives. For advertisers, this replicated their commercials' vision of the new woman who could (as a character in one commercial put it) "bring home the bacon/fry it up in a pan/and never let you forget you're a man/'cause I'm a *woman*."[31] For upscale working women, Lifetime's vision would seem to reiterate the emerging ideology of "having it all"—working outside the home as a professional, marrying and having children, and shouldering responsibility for domestic labor in the household. In this way, Lifetime's formula addresses lived experience in its frustrations and rewards, but only in terms of the personal, the emotional, the domestic. By not challenging the assumptions about labor, sexuality, and power that underlie the model of "having it all," Lifetime remains commercially viable, presenting television that provides role models for a way of life made possible by second wave feminism, but which Lifetime defines as feminine, never feminist.

Notes

1. Quoted in Michael Burgi, "If at First You Don't Succeed . . . " *Channels* September 1989: 66. Research for the project from which this article comes has been funded by the Office of the Vice President for Research and Sponsored Projects and the Graduate School and from the Humanities Center at Wayne State University and from the Office of the Vice President for Research and the Office of the Dean of Fine Arts at the University of Arizona.

2. On the gendering of genres, see Jackie Byars, *All That Hollywood Allows: Rereading Gender in 1950s Melodrama* (Chapel Hill and London: U of North Carolina P, 1991) and Christine Gledhill, ed. *Home Is Where the Heart Is: Studies in Melodrama and the Woman's Film* (London: British Film Institute, 1987). On the gendering of narrative forms, see Byars (above) and Rachel Blau DuPlessis, *Writing Beyond the Ending: Narrative Strategies of Twentieth-Century Women* (Bloomington: Indiana UP, 1985). On the gendering of technology, see Laura Mulvey's classic essay arguing that "the gaze" is male (or at least masculine), "Visual Pleasure and Narrative Cinema," *Screen* 16.3 (Autumn 1975); Mulvey's "Afterthoughts on 'Visual Pleasure and Narrative Cinema' Inspired by *Duel in the Sun* (King Vidor, 1946)," *Framework* 15-16-17 (Summer 1981); E. Ann Kaplan's introduction ("Is the Gaze Male?") to *Women and Film* (New York: Methuen, 1983); Byars's response in *All That Hollywood Allows;* Teresa de Lauretis, *Technologies of Gender* (Bloomington: Indiana UP, 1987). There are, of course, numerous other equally wonderful sources too numerous to list in a note.

3. Historically, the ratings industry has been controlled by a single entity, ranging from the initial monopolist, the Cooperative Analysis of Broadcasting (founded by the Association of National Advertisers in 1930), which was replaced by the C.E. Hooper company in the early 1930s, to the current monopolist, the A.C. Nielsen Company, which achieved an effective monopoly over television and radio ratings in the 1950s. In 1963, political pressure was brought to bear on the Nielsen monopoly, and the firm relinquished control over radio ratings while tolerating the appearance of competition in television ratings. For details, see E.R. Meehan, "Why We Don't Count," in Patricia Mellencamp, ed. *Logics of Television* (Bloomington: Indiana UP and London: British Film Institute, 1990) 117–137.

4. E.R. Meehan, "Heads of Households and Ladies of the House: Gender, Genre, and Broadcast Ratings, 1929–1990," in William S. Solomon and Robert W. McChesney, eds. *Ruthless Criticism: New Perspectives in US Communication History* (Minneapolis: U of Minnesota P, 1993) 204–221; Karen S. Buzzard, *Chains of Gold: Marketing the Ratings and Rating the Markets* (Metuchen, NJ: Scarecrow Press, 1990). Also see Erik Barnouw, *Tube of Plenty: The Evolution of American Television,* 2nd rev. ed. (New York and Oxford: Oxford UP, 1990) 471, for a CBS brochure entitled "Where the Girls Are" that was designed to assist advertisers in matching the demographics of product purchasers. The use of demographics is discussed from pp. 469–474. While the title of the brochure may strike one as indicative of "the bad old days," the brochure was issued in the early 1970s.

5. Standard histories include Erik Barnouw, *Tube of Plenty,* 1970, and the second revised edition, 1990; the three volume set includes *A Tower of Babel: A History of Broadcasting in the United States to 1933; The Golden Web: A History of Broadcasting in the United States, 1933–1953;* and *The Image Makers: A History of Broadcasting in the United States from 1953* (all New York and Oxford: Oxford UP). See also Muriel Cantor, *Prime-Time Television: Content and Control* (Beverly Hills, CA: Sage, 1980) and J. Fred MacDonald, *Don't Touch That Dial: Radio Programming in American Life From 1920 to 1960* (Chicago: Nelson-Hall, 1979). For book-length analyses of soap operas, see Muriel Cantor and Suzanne Pingree, *The Soap Opera* (Beverly Hills, CA: Sage, 1983); R. W. Steadman, *The Serials: Suspense and Drama in Installments* (Norman: U of Oklahoma P, 1977); R. W. Steadman "A History of the Broadcasting of Daytime Serial Drama in the United States," University of Southern California diss., 1959; and Robert C. Allen, *Speaking of Soap Operas* (Chapel Hill: U of North Carolina P, 1985).

6. Tania Modleski has illustrated how this rhythmic pattern translates into daytime television programming on the major networks and their affiliates, which concentrates on game shows and soap operas, program types characterized by segmentation and repetition; see her "Rhythms of Reception: Daytime Television and Women's Work," in E. Ann Kaplan, ed. *Regarding Television* (American Film Institute/University Publications of America, 1983) 67–75.

7. Herta Hertzog, "What Do We Really Know About Daytime Serial Listeners?," in Paul F. Lazarsfeld and Frank Stanton, eds. *Radio Research 1942–1943* (New York: Duell, Sloan, and Pearce, 1944) and "Motivations and Gratifications of Daily Serial Listeners," in Wilber Schramm, ed. *The Process and Effects of Mass Communication* (Urbana: U of Illinois P, 1961).

8. Michelle Hilmes, "Making Myths, Creating Monsters: Mary Margaret McBride and Daytime Broadcasting," paper presented at Console-ing Passions, 9 April 1995, Seattle, WA.

9. For accounts of the evolution of the flow of evening programming see Erik Barnouw, *Tube of Plenty;* Laurence Bergreen, *Look Now, Pay Later: The Rise of Network Broadcasting* (Garden City: Doubleday, 1980); and E.R. Meehan, "Heads of the Household and Ladies of the House."

10. Ruth Goldsen, *The Show and Tell Machine: How Television Works and Works You Over* (New York: Dial Press, 1977); Ruth Goldsen, "Throwaway Husbands, Wives, and Lovers," *Human Behavior* 35 (December 1976): 64–69; Bradley Greenberg, Robert Abelman, K. Neuendorf, "Sex on the Soap Opera: Afternoon Delight," *Journal of Communication* 31 (1981): 83–89; Bradley Greenberg, K. Neuendorf, N. Buerkel-Rothfuss, and L. Henderson, "What's on the Soaps and Who Cares?," *Journal of Broadcasting* (1982): 519–536; D.T. Lowry, G. Love, M. Kirby, "Sex on the Soap Opera: Patterns of Intimacy," *Journal of Communication* 31 (1981): 90–96; Muriel Cantor and Suzanne Pingree, *The Soap Opera.*

11. Although the primary target for soap operas continues to be women, the producers of soaps are quite aware that the number of faithful male viewers has increased significantly, particularly among college-aged males, and characters and plot lines reflect this awareness.

12. By "the networks" we are referring to the three still barely dominant broadcast networks—ABC (American Broadcasting Corp.), CBS (Columbia Broadcasting System), and NBC (National Broadcasting Co.). FOX, the up-and-coming broadcast network, still competes primarily in primetime. CBS and NBC soap operas are still owned by their sponsors.

13. For a full-blown analysis of the talk show phenomenon, see Jane Shattuc, *The Talking Cure: Women and TV Talk Shows* (Routledge, 1996).

14. *The Jenny Jones Show* frequently used a "secret admirer" format in which one person confessed an infatuation to the unwitting object of that affection on the air. The admired's sexual orientation and gender did not limit the program's creation of such ambushes. *Jones* recruited Jonathan Schmitz, a 24-year-old waiter from Orion Township, Michigan, as an admired guest for a show taped on 6 March 1995. *Jones* has stated that Schmitz was warned that the admirer could be either gender; Schmitz's family has stated that he told them that the show had identified his admirer as female. When called on stage, Schmitz found two acquaintances waiting for him—Donna Riley and Scott Amedure. Schmitz took Riley for the admirer until Amedure confessed his infatuation with Schmitz. Stating that he was heterosexual and not interested, Schmitz seemed to play the role of "good sport." On 9 March, Schmitz turned himself in to police, stating that he had shot and killed Scott Amedure. *Jones* disavowed all responsibility. While criminal charges have been filed against Schmitz and the Amedure family has filed a civil case against him, no suit has been brought against *Jones* despite the news media's coverage that suggests that *Jones* acted unwisely at best.

15. Barry Bluestone and Bennett Harrison, *The Deindustrialization of America* (New York: Basic Books, 1992).

16. Throughout the advertising, broadcasting, and cable industries, the terms "upscale" and "downscale" have been adopted as designations of consumers' economic status. This rhetoric of scales avoids issues of class structure, class differentiation, and economic exploitation. The terminology also manages to disparage those who are "downscale"—that is, people in the working class—and to subtly reinforce class-based prejudices. Although important in terms of capitalist ideology, such prejudices are irrational in economic terms when advertising products that are inexpensive, ubiquitous, and socially necessary (e.g., hand soap, tampons, toothpaste).

17. Julie D'Acci, *Defining Women: Television and the Case of "Cagney & Lacey"* (Chapel Hill and London: U of North Carolina P, 1994).

18. Barnouw 558.

19. The pattern of developing channels based on programming strategies used in network television and by local stations in programming off-network times has been noted by E.R. Meehan in "Technical Capability vs. Corporate Imperatives: Toward a Political Economy of Cable Television," in Janet Wasko and Vincent Mosco, eds. *The Political Economy of Information* (Madison: U of Wisconsin P, 1988): 167–187. Where Meehan argues that cable television means "more of the same for slightly fewer," Oscar H. Gandy argues in *Beyond Agenda Setting: Targeting Information Subsidies and Public Policy* (Norwood, NJ: Ablex, 1983) that media corporations will use "new" technologies like cable television to target narrower audiences with carefully drawn messages that have been crafted for highly specified demographics and psychographics. Suffice to say, that debate continues as such cable channels as Nickelodeon target children in a manner similar to the networks' Saturday "kid video" or stations' after-school mix of reruns and cartoon shows; or as religious channels like the old Christian Broadcasting Network (now the Family Channel) or Eternal Word Network or the Inspiration Channel target Christians a la the Sunday morning religious ghetto on networks and independent television stations. Similarly, networked or syndicated "teen shows" like *American Bandstand, Dance Party,* or *Lloyd Thaxton* are spun into entire channels that are differentiated in the same manner as radio stations: MTV for hard rockers, VH-1 for soft rockers, MTV-Latino for Spanish-language rockers. One finds dozens of examples: ESPN 1 & 2, as well as regional sports channels, for sports fans; the Science Fiction Channel for fans of old SF movies, serials, and series; the Country Music Channel for fans of country music and westernalia; The Learning Channel and Arts & Entertainment for fans of PBS programming.

20. Gandy, *Beyond Agenda Setting.*

21. United States Bureau of the Census, *Statistical Abstract of the United States* (Washington, DC: GPO, 1994): 567.

22. Mark R. Levy, "Home Video Recorders: A User Survey," *Journal of Communication* 30.4 (Autumn 1980): 23–27; Mark R. Levy, "Program Playback Preferences in VCR Households," *Journal of Broadcasting* (1980): 327–336; and Mark R. Levy, "Home Video Recorders and Timeshifting," *Journalism Quarterly* 58 (1981): 401–405. Levy found that people tape programs that they often don't get around to watching, unless there's some compelling reason to watch the tape—like it's a soap.

23. Douglas W. McCormick, Lifetime's President and Chief Executive Officer, personal interview, 3 March 1995.

24. Meredith Wagner, Senior Vice President for Public Affairs for Lifetime, described Lifetime's policy as quite conscious. In about 1992, Lifetime executives began to feel that they could go public as a women's network, and in July of 1994 they began to refer to the network as television for women, but it was not until February of 1995 that the promotional campaign "Lifetime: Television for Women" was launched in women's magazines, in press kits, and finally, in on-air promotions (personal interviews, 14 January 1995 and 24 May 1995).

25. *Ad Age* 11 April 1988: S8–9.

26. Although Lifetime runs many made-for-TV movies originally broadcast on network television, it is rare for a Lifetime movie to be picked up by a network. *Stop*

at Nothing and *Stolen Babies* are notable exceptions, probably because they star extremely well-known actresses who have starred in major network series.

27. While interviewing Bari Carrelli, Lifetime's Director of Original Movies, we revealed that part of our presentation at the second Console-ing Passions conference (USC, Los Angeles) consisted of a comparison of the two versions of *Notorious.* She was quite concerned, because she—and others at Lifetime—considered the film atypical of Lifetime movies (personal interview, 4 April 1993). Carrelli has since left Lifetime to work with NBC's original movie division; her move illustrates not simply that she's good at her job and that there is quite a lot of movement within the industry but also that most made-for-television movies target a female audience.

28. Referring to the earlier (1946) version as "Hitchcock's *Notorious*" and referring to the later (1992) version as the Lifetime version is not an unselfconscious decision; in "classic Hollywood cinema," authorial credit traditionally goes to a film's director, and when Hitchcock was the director, the credit is fully deserved. In the case of the Lifetime version, authorial credit cannot reside fully with the director, as executive producer Ilene Berg, in dialogue with Lifetime's executives, had a very active role in the production process. The 1946 version, as we have noted, was directed by Alfred Hitchcock and written by Ben Hecht. It starred Cary Grant, Ingrid Bergman, Claude Raines, and Madame Konstantin. The 1992 version, directed by Colin Bucksey and produced by Sophie Rivard, starred John Shea, Jenny Robertson, Jean-Pierre Cassel, and Marisa Berenson. The teleplay by Douglas Lloyd McIntosh was based on the story and screenplay by Ben Hecht.

29. Because of this essay's focus, we generally ignore aesthetic elements such as the fact that the Hitchcock version is shot entirely in black and white, while the Lifetime version begins in black and white—in the courtroom—and shifts to color as Alicia Valcones exits the courtroom. It's interesting but not particularly relevant to this discussion, and equally irrelevant are the numerous cost-saving decisions made by a made-for-TV movie director that make the Lifetime film less aesthetically stimulating than the Hitchcock film (though the camerawork is remarkably similar to that of the Hitchcock version in many of the most crucial scenes).

30. Various changes in what is acceptable in entertainment that have occurred over the past forty years become evident in comparing the two versions of *Notorious.* For example, the language in the Lifetime is considerably "rougher"; never, in the Hitchcock version, does Alicia curse. Other differences in the Lifetime version include more sexual explicitness (lots more skin showing) and, thanks to the demise of the Production Code, the ability of married couples to sleep in double beds.

31. In the commercial, for a perfume called Enjoli, a tall, thin woman wearing a body-tight evening gown removes her jacket, swings it over her shoulder and walks toward the camera singing these words, words that naturalize the construction of the working woman who has "everything," who works outside the home in a "job" and inside the home in every room of the house, especially the kitchen and the bedroom.

Television Production
Techniques
as Communication

DAVID BARKER

Some scholars of mass communication have begun to approach the television message as a visual text and interpretation of this text as a process of "decoding" (Fiske and Hartley, 1978; Silverstone, 1981). Perhaps the foremost proponent of this approach is Stuart Hall, who identifies this process of "decoding" as a "determinate moment" in television discourse (1980: 129). Yet, Hall makes it quite clear that the process of "encoding" is equally determinate:

> A "raw" historical event cannot, *in that form*, be transmitted by, say, a television newscast. Events can only be signified within the aural-visual forms of the television discourse. . . . The "message form" is the necessary "form of appearance" of the event in its passage from source to receiver. Thus, the transposition into and out of the "message form" is a determinate moment. (129)

Within the growing body of work based upon the encoding/decoding model, however (e.g., Brunsdon and Morley, 1978; Morley, 1980; Wren-Lewis, 1983), discussion has been restricted almost exclusively to only one of these "determinate moments": decoding. Indeed, the process of encoding, despite its homologous position in the model, has by comparison, been virtually ignored.[1]

From *Critical Studies in Mass Communication*, Barker, David. "Television Production Techniques in Communication." September 1985. Pages 234–246. Copyright by the Speech Communication Association. Reprinted by permission of the publisher.

The purpose of this study is to examine this process of encoding or, more specifically, the relationship between narrative structure and production techniques, as it is manifested in entertainment television. It is the thesis of this essay that the communicative ability of any television narrative is, in large part, a function of the production techniques utilized in its creation.[2]

The two programs chosen for this study were *All in the Family (AITF)* and *M*A*S*H*. The decision to examine these particular programs was based on two factors. First, both programs were pivotal to their own specific narrative traditions. *AITF* represents the tradition of domestic situation comedies that revolved around a single axial character—in this case Archie Bunker. Archie was axial inasmuch as plot lines were usually built directly upon his character, and most other characters in the program were usually defined not so much by their own idiosyncrasies as by their relationship with him. We can find many of the seeds of *AITF* in *The Life of Riley, Make Room for Daddy, The Honeymooners,* and *Father Knows Best.*

M*A*S*H, on the other hand, was pivotal to a tradition of what might be termed ensemble comedies in which each character had a persona of his or her own, distinct from the rest of the ensemble. Yet the interplay and conflict among such characters worked to strengthen the personalities of all concerned, making the ensemble comedy very much more than the sum of its parts. Foreshadowings of *M*A*S*H* can be found in *Burns and Allen, The Addams Family, Gilligan's Island,* and *Hogan's Heroes.*

Prior to *AITF,* network situation comedy in general had become entrenched in what could be called "1960s telefilm values," which were characterized by a highly utilitarian approach to the communicative abilities of even the most basic production techniques. As exemplified by such programs as *My Three Sons* or *Leave it to Beaver,* this was a production style based on a highly repetitive and predictable shooting pattern: an exterior establishing shot (e.g., the Cleaver home as Ward pulls into the driveway) followed by sequences of alternating medium shots as the narrative progresses (e.g., Ward comes in the front door to be greeted by June who proceeds to inform him of the daily crises; Ward then decides on a course of action and initiates it). This pattern was occasionally punctuated with a tighter shot, such as a medium close-up (bust shot), but close-ups were virtually never used. Similarly, performer movement (blocking) was utilized only as a way to move characters into and out of an environment: Beaver walks into his bedroom and throws himself on the bed or Wally walks into the kitchen and stands by the sink. As Millerson (1979: 287) has pointed out, there is a great deal of meaning in such production variables as shot selection and performer blocking. Programs produced with these 1960s telefilm values suggest that reinforcing the structure of the program narrative (e.g., the ebb and flow of conflicts) with particular production techniques was not a fundamental concern for the producers.

With *AITF* and *M*A*S*H*, however, close analysis of a number of episodes indicated that, for these two series, the relationship between narrative structure and production techniques was quite different. Thus, the second reason for choosing these two programs was that both were also products of conscious decisions by their respective creators, Norman Lear and Larry Gelbart, to utilize specific production techniques in specific ways.

In preparation for this study, twenty episodes selected at random of each series were analyzed for their use of particular production techniques, and it soon became clear that a number of these techniques—among them, control of screen space, lighting and set design, layers of action, and parallel editing—were manipulated significantly for narrative as well as aesthetic reasons. This analysis made it possible to draw some general observations about the role each of these techniques played in the communication of the particular narrative structures of *AITF* and *M*A*S*H*. As a way of providing specific examples for these observations, one randomly chosen episode from each series was videotaped and subjected to a rigorous shot-by-shot analysis.[3]

Before moving to a discussion of the way these variables were manipulated in relation to the program narratives, it would be useful to explore the nature of the narratives themselves. In Archie Bunker, Lear had an axial character whose persona was often patriarchal in the sense he was myopic and tyrannical.[4] Lear has stated that Archie reminded him a great deal of his own father (Adler, 1979: xx) and that much of *AITF* was intended to portray the patriarch as buffoon.[5] Lear thus decided to shoot *AITF* in proscenium. This meant that the cameras (and thus the viewing audience) would maintain a distinct distance; they would not be allowed to move into the set—into Archie's domain—for reverse angles. This, and the fact that the program was produced live-on-tape in front of an audience, created a great sense of theatricality. There were practical economic reasons for such a decision (Adler, 1979: xxii), but there were equally important narrative reasons as well: shooting in proscenium helped maintain Archie not only as the axial character but as the buffoonish patriarch. By preventing the cameras from moving into the set for reverse angles, viewers were allowed only to look at Archie, not with him.

Lear's decision to shoot *AITF* in proscenium with multiple cameras pulled situation comedy back to its roots. He essentially employed an updated version of the Electronicam system, a multiple film camera system Jackie Gleason had employed successfully on *The Honeymooners* some twenty years earlier (Mitz, 1983:123). But if *AITF* pulled situation comedy back to its roots, *M*A*S*H* pushed it forward into the somewhat more complicated aesthetic realm of the contemporary cinema. When Gelbart first saw the movie version of *M*A*S*H*, he realized the intrinsic role director Robert Altman's reflexive shooting style played in the film's narrative (Gelbart, 1983). Altman was not dealing with the all-pervasive influence of a single axial character, but with the nuances of an ensemble of characters, and the apparent aimlessness of his camera movements, the sheer "busyness" of his shots, actually helped define the characters and their relationships.[6] Thus a shooting style similar to that employed by Altman would be important in maintaining the spirit of the ensemble: a single camera with multiple setups, unimpeded by spatial or psychological boundaries, able to capture visual patterns of great complexity. In short, one might say that a more "aggressive" use of the camera than had been the norm for situation comedies would be necessary; programs like *Leave it to Beaver* had employed a single camera, but little effort had been made to use the camera (or any production variable) to reinforce the narrative.

Theoretical Approach

Effective control and manipulation of screen space is one of the most crucial elements of television aesthetics. While there are many ways of delineating such control (Arnheim, 1974; Burch, 1973; Heath, 1981; Zettl, 1973), for the purposes of this study I distinguished between two broad categories: camera space and performer space.

Camera space is composed of two elements: horizontal field of view and what I have termed "camera proximity." Horizontal field of view is the type of shot: CU (close-up, head and shoulders), MCU (medium close-up, taken at the bustline), MS (medium shot, taken at the waist), WS (wide shot, which encompasses the entire body or set), and so forth. The importance of field of view is underscored by Wurtzel and Dominick (1971) who argue that much of the perceived effectiveness of a television program depends on the way the director chooses the shots the audience is to see:

> The viewer, as represented by the camera, does not remain in one viewing position. He sees the action from both close-range and at a distance. (104)

The second component of camera space, camera proximity, is the location of the camera in relation to the performer—in front of them, behind them, and so forth. In *AITF*, camera proximity and, to a somewhat lesser extent, field of view, worked together to establish definite "geographical" boundaries for the cameras that were rarely violated. As will soon become evident, each performer in *AITF* had his or her own space that the other performers (to a greater or lesser degree) could move into and out of freely. But the camera could do so only at the risk of making the viewer uncomfortable. Such movement could be used for dramatic effect or to change the meaning of the narrative (e.g., the episode in which Archie and Mike were trapped in the basement and a camera was pulled into the set for a tight 2-shot as their usual antagonism gave way to a momentary rapport). In *M*A*S*H,* on the other hand, geographical boundaries for the camera were loosely defined if at all. The camera was allowed to move at will without fear of the movement necessarily affecting a change in the narrative.

The second type of television space distinguished here is *performer space.* This is primarily a function of performer blocking (positioning and movement) along axes. These axes are defined in relation to the camera: the horizontal *x*-axis perpendicular to the camera's line of sight and the *z*-axis of depth toward and away from the camera or parallel with the camera's line of sight (Zettl, 1973: 174). Each of the cameras in multiple camera shooting or each new set-up of the camera in film style shooting has its own x- and z-axis. The distinction to be made concerns the way these axes are utilized.

Axis utilization is perhaps best described in terms of vectors. Zettl defines vectors as "directional forces [within the screen] which lead our eyes from one point to another within, or even outside of, the picture field" (1973: 140). Further, Zettl distinguishes among three types of vectors: graphic (created by stationary objects arranged in such a way that they lead the viewer's eyes in a particular direction (e.g., a row of smokestacks), index (something that points unquestionably in a specific direction, e.g., a person looking or pointing), and motion (created by an object that is actually moving or perceived as moving onscreen) (Zettl, 1973: 140–42). In discussing performer blocking the most important of these vectors is, of course, the motion vector.

Comparative Analysis

In *AITF,* performers were blocked almost exclusively along the x-axis as they moved from the front door through the living and dining rooms to the kitchen and back again. The only time there was a real potential for movement toward or away from the cameras occurred when a character moved upstage to the stairway or downstage to the television set. *M*A*S*H,* on the other hand, utilized a great deal of movement along z-axis motion vectors. Because the camera was free to move into the performers' space for shot-reverse shot sequences, performers could move toward and away from the camera as easily as they could move perpendicular to it. In the episode of *AITF,* the vast majority (92 percent) of performer blocking was along x-axes. In *M*A*S*H,* the majority (78 percent) of performer blocking was along z-axes.

It is significant how the two components of space—camera and performer—worked together to reinforce the communicative ability of their respective narrative structures. In terms of space, the proscenium technique such as the one utilized in *AITF* would seem to favor an axial, somewhat patriarchal narrative structure in that it allows the viewer to only look at a character rather than with them. This is especially true when the patriarchal status of a character is the object of derision, as was the case with Archie. Such a status would be undercut somewhat if viewers were allowed to encroach upon that character's space proximally. Befitting a proscenium approach, the cameras thus became a fourth wall, allowing viewers to approach Archie's space from essentially only one direction.

Viewers could, and did, encroach upon Archie, however, through field of view: close-ups of Archie were often used for dramatic or comedic effect. This was especially true for reaction shots. In the particular episode under discussion here, there were six reaction shots; all were of Archie. Much of Archie's patriarchal stance, and the humor derived from making fun of such a stance, was a result not so much of what Archie said as the way he reacted to the words and actions of others. He appeared as the long-suffering father figure enduring the ignorance of the "children" about him (e.g., his reaction to Edith's news that she had promised their house for Florence and Herbert's wedding or his reaction to Edith's piano playing and singing during the wedding). Indeed, such reactions almost became narrative conventions within the series itself, aided considerably by the somewhat plastic quality of Carroll O'Connor's face and his remarkable ability to use it to show numerous inflections. Significantly, too, such reaction shots just as often showed Archie losing face, as he once again became the buffoon.

Reaction shots on *M*A*S*H*, however, were rare—the selected episode had none at all. Arguably, this was due to the fact that, in an ensemble comedy, the emotional reaction of any one character is in large part defined by the corporate reaction of the entire cast (witness the fact that in those episodes where a facial reaction of some sort was necessary the camera often panned across the faces of the entire cast).

The use of screen space to define a character in *AITF* was perhaps most conspicuous with regard to Archie and his chair. It was no accident that this particular chair occupied the point in the set where the *x*-axis vectors intersected the only real *z*-axis vector, that running from the television to the staircase. The action of *AITF* for the most part revolved around this throne; in fact, the space it usually occupied was the exact spot where Florence and Herbert said their vows. Normally, this was space Archie guarded zealously. Thus, the audience was never allowed to circle his chair or sneak up on it from behind, assuming Archie's place through a POV (point-of-view) shot.

The use of camera and performer space to reinforce the narrative was equally evident in *M*A*S*H,* where a large proportion of performer movement was employed as a transition device, to move the story from one subplot to another. In the sample episode, this was evident from the opening scene, which took place in the operating room (OR). In this scene, all three of the plotlines for the episode were laid out in dialogue between Hawkeye, Charles, B. J., and Potter. As they talked, Father Mulcahy paced back and forth, establishing a motion vector between them, asking questions that stimulated necessary plot information. The camera panned with Mulcahy as he moved, his movement acting not only as a transition between the surgeons but between the plotlines as well. More typically, however, movement-as-transition was achieved by having two characters moving along converging vectors meet, converse, then move on. The camera would pan or truck to follow them until they converged with another couplet standing still or moving in the opposite direction. The first couplet would "hand off" the story to the second and the camera would begin a new sequence with the second couplet.

This type of transition was seen when the Canadian leaves the *M*A*S*H* compound. Klinger escorts him to his truck and tells him goodbye. Klinger then continues across the compound along a *z*-axis until he converges with Hawkeye moving along the *z*-axis from the opposite direction. They stop, converse, and move on. Similar movement was used earlier in the episode when a nurse who had been talking to Hawkeye rises from their table and starts across the mess tent on the *x*-axis. The camera panned to follow her and came to rest on Klinger and the Canadian moving through the chow line on the z-axis.

This performer movement occurred in several planes simultaneously, thereby layering the action between foreground, middleground, and background. People were constantly moving in and out of the frame, past doorways and windows, between the camera and the subject of the shot, behind the subject, crowding the screen with visual information. To a very great extent, this layering was a result of the extensive use of z-axis motion vectors. As Zettl points out, "By placing objects and people along the z-axis in a specific way . . . we can make the viewer distinguish between foreground, middleground, and background rather readily . . . " (1973: 207). This can of course be compared with *AITF*, where extensive use of x-axis motion vectors resulted in the action usually being carried out on only one plane as opposed to three or four.

The use of performer movement as a transition device and the layering of that movement into multiple planes was obviously tailor-made for an ensemble comedy like *M*A*S*H* which utilized interweaving characters and plots. The movement itself acted very much as a needle and thread, sewing the narrative together. But the multiple-plot narrative structure of *M*A*S*H* also benefited from parallel editing (the intercutting of two activities occurring at roughly the same time in different locations) which was used to enhance the program narrative by playing the dialogue and actions in one subplot of the narrative off those in another. Put another way, parallel editing was used to help establish comedic relationships.

The comedic relationships in *M*A*S*H* were sometimes obvious. For example, there was a cut from Hawkeye berating Klinger for paying off a five dollar debt with a bottle of wine to Charles begging Hawkeye to tell him where he got the wine. In another example, there was a cut from Potter and Klinger pouring Charles's wine into their stranded jeep to Hawkeye pulling the cork from a wine bottle in preparation for his tryst with the winner of his essay contest. Other times, however, the relationships were far more subtle, as when Charles, who has been talking to Hawkeye and B. J., turns his head towards the door of the Swamp and we cut to a moment later that day as Hawkeye and B. J. leave the Swamp and walk outside. In either case, however, it was the preciseness with which these words and actions were matched through editing (and judicious shot selection) that allowed the viewer to not only jump across space and time with no loss of orientation but to likewise make the comedic connection between a stranded Potter and Klinger and an amorous Hawkeye. These techniques also enabled the divergent strains of an ensemble comedy like *M*A*S*H* to converge into a unified narrative structure rather than collapse into a series of isolated vignettes.

The establishment of comedic relationships also owed a great deal to timing. This was particularly true with regard to *AITF*. Inasmuch as *AITF* was shot live-on-tape with multiple cameras, most "editing" as such was done on the spot by switching between the cameras. Thus, postproduction editing, while usually necessary, was not the process of shot-by-shot assembly that an episode of *M*A*S*H* entailed. Nevertheless, in *AITF* the establishment of comedic relationships and the proper coordination of dialogue and movement were just as essential. Due to the factors of shooting in real time, comparatively fixed camera positions, and a lesser degree of postproduction editing, however, the comedy had to be played and the comedic relationships made clear by the performers themselves. This meant that split-second timing was paramount to the success of *AITF* (Lynch, 1973: 267–71).

By contrast, the single-camera film-style technique utilized in *M*A*S*H* did not require the performers to say their lines in real time to the extent the multiple-camera live-on-tape technique utilized in *AITF* did. In a shot/reverse-shot sequence, for instance, since only one camera was used, one member of the couplet would say all their lines for that camera position; then the camera would have to be moved for the lines of the second member of the couplet. Timing, so very important to the proper execution of comedy, was thus partially suspended, and only completely restored again when the editor assembled the film itself. Thus, performers in an ensemble comedy shot film-style must learn to set up their timing somewhat differently than those performers in a comedy like *AITF* shot in real time.[7]

Since the matter of timing was so crucial in *AITF*, every character had to know his or her blocking precisely, but this was especially true in Archie's case; it was through Archie's blocking that his role as the axial character within the narrative structure of *AITF* manifested itself so visibly. During the wedding ceremony for Florence and Herbert, Archie was constantly in motion, pulling one character after another about the set from one group and comedic situation to the next. It begins with Archie pulling a reluctant Herbert down the stairs and through the guests. Leaving him, he crosses the room to Edith and pulls her to the priest in an effort to get the ceremony started. He then pulls Edith to the piano, pushes her onto the bench and tells her to start playing, only to return once again to tell her to stop. Archie then goes up the stairs and returns with Florence, depositing her next to Herbert. He crosses back to the piano, picks up Edith, and pulls her over to Florence and Herbert. The scene continues in a similar manner, with Archie orchestrating virtually every movement.

While this particular episode was exceptional in the number of people involved in this last scene and the degree of their movement, it was an exception that illustrates the point. In a scene this involved, precise execution of blocking and dialogue—both matters of timing—was essential. Any lapse in this execution would have prevented the director from getting the necessary shot. Further, the degree to which the timing in the scene depended on Archie's blocking was reflective of his axial status within the series as a whole.

The control of screen space through field of view, camera proximity, performer blocking, parallel editing, and timing all move a great distance towards explaining why *AITF* and *M*A*S*H* "looked" the way they did. But much of the particular "look" of these two programs, especially with regard to the division of the visual field into planes and the articulation of depth, was also a function of lighting and set design.

Lighting and Set Design

As Millerson (1982) points out, television is inherently a two-dimensional medium and the careful control of light and shadow is essential for creating the illusion of a third dimension. Zettl (1973) distinguishes two types of television lighting techniques. The first, chiaroscuro, is lighting for light-dark contrast. "The basic aim is to articulate space," writes Zettl, "that is, to clarify and intensify the three-dimensional property of things and the space that surrounds them, to give the scene an expressive quality" (38). The second type of lighting, Notan, "is lighting for simple visibility. Flat lighting has no particular aesthetic function; its basic function is that of illumination. Flat lighting is emotionally flat, too. It lacks drama" (44).

Notan lighting was obviously utilized on *AITF,* where the set was lit flatly and evenly. There was no regard for time of day—it was as bright inside the Bunker house at night as it was during the day. Similarly, there was no regard for light source—when it was day there was no appreciable difference in the amount of light coming through the windows than when it was night. Most importantly, shadows were virtually nonexistent. Thus, the fact that action occurred on only one plane was reinforced by a lighting design that, through the absence of shadow, helped to create an environment of only one plane.

M*A*S*H, however, utilized chiaroscuro lighting, primarily in the form of source-directed lighting: during the day the sets were bright with "sunlight" streaming through windows while, at night, shadows increased markedly, the sets becoming dimmer, with darkened windows and light provided by lamps or overhead fixtures. Yet even during daylight hours, many depth clues were offered by shadows. As an example, in the mess tent, as Klinger glances at Hawkeye, there is a shot of Hawkeye sitting at his table. Even though there is nothing between the camera and Hawkeye to act as a point of reference, it is still obvious that Hawkeye is completely across the tent from Klinger. The fact that the shadows deepen as they move toward Hawkeye articulates the amount of space that exists between him and Klinger.

Set design can likewise articulate space and, through the use of depth clues, degrees of depth in the televisual image. Zettl (1973: 179) suggests a number of these clues, but three are of particular importance to the discussion here: overlapping planes, relative size, and height in the plane.

M*A*S*H utilized sets of great depth, and these three depth clues were all conspicuously evident. Overlapping planes (in which one object partially covers another so that it appears to be lying in front) were used in numerous shots. For example, shooting across a bunk when Hawkeye and Charles were in the Swamp arguing over the wine or shooting through the jeep windshield as Potter and Klinger return with the curare. Relative size (guessing how large something is or how far away it is by the size of its screen image) was also used a great deal due to the placement of set pieces in relation to the set and the camera (e.g., in the mess tent, shooting across one table at Hawkeye sitting next to the window with Klinger and the Canadian sitting in the background) or movement in various planes (e.g., Hawkeye and B. J. leaving the Swamp and walking towards the camera with jeeps and trucks passing behind them and nurses walking between them and the camera). There were also several occasions when height in plane (the higher something is in the picture field the further away it is) was used (e.g., Klinger turning around as the Canadian leaves to see Hawkeye approaching from across the compound).

Another conspicuous characteristic of the set design on $M^*A^*S^*H$ was the almost constant presence of the outside world. In the mess tent or in the "swamp," flaps were tied back, allowing viewers to watch the external as well as the internal workings of the camp: people walking by, jeeps passing, conversations being carried on, ballgames being played. Yet this presence in no way de-emphasized the importance of interiors. The more ensemble nature of $M^*A^*S^*H$ necessarily required an environment of diversity, and despite the superficial similarity of green canvas and tent poles, each of the sets on $M^*A^*S^*H$ maintained the distinct personality of its occupant. Character traits were conspicuously evident: the World War I memorabilia in Potter's office, the draped nylons and lace doilies in Margaret Houlihan's tent, the teddy bear tucked in Radar's bunk. In this regard, the most diverse habitat of all was the "swamp," where a still for making homemade hooch squatted side-by-side with a phonograph and recordings of Rachmaninoff. The diversity here was of course due to the diversity of the occupants: at various times Hawkeye, Trapper John, Frank, B. J., and Charles.

The great use of depth in the set designs for $M^*A^*S^*H$ stands in sharp contrast to the designs for *AITF*, where sets tended to be long and shallow. But because there was comparatively little movement toward or away from the camera, sets with any degree of real depth were unnecessary (this can also be seen on other situation comedies like *One Day at a Time, Maude, The Jeffersons*, and *Alice*). It should come as no surprise then, that the depth clues identified by Zettl were all missing from the particular episode of *AITF* under discussion here and were comparatively rare in any of the episodes analyzed in preparation for this essay. Indeed, the only time any of the depth clues even came close to utilization were the occasional instances of shooting across the television set.

In contrast to the efforts to include the outside world in $M^*A^*S^*H$, in *AITF* curtains were usually drawn over windows or, were they opened (e.g., the window in the Bunker's diningroom), the only thing visible through them was light, creating a sense of what Zettl calls "negative space" (1973: 177). Similarly, when front or back doors were opened, the audience saw painted backdrops and an occasional artificial bush or tree.

Up to a certain point, set design on $M^*A^*S^*H$ and *AITF* was a function of performer blocking. As Alan Wurtzel reminds us, sets physically define the limits of performer blocking (1983: 424), and $M^*A^*S^*H$'s orientation towards z-axis blocking necessitated sets of great depth as much as *AITF*'s orientation towards x-axis blocking necessitated sets that were long and shallow. But, as Horace Newcomb has pointed out, one must also consider the degree to which sets reinforce the program narrative by "delineating a great deal of formulaic meaning" (1974: 28).

The two-dimensional treatment of the outside world in *AITF* led to little or no sense of space beyond the confines of the Bunker home. This sense was further compounded by the great degree of homogeneity from one *AITF* set to another. The living/dining area, the kitchen, Archie and Edith's bedroom, and Mike and Gloria's bedroom all looked very much alike. While movement from one of these environments to another sometimes occasioned rhetorical shifts in the narrative (e.g., Archie and Mike often seemed more vulnerable, less defensive when in their respective bedrooms), together these sets provided a dramatic gestalt, a sense of psychological closure.

Metallinos (1979) states that psychological closure is "one of the most crucial forces operating within the visual field" and recounts Zettl's definition of it as "the perceptual process by which we take a minimum number of visual or auditory cues and mentally fill in nonexisting information in order to arrive at an easily managed pattern" (211). The basically two-dimensional set design of *AITF*—drab and nondescript—and the minimal visual information provided concerning the outside world, encouraged the viewer to focus attention on those things inside the Bunker house that were three-dimensional: the characters and their confrontations.[8]

This focusing of attention had a narrative function as well as a physiognomic one, however. Inasmuch as *AITF* revolved about an axial character, the true essence of the program was that the world began and ended with Archie. It was essential, then, that *AITF* employ a narrative gestalt to a much greater degree than *M*A*S*H*, and a great part of that narrative gestalt was the creation through specific set design and lighting techniques of a physical environment that was itself a complete, self-contained unit, apart from the outside world.

The need for narrative gestalt in *AITF* made it very much a drama of interiors. But in *M*A*S*H*, as much of the outside world as possible was included. I would argue that this was due to the fact that, unlike those in *AITF*, the characters in *M*A*S*H* were very closely tied to the outside world. So much of what happened in their lives was dictated by the ebb and flow of conflicts beyond their compound and beyond their control. Thus, a narrative heavily dependent on external realities was reflected in set designs that were open and emphasized the outside world.

Conclusion

It has been the thesis of this essay that the communicative ability of any television narrative is, in large part, a function of the production techniques utilized in its creation. While I think it quite clear that *AITF* and *M*A*S*H* support this thesis, one must be careful not to overemphasize the role of production techniques in the communication of entertainment television narratives based only upon the experience of two series. It would, however, seem appropriate to conclude that, at least in the case of *AITF* and *M*A*S*H,* the creators of the two shows, faced with a number of options (including the standard "1960s telefilm values"), made some deliberate production choices that, while gambles of sorts, were obviously felicitous—witness the influence the two shows have had on subsequent programming. *AITF's* proscenium style has dictated the course of situation comedy ever since, as the vast majority of sitcoms in the past decade have utilized multiple camera, live audience configurations. Similarly, *M*A*S*H* has exerted a tremendous influence but, unlike *AITF,* not on programming within its own genre. The visually complex influence of *M*A*S*H* can best be seen in recent hour-long comedy-dramas like *St. Elsewhere* and *Hill Street Blues,* an influence Robert Butler, who directed the pilot for *Hill Street Blues* called "making it look messy" (Gitlin, 1983: 293). Indeed, this influence can first be seen somewhat earlier in *Lou Grant,* when *M*A*S*H* producer Gene Reynolds teamed up with James Brooks and Alan Burns of MTM, the production company later responsible for *St. Elsewhere* and *Hill Street Blues.*

This is not to say that other production techniques could not have been utilized on *AITF* or *M*A*S*H* as, in fact, they were (e.g., the episodes where Mike and Archie were locked in the basement, where Gloria was molested, where the members of the 4077 were interviewed by a newsreel crew, where a subjective camera was used to show the 4077 from the point of view of a wounded soldier, etc.). These, however, were the rare exceptions rather than the rule and it is significant that such changes in production technique were not just the result of changes in narrative structure but were in large part responsible for the dramatic and emotional impact of these particular episodes.

In assigning meaning to specific production techniques, one runs the risk of overstating the importance of the television apparatus itself. Nonetheless, as Stuart Hall concedes, the way a message is encoded into televisual discourse has a great impact on what the message becomes and the way it is decoded. Indeed, the acknowledgement that the techniques of television production themselves have meaning questions the validity of looking at the production process as a given or, due to its often assembly-line, commercialized nature, as an endeavor unworthy of scholarly consideration. It argues, instead, that this process is an important link in human communication.

Notes

1. There is a body of research that, while not working from the perspective of the encoding/decoding model, nonetheless deals with various production techniques. It has tended to fall into two categories. The first of these has dealt with television as a medium for instruction or information (e.g., McCain, Chilberg, and Wakshlag, 1977; Schlater, 1969, 1970; Tiemens, 1970; Williams, 1965). The second category, on the other hand, has dealt more closely with television as a medium of entertainment, most often focusing on questions of aesthetics or semiotics (e.g.,

Herbener, Tubergen, and Whitlow, 1979; Metallinos, 1979; Metallinos and Tiemens, 1977; Porter, 1980, 1981, 1983). To varying degrees, the vast majority of this research—the current study included—owes a debt to the seminal work of Herbert Zettl, whose articulation of many of television's aesthetic tenets (1973, 1977, 1978) has provided it a foundation upon which to build.

2. In this context, I define "communicative ability" as the degree to which an encoded text determines its own decoding.

3. The episode of *AITF* concerned a conflict between Archie and Edith. Archie had planned a weekend fishing trip for himself and Edith along with Archie's friend Barney and his wife. Unbeknownst to Archie, Edith had agreed to have a wedding ceremony in their home for two octogenarians from the Sunshine Home, Florence and Herbert. The wedding was to take place the same day Archie wanted to leave on the fishing trip, the problem being how to schedule both to the detriment of neither.

The episode of *M*A*S*H* interwove three plots: procuring a drug, curare, used as a muscle relaxer prior to surgery; Klinger exchanging fruit cocktail with a Canadian M*A*S*H unit for several bottles of French wine; and Hawkeye holding an essay contest for the nurses with himself as prize.

4. My use of the term "patriarchal" in this context should be qualified, inasmuch as the term has gained a number of connotations, perhaps chief among them that of an historical system of male domination, though recently it has taken on a more Marxist bent, particularly in feminist film criticism. My use of it in reference to *AITF* is based upon the fact that while Archie is indeed a character axial to the narrative, his centrality has a blatantly oppressive, vituperative component to it (exemplified by his treatment of his family, particularly Edith) not necessarily associated with characters just because they are axial. Beyond this, however, further connotations of patriarchy are not intended.

5. During much of *AITF's* first few seasons a debate raged as to whether or not the program endorsed bigotry or defused it by making it the object of ridicule. For a selection of literature from both sides, see Adler (1979).

6. Diane Jacobs (1977) calls this aspect of Altman's style "actualism." For further discussion of Altman's *mise en scène* and camera movement, see Rosenbaum (1975) and Tarantino (1975).

7. For an interesting discussion of playing comedy for a single camera versus playing it for multiple cameras, see Kelly (1981), pp. 28–35.

8. Indeed, Lear had originally intended to shoot *AITF* in black-and-white. When CBS balked, he compromised and made the sets a drab brown and as nondescript as possible.

References

Adler, R. (1979) *All in the Family: A Critical Appraisal.* New York: Praeger.
Arnheim, R. (1974) *Art and Visual Perception.* Berkeley: University of California Press.
Brunsdon, C., and D. Morley (1978) *Everyday Television: "Nationwide."* London: British Film Institute.
Burch, N. (1973) *Theory of Film Practice.* Princeton: Princeton University Press.
Fiske, J., and J. Hartley (1978) *Reading Television.* London: Methuen.
Gelbart, L. (1983) "Its creator says hail and farewell to *M*A*S*H.*" *New York Times.* February 27.

Gitlin, T. (1983) *Inside Prime Time.* New York: Pantheon.

Hall, S. (1980) "Encoding/decoding," pp. 128–38, in S. Hall, D. Hobson, A. Lowe, and P. Willis (eds.) *Culture, Media, Language.* London: Hutchinson.

Heath, S. (1981) *Questions of Cinema.* Bloomington: Indiana University Press.

Herbener, G., G. Tubergen, and S. Whitlow (1979) "Dynamics of the frame in visual composition." *Educational Technology and Communications Journal 27* (Summer): 83–88.

Jacobs, D. (1977) *Hollywood Renaissance: Altman, Cassavetes, Coppola, Mazursky, Scorsese, and Others.* New York: A. S. Barnes.

Kelly, R. (1981) *The Andy Griffith Show.* Winston-Salem: John F. Blair.

Lynch, J. (1973) "Seven days with 'All in the Family': Case study of the taped TV drama." *Journal of Broadcasting* 17 (Summer): 259–74.

McCain, T., J. Chilberg, and J. Wakshlag (1977) "The effect of camera angle on source credibility and attraction." *Journal of Broadcasting* 20 (Winter): 35–46.

Metallinos, N. (1979) "Composition of the TV picture: Some hypotheses to test the forces operating within the television screen." *Educational Technology and Communications Journal 27* (Fall): 205–14.

Metallinos, N., and R. Tiemens (1977) "Asymmetry of the screen: The effect of left versus right placement of television images." *Journal of Broadcasting* 20 (Winter): 21–33.

Millerson, G. (1979) *The Technique of Television Production* (10th ed.). London: Focal Press.

———. (1982) *The Technique of Lighting for Motion Pictures and Television* (2d ed.). London: Focal Press.

Mitz, R. (1983) *The Great TV Sitcom Book.* New York: Perigee Books.

Morley, D. (1980) *The 'Nationwide' Audience.* London: British Film Institute.

Newcomb, H. (1974) *TV: The Most Popular Art.* Garden City, N.Y.: Anchor Books.

Porter, M. (1980) "Two studies of Lou Grant: montage style and the dominance of dialogue." Unpublished paper.

———. (1981) "The montage structure of adventure and dramatic prime time programming." Unpublished paper.

———. (1983) "Applying semiotics to the study of selected prime time television programs." *Journal of Broadcasting* 27 (Spring): 63–69.

Rosenbaum, J. (1975) "Improvisations and interactions in Altmanville." *Sight and Sound,* 44 (Winter).

Schlater, R. (1969) "Effect of irrelevant visual cues on recall of television messages." *Journal of Broadcasting* 14 (Winter): 63–69.

———. (1970). "Effect of speed of presentation on recall of television messages." *Journal of Broadcasting* 14 (Spring): 207–14.

Silverstone, R. (1981) *The Message of Television: Myth and Narrative in Modern Society.* London: Heinemann.

Tarantino, M. (1975) "Movement as metaphor: The long goodbye." *Sight and Sound,* 44 (Spring).

Kodak's "America"

Images from the American Eden

HAL HIMMELSTEIN

"The illiterate of the future," it has been said, "will not be the man who cannot read the alphabet, but the one who cannot take a photograph." But must we not also count as illiterate the photographer who cannot read his own pictures? Will not the caption become the most important component of the shot?

Walter Benjamin, "A Short History of Photography" (25)

Anything can be associated with anything else for a viewing subject who is structured by the rhetoric of the commercial.

Mark Poster, "Foucault, the Present and History" (120)

During 1984 and 1985, the J. Walter Thompson U.S.A. advertising agency conceived and produced the "Because Time Goes By"[1] national television advertising campaign for the Eastman Kodak Company. J. Walter Thompson has serviced the Kodak account, its second oldest account, since 1930.

The campaign comprised nine spots. Five were produced in 1984: "Reunion," "Music Makers," "Baseball," "Olympics," and "The Gift." Four others were produced in 1985: "America," "Henry, My Best Friend," "Old Lovers," and "Summer Love."[2] The campaign was "transitional" for the client. It marked a return to Kodak's tradition of warm, often lyrical "emotional appeals" commercials without completely abandoning the "product benefits" focus of recent campaigns.[3] Among those featured in the new spots were: young lovers on the beach sharing their memories in photographs as their summer of love comes to an end; elderly couples expressing their continued love; a little boy whose puppy quickly grows to a giant dog while the boy grows very little; and a Christmas commercial featuring a young child giving a gift to an elderly black man.

From *Journal of Film and Video*, vol. 41, no. 2 (Summer 1989). Reprinted by permission of the author.

The following discussion focuses on one of these spots, "America," which was first aired in the Spring and Summer of 1985 in both a sixty-second and a thirty-second version. "America" was chosen for study because it represents a dominant strain in television commercials from the period which employed themes of American patriotism and restoration. It was also chosen for study because the apparent rupture between its seamless aesthetic and its socially provocative imagery opens up an important discourse on the process and power of symbolization and mythification in our public imagery.

The resulting analysis is grounded in both a close reading of the text of "America," and a series of telephone interviews conducted in 1987 with key individuals in the agency's creative department and the client's Consumer Products Division's Marketing Communications Department who were intimately involved in the creation of the spot.[4] The interviewees were very open in their responses to all questions regarding the creative and administrative aspects of the commercial's production. At Kodak's request, financial information regarding the cost to produce the commercial was not forthcoming.[5] While the interviews provide important insights into the "mind" of the commercial and the minds of those who conceived it, one must be careful to separate creator intentionality and the text itself as viewed.

The Social Context of "America"

The "America" spot was part of an advertising trend. The advertising industry's success is dependent in large measure on its ability to interpret a "complex, multi-layered, fast-changing society," and to follow the society's emotional mood as quickly and accurately as possible (Stevenson D4). This is especially true for commercials seeking a heterogeneous national audience. When an ascending mood is perceived, agencies and their clients jump on the bandwagon; when it passes, they jump off. Themes and symbols representative of those themes are appropriated from the store of existing public imagery to tap the perceived mood. The confluence of two national events in 1984—the Summer Olympic Games in Los Angeles and Ronald Reagan's presidential re-election campaign—provided advertisers a clear signal that a patriotic mood was sweeping the country.

The swell of national pride surrounding the 1984 Los Angeles Games was an extension of the patriotic fervor generated by the underdog American ice hockey team's unexpected victory over the Soviet team four years before in the 1980 Winter Olympic Games in Lake Placid. Olympic competition, always a source of nationalism among competing countries, has for years been a forum for Cold War ideological warfare between the United States and the Soviet Union. The U.S. boycott of the 1980 Summer Olympics in Moscow, following the Soviet invasion of Afghanistan, and the Soviets' reprisal boycott of the Los Angeles Games are clear examples of the intrusion of international politics into sports.

Motivated by national ideology, the Carter administration in 1980 took the moral high ground of a nation of "free" people supporting the cause of a nation oppressed by a totalitarian regime. The 1984 Los Angeles Games provided Americans another opportunity to promote the American way of life in relation to the Soviets. In this case the ideological frame was economic. Rather than massive government support for the construction of sport facilities for the Games, American private enterprise contributed large sums of money for such construction. Corporate public relations considerations aside, the privatization of the Los Angeles Games provided a convenient symbol of the contrast between the Soviet athletic program, with its well-financed yet subservient athletes carrying out the goals of the state on the playing fields, rinks, and arenas, and the American program in which athletes are autonomous "free spirits" nurtured by free enterprise. This contrast became a subtext of many products' advertising campaigns saluting America's Olympic athletes.

The Reagan political spots drew heavily on the theme of national revitalization reflected in the American entrepreneurial spirit. The campaign's optimism seemed myopic to many, given evidence to the contrary of America's waning economic empire. Americans continued to lose jobs in the heavy manufacturing and high-technology electronics sectors of the economy to overseas competitors, foremost among them the Japanese; and, ironically, the farm crisis in America's heartland was reaching devastating proportions just as the Reagan commercial campaign was presenting images glorifying rural American life. Compounding the individual despair caused by unemployment in the industrial and high-technology sectors, and the increasing loss of family farms, was a general perception of America's loss of international prestige. Viewed in the context of the American military defeat in Vietnam and its embarrassment in the Iranian hostage debacle, America's economic decline took on added psychological importance. The central theme of the Reagan advertising campaign, that "Life is better . . . America's back . . . and people have a sense of pride they thought they'd never feel again (Stevenson D4), became the anthem for a nation gripped by malaise and apprehensive of its future.

Suddenly product campaigns extolling patriotic values cluttered the electronic landscape. Notable among them were Chrysler's "The pride is back, born in America," and Miller Beer's "Made the American way, born and bred in the U.S.A.," both of which drew directly on the Reagan campaign theme. Kodak's "America," while eschewing the overt symbolism of Chrysler's giant American flag and the equally overt lyrics of both the Chrysler and Miller spots, nonetheless drew heavily on the Reagan message, and for good reason, as we shall see.

Conceiving the Spot

In 1984, according to a J. Walter Thompson account supervisor, Eastman Kodak "was feeling somewhat vulnerable" because 10 percent of its film business in the United States had been taken away by Fuji Photo Film USA Inc., a Japanese film and videotape manufacturer that had entered the U.S. market in 1970.[6] Fuji had developed a film stock with color reproduction characteristics different from Kodak's. While Kodak had maintained its emphasis on the faithful rendition of skin tones, Fuji emphasized the bright colors (some people at Kodak called them "garish") to which the viewers of color television had become accustomed. Fuji had also taken the lead in product marketing, introducing multi-roll packages of film and huge, brightly colored point-of-sale advertising displays.

There was a difference of opinion in two camps within Kodak's Marketing Communications Department as to whether a new campaign should stress product benefits or brand image.[7] Kodak's top management historically "had a clear prejudice for brand image maintenance. It was proud of its image."[8] Central to Kodak's decision to stress brand image in the campaign was the reality that Fuji had a more successful product on the market—"Quite honestly, Kodak wasn't in a position to make grand product performance claims because Fuji, at the time, had surpassed Kodak in product quality"—and the agency's belief that "nine out of ten Americans shoot film to save their memories, not to worry about the industrial quality of film stock."[9]

Kodak decided to take the high ground, a smart move since its major competition was Japanese and the campaign coincided with the political window during which a patriotic theme would be well received. The "America" spot would "ride the tide of the new patriotism, a place that only Kodak could be."[10] The patriotic approach would allow Kodak to capitalize on the "heritage" of the brand.

Market research indicated that viewers had come to expect emotional appeal advertising from Kodak, spots with themes such as a mother's love for her son. At the same time, Kodak was trying to avoid the "trap of being [perceived as] a sentimental brand." It was committed to "moving its image forward without becoming high-tech or punk."[11]

Kodak's headquarters are located in Rochester, New York, a "stable environment out of the cultural 'firing line' of New York City," and this may account in part for its conservative mindset. According to a former advertising agency executive and long-time observer of the industry, Kodak has a "deeper sense of responsibility about the country as a whole" than a company headquartered in New York City or Los Angeles, which tends to be "more cynical." "A company's personality," he added, "is the key to the way commercials are [ideologically and aesthetically] constructed."[12] An account director for J. Walter Thompson, who was assigned the Kodak account after "America" had been shot, described Kodak's corporate philosophy:

> The company has a Midwestern mentality, a general outlook on life and conception of American society that is safer than most New York City-based companies, Kodak takes a more conservative approach. It is willing to be a little more provocative in terms of shooting style, but not in terms of politics. It reminds me of my Dow Chemical account in Indianapolis. It's not New York City.[13]

Kodak's Director of Marketing Communications for Consumer Products agreed with this assessment, saying Kodak "goes out of its way not to be controversial." If controversy arises, he added, it is "by accident."[14]

Not only does Kodak eschew the high-tech look which has become a signature of many contemporary brand image commercials; it also does not want to be perceived as a "funny" company. A recent example offers proof of this mindset at work. In 1985, J. Walter Thompson shot a spot called "Ostriches" as part of a campaign for Kodak's 400 film. The spot started on a close-up shot of jockeys lining up for the start of a race. As the race began, the shot widened to reveal the jockeys astride ostriches, not horses. While the spot post-tested very well, Kodak's Director of Marketing Communications for Consumer Products insisted that "humor is not an emotion" in Kodak's lexicon. The spot never aired.[15]

Kodak's cautious corporate philosophy is reflected in its formal, highly-structured commercial approval process. It was through this process that the "Because Time Goes By" campaign and the "America" spots were transformed from ideas to completed commercials. Kodak's formal approval process, while rare in the advertising milieu of the 1970s,[16] has become far more common in the 1980s where, with increasing conglomeration, there is "a less clear [corporate] attitude toward larger visions of America" and an increased bottom-line consciousness.[17] In Kodak's case, television advertising is "so important for presenting an image of the company" that all the various levels of Kodak's management are involved in deciding the thrust of a campaign.[18]

In developing television spots for its film products, Kodak's first decision-making level is the Marketing Communications Director for Film,[19] who oversees the advertising production process for commercials, print, and outdoor advertising of all film products. Generally in attendance at this initial meeting between client and agency staff are, for the client, the Marketing Communications Director for Film and "communications specialists" who will oversee the actual production of the spots and monitor costs, and for the agency, several key members of the creative team. This meeting is intended to narrow down a number of ideas for the proposed spots to those that have special merit.

The Marketing Communications Director for Film makes a recommendation to Kodak's Director of Marketing Communications for Consumer Products (including, but not limited to film products). This stage is "the most important buy-in. Management above [this level] will usually buy the Marketing Communications Director's judgment."[20] It was at this level that the debate between brand image and product-benefits approaches for the campaign took place, with brand image carrying the day.

The next level of decision-making resides with Kodak's Marketing General Manager for Film. Here we move from Marketing Communications to overall marketing management. Storyboards and related creative materials are presented by the agency. A "go-ahead" is given for the shoots. The succeeding stages of Kodak management decision-making are generally "for review only." These include Kodak's General Manager for the Consumer Products Division, and the Group Executive Vice-President for the Photographic Products Group. Once the spot is completed, it is presented to

Kodak's Chairman, Vice-Chairman, and President for *pro forma* approval. This is often done the day before the spot is scheduled to premiere. The purpose of the review is to familiarize the corporate officers with the spot or spots so that they can intelligently respond to any feedback they might receive from viewers. Of course, "a look from the Chairman" is worth a thousand words. If he doesn't like it, it won't air.[21]

The team assembled by the agency to produce a spot generally includes: a Vice President and Creative Supervisor, primarily an administrator, who assigns creative people to the account and acts as liason with the client; an Account Supervisor; a Group Creative Director who develops ideas for the spot (in the case of "America," the Group Creative Director was selected to direct the shooting of the spot; J. Walter Thompson often goes outside the agency to hire commercial directors); another Group Creative Director who writes music and lyrics for the spot; an Executive Producer who supervises the production, hires a production house to do the shooting, and monitors production costs (on the "America" shoot, the Executive Producer functioned as the Second Unit Director and also shot stills that were used in the spot); and an Art Director who does most of the casting for the spot.

It is difficult to credit any individual in a group creative effort, such as that which resulted in "America," as the sole originator of an idea or theme. We know that in a collective endeavor, ideas are generated by numerous informal dialogues among key participants as well as in more formal meetings. This is especially true in the creative departments of advertising agencies. According to one observer with many years of first-hand agency experience as an executive of one of the country's leading agencies:

> One probably won't get an answer as to the exact process in which an idea is constructed, because decisions get made in a non-decisional way at most agencies. The crystallization of the decision-making process is announced in a very brief memo from the agency's account executive: "We've decided to go forward with this idea." No one knows exactly who "we" was.[22]

Recognizing this difficulty, the author conducted telephone interviews, ranging in length from twenty minutes to an hour-and-a-half, with seven key players involved in the creation of "America" in an attempt to develop as clear a picture as possible of the gestation of the images, music, and lyrics that constitute the finished product. These interviews occurred two years after the spot's completion and may suffer to some extent from the problem of participant recall of specific facts and the exact sequence of events. In addition, as with any highly successful group creative effort, some participants may claim credit for others' ideas. The author sought to avoid this potential problem by cross-checking participant accounts and asking follow-up questions. In each instance of an unresolved discrepancy, and there were but three such cases, the author accepted as the accurate account that on which two or more participants concurred. Through this process a clear portrait of the spot's development emerged.

The J. Walter Thompson creative team was in California working on another project when word came from New York to develop an idea with a "patriotic theme" for the "America" spot. According to Greg Weinschenker, who had been assigned to direct "America," "they sent back an idea with people saluting the American flag." Weinschenker found that idea "boring." He suggested instead a motorcycle journey across the United States. His suggestion was autobiographical. In 1970 Weinschenker had travelled across the country on a motorcycle from New York City to Albuquerque, New Mexico, with his dog. Unlike "America," Weinschenker's journey "was not that romantic. In fact it was physically painful. It took two or three weeks."[23] According to Weinschenker, Kodak wanted the spot to show more color than the previous spots in the campaign, most of which were shot indoors, so the idea of an outdoors shoot was appealing.

Kodak's Marketing Communications Director for Film at the time, Bruce Wilson, was clear from the outset of discussions with agency staff as to the "concept and feeling" Kodak sought to achieve with "America," as well as its style. It was to be a "vignette" spot. Rather than a coherent narrative, a vignette commercial is a sequence of "slightly interlocking little scenes and situations" (Arlen 7).

The agency's creative team went to work developing a storyboard based on Weinschenker's and Kodak's conceptions. Weinschenker sat down with Linda Kaplan, an agency Group Creative Director and lyricist, to flesh out the idea. Kaplan and Weinschenker had worked closely on many projects prior to "America." Kaplan proposed the idea of a Vietnam draft evader returning from Canada following years of exile to see his family and reunite with his old girlfriend. Not only did Weinschenker find this idea too controversial, but he said "the rider would be too old." He wanted the rider to be "youthful, not jaded." According to Weinschenker, "the character was to have no pre-conceived notions about anything."[24] Had the agency proposed the draft evader idea to Kodak, it would never have entertained such a storyline, according to Kodak's Bruce Wilson.[25]

The "board" that emerged showed a young motorcycle rider going across the country, meeting different people. One original concept had the cyclist coming into a big city, Los Angeles, at the end of his journey. In contrast to the warmth and friendliness of the "country" he had seen, Los Angeles was a "cold place." Sitting on Hollywood Boulevard with tears in his eyes, the motorcycle rider internalizes the contrast.[26]

The precise storyboard for the spot was not that important to Kodak in giving the go-ahead to begin production. Director Weinschenker's "loose" shooting style, developed in many successful Kodak spots prior to "America," was well known to the client, which voiced no objection to such an approach. Kodak allowed the agency creative group sufficient latitude to pick up shots on location as opportunities for unplanned scenes became available. Because "America" was part of a larger "marketing package"— stills from the shoot were to be used for print advertisements in magazines in addition to their use in the commercial—the precise budget for the shoot was not of critical concern to Kodak.[27]

Shooting the Spot

Director Greg Weinschenker emphasized seeking "real people" rather than actors for the vignettes that would comprise the spot. The motorcycle rider protagonist would be a professional actor. The people he encountered on his journey across America would for the most part be cast from non-actors who lived in the places he visited.

Casting began. Greg Blanchard, the actor chosen to play the cyclist, was cast in Los Angeles. He "had the right spirit" according to Weinschenker. Blanchard's youthful, clean-cut appearance was ideally suited to the 'depoliticized" image both agency and client sought. The "clean cyclist" would maximize the viewer's identification and provide a functional hero, an ego-ideal. Conversely, the viewer's potential anxiety and defensive response to the iconography of the cyclist-as-anarchist, cultivated through decades of B-grade motorcycle gang movies and culminating in the anti-establishment, pot-smoking anti-heroes of *Easy Rider,* would be minimized (Steinbock 64–66). A professional motorcycle rider was cast as Blanchard's double. He would appear in panorama shots picked up by the Second Unit, headed by Executive Producer Sid Horn.

Sites for shooting were selected by agency Art Directors Kathy McMahon and Marisa Acocella. Primary sites were Oregon, Arizona, and Los Angeles. The rural locations would provide the palette of outdoor colors that Kodak desired—the lush greens and golds of the Oregon countryside, and the earthy browns and reds of the Arizona desert and mesas. Los Angeles would provide the contrasting image of big city "coldness."

These West Coast locations offered additional economic benefits. Agency Executive Producer Sid Horn had hired Ron Dexter, of Dexter, Dreyer and Lai, a Los Angeles-based film production house, as Director of Photography for "America." Art Directors McMahon and Acocella went out into the field two weeks before the crew to do the initial pre-casting of the "real people" Weinschenker sought. Weinschenker asked them to "just find the right people and the right look" for the scenes he had planned. Most of the final casting decisions were made by the director on site.

Weinschenker and Dexter headed the First Unit, which shot all the scenes featuring interactions between Greg Blanchard and the characters he encountered in Oregon, Arizona, and Los Angeles. Kodak Marketing Communications Specialist Ann Winkler, the client's representative on the shoot, worked with the First Unit. Executive Producer Sid Horn headed the Second Unit, which travelled south from Oregon to Monument Valley, Utah, picking up shots of Blanchard's double riding through the countryside. In addition to the film footage shot for the spot, Weinschenker, Horn, and a Kodak photographer shot stills, which were subsequently used in the spot and in magazine advertisements.

The persons appearing in the spot, and those who were cast and shot, but did not appear in the final version (the "out-grades"), were paid between $300 and $600 a day, depending on the length of the shooting day. Because the spot was so successful, airing over the course of many months in the national market, those appearing in major roles in the spot's final version made between $15,000 and $20,000 with residuals.[28]

The motorcyclist's first human encounter in the spot, with the elderly woman, was not storyboarded. While the crew was shooting the Oregon school bus scene (which became the spot's concluding vignette) the elderly woman wandered out of her house to see what was happening, then disappeared back into the house. Weinschenker spotted her, stopped the shoot, and ran after her. Her daughter, who lived in the house, talked with the director and got her mother to play in the spot. The elderly woman was totally deaf. As it turned out, the elderly woman's great-granddaughter was one of the children getting off the school bus. Weinschenker set up the two-shot of Blanchard and the elderly woman at the rural mail box. Blanchard began to point, and the elderly woman, picking up the cue, also pointed. The shot was in the can. According to Weinschenker, the elderly woman "never did know what was going on."

The scene of the motorcycle rider sitting with a bearded man on a bench in front of a country store and reaching out to shake the collie's paw was shot in an old Arizona town fallen on hard times. The town, once thriving because of its proximity to the mining industry, was now a virtual ghost town. The shot had the look of the "old west" we have come to expect in our popular imagery of the area.

The pick-up truck scene with Blanchard and the two black men was storyboarded before the shoot began. It was shot in Oregon. The original concept for this vignette had the three men sitting in the truck bed filled with hay. One of the black men was playing a harmonica, while Blanchard played guitar. This was shot, but Kodak's Winkler did not like it. She felt that "portraying blacks as musicians was a cliche."[29] Kodak was very careful not to represent groups in ways that some might consider stereotyped or demeaning. The scene was reconceived at the site. Weinschenker had the three men begin to unload the hay, which quickly turned into the playful hay-tossing scene used in the completed spot. Another version of the scene was shot, but not used. In this version, some black teen-agers had gotten their pick-up truck stuck in the mud. Blanchard stopped to help them free the truck. The consensus among the crew was that this shot didn't work.

When asked about the appropriateness of casting blacks in such a setting, Weinschenker replied "We had to have blacks in the commercial. If you have six people in a spot, one has to be black."[30] This statement should not be taken literally as evidence that racial quotas are employed by the agencies or clients. It does, however, generally reflect agency and client sensitivity to demographics. One longtime agency insider noted that "everyone in the ad business is very familiar with and sensitive to demographics," and that there is a "racial mindset" at the agencies.[31]

The question of the portrayal of blacks resurfaced a year later at Kodak. J. Walter Thompson had cast a black saxophone musician in one of the spots in Kodak's "The Color of Life" campaign. Before giving the go-ahead for the shoot, Kodak insisted that the role be recast with a white musician in the role, arguing, as had Winkler on the "America" shoot, that the black musician was a cliché.[32]

The scene of the cowboy greeting the motorcycle rider along the roadside was shot in Arizona. The cowboy was a real cowboy cast at the site. Similarly, three Vietnam veterans were lined up at a veterans hospital in Portland, Oregon, as possible actors in the scene where the motorcyclist offers a friendly handshake to a disabled veteran confined to a wheelchair. (None of the veterans who were actually physically disabled would agree to appear on camera in a wheelchair.) It rained constantly in Oregon during the time scheduled to shoot the scene, so the veteran's shoot was moved to Arizona.

The First Unit found Richard, the veteran who appeared in the scene, in a Phoenix, Arizona, veterans clinic. He was the only veteran who wanted to do the shot. While not physically disabled, he did have emotional problems. Like the other veterans, Richard didn't want to appear in a wheelchair but, said Weinschenker, "he needed the money." Weinschenker added, "he was a nice guy who couldn't cope with society. He had done drugs." Winkler was not comfortable with placing a veteran who was not physically disabled in a wheelchair (the contradiction between the artifice of such a representation and Weinschenker's professed desire to use "real people" in the spot was all too apparent—the veteran was "real," the nature of his injury was not). Winkler suggested the scene be shot two ways, one in the wheelchair and one not, and that the decision on which to use be made in editing. Weinschenker did a number of takes of Richard in the wheelchair, but before he could get the second shot without the wheelchair it started to rain, so that shot was never done. Winkler said, partly in jest, partly with conviction, "Greg must have planned it that way."[33] During the shooting of the scene, Weinschenker said, the veteran started to cry, although this version is not the one used in the completed spot.[34]

The Native American was cast in Arizona. McMahon wanted to use Will Sampson, the powerful Indian who starred in the film *One Flew Over the Cuckoo's Nest,* but he was unavailable. Instead, she found an Indian actor friend of Sampson's. The Indian was the head of an entertainment family who travelled the world doing tribal dances. He also worked with Indians with alcohol problems. During the shoot, Weinschenker wanted the Indian to hug the motorcyclist, but he discovered that Indians "don't like to hug." Instead, the scene as shot became a lighthearted conversation between the two men seated on a grassy hilltop.

The scene of the farmer on the old tractor following the cyclist down the two-lane rural highway was shot in Oregon. The final scene in the spot is a shot of the motorcyclist stopped on a country road as children alight from a yellow school bus and cross in front of him. The last child off, a small blond-haired boy carrying a lunch pail, stops in the middle of the road and turns toward the cyclist, who gives the boy a military salute. This scene, like one featuring the elderly woman, was not storyboarded. The idea for the scene was generated by Ann Winkler, Kodak's Marketing Communications Specialist, during the shoot. At that point in the shoot, Winkler pointed out to Weinschenker, no kids had been cast for the spot. Winkler and Kodak "wanted kids and dogs."[35] Weinschenker and the crew hated Winkler's suggestion, but shot the scene anyway. Weinschenker set up the scene with the children crossing in front of Greg Blanchard, the motorcycle rider. While they were shooting, one little boy stopped on his own to look at the cyclist. Weinschenker liked that image, and re-created the scene, directing Blanchard to salute. At the time of the shoot, this scene did not particularly stand out from the others, and it was not being considered as an ending. According to Kodak's Bruce Wilson, the agency creative people "felt the image was 'hokey,' but during editing it turned out to be a very powerful ending."[36]

Two alternative endings were shot, but neither was used. Weinschenker felt that the Hollywood Boulevard ending described earlier was poignant, but not right for the spot as it developed in editing, where the decision was made to confine the vignettes to the "country" with the possibility that the city footage shot, including the Hollywood Boulevard scene, might comprise a totally separate spot. (This, however, never materialized.) The other ending, which was not storyboarded, was shot in the same Arizona "ghost town" as the scene featuring the bearded man and collie. In it, the protagonist-rider meets an aging biker. After circling one another, Blanchard catches up with the aging biker and the two exchange greetings. According to Executive Producer Sid Horn and Kodak's Ann Winkler, although the scene was shot in numerous takes, upon viewing the dailies it was obvious that the scene "did not click."[37] It was discarded.

Lyricist Linda Kaplan, working separately from Weinschenker while he was on the shoot, wrote the lyrics for "America," then waited for the footage to see if the lyrics and images worked well together. If they didn't, Kaplan would adjust the lyrics to fit the images. According to Kaplan, they ended up matching well. Kaplan chose to establish a "Christopher Cross" feeling in the music, rejecting rock and roll.[38]

The First and Second Units together shot "between 40,000 and 50,000 feet of film" for the spot.[39] This resulted in a shooting ratio of about 450 feet shot for every foot actually used—a very high ratio by normal nationally-distributed commercial standards.

The respective skills of director Weinschenker and director of photography Ron Dexter, who led the First Unit, complemented one another. Weinschenker, who generated the ideas for most of the scenes shot, was particularly adept at working with actors. Dexter, who had an excellent sense of color and composition, was very good at picking up the perfect shot, and brought the "look" of the spot together.[40] Sid Horn's Second Unit brought in many very effective panorama shots.

Editing was done in New York City, with Weinschenker in charge. Kodak's Ann Winkler watched the editing for a few days. She had become emotionally involved in the spot, as had the other participants on the crew, and was reluctant to "let it go" at that time. At various points Weinschenker asked her for "suggestions" as to which scenarios she preferred, but she stayed out of the decision-making process.[41]

The edited spot was post-tested. According to Kodak's Bruce Wilson, Kodak "was trying to be a little more contemporary than in previous campaigns." "America" appeared to achieve this. The spot "tested more positive among younger people than older people, yet it did not test as more 'emotional'." According to the research, the youth and patriotism theme of "America" was relevant to younger, single viewers who saw the spot. "They could relate," added Wilson.[42]

The spot began airing during Kodak's peak advertising period, the time of year most Americans take their vacations, Spring and Summer 1985. "America" won numerous creative awards, including a 1986 Clio award for Best Original Music with Lyrics; a 1986 *Advertising Age* award for Best Commercial, "Leisure Entertainment" category; Mobius awards for Best Direction, Best Music, and Best Cinematography; an Art Directors Club Certificate of Merit; and a Silver award for Best Original Music with Lyrics at the 1985 International Film and TV Festival.

Viewer Responses

According to Kodak's Bruce Wilson, "the motorcycle community was absolutely ecstatic" about the portrayal of the motorcyclist. Kodak "received hundreds of letters in appreciation of the spot."[43] Ann Winkler noted that Kodak received "less than five negative letters."[44] The response received at the agency was similar. According to Vice President and Creative Supervisor Geraldine Killeen, more letters were received on "America" than for any spot she can remember. Especially praiseworthy were motorcycle riders and motorcycle magazines, who noted the clean-cut image of the cyclist which "reflected the majority of weekend motorcycle enthusiasts."[45]

While Bruce Wilson indicated Kodak did not receive "a single letter regarding the Vietnam veteran image," agency lyricist Kaplan noted that the agency did receive a few letters expressing the feeling that viewers did not want to be reminded of the war.[46]

Interpretive Contexts

The "story" embedded in the images, lyrics and music of "America" may appear at first glance to be seamless. Its lush greens and highly-saturated golds and reds, its majestic panoramas, slow-motion action and slow lapdissolves, its "kids and dogs" and other warm, friendly, compassionate, funloving denizens of rural America, all produce an almost hypnotic, transcendental vision of an American Eden in which the proud "American family" celebrates the sacrosanct American value of individual freedom, represented by the cyclist's journey of personal and geographic discovery. Nonetheless, as John Berger wrote:

> No story is like a wheeled vehicle whose contact with the road is continuous. Stories walk, like animals and men. And their steps are not only between narrated events but between each sentence, sometimes each word. Every step is a stride over something not said. (284–85)

While the "America" director Greg Weinschenker insisted that there was "no story" in the spot, and that the motorcycle rider "was to have no preconceived notions about anything," it is clear from the creators' own descriptions of the spot's gestation that narrative "strides" were taken; specific, conscious decisions were made regarding what to include in the spot and what to withhold. On one level, these decisions in practice appear to be more "negative reactive" than active. For example, the alternative ending, with the motorcycle rider sitting on Hollywood Boulevard, tears welling in his eyes as the stark contrast between the purity of the country and the coldness of the big city comes to consciousness, was rejected in favor of the theme of the celebration of the heartland.

The conceptualization process in commercial-making is essentially inductive, with the creators trouble-shooting individual scenes, rejecting representations that might offend sub-groups within the commercial's target audience. On another level, however, the decisions can be seen as ideologically grounded. For example, Weinschenker rejected the possible draft evader scenario at the outset. However, he subsequently made reference to Vietnam in the scene, filled with pathos, in which the cyclist meets and shakes hands with the disabled Vietnam veteran. In what was to become the concluding vignette in the spot, the scene Kodak's Bruce Wilson called the spot's "central image," Weinschenker directed the motorcyclist to throw a military salute to the young boy, last off the school bus, who stopped to stare at the rider.

The inclusion of the Vietnam veteran vignette and the image of the cyclist's military salute in the final version of the spot is significant when considered in the context of the experiences of the two men most responsible for the spot's creation: director Weinschenker and Kodak's Marketing Communications Director for Film, Bruce Wilson. Weinschenker characterized himself as a "protester during Vietnam." He did not go to war; his draft lottery number never came up. A friend of Jeff Miller, one of the students killed at Kent State, he had "animosity toward the establishment." He felt his 1970 motorcycle journey across America, the basis for his idea for the spot's theme, produced a change in him, resulting in "a great love for the country and its people."[47] Wilson, who felt the veteran image was "powerful and appropriate," and was concerned only that the handicapped person was presented in a "natural way," served in the Army for four-and-a-half years, although not in Vietnam, and indicated he was in favor of the war.[48]

The "things not said" are part of the story of "America." So too are those things which, having been said, are then wrenched from the hands of their creators and entered into the larger cultural discourse. "Cultures are dramatic conversations about things that matter to their participants, [arguments] about the meaning of the destiny its members share" (Bellah et al. 153). The creators never have the final word. Their work is alive in the culture, part of its "constituted narrative," appropriated by professional critics and regular viewers alike. It is therefore both intensely personal and political.

One of the most significant applications of themes and symbols by the advertising and public relations storytellers is "the power to create support for ideas and institutions by personalizing and humanizing them" (Fleischman and Cutler 144). Advertising, like all fictional narrative,

> is a mode constantly susceptible to transformation into myth. The creation of a narrative almost always entails the shaping of awkward materials into a smooth, closed structure. And this is the essence of myth. Like bourgeosis ideology most narrative . . . denies history, denies material reality as contradictory, and denies the fact of its own production. (Davies 70)

The apparent seamlessness of "America" may be interpreted in such a mythic context.

Shortly after "America" began its run in the national television market, one critic, reviewing the spot in *Advertising Age,* the industry's most respected trade publication, undertook to demythologize the spot. The review begins by comparing "America" with a scene from the film *Cabaret,* in which a blond-haired German youth, wearing a Nazi uniform, sings the song "Tomorrow Belongs To Me." The review continues:

> What distinguishes the Kodak campaign, entitled "Because Time Goes By," [from other patriotic commercials] is that it manipulates the concept of time as a means of political propaganda. . . .
> If the definition of a reactionary is one who tries to reconstruct a romanticized past for an uncertain future, then the Kodak campaign is the most ultra-conservative selling job of the '80s. . . .
> "America" . . . shows a young white man on a motorcycle "setting off to find America." Set in the present, the spot shows little but rustic surroundings and human symbols of a sanitized past.
> It's bad enough to show our grinning Everyman encountering a fluffy collie, a weatherbeaten cowboy and a little old lady at a roadside mailbox. But when he starts shaking hands with a crippled Vietnam veteran or yukking it up with a deliriously happy Indian, the spot crosses the line from mere nostalgia to pure demagoguery.
> The implication that all past ugliness can be whitewashed for a brighter future is driven home by the final image: As the cyclist stops for a little boy carrying a lunch box, he raises his hand to his forehead and flashes the boy a military salute. It's as if he is saying to his diminutive comrade: "Tomorrow belongs to us."
> . . . freezing moments in time has less to do with sentimental glory than precisely documenting the past. Tomorrow has never belonged to those who misremember yesterday. (McWilliams 52)

The critic, Michael McWilliams, had been reviewing spots on a free-lance basis for *Advertising Age* for about a year prior to his review of "America."

McWilliams was a conscientious objector during the Vietnam War. He had been drafted and performed two years of alternative service. The issue, argued McWilliams, is "simply that fifty-five thousand men died there. And that's what's important. Nothing else."[49]

The *Advertising Age* review prompted a strong rebuttal in the "Letters" column of *Advertising Age* from Stephen G. Bowen Jr., at the time Executive Vice President and General Manager, New York, J. Walter Thompson U.S.A. (Bowen was appointed President of J. Walter Thompson U.S.A. in May 1987.) Bowen wrote that McWilliams "has an extraordinarily fertile imagination reminiscent of the defeatists' laments of the national Democratic party during the past two elections." Bowen implied that McWilliams was out of touch with American values that helped elect Ronald Reagan, who campaigned on a platform of optimism and "for a healing of the wounds that kept our society from living up to its promise in the 60s and 70s." Bowen concluded that if McWilliams became enlightened and had an insight, "he should be sure to get it to Ted Kennedy first. He needs it . . . "(20).

Kodak would have preferred that Bowen not respond to the review. Kodak's own public position was not to respond, a company policy regarding any public debate in reference to one of its commercials. Internally, "no one [at Kodak] understood" how McWilliams could interpret "America" in this way. The Marketing Communications staff thought McWilliams was "a crackpot."[50] Director Greg Weinschenker expressed anger at the review, indicating he could not see how the spot could be interpreted as "Nazi propaganda."[51]

According to McWilliams, "Not a word or a comma was ever changed in any of my *Ad Age* reviews. My editor, Fred Danzig, who had been with *Ad Age* for many years, stood behind me in the whole affair."[52] Shortly after the appearance of his "America" review, McWilliams found his work was no longer being accepted for publication by *Advertising Age,* and he began writing about television for *Rolling Stone.*

The deeply personal nature of the varied responses to the images of the Vietnam veteran and the cyclist's military salute in the spot's final scene were brought into clearer focus by a colleague to whom the author showed the sixty-second version of "America." The colleague, himself able to avoid military service through a student deferment, found the imagery in the spot "profoundly troubling, calling into question one's own actions and decisions made during the war. It revives unresolved conflicts about personal ethics."[53]

These varied responses to the Vietnam War in particular, and to militarism in general, point to the power of public imagery to evoke cultural discourse which is profound, contentious, and psychologically complex. In a commercial, as in a photograph,

> The *seen,* the revealed, is the child of both appearances and the search. . . . appearances . . . go beyond, they insinuate further than the discrete phenomena they present, and yet their insinuations are rarely sufficient to make any more comprehensive reading indisputable. The precise

meaning . . . depends on the quest or need of the [viewer]. . . . The one who looks is essential to the meaning found, *and yet can be surpassed by it.* (Berger and Mohr 118)

While multiple readings must be acknowledged and respected as representing differences in individual perspective, one must nonetheless, in the words of Stuart Hall, guard against an undue "emphasis of difference—on the plurality of discourses, on the perpetual slippage of meaning . . . on the continuous slippage away from any conceivable conjuncture" ("Signification" 92–93). As a communicative form, "America" posits, through its codes, an organized system of core values and mythic constructs that circumscribes an American ethos. The mythic constructs of "America" are grounded in ideology. As Hall wrote, "Ideologies are the frameworks of thinking and calculation about the world—the 'ideas' which people use to figure out how the social world works [and] what their place is in it . . . " ("Signification" 99). Myth transforms the common sense of ideology into the society's "sacred social discourse." Myth, a living tradition, is suspended in time; it is both "primordial" and "indefinitely recoverable" (Eliade 5–6). Myth is, above all, discourse about power, about founding and maintaining a way of life, about a fundamental order of being.[54]

The mythology in "America" surpasses not only the cursory readings of McWilliams and Bowen, but also the intentions of the spot's creators. As Hall noted, "Just as the myth-teller may be unaware of the basic elements out of which his particular version of the myth is generated," so may he be unaware that "the frameworks and classifications . . . [he is] drawing on reproduced the ideological inventories of [his] society" ("Rediscovery" 72). A closer examination of the signification, representation, and ideology embedded in the mythic constructs of "America" will reveal the discursive practices in the text, its "ideological work."

Kodak is "about" photography. "Photographed images do not seem to be statements about the world so much as pieces of it, miniatures of reality that anyone can make or acquire" (Sontag 4). Kodak's vision, to create a nation of casual snapshooters and "serious amateur" photographers, relies heavily on this distinction between "making statements" and the capturing and preserving of raw "reality." The photograph "seems to have a more innocent, and *therefore more accurate*, relation to visible reality than do other mimetic objects like painting and drawings" (Sontag 5–6; emphasis added). Beyond this appearance of the accurate reporting of reality, "photographs actively promote nostalgia. Photography is an elegiac art, a twilight art. Most subjects photographed are, by virtue of being photographed, touched with bathos" (Sontag 15).

The combination of the seemingly real and the sentimental mystifies that which is photographed. The camera "can bestow authenticity upon any set of appearances, however false. The camera does not lie even when it is used to quote a lie. And so this makes the lie *appear* more truthful" (Berger and Mohr 96–97). In advertising "the lie is constructed before the camera" (Berger and Mohr 96).

The mystifying power of the photograph is ideally suited to the construction of mythology. The elegiac quality of "America," its bathos, is firmly rooted in the mythology of the American Eden. Kodak celebrates the Jeffersonian ideal of the honest ordinariness of the rural American, whose "good" labor and desire for community are morally superior to the vices of idleness, diversion, and intemperance of his urban brothers. Jefferson's ideal citizen was the diligent democratic husbandman, who could earn an independent living and participate in the civic life of a community of self-governing relative equals. Like the Puritans, Jefferson feared and abhorred the utilitarian individualism associated with the economic man of cities and industrialization and characterized by the "spirit of enterprise and the right to amass wealth and power for oneself" (Bellah et al. 28).

The mythic hero in American culture "must leave society [the Metropolis], alone or with one or a few others, in order to realize the moral good in the wilderness, at sea, or on the margins of settled society" (Bellah et al. 144). While Kodak's hero, the cyclist-wanderer, sets off to find America, and to "realize the moral good in the wilderness," he comes from nowhere. Existing outside history, he does not bear the taint of the Metropolis, of the American technological and military hegemony which was used for class subordination in the industrial city, projection of class war outward into racial war against Native Americans on the borders, and subsequently for creation of a vast international economic and political empire following World War II (Slotkin 51–52). References to the city as a "cold place" with its implicit socio-political implications of unbridled commercial power, class and race warfare, and lack of community were removed from the spot by eliminating the Hollywood Boulevard ending.

The history of the nineteenth-century conquest of Native Americans and the mythic ideological frame that rationalized it is glaringly absent from the discourse of "America." This complex mythic ideological system, consisting of two dominant readings of history, agrarianism and progressivism, provided an intellectual justification for American expansionism. The agrarian ideology of the Jeffersonians was "an antidote to the class antipathies generated by industrialization," substituting "the cultivation of the land, the interaction of man with pure and inanimate nature, for the human conflict of Indian dispossession" (Slotkin 52). The accompanying literary mythology of agrarianism saw the brutal Indian wars of the eighteenth and nineteenth centuries as an unpleasant prelude to the story of clearing and cultivating the soil by democratic farmers. The literary mythology of the Progressives, on the other hand, saw "the naturalness and inescapability of violence arising when two countries or races compete for the same territory" (Slotkin 52).

In either case, Native Americans' claims to the vast frontier and wilderness lands were invalidated in the name of progress and "manifest destiny." True, Jefferson promised Native American leaders in 1809 that:

> we will never do an unjust act toward you. On the contrary, we wish you
> to live in peace, to increase in numbers . . . and furnish food for your

increasing numbers. . . . We wish to see you possessed of property, and pro-
tecting it by regular laws. . . . all our people . . . look upon you as brethren,
born in the same land and having the same interests. (1267)

But there was a price. Native Americans would have to shift from hunting
to farming, thereby reducing the land holdings they would need to support
their own increasing population while opening frontier lands to accommodate the increasing white settler population.[55] Jefferson's desire to accomplish this land transfer justly and nonviolently ignored both Native Americans' sacred ties to the land and the drives of the Metropolitan machinery
of capitalism for continual resource exploitation.

Native Americans' status as marginal people living on the social and cultural periphery of Anglo America continues to the present. In the mid-1950s,
under a U.S. government policy of "relocation," Native Americans began
moving en masse from the reservations to selected cities, among them Los
Angeles, Seattle, San Francisco, and Minneapolis, in anticipation of receiving
education and job training. Many of those who signed up for these programs
were placed in run-down Army barracks and given little or no training. Many
didn't speak English. The problems of the reservations—poverty, poor
health, alcoholism, and suicide—followed Native Americans to the cities.
Today, over half of the 1.4 million Native Americans live in metropolitan
areas, where they have assumed the status of an urban underclass. There are
great fears in the Native American community that these displaced persons
are losing the "spiritual path" as they become assimilated into urban culture.

The nineteenth-century visual representations of Native Americans portrayed them as the colorfully primitive, gloriously doomed uncivilized (Dorris 27, 36).[56] Kodak's "America," in its own mystifying, portrays the Native
American as an ideal Jeffersonian citizen living in Edenic bliss, unproblem-
atically anchored in the vast space of the American wilderness.

"America" is equally mystifying in its representation of the American
farm. Images of lush farmland are combined with a shot of a farmer sitting
high atop an anachronistic tractor, following the cyclist down a winding two-
lane country road. The images evoke memories of the family farm and a simple agrarian life. These images belie not only the contemporary economic and
political struggles of family farmers, but also the social history of American
agriculture. In fact, the images of the farm and farmer offered by the spot
accomplish their ideological work by mythologizing a pre-existing myth.

The continued expansion of the "corporate farm" and its subsumption
of the small family farm, excluded from Kodak's vision of the heartland, is
not unique to the twentieth century. Nineteenth-century American bourgeois development belied the extant mythology linking national prosperity
with the pioneer farmer. In reality, according to historian Richard Slotkin,
"the special environment of some frontiers . . . gave . . . agricultural enterprises a particularly monopolistic and tyrannical form that was inimical to
the 'individualism' of entrepreneurs" (43–44). This was especially true of
farmers in regions dominated by railroad land companies and small ranch-

ers on range land desired by land-owning "oligarchies." Not only did the railroads sell land at vastly inflated rates to individual settlers or organized colonies, they also controlled the best land of the plains region and kept farm holders continually in their debt through manipulation of freight rates. In the South, the main cash crop, cotton, was instrumental in the organization of farming into a system of large plantations. The work of harvesting cotton was accomplished through the institution of slavery. Today's rural working class, among them tenant farmers and migrant farmworkers, is largely ignored in contemporary accounts of the "farm crisis." Also ignored is the exploitative relationship between migrant workers and the family farmers glorified in populist mythology. This relationship was exposed more than a quarter-century ago in the *CBS Reports* documentary *Harvest of Shame*.

In the process of producing the mythology of the American Eden, Kodak's "America" falls victim to "the general impulse toward . . . malignant possessiveness [which] shows signs of being stronger than ever in American life." According to psychiatrist Robert Jay Lifton, this impulse

> is populist in its rural, common-man, anti-cosmopolitan tones, nativist in its easy rage toward whatever is "foreign" and "alien," chauvinistic in its blindly "patriotic" distinction between "us" and "them." It is an impulse that not only runs deep in the American grain but in the universal grain as well. For it is associated with a broader image of restoration—an urge, often violent, to recover a past that never was, a golden age of perfect harmony during which all lived in loving simplicity and beauty. ("Introduction" 4)

The need for restoration is grounded in "symbolizations around national virtue and military honor" (Lifton, *Home* 132). One of the most powerful of these is that of the "warrior as hero" who functions as "a repository of broad social guilt. Sharing in his heroic mission could serve as a cleansing experience of collective relief from whatever guilt had been experienced over distant killing, or *from the need to feel any guilt whatsoever*" (132; emphasis added). The insistence on "the continuing purity and guiltlessness of American warriors" (132–33) is transferred to American society as a whole.

The American ethos has always contained a strong strain of self-righteousness. "In matters of war and national destiny," Lifton wrote, "Americans have always felt themselves to be a 'blessed' or 'chosen people'" (*Home* 158). America's post-World War II economic, technological, and military power rendered unpalatable our defeat in Vietnam at the hands of a "third rate" military power. Those who called into question the American warrior-hero's "purity of mission" were considered by many if not most Americans as disloyal to the American vision.

The draft-evader scenario rejected by Weinschenker at the outset of the conceptualization process would have raised troubling questions regarding the war, reawakening nagging questions of collective guilt. The scenario which did evolve substitutes a recruit for warrior-hero symbolization. This symbolization functions in the spot on both levels described by Lifton. The first level—the cleansing experience of collective relief from the guilt that has been experienced—is contained within the scene featuring the cyclist and the Vietnam veteran in the wheelchair. This scene presents the cyclist's mission as one of reconciliation. He becomes the agent of adjustment, restoring harmony to a country torn apart by the war, welcoming the tainted veteran back into company of "good men."[57] This scene is placed at the temporal center of the sixty-second spot (0:27–0:31). The second level—the cleansing experience of collective release from the need to feel any guilt whatsoever—is contained in the spot's final image, the freeze-frame of the cyclist's military salute to the young school boy. Is this young boy another echo of the "warrior-hero-to-be," carrying the American purity of mission into the future?

The warrior images in "America" are a far cry from the narrative of revenge exploited in mainstream theatrical films such as *Rambo,* in which the soldier-hero's retributive actions are decidedly individualistic and ultimately anti-social (Hallin 22). Nonetheless, in its quiet way the iconography of redemption in "America" seeks to build ideological consensus around the notion of the retrieval of America's greatness, a legacy of power and control re-established. By implication, war in general, and the Vietnam War in particular, are legitimized.

The warrior-hero iconography is a distinctly male iconography. Pure, rational, and strong, the male is the culture's source of stability. His journey is that of the "straight path." "America" is a commercial about the actions of men. The only women in the spot, the elderly woman and the young girls in the school bus scene, signalize the spot's main action, but are not integral to it. The four young school girls who run past the cyclist prior to the little boy's entrance in the frame do not acknowledge the cyclist's presence, and therefore cannot bond with him. On the other hand, the school girls' presence in the shot serves to announce and frame the subsequent militaristic bonding that does occur between the young boy and the cyclist. The elderly woman's pointing gesture directs the cyclist to the various men with whom he subsequently connects in the remainder of the spot.

The restorative impulse which motivates "America" is inscribed, in the "Because Time Goes By" caption, over the spot's final image. Benjamin's epigraph, quoted at the beginning of this essay, focuses on the power of captions to direct meaning and thereby to liberate the photographic object from its aura. For me, the "Because Time Goes By" caption works *against* the mystifying and depoliticizing practices inherent in the commercial while appearing at first reading to reinforce them. For a critical viewer in post-Vietnam America, the images in this commercial are not innocent ones.[58] This is so precisely because in spite of the passage of time, the real social relations and human connections evoked in the mythology of this spot are haunting. They refuse to be turned entirely into "art." Benjamin views history as a process of mourning, not in the elegiac sense, but rather as the history of the oppressed brought to present consciousness. Here the dialectic of official or dominant ideology and the "other" history of oppression becomes the source of emergent oppositional ideology. The photographer, a soothsayer predicting the future from remnants of the past, uncovers guilt and names the guilty in his pictures. "America," in spite of its massive, corporate attempt to cover and sanitize the past, ultimately succeeds, for a critical viewer, in doing just the opposite. The restorative impulse in "America" runs counter to the model of "transformation" proposed by Lifton: a model according to which we *confront*, through sustained questioning, the values and symbols that lead to acts of violence; *reorder* our values; and *renew* ourselves through the creative exploration of alternative social forms (*Home* 388–406). These "animating" principles both expose and refute the denial associated with the restorationist impulse.

Notes

The author wishes to thank Bernard Timberg for his many helpful editorial suggestions.

1. The "Because Time Goes By" theme is an appropriation of a memorable and still resonant older popular culture coding, the nostalgic "As Time Goes By" lyric in the film *Casablanca* (1942). The lyric evokes the memory of a brief, passionate love affair between Rick Blaine (Humphrey Bogart) and Ilsa Lund (Ingrid Bergman) in Paris just prior to the Nazi occupation. As Prefect of Police, Capitaine L. Renault reminded Rick, "under that cynical shell, you're at heart a sentimentalist." A similar appropriation, but with a sardonic twist, is the theme song of the 1970s social comedy *All in the Family*, "Those Were the Days."

2. Conversation with Sid Horn, former Executive Producer, J. Walter Thompson U.S.A., and Second Unit Director, "America," October 8, 1987. (Horn left the agency at the end of 1987.)

3. Conversation with Ann Winkler, Marketing Communications Specialist, Eastman Kodak (1980–86), October 14, 1987. Since these spots were introducing Kodak's Kodacolor VR film, the product-benefits approach could not be completely ignored.

4. The only key person directly involved in the spot's creation who declined an interview was the Director of Photography, Ron Dexter. Dexter indicated his busy production schedule prevented his participation in the study.

5. "America" is clearly a very high cost commercial by contemporary standards. Its six-week shooting schedule and 450:1 shooting ratio lead the author to estimate the cost to produce the spot in excess of $500,000.

6. Conversation with Warren Milich, Account Supervisor on "America," J. Walter Thompson U.S.A., May 8, 1987.

7. Bruce Wilson, at the time Kodak's Marketing Communications Director for Film, believed that the political climate in the country was right for an emotional approach. His immediate supervisor, Jack Powers, at the time the Director of Marketing Communications for Consumer Products, felt on the other hand that a product-benefits approach would be more successful. Wilson's view prevailed in the ensuing discussions. The spots would be produced to appeal more to emotions, with less emphasis on touting the specific benefits of Kodak films.

8. Conversation with Warren Milich.

9. Conversation with Warren Milich.

10. Conversation with Warren Milich.

11. Conversation with Warren Milich.

12. Conversation with Loomis Irish, Professor of Television and Radio, Brook-

lyn College of The City University of New York, and an executive for many years with Batten, Barton, Durstein and Osborne, April 29, 1987.

13. Conversation with Mitchell Brooks, Account Director on the Eastman Kodak account, J. Walter Thompson U.S.A., May 6, 1987.

14. Conversation with Bruce Wilson, Director Marketing Communications and Support Services for Consumer Products, Eastman Kodak, May 8, 1987. Kodak's marketing philosophy should not be generalized to all "heartland" companies, however. Some practitioners note that certain heartland companies, such as 3M and B. F. Goodrich, have supported controversial programs on Vietnam and China, while more "urban" East Coast companies such as General Electric and DuPont have scrupulously avoided controversy.

15. Conversations with Sid Horn and Ann Winkler.

16. Traditionally in the advertising business an idea on how to proceed with a campaign oftentimes was agreed upon by agency executives and clients over a game of golf or on a fishing trip. This was particularly true with family-owned clients and publicly-owned companies with a very secure senior management which had a clearly-articulated company philosophy on the perception of the American "reality."

17. Conversation with Loomis Irish.

18. Conversation with Bruce Wilson.

19. Kodak's organization of its marketing division is highly unusual for a large corporation. The division is divided into two distinct units—marketing and marketing communications. Marketing's primary functions include pricing of products, developing sales programs, and financial planning. Marketing communications, on the other hand, employs "communication specialists" working solely on advertising for all "paid communication." These communication specialists are involved in overseeing the advertising production process.

20. Conversation with Bruce Wilson.

21. Ibid. In *Thirty Seconds,* an eyewitness account of the "Reach Out" campaign for American Telephone & Telegraph, author Michael J. Arlen indicates final approval of the spots was given by an AT&T corporate vice-president in charge of public relations. Although the lines of decision-making authority may differ from corporation to corporation, it is clear that the ultimate decision to air or not air a spot is made at the highest level of the client management structure—in Kodak's case, at the very top.

22. Conversation with Loomis Irish.

23. Conversation with Greg Weinschenker, Director, "America," J. Walter Thompson U.S.A., April 11, 1987.

24. Conversation with Greg Weinschenker.

25. Conversation with Bruce Wilson. In all fairness, it is hard to imagine that any client would accept such a draft-evader scenario.

26. Conversation with Sid Horn.

27. Conversation with Bruce Wilson and Ann Winkler. The client pays the cost to shoot the commercial. Kodak Marketing Communications Specialist Ann Winkler was on the shoot and monitored production costs along with J. Walter Thompson Executive Producer Sid Horn. Horn is highly-regarded by Kodak as being "very budget-conscious."

28. Conversation with Sid Horn.

29. Conversation with Ann Winkler.

30. Conversation with Greg Weinschenker.

31. Conversation with Loomis Irish.

32. Conversation with Sid Horn.

33. Conversation with Ann Winkler.
34. Conversation with Greg Weinschenker.
35. Conversation with Ann Winkler.
36. Conversation with Bruce Wilson.
37. Conversations with Sid Horn and Ann Winkler.
38. Conversation with Linda Kaplan, Group Creative Director and Lyricist, J. Walter Thompson U.S.A., March 4, 1987.
39. Conversation with Greg Weinschenker.
40. Conversation with Sid Horn.
41. Conversation with Ann Winkler.
42. Conversation with Bruce Wilson.
43. Conversation with Bruce Wilson.
44. Conversation with Ann Winkler.
45. Conversation with Geraldine Killeen, Vice President and Creative Supervisor, J. Walter Thompson U.S.A., April 13, 1987.
46. Conversations with Bruce Wilson and Linda Kaplan.
47. Conversation with Greg Weinschenker.
48. Conversation with Bruce Wilson.
49. Conversation with Michael McWilliams, April 29, 1987.
50. Conversation with Ann Winkler.
51. Conversation with Greg Weinschenker.
52. Conversation with Michael McWilliams.
53. Conversation with Drewery McDaniel, Professor of Telecommunications, Ohio University, October 10, 1986.
54. Sheldon Wolin, "The Modern Political System: Myth Without Ritual." International Conference on the Presence of Myth in Contemporary Life. New York City, October 12, 1983.
55. Advocating the westward expansion of white settlers, and recognizing its inevitability, Jefferson nevertheless vowed to protect the Native American against the exploitation of unscrupulous whites, who made a practice of plying Indians with alcohol and getting them to sign over their land. Unlike the Puritans, who saw armed conflict with Native Americans as the inevitable struggle between God-fearing Christians and immoral heathens according to divine order, Jefferson, echoing French policy, envisioned the Indian and Caucasian intermarrying and forming a single community of noble farmers.
56. See also Slotkin, *The Fatal Environment*. Slotkin explores the "industrial and imperial version of the Frontier Myth whose categories still inform our political rhetoric of pioneering progress, world mission, and eternal strife with the forces of darkness and barbarism" (12).
57. The symbolization of reconciliation is firmly rooted in American history. In *The Fatal Environment*, Slotkin describes the Fourth of July celebration held in conjunction with the 1876 Centennial Exposition in Philadelphia, which "carried these themes of [national] growth and reconciliation into the realm of civic ritual. . . . The great parade . . . included a prominent contingent of former soldiers and officers of the Southern Confederacy—a display that was meant to symbolize the binding up of the wounds from the terrible Civil War that had torn the nation apart in four years of battle and twice that many of rancorous and uneasy peace. . . . But the imagery was a mask, the oratory hollow. The United States in 1876 was in the midst of the worst economic depression in its history, and of a crisis of cultural morale as well. The reality outside the fairgrounds put the Exposition's triumphant pageantry in a context that was corrosively ironic" (5).

58. My own reading is informed by my experience of six years in the U.S. Army Reserve during the period of the Vietnam War. That experience was marked by my disapproval of the war, a critical awareness of the contradictions of my role in the army, and the resultant feelings of guilt that I had not taken alternative action, such as evading the draft by going to Canada or claiming conscientious objector status and thereby refusing to participate in any manner, no matter how tangential, in the machinery of killing.

Works Cited

Arlen, Michael J. *Thirty Seconds*. New York: Farrar, Straus & Giroux, 1980.

Bellah, Robert N., et al. *Habits of the Heart: Individualism and Commitment in American Life*. Berkeley: University of California Press, 1985.

Benjamin, Walter. "A Short History of Photography." *Screen* 13:1 (1972): 5–26.

Berger, John, and Jean Mohr. *Another Way of Telling*. New York: Pantheon, 1982.

Bowen, Stephen G. Letter to the Editor. *Advertising Age*, 23 September 1985: 20.

Davies, Gil. "Teaching About Narrative." *Screen Education* 29 (Winter 1978–79): 56–76.

Dorris, Michael. "Mythmaking in the Old West." *New York Times*, 21 September 1986: 27, 36.

Eliade, Mircea. *Myth and Reality*. New York: Harper & Row, 1963.

Fleischman, Doris E., and Howard Walden Cutler. "Themes and Symbols." *The Engineering of Consent*. Ed. Edward L. Bernays. Norman: University of Oklahoma Press, 1955. Pp. 138–55.

Hall, Stuart. "The Rediscovery of 'Ideology': Return of the Repressed in Media Studies." *Culture, Society and the Media*. Ed. Michael Gurevitch et al. London: Methuen, 1982, Pp. 56–90.

———. "Signification, Representation, Ideology: Althusser and the Post-Structuralist Debates." *Critical Studies in Mass Communication* 2.2 (1985): 91–114.

Hallin, Daniel C. "Network News: We Keep America on Top of the World." *Watching Television*. Ed. Todd Gitlin. New York: Pantheon, 1986. Pp. 9–41.

Jefferson, Thomas. "Speech to the Chiefs of Various Indian Tribes." *Modern Eloquence: Political Oratory*. Vol. 13. Ed. Thomas B. Reed. Philadelphia: John D. Morris, 1903.

Lifton, Robert Jay. "Introduction." *America and the Asian Revolutions*. Ed. Robert Jay Lifton. New York: Aldine, 1970. Pp. 1–9.

———. *Home From the War: Vietnam Veterans—Neither Victims nor Executioners*. New York: Simon and Schuster, 1973.

McWilliams, Michael. "Kodak Ads Strain Credulity." *Advertising Age*, 26 August 1985: 52.

Poster, Mark. "Foucault, the Present and History." *Cultural Critique* 8 (Winter 1987–88): 105–21.

Slotkin, Richard. *The Fatal Environment: The Myth of the Frontier in the Age of Industrialization, 1800–1890*. Middleton, Conn.: Wesleyan University Press, 1985.

Sontag, Susan. *On Photography*. New York: Delta, 1977.

Steinbock, Dan. *Television and Screen Transference*. Helsinki: Finnish Broadcasting Company, 1986.

Stevenson, Richard W. "Red, White and Blue is Out." *New York Times*, 16 March 1987: D1, D4.

Civic Visions
Forms of Documentary

JOHN CORNER

A narrow definition of "documentary" might indicate that, assessed in terms of their frequency and positioning in channel schedules and the audience figures they routinely attract, documentary programs are not a major area of popular television output. However, a broader definition would see "documentarism" as one of the medium's defining modes. Programs which offer depictions of actuality, with or without exposition, have always been central to television's appeal. The popular "documentarism" of the travel program, certain kinds of sports footage and the wildlife series has now been joined by that of the "video diary" or the "real life drama" series, to constitute an outer ring of documentarist production, surrounding a core of non-fiction output to which the generic label "documentary" is routinely applied by the industry itself. "Current affairs" programming is sometimes uncertainly placed between having its own identity and being a subgenre of documentary. Core documentary on television, however entertaining it is also required to be, almost always works with a "serious" expositional (and frequently journalistic) purpose and, in Britain at least, this purpose has often been that of social inquiry set against a recognized (and visualized) context of economic inequality, social class difference and social change, together with the consequent "problems" thus produced.

The term "documentary" has widely been regarded as an unsatisfactory one since the pioneer filmmaker John Grierson first used it of *Moana*—a film made about life on a South Sea Island—in 1926.¹ His coinage was partly derivative from the French "documentaire," a term frequently used of travel films. However, although the extraordinarily wide range of different production methods, forms and intentions which it now covers often makes it a hazardous classification, there is enough "family resemblance" discernible between the different types of film-making activity subsumed under its label to ensure its continued use both within the industry and among the public and critics. While in cinema studies, given the dominance of fictional work, the use of a term like "non-fiction film" may be a useful, more forthright alternative, the idea of "non-fiction programming" is far too broad to be usable as a critical notion in relation to television.

Grierson himself recognized the term lacked precision but, like everyone else since, he had difficulty in coming up with anything better. "Documentary is a clumsy term, but let it stand" he wrote.² "Documentary" meant that a particular film was to be regarded primarily as a "document," a text whose interest lay in its referentiality, in what it indicated about the world through its sounds and images. Within Grierson's critical vocabulary, such documentation was in contrast both to the form and the content taken by the majority of acted and scripted feature films, with what he viewed disapprovingly as their elaborately "escapist" appeal and their often marked unreality of setting. Film can, of course, "document" through dramatic reconstruction, through interviewee accounts or through the speech exposition of a presenter, all of which are communicative modes widely used throughout the history of documentary film and television. However, the core mode of documentation from the 1930s through to today is the employment of the *recorded images and sounds of actuality* to provide the viewer with a distinctive kind of "seeing" and "hearing" experience, a distinctive means of knowledge. Documentary was grounded in an appeal to *sensory evidence*.

Various ideas of "truth" and "reality" have gathered around definitions of documentary principle and practice, sometimes attracting counter-ideas of "deception" and "artifice," but the notion of the "evidential" provides the best place from which to start an examination of this type of program making. The evidentiary properties of television and of film are related to their capacities, as recording technologies, to produce a "trace" of the physical world in sounds and images. They thereby have an "iconic" status which (though it is being undercut by the electronic technology of image processing) carries with it a level of *referential guarantee*. Within many documentary productions, this iconicity is used to implicate the viewer, both imaginatively and cognitively, as a witness to a heard and seen "real." It is on the basis of this relationship to apprehended realities that the other discourses of documentary—commentative, investigative, evaluative—are built. The way in which the base is established and the building work done across the broad range of documentary methods and styles involves a *series of transformations*. "Transformation" was the term Stuart Hall employed as a central idea in his analysis of how television worked as a *medium,* acting as an agency of change as well as of continuity and of connection. It is a notion which is well suited to an analysis of the phases of documentary production.

Documentary Production as a Series of Transformations

In the diagram below, the documentary process is depicted as one occurring across four stages, linked together by three moments or phases of production.

realities → pro-filmic events → recorded material → program

    ↑   ↑   ↑

scripting/organization   shooting   editing

If we take the three production phases in turn, we can examine how each does its transformative work.

Phase 1. Scripting and Organization

Out of the range of possible kinds of reality open to documentary treatment, a topic is chosen as the subject of a film or program. But how will this topic be depicted in particular images and sounds? The initial decision here concerns what to film, who to film and what kinds of sound (including speech) to record. No matter whether the topic is an abstract one (for example, loneliness in student communities) or a physically grounded one (for example, the problem of heavy traffic in rural areas), a *strategy of representation and of visualization* is required. Within this strategy, certain people, events, places, etc. will be selected for filming as being somehow "typical" of more general circumstances, even if this typicality is only implicit in the program rather than a declared premise of it. Unless the program is to consist entirely of interview segments linked by commentary, the selection needs to be thought through in terms of the pictures (of places, of things, of actions) which will best objectify the abstract and instantiate the general. What results from this set of decisions, once availability and practical considerations have been taken into account, is a selection of entities from the physical and human world at which or at whom the camera and the microphone will be pointed. This is the basis of what can usefully be identified as the *pro-filmic* stage of documentary making, by which time much creative selectivity has already been exercised. The expansiveness of "the real" (even around a quite specific topic) is already being got into shape for its transformation into coherent data, grounded in "the seen."

Phase 2. Shooting

Although previous (Phase 1) work will have established what to shoot, where and when, the direction of the shooting itself will also usually involve some management of the pro-filmic. So, for instance, an unemployed man might be "directed" in the timing and movements involved in a trip to the mailbox with a job application letter or a refugee mother might be "directed" as she prepares and serves a meal for her family. The degree of spatial and temporal management of pro-filmic activities (ostensibly activities which are only "observed" by the documentary team) will vary considerably in relation to their nature and complexity and to the type of depiction of them which the program seeks to offer. Its projected naturalism and continuity, its duration and its possible intercutting with other material or its mixing with voiced-over speech will be factors here. Certain sequences may have to be rehearsed and, as in fiction filming, many actions may have to be repeated in order for a one-camera production team to get visual continuity by combining shots taken from several viewpoints. The people being filmed are thereby positioned as "actors of themselves" within these adjustments, designed to fine-tune reality for photographic or electronic "capture." Almost certainly they will be encouraged not to recognize the camera's presence, since the illusion of unseen onlooking is central to conventional documentary aesthetics.

All these activities can be regarded as contributing to the realization of pro-filmic events and circumstances, the initial features of which were decided in Phase 1. However, the principal business of Phase 2 is that of "recording" itself. Here, a whole range of decisions about the position, angle and movement of the camera, the type and number of shots to be taken, the lighting to be used and the kind of sound recordings to be made will be implemented. It is at this point that an *aesthetics* of representation becomes active, as a (by now, managed) reality-in-process is turned both into data and expression; a stabilization, on film or video, of sights and sounds and also, inscribed within the making of the likenesses, a *way* of seeing and hearing. Perhaps the most important, creative (and often most controversial) stage is still to come, but a fundamental and irreversible translation has occurred and bits of reality are now in cans and boxes as *raw material.*

Phase 3. Editing

This phase, more comprehensively regarded as "post-production," leads up to the final, transmitted program. The various shots taken on location are selectively worked into sequences, with synchronized sound or voice-over and, in some cases, with a music soundtrack. Any pre-shot material (e.g. library film) is added, as the overall communicative organization, already there on paper, is implemented, often with considerable amendments in the light of the "strength and direction" of the material obtained. The proportion of argument to evidence, the movement across space and time (the latter perhaps involving chronological sequences), the introduction of conflicting viewpoints, the "weighting" of the program, explicitly or otherwise, in its findings and evaluations, all are interlinked matters of concern here. Final decisions are made about how to deploy material across the length of the program (certain scenes perhaps being returned to; interviews perhaps being "sliced" into sections and dispersed to several points). In particular, the question of how to "open" is posed. What resonant shot or section of interview comment or phrase of spoken commentary provides the most engaging way in? And then, how to close? Where to leave the viewer at the end, in terms both of knowledge and of feelings about the topic as it continues to exist in the world, outside the temporary, intensive framing of the documentary "window"?

Such a broad outline ignores the often radical differences of method and form to be found in current documentary, but it brings out well the elements which are common to many and it highlights some of those aspects which have made documentaries so controversial a form of program making. In fact, the scheme could be extended beyond the fourth stage—the screened program—to a fifth—the understanding and significance given to it by viewers. This would involve a further phase of transformation—the interpretative activities of the viewers, drawing on their previous knowledge, dispositions and values. That programs "mean" different things to different viewers, both at the level of primary comprehension and at the level of attributed significance, is well established in media research. Many disputes over the "fairness" and truthfulness of documentary programs involve differences of opinion as to actually what was being "said." This is also true of disputes about news. However, documentary is a more symbolically expansive form than news, able to develop a range and density of depiction which becomes more open to interpretative variation as it extends beyond direct exposition into the implicit and the associational, often in the process touching on imaginative territories more closely associated with narrative fiction. I shall say something about the characteristic form taken by public disputes over documentary portrayal at the end of this chapter.

I want to consider both established and emerging aspects of documentarism by using a number of subheads which help to identify some its interrelated components. First of all, though, given its lineage in cinema and radio, it is worthwhile considering briefly the social history of documentary as a major genre of public communication.

The Formation of Television Documentary

Documentary on television now draws on internationally familiar conventions. These conventions constitute a subgeneric system of socio-aesthetic "recipes," each of which carries its implications for the particular kind of "hearing and looking" experience offered to the viewer. The nature of television sound and image and the character of the medium as a domestic service most frequently operating through scheduled programming have influenced the way in which the documentary has been able to develop within it. However, the precedents of cinema and of radio documentary were strong ones in the formation of television work and they still show through in contemporary developments.

The Precedent of Documentary Cinema

The British documentary cinema movement of the 1930s, centered on John Grierson and the team of directors who worked with him successively at the Empire Marketing Board, the GPO Film Unit and at the Crown Film Unit, provided what was undoubtedly the most powerful direct influence on television documentary.[3] Although it could be disputed what precisely should be included in the "canon," major pre-war films would include *Song of Ceylon* (1933), *Industrial Britain* (1931), *Coalface* (1935), *Housing Problems* (1935) and *Nightmail* (1936). The 1930s movement has been the subject of intensive recent scholarship and any analysis of its work is obviously beyond both the scope and purpose of this chapter. It may nevertheless be useful to identify the principal aesthetic and social principles which it established as central to the "documentary approach," principles which have so often been cited, defended and attacked in relation to subsequent films and programs as well as in relation to these pioneering productions themselves.

The films made by those involved in the 1930s "movement" were the result of what now seems a rather strange mix of motives, very much of the period. There was, first of all, a very strong interest in developing film as an art form, and (following European examples) in doing so by taking "real life" subjects as the basis for "creative interpretation." This aesthetic impulse, broadly realist in orientation but also influenced by modernist form (so not at all committed to the idea of a simple "transparency" and quite prepared to use the images and sounds of the real as the elements of a "film language"), was related to a belief in film's capacities as a medium of social revelation and of democratic development. Film could engage people with, and *in,* the political and social adventure of modern industrial society, an adventure which involved recognition of new levels of economic interdependency between social groups and which brought with it the need for a revised sense of national community. There was a new respect for the various work skills by which a modern society sustained itself, and a declared belief in modern citizenship, unprejudiced by older, class hierarchic values and newly committed to exploring "ordinary life" as part of a proper representation of community and nation.

However, yet another element in the mix was an interest in the new role played by promotion and publicity within the modern political and social order. One aspect of this is apparent in the use of film as an agency of popular, civic education. Such films were to be devices not only of instruction and revelation but also of persuasion, they were to be *propagandist* in the cause of democracy. But the interest in promotional communication, together with the broadly optimistic perspective on national development held by many of the film makers ("a modern Britain in a changing world"), also fitted in well—perhaps too well—with the requirements of the funding base which the movement relied upon. This base was essentially provided from organizations (including those of the State) seeking to promote their product and their corporate image through the films, albeit indirectly. So the overall socioaesthetic character of the documentary movement was partly made up of tensions, ones not always successfully reconciled in the films themselves. Realist in general philosophy yet also interested in modernist "experiment," ethnographically exploratory yet didactic, democratic yet propagandist, egalitarian yet often condescending, analytic yet often celebratory—the tensions are multiple. They are also often productive in giving many of the documentaries an ambivalence which is one source of their continuing distinctiveness and interest, putting them at some distance from the dullness and complacency of standard "official information" films of the period.

But perhaps the most important tension at work within the movement (one that gets implicated in most of the others) is the one between "documentary as art" and "documentary as report." The play-off between form-led aesthetic experimentation and a topic-led concern to address social reality and social problems (a play-off with implications not only for communicative form but for communicative aims and intended audiences) was a major factor in determining differences of directorial practice. Finally, it figured in disagreements which developed between group members about overall documentary direction (the contrast between an aesthetically self-conscious film like *Coalface* and a "reportage" work like *Housing Problems* is illuminating here). This issue, though rarely so pronounced, has been a continuing one in the formation of documentary television, negotiated in various ways in relation to technological change and the shifts of generic development.

Radio Features and the Accessed Voice

The film documentaries made under corporate sponsorship during the 1930s, and then as part of the Government's Home Front propaganda during World War II, thus provided television with a number of models for turning the camera into a "public eye," for its visualization of the social world. Many of those who had worked in documentary film subsequently became members of the BBC's documentary department after the war and, at least initially, saw the television documentary as continuing directly in the tradition established by the film movement. The distinguished film maker Paul Rotha, appointed Head of Documentaries in 1953, noted the "paramount importance" which nightly access to a mass audience had for "those who still believe that documentary has a specific social job to do."[4]

But there was another important influence at work in early television documentary. During the 1930s, members of the features department of BBC radio had developed ways of building programs around actuality sound and speech which were finally to be as important a point of reference and creative stimulus for television documentary as the cinematic precedent. With few exceptions (*Housing Problems* being notable here) documentary cinema had not used the interview as a primary informational device. This was largely due to technical limitations, and consequent practical difficulties, in the recording of synchronized sound on location. However, the result was an aesthetic of documentation which, while it sought to *depict* social realities, was unable to explore social experience except insofar as this could either be visually rendered or reported at second-hand. A degree of "distance" inevitably opened up between depicted world and viewer, a distance which could only be further underlined by the use of a spoken commentary coming, as it were, from "outside the frame" and objectifying that which was seen within it.

By the very need to work primarily through speech, radio features' producers had pioneered location interviews and had, within a variety of innovative programs, placed "ordinary talk" recorded on location right at the center of their program design.[5] Even though such early examples of the interview (often broadcast as direct "testimony") sometimes sound nervous and stilted alongside the speech of broadcasting today, the use of participant talk realigned the relationship between portrayed subject and listener. It allowed the mediation of a world which was at least partly described and reflected upon in the terms of those portrayed rather than those of the portrayers. The documentary perspective moved from one model (the cinematic), which was emphatically visual and external, to another (radio features), which had a degree of access to the "interior" of social process, including ordinary experience. The public character of the relationship between portrayers, portrayed and audience underwent a change as a consequence; "access" of one kind or another became written into expectations about what broadcast documentary did. Many of the important developments in television documentarism, in the formative period and since, differ from the cinematic tradition in that, like radio features, they too are grounded in the use of ordinary speech, either in forms of interview or in "overheard" exchange.

The Generic System of Television Documentary

Quite quickly, the conditions of documentary production within television established an aesthetic order different from that of cinema. Programs were frequently made within a series format. Along with this went the use of regularly scheduled spots, a named reporter/presenter who appeared (and often "featured") within the program, a style of more personalized, intimate address and a recognition of the fact that most viewers were sitting at home and, depending on the placing of the program in the schedule, might be pleased to see the topic treated in a "lively" way as well as informatively. The arrival of competition in 1955, with ITV's network being available to viewers as well as the BBC, pushed the development of documentary television further into innovation across a wide range of different formats and styles, creating inter-generic links with drama, with news and current affairs, and with the various "magazine" programs then being devised as a way of mixing "serious" and "light" elements.[6]

One of the most important determinants of the social and aesthetic range of documentary in this period was the extent to which it was regarded within broadcasting institutions as a form of journalism. Seen thus, certain kinds of news-related subjects began to seem more appropriate than less topical themes and documentary styles organized around the "quest" of a presenter/reporter, often delving "behind the headlines," became dominant. For those who regarded the documentary as essentially a director's form, as a space for authoring a kind of "visual essay," the aesthetic limitations imposed by journalistic conventions were often regarded as a threat. Two subgenres which created space for extending documentary language beyond the journalistic were drama-documentary and the "fly-on-the-wall" style of observationalism, the latter developing (with considerable modification) out of the 1960s *cinema verité* movement in France.[7] Both gained large audiences and critical prominence in the 1960s and both relied extensively, though in different ways, on the extended opportunities for "location naturalism" which lightweight 16 mm cameras brought with them.

Though no longer so controversial *per se,* partly because of their development into a conventional subgenre, drama-documentaries still find a regular and high-profile place in the broadcast schedules. "Fly-on-the-wall," on the other hand, is the broad designation (less pretentious than *vérité* though perhaps equally misleading) for one of the most successful and long-running strands of documentary television. It is a strand which has gone through a number of phases of innovation and development. These have left its basic communicative idea and appeal largely unchanged however, if a good deal less novel than when the first such programs appeared on the screen.

I have outlined briefly the general transformative processes involved in producing documentary television and noted some of the influences at work as the distinctive identity and range of television documentary came to be established. I now want to explore further five aspects of communicative principle and practice—observation, interview, dramatization, *mise-en-scène* and exposition—which have given documentary work such public appeal, influence and controversiality.[8]

Elements of Documentary

Observation

The idea of unseen observation, and then the communicative organization of this through a variety of devices, are central to documentary aesthetics. Such an idea has implications both for the pleasure of watching documentaries and for the kinds of knowing which they generate. Unseen observation is, as I shall argue in more detail later, the "enabling fiction" upon which many documentaries depend. Sequences of observation are common to most kinds of documentary program, while in some an observational mode becomes the principal if not exclusive means of portrayal. Grounded, with few exceptions, in the pretense that those portrayed are unaware of the camera's presence, the observational mode provides viewers with a vicarious experience of the real—an experience of witness—against which to form a response. This does not require that they believe that somehow the camera *was* unseen (although the watching of observational sequences certainly encourages the temporary illusion that this is so, together with some of its voyeurist consequences). What they have to believe is that nothing significant would have changed had the camera not been there, thereby legitimating the way in which its absence is pretended. This is a belief in the event-which-might-have-been, one which the very production of the "profilmic" makes a matter solely for speculation and trust since what *might* have happened had the camera not been there is not available and never can be for a television audience.

What would be the consequence of *allowing* the recognition of the camera by participants? First of all, it would have the effect, in many instances, of de-objectifying the documentary "look" at the world, thereby implicating the production team and, via the camera lens, the viewer, in an uncertain relationship of mutual subjectivity with participants. Within a framing of mutual observation, the action of the participants would implicitly take on an aspect of "display" such as to render certain observed activities (for instance, casual asides in a shop while making a purchase, an exchange between two policeman on the beat) awkwardly false, an act in dissonance with a pro-filmic which, elsewhere, was openly proclaiming its status *as performance.*

Paradoxically, the observational mode places the viewer in relationship to "real action" much closer to that of screen fiction than to that of primary perception. In most cases in everyday life, the *acknowledgment* of an observer by the observed would very much be expected, to the point of stopping ongoing behavior or changing its nature. The "trick" of observationalism thus allows distinct kinds of opportunity for depiction. The director can choose either to let significance be delivered self-evidently (perhaps with recorded speech between participants framed as "overheard" and naturally occurring within the observed scene) or to run voice-over speech across the image track, thereby inserting a "bridge" of direct address between observed scene and viewer. This latter procedure increases the informational productivity of the sequence at the same time as it reduces the spectatorial intensities of observational viewing, risking a diminishing of what is shown to a mere illustration of what is being said. Another option, the use of participant voice-over across observed sequences, is less intrusive insofar as it has a generation point within the frame, though it, once again, risks compromising the space for scrutiny, and the space for viewer self-sufficiency, ostensibly made available by unaccompanied observationalism. However, whereas presenter voice-over further reinforces the objectification of depicted persons and events, making them a matter of openly "public" scrutiny, participant voice-over can powerfully subjectify and interiorize what is in the image, perhaps displacing it from immediacy and making it a basis for speaker self-reflection.

Visually, although the plane of the observed action shares features with the plane of action in narrative fiction, there are important differences. In much observational documentary, all persons are equally objectified by the camera, precisely as objects of observation. In narrative fiction, extensive use of close-up, shot-reverse-shot in conversational exchange and the use of the point-of-view shot to align viewing with the gaze of one of the people within the action, all work to subjectivize aspects of setting and circumstance. This has often powerful consequences for the viewing relationships which viewers develop with those portrayed on the screen.

However, despite the gap between documentary representations of persons and the portrayal of "characters" in fiction, some recent observational programs have attempted to construct visualizations which draw on modified elements of fictional language. There are clear points of risk here. For instance, to bring the viewer too comprehensively into the space of observed action, dispersing viewpoints and shots in accordance with its movement, would be to break precisely with that sense of "onlooking" which certifies what is seen as evidential (not manufactured for the cameras) and which is necessarily experienced imaginatively as viewing "at a distance," however small this distance may sometimes be. With large public events (for instance, a rally or a riot) the question of how onlooking distance squares with the evidential trustworthiness of what is seen hardly arises. The more intimate the sphere of life made available to the public gaze however (for instance, a family argument in a kitchen), the more this relationship becomes a potential problem. So although observational scenes of domestic life are now routine on British television, scenes between observed subjects taking place in cars, for instance, or in bedrooms, would raise to a possible crisis point the question of the credibility of the image.

Similarly, to adopt too striking a *styling* of the observational image, using tracking shots, slow pans, zooms, etc., works against the idea that the image has been "captured" adventurously and perhaps somewhat furtively from the ongoing real. Short observational sequences in documentaries constructed within a spoken, direct address structure can develop as highly stylized "little scenes from life" with more impunity than programs whose primary mode is observational. Within the former structure, the "little scene" becomes illustrative (secondary to the exposition; a kind of moving tableau) rather than evidential (the actual basis for exposition and, perhaps, self-sufficient as communication without it). In a structure grounded in observationalism, depictive integrity (the grounds for viewer *trust*) is certified in the uneven, awkward framing of action; the slight delays in following its movement; the necessary distance from it and the general unavailability of cutaway shots to anticipate what is to come (e.g. doors, hands, objects to be used). That the viewer is intermittently aware of a camera at work in the production of the "view" does not disrupt engagement with the viewed. But too frequent a noting of just *how* this "view" is being constructed may well do.

As I noted earlier, the observational mode has become central to a whole range of documentary styles (and also to the documentarist elements in other forms, for example in news reports and in travel programs). Its apparent discursive minimalism provides programs with a strongly "evidentiary" or possibly "illustrative" (see above) level of visualization. Around this core, secondary elements, interpretative and evaluative, can be organized. What it offers for viewers is the spectatorial appeal of observing present-tense realities from a "safe" position (a position whose presence has been aesthetically erased from the plane of observation). This is an experience which gives distinctive onlooking pleasures, of a kind related to those involved in attending to dramatic performance, as well as the satisfactions of independent judgment in relation to presented evidence.

Observation is both a "direct" and an "indirect" communicative mode: "indirect" in its placing of viewers as witnesses of speech and action which they are largely left to construe into significance through their own interpretative work; "direct" insofar as, assuming an "intention-to-mean" on the part of the production team, such a method might be seen as merely a strategy of "soft sell," avoiding the risks of perceived partiality carried by more direct exposition but nevertheless effectively supporting certain evaluations and prompting particular ways of classifying and relating what is said and shown. To take this latter approach, however, assumes a more self-consciously propositional "core" to depiction, a narrower agenda concerning both the topic and the materials of its representation, than most documentarists working in this way declare themselves to have. Notwithstanding such denials of implicit "point making," wherever observationalism is used *illustratively*, embedded as a sequence within an exposition using other modes of address, the suspicion will linger that the requirement for it to "fit in" with what is proposed more directly elsewhere is one which overrides all other criteria brought to its selection, shooting and editing.

The observational mode, variously combined with expositional forms (interview, voice-over, to-camera presentation), becomes the central principle of *vérité*-style programs, to the point that in many such programs all discourses external to the plane of observed action (for instance, presenter speech of any kind and speech in response to interview questioning) are excluded. Additionally, directors working within such formats, though they vary considerably in philosophy, have generally eschewed any directorial management of the action to be "observed," thus imposing quite strict limitations on the kind of scene which is likely to be available for recording (unlike in the more conventional, short "observational" sequences of mainstream documentary which, as I noted above, can be, and often are, fully managed and rehearsed for the camera).[9] As many commentators have observed, the "purist" approach, when sustained across the full length of a program, may run into a number of difficulties with its viewers. Dependence on the close observation of the particular without expositional support increases the possibility of incoherence and boredom, in relation both to observed particularity ("what is going on here?") and to the significance of *this* particularity for the general *topic* (for instance, "loneliness," naval training, the operations of the vice squad) into which it is an exploration. Ironically, anxiety about this may drive the "purist" production team into putting greater emphasis on the hidden transformations of post-production, using high ratios of film shot to film screened (30:1 is not uncommon in this kind of work) to edit the piece into coherence and watchability through a set of practices which are finally every bit as *authorial,* if differently so, as those of heavily directed shooting.

Perhaps it is for this reason that recent British television *vérité* has begun to introduce both presentational and interview elements into the flow of its observational depictions, sometimes affording them a degree of "naturalization" within the frame of observed action (for example, in-shot interview speech while the interviewee is driving a vehicle, thereby avoiding the problem of their own "look" and also embedding their speech, directed out of frame, in a context of in-frame action).

As I write, the most recent attempt to rework observationalism in Britain is the BBC series *The Living Soap,* in which students sharing a house are filmed in their weekly activities. This draws on precedents for domestic *vérité* (such as the BBC's *The Family,* 1972) but introduces elements of "access" programming too, insofar as the students themselves voice-over much of the material and also do short to-camera pieces from a room in the house rigged for this purpose. The mixing of modes, involving varying kinds of relationship with what is going on but implicating the subjects deeply in their portrayal, has received a mixed reception by critics and audiences. As a result of its year-long run and the transmitting of earlier episodes while later ones are being made, the series has begun to feature reactions to itself. Not only have some of the students developed self-consciously "star"-like personas (along the lines of soap celebrities) but local prejudice against them has resulted in abuse and attacks on the house. All in all, this has turned out to be an extremely awkward venture in the revision of documentary viewing relations.

Interview

Interview speech is a major mode of television documentarism. It contrasts directly with the observational mode in that it is openly interventionist. This intervention is signalled both verbally and visually. Speech is elicited by questioning and the speaker usually either addresses an in-shot interviewer or looks "out" in three-quarter profile. When interview speech is used as voice-over across sequences of participant action, the talk relates to (and perhaps describes) what is in the pictures. Nevertheless, the communicative address is still outwards, as direct address to a viewer. But although the interview breaks with the idea of a plane of ongoing action simply present to an unacknowledged camera, its general mode of presentation depends on a sensitive play-off between its status as public speaking and its status as an overheard exchange between two individuals. In respect of the latter, the fact that is *calculatedly and self-consciously* overheard makes it communicatively different from speech in the observational mode, where no such calculation is presumed and, indeed, where it would undercut the efficacy of that mode were it to be so. Clearly, interviewees will vary in the extent to which they feel able to move from supplying "answers" produced within the professionalized conventions of overhearing to supplying answers which attempt a more direct communication with the audience. Private citizens questioned on matters of direct personal concern are far less likely than politicians to make such shifts, which can either be carried out as an implicit "tactical switch" or explicitly marked as a temporary and partial reconfiguration of the communicative relationship (as in phrases like "I'm sure many people listening to that question will want to ask . . . ").

The interview as a *method* for eliciting speech for documentary is not the same as the interview as a mode of discourse within the finished program. The relationship of the one with the other varies and with this go variations in the kinds of social relations obtaining between speakers and viewers. At one extreme, there is the use of fragments of interviewee utterance at several different points throughout a program, with no indication of the kind of questions used to prompt such talk and little sense of the context in which the talk was produced (no sense at all in the case of speech being used entirely as voice-over). At the other, there is the presentation of the interview itself as a social episode within the documentary, involving an initial encounter (perhaps an exchange of greetings) between interviewer and interviewee and a full depiction of the setting and circumstances within which subsequent talk takes place.[10] This latter mode of presentation moves towards a modified form of "observationalism" although, unlike the kinds of production in that mode discussed above, it is one in which what the viewer is invited to observe is essentially a "television event" (the status of which is grounded in the visible presence of the presenter) rather than extratelevisual reality. However naturalistically such an interview may be depicted (location settings, continuity of action, markers of the passage of time etc.) the question of television's intervention exerting a modifying effect on behavior (including speech) does not arise at all. It has no grounds for doing so, given that the action is television initiated from the start and there is little or no behavior depicted which has its immediate motives *outside* of television's own requirements.

It is interesting to consider what alternatives exist to the duality of the interview as public speaking organized as private exchange. Two options present themselves immediately. First of all, a reporter could simply give an account of what people had said. This would deny visual depiction to those whose speech was used, present difficulties of communicative organization (for instance, judging the length of such accounts that viewers would find it acceptable to listen to) and pose questions not only about the accuracy of reported speech summary but, if citation of direct speech were used, about the accuracy of this to the original utterances (the pauses, the stressing, the cadences, etc.). It would also radically, and perhaps catastrophically, reduce the evidentiary status of the material. Alternatively, the interviewee could be invited directly to address the camera and the viewer rather than to the interviewer. But this option runs into two problems. First of all, "ordinary" interviewees usually have no *specific* communicative project other than their willingness to answer questions about their experiences or views. In this sense, their utterance is "dependent speech" and its obvious and most appropriate form is an answer to the person who asked the question. Secondly, the delivery of speech to a camera lens requires an interviewee to have an ease and competence in a kind of professional public address which would frequently be found wanting. This could serve only to reduce the effectiveness of what was said and, in most cases, it would act as a considerable constraint on the interviewee's expressive opportunities. So the "duality" of the interview, together with its semi-fraudulent aesthetics, is likely to remain a central feature of documentary language and thereby an indispensible element of public communication.

This allowed, the precise form of the conduct and representation of interview sequences has been the focus of recent development. For instance, the visualization of interviews raises a number of pressing questions about *personal* depiction in documentary. Among these are questions about the communicative status of interviewees within the documentary as a whole, the settings in which they speak and the way in which they are established and shot as speakers within these settings.

In strongly presenter-led programs, interviewees can be heavily subordinated to the exposition, appearing merely to lend eye witness or brief experiential corroboration to an account fashioned essentially from other information sources. Such programs sometimes give the impression of simply "appropriating" the speech of the interviewee for a project grounded elsewhere, a project of which the interviewee is unaware. Given the scale of revision to which treatments are sometimes subjected in post-production, it is not hard to see why interviewees are occasionally surprised and angry to find themselves speaking on screen within the framing terms of a topic or subtopic other than that which they had been invited to believe provided the grounds for their interview. It is important for the public integrity of the form that documentary makers do not routinely become agents of interviewee interests (an impossible task anyway, given the various directions these might take within any one documentary). However, the emergence of "access documentaries," in which the expression of ordinary and often marginalized experience becomes the primary directorial goal, has considerably developed the aesthetics of interviewee portrayal (for instance, in respect of settings, compositions and forms of editing) and, at the same time, "access" approaches have tried to be more open about the social relations of the interview method. Such films frequently feature a sequence of caption-identified interviewees right at the start, establishing them as central within the structure and aims of the piece.[11] Depending on the subject of their speech, a reinforcement of their status is achieved through allowing what would, by convention, be regarded as "extended" periods of talk, with opportunities for self-correction, repetition and the exercising of a local control over the direction of the topic not normally extended in mainstream shooting and post-production practice. Moreover, the visual framing of the speaking itself often works "with" rather than "upon" what is said, eschewing that kind of objectifying surveillance of the face, tightening up around emotional display and "meaningful" cutaways (nervous hands, awkward posture) which are to be found in many mainstream productions.

It is likely that some aspects of this kind of more supportive representation of accessed speakers will become assimilated into a broader range of output. As I remarked earlier, however, it would clearly be a mistake to suppose that the public project of documentary is best served by privileging accessees over any sense of the independent integrity of the topic or of responsibilities to the viewer.

In my scheme of documentary transformation, I referred to the way in which the use of interviews within the structure of a program can vary considerably, even given the same practice at the time of preparation and shooting. The edited interview can be used in its entirety at one place in the program or it can be divided into a number of sequences, even down to one-phrase units, placed at different points according to the logic of exposition being followed. The more it is used in dispersed form, the less opportunity there is for what is said to achieve a significance which is informed by the *terms of the interviewee* and the more likely it is that interviewees will regard their final "performances" as, intentionally or otherwise, to be taken "out of context." However, preserving the integrity of interview-as-method in interview-as-screened, by eschewing "slicing" and only using an interviewee once, dictates a logic of structure in which the sequential treatment of multiple themes, or the development of a chronology of events across a number of witnesses, is seriously restricted in its portrayal. Subordination of interviewees to program logics is a continuing requirement in documentaries other than those in which "access" is the principal communicative goal. Even here, of course, subordination may well occur.

Dramatization

"Dramatization" is a level of nearly all documentary production in the sense that it is a consequence of that "enabling fiction" referred to above, by which things appear to be occurring naturally in front of the camera and unaware of its presence. Within this routine dramatization, there occurs what the documentary scholar Bill Nichols has called "virtual performance" (Nichols, 1991, p. 122), as people play themselves before the cameras with greater or lesser degrees of motivated adjustment. However, the idea of "dramatization" is most often associated with programs in which the generic conventions of documentary *exposition* are put in some combination with those of dramatic *narrative*. Although there are now a number of "recipes" for drama-doc combination established on both sides of the Atlantic, it is useful to distinguish between those which give primacy to a documentary base, which then receives a dramatic realization (dramatized documentaries), and those which are primarily playscripts, receiving a treatment drawing variously on documentary's depictive conventions and the viewing relations associated with these (documentary dramas).

The latter became the center of much academic and public debate in Britain during the 1960s and 1970s, when a number of politically radical writers and directors were involved in different kinds of realist drama production, all of which projected politically and socially controversial themes. Given the general adoption, in this work, of a "heightened naturalism" of shooting style, acting and scripting, together with frequent imitation of newsreel and *vérité*-style sequences, the precise nature of the truth claims being made in the dramas was turned into an issue by politicians and by some television critics.[12] Since the content of most programs was left-wing in general orientation, there was inevitably a certain amount of disingenuousness about Conservative complaints that it was primarily the *form* of such productions which was unacceptable.

At the center of such complaints was the charge that drama-doc mixes were likely to lead to confusion among the audience about precisely what they were watching. Anxiety about this was the reason given for the Government banning Peter Watkin's BBC drama-doc about nuclear disaster, *The War Game*, in 1966, although concern about the likely impact of the program on "deterrence policy" seems to have been more decisive. It is also the case that many of the programs which were found so controversial either concerned historical events (a notable instance was the *Days of Hope* series of films about working class experience, directed by Ken Loach, scripted by Jim Allen, and first broadcast by the BBC in 1975) or involved the portrayal of quite intimate ongoing action and speech between characters (as in the "classic" Loach/Sandford *Cathy Come Home*, 1966). It's hard to see fundamental confusion as a real risk here. Certainly, a "playing" with established conventions, pointing up the inadequacies of sharp generic distinction, was generally part of production aims. This was designed to rub up against audience expectations and to generate a fresh kind of response. But for viewers to believe that they were watching actuality footage of Great War trench conversations or contemporary marital argument would have required a quite astonishing naivety about what television documentary can do. However, an uncertainty about the *extent* to which what was depicted was "based on fact" is more understandable and more likely. In the case of *Cathy*, for instance, just how far one particular real incident had been the model for the script (in other words, whether there was a "real Cathy") seemed to be a matter of concern and confusion for a number of viewers at the time and continues to be an issue with student audiences today, despite the explicitness of the closing captions.

While, as I have noted, it was precisely part of the whole project to call into question the neatness of the convention that fiction was "false" and documentary "true," the tactic of mixing depictive conventions to produce an account indeterminate in its specific referentiality is one which still produces public argument and is by no means settled by pointing to the inadequacies of conventional categorization. Many drama-based productions used documentary-style presentation in order not only to put the socioaesthetic conventions of television under stress but also to get the double benefit of documentary credibility and creative license. For unlike mainstream documentary, documentary-drama operated with a playwright's freedom to construct characters, dialogue and action precisely as wished, and then placed these within a strongly developed context of historical or contemporary realities, sometimes including the portrayal of real (and "famous") people.

The move in the other direction, towards the dramatization of material initially researched within the documentary frame (and often in documentary departments), has a long history in television, being one of the methods used when the lack of lightweight equipment made access to certain kinds of location impossible for orthodox documentary representation.[13] There are considerable variations in the means and models adopted for dramatizing the documentary "core" material, which is often of a kind—papers, tape recordings, private interviews—not visible to the audience at all. But the overall style of such programs is generally very different from that of documentary drama. The claim to documentary credibility is based on the specific referentiality which the script, via research, has to actually occurring events (a claim whose strength may vary from program to program) and so there is no need for the producers to go for a documentary "likeness" in the manner of portrayal itself. Indeed, in some recent examples in Britain [Lockerbie (Granada 1990) about the PanAm/Lockerbie disaster, and Valdez (BBC 1991) about the Alaskan oil spill] the international thriller and the disaster movie have provided the stylistic model.

It is interesting that "based on fact" films continue to be a major genre in cinema but they do not arouse anything like the heated debate which has followed many drama-documentary programs (of both kinds discussed above) on television. This is partly due to the particular, public character of the "truth ethics" of television, and the way in which both dramatized documentaries and documentary dramas play off the strong presence in television schedules of mainstream documentary output. In the cinema, the public anticipates a film which is primarily concerned with delivering a form of dramatic entertainment, whatever historical referentiality it also wishes to claim. Therefore even when questions of accuracy arise in public discussion [as for instance in relation to J.F.K. (1991) or Malcolm X (1993)], they generally do so in a climate which shows considerably more tolerance towards the film maker's license in the context of a fully commercial entertainment industry.

The types of research and documentation upon which drama-documentary forms are based continue to be a point of development in contemporary television, as do the different possibilities of dramatic form which are employed in turning the result into screen narrative. The various approaches to documentation and depiction also continue to present research with a key intersection point of different television practices and kinds of realism. Drama-documentary is now to be found as a part of programs using other conventions. In Britain, the United States and Europe, dramatic reconstruction has been assimilated within many different genres to become an accepted, if still sometimes controversial, component of public television.

Mise-en-scène

The term *mise-en-scène* is taken from the critical language of fictional cinema (and before that, of theatre), but it has always been useful for the analysis of work in documentary and is particularly relevant to recent developments in television. In cinematic criticism, it means "putting into shot" and describes the way in which a director organizes the composition of a scene and the placing of people, action and props within it. Although the expressive opportunities for non-fiction directors have often been more limited than for their counterparts in feature film making—a matter of budgets and production time as well as of generic convention (the relatively narrow circumscription of documentary discourse in relation to "topic" as opposed to the expansive possibilities of "story")—*mise-en-scène* points to an important dimension of documentary assembly. In the self-consciously experimental films of the 1930s, realist settings were often combined with more symbolic renderings of place and space [the depiction of the mining village and its surrounding landscape in *Coalface* (1935) would be a good example, while Humphrey Jennings's wartime classic *Listen to Britain* (1942) works from a base in realist representation to make emblematic certain parts of wartime Britain, particularly the buildings of London].

The emergence, and then the dominance, of the journalistic in television documentary depiction had consequences for visual treatments. It encouraged containment of the range of visualizations within the terms of the literal and the naturalistic. Often, the visualization of setting offered no more than a framing for inquiry, for interview, for observed social action. There has always been a place (often under the aegis of "arts" output) for documentaries taking a more indirect route to their subject, allowing the play of associations and giving visual depiction (sometimes accompanied by music) a dominant communicative function, but this place has often been marginal. The work of Denis Mitchell for the BBC and Granada is notable here [particularly in prize-winning films like *Morning in the Streets* (BBC 1959), about aspects of working-class life in the inner cities of Manchester and Liverpool].

Recently, this established television tendency towards a "literalization" of the documentary image, the visual rendering kept flat and spare, consonant with the terms of an observed, objectified and mundane social reality, has given way to the emergence of much more symbolically dense ways of rendering place and action, and relating them both to the human subjects of the documentary and to the development of topic. This shift, observable across a range of programs, is one which seems to have been largely prompted by the influence upon documentary production of other generic forms, many of which have themselves undergone quite radical shifts in depictive mode. The newer approaches to visualization in television advertising (for instance, towards the appeal of the "strange" and the "bizarre") and the range of image types explored by pop video are two of the most obvious sources of a rethought documentary *mise-en-scène*, although behind both of these are shifts in the set design, lighting and visual styling of mainstream cinema. These influences continue to work their way into the production of the documentary image in a number of different ways, as part of a more general process of inter-generic blurrings, borrowings and adaptations within television. One of the most significant changes, first of all to be found in the work of small independent companies but now observable more generally, has been the use of a lighting style and mode of composition which produces what I think can best be called an effect of "hallucinatory realism" or "displaced realism." The image is still firmly referential in its depiction, nor is there any rearranging of the pro-filmic to create supplementary non-referential effects. However, by "theatrical" lighting and a camera style which holds and explores the scene with a more obvious, confident control than is usual in documentary (e.g. crane shots, slow tracking shots, the visual marking of certain things as "significant") the setting is displaced from conventional referentiality and is (however lightly) "defamiliarized" in the direction of the fictional.

Sometimes the use of color filtering (particularly, the use of blue—widespread in television advertising) gives a further objectifying distance and coolness, a further suggestion of a level or dimension of artifice uncertainly placed between being somehow a property of the real itself and being a function of self-conscious depictive style. This may be the way in which a documentarism aware of post-modernist debate chooses to put its reality into inverted commas while remaining true to the physical contours of pro-filmic appearance. The result is often not so much a subversion of the normative, however, as a heightening of its interest. As I suggested, the newer, ironic styling of international television advertising and, behind this, certain shifts in the look and movement of feature film, seem to be factors in many of these revised practices of visualization.

A concern with developing a semi-detached aesthetic for documentary (one which is not directly subordinate to what it represents but which still grounds its project in the depiction and exposition of a referent) can also be noticed at work in interview sequences, a point already touched on. For instance, there has been a move, though not yet a pronounced one, towards placing the interviewee in "striking" or "provocative" settings, as long as these do not break entirely with realist plausibility.

A good example of this kind of shift away from the conventions of contextual literalism can be taken from the film *When the Dog Bites* (Penny Woolcock, Trade/Channel Four 1988), whose degree of commitment to the extension of documentary language was controversial when it was first shown. An unemployed man is interviewed in the local swimming bath, the camera portraying him with the water-line at midpoint in the frame, the submerged lower half of his body partly visible. The whole aesthetic of the shot is based upon this "split" depiction, together with the uneven and shifting light patterns caused by reflections from the water. The effect of such an approach is immediately to strengthen the visualized context of speech, though whether this is complementary to what is said or a detraction from it is open to dispute. The introduction of a more symbolically expansive approach to documentary depiction increases the visual appeal of work in the genre (in contrast, say, to the minimalism and visual banality of much *vérité*), at the same time as it risks a similar kind of "aesthetic displacement" to that which certain documentaries of the 1930s are sometimes accused of displaying. This is a displacement whereby the specific realities, ostensibly the subject of documentation, become secondary to the discursive effects generated from them.

It is interesting that at the same time as a more aesthetically ambitious, self-consciously stylized approach to documentary has been making progress in the British schedules, there has also been an attempt to revivify the appeal of the undermediated, or even of the apparently *un*mediated. This has taken the form of do-it-yourself documentaries (notably, the highly successful *Video Diaries* and *Teenage Diaries* series on BBC) and a number of experiments involving concealed cameras. The footage produced by such initiatives often sets a new standard for "raw" television (undercutting in this respect the increasingly familiar repertoire of *verité* observation). To continue with the culinary metaphor (see Levi-Strauss, 1970), it is tempting to see its appeal as being gained by contrast with (though perhaps, finally, in complement to) the newer forms of the "cooked" now available in documentary television.

Exposition

"Exposition" (description and commentary) in relation to a body of visualized evidence is what the vast majority of television documentaries provide. Frequently, this exposition takes the form of an inquiry, the conduct of which may be more or less explicit. I discussed earlier how, in programs made primarily or even exclusively in the observational mode, exposition is indirect, implicit and open both to uncertainties of intention and to considerable interpretative work by the viewer.

But even in the most "purist" of fly-on-the-wall documentaries, the imaged particularism of local action and behavior, however fascinating and "watchable" in itself, must be filtered upwards by the viewer to a more general level of significance, must be seen to "say" something about the *kind* of events and people being observed. Action must be connected to topic. This "saying" may, with varying emphasis, be attributed to the *intentions* of the program makers.[14] Production teams working on such films edit them according to criteria of relevance and significance in relation to their revelatory yield at this general level (as well as to their "watchability") however non-dogmatic and provisional such criteria might be.

In many British observational series, the focus for "implicit exposition" of this kind has been an institution (series titles have a strong tradition of making this very clear, e.g. *Sailor, Police, The Family, The Duty Men, Redbrick, Murder Squad*). Bound by its procedures to the depiction of present-tense action and able to use only those forms of logic, explanation and argumentation which arise plausibly from such depiction, the observational program can only work effectively where "top-down" classifications of this kind can be used to organize local meanings. As a form for the revelation of contemporary social process, this "weak exposition/strong evidence" format achieves optimum force and focus. But, of course, this is by no means the only type of communicative task which television documentary undertakes. It also requires to address topics (say, of an abstract or historical character) which cannot easily be particularized around present-tense action, or benefit from the constraints of space and time which provide observationalism with its density and power.

At the other extreme from the reticence of observational exposition is the continuous use of presenter voice-over to introduce, to describe and to connect parts of the account and perhaps to conclude it. This has been well-dubbed the "voice of God" mode and, although it was extensively used in documentary cinema from the 1930s onwards, it has been sparingly employed as a structuring device in contemporary television. Risking a negative reaction from a viewer willing to be told things but unwilling to be the subject of continuous expositional address, full commentary inevitably closes down the possibilities for the development of a visual exploration of the theme, since "under" its discourse there is a strong tendency for images to become merely illustrative and to be edited at a pace which does not allow room for the viewer to give much attention either to what they show or how they show it. The old cinema newsreels illustrate this tendency to what now seems an almost parodic degree.

One exception to the gradual shift away from commentary in television was the *World in Action* series, started on Granada television in 1962. From the start, the series made regular use of the commentary style. However, instead of those tones of authoritative knowing from which it was hard for the older style of commentary to escape, *World in Action* carried the clipped and urgent voice of a reporter, taking the viewer through a program structured entirely in terms of investigative immediacy and imminent revelation (sometimes one directly visualized, sometimes not).[15] The voice issued from "within" the inquiry (often using present-tense description) rather than from "above" it, and its use differed from that of earlier styles of commentary film in the interspersing of commentary with sequences of interview.

Although many documentarists today prefer, where possible, to have a revelatory rather than a descriptive structure to their accounts, the use of commentary voice at points within a program is still indispensable for providing the viewer with certain kinds of information and explanatory background and for linking between sequences. By convention, the journalistic account (unlike the more indirect kinds of documentary exploration) often requires a summary and a reportorial assessment at the end. Here, the viewer is presented, if not usually with hard conclusions, then with pointers to what factors are important in *coming* to a conclusion. This kind of rational, argumentational work is best suited to direct speech, either in voice-over or camera address.

I looked, earlier, at the function of interviews in documentary discourse and noted both their variety and widespread use in television. Interviews are another way of organizing exposition as well as being a component of it. The "string-of-interviews" model is now more prevalent in television than the commentary-over-film model and just as common as the varieties of observationalism. A structure based on interviews produces a looser, more dispersed logic of development than either the focused particularity of observationalism or the highly defined, verbal order imposed on a documentary by a full commentary.

In documentaries seeking to develop a general theme primarily by a sequence of interviews, where there is some choice as to the interviewees used there is also frequently considerable effort put into selecting personable subjects, ones who will project engagingly to the viewer and who are able to give their responses in a way which will *seem* both authentic and coherent.

It is not uncommon in interview-based programs for one or more of the interviewees to take on the role of a "presenter substitute," being featured regularly in order to make key links and to offer voice-over commentary outside the confines of "personal experience," the primary category of knowledge which interviewees are used to develop. In several recent films, speaking subjects who might have conventionally been placed in the program as interviewees, have actually been shot in observational mode, delivering their accounts to groups. For instance, the Oscar-nominated 1992 film, *Liberators*, about the all-black U.S. Army units which fought in World War II, makes intercut use of a lecture to achieve expositional continuity. Such a method immediately allows a far more formal and explicit presentation than interview response and it also has the effect of "socializing" the spoken testimony outwards to include, rather than the mediating figure of an interviewer, an actual audience. An awkward duality between the speaking requirements of the occasion and the speaking requirements of the program may remain, however, making it difficult to classify the speech as being *simply* an address to a primary audience eavesdropped on by the camera crew. (The management of this kind of tension is now a routine element of political speech making.)

Within the various combinations of image and speech deployed in recent documentary exposition, *archive* material has frequently been given a major function in the overall design. This function has often been a dynamic one insofar as it has not been to set up an authoritatively visualized "then" over which the interpretative commentary of "now" can be offered, but to raise questions about both "then" and "now" by juxtaposition, often interrogating both the forms of official memory and the character of popular experience in relation to this.

An influential example of this *diacritical* use of archive material as a primary component of structure is to be found in Connie Field's much-discussed film, *The Life and Times of Rosie the Riveter* (1980).[16] Throughout *Rosie*, which concerns itself with the experience of women working in different sectors of U.S. industry during World War II, footage from old government propaganda material provides an intercut contrast with the testimony of selected interviewees, talking of their own working lives. The promotional excesses and insincerities of the archive material provide the film as a whole with a number of devices crucial to its structure. They give a contrast by which the women's testimony is enhanced as well as the means by which the film develops an edge of wit and critical humor and by which the more general questions of propaganda and of gender inequality are raised. The couplet of archive/testimony, in its varying degrees of non-alignment and contradiction, is used by the film as the means through which to develop a critical historical narrative.

A "light" form of dramatization is brought into the combination at one point, resituating the film's respondents back in the historical moment which was to be of such significance in determining the pattern of their lives over the next few years—the Japanese attack on Pearl Harbor. This sequence begins with the in-shot testimony of an interviewee who tells how, serving as a maid at the time, she was asked by her employer to come into a room and listen to an important news flash being broadcast on the radio. As the news broadcast begins on the soundtrack, the sequence moves to a clip from an old feature film in which a couple listen in on their bedside radio, cutting to other feature film and archive shots of various groups of people responding to the broadcast in their cars and in public spaces. As the soundtrack shifts to a recording of President Roosevelt's speech containing the declaration of war, all five women interviewees are depicted in a series of shots which places them, too, as "listening in." The sequence finishes with archive film of Roosevelt making his speech. The effect is to re-enact "then" within "now," a depictive interfusion of the two times and yet also a recognition and underlining of their separateness.

Such a mixing of modes in post-production produces an expositional system which is able to achieve a wide range of affective as well as cognitive effects. The inter-discursive use of archive materials (their use as other than unproblematic historical *reference*) was pioneered in independent cinema. For instance, the U.S. documentarist, Emile De Antonio, explored recent archive footage as a tool of critical documentary in his Vietnam film *In the Year of the Pig* (1969), where much of the visualization is constructed by the juxtaposition of archive clips, with their various soundtracks also providing a major contribution to the film's project.

I have already mentioned how "mixed" expositional structures have started to appear more frequently in the British schedules. A good case in point is the series *Disguises*, launched by Granada in 1993. The basic idea of this format was the use of hidden cameras as an aid to reporting areas of public controversy. The "core" footage, often taking up a small amount of the total program time, was the *vérité* material thus shot. Since *this* was taken without the knowledge of those in shot, it had a referentiality of an even stronger kind than that obtained in conventional *vérité:* that of the "poor image"—cramped, badly lit, lacking composition and consistent framing and often in unplanned motion, with accompanying actuality sound often so poor that speech has to be subtitled.

Around this point of innovation, another novel dimension was organized—that of reportorial disguise and reportorial participation. This was primarily a prerequisite for obtaining the clandestine shots, but it was also more. A reworked version of the reportorial quest became the principal narrative of each program, a quest in which "becoming disguised," "being disguised" and sometimes "removing disguise" became episodes of marked journalistic self-dramatization, playing knowingly with the idea of uncertainty and risk as well as with the pleasures of "dressing up," "pretence" and "spying."

However, the programs still required visualizing from conventional sources (location camera teams) in order to provide an expositional context within which the clandestine material could fit and make sense. With some variation as to topic, they also required the use of voice-over, to render the events depicted fully comprehensible; and direct presenter address, to get the personalized "out-of-role" alignment with the viewer upon which the thrills of "in-role" disguise partly depended. In some cases, interview material was also used. In its combined expositional form, *Disguises* seemed in many ways to be very much a product of its times. It went for a new form of "revelatory" account, a new form of documentation (inescapably action-based in its focus) and for a new kind of documentary appeal, a new "buzz" for the viewer, drawing extensively on the fly-on-the-wall tradition and a kind of theatricalized reporting owing something to current styles in "features" (as seen in the newer youth programs as well as in a range of special interest formats being applied, for instance, to cooking, travel and motoring series).

My own judgment is that the *Disguises* mix was pushed too far in the entertainment direction and that the informational yield of the hidden camera material was often insufficient to justify the elaborate setting up of disguised behavior. This produced a discordance between aims and means which sometimes showed itself as uncertainty of tone in the reporting itself. But the series is best seen as indicative of some of the elements at work in what is only the "first wave" of a broad and diverse movement towards rethinking the terms of television documentary. I suggested that this trend draws on a new intergeneric awareness, but in Britain it is also directly determined by the need for documentary to reconsider its relationship with audiences under the conditions of extended channel choice and increased competition for revenue and funding.

Contested Optics: The Disputability of Documentary Form

At the start of this chapter I discussed how documentary had its origins in ideas about progressive citizenship in industrial society. Some of these ideas were democratic and critical of an older order of informational inequality and political control. But the "solution" which documentary offered to the problem of the limited availability of public knowledge and the increasing commercialization of the press was itself shot through with authoritarian strands. Not for the first time nor the last, ostensibly democratic initiatives became less straightforward when it came to their implementation and the selection of means. It is also the case that pioneer documentarists, not unlike many contemporary broadcasters in this respect, had to keep their work within certain "givens" compatible with regular and adequate funding.

However, as I noted, most of television documentary's accounts are institutionalized as "public" by their proximity to the publicly accountable activity of journalism. In many countries, this is further underwritten by their production as part of a broadly "public service" dimension to the national television system. It is clear that this latter context is now rapidly changing towards one in which market factors will identify viewers more strongly as "consumers" (even allowing for the necessary, minimum "public" status which journalism has usually to claim as a professional condition of its activity). Although the early 1990s has seen a remarkable amount of innovation in topics and treatments, the effects of these larger changes upon documentary television internationally may well turn out finally to be strongly negative.

The consequences for television documentary of having an institutionalized public identity have been both limiting and enabling. The limitations have followed from the relatively tight circumscription of documentary "impartiality" within a code of practice drawn up without much, if any, direct recognition of the contexts of political power and of economic inequality within which television operates. To that degree, documentary television (particularly in Britain) has always risked being over-polite, cautious and complacent while at the same time being celebratory about its own boldness. It has also risked a degree of patrician condescension in its tones, echoing in this respect some of the pioneer documentary films. The history of explicit and of covert interference in documentary production by government agencies as well as by national television managers suggests that such limitations, and the "climate" they characterize, are partly the product of effectively maintained parameters external to television itself.

The complementary strengths which "public" status has brought to documentary have resulted from the need to engage the popular audience and to develop an investigative integrity of evidence, and of precision and clarity in its analysis, by which to resist "official" pressures either during production or after screening. This has worked to give the best documentary teams and departments a discipline of thoughtful practice which has often served to trim stylistic self-indulgence as well as to restrain any moves towards an over-speculative use of data or the premature judgement of causality.

Both the limitations and strengths can be contrasted to the relative "freedoms" of the independent documentary movement in contemporary cinema, far stronger in the U.S.A. than in Britain. Here, given the circumstances of distribution and exhibition, formal innovation has not felt so tied to the requirements of market popularity. The result has been that a far richer, more complex and more self-consciously authored language of documentary has been developed, one often matching the density and "difficulty" of art cinema.[17] Along with this has gone freedom from the requirements of balance and impartiality, allowing film makers to develop expositions which have far more polemical edge and depth of critique. Self-identified as "interventions" in the public arena rather than as "commentaries" upon (mostly predefined) "issues," the films of independent documentary cinema have no obligation to be fair and they can therefore generate a calculated *un*-evenhandedness of treatment which some have seen as a necessary corrective to the economic, social and communicative inequalities which broadcasting tends to reproduce as much as it questions.

The reverse side of this opportunity is the increased danger not only of "preaching to the converted" (a matter as much of distribution as of form in the first instance) but of becoming "promotional" in a particular cause to the point of losing the self-critical controls of argument. If a belief in the routine professional availability of "objectivity" has been an obstacle in the development of an adequate level of self-reflection both in television documentary and in television news, the belief that "objectivity" is an entirely illusory quality has limited the force and relevance of much work from independent cinema, reinforcing the marginality of its social significance.

Across both television and cinema, two simple notions which can be useful to a discussion of documentary's controversiality are "openness" and "closure." In television, the origin of much documentary practice within the framework of current affairs journalism means that many programs are built around a spine of investigated circumstances presented as the factual basis for opinion and argument. This is "closed" insofar as most viewers are unlikely to have access to alternative information with which to challenge its account, even though they might entertain scepticism as to its reliability.

A routine exception to this occurs where a program concerns itself with a particular group of people, defined in terms of common characteristics such as socio-cultural background (for instance, London's Afro-Caribbean community, Liverpool Irish, first-year undergraduates), recreational interest (for instance, golfers, football supporters) or social problems (alcoholics, the homeless). The interpretations of the documentary fact-base made by people in the groups which form the subject of the program are then likely to be actively critical (even if finally positive) when compared with those of other members of the audience.

It would be very useful to know more about the judgments made by groups or individuals who have been the subject (and, in one sense, the object) of documentary representation. This would not entail a simple privileging of their accounts against those of the documentarist—after all, their own anxieties about portrayal and closeness to the topic may well produce a version of what is finally "fair" and "unfair" at least as skewed as a documentary account. Where professional groups (for instance, doctors, teachers, police) have publicly complained about their depiction, it is often clear, despite declarations to the contrary, that a highly selective and positive self-concept has been used as the criterion for their judgment. Documentary makers need a way of maintaining responsibility for their own accounts (not routinely ceding this to subject groups out of some misplaced notion of representational democracy) while at the same time dissuading their audience from taking this account as unproblematic. They need to retain sufficient "closure" on their material to present a clear and coherent exposition, underpinned by visual material, but sufficient "openness" to allow viewers to exercise a critical independence.

These basic questions about the *democratic character* of documentary discourse do not easily and directly correlate with particular forms. For instance, a commentary film, ostensibly a traditional closed form in which discursive management is direct and often continuous, can be constructed in such a way in relation to the various other voices it uses, and in its combination with visuals, as to present viewers with a thoughtful and questioning viewing experience. On the other hand, a fly-on-the-wall program, despite its apparent openness, can work with a very tightly managed sense of the significance of what is going on. This sense may have an implicit presence at every stage of the production process and be projected for "sharing" by the viewer without at any time being a matter of explicit address.

Although critics have often overestimated the gullibility of viewers in response to visualization, there is no doubt that one of the most effective means by which documentaries seek to naturalize their accounts, to remove them from the contingencies of their own production, is by the use of images to provide a level of self-evident support. This can have the effect of closing the account neatly down around its own selected data and classifications (e.g., "types" of people, "types" of problem, "types" of circumstance).

Documentary television does not have available to it the space for self-reflexivity which independent cinema frequently allows itself. But there are ways of hanging on to the primariness of theme while being more open about the extent to which this is a construct of the production agenda and chosen form (of voice-over, of interview, of the observational scene, of particular combinations of sound and image). Developing these ways is one of the most important requirements for any reimagining of television documentary as a civic enterprise.

"A good documentary stimulates discussion of its subject, not itself" (Nichols, 1991, p. x). In his invaluable discussion of documentary theory, Bill Nichols cites this remark of a director, probing at the issues it raises. Clearly, in one sense it is self-evidently true—a "good" documentary must always, by definition, have the primary aim of directing its viewers down its *referential axis* towards "real world" concerns. Yet, as we have seen, there is an *aesthetic axis* too—a documentary "poetics." This does not merely comprise a set of presentational skills; it is centrally implicated in the production of the referential, and can be admitted to be so without distracting from the latter's primacy.

We return again to the documentary pioneers of the 1930s, for whom the debates about "art" and "reportage," the tensions and the complementarities, were fundamental. I have suggested that their attempted resolutions of this debate in documentary practice were often characterized by a certain ambivalence, a degree of instability and, indeed, of uneasiness. Given the nature of what is involved communicatively and socially, it may very well be that these qualities will continue to be present in much of the most imaginative and most socially engaged work in documentary.

Notes

1. A good discussion of Grierson's ideas about the documentary genre, placed in their contemporary intellectual context, is contained in Aitkin (1990).
2. The opening sentence of "First Principles of Documentary" (1933), in Hardy (1979).
3. See, for instance, Miles and Smith (1987) and Aitkin (1990). The latter includes an extensive bibliography. Hillier and Lovell (1972) is still a valuable, pioneering study, with a good general account as well as perceptive commentary on individual films. In my own discussion of the "documentary movement" I have drawn on the wide range of articles now available on formal and social aspects of the work, though a major study of the films is still awaited.
4. Unpublished BBC memo, 29 October, "Television and the future of broadcasting." I am indebted to Elaine Bell for this quotation. See her essay "The Origin of British Television Documentary" in Corner (1991d, pp. 65–80).
5. Paddy Scannell is the major historian of British radio form. See his "The Stuff of Radio" in Corner (1986, pp. 1–26).
6. For a more detailed study of the emergence of documentary as a television genre, see John Corner, "Documentary Voices" in Corner (1991d, pp. 42–59).
7. Vaughan (1976) is illuminating on the origins of television work, while Goodwin et al. (1983) brings together a number of valuable items on drama-documentary forms.
8. In doing so, I draw on two extremely rich bodies of work on documentary, that of Dai Vaughan (see Vaughan, 1976, 1992) and that of Bill Nichols, whose theoretical study (1991) is a major text in documentary analysis, although it is concerned primarily with cinema.
9. Richard Collins discusses the question of "intervention" in *vérité*, at both shooting and editing stages, in his article "Seeing Is Believing" in Corner (1986, pp. 125–138).
10. Early instances of presenting the documentary interview as a social encounter are discussed in Corner (1991c).
11. One widely shown film which adopts this approach is Connie Field's *The Life and Times of Rosie the Riveter* (1980), referred to elsewhere in this chapter.
12. This debate about drama-documentary "naturalism" is well discussed in Goodwin et al. (1983) and in Paget (1990). Caughie (1980) explores the conventions of the "new" documentary-drama, making the distinction between it and dramatized documentary.
13. Elaine Bell's work on "Origins" (see note 4) discusses how early drama-doc was often a response to technical limitations. Nowadays, it is often a response to the limitations on access to certain kinds of institution and event.

14. For a study of how viewers variously attribute intentions to documentary material where such material present itself as "neutral," see Richardson and Corner (1986).

15. An assessment of the form of this series by a writer who was also a pioneer documentary director is given in Swallow (1966).

16. Nichols (1983) discusses this film in some detail, as an innovative mixture of interview and archive materials.

17. The range of independent cinema work in the U.S.A. is clear from the critical commentary of Nichols (1991).

References

Aitkin, I. (1990) *Film and Reform.* London: Routledge.

Caughie, J. (1980) "Progressive Television and Documentary Drama," *Screen* 21:3.

Corner, J. (ed.) (1986) *Documentary and the Mass Media.* London: Edward Arnold.

———. (1991c) "The Interview as Social Encounter," in Paddy Scannell (ed.) *Broadcast Talk.* London: Sage.

———. (ed.) (1991d) *Popular Television in Britain: Studies in Cultural History.* London: British Film Institute.

Goodwin, A. et al. (eds.) (1983) *Drama-documentary: B.F.I. Dossier 19.* London: British Film Institute.

Hardy, F. (ed.) (1979) *Grierson on Documentary.* London: Faber.

Hillier, J. and Lovell, A. (1972) *Studies in Documentary.* London: Secker and Warburg.

Levi-Strauss, C. (1970) *The Raw and the Cooked.* London: Cape.

Miles, P. and Smith, M. (1987) Chapter 6 of *Cinema, Literature and Society.* London: Croom Helm.

Nichols, B. (1983) "The Voice of Documentary," *Film Quarterly* 36:3, 17–30.

———. (1991) *Representing Reality.* Bloomington: Indiana University Press.

Paget, D. (1990) *True Stories? Documentary Drama on Radio, Screen and Stage.* Manchester: Manchester University Press.

Swallow, N. (1966) *Factual Television.* London: Focal Press.

Vaughan, D. (1976) *Television Documentary Usage.* London: British Film Institute.

———. (1992) "The Aesthetics of Ambiguity," in P. Crawford and D. Turton (eds.) *Film as Ethnography.* Manchester: Manchester University Press, pp. 99–115.

Part II

TELEVISION TEXTS

Many individuals, strong critics and outstanding scholars among them, quarrel with the reference to television as a "text." The term, they suggest, should be reserved for the printed word, for those forms of communication experienced most often by individuals encountering a specific artifact that is used privately, indeed, intimately.

As editor of a most influential book review, Charles McGrath is fully aware of these distinctions. The fact that he chooses to entitle his essay on television "The Triumph of the Prime-Time Novel" is no coincidence. McGrath finds in contemporary television not only the traits and characteristics of high literary art. He also suggests that much of television surpasses contemporary prose fiction in significant ways. And though he concentrates on the writing in those television programs, it is impossible to consider the value and power of the writing without acknowledging the visual component, the economic context, the technological production techniques, and the performances which surround and enrich those words.

But McGrath's work also suggests how far removed such a thoughtful critic can be from the large body of material now available in more systematic approaches to "television studies." McGrath's notice of the novelistic aspects of television, for example, is presented as a wide-eyed discovery, rather than recognition of a perspective common among television scholars and academic critics for more than twenty years. And his suggestions that it is "ironic" that "TV of late has . . . become much more of a writer's medium than either movies or Broadway" or that the fact that "the people who create and who produce most shows are also the people who write them" is "accidental" seem cheerfully unaware of many studies of the television industry (or of the structures of the industry itself). Still, his essay provides a provocative contrast to the (mostly) academic essays in this collection. Stylistically distinctive, it provides an excellent model of writing about television by a non-specialist.

Adrienne L. McLean's essay on *The X-Files* is equally provocative in other ways. Foregoing any specific, detailed analysis of the ongoing plots of this series, or of the huge and varied fan responses so often noted, she suggests that one aspect of the show's significance lies in more complicated relations to contemporary culture. Paralleling *X-Files* motifs and plots with Marshall McLuhan's "probes" of 20th century life, she suggests reconsiderations of the television program, of television itself, of McLuhan, and the social and cultural structures within which we experience all these matters. Citing concerns shared by *The X-Files* and McLuhan, concerns for "the decay of meaning in our lives," McLean suggests that both sources also urge us to create new meanings. Her essay, as provocative criticism, is a "probe" in exactly that direction.

Milly Buonanno's study of *Il Maresciallo Rocca*, an Italian police series, reminds us, however, that old meanings do exist, and that culturally resonant meanings still form the basis of much television. This essay illuminates numerous topics in television studies. It is particularly helpful in pointing out how countries that have long depended on imported fiction programs are now developing specific types of television to fill schedules. In this sense it is a valuable insight into the processes of international broadcasting strategies. In this regard it should be read in conjunction with James Hay's exploration of the Italian media landscape. Buonanno's discussion of the "sense of place" in *Il Maresciallo Rocca* is especially instructive in this comparison.

But it is also a strong genre study, pointing to the ways in which a particular program draws on and modifies characteristics developed in previous programs. It thus demonstrates how indigenous genre programming must draw on patterns of deep cultural experience to create distinctive content. As a result, the essay provides an excellent opportunity for readers in other social and cultural contexts to contrast and compare this program with police programs from their own traditions.

The title of Herman Gray's essay, "The Politics of Representation in Network Television," could be applied to an entire body of work within the field of television studies. Even though his study focuses on the representation of African Americans, the topic has been of central concern to many other television scholars. Gray's essay serves as a model for exploring that topic. He succinctly traces the history of representational practices as related to African Americans, he points to an especially significant "turning point" ("the Cosby moment") in that history, and goes on to outline three major discursive strategies of representation: assimilationist, pluralist, and multicultural. He concludes this chapter of a larger study by suggesting that:

> At their best, such representations [of African Americans] fully engage all aspects of African American life and, in the process, move cultural strug-

gles within television and media beyond limited and narrow questions of positive/negative images, role models and simple reversals to the politics of representation.

In some ways, then, this essay can be seen as an introduction to several that follow. Readers should decide whether or not this tripartite approach to representation can apply to other cases.

For example, Pat Kirkham and Beverley Skeggs examine the British comedy *Absolutely Fabulous* in part to "draw attention to" issues such as "mother/daughter relations, the relationship between female best friends, and comedy based on women's appearance, the body and aging." Here comparisons are available with Gray's approach to issues related to African American representations, but also with comedies from other broadcasting traditions. Readers may ask why *Roseanne* would wish to license the format of *Absolutely Fabulous* for an American adaptation—and ask why that program has not yet been made in the U.S. They may also wish to compare *AbFab* with *Cybill* as a site of many of the same issues.

Another comparison is possible with a turn to another social group, adolescents. Douglas Kellner finds in *Beavis and Butt-Head* the source of "complex media effects" that "crystallize the experiences and feelings of alienation and hopelessness produced by a disintegrating society. . . . " The representations offered in this controversial cartoon have been explored from multiple perspectives. Kellner's critique is one of the stronger readings, connecting the program to far larger patterns of social experience. As with a number of essays in this section, the more significant question may rise in Kellner's assertion that "[p]revious studies of media effects seem blind to the sort of complex effects of media culture texts" of the sort presented in his essay. The effects he cites depend upon the "use" of television, the transformation of a "media sensation" into a "new resource for pleasures, identities, and contestation."

América Rodriguez is also concerned with complex media effects, especially those created by a specific professional group within a specific ethnic context. Her topic is the news program *Noticiero Univisión*, the nightly national news as broadcast on Univision, the largest Spanish language television network in the U.S. Her conclusion that the program "symbolically denationalizes its intended audience of recent Latin American immigrants to the United States as it renationalizes them as U.S. Hispanics" rests not only on a "reading" of the content of this program, but more importantly on a detailed study of its production practices. This essay is a model of how to conduct this sort of production research (and indeed could have been included in Part I of this collection). The interview and observational techniques, combined with careful study of the content of news broadcasts, could be applied by readers to topics presented in local contexts, on campuses, and with media other than television.

The essays introduced to this point have focused primarily on the most conventional programs in prime-time television, fiction and news. The essays that follow explore other forms of television, forms that have increasingly

become central and significant in the programming strategies of broadcasting systems around the world.

Bernard Timberg's outline of the generic features of television talk shows
provides tools for analyzing what has become in recent years one of the most
discussed types of television programming. Talk shows have proliferated. But
as Timberg points out, most of the central features, the "rules" in these shows
remain very familiar, even formulaic. The most useful application of this essay
will be in both identifying the presence of these elements and in showing how
each program attempts to modify them in some specific manner. The modifications are crucial in successful applications of Timberg's Rule No. 4,
"Words = Dollars." Unless new talk shows can somehow distinguish themselves they have only the rarest chance of financial success, yet if they do away
with the rules altogether, they reduce those chances further. And since the
ubiquity of talk shows results in part from their economy—they are far
cheaper than other forms of television—this sort of creative conservatism is a
fundamental aspect of the "business" of TV.

Similarly, game shows have come to occupy many slots in television
schedules around the world. Again, a primary cause for this prevalence is the
economic advantage offered by the genre. But there are other appeals as well,
culturally and socially distinct appeals that can vary in national contexts.
Michael Skovmand's comparative study of *Wheel of Fortune* in four different
countries is a rare example of international comparative analysis of television.
Equally important, however, is the analysis of what such a program might
mean in the context of public service broadcasting as opposed to (or, indeed,
growing from) its presentation in a strictly commercial television system.

Ib Bondebjerg offers another international comparison, this time of
"reality programming." As with talk and game shows, and for many of the
same economic reasons, so-called "reality" shows have become staple broadcasting units. But as Bondebjerg's analysis makes clear, there are implications that exceed the economic in the use of this programming strategy. His
primary critical concern is with the blurring of boundaries: reality and fiction, public and private, public service broadcasting and commercial broadcasting. In another comparison with game and talk shows we should recognize that these "hybrid" realities are also still dependent on some degree
of distinction and differentiation. Is *COPS* more like or unlike *Rescue 911?*
Is either more like the news or a dramatization? Bondebjerg's analysis probes
the generic and, perhaps more significantly, the ethical implications of such
comparisons.

Talk, game, and reality programs have proliferated in the period following the end of strongly consolidated network television. Whether we
speak of the three commercial networks in the U.S., the restricted number
of BBC channels, or the single channel broadcasting systems of Israel and
some Nordic countries, we speak of an era now gone. The increasing number of channels has meant a scramble for programming. Dollars for programs have been stretched thin. Cheaper forms—talk, game, reality—have
emerged among other responses to the new delivery systems.

In such systems audiences are dispersed, familiar as migratory viewers armed with remote control devices. The point of Daniel Dayan and Elihu Katz's discussion of "media events" is that precious few television programs can attract the massive numbers of an earlier television era. Occasionally, however, television once again becomes the site of collective viewing. Occasionally an event so powerful that it drives out other forms of television occurs. The most recent media event of this magnitude was the death and funeral of Princess Diana. While that terrible occasion does not meet every defining criterion outlined in the Dayan and Katz essay, their analysis nevertheless characterizes elements of the televisual and audience response in precise detail.

For some users of this collection, the sense that television once nightly provided programs that attracted massive audiences will seem utterly strange. Contemporary experience is far more familiar with a fragmented schedule, with instant change to multiple channels, with programming straining to distinguish itself among the welter of offerings (as John Thornton Caldwell describes in "Excessive Style" in the final section of the book). Even in this context, however, it is possible to gain a critical perspective, to stand away from individual programs, from genres, from program schedules. The essays in this section offer multiple strategies and approaches for doing so. They should be applied and tested in varying contexts, with varying examples. From those applications and tests, users should develop their own critical systems.

The Triumph of the Prime-Time Novel

CHARLES McGRATH

New York City, perhaps more than any other place on earth, harbors large pockets of people who brag about being too busy to watch TV. Many of them are lying—at least a little. On average, 54.4 million Americans tune in every night, remember. Some of them are even card-carrying intellectuals who, if they haven't graduated yet to a 60-inch screen with wall projection and Dolby sound, nevertheless keep a little cable-ready Sony wedged up there in the bookcase, next to Rilke and Heidegger. If you're telling the truth, though—if you *really* haven't looked lately—you should give it another chance. You're missing out on something. TV is actually enjoying a sort of golden age—it has become a medium you can consistently rely on not just for distraction but for enlightenment.

I should quickly explain here that by TV I don't mean all TV, or even most of it. I don't mean the tabloid exposés of Sally, Ricki, Geraldo and the rest. I don't mean the sitcoms, which, with a few exceptions like "Home Improvement," seem increasingly devoted to the theme of dysfunction and to be stuck on the premise of cramming as many unlike people as possible into a single household. I don't mean the prime-time soaps, like "Melrose Place" and "Beverly Hills 90210," though I watch them faithfully.

And I especially don't mean highbrow TV like "Masterpiece Theater," with its attempts to translate three-decker Victorian novels onto the tube. As last season's "Martin Chuzzlewit" demonstrated—not to mention the disas-

---

trous "Middlemarch" of the season before—TV, no matter how well intentioned or generously budgeted, probably isn't capable of successfully dramatizing such large-scale literary creations, at least not in just a few hourly installments. In the case of "Chuzzlewit," great chunks of the plot fell out, and the characters, even one-dimensional types like Pecksniff, turned into caricatures of themselves; it was Dickens's illustrator, Cruikshank, rather than Dickens himself, who became the real inspiration for the series. George Eliot fared even worse. What disappeared in Andrew Davies's TV adaptation of "Middlemarch" was not just the usual "complexity" but politics (one of the big themes in the novel) and—astonishingly—sex. Rosamond became a simp, not a predator, and Casaubon was so desiccated in Patrick Malahide's characterization that his slimy reptilian side—the side that was interested in Dorothea for more than just her footnoting ability—was all but lost sight of.

The TV shows I have in mind are the weekly network dramatic series. These shows are flourishing in a way that they haven't since the very early days of the medium, and have grown in depth and sophistication into what might be thought of as a brand-new genre: call it the prime-time novel.

To watch network TV still requires a fair amount of patience. Even when you tune in to the best shows you have to endure the constant onslaught of commercial interruptions, and commercials, it has to be said, have not improved over the years. (It helps if you picked up the television habit back in your childhood, during those blissful, cartoon-saturated Saturday mornings spent in front of the old cathode-ray-tubed RCA, while your mother banged the vacuum around your feet and sighed about all the fresh air you · were missing—you learned how to tune out.) Yet for all its commercialism, network TV now is less under the thumb of the money men than either the movies or the Broadway theater, if only because with any given episode there's so much less at stake financially. TV, as a result, is frequently more daring and less formulaic than either the stage or the big screen, both of which have to make back huge investments very quickly. Television can afford to take chances, and often enough it does. And TV of late has, ironically, become much more of a writer's medium than either movies or Broadway, which are more and more preoccupied with delivering spectacle of one kind or another. (TV is more of a writer's medium than a lot of magazines, for that matter.)

This state of affairs has come about not through any great wisdom or cultural aspirations on the part of the executives who run the networks—these people have M.B.A.'s, after all, not degrees in comp lit. It has happened, rather, because of the very nature of the medium (spectacle doesn't show up well on the small screen, and it's too expensive anyway) and because of the almost accidental fact that the people who create and who produce most shows are also the people who write them, or else they're former writers. In any case, it's generally the writers, not the directors or the editors, who have the final cut. Think of what Hollywood would be like if the novelist Richard Price, say, got to tell Spike Lee what to do.

TV will never be better than reading, thank goodness. It's hard to imagine a tube, however small, that could approximate the convenience and portability—the companionability—of a book. And images and spoken words, no matter how eloquent, lack the suggestiveness, the invitation to something deeper, of words on a page. But on television these days, if you listen hard enough, you can often hear dialogue of writerly quality—dialogue, that is, that's good enough to be in a book. And there are ways in which TV has actually taken over some of the roles that books used to fill. A few of the more inventive TV series, for example, have become for our era the equivalent of the serial novel, unfolding epic stories installment by installment, and sweeping all of us up in shared anxiety and in a lot of group sighing and head shaking over what fate or (it's the same thing) the author has in store.

TV drama is also one of the few remaining art forms to continue the tradition of classic American realism, the realism of Dreiser and Hopper: the painstaking, almost literal examination of middle- and working-class lives in the conviction that truth resides less in ideas than in details closely observed. More than many novels, TV tells us how we live now.

Much of the TV drama I'm talking about—shows like "E.R.," "Chicago Hope," "Homicide: Life on the Streets," "N.Y.P.D. Blue," "Law and Order," "Picket Fences" and the lamentably canceled "My So-Called Life"—is rooted in the formulas set down in the earliest days of the medium: the cop show, for example, or the doc show. The first generation of great TV writers, the Gore Vidals and Paddy Chayefskys, consciously based their work on literary models, and on classical dramatic principles in particular. The current generation is no less literary ("Homicide"'s Henry Bromell used to write short stories for The New Yorker), but to a considerable extent the best new shows owe their form and content to nothing other than TV itself. You could make a case, I suppose, that the great innovation of contemporary TV—the device, first used by "Hill Street Blues" in 1981, of telling several stories at once—was inspired at least in part by Elmer Rice's 1929 play, "Street Scene," which simultaneously told the stories that unfolded in a single day in the life of several families living in a New York tenement. You could also argue, much more convincingly, that some of the better writing on the good shows now could never have happened without the example of novelists like Elmore Leonard and George V. Higgins. The real influence, however, is simply earlier cop and doc shows like "Naked City" and "Ben Casey," whose tricks the latest crop of writers have borrowed and whose formulas they've enriched and complicated. Many of these shows, in fact, work by combining several familiar TV genres: doc show plus soap opera, for example ("E.R."), or cops-and-robbers plus midlife-crisis comedy ("N.Y.P.D. Blue").

What's surprising is that by operating within the ancient conventions, and sometimes right at the very edges of them, these shows often manage a considerable degree of originality. And they frequently attain a kind of truthfulness, or social seriousness, that movies, in particular, seem to be shying away from these days. A TV executive I know is fond of pointing out that an issue-oriented film like "Silkwood" or "Norma Rae" could not be made today, that nobody would finance such a project; his implication is that people who care about radiation and about the labor movement are now working for TV instead of for Hollywood. In truth, TV might not make "Silkwood" or "Norma Rae" either, and yet in some series characters like Norma Rae and Karen Silkwood would not seem the least out of place.

Few shows have ever been as issue-oriented as "Law and Order" (NBC, Wednesday night). Its seriousness, in fact—its way of looking at contemporary issues from several sides at once—is what most recommends this program, which in other respects has an almost antediluvian quality. No jumpy, hand-held-camera shots, that is; no overlapping dialogue; no complicated ensemble plots. Each episode proceeds in a stately Aristotelian fashion, following the two-part formula invoked by the introductory voice-over: "In the criminal justice system, the people are represented by two separate yet equally important groups: the police, who investigate crime, and the district attorneys, who prosecute the offenders. These are their stories."

Apparently unburdened by personal lives, the detectives here (played by Jerry Orbach and Benjamin Bratt) wear nice suits and topcoats and drink their coffee out of mugs, not out of those Grecian-frieze paper cups that have become a signature detail on some of the hipper shows. And they go about their business in an efficient, bantering manner, an updated version of the style that prevailed on the old Jack Webb "Dragnet." The district attorneys, on the other hand (Jill Hennessy and a boyishly tousled Sam Waterston), quiver with conviction and with passion for justice, and have to be periodically brought to earth by an avuncular old counselor (Steven Hill).

What these characters (the lawyers especially) mostly do is talk. They talk about "perps" and victims and witnesses, naturally, but they also talk a lot about rights and about the system and about the urgent and sometimes unresolvable dilemmas that the writers send their way with such uncanny regularity. "Law and Order" depends on stories more than characters, and it's known in the industry for its speed in responding to real-life events and incorporating them into the show's plots; sometimes it takes as little as eight weeks for a script to be developed and to make its way onto the air. Last season alone there were stories involving abortion rights and affirmative action; a murder, very similar to a famous Westchester case, in which a young man, suffering an alcoholic blackout, killed two people he mistakenly took to be his parents, and the apprehension and conviction of a Katherine Ann Power-like fugitive (who, in a nice touch, was represented by William Kunstler himself, his shaggy gray locks streaming behind him and his glasses perched unslippably on that majestic furrowed dome). Still unresolved (though a solution has been promised this season) is a two-year-old murder case eerily reminiscent of the Malcolm X assassination. This one also includes characters modeled on Louis Farrakhan and Coretta Scott King. It has raised the specter of race riots in New York, and turns on the issue of a lone gunman versus a conspiracy of shooters. It has everything except the Michigan militia.

The very best of the TV dramas, however, aren't quite as earnest and explicit as "Law and Order" tends to be; they're informative in another, more subliminal way. For instance, if you watch enough "E.R.," the hit show set in the busy emergency ward of a Chicago hospital (NBC, Thursday night), you can, without even knowing it, learn a lot about medicine. I'd like to think that in a personnel shortage I could pitch right in. Let's say you were to come speeding down the corridor right now on a gurney (the show does great gurney shots, tracking the ceiling lights overhead and the dramatic moment when those swinging double doors pop open), and let's say you were "presenting" with, oh, an aluminum rod sticking through your chest, the way one poor guy was in an episode directed last season by Quentin Tarantino. From hours of watching, I know that the first thing to do is to get a "line"—an IV—into you and to order up a 125-milligram Solumedrol push. And let's have, what the heck, 5 of morphine. That should make you feel better right away. (The best way to install a line, by the way, is to use a No. 16 needle; pull the skin tight, so the veins don't roll, and go in slow.)

All right, let's type and crossmatch, let's get a blood gas, and I want chest film. Come on, let's move! I can't remember whether it's the McGill forceps or the Foley catheter I'm supposed to use to remove the bar, but I'm not going to worry about that right now, because I've got a little problem here. Your B.P. is 50 over 30 and, oops, the monitor is starting to beep. Better give me some "epi," *stat*, and—sorry, I forgot to do this earlier—I've got to tube you and bag you so we can clear a passage and force a little air into your lungs. Oh *no!* You're flat-lining! Clear, everybody, I'm going to use the paddles! O.K., let's try that again! I'm charging. Now . . . clear! *Whap!* Nothing? All right, all right—I'm going in! I'm just going to make a little incision here, and I'm going to spread a couple of ribs, and I'm going to massage your heart. Nothing to it—I do this all the time. . . .

Well, you get the idea. You'll be going home, by the way, in less than an hour. Though "E.R." follows the "Hill Street"-honed formula of overlapping several self-contained plots with one or more longer-running stories that take several weeks to unfold, it somehow manages a nearly opposite effect with time. Instead of slowing TV time down, as "Hill Street" did, and making it resemble novelistic time, a typical episode of "E.R." crams into 48 minutes so much incident and so many people that the effect is a kind of hyper-reality, an adrenaline rush. "E.R." has lots of compelling characters: Dr. Benton, the intense, dignified black surgeon who can cure everything, it seems, except his own inner hurt; Dr. Greene, the sensitive resident whose marriage is falling apart and whose career suddenly looked bleak after he botched a delivery; Dr. Ross, the womanizing pediatrician; Nurse Hathaway, troubled and depressed and for a while sneaking too many pills from the drug cabinet. But mostly we get to know them not, as on the old "St. Elsewhere"—which used to be *the* state-of-the art medical drama—by spending a lot of quality time, so to speak, hanging out with them, but, rather, by catching up with them in snatches as they race from one crisis to the next. The result, often, is a kind of intensity delivered on the run.

A small episode in last season's finale, involving an end-stage AIDS patient, his mother and his lover, and their letting him go, can't have taken up more than a few minutes of air time; yet in its brevity and directness, and in the honesty of its details, it was a more affecting evocation of the AIDS crisis than Jonathan Demme's overblown "Philadelphia," say. Its power came from the fact that this little moment happened in the middle of a lot of other moments—almost as in life. Similarly, a brief, silent stretch at the end of the botched-delivery episode, when Dr. Greene, exhausted, fighting tears, rides the El home in a cold winter dawn, achieved a remarkably understated eloquence. The show has a knack for dramatizing private moments—for sneaking up on them when both we and the characters are most worn down and vulnerable.

But the real reason for "E.R."'s success, I think, is that it recognizes that such private moments are so few and so hasty, and that most of us are overinvolved in an activity that has traditionally been given short shrift on TV, and in print and on the movie screen as well. I mean work, of course. In movies these days, if people have jobs at all it's in fields like architecture or publishing—professions, it would seem, that don't demand you do very much. In contemporary American novels, what people mostly do, besides sort out their relationships, is write or teach. Not the least of the qualities recommending Richard Ford's new novel, "Independence Day," is that, for a change, the protagonist actually goes to the office every day and toils at an ordinary middle-class desk job—or desk-and-car job. (He's a real-estate agent.)

Work, along with class, has somehow become an overlooked little secret in a lot of American art, popular or high, something to be avoided or ignored. Robert Benton's "Nobody's Fool" is one of the few recent Hollywood movies with a working-class theme, and though it was in many ways a careful and thoughtful effort, by casting Paul Newman as the story's hero, a hard-drinking underemployed construction worker, it inevitably invested blue-collar life with a sheen of glamour. Newman's work clothes looked like something he had ordered from the Land's End catalogue.

TV sitcoms like "Roseanne" and "Married With Children" have lately embraced both work and class, offering us a raucous, newly liberated view of blue-collar family life. But shows like "E.R." have gone one step further. They've remembered that for a lot of us work is where we live most of the time; that, like it or not, our job relationships are often as intimate as our family relationships, and that work is often where we invest most of our emotional energy. Even if we don't work in hospitals or in station houses, we can recognize these TV workplaces as being very similar to our own— with their annoyances and reassuring rituals, crises and the endless time between filled with talk of everything and nothing.

The workplace where I've found myself most at home lately—after my day job, that is—is the 15th Precinct, the home of "N.Y.P.D. Blue," the Emmy winner created by Steven Bochco and David Milch, who also worked together on "Hill Street Blues." (Bochco, now the chief guru of TV drama, has to his own credit such ground-breaking shows as "Doogie Howser, M.D." and "L.A. Law," not to mention the short-lived turkey "Bay City

Blues" and the unspeakable "Cop Rock.") "N.Y.P.D. Blue" (ABC, Tuesday night) is filmed almost entirely in Hollywood, but by using some well-
chosen New York City exteriors and just a few station-house sets—a poorly
lighted stairwell, a squad room, a room where suspects are interviewed and
a dingy men's room (where many of the most intimate and revealing scenes
take place)—the show has managed to evoke the authentic look and feel of
New York and its police force.

"N.Y.P.D. Blue" is full of cases, many of them based on the recollec-
tions of Bill Clark, a retired New York City detective who works as a consultant on the program and has also collaborated with Milch on a book
about the series' beginnings. The show has perfected the old "Hill Street"
formula of braiding into one 48-minute installment one or two self-
contained subplots and a longer story that may take several episodes to
unfold, so that the viewer is simultaneously satisfied and left hanging. In
any given week the show overflows with narrative—stories about "skels,"
"mungo guys," junkies, rapists and thieves, and about the private lives of
the cops who pursue them.

It is not plot, however, that drives the show as much as it is characters,
in particular Andy Sipowicz, the bald, thick-chested, volatile but repressed
detective who, in Dennis Franz's masterly portrayal, has invested both the
wisecrack and the slow burn with a rare kind of eloquence. Franz, it should
be noted, is not exactly breaking new ground here: this is the 27th time he
has played a cop. According to Milch, everyone on the set marvels at how little he needs to prepare for his scenes, how he never has to think about them.
Effortlessness, or the appearance of effortlessness, is actually a hallmark of the
best TV acting, as opposed to movie acting, in which so often we're meant
to see (or, at any rate, are never allowed to forget) the personality of the actor
underneath the role. Think of Meryl Streep in just about any of her pictures
or, at another extreme, Bruce Willis in just about any of his. Franz *is* Sipowicz, and the difference is that TV allows him to inhabit the role in ways that
the big screen would not—in dozens and dozens of small moments, for example, and by reacting to other characters as well as by being the focus of a scene.
Sometimes, for minutes on end, all he does is *listen*—in anger or disbelief or
with enormous weariness. The difference, in its way, is as great as the difference between screen acting and stage acting.

Over the last two years, I've come to think of Andy almost as a friend—
someone I know nearly as well as the people I actually work with, somebody I can count on. But his character's centrality hasn't always been so
clear. In the first season it was Sipowicz's sidekick, John Kelly, the straight-
shooting heartthrob played by the orange-haired David Caruso, who commanded most of the attention. And when, at the end of that year, Caruso
and the producers parted over a contract dispute, a lot of viewers feared
that the show's chemistry would be irreparably altered.

From Milch's book, "True Blue: The Real Stories Behind N.Y.P.D.
Blue," it emerges that, in fact, he, Bochco and virtually everyone in the cast
were glad to be rid of Caruso, who had become a prima donna. It also turns

out that Jimmy Smits, who replaced Caruso, had been Bochco's first choice all along. In any event, we needn't have worried, though the show cleverly toyed with our anxieties by incorporating them into the plot of last season's premiere: Sipowicz immediately began to protest to Lieutenant Fancy, the boss of the 15th, that he and his new partner would never get along. "Don't get me started," he says at one point, explaining what's wrong with the new guy. "It's a whole attitude. 'How you doin'?'—this type of thing."

The matter began to be resolved in a conversation about pets, of all things—one of those dialogues that "N.Y.P.D. Blue" does with such ease and confidence, in which the writers seem, without stepping out of character, to be winking slightly at the viewer, as if to say, "Don't miss this!" Sipowicz's new partner, Detective Bobby Simone (Smits), whom we have discovered to be the sensitive-loner type, talks about his racing pigeons and their ability to find their way home across long distances. Sipowicz, who raises tropical fish, says: "I got a clown-fish couple just had eggs. In the morning while I'm having coffee, that male cleans each egg with his mouth. He never breaks one. The whole day while I'm working, him and his wife guard that nest and fan water over their eggs." He pauses and looks at Simone. "Those are dedicated fish. You see that kind of thing in pigeons?"

What makes Sipowicz so affecting—and so funny—is not just his lumbering dignity but the fact that we have seen him change. Down a long corridor of Tuesday nights, we've watched him struggle with the bottle, with rage (especially in cases involving children) and with his own barely concealed racism and homophobia. We've seen him make peace with his estranged son, and we've seen him, with agonizing slowness and one terrifying drunken slip-up, fall in love with, move in with, and even propose to and marry, Sylvia Costas, the long-suffering assistant district attorney whom he insulted in the show's very first episode after she failed to convict a mobster he had arrested and then implied that the problem, in part, was that Sipowicz had lied on the stand. (When she upbraids him, his response is to grab his crotch.)

And it's not just Sipowicz who changes, of course. Detective Medavoy, a bundle of nerdish anxieties, becomes, after an uncharacteristic moment of boldness, more and more silent, flushed and awkwardly neurotic, and eventually blows his romance with the sultry but bighearted station-house receptionist, Miss Abandando. Detective Martinez, the young rookie, screws up his courage over an entire season and is eventually rewarded by getting a date with Detective Lesniak. Lieutenant Fancy and his younger brother, who are black, quarrel and then reconcile over the issue of how best to get along in a police force run by white folks.

All these alterations, some great, some small, happen incrementally, over weeks of episodes—the way such things happen in life, and not the way they typically happen in movies, for example, or even in books. To think of a character in recent American fiction who actually evolves this way—who ages and changes before our eyes—you may have to go back to Harry Angstrom, in Updike's "Rabbit" novels. In so many contemporary books, you get just a few days or weeks in the lives of the characters, or a year or two at most. There isn't room enough for a whole lot to happen.

Milch, who as an undergraduate at Yale studied writing with Robert Penn Warren, has said on several occasions that Warren's greatest lesson was that the secret subject of any story is what we learn, or fail to learn, over time. And it's time—hours and hours of it, stretched out over a 22-week season—that is both the great advantage of "N.Y.P.D. Blue" (compared with the two or three hours at most that are available to plays or to movies) and its great discovery. The show uses time the way serial novels used to, incorporating the intervals between installments, and the tension between what we've learned and what we fear or hope, into the experience of the story itself.

I had several morning-after conversations last year with a friend of mine, another faithful viewer, about whether or not Simone's new girlfriend, Detective Russell, was a secret alcoholic—discussions not dissimilar, I imagine, to the ones serial readers must have had in 1841 while they waited for the news about what had happened to Dickens's Little Nell.

The first time they met, didn't she have a wine cooler with lunch?

Yes, but if she were a man would you have even noticed? Why can't a woman have a drink on TV without everyone's suspecting something?

All right, then why is she always going into the bathroom and locking the door? Answer that. *Sipowicz* thinks she has a problem.

Sipowicz is in A.A., remember? People in A.A think everybody is a drunk.

Like most people—like Bobby Simone himself, in fact—I guessed the truth a week or two before I knew it for certain, and the slow unraveling only served to heighten the poignancy.

The other trick "N.Y.P.D. Blue" may have learned from the serial novel, and from Dickens in particular, is that lesser characters can sometimes claim center stage without necessarily taking on new attributes. They can do it, in fact, by simply becoming truer to their limited natures, as happened last season with Medavoy and Abandando, who, as Milch says, took even the writers by surprise. Nobody was prepared for this unlikely romance, or for how low the self-immolating Medavoy would eventually sink. "N.Y.P.D. Blue" has erased some of the traditional boundaries between subplot and main plot—the show is all one big plot that takes weeks and weeks to resolve—but it has also learned how to play characters who change against those who cannot. It has learned, in fact, a great Dickensian lesson: it is in the nature of adversity to turn most of us into caricatures.

"E.R." and "N.Y.P.D. Blue" are still TV shows, to be sure. People occasionally die on "E.R.," but more often they get better; in any case, few suffer much. The wards are always humming, the nurses and orderlies cheerful and polite. Nobody is seen paying a bill, or even filling out an insurance form, for that matter. And the cases on "N.Y.P.D. Blue" are almost always "cleared," as the cops say, and most often not by means of tedious, time-consuming legwork but, rather, by the much more efficient expedient of picking up a couple of skels and then playing good cop-bad cop with them until they break down and confess. I've never seen anybody on this show exercise his constitutional right and clam up until he can consult a lawyer. It almost goes without saying that neither "E.R." nor "N.Y.P.D. Blue," for all their daring in other ways ("N.Y.P.D.," in particular, has repeatedly pushed the network censors way over the usual line when it comes to language and nudity), has dramatized one of the most basic and elemental acts of private life in America—namely, TV watching itself. Except for Sipowicz (who shoots the tube out one night in a drunken rage), nobody on these shows seems to even own a television set; I've never seen a character looking at one, not even the poor sick kids, bored silly, in the "E.R." children's ward. (They have to make do with Gameboys instead.)

The only way TV makes its presence known in these prime-time dramas is in the form of newspeople pushing their way into the station-house lobby or clamoring, vulturelike, outside the emergency-room entrance; in all of these confrontations, the camera is always seen as an antagonist, a disrupter of business and a falsifier of truth. In one episode of "Homicide: Life on the Street"—the innovative cop drama that the film director Barry Levinson is the co-producer of—the show's writers even experimented with the device of having obnoxious newscasters, with hand-held cameras, seem to waylay the characters with pointless questions between scenes.

The failure of TV drama to take itself into account is one of the great oddities of the medium. It's only on the comedies like "Roseanne" that the characters regularly do what the rest of us do: come home, give a quick wave to the spouse and the kids and then grab the newspaper to see what's on that night.

The most realistic TV family of all, of course, is Homer and Marge and the gang: the Simpsons, who not only put in hours in front of the tube, while pizza crusts and spent soda and beer cans mount up around them, but have formed most of their ideas about the world from what they see on television. TV may, in fact, be all that holds the Simpson family together.

Watching television is in many ways a private, solitary activity—almost like reading. But watching television is also what we do as a nation; millions and millions of us tune in together, like Homer and Marge, at the same time, to the same shows. Television is something, maybe the only thing, that all of us have in common. In my own case, I was never so grateful for TV as when, during a period in my life not long ago, I was working at a job that required me to spend 12 or 14 hours a day reading, or else talking to people about what they had written. By the time I got home, cranky and bleary-eyed, my wife and children were often asleep, but my faithful companion in the den never failed to brighten at my arrival. It gave me the news and the scores, sang all the new songs to me and generally kept me abreast of all the life I was missing. Most of all it told me stories. When I went back to work the next day I had something to talk about—how Andy was doing, whether Doc Greene and his wife would get back together—and I felt connected.

It's tempting to imagine a time when TV, which is one of the things routinely blamed for the breakup of the American family, could bring us all together again, the way it did a few years ago when we paused as a nation to consider who really killed J. R. TV could give us the news not just by reporting but by telling us even better, more affecting stories and by introducing us to richer, more complicated characters, about whom we could care even more deeply. It could happen.

But I'm not holding my breath. Like most viewers, I've been anxiously and hopefully watching the early installments of Bochco's new masterwork, "Murder One," which is supposed to be TV drama at its most artful yet. It's still too early to say for sure, but I already have glum forebodings. Taking on contemporary social issues is one thing, but do we really want to be reminded of the O.J. case for 18 more weeks?

And much about the show suggests that Bochco et al. may have entered a baroque, mannerist phase: the portentous, harpsichord-like theme song; the dark palette and Rembrandt-esque shadows; even Daniel Benzali, the show's star, who with his enormous smooth head resembles a kind of giant, middle-aged putto—a cherub grown old and overripe. "Murder One" raises the awful possibility that TV, without our even knowing it, may already have passed through its golden age and be embarked upon a descent into self-consciousness and affectation. Or, worse, that TV, if it's good, is good when nobody expects too much of it.

Media Effects
Marshall McLuhan, Television Culture, and "The X-Files"

ADRIENNE L. McLEAN

Since its premiere in 1993, the Fox network television series "The X-Files" has gone from being what *USA Today* called a "weekly creep show" with a small cult following to a lauded, respectable, and profitable prime-time drama complete with Emmys, Golden Globes, and a top-twenty audience share in the United States and some 60 foreign countries. In addition to a forthcoming movie and assorted novelizations, guidebooks, and official and unofficial tie-in merchandise, the series—which one fan writer describes as "part police procedural, part suspense thriller, part action adventure, part medical drama, part science fiction and part horror"—has also already generated its own book-length collection of scholarly essays.[1] "The X-Files" stars previously unknown actors Gillian Anderson and David Duchovny as Dana Scully and Fox Mulder, FBI agents who have an extremely close and interesting relationship with each other—interesting (and unusual, for television) because it is strictly platonic. Each week the two labor, together and separately, to disentangle and understand what appears to be, at this writing, a giant government conspiracy involving alien/human hybridization, in which they themselves are somehow implicated.

Both the relationship and the conspiracy are the subjects of intense speculation by what *Entertainment Weekly* calls the show's "extreme, obsessed, hyperscrutinizing fan base"—or "X-Philes," as they refer to themselves on the Internet.[2] And, in turn, the fact that the X-Philes were among the first

to use cyberspace to create their own virtual fan culture and specialized interest groups (there are now nearly 500 websites devoted to "The X-Files")
has itself resulted in considerable journalistic and scholarly attention.[3] In
short, "The X-Files" is a popular culture phenomenon because of its bizarre
subject matter and genre-bending, its cult status and obsessive fans; because
the relationship of its main characters departs from television's usual gender stereotypes; and because it may represent, in the words of Michele
Malach, "part of a continuing cultural dialogue about law and order, freedom and safety, right and wrong, truth and falsity" during a period of PMT,
or "premillennial tension."[4]

I began to ponder another side to the "The X-Files" and its popularity
while teaching a course on visual culture and reading some of the recently
reissued works of media critic Marshall McLuhan (1911–1980).[5] Certainly
the rise and fall and rise of McLuhan's reputation might easily be written into
one of the show's "the truth is out there" plot lines. Upon the publication of
his second book, *Understanding Media*, in 1964, the *New York Herald Tribune* hailed McLuhan as "the most important thinker since Newton, Darwin,
Freud, Einstein and Pavlov," and McLuhan's name and many of his aphorisms—"the medium is the message," "global village," "the age of information"—became part of our permanent lexicon. But what Andrew Ross refers
to as McLuhan's "unremittingly formalist scheme," or his apparent refusal to
treat any mass medium as a specific practice imbricated in existing and interested economic and political power structures, kept the "High Priest of
Popcult and Metaphysician of Media," as *Playboy* called him in 1969, from
being taken seriously by many academic scholars after the mid-1970s.[6] In
1974 Hans Magnus Enzensberger harshly dismissed McLuhan as an apolitical "charlatan" who was "incapable of any theoretical construction" and who
wrote with "provocative idiocy," and Enzensberger was hardly alone in his
opinion.[7] After McLuhan's death in 1980, his name and reputation, as Lewis
Lapham writes, were "sent to the attic with the rest of the sensibility . . . that
embodied the failed hopes of a discredited decade."[8]

The current resurgence of interest in McLuhan does seem to be driven
less by an interest in his theorizing than by his apparent ability to predict the
electronic future. The emergence of the Internet and its role in the formation of a new global village, and the rise of home computers, video recorders,
cable and satellite networks, cellular phones, and other technologies of electronic communication and, by implication, surveillance, have given McLuhan
validity as a prophet of the condition that cultural critics variously describe as
postmodernism or postmodernity. What was once dismissed as typical
McLuhan jeremiad is now accepted as the common denominator of our
collective lives—that, as he wrote in 1967, the electronic media are "so pervasive in their personal, political, economic, aesthetic, psychological, moral,
ethical, and social consequences that they leave no part of us untouched, unaf-
fected, unaltered."[9]

McLuhan did not only predict the future, however. He helped to chart
its discursive course. In fact, his work is now being acknowledged as visionary

for what scholars had heretofore dismissed with contempt as formal and theoretical faults. The aphoristic and fragmentary nature of McLuhan's discourse, its "weird and hybrid dabbling" in "scientific mysticism," as Lapham puts it, have all become familiar as a post-modern *style* of writing and, equally important, historical investigation.[10] In a climate in which historians desire to "free themselves," Robert Rosenstone claims, "from the constricting bonds of metanarratives and the Historical discipline (the way history is taught in schools),"[11] the fragmentary theorizing of McLuhan no longer seems so idiotic. Although in 1975 it made sense for Raymond Williams to declare that "as descriptions of any observable social state or tendency" McLuhan's images of society were "ludicrous," clearly this is no longer the case.[12]

My own appropriation of McLuhan to illuminate the workings of a particular television text is itself a postmodern stance, and marks me as what Anne Friedberg and others call a cultural *flâneuse*.[13] The connection that I make between McLuhan and "The X-Files" is at once arbitrary (they have nothing historically to do with one another, yet I choose to connect them) and theoretically sound (I believe that McLuhan's work on media effects does help us to understand "The X-Files" and, by implication, other popular television shows, both as representations in a precise cultural moment and as links to past television practice). This postmodern posture, however, is one which McLuhan himself regularly employed in his search to understand the effects of a media form like television on the culture which had called it into being. The aphorisms which have come down to us as McLuhan's theories were in fact actually his "probes," the "tentative statements" or "keywords" that McLuhan repeated, recast, revised, and "stretched" in order to investigate meaning. Probes are thus "drills," in the words of McLuhan biographer W. Terrence Gordon, that helped McLuhan to "blast" through what Arthur Kroker calls the "deep, invisible assumptions," the "silent structural rules" of the technology within which we are situated and which has taken us over.[14]

The point of the probes and their humor, jest, paradox, and irony is not, as Gordon points out, to "finish" the hole that the drill makes. Rather, it is what the drill "churns up" that matters.[15] Here, I use several of McLuhan's aphorisms about television culture and the effects of electronic media on our collective "sensorium"—our minds, our bodies, our nervous systems, our experience of time and space—as a set of probes with which to "pierce the crust" of "The X-Files."[16] Before drilling, however, I want to explore the general landscape of which "The X-Files" is a feature, to examine not only the show's obvious surface but the programming context into which it fits. Only then can I turn to the McLuhanesque aspects of the show, its literalization of some of his most famous speculations: that television is a cool medium which thrives on cool characters and involves the casual participation of all of the senses; that it substitutes a vague insight for a real point of view; and that it produces a collective anxiety which is dominated by a free-floating terror in which "everybody is so profoundly involved with everybody else [that] nobody can really imagine what private guilt can be anymore." In conclusion, I will address, if not completely answer, the question that people repeatedly put to me when they learn of my interest in "The X-Files": namely, whether I am for it, or against it.

From its pilot forward, "The X-Files" has regularly featured and referred to mythology, ritual, and history ancient and modern. "The mythology" is also the official name for what series creator Chris Carter calls the "conspiracy" episodes that form the "scaffolding on which the series hangs."[17] The Lévi-Straussian dimensions of this phrase are hard to miss, as are the show's obvious pairs of binary opposites (good/evil, male/female, alien/human, belief/skepticism, spooky/normal, truth/lies, etc.). In addition, its hermeneutics of lack, loss, and need and its intermittently appearing and disappearing helpers and villains and sought-for persons make it always already folkloric in the Proppian sense as well. The question is what this self-conscious mythology, this spectacle or deployment of myth and folktale structure, obscures or plays with.

Like all television shows, "The X-Files" is polysemic and readable from what John Fiske calls "relations of subordination or opposition to the dominant meanings proposed by the text."[18] It may be that a concern with the fantastic and mythical is simply a dominant meaning of "The X-Files." But this concern marks other recent television shows as well. John Thornton Caldwell has identified a trend, a counterstrategy in American broadcast programming since the 1980s which he calls "televisuality" that not only foregrounds a "visually based mythology, framework, and aesthetic based on an extreme self-consciousness of style" but often utilizes "self-contained and volatile narrative and fantasy worlds."[19] Televisuality is "both a pretext for economic intervention and a programming tool used to flaunt and throw around ontological distinctions: history/text, news/film, reality/fiction."[20] Televisuality employs style to attract to faltering networks the discriminating viewers who belong to the 18-to-49 demographic that is so important to advertisers. In other words, relations of subordination or opposition might easily be structured into the plot of "The X-Files" both as authorial expression and as a marketing strategy. And this would not be remarkable.

I want to suggest that Caldwell's description of televisuality bears a startling resemblance to McLuhan's claims about the hybrid nature of television and its effects on our minds and bodies. To McLuhan, television was obviously an "integral medium, forcing an interaction among components of experience which have long been separate and scattered." Through its ability to link, instantaneously, simultaneously, and nonlinearly, "anything with anything else," television restructures us into beings whose sense of the world is based on a discarnate involvement with process, with style, with visual mythology, with fantasy worlds. The only difference between television and televisuality is the increase in self-reflexivity that the new term implies. Television now "knows" just what we know, so that it often serves as a substitute for lived experience, or translates reality for us. Television's own hidden ground has become the content of the medium itself.

Here we are obviously arching towards McLuhan's most famous aphorism and foundational probe, namely that "the medium is the message." What McLuhan discovered through repeated applications of this probe is that the major effect of any medium is never its content but, instead, the "revolutionary environmental transformations" that the medium subliminally induces. That television is cool rather than hot refers to the different environmental transformations and sensory effects McLuhan associates with media of higher or lower definition. Hot media, in which he situates radio, photography, and cinema, contain relatively complete visual or aural information (they tend to "extend" one sense over others) and thus require less involvement of the user in making meaning from them. Cool media, on the other hand—the telephone, cartoons, television—supply less visual or aural information and thus require much greater sensory participation by the user.

To agree that television is a cool medium does not mean that we have to accept all of McLuhan's speculations about its neurological effects (television's sequential electronic scanning process may or may not create a "mosaic-like" tactile image that becomes "inscribed on our skins"). What matters here is McLuhan's insistence on the meaning of television's ubiquity, its usurpation of our psychic processes, and its potential to leave us in an "exhausted slump" of sensory overload. Television is at once a medium that requires audience participation and one which creates numbness and dulls our perceptions as well. This is what McLuhan describes as the "paradoxical feature of the 'cool' TV medium. It involves us in moving depth, but it does not excite, agitate or arouse."

In light of television's increasing televisuality, however, does the appellation "cool" remain useful? Does content really *not* matter in an age of cult shows, cult stars, audiences who schedule their lives around talk shows, soap operas, or "The X-Files"? Certainly television is becoming more and more like movies, fulfilling another McLuhan aphorism that all media tend to heat up over time. But this is because television, McLuhan would undoubtedly point out, has been superseded by a new "environmental" medium—the computer-linked Internet. Like print, the telegraph, the photograph, and cinema before it, television is now being reprocessed into a "harmless consumer commodity." It is no longer regarded as "corrupt or degrading" because that designation is "always reserved," McLuhan believes, for "whatever is actively environmental." At present, with television the acknowledged subliminal ground of middle-class life, the computer and the Internet are becoming the new cool media, provoking in us that psychic and social disturbance that was once created by the TV image.

It is therefore hardly surprising to find "The X-Files," like many other televisually oriented programs, often described as movie-like, or to realize that many movies scarcely signify as theatrical releases but as the television shows which, through video, they eventually become. What I am claiming, then, is also paradoxical: that even though "The X-Files" is movie-like formally and stylistically, it has chosen to remain cool in the McLuhanesque sense.[21] "The X-Files" literalizes coolness, making what Arthur Kroker calls the "inner, structural code of the technological experience" an element of its content as well as its electronic form.[22] When we drill into "The X-Files," it is our lives under television that get churned to the surface.

One of the best-known features of "The X-Files" is the degree of audience involvement and participation that the show's elliptical yet serial narrative structure fosters. The first McLuhan probe I employed, therefore, is that the "cool TV medium promotes depth structures in art and entertainment alike, and creates audience involvement in depth as well." By withholding plot and character information from audiences for weeks or even months at a time, slowly doling out pieces to a puzzle that grows larger with each episode, "The X-Files" forces depth participation to the surface. The murky visual design of the show, its strange colors and expressionist lighting, also force us to participate in creating sense from what we often cannot actually see.

Nor is understanding made easy by the language of "The X-Files," which is frequently itself aphoristic—e.g., "The truth is out there," "Believe the lies," "I want to believe," "All lies lead to the truth." One of the reasons McLuhan chose aphorism as his favored means of expression is that aphorism—like television—is by nature incomplete. Aphorism requires "participation on the part of the person regarding it or thinking about it," and is therefore the language, he believes, of teaching. What does "The X-Files" teach? The show obviously aims to "deeply involve [us] in the process of learning, illustrating graphically the complex interplay of people and events, the development of forms, the multileveled interrelationships between and among such arbitrarily segregated subjects as biology, geography, mathematics, anthropology, history, literature and languages." Yet this last quotation refers to McLuhan's vision for the role of television in the classroom. What does it mean that we can have this vision fulfilled by a prime-time creep show?

When I first encountered "The X-Files," I was greatly upset by its violence. People and animals were killed all the time, and they tended to be graphically scarified in the process. But I quickly became acclimated to the violence because "The X-Files" does consistently involve us, through its thematics of investigation, in making "multileveled" connections between "arbitrarily segregated subjects." On "The X-Files" one learns what standing inside an eviscerated elephant is like, what the Coriolis force is, how a succubus or a wraith is supposed to behave, how long it would take a python to digest a human, what escalating serial fetishism is, how cows look when they've been struck by lightning. One learns what happens to human flesh when you boil it, crush it, embalm it alive, freeze it, irradiate it, slice it with a razor blade, burn it, mutate it. Yet the visual depiction of these things seldom stirs up more than a faint, brief, queasiness, because it is the appeal of knowledge and process that involves us more than the imagined effects of violence on actual human or inhuman organisms. "The X-Files" literalizes McLuhan's suggestion that not only "deeper, but further, into all knowledge has become the normal popular demand since TV." Like television itself, "The X-Files" "compels commitment and participation, quite regardless of any point of view."

The McLuhan probe which best explains how "The X-Files" can at once create knowledge in depth and fail to produce a coherent point of view comprises two remarks. The first is that the cool medium of television rewards "spontaneous casualness" and "compatible coolness and indifference" in its actors (which also allow the viewer to "fill in the gaps with his [or her] own personal identification"); the second that the "cooling system" of television often "brings on a lifelong state of psychic rigor mortis, or of somnambulism, particularly observable in periods of new technology." The manner in which the two protagonists of "The X-Files," Scully/Anderson and Mulder/Duchovny, embody each of these aphorisms has been the subject of a striking amount of fan and audience discourse. Because Anderson and Duchovny became stars by being Scully and Mulder, they also literalize McLuhan's statement that fans of television prefer to think about and relate to TV stars *as* their roles, rather than as "real people."

Clearly the boundaries between forms of fan discourse are much more fluid now than they were when McLuhan was writing, but it is hard to imagine Scully and Mulder played by well-known actors with preexisting or well-defined and filled-in extratextual identities. In fact, "The X-Files" encourages role/performer confusion by using what *Entertainment Weekly* calls a "Who-*is*-that-guy" casting strategy.[23] But even though the show openly foregrounds its own coolness (as when Mulder wonders whether he can get something disgusting off his fingers "without betraying [his] cool exterior"), does this mean that Mulder and Scully are cool in the McLuhanesque sense? Absolutely, indeed programmatically.

The comments of reviewers are useful in this regard. *The Village Voice* remarked early on Duchovny's "wonderful deadpan poise," and *Gentlemen's Quarterly* the fact that he is "as murky as swamp water."[24] *Entertainment Weekly* admires Anderson's "open, blank stare" and Duchovny's "pin-eyed zombie cool," *The New Yorker* the show's "deadpan aplomb in the face of man-size flukes and alien fetuses."[25] Although at this point we might claim any number of other antecedents for an intense but low-key or unemotional acting style—film noir, Method acting, particular star images—the obvious influence would seem to be television itself, which changed adolescence from what McLuhan called a "time of fresh, eager, and expressive countenances" to one in which the "child of the TV age" sports a "dead and sculptural pan." In short, one of the ways that we adjust to the violence of "The X-Files" is by acquiring what Scully and Mulder have, the "casual and cool nonchalance of the playful and superior being," and incorporating their viewing strategy, their attitude of grave indifference toward virtually all that they encounter, as our own. Whether confronted with horrific and graphically presented brutality, paranormal threats, family crises, or good news, Scully and Mulder exhibit the somnambulism and numbness that television invokes in all of us. When I watch them, I too become numb. As does reviewer James Wolcott, in whom "The X-Files" induces "a lush, becalmed spirit of voyeurism so pure and intent that it borders on a trance state."[26]

The third probe, which speaks to television's paradoxical alliance of numbness and participation, is McLuhan's characterization of the technological present as a new Age of Anxiety. Unlike modernist anxiety, in which the individual and his or her own interior are alienated from society, McLuhan's "anxiety of indifference" is generated by what Glenn Willmott calls the "denial (or penetration by the media, and so by everyone else) of any margins of solitude or alienation."[27] This loss of margins leads inevitably, McLuhan believes, to a perpetual—and perpetually doomed, in a media-driven environment—"questing for lost identity." Do "the hermeneutics of faith practiced by Mulder and the hermeneutics of suspicion practiced by Scully" provide, therefore, what Jimmie L. Reeves, Mark C. Rodgers, and Michael Epstein call a "bifocal outlook on unexplained phenomenon that is characterized by a sincerity that stands in stark contrast to the mockeries" of "Twin Peaks," "Beavis and Butthead," and others?[28] Or is the "quest for *anything*," as McLuhan puts it, including knowledge-seeking itself, undertaken because it is the only pure thrill left?

The quests that engage Scully and Mulder on "The X-Files" are intensely focused on foundational identity issues: the meaning of family socially and individually; of where and how one belongs in the world in an existential sense. A number of episodes, for example, center on Scully's search for who or what killed her sister, for the approval of her father, the identity of whoever abducted her for a month and stole her ability to bear children, whoever gave her (and then cured) her terminal cancer. Mulder seeks his abducted sister and the rogue FBI agent who may have killed his father (even as questions are raised about who his father actually is). So ritualized and Freudian is this focus on family relationships that it seems linked to the extreme potency with which these issues are charged in melodrama. The omnipresence of music on "The X-Files," the way it is used to create mood and mark climaxes, also suggests an affinity with melodrama.

Yet on "The X-Files," families scarcely matter except as plot devices. Although Scully's family is said to be important to her, there is little emotional affect in her relationship to its members. Her family obviously bores her, and she them. While Mulder is supposed to be searching for his sister, finding her (which he has done now several times) does not alter his cool demeanor, nor does it deter him from doggedly pursuing the truth. The most important relationship on "The X-Files," the only one which *does* carry emotional weight, is the relationship between Mulder and Scully themselves.

Under its surface mythology of conspiracies and shadow governments, aliens and monstrosity, or even what Rhonda Wilcox and J. P. Williams call "liminality and gender pleasure," "The X-Files" and its popularity can be read as literalizing the ways in which our lives and relationships have been changed by television.[29] What is often perceived as the "lack" in the relationship of Scully and Mulder—its sexual and legal component—makes sense, then, in McLuhanesque terms. Scully and Mulder cannot be joined sexually or legally because they are both literally and figuratively alienated, penetrated, and probed to the molecular level by omniscient and omnipotent forces who have infiltrated, like television and, now, computers, virtually everything in our lives. In other words, were they to become lovers, they would cease to signify this and would instead become conventional representatives of what Kroker characterizes as the "imposed assumptions" of an outmoded set of social relations.

Scully and Mulder trust each other, and they trust what they do. Yet virtually everything they think they know is wrong. Television has taught them the arts of insight, but not how to formulate a point of view. It has sent them on a quest for identity, but taught them also never to trust what they find as a result of it. The media-driven milieu of "The X-Files" suggests that the whole world is now the same place, all of it accessible, all of it at once safe, dangerous, restricting, liberating. The North Pole is no more or less threatening than the New Jersey woods or a cheap motel room. A shopping mall, home, office building, or computer may harbor a mutant or alien; a kindly doctor or schoolteacher may inject you with a lethal virus; someone who looks like your sister or like your partner may turn out to be a shape-shifter or a clone. The psychic and physical collide in flashbacks that lie, in point-of-view shots that turn out to be "wrong," in montage sequences that link events "incorrectly." We cannot believe what we see on television, what we download from computers, what we hear on our cell phones. And yet just as Scully and Mulder believe in their relationship to each other and that there is truth *somewhere*, we do believe, all the time. We *have* to believe in the reality of *something*, even if that something is the paranoia induced by television itself.

In "The X-Files," the extent to which we see, feel, and experience everything through technology, through literal "mediation," is what McLuhan's probes churn into a vortex of simultaneous paranoia, humor, and comfort. Paranoia is the only emotional tone that makes sense in a world in which we have let television and computers become substitutes for our nervous systems and our bodies. Yet because the paranoia is free-floating, as McLuhan points out, originating in media which are "both inside and outside," it is also soothing. If, as "The X-Files" suggests, aliens and mutants are everywhere, one need not worry about them. Since an invisible shadow government controls everything from baseball to the media to our national destiny, real paranoia (much less political action) would be beside the point. Even terminal illness and death are rarely more than temporary plot divagations.[30] Does this represent what Reeves, Rodgers, and Epstein call a "reinvigoration of consensus culture and a renunciation of the excesses and exclusions of postmodernism"?[31] Does "The X-Files" really acknowledge and affirm what its mythology overtly declares *should* matter to us—the ineffable, the spiritual, the other—or is it a televisual display of ideological virtuosity, the shape-shifting of its mutants and aliens no less and no more difficult than the easy mutability it posits among the markers of gender, race, nationality, or mortality?

The reason I am still *for* "The X-Files" is that it elicits so many passionate yet wildly variable reactions, that it has no strong consensus response. The most beneficent interpretation of the show would be that, through its foregrounding of coolness and style, it helps us achieve what McLuhan calls a consciousness of the "revolutionary transformations caused by new media," thus giving us the means by which to "anticipate and control them" rather than being their slaves. Its Internet communities, though relatively exclusive in terms of educational, financial, and leisure resources, also bespeak a need for real connection, a connection which often extends beyond membership in the Gillian Anderson Testosterone Brigade or the Smart Young

X-Philes. McLuhan would undoubtedly approve of the fact that one elementary school teacher uses the popularity of "The X-Files" among her students to get them interested in real science, but he would also agree with the scientist who fulminates against the show for being "pernicious because week after week it promotes the idea that a supernatural explanation should be favored over a rational one."[32]

What I am against in the show, however, is also its coolness, its blankness, its humor in the face of any and all killing, its increasing "flaunting of ontological distinctions" involving politics, power, and mortality.[33] What "The X-Files" and its popularity suggest is that we would all like to be like Mulder and like Scully, that we all want *not* to be excited, agitated, or aroused by everything we see and experience, and certainly not by everything that we see and experience on television. We, too, would like to be able to "cool off" what McLuhan calls the "hot situations of actual life" by "miming" them with humor and play.[34] Yet, as Kroker writes, for McLuhan television was a new technological sensorium, an "artificial amplification, and transferral, of human consciousness and sensory organs to the technical apparatus, which now, having achieved the electronic phase of 'simultaneity' and 'instantaneous scope,' returns to take its due on the human body."[35] A show that repeatedly foregrounds this process, whether consciously or inadvertently, might easily appear, as "The X-Files" does to so many, to be a whole new form of television.

The literal conjunctions of "The X-Files" and McLuhan's probes into the environmental effects of television form what I have argued to be the show's own invisible assumptions. "The X-Files" and its worldwide following represent, indeed embody, a McLuhanesque view of the changing nature of meaning itself in a media-driven universe. Created by a California surfer out of the bits and pieces of his own mass-mediated past, "The X-Files" is meant, Chris Carter claims, to scare us.[36] The truly frightening thing may be that we have already reached the state of psychic rigor mortis that McLuhan predicted television would eventually induce. Yet McLuhan also observed that television seemed to prompt in its audience "a strong drive toward religious experience with rich liturgical overtones," and this "The X-Files" supports as well. In the end, both Marshall McLuhan and "The X-Files" are concerned with the decay of meaning in our lives, and both urge us to create for ourselves what we may no longer be able to find.

Notes

1. The quotation is on p. 2 of the anthology (David Lavery, Angela Hague, and Marla Cartwright, eds., *Deny All Knowledge: Reading* The X Files [Syracuse, N.Y.: Syracuse University Press, 1996]).

2. *Entertainment Weekly* (29 November, 1996), p. 38.

3. See, for example, Jimmie L. Reeves, Mark C. Rodgers, and Michael Epstein, "Rewriting Popularity: The Cult *Files*," pp. 22–35, and Susan J. Clerc, "DDEB, GATB, MPPB, and Ratboy: *The X-Files'* Media Fandom, Online and Off," pp. 36–51, in Lavery, Hague, and Cartwright, op. cit.

4. In Lavery, Hague, and Cartwright, op. cit., p. 20. The "PMT" is from "We All Love X. But Why?," *New Statesman and Society* (23 August, 1996), p. 26.

5. Among them Eric McLuhan and Frank Zingrone, eds., *Essential McLuhan* (New York: Basic Books, 1995); Marshall McLuhan, *Understanding Media: The Extensions of Man* [1964] (Cambridge, MA: MIT Press, 1996); Marshall McLuhan and Quentin Fiore, *The Medium Is the Message: An Inventory of Effects* [1967] (San Francisco: Hardwired, 1996). All of these have been reprinted in several foreign languages as well. Recent books about McLuhan include Glenn Willmott, *McLuhan, or Modernism in Reverse* (Toronto: University of Toronto Press, 1996); Paul Benedetti and Nancy DeHart, eds., *On McLuhan: Forward Through the Rearview Mirror* (Cambridge, MA: MIT Press, 1997); W. Terrence Gordon, *Marshall McLuhan: Escape into Understanding, A Biography* (New York: Basic Books, 1997).

6. Andrew Ross, *No Respect: Intellectuals and Popular Culture* (New York: Routledge, 1989), p. 114. The *Playboy* quote is in McLuhan and Zingrone, *Essential McLuhan*, p. 233.

7. Hans Magnus Enzensberger, "Constituents of a Theory of the Media" [1974], in John C. Hanhardt, ed., *Video Culture: A Critical Investigation* (New York: Visual Studies Workshop, 1986), pp. 114–115. For summaries of the academic reaction to McLuhan during his lifetime, see Ross, *No Respect*, and Gordon, *Marshall McLuhan*.

8. Lewis Lapham, introduction to McLuhan, *Understanding Media*, p. xi.

9. From *The Medium Is the Message* (New York: Bantam Books, 1967), p. 26. Unless otherwise noted, all other quoted McLuhan aphorisms are taken either from McLuhan, *Understanding Media*, or McLuhan and Zingrone, *Essential McLuhan*.

10. Lapham, in McLuhan, *Understanding Media*, p. xiii.

11. Robert A. Rosenstone, "The Future of the Past: Film and the Beginnings of Postmodern History," in Vivian Sobchack, ed., *The Persistence of History: Cinema, Television, and the Modern Event* (New York: Routledge, 1996), p. 215.

12. Raymond Williams, *Television: Technology and Cultural Form* [1975] (London: Routledge, 1990), p. 128.

13. See Anne Friedberg, *Window Shopping: Cinema and the Postmodern* (Berkeley, CA: University of California Press, 1993). McLuhan's "hybrid dabbling," of course, obviously makes him a *flâneur* as well.

14. Gordon, *Marshall McLuhan*, pp. 105, 179, 302; Arthur Kroker, *Technology and the Canadian Mind: Innis/McLuhan/Grant* (New York: St. Martin's Press, 1984), p. 55.

15. Gordon, op. cit., p. 302.

16. Ibid.

17. *Entertainment Weekly* (29 November, 1996), pp. 38–39.

18. John Fiske, *Television Culture* (London: Methuen, 1987), p. 93. See also his "Television: Polysemy and Popularity," *Critical Studies in Mass Communication* 3 (December 1986), pp. 391–408.

19. John Thornton Caldwell, *Televisuality: Style, Crisis, and Authority in American Television* (New Brunswick, N.J.: Rutgers University Press, 1995), pp. 4, 261. For more on the aggressively eclectic style of one of the best-known precursors to "The X-Files," David Lynch's "Twin Peaks," see also Jim Collins, "Postmodernism and Television," in Robert C. Allen, ed., *Channels of Discourse, Reassembled: Television and Contemporary Criticism*, 2nd ed. (Chapel Hill, N.C.: University of North Carolina Press, 1992), pp. 327–349.

20. Caldwell, op. cit., p. 233.

21. For more on the forthcoming movie version of "The X-Files," whose plot,

stars, writers, and production personnel are virtually all connected with the television show but "much bigger," see James Sterngold, "'X-Files' Looks for the Room to Stretch Out," *New York Times* (21 September, 1997), pp. 9, 14.

22. Kroker, op. cit., p. 17.

23. Mike Flaherty, "Unseen Forces," *Entertainment Weekly* (29 November, 1996), p. 50.

24. Erik Davis, "Earth's Most Wanted," *Village Voice* (26 October, 1993), pp. 49–50; Allison Glock, "Darkman," *Gentlemen's Quarterly* (January 1997), p. 94.

25. Ken Tucker, "Spooky Kind of Love," *Entertainment Weekly* (29 November, 1996), p. 36; *Entertainment Weekly* (24 October, 1997), p. 42; James Wolcott, "Too Much Pulp," *The New Yorker* (6 January, 1997), p. 76.

26. Wolcott, op. cit., p. 76.

27. Willmott, op. cit., p. 170.

28. Reeves, Rodgers, and Epstein, op. cit., p. 35.

29. For contrasting discussions of the representation of gender in "The X-Files," see Rhonda Wilcox and J. P. Williams, "'What Do You Think?' The X-Files, Liminality, and Gender Pleasure," pp. 99–120; Lisa Parks, "Special Agent or Monstrosity? Finding the Feminine in *The X-Files*," pp. 121–134; Linda Badley, "The Rebirth of the Clinic: The Body as Alien in *The X-Files*," pp. 148–167; Elizabeth Kubek, "'You Only Expose Your Father': The Imaginary, Voyeurism, and the Symbolic Order in *The X-Files*," pp. 168–204, in Lavery, Hague, and Cartwright, *Deny All Knowledge*. Of course, television watching, "normal" or otherwise, has itself been featured in "X-Files" episodes, along with computers and other forms of electronic technology. A McLuhanesque detail of the show is its reliance on cellular phones: " 'I don't think you could have done this series before cell phones,' says Chris Carter. 'We can have [Scully and Mulder] in two different places yet very connected' " (*TV Guide* [17–23 May, 1997], pp. 26, 28).

30. To paraphrase James Wolcott, nobody really dies on "The X-Files"; they may at any time be hybridized, reincarnated, regenerated, cloned, and so on (in Badley, "Rebirth of the Clinic," p. 164). During the 1996–97 season, Scully was given a terminal metastasizing brain tumor that was later cured by a computer chip that Mulder found in a government file drawer, and Mulder himself appeared to commit suicide during the season finale. The ideological implications of making these issues so mutable remain to be addressed.

31. Reeves, Rodgers, and Epstein, "Rewriting Popularity," p. 35.

32. James Williams, "Undercover Work," *Times Educational Supplement* (3 January, 1997), p. III; "We All Love X. But Why?" See also C. Eugene Emery, Jr., "Paranormal and Paranoid Intermingle on Fox TV's 'X-Files,'" *Skeptical Inquirer* (March/April 1995), pp. 18–19, and William Evans, "Science and Reason in Film and Television," *Skeptical Inquirer* (January/February 1996), pp. 45–48, 58. The *Skeptical Inquirer* loves to point out errors in the "science" of "The X-Files," such as that its description of the Coriolis force was not only backwards but applied to the wrong phenomenon entirely.

33. As Wolcott puts it, "the nadir was reached" during the 1996–97 season "in an episode where a trio of backwoods mutations savagely beat a black couple to death to the ironic strains of a Johnny Mathis tune" ("Too Much Pulp," p. 76). The show has also begun to incorporate more and more archival documentary footage into its fictional storylines, and to cull plots from topical news and events.

34. The relative lack of popularity of another Chris Carter series, "Millennium," which began to run on Fox in 1996, is interesting by comparison to "The X-Files."

"Millennium" tends to *lecture* to its audiences rather than creating a sense of what McLuhan calls "do-it-yourself-ness and depth involvement"; its single star, Lance Henriksen, not only has an appearance which "strongly declares his role and status in life" (and hence is "wrong" for television) but possesses very little "spontaneous casualness"; and it desperately needs "humor and play." Or, it could be that "Millennium" is, like "Twin Peaks" did, simply "drown[ing] in the puddle of its own drippy artiness" (Jonathan Ross, "Talking with Aliens," *Sight and Sound* [June 1995], p. 61).

35. Kroker, op. cit., p. 72.

36. Chris Carter regularly calls himself a California surfer in the popular press. Besides "Twin Peaks" and all of David Lynch's films, Carter cites as influences on "The X-Files" the television shows "Twilight Zone," "Kolchak: The Night Stalker," "The Avengers," "The Untouchables," the PBS series "Prime Suspect," and the films *Silence of the Lambs, All the President's Men, Alien* and *Aliens,* and anything by David Cronenberg.

Il Maresciallo Rocca
The Italian Way to the TV Police Series

MILLY BUONANNO

1. A Well-Tempered Success

It was only in 1996 that in Italy the police show returned to a popularity it had lost in the previous two decades. This renewed success is mainly due to a series produced by RAI (the state TV broadcaster) which was rated among the ten most watched programs in the 95–96 season and, more generally, among the most popular TV fictions produced in the 90s.

Unlike other European countries, such as France, Great Britain and Germany, where the police series has a solid tradition in terms of production and consumption practices, in Italy this genre, after quite a long period of latency, has just started to reemerge and is now experiencing a new and somehow original popularity. To be more precise, early Italian television had already produced several popular police series in the 50s and 60s, but the most recent productions redefine, more originally and consciously, the genre and the formula of the classical police series. They open the way to a peculiarly Italian version of this genre, a version which is rapidly creating and consolidating its own audience.

The "police series of the year" in 1996 was *Il Maresciallo Rocca* (Marshall Rocca), a series composed of 8 episodes, each lasting one and a half hours. According to Italian production practice a series rarely lasts more than 12 episodes. *Il Maresciallo Rocca* was produced by RAIDUE (the second channel of the Italian public television) and aired at prime time in January and February of 1996. It has reached higher and higher ratings, with a peak of 17 million people (60% share) for the last episode. Indeed, such high levels had not been reached since March 1989 when *La Piovra* (*The*

Octopus, until now the most popular TV fiction ever produced in Italy) closed its fourth series with the murder of its hero by the Mafia. Appreciated by critics as well as by viewers, *Il Maresciallo Rocca* represents something more than a simple TV hit; it is an authentic phenomenon of popularity which has succeeded in gathering dispersed members of Italian families around the TV set; it has become a subject of collective discourse and has revitalized the waning image of Italian TV fiction.

As typically occurs, such a phenomenon of popularity has ended up conflating the character and the actor: Gigi Proietti, an eclectic and brilliant theater actor with some TV experience is now widely identified and type-cast as "Marshall Rocca." Therefore, in the attempt to avoid being totally "cannibalized" by the character, the actor Proietti requested and obtained the postponement of the series reruns from Spring to Autumn 1996. He also decided to return to the theater before shooting the new episodes (planned for the end of 1997). This means that the new series will not be aired until two years after the previous one. Such a long discontinuity between the first and the second series may be somehow inconceivable abroad, but is perfectly normal in Italy where the TV industry and culture have not yet matured so as to assure immediate continuation of successful productions, dispersing and devaluating—as a consequence—their popularity and marketability.

On the other hand, however, it must be noted that *Il Maresciallo Rocca* is the well-tempered output of a process of transformation of marketing and production practices, a process which Italian TV fiction is currently undergoing in the attempt to overcome an artisan dimension and to experiment with new procedures and strategies. As a consequence of this process the creative phase of *Il Maresciallo Rocca* has been unusually accurate, both in terms of documentation (the *Carabinieri,* Marshall Rocca's corps, have been repeatedly consulted) and scriptwriting (story editors, professional figures basically unknown here, have been widely employed to check all scripts).

Moreover (also quite unusual for Italian media marketing practices) the series has been promoted almost in a movie-like fashion: huge posters have appeared on the sides of public buses and on the walls of widely crowded places such as railway stations. More interestingly, the series has been "drawn in" by the evening news which on the days of transmission ended with a short interview with the protagonist, inviting the audience to stay tuned to the "stories of common heroism of Marshall Rocca." The protagonist himself has appeared on TV during the break between the news and the series as a testimonial for a coffee brand in order to maintain the viewers' attention through the sequential flow of news, commercials and fiction.

The press coverage of *Il Maresciallo Rocca* has been remarkable. It has undoubtedly contributed to both creating and spreading a positive public opinion towards the program, which was quickly considered as the emblem of "good national fiction." Italian journalists, often accused of giving too much attention to TV, though not always in a competent and appreciative way, usually tend to adopt a schizophrenic position towards TV fiction: they either complain about the invasion of American productions (except for celebrating cult programs such as *ER* and *X-Files*), or mock soap operas and telenovelas, but they are never interested in giving a serious and well informed critical coverage of national TV fiction. They seem merely to be echoing the promotional practices of commercial networks, production companies and press agencies. *Il Maresciallo Rocca* has benefited from the initiatives taken by the powerful promotional machine of the press and, conversely, a significant part of the press coverage—consisting of critiques, opinions, comments, debates—has been activated by the enormous and partly unexpected success of the series.

The popularity of the series has certainly contributed to give greater visibility to the corps of the *Carabinieri* (which has lately received ten thousand extra applications) and, similarly, the popularity of the *Carabinieri* has probably increased the success of the series. Significantly, the hero of the first successful Italian police series in the last twenty years is not a policeman but a *carabiniere,* and that, for Italian society, makes a great difference. Between the *Carabinieri* (a branch of the army) and the police there has always been a partial overlap of functions as well as a historical antagonism which is reflected in the different way the two institutions and their members are perceived by people. Schematically speaking, the police tend to be seen as a repressive force whereas the *Carabinieri*—more diffusely located throughout the national territory—are considered a protective institution. It must also be mentioned that the *Carabinieri's* presumed dullness and simple-mindedness have inspired a whole literature of jokes which, however, people do not tell with mocking superiority, but rather with a sense of familiarity usually attributed to those figures one often feels closer to. On the whole, we can say that the *Carabinieri* are widely considered trustworthy and heroic officers and occupy a central position in popular *imagerie* and imagination; they have repeatedly appeared on the covers of popular magazines performing some courageous action and have been immortalized by the most popular actors of Italian comedy, such as Vittorio De Sica and Totó, as friendly and kind *marescialli* who, if necessary, may turn into daring heroes. Furthermore, thanks to an elegant black uniform decorated with red and golden motifs, the *Carabinieri* are also a symbol of physical attractiveness and male beauty: "you're as handsome as a *Carabiniere,*" a mother says to her son, a police inspector, in a previous, but not successful, Italian police series.

Of course, the reasons for a phenomenon of popularity like *Il Maresciallo Rocca* cannot be reduced either to effective marketing strategies or to the positive and familiar image of the institution its protagonist represents. It is in fact necessary to make a short journey through the history of the police series in Italy in order to see how *Il Maresciallo Rocca* redefines the genre, the structure and the texture of its formula, characters and *milieus*.

2. From the Global to the Local

The history of the Italian TV police series can be structured according to a three-period chronology: the first period coincides with the monopolistic phase of public television and goes from the mid-50s—RAI started broadcasting in 1954—to the mid-70s; the second period covers the 80s and is characterized by the emergence and affirmation of commercial networks and by the increasing competition between public and private television; the third period starts with the current decade.

The monopolistic phase is deeply inspired by a pedagogic ideology—TV as an instrument of education and cultivation of the audience—and is influenced by professionals with a strong literary-humanistic formation. As far as fiction is concerned, the interaction between this pedagogic project and high culture gives rise to the creation of a genre which soon becomes a specific and distinctly Italian product: the *sceneggiato*, a term still in use in Italy to name TV fiction in general. Also called *teleromanzo*, the *sceneggiato* is a mini-series (between four and seven episodes) based on an Italian or foreign literary work. During the years of RAI's monopoly, the most popular novels of the 19th century European and non-European literary tradition were turned into *sceneggiati* whose successes originate the first examples of TV stardom. Although they have not been produced for more than 20 years now, many *sceneggiati* are still vividly present in the memory of older viewers who sometimes may watch the re-runs shown late at night.

In addition to the historical-literary *sceneggiato*, early Italian TV cultivated a second, albeit less relevant, productive vein: the police series. On the one hand, the police series followed the same logic as the *sceneggiato*. In other words, it was mainly based on the European and North American literary "classics" of the so-called yellow fiction, which took its name from the color of the covers of a popular series of police short novels. *Philo Vance, Nero Wolfe, Maigret, Father Brown* were quite familiar to Italian viewers who became used to a genre offering stories which, although locally produced, were in fact conceived and set in nonlocal geo-cultural contexts (France, Great Britain, USA). Retrospectively, the international character of these early police series can be considered a kind of anticipatory socialization of Italians to the wave of foreign series (mainly from the US) which in the coming decades were to invade private and public networks. This preference for foreign police novels certainly reflects the common opinion that Italian authors and *milieus* would be hardly credible for this particular genre (up to relatively recent times Italian authors of yellow fiction have published their stories under North American pseudonyms).

On the other hand, the police series introduces at least two significant innovations in the structure of the *sceneggiato:* a contemporary setting and a serial format. Unlike a fiction mainly oriented towards a 19th century past, the police series opens unusual windows to the present; moreover, it breaks the dominance of the mini-series and paves the way to the first domestic productions modeled on foreign series (*Perry Mason, Alfred Hitchcock*) which, albeit limitedly, are just starting to be scheduled on Italian networks.

However, it must be noted that the series Italian TV takes from foreign police novels are not just mere and rigorous reproductions of them. On the contrary, they go through a process of re-adaptation and "domestication" which grafts or stresses all those elements closer to Italian culture. In *Maigret,* for example, the family life background of the inspector is more extended than in the original novels by Simenon, and Mrs. Maigret is no longer a dimmed and discreet figure, but rather a maternal and nurturing Italian wife.

Policemen's and detectives' personalities too are re-adapted so that they have more human and good-natured profiles. That is, for example, the direction followed by *Il Tenente Sheridan* (Lieutenant Sheridan), one of the most representative programs in the history of Italian TV, broadcast from the late 50s to the early 70s, although with long interruptions and a format alternating between series and mini-series.

The stories of *Il Tenente Sheridan* were based on scripts written by Italian authors who, for the reasons mentioned earlier, operated within a process of delocalization of the protagonist (a member of the San Francisco police) and his *milieus* by transferring them to the United States (of course production is not made on locations but entirely in TV studios). Unlike traditional series, these stories were contained in a program whose innovative and typically recombinant formula merged the police story with the quiz show. Titled *Il Club del Giallo* (The Yellow Club), each program included the participation of some players who were ritually welcomed and entertained by a host in a club setting; eventually, the episode of the day was shown and interrupted just a few minutes before the end in order to allow the players to guess secretly the *whodunit;* finally, the conclusion was shown and the criminal unmasked by Sheridan; the program ended with the awarding of prizes to those players who had guessed the perpetrator of the crime and his/her motive correctly.

This original and attractive formula assured an immediate success to the program; but the actual focus of interest of the *Club* was Sheridan, whom the Italian audience, despite his foreign name, recognized and appreciated as typically Italian. Always wrapped in a white raincoat, with a serious expression and sharp features à la Humphrey Bogart, Sheridan was a policeman whose sensitivity and amiability had nothing in common with either the aggressive character of US cops or the roughness of the Italian policeman stereotype; he conjugated honesty and professional morality with the passions and vices everybody experiences, and that made him more credible and closer to common people, and ultimately a very popular figure, an authentic national *pop-icon*. The character soon exceeded the text which created it and, endowed with an existence of its own, became a testimonial for commercials while the actor, definitely identified with Sheridan, was continuously requested to solve, like an actual policeman, real little enigmas, even many years after the end of the series.

Therefore, during the first period of its history the Italian police series clearly tried to acquire a distinctly international dimension: it adopted non-Italian authors and characters, told non-Italian stories and re-created non-Italian *milieus;* even when it was working on original scripts, it preferred to use foreign names and scenarios. However, this strategy of delocalizing a genre which supposedly did not belong to the Italian tradition in order to give it more credit did leave some margins or interstices where the ingredients for an Italian version of the police series may blend and start taking form and substance; for example, the notion of the mimetic hero, i.e. the protagonist as a common person.

During the second period the Italian *mediascape* underwent a deep and turbulent transformation: RAI created a third channel, the flow of programs was extended to cover the entire day and, more importantly, private networks started emerging, first locally and then nationally. The most immediate effect of this transformation was an enormous increase of the TV offerings and a dramatic need for new programs which domestic production could only partially satisfy. Private networks—which started producing their own fiction only in the mid 80s—gave way to a heavy importation of American productions and RAI, caught in the competition, was obliged to do the same; as a consequence, Italy became, and remained for many years, the major European importer of foreign (mainly from the US) fiction. During this period, which roughly covered 15 years, Italians familiarized themselves with new genres, such as the sitcom and the serial, but, more importantly, they were exposed to an unending TV offer and soon became heavy viewers of US police series. Although only a few of these series achieved a great popularity (others became cult products for a more restricted audience), basically there was no single US cop show which was not imported in Italy and adopted in the daily encyclopedia of TV titles, texts, characters and actors familiar to Italian viewers.

In the meantime, domestic production entered a period of increasingly deep decline which only started giving some signs of inversion in the mid-90s: producing programs was far more expensive than buying them, and moreover foreign programs were available in large quantities whereas Italian productions were more limited and, ultimately, insufficient in number to cover a prolonged TV schedule.

However, RAI did not entirely abandon the production of police series (it must be pointed out that private networks were and are not interested in the genre) but, although the series and mini-series produced in this period still achieved the success typically attributed to national fiction, they never actually became popular and today are mainly forgotten. Nonetheless, their role in the history, or rather in the process of transformation and elaboration of the Italian police series, is undeniably fundamental as they represent a kind of experimental laboratory for a new localization of the genre within national production. Unlike the previous period, the authors, the characters and the *milieus* were now distinctly Italian; the heroes—always rigorously nonviolent, endowed with human warmth, more intuitive and witty rather than rational or methodical—had Italian names such as Marshall *Arnaudi,* Inspector *De Vincenzi,* Inspector *Falchi,* Sergeant *Sarti,* Detective *Spada,* and operated in Italian cities. The difference from US cop shows could not be more evident, a difference constructed and cultivated intentionally, in search of a national way to the genre.

From the point of view of the relationship between the global and the local in media production and consumption practices, this fragment of Italian TV experience offers an interesting case for cultural analysis. Years and

years of importation, offer and consumption of US cop shows have undoubtedly left strong traces in the popular memory and collective imagery which
cannot be naively ignored; however, not only do the police series produced
in Italy during and after the invasion of US series deny any mechanistic
hypothesis of an irresistible cultural colonization, they also do not allow any
oversimplifying interpretation in terms of an Americanization of their style
and content. On the contrary, they re-elaborate the formulas and the narrative materials of the genre so as to create an original and peculiar expression of the Italian imagination.

All productions made in the early 90s have contributed to the accomplishment of this process. In the last decade there has been a growing interest in the national police series, while US police series are less dominant and
frequently relegated to daytime as, for example, *Murder She Wrote*. This new
period (the third one) starts with *L'Ispettore Sarti* (Inspector Sarti), based
on the short stories written by Loriano Machiavelli, one of the most popular and original contemporary writers of crime stories. Due to the fact that
it is aired late at night, the series has not achieved a great success. It has
certainly become, however, a cult program, largely covered by the press and
appreciated by critics, and its protagonist, a tragi-comic, at times even an
inept figure, has been elected "TV character of the year."

Two other police series must also be mentioned: *Il Commissario Corso*
(Inspector Corso) and *Un Commissario a Roma* (An Inspector in Rome).
Although they reach different ratings (only the second one has entered the
top ten), both these series cast cinema actors whom Italians know as interpreters of the so-called "commedia all'italiana." The presence of comic actors
is not only a source of success, but also an important factor contributing to
redefinition of the genre and the ways it addresses (and is consumed by)
viewers. *L'Ispettore Sarti* already, with its awkward and unlucky protagonist,
has started creating an audience for a kind of comic police series: following
this tendency, these two series definitely ratify it by casting actors whose
names evoke in the audience some sort of expectation about the brilliant
lightness and the pleasure of comedy.

Moreover, it is precisely with *L'Ispettore Sarti*, which has somehow set
the standards of the genre, that the police series of the 90s does more than
simply give some "humanizing" glances at the private life of these characters.
More substantially, it starts turning private life into a recurrent and important background, narrating it, at times even intertwining it with the crime
story. In other words, the typical themes and developments of the police series
are mingled with the typical themes and developments of the love and family genre in a way which witnesses the eclectic and combinatory vocation the
Italian police series seems to have possessed since its very beginning.

3. The Formula of the New Italian Police Series

Synthetically, it can be said that the Italian contemporary police series has
evolved into a formula whose peculiarity and identity are based on the com-

bination of four main ingredients relating to the genre, the setting, the themes and the subjectivity of the protagonists. It must be noted, however, that the term "formula" here does not indicate a codified and standardized model, but rather a relatively constant, yet always flexible, blend of ingredients differently combined in more or less original and effective dosages and treatments.

1) The first ingredient is the mixture between the comic and the dramatic. Jokes and gags, evoked and guaranteed by the presence of actors coming from the comedy tradition of cinema and theater (Diego Abantantuono, Nino Manfredi, Gigi Proietti), cross the new Italian police series contaminating it with comic elements. The drama of the crime is still there, of course, but somehow lightened and sweetened by frequent occasions for laughter and amusement.

In the attempt to provide the Italian police series with new vitality and originality, this was probably the best direction to follow. Within our national cinema comedy is in fact the only genre still capable of attracting large audiences, and private networks, after discovering this fact, have based almost their entire production of fiction on this genre. Public television instead, traditionally more oriented towards dramatic and melodramatic fiction, is only now entering the field, inserting comic elements into the police genre, and hence succeeding in attracting—at least with its best productions—larger portions of viewers who appear certainly more varied and composite than the *amateurs* of classical police stories or US cop shows. This operation has been in a way facilitated by the fact that the offer of US series has lately diminished, while the few police series imported from France and Germany do not constitute serious competition for national productions.

2) A second ingredient of the new formula is represented by the "distanciation" from the metropolitan *milieu,* as the police series of the 70s and 80s had already started to do, choosing their locations among the small Italian provinces. On the contrary, the traditional police story, rooted since its very beginning in the modern city, can instead be defined in all of its versions—literary, television and cinema—as a mostly metropolitan genre; the US series are always located in the big cities of the east and west coasts and initially the provincial setting of Italian productions is probably motivated by a need for distinction, if not of open opposition to them.

This initial tendency is further developed by the contemporary police series, but in two different directions. The first one simply chooses provincial settings, as is the case of *Il Maresciallo Rocca,* entirely located in a small city not far from the capital. The second direction, more elaborately and sophisticatedly, presents a kind of "provincialization" of the metropolitan space; from a formal point of view, the series is still located in a large city, such as Rome (*Un Commissario a Roma*), Milan (*Il Commissario Corso*), Bologna (*L'Ispettore Sarti*), but the metropolitan context has been reshaped so as to evoke the different aspects—external areas, rhythms of life, human relationships, typologies of crimes—of a provincial city and society. All this originates from the fact that Italy has never become a country of metropolises; indeed, lately, the population of large cities has tended to leave metropolitan areas and move to the smaller urban centers scattered throughout the national territory; as a result of this phenomenon the audience feels more "at home" if confronted with a provincial setting.

3) "Home" is precisely the third ingredient of the formula: the presence of the private/familiar sphere, i.e. the domestic dimension, in the narrative texture of the new police series. It is a well known fact that the private element, and the family in particular, have always occupied, both literally and symbolically, a central space in the Italian cultural tradition and social life. Despite all the undeniable transformations which in the last two or three decades have occurred in the structure and "feeling" of the family, Italy is the only Western country where traditional familial elements persist more manifestly and deeply than anywhere else: from the solidity of family and intergenerational ties to the mutual solidarity within the family network.

It is not surprising, therefore, that all protagonists of the new police series have a family (though not necessarily a "normal" or nuclear one) and a private life, and both are a significant part of the narrative. The reason for this domestic dimension being present only in recent productions can be explained by the fact that in its first phase the Italian police series was still subordinated to a non-Italian tradition, and in the second phase it was still laying the bases of a localization which did not dare to push the limits too much.

Several international productions too have lately offered some protagonists whose profiles have been enriched and diversified by the insertion of fragments of knowledge and representation of their private and family lives: Inspector Navarro, for example, the hero of the eponymously-titled French series (but many US cases could also be mentioned), after the mysterious departure of his wife, lives with a pre-adolescent daughter whom he lovingly interacts with when he comes home at the end of each episode.

The Italian police series, however, offers much more than fragments of private life or temporary intrusions in the domestic *milieu* and familiar affections of its protagonists; it presents the entire sphere of domesticity in its constitutive moments and details: from the collective preparation and consumption of meals to more intimate situations like chatting late at night in bed or walking about the house, *en deshabillé*, at breakfast time. By displaying a whole range of sentimental and educative themes, not only does the Italian police series enrich the traditional police story-line with new issues, but also, by framing such a line into a narrative scheme, modifies the very structure of the series (as we will see in the analysis of *Il Maresciallo Rocca*).

Evidently, the Italian version of the police series is influenced by a specifically local cultural element—the importance of the family and private sphere—either at the level of themes and narrative architectures or at the level of production and marketing strategies. In other words, the mixture of crime dramas with family stories creates the conditions, if not the guarantees, for a genre and a product which succeeds in appealing to larger and more varied fractions of an audience.

4) The fourth ingredient of this new formula can be traced back to the years when the Italian police series used to adopt and re-elaborate foreign

narrative models and characters. It concerns the subjectivity of the protagonists, anti-heroes symbolizing an average humanity endowed with common vices and virtues.

The construction of the typical protagonist of the Italian police series is based on a "discursive mimetic strategy." Building on a passage from Aristotle's *Poetics,* Northrop Frye[1] elaborated on a classification of literary works according to the different stature and power of action of the protagonists. Following Frye's scheme, James W. Chesebro[2] has identified (and applied to television textual analysis) five different discursive strategies or modes of construction of the hero. "Mimetic," in Chesebro's words (or "low mimetic" in Frye's) is that hero whose stature in terms of capacities, intelligence, and power to control circumstances can be perceived as basically similar to ours. "If not superior either to other men or to the environment, the hero is one of us; we are sensitive to his common humanity and ask . . . for obedience to the same canons of probability which are present in our own experience."[3]

Therefore, the typical protagonist of the Italian police series is a "common person" whose personality and intellectual resources as well as power to control circumstances are quite similar to ours. No particular gift or quality puts him above the normal human condition. His wittiest and most effective actions can be ultimately performed also by an averagely intelligent person since they do not require or presuppose an *animus,* nor an athlete's body, but just a simple, daily inclination to work in an honest, compassionate and nonviolent way veined by a sense of impatience for bureaucratic rules. It would be inappropriate to define this protagonist as a "man with no quality" since he does embody all those qualities Italians tend to appreciate: cunning, flexibility, intuition, knowledge of the world. However, it would be equally inappropriate to ignore his vices, the inclination to impulsiveness and improvisation, and in general a whimsical temper which tends to appear especially in his private life.

The sense and the value of the strategic construction of a mimetic hero, an "everyman" as it were, can be better understood if one considers the fact that Italian culture is somehow run through by a vein of incompatibility and resistance towards the typical hero of the traditional police series. With the exception of private or amateur detective, belonging more to a literary tradition rather than a TV one, such a hero is an institutional figure, the representative of a State Corps in charge of the respect of Law and Order; according to the conventions of the genre he is always a winner, one who unfailingly comes up with a solution to the enigma, unmasks the criminals and arrests them.

In Italy this ideal narrative structure collides with a civic culture which, however inconstant and uneven, is characterized by a suspicious, if not totally distrustful, attitude towards all state institutions and representatives. The recent scandals of *Tangentopoli*—a long series of judicial investigations and trials against a large number of corrupt politicians and businessmen—may have increased Italians' confidence in the Magistrature, but on the whole they still tend to be skeptical that law, order and justice institutions are capable of accomplishing their tasks effectively.

A second consideration that needs to be made is that a persisting tradition of medieval religiosity with its bloody martyrological universe as well as a long history of foreign invasions and dominations have not only caused one notion of power to be an overwhelming, cruel and corrupt force, but have also contributed to conditions for a deep conflation between heroism and martyrdom[4] being created and rooted in Italian collective culture. From past history (the martyrs of the Risorgimento or the antifascist heroes of World War II) to more recent events (the magistrates Falcone and Borsellino and the numerous victims of the Mafia), the ideal Italian hero is characteristically voted to sacrifice, to be a loser, from a practical point of view, but indeed a winner from a moral one. Significantly, before the appearance of Marshall Rocca, the pantheon of Italian TV heroes was dominated by the figure of Inspector Cattani, the protagonist of *La Piovra:* a lonely and desperate hero who, in the fight against organized crime, is finally killed by the Mafia.[5]

By creating a protagonist who is "like one of us" and by mediating between the Italian culture and the conventions of the genre, the Italian police series has contributed to the affirmation of a kind of character Italians wouldn't have accepted so easily. Although formally still representing a state institution, in fact the everyday life hero of the Italian police series embodies the common person and his victory over criminals becomes more credible to us since, in a way, it is also *our* victory.

4. The Stories of Common Heroism of Marshall Rocca

The contemporary formula of the Italian police series finds a perfect and, so to speak, geometric expression in *Il Maresciallo Rocca*. Light humor, provincial settings, family life situations and a common, everyday life hero (as the promotional campaign has defined Rocca): all the basic ingredients we have just described are there, combined as harmoniously as never before. The series, however, does not simply build and capitalize on previous experiences, but, working on the margins, introduces its own variations, as, for example, with the text which is characterized by a more evident turn towards the private/familiar spheres of the protagonist. We are faced with an authentic conflation of two genres, or better with a grafting of the familiar (and sentimental) comedy onto the police story—after all in the evolution and re-writing of genres this kind of operation occurs all the time: think, for example, of *Bonanza*'s grafting of the family story onto the western.

The protagonist of the series is a mature marshall of the *Carabinieri* working in Viterbo, a city 100 km away from Rome. Viterbo is one of the most beautiful medieval centers in Italy. It has a well preserved urbanistic structure and important monuments such as the Palace of the Popes, built in the second half of the 13th century as a pontifical residence. Nevertheless, in a country where artistically and historically interesting places abound, Viterbo is not one of the most popular and, more importantly, it is not linked to any particular and widely known iconic identification, as is for example the tower in Pisa, the square in Siena where the famous annual

horse race (the *Palio*) is run, the cathedral facade in Orvieto, etc. Consequently, many viewers have come to know only through the press that the
series is set in Viterbo. However, the nonpopularity of the setting, far from
being a disadvantage, has in fact given a higher representative quality to the
images of the city which have since become the visual marks of a distinctly
Italian place, with its ancient spots naturalized in the everyday life landscape.

Marshall Rocca is a widower with three children whose ages range from
childhood to youth, all living together in the apartment next to the *Carabinieri* station. By centering the text on the paternal figure, intertwining it
with the institutional role of the Marshall, the series connects, for the first
time, the police story with the recent tendency in Italian fiction to privilege
the representation and thematic treatment of paternity. However, it would
be wrong to consider the protagonist simply as a loving and sensitive father,
as a quite popular model in contemporary media imagination would suggest (a model which Hollywood shares too: a "paternal cycle" is present
since at least *Kramer vs. Kramer*). On the contrary, *Il Maresciallo Rocca*
reveals a particular ability in employing stereotypes creatively as it transforms
its protagonist into the embodiment of a kind of father rarely appearing in
contemporary TV fiction: a good father, of course, but most of all an authoritative and wise figure, respected both by his children and by his young
Carabinieri whom he also addresses with a paternal attitude. Much of the
popularity this figure has achieved is due to this strong and well-defined
paternal quality which makes Marshall Rocca a leader, the moral center of
the familiar and working *milieus*, and the gravitational point of the community as a whole. Although time, place and genre set *Il Maresciallo Rocca*
quite far from the Western, yet, by conflating the figure which guarantees
Law and Order with the figure symbolizing paternity, the protagonist seems
to evoke a sheriff, as the scriptwriters themselves must have intended.

The private life of Marshall Rocca, which frames the whole series, is
enriched since the very first episode by his falling in love with the new phar-
macist of the town, a sweet and discreet woman who has just come out
from a painful divorce (played by Stefania Sandrelli, a cinema actress with
a long and uninterrupted popularity).

Family, love, crime: combining these three thematic areas the series succeeds in recomposing the segmentation of the genre and the audience, appealing to diversified portions of it. As media professionals say, *Il Maresciallo
Rocca* has got "something for everybody": a love-story and family situations
for women, intergenerational relationships and young characters for young
people, and a crime-story for the amateurs (usually men) of the genre. Finally,
it must be pointed out that the representation of the normal processes of a
familial and sentimental life has an important reassuring function, especially
for a genre traditionally based on deviancy.

All these elements are formally translated into a narrative structure which
could be defined as open and closed at the same time, a *framed* serial formula
where the single and autonomous episodes are inserted into a narrative frame
which, following a linear and continuous development, provides the series

with history and memory. Each episode develops an issue-oriented police story—usury, incest, exploitation of immigrant workers—whose solution is due to the nonextraordinary, yet always effective and well-experienced, modes of investigation of Marshall Rocca. In the margins, and sometimes even in the central spaces of the police plot, we find, episode after episode, a family and a love story. The former employs the modes, the canons and the temporality of the domestic comedy: with little or no evolution at all, it offers situations and problems which typically belong to the daily interaction between a father and three children. On the contrary, the love story follows, albeit weakly, some kind of evolution; it has ups and downs, resentments and delays, until it consolidates into a real engagement, joyfully and movingly celebrated in the last episode. In other words, we can say that each episode is structured according to a three-level narrative scheme—the police story, the domestic situation and the sentimental relationship—and a double temporality—a repetitive one (the series) and a continuous one (the frame).

The plot of this police series is usually quite simple so that the audience can selfconfidently follow the investigations and even, thanks to repeated and often manifest clues, anticipate the solution. Significantly, in order to stress this collective participation in the investigations, several episodes end with a choral composition where the marshall's collaborators, friends and relatives gather around a table to celebrate and toast together: indeed, an unusual ritual for a police story, yet an important one since it both reveals the domesticity pervading the world of the series and expresses a common and widely recognized trait of Italian culture and tradition, i.e. the pleasure of eating and drinking together.

Domesticity contributes in creating and supporting the image of "an everyday life, a common hero," as the promos say stressing the peculiar characterization of the protagonist: a positive hero, but always quite normal in his common (in the double sense of diffused and ordinary) and solid virtues. In this series normality and everyday life acquire a distinctive thematic and representative space: scenes and situations of everyday life are scattered throughout the episodes, both in the private and professional spheres, hence contributing to give credibility to the story. The hero himself is often represented in a daily-life fashion through a precise narrative strategy. His average-person quality is favored by a certain play of character contrasts and a likely mixture of vices and virtues. Both these categories—alternately, prevailing one over the other, depending on the cases or the point of view—define the most evident characteristic of Rocca's profile, as his name (meaning "rock") also indicates: the stubbornness and the perseverance which animate his actions bringing him to make some (rare) mistakes which, however, he honestly and readily admits.

Always self-confident, friendly and ironic, yet resolute and effective, Marshall Rocca introduced in the world of the series, entirely revolving around him, a touch of lightness and optimism which Italian fiction had not offered for a long time, at least in such a convinced and convincing way, and also creates the conditions of possibility for a lasting presence of the series in the memory and imagination of Italian viewers.

5. *The Sense of Place*

Il Maresciallo Rocca is one of those rare TV fictions which has succeeded in permeating an entire TV season in such an intense and diffused way that the simple notion of success appears totally inadequate to describe it. Of course, every season has its own hits, but there is not a necessary equivalence between high audience ratings and the capacity a fiction has to penetrate and deeply resonate in the collective imagination. The popularity of *Il Maresciallo Rocca* cannot be properly grasped without taking into account, last but not least, another factor whose special nature goes beyond the considerations about the genre and the character we have made so far.

What makes this series a peculiar case is a rather distinctive quality which, while not being the only reason for its popularity, is definitely a very important component of it, a quality which can be defined as "the sense of place." In other words, *Il Maresciallo Rocca* is characterized by a blend of elements which cooperate in creating and communicating a strong "sense of place."

In media studies this expression designates the delocalization of social life; in this case "the sense of place" is evoked to argue that electronic media are ultimately undermining it, by giving us the possibility to participate in situations and experiences remotely located from the place we live in[6]. But the expression has been also employed in TV studies, particularly by Horace Newcomb[7], to evoke the quality—always elusive from an analytical point of view, yet empirically perceptible—some texts or programs have to suggest accents, atmospheres and resonances clearly belonging to the lived reality *and* collective imagination of a particular place or country.

Several compositive elements contribute to create this "sense of place"— the themes, regional inflections, profiles of the characters, visual materials, and iconic signs of identification—all of them working in isolation or mixed together. For example, the importance of visual materials and iconic signs of identification does not imply that an accurate photographic representation of the locations, nor a repetition of metonymic images—the Eiffel Tower *for* Paris, the Imperial Fora *for* Rome and so on—are sufficient to evoke "the sense of place" which in fact results from the intersection between landscapes and emotions and operates more through suggestion than through objective reproduction. Similarly, it is insufficient to see the notion of "recognizability" as merely linked to traditional stereotypes of places, milieus or culture since "the sense of place" more often implies a creative use of the stereotypes.

We can distinctly feel the highly communicative and attracting presence of this particular quality whenever a fiction succeeds in familiarizing us with the physical/social spaces and the human types it narrates, although they do not belong directly to our lived experience. To better grasp what is being argued here, think for example of a genre (the Western) where "the sense of place" is clearly a constitutive factor. While being fundamental in creating an atmosphere and evoking a mood for intense tunings, the "sense of place" is not necessarily a guarantee of quality. For instance, the hospital series *ER* is connoted by codes and atmospheres of place which are nothing but the simple representation of a US hospital, yet its artistic quality is quite superior to that of *Dallas* where modern Texas and its oil richness are accurately represented in a Wild West fashion.

The old walls of the houses, the little traffic-free streets quickly leading to the countryside, the fields of chicory, the little railway station; and also the private and the work-place family, both gathered around the same paternal figure, the domestic life scenes, even the cellular telephone so much ridiculed by some critics[8]: through figurative, thematic and symbolic elements like these, *Il Maresciallo Rocca* creates a microcosm pervaded by a deep and emotionally acute "sense of place," a place where we feel at home.

The "place," of course, cannot be identified *tout court* with Viterbo (where the series has been located) which in fact tells little or nothing to most of the viewers. It is rather a mental place—a metonymy for Italy as a whole—built with mixed fragments of geography, history, memory and imagination, regrets and expectations, all of them suggesting a world which could not be defined as traditional, or referred back to the 50s. On the contrary, it is a distinctly contemporary place not so much for the lifestyles and the typologies or modes of deviancy we are faced with, but rather for the horizon of values it suggests: honesty, attachment to work and family, human solidarity, i.e. all those values which Italians today tend to regard as fundamental for the moral growth of the country, as social research has demonstrated.

Standing out neatly from this horizon is Marshall Rocca's figure: like the sheriff in Western movies, he is the moral centre of the place, the *genius loci*, a *locus* he paternally and reassuringly makes more desirable and familiar to us. That is why *Il Maresciallo Rocca* far from evoking an Italy of the past is in fact appealing to a *deep Italy* of the present which, given its popularity, it has evidently, and in all senses, touched.

Notes

1. Northrop Frye, *Anatomia della critica*, Einaudi, Torino 1969, 45ff.
2. James W. Chesebro, "Communication, Values, Popular TV Series," in Horace Newcomb (ed.), *Television: The Critical View*. New York: Oxford University Press, 1987 (fourth edition).
3. Frye, *Anatomia della critica*, 46.
4. A. Montanari, *Eroi immaginari*, Liguori, Napoli 1995.
5. M. Buonanno, *La Piovra. La carriera politica di una fiction popolare*, Costa & Nolan, Genova 1996. For a more general view on the tendencies of Italian fiction see by the same author, *Narrami o diva*, Liguori, Napoli 1994, *Leggere la fiction*, Liguori, Napoli 1996 as well as the annual reports *La fiction italiana/L'Italia nella fiction*, published by RAI-VQPT.
6. J. Meyrowitz, *No Sense of Place*. New York: Oxford University Press, 1985.

7. I am grateful to Horace Newcomb for discussing with me, via e-mail, the meaning and the implications of the notion of "the sense of place."

8. Some critics have argued that it is rather unrealistic that a marshall of the Carabinieri has a cellular telephone. But that is not the point. The fact is that in Italy the visibility and the use of cellular telephones are today so evident that they represent an authentic phenomenon of national costume and a suggestive element which contributes to familiarize the audience with the place.

The Politics
of Representation
in Network Television

HERMAN GRAY

Along with the structural shifts, cultural discourses, and institutional trans-formations of the television industry, contemporary television representa-tions of blackness are linked to the presence and admittedly limited influ-ence of a small number of highly visible black producers, writers, directors, and on-screen talent in the entertainment industry. Within the institutional constraints and cultural traditions of a collaborative and producer-driven medium such as television, the successes of Bill Cosby, Oprah Winfrey, Stan Lathan, Arsenio Hall, Marla Gibbs, Keenen Ivory Wayans, Stanley Robert-son, Kellie Goode, Dolores Morris, Suzanne de Passe, Topper Carew, Frank Dawson, Sherman Hemsley, Quincy Jones, Thomas Carter, Carl Franklin, Michael Warren, Debbie Allen, and Tim Reid increased their individual abil-ities at studios and the networks to shape the creation, direction, and tone of television representations of African Americans (Gunther 1990; Horowitz 1989; O'Connor 1990; Zook 1994).[1]

Of course, there is nothing particularly remarkable about the presence of black producers, writers, and directors in network television. Indeed, directors and producers Michael Moye, Thomas Carter, Suzanne de Passe, and others have been central to the production of such critically acclaimed programming as *Equal Justice* and *Lonesome Dove* (Gunther 1990).[2] What is remarkable, however, is that these critically and commercially successful shows have not necessarily been organized around black themes and black cultural sensibilities. Television clearly needs more of this kind of black presence.

At the other extreme are television shows that traffic heavily in themes and representations about blacks, but that, by and large, operate under the creative control and direction of white studio and network executives. Successful comedies such as *Sanford & Son*, Norman Lear/Bud Yorkin staples *The Jeffersons* and *Good Times*, and more recent shows such as *Amen* and *227* come immediately to mind. To be sure, these shows employed black writers and actors, and they drew their creative direction, look, and sensibility from African American culture. But ultimately, the overall creative responsibility for these shows rested with white executive producers—Bud Yorkin, Norman Lear, the Carsey-Werner Company, Irma Kalish, Ed Weinberger, and Miller-Boyett Productions (Newcomb and Alley 1983).

In the final analysis, the creative vision of the white producers predominated even if situations and themes they explored were drawn from African American culture (Newcomb and Alley 1983; interviews with black writers from *227*, 1990). Although the programs were shows about blacks (rather than black shows), there were clearly boundaries concerning cultural representations, social themes, and professional conventions that they dared not transgress. As some of the black television writers from *227* explained to me, the nuances and sensibilities of African American culture that many of them found funny and attempted to bring to particular scripts or scenes became points of professional contention or were eliminated because white head writers and producers thought otherwise.[3] Black writers seldom had the same veto power over white characters, situations, and themes (interview with writers from *227*, 1990).

For many of the shows based on the situations and experiences of blacks, the conventions of television production (especially collaborative writing) serve to discipline, contain, and ultimately construct a point of view. Not surprisingly, this point of view constructs and privileges white middle-class audiences as the ideal viewers and subjects of television stories. In the producer-driven medium of television, a paucity of producers of color continues to be the rule. In a 1989 report issued by the National Commission on Working Women, researcher Sally Steenland (1989) notes that "minority producers constitute only 7% of all producers working on shows with minority characters. Minority female producers comprise only 2% of the total. Of 162 producers working on 30 shows containing minority characters, only 12 are people of color, while 150 (93%) are white. Of the 12 minority producers, 8 are male and 4 are female" (p. 11).

African American writers, directors, and producers in the television industry must still negotiate the rough seas of an institutional and cultural system tightly but subtly structured by race and gender (Dates 1990).[4] It is all the more remarkable, then, that a small number of visible and influential black executive producers, directors, and writers forced open creative spaces within the productive apparatus of television. And within this discursive and industrial space—between black invisibility and white-authorized representations of blackness—black producers such as Cosby, Wayans, Hall, and Jones have had some impact. Rather than simply placing blackness and black themes in the service of the creative visions of white producers or inserting blackness within existing aesthetic visions, these producers have helped to challenge and transform conventional television treatments of blackness by introducing black viewpoints and perspectives (Hampton 1989). In short, they have introduced different approaches and placed existing aesthetic and production conventions in the service of blackness and African American cultural perspectives (Gunther 1990; O'Connor 1990; Ressner 1990). By trying to construct and represent the experiences, nuances, and explicit concerns of African Americans, these producers offer not only different stories, but alternative ways of negotiating and realizing them. Indeed, Kristal Brent Zook (1994) argues quite convincingly that in the 1980s and 1990s television has been an especially important discursive and institutional space because it serves as a vehicle for intertextual and autobiographical dialogue for blacks.

In a business long criticized for the absence of people of color in decision-making positions and authority, efforts on the part of black executives to hire and train African Americans are, to say the least, hard to sustain.[5] In terms of hiring, training, and placement of black talent in all phases of the industry, Bill Cosby, Quincy Jones, and Keenen Ivory Wayans have been singled out. For example, Susan Fales, former executive producer of the *The Cosby Show* spinoff, *A Different World*, began her career in television as an intern with *The Cosby Show* (interview with Susan Fales, 1990).

The impact of this small cohort of influential black producers occasionally, but all too rarely, reaches beyond the generic and thematic boundaries of situation comedy and the thematic dominance of streetwise masculinity that pervades so much of contemporary television representations of blacks. *The Women of Brewster Place, Lonesome Dove,* and *Motown 25: Yesterday, Today, Forever, Polly,* and *The Mary Thomas Story* were all projects created, engineered, or produced by black women: Oprah Winfrey (Harpo Productions), Suzanne de Passe (Motown), and Dolores Morris (Disney Television). As core members of *A Different World*'s production team, black women such as executive producer Susan Fales, director and writer Debbie Allen, and writers Neema Barnette and Yvette Lee were all responsible for the creative look, feel, and direction of the program. As Jacqueline Bobo (1991) points out, these and other black women tell stories about black women that are different from those told by others, and they tell those stories differently. Thus, these black women contribute to the more general project of "fleshing out their female characters to become more multi-dimensional and like actual women and . . . experimenting with important issues and themes" (Steenland 1987:24).

Like their counterparts in cinema and literature, this recent cohort of black television producers has experienced growing visibility and success that has heightened the expectations of black audiences and critics. These heightened expectations have, in turn, produced conflict among and criticism from African Americans. For instance, heated public criticism has been directed toward Keenen Ivory Wayans, creator and former producer of *In Living Color,* for staging his irreverent humor at the expense of blacks; toward Arsenio Hall for his failure to place more blacks on the staff and technical crew of his late-night talk show; and toward Bill Cosby because his series often failed to address social issues facing black Americans (Braxton 1991; Christon 1989; Collins 1990; Dyson 1989; Fuller 1992; Gray 1989; Jhally and Lewis 1992).

The mere presence of a critical group of successful black producers, directors, and writers has, nevertheless, helped to bring different, often more complex, stories, themes, characters, and representations of blackness to commercial network television. Questions about the continuing presence of racism and sexism in the television industry as well as the social impact and cultural meaning of these stories are ongoing subjects of heated debate and study. The fact remains, however, that the variety and sheer number of stories about blacks proliferated in the 1980s to a degree perhaps unparalleled in the history of television (Siegel 1989a; Waters and Huck 1988).

The Historical and Discursive Formation of Television Treatments of Blackness

Alone, the argument that television representation of blackness is primarily shaped by changing industrial and market conditions that enabled a small number of black producers, directors, and writers to tell stories about black life from the perspective of blacks is reductionist. To avoid such reductionism, I want to argue also for a reading of the social meaning and cultural significance of television's representations of blackness in terms of their political, historical, and aesthetic relationship to earlier generations of shows about blacks. I contend that contemporary television representations of blacks depend heavily on shows about families, the genre of (black) situation comedy, entertainment/variety programming, and the social issue traditions of Norman Lear (Allen 1987; Dates 1990; MacDonald 1983; Spigel 1992; Taylor 1989).

Ultimately, then, I argue that our contemporary moment continues to be shaped discursively by representations of race and ethnicity that began in the formative years of television (Lipsitz 1990b; Riggs 1991a; Spigel 1992; Winston 1982). The formative period of television and its representation of race and ethnicity in general and blacks in particular is central to my argument in two crucial ways: first, together with dominant representations of blacks in film, radio, the press, and vaudeville, this inaugural moment helped to shape the cultural and social terms in which representations of blacks appeared in mass media and popular culture (Dates 1990); second, as illustrated by Marlon Riggs's (1991a) documentary film, *Color Adjustment,* this formative period is a defining discursive and aesthetic moment that enabled and shaped the adjustments that black representations continue to make. It remains the moment against which all other television representations of blackness have reacted. And it is the defining moment with which subsequent representations, including those in the 1980s and beyond, remain in dialogue (Dates 1990; Riggs 1991b; Taylor 1991; Winston 1982). In the early 1950s, programs such as *Amos 'n' Andy, Beulah, The Jack Benny Show*, and *Life with Father* presented blacks in stereotypical and subservient roles whose origins lay in eighteenth- and nineteenth-century popular forms (Cripps 1983; Dates 1990; Ely 1991; Winston 1982). Blacks appeared primarily as maids, cooks, "mammies," and other servants, or as con artists and deadbeats. These stereotypes were necessary for the representation and legitimation of a racial order built on racism and white supremacy. Media scholars and historians have clearly established the formative role of radio in the institutional and aesthetic organization of early television (Czitrom 1982). As Winston (1982), Barlow and Dates (1990), and Ely (1991) suggest, the networks, first with radio and later with television shows such as *Beulah, Amos 'n' Andy*, and *The Jack Benny Show*, played an active and crucial role in the construction and representation of blacks in American mass media.[6] In the televisual world of the early 1950s, the social and cultural rules of race relations between blacks and whites were explicit: black otherness was required for white subjectivity; blacks and whites occupied separate and unequal worlds; black labor was always in the service of white domesticity (*The Jack Benny Show, Life with Father, Beulah*); black humor was necessary for the amusement of whites.[7]

Culturally, because blackness served whiteness in this way, the reigning perspective of this world was always staged from a white subject position; when television did venture inside the separate and unfamiliar world of blacks—in, say, *Amos 'n' Andy*—viewers found comforting reminders of whiteness and the ideology of white supremacy that it served: here was the responsible, even sympathetic, black domestic in *Beulah;* there were the responsible but naive members of the world of *Amos 'n' Andy*. But seldom were there representations of the social competence and civic responsibilities that would place any of the black characters from these shows on equal footing with whites (Dates 1990:204). Black characters who populated the television world of the early 1950s were happy-go-lucky social incompetents who knew their place and whose antics served to amuse and comfort culturally sanctioned notions of whiteness, especially white superiority and paternalism. These black folk could be trusted to manage white households, nurture white children, and "restore balance and normalcy to the [white] household" (Dates 1990:262), but they could not be trusted with the social and civic responsibilities of full citizenship as equals with whites.

In the racially stratified and segregated social order of the 1950s United States, there was enough about these representations to both comfort and offend. So pervasive and secure was the discourse of whiteness that in their amusement whites were incapable of seeing these shows and the representations they presented as offensive. At the same time, of course, many middle-class blacks were so outraged by these shows, particularly *Amos 'n' Andy*, that the NAACP successfully organized and engineered a campaign in 1953 to remove the show from the air (Cripps 1983; Dates 1990; Ely 1991; Montgomery 1989). As racist and stereotypical as these representations were, the cultural and racial politics they activated were far from simple; many poor, working-class, and even middle-class blacks still managed to read against the dominant discourse of whiteness and find humor in the show. However, because of the charged racial politics between blacks and whites, as well as the class and cultural politics within black America, the tastes, pleasures, and voices in support of the show were drowned out by the moral outrage of middle-class blacks.[8] To be sure, although blacks and whites alike may have found the show entertaining and funny, these pleasures meant different things. They were situated in very different material and discursive worlds. The social issues, political positions, and cultural alliances that shows such as *Amos 'n' Andy* organized and crystallized, then, were powerful and far-reaching in their impact, so much so that I believe that contemporary representations remain in dialogue with and only now have begun to transcend this formative period.[9]

By the late 1950s and throughout the 1960s, the few representations of blacks that did appear on network television offered more benign and less explicitly stereotypical images of African Americans. Shows such as *The Nat "King" Cole Show* (1956–57), *I Spy* (1965–68), and *Julia* (1968–71) attempted to make blacks acceptable to whites by containing them or rendering them, if not culturally white, invisible.[10] In these shows the social and cultural "fact of blackness" was treated as a minor if not coincidental theme—present but contained. In the racially tense and stratified United States of the middle 1960s, Diahann Carroll and Bill Cosby lived and worked in mostly white worlds where whites dare not notice and blacks dare not acknowledge their blackness. Where the cultural and social "fact of blackness" was irrepressible, indeed, central to the aesthetics of a show, it had to be contained. (Whiteness also operated as the dominant and normative place of subjectivity both on and off the screen. In this racialized world of television common sense neither whites nor blacks had any need to acknowledge whiteness explicitly.)

This strategy of containment was used with Nat Cole, the elegant and sophisticated star of *The Nat "King" Cole Show*.[11] An accomplished jazz—read black—pianist, Cole was packaged and presented by NBC to foreground his qualities as a universally appealing entertainer. Cole was the host of a television variety show that emphasized his easy manner and polished vocal style, and the containment of his blackness was clearly aimed to quell white fears and appeal to liberal white middle-class notions of responsibility and good taste. In the social and cultural climate of the times, NBC thought it necessary to separate Cole from any association with the black jazz life (an association made larger than life with the sensational press coverage of Billie Holiday, Charlie Parker, Charles Mingus, and Miles Davis), equating black jazz artists with drugs, sex, rebellion, and social deviance. Despite this cautious strategy, the network's failure to secure national sponsors for the show, especially in the South, resulted in cancellation of *The Nat "King" Cole Show* after only one season. Sanitized and contained representations of blacks in the late 1950s and the 1960s developed in response to the stereotypical images that appeared in the early days of television. They constitute signal moments in discursive adjustment and readjustment of black representations in commercial television (MacDonald 1983; Montgomery 1989; Winston 1982).

Against this discursive backdrop as well as the social rebellions of the 1960s, the representations of black Americans that appeared throughout the 1970s were a direct response to social protest and petitions by blacks against American society in general and the media in particular for the general absence of black representations (MacDonald 1983; Montgomery 1989; Winston 1982). Beginning in 1972, television program makers and the networks produced shows that reached for "authentic" representations of black life within poor urban communities.[12] These programs were created as responses to angry calls by different sectors of the black community for "relevant" and "authentic" images of black people.

It is easy to see now that both the demand for relevant shows and the networks' responses were themselves profoundly influenced by the racial and cultural politics of the period. The new shows offered were designed to contain the anger and impatience of communities on the move politically; program makers, the networks, and "the community" never paused to examine critically the notions of relevance or authenticity. As a visible and polemical site of cultural debate, television moved away from its treatment of blacks in the previous decade. The television programs involving blacks in the 1970s were largely representations of what white liberal middle-class television program makers assumed (or projected) were "authentic" accounts of poor black urban ghetto experiences. *Good Times* (1974–79), *Sanford & Son* (1972–77), and *What's Happening!!* (1976–79), for example, were all set in poor urban communities and populated by blacks who were often unemployed or underemployed. But more important, for the times, these black folk were good-humored and united in racial solidarity regardless (or perhaps because) of their condition. Ironically, despite the humor and social circumstances of the characters, these shows continued to idealize and quietly reinforce a normative white middle-class construction of family, love, and happiness. These shows implicitly reaffirmed the commonsense belief that such ideals and the values they promote are the rewards of individual sacrifice and hard work.

These themes appeared in yet another signal moment in commercial television representations of African Americans—in the hugely successful miniseries *Roots*. Inhabiting the televisual space explored three years earlier in the miniseries *The Autobiography of Miss Jane Pittman*, *Roots* distinguished itself commercially and thematically as one of the most-watched television shows in history. Based on Alex Haley's book of the same name, *Roots* presented the epic story of the black American odyssey from Africa through slavery to the twentieth century. It brought to millions of Americans, for the first time, the story of the horrors of slavery and the noble struggles of black Americans. This television representation of blacks remained anchored by familiar commitments to economic mobility, family cohesion, private property, and the notion of America as a land of immigrants held together by shared struggles of hardships and ultimate triumph.

There is little doubt that the success of *Roots* helped to recover and reposition television constructions and representations of African Americans and blackness from their historic labors in behalf of white racism and myths of white superiority. But the miniseries also contributed quite significantly to the transformation, in the popular imaginary, of the discourse of slavery and American race relations between blacks and whites. That is to say, with *Roots* the popular media discourse about slavery moved from one of almost complete invisibility (never mind structured racial subordination, human degradation, and economic exploitation) to one of ethnicity, immigration, and human triumph. This powerful television epic effectively constructed the story of American slavery from the stage of emotional identifications and attachments to individual characters, family struggles, and the realization of the American dream. Consequently, the social organization of racial subordination, the cultural reliance on human degradation, and the economic exploitation of black labor receded almost completely from the story. And, of course, this quality is precisely what made the television series such a huge success.

From the distance of some seventeen years, I also want to suggest another less obvious but powerful effect of *Roots,* especially for African American cultural struggles over the sign of blackness. My criticisms of the dominant labors of the series notwithstanding, I want to propose that for an entire generation of young blacks, *Roots* also opened—enabled, really—a discursive space in mass media and popular culture within which contemporary discourses of blackness developed and circulated. I think that it is possible to locate within the media discourse of blackness articulated by *Roots* some of the enabling conditions necessary for the rearticulation of the discourse of Afrocentric nationalism. In other words, I would place *Roots* in dialogue with the reactivation and renewed interest in black studies and the development of African-centered rap and black urban style, especially their contemporary articulation and expression in popular culture and mass media. It seems to me that *Roots* enabled and facilitated the circulation and saturation of the popular imaginary with television representation of Africa and blackness. Finally, relative to the televisual construction of African Americans and blackness in the 1950s and 1960s, *Roots* helped to alter slightly, even momentarily interrupt, the gaze of television's idealized white middle-class viewers and subjects. However minimal, with its cultural acknowledgment of black viewers and subjects, the miniseries enabled a temporary but no less powerful transitional space within which to refigure and reconstruct black television representations.[13]

In black-oriented situation comedies of the late 1970s and early 1980s, especially the long-running *The Jeffersons,* as well as *Benson, Webster, Diff'rent Strokes,* and *Gimme a Break,* black upward social mobility and middle-class affluence replaced black urban poverty as both setting and theme (Gray 1986).[14] Predictably, however, the humor remained. Even though these situation comedies were set in different kinds of "families"—single-parent households, homes with cross-racial adoptions—that were supposed to represent an enlightened approach to racial difference, in the end they

too were anchored by and in dialogue with familiar themes and emblems
of familial stability, individualism, and middle-class affluence (Gray 1986).
Although blackness was explicitly marked in these shows, it was whiteness
and its privileged status that remained unmarked and therefore hegemonic
within television's discursive field of racial construction and representation
(Kelley 1992). As with their predecessors from the 1950s and 1960s, blacks
in the shows from the 1970s and early 1980s continued to serve as surrogate managers, nurturers, and objects of white middle-class fascination
(Dates 1990; Steenland 1989). Furthermore, as conventional staples of the
genre, they required unusual and unfamiliar situations (e.g., black children
in white middle-class homes) for thematic structure and comedic payoff. In
appearance, this generation of shows seems more explicit, if not about the
subject of race, at least about cultural difference. However, because they
continued to construct and privilege white middle-class viewers and subject
positions, in the end they were often as benign and contained as shows
about blacks from earlier decades.

The Cosby Moment

Discursively, in terms of television constructions of blackness, *The Cosby Show*
is culturally significant because of the productive space it cleared and the
aesthetic constructions of black cultural style it enabled. Pivotal to understanding the social position and cultural significance of contemporary television representations of blackness is what I shall call the Cosby moment.
Like the miniseries *Roots, The Cosby Show* reconfigured the aesthetic and
industrial spaces within which modern television representations of blacks
are constructed.

Indeed, under Bill Cosby's careful guidance the show quite intentionally presented itself as a corrective to previous generations of television representations of black life. In countless press interviews, Cosby voiced his
frustrations with television's representation of blacks. Here is just one:

> Run down what you saw of black people on TV before the Huxtables. You
> had "Amos 'n' Andy," one of the funniest shows ever, people say. But who
> ever went to college? Who tried for better things? In "Good Times," J. J.
> Walker played a definite underachiever. In "Sanford & Son," you have a
> junk dealer living a few thousand dollars above the welfare level. "The Jef-
> fersons" move uptown. He owns a dry-cleaning store, lives in an integrated
> neighborhood. Where are the sociological writings about this? (quoted in
> Christon 1989:45)

Positioning *The Cosby Show* in relation to the previous history of programs
about blacks helps explain its upper-middle-class focus. More significantly,
the show's discursive relationship to television's historical treatment of
African Americans and contemporary social and cultural debates (about the
black underclass, the black family, and black moral character) helps to explain
its insistent recuperation of African American social equality (and competence), especially through the trope of the stable and unified black middle-

class family (Dates 1990; Downing 1988; Dyson 1989; Fuller 1992; Jhally and Lewis 1992).

In *The Cosby Show*, blackness, although an element of the show's theme, character, and sensibility, was mediated and explicitly figured through home life, family, and middle-classness. Cosby explained the show's treatment of race: "It may seem I'm an authority because my skin color gives me a mark of a victim. But that's not a true label. I won't deal with the *foolishness* of racial overtones on the show. I base an awful lot of what I've done simply on what people will enjoy. I want to show a family that has a *good* life, not people to be jealous of" (quoted in Christon 1989:7; emphasis added).[15] The Huxtable family is universally appealing, then, largely because it is a middle-class family that happens to be black (Dates 1990; Dyson 1989; Fuller 1992; Gray 1989; Greenly 1987; Jhally and Lewis 1992).

In an enactment of what Stuart Hall (1981b) calls the "politics of reversals" in black-oriented shows from the 1970s, the merger of race (blackness) and class (poverty) often provided little discursive and textual space for whites and many middle-class blacks to construct meaning for the shows that was not troubling and derisive. *The Cosby Show* strategically used the Huxtables' upper-middle-class status to invite audience identifications across race, gender, and class lines. For poor, working-, and middle-class African Americans, Asian Americans, latinos, and whites it was impossible simply to laugh at these characters and make their blackness an object of derision and fascination. Rather, blackness coexisted in the show on the same discursive plane as their upper-middle-class success (Dyson 1989; Jhally and Lewis 1992).

In this respect, *The Cosby Show* is critical to the development of contemporary television representations of blacks. The show opened to some whites and affirmed for many (though by no means all) blacks a vast and previously unexplored territory of diversity within blackness—that is, upper-middle-class life.[16] On the question of *The Cosby Show*'s importance to the representation of differences within blackness, Michael Dyson (1989) perceptively notes:

> *The Cosby Show* reflects the increasing diversity of African American life, including continuous upward social mobility by blacks, which provides access to new employment opportunities and expands the black middle class. Such mobility and expansion insures the development of new styles for blacks that radically alter and impact African American culture. *The Cosby Show* is a legitimate expression of one aspect of that diversity. Another aspect is the intra-racial class divisions and differentiation introduced as a result of this diversification of African American life. (p. 29)

Discursively, the show appropriated the genre of situation comedy and used it to offer a more complex representation of African American life than had been seen previously.

This ability to organize and articulate different audiences together successfully through televisual representations of upper-middle-class African Americans accounts for *The Cosby Show*'s popularity as well as the criticisms and suspicions it generated (Dyson 1989; Gray 1989; Jhally and Lewis 1992). If, to its credit, the program did not construct a monolithic and one-dimensional view of blackness, then, as Dyson points out, its major drawback was its unwillingness to build on the very diversity and complexity of black life that it brought to television. That is to say, the show seemed unwilling to critique and engage various aspects of black diversity that it visually represented. In particular, *The Cosby Show* often failed even to comment on the economic and social disparities and constraints facing millions of African Americans outside of the middle class.

The show seemed unable, or unwilling, to negotiate its universal appeals to family, the middle class, mobility, and individualism on the one hand and the particularities of black social, cultural, political, and economic realities on the other. While effectively representing middle-class blackness as one expression of black diversity, the show in turn submerged other sites, tensions, and points of difference by consistently celebrating mobility, unlimited consumerism, and the patriarchal nuclear family (Dyson 1989; Gray 1989). Notwithstanding its political and cultural desires, *The Cosby Show* seemed nevertheless underwritten by the racial politics of "unity," which comes at the cost of subordinating key differences within that unity. In the social climate of the Reagan and Bush years and amid debates about affirmative action and the urban underclass, the show as Dyson (1989) puts it,

> presented a black universe as the norm, feeling no need to announce the imposition of African American perspectives since they are assumed. Cosby has shown us that we need not construct the whole house of our life experience from the raw material of our racial identity. And that black folk are interested in issues which transcend race. *However, such coming of age progress should not lead to zero-sum social concerns so that to be aware of race-transcending issues replaces or cancels out concerns about the black poor or issues which generate interracial conflict.* (p. 30; emphasis added)

As Dyson suggests, *The Cosby Show*'s strategic stance on the "foolishness of racial overtones" has its limits. This was made painfully obvious in April 1992 with the entirely coincidental, but no less poignant, juxtaposition of the show's final episode with news coverage of the Los Angeles riots. The televisual landscape that evening dramatically illustrated that no matter how much television tries to manage and smooth them over, conflict, rage, and suspicion based on race and class are central elements of contemporary America. Next to the rage that produced pictures or Los Angeles burning, the representations and expressions of African American life and experience on *The Cosby Show* (and so much of contemporary television) seemed little more than soothing symbolic props required to affirm America's latest illusion of feel-good multiculturalism and racial cooperation.

Many of the same contradictions and labors of blackness found in the representations of African Americans on *The Cosby Show* were also present in other black-oriented shows that appeared in the aftermath of the show's success. *Amen, Homeroom, 227, Snoops, Family Matters,* and *True Colors* all provided familiar (and comfortable) renderings of black middle-class family life in the United States. The cultural traditions and social experiences and concerns of many African Americans, although much more explicit, nevertheless functioned in these programs as comedic devices, to stage the action or signal minor differences. Although often staged from a black normative universe, these shows seldom presented black subjectivities and cultural traditions as alternative perspectives on everyday life.[17] That is to say, as a cultural and experiential referent, blackness was seldom privileged or framed as a vantage point for critical insights, guides to action, or explanations for what happens to African American people in modern American society.

By contrast, *Frank's Place*, some of the programming on the Black Entertainment Television cable network, *A Man Called Hawk*, early programs on *The Arsenio Hall Show*, *Yo! MTV Raps*, *Pump It Up*, *Rap Street*, *A Different World*, and *In Living Color* often deployed race and class in different ways.[18] These shows present visions and perspectives in which African American social locations and experiences are more central to the programs' structure and viewpoint. Of course, all of these shows operate squarely within the conventional and aesthetic boundaries of their particular genres—situation comedy, variety, talk, or whatever. But, as I suggest below, in significant respects these shows are different from the others, including *The Cosby Show*. At the same time, however, they are dependent on *Cosby* and the shows that preceded it for representations of black experiences in America. That is, how they construct black subjects can be read only against previous shows. In this respect, I regard *The Cosby Show* as a critically important moment, a transitional point, if you will, in the development of television representations of blacks. *The Cosby Show* and some of the innovative shows that followed it (e.g., *Frank's Place*, *Roc*, *A Man Called Hawk*) form part of a continuing discourse of adjustment and dialogue with the history of television representations of blacks.

The Cosby Show's most significant contribution to television's representations of blacks and the ongoing discursive adjustments that are central to such a project has been the way that it repositioned and recoded blackness and black (middle-class) subjectivity within television's own discursive and institutional practices. To be sure, the limitations and criticisms of the show, especially the cultural labors it performed in the rearticulation of a new, more "enlightened" racism, as well as the consolidation of Reaganism on the question of race and morality, must be registered (Gray 1993a; Jhally and Lewis 1992; Miller 1988). However, coming as it did in the midst of neoconservative assaults, African American cultural debates, and the transformation of the television industry, the show has also had an enabling effect within television. Indeed, *The Cosby Show* itself became the subject of parody and imitation. In its last few seasons the show turned its thematic gaze away from its narrow preoccupation with familial domesticity to pressing social issues, including education and employment, affecting urban black youth.[19]

For most of its run I remained ambivalent about *The Cosby Show*. As a regular viewer, on many occasions I found pleasures in the predictable humor and identified with the idealizations of family, mobility, and material security represented on the show. I took particular delight in the program's constant attempt to showcase black music and such musicians as John Birks (Dizzy) Gillespie, B. B. King, Mongo Santamaria, and Betty Carter. On the other hand, in my classes, at conferences, and in print I have criticized the show for its idealization of the middle class and its failure to address issues that confront a large number of African Americans. I have often regarded this ambivalence as my unwillingness to stake out a position on the show, to make up my mind. But this unwillingness, I am increasingly convinced, is part of the show's appeal, its complexity in an age of racial and cultural politics where the sign of blackness labors in the service of many different interests at once. As I have been arguing, *The Cosby Show* constructed and enabled new ways of representing African Americans' lives. But within black cultural politics of difference the strategy of staging black diversity within the limited sphere of domesticity and upper-middle-class affluence has its costs.

Discursive Practices and Contemporary Television Representations of Blackness

Having mapped the institutional and discursive history of commercial network television representations of blackness, I now want to suggest that contemporary images of African Americans are anchored by three kinds of discursive practices. I shall refer to these as assimilationist (invisibility), pluralist (separate but equal), and multiculturalist (diversity). In each of these discursive practices, I am interested in how the strategies of signification employed in representative television programs construct, frame, stage, and narrate general issues of race and, more specifically, black subjectivity and presence in contemporary U.S. society.

These practices are historically and discursively related to one another and to contemporary social discourses about race. Thus, the dominance and primacy of a particular set of images and representations from each of these television constructions and representations of blackness are contingent on the social, technological, and institutional conditions in which they are situated. Through reruns, cable networks, syndication, and independent stations, viewers have virtually unlimited access to the complete body of television representations of blacks. Thus, these programs constitute a vital part of the contemporary television landscape and should be examined by media and television scholars in terms of the shifting meanings and pleasures they offer in our present moment (see Butsch 1990).

Assimilation and the Discourse of Invisibility

Assimilationist television discourses treat the social and political issues of black presence in particular and racism in general as individual problems. As complex social and political issues, questions of race, gender, class, and power are addressed through the treatment of racism and racial inequality as the results of prejudice (attitudes), and through the foregrounding of the individual ego as the site of social change and transformation. I consider shows assimilationist to the extent that the worlds they construct are distinguished by the complete elimination or, at best, marginalization of social and cultural difference in the interest of shared and universal similarity. These are noble aspirations, to be sure, but such programs consistently erase the histories of conquest, slavery, isolation, and power inequalities, conflicts, and struggles for justice and equality that are central features of U.S. society (see Lipsitz 1990b). Programs organized by such assumptions are framed almost entirely through codes and signifying practices that celebrate racial invisibility and color blindness (see Gray 1986). Beginning with *I Spy* and continuing with *Julia, Mission: Impossible,* and *Room 222,* these early shows integrated individual black characters into hegemonic white worlds void of any hint of African American traditions, social struggle, racial conflicts, and cultural difference.

Contemporary variations on this theme remain with us today. In the 1980s, assimilationist television representations of African Americans could be found in daytime soaps, advertising, and local and network new programs as well as in such prime-time shows as *Family Ties, The Golden Girls, Designing Women, L.A. Law,* and *Night Court.* Without a doubt, some of these shows, including *L.A. Law, The Golden Girls,* and *Designing Women,* featured episodes that explicitly addressed issues of contemporary racial politics, but I nonetheless maintain that where such themes were explicitly addressed they were underwritten and framed by assumptions that privilege individual cooperation and color blindness. In other words, at their best these shows acknowledged but nevertheless framed cultural distinctions and conflicts based on race in ways that ultimately appealed to visions of color blindness, similarity, and universal harmony. In terms of black participation (and inclusion), black characters' acceptance seemed to be inversely related to the degree of separation from black social life and culture. Unique individual black characters (such as Anthony in *Designing Women*) seemed to demonstrate the principle of racial exceptionalism. That is, they seemed to be appealing because of their uniqueness and their neatness of fit into a normative television universe.

Assimilationist programs construct a United States where the historic and contemporary consequences of structured social inequality and a culture deeply inflected and defined by racism are invisible and inconsequential to the lives of its citizens. Seldom on these shows is there ever any sustained engagement with the messiness, confusion, and tension caused by racism and inequality that punctuate the daily experience of so many members of our society. In these televisual worlds American racial progress is measured by the extent to which individual citizens, regardless of color, class, or gender, are the same and are treated equally within the existing social, economic, and cultural (and televisual) order. When they exist, race, class, and gender inequalities seem quite extraordinary, and they always seem to operate at the level of individual experience. Put differently, to the extent that these tensions and conflicts are addressed at all, they figure primarily through individual characters (white and black) with prejudiced attitudes, who then become the focus of the symbolic transformation required to restore narrative balance.

In keeping with television's conventional emphasis on character and dramatic action, assimilationist television discourses locate the origins and operation of prejudiced attitudes at the level of the individual, where they stem from deeply held fears, insecurities, and misunderstandings by individual whites who lack sufficient contact with blacks and other peoples of color. For blacks, on the other hand, they are expressed as the hurts and pains of exclusion that have inevitably hardened into victimization, anger, and irrationality. Typical examples from episodes of *Family Ties* and *The Golden Girls* used the presence of black neighbors and a potential romantic interest, respectively, to identify and draw out white prejudices and suspicions about blacks. In the end, misunderstandings and mistrust were revealed as the source of fear and suspicion. With television's conventional reliance on narrative resolution, once identified, such troubling issues as racial prejudice are easily resolved (or contained) in the space of thirty minutes.

One other characteristic defines shows embedded in an assimilationist discourse: the privileged subject position is necessarily that of the white middle class. That is to say, whiteness is the privileged yet unnamed place from which to see and make sense of the world. This very transparency contributes to the hegemonic status of this televisual construction of whiteness, placing it beyond critical interrogation. Indeed, relative to the hegemonic status that whiteness occupies in this discourse, blackness simply works to reaffirm, shore up, and police the cultural and moral boundaries of the existing racial order. From the privileged angle of their normative race and class positions, whites are portrayed as sympathetic advocates for the elimination of prejudice.

Pluralist or Separate-but-Equal Discourses

Separate-but-equal discourses situate black characters in domestically centered black worlds and circumstances that essentially parallel those of whites. Like their white counterparts, these shows are anchored by the normative ideals of individual equality and social inclusion. In other words, they maintain a commitment to universal acceptance into the transparent "normative" middle class. However, it is a separate-but-equal inclusion. In this television world, blacks and whites are just alike save for minor differences of habit and perspective developed from African American experiences in a homogeneous and monolithic black world. In this televisual black world, African Americans face the same experiences, situations, and conflicts as whites except for the fact that they remain separate but equal.

I have in mind such programs as *Family Matters, 227, Amen,* and *Fresh Prince of Bel Air;* earlier shows with predominantly black casts that currently run in syndication from previous seasons, such as *The Jeffersons, What's Happening!!, Sanford & Son,* and *That's My Mama;* as well as some of the programming featured on Black Entertainment Television.[20] What makes these shows pluralist and therefore different from the assimilationist shows is their explicit recognition of race (blackness) as the basis of cultural difference (expressed as separation) as a feature of U.S. society.[21] As in so much of television, the social and historical contexts in which these acknowledged differences are expressed, sustained, and meaningful are absent. The particularity of black cultural difference is therefore articulated with(in) the dominant historical, cultural, and social discourses about American society. It is possible, then, to recognize, indeed celebrate, the presence of African Americans, latinos, Asians, Native Americans, and women and the particularly distinct tradition, experiences, and positions they represent without disrupting and challenging the dominant narratives about American society. In other words, race as the basis of inequality, conquest, slavery, subordination, exploitation, even social location is eliminated, as are the oppositions, struggles, survival strategies, and distinctive lifeways that result from these experiences. In this manner cultural difference and diversity can be represented, even celebrated, but in ways that confirm and authorize dominant social, political, cultural, and economic positions and relationships. From the separate-but-equal televisual world inaugurated by *Amos 'n' Andy,* a large number of black representations remain separate, even if they have gained, symbolically at least, a measure of equality.

Contemporary black-oriented shows and the representations they offer occupy a discursive space still marked by their relationship to an unnamed but nevertheless hegemonic order. Like assimilationist representations, pluralist representations are constructed from an angle of vision defined by that normative order. The assumptions organizing pluralist representations of black life offer variations and modifications of the representations in the assimilationist paradigm. These shows are also tethered to this hegemonic white middle-class universe in yet another way—through the conventional formulas, genres, codes, and practices that structure their representations. Hence, on the face of it, shows from *227* to *Family Matters* present themes, experiences, and concerns that seem, and in some instances are, "uniquely African American"—for example, the black church (*Amen*) and black women's friendships (*227* and, more recently, *Living Single*). Of course, the images of black life in these shows do represent one mode of black participation in American society. However, representations of blackness in these separate-but-equal worlds depend on an essential and universal black subject for their distinction from and similarity to the normative center. On programs such as *Amen, 227,* and *Family Matters,* black people live out simple and largely one-dimensional lives in segregated universes where they encounter the usual televisual challenges in the domestic sphere—social relations, child rearing, awkward situations, personal embarrassment, and romance.

Culturally, these shows construct a view of American race relations in which conflict, tension, and struggles over power, especially claims on blackness, depend on the logic of a cultural pluralism that requires a homogeneous, totalizing blackness, a blackness incapable of addressing the differences, tensions, and diversities among African Americans (and other communities of color).[22] Shows organized by such pluralist logic seldom, if ever, critique or engage the hegemonic character of (middle-class constructions of) whiteness or, for that matter, totalizing constructions of blackness. Discursively, the problem of racial inequality is displaced by the incorporation of blacks into that great American stew where such cultural distinctions are minor issues that enrich the American cultural universe without noticeably disturbing the delicate balance of power, which remains unnamed, hidden, and invisible. Obscured are representations of diversity within and among African Americans, as well as the intraracial/ethnic alliances and tensions that also characterize post-civil rights race relations in the United States. Together with assimilationist discourses, these television programs effectively work for some viewers to produce pleasures and identifications precisely because their presence on commercial network television symbolically confirms the legitimacy and effectiveness of the very cultural pluralism on which America's official construction and representation of itself depend. Obscured in the process is the impact (and responses to it) of structured social inequality and the social hierarchies that are structured by it.

Multiculturalism/Diversity

I argued earlier in this chapter that *The Cosby Show* reconfigured representations of African Americans in commercial network television. Although this program marked an aesthetic and discursive turn away from assimilationist and pluralist practices, key elements of both continued to structure and organize aspects of *The Cosby Show*, which remained rooted in both sets of discourses. In style and form, the show operated from the normative space of a largely black, often multicultural world that paralleled that of whites. It appealed to the universal themes of mobility and individualism, and it privileged the upper-middle-class black family as the site of social life.

At the same time, the show moved some distance away from these elements through its attempt to explore the interiors of black lives and subjectivities from the angle of African Americans. *The Cosby Show* constructed black Americans as the authors of and participants in their own notion of America and what it means to be American. This transitional moment was most evident in the show's use of blackness and African American culture as a kind of emblematic code of difference.

More central to the transition from assimilationist and pluralist discourses to an engagement with the cultural politics of difference, however, are *Frank's Place* and, more recently, *Roc* and *South Central*. The short-lived *Frank's Place* was coproduced by Tim Reid and Hugh Wilson and aired on the CBS television network during the 1987-88 season. The show was distinguished by its explicit construction and positioning of African American culture at the very center of its social and cultural universe. From this position the show examined everyday life from the perspective of working-class as well as middle-class blacks. It seldom, if ever, adjusted its perspective and its representation of African American cultural experiences to the gaze of an idealized white middle-class audience. The discursive practices that structured *Frank's Place* (and *Roc*) are also distinguished by an innovative approach to television as a form—the program's explicit attention to African American themes, the use of original popular music from the African American musical tradition (i.e., blues), the blurring of genres (comedy/drama), the lack of closure and resolution, the setting and location, and the use of different visual and narrative strategies (e.g., a cinematic look and feel, lighting, and production style). (In the case of *Roc*, I would add to these the use of live/real-time production.)

In addition to *Frank's Place* I would count some of the very early seasons of *The Arsenio Hall Show, A Different World,* and *In Living Color* as representative programs that have explicitly engaged the cultural politics of diversity and multiculturalism within the sign of blackness. Television programs operating within this discursive space position viewers, regardless of race, class, or gender locations, to participate in black experiences from multiple subject positions. In these shows viewers encounter complex, even contradictory, perspectives and representations of black life in America. The guiding sensibility is neither integrationist nor pluralist, though elements of both may turn up. Unlike in assimilationist discourses, there are Black Subjects (as opposed to black Subjects), and unlike in pluralist discourses, these Black Subjects are not so total and monolithic that they become THE BLACK SUBJECT.

The issue of cultural difference and the problem of African American diversity and inclusion form the social ground from which these shows operate. As illustrated by *The Cosby Show*, the discourse of multiculturalism/diversity offers a view of what it means to be American from the vantage point of African Americans. But, unlike *The Cosby Show*, this is not a zero-sum game. The social and cultural terms in which it is possible to be black and American and to participate in the American experience are more open. Although these terms often continue to support a "normative" conception of the American universe (especially in its class and mobility aspirations), in other respects shows such as *Frank's Place* and *Roc* stretch this conception by interrogating and engaging African American cultural traditions, perspectives, and experiences.[23]

In shows that engage cultural politics of difference within the sign of blackness, black life and culture are constantly made, remade, modified, and extended. They are made rather than discovered, and they are dynamic rather than frozen (Hall 1989). Such programs create a discursive space in which subject positions are transgressive and contradictory, troubling, and pleasurable, as are the representations used to construct identity (see Lipsitz 1990b), a space that is neither integrationist nor pluralist—indeed, it is often both at the same time. Not surprisingly, black middle-class cultural perspectives and viewpoints continue to shape and define these shows; however, they are driven less by the hegemonic gaze of whiteness. (This gaze is detectable in the assimilationist attempt to silence cultural difference and in the pluralist attempt to claim that African American cultural experiences are parallel to white immigrant experiences.)

It is not that the representations that appear within this set of discursive practices and strategies simply offer a more culturally satisfying and politically progressive alternative to assimilationist and pluralist discourses. Indeed, they often do not. They do, however, represent questions of diversity within blackness more directly, explicitly, and frequently, and as central features of the programs. *A Different World, Frank's Place, Roc,* and *In Living Color* have consistently and explicitly examined issues of racism, apartheid, discrimination, nationalism, masculinity, color coding, desegregation, and poverty from multiple and complex perspectives within blackness.

In these shows, differences that originate from within African American social and cultural experiences have been not just acknowledged, but interrogated, even parodied as subjects of television. *In Living Color* and *A Different World,* for instance, have used drama, humor, parody, and satire to examine subjects as diverse as Caribbean immigrants, black fraternities, beauty contests, black gay men, the Nation of Islam, Louis Farrakhan, Jesse Jackson, Marion Barry, racial attitudes, hip-hop culture, and white guilt. The richness of African American cultural and social life as well as the experience of otherness that derives from subordinate status and social inequality are recognized, critiqued, and commented on. The racial politics that helps to structure and define U.S. society is never far from the surface.

Watching Television, Seeing Black

In many of the programs located in both pluralist and multiculturalist discourses, African American culture is central to the construction of black subjects as well as program content, aesthetic organization, setting, and narrative. These discourses, especially those that I regard as multiculturalist, operate at multiple levels of class, gender, region, color, and culture, and though fractured and selective, their dominant angle of vision, social location, and cultural context are African American (Fiske 1987; Hall 1980, 1989; Newcomb 1984). In all of the television representations of cultural difference there remains a contradictory character, one where the leaks, fractures, tensions, and contradictions in a stratified multicultural society continue to find expression.

Although contained within the larger hegemonic terms of the dominant American discourse on race and race relations driven by the narrative of inclusion, many of the shows circulating within these various discursive practices provide different representations of African Americans on commercial network television (Hall 1981b). Within commercial television representations of African American culture, the most compelling and powerful representations mark, displace, and disarticulate hegemonic and normative cultural assumptions and representations about America's racial order. At their best, such representations fully engage all aspects of African American life and, in the process, move cultural struggles within television and media beyond limited and narrow questions of positive/negative images, role models, and simple reversals to the politics of representation (Fregoso 1990a; Hall 1989).

Contemporary television representations of blackness require a sharper, more engaged analytic focus on the multilayered, dialogic, intertextual, and contradictory character of racial representations in commercial network television. I do not claim, of course, that these representations are inherently resistant or oppositional. The hegemonic terms and effects of racial representation are no longer hidden, silenced, and beyond analytic and political interrogation. To make sense of television representations of blackness politically, we must theorize and understand them in relation to other television representations and to discourses beyond the television screen. The readings, affirmations, and interrogations that follow attempt just such a critical practice.

Notes

1. One of the very specific ways in which the presence of these limited spheres of individual influence has been expressed in the organization and production of television programs about blacks is through the use of black professionals as consultants and advisers in the development of programs featuring blacks. For an interesting discussion of this phenomenon in the cases of women, Mexican Americans, and blacks in television, see Kathryn Montgomery's *Target Prime Time* (1989).
2. See Horowitz (1989) for a detailed discussion of the role of black film executives in the production of several commercially successful films in the 1980s.
3. In some instances, black actors and actresses exert some influence on the creative vision and direction of black representations. These actors and actresses, however, do not or may not choose to receive production and writing titles (interview with Marla Gibbs, 1990; see also Zook 1994).
4. My interview data confirm observations made by Gitlin (1983), Horowitz (1989), and Steenland (1987, 1989).
5. Black studio and network executives with whom I spoke reported that black executives are concentrated at the middle levels of the management structure, where they often have the power to stop a project, but few are positioned at the very top, where they can "green-light" a project (interviews with Stanley Robertson, Dolores Morris, and Frank Dawson, 1990). See also Horowitz (1989).
6. See *Black Film Review* (1993) for a discussion of the crucial role of black filmmakers such as Oscar Micheaux in generating counterrepresentations of blacks.
7. Also, black women were big, loud, and dark, and fulfilled the role of the nurturing caretaker of the white home (e.g., *Beulah*).
8. In 1952, *Amos 'n' Andy* received an Emmy Award nomination (Ely 1991).
9. Many of the criticisms leveled at rap music and programs such as *In Living Color* have their roots in the black cultural politics of this period. Concerns about racial embarrassment, black perpetuation of stereotypes, and so on were as urgent, especially for the black middle class, then as they are now.
10. Another show from the period that followed this pattern for the social construction and representation of blackness was *Room 222*.
11. Other variety shows of the period featuring black hosts included *The Leslie Uggams Show* (1969), *The Flip Wilson Show* (1970–74), and *The New Bill Cosby Show* (1972–73).
12. In the early 1970s, *The Flip Wilson Show*, a comedy-variety show starring comedian Flip Wilson, enjoyed a four-year run. The show has been characterized as a breakthrough in commercial television because it was the first black-led variety show to rate consistently among the top-rated shows in television. This show included, among other things, the kind of black-based parody and humor that would

reappear in the late 1980s with the explosion of black comedy and variety (see Kolbert 1993).

13. See Dates (1990:257) for an inventory of black-oriented miniseries that aired following the commercial success of *Roots.*

14. *The Jeffersons* originally aired in 1975 and enjoyed a ten-year run. I place the series in relationship to these other programs because of the centrality of the mobility narrative in the show. Discursively, the series is important to the shows set in poverty because it serves to reinforce (rather than simply realize) the mobility myth.

15. African American writers from *227* told me that in the culture of the industry, black-oriented programs that explicitly attempt to address issues of inequality and racism or that seem to have a didactic function are regarded as "message shows." They also suggested that from the perspective of studios and the networks, such shows are perceived as risky and difficult to bring to the screen without stirring up trouble or offending some primary constituent (e.g., producers, networks, advertisers) in the production process (interviews with writers, 1990).

16. *The Arsenio Hall Show* is similar in this respect. The chatty format is really about the class and mobility aspirations of a new generation of young blacks and whites.

17. One of the executive producers at *227* described the show as a "reality-based show about a nice middle-class black family," therefore not a show with "messages or anything of that nature." She also conceded that the primary interest of the show is comedy (interview with Irma Kalish, 1990).

18. During the 1992–93 season, shows such as *Roc* and *Where I Live* continued this approach to programs about blacks.

19. Although designed to showcase the individual stars of the show, aesthetically *The Cosby Show's* style also moved through subtle but noticeable changes, the most remarkable being the slow evolution of the show's opening strip over successive seasons. The background setting and theme music for the show's opening moved steadily from an empty blue screen (accompanied by jazz) background to a tropical island setting (accompanied by steel pans and Caribbean music) to a grafitti-filled wall on an urban street corner (accompanied by urban-based funk).

20. The continued circulation and availability of many of these older programs through reruns and cable are central to my claim that these programs are structured by pluralist discourses.

21. See Dates and Barlow (1990) for discussion of the formation, operation, and impact of black media organizations and black participation in mass media in the United States.

22. See Fregoso (1990a:264). The special issue of *Cultural Studies* published in October 1990 represents an important intervention by Chicana/o scholars on the issue of identity, racial politics, and cultural representation (Chabram and Fregoso 1990). See also Hall (1988).

23. Paul Gilroy (1991b) has written rather persuasively about the cultural impress of blacks in England on the normative notions of what it means to be British, especially black and British. George Lipsitz (1990a) makes a similar argument.

References

Allen, Robert, ed. (1987) *Channels of Discourse: Television and Contemporary Criticism.* Chapel Hill: University of North Carolina Press.
Bobo, Jacqueline. (1991) "Black Women in Fiction and Non-Fiction: Images of Power and Powerlessness." *Wide Angle* 13, nos. 3–4: 72–81.

Braxton, Greg. (1991) "To Him Rap's No Laughing Matter." *Los Angeles Times* July 14, Calender, 4, 82, 84.

Butsch, Richard. (1990) "Home Video and Corporate Plans: Capital's Limited Power to Manipulate Leisure." In Richard Butsch (ed.) *For Fun and Profit: The Transformation of Leisure into Consumption,* 215–35. Philadelphia: Temple University Press.

Chabram, Angie C. and Rosa Linda Fregoso (eds.) (1990) *Chicana/o Representations: Reframing Alternative Critical Discourses.* Special Issue, *Cultural Studies* 4 (October):

Christian, Barbara. (1988) "The Race for Theory." *Feminist Studies* 14, no. 1: 69–79.

Christon, Lawrence. (1989) "The World According to the Cos." *Los Angeles Times,* December 10, Calender, 6, 45–47.

Collins, Patricia Hill. (1990) *Black Feminist Thought: Knowledge, Consciousness and the Politics of Empowerment.* New York: Routledge.

Cripps, Thomas. (1983) "Amos 'n' Andy and the Debate over American Racial Integration." In John E. O'Connor (ed.) *American History, American Television: Interpreting the Video Past,* pp. 33–54. New York: Frederick Ungar.

Czitron, Daniel. (1982) *Media and the American Mind: From Morse to McLuhan.* Chapel Hill: University of North Carolina Press.

Dates, Jannette. (1990) "Commercial Television." In Jannette Dates and William Barlow (eds.) *Split Image: African Americans in the Mass Media.* Washington, D.C.: Howard University Press.

Dates, Jannette and William Barlow (eds.) (1990) *Split Image: African Americans in the Mass Media.* Washington, D.C.: Howard University Press.

Downing, John. (1988) "The Cosby Show and American Racial Discourse." In G. Smitherman-Donaldson and T.A. Van Dijk (eds.), *Discourse and Discrimination,* p. 46–74. Detroit: Wayne State University Press.

Dyson, Michael. (1989) "Bill Cosby and the Politics of Race." *Z Magazine,* September, 26–30.

Ely, Melvin Patrick. (1991) *The Adventures of Amos 'n' Andy: A Social History of an American Phenomenon.* New York: Free Press.

Fiske, John. (1987) *Television Culture.* London: Methuen.

Fregoso, Rosa Linda. (1990a) "Born in East L.A.: Chicano Cinema and the Politics of Representation." In Angie C. Chabram and Rosa Linda Fregoso (eds.), *Chicana/o Representations: Reframing Alternative Critical Discourses* (special issue). *Cultural Studies* 4 (October): 264–81.

Fuller, Linda K. (1992) *The Cosby Show: Audiences, Impact, and Implications.* Westport, Connecticut: Greenwood.

Gilroy, Paul. (1991b) *There Ain't No Black in the Union Jack: The Cultural Politics of Race and Nation.* Chicago: University of Chicago Press.

Gitlin, Todd. (1983) *Inside Prime Time.* New York: Pantheon.

Gray, Herman. (1993a) "African American Political Desire and the Seductions of Contemporary Cultural Politics." *Cultural Studies* 7: 364–74.

———. (1989) "Television, Black Americans, and the American Dream." *Critical Studies in Mass Communication* 6: 376–87.

———. (1986) "Television and the New Black Man: Black Male Images in Prime Time Situation Comedy." *Media, Culture and Society* 8: 223–43.

Greely, Andrew. (1987) "Today's Morality Play: The Sitcom." *New York Times,* May 17, Arts and Leisure, 1, 40.

Gunther, Marc. (1990) "Black Producers Add a Fresh Nuance." *New York Times,* August 26, Arts and Leisure, 25, 31.

Hall, Stuart. (1989) "Cultural Identity and Cinematic Representation." *Framework* 36: 68–92.

———. (1981b) "Whites of Their Eyes:Racist Ideology and the Media." In George Bridges and Rosalind Brunt (eds.) *Silver Linings*. London: Lawrence & Wishart.

———. (1980) "Encoding/Decoding." In S. Hall et al. (eds.) *Culture, Media, Language*. London: Hutchinson.

Hampton, Henry. (1989) "The Camera Lens as a Two-Edged Sword." *New York Times*, January 15, H29, H37.

Horowitz, Jay. (1989) "Hollywood's Dirty Little Secret." *Premiere*, March, 56–59-64.

Jhally, Sut, and Justin Lewis. (1992) *Enlightened Racism: The Cosby Show, Audiences, and the Myth of the American Dream*. Boulder, Colorado:Westview.

Kelley, Robin D. G. (1992) "Notes on Deconstructing 'the Folk.'" *American Historical Review* 97: 1400–1406.

Kolbert, Elizabeth. (1993) "From 'Beulah' to Oprah: The Evolution of Black Images on TV." *New York Times*, January 15, B4.

Lipsitz, George. (1990b) *Time Passages:Collective Memory and American Popular Culture*. Minneapolis: University of Minnesota Press.

MacDonald, J. Fred. (1983) *Blacks and White TV: Afro-Americans in Television Since 1948*. Chicago: Nelson-Hall.

Miller, Mark Crispin. (1988) "Cosby Knows Best." In Mark Crispin Miller (ed.) *Boxed In: The Culture of TV*. Evanston, Illinois: Northwestern University Press.

Montgomery, Kathryn. (1989) *Target Prime Time*. New York: Oxford University Press.

Newcomb, Horace. (1984) "On the Dialogic Aspects of Mass Communication." *Critical Studies in Mass Communication* 1: 34–50.

Newcomb, Horace and Robert S. Alley. (1983) *The Producer's Medium: Conversations with Creators of American TV*. New York: Oxford University Press.

O'Connor, John J. (1990) "On TV Less Separate, More Equal." *New York Times*, April 29, sec. 2: 1, 35.

Ressner, Jeffrey. (1990) "Off Color TV." *Rolling Stone*, August 23, 50.

Riggs, Marlon. (1991a) *Color Adjustment* (film). San Francisco: California Newsreel.

———. (1991b) "Confessions of a Snap Queen." In Valery Smity, C. Billops, and A. Griffin (eds.) Special Issue: *Black American Literature Forum* 25, no. 2.

Siegel, Ed. (1989a) "The Networks Go Ethnic." *Boston Globe*, September 16, Living/Arts, 7, 14.

Spigel, Lynn. (1992) *Make Room for TV: Television and the Family Ideal in Postwar America*. Chicago: University of Chicago Press.

Steenland, Sally. (1989) *Unequal Picture: Black, Hispanic, Asian, and Native American Characters on Television*. Washington, D.C.: National Commission on Working Women.

———. (1987) *Prime Time Power: Women Producers, Writers, and Directors in TV*. Washington, D.C.: National Commission on Working Women.

Taylor, Ella. (1989) *Prime-Time Families: Television Culture in Postwar America*. Berkeley: University of California Press.

Waters, Harry F. and Janet Huck. (1988) "TV's New Racial Hue." *Newsweek*, January 25, 52–54.

Winston, Michael R. (1982) "Racial Consciousness and the Evolution of Mass Communication in the United States." *Daedalus* 111: 171–82.

Zook, Kristal Brent. (1994) "How I Became the Prince of a Town Called Bel Air: Nationalist Desire in Black Television." Doctoral Dissertation, University of California, Santa Cruz.

Absolutely Fabulous
Absolutely Feminist?

PAT KIRKHAM and BEVERLEY SKEGGS

Much work on television fiction has focused on questions about the ways in which programs appeal to and affect different audiences. Feminist work in particular has focused on the way in which the soap opera genre has appealed to both feminine and feminist feelings to develop its pleasurable possibilities. Less work has been done on comedy and this essay therefore offers a study of a popular British television comedy which features four women characters spread across three generations. We are interested in the possibilities opened up by a situation comedy and in particular we want to explore the complex pleasures for women viewers which this conjunction of femininity, feminism and comedy offers.

This essay will first interrogate the contexts of the textual production of *Absolutely Fabulous,* outlining the historical positions and traditions on which it draws and the knowledge(s) required to understand it. It will focus on a number of interlinking areas: conduct and behavior; responsibility; femininity and masquerade. In doing so it will draw attention to the central motifs through which the program explores these issues: mother/daughter relations, the relationship between female best friends, and comedy based on women's appearance, the body and aging.

Written by the comedian Jennifer Saunders (who achieved fame and commercial success in Britain in a comedy partnership with Dawn French), directed by Bob Spiers and produced by Jon Plowman, *Absolutely Fabulous* is a situation comedy based on four central women characters. Saunders herself stars as PR executive Edina Monsoon, with Joanna Lumley as her best friend and fashion editor Patsy Stone, Julia Sawahla as her school student daughter Saffron, and June Whitfield as her mother. The series is set mainly in the "designer" kitchen of Edina's large London house, which is equipped with 1980s and early 1990s designer gadgets and furniture as well as examples of "ethnic chic" and modern art. The other main location is Edina's equally "designer" office, although there are occasional location episodes based on holidays in Provence, Marrakesh and skiing in the Alps.

First broadcast in Britain in the autumn of 1992, the series began in a midevening slot (9:30–10:00 p.m.) on the more "highbrow" of the two BBC channels and attracted audiences of up to 10 million, winning somewhat unusually (for such a large audience) a cult following and high critical praise. It won the 1993 British Film and Television Award for best comedy series. This popularity ensured that the second series in 1994 was moved to the same time slot on the more popular BBC1 channel, where it retained audiences of 11 million and quadrupled its budget. Guest appearances from celebrities such as Germaine Greer, Britt Ekland and Miranda Richardson confirmed its cult status. The third and final series began in April 1995 on BBC1, although two 45-minute "special" episodes were shown on BBC1 in November 1996. Jennifer Saunders has sworn this is the end for Patsy and Edina, though a final, final comeback would be welcomed by fans.

Plans to show the series in the USA met with problems because it was regarded as too vulgar and too pro-drug, as were the scripts for an "American remake" submitted to ABC TV after Roseanne Barr acquired the rights.[1] In the end, the first British series was screened in the USA in 1994 and met with success, winning two Emmys (television's equivalent of Oscars). It achieved a cult status in the USA, as it did in Australia where "Patsy lookalikes" first appeared in the Sydney Mardi Gras parades in 1994.[2]

Historical and Sociopolitical Contexts

The original idea for the program came from Ruby Wax (famous for her irreverent, anarchic, surreal humor) who wanted to interview Joanna Lumley on her TV program by setting her up (obviously with her knowledge) as a completely drunken cook. The basic structural gag was thus initiated around a woman who refused to accept the need to behave "appropriately." The series draws on 1960s hippiedom, 1970s hedonism, 1980s Thatcherism and 1990s righteousness. The central character, Edina, is allegedly modeled on a very successful PR executive, Lynn Franks. Edina and the hard and cynical Patsy represent aspects of 1980s Thatcherism: they are bullish, selfish and hideously materialistic. This aspect, however, is set against the remnants from their late 1960s/1970s laid-back and lazy lifestyle, represented mainly by Buddhist chanting and the use of drugs, both 1970s "dope" and 1980s "coke." The past and the Thatcherite present are, at times, played off against each other to produce comedy and social comment while at other points they meld together in hilarious confusion. Even Edina's surname—Monsoon—with its connotations of hippie Eastern travels is also the name of a fashion retailer of middle-of-the-range hippie clothes. Patsy's name—Stone—refers both to the past (to being stoned and the Rolling Stones) and to the present hardness of her character.

The critique of the materialist values of Thatcherism is made apparent in most episodes. As a PR executive it is Edina's job to work out the marketing angles on ultimately non-functional commodities, such as "pop specs." This emphasis on profits at all costs is taken to its limits in the Romanian baby episode, where she imports Romanian babies and works out the sales angles available as if they were simply another commodity. This lack of ethical and collective values, arguably a central Thatcherite project, is made explicit by setting it against the characterization of the daughter Saffy, who is used to represent a caring 1990s student, anti-materialist, into ecology and social issues. "Mum," she comments in a typically exasperated moment, "people don't get more interesting the more money you spend."

The fit and muscular values of Thatcherism are also associated with the current preoccupation with health and care of the self and body. This enables the body to be more Darwinistic ("survival of the fittest") and hence more productive in the labor market, but in *Absolutely Fabulous* it is ridiculed through the excessive drinking and drug-taking of Edina and Patsy, which again is set against lemonade-drinking Saffy.

The other acquisitive Thatcherite and neocolonial value exposed in the program is the use of ethnic objects to signify distinctive taste and thus a lifestyle. This is expressed in the decor of the set and is made obvious in lines by Edina such as:

> I got a load of those lip plates from dead Amazonian Indians, I thought could be ashtrays. [*to Saffron*] Don't look at me like that, we can take the lips off. Lots of kitchen pots and pans from Somalia. They don't need them, they've got no food to eat. But, best news of all, you know all the villages that were deserted by the Kurds . . . *I've* got the franchise. (Saunders, 1993: 144)

This delight in "Third World chic" and global commodification not only suggests that nothing is sacred from capitalism ("the franchise") but also that nothing is sacred from comedy.

Finally, but crucially, feminism of the 1960s and 1970s provides the context for much of the humor of *Absolutely Fabulous*. Again this is handled through contradiction and contrast. The emphasis on women as best friends, the flirtation with lesbianism, the way in which Edina and Patsy pursue their own goals seem to stem from feminist positions of independence and female worth, but in their obsession with fat (featured in an episode actually called "Fat" but present throughout in comments and jokes) the two central characters continually fly in the face of the notion that "fat is a feminist issue." The feminist context also helps to explain the way in which the obsession with fashion (Edina literally prostrates herself before a fashion designer in the final episode) is offered both as a source of identification and mockery.

Comedic Traditions

The historical and social contexts of *Absolutely Fabulous* operate within the wide range of comedic traditions on which the program draws. Much of the originality and freshness of *Absolutely Fabulous* lies in its particular mix of comedic devices. Visual, verbal, physical, situation and character comedy are all present and the interplay between the different aspects is important. The verbal jokes about hedonism are frequently played out in the physical—a device which works, for example, to highlight the tensions between smoking and drinking as sophisticated social tools and as indulgences which wreck the mind and body. Similarly, narrative situations such as moments of crisis which disrupt the normal are made the more comic by the additional elements of visual and physical humor. The visual parody of fashion is made largely through Edina's clothes (the ridiculousness of her outfits contrasts with Saffy's unassuming dress and the sophistication of Patsy's). This is augmented by physical comedy, most notably when Saunders uses her "too large" body to fit into "too small" clothes, clothes that were deliberately bought a size too small in the manner of Charlie Chaplin and Norman Wisdom.[3] The wearing of clothes is also a comic device in the treatment of Patsy. She wears beautiful and expensive clothes which hang and fit perfectly on her model size body, but this image is deflated when they become out of place, disrupted and dishevelled, drawing attention to her feminine constructions. One episode involves a scene of arrival at Marrakesh airport in which the comic effect is based on this contrast. Patsy, beginning as the model of sophistication, gets progressively drunk and aggressive on the plane and, in a brilliant piece of physical comedy, she gets stuck on the revolving luggage deposit. She finally emerges from the airport as a complete mess with clothes dishevelled and high hair lopsided.

As this incident shows, at the heart of *Absolutely Fabulous* is the question of "making a spectacle" of oneself and the show can be seen to operate within the general modes of ritual spectacle, comic verbal compositions, curses and oaths, disruption of order and general unruliness reminiscent of those described by Bakhtin (1984) in relation to carnival. A central feature of *Absolutely Fabulous*'s comedy is what happens to people when they step outside of their place, when they transgress the social limits which circumscribe their actions. Banks and Swift (1986) argue that for humor to be maintained, characters can never achieve their ideals and are always reminded of what they really are. Much of the verbal interplay of *Absolutely Fabulous* consists of reminding characters of their place. This form of wit could not be achieved without the buddy relationship of the two female central characters. Patsy and Edina encourage each other to reach for impossible desires, neither exercises a limit on the other and they turn to each other for bickering solace with every failure.

Other long and rich traditions on which the program draws include ridiculing the rich and the ruling classes, political and personal satire, unruly women, "the Fool," the "kill joy," the dupe, role reversals, juxtaposing the unexpected, anarchic comedy and comedies of manners. The play on the "grotesque woman" is frequently used (Russo, 1986). The "one liners" of *Absolutely Fabulous*, including quick put-downs, sharp and often vituperative satirical stabs, verbal deflations and repartee which approaches mutual heckling, and the double acts of comic and "straight guy," naïve simpleton and clown (Edina and Saffy, Edina and her mother, Patsy and Saffy) can be traced back to and contextualized within these traditions.

Many of these older aspects of comedy were given more specific configuration within the nineteenth- and twentieth-century traditions of music hall and variety shows which featured individual performers and double acts. In the overall narrative, therefore, individual set-pieces such as Patsy's drunkenness or Edina's self-denigration are important elements in the comedy. More recent influences include the British comics Tony Hancock, Harry H. Corbett and Wilfred Bramble (Steptoe and his son) and John Cleese. The Cleesian influence is most apparent in the physical clowning and the comic use of the body. The send-up of bourgeois pretensions draws on the famous *Hancock's Half Hour* radio series and the subsequent television shows; the gag of the grown-up child playing parent to the disreputable parent was the basis for the television series *Steptoe and Son*. Although it is not unusual to have women as the focus of comedy of middle-class pretensions, the Cleese and the Steptoe comparisons remind us that the effect of making oneself ridiculous through the body or behaving in other vulgar and outrageous ways when old is all the more striking when the protagonists are women.

Until recently there has been very little comedy on our television screens of women behaving in vulgar and unruly ways, and the debt of *Absolutely Fabulous* to Roseanne Barr should not be ignored. It was she who, writing and playing in the US sitcom *Roseanne*, made a comedy heroine of the unruly and irreverent woman and broke down many of the unwritten codes about the comic depiction of the behavior of mothers and of women over 30 (Rowe, 1995). A further influence is another US sitcom, *The Golden Girls*, which featured four or five older women, some of whom seriously transgressed "appropriate" behavior in relation to age. It contained a brilliant example of a mafia-style mother whose long-suffering daughter tried to keep her out of trouble—surely one model for the mother–daughter role reversal which is at the heart of *Absolutely Fabulous*.

Absolutely Fabulous also needs to be contextualized against the phenomenal growth of alternative comedy in Britain in the 1980s and the space created within that by and for female and feminist comics; Jennifer Saunders came up through that route to *Absolutely Fabulous*, as is indicated by her previous television shows, *Girls On Top*, *French and Saunders* and *The Comic Strip Presents*. Her presence reinforces the use of sketches and draws on traditions established from variety performances and radio shows which used "real" characters alongside recognizably straight actors in supporting roles. *Absolutely Fabulous* is clearly alternative in its use of one-liners, its social observation and its political comment.

Saunders's very presence announces the fact that *Absolutely Fabulous* is a "comedian's comedy" (Jenkins, 1992: 232); her being there signals for us to laugh. Yet intriguingly she is the one character who is cast neither for nor against type, probably because her chameleon-like ability to take on a huge variety of roles means that she is not typecast. By contrast, Joanna Lumley, the epitome of upper-middle-class British white femininity, was cast against type to great comic effect. This former boarding school girl from a colonial family, a former model (with a passing resemblance to Princess Diana) and a reputed supporter of the Conservative government, plays the aging, dissolute and drunken best friend who not only burns the innocent Saffy with a cigarette but also sells her off in Morocco because she spoils the fun Patsy likes to have with Edina. Neither her role as Purdy in *The New Avengers* nor as a "James Bond Girl" prepared the public for this role and the juxtaposition of the haughty "English rose" image with the outrageous character of Patsy creates a frisson which is absolutely central to the comedy.

June Whitfield and Julia Sawahla were by contrast much more in tune with the parts they played. Part of the strength of Saffy's "straight guy" character comes directly from Julia Sawahla's previous television roles, particularly the squeaky clean teenager in spectacles in *Press Gang*. June Whitfield is a famous comedy actress. She performed in the BBC light entertainment programs such as *Love From Judy* and *Take It From Here* in the 1940s and was probably best known for her television role as the sweet and innocent suburban woman in the sitcom *Terry and June*. However, there is another side to Whitfield—she played Margaret Thatcher on the radio and this dualism is cleverly developed in *Absolutely Fabulous*. Gran is an older "straight" character whom Saunders could use in a second layer of the mother–daughter reversals and also a character who on occasions matched her daughter, Edina, for maliciousness.[4]

Some humor which results from the program's roots in situation comedy comes from working within those traditions, but much comes from stretching them to their limits. The family is central to situation comedy but the family presented here is strange both in its structure and the degree of its dysfunctionality. Firstly, Edina is a single parent and Saffy's father is gay. Secondly, the traditional roles of mother and daughter are reversed in Edina and Saffy, and Edina's relationship with her own mother is shocking in the lack of filial affection. Juxtapositions, oppositions and role reversals all work to heighten the bizarre nature of the family which is never as strong a unit as the best friend dyad of Edina and Patsy. The main "outsider" role of Patsy is a co-starring one which thus decenters the family, as does the way in which she constantly pulls Edina away from the home to indulge in non-domestic pleasures.

Another outsider to the family, Bubble (Edina's assistant played by Jane Horrocks), strengthens this depiction of Edina's world beyond the home, the world of fashion at which Saunders's scripts take numerous swipes. Like

Gran, Bubble is in the tradition of "the Fool," part of whose function is to expose the pretensions of the serious. Like Gran, though, Bubble is a hybrid character incorporating aspects of the village idiot, clown, working-class and dumb blonde stereotypes—all of which add up to a general wackiness. Nevertheless, the very battyness and naïveté of both these characters is used to highlight the constructed nature of all claims to seriousness. Bubble and Gran represent different generations and embody different value systems which, together with Saffy's moral code, work as foils to expose the more preposterous values endorsed by Patsy and Edina. Saffy's moral positions point to the immorality of her mother and Patsy. Bubble's naïveté points to the calculating manipulations of Edina and Patsy, and Gran's innocence points to their knowingness. Juxtapositions have long been a staple of comedy and here they enable ethical explorations to be made.

Comedy, particularly that in which the freedom of the clown to act outrageously is usurped by women, can be liberating (Jenkins, 1992), but these effects can be dampened and closed down by censure such as that exercised by Saffy and Gran. The liberating effect can also be counter-balanced by closure, by the program returning the viewer to the safe values of the *status quo*. However, *Absolutely Fabulous,* more than most comedies, rarely achieves closure; the viewer is only ever given a glimpse of normality for it to be ripped away again. We wait for Edina to be nice to her daughter, but if we get such a moment occasionally it is only to have it immediately snatched away. The degree to which the program resists closure is new and accounts in part for its impact. It continually shifts between liberation and censure and moral closure is rarely achieved. The codicils at the end often put a final sting in the tale; Edina and Patsy save Saffy from a disastrous marriage and promptly steal the tickets for her honeymoon trip . . .

Feminine Conduct

As the previous section has indicated, much of the comedy of *Absolutely Fabulous* centers on questions of female conduct and appropriate behavior. Debates over correct conduct with women as central signifiers have been waged for centuries in England. These struggles are based on establishing and marking the distance between the "respectable women" and the sexualized others, whose behavior was so lacking in respectability and authority that they could have no claim to power and authority. Black and white working-class women (usually signified as prostitutes, malignant and contagious) have been used as the deviant others against which correct and appropriate feminine behavior could be defined (Gilman, 1992). Vron Ware (1992) notes how definitions of white femininity were generated through the designation of the black sexualized other and Lury (1993) argues that the ability for women to comment or look, particularly in a sexual context, was compromised and circumscribed by an adherence to feminine characteristics of respectability. She traces the emergence of gendered notions of propriety in the late eighteenth and nineteenth centuries, which suggested that women's respectability would be compromised by their ability to look, to use their gaze. The promotion of feminine characteristics was reproduced through representations of women's bodies. As women's bodies came to signify femininity, so notions of appropriate feminine conduct operated as processes of monitoring and self-surveillance which enabled distinctions between different groups of women to be maintained.

This was further consolidated by the responsibilities which women were given. Women could show their respectability by carrying out particular responsibilities but not others, and labor and self-regulation were tightly linked to self-presentation. It was not just the dispositions and characteristics of respectability which signified an appropriate femininity but the performance of duty and obligation (Skeggs, 1997). As part of this process, sexual behavior had to be placed and contained within family values, as Foucault notes:

> the first figure to be investigated by the development of sexuality, one of the first to be "sexualised," was the "idle" woman. She inhabited the outer edge of the "world," in which she always had to appear as a value, and of the family, where she was assigned a new identity charged with conjugal and parental obligation. (1979: 121)

In the moralizing of the social order which designates care for others and care for self as feminine responsibilities, new guilts and new shames are produced (Elias, 1982). It is these (self and other) controls and responsibilities which *Absolutely Fabulous* irreverently addresses.

As a mother, Edina constantly refuses maternal responsibility: "As your mother I cannot be responsible for your well being" she tells Saffy. The whole program is structured around the irresponsible mother and best friend. A whole sketch centers on Edina's refusal to take responsibility for family finances. When she misses Saffy's birthday, she remonstrates with her saying, "Don't get at me darling, I'm the one who gave you birth, I'm the one who uncrossed her legs for you." This is not just a refusal of maternal responsibility, but also of the guilt that usually accompanies it (Wearing, 1984; Donzelot, 1979). Edina also fails to respect the maternal position more generally. When a friend who is a new mother (Miranda Richardson) comes to stay, Edina has sex with the husband (the audience hears it over the baby intercom), while the mother/wife bemoans her maternal duties. Edina is thus completely amoral in the face of possible pleasure. In addition, she ignores her duties in other relationships, refusing to behave responsibly towards her own mother and her friends. After a call from a distressed friend, she complains, "she was crying so much I had to put the phone down."

Edina, however, does not completely eschew responsibility for herself, but pays for it rather than labors at it. She pays for self-care, while refusing to take care of the self. Although she is locked into the discourse of the care of the self, anything which takes time from shopping or drinking is considered a distraction. She is constantly finding new schemes, such as Japanese chanting or crystals, which will enable her to get in touch with some spurious notion of "herself." The whole discourse of feminine self-care is thus sent up and trivialized through Edina's many attempts to try on new forms of self-understanding. She continues to drink and take drugs in vast amounts, while also having colonic irrigation, undergoing fat-reducing sessions by being wrapped in mud, and trying aromatherapy and rebirthing. Edina's responsibility for her body is explicitly commodified. At the same time, Patsy exemplifies the excessive self-regulation encouraged by dieting. In one sketch, Patsy holds her stomach and Edina asks "have you eaten something?" "Not since 1973," replies Patsy. This points to the differences between the two women's bodies. Patsy is the 1970s model, who has retained the same body, controlling it through drugs and cigarettes; Edina's body, in the tradition of grotesque realism, is completely out of control; both are a response to political contexts and interpretations of femininity.

Regulation is constantly set against the hedonism in which Patsy and Edina delight. They are rarely in control and their excesses make explicit the controls and regulations upon women's conduct. They drink too much and take drugs in inappropriate places, places of labor and responsibility, such as the office and the kitchen. Patsy and Edina are unashamedly hedonistic, not a term associated with women, for as Kaplan (1992) notes, women's love of pleasure is deeply stigmatized as the sign of their degradation. Patsy's and Edina's hedonism provides commentary not on just regulations, but also on pretension. Although the two claim to be knowledgable consumers, the audience is encouraged to find their excessive expenditure and their Thatcherite hippiedom vulgar. In Bourdieu's terms, they operate at the level of the profane; while they claim to be culturally superior, theirs is hardly "the sacred sphere of culture . . . of those who can be satisfied with the sublimated, refined, disinterested, gratuitous, distinguished pleasures for ever closed to the profane" (Bourdieu, 1986: 7). Thus it can be argued that the program offers to certain viewers the satisfaction of looking down on this vulgar hedonism, a satisfaction largely based on the viewer's own access to the cultural capital derived from "high" culture. Many viewers, however, may not have access to this "high cultural" knowledge to be able to critique it.

This commentary and comedy is thus double-edged. The textual critique of pretensions is contradicted by the display and use of what are already coded as desirable objects. What Patsy and Edina hedonistically consume—whether it be designer clothes, holidays or drink (characteristically referred to as "Bolly" and "Stolly")—is very desirable to most viewers. As Patsy and Edina playfully try to pass as knowing, consuming, global bourgeoisie and as successful, cultured, glamorous women, they laugh at themselves. But the comedy of all this depends on whether the audience is positioned to read their pretensions and passings as ironic. For those who have yet to gain access to time and space to play, playfulness around consumption may remain unthinkable, the clear parody of excessive consumption coming up against the reality of viewers' lives and experiences. Access is the key issue and here we come up against the limits of textual analysis; further work is needed to analyze how different audiences handle such issues.

The parody of consumption may also have backfired in another way. *Absolutely Fabulous* was lauded and hyped by the very world it sought to satirize, as was evidenced by the stars and celebrities queuing up to make guest appearances. It marketed as desirable the very objects it sought to deride. While *Absolutely Fabulous* may serve to legitimize women's refusal to fit into appropriate modes of conduct, it can also be seen as presenting traditional femininity and excessive materialism and greed as desirable.

Despite this, we would suggest that that the program does adopt a feminist mode in the way in which it contests the male view as dominant. It contributes to the challenges of the male gaze that are being made across the various sites of popular culture. In *Absolutely Fabulous,* use is made of the female gaze to scrutinize, assess and humiliate in a humorous tradition which can be found in many areas of women's culture outside of the visual (Skeggs, 1991). Patsy and Edina look, they laugh, they judge and are irreverent about the male gaze. It no longer has the power, once suggested, to control and fix women as objects to be looked at.

Femininity as Masquerade?

The feminine masquerades of Patsy and Edina are a humorous exposé of the impossibility of femininity. Their efforts show that it is impossible to "do" femininity properly. It is significant that both have female names and nicknames based on male forms (Pats and Eddy) and use a variety of endearments and modes of address; both have moments of self-doubt which they occasionally reveal to each other but which are soon covered up; both display an endless concern for presentation and appearances while being aware always that they are playing. Even sexuality is a form of teasing as the hints about a lesbian relationship are undercut by arguments about who puts out the light when they share a bed. Edina and Patsy's spectacular displays challenge propriety, care of the self, female responsibility and respectability by parading femininity as a mode to be put on and off rather than something which comes naturally. But, as with the parodying of consumption, this presentation of femininity as masquerade has its limitations which we can see by contrasting the two main characters.

Patsy represents an old symbol of old white English femininity, the vain, sexually frank, non-income generating, decadent, licentious female that disrupts the domestic containment of women in particular and the social order in general. But with her imperious presence, she also resembles the form of white English femininity given renewed symbolic legitimacy through, for example, Princess Diana. Joanna Lumley's connections with the British aristocracy are well publicized. In a deeply class-divided society, Patsy represents aristocratic femininity. Because of her class, she has fewer constraints on her behavior than other women and because of the associations between feminine and aristocratic modes of behavior (see Nead, 1988 and Ware, 1992), Patsy can achieve the feminine standards established. She has access to the "right" accoutrements of femininity and the styling of her body. In this sense Patsy is a sign of femininity as simulation. She presents her body as if she (and it) has submitted to ideas about what a certain kind of upper-middle-class women should be.

This simulation is made especially apparent when we learn in the second series that Patsy had a sex change in Morocco in the 1970s and was previously a man. Patsy is able to flaunt femininity in order to hold it at a distance and make it an object of ridicule while being very successful at it. However, setting up femininity as a masquerade to be laughed at only works with Patsy because she operates as such a strong signifier of upper-class femininity, and the strength of this signifier cannot be destroyed through the way in which it is played with through her performance. Her glamour overrides ridicule and even if it is a masquerade it is a very good one, one to which many would aspire and one which has been promoted as ideal in women's and TV listing magazines.[5]

Edina is not in the same position. Her social and cultural location is not of the aristocracy, but of lower middle class made good, precisely the social location that was offered inducements through Thatcherism in return for its votes. Edina cannot successfully play at femininity because she does not begin from the right location with the right objects and the proper body. Edina repeatedly gets it all wrong. For her femininity is a form of visible labor. She works at it continually but fails to get it right. Her body is out of control, her accoutrements are over the top. Even though she wears the "right" designer labels, she puts them together in such a way as to look ridiculous. Her knowledge is not the right class-based knowledge. Watching Edina, we feel embarrassed by her very performance, the masquerade made explicitly spectacular by the colors and tightness of her clothing. Femininity as masquerade may only operate as a critique for those who can actually access it effectively when necessary. As Tyler argues:

> Theories of mimicry reinscribe white, middle-class femininity as the real thing, the (quint)essences of femininity . . . Miming the feminine means impersonating a white middle-class impersonation of an "other" ideal of femininity . . . Feminist theorists of mimicry distinguish themselves from "other" women even as they assimilate the latter by romanticizing them, assuming the other has a critical knowledge about femininity because of her difference from what counts as natural femininity: white, Anglo, bourgeois style. It is only from a middle-class point of view that Dolly Parton looks like a female impersonator. (1991: 57)

Both Patsy and Edina make visible the invisible, the masquerade, the labor and ridiculousness of femininity, but it is only in Edina where femininity is made really undesirable. Because Patsy is so close to ideological ideals and representations of femininity, she does not generate distance from it and her character therefore hinges on a critique of a particular form of conduct rather than on femininity itself. Although in both cases femininity is presented as a construction, it is never entirely undermined. Edina's pathetic attempts and Patsy's assured assumptions of the trappings may ultimately make achievement of the feminine ideal more distant but also more desirable.

Conclusion

Absolutely Fabulous has been understood to offer a mocking critique of both the greed and commodification of 1980s. Thatcherite political values and a celebration of unruly women who kick against the restrictions of British society. But the critiques of the vulgarity of Thatcherism and the follies of the class system work only if the objects used in making the critique are not still seen as desirable by those not privileged enough to abandon them. The program may in fact serve to reproduce the very desires and longings it mocks and works against, desires and longings in the audience based precisely on their persistent exclusion from the possibilities which Patsy and Edina parody. This is why it needs to be studied within its historical and national context. It is a program that could only have been generated from the class-divided 1980s when aristocracy and anarchy, feminism and femininity, contributed to produce a form of comedy which enabled the pretentious not only to laugh at themselves but, in the strong traditions of British comedy, to be laughed at by others.

Notes

1. See *TV Guide*, Indiana Edition, 23–29 July 1994. Thanks to Ellen Seiter for information.
2. We are grateful to Jackie Cook and Karen Jennings for information.
3. For a discussion of dress and *Absolutely Fabulous* see Angela's Hogan interview with costume designer Sarah Burns, "Dressed to Spill," *TV Times*, 22–28 January 1994, pp. 8–9.
4. For an indication of June Whitfield's persona during the period of the program, see Vanessa Berridge, "June Whitfield," *Women and Home*, February 1994, p. 56 and Alan Franks, "Sainted Aunt," *Times Magazine*, 11 January 1997.
5. See *TV Quick*, 22–28 January 1994, Issue 3; *TV Times* 22–28 January 1994.

References

Bakhtin, M., 1984: *Rabelais and His World*, trans. H. Iswolsky. Bloomington: Indiana University Press.

Banks, M. and Swift, A., 1986: *The Joke's on Us: Women in Comedy from Music Hall to the Present Day*. London: Pandora.

Bourdieu, P., 1986: *Distinction: A Social Critique of the Judgement of Taste*. London: Routledge.

Donzelot, J., 1979: *The Policing of Families: Welfare versus the State*. London: Hutchinson.

Elias, N., 1982: *Power and Civility: The Civilising Process, Vol. 2*. New York: Pantheon Books.

Foucault, M., 1979: *The History of Sexuality, Vol. 1: An Introduction*. London: Penguin.

Gilman, S., 1992: "Black bodies, white bodies: towards an iconography of female sexuality in late nineteenth century art, medicine and literature." In J. Donald and A. Rattansi (eds), *"Race," Culture and Difference*. London: Sage/Open University Press, 171–98.

Jenkins, H., 1992: *What Made Pistachio Nuts? Early Sound Comedy and the Vaudeville Aesthetic.* New York: Columbia University Press.

Kaplan, E. A., 1992: *Motherhood and Representation: The Mother in Popular Culture and Melodrama.* London: Routledge.

Lury, C., 1993: *Cultural Rights: Technology, Legality and Personality.* London: Routledge.

Nead, L., 1988: *Myths of Sexuality: Representations of Women in Victorian Britain* Oxford; Blackwell.

Rowe, K. K., 1995: *The Unruly Woman: Gender and the Genres of Laughter.* Austin: University of Texas Press.

Russo, M., 1986: "Female grotesques: carnival and theory." In T. de Lauretis (ed.), *Feminist Studies/Critical Studies.* Bloomington: Indiana University Press, 213–29.

Saunders, J., 1993: *Absolutely Fabulous.* London: BBC Books.

———, 1994: *Absolutely Fabulous 2.* London: BBC Books.

Skeggs, B., 1991: "A spanking good time." *Magazine of Cultural Studies*, 3: 28–33.

———, 1997: *Formations of Class and Gender Becoming Respectable.* London: Sage.

Tyler, C-A., 1991: "Boys will be girls: the politics of gay drag." In D. Fuss (ed.), *Inside Out: Lesbian Theories, Gay Theories.* London: Routledge.

Ware, V., 1992: *Beyond the Pale: White Women, Racism and History.* London: Verso.

Wearing, B., 1984: *The Ideology of Motherhood.* Sydney: Allen and Unwin.

Beavis and Butt-Head
No Future for Postmodern Youth

DOUGLAS KELLNER

Animated cartoon characters Beavis and Butt-Head sit in a shabby house much of the day, watching television, especially music videos, which they criticize in terms of whether the videos are "cool" or "suck." When they leave the house to go to school, to work in a fast food joint, or to seek adventure, they often engage in destructive and even criminal behavior. Developed for MTV by animated cartoonist Mike Judge, the series spoofs precisely the sort of music videos played by the music television channel.[1] *Beavis and Butt-Head* quickly became a cult favorite, loved by youth, yet elicited spirited controversy when some young fans of the show imitated typical Beavis and Butt-Head activity, burning down houses, and torturing and killing animals.[2]

The series provides a critical vision of the current generation of youth raised primarily on media culture. This generation was possibly conceived in the sights and sounds of media culture, weaned on it, and socialized by the glass teat of television used as pacifier, baby sitter, and educator by a generation of parents for whom media culture, especially television, was a natural background and constitutive part of everyday life. The show depicts the dissolution of a rational subject and perhaps the end of the Enlightenment in today's media culture. Beavis and Butt-Head react viscerally to the videos, snickering at the images, finding representations of violence and sex "cool," while anything complex which requires interpretation "sucks." Be-

reft of any cultivated taste, judgment, or rationality, and without ethical or
political values, the characters react in a literally mindless fashion and appear
to lack almost all cognitive and communicative skills.

The intense alienation of Beavis and Butt-Head, their love for heavy
metal culture and media images of sex and violence, and their violent cartoon
activity soon elicited heated controversy, producing a "Beavis and Butt-
Head" effect that has elicited literally thousands of articles and heated debates, even leading to U.S. Senate condemnations of the show for promoting mindless violence and stupid behavior.[3] From the beginning, there was
intense media focus on the show and strongly opposed opinions of it. In a
cover story on the show, *Rolling Stone* declared them "The Voice of a New
Generation" (August 19, 1993) and *Newsweek* also put them on its cover,
both praising them and damning them by concluding: "The downward spi-
ral of the living white male surely ends here: in a little pimple named Butt-
head whose idea of an idea is, 'Hey, Beavis, let's go over to Stuart's house
and light one in his cat's butt'" (October 11, 1993). "Stupid, lazy, cruel;
without ambitions, without values, without futures" are other terms used in
the media to describe the characters and the series (*The Dallas Morning News*,
August 29, 1993) and there have been countless calls to ban the show.

Indeed, a lottery prize winner in California began a crusade against the
series, after hearing about a cat that was killed when kids put a firecracker
in its mouth, imitating Beavis and Butt-Head's violence against animals and
a suggestion in one episode that they stick a firecracker in a neighbor boy's
cat (*The Hollywood Reporter*, July 16, 1993). Librarians in Westchester, New
York ranked *Beavis and Butt-Head* high "on a list of movies and television
shows that they think negatively influence youngsters' reading habits," because of their attacks on books and frequent remarks that books, or even
words, "suck" (*The New York Times*, July 11, 1993). Prison officials in Oklahoma banned the show, schools in South Dakota banned clothing and other
items bearing their likeness (*Times Newspapers Limited*, October 11, 1993),
and a group of Missouri fourth graders started a petition drive to get the
program off the air (*Radio TV Reports*, October 25, 1993).

Yet the series continued to be highly popular into 1994, and it has
spawned a best-selling album of heavy metal rock, a popular book, countless consumer items, and movie contracts in the works. *Time* magazine critic,
Kurt Anderson, praised the series as "the bravest show ever run on national
television" (*The New York Times*, July 11, 1993) and there is no question
but that it has pushed the boundaries of the permissible on mainstream television to new extremes (some critics would say to new lows).

In a certain sense, *Beavis and Butt-Head* is "postmodern" in that it is
purely a product of media culture, with its characters, style, and content
almost solely derivative from previous TV shows. The two characters Beavis
and Butt-Head are a spin-off of Wayne and Garth in *Wayne's World*, a popular *Saturday Night Live* feature, spun off into popular movies. They also
resemble the SCTV characters Bob and Doug McKenzie, who sit around
on a couch and make lewd and crude remarks while they watch TV and

drink beer. Beavis and Butt-Head also take the asocial behavior of cartoon character Bart Simpson to a more intense extreme. Their comments on the music videos replicate the popular Comedy Central channel's series *Mystery Science Theater 3000,* which features two cartoon stick figures making irreverent comments on god-awful old Hollywood movies and network television shows. And, of course, the music videos are a direct replication of MTV's basic fare.

Beavis and Butt-Head is interesting for a diagnostic critique because the main characters get all of their ideas and images concerning life from the media and their entire view of history and the world is entirely derived from media culture. When they see a costumed rapper wearing an eighteenth-century-style white wig on a music video, Butt-Head remarks: "He's dressed up like that dude on the dollar." The 1960s is the time of hippies, Woodstock and rock 'n' roll for them; Vietnam is ancient history, collapsed into other American wars. Even the 1950s is nothing but a series of mangled media cliches: on Nelson, the twins of 1950s teen idol Ricky Nelson, Butt-Head remarks that: "These chicks look like guys." Beavis responds: "I heard that these chicks' grandpa was Ozzy Osbourne." And Butt-Head rejoins: "No way. They're Elvis's kids."

The figures of history are collapsed for Beavis and Butt-Head into media culture and provide material for salacious jokes, which require detailed knowledge of media culture:

> *Butt-Head:* What happened when Napoleon went to Mount Olive?
> *Beavis:* I don't know. What?
> *Butt-Head:* Popeye got pissed.

Moreover, Beavis and Butt-Head seem to have no family, living alone in a shabby house, getting enculturated solely by television and media culture. There are some references to their mothers and in one episode there is a suggestion that Butt-Head is not even certain who his father is, thus the series presents a world without fathers.[4] School is totally alienating for the two, as is work in a fast-food restaurant. Adult figures who they encounter are largely white conservative males, or liberal yuppies, with whom they come into often violent conflict and whose property or goods they inevitably destroy.

There is a fantasy wish-fulfillment aspect to *Beavis and Butt-Head* that perhaps helps account for its popularity: kids often wish that they had no parents and that they could just sit and watch music videos and go out and do whatever they wanted to (sometimes we *all* feel this way). Kids are also naturally disrespectful of authority and love to see defiance of social forces that they find oppressive. Indeed, Beavis and Butt-Head's much maligned, discussed, and imitated laughter ("Heh, heh, heh" and "Huh, huh") may signify that in their space *they rule,* that Beavis and Butt-Head are sovereign, that they control the television and can do any damn thing that they want. Notably, they get in trouble in school and other sites of authority with their laugh, but at home they can laugh and snicker to the max.

And so the series has a utopian dimension: the utopia of no parental authority and unlimited freedom to do whatever they want when they want to. "Dude, we're there" is a favorite phrase they use when they decide to see or do something—and they never have to ask their (absent) parents' permission. On the other hand, they represent the consequences of totally unsocialized adolescent behavior driven by aggressive instincts.[5] Indeed, their "utopia" is highly solipsistic and narcissistic with no community, no consensual norms or morality to bind them, and no concern for other people. The vision of the teenagers alone in their house watching TV and then wreaking havoc on their neighborhood presents a vision of a society of broken families, disintegrating communities, and anomic individuals, without values or goals.

Beavis and Butt-Head are thus left alone with TV and become couch-potato critics, especially of their beloved music videos. In a sense, they are the first media critics to become cult heros of media culture, though there are contradictions in their media criticism. Many of the videos that they attack are stupid and pretentious, and in general it is good to cultivate a critical attitude toward culture forms and to promote cultural criticism—an attitude that can indeed be applied to much of what appears on *Beavis and Butt-Head*. Such critique distances its audience from music video culture and calls for making critical judgments on its products. Yet Beavis and Butt-Head's own judgments are highly questionable, praising images of violence, fire, naked women, and heavy metal noise, while declaring that "college music," words, and any complexity in the videos "suck."

Thus, on one level, the series provides sharp social satire and critique of the culture and society. The episodes constantly make fun of television, especially music videos, and other forms of media culture. They criticize conservative authority figures and wishy-washy liberals. They satirize authoritarian institutions like the workplace, schools, and military recruitment centers and provide critical commentary on many features of contemporary life. Yet, the series undercuts some of its social critique by reproducing the worst sexist, violent, and narcissistic elements of contemporary life, which are made amusing and even likeable in the figures of Beavis and Butt-Head.

Consequently, *Beavis and Butt-Head* is surprisingly complex and requires a diagnostic critique to analyze its contradictory text and effects. There is no denying, however, that the *Beavis and Butt-Head* effect is one of the most significant media phenomena of recent years.[6] Like Linklater, Judge has obviously tapped into a highly responsive chord and created a media sensation with the characters of Beavis and Butt-Head serving as powerfully resonant images. In 1993, while lecturing on cultural studies, wherever I would go audiences would ask me what I thought of *Beavis and Butt-Head* and so I eventually began to watch it and to incorporate remarks on the series into my lectures.[7] If I was critical or disparaging, young members of the audience would attack me and after a lecture at the University of Kansas, a young man came up, incredulous that I would dare to criticize the series, certain that Mike Judge was a great genius who understood exactly how it was for contemporary youth, with no prospects for a job or career, and little prospect for even marriage and family and a meaningful life. In this situation, I was told, what else can young people do except watch MTV and occasionally go out and destroy something?

In a sense, the series thus enacts youth and class revenge against older, middle-class and conservative adults, who appear as oppressive authority figures. Their neighbor Tom Anderson—depicted as a conservative World War II and Korean war veteran—is a special butt of their escapades and they cut down trees in his yard with a chain saw, which, of course, causes the tree to demolish his house, assorted fences, power lines, and cars. They put his dog in a laundromat washing machine to clean it; they steal his credit card to buy animals at the mall; they lob mud baseballs into his yard, one of which hits his barbecue; and otherwise torment him. Beavis and Butt-Head also blow up an Army recruiting station with a grenade, as the officer attempts to recruit them; they steal the cart of a wealthy man, Billy Bob, who has a heart attack when he sees them riding off in his vehicle; and they love to put worms, rats, and other animals in the fast food that they are shown giving to obnoxious white male customers in the burger joint where they work.

Beavis and Butt-Head also love to trash the house of their "friend" Stewart whose yuppie parents indulgently pamper their son and his playmates. Stewart's permissive liberal parents are shown to be silly and ineffectual, as when his father complains that Stewart violated his parents' trust when he let Beavis and Butt-Head in the house after they caused an explosion which blew the wall out. The mother gushes about how cute they are and offers them lemonade—in fact, few women authority figures are depicted.

The dynamic duo also torment and make fun of their liberal hippie teacher, Mr Van Driessen, who tries to teach them to be politically correct. They destroy his irreplaceable eight-track music collection when he offers to let them clean his house to learn the value of work and money. When he takes them camping to get in touch with their feelings and nature, they fight and torment animals. In fact, they rebel against all their teachers and authority figures and are thus presented in opposition to everyone, ranging from conservative males, to liberal yuppies, to hippie radicals.

Moreover, the series presents the revenge of youth and those who are terminally downwardly mobile against more privileged classes and individuals. Like the punk generation before them, Beavis and Butt-Head have no future. Thus, while their behavior is undeniably juvenile, offensive, sexist, and politically incorrect, it allows diagnosis of underclass and downwardly mobile youth who have nothing to do, but to destroy things and engage in asocial behavior.

From this perspective, *Beavis and Butt-Head* is an example of media culture as popular revenge.[8] Beavis and Butt-Head avenge youth and the downwardly mobile against those oppressive authority figures who they confront daily. Most of the conservative men have vaguely Texan, or Southwestern, accents, so perhaps the male authority figures represent oppressive males experienced by Judge in his own youth in San Diego, New Mexico and Texas. Moreover, Beavis and Butt-Head's violence is that of a violent society in which the media present endless images of the sort of violent activities that the two characters regularly engage in. The series thus points to the existence of a large teenage underclass with no future which is undereducated and potentially violent. The young underclass Beavis and Butt-Heads of the society have nothing to look forward to in life save a job at the local 7-Eleven, waiting to get held up at gunpoint. Consequently, the series is a social hieroglyphic which allows us to decode the attitudes, behavior, and situation of large segments of youth in contemporary U.S. society.

For a diagnostic critique, then, it is wrong to simply excuse the antics of Beavis and Butt-Head as typical behavior of the young. Likewise, it is not enough simply to condemn them as pathological.[9] Rather the series reveals how violent society is becoming and the dead-end futures of downwardly mobile youth from broken homes who are undereducated and have no real job possibilities or future. Indeed, the heavy metal culture in which Beavis and Butt-Head immerse themselves is a way for those caught up in dead-end lives to blot everything out, to escape in a world of pure noise and aggression, and in turn to express their own aggression and frustrations through heavy metal "head-banging." Thus, when Beavis and Butt-Head play the "air guitar," imitating heavy metal playing during the music videos, they are signalling both their aggression and the hopelessness of their situation.

Beavis and Butt-Head's narcissism and sociopathic behavior is a symptom of a society that is not providing adequate nurture or support to its citizens. It is indeed curious that many of the most popular media culture figures could easily be clinically diagnosed and analyzed as narcissistic: Rush Limbaugh, Andrew Dice Clay, Howard Stern, and other popular media figures are examples of empty, insecure, and hostile individuals who resort to extreme behavior and assertions to call attention to themselves. In turn, they tap into audience aggression and frustrations and become popular precisely because of their ability to articulate inchoate social anger. Indeed, compared to a Rush Limbaugh, Beavis and Butt-Head are relatively modest and restrained in their narcissism.

Beavis and Butt-Head, Rush Limbaugh, and other figures of contemporary U.S. media culture also think they know things, but are know-nothings in the good old tradition of American anti-intellectualism. These figures are basically buffoons, sometimes entertaining and often offensive, who in the classical syndrome of narcissism are empty, insecure, and aggressive. They masquerade their emptiness and insecurity in verbal bravado and aggressiveness and attention-seeking action. They also display classic symptoms of fear of women, who they continually objectify, and engage in puerile and infantile sexual jokes and gesture. Beavis and Butt-Head are classic teenagers whose hormones are out of control and who cannot control them, and their elders like Howard Stern and Andrew Dice Clay exhibit similar symptoms. These figures of popular entertainment are all white boys, incapable of taking the position of the other, of empathizing with the other, or of respecting differences. They are all extremely homophobic, though Beavis and Butt-Head are obviously repressing homosexual proclivities signalled in all the "butt" jokes, "suck" references, and Butt-Head's injunction: "Hey, Beavis pull my finger."

In a sense, *Beavis and Butt-Head* is an example of what has been called "loser television," surely a new phenomenon in television history. Previous television series tended to depict wealthy, or secure middle-class, individuals and families, often with highly glamorous lives. It was believed that advertisers preferred affluent environments to sell their products and so the working class and underclass were excluded from network television for decades. Indeed, during the Reaganite 1980s, programs like *Dallas, Dynasty,* and *Life Styles of the Rich and Famous* celebrated wealth and affluence. This dream has been punctured by the reality of everyday life in a downsliding economy, and so a large television audience is attracted to programs that articulate their own frustration and anger in experiencing downward mobility and a sense of no future. Hence, the popularity of new "loser television," including *The Simpsons, Roseanne,* and *Beavis and Butt-Head.*

Thus, the MTV show *Beavis and Butt-Head* allows a diagnostic critique of the plight of contemporary youth in disintegrating families, with little education, and with no job possibilities. Beavis and Butt-Head's destructiveness can be seen in part as an expression of their hopelessness and alienation and shows the dead-end prospects for many working-class and middle-class youths. Moreover, the series also replicates the sort of violence that is so widespread in the media from heavy metal rock videos to TV entertainment and news. Thus, the characters' violence simply mirrors growing youth violence in a disintegrating society and allows the possibility of a diagnostic critique of the social situation of contemporary youth.

Yet the show *is* highly violent and has already had spectacular violence effects. In the *Liquid Television* animated short that preceded the series, Judge shows Beavis and Butt-Head playing "frog baseball," splattering frogs and bashing each other with baseball bats (an image immortalized on one of many Beavis and Butt-Head t-shirts). In other shows, they use lighters to start fires, blow up a neighbor's house by sniffing gas from the stove and then lighting it, and engage in multifarious other acts of mayhem and violence. A Los Angeles area school teacher discovered that about 90 percent of her class watched the show and invited a local fire department official to speak to her class:

> after several students wrote about playing with fire and explosives in their autobiographical sketches. Some examples: "A major 'Beavis and Butt-Head' fan, Jarrod Metchikoff, 12, used to 'line them (firecrackers) up in a tube and shoot them in the sewer pipe' until his mother found out. Brett Heimstra, 12, said he set off firecrackers in manholes and sewers until his mother discovered them and he 'heard some stuff about how it's dangerous.' Elizabeth Hastings, 12, said she knows a boy who lights firecrackers in portable toilets" (*Los Angeles Times,* October 16, 1993)

The fire official told the students "about a 10-year-old Orange County boy who lost use of his hand after an explosion caused by WD-40 and a cigarette lighter" (ibid.). After the initial reports of cruelty to animals and fans of the show starting fires, many more such reports came in. The fire chief in Sidney, Ohio, "blamed MTV's cartoon for a house fire started by three girls" (*The Plain Dealer*, October 14, 1993). Further: "Austin, Texas, investigators say three fires started by kids may have some connection to the show" (*USA Today*, October 15, 1993). And Houston teenage fans of the show were blamed for setting fires near the Galleria mall (*Radio TV Reports*, October 25, 1993).

Intense criticism of the show's violence—and Congressional threats to regulate TV violence—led MTV to move back its playtime to later in the evening and there was a promise not to replay the more violent episodes, or to show Beavis and Butt-Head starting fires, or Beavis shouting "Fire! Fire!" but the series had already become part of a national mythology and its popularity continued apace.[10] Indeed, media culture is drawn to violence and taboo-breaking action to draw audiences in an ever-more competitive field. Thus, the program's excesses are directly related to a competitive situation in which commercial media are driven to show ever more violent and extreme behavior in the intense pressures for high profits—a trend that many believe will accelerate as the number of TV channels grows and competition becomes fiercer.

And so we see how media culture taps into its audience's concerns and in turn becomes part of a circuit of culture, with distinctive effects. Media cultural texts articulate social experiences, transcoding them into the medium of forms like television, film, or popular music. The texts are then appropriated by audiences, which use certain resonant texts and images to articulate their own sense of style, look, and identity. Media culture provides resources to make meanings, pleasure, and identity, but also shape and form specific identities and circulate material whose appropriateness may insert audiences into specific positions (i.e. macho Rambo, sexy Madonna, disaffected Slackers, violent Beavis and Butt-Head, and so on).

The *Beavis and Butt-Head* effects were particularly striking. Not only did the show promote acts of violence and copious discussion of media effects, but the characters became models for youth behavior, with young people imitating various of their tics and behavior patterns. Of course, the series generated a large consumer market of "Beavis and Butt-Head" products, which in turn proliferated its images and effects. For example: "Maskmaker Ed Edmunds of Distortions Unlimited says he's sold 40,000 Beavis and Butt-Head masks, his top sellers for this Halloween season" (*U.S.A. Today*, October 26, 1993). In 1994, Beavis and Butt-Head combs, calendars, and even day-planners were on the market.

The show also strongly influenced musical tastes and sales, providing a boon for heavy metal rock. Studies showed that sales jumped of every video played on the show, including ones Beavis and Butt-Head panned.[11] The *Beavis and Butt-Head* effect even became part of political contestation:

> It was only a matter of time before "Beavis Clinton" and "Butt-Head Gore" T-shirts began appearing on the streets of Washington. The hapless, ugly, dumb cartoon characters have been altered to look like the leaders of the

free world, thanks to local political entrepreneurs and T-shirt creators Kathleen Patten, Beth Loudy and Chris Tremblay. On the shirts, Beavis is sporting a Fleetwood Mac T-shirt and is seen asking Butt-Head, "Eh, do you think we'll get re-elected?" To which the veep, wearing the Greenpeace whale logo, says: "Huh . . . nope." (*Washington Times,* October 26, 1993)[12]

Previous studies of media effects seem blind to the sort of complex effects of media culture texts of the sort I have discussed in analyses of the *Rambo* effect, the *Slacker* effect, and the *Beavis and Butt-Head* effect. In each case, figures and material were taken from these texts and were used to produce meaning, identities, discourse, and behavior. The media provide symbolic environments in which people live and strongly influence their thought, behavior, and style. When a media sensation like *Beavis and Butt-Head* appears, it becomes part of that environment, and in turn becomes a new resource for pleasures, identities, and contestation.

Thus, it is totally idiotic to claim that media culture has no discernible effects, as in the dominant paradigm from the 1940s, which lasted several decades.[13] Yet it is equally blind to blithely claim that audiences simply produce their own meanings from texts and that the texts do not have their own effectivity. As my discussions have shown, media culture has very powerful effects, though its meanings are mediated by audiences and even a figure like Rambo can be a contested terrain in which different groups inflect its meanings in different ways.

The *Slacker* and *Beavis and Butt-Head* effects that I have just discussed crystallize the experiences and feelings of alienation and hopelessness produced by a disintegrating society and shape these experiences into identification with slackers, rockers, heavy metal and nihilistic violence of the sort engaged in by Beavis and Butt-Head. Popular media texts tap into and articulate feelings and experiences of their audiences and in turn circulate material effects that shape thought and behavior. The texts of media culture thus have very powerful and distinctive effects and should thus be carefully scrutinized and subject to diagnostic critique.

Notes

1. *Beavis and Butt-Head* was based on an animated short by Mike Judge, in which the two characters play "frog baseball," shown at the Sick and Twisted Animation festival and taken up by MTV's animated series *Liquid Television.* The series itself premiered in March 1993, but because there were only four episodes, the show went on hiatus, returning May 17 after Judge and his team of creative assistants put together thirty-two new episodes (*The San Francisco Chronicle,* June 29, 1993). The series tripled MTV's ratings and MTV ordered 130 more episodes for 1994 (*The New York Times,* October 17, 1993).

2. An October 9, 1993, story in the *Dayton Daily News* reported that a 5-year-old boy in Dayton, Ohio, ignited his bedclothes with a cigarette lighter after watching the pyromaniac antics of Beavis and Butt-Head, according to his mother. The boy's younger sister, aged 2, died in the ensuing blaze. The mother said her 5-year-old son had become "obsessed" with *Beavis and Butt-Head* and imitated the char-

acters' destructive behavior. I provide more examples of the *Beavis and Butt-Head* effect throughout this section.

3. An October 23, 1993, Senate Hearing on TV violence focused media attention on the show, though U.S. Sen. Ernest Hollings (D-SC) botched references to it, saying: "We've got this—what is it—Buffcoat and Beaver or Beaver and something else . . . I haven't seen it; I don't watch it; it was at 7 o'clock—Buffcoat—and they put it on now at 10:30, I think" (*The Hartford Courant,* October 26, 1993). Such ignorance of media culture is often found in some of its harshest critics.

4. Their family genealogy in a book on the series puts a question mark in the place of both of their fathers (Johnson S. and Marcil E. *Beavis and Butt-head. This book sucks* (New York: Pocket Books) 1993). So far, their mothers have not been shown, though there are some references to them. It is also unclear exactly whose house they live in, or are shown watching TV in, and whether they do or do not live together. One episode suggests that they are in Butt-Head's house and that his mother is (is always) out with her boyfriend, but other episodes show two beds together in what appears to be their highly messy bedroom and as of early 1994, their parents have never been shown.

5. Psychoanalysts like to identify Beavis and Butt-Head with the Freudian Id, with uncontrolled aggression and sexual impulses that they cannot understand or control (they were often shown masturbating, or talking about it, and Beavis uncontrollably "moons" attractive female singers while watching music videos). There is also a barely repressed homo-erotic element to their relationship, expressed in the endless "butt" jokes and references, their constant use of "sucks," and other verbal and visual behavior ("Hey Beavis, pull my finger.").

6. Margot Emery was taking a midterm examination in a mass communications theory course for master's degree candidates at the University of Tennessee at Knoxville when she found, on the last page, a question about . . . Beavis and Butt-Head. Novelist Gloria Naylor, Hartford Stage Company artistic director Mark Lamos and other distinguished panelists were discussing stereotypes in art, especially the depiction of Jews in "The Merchant of Venice," when unexpectedly the talk swung around to . . . Beavis and Butt-Head. Fred Rogers of "Mister Rogers' Neighborhood" was being honored for his work by the Pittsburgh Presbytery and wound up discoursing upon . . . Beavis and Butt-Head. Thomas Grasso, a prisoner whose main problem these days is deciding whether he'd rather have the state of Oklahoma execute him or the state of New York imprison him for a very long time, recently wrote a poem comparing Gov. Mario Cuomo and a New York corrections official to . . . Beavis and Butt-Head. In fact, it has become so rare to read 10 pages of a magazine, to browse one section of a newspaper or to endure 30 minutes of television or radio talk without bumping into some knowing reference to the animated MTV dullards. (*The Hartford Courant,* October 26, 1993)

7. Via MTV marathons of the series in summer 1993, January 1994, and Steve Best's collection, I was able to see almost every episode of the series. I also did extensive Nexis data-base searches for mainstream media references to and debates over the series and through the Fall of 1993 and into 1994, there were literally hundreds of references to the series. There also appeared a best-selling album of the heavy metal that Beavis and Butt-Head celebrate, a best-selling book, and movie deals in the works. Consequently, one can also easily speak of the *Beavis and Butt-Head* effect.

8. On this concept and a wealth of examples, see Kellner "Ideology, Marxism and Advanced Capitalism." *Socialist Review,* **42:** 37–65, 1978.

9. After a Washington, D.C. psychologist said that Beavis and Butt-Head's humor sounded like the antics of normal youth, she frantically called back the reporter after seeing that night's episode, leading her to comment on voice mail. "I totally condemn this program. I do not see any shred of normal adolescent behavior here. It's one of the most sadistic, pathological programs I've ever seen. I would not recommend it to anyone of any age" (*The Washington Times,* October 17, 1993). The same story noted that an advocate of People for the Ethical Treatment of Animals stated: "Psychiatrists will tell you that almost every major serial killer has animal abuse in their background. Beavis and Butt-Head not only torture animals, but they are preoccupied with fire, and those are two of the three predictors of adult criminal behavior."

10. MTV's parent company Viacom was engaged at the time in a much-publicized battle to merge with Paramount and the conglomerate obviously did not want too much bad publicity. Thus, MTV had to walk the line between preserving its most profitable and popular product and avoiding excessive media criticism. The result was compromises that softened the edge of *Beavis and Butt-Head,* while attempting to preserve the show's popularity. As of spring 1994, the MTV strategy has worked with the show continuing to be highly popular with controversy diminishing.

11. The group White Zombie's album *La Sexorcisto: Devil Music Vol. 1,* for example,

> wasn't selling enough to make the nation's Top 100 charts, averaging only about 2,000 copies a week. But the group's video has been a fixture on "Beavis and Butt-Head" since the summer, and the exposure—along with the bratty teens' words of praise—have propelled the album into the national Top 30. Estimated sales now: more than 500,000 copies. . . . Rick Krim, MTV's vice president of talent and artists relations, explains the response to the "Beavis and Butt-Head" exposure. "We had liked the Thunder video and supported it with play on the various specialty shows" he says. "That never really sparked significant album sales, the Beavis and Butt-Head exposure sure did. The sales response was pretty immediate. . . . Almost everything that gets played on the show gets some sort of sales bump from it" (*Billboard,* September 4, 1993).

12. Such an anti-Clinton move could backfire as younger voters might interpret the association to suggest that Clinton and Gore are "cool" and thus come to support them.

13. I am speaking of Lazarsfeld's "two step flow" model which claimed that media culture had no direct effects, that its effects were modest and minimal, and mediated by "opinion leaders" who had the more important effects on consumer and political behavior, social attitudes, and the like (see Katz E. and Lazarsfeld P. F. *Personal influence* (New York: The Free Press) 1955 and the critical discussion of its effects in Gitlin T. "Media sociology: the dominant paradigm." *Theory and Society* **6:** 205–53, 1978).

Objectivity and Ethnicity in the Production of the *Noticiero Univisión*[1]

AMÉRICA RODRIGUEZ

The U.S. trained journalists of the *Noticiero Univisión,* the nightly national newscast of the largest Spanish language television network in the United States, daily recreate a defining tension between their fealty to the professional code of objectivity and their commitment to their ethnicity and that of their imagined audience[2] of U.S. Latinos.[3] Nightly, *Univisión* journalists produce a discursive (see for example Siefert, 1994) construction of U.S. Latino ethnicity. The structures of discourse of the *Noticiero Univisión*—the particular Spanish language employed, as well as the purposeful framing and presentation of news stories—daily produce a unified narrative of world events. The production of this national news program offers a particular terrain in which to examine issues of meaning and power (Hall, 1980, 1982) regarding communities the U.S. Census Bureau predicts will be the nation's largest ethnic minority group by the year 2020.

Univisión journalists are deeply imbedded in the national journalistic culture and the broader national "American" culture (Schudson, 1995, pp. 1–36; Carey, 1986). However, in contrast to many national journalists who have only a "vague image" of their audience (Gans, 1979, p. 230), *Univisión* journalists have detailed conceptualizations of their audience. Their presumptive audience is a culturally distinct, often oppressed and exploited people. *Univisión* journalists have also suffered racism and injustice, both personally and professionally. The journalists' conceptualization of and iden-

From *Critical Studies in Mass Communication,* March 1996. Copyright © 1996 by the National Communication Association. Reprinted by permission of the publisher.

tification with their audience is a central force shaping the production of the *Noticiero.*

In addition to its defining role in the journalistic practice of the *Noticiero,* the newscasts' presumptive audience is at the center of the economic analysis of the production of this alternative (Williams, 1980, p. 14) U.S. national news program. Like other U.S. commercial media, the *Noticiero* must attract and maintain an audience which can be sold to advertisers through the mediation of audience measurement ratings systems (Ang, 1991; Barnes and Thomson, 1994). The process of strategically defining and then selling U.S. Spanish speakers as a commodity has historically been fraught with political and cultural obstacles (Rodriguez, 1995). Today, the nexus of U.S. Spanish language media "audiencemaking" (Ettema and Whitney, 1994, pp. 1–19) is the notion of U.S. Latino panethnicity—a commercially viable marketing stratagem that constructs the financial foundation of *Univisión,* and so its nightly newscast.

U.S. Latino panethnicity is a contested notion in the newsroom, dismissed by the journalists as "business talk," yet the touchstone of editorial decisions. U.S. Latino panethnicity holds that all U.S. Latinos, Latin American immigrants and their descendants, are one unitary group, regardless of differences of national origin, race, class, or U.S. immigration history. U.S. Latino panethnicity, and its hemispheric complement, panamericanism, construct the "Hispanic market," and are the "symbolic glue" (Kaniss, 1991) that holds together the *Noticiero Univisión* audience for national advertisers.

This essay combines a detailed ethnography of *Noticiero Univisión* production and an extensive comparative content analysis of the *Noticiero* and ABC's *World News Tonight with Peter Jennings.*[4] The content analysis shows the deep similarities in form and newsmaking routines, and thereby in content of the two programs. It also highlights the striking differences between the two newscasts' mapping of the world. The production ethnography focuses attention on the concrete professional and economic "contexts and constraints" (Morley, 1986) of this cultural production process.[5] The quantitative unit of the content analysis is the story. However, informed by the ethnography, the discussion of the findings more often focuses on multiple stories, common themes, and coverage of particular issues. The multi-method study examines the mutually reinforcing cultural and economic dimensions of ethnicity and objectivity in the production of the *Noticiero Univisión.*

"Objectivity" in this essay references the dominant ideology and practice of U.S. journalism, what Hallin (1986) has called "conservative reformism." Objectivity is the nexus of the cultural and ideological commonality that the *Noticiero Univisión* shares with English language U.S. journalism. The production of the *Noticiero Univisión* is a highly routinized, professionally self-protective process (Tuchman, 1972); the result of mutually beneficial elite interactions (Sigal, 1973) that create a nightly capsule of global reality. For *Univisión* journalists, like their general market counterparts, objectivity is the emblem of U.S. journalism (Schudson, 1978, pp.

9–10). However, for *Univisión* journalists, objectivity, especially its non-partisan dimension, has special salience.

Many key *Univisión* journalists[6] were once employees of *Televisa,* the monopolistic Mexican entertainment conglomerate that is commonly referred to as the Ministry of Culture of the Mexican ruling party known by its Spanish acronym, the PRI. *Televisa* journalists have rarely been less than fawning in their reporting of Mexican government policies, while at the same time ignoring government critics.[7] For these journalists, as well as their colleagues who are immigrants from other authoritarian Latin American regimes (e.g., Cuba, Argentina) the U.S. constitution's First Amendment is, as one put it, "like a religion for me." (In practice, as will be discussed below, the purity of this idealized political neutrality is constrained by *Univisión*'s ethnocentric coverage of U.S. Latino politics.) The practice of U.S. professional objectivity, in other words, is what makes *Univisión* journalists U.S. journalists.

Additionally, journalistic objectivity confers professional credibility on these ethnic minority journalists both in the eyes of their audience and general market peers; objectivity legitimizes the journalists' "expert" positioning relative to the audience (Gans, 1979; Schudson, 1978). Closely related to this last authoritative dimension of objectivity is its function as a marketing tool (Schiller, 1981). As the first (and in many communities still the only) U.S. Spanish-language national television newscast, *Univisión* journalists' cultural embrace of objectivity reinforces the program's distinctiveness and reliability, particularly for its presumptive audience of recent Latin American immigrants.

U.S. Latino ethnicity in this essay is conceived of as an ongoing social process; a dynamic, identifying manifestation of the complex, often contradictory experiences of Latin American immigration to the United States. The *Noticiero Univisión* reproduces its particular vision of and prescription for (Geertz, 1973, p. 44) U.S. Latino ethnicity for its two "publics": the presumptive audience and advertisers. Obviously enough, the self-conscious ethnicity of the *Noticiero Univisión* is what distinguishes it most clearly from other U.S. national newscasts. Largely white European-American general market journalists rarely think about their ethnicity, or that of their audience.[8] In sharp contrast, *Univisión* journalists daily reproduce their U.S. Latino ethnicity. This study analyzes the production of the *Noticiero* as an interaction between the demands of the commercial enterprise *Univisión,* the professional ideals of the U.S.-trained journalists, and the Latino ethnic identification of the journalists and their imagined audience.

To contextualize the production of the *Noticiero Univisión,* I consider the foundational role of U.S. Latino panethnicity in the commercial and cultural enterprise *Univisión,* first examining the economic structures of the transnational corporation, and then the journalistic role of panethnicity. Subsequent sections examine the cultural, professional and economic process of creating the newscast through textual analysis as well as an examination of the story selection and narrative stance of *Noticiero Univisión* journalists.

The Commercial Imperative: U.S. Latino Panethnicity and the Hispanic Market

The *Noticiero Univisión* is the fifth most watched program on U.S. Spanish language television[9] *Univisión* is the preeminent U.S. Spanish language television network; about 85 percent of the Spanish language television audience in the United States watches *Univisión,* about 15 percent watches its rival, *Telemundo.*[10] *Univisión* was founded 25 years ago (as SIN, the Spanish International Network) and today commands most of the advertising dollars of the U.S. Spanish language television industry. *Univisión* executives say their first job, a quarter century after the creation of U.S. Spanish language television, is to persuade advertisers that U.S. Spanish speakers are an audience worth targeting.[11] Fifty percent of *Univisión* is owned by Jerry Perrenchino, an entertainment financier perhaps best known as one of the early backers of Norman Lear. Twenty five percent of *Univisión* is owned by the Cisneros brothers, owners of *Venevisión,* a Venezuelan broadcasting company. The remaining 25 percent of the network is owned by *Televisa,* the monopolistic Mexican entertainment conglomerate and founder (in 1961) of U.S. Spanish language television.

Except for a brief interlude,[12] *Televisa* has dominated U.S. Spanish language television from its inception. The U.S. television market, from the perspective of the U.S. commercial interests is small; it is "narrowcasting." Seen from the point of view of Latin American entrepreneurs, U.S. Hispanics represent the richest Latin American market.[13] Understood within the Latin American media context, it therefore is not surprising that *Televisa's* current minority ownership status understates its defining role in *Univisión.*[14] After *Televisa's* latest repurchase of *Univisión* in 1992, the *Noticiero* bureaus in Chile and Argentina were closed. Consequently, there is somewhat less Latin American news on the program, but otherwise, there is little discernible difference in this program under its new ownership structure.

The *Noticiero,* because it is profitable and because of its prestige as the flagship news program, has established some distance from network ownership. The *Noticiero Univisión* is obligated not only to make a profit, but also to maintain its credibility with the audience, as well as its privileged role within an entertainment-oriented organization (Hallin, 1985). All other U.S.-produced *Univisión* programming is aggressively marketed and broadcast throughout Latin America.[15] While the *Noticiero* (more often, pirated segments of the program) is seen in Latin America, unlike other *Univisión* programs, the Latin American market is not a central part of the production rationale. This, however, is not to minimize the role of the newscast in the economic success of *Univisión:* a nightly national news program was very much part of the strategy for expanding and solidifying a national, panethnic U.S. audience when *Univisión* began to transmit its programming via satellite in 1981 (Rodriguez, 1995).

Univisión is both a product and a producer of U.S. Latino panethnicity. *Univisión* conceived, created and legitimated a U.S. Hispanic market and a national U.S. Spanish speaking audience as it commercially exploited it. U.S. Latino panethnicity has dual origins, as an administrative convenience for the U.S. government, specifically the Census Bureau (Melville, 1988; Sommers, 1991), and as a commercial construction for advertisers seeking "new" markets. By commissioning the first national Hispanic market research,[16] *Univisión,* then known as SIN, helped initiate the process of commercially defining Latin Americans and their descendants in the United States as a unitary market, a national audience.

Univisión and its 600 affiliated television stations are a "bridging institution" (Espiritu, 1992), a source of symbolic reinterpretation of the U.S. Latin American immigration experience—an element of the process of social change that transforms Cuban, Mexican, Puerto Rican, Central and South American immigrants into U.S. Hispanic "ethnics." Until SIN produced a nationally conceived and distributed news program in 1981, U.S. Spanish language immigrant news (radio and newspapers) had been more narrowly delimited, usually by city or town, occasionally by region, which in the case of U.S. Latinos roughly coincides with national origin (i.e., Puerto Ricans in New York City, Cubans in south Florida, Mexicans and Mexican Americans in California and the Southwest). Similarly, until the 1980's Hispanic national advertising campaigns were actually three separate campaigns, with separate iconography: advertisements that targeted Puerto Ricans featured *salsa* music and cityscapes; for Mexicans and Mexican Americans, the music was *ranchera,* the landscape featured cactuses; for Cubans, cigars and palm trees.[17]

Beginning in the mid 1980's, Hispanic advertising largely eschewed national origin symbolism for a denationalized, panethnic "Walter Cronkite Spanish," and a "Hispanic USA" advertising strategy. Today, the commercial imperative of U.S. Latino panethnicity has been broadened in the construction of panamericanism, the notion that the U.S. Hispanic market is one segment—albeit the wealthiest segment—of a hemispheric market that embraces Spanish speakers in North, Central and South America. In addition to *Univisión, Telemundo,* NBC, CNN, and MTV are producing Spanish language programming in the United States for broadcast in Latin America. Similarly, U.S. advertising agencies are producing campaigns for the Hispanic market that are distributed—with minor adaptations—to diverse Latin American nations.

Univisión national newscasts are predicated on the existence of a national panethnic Hispanic market, as well as a panethnic community of interest. U.S. Latino panethnicity is implicit when *Univisión* journalists produce stories about the Puerto Rican community in the Bronx for the *Noticiero Univisión;* the presumption is that Mexican-Americans in Los Angeles and Cubans in Miami will also be interested in a story about their fellow Hispanics. However, the presumed panethnic identity of the *Noticiero* audience is a contested one. Simply put, no one is born "Hispanic"—which is not to dismiss the cultural power of this categorization amongst U.S. Latinos. Organized U.S. Latino political groups often adopt "Latinismo" for strategic purposes (Padilla, 1985; Sommers, 1991). The naming "Hispanics" has tremendous resonance throughout U.S. public culture (think of the phrase "blacks and Hispanics"), and is reinforced by countless social service agencies and by local and national media—both mainstream and ethnically oriented media.

Nonetheless, studies of U.S. Latino ethnic identity show clearly that national origin identification as well as class differences, and differences in U.S. immigration histories, override the unifying power of language in determining Hispanic self-identification (Hart-González, 1985; López and Espiritu, 1990, de la Garza, 1992). *Univisión* journalists have personal and professional knowledge of the a historical nature and lack of authenticity in notions of U.S. Latino panethnicity. Nevertheless, as will be detailed below, it is a constitutive force in the news production process.

The Journalists and Their Imagined Audience

The primary characteristic of *"Hispanos"* as an imagined audience is, obviously enough, that they understand the Spanish language. Moreover, the journalists' presumption is that the audience's interests are *represented* by the Spanish language. This is an understanding of language that expands upon the fundamental social function of language as a narrowly communicative tool. It is a conceptualization of language as a symbol system that embodies essential characteristics of the ethnic group (Edwards, 1975, p. 17; Fishman, 1989, p. 32). From the journalists' point of view, the *Noticiero Univisión* audience's demonstrated preference for the Spanish language defines them as a language community, and therefore a community of interest (Anderson 1986, p. 29). News director Guillermo Martínez explains,

> . . . they are first interested in *su patria chica* [their hometown], *su nación* [their country], and *su patria grande que es el continente* [their larger country which is the continent, Latin America] . . . Salvadorans are more interested in whether there is corruption in Mexican government or not than they are in the fact that Margaret Thatcher fell in London.

Similarly, one of the constitutive beliefs of the *Noticiero Univisión* journalists is that their imagined audience is more interested in news of other U.S. Latino communities than of say, that of African-American or European-American communities (of which more below).

In *Univisión* entertainment programming and advertising, intra-ethnic rivalries are masked, and the illusion of U.S. Latino panethnicity is achieved by eliminating specific national origin cultural cues. News, in contrast, is mostly about politics. Differing political ideologies are at the root of most Latino intra-ethnic tensions and are not as easily disguised. *Univisión* journalists are simultaneously pulled toward two poles. The panethnic pole motivates production for a broad, unified community of interest; the imagined community that is interested in news of other U.S. Latinos and more interested in Latin American news than European news. The other, counter-panethnic pole pulls the journalists towards production for a more diversified imagined community of interest: Mexicans and border issues, Puerto Ricans and the island's referenda, Cubans and the Castro government.

While all national origin U.S. Latino groups are represented in the national newsrooms and amongst U.S.-based correspondents, Cuban Americans are overrepresented in news management positions (i.e., vice president for news, executive producers). Recent controversies concerning intra-ethnic tensions playing themselves out on the *Noticiero* terrain have made the journalists exceedingly aware of the precariousness of their panethnic project.[18] Their response has been offer the *Noticiero* as a bridge that spans but does not deny the material and political differences that characterize the audience, as *Noticiero* co-anchor Jorge Ramos elaborates,

> I don't think most Hispanics think of themselves as Hispanics. They think of themselves as Cuban-Americans or Cubans, Mexican-Americans or Puerto Ricans or whatever. I don't think there is a consciousness that we are Hispanics. I think there is an idea that we share something . . . language . . . the desire to do something in this country better than where we were before. . . . I don't think we are a homogenous minority.

Ramos's statement is not a contradiction of Martínez's description of an imagined community of Latino interest, but rather an expression of the contested nature of *Univisión*'s journalistic panethnicity. In the *Noticiero Univisión* newsrooms, as in the larger society, U.S. Latino political and cultural identity is neither unitary or static, but rather continuously negotiated.

U.S. Latino intra-ethnic political differences, which are signs of deep divergences of class, racial and U.S. immigration histories (see especially Nelson and Tienda, 1985; Portes and Truelove, 1987) have the potential to tear the panethnic fabric of the *Noticiero Univisión*. The journalists, many of whom consider themselves and their families refugees from a myriad of Latin American political upheavals, are keenly aware of this, and so strive to avoid intra-ethnic tensions. In their daily news production routines, *Univisión* journalists self-consciously try to be what they call national origin "balanced." The almost daily stories from the New York bureau tend to feature news of particular interest to that city's largely Puerto Rican population, those from the southwest bureaus, news of Mexican Americans, etc. Care is taken not to overload the Miami based newscast with Cuban-American news. The content analysis shows that the national origin of *Noticiero* U.S. Latino soundbites or news actors roughly approximates the national population distribution (which according to *Univisión* audience research, roughly fits the network's audience profile).[19]

While the efforts to avoid intra-ethnic favoritism in domestic coverage tend to be routinized, not explicitly acknowledged, and organizationally masked, largely by the location of bureaus, the international news production guidelines are explicit (see discussion of Latin American news below). In addition to these professional practices, the journalists, whose offices are in the same building with the sales and promotion staff, are constantly reminded by posters and videos in the lobby, by marketing staffers dropping into the newsroom, and by promotional spots that they participate in, that the *Univisión* network, their employer, is predicated on the notion of a national, panethnic Hispanic market. "*Somos el lazo que une a los Hispanos,*" "We are the tie that joins Hispanics," was one network musical jingle.

Language

The Spanish language often has a counter-panethnic function; particular Spanish language accents and diction, while mutually intelligible, identify the speaker's particular national origin. *Univisión* journalists are committed to using a Spanish language that will appeal to and be understood by all Hispanics. They are adamant in their condemnation of "Spanglish," a slang combination of Spanish and English, completely rejecting it for use in the *Noticiero Univisión*. *Noticiero* producer Patsy Lorris Soto explains, "We are committed not only to maintaining the Spanish language, but to improving it, and teaching it."[20]

Panethnic Spanish is not only a question of vocabulary, but also of accent and intonation. *Noticiero* correspondents and anchors speak "accentless" Spanish, a product of their interaction with Latinos of various national origin groups and their professional training. For those who immigrated to the United States as adults, losing their national accents and replacing them with an "*Univisión*" accent was a conscious effort. Mexican born *Noticiero* co-anchor Jorge Ramos reports that his "Walter Cronkite Spanish" accent is achieving its panethnic goal,

> People think I am from their country; if they are from Peru they think I am Peruvian; from Colombia, Colombian, or that I was born in the States. . . . Many people look at me as their own, from their own country. . . .

Like the *Noticiero Univisión* nationality-neutral Spanish accent, the journalists' use of the collective personal pronoun, *nosotros* ("we"), and *ustedes* ("you," or "your") is a symbolic bridge between audience members, as well as between the audience and the *Noticiero Univisión* journalists.[21] The use of collective personal pronouns in U.S. media is hardly unusual; *U.S.A. Today* and various network promotional campaigns come to mind. There are exceptions to this rule made in mainstream broadcast news during wartime, or national celebrations, such as the Olympics. The use of "we" on these occasions marks the events as special. In the context of the *Noticiero Univisión,* that of a multinational, panethnic minority cultural production, the symbolic salience of these pronouns is worth particular note. "*Nosotros*" and "*ustedes*" reference a particular unitary group, U.S. Hispanics. Examples include: *Nosotros en este pais . . .* (We in this country); *Tenemos que prepararnos . . .* (We need to prepare ourselves). Every evening, among the first words of the *Noticiero* is "*su,*" or "your." An announcer says: "*Esta es su Noticiero Univisión con Jorge Ramos y Maria Elena Salinas.*" Translation: "This is *your* Univisión newscast . . ." The word "*su*" ("your"), in the initial seconds of the *Univisión* newscast is an invitation and a declaration of ownership—to the audience. *Univisión*'s use of collective, personal pronouns signal that journalists and panethnic audience together are the insiders, the legitimated actors in this newscast.

What Is Univisión News? How Is It Presented?

The selection and framing of stories for the *Noticiero Univisión* is a response to the economic logic of the television production process; each night the *Noticiero* needs to make 22 minutes of national news in order to attract a national audience (Epstein 1973, p. 264). A significant portion of that effort is the transformation of local stories, which for this newscast means national origin specific stories (e.g., Puerto Ricans in New York, Cubans in Florida), into national panethnic stories. This is largely a discursive practice, that is, U.S. Latinos are created and recreated each night as a national minority by the framing and presentation of news stories. This process blunts the distinctive national origin edge the story may have had if it were produced for local consumption. Each night the *Noticiero* needs to elaborate stories about "issues with the symbolic capital necessary to unite the fragmented . . . audience" (Kaniss, 1991, p. 4). The cultural and economic imperatives of nightly *Noticiero* production are to make news that spans the diverse immigration histories of U.S. Latinos as well as the racial, class, and deeply held political differences that characterize this diverse population.

Figures 1 and 2 illustrate the sharply contrasting contours of the story selection process of the *Noticiero Univisión* and ABC's *World News Tonight with Peter Jennings,* showing with broad strokes the most obvious difference between these two national newscasts. Focusing first on the category "U.S." note that this is, predictably, the largest categorization of ABC stories. When this category is combined with "Washington, D.C.," the content analysis reveals that despite its name, *World News Tonight with Peter Jennings,* over three quarters (79%) of the program is about the United States. The same calculations for the *Noticiero Univisión* show that less than half (43%) of this U.S. national newscast is about the United States. The *Univisión* newscast contains slightly more news about Latin America than about the United States. Much of the *Noticiero* audience and most of the journalists who produce it are either immigrants or recent (first or second generation) U.S. residents. For them, the social process of immigration is not a distant memory (or something read about in textbooks), but rather ongoing. The resultant world view is therefore somewhat bifurcated: *Univisión* journalists and their imagined audience are of two worlds, not fully removed from one, yet not fully a member of either.

There are equally significant similarities between the two programs that illustrate the fundamental professional commonalities of the *Noticiero Univisión* and ABC's nightly national news program. As discussed in the introductory section of this essay, *Univisión* journalists embrace the U.S. journalistic ideal of objectivity in its various dimensions. The similarities in the two organizations routine practices—the building blocks of professional ide-

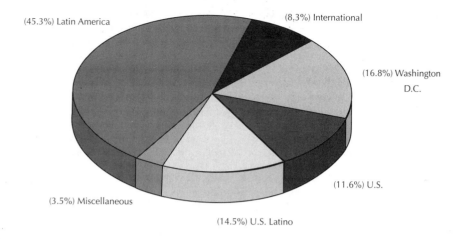

FIGURE 1

UNIVISIÓN TOPICS

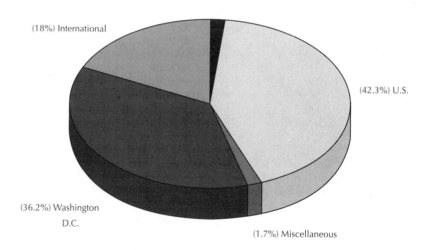

FIGURE 2

ABC TOPICS

ology—are evidence of a deep cultural affinity. For both newscasts the largest single U.S. subcategory is stories produced in the networks' Washington, D.C., bureaus. For both networks, these are their largest bureaus, reflections of the nation's capital-centered political culture, headquarters of the legislative, judicial and executive branches of the federal government. The government orientation of both journalistic organizations is also shown in the soundbite analysis: 41% of ABC soundbites are of government officials, and an identical proportion, 41%, of the *Noticiero Univisión* soundbites are of government officials.[22] The privileging of government officials as news actors within the *Noticiero Univisión* is one indication of the political orientation of the program; despite cultural differences, *Univisión* is a participant in the "nationalization of newsroom culture," where national news organizations are in continual interaction (Schudson, 1991, p. 271). This interplay reaffirms and reinforces the tacit social consensus amongst national journalists about what news is and how it should be represented.

    Univisión institutional news sources for U.S. and international news (with the exception of U.S. Latino and Latin American news) are the same as the general market networks and those of the larger national news culture. *Univisión* journalists begin their working days listening to all-news radio, watching CNN, reading *The New York Times* and the *Wall Street Journal.* (Bureau producers and correspondents read their local newspapers also, both English and Spanish language.) They also regularly read *Time, Newsweek,* and *U.S. News and World Report.* In the *Univisión* national newsroom in Miami, the Associated Press wire is next to the Reuters one, which is a couple of steps away from the ABC video newswire. CNN and C-Span are tuned in on producers' desks. Signs that this national newsroom is somewhat different than others are the Spanish language *Noti-Mex* newswire from Mexico, the *Imevisión* video newswire (also from Mexico), and the (U.S. and Latin American) Spanish language newspapers on the assignment editors' desk. The national (video and print) news services' interpretation of U.S. and international news is wholly accepted by *Univisión* journalists. These are among what Tuchman (1978) calls U.S. journalists' "web of facticity," that is, what the journalists believe to be factually "true." *Univisión* journalists might quibble with style and emphasis but, actively accepting the prestigious mantle of mainstream journalistic practice, they do not question the fundamental framing or analysis presented by U.S. national news services.

    Nor do they question the visual presentation conventions of U.S. television news, the stratagems that bring dramatic unity to the plot and narrative of news stories—what makes them, in the journalists' eyes, compelling television (Carey 1986, p. 148). *Univisión* journalists consider "American network" news (ABC, NBC, CBS, CNN), the "best in the world." The presentation norms of the *Noticiero* are emblematic of this self-conscious mimicry. The daily production meeting, where that evening's program is outlined, is one of the very few times the journalists will, without any embarrassment, speak "Spanglish:" "*el* kicker," (a light feature, traditionally the last one in the newscast), "*los* supras," (the captions that identify soundbites), and the most damning word in this lexicon: "boring!" The *Noticiero Univisión,* without the soundtrack, is indistinguishable from a general market newscast: from the physical attractiveness of the anchors, to the shots of Washington correspondents signing off in front of iconic buildings, to the "quick cut" pace of the editing and the framing of "head shots," the *Noticiero* looks like a U.S. news program.

Furthermore, pointing up the arbitrary distinction between form and content, the narrative structure of the reports on the two networks is identical. This speaks to the formulaic nature of U.S. national television news and of *Univisión*'s embrace of it. The 100-second dramas (or "wraps") are identically structured and in many of the Washington, D.C., stories, feature the same cast of characters. In addition to the aforementioned identical reliance on government officials for their U.S. coverage, the two newscasts employ a similar proportion of "unknowns," (Gans, 1979) or otherwise anonymous people to "humanize" news coverage; 28% of *Univisión* soundbites are of "unknowns," while 27% of ABC's are. The similarity of the presentation norms and the narrative structure and so the content of the two national newscasts highlight the journalistic and commercial imperatives that shape both programs. Moreover, they illustrate how U.S. journalistic objectivity has been naturalized into the "common sense" of U.S. journalistic discourse. As Michael Schudson has written,

> The power of the media lies not only (and not even primarily) in its power to declare things to be true, but in its power to provide the forms in which the declarations appear. News in newspaper or on television has a relationship to the real world not only in content but in form: that is, in the way the world is incorporated into unquestioned and unnoticed conventions of narration, and then transfigured, no longer a subject for discussion but a premise for any conversation at all (1982, p. 98).

Both ABC's *World News Tonight with Peter Jennings* and the *Noticiero Univisión* attempt each evening to maximize their audience by producing—within the boundaries prescribed by journalistic objectivity—a largely inoffensive, professionally consensual news program.

Nonetheless there are distinctive differences between these two national newscasts, differences that can be traced to the social and economic status of the *Univisión* audience. Two examples illustrate this defining difference. While both ABC and *Univisión* produce comparably framed (strategic, inside the Beltway) stories about Zoe Baird, President Clinton's failed nominee for attorney general, *Univisión* produced extended interviews with the undocumented workers and used the controversy as a "peg" to begin a series on U.S. Latino domestic labor. This example, and others discussed below, are representations of ethnicity as a point of view, a distinct cultural lens through which "news" is produced. In a daily example, immediately following the report of the Dow Jones average, *Univisión* reports on the day's dollar exchange rate for the currencies of nine Latin American nations. As will be discussed in detail below Latin America, particularly Latin American immigration to the United States are continual features of the *Univisión* national newscast.

Univisión's coverage of Latin America and U.S. Latino communities discursively reproduces U.S. Latino ethnicity, highlighting the social ambivalence of this ethnic minority group who are marginalized participants in two worlds. Moreover, the construction of these stories—topics not routinely included in general market national newscasts—illustrates how *Univisión* journalism is a special case of the dominant U.S. professional ideology. The unifying theme of these defining aspects of the *Noticiero Univisión* is their symbolic reproduction of the *inclusion* of this ethnic minority group, and issues of presumed interest of them, in U.S. society. The production of these stories—which combined make up more than half of the newscast—clearly express the tension that exists between the two constitutive ideals of *Univisión* journalism, ethnicity and objectivity, a tension that is not finally resolved, but rather is daily reproduced.

U.S. Latino News

Unlike U.S. news, there is no professional journalistic consensus about what national U.S. Latino news is. To the extent that this question has been addressed by mainstream national journalists, the consensus is that generally, news about U.S. Latinos is not national news.[23] *Univisión* journalists reject this exclusion and adapt—but do not fundamentally alter—mainstream routines and conventions for their creation of national U.S. Latino news. The journalists' recognition of the social marginalization of their audience (*vis à vis* general market audiences) construct the alternative vantage point from which news is made. This section examines the intersection of traditional U.S. journalistic values and a decidedly untraditional news topic: U.S. Latinos.

As shown in Figure 1, the *Noticiero Univisión* dedicates approximately one-seventh of its air time to news of U.S. Latino communities, slightly more time than it gives to news that emanates from the nation's capital, the traditional center of U.S. news production. These stories tend to be more nuanced and thoughtful, less cut and dried than other U.S. reporting.[24] The social status of the U.S. Latinos that populate these stories is markedly different than that of the general U.S. news actor population; U.S. Latinos tend not to be "newsmakers."

An analysis of the content of the *Noticiero*'s U.S. Latino stories groups them into two broad categories. In the first, Latinos illustrate traditionally conceived U.S. news stories, such as those about the national economy, public school education, or new discoveries in the health sciences. The second group of stories, principally concerning immigration and U.S. Latino civil rights, are rarely included on the mainstream national news agenda.

The most frequently produced type of *Univisión* U.S. Latino story uses U.S. Latinos and U.S. Latino communities to illustrate an otherwise traditionally conceived story. For example, instead of interviewing European-Americans in suburban Chicago about a federal study on the increasing incidence of measles, as ABC did, the *Noticiero Univisión* sent a correspondent to a Latino neighborhood in San Francisco. This inclusive gesture draws U.S. residents of Latin American descent into the public sphere of U.S. civil society, in this case as a group which will be affected by government policies that have been developed in response to a potential measles epidemic.

This particularizing of the news for the Latino audience does not alter the mainstream conceptualizations of "newsworthiness" that shape these stories. *Univisión* news director Guillermo Martinez declares, "We only cover Hispanics when they make news." In this instance the Latinos who were "making news" were physicians, public health officials and parents of young children.

The *Noticiero's* coverage of Latinos in the electoral arena of U.S. politics, as voters, candidates and elected officials, is a special case of the inclusive mode of *Univisión* U.S. Latino news. *Univisión* journalists are supporters of U.S. electoral processes. In this they are no different than their general market colleagues. However, the *Noticiero's* unblushing advocacy of the inclusion of U.S. Latinos in U.S. electoral politics sets it apart from its mainstream counterparts. Some examples: Coverage of Latino candidates is unabashedly favorable; a recurring theme of this political coverage bemoans low Latino voter registration rates; the *Noticiero* demonized California Governor Pete Wilson for his advocacy of Proposition 187, which would have denied many government services to undocumented immigrants, in much the same manner as the English language networks (as well as *Univisión*) demonized Saddam Hussein. Nonetheless, the journalists are careful to make ritual nods to objectivity; a soundbite of the non-Latino opposing candidate is featured in each of these reports.

Univisión's U.S. Latino electoral political coverage somewhat submerges the panethnic ideal. It explicitly recognizes the divergent political orientations of the three major national origin groups; to do otherwise would bring into doubt the journalists' credibility. Like ABC, *Univisión* employed an national election pollster in 1992. The polls' respondent categories were: "*votantes de descendencia anglosajona,*" voters of Anglo-Saxon ancestry and *negros,* blacks. *Hispanos,* Hispanics was subdivided into three groups: "*Cubano-americanos,*" Cuban-Americans; "*Mexico-americanos,*" Mexican Americans; and "*Puerto-riqueños,*" Puerto Ricans. Consistently throughout the presidential election season, the poll results showed significant differences among the three groups, with Clinton leading by wide margins among Puerto Ricans and Mexican-Americans, and Bush ahead by somewhat smaller percentages among Cuban-Americans.

Where *Univisión* "Hispanic vote" coverage highlights the desirability of Latino participation in U.S. political processes and institutions, the majority of *Univisión* coverage of immigration issues focuses on the exploitation of Latinos by those same institutions and practices. In these stories, the journalists position themselves, in the Nineteenth century progressive tradition, as populist muckrakers. These stories, while often critical of aspects of U.S. society, are not oppositional. They do not seek to change the rules or ideals that govern U.S. society. Rather, *Univisión* journalists aim to expose rule-breaking for the benefit of their audience.

A key presumption of the construction of the *Noticiero Univisión* panethnic audience is that a heritage of immigration—second only to the Spanish language—is the basis of a profound sense of commonality among U.S.

Latinos. Further, the imagined audience's interest in immigration is broadly conceived; they are interested in Haitian immigration to the United States and Latin American immigration to Spain, as well as the primary focus, Latin American immigration to the United States. One 1992 *Noticiero* opened with these words:

> We begin this newscast today with the story of the tragedy of all of those who flee their country. Today this touches us particularly closely because we are talking about people from Cuba and people from Mexico. People who are fleeing because of political or economic reasons and whose goal is almost always the same: the United States. We have two reports.

One report was about the increasing number of Cuban nationals arriving in south Florida on home-made rafts. The second concerned the enslavement of a group of Mexican immigrant men in Texas. In both reports, the immigrants, whose health was seriously compromised by the circumstances of their immigration, were framed with respect, if not admiration. "We are telling truths that are not usually told," remarked one *Noticiero* journalist, referring to a report about unauthorized Mexican immigrant garment workers in Texas who organized a strike and, at great risk to themselves and their families, forced the repair of their work place.

A series of "special reports" that aired in October, 1992 (during "sweeps week") was entitled: "Scapegoats." It was introduced with these decidedly unobjective words:

> We are going to discuss how immigrants are used as the scapegoats for the economic ills of the United States, and the intensification of racism against Hispanics as the economic situation worsens.

The series, anchored from Los Angeles (*Univisión*'s largest market), included reports on the "militarization of the border with Mexico." Again, the journalists self-consciously embrace the rudiments of journalistic objectivity: in each of these reports, the views of the relevant government agency, xenophobic community leader, or anti-immigrant political candidate were represented. With these stories, which are produced in accordance with traditional journalistic guidelines, the issues divided into "two sides," with both represented, *Univisión* journalists posit themselves as defenders of Latin American immigrants in the United States, many of whom do not have a public voice.

While *Univisión* journalists' personal and professional experience prevents them from wholly embracing the "contemporary ideology of American racial openness,"[25] their ethnocentrism and professional ideology constrain their challenge of it. The soundbite analysis shows a larger proportion of people of color overall on *Univisión* than on ABC. Thirty five percent of *Univisión* soundbites were of Latinos, as compared with less than 1% of ABC soundbites.[26] Yet, news actors who were African or Asian American are 50% *less* represented on *Univisión* than they are on ABC.[27] In other words, the *Noticiero Univisión*, while modifying the white ethnocentrism of general market newscasts is primarily shaped by its own ethnocentrism, and does not fully confront the racial myopia of the dominant society.

Latin American News

Like U.S. Latino news, news of Latin America is not a regular feature of U.S. national television news. As with their coverage of Latino communities, *Univisión* journalists embrace traditional U.S. journalistic ideology in their Latin American reporting—with modifications. Nearly half, 45%, of each *Noticiero Univisión* is about Latin America, while just under 2% of ABC's *World News Tonight with Peter Jennings* is taken up with news of Latin America. This enormous disparity in story selection is the clearest direct evidence of the distinct world views of these two U.S. television networks. Moreover, 48% of the *Noticiero Univisión* lead stories, the story journalists consider to be the most important story of the day, are Latin America stories. The significance of these reports is their inclusion and prominence in a U.S. newscast; they declare simply and unambiguously that in *our* world Latin America matters. Moreover, the production of Latin American news is key to *Univisión* journalists' professional self-concept as objective journalists. As mentioned above, many are daily reinforcing their rejection of what they believe is severely compromised Latin American journalistic practice, relishing the opportunity to work free of government interference and censorship.

For the journalists' imagined U.S. immigrant audience, these reports offer news of their "*patria grande*," of the panamerican hemisphere. Perhaps this is to be expected of a national news program that is produced for an audience made up largely of Latin American immigrants and their descendants. However, it seems simplistically misleading to conclude that of course *Univisión* would give prominence to news of "home." This is but one defining element of Latin American news in the *Noticiero*. "Home" too, is an imagined community and just the beginning of the analysis.

Univisión's coverage of Latin America constructs the intended audience as residents of a hemisphere, what the journalists call "*el continente americano*," the American continent. The journalists assume that U.S. Latinos are interested in Latin American politics as well as the Latin American Olympic medal count, and the deaths of Latin American actors and artists. Mainstream U.S. national newscasts configure their global maps with the United States at the center, Asia at one periphery and Europe on the other, along an east-west axis. The *Univisión* global axis runs north-south, through the United States to Mexico, Central and South America. This journalistic cartography prompts the *Noticiero Univisión* to have bureaus in Mexico City, Lima, Bogotá, Managua and San Salvador. *Univisión* does not have correspondents in London, Paris, Tokyo, Beijing or Moscow.

As discussed earlier, the *Noticiero* privileges news of the United States; the presumptive audience comprises *U.S. Latinos*. Nevertheless, by committing almost half its air time to Latin American news, the journalists of the *Noticiero*, many of them immigrants themselves, are acknowledging the duality of immigrant, especially recent immigrant, life. Immigrants are between two countries, of two countries, and not fully present in either. This is especially true of contemporary Latin American immigrants, many of whom, after settling in the United States, maintain close contact with their native countries, in many instances visiting frequently (Cornelius, 1992). Often times, this national duality is evidenced in the selection of the lead story for a given day's program: a single lead story is *not* selected; two are. For example on March 17, 1992, the *Noticiero* began,

> Jorge Ramos: Good evening. The primary elections today in Illinois and Michigan could decide which candidates will continue on to the finish line.

> Maria Elena Salinas: We will have extensive coverage of these elections later. But first, we go to Buenos Aires, Argentina where this afternoon there were war-like scenes. . . . The Israeli embassy in Buenos Aires suffered a dynamite explosion that demolished the building. . . . Our correspondent Oswaldo Petrozino has this report from the scene.

This story was not motivated by a desire to cover news from "home;" there are relatively few Argentineans in the United States. From the point of view of a Mexican immigrant, the largest national origin Latino group, the *Noticiero Univisión* offers little news from home. Of the 25 or so stories on each newscast, perhaps one or two will be about Mexico. While Mexico is the most represented of Latin American countries on the *Noticiero* (22 percent of Latin America stories), the news is largely about the politics of the federal government in Mexico City, which may or may not have bearing on an immigrant's life, or that of her family in Mexico.

The two other Latin American countries with large U.S. immigrant populations, Cuba, and Puerto Rico, are the topic of relatively little news. Cuba makes up 3% of the *Noticiero*'s Latin America coverage; Cubans are about 10% of *Univisión*'s news audience. This is attributable to logistical difficulties and to the Cuban-born news managers' efforts to refute critics' "Cubanization" charge. Puerto Ricans constitute about 10% of the nation's Latino population; news about Puerto Rico in the period analyzed in the content analysis is negligible (although since the Goya boycott mentioned earlier, it has increased).

The notion of "home" for *Univisión* journalists is shaped by commercial and professional considerations. To illustrate, in the fall of 1991, the journalists noticed that whenever the lead story of the West coast edition was about Central America, *Noticiero* ratings increased. Salvadorans and Nicaraguans are among the fastest growing Latino immigrant groups in the United States; as recent immigrants they are potential members of *Univisión*'s core mass audience.[28] The commercial imperative to maximize audience is interacting in this instance with the journalistic propensity to produce a "good story." The civil wars and their aftermaths in El Salvador and Nicaragua presented a continuing, almost daily, series of traditionally conceived "newsworthy" events to report on.

There is not a sizable Peruvian community in the United States; relative to other Latin American immigrant groups, the Colombian community is small. Yet the second largest group of Latin American stories (after Mexico) is news of those two countries.[29] Here again, commercial and professional imperatives are mutually reinforcing: guerilla insurgencies, illicit drug trafficking, and ongoing efforts to "democratize" these countries make for a steady supply of breaking and dramatic, and therefore presumably audience-maximizing, news stories.[30]

Moreover, *Univisión*'s emphasis on Latin American news is part of its larger panethnic, de-nationalizing project. The journalists believe that it is "natural," incontrovertible, that U.S. Latinos would be interested in news of "*el continente americano*," the American continent—that a Mexican immigrant would be almost as interested in news of El Salvador, as she would Mexican news. *Univisión* journalists believe the unifying force of this hemispheric identity is a bridge that blurs differences amongst the *Univisión* audience, thereby constructing a unitary "imagined community."

However, daily news production is not generally organized around regional issues, but rather news of particular Latin American countries, most often "breaking" political and economic news regarding national governments. These stories are considered news by *Univisión* journalists because they relate events that happened yesterday, today or tomorrow and because they involve high ranking and/or powerful government officials. By incorporating mainstream forms such as the temporal frame and deference to government authorities, *Noticiero* journalists are able to preserve their objective narrative stance while presenting news of what—in the U.S. context—are unconventional topics. These daily news routines are largely unacknowledged by the journalists; they are habitual, workaday response to the pressures of producing a daily news program. However, another key *Noticiero* Latin American news routine is highly self-conscious.

Seventy-four percent of the *Noticiero*'s Latin American news is about politics.[31] These political stories often inspire strong emotion among the *Noticiero* journalists, many of whom consider themselves to be political refugees. Cuban-born news director Guillermo Martínez makes no secret of his disdain for Cuban leader Fidel Castro. Mexican-born co-anchor Jorge Ramos left his native country because he was censored by the Mexican ruling party, the PRI. Melding U.S. Latino panethnic and U.S. journalistic objectivity considerations, political news about Mexico is routinely edited by Cuban-Americans and news about Cuba is edited by Mexican Americans. As Martínez explains, "I don't have an axe to grind in Mexico, and they [Mexican and Mexican American *Univisión* journalists] don't have an axe to grind in Cuba."[32]

Unlike other U.S.-produced international news (including *Univisión*'s coverage of Europe, Africa and Asia), the *Noticiero*'s reporting on Latin America is not primarily concerned with the United States. *Univisión* dedicates considerable resources to reporting U.S. military and diplomatic relations with various Latin American countries. Most often, however, events in

Latin America do not need a U.S. "angle" to qualify as *Univisión* news. For example, the forced resignation of a member of the Argentinean cabinet is presented in much the same way as a U.S. presidential cabinet reshuffle.

The *Noticiero Univisión*'s coverage of Mexico is the clearest example of this newscast's distinctive charting of the globe. Mexico is not invariably considered to be "foreign" to the United States. Although consciousness of political cartography is heightened in the *Noticiero* reporting on unauthorized Mexican immigration to the United States, the arbitrariness of the United States-Mexico border is also highlighted in this coverage. In many feature and arts stories issues of nationhood are masked, seemingly irrelevant. A transnational comradeship is symbolically created and recreated each year when, to cite two examples, the *Noticiero* broadcasts consecutive stories about celebrations of Mexican independence day, and commemorations of *la Virgen de Guadalupe*, Mexico's patron saint, on *both* sides of the United States-Mexico border.

In its reporting on Latin America, the *Noticiero Univisión* creates a history, a collective memory for its imagined audience. Daily, news stories offer U.S. Latino immigrants a sense of where they came from. Hobsbawm (1983, pp. 9–12) writes of the intentionality of "invented traditions," common histories created by social institutions so as to legitimate themselves. In the case of *Univisión* news, the reporting on Latin America constructs a shared past for its audience of Latino immigrants—who are the core "mass" audience for the network. However, as has been argued throughout this essay, the role of the *Noticiero Univisión* in the U.S. public sphere is more complicated than its economic function of helping legitimate the broadcast enterprise. It also seeks to educate its imagined community and in so doing, disseminate a panethnic, Latino identity.

Conclusions

The *Noticiero Univisión* is an example of a cultural production of transnational economic structures and their principal products, transnational audiences. Professional and cultural imperatives integrate the commercial profit motive in the complexity of the production process. The result of this melding, is an audience-centered, objective, ethnic minority national newscast. Structurally, the same cultural, commercial and professional processes homogenize the presumptive general market audience and naturalize objectivity in the production of mainstream national news. The significance of these processes as they are constructed in the production of the *Noticiero Univisión* turns on its imagined audience. In its simultaneous embrace of journalistic objectivity and U.S. Latino panethnic identity, this newscast is a resource for Latinos in their acculturation to U.S. society.

The *Noticiero Univisión* legitimizes U.S. Latinos' use of the Spanish language as a language of U.S. political discourse. In so doing, the journalists reflect a panethnic vision of the audience back to itself. Their self-conscious inclusion of Hispanics in U.S. civic culture, and the extended coverage of

Latin America, affirm both the ethnic minority group and U.S. political processes. The Spanish language is the broadest, most encompassing symbol in the *Univisión* symbol system, embodying the audience-centered news production process and the consequent world view of the *Noticiero Univisión*. It is also an apt proxy for the *Univisión* audience, key to "streamlining" (Ang, 1991) U.S. Latinos into a commodity to be bought and sold in the narrowcasting Hispanic market. Again, the cultural and economic imperatives that motivate the *Noticiero Univisión* are mutually reinforcing, melded in the newsmaking production process.

The *Noticiero Univisión* reproduces a social world, that of U.S. Latino communities and Latin America, that is rarely seen on say, ABC news programs. However, the *Noticiero* does not seek an alteration of the precepts and foundations of U.S. journalism, rather, it claims a space within U.S. journalistic ideology—a commercially viable space—to project a particular mapping of the world and the United States—a professionally objective portrayal. The embrace of the U.S. Latino ethnic minority group in the newscasts' conceptualization of U.S. nationhood activates the newscasts' professional, cultural and commercial imperatives. The nationality of the imagined audience is thus fluid, blurred by both the social dynamism of immigration, and by the globalized culture industries that reproduce it.

Ultimately, the commercially and culturally unifying forces of panethnicity and objectivity constrain the journalists' reproduction of U.S. Latino diversity. The production of the *Noticiero Univisión* symbolically denationalizes its intended audience of recent Latin American immigrants to the United States as it renationalizes them as U.S. Hispanics. In this way the journalists' professional ethic of "conservative reformism" responds to the commercial imperative of panethnicity. Thus, the *Noticiero Univisión* audience is constructed as communities which are seeking a just and secure place within U.S. culture, not apart from it, not desirous of any fundamental change in its defining structures.

Notes

1. Funding for the research of this article was provided by the Spencer Foundation, the Center for U.S.-Mexican Studies at the University of California, San Diego and a Mellon Research Grant facilitated by the Institute for Latin American Studies at the University of Texas at Austin. The writing was funded in part by the University Research Institute of the University of Texas at Austin.

2. I rely here on an adaptation of Benedict Anderson's *Imagined Communities* (1986), particularly Anderson's defining concept that nationalism is the cultural product of the interaction of societal institutions, including the mass media. Similarly, this essay argues that ethnicity and ethnic identifications such as "Hispanic" are created by the interaction of media institutions (in which I include advertisers and marketers) with other societal institutional actors such as government.

3. "U.S. Latinos," refers to Latin Americans or people of Latin American descent who reside in the United States. "Hispanic" references the prevailing commercial and US government categorization of US Latinos (see for example, Oboler, 1995).

4. A total of 782 stories—407 ABC, 375 *Univisión*—broadcast on alternate weekdays in May, 1991, and June, 1992, were studied. 150 dimensions of each story were coded by a single coder, the author. In addition, 352 *Univisión* soundbites and 466 ABC soundbites from the same programs were analyzed. The particular months were chosen for analysis because of the absence of major continuing stories (e.g., the Persian Gulf War, the arrival of thousands of Cuban boat people in south Florida) in these periods. This exclusion permitted the analysis of routine news coverage. For a more detailed presentation of the parameters of the content analysis, see part two of Rodriguez (1993).

5. The ethnography consisted of some 100 hours of interviewing and observing *Univisión* journalists—correspondents, producers and editors—in the network's national newsrooms in California and Miami. Extended, unstructured interviews with *Noticiero Univisión* journalists were conducted in Laguna Niguel, California in November and December, 1991, and in Miami, Florida in June, 1992. All interviews were conducted in English, unless otherwise noted. Citations from newsroom observations and from the broadcast text have been translated from the original Spanish by the author.

6. Including *Noticiero* co-anchor Jorge Ramos, the newsroom's intellectual leader, who was fired by *Televisa* for his reporting.

7. In its coverage of the 1992 Mexican presidential contest, *Televisa,* for the first time in its history, gave minimal coverage to opposition party candidates.

8. I am reminded here of the adage, "What does a fish know about water?"

9. *Hispanic Business,* December, 1994. Unless otherwise noted, information about the "Hispanic market" is based on trade journal reporting which in addition to *Hispanic Business* includes *Electronic Media, Broadcasting, Variety,* as well as *The New York Times,* the *Wall Street Journal,* and the *Los Angeles Times.*

10. *Hispanic Business,* December, 1994.

11. Personal interviews with several *Univisión* sales and marketing executives, Miami, Florida, November, 1994. *Univisión*'s largest advertisers are Anheuser-Busch (Budweiser), Colgate Palmolive, Procter and Gamble, and Toyota. Hispanics make up approximately 9 percent of the U.S. population and about 4 percent of the nation's TV viewers. In 1992, advertising on U.S. Spanish language television accounted for about 1% of U.S. television advertising (*Hispanic Business,* December 1992).

12. In 1986 a Federal Communications Commission (FCC) administrative judge ruled, in response to complaints by minority shareholders, that *Televisa* was in violation of a key provision of U.S. communications law that prohibits foreign ownership of U.S. broadcast stations. The FCC ordered the sale of the Spanish International Network (SIN), and its stations. Hallmark Cards of Kansas City, Missouri bought the network and renamed it *Univisión.*

13. Interview with Lionel Sosa, of Sosa and Associates, a leading U.S. Hispanic and Latin American market research and advertising firm, February, 1995, Austin, TX.

14. *Televisa,* the world's largest producer of Spanish language television programming, supplies the majority of *Univisión* programming, and *Televisa* has a controlling interest in PanAmSat, the satellite which distributes *Univisión* programming.

15. These include *Sábado Gigante* (Giant Saturday, a variety program), *Cristina* (a talk show), as well as other entertainment and sports programming.

16. "Hispanic USA" by Yankelovich et al., 1979.

17. Interviews with Hispanic marketers and advertising executives meeting at the annual "*Se Habla Español,*" trade conference, Chicago, September, 1989.

18. Examples include charges of "Cubanization" leveled at the network by newsroom employees of its owned and operated Los Angels affiliate, KMEX, and

an advertising boycott by Goya, a Puerto Rican manufacturer of Latino style food that alleged racism and sexism against Puerto Rican women by a network news commentator (Rodriguez, 1993).

19. About two thirds of the soundbites were of Mexicans or Mexican Americans, about ten percent of Cubans or Cuban Americans, and an equal amount of Puerto Ricans, with the remainder of other Latin American nations. The author acknowledges that these numbers are subjective, based on the author's ability to identify various national origin accented Spanish.

20. Interview conducted in Spanish, translation mine.

21. For a comparative analysis of the use of pronouns in Italian and U.S. television news see D. Hallin and P. Mancini (1984).

22. This study thus joins the long list of those echoing the findings of Sigal (1973).

23. The content analysis shows that ABC dedicated just over one percent (1.3%) of its airtime to news about U.S. Latinos or U.S. Latino communities. See also Martingale (1995).

24. U.S. Latino stories are longer than other *Noticiero* stories, a mean of 143 seconds compared to 26 seconds for other *Univisión* stories; they use roughly three times as many soundbites as other *Noticiero* stories; these soundbites are three times the average length of *Univisión* soundbites generally.

25. "... [a]n open class structure, racial tolerance, economic mobility, the sanctity of individualism and the availability of the American dream." (Gray 1989, p. 376).

26. The racial categorization "Latino" is problematic. Many U.S. Latinos are multiracial; of African, Native, Caucasian or mixed race heritage. See for example Rodriguez (1989).

27. Five percent of *Univisión* soundbites were of African-Americans, while 10 percent of ABC's were. Similarly, 1 percent *Univisión*'s soundbites were of Asian-Americans, while ABC had 2 percent Asian-American soundbites.

28. El Salvador stories make up 10 percent of *Univisión* stories; Nicaragua, 6 percent.

29. Peruvian and Colombian stories were both 12% of the total number.

30. Six percent of the *Noticiero* is about Chile, 4% is about Argentina, 3% about Brazil. There are not sizable immigrant communities from these countries in the U.S. In the period studied there were however, *Univisión* news bureaus in these Latin American countries each providing twice weekly standard coverage of government and economic activities, as well as feature reports.

31. Specifically, 29% about economics, 23% about war (in which is included peace negotiations), 21% about government personnel reshuffles, 6% about human rights, 4% about elections and 2% about labor strikes.

32. The animosity stems largely from the Mexican government's support of Cuban leader Fidel Castro. Many Cuban Americans identify themselves as political refugees from Castro's Cuba.

References

Anderson, B. (1986). *Imagined Communities: Reflections on the Origin and Spread of Nationalism*. London: Verso Editions and NLB.

Ang, I. (1991). *Desperately Seeking the Audience*. London: Routledge.

Barnes, B. E. and Thomson, L. M. (1994). Power to the People (Meter): Audience Measurement Technology and Media Specialization, in *Audiencemaking: How the Media Create the Audience,* J. S. Ettema and D. C. Whitney, eds., Thousand Oaks, CA: Sage.

Carey, J. (1986). The Dark Continent of American Journalism, in *Reading the News,* R. K. Manoff and M. Schudson, eds., New York: Pantheon.

Cornelius, W. A. (1992). From Sojourners to Settlers: The Changing Profile of Mexican Immigration to the United States, in *U.S.-Mexico Relations: Labor Market Interdependence,* Jorge A. Bustamante, Clark W. Reynolds, and Raúl A. Hinojosa Ojeda, eds. Stanford: Stanford University Press.

de la Garza, R. (1992). *Latino Voices: Mexican, Puerto Rican and Cuban Perspectives on American Politics.* Hartford: Westview Press.

Edwards, J. (1975). *Language, Society and Identity.* London: Basil Blackwell in association with Andre Deutsch.

Epstein, E. J. (1973). *News From Nowhere.* New York: Vintage.

Espiritu, Y. L. (1992). *Asian American Panethnicity: Bridging Institutions and Identities.* Philadelphia: Temple University Press.

Ettema, J. S. and D. C. Whitney, eds. (1994). *Audiencemaking: How the Media Create the Audience.* Thousand Oaks, CA: Sage Publications, Inc.

Fishman, J. (1989). *Language and Ethnicity in Minority Sociolinguistic Perspective.* Claredon, England: Multilingual Matters Ltd.

Gans, H. J. (1979). *Deciding What's News: A Study of CBS Evening News, NBC Nightly News, Newsweek and Time.* New York: Vintage.

Geertz, C. (1973). *The Interpretation of Cultures.* New York: Basic Books.

Gitlin, T. (1980). *The Whole World is Watching: Mass Media in the Making and Unmaking of the New Left.* Berkeley: University of California Press.

Gray, H. (1989). Television, Black Americans, and the American Dream, *Critical Studies in Mass Communication.*

Hall, S. (1979). Culture, Media and the 'Ideological Effect' in *Mass Communication and Society,* J. Curran, M. Gurevitch and Janet Woollacott (eds.), London: Sage.

Hall, S. (1990). Cultural Identity and Diaspora, in *Identity: Community, Culture, Difference.* J. Rutherford (ed.), London: Lawrence and Wishart.

Hallin, D. C. (1985). The American News Media: a critical theory perspective in J. M. Forrester (ed.), *Critical Theory and Public Life.* Boston: MIT Press.

Hallin, D. C. (1986). We Keep America on Top of the World, in *Watching Television,* T. Gitlin (ed.), New York: Pantheon Books.

Hallin, D. C. (1994). *We Keep America on Top of the World: Television Journalism and the Public Sphere.* New York: Routledge, 1994.

Hallin, D. C. and P. Mancini (1984). Speaking of the President: Political Structure and Representational Form in U.S. and Italian Television News, *Theory and Society 13,* 4, p. 829–850.

Hart-González, L. (1985). Pan Hispanism and Sub-Community in Washington, DC, pp. 73–89 in *Spanish Language Use and Public Life in the United States,* L. E. Olivares, et al, (eds), New York: Mouton Publishers.

Hobsbawm, E. (1983). Introduction: Inventing Traditions in *The Invention of Tradition,* E. Hobsbawm and T. Ranger (eds.) Cambridge: Cambridge University Press.

Kaniss, P. (1991). *Making Local News.* Chicago: University of Chicago Press.

López, D. and Y. L. Espiritu (1990). Panethnicity in the United States: A Theoretical Framework, *Ethnic and Racial Studies,* 3, 2.

Martingale, C. (1995, August). Only in Glimpses: Portrayal of America's Largest Minority Groups by *The New York Times,* 1934–1994. Paper presented at the meeting of the Association for Education in Journalism and Mass Communication, Washington, DC.

Melville, M. B. (1988). Hispanics: Race, Class or Ethnicity? *Journal of Ethnic Studies,* 16, 67–83.

Morley, David (1986). *Family Television: Cultural Power and Domestic Leisure* London: Routledge.

Nelson, C. and M. Tienda (1985). The Structuring of Hispanic Ethnicity: Historical and Contemporary Perspectives, *Ethnic and Racial Studies 8,* 1, pp. 49–74.

Oboler, Suzanne (1995). *Ethnic Labels, Latino Lives: Identity and the Politics of (Re)presentation in the United States.* Minneapolis: University of Minnesota Press.

Padilla, F. M. (1985). *Latino Ethnic Consciousness: The Case of Mexican Americans and Puerto Ricans in Chicago.* South Bend, IN: University of Notre Dame Press.

Portes, A. and C. Truelove. (1987). Making Sense of Diversity: Recent Research on Hispanic Minorities in the United States, *Annual Review of Sociology, 13.*

Rodriguez, A. (1993). Made in the U.S.A.: The Constructions of the *Noticiero Univisión,* La Jolla, CA: Ph.D. dissertation.

Rodriguez, A. (1995). Creating an Audience and Remapping a Nation: A Brief History of U.S. Spanish Language Broadcasting, 1930–1980, forthcoming in *Quarterly Review of Film and Video.*

Rodriguez, C. (1989). Puerto Ricans: The Rainbow People in *Puerto Ricans: Born in the U.S.A.,* New York: Unwin Hyman, Inc.

Schiller, D. (1981). *Objectivity and the News.* Philadelphia: University of Pennsylvania Press.

Schudson, M. (1978). *Discovering the News: A Social History of American Newspapers.* New York: Basic Books.

Schudson, M. (1982). The politics of narrative form: the emergence of news conventions in print and television, *Daedalus,* vol. 111, no. 4.

Schudson, M. (1991). National News Culture and the Rise of the Informational Citizen in *America at Century's End,* A. Wolfe (ed.), Berkeley: University of California Press.

Schudson, M. (1995). *The Power Of News.* Cambridge: Harvard University Press.

Shils, E. (1975). The Integration of Society in *Center and Periphery,* E. Shils (ed.), Chicago: University of Chicago Press.

Siefert, M. (1994). The Audience at Home: The Early Recording Industry and the Marketing of Musical Taste in *Audiencemaking: How the Media Create the Audience,* J. S. Ettema and D. C. Whitney (eds.), Thousand Oaks, CA:Sage.

Sigal, L. V. (1973). *Reporters and Officials: The Organization and Politics of Newsmaking.* Lexington MA: DC Health and Company.

Sommers, L. K. (1991). Inventing Latinismo: The Creation of 'Hispanic' Panethnicity in the United States, *Journal of American Folklore,* 104.

Tuchman, G. (1972). Objectivity as Strategic Ritual: An Examination of Newsmen's Notions of Objectivity, *Journal of Sociology,* 77, 4.

Tuchman, G. (1978). *Making News: A Study in the Construction of Reality.* New York: The Free Press.

Williams, R. (1980). *Problems in Materialism and Culture.* London: Verso Press.

Yankelovich, D. et al. (1979). *Hispanic USA.* New York: Yankelovich, Skelly and White.

The Unspoken Rules
of Television Talk

BERNARD TIMBERG

The talk show, like the daily newspaper, is often considered a disposable form. When *Tonight* show host Jack Paar mentioned to director Hal Gurnee in the early 1960s that he was going to throw away the taped masters from the first years of his show, Gurnee's response was quick: "You're not going to throw away the hubs, are you?" (The aluminum hubs of the two-inch video masters were worth $90 at the time.)[1] The first ten years of Johnny Carson's *Tonight* shows were erased by NBC without any thought to future use. The producers of television talk had no idea that what they were sending out over the airwaves might have future value.

The academic industry has similarly neglected talk shows. While there has been an explosion of interest in television on the part of scholars and critics in the 1980's, most of that interest had been directed toward news and dramatic programming. With news and drama, critics from the arts, humanities, and social sciences had a place to start: historical and sociological studies of news production and a tradition of narrative studies in literature and film that could be transferred to the small screen.

Talk shows came out of a series of less well defined traditions— Chatauqua, vaudeville, newspaper opinion and gossip columns, radio panel and information shows, variety and musical theater. Talk shows also crossed wildly uneven informational terrain, from entertainment talk shows with

---

From *Television Talk*, The University of Texas Press (forthcoming 1994). Reprinted with permission.

stars and celebrities to talk shows that feature headline news and current events to specialized talk shows on things like home repair and cooking.

Talk shows of one kind or another made up 24 percent of all radio programming from 1927 to 1956, with general variety talk, audience participation, human interest, and panel shows comprising as much as 40 to 60 percent of the daytime schedule.[2] Network television from 1949 to 1973 consistently filled over half its daytime program hours with talk programming of one kind or another, and devoted 15 to 20 percent of the evening schedule to talk programming.[3] As the networks went into decline in the 1980s, talk shows continued to expand. How was scholar or critic to make sense of such a massive array of material? What exactly was the worth of this incessant flow of words?

We are beginning to learn that yesterday's trash is today's history. Over time, through Peabody and Emmy awards, books, articles, and critical acclaim, the talk show has begun to receive recognition for its role in defining social, cultural, and political life in America over the past four decades. Politicians have always known the power of television. Adlai Stevenson was probably the last Presidential candidate to disdain its use. Since the media-created campaign of Ross Perot and his announcement of candidacy on *Larry King Live* in 1992, Presidential candidates have made television talk shows central to their campaigns.

In circumstances such as these the hosts of television talk shows have become increasingly powerful. They speak to cultural ideas and ideals as forcefully as politicians or educators, and their impact may at times be greater.[4] National talk show hosts become surrogates for the citizen. Interrogators on the news or clown princes and jesters on entertainment talk shows, major television hosts have the license to question and mock—as long as they play within the rules.

Some names stand out in any account of television talk—Steve Allen, Ernie Kovacs, Jack Paar, Johnny Carson, David Letterman in entertainment talk; Edward R. Murrow,[5] Ted Koppel, Bill Moyers, Phil Donahue, and Oprah Winfrey in news and public affairs. These hosts have become part of the history and folklore of television. They are the titans of talk.

Just as the titans of television talk shape the talk show as it emerges in the network era,[6] so these titans are themselves shaped by previous talk show traditions—by sponsors, network officials, professional writers, producers and directors trained on other shows, and by generations of Americans who have enjoyed the form. An investigation of the television talk show must look at the landmark figures who have established the talk show as a form, but it also must describe the intricate web of forces, the people and passions, that put a talk show on the air.

Though hosts and shows change over time, the principles remain the same. The talk show is host-centered, forged in the present tense, spontaneous but structured, churned out within the strict formulas and timed segments of costly network time, and designed to play to the hottest topics of the day. Whoever may be the host, these are the operating principles of the television talk show.

If you had been watching the Letterman show the evening of October 15, 1986, you would have heard Letterman conclude his opening remarks by asking director Hal Gurnee: "The last we heard the ballgame between the Astros and the Mets is tied 3–3 in the bottom of the tenth? Is that right?" Looking up to an undefined space in the sky, Letterman continues, "Hal, oh Hal—this will be our director Hal Gertner—can you keep us posted if there are any developments in that ball game?"

Letterman is talking about the National League playoff game between the New York Mets and the Houston Astros, a hard fought contest that has gone into extra innings. The Mets have not been in a World Series since 1973 and have not won a pennant since the "Miracle Mets" of 1969.

Letterman's voice at this moment is reminiscent of Jack Benny's invocations of his "valet" Rochester. Gurnee, or "Gertner," as Letterman calls him, is, like Rochester, the formally obedient servant who is not the least cowed by his master's voice. "Yeah, Dave," the off-screen Gurnee replies, "by the way, it's 3–3 in the tenth."

Letterman shoots back: "I just announced that Hal." The director calmly replies that he just wanted to be sure everyone knew. A suspicion forming on his brow, Letterman asks, "Are you watching the game in there?" The director's response is instantaneous, "Sure we are!" The studio audience breaks into laughter, and Letterman himself begins to laugh at the thought of his director, feet on the console, paying more attention to the Mets game than his star.

"But that shouldn't affect the quality of tonight's show, should it?" Letterman asks.

"Not at all, Dave. Craig Reynolds is up, by the way."

"OK, OK," Dave attempts to break off and go back to the show, but he can't get his vagrant director off his mind. "Do you guys have snacks in there?"

"They're on their way," Gurnee replies, followed by another explosion of laughter from the studio audience. Letterman himself cackles at this latest effrontery. "Well, just let us know what happens," he trails off.

When Letterman announces his first guest, NBC news anchor Tom Brokaw, Gurnee/Gertner interrupts again. His voice is quiet, polite, assured. "Excuse me, Dave. He fouled one off." (A new roar of laughter from the studio audience.)

Letterman waits for the laughter to die down. "All right, fine, Hal." Then, his voice dripping with sarcasm, "let us know if there are any broken bats, too, all right?"

Things run smoothly through the first guest interview. Then, just as Letterman comes back from the commercial break, the director intercedes again, "Excuse me, Dave."

"That's our director," Letterman explains to his viewers. A look of uneasy amusement crosses his face.

"Keith Hernandez is up now, Dave."

"OK," Letterman replies quickly, seeking to go on.

"I'm sorry, he just stepped out of the box."

"OK, Hal." The emphasis on the word "OK" telegraphs Letterman's impatience. Gurnee is not deterred and continues, "Looks like he has something in his eye."

"Uh-huh." Letterman says. A scowl crosses his face. He is clearly no longer amused. "*OK, Hal.*"

This brings a moment of silence, and though it appears that the host has finally shaken a director more concerned with the baseball game on a competing channel than directing his show, just as Letterman is about to launch his discussion with his second guest, a familiar voice is heard over the intercom.

"By the way, Dave, I thought you might want to know, it's still 3–3."

"3–3, what inning?" Letterman asks.

"Bottom of the eleventh," the director replies.

"Bottom of the eleventh," the host repeats. Mechanically consulting his blue sheet of notes, Letterman turns to the next item of business, "OK. Tomorrow on the program we have—"

Before he can get the next words out of his mouth, the familiar voice returns, "Excuse me, Dave. Billy Hatcher's up."

"Uh?" Letterman is startled. (A small laugh builds in the studio audience.)

"He just stepped out," Gurnee continues. "He's knocking some dirt off his spikes."

"I'll knock some dirt off your spikes, Hal." Letterman mutters under his breath. (A small titter rises in the audience.)

"Excuse me?" the director replies. This act of chutzpah elicits a huge, four-second roll of laughter from the audience.

Letterman, caught off guard, retreats. "Nothing, Hal. You go back to your corn dogs and beer. Don't let *us* interrupt anything out there."

The entire exchange has taken one minute and forty-five seconds of air time.

Highlighting the Rules by Breaking Them

This scenario is not just amusing. It illustrates, by challenging but ultimately reaffirming them, a set of talk show rules and principles that govern virtually all television talk shows. These are the principles of "fresh talk"[7]—talk that is not scripted or canned but generated moment to moment.

What distinguishes the fresh talk of one talk show from another is the personality of the host, the topics addressed, and the talk traditions within which the host operates. Certain hosts have redefined what talk shows do and have been enormously successful at it. They are the titans of television talk, and they have almost always come from news and entertainment shows. We'll take a quick look at those rules now, and then take a closer look at them in the following pages.

Letterman took the entertainment talk show on television in new directions by "problematizing" it—questioning its rules and playfully subverting them on the air in each show. In the incident above, five basic unspoken rules of television talk are brought into question.

The first is the host's centrality and control of the show. The primary rule of television talk is that the host is the master (or mistress) of ceremonies. From the beginning, emcees and femcees have centered television talk.

The second rule brought into question concerns the present-tense flow of a television talk show and the unspoken understanding that no one is entitled to stop it. It is this present-tense flow, orchestrated skillfully and unobtrusively by the host, that is so abruptly halted by the director's interventions. The viewer is made uncomfortably aware of how little it takes to stop the smooth technological operation of a television talk show. When Gurnee intercedes and threatens to redirect the show at his own whim, he pointedly breaks its flow.

Gurnee also willfully ignores Letterman's special role, as talk show host, of speaking to and amusing millions as if engaged in a private conversation with them. The private conversations that take place on the show are of course destined for a wide viewing audience—some three or four million viewers each night. That unspoken compact between talk show host and viewer is violated by a purely private intervention—what the director and his crew choose to do at the moment.

Fourth, the commodity function of the show is interrupted. This is the most important function of television talk to its network management (in this case NBC). It is the commercial imperative to reach the biggest possible audience in the show's time slot with the commercials that accompany the program. This purpose is clearly subverted here by a technical team that prefers to watch a competing show (with its commercials).

Finally, the conscious structuring and crafting of what seems "spontaneous" in television talk is brought to light in the director's actions. For the seamless functioning of a talk show, the invisible hands and eyes of the technical crew must be unquestioningly trained to their tasks. Wandering off to see another show, even if it only occupies part of the technical crew's time and attention, is not acceptable—treasonable even, when the crew's job is to fashion the sound and picture images that put the show out over the air.

Indeed, this comedy bit on the Letterman show has called into question the unspoken rules that distinguish television talk from the kinds of talk that occur in the street, on the playground, or in the house, and are silently assumed in the creation of all television talk shows.

While some talk show hosts are innovators who, like Letterman and Donahue, take the television talk show in new directions, others, like Johnny Carson, are synthesizers of previous talk show traditions. Taking over the *Tonight* show from Steve Allen, Ernie Kovacs, and Jack Paar (all significant innovators) in 1963, Carson's long reign as "king of late night talk" institutionalized the late night comedy/variety talk show. He set a standard for his competitors as well as successors in late night talk.

When Carson appeared on the air for the last time on May 22, 1992, fifty million people watched the show, a talk show record. Carson's retirement was front page news across the country, with publicity that built steadily in the week before his final appearance. In the week of his retirement after thirty years on the air, Carson was hailed as a cultural institution. Though Letterman rose to prominence in the 1980s as the host who took late night comedy talk in new directions, Carson was the host who more than any other consolidated its traditions. When we look at the unspoken rules of television talk in depth in the next section, we will be referring back to Carson as a standard.

When I speak here of "television talk" rather than "television talk shows," I am referring to a special kind of talk that occurs in front of the camera. It is often directed to an individual in the studio (host, guest, or sidekick) but also, simultaneously, to a national television viewing audience of millions. On entertainment talk shows and on entertainment/public affairs shows like *Donahue,* and occasionally on shows oriented toward hard news like Ted Koppel's electronic town meetings, a studio audience serves to varying degrees as a surrogate for the viewing audience at home.

Television talk is always present tense, though it is produced in varying degrees of "liveness": truly live, taped as-if-live, or filmed or taped and edited afterwards. TV talk is also produced, and played back, with different degrees of frequency. There are daily shows, weekly shows, and talk shows recorded at irregular intervals, like Bill Moyers *Conversations with . . .* series. However frequently produced, talk shows become a regular viewing habit at the times they are broadcast. It is common, for instance, for a weekly or monthly show to be "stripped" as a daily show in syndication.

In practice, however blurred these differences are in a viewer's experience of television talk, they play a part in how viewers form relationships with talk show hosts. Letterman, for instance, was taped as-if-live daily at 5:30 PM for a 12:30 EST broadcast and was careful never to stay on the air too long with reruns. Whatever the degree of "liveness" or frequency of a talk show on the air, the basic rules or principles remain the same.

Unspoken Rules

Rule No. 1: Television Talk Is Host-Centered

Even though much television talk is planned or scripted by an off-screen team (indeed, as we will later see, Gurnee's interruptions were planned in advance), television talk invariably centers, in one way or another, on the host. In every talk show explored [here] the host turns out to have a high degree of control over the show and over the production team that builds the show. From a production point of view, the host is frequently the managing editor of the show. From a marketing point of view, the host is the label that sells the product. A successful talk show host also becomes the fulcrum of the show's power in negotiations with the network. He or she is the one irreplaceable part. Without the "brand-name" host, the show may continue (as, for instance, the *Tonight* show continued when Leno replaced Carson), but network executives are fully aware that the success of the show hinges on the host.

Early talk had an array of formidable hosts. Eleanor Roosevelt had a show in New York from 1950 to 1951 called *Mrs. Roosevelt Meets the Public*.[8] Albert Einstein was her first guest. Women were frequent hosts and among television's first prominent talk personalities beginning in 1948. Then came a shakedown in the industry. The highly verbal panel and game shows that early television had inherited from radio days gave way to entertainment and variety talk. During the 1960s and 1970s the networks grew in power, higher rates were charged and talk time became more costly. Television talk was institutionalized.

Johnny Carson rose to power during this time. The *Tonight* show was inexpensive to produce, guests being paid little or nothing to appear on the show, and *Tonight* became a steady profit center for the network. Such consistency was a rare in an industry where booms and busts in program cycles were the norm. Carson also set a standard by his astute management of the show. Through well-publicized walkouts and thorny negotiations with the networks when his contracts came up, Carson gradually established better conditions for himself, leading to his famous four- and three-day work weeks. With each contract he assumed greater degrees of and control and ownership over his show. Carson set a standard. By the 1980s, major news talk and entertainment talk show hosts, aided by personal managers and agents, commanded multi-million dollar salaries and significant degrees of control over their shows.

Along with making business decisions about their shows, successful talk show hosts work closely with their producers to select and manage their writer/producer teams. From the earliest days, talk show hosts had writers and producers who worked for them. Steve Allen generally had two writers on his staff—one of them, Herb Sargent, going on to write with a much younger team of writers twenty-five years later on *Saturday Night Live*. Carson listed eight writers on his final *Tonight* show. Letterman expanded his writing staff from nine to twelve in his first ten years on the air. There was never any question for whom the writers wrote or to whom they were responsible.

This was true of talk show producers by and large as well. Jack Paar went through three producers in his first two years. Letterman switched producers after five years on the air and then added another one (Peter LaSally from the *Tonight* show) when Carson went off the air. Carson had two producers before Fred de Cordova's long stewardship in the 1970s and 1980s. De Cordova, a veteran producer-director who had worked with such major show business figures as Fred MacMurray, Jack Benny, and George Burns, always took his orders directly from Carson. Carson oversaw every detail of the show and his control over his writers was absolute. Carson's writers were always on six-week renewable contracts.

Johnny Carson followed time-honored talk show traditions here. Talk show writers are almost always anonymous and are almost always on short-term contracts. Letterman varied that tradition by allowing his writers to be pictured with him in publicity shots and assume speaking roles in skits,[9] but he too left most of his writers' work invisible. During Carson's final show, which stood to some extent as a commemoration of everyone who had worked on the show for thirty years, none of the writers was mentioned by name. Only in the final credits at the very end could the viewer catch the names of Carson's writers, a form of recognition that did not occur on the nightly show.

Television talk begins and ends with the host. Talk shows are, to use the words of one producer, "he" or "she" shows.[10] The producers and talent: coordinators line up guests and topics for "him" or "her"; the writers write lines that will work for "him" or "her," to be spoken as he or she would speak them. The tone and pacing of everything that happens within the show is set by the host.

Rule No. 2: Television Talk Is Produced and Experienced in the Present Tense

Videotaped, live, or taped as-if-live, television talk shows take place in the present tense. By 1992 most were videotaped before they went on the air. Talk shows go to reruns from time to time, notably when hosts go on vacation breaks. Some shows, like Johnny Carson's *Best of* series, have been packaged as syndication reruns. Yet even "reruns" participate in the illusion of the talk show present. Talk shows are conducted, and viewers participate in them, as if talk show host and guest and viewer *occupy the same moment*—the moment the show goes on the air.

This should not be surprising. Television is a present-tense medium. In the early 1950s viewers were thrilled to see the first coast-to-coast cable transmission as both the Pacific and Atlantic Oceans appeared together on Edward R. Murrow's *See It Now*. Television's most exciting moments in news, politics, and sports still take place in an electronically instantaneous present. This kind of present-tense immediacy distinguishes television from film and photography, which capture images and relay them back later. Film and photography render a frozen present tense, bringing a present-tense moment back to us at a later time. News, sports, and talk shows alone require viewers to "suspend disbelief" and think of the host as speaking directly to them.

Rule No. 3: Talk Show Hosts Speak Intimately to Millions

Talk show hosts sustain a sense of history, continuity, and intimacy with millions simultaneously. On his last show in May 1992, Carson was clearly aware of the history and continuity of his relationship with his audience. Before launching his last monologue, Carson brought a stool on stage. This was the stool with which he had begun the show in 1962, inherited from Jack Paar before him. "We'll end this show as we began," he said, surrounded by "the same shabby set and props." Several times his voice choked with emotion as he spoke. This indeed was a form of present tense immediacy through the camera, a private conversation to a very public audience.

Rule No. 4: Words = Dollars

Johnny Carson's monologue on his last show included a joke about the proliferation of talk shows on television in the early 1990s. "When we started this show," he said, "the total population of the earth was 3 billion, 100 million. This summer it is 5 billion, 500 million people, which is a net increase of 2 billion, 400 million people. . . . A more amazing statistic is that half of those 2 billion, 400 million people will soon have their own late night talk show."

Carson's joke about multiplying talk shows suggested that even on the eve of his retirement he had his eye on the competition. Talk shows were, as they had always been, relatively cheap to produce in 1992, often costing less than $100,000 a show compared to upwards of a million dollars or more for a prime time drama. That, combined with the insatiable demands of the entertainment industry to promote its products and a larger number of new outlets through satellite and cable TV, had given rise to the new cycle of talk shows to which Carson referred.

With all that was new, however, commercials still funded most TV talk shows. Carson referred to this too on his final broadcast, catching himself as he reminisced with sidekicks Ed McMahon and Doc Severinsen and almost forgot a commercial break. Should he go to a commercial, he asked his old staff members, and then, shaking his head as if that were a silly question, he said, "Of course, 'the dollar.'" As McMahon and Severinsen nodded assent, Carson muttered "some things never change" and went dutifully into the commercial.

Some things do not change on commercial television. Television talk is a commodity. Carson's joke on the proliferation of talk shows, which was comprised of seventy-five words and ran only thirty seconds on the screen, was a $150,000 joke—the cost to advertisers of a thirty-second "spot" on Carson's last show. Each word of that joke cost approximately $2,000.[11]

Although the rates on Carson's last show were particularly high that evening,[12] commercial time on television is invariably costly. An industry of network and station "reps," time buyers and sellers, manages the fluctuations of advertising time in the talk show market.

Hosts are commodities, too. Their worth to networks and advertisers is reflected in their yearly salaries. In 1991 NBC paid Carson approximately $30 million.[13] The only talk show host to exceed Carson's salary was Oprah Winfrey, whose syndication contracts brought her an annual $42 million. In 1991 Arsenio Hall received $12 million dollars for his role as host, Phil Donahue $8 million, David Letterman, $6 million (jumping to $14 million

Major National Talk Show Hosts on Television (1948–92)
By Robert Erler and Bernard Timberg

Talk Show Host	Years of National Talk Prominence
Faye Emerson (1948–60)	12
Arthur Godfrey (1948–61)	13
Arlene Francis (1949–75)	26
Dave Garroway (1949–61)	12
Garry Moore (1950–77)	27
Art Linkletter (1950–70)	20
Steve Allen (1950–84)	34
Ernie Kovacs (1951–61)	10
Mike Wallace (1951–)	41
Merv Griffin (1951–86)	35
Hugh Downs (1951–)	41
Edward R. Murrow (1951–59)	8
Dinah Shore (1951–62, 1970–80)	21
Jack Paar (1951–65, 1973)	15
Mike Douglas (1953–82)	29
Johnny Carson (1954–92)	38
David Susskind (1956–86)	30
Barbara Walters (1963–)	29
William Buckley (1966–)	26
Dick Cavett (1966–)	26
Joan Rivers (1969, 1983–)	10
Phil Donahue (1970–)	22
Bill Moyers (1971–)	21
Tom Snyder (1973–82)	9
Geraldo Rivera (1978–)	14
Robert McNeil and Jim Lehrer (1979–)	13
Ted Koppel (1979–)	13
David Letterman (1980–)	12
John McLaughlin (1982–)	10
Larry King (1983–)	9
Oprah Winfrey (1986–)	6
Arsenio Hall (1987–)	5

Note: Hosts associated exclusively with game shows, even when those shows have centered around clever forms of talk (for example, Groucho Marx in *You Bet Your Life* or John Daly and the panelists of *What's My Line?*), have not been included in the list. Neither have we included long-standing hosts of talk shows that have centered on special topics, like Oral Roberts and Pat Robertson, who had successful religious talk shows; Dick Clark, who has been on the air almost continuously since the 1950s with his shows on music; or Ruth Westheimer with her highly successful shows on sexual topics.[17]

in his deal with CBS the next year), Jay Leno, $3 million.[14] These figures were supplemented by income from host-owned production companies that produced films and other television shows, and from real estate and other investments. Oprah Winfrey's net worth in 1991 was an estimated $250 million. That made her, along with Carson, one of America's wealthiest 400 people, according to *Forbes* magazine's annual survey. Television talk makes money for those who own it and produce it. Money is the fuel that drives the machine.

Rule No. 5: Television Talk Structures Spontaneity

Talk on television is by necessity highly planned. It must fit the format, commercial imperatives, and time limits of commercial television. Though it can be entertaining, even "outrageous," it must never permanently alienate advertisers or viewers.

A good example of the limits of television talk can be seen in the career of talk show host Morton Downey, Jr. Confrontational and abrasive, an "in-your-face" kind of host, Downey had a loyal following for his 1980s syndicated show out of New Jersey. Though critics were frequently repelled by Downey as a personality, they also found him provocative and a welcome change from the blandness of most television. When Downey blew cigarette smoke into the camera and leered challenges at viewers and guests, "blue chip" advertisers did not want their products associated with his show and it was taken off the air.[15]

Downey represents an extreme example, but all television talk shows are regulated by invisible rules of acceptability. Guests are carefully chosen, questions prescreened. In the comedian Richard Pryor's appearance on the Letterman show in 1986, as much as 80 percent of the interview was set up in advance. This was standard procedure in the preparation of guest interviews. The questions, the order of the questions and Pryor's possible responses were discussed by Letterman with segment producer Robert Morton, who prepared the interview. Morton's notes were in front of Letterman throughout and structured his replies.[16]

The give and take on a show like Carson's or Letterman's is structured by scores of such invisible hands. Carson's final show lists two executive producers, a line producer, a director, a co-producer, two writing supervisors, six writers, a music supervisor, a musical conductor and assistant musical conductor, three talent coordinators, a commercial administrator, two production managers, an associate director, an art director, a production assistant, two stage managers, a technical director, a lighting director, two audio technicians, a video engineer, three videotape editors, a head carpenter, a prop master, a head electrician, a production staff of five, a makeup person, a hairdresser, a graphic arts department, a wardrobe supervisor, and various assistants to the producers. Fifty-five names appeared in all, and this represented only the employees of Carson Productions, not the NBC camera crews and studio technicians in Burbank who taped the show. Nor do we see in the credits the scores of network officials who oversaw, budgeted, did legal work, and publicized the show. Over a hundred talk show professionals put a show like *Tonight* on the air each evening.

The rules of television talk are clear. They have been formulated over forty years of television practice, an inheritance of radio and performance traditions that preceded television by many years. Host-centered, a commodity in competition with other commodities, topical and spontaneous within professionally prescribed limits, these are the unspoken rules that guide television talk.

Notes

1. Hal Gurnee made these remarks in a seminar co-sponsored by the Museum of Television and Radio and the Directors Guild at the Museum of Television and Radio on May 26, 1992. Gurnee was the person responsible for my unusual access to the Letterman show 1983–86.

2. These figures come from Christopher H. Sterling and John M. Kitross, *Stay Tuned: A Concise History of American Broadcasting*, Belmont, Calif.: Wadsworth Publishing, 1978, Programming Charts: pp. 519–26.

3. Ibid., pp. 528–32.

4. See Frank Mankiewicz, "From Lippmann to Letterman: The 10 Most Powerful Voices," *Gannett Center Journal* 3:2 (Spring 1989), p. 81. In Mankiewicz' decade by decade summary, television hosts and news anchors have progressively assumed the role once played by nationally syndicated newspaper columnists, cartoonists, and radio commentators as influencers of public opinion.

5. With his celebrity interview show *Person to Person* from 1951–61, Edward R. Murrow was a founder of entertainment talk as well as news talk. Murrow resisted the celebrity orientation of *Person to Person* at first. One of his early shows featured a mail carrier in Harlem, for instance. But non-celebrity interviews did not do well in the ratings and were abandoned. (Joseph Persico, *Edward R. Murrow: An American Original*, New York: McGraw-Hill, 1988, p. 345.) *Person to Person* was a forerunner of the Barbara Walters specials and other talk shows based on one-on-one celebrity visits and the work of the so-called lower Murrow established some of the earliest traditions of entertainment talk on television.

6. Thomas Schatz uses de Saussure's terms *parole* and *langue* to describe the impact of certain Hollywood films on the "language structure" of Hollywood film genres. The same could be said of the impact of certain talk show hosts. Their shows redirect the development of the "language" of the television talk show.

7. The term is borrowed from Erving Goffman's *Forms of Talk*, Philadelphia: University of Pennsylvania Press, 1981. The different kinds of fresh talk on television correspond in interesting ways to the four "aims" of discourse theorists have posited for social speech: aims of information, entertainment, persuasion, and, more recently, self-expression. Television talk exhibits, in one form or another, all four of these aims. As is the case in written or spoken language, these aims frequently overlap. Each of the major traditions of television talk—that of the news, the entertainment talk/variety show, the reframed event, and the sales pitch—privileges one or another of these four major aims of speech. For a detailed discussion of the dis-

course aims of television talk shows, see *Titans of Talk*, Chapter 2, "The Range and History of Television Talk Show," Austin: University of Texas Press, 1994. For more detailed general discussion of the aims of discourse and their history in written and spoken speech, see James L. Kinneavy, *A Theory of Discourse*, Englewood Cliff, N.J.: Prentice-Hall, 1971.

8. *Mrs. Roosevelt Meets the Public*, originally titled *Today with Mrs. Roosevelt*, ran from February 12, 1950, to July 15, 1951.

9. He also allowed his writers to do outside work, and many went on to other writing jobs after two or three years with the show.

10. Tony Geiss, who was an associate producer on *Late Night with David Letterman* in its first year on the air.

11. Figures supplied July 28, 1992, by Gene Cunningham, research director for Blair Television, from sources in the NBC Sales Department. Admittedly, the cost of advertising time was especially high during Carson's final week. The NBC sales department hiked the rate considerably; normally a thirty-second spot would cost from $30,000 to 35,000 and this would have been a $30,000 joke.

12. The show had a record audience that night, with approximately 50 million viewers tuning in.

13. These figures are from a 1992 *Forbes* magazine article.

14. Ibid.

15. The source of this information is Fred Gold, Research Director of WWOR-TV at the time of the Downey show.

16. Chapter 9 of *Titans of Talk*, in the part of the book that goes behind the scenes to show how a talk show is produced from the control room and the studio floor, describes the detailed preparation that goes into a show of this kind.

17. Other prominent hosts of special topic talk shows include Julia Childs with her cooking shows and Bob Vila of *This Old House* on PBS. Among the hosts who upped the ante of confrontation on television talk shows were Joe Pyne, Alan Burke, Les Crane, and Morton Downey, Jr. The confrontational talk show hosts tended to have only a regional impact or did not last for long as national shows (sometimes because of sponsor decisions).

The decision to exclude some of the most prominent hosts of game shows was a particularly difficult one for us, since game show hosts sometimes represented some of the most entertaining and original forms of fresh talk on the air at the time. Certainly, the talk of Groucho Marx on *You Bet Your Life* was as important as the game, and, as David Marc and Robert Thompson point out in *Prime Time, Prime Movers* (Boston: Little, Brown, 1992), *What's My Line?* was as much a talk show as a game show, featuring such well-known raconteurs as book publisher Bennett Cerf, syndicated columnist Dorthy Kilgallen, and poet Louis Untermeyer. Ultimately, however, we decided that the talk of the game show revolves around the game that is central to the show's format, and the ratio of talk to game, as well as the role of the host or master of ceremonies of a game show, should be left to a book that centers on that genre. Similarly, though hosts of special topic talk shows do take on national prominence and certainly influence the form of television talk—Dr. Ruth Westheimer and her appearance as a guest on national talk shows signalled a new openness and legitimacy to discussions of sexual topics, and Pat Robertson became a national figure through his discussions of political and cultural issues as well as religion—these hosts are primarily identified with the topics that are their special concern rather than general news and entertainment programming.

Barbarous TV International

Syndicated Wheels of Fortune

MICHAEL SKOVMAND

Since the beginning of regular radio broadcasts, game shows have been a habitual and popular part of the media fare in our part of the world. Generations of listeners and viewers have spent hours and hours participating in games testing their memory, intelligence, and specialized or general knowledge. And yet, it seems to me, very little research, or scholarly debate, has been devoted to this particular branch of the media. I would suggest that there are historical and institutional reasons for this.

One obvious reason for this neglect is that game shows have simply not been found worthy of sustained scholarly attention. Generically, TV game shows are a carry-over from radio shows, whose concepts, in turn, were borrowed from or inspired by a variety of parlor games. So, as a genre, game shows seem not innovative at all, but part of an unbroken and unproblematic historical continuum of cultural practices.[1]

Another reason is that game shows are generally perceived as culturally insignificant and/or politically innocuous. Unlike such genres as news, documentaries, or drama, game shows are unlikely vehicles for contemporary commentary or debate. Consequently, they have not been the focus of the discussion of novel or disruptive issues, nor have they been seen to be the site of particular social or institutional bias. Although the famous quiz scandals in US television in the fifties brought TV prize games into temporary disrepute, game shows as a genre continued in modified forms—or, as in the case of *The $64,000 Question,* were resumed after a suitable pause. Game shows may have been looked upon as a contributing factor in the "narcotizing dysfunction" of TV in general, or as a part of the "waste land" of Western or Westernized broadcasting, but they are hardly ever singled out for particular mention, or reviewed, except perhaps as the backdrop for the antics of some glamorous TV personality. Game shows form a continuing series: they are part of the televisual furniture (Welch 1958).

Mike Clarke, in his book *Teaching Popular Television,* makes some interesting comments on the status of the game show. One of the reasons why the game show ranks even lower than soap opera and crime series, according to Clarke, is "that it has no ready equivalent in literature or on the stage." Practitioners of television criticism are habitually recruited from the Humanities departments of universities. They are intellectuals steeped in traditions of literary analysis, who find it difficult to recognize game shows, indeed the whole range of non-fictional "live" entertainment, as "texts for analysis."

Text or Cultural Practice?

There are good reasons why intellectuals find it so difficult to perceive game shows as "texts for analysis." To use a rather appropriate metaphor, game shows are "hard to pin down"—in the sense that they are not inert matter, like a dead insect. They keep wriggling.

Game shows foreground the fact that they are a *cultural practice* rather than a "text." Unlike a "text," a cultural practice is not "authored." There is no authority, no *auteur,* whose personal/institutional choices have organized the production of the text. Instead, there are rules and conventions, traditionally accepted by the participants, and roles, provisionally distributed.

What is more, game shows are "live," or rather, they function as live television. Although they are made in bundles of between three and five a day, and have been recorded weeks in advance of the actual screening, they are presented as live, and are so for all practical intents and purposes, in the sense that the game component as such is almost 100 percent unedited, with ad breaks and presentation of prizes as the only post-production inserts. It is, in other words, time-shifted, but functionally live, and tell-tale references to current or seasonal events are carefully avoided to maintain that sense of liveness.

This notion of liveness again militates against the idea of its being a "text for analysis." There is no "central consciousness" or organizing perspective. There is no stable role distribution. There is, on the contrary, an element of surprise and improvisation which makes the actualized narrative structure unpredictable—always, of course, within the given game format. One program may chronicle the fortunes of the heroic failure, another the lucky streak of the mediocre contestant. There is no telling in advance, because neither an absent *auteur* nor the host of the show wields a determining influence on the course of events.

The study of "participatory" forms of television radicalizes the discussion about television as a social and cultural site, or forum. This is why any approach to a show like *Wheel of Fortune,* and to TV game and quiz shows in general, should be a two-pronged one: on the one hand, these shows should be seen as part of the category of "live" television entertainment, that is to say as part of the wider category of popular television programming. On the other hand, game and quiz shows should be seen as part of a field of *cultural practices* which are not necessarily communicated by way of television at all, a field of practices which include parlor games, bingo, fairs, and gossip.

In an interview from 1984 (Modleski 1986), Raymond Williams points in a similar direction, towards an overlooked interface between popular culture in general and popular television programming:

> Popular culture now sometimes means to some of its practitioners that which represents a certain kind of interest or experience, as against the modes of an established culture or against a power . . . But the other meaning, in which I've been particularly interested lately, takes up a whole range which never got recognized as culture at all within an old dispensation: that of a very active world of everyday conversation and exchange. Jokes, idioms, characteristic forms not just of everyday dress but occasional dress, people consciously having a party, making a do, marking an occasion. I think this area has been very seriously under-valued, and it isn't only that it is undervalued in itself. We're not yet clear about the relation of those things to certain widely successful television forms. (Modleski 1986: 5)

In recent decades, it is probably the divergent attitudes to "mass culture" among intellectuals which have drawn the most irreducible dividing lines within the intellectual community.

The two major instances, the people and the major means of communication, seemed poles apart, and in particular the reductionist rhetoric of structuralist analysis of the 1970s seemed incapable of moving beyond stating what appeared to be the obvious: that the mass media were a major reproductive agency of dominant ideas, most insidiously at work in their "popular" guises. John Tulloch's analysis of British TV quizzes, "Gradgrind's Heirs" (1976), is no exception:

> One programming form that explicitly concerns itself with "knowledge" whilst claiming at the same time the status of "entertainment" is the television quiz. Bearing in mind Murdock and Golding's dictum that "it is not sufficient simply to assert that the mass media are part of the ideological apparatus of the state, it is also necessary to demonstrate how ideology is produced in concrete practice," I will attempt to indicate how that ideology is reproduced in two current quiz programmes. My principal assumption is that even seemingly trivial broadcast forms—forms that invite and depend on us taking them for granted—play an important part in structuring consciousness and thereby ensuring the continued reproduction of social contradiction. (Tulloch 1976: 3)

Media analyses of popular television programming in the early and midseventies would typically set out with intentions similar to Tulloch's, i.e. they would be "demonstrations of how ideology is reproduced in concrete practice," and the result would almost inevitably demonstrate "the continued reproduction of social contradiction."

John Fiske, in his *Television Culture* (1987), manages to combine the determinacy of this position with an extremely voluntarist notion of audience. As he puts it,

> Quiz shows, like advertising, are undoubtedly part of commodity capitalism, and use many of the similar cultural strategies. For instance, glamorous models are used to display the prizes and thus associate commodities with sexuality, thereby linking buying with sexual desire and satisfaction . . .

But, he goes on to say,

> the motivations of producers of quiz shows that determine the main characteristics of the genre do not necessarily determine the ways that they are read or used by the viewers . . . quiz shows produce particularly active, participatory viewers. Their mini-narratives are structured around the hermeneutic code which poses and then resolves enigmas. But unlike typical narratives, quiz shows are not presented as enacted fiction, but as live events. (Fiske 1987: 272)

Fiske sums up his position by appropriating a version of Stuart Hall's concept of "articulation."

> So, while quiz shows may articulate (speak) consumerism as they carry the voice of their producer, they may also articulate (speak) responses to that consumerism in accents that speak the interests of the consumer. (Fiske 1987: 273–4)

In my view, the challenge to any analysis of popular television lies not simply in pointing to these abstract contradictions, but in demonstrating through theoretically informed concrete studies just how these contradictions are negotiated as part of a much more complex and historically specific communicative practice. The following analysis of game shows in general and *Wheel of Fortune* in particular is an attempt in this direction.

Games of Distinction and Games of Participation

In *Television Culture,* John Fiske presents a useful "hierarchy of quiz shows," organized in relation to the social and cultural currency accorded to the various competences required for participants in the shows, either directly as contestants, or vicariously, as audience. At the top, Fiske places extreme demonstrations of factual knowledge, as we know it from quizzes such as *Mastermind* or *The $64,000 Question*. Below that is the transitional category of "everyday knowledge," displayed in such shows as *The Price Is Right* and *Wheel of Fortune*. As we move downwards in the hierarchy, we pass into the category of what Fiske calls "human knowledge," involving knowledge of people in general (*Family Feud*), and, at the bottom of the hierarchy, the competences involved concern knowledge of specific people, for example between spouses (*The Newlywed Game, Mr. and Mrs.*).

Fiske's hierarchy is based on the relative social value attached to the competences displayed in the shows. In this, he draws on Pierre Bourdieu's concept of cultural capital, as competences acquired through education and upbringing which are in a complex, but ultimately subordinate, relation to economic capital. However, just as rewarding in this context are Bourdieu's *dynamic* concepts of distinction and participation (Bourdieu 1984). Games like *Mastermind* and *Trivial Pursuit* are essentially games of distinction, in which the successful contestants distinguish themselves by displaying valued competences to the exclusion of others.[2] Games of distinction are a complex phenomenon: they are deliberately distanced from sordid notions of direct material gain, and yet socially or culturally profitable, i.e., ultimately, "work" by other means. Games of participation, by contrast, are seen as vulgar and barbarous in their direct relation to tangible sentiment, or gain, and scandalous because they are culturally and socially unprofitable, "a waste of time."

Games like *The Newlywed Game* and *Wheel of Fortune* are games of participation, in which the display of competences includes the other contestants in playful interaction. If we look beyond television, Bingo, simple card games, and children's games are cultural practices which are inclusive rather than exclusive. They are basically games in which distinction is not conferred upon the individual as a recognition of the possession of a permanent competence of marketable cultural value. Luck, chance, or a provisional role distribution include the contestants in a sense of collectivity and participation, as opposed to the games of distinction, in which individuality and exclusiveness are at a premium.

It should be emphasized, however, that Bourdieu's categories are not categories defining essences. Most games are capable of being transformed from distinctive into participatory games, or vice versa. Arguments over ball games or card games are typically of this nature—contestants are accused of not "taking the game seriously," i.e. trying to turn a "distinguishing" game into a participatory one, or vice versa.

Wheel of Fortune is tendentially a participatory game. It is underscored by the hosts that it is the kind of game in which "everybody wins." (In the Danish and Scandinavian versions, for instance, contestants without winnings are given an inexpensive watch in order to underline the idea that nobody leaves the game empty-handed.) The added appeal of popular "audience participation" shows lies in the extra bonus of simply appearing on television. The prevalence of this philosophy is substantiated by several sources.[3]

This basic participatory quality of the show is demonstrated most clearly in limited cases in which this atmosphere is challenged by contestants who appear exceptionally clever and/or too greedy, thereby upsetting the delicate balance of comradeship and exciting competitiveness. It is then the role of the otherwise low-key host to step in and attempt to correct this by bringing the culprit in line with the other contestants.

The Invention of the Wheel

The history of the success of *Wheel of Fortune* is interesting in its own right, and in addition underscores some general points about the genre and its position within mainstream popular TV production.

The game was invented by Merv Griffin, the American singer and TV host. He modelled it on the traditional game of "Hangman," but gave it a less morbid form, and combined the wordgame with the roulette-like feature of the spinning wheel of fortune. It was launched in 1973 by Merv Griffin as a daytime show for NBC, syndicated since 1983 by King World Productions; syndication rights had been bought in 1982 for $50,000. In 1986 Griffin sold the show to the Coca-Cola Company for $250 million, a sensational price at that end of the business. The production price per episode is remarkably cheap and entirely predictable, and is said to be about $25,000 (Pollan 1986: 24). Actually, the chances are that it is appreciably less, since the advertising value of providing prizes for the show would be more than sufficient to sponsor the production. Four or five episodes are produced consecutively in daily production runs, adding up to 195 episodes per year plus 65 reruns (Pollan 1986: 24). At present, the show is produced under contract in eight European countries.

There has been no shortage of attempts to explain the spectacular success of *Wheel of Fortune* in the United States. Like most other successes, it seems to hinge on a combination of external and internal factors.

The Cinderella story of Vanna White, the mute, wildly applauding cheerleader hostess whose presence on the show propelled her from total anonymity to superstardom overnight, was a consequence of the success of the show, but the Vanna White story in turn increased the show's momentum. For Pat Sajak, the male host of the show, *Wheel of Fortune* has also been a career-maker. So far, his success on the *Wheel* has earned him a talk show of his own.

Generally, in the choice of hosts, participants, prizes, and decor, it is the emphasis on relative ordinariness which characterizes the show. The aggressive competitiveness of other comparable game or quiz shows is virtually non-existent on the *Wheel*. Instead, there is a laid back, relaxed atmosphere of friendliness and mutual supportiveness. Institutionally, the unusual move to place a game show like *Wheel of Fortune* in the prime-time access slot (the legally stipulated non-network period preceding network prime time) proved to be an important factor in making it take off. Awakening from twelve years of daytime doldrums, within two years it had a following of 43 million viewers in that slot (as opposed to 8 million in the daytime). Success within the US media system creates its own momentum. Once a show demonstrates exceptional attractiveness, its market value is further increased because of its usefulness as a lead-in or lead-out to boost the ratings of neighboring shows. The profitability of local stations depends less on the size of their prime-time audience than on the two hours that precede prime time, i.e. "early fringe" and "prime-time access," and there are several examples showing how the *Wheel of Fortune* has been decisive in boosting the flagging economy of local stations (Pollan 1986: 24). The *Wheel* was increasingly bought not only by minor local stations, but by stations in the major US markets owned and operated by the networks, functioning specifically, and very effectively, as a lead-in or lead-out to what was coming into increasing prominence: their local news bulletins.

The demographic appeal of *Wheel of Fortune* is remarkably similar in Europe and the US: it has a broad, generally lower-middle-class appeal, with a bias towards the demographically interesting target group of women between 25 and 54. The Achilles heel, however, of a show like the *Wheel* tends to be the (slight) age bias of its audience, which may make it vulnerable in a media system like the American one, in which there is a premium not just on ratings, but on the purchasing power of the audience. Nevertheless, it remains the most successful syndicated game show in recent US TV history,[4] having been consistently at the top of the polls of syndicated shows since the mid-eighties. Its success, followed up by the successes of *Jeopardy* (a highly competitive quiz show) and *The Oprah Winfrey Show* (a talk show with a dynamic black hostess), has turned King World Productions into one of the major players in the syndication business.

The success of *Wheel of Fortune* was exported during the 1980s, to Britain, France, Germany, and Scandinavia, among other countries. The varied reception of the *Wheel* reflects the differences of the existing media systems and traditions. The Danish experience is a case in point.

In Denmark, the *Wheel* was used as part of the launching, in October 1988, of the second Danish channel, a public-service channel partly financed by advertising, partly by license fees. The *Wheel* came to signify a more brash, populist, and Americanized approach to live entertainment, contrasting strongly with the staid, paternalist stance of Channel 1. Within weeks the *Wheel* became a hit with the Danish audience, consistently scoring rating points of 30 percent or more. Furthermore, the *Wheel* became a pawn in a hostile game of competitive scheduling of the main evening news bulletin between the two channels. The popularity of the *Wheel* meant that it could be placed practically anywhere without significant loss of rating points: it could even challenge the long-established success of the main evening news on Channel 1. So, as in the US, it was not only the intrinsic qualities of the *Wheel*, but also its usefulness as a scheduling pawn which made it so attractive a purchase.

But what are the intrinsic qualities of *Wheel of Fortune*? It is important to point out that the *Wheel* is not a stable entity. In the US and elsewhere it has been modified over time, and there are important national variations between, say, the American, the German, and the Danish versions. Nevertheless, the contracting producers of the *Wheel* are under an obligation to present a fairly homogeneous product, and there is indeed a shared structure and a shared visual aesthetic, as well as a shared sense of mood and tone, for all the national variations.

The sets share a basic design: a large, flashy vertical display board bearing blank tiles behind which the letters of the word puzzle are hidden, plus a large, multi-colored roulette-like wheel with wedges, all marked with numbers except two which say "Bankrupt" and "Lose a Turn."

The wheel indicates the rewards earned by picking a correct letter, and the person who solves the word puzzle is allowed to spend his accumulated winnings by "going shopping" among a range of commodities, ranging from necklaces and expensive kitchen utensils to VCRs and cruises. The "shopping" is done in identical fashion in all versions of the *Wheel:* the face of the winner is inserted in the corner of the frame, making choices of commodities, while the camera glides lovingly up and down the glittering display of wares. (The shopping element has been reduced considerably in recent years in the US version, in favor of straight cash winnings.[5]) After the choices have been made, an off-screen melodious male voice gives a brief characterization of the goods chosen, including their price, while the camera again caresses the merchandise.[6] The top scorer goes on to a bonus round which offers prizes such as cars, cruises, and luxury stereos.

The serial character of the show is emphasized by having the winner appear on some of the following shows, for instance for a maximum of three in a row (the US), or by having a final play-off among the week's winners (Denmark).

There are, in other words, two distinct phases in the show: the game phase and the consumer phase. The game phase is structured by its two components, the board and the wheel, signifying the two elements of the game: skill and luck. Arguably one of the secrets of the success of the *Wheel* is precisely the balance struck between skill and luck. American critics have argued that one of the main appeals of the US *Wheel* is that it is precisely pitched at a level of difficulty at which the majority of its audience will enjoy the sense of superiority of being just a fraction quicker than the contestants at solving the word puzzle. Admittedly, the US version appears considerably easier to solve than most European versions. The US version uses longer phrases (which means fewer misses) and assists its contestants by supplying extra letters. This is in harmony with other features in the US version which emphasize the show's lack of competitiveness: the way contestants root for each other—it is everybody together against the wheel and the puzzle—and the way in which everybody is made a winner, since everybody keeps the amounts they have won, even from the rounds where they did not earn the right to go shopping.

The *Wheel,* like other serialized formats, has a core constituency, but unlike soap operas, with their narrative continuity, the audience figures are volatile, because a relatively large proportion of the *Wheel* audience is easily affected by the offerings of competing channels. Obviously, this is explainable by the fact that watching the *Wheel* is an everyday, low-key type of practice which can easily be missed now and then without detriment to the viewing experience. Interestingly, as Danish audience figures document, this means that the smaller the *Wheel* audience, the *higher* the quality assessment (on a scale from 1 to 5) given by the audience.[7] Indeed, this notion of low-intensity viewing applies also to the viewing of any individual episode of the *Wheel.* It is no coincidence that a program like the *Wheel* has a majority of women viewers, because although the program *may* be watched with rapt attention, the chopped-up structure and the low intensity of the show *accommodates* the kind of distracted, peripheral viewing of the majority of women, to whom the home is not only the site of the TV set, but their actual place of work.[8]

Four Wheels *Compared*

Wheel of Fortune is produced in many countries outside the United States under contract with King World Productions. To what extent is this show a stable entity when produced outside the United States? How well does it travel? Alongside the American version, I have taken a closer look at three *Wheels*, produced under very different circumstances from the US version: the German *Glücksrad,* produced by Sat1, *Lyckohjulet,* produced by pan-Scandinavian TV3, and *Lykkehjulet,* broadcast by TV2, the second Danish channel.

Glücksrad is broadcast by the pan-German commercial satellite station Sat1, owned by German media mogul Leo Kirsch, whose footprint covers a good deal of Central and Northern Europe. The game show is broadcast at 7 p.m. on weekdays only.

Lyckohjulet (7 p.m. on weekdays) is broadcast by the satellite station TV3, catering for the Scandinavian region and alternating between Swedish, Norwegian and Danish, although Swedish is the predominant language, which reflects the fact that the station is owned by the Sweden-based international media conglomerate Kinnevik. Like Sat1, it is a commercial channel whose revenue is based on the sale of advertising time.

Lykkehjulet is broadcast seven days a week, at 6:30 p.m. on weekdays and at 7:30 p.m. on weekends. It is produced by Nordisk Film for TV2, the terrestrial second Danish channel, a semi-independent TV station whose revenue derives partly from license fees shared with the Danish Channel 1, partly from limited block advertising and sponsoring agreements. Unlike the three other *Wheels* mentioned, this version is uninterrupted by advertising breaks. I am deliberately refraining from quoting audience figures for the four shows, because it would be almost impossible to treat these figures on a par. Suffice it to say that the US and Danish versions are exceptionally successful game shows, while the German and Scandinavian versions are an integral part of the programming of two satellite channels which are trying to get established with a multinational and extremely heterogeneous audience.

The following thumbnail sketch of the four versions attempts to answer the following question: is a game show like *Wheel of Fortune* exported wholesale, or is it remodelled substantially to accord with the local broadcasting culture?

My characterization of the four shows is based on (1) a comparison of four distinctive variables within the invariable format, plus (2) a quantitative assessment of the relative weight given to four narrative categories of the show. The four distinctive features I have singled out are:

(a) the participation/non-participation of the studio audience
(b) the applause/non-applause of the hostess and contestants

(c) the participation/non-participation of the hostess
(d) the décor of the set

The Participation of the Audience

The American *Wheel* is characterized by a high degree of involvement on the part of the studio audience, which includes family members of the contestants. The cheering of the audience is a marked feature throughout the game, and contestants are frequently, by gesture or gaze, in contact with family members in the audience. After the winner has emerged, family and friends spill on to the set to participate in the celebration.

The *Glücksrad* and *Lyckohjulet* both signal the presence of a studio audience through a token initial pan, but other than that there is little interaction except unobtrusive audience applause. There is no trespassing by the audience on to the set.

The Danish *Lykkehjulet* has no visual representation of its audience (which is very small because of the cramped studio conditions of Nordisk Film) either before, during, or after the show, and its reactions are audibly reinforced by synthetic means.

The Applause of the Hostess and Contestants

The supportive applause of Vanna White and all the contestants when the wheel is spun is a kind of "cheerleader" enthusiasm which appears slightly odd to European audiences, I would suggest. Neither *Glücksrad* nor *Lykkehjulet* has adopted this practice. *Lyckohjulet,* however, practises a very low-key version of the American way of applauding, carried out by the contestants with visible unease. This is compounded by the fact that *Lyckohjulet,* unlike any other version known to me, is essentially a two-person confrontation: it has two initial "national" rounds with two contestants of the same nationality in each round, whereupon two contestants of different nationalities meet in the final.

The Participation of the Hostess

The relative "competence" given to the hostess is a particularly interesting feature, which signals variant notions about gender and equality. Vanna White remains mute throughout the show, a representation of femininity which seems quaint even in the US media context, but which is adopted by *Glücksrad*'s hostess, whereas both Scandinavian hostesses exercise the faculty of speech. A mute hostess would probably, in a Scandinavian context, be taken as a controversial sexist feature, particularly in combination with a male host.[9] The Swedish hostess of *Lyckohjulet* engages in a brief pre-game chat with the Norwegian host, and announces the phrase categories. The Danish hostess goes even further than this, in that during the show there is occasional bantering between host and hostess, in which even the disembodied voice of the announcer of prizes is involved from time to time.

The Décor of the Set

The variation in décor seems to be in striking accordance with the crudest national stereotypes: the US *Wheel* décor spells gaudy, glittery vulgarity; the German décor is matter-of-fact, with contestants performing on a background of steely grey; the pan-Scandinavian *Lyckohjulet* is done in tasteful matching light blue and pink pastels; and the décor of the Danish *Lykkehjulet* is a rather child-like set of circles and staircases, done in feel-good primary colors.

The quantitative analysis, based on random sampling between November 1989 and May 1990, attempts to quantify the narrative constituents of the four variants, in four rough-and-ready categories: (1) the actual game component; (2) talk, including introductions and continuity within the show; (3) "shopping," i.e. the phase in which the contestants spend their hard-won money on the merchandise, and where the merchandise is portrayed by camera and voice-over; and (4) the interruptions made by advertising breaks.

The percentages are given with and without the ad sections included, in order that the Danish version (which has no ad breaks) may be comparable.

Quantitative Analysis

Wheel of Fortune (USA)

				minus ad blocks
game:	13 mins	38 secs	48.20%	65.23%
talk:	5 mins	24 secs	19.09%	25.84%
shopping:	1 min	52 secs	6.60%	8.93%
ad blocks:	7 mins	23 secs	26.10%	
total:	28 mins	17 secs		

Lyckohjulet (TV3, Scandinavia)

game:	15 mins	27 secs	49.41%	56.11%
talk:	6 mins	47 secs	21.70%	24.64%
shopping:	5 mins	18 secs	16.95%	19.25%
ads:	4 mins	44 secs	15.14%	
total:	32 mins	16 secs		

Glücksrad (Sat1, Northern Europe)

game:	9 mins	43 secs	31.67%	45.33%
talk:	5 mins	18 secs	17.27%	24.73%
shopping:	6 mins	25 secs	20.91%	29.94%
ads:	9 mins	15 secs	30.15%	
total:	30 mins	41 secs		

Lykkehjulet (TV2, Denmark)

game:	14 mins	15 secs	57%
talk/continuity:	5 mins	15 secs	21%
shopping/prizes:	5 mins	30 secs	22%
total:	25 mins		

The above figures, while open to many kinds of interpretation, seem to point towards the following conclusions, which are in part substantiated by my more qualitative analysis.

The US *Wheel* is the most game-orientated and participatory version among the four under examination, with the Danish *Lykkehjulet* in second place, and *Glücksrad* decidedly at the bottom. The "talk" component is remarkably stable across the board. The "shopping" component, which competes for time with the game part, is lowest in the US version, and indisputably highest in the German satellite version. In fact, *Glücksrad* comes across as saturated with commodities—if you add the "shopping" component, three quarters of which have an occasional *Werbung* (=advertisement) sign flashing, indicating that this is technically an ad, to the genuine ad block, you will find that more than fifty percent of your half-hour game show consists of undisguised advertising! This compares with slightly less than 33 percent in the US and pan-Scandinavian versions.

At the risk of oversimplification, I will venture the following conclusion, based on the above: *Wheel of Fortune* is a game show in which popular/participatory and consumerist modes of address compete. A popular/participatory game show requires a genuine sense of constituency for the show to work. There is that sense of constituency in the practice of the US and Danish versions. In the case of *Glücksrad* there does not seem to be such a sense, and consequently the show relies on its consumerist address and appears as primarily a vehicle for advertising. In the case of the pan-Scandinavian *Lyckohjulet* there is an attempt to create a "Scandinavian" sense of constituency and mode of address, but given the lack of cohesiveness of its actual satellite audience, the game show comes across as simply a slightly more up-market version of *Glücksrad*.[10]

The Wheel: *Rampant Advertorialism?*

The hybrid "advertorialism" is an attempt to describe the erosion of the barriers in print and electronic media alike between editorial matter and advertising. In the 1980s, MTV was perhaps the most obvious example of how these barriers virtually disappeared: on MTV, video clips, shown as "editorial" programming, function as advertisements for themselves, for the records, the artists, their concerts, and so on. The "sweet deal" between the television company and the advertisers, i.e. video producers, by which programming content is delivered free of charge in exchange for airtime, also exists, to an unknown extent, in the production of a program like *Wheel of Fortune*.

Regardless of the amount of legal restrictions attempting to prevent program producers from making unauthorized agreements with the companies delivering the prizes, the heart of the matter is that the commercial value of having one's wares exhibited on a show as successful as *Wheel of Fortune* is so enormous that it cannot be ignored, especially not by TV executives on the lookout for overall improvement in profitability. In a sense, this is a temptation lurking in the shadows of any major media production. The provision of cars and clothes for *Miami Vice,* the selection of the location for the next James Bond movie, the brand choice of whisky for a major feature film like *The Great Gatsby* all involve potential conflicts between "editorial" and financial considerations. There is nothing extraordinary in that, since this conflict exists abundantly already. However, in the case of "public," if not public-service media, such as daily newspapers and broadcast television, the threat to the integrity of the medium as a "forum" of public exchange is a real one when and if the audience find it impossible to determine the boundary lines between editorial and advertising content. The optimistic libertarianism of John Fiske (in *Television Culture*) would maintain that the problem does not exist, because however treacherous the producers of programs may be, the active audience will generally make their own, perhaps alternative, sense of the program. This argument, however, does not do away with the problem that the program makers may have to accept undue commercial interference with the program, precisely because the commodities are an integral part of the editorial content. One of the litmus tests of such potential interference could be to ask the following questions: could Jack (the off-screen male voice presenting the prizes) actually make fun of the goods without breaking the (perhaps tacit) consensus between programmers and purveyors? Would it be permissible for contestants openly to express displeasure with certain prizes? If not, why not?

Conclusion

Anyone attempting to draw bombastic, heavy-handed conclusions about an "interactive" game show like *Wheel of Fortune,* or indeed any genre of popular television, should recall the extreme caution of a study such as McQuail *et al.* (1972). One of the main conclusions of their study, which included quizzes, a radio serial, a TV soap opera, two TV action series, and TV news programs, was quite simply that

> people can look to quite different kinds of material for essentially the same gratification and, correlatively, find alternative satisfactions in the same televised material. (1972: 153)[11]

Does this view not coincide perfectly with that of John Fiske, who sees no contradiction between doing an ideological critique of the producers of popular television, while at the same time celebrating the "openness" of "the popular text" and the active independence of its audience? I do not think so. On the contrary, my attempt at a comparative analysis of national versions of a game show like *Wheel of Fortune* is making the rather anti-essentialist point that "popular television" is not a stable entity, geographically or over time. It also draws conclusions about live, interactive programs such as *Wheel of Fortune* which cannot be applied to popular fictional programming such as soaps or sitcom, which are not remade under contract, but exported wholesale. In fact, one conclusion of the above analysis might be that one should be extremely wary of operating with a general concept such as "the popular text": any programming, but certainly live participatory programming, should always be seen as relative to the way in which the broadcasting system in point relates to its actual and imaginary audience, and relative to the range of other popular cultural practices which may or may not take on televisual forms.[12]

Notes

1. See, for example, Johan Huizinga's broadly anthropological approach to man as a "playing animal" in *Homo Ludens* (1944).

2. One should, however, be aware of gradations of competences involved and the way they are displayed. There are differences of cultural valuation ascribed to, for instance, the demonstration of encyclopedic knowledge of the complete works of Shakespeare and, say, the autistic total recall of telephone directories. And even the wizard contestants on game shows like *Mastermind* are still just clever amateurs compared to those really in the know who host the show, make up the questions, and sit in judgment.

3. In January 1990, I had an opportunity to witness the briefing session before the daily production run of the three episodes of the Danish version of *Wheel of Fortune*. It was repeatedly emphasized by the Danish host that the contestants should stop worrying about prizes: they were already winners in having been selected for the show. Everything else, including prizes, should be enjoyed simply as a "bonus." And in actual fact, this attitude, from my experience with contestants, seems to be the prevailing one. A quite similar finding is reported by Alexander Cockburn in *American Film* (Cockburn 1986: 26).

4. In its heyday in the mid-1980s, *Wheel of Fortune* consistently scored a rating of 20 percent or more. In 1989–90 it dropped to between 14 and 15 percent, which still leaves it at the top of the polls for bartered series of shows. Of course, with the advent of new networks, plus the proliferation of additional offerings on cable or satellite, ratings are not what they used to be. By comparison, the quiz show *The $64,000 Question*, in July 1955, within a month of its introduction, scored a Nielsen rating of 41.1, the highest in the nation, equalling an audience of 13,423,000 households.

5. In fact, one should be cautious of static forms of analysis of popular serial forms, as there are real shifts in emphasis taking place over time, within each individual show and across the range of, for example, quiz and game shows. Gary Whannel makes that point in his discussion of the changes taking place in British television in the eighties, between early and late Thatcherist populism (Whannel 1990: 107).

6. Within the last couple of years, the US version has done away with the extended and time-consuming shopping spree and restricted itself to money prizes and a few luxury items such as cruises and kitchens, plus of course the final bonus, usually a car.

7. See AIM TV-Undersøgelser (Danish TV Audience Research Institute), for the period November 1989 to May 1990.

8. For a much more detailed development of this argument, see Morley 1986.

9. In an interview with me, Bent Burg, the Danish host of *Lykkehjulet*, pointed out that they wanted a blonde, but not a dumb blonde, as hostess, as this went against "Danish mentality."

10. The rather vague term "sense of constituency" is indebted to Newcomb and Hirsch's idea of TV as a "cultural forum" (Newcomb and Hirsch 1986).

11. This finding is supported and sophisticated by much subsequent research, most recently by Wernblad *et al.* (1990), whose reception analysis of the Danish version of *Wheel of Fortune* focuses on "ideal types" among the Danish audience, whose relations with the show are analyzed in parallel to the gratification patterns demonstrated by McQuail *et al.* (1972), i.e. "self-rating appeal," "basis for social interaction," "excitement" (the fourth category, "educational appeal," is more relevant to the quiz shows than to a game show like *Wheel of Fortune*, although a whole generation of Americans claim to have learned how to spell from watching the *Wheel*).

12. Charlotte Brunsdon makes a similar point very succinctly in her essay "Text and Audience."

> The need to specify context and mode of viewing in any textual discussion, and the awareness that these factors may be more determining of the experience of a text than any textual feature, do not, in and of themselves, either eliminate the text as a meaningful category, or render all texts the same . . . The recognition of the creativity of the audience must, I think, be mobilized back in relation to the television text, and the demands that are made on program makers for a diverse and plural programming which is adequate to the needs, desires and pleasures of the audience. Otherwise, however well intentioned, our work reproduces and elaborates the dominant paradigm in which the popular is the devalued term.
>
> (Brunsdon 1989: 125–6)

References

Bourdieu, P. (1984) *Distinction*, London and New York: Routledge.

Brunsdon, C. (1989) "Text and Audience," in Ellen Seiter *et al.* (eds), *Remote Control*, London: Routledge.

Clarke, M. (1987) *Teaching Popular Television*, London: Comedia.

Cockburn, A. (1986) "The Money Pit," *American Film*, July/August.

Fiske, J. (1987) *Television Culture*, London: Routledge.

Grossberger, L. (1986) "Triumph of the Wheel," *Rolling Stone*, 4 December.

Huizinga, J. (1944) *Homo Ludens*, Basel: Pantheon.

McQuail, D., Blumler, J., and Brown, R. (1972) "The Television Audience, A Revised Perspective," in D. McQuail (ed.), *The Sociology of Mass Communications*, Harmondsworth: Penguin.

Modleski, T. (ed.) (1986) *Studies in Entertainment*, Bloomington, Indiana: Indiana University Press.

Morley, D. (1986) *Family Television: Cultural Power and Domestic Leisure*, London: Comedia.

Newcomb, H. M. and Hirsch, P. M. (1986) "Television as a Cultural Forum: Implications for Research," in W. D. Rowland and B. Watkins (eds), *Interpreting Television*, London: Sage Publications.

Pollan, M. (1986) "Jackpot," *Channels*, 22 June.

Seiter, E. *et al.* (eds) (1989) *Remote Control: Television, Audiences and Cultural Power*, London: Routledge.

Tulloch, J. (1976) "Gradgrind's Heirs—The Quiz and the Presentation of Knowledge by British Television," *Screen Education*, Summer.

Welch, P. E. (1958) "The Quiz Program: A Network Television Staple," *Journal of Broadcasting* 2. 4.

Wernblad, G. *et al.* (1990) "Der skal også vuære noget for de små i samfundet—en receptionsanalyse af Lykkehjulet," Institut for Informations- og Medievidenskab, Aarhus Universitet.

Whannel, G. (1990) "Winner Takes All: Competition," in A. Goodwin and G. Whannel (eds), *Understanding Television*, London: Routledge.

Public Discourse/ Private Fascination

Hybridization in "True-Life-Story" Genres

IB BONDEBJERG

Hybridization—Decline of Public Television?

As a shared environment, television tends to include some aspect of every facet of our culture. . . . However, there is little that is new about any of the information presented on television; what *is* new is that formerly segregated information systems are integrated. (Meyrowitz, 1985:87).

12 June 1994 is not just a dramatic date in the life of one famous American football star, O. J. Simpson, but also a symbolic climax in the hybridization of public and private discourse on television. What millions of viewers could witness live was not a manhunt in a fiction crime series, but a live news broadcast, and what has followed since is neither a soap opera nor a courtroom drama, but an unfolding news story. In American culture, this courtroom drama has already exceeded all other major symbolic media-events, and is practically flooding most American media, both printed and visual. A cheap drama-doc production of O. J.'s life is already out on video, following his bestselling autobiography written in jail. The O. J. Simpson trial is by now a global true-life story bestseller on world television. But this piece of true life has all the qualities of fictional narrative and points to the rise of other dramatized factual forms on crime and social problems, in not just American but also European television.

From *Media, Culture and Society,* January 1996. Copyright © 1996 by Sage Publications. Reprinted by permission of the publisher.

Seminal American forms are: *Rescue 911,* where accidents are reconstructed and dramatized, *America's Most Wanted* or *Manhunter,* where crime investigations invite the viewer to play cop, talk shows like *Oprah Winfrey,* where family life and soft news items of human interest are brought to a public forum, or journalistic magazines like CBS's *48 Hours,* with dramatic crime themes and investigation of social distress in melodramatic form. From America, "true-life-story" genres have been exported and adapted to European formats, even in formerly very traditional public service cultures. Good examples are the Swedish magazine on accidents *SOS-liv eller död* (SOS—life or death), or the very successful British equivalent *999,* ZDF's crime-magazine *Actenzeichen XY—ungelöst* (started originally in 1967, but relaunched in the 1990s), the British *Crimewatch UK* (started 1984), the Danish and Swedish equivalents *Sagen uopklaret* (Case unsolved) and *Brottsplats* (Crime scene). One can add human interest or social documentaries, a rising genre on almost all European channels, or the true-life story journalistic magazines like the Danish *Damernes magasin* (Ladies magazine). The last form is part of an equally popular rise in more "open access" program types, a whole range of talk shows or more intimate talk-magazines focusing on private life and family matters, and often linked to a female host.

In all of these examples, tabloid journalism or soft, human interest journalism has arrived on television and private life stories have been lifted into public discourses, changing the established forms of journalism. At the same time new forms of television documentary—building on the documentary film tradition—have emerged, where hybridization of factual forms and fictional elements are found. It can either take the form of observational, voyeuristic images of "back stage" (Meyrowitz, 1985), social and private life, dramatized true-life narratives or highly meta-communicative forms of play with factuality and objectivity. The increase in forms with blurred borderlines and hybrid genre formats makes it all the more necessary to take a look at the interaction between private and public discourses and at the pragmatic dimension of reception.

Even though we need the distinction between fact and fiction, and it is very fundamental in our social and communicative behavior, it is also true that the difference is not basic on all levels. At a textual level, within segments of a text, it may be hard to draw a clear line, and even though the context, the communicative situation and the act of reference are different in most cases, it is also important to note that we use our real life categories and our basic experiences and schemas when we relate both to fictional and factual forms. Our use of, and response to, programs of a hybrid nature may influence both our public knowledge of social matters and our emotional, interpersonal understanding of life. Programs like these raise the question of how public discourse and private fascination are combined on the textual and experiential level of interaction between program and viewer (Bondebjerg, 1994).

On a macro-level, hybrid genres point to the possible and much discussed transformation of the public sphere. In the Habermas tradition, the hybridization of private and public discourse is often seen as a sign of simple decline, where the commercial powers of the system suppress the forces of the lifeworld (Habermas, 1987, 1989). But the development could also be seen as a result of the democratic impact of visual media on public discourse through a new *integration* of forms of public and private interaction which used to be clearly separated. Visual communication also consists of "displayed interactions" (Scannell, 1994) where social roles, forms of interaction and ways of talking and behaving are *publicly* broadcast to *private* viewers. The all-pervasive nature of television in public and private life over the last two decades, the growing tendency of being linked "live" to the world stage, both front and back (Meyrowitz, 1985), have changed the very concept of public and private. The hybridization of fiction and factual forms is not simply a question of the decline of public discourse, it is the arrival of old discourses in a new medium, and the creation of new public images of old forms of life-narrative and of talk.

In a way, then, it could be argued that what we are witnessing through hybridization and new reality and access genres is the democratization of an old public service discourse, dominated by experts and a very official kind of talk, and the creation of a new mixed public sphere, where common knowledge and everyday experience play a much larger role (Livingstone and Lunt, 1994). But in spite of this, there is a need for critical perspectives: dramatizing crime, personal problems and social issues in fascinating forms does not necessarily create the basis for public knowledge. There is still the question of balance, relevance and the question of putting things into appropriate perspectives and contexts. The blurred boundaries between factual forms and fiction, between private and public, should not be an invitation to relativism.

Crime: The Public and the Private Eye

In his new book, Norman Fairclough (Fairclough, 1995: 150ff) analyzes *Crimewatch UK* as a prototype of the kind of crime-magazines where crime reconstruction is used as a way of getting the public to help the police solve cases and be more on the alert against possible criminal acts. He has three main points in his analysis: first of all, that the generic formula is indeed a hybridization, where information, fact and public appeal are mixed with dramatization and fiction; second, that the programs offer a new kind of mixture of voices and discourses, where official, public language and *arguing* is merged with very private, everyday language and *experience,* with a tendency to push things towards the personal narratives (in reconstructions and interviews with victims, relatives and witnesses) as the core of the program. The third point follows from this mixing of discourses and linkage between a rhetoric of the factual and a more personal narrative:

> the ambivalent mix of reconstruction and re-enactment, and the mixing together of dramatized narrative and public appeal, resituate police work in the familiar and homely world of television entertainment. And the salience of a lifeworld discourse within the re-enactment, in the biograph-

ical elements and the dialogue, but also in the actual recounting of events in the testimony of witnesses, links policework with ordinary people and ordinary experience. (Fairclough, 1995: 168)

The program can be seen as a new way of restoring the eroded and crumbling relations between ordinary people and the state and official public sphere. In a positive view then, we have a new public sphere based on a broadening of discourses and representational forms of reality, a "truer" integration made possible by electronic means. But a more pessimistic view would point to this as mere legitimation and entertainment: only crimes of a certain kind are taken up, and a more critical context and perspective on crime in society is not presented here. What we get is a few cases of solved crimes, but for most of the audience this is just a fascinating thrill of witnessing what *could* happen to any person in everyday life, but luckily has not yet happened to you.

Crimewatch UK is clearly a public service crime magazine insofar as it does not overdo the dramatization sequences and is legitimized through the purpose of getting help from the public to solve crime (Schlesinger and Tumber, 1993, explore this aspect fully). The program does contain informational parts, that help us better understand both the nature and reason for crimes and the process of investigation, and it does try to contribute to the education of the public in stronger responsibility, participation and watchfulness. All these elements could also be found in news-programs or public appeals through other channels. The *Crimewatch UK* format is based on a few main cases, which are reconstructed according to a pretty firm and stable pattern: direct introduction by presenter, reconstruction of the case, interview with police, and concluding remarks from the presenter in which an appeal to the public is made. During the reconstruction (where actors are used) the voice of personal testimony is heard. In this way we get both the public official voice and the involved voices, and we see with both the public and the private eye so to speak; a private eye, not just of the amateur detective, neither just the safe, distant and anonymous TV-voyeur, but the private eye of those involved, the victims and their relatives whose stories are dramatized in front of us.

But apart from these reconstructions we also get the sense of a program at work, we get updates on earlier cases, and, usually at a later time the same day, a *Crimewatch Update*. This leaves the audience with the feeling of actually being part of an investigation, where interventions do matter. Throughout the program we also get shorter features called "Photocall," "Incident Desk" and "Aladdin's Cave," short segments where police present other cases without reconstructions, but with various forms of documentation. "Aladdin's Cave" is like the soft item at the end of a news program, in this case in the form of a presentation of stolen or unclaimed objects. Another program of this type is the long running German program *Aktenzeichen XY . . . Ungelöst,* a program that since 1967 and until the beginning of 1990 was one of the most popular programs in the ZDF Friday prime time schedule. The program is lead by a main presenter, Eduard Zimmermann from the Munich Studio, but with three other presenters in other studios. The formula is based on an update, a presentation of new cases either in short form or through longer reconstructions and a final summation given by the main presenter. Over the years, this program has often been criticized for causing more anxiety about crime in everyday life than necessary and for encouraging people to overreact as "stool pigeons." However, the program makers always point to the very high percentage of solved cases.

In 1989, just one year after the introduction of the new Danish channel TV2, a program like the British and German one appeared on the Danish channel 1, DR. The title was *Sagen uopklaret* (Case unsolved) and the formula was basically the same. In one of the first programs, from 30 April 1990, we follow three cases: arson on board the Danish ship, Scandinavian Star, where more than 100 people were killed, a robbery of a jewelery store and a bank robbery. The program opens with a very long introduction by the presenter, Hans Georg Møller, a well respected Danish journalist, placed in a studio which looks like a mixture of a public office and a police office.

The program's logo is very subdued when compared to both other European public service magazines and especially when compared to the American programs. The program is clearly linked to the News and Current Affairs Department and the address of these programs is used. The introduction clearly indicates this, we are carefully told about the structure and the aim of the program and the dominance of news codes is clear. The presenter is a classical anchor-person, just like Zimmermann in the German version, and he delegates exposition to several reporters, who guide us through the various cases and the interviews, visual investigations or later updates on the result of the appeal to viewers.

The first case, the arson, does not include any reconstructed scenes at all, probably the result of an ethical decision. Instead, we get what could have been an item in a news program or a longer thematic current affairs program. The reporter is at the scene of the crime, we get a tour through the burned-out premises, we talk to experts in fires, policemen on the case and we finish with an interview with two of the leading investigators in the studio. However, in the two following cases we get small reconstructed dramas, not very long and only briefly without the voice-over of the reporter. The fictional world is all the time controlled, and we are hardly allowed the uncommented-on experience of a closed, diegetic narrative universe. The fictional element is used as a form of illustration and information, and there is no direct confrontation with the witnesses or the victims. What they have to say is filtered through the more authoritative voice of the reporters.

This first Danish example clearly shows the still very controlled aesthetics of a traditional public service TV-culture, but nevertheless this new form of program was widely discussed, coming as it did directly after the breaking of monopoly and the introduction of commercial television in Denmark. Now, five years later, a much wider range of hybrid programs is not controversial, and on the new Danish channel TV2 (partly financed by license and partly by commercials) and the totally commercial TV3 (broadcasting from London and outside the jurisdiction of Danish law) a number of American programs have been introduced.

In programs on crime, a new series, *Sagen opklaret* (Case solved, 1995), went one step further in fictionalization. This time the program was not legitimized by the appeal to public participation in the solving of crimes, but authentic cases were used simply to tell dramatic stories and to tell about policework. The program does not differ very much from the kind of fictional crime series earlier made by the same department, Provinsafdelingen (the Provincial Department) of DR, a public service station. The episode of January 1995 called "Mordet i landsbyen" (The murder in the village) is typical. The opening sequences show the blue, blinking lights of a police car, then we see a number of items belonging to police and detective work. After this we are directly in a "reconstruction." The presenter, however, is seen addressing us both from the "outside," as an authoritative narrator, and from "inside," as an "on the spot" reporter.

We witness neighbors (like the rest of the reconstruction, all people are played by local amateur actors) finding the local grocer (an elderly woman) murdered by wounds in the head, and her grown-up grandchild very badly hurt upstairs in bed. After this the title comes up and a text is printed on the screen which in translation reads. "This program is based on police files on authentic cases. The criminal and the victims are played by local actors. But the policemen and women tell and act in their own stories." The focus then is on policework. Only the presenter steps outside the reconstruction of events as a narrator at the different sites of the crime, leading us from one scene to another, supplying comments. In the last part of the program the narrator acts as a reporter from the court where the son-in-law, who turns out to be the murderer, is sentenced to life imprisonment. The trial is not reconstructed but we get a reconstruction of the murder in the last part, this time with the actual encounter between murderer and victim.

It is perhaps characteristic that we don't see the actual killing. At the beginning of the piece this could be explained by the need for suspense, but at the end this is not the case. Compared to an American/European crime series the fictional story is guided by a more puritan and non-violent aesthetic. We don't get very many red herrings, the story and the policework quickly focus on one suspect, but the question is *how* they prove it and also the psychological motive for the crime. Basically, this is an educational case history, with a semi-factual narrator and with inter-textual loans from family melodrama and police-crime series.

Crime the American Way

This tendency in European public service television to use real crime cases to create docudrama and the aesthetic form of reconstruction is, however, much stronger on American television and on the more commercial European channels, which often carry these programs. In 1987 NBC launched the first of these crime hybridization programs called *Unsolved Mysteries*, but the new network Fox soon followed with *COPS* (1989–) and *America's Most Wanted* (1988–) continued with the same host, John Walsh, in *Manhunter* (1994–). *COPS* was clearly a new step towards involved reality television: a production team followed actual cops on their rounds, often at night and often in the worst neighborhoods. The tapes were edited to a format of 22 minutes without any narrator but with the actuality sound from the tapes and the voices of the police and the suspects involved, in a sense a piece of "television verité." There is actually no hybridization at work here, apart from the fact that the editing has a narrative structure, but this is the "real stuff" as it was recorded and then condensed, and it showed the most horrible side of violent criminal acts.

The voyeuristic qualities of such a program are obvious and it could be criticized for just this character of being "private eye on public affairs," without perspective, discussion or context. *Unsolved Mysteries* was the American equivalent to *Crimewatch UK* but, unlike this series, it not only dealt with crime, but also with reuniting missing persons, with supernatural things (like UFOs) and other mysteries and misfortunes. Normally the re-enactments were done according to Hollywood conventions, for instance in one elaborate recreation of the famous and still unsolved mystery of what became of the people behind the 1962 Alcatraz prison escape.

Often the American genres have a faster rhythm and less ethical reservations about what to show and how to show it: the aim is clearly more to entertain than to give information. A distinction could be made between a documentary program like *48 Hours* (CBS, 1988–) in which reconstruction is not normally a part, and where the aim is a journalistic, in-depth analysis of current affairs with a strong element of television verité in the reporting style, and a program like *Manhunter,* where dramatization and reconstructed crimes dominate. The host and anchor person in *48 Hours* is the CBS News anchor person Dan Rather. Speaking from a special news-desk he links together reporters on the case in various locations. The topic could be anything, but lately there has been a clear tendency to choose more sensational crime stories to investigate. However, this is nothing compared to the focus in *America's Most Wanted* and later *Manhunter,* where the host John Walsh is himself a professional manhunter for the FBI and has a personal background the main points of which are repeated at the start of each *Manhunter* episode. In 1981 his own six-year-old boy was kidnapped and murdered, and he decided to become a manhunter: in true American style the idea of public justice is here dramatically mixed with private revenge.

"Childhunter" (broadcast on the Danish TV3 1994) is a typical *48 Hours* episode of 50 minutes. It starts with a short montage of visual fragments and interviews from the program we are about to see, then follow the permanent logo and title sequence of the program, focusing on the reporters and Dan Rather, who gives his introduction from the news-desk. The program is divided into chapters of a metaphorical nature: "Cold Comfort," telling us about the Woods family and volunteers digging in the snow for clues that might lead to the finding of the body of their missing daughter, but also to the arrest of a possible suspect, the serial killer called "Child Hunter"; "Pied Piper," looking into the past of this serial killer, a nice guy whom nobody would suspect, but who suddenly began to show traces of a split personality; "Family Secret," getting us really close to an on-camera confession by his relatives about the sexual abuse they have all been victims of, abuse committed by the suspected killer's father.

The journalistic research, as can be seen, is clearly organized into a dramatic narrative, where "Family Secret" is the main clue. The last three chapters, "Shared Grief," "Teach Your Children" and "Cold Comfort" (once more), all function as concluding parts, setting the story in perspective and drawing from the case to reflect on more general public matters. The necessity to create family networks is stressed, the need for public education of children is underlined and in general family values are supported as a defense against this type of crime. The program is thus a classical, documentary program with human interest focus. It uses some elements of dramatic, narrative sequencing and the emphasis is very much on strong melodramatic moments, where investigators succeed in *breaking into* the private life of suspect and victim, revealing the psychological and emotional dimension behind a news headline. In this sense, the program fits into the overall tendency to mix discourses and to let the official voices and the voices of everyday life meet. However, this hybridization is done within the overarching formats of television verité and investigative journalism.

Manhunter, on the other hand, is clearly marked by strong hybridization and although the host, John Walsh, steps forward as an on-the-spot reporter, he is very much *staged* like a fictional character, embodying the action values of the crime fiction series. He speaks both as a public and private eye: "A manhunter is a hunter of men and women who have chosen to live on the wrong side of the law, I hunt criminals, I became a manhunter as . . . I track down people who escape without mercy. . . ." This media figure is both "one of them up there," he is tough, professional and efficient, but he is also "one of us," because it has *happened to him,* he knows what it is like through personal experience.

Apart from the focus on the reporter, the opening sequences of *Manhunter* use a very dramatic and fast paced montage of crime and manhunt as a signature for the program. In the episode "Inside Folsom Prison" (transmitted on Danish TV3, 1994), we focus on two escapes and the criminal acts committed by the two escapees. There is a use of reconstruction both of the crimes and the escape, occasionally accompanied by voice-over narration, by on-site commentary by Walsh or by interviews. Since the intention here is not actually to appeal for public help, but rather to tell a good action story with Walsh as the guide and hero, the reconstruction and format are different from the European crime magazines: this is entertainment lightly masked as journalism. However, the program also has genuine journalistic elements. Part of it is about Folsom Prison, where we follow the routines of the day and hear interviews with prison guards and inmates.

It is not surprising, seen in this perspective, that the O. J. Simpson case has had such an impact on American television and the American public, and that commercial European channels have been eager to broadcast this ultimate reality courtroom drama. In Denmark it is TV3 that broadcasts a program once a week called *Åben Rettergang* (Open Court), which for the last six months has been a concentrated version of the live TV-version of the trial. The transmissions started in January 1995, and in the first edition of the program, with Paul Gazan (a Danish journalist, originally from the Danish tabloid newspaper *Ekstrabladet*) as host, we see a clear shift in the rhetoric, a hybridization of public discourse on television. Paul Gazan's opening speech is in itself a piece of tabloid rhetoric: "Over the cafe-tables, at work and at home, everywhere people ask the same question: did this celebrated, black sports hero really murder his ex-wife, the mother of his children, that fateful June night in LA last year?"

The discourse is narrative, in dramatized present tense, it links up to everyday language but it also uses hyperbolic, literary language, and as he continues he combines sales talk and generic buzzwords: we can expect "intense drama, emotional outbursts, shocking details about the bestial murder etc . . . " and the lawyers are clearly staged and fictionalized as fictional TV stars, O. J.'s lawyers, for instance, are given the name "The Dream Team." Metaphors are strongly present in this case; later, when O. J. was trying the bloodstained gloves from the murder site to see if they would fit (they did not!) the press named it instantly "the Cinderella test."

Although only for the first week was the camera able to move and perform zooms, then being made immobile because by accident one of the jury members was filmed, the whole process of depiction seems to reflect with media saturated, mythical images and discourses linked to racial questions, family values and sexuality. As John Fiske has pointed out (Fiske, 1994), this case is a media event with strong ties to all the most pervasive public images in America of the 1990s, and it is the only known "not public" incident to have caused a break in all the major networks' planned schedules. The trial somehow seems to be the *ultimate* crime reality TV, with a strong element of meta-textual ritual where the whole hybridization of public and private is on trial.

The opening statement of the prosecution counsel strongly addressed this theme and made it central:

> He may be the best running back in American football—we have watched him run after planes in Hertz commercials. We have watched him with fifty-inch afrohair in *Naked Gun 3½*. We have seen him again and again, and we have come to think, that we know him. But what we have been seeing, Ladies and Gentlemen, is only the public persona, the face of the athlete, the face of the actor. It is not that public face that is on trial today. Like many men in public they have a public face, a public persona—and they also have a private face. And that is the face we will expose to you in this trial. The other side of O. J., the side you never met before. (quoted from the tape on Jan. 24 1995)

Just as these last words are spoken, we get a reaction shot of O. J.'s face, a clear fictional intervention from the supposed neutral witness: the camera.

This is also the case when the female prosecutor finished her part of the presentation and with deep sighs of emotion concluded on the *private* side of O. J., the dark other side of the male oppressor:

> On June 12 1994, after a violent relationship in which the defendant beat her, humiliated her and controlled her, after he took her youth, her freedom and her self-respect—just as she was trying to break free—O. J. Simpson took her very life as a last final act of ultimate control. (Quoted from same tape as above)

Just like other forms of hybridization in crime reality genres on TV, the transmission and the whole discourse surrounding the O. J. Simpson case point to a blurring of public and private spheres. This is not a new phenomenon, but it has been magnified by the centrality and reach of television in modern society on both a national and a global scale. O. J. has become a sort of fictional figure in the public European mind, without ever being a public hero in our private and local lives—he becomes a general media symbol. The effects of the trial are a symptom of the processes in the change of the public sphere analysed by Joshua Meyrowitz (Meyrowitz, 1985). As the discourse of the O. J. Simpson prosecutors indicates it *is* very difficult to separate the public and private in a culture dominated by visual mediation. Well-known people who appear in public seem to be persons in *another* way than before, where the public and the private person were more clearly separated.

The difference between public and private is blurred, and the discourses separating front stage behavior and backstage behavior become more and more complicated, since the private side is more open for inspection and private human qualities (bad or good) are more visible. The public sphere becomes a middle region, a place where a hybridization of public and private takes place and, as a consequence, the front stage behavaior must be managed more carefully and the back stage becomes more a "deep back stage." The O. J. Simpson case, with its whole symbolic rhetoric about who's on trial and its focus on the deep back stage persona of O. J. makes this process obvious, and that makes it a fascinating object for both the public and the private eye of an audience already used to hybridization. We know that the staging and dramatization and narrative reconstruction taking place in reality TV are just part of a construction taking place *all* the time, but still we are looking for a deeper, authentic dimension of reality. Fictional strategies in factual forms make it easier to get close to this other, deep, backstage reality.

Disaster, Illness, and Accidents: The Melodrama of Real Life

Just as American channels were the first to develop new reality genres concerning crime and to develop the format to the extreme in both entertainment and verité form, it was also the Americans who started the reality series on the melodrama of ordinary people hit by random disaster. These programs deal with the victims and the heroic deeds of those that saved them, both people with this as their job (police, firefighters, doctors, ambulance squads, etc.) and the ordinary heroes who happened to be there when fate struck. The seminal program is *Rescue 911,* created by CBS in 1989 and with William Shatner as its world-famous host. It is now broadcast in more than 50 countries all over the world, and has inspired a number of nationally produced programs, including the British *999* (started in 1992, BBC1).

The criminal reality magazines draw on formulas like action, adventure and crime fiction, in which there is a clear moral duality between good and bad and a clear structure for cleaning up and tracking down the bad. As audience we can actively take part, either directly or by identification with the hero, while at the same time experiencing the voyeuristic thrill of seeing the evil. The disaster reality program draws on melodrama. The identification here is basically the identification with an innocent victim, a victim who might be oneself, caught by random forces (nature, sickness etc.) which we cannot control. The fact that these programs deal with real people and real stories does not radically alter their psychological dimension.

The difference is, that being told that this is real, our identification and whole attitude towards the program makes the experience much stronger. In fiction we can identify more freely, because there is a distance: we know that what we see is just a metaphor for what might be reality. The difference is a difference in degree, not in kind. We relate to real people and real events in many factual genres with the same emotional and cognitive schemas as in fictional genres, though with a difference in the precise character of the relationship (see Bondebjerg, 1994; Branigan, 1992). Not even narrative structure makes a clear difference, since many things point to the existence of narrative structure as a deep-rooted structure in human understanding and problem solving (Mandler, 1984; Schank, 1990).

If, as I indicate here, fictional and factual formats are blurred in the way our mind, language and culture work, if we can easily switch from actual to hypothetical mode, and if even rational and scientific processes are often guided by metaphoric structures (see Johnson, 1987; Bondebjerg, 1994), then this puts a new light on hybridization. This is not necessarily a question of decline: factual genres and fictional ones are both rhetorical constructions that interpret reality according to certain rules. Reality exists and is out there, but we can only reach it on the basis of pragmatic rules in context. Both fact and fiction are important ways of talking about reality, and we need them and the difference between them in order to function. Therefore the way they are combined is important, but it is not in itself problematic to combine the two—on the contrary.

That the producers of programs like this basically see the combination as a means of getting hold of a bigger audience is beyond doubt, even in public service television. The appearance and growth of such programs are linked to the rise of commercial competition in broadcasting in the 1980s and 1990s. The producer of *999* put it very clearly from the start:

> We are using all the available film techniques to make engaging films that include non-documentary drama techniques. Once you would have done

it in a straight documentary way, but this is a way of making factual television more accessible to a big audience. (Powell et al., 1992: 32)

Kilborn (1994), who uses this quotation, examines the BBC's defense against criticism of programs like these for indicating a move towards commercialism; the defense is a compromise between public service and populist imperatives (Kilborn, 1994: 433). The question of documentary techniques and fictionalized techniques could also be seen from a reception point of view. Empirical, cognitive reception studies done by the Swedish researcher Birgitte Höijer (1992, 1992a, 1992b) indicate that there is a quite striking similarity between the kind of schemas and involvement used by viewers confronted with nationally-located realistic TV-fiction and nationally-located documentary programs.

All this does *not* mean that questions of trying to be accurate in factual programming and to be clear when using *either* one textual strategy *or* the other in a program using hybridization are unimportant. The pragmatic contract between the sender and receiver of the program is very important, and the credibility of communication is at stake here if television violates the pragmatic rules. But these rules do not per se prohibit certain forms of hybridization; it is a question of use in the particular program, and content and intentions are just as important as aesthetic form itself.

Rescue 911 normally can include both authentic sound—the actual call to the 911 number is almost always used—even if the rest of the story is reconstructed, and authentic visual material as well as reconstructed material. The contract with the viewer is secured at the beginning of the program, where a voice-over and texts tell us that: "This program contains true stories of rescues. All of the 911 calls you hear are real. Whenever possible the actual people have helped us reconstruct events as they happened." This means that normally we both see and hear the actual people involved in the reconstructions, they tell their own stories, often as voice-over narrators to reconstructed images. We are confronted with real people in narrated, fictional structures, a strong way of creating empathy, but they also speak to us in testimony, authentic voices facing the camera in interview position. The use of testimonial voices looking back on "then," the recreation of a fictional present tense "then," combined with the actual people "now" speaking about "then," creates both a dramatic tense and a security. The mode of the program is a combination of the emotionally charted portrayal of events (as in fictions with an unknown end) and, at the same time, the knowing of *what* happened and *how* things are dealt with and in the future might be avoided, as is usual in the telling of factual stories (see Corner, 1995: 28 ff).

The written contract at the start of the program is followed by the visual signature of the program, a careful mix of dramatic rescue pictures filmed with changing camera movements and fast paced montage. The music is exciting and the moment the title *Rescue 911* comes on the screen we are *in* the car driving to a rescue—the whole montage has a dramatic curve of its own, closing with an image of a mother hugging her child: we are safe, *everything went well.* The melodramatic effect of placing people at the near edge of disaster, followed by a last minute rescue is very strong here. Everyday life is given a much stronger dimension and meaning, often expressed in the final statement of the people involved: they have come closer to each other, they have learned to value life and to take care of what they have. This reworked perspective on the individual and everyday experience is the essence of melodramatic experience and aesthetics (see Elsaesser, 1987).

It is a dimension constantly recalled in the comments by the host, William Shatner, who walks towards us from his newsroom. The use of the newsroom, of course, indicates factuality: a factuality in which *ordinary* people, in contrast to their placing in hard news, are important. The hybridization, however, is also obvious, since this factual program is actually produced, as the credits tell us, by the CBS Entertainment Group. But Shatner's comments indicate how the powers of ordinary people can *grow* with the task, or how little things can become of very great importance. Before the first story in the episode used here (originally from 1993, broadcast 1994 on the Danish TV2) his comment is: "In an emergency situation an innocent error may quickly prove fatal"; before the second story: "when life is at stake, we may do things we have never done before."

The selected stories have a fairly predictable structure and quality: the American stories are not very often about accidents linked to work situations but most often take place in the private world, and they very often involve children. The structure follows the same pattern: first a fairly normal and idyllic situation, then suddenly everything is changed, we follow the panic, then the *heroic* powers of the ordinary are involved, after which professionals take over, and finally we have the conclusions and afterthoughts. In this particular episode we have three stories: a boy breaking his neck driving his three-wheel motorcycle, saved by his own brother and afterwards by supreme medical skills; a baby left alone for a short moment and almost drowned in the bathtub, but saved first by the mother guided to first aid over the phone and then again by doctors, and finally the story of how a mad bank robber taking hostages is caught without any shooting and killing thanks to one man's heroic deed.

In all the stories ordinary people play a crucial role before the professionals arrive, but then the professionals are also very much treated as people like us. This is most strongly shown in the second story about the drowning baby, where the 911 female phone operator receives the call, and calmly guides the emotionally distressed mother through the first-aid procedure. Her own testimonial is very powerful and she weeps in front of the camera. The affective dimension is strong in the program, but to call the program informational, as is done in Brooks and Marsh's directory of prime-time network programs (Brooks and Marsh, 1992) can also be defended. Information on a general human level is first of all imbedded in the emotional reliving of these incidents in itself, but, on top of that, all the stories contain more or less direct information and public guidance. In the first one the message is not to drive three wheelers, in the second one there is a public appeal for parents to take a first-aid course, and in the last story a warning *against* playing the foolhardy hero in criminal situations.

If we compare the American version with the European, public service versions, this is probably where they differ. *999* and the Swedish version *SOS—på liv eller död*, generally stress the informational side much more. In the 5 May 1995 episode of *999* this can be demonstrated in connection with almost all of the stories. The presenter and host Michael Buerk is much more active and thorough in his introduction and remarks, which also points to the dominance of the more factual codes. But also the way the stories unfold is generally more informational. The first story, about a man who is stabbed in the heart on the street and is actually almost dead by the arrival of the ambulance helicopter, develops into a story about the *techniques* of open heart surgery. The doctor who performed this first on-the-street oper-ation is portrayed in great detail, and he is on screen several times showing us on a model figure exactly *how* the surgery was done. A medical science genre merges with the true-life-story format.

This very strong element of popular scientific information is not in the other stories, but here we have a strong element of public appeal. In the second story, about a babysitter who saves a child because she has taken a first-aid course, the story in itself spells out the moral: take a first-aid course yourself and make sure you never leave your child in the care of someone who has not taken this course. This point is demonstrated in great detail with pictures and interviews with people on such a course. The same goes for a part of the program, following right after the story of a man who nearly drowned, called "Surf Rescue, Surf Patrol," where the public and children in particular (with the use of "Baywatch aesthetics"!) are urged to learn to swim and be able to do life-saving in the water. In the only Scandinavian version of this program so far, produced by the commercial channel TV4, the same tendency is clear. Although not produced by a public service sta-tion, the stories are muted and selective in dramatization and the part about the work of the professionals is detailed.

"Soft Items" in Female Discourse and Verité Style Documentary

Magazines on crime and rescue are not the only new type of reality pro-gramming on TV to rise to popularity in the 1980s and 1990s, and they are not the only way in which everyday life has taken a new position on television. If soft news and human interest used to be at the lower end of the prestige range then this has begun to change dramatically. Soft items on lifestyle, family problems, culture, private life, the bizarre, the perverted and social issues concerning all the "losers" of society play a much larger role in talk shows or other talk format magazines and new types of docu-mentary on television.

The melodrama of everyday life is also in focus in talk shows, like the *Oprah Winfrey Show* or the very successful Danish magazine *Damernes Ma-*

gasin inspired by the aesthetics of a serious women's weekly, and the features on private life and social problems which you can find in these weeklies. A whole series of female hosts has appeared on the Danish screens lately, often with a more bizarre and daring style than the normal talk shows. The same host as in *Damernes Magasin*, Camilla Miehe-Renard, later appeared in a Friday late-night talk show, *Ikke i aften, skat!* (Not tonight, Darling) on sexual behavior, and an already very well-known provocative female writer, Synnøve Søe, set a new standard in personal self-exposure on television, in which the intimate, personal form of the host's presentation created a new kind of private discourse in public form. On Italian television this tendency to make deep back-stage behavior and discourse visible and public on television has created a number of commercial programs with clear ethical problems. In *Lui, lei e l'altro* (He, her and the other) couples who have broken up are confronted, often with the person who was the cause for the divorce, and the interviewer will try to get the most private and detailed information "on the table" to provoke a confrontation. In *Perdonami* (Forgive me), following the cultural tradition of religious confessing, people are asked to confess bad actions or crimes on screen, and they are then confronted with the victims for a scene of forgiveness.

New forms of access programs will always run the risk of being brought over the ethical threshold (see Corner, 1994), but the question is whether these programs as a whole represent a danger or a step forward in the creation of a new kind of public forum. In Denmark a new documentary group was formed in DR in 1988 as a result of the stronger competition ahead. Since then, they have created a number of prize-winning documentaries, both on hard news topics like ordinary crime, financial crime, political scandals, institutional mistreatment of certain groups and on more social and human interest areas like drugs, alcohol misuse, prostitution, neglected children, the poor, the unemployed, the old and the lonely etc. Like the series of documentaries in Britain, *Breadline Britain,* on poverty (see Meinhof and Richardson, 1994), these programs gave a voice to people normally not heard in the media, but they were also criticized for staging and stereotyping social distress in a very individualized perspective with no general context.

The same discussion has also followed the series of programs made by the Dane Lars Engels on life in the hard urban neighborhood of Vesterbro, Copenhagen (see Bondebjerg, 1994: 77 ff). Together his five programs give a verité style but impressionistic image of the life of people on the not-so-sunny-side of the street. It is not claimed to be the whole truth, but aspects of authentic life told without any voice-over narration or explanations from a presenter, expert or authoritative narrator. In one of the programs, *Natlaeger* (Emergency doctors), we are pretty close to the authentic, observational equivalent of the rescue programs. We simply follow an emergency doctor on his nightly routine, we hear him commenting on what he sees, and we witness his visits to patients belonging to the most miserable clients in society. It is a very strong social document, in its form like a naturalistic fictional narrative, unfolding an impressionistic mosaic of voices, scenes, characters, dialogue, monologue etc. It could be a fictional film made in documentary style, but it is the edited version of actuality material.

These verité-style programs give access to the voice of the publicly invisible and to a degree go beyond the threshold of deep private space, just as the Italian ones do, however the intention and the ethical standard seem different: there seems to be a fundamental solidarity and social intention at work here, rather than the intention of sensation and entertainment. But we are walking a thin line, as we are in some of the talk shows and talk-magazines that deal with very private matters. The popularity of *Oprah Winfrey* lies in the way she makes ordinary people talk to each other about problems that are often publicly invisible or underestimated. Her focus is often on female problems and family life and therefore her program aims at the same public as soaps, and the problems that soaps often deal with are put into factual form here. There is no direct hybridization as far as "fact" and "fiction" go, but she unites the discourse of experts and ordinary people and one could say that she creates mini-narratives on the basis of ordinary life. The show thrives on the same fuel that fiction is made of.

This is also one of the elements in focus in Livingstone and Lunt's book *Talk on Television,* where they point to storytelling as one of the basic rhetorical structures in talk shows and audience participation programs. They even go so far as to indicate that the whole program can be seen in a fictional, narrative structure, with the host as hero and helper in relation to "our own" stories (Livingstone and Lunt, 1994: 54ff). The discourse of ordinary people *is* the story rather than the expert argumentation, and often the debate will take the form of examples. This is also the guiding principle in *Damernes magasin* on the Danish public service channel DR. The host, Camilla Miehe-Renard, is placed in a studio resembling a private apartment and the basic formula is the case history, where people with a special problem or a special experience are interviewed in a very intimate tête-à-tête form. There is only one case per program and sometimes only one person, but often the story from this person is set in perspective by interviews with close friends and relatives.

In the episode on alcoholics (January 1991) the main character is Anders, an alcoholic now well out of his misuse, but we also get interviews with his wife and a man whose wife was an alcoholic. The program lasts for half an hour, most of the time dedicated to the interviews. A controversial part of the program is interruptions, with short life-style segments on food, clothing etc., features that imitate the ads in a women's weekly. The stories, however, come out strongly, based as they are on a life-story format, where all the details, feelings and facts are laid open in front of us by people who have "come through to the other side" and therefore are experienced experts in particular everyday life problems. We *never* meet professional social workers, psychologists etc., and the interviewer is clearly a helper trying to be on the level with the people she is interviewing. Everyday experience is transformed from a private to a public forum.

The Private in the Public, the Public in the Private: Concluding Remarks

It is not possible to formulate one very negative or very positive conclusion on the true-life-story formats and the hybridization of recent television genres. One element in the explanation and evaluation of developments is clearly that what is taking place here is an updating of a paternalistic public service discourse to include a more democratic selection of topics and voices outside the traditionally defined area of public interest. The development of a more and more global and permanent electronic public sphere makes it obvious that "information once shared only among people of a certain age, class, religion, sex, profession or other subgroup of the sub culture has now been thrown into a public forum" (Meyrowitz, 1985: 87). The dominant middle-class, middle-of-the-road public service culture is doomed in this development.

On the other hand, these tendencies are also clearly a product of commercialism, of the exploitation of all areas of life for entertainment and for the benefit not of citizens but consumers. It is not easy to point to specific aesthetic tendencies that should be banned or that can only be connected with speculative, non-ethical purposes. Aesthetic formats and generic formulas can be used for a number of different purposes, and what may appear problematic in the version on one channel, could be judged perfect for versions on other channels. Different genres allow different forms of valuable knowledge and ways of combining fact and fiction, emotion, empathy and reflection, private and public. We should not criticize fictional elements in factual genres, just because they are fictional—both modes co-exist in our mind and our interpretation of the world.

If people become victims or targets of objectifying strategies and the conditions for communication are not clear we have ethical problems (see Corner, 1994). But even the most fictionalized factual programs can be of high ethical standard. To give access to many voices and discourses is of vital importance for public television, but this democratic goal should neither lead to populist disregard for the need for intellectual debate and factual precision, nor to a simple division of programs along class and educational lines. Hybridization programs are fascinating and important to discuss: they frequently try to bridge the gap between different discourses, genres and between the public in private and the private in the public.

References

Bondebjerg, Ib (1994) "Narratives of Reality: Documentary Film and Television in a Cognitive and Pragmatic Perspective," *Nordicom Review* 1: 65–87.

Branigan, Edward (1992) *Narrative Comprehension and Film*. London: Routledge.

Brooks, Tim and Earle Marsh (1992) *The Complete Directory to Prime Time Network Shows 1946–Present*. New York: Ballantine Books.

Corner, John (1994) "Mediating the Ordinary: The 'Access Idea and Television

Form,'" in M. Aldrich and N. Hewitt (eds) *Controlling Broadcasting*. Manchester: Manchester University Press.

Corner, John (1995) *Television Form and Public Address*. London: Edward Arnold.

Elsaesser, Thomas (1987) "Tales of Sound and Fury: Observations on the Family Melodrama," in Christine Gledhill (ed.) *Home Is Where the Heart Is*. London: BFI.

Fairclough, Norman (1995) *Media Discourse*. London: Edward Arnold.

Fiske, John (1994) *Media Matters*. Minneapolis: University of Minnesota Press.

Habermas, Jürgen (1987) *The Theory of Communicative Action 1–2*. Boston: Beacon Press.

Habermas, Jürgen (1989) *The Structural Transformation of the Public Sphere: An Inquiry Into a Category of Bourgeois Society*. Cambridge, MA: MIT Press.

Höijer, Birgitta (1992) "Socio-Cognitive Structures and Television Reception," *Media, Culture & Society* 14: 583–603.

Höijer, Birgitta (1992a) "Reception of Television Narration as a Socio-Cognitive Process: A Schema-Theoretical Outline," *Poetics* 21: 283–304.

Höijer, Birgitta (1992b) *TV-uppleverlser av fakta och fiktion*, Sveriges radio/PUB.PM report.

Johnson, Mark (1987) *The Body in the Mind: The Bodily Basis of Meaning, Imagination and Reason*. Chicago: Chicago University Press.

Kilborn, Richard (1994) "How Real Can You Get?: Recent Developments in 'Reality' Television," *European Journal of Television* 9: 421–39.

Livingstone, Sonja and Peter Lunt (1994) *Talk on Television*. London: Routledge.

Mandler, Jean Matter (1984) *Stories, Scripts and Scenes: Aspects of Schema Theory*. Hillsdale, NJ: Lawrence Erlbaum.

Meinhof, Ulrike H. and Kay Richardson (eds) (1994) *Text, Discourse and Context*. London: Longman.

Meyrowitz, Joshua (1985) *No Sense of Place*. New York: Oxford University Press.

Powell, R. et al. (1992) "Real to Real," *Broadcast* 9 April: 32.

Scannell, Paddy (1994) "Kommunikativ intentionalitet i radio og fjernsyn," *Mediekultur* 22: 30–40.

Schank, Roger (1990) *Tell Me a Story*. New York: Scribner.

Schlesinger, Philip and Howard Tumber (1993) "Fighting the War Against Crime," *British Journal of Criminology* 33(1): 19–31.

Defining Media Events

High Holidays of Mass Communication

DANIEL DAYAN and ELIHU KATZ

This [study] is about the festive viewing of television. It is about those historic occasions—mostly occasions of state—that are televised as they take place and transfix a nation or the world. They include epic contests of politics and sports, charismatic missions, and the rites of passage of the great—what we call Contests, Conquests, and Coronations. In spite of the differences among them, events such as the Olympic Games, Anwar el-Sadat's journey to Jerusalem, and the funeral of John F. Kennedy have given shape to a new narrative genre that employs the unique potential of the electronic media to command attention universally and simultaneously in order to tell a primordial story about current affairs. These are events that hang a halo over the television set and transform the viewing experience.

We call them collectively "media events," a term we wish to redeem from its pejorative connotations. Alternatively, we might have "television ceremonies," or "festive television," or even "cultural performances" (Singer, 1984). These telecasts share a large number of common attributes which we shall attempt to identify. Audiences recognize them as an invitation—even a command—to stop their daily routines and join in a holiday experience. If festive viewing is to ordinary viewing what holidays are to the everyday, these events are the high holidays of mass communication. Conceptually speaking, this [study] is an attempt to bring the anthropology of ceremony (Durkheim, 1915; Handelman, 1990; Lévi-Strauss, 1963; Turner, 1985) to bear on the process of mass communication.

Television Genres

Until very recently, television was thought to be saying nothing worthy of humanistic analysis. To propose that television—like the other media—deals in "texts" and "genres" seemed to be conferring too much dignity. Viewers were thought to be watching not programs but television. They were assumed to be passive and unselective, satisfied with stories intended for an undifferentiated audience with a short attention span. Social scientists studied television the way they had studied radio; they searched for mass response to persuasion attempts, or to the images of race, sex, or occupation, or to acts of violence. Some concentrated on long-run effects, taking note of the substitute environment with which TV envelops heavy viewers. Others focused on the effect of television on social institutions, such as politics.

Yet producers and audiences alike routinely assume the existence of television genres. The broadcasters themselves, and the TV listings in newspapers and magazines, regularly classify programs by type: news, documentary, sports, action, adventure, Western, situation comedy, soap opera, variety show, game show, talk show, children's cartoon, and the like. Researchers in mass communications employ these categories too, almost as uncritically. With the exception of soap opera that dates to radio (Herzog, 1941; Arnheim, 1944; Warner, 1962; Katzman, 1972; Modleski, 1982; Cassata, 1983; Cantor and Pingree, 1983; and Allen, 1985), very little serious work has been done on the characteristics of these forms, how they differ from one another, how they relate to corresponding forms in other media, what their messages are, and how these messages are communicated.

Systematic study of the news as a genre of broadcasting has recently begun to rival interest in the soap opera (Epstein, 1973; Tuchman, 1978; Fiske and Hartley, 1978; Schlesinger, 1978; Gans, 1979; Graber, 1984; Morse, 1985). Certain political forms—national conventions, presidential debates, political advertising—have also gained attention, and the situation comedy is having its day (Marc, 1989; Taylor, 1989). Still, until recently, and with only occasional exceptions, social studies of television have treated the medium as a whole or in terms of discrete stimuli, without paying serious attention to its component forms. The publications of Horace Newcomb (1974) in the United States and Raymond Williams (1975) in England represent major turning points in the mapping of television territory.

It is striking how different is the study of film. Cinema studies approach film with a literary perspective, as texts to be classified and decoded, sociologically, politically, and psychoanalytically.[1] The same kind of classificatory effort has been applied—although not always uncondescendingly—to the other genres of popular culture. In *Adventure, Mystery, Romance* (1976) John Cawelti elaborates on the dominant genres (he prefers to speak of formulas) of popular fiction. In adventure stories—chivalric tales, war novels, mysteries—Cawelti finds the message of triumph over death, injustice, and the dangerous enemy. The classic detective story stands out in his category of mystery and leads the reader to a desirable and rational restoration of order and of pacification of the unknown. Romance teaches the all-sufficiency of love, celebrating monogamy and domesticity.

Following Cawelti, Newcomb (1974) attempted to delve into the formulas of television. This was the first time, to our knowledge, that a scholar classified television programs systematically: he analyzed the programs in each category and generalized about what they had in common. In the process he proposed a much broader generalization: that television, as a medium, imposes an element of "familism" on each of the genres which it has inherited from the other media of popular culture. In other words, says Newcomb, the Western, the action adventure, and the detective story, not just the soap opera or the situation comedy, is domesticated by television as if to attune the medium as a whole to the nuclear family, television's original viewing group.

Television with a Halo

Even those like Williams and Newcomb, who pioneered in the classification of television genres, approach the viewing experience not in terms of discrete programs but in terms of the patterned sequences of stimuli (images, issues, messages, stories) that constitute an evening's viewing. They prefer to speak of "strips" (Newcomb and Hirsch, 1983), "flow" (Williams, 1975), compounded interruption (Houston, 1984), relentless messages (Gerbner et al., 1979), moving wallpaper, and mindless chewing gum (Hood, 1967; Csikszentmihalyi and Kubey, 1981).

Even if it is true that most of television melds into some such seamless "supertext" (Browne, 1984), there are certain types of programs that demand and receive focused attention (Liebes and Katz, 1990). Media events are one such genre. Unique to television, they differ markedly from the genres of the everynight.

Readers will have no trouble identifying the kinds of broadcasts we have in mind.[2] Every nation has them. Our sample of a dozen of these events, internationally, includes the funerals of President Kennedy and Lord Louis Mountbatten, the royal wedding of Charles and Diana, the journeys of Pope John Paul II and Anwar el-Sadat, the debates of 1960 between John Kennedy and Richard Nixon, the Watergate hearings, the revolutionary changes of 1989 in Eastern Europe, the Olympics, and others. We have studied accounts and video recordings of these events, and have ourselves conducted empirical research into five of them.[3]

The most obvious difference between media events and other formulas or genres of broadcasting is that they are, by definition, not routine. In fact, they are *interruptions* of routine; they intervene in the normal flow of broadcasting and our lives. Like the holidays that halt everyday routines, television events propose exceptional things to think about, to witness, and to do. Regular broadcasting is suspended and preempted as we are guided by a series of special announcements and preludes that transform daily life into something special and, upon the conclusion of the event, are guided back again. In the most characteristic events, the interruption is *monopolistic,* in that all channels switch away from their regularly scheduled programming in order to turn to the great event, perhaps leaving a handful of independent stations outside the consensus. Broadcasting can hardly make a more dramatic announcement of the importance of what is about to happen.

Moreover, the happening is *live.* The events are transmitted as they occur, in real time; the French call this *en direct.* They are therefore unpredictable, at least in the sense that something can go wrong. Even the live broadcast of a symphony orchestra contains this element of tension. Typically, these events are *organized outside the media,* and the media serve them in what Jakobson (1960) would call a phatic role in that, at least theoretically, the media only provide a channel for their transmission. By "outside" we mean both that the events take place outside the studio in what broadcasters call "remote locations" and that the events is not usually initiated by the broadcasting organizations. This kind of connection, in real time, to a remote place—one having major importance to some central value of society, as we shall see—is credited with an exceptional value, by both broadcasters and their audiences (Vianello, 1983). Indeed, the complexity of mounting these broadcasts is such, or is thought to be such, that they are hailed as "miracles" by the broadcasters, as much for their technological as for their ceremonial triumphs (Sorohan, 1979; Russo, 1983).[4]

The organizers, typically, are public bodies with whom the media cooperate, such as governments, parliaments (congressional committees, for example), political parties (national conventions), international bodies (the Olympics committee), and the like. These organizers are well within the establishment. They are part of what Shils (1975) calls the center. They stand for consensual values and they have the authority to command our attention. It is no surprise that the Woodstock festival—the landmark celebration of protesting youth in the sixties—was distributed as a film rather than as a live television event.

Thus, the League of Women Voters and the two major political parties organized the presidential debates in 1976 and 1980; the palace and the Church of England planned and "produced" the royal wedding; the Olympics are staged by the International Olympics Committee. There may be certain exceptions to this rule: the European Broadcasting Union organizes the annual Eurovision Song Contest, for example, and the Super Bowl—the American football championship—involves a direct organizational input on the part of American broadcasters. But on the whole, these events are not organized by the broadcasters even if they are planned with television "in mind." The media are asked, or ask, to join.

Of course, there may well be collusion between broadcasters and organizers, as was evident in the Gerald Ford–Jimmy Carter debate in Philadelphia, for example, when the TV sound failed and the ostensibly local meeting in a hired hall was suspended until the national broadcast could be resumed. And a state-operated broadcasting system (Poland, for example; *not* England or Israel) may be indistinguishable from the organizers. But the exceptions only serve to prove the rule.

These events are *preplanned,* announced and advertised in advance. Viewers—and, indeed, broadcasters—had only a few days notice of the exact time of Sadat's arrival in Jerusalem (Cohen, 1978); Irish television advertised the Pope's visit to Ireland a few weeks in advance (Sorohan, 1979); the 1984 Los Angeles Olympics were heralded for more than four years. Important for our purpose is that advance notice gives time for anticipation and preparation on the part of both broadcasters and audiences. There is an active period of looking forward, abetted by the promotional activity of the broadcasters.

The conjunction of *live* and *remote,* on the one hand, and *interrupted* but *preplanned,* on the other, takes us a considerable distance toward our definition of the genre. Note that live-and-remote excludes routine studio broadcasts that may originate live, as well as feature programs such as *Roots* or *Holocaust.* The addition of interruption excludes the evening news, while preplanned excludes major news events—such as the attempted assassination of a pope or a president, the nuclear accident at Three Mile Island, and, at first glance (but we shall reconsider this), the so-called television revolutions in Romania and Czechoslovakia. In other words, our corpus is limited to ceremonial occasions.

Returning to the elements of definition, we find that these broadcast events are presented with *reverence* and *ceremony.* The journalists who preside over them suspend their normally critical stance and treat their subject with respect, even awe. Garry Wills (1980) called media coverage of the Pope, including that of the written press, "falling in love with love" and "The Greatest Story Ever Told." He was referring to the almost priestly role played by journalists on the occasion, and we find a reverential attitude characteristic of the genre as a whole. We have already noted that the broadcast transports us to some aspect of the sacred center of the society (Shils, 1975).

Of course, the very flow of ceremonial events is courtly and invites awe. There is the playing of the national anthem, the funereal beat of the drum corps, the diplomatic ceremony of being escorted from the plane, the rules of decorum in church and at Senate hearings. The point is that in media events television rarely intrudes: it interrupts only to identify the music being played or the name of the chief of protocol. It upholds the definition of the event by its organizers, explains the meaning of the symbols of the occasion, only rarely intervenes with analysis and almost never with criticism. Often advertising is suspended. There are variations: the live broadcast of Sadat's arrival in Jerusalem was treated differently by Israeli television than by the American networks, which had more explaining to do (Zelizer, 1981). While we shall have occasion to point out these differences, they are outweighed by the similarities.

Even when these programs address conflict—as they do—they celebrate not conflict but *reconciliation*. This is where they differ from the daily news events, where conflict is the inevitable subject. Often they are ceremonial efforts to redress conflict or to restore order or, more rarely, to institute change. They call for a cessation of hostilities, at least for a moment, as when the royal wedding halted the street fighting in Brixton and the terror in Northern Ireland. A more permanent truce followed the journeys of Sadat to Jerusalem and the Pope to Argentina. These events applaud the *voluntary* actions of great personalities. They celebrate what, on the whole, are establishment initiatives that are therefore unquestionably *hegemonic*. They are proclaimed *historic*.

These ceremonials *electrify very large audiences*—a nation, several nations, or the world. They are gripping, enthralling. They are characterized by a *norm of viewing* in which people tell each other that it is mandatory to view, that they must put all else aside. The unanimity of the networks in presenting the same event underlines the worth, even the obligation, of viewing. They cause viewers to *celebrate* the event by gathering before the television set in groups, rather than alone. Often the audience is given an active role in the celebration. Figuratively, at least, these events induce people to dress up, rather than dress down, to view television. These broadcasts *integrate* societies in a collective heartbeat and evoke a *renewal of loyalty* to the society and its legitimate authority.

A More Parsimonious Approach to Definition

Despite its heaviness, we shall argue that the elements in our definition are "necessary," and that no subset of them is "sufficient" without the others.[5] This hypothesis does not mean that the elements cannot exist without one another, but they are not then what we call media events; they are something else.

Consider, for example, the *live* broadcasting of an event which is not *preplanned*—say, the live reporting of the leaking atomic energy plant at Three Mile Island (Veron, 1981). The leakage is a great *news* event, but not one of the great *ceremonial* events that interest us. Thus, we are interested here in the Kennedy funeral—a great ceremonial event—and not the Kennedy assassination—a great news event. The messages of these two broadcasts are different, their effects are different, they are presented in quite a different tone. Great news events speak of accidents, of disruption; great ceremonial events celebrate order and its restoration. In short, great news events are another genre of broadcasting, neighbor to our own, that will help to set the boundaries of media events.[6]

Consider an event that fails to *excite* the public or one that is not presented with *reverence* by the broadcasters. Such events do not qualify according to the definition, but they are particularly interesting because they suggest a pathology of media events, of which the former is an event "manqué" and the latter an event "denied" by the broadcasters. . . .

Thus, by converting the elements of the definition into a typology—where elements are variously present or absent, or present in varying degree—we can identify alternative genres of broadcasting that differ from one another by virtue of a particular element. Examination of these alternative forms and the conditions of their occurrence will help define our own events by providing boundary markers.

One additional operation, methodologically speaking, can be performed on the definition. By transforming the elements into variables, one can note which elements correlate with which others. Doing so, one might ask whether, say, the degree of *reverence* invoked by the presenter correlates with the degree of viewer *enthrallment*.

Presentation of the genre can be formulated more elegantly, by grouping the elements of the definition into broader categories. The linguistic categories of syntactics, semantics, and pragmatics are useful for this purpose.

Syntactically, media events may be characterized, first, by our elements of interruption, monopoly, being broadcast live, and being remote. These are components of the "grammar" of broadcasting. The cancellation of regularly scheduled programs and the convergence of channels are the most dramatic kinds of punctuation available to broadcasters. They put a full stop to everything else on the air; they combine the cacophony of many simultaneous channels into one monophonic line. Of course, these elements also carry semantic meaning: they speak of the greatness of the event. And they have a pragmatic aspect as well: the interruption of the sequence of television puts a stop to the normal flow of life.

The live and remote broadcast takes us back and forth between the studio and some faraway place. Such broadcasts employ special rhetorical forms and the technology required to connect the event and the studio. The language is the language of transportation—"We take you now to . . . " Both pictures and words are slowed to a ceremonial pace, and aesthetic considerations are unusually important. The pictures of media events, relative to their words, carry much more weight than the balance to which we are accustomed in the nightly news, where words are far more important than pictures (Altman, 1986; Katz, Adoni, and Parness, 1977). The centrality of these various elements of syntax is immediately apparent when one compares the event itself to each subsequent representation of the event—the wrap-up, the news, and the eventual anniversaries: length is drastically cut; pace is speeded up; words reassert their importance; references to the heroic logistics of the broadcast disappear. Syntactic unpredictability (that matches the semantic uncertainty) is smoothed over.

The fact that the event is situated *outside* broadcasting organizations, both physically and organizationally, implies a network of connections that differ from the everyday. The specialists of outside broadcasting deploy their OB units—as the British call them—and the studio now serves as intermediary between its people in the field and the audience, allowing some of the dialogue of stage directions between studio and field to become part of the spectacle. Their cadence is *reverential* and *ceremonial*.

The interruption, when it comes, has been elaborately advertised and *rehearsed.* It entails a major commitment of manpower, technology, and resources on the part of organizers and broadcasters. It comes not as a complete surprise—as in major newsbreaks—but as something long anticipated and looked forward to, like a holiday. In order to make certain that the point of this ritual framing will not be lost on the audience, the broadcasters spend hours, sometimes days, rehearsing the audience in the event's itinerary, timetable, and symbolics. Even one-time events can be ritualized in this way.

The meaning of the event—its semantic dimension—is typically proposed by its organizers and shared by the broadcasters—although this point requires elaboration. . . . Of course, each event is specific in this regard. For example, the royal wedding was proposed as a Cinderella story, the moon landings as the new American frontier, and the papal diplomacy as a pilgrimage. Regardless of the specifics of each event, the genre as a whole contains a set of core meanings, often loudly proclaimed. Thus, all such events are hailed as *historic;* they strive to mark a new record, to change an old way of doing or thinking, or to mark the passing of an era. Whether it is the Olympics or Watergate, Sadat or the Pope, the turning-point character of the event is central.

The event features the performance of symbolic acts that have relevance for one or more of the core values of society (Lukes, 1975). By dint of the cooperation between organizers and broadcasters, the event is presented with *ceremonial reverence,* in tones that express sacrality and awe.

The message is one of *reconciliation,* in which participants and audiences are invited to unite in the overcoming of conflict or at least in its postponement or miniaturization. Almost all of these events have heroic figures around whose *initiatives* the reintegration of society is proposed.

Pragmatically, the event *enthralls very large audiences.* A nation or several nations, sometimes the entire world, may be stirred while watching the superhuman achievement of an Olympic star or an astronaut. Sadat electrified the people of Israel, and the Pope revived the spirit of the Polish people. These are thrilling events, reaching the largest audiences in the history of the world. They are shared experiences, uniting viewers with one another and with their societies. A *norm of viewing* accompanies the airing of these events. As the day approaches, people tell one another that viewing is obligatory, that no other activity is acceptable during the broadcast. Viewers actively *celebrate,* preferring to view in the company of others and to make special preparations—unusual food, for example—in order to partake more fully in the event.

The genre is best defined, then, at the intersection of the syntactic, the semantic, and the pragmatic. And, as was argued above, we shall contend that all three elements are "necessary." If we chose to apply the pragmatic criterion alone, the events so defined would include television programs that enthralled very large audiences, such as the early miniseries or perhaps even key episodes of programs such as *Dallas.* They might also include films that attracted large, sometimes cultish audiences such as the *Rocky Horror Picture*

Show or *Woodstock;* these were indeed compulsory viewing for certain segments of the population and invited widespread participation. If syntactics were the sole criterion, major news events would demand to be included. By the same token, if the genre were defined in terms of the semantic alone, we should number among media events all those films and programs that claim to be historic, preach reconciliation, celebrate initiative, and are produced and presented with reverence. Films of the Olympics by Leni Riefenstahl, Kon Ichikawa, or Claude Lelouch, for example, might therefore qualify.

Hence our insistence on defining the corpus of events in terms of all three linguistic categories, an insistence further justified by the fact that we are dealing with ceremonial performances and that no such performance can be described in terms of its text alone. A ceremony interrupts the flow of daily life (syntactics); it deals reverently with sacred matters (semantics); and it involves the response (pragmatics) of a committed audience.

Why Study Media Events?

Implicit in this definition of the genre are answers to the question, Why study media events? The student of modern society—not just of television—will find a dozen or more powerful reasons for doing so. Let us spell them out.

1. The live broadcasting of these television events attracts the *largest audiences in the history of the world.* Lest we be misunderstood, we are talking about audiences as large as 500 million people attending to the same stimulus at the same time, at the moment of its emission. It is conceivable that there were cumulative audiences of this size prior to the electronic age— for the Bible, for example. Perhaps one might have been able to say that there were several hundred million people alive on earth who had read, or heard tell of, the same Book. But it was not until radio broadcasting—and home radio receivers—that simultaneity of exposure became possible. The enormity of this audience, together with the awareness by all of its enormity, is awesome. It is all the more awesome when one realizes that the subject of these broadcasts is ceremony, the sort which anthropologists would find familiar if it were not for the scale. Some of these ceremonies are so all-encompassing that there is nobody left to serve as out-group. "We Are the World" is certainly the appropriate theme song for media events. To enthrall such a multitude is no mean feat; to enlist their assent defies all of the caveats of media-effects research.[7]

2. The power of these events lies, first of all, in the rare *realization of the full potential of electronic media technology.* Students of media effects know that at most times and places this potential of radio and television are capable of reaching everybody simultaneously and directly; their message, in other words, can be total, immediate, and unmediated. But this condition hardly ever obtains. Messages are multiple; audiences are selective; social networks intervene; diffusion takes time. On the occasion of media events, however, these intervening mechanisms are suspended. Interpersonal networks and diffusion processes are active before and after the event, mobi-

lizing attention to the event and fostering intense hermeneutic activity over its interpretation. But during the liminal moments, totality, and simultaneity are unbound; organizers and broadcasters resonate together; competing channels merge into one; viewers present themselves at the same time and in every place. All eyes are fixed on the ceremonial center, through which each nuclear cell is connected to all the rest. Social integration of the highest order is thus achieved via mass communication. During these rare moments of intermission, society is both as atomized and as integrated as a mass-society theorist might ever imagine (Kornhauser, 1959).

3. Thus, the media have power not only to insert messages into social networks but to create the networks themselves—to atomize, to integrate, or otherwise to design social structure—at least momentarily. We have seen that *media events may create their own constituencies*. Egypt and Israel were united for Sadat's visit not only by images of the arrival of the leader of a theretofore hostile Arab nation, but by means of an ad hoc microwave link between the broadcasting systems of the two countries.[8] Similarly, the royal wedding reunited the British Empire, and Third World nations joined the first two worlds for the Olympics. That media events can talk over and around conventional political geography reminds us that media technology is too often overlooked by students of media effects in their distrust of hypotheses of technological determinism. Papyrus and ancient empire, print and the Protestant Reformation, the newspaper and European nationalism, the telegraph and the economic integration of American markets are links between attributes of communication technologies and social structures. They connect portability, reproducibility, linearity, simultaneity, on the one hand, to empire, church, nation, market, on the other.

By extension, it can be seen that the "center" of these media-engendered social structures is not bound by geography either. In the case of media events, the center—on which all eyes are focused—is the place where the organizer of a "historic" ceremony joins with a skilled broadcaster to produce an event. In this sense, Britain is often the center of the world; one has only to compare the broadcast funeral of the assassinated Mountbatten with the broadcast funeral of the assassinated Sadat or India's Indira Gandhi to understand why.

4. Conquering not only space but time, media events have the power to declare a holiday, thus to play a part in the *civil religion*. Like religious holidays, major media events mean an interruption of routine, days off from work, norms of participation in ceremony and ritual, concentration on some central value, the experience of communities and equality in one's immediate environment and of integration with a cultural center. The reverent tones of the ceremony, the dress and demeanor of those gathered in front of the set, the sense of communion with the mass of viewers, are all reminiscent of holy days. The ceremonial roles assumed by viewers—mourner, citizen, juror, sports fan—differentiate holiday viewing from everyday viewing and transform the nature of involvement with the medium. The secret of the

effectiveness of these televised events, we believe, is in the roles which viewers bring with them from other institutions, and by means of which passive spectatorship gives way to ceremonial participation. The depth of this involvement, in turn, has relevance for the formation of public opinion and for institutions such as politics, religion, and leisure. In a further step, they enter the collective memory.

5. *Reality is uprooted* by media events. If an event originates in a particular location, that location is turned into a Hollywood set. The "original" is only a studio. Thus conquering space in an even more fundamental way, television causes events to move off the ground and "into the air." The era of television events, therefore, may be not only one in which the reproduction is as important as the original, as Benjamin (1968) proposed, but also one in which the reproduction is more important than the original.

Sometimes the original is inaccessible to live audiences because it is taking place in London, or because it is taking place on the moon, for example. Even more fundamental are those events that have no original anywhere because the broadcast is a montage originating in several different locations simultaneously. The "reality" of Kennedy's debating Nixon when one was in New York and the other in California is not diminished for its being in the air, and in the living room. Prince Charles, at the church, is waiting for Lady Diana as her carriage is drawn through the streets of London. This is reality. But it is an invisible reality that cannot be apprehended as such because it is happening simultaneously at different places. No one person can see all of it, that is, except the television director and hundreds of millions in their homes.

6. The process of producing these events and telling their story relates to the arts of television, journalism, and narration. Study of the rhetorical devices for communicating festivity, enlisting participation, and mobilizing consensus demands answers to the questions of how television manages to project ritual and ceremony in the two-dimensional space of spectacle. Essential to an understanding of these events—in addition to the readiness of the audience to assume ceremonial roles—is an analysis of how the story is framed, how interest is sustained, how the event aggregates endorsements, how the broadcasting staff is deployed to give depth to the event, how viewers interact with the screen, what tasks are assigned to the viewers. Media events give insight into the *aesthetics of television production,* together with an awareness of the nature of the contract that obtains between organizers and broadcasters.

The audience is aware of the genre of media events. We (and certain fellow researchers) recognize the constituent features of this rare but recurrent narrative form, and so do producers and viewers. The professional networks of producers buzz with information on the extraordinary mobilization of manpower, technology, aesthetics, and security arrangements required to mount a media event.[9] At the same time, the networks of viewers carry word of the attitudes, rehearsals, and roles appropriate to their celebration. The expectation that certain events in the real world will be given media-events treatment is proof of public awareness of the genre. Israelis appealed to the High Court of Justice demanding that the war-crimes trial of John Demjanjuk be broadcast live.[10]

7. Shades of *political spectacle.* Are media events, then, electronic incarnations of the staged events of revolutionary regimes and latter-day versions of the mass rallies of fascism? We think not, even if they might seem to be. It is true that media events find society in a vulnerable state as far as indoctrination is concerned: divided into nuclear cells of family and friends, disconnected from the institutions of work and voluntary association, eyes and ears focused on the monopolistic message of the center, hearts prepared with room. This is reminiscent, *mutatis mutandis,* of the social structure of a disaster that strikes at night, or of a brainwashing regimen. The threshold of suggestibility is at its lowest the more isolated the individual is from others, the more accessible he or she is to the media, the more dependent the person is, the more the power to reward conformity or punish deviation is in the hands of the communicator.

Nevertheless, media events are not simply political manipulations. Broadcasters—in Western societies—are independent of, or at least legally differentiated from, government. They can, and sometimes do, say no to an establishment proposal to mount an event. Journalists need convincing before suspending professional disbelief, and even commercial interest sometimes acts as a buffer. Second, public approval is required for an event to succeed; official events cannot be imposed on the unwilling or unbelieving. Third, individuals are not alone, not even alone with family, but in the company of others whom they invite to join in the thrill of an event and then to sit in judgment of it. Some societies provide public space for such discussion and interpretation; others provide only living rooms and telephones. Family friends, home, and living-room furniture are not a likely context for translating aroused emotion into collective political action. Fourth, the audience, too, has veto power. Oppositional readings are possible and hegemonic messages may be read upside down by some. These checks and balances filter the manipulative potential of media events and limit the vulnerability of mass audiences.[11]

Still, the question of hegemonic abuse must be asked continually. Almost all of these events are establishment initiated, and only rarely, one suspects, do the broadcasters say no. Instead, journalists—sometimes reluctantly—put critical distance aside in favor of the reverent tones of presenters. Broadcasters thus share the consensual occasion with the organizers and satisfy the public—so we have hypothesized—that they are patriots after all.

8. When media events are seen as a *response to prior events* or to social crisis, the link to public opinion is evident. Thus, certain media events have a commemorative function, reminding us—as on anniversaries—of what deserves to be remembered. Others have a restorative function following social trauma. The most memorable of them have a transformative function inasmuch as they illustrate or enact possible solutions to social problems, sometimes engendering yet further events which actually "change the world."

In the restorative domain, media events address social conflict—through emphasizing the rules (as in Contests), through praising the deeds of the great in whom charisma is invested (Conquests), and through celebrating consensual values (as do Coronations).

9. At the same time, certain events have an *intrinsically liberating* function, ideologically speaking; they serve a transformative function. However hegemonically sponsored, and however affirmatively read, they invite reexamination of the status quo and are a reminder that reality falls short of society's norm. Taking place in a liminal context, evoking that climate of intense reflexivity which Victor Turner characterized as the "subjunctive mode of culture," their publics exit the everyday world and experience a shattering of perceptions and certainties. Even if the situations in which they are immersed are shortlived and do not institutionalize new norms, at least they provoke critical awareness of the taken-for-granted and mental appraisal of alternative possibilities. They possess a normative dimension in the sense of displaying desirable alternatives, situations which "ought to" exist but do not. These are previews, foretastes of the perhaps possible, fragments of a future in which the members of society are invited to spend a few hours or a few days. Activating latent aspirations, they offer a peek into utopia.

10. One wonders whether the media-events genre is not an expression of a *neo-romantic desire for heroic action* by great men followed by the spontaneity of mass action. In this sense, media events go beyond journalism in highlighting charisma and collective action, in defiance of established authority. The dissatisfaction with official inaction and bureaucratic ritualism, the belief in the power of the people to do it themselves, the yearning for leadership of stature—all characterize media events. We can join Sadat or the Pope and change the world; the people can unite to save Africans from starvation by supporting "Live Aid." The celebration of voluntarism—the willful resolve to take direct, simple, spontaneous, ostensibly nonideological action—underlies media events, and may indeed constitute part of their attraction. The desire for spontaneous action, of course, recalls the erratic rhythm of arousal and repose predicted by the theory of mass society (Kornhauser, 1959). In the telling of media events, establishment heroes are made to appear more defiant than they actually were. But media events and collective action may be more than a dream. The escalation of interaction among public opinion, new or old leadership, and the mass media fanned the revolutions of Eastern Europe in the fall of 1989.[12]

11. The *rhetoric of media events* is instructive, too, for what it reveals not only about the difference between democratic and totalitarian ceremonies, but also about the difference between journalism and social science, and between popular and academic history. The media events of democracies—the kind we consider here—are persuasive occasions, attempting to enlist mass support; they take the form of political contests or of the live broadcasting of heroic missions—those that invite the public to embrace heroes who have put their lives and reputations on the line in the cause of a proposed change.[13] The ceremonies of totalitarian societies (Lane, 1981)

are more commemorative. They also seek to enlist support, but for present and past; the First of May parade was a more characteristic media event in postwar Eastern Europe (Lendvay, Tolgyesi, and Tomka, 1982) than a space shot.[14] Terrorist events contrast with both of these in their display not of persuasion but of force, not of majesty but of disruption and provocation.

The rhetoric of media events contrasts—as does journalism, generally—with academic rhetoric in its emphasis on great individuals and apocalyptic events. Where social science sees long-run deterministic processes, journalism prefers heroes or villains who get up one morning resolved to change the world. Where academic historians see events as projective as underlying trends, journalists prefer a stroboscopic history which flashes dramatic events on and off the screen.

12. Media events *privilege the home.* This is where the "historic" version of the event is on view, the one that will be entered into collective memory. Normally the home represents a retreat from the space of public deliberation, and television is blamed, perhaps rightly, for celebrating family and keeping people home (Newcomb, 1974). When it is argued that television presents society with the issues it has to face, the retort, "narcotizing dysfunction"—that is, the false consciousness of involvement and participation—is quick to follow (Lazarsfeld and Merton, 1948). Yet the home may become a public space on the occasion of media events, a place where friends and family meet to share in both the ceremony and the deliberation that follows. Observational research needs to be done on the workings of these political "salons." Ironically, critical theorists, newly alert to the feminist movement, now see in the soap opera and other family programs an important "site of gender struggle," and their derision of the apolitical home is undergoing revision.

But there is more to politics than feminism, and we need empirical answers to the question of whether the home is transformed into a political space during and after a media event. In fact, we need basic research on who is home and when (in light of the growing number of one-and two-person households), who views with whom, who talks with whom, how opinion is formed, and how it is fed back to decision-makers. These everyday occasions of opinion formation should then be compared with media events. It is hard to believe, but nevertheless true, that the study of public opinion has become disconnected from the study of mass communication.

13. Media events preview the *future of television.* When radio became a medium of segmentation—subdividing audiences by age and education—television replaced it as the medium of national integration. As the new media technology multiplies the number of channels, television will also become a medium of segmentation, and television-as-we-know-it will disappear. The function of national integration may devolve upon television ceremonies of the sort we are discussing here. By that time, however, the nation-state itself may be on the way out, its boundaries out of sync with the new media technology. Media events may then create and integrate communities larger than nations. Indeed, the genre of media events may itself

be seen as a response to the integrative needs of national and, increasingly, international communities and organizations.

Certain multinational interests have already spotted the potential of international events and may sink the genre in the process. Some combination of the televised Olympics and televised philanthropic marathons inspired the effort to enlist worldwide aid to combat famine in Africa. Satellite broadcasters already transmit live sports events multinationally (Uplinger, 1990; but see Mytton, 1991). Aroused collective feeling must be a great lure to advertisers, and one wonders whether the entry of the commercial impresario into the arena of these events does not augur ill for their survival as necessarily occasional, and heavily value-laden, "high holidays."

Notes

1. The typologies of relationship among storyteller, camera, actors, and audience have all been carefully dissected. And the ideological implications of changes within and among film genres—for continuity and change in values and social structure—have been the subject of continuous speculation. Somehow cinema studies have fallen to the humanist and broadcasting to the social scientist. The rich theorizing of the humanist and the careful empiricism of the social scientist are only now being combined in the analysis of television. The humanists have found interest (and at last legitimacy) in the study of television, and certain social scientists have responded by building conceptual bridges and methods to facilitate joint work (for example, Schudson, 1978). It was in the aftermath of the antiestablishmentarianism of the 1960s that this began to happen, with the politicization of media studies. It led to a renewal of the dialogue between humanists and social scientists that characterized the early days of the study of mass communication, and to renewed interest in critical schools of media studies such as the German-American Frankfurt School, American "cultural studies," and the work of the semiologists in France.

2. The earliest postwar examples include the American presidential conventions of 1948 and 1952, the return of General Douglas MacArthur from the Pacific in 1951, Senator Estes Kefauver's hearings on crime the same year, the inaugurations of Harry Truman and Dwight Eisenhower, Truman's guided tour of the White House in 1952, and, most memorable of all, the coronation of Elizabeth II on June 22, 1953. For details on the broadcasts of these events, see Russo (1983). The analysis by Lang and Lang (1953) of the MacArthur Day procession is the pioneering classic of media-events research.

3. We observed and collected relevant material on the occasion of the first presidential debates (Katz and Feldman, 1962), Sadat's journey to Jerusalem (Katz, Dayan, and Motyl, 1983), and the royal wedding (Dayan and Katz, 1982). We went to Poland to examine materials on the Pope's first visit (Dayan, Katz, and Kerns, 1984). One of our colleagues made an empirical study of the television audience of the 1984 Olympics (Rothenbuhler, 1985, 1988, 1989).

4. Russo's (1983) dissertation sketches the organizational and technological solutions to the problems of the live broadcasting of special events from remote locations. He shows, for example, how the series of space shots stimulated important developments in video technology that were subsequently employed in quite different contexts, such as coverage of the Kennedy assassination and funeral. We shall repeatedly draw on Russo's work.

5. Huizinga (1950) and Caillois (1961) face the same sort of problem with their multifaceted definition of play. Their definition is an overview of the different types of games. Thus, play is an activity (1) entered voluntarily (except when ceremonial roles or social pressures force participation); (2) situated "outside" ordinary life and accompanied by an awareness of its "unreality"; (3) intensely absorbing to the participants; (4) bounded in time and space; (5) governed by rules of order; (6) uncertain of outcome; and (7) promoting the formation of social groupings. Some of these elements also define media events; others are characteristics of ordinary television viewing (Stephenson, 1967). The problems of specifying the social conditions that give rise to play, the types of play, and the function of play for individual and society are closely related to the problems that confront the present project.

6. Russo (1983, p. 42) distinguishes three genres of television news—regular news, documentaries, and special events—but does not make the distinction between major news events and major ceremonial events that is central to our argument. "Special events broadcasting," Russo's subject, "refers to a genre or type of news coverage which deals with live origination of a major news story."

7. The appendix to [*Media Events,* Dayan and Katz, 1992] attempts to compare the effects of media events with those highlighted in the various traditions of research on media effects.

8. President Sadat's visit to Jerusalem was covered by an unprecedented number of newspapers and broadcasting organizations, mobilizing about 1,500 newsmen—580 from the United States alone. The live broadcast began at Ben Gurion Airport on Saturday night, November 19, 1977. Television followed the visitor and his hosts almost continually for most of the forty-four hours of his visit, to sites such as the Al Aqsa mosque, the Yad Vashem memorial, the Church of the Holy. Sepulchre, and, most important, to his address before the Knesset. The live pictures provided by Israeli television were relayed to Egypt and to Western broadcasting organizations, which supplied their own commentaries and experts including Abba Eban (ABC) and John Kissinger (NBC). American television journalists played catalytic roles, beginning with Walter Cronkite's parallel interviews with Menachem Begin and Anwar el-Sadat on the eve of the visit. While the visit was in progress, exclusive joint interviews of the two protagonists were broadcast by CBS (Walter Cronkite), NBC (John Chancellor), and ABC (Barbara Walters). Egyptian television produced a live broadcast of Sadat's triumphant return to Cairo, which was relayed to Israel over the microwave link, with a commentary in Hebrew by an Egyptian broadcaster. Audiences for the broadcasts included almost all Israelis; only 3 percent recalled that they did not view the arrival ceremony (Israel Institute of Applied Social Research [Peled], 1979). It is estimated that perhaps 3 million Arab viewers saw Israeli television from across the border, and Israeli radio claimed 50 million Arab listeners. In the United States, the Knesset speech attracted an estimated 30 million viewers (Nasser, 1978), and in France, 58 percent of a 1978 viewing panel reported having seen at least part of the trip (Centre d'Etudes d'Opinion, 1981). Two years later, 87 percent of Israelis thought that it was "important" for them to have seen the live broadcast, and 94 percent of them thought it a "historic moment" (Peled, 1979).

9. In anticipation of the Pope's visit in 1979, Irish television (Radio Telefis Eirann) consulted the prior experience of Poland and Mexico. Equipment valued at 12 million pounds and including forty-four cameras was assembled for the occasion, in the biggest collective effort RTE had ever made (Sorohan, 1979; Gleeson, 1979). Russo (1983, p. 320) estimated that the Kennedy assassination and funeral involved virtually all of the 2,000 employees of the three U.S. network news organizations,

at a cost of perhaps $32 million. The BBC's royal wedding required some sixty television cameras in the largest outside-broadcasting operation in its history (Griffin-Beale, 1981). Media events involve a huge amount of sharing and pooling of equipment among broadcasters. A great sense of pride in the "miracle" of accomplishment typically follows these events (Sorohan, 1979; Todorovic, 1980).

10. The trial of Adolf Eichmann, recorded on film by Alan Rosenthal, was later transferred to videotape but was not broadcast during the period of the trial.

11. Compare Martin's (1969, p. 93) discussion of the checks on divinely validated temporal power when the church—like the media, in the case of media events—has "the capacity both to compound and challenge . . . temporal authority." Martin points to "institutional checks," "symbolic checks," and, rather in despair, to the conclusion that restraint "is realized less in those who perform the acts of temporal and spiritual union than by those suffering and excluded groups who recognize that an ideal has been violated. It is the poor and meek of the earth who realize that crucial limiting concepts are available whereby they can assert the crown rights of the Redeemer against the rights of the crown." For a conclusion opposite to the one drawn here, see Zelizer (in press).

12. The Live Aid event was broadcast on July 13, 1985. It originated from multiple locations, including Wembley in the United Kingdom, Philadelphia, and Moscow. The event lasted sixteen hours and was diffused via thirteen satellites to 150 countries, including India and China. The international audience was estimated at 650 million (presumably based on some percentage of the 2 billion potential in the countries reached). The U.S. figure was 180 million. The event cost 3.7 million dollars and 4 million pounds, which was obtained through sale of TV rights and corporate donations. Estimates of money raised vary from $70 million to $147 million (Hickey, 1987).

13. Only in the fall of 1989 did Czech television openly defy the already crippled communist government by presenting live broadcasts of the mass rallies in Wenceslas Square. "If he [Jiri Hrabovsky, new anchor of Czech television] and a few hundred colleagues hadn't stuck their necks out earlier and broadcast the people's protests, Czechoslovakia's rout of communism might not have gone so far. People made this revolution. Television has spread it" (Newman, 1989). . . .

14. Yet there was a discussion over whether to risk publicizing failure in the live broadcasting of American space shots (Russo, 1983). Note also that, subsequent to the Challenger disaster, the Soviets offered a live broadcast of a space shot. . . .

References

Allen, R. C. 1985. *Speaking of soap operas.* Chapel Hill: University of North Carolina Press.

Altman, R. 1986. Television/sound. In T. Modleski, ed. *Studies in entertainment: Critical approaches to mass culture.* Bloomington: Indiana University Press.

Arnheim, R. 1944. World of the daytime serial. In P. F. Lazarsfeld and F. N. Stanton, eds. *Radio research: 1942–1943.* New York: Duell, Sloan & Pearce.

Benjamin, W. 1968a. The work of art in the age of mechanical reproduction. In Hannah Arendt, ed. *Illuminations.* Trans. Harry Zohn. New York: Harcourt Brace Jovanovich.

———. 1968b. What is epic theater? In Hannah Arendt, ed. *Illuminations.* Trans. Harry Zohn. New York: Harcourt Brace Jovanovich.

Browne, N. 1984. The political economy of television's supertext. *Quarterly Review of Film Studies* 9(3): 174–83.

Caillois, R. 1961. *Man, play, and games*. New York: Free Press of Glencoe.

Cantor, M. G., and S. Pingree. 1983. *The soap opera*. Beverly Hills: Sage.

Cassata, M. B. 1983. *Life on daytime television: Tuning-in American serial drama*. Norwood, N.J.: Ablex.

Cawelti, J. 1976. *Adventure, mystery, romance: Formula stories as art and popular culture*. Chicago: University of Chicago Press.

Centre d'Etudes d'Opinion. 1981. Les grands événements historiques à la télévision. *Cahiers de la Communication* (1)1: 51–61.

Cohen, N. 1978. President Sadat's visit to Jerusalem: Broadcasting aspects. *EBU Review* 29: 8–12.

Csikszentmihalyi, M., and R. W. Kubey. 1981. Television and the rest of life: A systematic comparison to subjective experience. *Public Opinion Quarterly* 45: 317–28.

Dayan, D., and E. Katz. 1982. Rituel publics à usage privé: métamorphose télévisée d'un mariage royal. *Les Annales: Economie, Société, Civilisation*. Abridged and revised in English as Electronic ceremonies: Television performs a royal wedding. In M. Blonsky, ed. *On signs*. Baltimore: Johns Hopkins University Press, 1985.

———. 1992. *Media events: The live broadcasting of history*. Cambridge: Harvard University Press.

Dayan, D., E. Katz, and P. Kerns. 1984. Armchair pilgrimages: the trips of Pope John Paul II and their television public. *On Film* 13: 25–34. Reprinted in M. Gurevitch and M. Levy, eds. *Mass communication review yearbook*. Vol. 5. Beverly Hills: Sage. 1985.

Durkheim, E. 1915. *The elementary forms of the religious life: A study in religious sociology*. Trans. J. W. Swain. London: Allen & Unwin.

Epstein, E. J. 1973. *News from nowhere: television and the news*. New York: Vintage Books.

Fiske, J., and J. Hartley. 1978. *Reading television*. London: Methuen.

Gans, H. J. 1979. *Deciding what's news: a study of CBS Evening News, NBC Nightly News, Newsweek, and Time*. New York: Pantheon Books.

Gerbner, G., L. Gross, N. Signorielli, M. Morgan, and M. Jackson-Beeck. 1979. The demonstration of power: Violence profile no. 10. *Journal of Communication* 29(3): 177–96.

Gleeson, P. 1979. The chieftains, Bernadette, and a choir of 6,000. *Irish Broadcasting Review*, pp. 42–43.

Graber, D. A. 1984. *Processing the news: how people tame the information tide*. New York: Longman.

Griffin-Beale, C. 1981. The royal wedding day on ITV. *Broadcast* (UK), July 27, no. 1118: 15–17.

Handelman, D. 1990. *Models and mirrors: Towards an anthropology of public events*. New York: Cambridge University Press.

Herzog, H. 1941. On borrowed experience: An analysis of listening to daytime sketches. *Studies in Philosophy and Social Science* 9: 45–65.

Hickey, N. 1987. The age of global TV. *TV Guide*, October 3, pp. 5–11.

Hood, S. C. 1967. *A survey of television*. London: Heinemann.

Houston, B. 1984. Viewing television: The metapsychology of endless consumption. *Quarterly Review of Film Studies* 9(3): 183–95.

Huizinga, J. 1950. *Homo ludens: A study of the play element in culture*. New York: Roy.

Jakobson, R. 1960. Linguistics and poetics. In T. Sebeok, ed. *Style in language.* New York: Wiley.

Katz, E., and S. Feldman. 1962. The Kennedy-Nixon debates: A survey of surveys. In S. Kraus, ed. *The great debates: Background, perspectives, effects.* Bloomington: Indiana University Press.

Katz, E., H. Adoni, and P. Parness. 1977. Remembering the news: What the picture adds to recall. *Journalism Quarterly* 54: 231–39.

Katz, E., D. Dayan, and P. Motyl. 1983. Television diplomacy: Sadat in Jerusalem. In G. Gerbner and M. Seifert, eds. *World communications.* New York: Longman.

Katzman, N. 1972. Television soap operas: What's been going on anyway? *Public Opinion Quarterly* 36: 200–211.

Kornhauser, W. 1959. *The politics of mass society.* New York: Free Press of Glencoe.

Lane, C. 1981. *The rites of ruler: Ritual in industrial society—the Soviet case.* New York: Cambridge University Press.

Lang, K., and G. E. Lang. 1953. The unique perspective of television. *American Sociological Review* 18: 3–12.

Lazarsfeld, P. F., and R. K. Merton. 1948. Mass communication, popular taste, and organized social action. In L. Bryson, ed. *Communication of ideas,* pp. 95–118. New York: Harper & Row.

Lendvay, J., J. Tolgyesi, and M. Tomka. 1982. First of May: A Hungarian media event. Paper presented at the World Congress of Sociology, Mexico City.

Lévi-Strauss, C. 1963. The effectiveness of symbols. In C. Lévi-Strauss, *Structural anthropology.* Vol. 1. New York: Basic Books.

Liebes, T., and E. Katz. 1990. *The export of meaning: Cross-cultural readings of Dallas.* New York: Oxford University Press.

Lukes, S. 1975. Political ritual and social integration. *Sociology* 9(2): 289–308.

Marc, D. 1989. *Comic visions: Television comedy and American culture.* Boston: Unwin Hyman.

Martin, D. A. 1969. *The religious and the secular: Studies in secularization.* London: Routledge and Kegan Paul.

Modleski, T. 1982. *Loving with a vengeance.* Hamden, Conn.: Action Books.

Morse, M. 1985. Talk, talk, talk: The space of discourse on television. *Screen* (26)2: 2–17.

Mytton, G. 1991. A billion viewers can't be right. *InterMedia* 19/8: 10–12.

Nasser, M. 1979. Sadat's television manipulation. Unpublished. Annenberg School for Communication, University of Southern California, Los Angeles.

Newcomb, H. 1974. *TV: The most popular art.* New York: Anchor.

Newcomb, H., and P. Hirsch. 1983. Television as a cultural forum: Implications for research. *Quarterly Review of Film Studies* 8: 48–55.

Newman, B. 1989. Switching channels: Czechoslovakia's TV in a flash became free as it covered uprising, and other articles. *Wall Street Journal,* November 27, December 5.

Peled, T. 1979. Dynamics of public opinion from Sadat's visit to Jerusalem through President Carter's announcement of the Israeli-Egyptian agreement. Jerusalem: Israel Institute of Applied Social Research (research report for ABC News).

Rothenbuhler, E. 1985. Media events, civil religion, and social solidarity: the living room celebration of the Olympic Games. Ph.D. dissertation, Annenberg School for Communication, University of Southern California, Los Angeles.

———. 1988. The living room celebration of the Olympic Games. *Journal of Communication* 38: 61–81.

————. 1989. Values and symbolism: public orientations to the Olympic media event. *Critical studies in mass communication*. Vol. 6, pp. 138–57.

Russo, M. A. 1983. CBS and the American political experience: A history of the CBS News special events and election units, 1952–1968. Ph.D. dissertation, New York University; Ann Arbor: University microfilm.

Schlesinger, P. 1978. *Putting reality together: BBC News*. London: Constable.

Schudson, M. 1978. *Discovering the news: A social history of American newspapers*. New York: Basic Books.

Shils, E. 1975. *Center and periphery: Essays in macrosociology*. Chicago: University of Chicago Press.

Singer, M. 1984. *Man's glassy essence: Explorations in semiotic anthropology*. Bloomington: Indiana University Press.

Sorohan, J. 1979. Pulling off a broadcasting miracle with nine weeks' notice. *Irish Broadcasting Review*: 46–47.

Stephenson, W. 1967. *The play theory of mass communication*. Chicago: University of Chicago Press.

Taylor, E. 1989. *Prime-time families: Television culture in postwar America*. Berkeley: University of California Press.

Todorovic, A. 1988. The funeral of Marshal Tito. *European Broadcasting Union Review* 31: 25–28.

Turner, V. 1985. Liminality, Kabbala, and the media. *Religion* 15: 205–17.

Uplinger, H. 1989. Global TV: What follows live aid? *InterMedia* 17(6): 17.

Veron, E. 1981. *Construire l'événement: Les médias et l'accident de Three Mile Island*. Paris: Minuit. (With the collaboration of J. Dana and A. F. de Ferrière.)

Vianello, R. 1986. The power politics of live television. *Journal of Film and Video* 37(3): 26–40.

Warner, W. L. 1962. *American life: Dream and reality*. Chicago: University of Chicago Press.

Williams, R. 1975. *Television: Technology and cultural form*. New York: Schocken Books.

Zelizer, B. 1981. The parameters of broadcast of Sadat's arrival in Jerusalem. Master's thesis, Communications Institute, Hebrew University of Jerusalem.

————. In Press. From home to public forum: media events and the public sphere. *Journal of Film and Video*.

Part III

THE RECEPTION CONTEXTS OF TELEVISION

Studies of the reception of, uses of, and responses to television continue to grow in number. As the studies proliferate, issues, debates, and controversies surrounding audience activity arise in comparable degree. Early perspectives suggesting that television audiences were empty vessels, passive absorbers of televisual content and processes gave way to notions of active audiences. From this perspective, individuals and groups were considered quite capable of viewing more analytically and critically, making decisions, accepting or rejecting ideas and ideologies presented by TV and "ethnographic" observations and interviews with audience members seemed to confirm this point. For some researchers and critics, however, the pendulum swung too far as audiences were granted enormous powers of resistance to mediated messages and meanings, and "resistance" to textual properties was translated into political significance.

Many scholars and critics have moved away from more extreme notions of audience power and have exhibited more temperate, nuanced, and precise formulations of these processes. Fortunately, too, the resulting retreats have not indicated an abandonment of concepts of active audience engagement. As with many features of television studies, the topic has been made more complex as more and more specific studies are produced and more types and levels of influence are factored into the analysis. The essays in this section add to that complexity.

The first two essays do not, in fact, address conventional notions of what has come to be known as "reception studies" in a direct manner. Both focus instead on questions of "media literacy" and are primarily concerned with how students at all levels should be instructed to view, interpret, and understand—to "read," television. The essays are certainly valuable in that regard and students using this collection should be able to sharpen their analytical skills by applying questions and directives presented here. Moreover, the approaches offered in these two essays should be explored alongside those presented by David Barker, Hal Himmelstein, and América Rodriguez in other parts of this book. There, too, in the descriptions and analyses of professional decision-making, various assumptions about media literacy are clearly at work. But in their focus on "literacy" these essays also provide extremely valuable tools and approaches with which to pursue audience research.

Joshua Meyrowitz addresses the question of literacy by constructing three metaphors, each of which suggests different emphases. Media as "conduits" carrying messages lead to a focus on "media content literacy," which traces out meanings presented from many elements. Media as "distinct languages" require a focus on "media grammar literacy." Here the primary concern is with understanding "production variables" within different media. Finally, the notion of media as "environments" deals with the "influence of the relatively fixed characteristics of each medium."

While acknowledging the need for these specific types of analysis, Justin Lewis and Sut Jhally add a focus on contexts surrounding the production and reception of media texts and messages. They argue that "mass media . . . should be understood as more than a collection of texts to be deconstructed and analyzed." They should also be studied as "sets of institutions with particular social and economic structures that are neither inevitable nor irreversible." One purpose of media literacy training in their view should be to teach students to "engage media texts," but also to teach them to "engage and challenge media institutions."

Media literacy as presented in these two essays involves study of the constant interplay of cultural patterns, institutions, individuals, and power. They thus offer a set of resource topics and questions with which to conduct audience research and, for present purposes, to examine studies already completed. In these existing studies we can ask what elements have been focused on by the researcher—text, medium, institution, program, genre, etc.? In ethnographic studies, what elements are found to have interested and attracted audiences? Do they discuss the "medium" at large? Do they critique the television industry? Is that critique informed by knowledge (a "literate view") of the industry or by commonly shared dissatisfaction? Are audiences aware of technical and aesthetic choices such as camera angles and editing patterns? All these questions and many more could be developed from the media literacy perspective and applied to and in audience studies.

Anna McCarthy's essay is certainly susceptible to such comparative questions, but in a new and quite exploratory context. Her study of the placement of television sets in public places, primarily in taverns, during the early years of television broadcasting in the United States adds a much needed dimension to both audience studies and television history. Her work is directly related to Lynn Spigel's analysis of the role of television in the home in this volume. McCarthy demonstrates once again, in a distinctive context, that viewers *learned* how to interact with the new medium. Most importantly, she also shows that even in these earliest settings, television was woven into the dense fabric of social structures and influences. The study of public viewing of television in taverns requires exploration of the role and regulation of leisure (and therefore of labor), of matters related to class, gender, and race, of institutions as (apparently) disparate as television set manufacturers and baseball club owners.

It is worth noting that many of the events viewed in taverns were sports related and engaged active "fans." Television programs of all sorts, of course, have fans, and in their activity audience studies have found some of the richest topics for research. Henry Jenkins's exploration of the creative work of *Star Trek* fans is one example of this body of work. His essay shows how fans have made this program a significant aspect of their own lived experience. And in rewriting the "story" of *Star Trek*, fans demonstrate not only an engagement with television, but competencies in multiple media literacies. In so doing they actually establish critical, analytical questions that should be pursued by users of these essays. What happens to characters when they "move" from one medium (television) to another (literature)? What happens to the "text?" What is the nature of "authorship" in each medium? And how does individual appropriation of these meanings, stories, structures, and characters demonstrate a critical involvement with the material and an appropriation of ideas and images constructed by powerful institutions?

Ellen Seiter's essay turns the critical question back toward the researcher. Her account of a "troubling" interview conducted as part of a larger audience study raises issues that cut across most scholarly endeavors, even those that do not involve direct engagement with audiences. The troublesome issues arise from the recognition—so necessary in any research—of varying degrees of cultural capital. As "protected" academic researchers, Seiter and her colleagues encountered a range of social attitudes toward television and those who view it. As a result of those encounters she asks that researchers recognize their "own dominance and class interests with the system of cultural distinctions." Just as television viewing in taverns, then, requires the critic to examine what it meant to drink alcohol in public in the 1950s, so this essay asks what it means to enter the homes of television viewers and probe their attitudes. The transcript of the interview is presented with this essay so that users of this collection can form their own judgments about the events and the resulting analysis.

Almost all the issues addressed in previous essays become part of Jostein Gripsrud's discussion of the appearance of *Dynasty* in Norway. His essay on public and individual responses to the program, responses that erupted into "The Cultural Debate of the Ages," demonstrates precisely how "reception" takes place within contexts ranging from national history to broadcasting policy to religious conviction to scholarly perspectives. This essay, then, exemplifies the ways in which matters of television viewing spill out of the domestic and into the public realms, reminding us of McCarthy's discussion of public TV viewing in the early 1950s. It demonstrates the power of personal response and resonates with Jenkins's discussion of active fans. It self-consciously addresses the role of the scholar who is pulled into the debate, echoing concerns expressed by Seiter. And it clearly demonstrates the presence of multiple types of media literacy, ranging from evaluation of production values to discussions of media policy by concerned citizens.

In some ways, then, this very visible "debate" confirms notions of active viewers, even as it demonstrates the unequal distribution of the real power needed to effect changes in television. Students wishing to model their own critical work on such a synthetic approach would do well to examine current controversies such as, in the United States, the response to Ellen Degeneres's coming out as a lesbian in her television show, *Ellen,* or in discussions of the propriety of television news and documentary discussions of the Clinton/Lewinsky events.

As all these essays show, the continuing attention to television audiences is now a major aspect of critical television studies. While each new project may seem to confound previous conclusions, these developments should be seen as part of the growing complexity of this field of inquiry.

Multiple Media Literacies

JOSHUA MEYROWITZ

What is *media literacy?* Discussions of this concept typically focus on how to redefine literacy to fit our current media environment. Less attention tends to be given to different definitions for the other half of the phrase. After all, surely everyone knows what "media" are! Indeed, it is the pervasiveness of a wide array of media—movies, radio, television, computers, and so forth—that has stimulated the debate over how to reconceptualize literacy in the first place.

Yet, I argue that there is less consensus about what we mean by media than many researchers, parents, and teachers may at first imagine. Also, different ways of thinking about media lead to different conceptions of the competencies, or literacies, that may be desirable in the educated and aware citizen.

In this essay I outline one typology of multiple media literacies, based on three distinct metaphors for what a medium of communication is. Each metaphor leads to a different set of questions about media, to different approaches to doing media research, and to a different way of defining basic media literacy. Yet, the different conceptions of media described here are not entirely unrelated. The visual models included in this article, therefore, attempt to portray both the differences and the relationships among three types of knowledge about media.

From *Journal of Communication*, Winter 1998. Copyright © 1998 by Oxford University Press. Reprinted by permission of the publisher.

Media Content Literacy

The most common conception of media is that they are conduits that hold and send messages. This conception has fostered many ways of discussing and studying the content of media. Within this general view of media, basic media literacy involves being able to access and analyze messages in a variety of media. Content literacy takes many forms. These include being able to decode and follow the intended manifest message; exploring intended and unintended latent messages; being aware of different content genres; being aware of the cultural, institutional, and commercial forces that tend to lead to certain types of messages being constructed while others are avoided; and understanding that different individuals and groups tend to "read" the same "texts" differently.

As the list of content elements in Table 1 suggests, media content dominates most debates and studies of media. Indeed, the explicit or implicit view of media as conduits is shared among many media critics and researchers

Table 1 Media Content Elements

The media-as-conduits metaphor focuses attention on those elements that move relatively easily from medium to medium and between live interaction and media, such as:

ideas
themes
topics
information
values
ideologies
persuasive appeals
settings
objects
characters or roles
actions or behaviors
narratives
genres (thematically or topically defined)

Typical questions about media-content elements explore:

structure/pattern of above content elements
motivations of producers of content
influence of media industry structure on content
economic and political influences on content
variations in individual and group perception of content
correlations between media content and reality
the effects of content
the types of messages that rarely if ever appear in mainstream media

> The importance of media content is most visible when other elements of mediated communications are ignored and when one content element, **A**, is contrasted with another real or hypothetical content element, **B**.
>
> # A vs. B
>
> ## CONTENT ELEMENT **A** vs. CONTENT ELEMENT **B**
>
> *For example:*
>
> violent vs. peaceful content
> sexist vs. egalitarian content
> routine reporting vs. investigative journalism
> unrealistic vs. realistic content
> one genre vs. another genre

Figure 1 Analysis of content.

who otherwise have little in common. These include ministers who condemn the immoral nature of much TV-portrayed behavior; activists who protest the limited and stereotyped portrayal of women, gays, African Americans, or other minorities in the media; and a wide range of researchers who study manifest and latent content in news and entertainment through a plethora of quantitative and qualitative methods.

Further, although the early stimulus-response, conveyor-belt theory of media effects has long been abandoned in academic circles in favor of generally much more sophisticated and subtle models of media influence and transaction, the majority of current approaches have not actually strayed that far from one of the original assumptions: that there is something inside, and somehow separable from the medium, that can be analyzed and studied. As Wilbur Schramm (1973), an icon of one form of content study, once put it, "The message is the message, and the medium is the medium" (p. 128).

The focus on media content is popular for several reasons. For one thing, media content—in it smanifest form, at least—tends to be the most obvious aspect of mediated communications. This makes media content important to study. Further, media content concerns tend to focus on aspects of communication that are not specific to specific media. Indeed, most content elements involve behaviour, themes, and topics that cross easily from medium to medium and between mediated and unmediated interaction. For example, popular content concerns (e.g., violence, sexism, racism, ideological bias) all exist within most communication forms, including face-to-face interaction. Thus, in a media-saturated society, media content questions draw the attention of anyone with a strong concern about any aspect of social life. Because media content elements can be separated, at least analytically, from the particular media that contain them, discussions of the content from any medium can be presented in any other medium. Media content can be relatively easily coded, counted, and verbally analyzed. The ease with which one can speak and write about media content, regardless of the medium in which the content is found, makes it a favorite topic of pundits, preachers, politicians, and professors.

To set the stage for visualizing the relationship between content literacy and other forms of media literacy, I suggest using letters A, B, C, and so on to symbolize media content elements (see Figure 1). Content questions generally focus on the analysis of some aspect of content element A contrasted, explicitly or implicitly, with a real or hypothetical content element B.

Knowing how to access, interpret, and evaluate content from a variety of media is an essential ingredient of any conception of media literacy. One could argue, for example, that every citizen needs to know a great deal about news in order for democracy to function. Basic media content literacy could go beyond simply "keeping up" with the news. It could also involve understanding how news tends to be constructed and how political, economic, and institutional constraints lead certain forms of news to dominate, regardless of the medium through which the news is conveyed. The last few decades have seen the growth of an excellent literature on critical analysis of news that could easily serve as a foundation for news-content literacy (e.g., Altheide, 1976; Gans, 1979; Hallin, 1994; Herman & Chomsky, 1988; Manoff and Schudson, 1986; Schudson, 1995; Sigal, 1973, Tuchman, 1978). A similarly powerful (and in some ways related) case could be made for basic understanding of how much of our media content serves as explicit or implicit advertising (e.g. Barnouw, 1978; Savan, 1994).

However, media content issues, as important as they are, do not exhaust the basic skills that we should all have with respect to media. Indeed, in some ways, this most popular approach to media is not really about media. That is, when content is the focus, not much attention tends to be given to the particular characteristics of the medium through which the messages examined are conveyed. In the next two sections I outline conceptions of media that suggest the need for two additional forms of media literacy.

Media Grammar Literacy

Another conception of media involves seeing each medium as its own language. This view of media leads to a focus on the unique "grammar" of each medium and the ways in which the production variables of each medium—or what Zettl (1990) calls the medium's "aesthetic" aspects—interact with content elements. Unlike most content elements, which cross easily from medium to medium and from mediated to nonmediated interaction, media grammar variables are peculiar to media. Although one can exhibit violence, sexism, or racism in real life, for example, it is difficult to "cut to a close-up" or "dissolve to the beach" in everyday interactions. One person cannot sing the harmony and the melody at the same time without the medium of audio recording, nor can we change typefaces in speech.

Basic media literacy, within this conception of media as languages, entails understanding and recognizing the standard range of production variables within each medium, as well as recognizing the ways in which the variables are typically used to attempt to shape perception and response to mediated communications. More advanced forms of media grammar literacy involve knowledge of a wider range of variables within each medium, being able to manipulate the variables skillfully in one's own media productions, understanding what cultural and institutional forces tend to encourage some uses of grammar variables rather than others, and recognizing that responses to production variables may vary individually and culturally.[1]

Table 2 outlines some of the key grammar variables that can be manipulated in a few sample types of media to create certain impressions. As noted, some variables operate in more than one medium. Television and film incorporate most of the variables of still photography and audio. When photography and print, or film and print, are mixed (as in magazines or in movie titles), many variables from more than one column come into play. Computer programs and web sites are increasingly incorporating many of the

Table 2 Sample Grammar Variables for Various Media

Production variables can be manipulated within each medium to alter perception of message content.

Print Media	*Still Photography*	*Radio/Audio*	*TV/Film*
size/shape of page	framing (CU/MS/LS)	mike pickup pattern(s)	(most photo variables)
color(s) of paper	angle (low/high/level)	sound perspective	(all audio variables)
thickness of paper		electronic volume	visual fade in/out
texture of paper	front/back/profile	electronic tone	cuts
size(s) of type	selection of focus	frequency filter(s)	dissolves
typeface design(s)	depth of focus	fade up/fade out	cross-cutting
color(s) of type	lens (wide → telephoto)	cross-fade	length of shots
use of italics/bold		multitracking	zooms vs. dollies
widths of columns	exposure	segue/silence	pans vs. trucks
spacing	aperture opening	echo	tilts up/tilts down
paragraph breaks	shutter speed	speed changes	still or shaking camera
punctuation	type of film	backwards	objective vs. subjective shots
use of blank space	filter(s)	channel separation	
mosaic of text & graphics	double exposure	channel balance	split screen & multi-image
	color balance		rack focus
	contrast		follow focus
	type of paper		juxtapositions of sound & image
	cropping		
	size/shape of image		

variables of text, photography, sound, and motion. Yet, despite some crossover in variables, each medium tends to offer its unique mix of variables. Even TV and film, which are listed together on the table for simplicity, achieve the same effect (such as a dissolve) through different physical means, and each has some variables not shared with the other (such as the wide spectrum of electronic visual effects available in TV).

Unlike media content literacy, media grammar literacy demands some understanding of the specific workings of individual media. There is no space here to discuss the uses of many variables in many media. So, to illustrate the type of knowledge that media grammar literacy entails I will focus on a very brief outline of a few of the basic visual variables that operate in the typical television program or movie.

The selective use of close-ups, medium shots, and long shots can reshape the perceptions of both fictional and nonfictional sequences. Shot framing often draws on the culturally patterned uses of interpersonal distances in real-life interactions (Meyrowitz, 1986). Close-ups simulate intimate distances and encourage viewers to feel a personal connection to the pictured person. Generally, the main character in a program or movie is the first person seen in frequent close-ups. Persons seen at greater distances are more likely to be perceived in terms of their social roles. Media grammar literacy, then, might include awareness of how viewers may react differently to violent acts depending on the way the perpetrators and victims are photographed. Similarly, the viewer aware of media grammar is more likely than other viewers to observe how nonfiction sequences (e.g., news and documentaries) are carefully crafted to look as if they are not crafted, but simply real—what Gaye Tuchman (1978) calls the creation of an "aura of representation." For example, the media grammar literate viewer might observe that, although some people who are the subjects of television news are shown in tight closeups, journalists themselves rarely are (in order to maintain the impression of impersonal objectivity).

Camera angles also tend to be used in particular ways. Low-angle shots (camera below subject) are often used to suggest power and authority, though extreme low angles can be used to mock someone's sense of self-importance. Level shots are typically used to suggest someone is a "peer" or is "on the level," which is why this is another technique typically used by journalists on themselves. High-angle shots (camera above subject) are typically used to suggest that someone is small or weak.

Wide-angle lenses tend to stretch the apparent distance between foreground and background, whereas long (telephoto) lenses tend to compress foreground and background. News reports on highway crowding, for example, typically use long lenses to make it appear that the cars are squashed together. In contrast, car ads typically use wide lenses to impress viewers with the spacious interior of the vehicle and to convey the appeal of the wide-open road.

Media grammar literacy could go far beyond these basic variables to entail awareness of how manipulation of production variables may be subtly reflecting and influencing the public's perception of people, places, and events. Media grammar literacy could include understanding how visual grammar variables can be used to guide the public's attention (such as through editing structure, selective primary focus, and focus depth); encourage alignment with one side versus the other in war movies, news, and documentaries (through camera placement, shot framing, whole-camera movement vs. lens zooming and panning); depict people in a particular country as part of a crowded mass as opposed to individual human beings (through long lenses or bird's-eye views or both); portray some news sources as stable and authoritative (with tripod-steadied medium shots), and other sources as unstable, threatening, and untrustworthy (with shaking cameras or tight closeups, in which natural body shifts lead to what appear to be attempts to escape the scrutiny of the camera); and so on. Media grammar literacy should also involve awareness of the impact of media variables that are not as easily "seen," such as the impact of sound-track elements, which include different sound perspectives (the aural equivalents of different shot framings), different microphone pickup patterns, and sound equalization filters.

Of course, there can be no meaningful manipulation of media grammar variables without some media content to work with. However, the grammar is most visible when a content element is held constant. In Figure 2, therefore, grammar concerns are represented schematically by showing a sample content element A within two different polygons (a square vs. a triangle), which are used to represent grammar variables.

The impact of media grammar is most visible when a content element, A, is held constant and one grammar variable is contrasted with another.

GRAMMAR VARIABLE □ vs. GRAMMAR VARIABLE △

For example:

MURDER
shown from perspective of victim vs. perspective of murderer

FEMALE EXECUTIVE
portrayed in "professional," low-angle medium shot
vs. "intimate," level-angle closeup

STREET IN BAGHDAD
shown with "crowding" long lens vs. "spacious" wide angle lens

Figure 2 Analysis of grammar.

Media grammar tends to receive significantly less attention than media content for several reasons. For one thing, many people are simply not aware that a wide range of production variables are at play most of the time in most of the media to which they attend. Producers, after all, generally want audiences to be aware of content elements, but not to be aware of grammar elements. A television or movie producer would prefer that audience members consciously feel empathy for a character, rather than be aware of their response to the use of prolonged close-ups. Similarly, the editors of a prestigious newspaper do not want their readers to consider how much of the paper's credibility might be lost if the same stories were in a different typeface and format.

Ironically, then, powerful content and powerful grammar typically have opposite effects on audience awareness: The more effective media content elements are, the more that audiences are likely to be aware of, and think about, the content. The more effective the media grammar elements are, the less the average audience member will even notice them.

Even those who study media often shy away from writing and speaking about media grammar because of how difficult it is to convey a description of grammar from the medium of production to the medium of description. Media grammar elements need much more translation than media content elements, and one can never be sure how aware one's audience is of the variables being described. For example, I find it easy to tell you here in words that in the movie *Wall Street,* Bud Fox, the young stockbroker portrayed by Charlie Sheen, eventually comes to feel imprisoned by the same games of high finance that once made him feel empowered (a content description). However, if I try to describe here how this content theme is reinforced through many subtle shifts in shot structures as the movie evolves, including the use, at a pivotal moment, of a smooth combination of zoom-in on Sheen as the camera dollies out, thereby making it appear that the Wall Street buildings behind the character are literally closing in on him as he just stands still, those readers unfamiliar with the visual impact of such a combination of techniques are likely to be lost. The most interesting and clearest way to explain these techniques would entail displaying them (repeatedly, and in slow motion, perhaps) within the original medium of presentation.[2]

Although those who have no formal training in media production techniques are often unaware of them, once someone has been taught about grammar variables, they are hard to miss. The variables listed in Table 2 are, after all, clearly visible or audible once one knows to look or listen for them. Even more challenging, then, is the third conception of media literacy, described in the next section, which entails understanding the least overt aspect of mediated communications.

Medium Literacy

A third conception of media is that each medium is a type of setting or environment that has relatively fixed characteristics that influence communication in a particular manner—regardless of the choice of content elements and regardless of the particular manipulation of production variables.

This approach is most often associated with Marshall McLuhan (1964), but others before McLuhan, and many since, have also developed aspects of this perspective, which I have called "medium theory" (Meyrowitz, 1985, pp. 16–23; 1994). I use the singular, medium, because unlike most media theory, this approach focuses on the particular characteristics of each medium.

Table 3 lists sample characteristics that can be used to distinguish one medium from another (e.g., radio vs. television), or to show how one gen-

Table 3 Sample Medium Variables

Medium analysis focuses attention on those relatively fixed features of a given medium (or of a general type of media) that make it a unique communication setting and distinguish it from other media and from face-to-face interaction.

type of sensory information conveyed; unisensory or multisensory
(*visual, oral, olfactory, etc.*)

the form of information within each sense
(*e.g., picture vs. written word; clicks vs. voice*)

degree of definition, resolution, fidelity (*e.g., a radio voice is closer to a live voice than a TV closeup is to a live face*)

unidirectional vs. bidirectional vs. multidirectional
(*e.g., radio vs. telephone vs. on-line computer conference*)

simultaneous vs. sequential bidirectionality (*e.g., hearing other person's response as one speaks over telephone vs. CB turn taking*)

speed and degree of immediacy in encoding, dissemination, and decoding

relative ease/difficulty of learning to encode and decode and number and types of stages of mastery (*e.g., learning to read vs. learning to listen to the radio*)

ratio of encoding difficulty to decoding difficulty

physical requirements for engaging the medium (*Does one have to be in a certain place, hold something, stand still, look in a certain direction, use special lighting, stop live interaction, etc.?*)

degree and type of human manipulation (*e.g., painting a picture vs. snapping a photograph*)

scope and nature of dissemination (*e.g, how many people can attend to the same message at the same moment*)

---

eral type of media is different from another type of media (e.g., electronic media vs. print media).

Medium literacy involves understanding how the nature of the medium shapes key aspects of the communication on both the micro-, single-situation level and on the macro-, societal level. Microlevel medium literacy, for example, could entail understanding why a particular type of interaction (e.g., contacting someone for a date, ending an intimate relationship, inquiring about a job, selling a particular product, negotiating a peace treaty, etc.) might work differently in one form of communication (face-to-face, phone, letter, E-mail, etc.) than another.

Many people, for example, might avoid using the telephone to try to end an intimate relationship because, with the phone, one's verbal message may be overwhelmed by one's emotional vocal overtones, and one is interrupted and influenced by the words and sounds of the other person. A "Dear John telephone call," therefore, is often inherently paradoxical. Because the telephone offers vocal, bidirectional, and simultaneous communication, it tends to maintain an informal, intimate, and fluid relationship, even as one tries to end such a relationship. A Dear John letter, however, allows one to "have one's say" without conveying emotional vocalizations or dealing with interruptions or responses from the other party. Further, unlike an ongoing phone call, letter writing allows the sender to write and rewrite a letter until it captures the right tone. For similar reasons, the phone is often much better than a letter for initiating an intimate relationship. Its simulation of close conversational distance allows for a testing of intimacy through the vocal channel only, without the initial intensity of bodily proximity, sight, and smell.

On the macrolevel, medium literacy entails understanding how the widespread use of a new medium may lead to broad social changes. For example, macrolevel medium theory explores such issues as how the addition of a new medium to the matrix of existing media may alter the boundaries and nature of many social situations, reshape the relationships among people, and strengthen or weaken various social institutions.

For example, macrolevel medium literacy could involve understanding theories about (a) the ways in which the widespread use of the telephone changed dating rituals and business practices in general, including the decline and changing role of letter writing; (b) the ways in which changes in dominant media alter social conceptions of what it means to be educated and competent; (c) whether the spread of television, with its presentation of the sounds and images of distant others, has fostered the increasing focus on the appearance, style, and intimate life details of public figures; (d) whether the increasing use of place-insensitive electronic media has reduced the significance of national boundaries and stimulated the process of globalization; and (e) whether the increasing use of the internet, with its many alternative sources of information, including historical facts that are routinely excluded from the explanatory stories in the mainstream news media, will force the dominant, corporate news media to alter their reporting practices in order to maintain credibility with the public.

Medium analysis does not suggest that media come into being on their own. Medium literacy also involves consideration of how political, economic, and social forces encourage the development of some media over others. Also significant is the question of why particular forms of various media evolved. Why did television, for example, develop as a unidirectional mass medium as opposed to an interactive community medium? Such analyses could easily be linked with the discussions of the commercial nature of our media systems and their ties to corporate and governmental elites.

As Figure 3 indicates, medium analysis involves explicit or implicit comparison of one medium of communication with another medium of communication (or with unmediated interaction). Because it is impossible for a medium to have any influence without content, and because most media messages also involve the conscious or unconscious manipulation of gram-

Media environments are most visible when content elements are held constant and one looks beyond the range of grammar choices within each medium to the differences between using one medium vs. another medium (or vs. no medium at all).

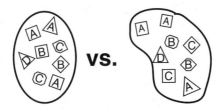

MEDIUM ENVIRONMENT ◯ vs. MEDIUM ENVIRONMENT

For example:

e-mail message vs. telephone call
political debate on radio vs. TV
news via TV vs. newspaper
policy discussion on network TV vs. interactive community TV
education in a "print culture" vs. an "electronic culture"
(also: any medium vs. face-to-face)

On the micro, single-situation level, medium analyses look at the implications of choosing one medium versus another for a particular communication. Macro, societal-level medium analyses explore how the widespread use of a new medium leads to broad social changes.

Figure 3 Medium analysis.

mar variables, each media environment (a surrounding, curved-line shape) contains content elements (letters) and grammar elements (polygons) as well.

Medium theory is the least common form of media analysis. This may be because the environment fostered by a medium is much less directly observable than the content and the grammar of media. The medium environment is most visible when the medium is just beginning to be used by a significant proportion of the population. For example, the current discussions of cyberspace generally support the medium-theory perspective that each medium is a new type of social "place" whose influence cannot be reduced to the content of the messages that flow through the net. Once a new generation is born into a world where use of the Web is widespread, however, awareness of cyberspace as a new social setting will no doubt recede. Ironically, then, the environment of a medium is most invisible when its influence is most pervasive.

Summary and Conclusion

This article has suggested that there are at least three different types of media literacy, each linked to a different conception of media. The idea that media are conduits that bring us messages suggests the need for media content literacy. The notion that media are languages with distinct grammars highlights the need to be literate in media production variables (media grammar literacy). The conception of media as environments points to the need to understand the influence on both the micro- and macrolevel of the relatively fixed characteristics of each medium, or of each general type of media (medium literacy).

Although the third conception of media is the least commonly drawn on at the present time, it offers some special self-reflexive insights for those interested in media literacy. Macrolevel medium literacy, for example, provides a way of understanding how the shift from oral to literate forms of communication supported new educational institutions and educational practices, which are now themselves being reshaped by the addition of various electronic media—leading to the calls for new forms of literacy.

Ironically, awareness of medium influence also leads to some insight into factors that make it difficult for many people to perceive this level of influence. Understanding particular characteristics of new media is hindered, for example, by the tendency to describe new media using concepts drawn from older media. This point leads to a critique of some of the common terminology that I also have drawn on in this article. The use of the term *literacy* to refer to skills with a variety of media and the use of the term *texts* to refer to the content of nontextual media, for example, make it even more difficult than it already is for many people to discern the very differences among media that the medium-theory perspective attempts to highlight.

Watching television, for example, has very little to do with traditional literacy (Meyrowitz, 1985, pp. 73–114). Television is mostly a presentational analogic system, whereas text information is discursive and digital. Young children are able to watch television long before they can learn to read. Further, although a child typically needs to learn to read simple books before reading more complex books, there is little, except an intervening adult, programmed V-chip, or sleep schedule, that demands that a young child watch *Mr. Rogers' Neighborhood* before watching *NYPD Blue*. Young children may not understand television in the same way that adults do (just as they may process live events differently), but television does not have the same sort of initial screening device that books do. Using the notion of literacy to describe engagements with all media tends to obscure the fact that there are different skills required for mastering different media.

Macrolevel medium theory also offers one way of explaining why our schools now seem to be in perpetual crisis. Until recently, the school system played the primary role in giving young children access to general social information and in teaching children the basic skills they would need to gain access to nonlocal experience throughout the rest of their lives—text literacy. The many relatively new, nonreading ways to gain access to information now weaken the informational power of the school and diminish the incentives to learn to read and write well. Many schools now feel the need to redouble their efforts to teach traditional literacy skills, while attempting to help students process the information they receive through nontextual media. Yet the added staff, time, and resources that would be needed to work on these two fronts are rarely forthcoming.

Meanwhile, as schools are struggling to do more, nontextual media also threaten the basic structure of the school system and the traditional authority of teachers. The system of separating students by chronological age developed only with the spread of print literacy (Meyrowitz, 1985, pp. 258–265). The system was based on the assumptions that most of what a child knows can be correlated closely with his or her age and reading ability, and that the teacher always knows more than the young student (Meyrowitz, 1985; Papert, 1993). The vast range of experiences that children now have through nonprint media make age and reading ability much weaker predictors of children's knowledge and more often give even young children experience with topics and issues unfamiliar to their teachers.

Ironically, then, the medium-theory perspective clarifies one of the perplexing paradoxes of the media literacy movement: why there are so many fine efforts underway to incorporate media literacy in school curricula, and why so little formal and successful implementation of such programs has thus far been accomplished.

The model of multiple media literacies outlined here also suggests that there is no finite set of knowledge that will make someone media literate, and that it is unrealistic to expect any given media literacy program to teach all that we could hope children and adults would know about media. Nevertheless, wider awareness of these three general types of media literacy may enhance the ability of citizens to understand and participate more fully in a media-saturated society.

Notes

1. One can also use the production process as a means of gaining the initial awareness of content and production variables. My former student, Karen Webster, now a graduate student at the University of Utah, demonstrated this in her news production work with 4th and 5th graders on the Oyster River Media Education Project from 1990 to 1993 (Webster & Meyrowitz, 1995).

2. The spread of web publishing may lead to a surge of new media grammar research and publications, because, assuming that copyright and fair use issues can be resolved, web articles can contain audio and visual samples from the works being studied. This possibility is an example of a "medium" argument, which grows from the third media metaphor discussed in this essay.

References

Altheide, D. L. (1976). *Creating reality: How TV news distorts events.* Beverly Hills, CA: Sage.

Barnouw, E. (1978). *The sponsor: Notes on a modern potentate.* New York: Oxford University Press.

Gans, H. J. (1979). *Deciding what's news.* New York: Vintage.

Hallin, D. (1994). *We keep America on top of the world: Television journalism and the public sphere.* New York: Routledge.

Herman, E. S., & Chomsky, N. (1988). *Manufacturing consent: The political economy of the mass media.* New York: Pantheon.

McLuhan, M. (1964). *Understanding media: The extensions of man.* New York: Signet.

Manoff, R. K., & Schudson, M. (Eds.). (1986). *Reading the news.* New York: Pantheon Books.

Meyrowitz, J. (1985). *No sense of place: The impact of electronic media on social behavior.* New York: Oxford University Press.

Meyrowitz, J. (1986). Television and interpersonal behavior: Codes of perception and response. In G. Gumpert & R. Cathcart (Eds.), *Inter/media: Interpersonal communication in a media world* (3rd. ed., pp. 253–272). New York: Oxford University Press.

Meyrowitz, J. (1994). Medium theory. In D. Crowley & D. Mitchell (Eds.), *Communication theory today* (pp. 50–77). Cambridge, England: Polity Press.

Papert, S. (1993). *The children's machine: Rethinking school in the age of the computer.* New York: Basic Books.

Savan, L. (1994). *The sponsored life: Ads, TV, and American culture.* Philadelphia: Temple University Press.

Schramm, W. (1973). *Men, messages, and media: A look at human communication.* New York: Harper & Row.

Schudson, M. (1995). *The power of news.* Cambridge, MA: Harvard University Press.

Sigal, L. (1973). *Reporters and officials.* Lexington, MA: Heath.

Webster, K., & Meyrowitz, J. (1995, July/August). Whose views make news? *Cable in the classroom,* pp. 10–11.

Zettl, H. (1990). *Sight-sound-motion: Applied media aesthetics* (2nd ed.). Belmont, CA: Wadsworth.

The Struggle
Over Media Literacy

JUSTIN LEWIS and SUT JHALLY

The argument we wish to make is, in essence, a simple one: Media literacy should be about helping people to become sophisticated citizens rather than sophisticated consumers. The mass media, in other words, should be understood as more than a collection of texts to be deconstructed and analyzed so that we can distinguish or choose among them. They should be analyzed as sets of institutions with particular social and economic structures that are neither inevitable nor irreversible. Media education should certainly teach students to engage media texts, but it should also, in our view, teach them to engage and challenge media institutions.

Although we see textual analysis as an integral part of media education, we suggest that in any media system, the reason why we see some messages and not others raises the question of power and the active construction of the social world. Our arguments here are prompted by comments made by a pioneer in the U.S. media literacy movement, Renée Hobbs, following the National Media Literacy Conference held in Los Angeles in October 1996. Hobbs was concerned that "for some participants, media literacy has been either deliberately or accidentally conflated with activism around media reform issues." In her view, "it is inappropriate to lump media activism together with media literacy." Instead, she argued that "at the heart of the media literacy movement is the open, questioning, reflective, critical stance towards messages." Hobbs (1996) defined *media literacy* as "the process of

From *Journal of Communication*, Winter 1998. Copyright © 1998 by Oxford University Press. Reprinted by permission of the publisher.

accessing, critically analyzing media messages and creating messages using media tools. The goal of media literacy is to promote autonomy through the development of analysis, reasoning, communication and self-expression skills" (p. iii).

We argue that such avoidance of thorny political territory sidesteps widespread citizen concerns and misses an opportunity to demonstrate the valence and necessity of not merely understanding the world, but of changing it. In making this argument, we take our lead from the work of Len Masterman, for whom,

> The democratization of institutions, and the long march toward a truly participatory democracy, will be highly dependent upon the ability of majorities of citizens to take control, become effective change agents, make rational decisions (often on the basis of media evidence) and to communicate effectively perhaps through an active involvement with the media. (Masterman, 1997, p. 60)

This is particularly important in a media system in which most messages are either explicitly or implicitly commercial—either straightforward advertisements or content designed to deliver audiences to advertisers in the most efficient and profitable way (see Barnouw, 1978; Jhally 1990). The mass media may be producing art, but they are also producing commerce. We feel that it is impossible to understand one fully without comprehending the other. Unlike some of the more public service-oriented broadcasting systems in Europe and elsewhere, the goals of a loosely regulated, commercial media have no educational, cultural, or informational imperatives. As much of the literature on the political economy of the media suggests, they are there to maximize profits and to serve a set of corporate interests. These imperatives provide a framework that helps to shape both the form and content of media texts (Bagdikian, 1997; Garnham, 1990; Herman & Chomsky, 1988; Schiller, 1984, 1989, 1996).

We therefore argue for a contextual approach to media education, one in which the media text is a stage in a process of ideological production. As Richard Johnson (1986–87) suggested in his classic introduction to British cultural studies: Although we may be able to distinguish between a series of analytical moments (i.e., production of text, the text itself, reception of text), we need to be able to understand the determinations and connections between them. Like Johnson, we urge those involved in media education to think of the circuit of cultural production.

In what follows, we first argue, as briefly as we can, for a contextual rather than a text-centered approach. Such a perspective allows students to imagine ways of changing media systems and creates the possibility of a more democratic media. We next propose an emphasis on political economy in the face of the current trend towards text-centered approaches. Having stressed the importance of the production end of the circuit, we then consider the role in media education of teaching production skills. We conclude with a more practical consideration of the politics of media literacy, arguing against the pragmatism of text-centered approaches.

Textual Versus Contextual Approaches

The notion of literacy, particularly in relation to forms like television, is a complex one. The call for media education is in response not to a functionally illiterate media public, but to a public who are already voracious readers, viewers, and listeners. Media literacy is more than a matter of basic comprehension. Few people, after all, need to be taught how to make sense of television or, in most cases, to appreciate its "preferred meanings" (Hall, 1980; Morely, 1980, 1986). On the contrary, the fact that so many have the ability to make sense of a barrage of disconnected, split-second images amidst a sophisticated range of realist conventions implies that—in one, restricted sense at least—a high degree of literacy already exists.

Media literacy is, therefore, more than a question of comprehension: It is concerned with the form and scope of that comprehension. Media literacy is not a simple matter of reading media well, whether in the traditional Leavisite sense (of distinguishing between "good" and "bad" texts, see Leavis, 1950), or in the more deconstructive sense of understanding textual strategies, possibilities, or pleasures (Barthes, 1974, 1975, 1988). There is more to media education than a framework for appreciating the finer nuances of the *Seinfeld* narrative, the montage of the opening credits of *ER,* or ways in which the extreme close-up shot in *60 Minutes* situates the spectator.

The distinction we would like to make is between a text-focused form of media literacy and a contextual approach, in which the unraveling of media texts takes place in the context of their production and reception. This is not to downplay the importance of textual analysis. It is at the level of the text, after all, that vital issues of representation are played out, and a sophisticated textual analysis can tell us something about both encoding and decoding (Hall, 1993). However, a textual analysis that takes place without examining the institutional, cultural, and economic conditions in which texts are produced and understood is necessarily limited.

Media literacy, in short, is about more than the analysis of messages, it is about an awareness of why those messages are there. It is not enough to know that they are produced, or even how, in a technical sense, they are produced. To appreciate the significance of contemporary media, we need to know why they are produced, under what constraints and conditions, and by whom.

Raymond Williams (1977) has documented the way in which early struggles over literacy were bound up with questions of power and control. In the early years of industry, workers were trained to read, but not to write. This allowed them to follow orders or read the bible for moral instruction, but not to express their own needs or interests. Although contemporary television audiences are not so consciously deprived, their situation is in many ways analogous. They are expected to consume rather than produce— to pick from the display offered by commercial television rather than debate the terms and conditions in which broadcasting takes place.

We therefore need to differentiate between a text-centered approach that restricts itself to proficiency in reading and Williams's (1974, 1980) more general form of cultural criticism in which both the reading and the production of texts are understood within sets of social relations. So, for example, Janice Radway's (1994) work on romances and the Book of the Month Club engages with determinations at every stage in the circuit of production and reception.

As both Williams's (1974, 1980) and Radway's (1994) work suggests, an analysis of political economy should not be restricted to a narrow set of economic relations. The media are determined by a set of social and economic conditions that involve the key dividing lines of our culture, whether they be race, class, gender, sexuality, age, or mobility. This may be a complex point, but we are concerned that media education in the United States will flounder if it cannot locate media texts in a broad set of social realities.

Roland Barthes's (1977) well-known announcement of the Death of the Author is illustrative here. His argument is, in many ways, a celebration of textual analysis in which a focus on production or reception becomes a constraint on the practice of reading. Barthes's argument works because he is engaged with a particular site (i.e., traditional literary criticism) in which the politics of production are less central. He is concerned with the way literary texts, many of which have been around for some time, are read and understood, not with the production, marketing, and distribution of contemporary fiction.

Media studies, on the other hand, is forced to deal with limits and constraints, to explain absences, such as, for example, the comparative absence of a Black working class on U.S. television (Jhally & Lewis, 1992), and the consequences of those absences. To do so, it is required to go beyond the text.

If this contextual approach makes media literacy less "safe," it also makes it more enticing. So, for example, asking high school students to critique an advertisement by the Campaign for a Drug Free America may or may not encourage a vague cynicism about how those in authority view (or attempt to situate) American youth. This kind of cynicism is, on its own, unhelpful to both high school students and their teachers. If the teacher is able to go beyond the text, to point out that the Campaign for a Drug Free America is a consortium funded by America's leading alcohol, tobacco, and pharmaceutical companies (Cotts, 1992), the students are confronted with a more concrete political reality. The conclusions they draw may still be cynical, but it is likely to be a more directed cynicism, one born of analysis rather than attitude. Students can do more than play textual games, they can question the rules.

Similarly, an analysis of the news should be concerned not only with the way stories are constructed, but also with who is and who is not allowed to speak (Herman & Chomsky, 1988). A purely textual critique of television news is more speculative. For students to evaluate a news story seriously, they need to be able to go beyond the text, to consider the various stories that surround it, and thereby place it within a context that enables them to see the choices ABC or CNN have made.

Political Economy and Citizenship

If the political economy of the media seems a rather dry subject for students to consider, it need not be so. In our experience, students often find this level of analysis easier to grasp than a text-focused analysis. There is, in this respect, a healthy literature on political economy from which to draw (Bagdikian, 1997; Herman & McChesney, 1997; Schiller, 1984, 1989, 1996), much of which is extremely useful in allowing students to appreciate issues raised by a textual analysis. Pedagogically, this is less complex or arduous than it sounds. When automobile ads invariably show cars driving along empty roads, often across pristine landscapes with cloudless skies, we might ask students not only what is being left out of these images (traffic, pollution, smog), but why? In whose interest is it to see the automobile as a symbol of freedom, exploring rather than despoiling the U.S. landscape? What role do these interests have in media production? What are the consequences of seeing the automobile in only these terms?

Our experience indicates that students find it difficult to make sense of media messages as part of a vast, complex, and contradictory panorama made up of authorless ideologies. The politics of media texts become more tangible if they are seen as produced by real people for specific purposes. If this seems a perilously political approach, it is no less so than allowing students to see the media only on their own terms. It is a little like teaching a literary canon without allowing students to question the limits or foci of that canon. This is all the more troubling, perhaps, when the media canon is a product of a purely commercial rationale.

This approach undoubtedly has political consequences. Just as political education allows citizens to think more critically and constructively about politics, media literacy can provide people with the wherewithal for thinking about the limits and possibilities of media systems. This is, needless to say, no small task, particularly in the United States, where exposure to foreign media is as limited as it is anywhere in the world.

U.S. broadcasting is highly distinctive. Unlike the public service models that influence broadcasting in most other industrialized countries, the history of radio and television in the U.S. is one of rampant commercialism (McAllister, 1996). In the United States, media corporations have, since the 1930s, been unusually successful in promoting an idea of broadcasting in economic rather than cultural terms, that is, as a business rather than a public service (McChesney, 1993). Media regulation in the U.S., particularly since the Reagan era, is conspicuous by its absence, yet many Americans find it difficult to imagine how it could be any other way.

This conceptual limitation has little to do with preference. Surveys do not suggest that Americans are especially happy or uncritical about television (Times Mirror, 1993). It is more a matter of education than imagination. It is difficult to propose changes to a system that is regarded as both inevitable and ubiquitous, and when the only alternative ever presented is the dull, propagandist fare of totalitarian regimes. Indeed, it could be argued that one of the successes of commercial broadcasting in the U.S. has been persuading Americans that there is no alternative, and that the American system is the only conceivable model in a society that values free speech and free expression. The European concept of public service broadcasting, with its possibilities of public funding, cross subsidy, and regulations to promote education and diversity, remains a well-kept secret. If the British system is capable of offering a wide range of quality programs with a comparatively small number of channels, one can only imagine the breadth and range of a public service system in a country with a media market as large and bountiful as the United States.

As we have suggested, this implicates the notions of citizenship and cultural democracy. When the British government sanctioned a fourth network (Channel Four) at the beginning of the 1980s, it was at the center of a public debate about the funding, remit, regulation, and purpose of a new television network. Although some were critical of the scope of that discussion (Blanchard & Morley, 1982; Lambert, 1982), most recent changes in the North American broadcasting landscape have occurred with little or no public input. The lack of public debate surrounding the passage of the Telecommunications Act of 1996 is a graphic example of how a major restructuring of the media environment disappeared from public view. For us, what is most worrisome about this absence is less the lack of consultation and discussion than an ideological climate in which the public is so accustomed to being interpolated as mere consumers in a corporate world that any notion of democratic input seems difficult to grasp.

A brief anecdote told to us by our colleague, Michael Morgan, suggests the extent of the problem. During an exam, students were asked to identify which type of media system was most common in countries worldwide: (a) a government-run or public service model or (b) a commercial model. Before the exam, students were told that when they came to this question, they should not even bother to read it, since the correct answer was "a." Despite this apparently unambiguous advice, half his students proceeded to get the answer wrong. This is not a question of dullness (the students performed well enough overall), it suggests that the correct answer ran so counter to their own preconceptions that many disregarded not only what they had learned, but an answer they had just been told was correct. They were simply unable to imagine a world in which the U.S. model was atypical.

The blinkered, ideological assumptions behind this premise are fairly deep-rooted, and it will undoubtedly take more than a few media literacy classes to open American minds to other possibilities. Nevertheless, a media literacy curriculum in which issues of representation and content are taught alongside questions of political economy presents a challenge to regulators who have, in recent years, offered little more than the further deregulation of an already lightly regulated system. Debates about the regulation and subsidy of broadcasting can become public debates, rather than esoteric, lopsided discussions among media corporations, legislators, and a few poorly funded pressure groups.

Those currently campaigning for media reform—whether to regulate childrens' programming so that it is not simply a marketing vehicle for the toy industry, or for a viable public television service, or for restrictions to monopoly ownership—are stymied not because their ideas are unpopular, but because, at a fundamental level, their relevance is not appreciated. Americans have become used to a system of top-down control, where a citizen's input is restricted to being a blip in the Nielsen ratings and where commercial considerations are inexorably paramount. Media literacy is, therefore, a way of extending democracy to the very place where democracy is increasingly scripted and defined.

The Use and Abuse of Technology

If we have focused on political economy, it is because we see a danger of the circuit of cultural production and reception becoming excluded from the discussion. Our argument, nevertheless, is not about teaching one thing rather than another, but about the integration of these levels of analysis. A focus on media production that excluded textual analysis would, in our view, be as problematic and fragmented as a purely text-centered approach.

In our experience, the way in which high school teachers may, without guidance, interpret the idea of media literacy suggests that this is a particular risk when teachers are fortunate enough to have the technology for practical classes in media production. There are instances when the seductive and pseudo-empowering nature of the technology works to exclude both a broad political economy and a critical textual analysis (Frechette, 1997).

For teachers with access to cameras and editing facilities, this technology can be an indispensable component of an educational practice that highlights the question of representation. As Stuart Ewen (1996) put it,

> Media literacy cannot simply be seen as a vaccination against PR or other familiar strains of institutionalized guile. It must be understood as an education in techniques that can democratize the realm of public expression and will magnify the possibility of meaningful public interactions. (p. 414)

In this ideal form, teaching production skills can be a vibrant part of a media literacy project. However, we would caution against an unthinking embrace. Although media production offers several pedagogical opportunities, it may close down as many analytical paths as it opens.

It is sometimes assumed, for example, that a practical knowledge of video production will help demystify the world of television and promote a more analytical, critical perspective. There is, however, little evidence to support such an assumption. To the contrary, we have found that students are apt to be seduced by the form, to try to imitate commercial television, and, when their efforts fall short, regard the work of professionals purely in terms of their aesthetic or technical prowess. At best, teaching production as purely a set of technical skills leads to an analytical immersion rather than a critical distance.

Unless the educational limits of teaching production are stressed, well-resourced schools might answer the call for media literacy simply by offering classes in media production. This would, in our view, blunt the critical edge of media literacy and allow it to be co-opted into a system of existing educational inequities. If media education is seen as dependent upon the purchase of video cameras and editing equipment, only those schools with sufficient means will be able to participate. Once media literacy is tied to the size of a school's capital budget, it risks becoming yet another symbol of cultural capital.

This is not to say that teaching production cannot or should not be a component of a media literacy project. It certainly is possible—even desirable—to incorporate production classes into a media literacy context, particularly with groups who already feel marginalized by mainstream media. The Educational Video Center in New York is a good example of such an initiative. Students are encouraged to use video technology to tell stories that are rarely heard on commercial television. This both enhances and develops their sense of critical reflection because they are not so much copying the medium as exploring its potential. This is possible because, at the EVC, production has been integrated into an overall theoretical approach that highlights the question of power.

The Politics of Media Literacy

As we have suggested, this approach to media education inevitably raises challenging political questions that, in some respects, it would be safer to avoid. Yet, we would argue, the feelings of frustration and dissatisfaction that many parents, teachers, and citizens feel is an explicitly political form of discontent—one that gives media literacy its sense of urgency and relevance.

Educators, whether parents or teachers, are tired of competing with television. They are tired of dismissing it as a mere distraction or else resenting it as the "evil twin" of universal education, the proverbial devil with little substance and all the best tunes. They are also tired of being offered the rather smug retort to their complaints that if parents or citizens are unhappy with what's offered, they can always turn it off. Most of us, after all, like watching what we consider to be worthwhile, informative, or entertaining. We don't want it to go away. Most educators are aware that the bumper-sticker invocation to "kill your television" has an ostrich-like impracticality. We want to improve it.

In the current political climate, the political options generally presented to deal with television have been, at best, fairly limited reactions to television's perceived excesses. Calls for censorship, boycotts, or parental control of television viewing via new technologies such as the V-chip all take a fairly negative stance, one in which the basic political economy of loosely regulated commercial television remains intact. If we are to have a television system whose goals have more to do with public service than commerce—whether that means a greater diversity of images and representations, less commercial interruption, more documentary programming, or more educational children's programs—we need to develop a citizenry that appreciates the politics of regulation and funding, to thereby imagine what television might be, and how the system might be changed to make it so. The challenge for media literacy, we would argue, is to make this possibility seem less remote.

Conclusion

Whatever this desire for change involves, it will never be fully addressed by a text-centered approach to media education. The demands that give the campaign for media literacy a certain urgency require an approach that addresses questions about social context and social impact. Parents concerned about violence or gender stereotyping in children's programs are unlikely to be mollified by the thought that the Power Rangers can be read on a number of different levels, or even that their children may eventually come to understand the limits of such stereotypes. They want to know what influence such programming may have and how media producers might be persuaded to offer something less pernicious. They are, in short, concerned not just with the nature of the visual environment, but the forces that shape it. A contextual approach to media literacy allows students to see the media within a framework of interests and power relations. If some see a danger here of making media literacy an overtly political project, we take the opposite view. A text-centered approach that fails to address current concerns and dissatisfaction with the media risks losing the political impetus that gives it its current purchase.

For the past four years we have been involved with the Five-College Media Literacy Institute, which introduces teachers to the field of media literacy from the contextual, cultural studies perspective we have briefly outlined. As many in the field are aware, when teachers return to their schools, there is little financial, pedagogical, or structural support for the integration of critical questions around media into the existing curriculum. Creating these supportive environments is a political task, one that, as Wally Bowen (1994) argues with unapologetic vigor, needs to

> connect to the interests and concerns of a broad range of scholars, teachers, health educators, parents and citizens who are seeking ways to critically challenge a media system that exploits children, reduces citizens to consumers, rewards those who poison public discourse, and perpetuates a high-consumption lifestyle that is slowly strangling the planet's life-support systems. (p. 2)

The implementation of media literacy as a component of the K–12 curriculum will require enthusiastic community support. If a text-centered approach seems the politically safer option, it is also one, in our view, that is less likely to enthuse teachers and parents.

We acknowledge, however, that a contextual approach with an emphasis on political economy is likely to be less acceptable to some elements within the media literacy coalition than a text-centered approach. Indeed, there is no doubt that advocates for a certain form of text-centered media literacy have been successful in broadening support for media education, and there is certainly an argument that such pragmatism may be more likely to lead to the widespread implementation of media literacy.

As we have stated, this risks diluting the enthusiasm created by the desire for a public voice in decisions about media programming. The rush to embrace media literacy may also lead to its suffocating under the weight of its own incoherence. Even the commercial media industry—perhaps sensing that, in a period of minimal political interference or regulation, the only real danger to its unrestricted growth and profit maximization is a critically informed public—is moving to initiate its own version. Thus, in the inaugural issue of *Better Viewing* magazine, Continental Cablevision (now MediaOne) invokes media literacy and the general empowerment of its viewers. In this self-serving appropriation, informed citizenship means little more than a weekly perusal of *TV Guide*. It is safe to assume that Continental Cablevision's notion of empowerment does not extend to the regulation of media monopolies or subversive notions about public service broadcasting (Cowie, 1995).

If this attempted colonization is breathtaking in its audacity, it is possible because the phrase itself, with its irresistible invocation of the most basic of skills, is noncommittal on how it applies to the comprehension of mass media. Norman Cowie (1996) described how, in the United States,

> there is an uneasy consensus among media literacy proponents around a definition that was formulated in Canada in 1989, as "the ability to access, analyze, communicate and produce media in a variety of forms." While this definition appears to serve as a rallying point for coalition building, there is a decided lack of consensus around its terms and practices. (p. 1)

In the face of attempts to build up a critical mass for reform, it is not surprising that the media literacy movement has avoided hard questions and debate around its core concerns. This avoidance of principle, however, comes at a price. It risks sapping the movement's vitality and replacing it with a vapid ambiguity.

Our advocacy of a contextual approach to media education is influenced by our experience of teaching these issues at the college level, where media analysis thrives in several disciplines in the humanities and liberal arts. The bureaucratic and political contexts of the K–12 situation are very different, and it is easy to see why a more limited, text-based "visual literacy" worked so well in the confines of this environment. As Wally Bowen (1994) put it:

> The inherent conservatism of U.S. public school bureaucracies discourages the broader examination of media culture inherent in a cultural studies approach, with its emphasis on questions of political economy, power relations, hegemonic influence. . . . The conventional wisdom said that entry into the politically charged minefield of the public school curriculum is

achieved by slipping media literacy into the language arts "critical skills" curriculum. (pp. 1–2)

This defensive posture is perfectly understandable in those places where there is little existing institutional support to create an entirely new field. It has also led to the uneasy consensus that Cowie (1996) described among a disparate group of interests. When your numbers are small, why separate over internal doctrinaire disputes? The sheer scale of the U.S. educational system has meant that the focus on diversity of approaches, which Hobbs (1996) argued is the strength of the media literacy, is also our greatest weakness. We would argue with Cowie that, "the pluralism that underwrites this diversity has had a depoliticising effect on the very issues that media literacy seeks to address" and that "when one surveys the work that has been accomplished on the basis of a meaningful consensus in countries such as Canada, Western Europe and Australia, it is difficult to feel that our enduring lack of a consensus is viable" (p. 1).

For us, the risk lies in depriving students of a political education that is essential if they are to be capable of making rational decisions amidst a deluge of media messages. To evaluate those messages, students must learn to see them not simply as true or false, realistic or misleading, stereotypical or positive, but as authored voices with certain interests or assumptions about the world, voices that could be influenced or replaced. As Noam Chomsky (1989) noted, "Citizens of the democratic societies should undertake a course of intellectual self-defense to protect themselves from manipulation and control, and to lay the basis for meaningful democracy" (p. viii). It is important to note that we are not advocating propagandizing in schools for a particular political perspective. We are advocating a view that recognizes that the world is always made by someone, and a decision to tolerate the status quo is as political as a more overtly radical act.

References

Bagdikian, B. (1997). *The media monopoly.* Boston: Beacon Press.

Barnouw, E. (1978). *The sponsor: Notes on a modern potentate.* New York: Oxford University Press.

Barthes, R. (1974). *S/Z.* New York: Hill & Wang.

Barthes, R. (1975). *The pleasure of the text.* London: Jonathan Cape.

Barthes, R. (1977). *Image-Music-Text.* Glasgow, Scotland: Fontana.

Barthes, R. (1988). *Mythologies.* New York: Noonday Press.

Blanchard, S., & Morley, D. (1982). *What's this Channel Four?* London: Comedia.

Bowen, W. (1994). Can U.S. media literacy movement open door to more points of view? *The New Citizen, 2*(1). (http://www.main.nc.us/cml/new_citizen/ v2n1/win94c.html)

Chomsky, N. (1989). *Necessary illusions: Thought control in democratic societies.* Boston, MA: South End Press.

Cotts, C. (1992). Hard sell in the drug war. *The Nation,* pp. 300–303.

Cowie, N. (Summer/Fall, 1995). The future of media literacy in the age of corporate sponsorship. *Video & Learning,* pp. 5–6.

Cowie, N. (1996, May 9). *Media literacy: From the creation of "critical consumers" to the formation of (radical) political subjects*. Paper presented at the conference on Alliance for Community Media, Burlington, VT.

Ewen, S. (1996). *PR: A social history of spin*. New York: Basic Books.

Frechette, J. (1997). *The politics of implementing media literacy into the United States: A look at the objectives and obstacles facing the Massachusetts public school teacher*. Unpublished master's thesis, Department of Communication, University of Massachusetts at Amherst.

Hall, S. (1980). Encoding/Decoding. In S. Hall, D. Hobson, A. Lowe, & P. Willis (Eds.), *Culture, media, language* (pp. 128–138). London: Hutchinson.

Hall, S. (1994). Reflections upon the encoding/decoding model: An interview with Stuart Hall. In J. Cruz & J. Lewis (Eds.), *Viewing, reading, listening: Audiences and cultural reception* (pp. 253–274). Boulder, CO: Westview.

Herman, E., & Chomsky, N. (1988). *Manufacturing consent: The political economy of the mass media*. New York: Pantheon.

Herman, E., & McChesney, R. (1997). *The global media: The new missionaries of corporate capitalism*. London: Cassell.

Hobbs, R. (1996). Media literacy, media activism. *Telemedium, the Journal of Media Literacy, 42*(3).

Garnham, N. (1990). *Capitalism and communication*. London: Sage.

Jhally, S. (1990). *The codes of advertising: Fetishism and the political economy of meaning in the consumer society*. New York: Routledge.

Jhally, S., & Lewis, J. (1992). *Enlightened racism: Audiences, the Cosby show and the myth of the American dream*. Boulder, CO: Westview.

Johnson, R. (1986–87). What is cultural studies anyway? *Social Text, 16,* 38–80.

Lambert, S. (1982). *Channel 4: Television with a difference?* London: British Film Institute.

Leavis, R. (1950). *The great tradition: George Eliot, Henry James, Joseph Conrad*. London: Chatto & Windus.

Masterman, L. (1997). A rationale for media education. In R. Kubey (Ed.), *Media literacy in the information age* (pp. 15–68). New Brunswick, NJ: Transaction.

McAllister, M. (1996). *The commercialisation of American culture: New advertising, control and democracy*. Thousand Oaks, CA: Sage.

McChesney, R. (1993). *Telecommunications, mass media and democracy: The battle for the control of U.S. broadcasting 1928–1935*. New York: Oxford University Press.

Morley, D. (1980). *The nationwide audience*. London: British Film Institute.

Morley, D. (1986). *Family television*. London: Comedia.

Radway, J. (1994). Romance and the work of fantasy: Struggles over feminine sexuality and subjectivity at century's end. In J. Cruz & J. Lewis (Eds.), *Viewing, reading listening: Audiences and cultural reception*. Boulder, CO: Westview.

Schiller, H. (1996). *Information inequality: The deepening social crisis in America*. New York: Routledge.

Schiller, H. (1984). *Information and the crisis economy*. Norwood, NJ: Ablex.

Schiller, H. (1989). *Culture Inc.: The corporate takeover of public expression*. New York: Oxford University Press.

Times Mirror Center for the People and the Press (1993, March 24). Poll.

Williams, R. (1974). *Television, technology and cultural form*. London: Fontana.

Williams, R. (1977). *Marxism and literature*. New York: Columbia University Press.

Williams, R. (1980). *Problems in materialism and culture*. London: New Left Books.

"The Front Row Is Reserved for Scotch Drinkers"

Early Television's Tavern Audience

ANNA McCARTHY

The early history of television viewing in the United States is generally examined in relation to certain postwar trends: the housing boom, suburbanization, growing consumption, increased leisure time, and an "affluent" working class.[1] Numerous sociological studies of middle-class populations at the time depicted these trends as a series of profound transformations in the relation between public and private spheres.[2] Drawing upon these studies, Robert Fishman describes television in terms of the evaporation of public life, arguing that TV constituted the postwar suburb's "perfect medium," bypassing "the old centers of community . . . to go directly to the home."[3] More recently, broadcast historians have shown that TV's impact on community life was hardly this simple. Indeed, as Lynn Spigel and others have argued, the medium provided a focus for cultural anxieties about these transformations.[4] Suburbanization, Spigel points out, did not necessarily entail the disappearance of community; rather, it was a specific configuration of a middle-class communal ideal in which communications forms such as TV meant that "people could keep their distance from the world but at the same time imagine that their domestic spheres were connected to a wider social fabric."[5] Furthermore, discourses on TV as home entertainment in the postwar years often articulated the ambiguities inherent within the bourgeois distinction between public and private: "Television was caught in a contradictory movement between public and private worlds, and it often

From *Cinema Journal* 34:4, pp. 31–49; by permission of the author and the University of Texas Press. All rights retained by the University of Texas Press.

became a rhetorical figure for that contradiction."[6] Spigel fully explores the dynamics of this contradiction within the physical space of the home and in the social milieu of suburban *arrivistes,* a population negotiating and adapting to a life of housing developments, automobiles, and new families. As several critics observe, advertisements for television receivers offered to reconfigure this "lonely crowd" as a "family circle": kids on the floor, parents in armchairs, and a ballerina on the screen.[7] This image of early TV viewership is unquestionably the most prevalent one in popular memory, perhaps leading to the impression that the middle-class suburban living room was the only social space where TV was viewed.

This essay aims to expand this impression of the early TV audience by investigating the medium's emergence outside the home and within a larger urban geography. I approach TV as a form of public amusement, examining the widespread installation of TV sets in barrooms between 1946 and 1949. My goal is to locate the horizons of the barroom viewing experience both within the discursive regimes of larger institutions and within the local protocols and practices of the tavern itself. Like the middle-class home, the neighborhood tavern embodied a particular social history. Television's integration into urban, working-class life via the barroom was, I argue, less determined by the contradictory ideologies of domesticity than by a historically constructed *habitus* in which institutionalized spaces of recreation, like saloons and movie theaters, lent a semblance of autonomy to working-class leisure pursuits. At the same time, this apparent autonomy was continually compromised, as reformists and commercial interests sought to define or regulate tavern TV viewing.

Tavern TV installation was considered to be just a phase in TV's conquest of the home, even when barstool viewers greatly outnumbered the home audience.[8] In 1947, industrial surveys estimated that most viewers, particularly sports fans, watched from the tavern and not the living room.[9] This audience's thirst for both television and refreshments led *Sponsor* to conclude in 1948 that "the product using TV most successfully to date is beer."[10] Broadcasters found that bar patrons and householders preferred different types of programming; the fact that both were most likely to watch in the evenings made scheduling difficult. "The bar and grill set prefers sporting and news events," an article in *Business Week* reported, "and there aren't enough . . . to fill television's broadcasting hours." Noting that "the studio programs designed for home listening do not appeal to the watchers in saloons," the article concluded that the audience manifested a "split personality."[11] *Newsweek* reached a similar conclusion: "Other television shows feature fashion shows and special events, but bar owners find sports telecasts more popular."[12] These analyses of "television's audience problem" were clearly gendered: the bar was considered the province of male viewers, while women were presumed to make up the domestic audience. *Business Week* further surmised that the two audiences occupied different class positions. Working-class people watched in bars, while those with "more comfortable incomes" watched at home.

I find these characterizations less valid as empirical conclusions than as instances of the bourgeois ideology of "two spheres" that served, Lynn Spigel points out, as the historical backdrop for the domestic installation of television.[13] In this particular case, the discursive separation of audiences according to gender and class also indicates that from its inception the industry conceived of television as a gendered apparatus, both in programming and in the spaces where the programming was viewed.[14] It seems likely, however, that the audience watching in public drinking establishments was, as a whole, far more diverse than such portrayals suggest.[15] While the TV audience within one kind of bar was probably quite homogeneous, television was installed in all types of establishments and thus reached a range of social groups, from fairly wealthy men and women to transient, mostly male, "down and out" communities.[16] Journalistic coverage of TV in bars tended to focus, however, on its installation in neighborhood taverns, a type of public drinking place that outnumbered all others in the forties.

The word "tavern" became popular after Prohibition as a way of avoiding the undesirable connotations of "saloon," which brought to mind "disreputability, low-lifes, 'Father, dear Father, come home with me now,' and that sort of thing."[17] In the press it generally described a low-key, beer-serving, male-oriented, working-class neighborhood drinkery, offering its core of regulars a few amusements and perhaps some food. To a lesser extent, the word also designated downtown bars frequented by businessmen; slippage between the two appears to stem from the fact that both catered to a regular, predominantly male patronage and served primarily beer. In Manhattan, the phrase "bar and grill" appeared to cover both types of place.[18] H. L. Mencken noted that although words like "tavern," "taproom," and "stube" were intended to minimize the association with the saloon, the establishments they designated had changed little.[19] In forties usage, then, "tavern" differentiated primarily neighborhood bars from other places where alcohol was consumed at the time.

A sociological study completed in 1950 divided urban drinking holes into five or six major categories based on class, location, and social function: "drink and dine," nightclub (or cocktail lounge), downtown bar, skid row bar, and neighborhood tavern.[20] The first three attracted a significantly larger proportion of women and middle-class people than the tavern; in the study cited above, almost half the patrons of nightclubs were found to be women. In contrast, of all women who went regularly to bars, only one-fifth stated that they patronized taverns.[21] Quite likely, the amount of female patronage probably varied from space to space, and some taverns were certainly equally patronized by men and women. In fact, the same study found that "women were more likely to affirm the importance of the tavern in providing a meeting place and satisfying unmet social needs." One woman even stated, "If my daughters are eventually going to drink I would rather they go to the tavern than to go to private places."[22] In many cases, however, the presence of women was frowned upon by male customers.[23] Signs posted above the bar often explicitly attempted to regulate the activities of women customers or prohibit them altogether, as in the following examples collected in a 1947 survey of taverns in Manhattan and the boroughs of New York:

Danger! Women Drinking
Notice! No Back Room Here for Ladies
Good Ale, Raw Onions, and No Ladies
No Unescorted Ladies Permitted at Bar[24]

Although no legal interdiction barred women from taverns, such signs would severely limit their participation in tavern social life.

Working-class neighborhood bars, before and after Prohibition, were a hub of male (and sometimes female) recreation in community life.[25] In 1947, one observer characterized the tavern as a place "frequented by men and women who call each other by first names, who know what their drinking companions work at, the number of children each has, whether so-and-so is getting married, and who, in short, feel comfortable, natural, and at ease in each other's company."[26] Regular customers thought of their local taverns as informal social clubs rather than places to get drunk: "Many who wish to drink may do so at home or in other private ways," one patron noted. "Often [the tavern] is the only place a man can go unless he belongs to such clubs as Madison Club, Elks Club, et al., and including country clubs."[27] A "drink and dine" owner echoed the club analogy, adding that while formal clubs maintained restrictive membership requirements, "when [people] want to meet on common ground, they all meet at a neighborhood tavern or hotel bar."[28] Another proprietor also characterized the atmosphere of the tavern in terms of its egalitarianism: "A person sitting on the other side of the bar feels equal to his neighbor on the next stool."[29] This was echoed by a number of patrons, who felt that "everyone is equal in a tavern—whereas schools and churches all have their caste systems."[30] The tavern was thus an institution distinct from others, understood by its patrons as a nonhierarchical social space.

Jurgen Habermas has used the concept of the public sphere to designate a social institution in which private individuals congregate for convivial discussion, a discursive arena which is, in principle, open to all citizens and where outside social status is "bracketed" to one side.[31] At once a theoretical construct, a democratic ideal, and a historical description, the term "public sphere" does not apply uniformly to all nondomestic social spaces. Rather, in Habermas's formulation, it indicates the process by which discussions and civic debates—including literary or cultural ones—constitute forms of political participation. The classical public sphere was a bourgeois social formation which, for all its openness, actually excluded a great many people, particularly women, the working class, and minorities. It was, in other words, exclusionary rather than inclusive. Since Habermas's original formulation, however, social theorists have reoriented the concept in order to specify the discursive arenas of marginalized groups, discussing the potentialities and limits of a "proletarian public sphere" (Oskar Negt and Alexandre Kluge) or "subaltern counterpublics" (Nancy Fraser).[32] In the 1940s, when patrons described the conversational space of the tavern, they continually referred to the bar as a forum for discussion "about problems, politics, and common interests"; topics ranged from "sports and . . . families" to "problems of home, of work, of business" to "local and foreign problems."[33] In these conceptions, and in the belief that the tavern provided a barrierless space for exchange and communication, the outlines of a working-class public sphere begin to emerge.

Habermas was pessimistic about the possibility of the formation of a critical public in twentieth-century mass-cultural patterns of amusement and leisure. In particular, he argued, the foundation of the "classical" public sphere, in which privately conducted practices of reading and thinking informed public discussion, evaporated as the structure of work, leisure, and family life changed. Defined by a particular relation between public and private existence, the bourgeois public sphere lost its critical function when work, previously considered part of the private realm, became a public affair, and the private sphere that previously supported the public one shrank "into the inner areas of a conjugal family largely relieved of its function and weakened in its authority—the quiet bliss of homeyness."[34] Habermas placed much of the blame for the bourgeois public sphere's disappearance on mass culture. Critical debate was unnecessary, he argued, "when people went to the movies together, listened to the radio, or watched TV." Such activities were forms of absorption that required no reflection; passive consumption had replaced the discussion and interaction associated with the public sphere.[35]

In 1949, sociologist Herbert Bloch betrayed a similarly elitist attitude toward public recreation when he identified the tavern (more precisely the lounge) with "passive entertainment . . . the various forms of the mass spectacle . . . and commercialized recreational media." For Bloch, urbanization was at fault in the commodification of leisure: "the crawling, gargantuan, megalopolitan urban centers . . . [have] provided a ready market to those commercial purveyors of recreation emanating from Hollywood, Tin Pan Alley and the Corner Cocktail Lounge."[36] By most accounts, however, tavern and saloon life was hardly a form of passive absorption; conversation, community participation, and recreational activities were intertwined in the social history of such places. Insofar as working-class drinking spots constituted a public sphere, their community role rested upon an ability to offer both amusement *and* discourse.[37] People came to the bar not to escape but to do a number of things: "talk, exchange ideas, discuss their important problem, and have fun playing cards and shuffleboard and listening to the juke box."[38] In one sociologist's words, "in practically all of the functions of the tavern the patrons are not primarily observers, as they are when attending church, the theater, and various athletic events. Instead of being the audience they are participating actively; instead of having their thoughts and actions patterned for them, they are free to act and think as they wish."[39]

The crux of the tavern as an institution lay in the sense of autonomy and self-determination it lent to the activities that took place within its walls. In this capacity, it was a product of a larger historical process. Roy Rosenzweig, in his study of working-class leisure in a turn-of-the-century industrial city, demonstrates that leisure—"eight hours for what we will"—was a right working people fought for, and that the saloon was a particularly contested site in this struggle. The history of leisure and recreation in the United States, he argues, was not simply a progressive decay of agency through a commodified desire for passive amusement. Rather, it reflected a class conflict in which middle-class reformers and institutions sought to define appropriate forms of recreation for the working classes.[40]

This history of recreation and regulation was the backdrop for television's arrival in the public life of the tavern. When the television set was installed, it entered a space that was marked by diverse forms of regulation.[41] These included municipal and federal interdictions on children and gambling, the imposition of closing times, special licensing, and entertainment restrictions. In addition, certain activities were proscribed locally and individually (such as dancing, spitting, and swearing) and countless unwritten codes prevented women, minorities, and others from entering. The TV set thus inhabited a social space filled with discourses and practices that in one way or another placed limits upon the behaviors and practices taking place therein.

Television also placed the tavern in a new alignment with other commercial spaces in the geography of urban working-class leisure. The tavern's status as a place of amusement was the point of articulation in this discursive operation. Sports officials and theater operators viewed the tavern-going public as a rival mass audience, and moral guardians of youth who saw the tavern television set as a lure for juvenile delinquency attempted to provide "alternative" sites for youth viewers in more appropriate recreational spaces. These external discourses, together with localized and internal protocols, delineated the field of possible reception practices in the tavern. My analysis will move from "outside" to "inside" to trace the horizons of this experience.

Debates over televised sports in the late forties generally centered on whether the medium would create new fans or decrease stadium attendance.[42] In 1948 *Variety* ran an article that characterized the tavern sports audience as a potentially greater threat to gate receipts than home viewers. The article reported that baseball league executives had "expressed [the] conviction that tele, if confined to its rightful place in the home, could help them by converting some of the public into new fans. They voiced considerable misgivings, however, about the number of bars that advertise in bold window cards 'see the baseball games here.'"[43] To stave off "the competition tossed in their faces by tavern and bar sets," baseball owners announced that they would ask set manufacturers and distributors to warn bars against advertising games in their windows. If cooperation was not received, owners warned that "they might prohibit baseball telecasting in the future. And that . . . would cut a deep swath into the pull of taverns."[44]

In metropolitan areas like New York, which had three baseball teams at the time, bar viewers may have posed some threat to stadium earnings.

Tavern owners who hosted televised sports events experienced sales increases of up to 60 percent.[45] In 1947, a Chicago tavern owner told *Time,* " 'Bout coupla months ago we was losin' money but fast . . . I figure maybe dese guys is goin to hockey games or fights, an I say, why not bring hockey or fights here, so guys can see sports and drink atta same time."[46] This account points to the source of sports promoters' displeasure, namely, the fact that preexisting fans were drawn to the tavern as a more local and comfortable viewing environment than the stadium. The fear was that fans enjoyed watching from a barstool as much as, if not more than, from the bleachers.[47]

In contrast, some broadcasters and sports promoters believed that *home* viewers would be drawn to the ballpark to see for themselves what the stadium experience was like. One ad executive stated: "I've already gone to more games than I did last year. Television increased my interest in getting out to the park."[48] Boxing promoter Mike Jacobs's press agent claimed that a friend who once vowed never to see a fight became a fan when he bought a television set: "Since then, he's been to the Garden five times this summer."[49] Writing in *Variety,* ABC executive Paul Whiteman explained that it was the differences between the TV and the "live" experience that made new fans: "bellowing opinions is part of the fun of attending a ball game or a fight and I think that television will create fans who buy tickets."[50]

In the discourse on home and stadium sports spectatorship, the tavern emerged as a place where the televised event and the bleacher experience seemed to blend together. Journalists covering tavern television noticed that large groups of viewers acted like fans attending the event in person. The *New Yorker,* for example, offered the following account of tavern viewers of the 1946 Louis-Conn fight: "Along about the fourth round, some of the audience were carried away by the illusion that they were actually at the stadium. 'Hit him, Billy,' cried a partisan spectator. 'G'wan, you think he can hear you?' retorted a realist."[51] In their attempt to prevent bar owners from drawing fans by advertising games, baseball magnates tacitly acknowledged that the tavern provided a real form of crowd participation. The barroom was no longer simply a place for community leisure, it had become a place of public, mass amusement and a competitor to the stadium in the market of sports spectatorship. By bringing public amusements from outside the neighborhood into a community-centered space, taverns encroached on fixed audience markets, even though taverngoers undoubtedly continued to patronize other amusements.

Motion picture exhibitors shared the concerns of baseball owners. In 1948, a group of New Jersey theater owners called a meeting with legislators to discuss the "alarming threat" television posed for the film business. Their target was not the home audience but the tavern; a survey in the area had disclosed that, in *Variety*'s jargon, "most theaters are now surrounded by a belt of bistros which offer tele entertainment as a cuffo chaser to the drinks."[52] (Translation: a number of lounges and restaurants with television were located near theaters.) To stave off the possibility that people might settle for a night of TV and drinks instead of a movie show, exhibitors suggested that bars be required to purchase licenses as places of amusement. The effort was probably futile, as the IRS had ruled the year before that taverns with TV were not eligible for federal amusement taxes when the set was "not coupled with other amusements."[53] In all likelihood, these theater owners were motivated by the 1947 precedent set in Philadelphia, where the liquor board ignored the IRS ruling and instituted a one-hundred-and-twenty-dollar amusement tax on taverns with TV.[54] When tavern owners protested, the Pennsylvania Supreme Court held that "video was in effect motion pictures" and authorized the tax in a move which undoubtedly pleased both sports promoters and theater owners.[55] Such judicial rulings placed television within the legislative arena of public amusements, where municipal and commercial interests could jointly patrol the borders of the tavern as a space of recreation.[56]

There is a certain irony in the fact that TV led theater owners in the forties to rally against taverns: earlier in the century, saloon keepers had "protested excitedly against the nickelodeon as a menace to their trade."[57] Both saloon and theater were frequently targets of Progressive Era discourses on youth and recreation. They held a position of notoriety in the minds of most middle-class reform- and temperance-minded citizens who considered them unsanitary and unfit places for mothers and children.[58] According to one report, gangs of "juvenile delinquents" frequented movie theaters. Young crowds also congregated at the swinging door of the saloon, forming an audience for the spectacle of drunkenness inside.[59]

The goal of youth reform strategies in the Progressive Era was to reorganize spatially the recreation practices of young people. Many groups attempted to block the corrupting influence of both saloon and theater, opening special children's clubhouses and using structured play activities to instill a sense of responsibility and moral rectitude. One play reformer noted, "The immediate necessity is to get hold of the child, and in early years create such interests and ideals that the future man and woman cannot be drawn into the lower life of which the saloon is the exponent."[60] For adults, temperance groups established social clubs that replicated the social function of the saloon, sans alcohol, in spaces equipped with billiards, newspapers, and tables and chairs for conversation.[61] Progressive Era reformers thus mapped leisure in working-class communities along an axis that traversed inappropriate spaces, such as saloons; dubious ones, such as movie theaters; and appropriate ones, such as social clubs and playgrounds.

Television assisted a similar mapping procedure in the 1940s, when benevolent groups established their own TV sites as alternatives to the tavern. The Salvation Army in New York's Bowery began a long fundraising drive in 1947 to purchase a television for its Red Shield Club, "so that men who are determined not to drink will not be lured into barrooms by television."[62] The majority of alternative television sites, however, targeted youth who might sneak into taverns and stand outside barroom windows to see television.[63] To curtail such activities, numerous churches, park districts, civic groups, and private individuals established special television clubs for children. One minister praised television as a good way of occupying a child's mind, adding that "child welfare leaders have recognized that television has given them a 'natural' for attracting children to the church and to supervised clubs."[64]

Supervision was not a concealed strategy of youth viewing sites; rather, it was their announced intention. A successful Presbyterian TV club in Greenwich Village led a writer in the *Christian Century* to observe that while the site's "primary purpose was to get young people out of the taverns . . . the only places where most of them had a chance to see telecasts," it also allowed the church to "keep a watchful eye on the audience."[65] Several other reports noted television's disciplinary effect;[66] as one organizer exclaimed, "one has only to witness a group of vigorous, hard to handle boys sitting meekly before a televised professional or college football game to realize the interest value of this new form of entertainment."[67] Viewing clubs removed children from the unpredictable social arena of the tavern, where they might be exposed to the sight of drunken adults. Ideally, they assembled youth within one space and directed their energy and attention toward a single point, the TV screen. The goal was, clearly, to organize and standardize youth social activities, creating watchers who were themselves more easily watched.[68]

Whether this goal was achieved is quite another matter. In at least one instance, several factors combined to thwart a juvenile viewing site's "good intentions." The Louisville public library, which employed college students as "television sitters" to "keep the sets adjusted and protected, and to supervise the crowd," experienced problems with its youth TV scheme almost as soon as it was established.[69] A local newspaper article reported that "some of the kids are throwing things at the operators, the machines, and the windows." In addition, parents were using the library TV as a babysitter while they "went merrily to parties," not returning until late in the evening to collect their children. The article also claimed that drunks were crashing the show, a situation that surely ran counter to one of the general purposes of juvenile viewing sites: preventing children from witnessing the spectacle of adult drunkenness.[70] Furthermore, library board members complained that the programs children were watching were not suitable. Father Felix Pitt, secretary of the city's Catholic school board, expressed horror that the young viewers had been allowed to watch the movie *The Private Life of Henry VIII* on TV. Rather than discontinue the project, the library handed responsibility over to the city's recreation department, replacing the college student sitters with personnel trained in juvenile management.[71]

The most publicized youth viewing site was one that diverged considerably from the municipal model. In 1948, a Hoboken tavernkeeper, Patrick "Parkey" Radigan, became a minor celebrity when the *New York Times* publicized his daily practice of closing the bar for one hour and inviting children in to watch "Howdy Doody," "Small Fry Club," and "Junior Frolics."[72] When asked about his motivation, Radigan replied, "Most of [the kids] come from poor families and can't afford to see a big ball game, or, for that matter, too much of any kind of entertainment. And besides, it seemed like a good way to keep them off the streets."[73] After the New Jersey Alcoholic Beverage Commission put a stop to the "children's hour," an area veterans group carried on the custom by adding a TV club room to their lodge. Radigan's intention, to keep kids off the streets, was shared by most church and civic groups at the time and lauded by the press and the state liquor board. The latter's reproof centered less on the illegality of the arrangement than on the idea that the physical space of the tavern, with or without patrons, was a corrupting influence. As one official put it, "A barroom hardly constitutes the proper setting for a 'Children's Hour' . . . Longfellow would turn in his grave."[74]

Radigan's scheme, while it aided the fight against juvenile crime by keeping children off the streets, brought them into a seemingly autonomous sphere of adult leisure. When his young viewers relocated to a civic locale, they entered the territory of an institutional gaze able to monitor them for signs of delinquency. At stake in the debate over the children's hour (and over working-class youth recreation in general) was not what children did but the need to assert repeatedly a sense of appropriate and inappropriate recreation spaces.[75]

This use of television to regulate youth recreation was aided by TV set manufacturers and distributors who occasionally donated receivers or established generous installment plans for charitable group viewing sites.[76] Such philanthropic gestures created goodwill for manufacturers; more important, they habituated young viewers so that they might eventually catalyze the parental decision to purchase a set for the household.[77] This was the explicit goal of the National Association of Broadcasters when it recommended that new television stations encourage viewership by establishing public youth viewing sites in theaters: "In effect, the theater would . . . [operate] as a public relations magnet to attract people to buy sets and to develop a station's audience."[78] The viewing sites established to counteract the pull of the tavern may not have shared this marketing goal, but they too helped promote receiver sales by exposing young viewers to television.

In the tavern, the receiver industry quickly recognized a distinct market for large screen sets. Several manufacturers developed projection or "direct view" systems for public viewing. While larger companies such as Dumont, RCA, Philco, and GE added these models to their existing lines of home sets, at least one company, the United States Television Manufacturing Corporation, specialized in receivers for public places and claimed to have supplied 95 percent of all projection sets in bars and hotels. One model, the Tavern Telesymphonic, had a twenty-five-by-nineteen-inch screen and retailed for two thousand dollars.[79] An RCA projection system was the centerpiece in a New York bar, billed as "the first cocktail lounge devoted to television," that featured "special chairs equipped to hold drinks and sandwiches."[80] Juke box manufacturers and operators also jumped on the tavern television bandwagon by marketing coin-operated devices capable of supplying six minutes of television, radio, or phonograph music for a nickel.

Promotional copy for one such machine, called the Solotone, emphasized its profit potential for tavern owners: "The mechanism . . . [keeps] people seated and therefore not so preoccupied that they forget eating and drinking. It also is said to eliminate 'floaters.' "[81] The likely meaning of the word "floater" is suggested in the ad copy for another coin-operated television set from the period. The device, the ad promised, would help bar owners avoid "the nonprofitable 'free show' customer."[82]

These references to people who visited the bar to watch TV without drinking suggest that with the advent of television, some aspects of the tavern as a social space were altered. In broaching this question, I want to reiterate that taverns themselves varied greatly in atmosphere, in the importance of amusements like pinball and radio in the social practices therein, in the bar's accessibility to strangers, women, and other outside groups, and numerous other factors. For this reason, it would be utopian to attempt a reconstruction of either the phenomenological conditions of tavern spectatorship or the "actual" reception practices of "real" individuals. Instead, I will delineate the "inside" horizons of tavern reception as a field of possibilities rather than a set of definitive characteristics. Central to my discussion is the question of whether the emergence of protocols for watching television in the bar in fact diminished the space's function as a convivial public institution in the community. In other words, to what extent did protocols for watching become protocols for socializing?

The historical emergence of standard protocols for viewing is, of course, one of the central questions in the study of preclassical American cinema. Miriam Hansen has argued that in early cinema, before classical Hollywood's standardized reception contexts and suturing narrative and visual codes, "the viewer is solicited in a more direct manner—as a member of an anticipated social audience and a public, rather than an invisible, private consumer."[83] Early cinema thus mobilized the specifically *public* dimension of spectatorship, which "is distinct from both textual and social determinations of spectatorship because it entails the very moment in which reception can gain a momentum of its own, can give rise to formations not necessarily anticipated in the context of production . . . Although always precarious and subject to ceaseless—industrial, ideological—appropriation, the public dimension . . . harbors a potentially autonomous dynamic."[84]

Roy Rosenzweig has argued convincingly that early movie theater audience conduct "was built on a long tradition of crowd behavior that could be found at a variety of earlier amusements from melodramas to saloons to Fourth of July picnics to working class parks."[85] Similarly, barroom television viewing was a practice defined by its location within a public, community-oriented space that appeared to form a self-determining social sphere. It derived from the working-class world of saloons and nickelodeons, corresponding with the latter's ability to provide a viewing experience "contingent on local conditions and constellations, leaving reception at the mercy of relatively *unpredictable*, aleatory processes."[86] It also shared many features with the crowd experience of stadium sports. Although Hansen's account of early cinema reception does not address this correspondence, the two clearly overlap as collective forms of active spectatorial engagement. Hansen's understanding of the early moviegoing public's relation to the spectacle is closely allied with the position of the stadium sports viewer described by Margaret Morse, whose primary identification "is not with [the] team but with the crowd itself."[87] Morse's assertion perhaps underestimates the extent of fan loyalty, however. More likely, stadium viewing is a mutually constructed, plural identification with *both* collectivity and spectacle. In this respect, it shares a bond with early silent film spectatorship, in which the viewer is "a participant in a concrete and variable situation of reception."[88] These connected ideas of viewership articulate the possible identifications of the tavern sports fan, a viewer publicly engaging with both spectacle and context.

This context-based reception structure would have been most keenly experienced by the "knothole brotherhood"[89] of children peering through the tavern window at the remote set. For these viewers, the meaning of the action on-screen would have depended greatly on the visibility of the audience inside. In such a scenario, the experience of watching was transmitted as much, or more, by the audience as it was by the broadcast. Such forms of engagement would also have emerged on nights when big fights or games were televised and huge crowds gathered in neighborhood taverns. On one fight night, a small New York bar counted 37 customers at 9:15, 162 when the bout ended.[90] Tavern owners did their best to make the screen as visible as possible. Although sets were initially placed directly on the bar, later it was more common to find them on shelves near the ceiling, a placement that made them easier to see and discouraged customers from fiddling with the knobs.[91] *Colliers* reported that "inventive taproom tycoons use mirrors to enlarge the screen's pictures and multiply the visible surfaces," although it was more common to see bar managers place magnifying lenses in front of the screen to make the picture larger.[92]

Viewing protocols emerged primarily around the contingencies of space, which was at a premium when big events were broadcast. In crowded bars, patrons were asked to remove their hats and stay seated during important broadcasts.[93] A sign on one tavern's set read, "You're not transparent. People back of you can't see the screen. Please don't stand there."[94] Tavern owners found ways to arrange crowds efficiently. According to the *New Yorker*, the owner of one bar seated the audience that gathered for the 1946 Louis-Conn bout in a predetermined pattern: "seventy in straight backed chairs on the floor, fifty more in booths along the wall, a couple of hundred standing at the bar, and several dozen outside peering through the window."[95] *Colliers* reported that one restaurant owner in the Bronx converted his back room into a television theater and claimed that a New Jersey publican had constructed wooden bleachers around the walls of the bar.[96]

Television changed the rules of socializing in a number of ways. First, tavern owners were interested in using TV to maximize revenues. Common strategies included raising prices, imposing drink minimums, and suspending draft beer sales in favor of bottles during important sports games. A bar in Brooklyn seated viewers during important games according to their drinks: "The front row is reserved for scotch drinkers, the second row for the bourbon, rye, and blend trade, third row for devotees of the grape, the last row and standing room for the ordinary and beer drinking fare."[97]

The second, related way in which television may have changed the social space of the tavern concerns its convivial function as a hub of community social life. In 1948, *Variety* reported that television had brought an unwelcome transformation in some bars, citing a report from Alcoholic Beverage Commission officers in New Jersey that stated, "Bar owners are jerking [TV sets] out as bad investments." Their reasons, the article claimed, were that people came to the bar to watch TV and not for the social drinking experience, that patrons drank too slowly, and that they tended to leave as soon as the show was over. "The novelty of TV has worn off and . . . nonpaying barflies keep customers from the bar . . . Patrons fail to agree on which programs they want to look at, with noisy debate resulting from such disagreement," the article noted.[98] Other sources reported that bartenders found TV viewers to be "small beer drinkers," and that the set drew too many strangers and made regulars feel unwelcome.

In the popular press, a recurrent complaint about television in the bar was that it killed conversation. Several journalists bemoaned the loss of talk and conviviality in the local tavern: "It used to be practically a barroom must to engage in badinage and raillery with a hapless, elbow bending neighbor. Television has invoked the silence of the tomb on the bar," one writer claimed. This silence was broken only by "the grunts, groans and roars emanating from a ten inch screen perched precariously over the far end of the bar."[99] Contrary to Leo Bogart's assertion that TV in bars "provided a common denominator of experience which may . . . have stimulated some conversation among people with little in common to talk about,"[100] these commentators asserted that conversations in taverns had become "furtive, sandwiched in between strikeouts, odes to cigarettes, and hysterical hymns to men of muscle."[101]

The tone of such pieces is well illustrated in the following "barroom lament" from the *New York Times.*

> The saloon . . . has been the favorite forum of the man with something on his mind. In it he could air his preferences, his prejudices, and his heresies; fulminate against his employers, his relatives, and the status quo, voice his grievances against mankind, calypso singers, and parking regulations . . .
>
> The saloon now harbors a horde of mutes. Thanks to the intrusion of a garrulous pictorial contraption called television, the thirsty talker has had his forum shot out from under him.
>
> As a business bait, television may offer momentary rewards; as a curb on freedom and continuity of speech it can only breed resentment.[102]

The tavern patron, in this depiction, was a sodden rambler to whom calypso singers and the status quo were equally irksome; he talked regardlessly, with or without listeners. In this and similar articles, despite the affirmation of talk and conviviality as public functions of the barroom, the general tone betrayed a disdain for the tavern and its patrons and a derisive dismissal of the possibility that it might serve a public sphere-like function in urban communities. As the above quote demonstrates, such articles tended to affect the rhetorical style of a hiccuping, W. C. Fieldsesque barstool philosopher. Another editorial, entitled "Video Kayoes the Barroom Bore," welcomed television's intrusion as a way of silencing such incessant talkers. It heralded the defeat of the drunk whose "bleary face, unrelenting elbow, and incoherent phrases disturb his suffering neighbor on the bar stool."[103]

This was the image of the working-class, tavern-going public in dominant journalistic accounts of television's impact on the bar. It offers little insight into the day-to-day role TV played in the lives of tavern patrons. Even so, less polemical descriptions of the tavern on the night of a big event—crowded floors, with enthralled, hatless sports fans seated in efficient rows—corroborate the idea that television brought social protocols governing both viewing *and* group interaction to the tavern. It is questionable, however, that these fixed spatial arrangements and the imposition of rules about removing hats and remaining seated were continually enforced. The more likely possibility is that viewing protocols applied only on special occasions such as championship bouts and not in more everyday forms of viewership. It would be more reasonable to assume that the spectrum of possible modes of reception in taverns (as at home) ranged from complete absorption and identification to selective or minimal attention; the spatial and social reorganization of the tavern via television would, correspondingly, have varied greatly depending on the context. Indeed, television viewing, according to some accounts, was completely integrated within the leisure and recreation activities of the tavern. One tavernkeeper's observations indicate the extent of this assimilation and highlight the importance of recreational activity for creating a semi-institutional and apparently autonomous working-class public sphere:

> [The tavern is] a working man's or poor man's club, a place for clean relaxation from business cares . . . a place to exchange political views and talk over local, state, and national affairs, a place for the housewives to sit and exchange home management, etc. over a beer, soft drinks, and popcorn. Some play a few hands of cards, others watch television, while still some others play their favorite songs on the jukebox.[104]

Both home and tavern as viewing spaces allowed for a range of possible forms of reception and involved a blurring of public and private experience. The tavern differed from the home, however, in its long association with working-class community recreation. This association dated from the late-nineteenth-century rise of the saloon as, in Roy Rosenzweig's words, "a distinctive . . . leisure institution—a separate and largely autonomous cultural sphere." As a space for viewing, the tavern fostered collective modes of reception that included public, convivial exchange—the type of audience formation previously associated with the nickelodeon. At the same time, however, the autonomy of the viewing experience was perhaps more perceptual than structural, as it was circumscribed from both within and without the social space of the tavern: through local protocols and customs and through the dominant organizing regimes of working-class recreation. It was also narrowly articulated, as the tavern tended to exclude a great many people, especially women. Indeed, the possibility that public social arenas are "alternative" in a genuine sense is always provisional; as Hansen notes, one must always ask "alternative for whom and at what historical juncture, in relation to which configurations of experience?"[105] It seems quite likely that television helped further the tavern's identification with masculinist pursuits by creating a space for sports viewing, an activity that probably appealed less to women than to men. The collective and participatory engagement of the working-class tavern TV audience was not, in other words, a utopian field of reception practices devoid of contradiction or untouched by conflicting tendencies. These contradictions derived from a specific history, however: that of working-class recreation. While this history overlaps with the complex lineage of domestic amusements that shaped discourses on home viewing, it also pinpoints the uniqueness of the tavern audience and widens our understanding of the conditions surrounding early TV spectatorship in general.

Two photographic images suggest the possibilities and limits of tavern viewing as mode of spectatorship and as a field of interaction. Both are press photographs of public youth viewing from the postwar era. The first depicts a group seated meekly in orderly rows within a fieldhouse looking down at a small monitor with an adult guardian standing on the side.[106] The other shows an interracial group of children and one adult passerby peering together through the frosted glass of a tavern. They appear to be laughing at something inside—either the TV or the patrons.[107] Taken together, the two photographic images articulate the social field within which tavern viewing took place, a historical context in which surveillant, regulatory, and commodifying regimes of social knowledge intersected with tactical appropriations of space based on mutuality, shared enjoyment, heterogeneity, and the pleasure of spontaneous interaction.

Notes

I wish to thank the following people for their comments and suggestions on this essay: William Boddy, Tom Gunning, Laura Kipnis, Chad Raphael, Pamela Robertson, James Schwoch, Lynn Spigel, Mimi White, Mark Williams, and Rick Wojcik.

1. Lynn Spigel, *Make Room for TV: Television and the Family Ideal in Postwar America* (Chicago: University of Chicago Press, 1992); Cecelia Ticchi, *Electronic Hearth: Creating an American Television Culture* (New York: Oxford University Press, 1991); Mary Beth Haralovich, "Sitcoms and Suburbs," in *Private Screenings: Television and the Female Consumer*, ed. Lynn Spigel and Denise Mann (Minneapolis: University of Minnesota Press, 1992); Denise Mann, "The Spectacularization of Everyday Life," in ibid.; George Lipsitz, *Time Passages: Collective Memory and Popular Culture* (Minneapolis: University of Minnesota Press, 1990), 39–75. See also Jurgen Habermas, *The Structural Transformation of the Public Sphere: An Inquiry*

into a Category of Bourgeois Society, trans. Thomas Burger (Cambridge: MIT Press, 1991), 157–58, 163; Lynn Joyrich, "All that Television Allows," in *Private Screenings,* ed. Spigel and Mann, 227.

2. David Riesman, *The Lonely Crowd* (New Haven: Yale University Press, 1950); William H. Whyte, *The Organization Man* (New York: Simon and Schuster, 1956); Herbert Gans, *The Levittowners: Ways of Life and Politics in a New Suburban Community* (New York: Pantheon, 1967).

3. Robert Fishman, *Bourgeois Utopias: The Rise and Fall of Suburbia* (New York: Basic Books, 1989), 201.

4. Spigel, *Make Room for TV.* See also Lipsitz, *Time Passages;* Haralovich, "Sitcoms and Suburbs."

5. Spigel, *Make Room for TV,* 101.

6. Ibid., 109.

7. Ibid., 36–72; Ticchi, *Electronic Hearth,* 42–62, passim.

8. Leo Bogart coined the phrase "Tavern Phase" in *The Age of Television: A Study of Viewing Habits and the Impact of Television on American Life* (New York: Frederick Ungar, 1956), 87–89.

9. In March 1947, Chicago TV station WBKB reported that two-thirds of its audience were customers of the 250 TV-equipped taverns in the city. Later that year, when there were 7,000 sets in the city, over half the audience watched in the 1,800 taverns with TV. In September, *Business Week* reported that while only 3,000 of the 43,000 sets in the New York metropolitan area were in bars, home and tavern audiences were roughly equivalent in size. *Time,* 24 March 1947, 63; *Newsweek,* 27 October 1942, 82; *Advertising Age,* 14 January 1948, 58; *Business Week,* 13 September 1947, 70. See also *Sponsor* (March 1947): 49.

10. *Sponsor* (July 1948): 75.

11. *Business Week,* 13 September 1947, 70.

12. *Newsweek,* 16 June 1947, 70.

13. Spigel, *Make Room for TV,* 11.

14. Concurrent "intrastore TV" experiments, which introduced television as a point-of-purchase merchandising aid in department stores, offer additional support for this argument.

15. Diversity had its limits, obviously. In the forties, in a city like Chicago, drinking places were heavily segregated according to race; the only acceptable intermingling would have been when African-American performers played to white audiences or to mixed groups within a jazz club. Little material from the period that might shed some light on the use of TV in African-American barrooms survives. I have come across display advertisements in the *Chicago Defender,* an African-American weekly, that in 1948 promoted televised sports events as part of a line-up that might include jazz, comedy, and burlesque. The particular mention of sports acquires extra significance when one considers that Jackie Robinson, the first black major league baseball player, signed with the Dodgers the year before.

16. *Colliers,* 27 September 1947, 28–30; *Time,* 24 March 1947, 63.

17. Roy Copperud, *American Usage and Style: The Consensus* (New York: Van Nostrand Reinhold, 1980), 43; see also H. L. Mencken, *The American Language: An Enquiry into the Development of English in the United States* (New York: Knopf, 1945), 219, 292; *Supplement I* (1945): 267.

18. *Colliers,* 27 September 1947, 28–32; *New Yorker,* 29 June 1946, 16–17.

19. Mencken, *The American Language,* 292.

20. Boyd E. Macrory, "The Tavern and the Community," *Quarterly Journal of Studies on Alcohol,* 13, no. 4 (December 1952): 625.

21. Ibid., 616.

22. Ibid., 634, 616.

23. Ibid., passim.

24. Bernard Rosenberg, "New York Bar Signs," *Quarterly Journal of Studies on Alcohol* 8, no. 2 (September 1947): 351.

25. On the saloon, see Roy Rosenzweig, *Eight Hours for What We Will: Workers and Leisure in an Industrial City, 1870–1920* (New York: Cambridge University Press, 1983), 35–64, 93–126; Kathy Peiss, *Cheap Amusements: Working Women and Leisure in Turn of the Century New York* (Philadelphia: Temple University Press, 1986), 17–21; John M. Kingsdale, "The Poor Man's Club: Social Functions of the Urban Working Class Saloon," *American Quarterly,* 25 October 1973; Madelon Powers, "Decay from Within: The Inevitable Doom of the American Saloon," in *Drinking: Behavior and Belief in Modern History,* ed. Susanna Barrows and Robin Room (Berkeley: University of California Press, 1991). For more on the tavern, see David Gottlieb, "The Neighborhood Tavern and the Cocktail Lounge: A Study of Class Differences," *American Journal of Sociology* 62, no. 6 (May 1957): 559–62.

26. Rosenberg, "New York Bar Signs," 348.

27. Tavern patron, quoted in Macrory, "The Tavern and the Community," 631.

28. Quoted in ibid., 632.

29. Quoted in ibid., 632.

30. Patron, quoted in ibid., 616.

31. Habermas, *The Structural Transformation of the Public Sphere,* 1–26.

32. Oskar Negt and Alexandre Kluge, "The Public Sphere and Experience: Selections," trans. Peter Labanyi, *October* 46 (fall 1988): 66–71; Nancy Fraser, "Rethinking the Public Sphere: A Contribution to the Critique of Actually Existing Democracy," *Social Text* 25, 26 (1990): 67–70.

33. Macrory, "The Tavern and the Community," 628, 634, 635.

34. Habermas, *The Structural Transformation of the Public Sphere,* 159.

35. Ibid., 163. For a critique of the reification of categories of public and private in bourgeois ideologies, a conceptual division that informs Habermas's theory of the public sphere, see Spigel, *Make Room for TV,* 100–101.

36. Herbert Bloch, "Alcohol and American Recreation Life," *American Scholar* 18 (January 1949): 65.

37. Kingsdale, "The Poor Man's Club," 480, 487; Rosenzweig, *Eight Hours for What We Will,* 44, 58; Powers, "Decay from Within," 113; Gottlieb, "The Neighborhood Tavern and the Cocktail Lounge," 560; Macrory, "The Tavern and the Community," 628.

38. Macrory, "The Tavern and the Community, 630.

39. Ibid., 631.

40. Rosenzweig, *Eight Hours for What We Will,* 1–5, 222–28.

41. I do not mean to suggest that the home was a space devoid of regulation. For a thorough analysis of TV's integration into existing domestic regimes, see Spigel, *Make Room for TV.*

42. For a description of the arguments on either side, see *Nation's Business* (March 1949): 46–48, 84.

43. *Variety,* 16 June 1948, 32.

44. Ibid.

45. Survey by *Beverage Media* (tavern trade journal), cited in *Colliers,* 27 September 1947, 28, and *Newsweek,* 16 June 1947, 64.

46. Al Schlossberg of the King's Palace, "quoted" in *Time,* 24 March 1947, 63.

47. A belief reiterated by the *New Yorker* (29 June 1946, 17) in terms of boxing.

48. Ben Duffy, *Variety*, 28 July 1948, 49.

49. *Colliers*, 27 September 1947, 32.

50. *Variety*, 28 July 1948, 26.

51. *New Yorker*, 29 June 1947, 17.

52. *Variety*, 28 January 1948, 5.

53. *Colliers*, 27 September 1947, 32. See also *Sponsor* (April 1947):48.

54. *Colliers*, 27 September 1947, 32. See also *New York Times*, 27 November 1948, 23; *Variety*, 16 February 1949, 33; *Broadcasting*, 3 February 1949, 5 December 1949, 64.

55. *Variety*, 16 February 1949, 88. The tax was eventually overturned by the state senate (*Broadcasting*, 25 April 1949, 66).

56. In a limited way, TV programmers also attempted to capture the tavern audience as a source of revenue. Film producer Hal Roach announced in 1948 that because television sponsorship fees were so low, his newly formed TV company would only license its programming for distribution to tavern and lounge viewers (presumably via closed circuit systems or scrambled broadcasts). *Variety*, 2 March 1949, 31.

57. Rosenzweig, *Eight Hours for What We Will*, 190–91.

58. Ibid., 202.

59. Kingsdale, "The Poor Man's Club," 485.

60. Raymond Calkins, quoted in Powers, "Decay from Within," 116. See also Rosenzweig, *Eight Hours for What We Will*, 204–5, 143–47.

61. Rosenzweig, *Eight Hours for What We Will*, 106.

62. *New York Times*, 19 July 1948, 12; see also 21 June 1948, 23; *Time*, 2 August 1948.

63. *Recreation* (February 1949): 494, (January 1948): 460; *Christian Century*, 2 February 1949, 143; *New York Times*, 2 October 1947, 56; *Broadcasting*, 24 March 1948, 24, 12 July 1948, 68, 17 January 1949; *Newsweek*, 27 October 1947, 24; *Chicago Daily News*, 17 September 1948; *Variety*, 24 March 1948, 31.

64. *Chicago Daily News*, 17 September 1948, 38.

65. *Christian Century*, 2 February 1949, 143.

66. The use of TV to tranquilize a captive audience would be a quite literal description of its experimental deployment in a psychiatric prison, which reported that because of television, "fewer sedatives [were] being used than at any other time in prison history" (*Variety*, 2 February 1949, 1).

67. *Recreation* (January 1948): 460.

68. See Michel Foucault, *Discipline and Punish*, trans. Alan Sheridan (New York: Vintage Books, 1979), esp. 147–51, 187.

69. *Library Journal*, 15 March 1949, 410.

70. One "television sitter" quit, the article claimed, after a wayward drunk pulled a knife on him.

71. *Louisville Courier-Journal*, 13 April 1949, sec. 2, 1.

72. *New York Times*, 4 July 1948, sec. 2, 7; *Time*, 2 August 1948, 43.

73. *New York Times*, 4 July 1948, sec. 2, 7.

74. *New York Times*, 21 July 1948, 25; 8 August 1948, sec. 2, 7.

75. See Lynn Spigel, "Seducing the Innocent," in William Solomon and Robert W. McChesney, eds., *Ruthless Criticism: New Perspectives in U.S. Communications History* (Minneapolis: University of Minnesota Press, 1993), 265–67 for a discussion of the larger debate on juvenile delinquency and television.

76. *Newsweek,* 27 October 1947, 82; *New York Times,* 2 October 1947, 56. See also a WBKB press release in *Broadcasting,* 29 March 1948, 24, which appears to solicit manufacturer donations.

77. See also Spigel, "Seducing the Innocent," 279–80.

78. *Variety,* 3 February 1949, 77.

79. *New York Times,* 1 January 1947, 43; 12 July 1947, 20; 16 June 1947, 64, XX 10, 27 March 1948, 22; 19 November 1947, 40; *Newsweek,* 16 June 1947, 64; *Colliers,* 27 September 1947, 30; *Illustrated Press* (New Orleans), 17–23 September 1948, 8.

80. *Variety,* 6 April 1949, 30.

81. *Broadcasting,* 24 January 1949, 36.

82. *New Orleans Times-Picayune,* 17 December 1948, sec. 4, 14. See also *Broadcasting,* 25 July 1949, 50.

83. Miriam Hansen, *Babel and Babylon: Spectatorship in Early Silent Film* (Cambridge: Harvard University Press, 1991), 15.

84. Ibid., 7.

85. Rosenzweig, *Eight Hours for What We Will,* 199.

86. Hansen, *Babel and Babylon,* 94.

87. Margaret Morse, "Sport on Television: Replay and Display," in *Regarding Television: Critical Approaches—An Anthology,* ed. E. Ann Kaplan (Frederick, Md.: American Film Institute/University Publications of America, 1983), 47.

88. Hansen, *Babel and Babylon,* 17.

89. *Colliers,* 27 September 1947, 30.

90. Orrin Dunlap, *The Future of Television* (New York: Harper and Brothers, 1947), 56.

91. *Colliers,* 27 September 1947, 30; interview with Mrs. Ziencek, Chicago tavern proprietor, 25 September 1993; interview with Joe Danno, proprietor of Bucket 'O' Suds, a Chicago tavern, 19 October 1993.

92. *Colliers,* 27 September 1947, 30; Ziencek interview, 25 September 1993.

93. This request recalls similar complaints about women's hats in the early years of cinema, a visibility problem solved humorously in D. W. Griffith's *Those Awful Hats* (1908).

94. *New Yorker,* 29 June 1946, 17.

95. Ibid.

96. *Colliers,* 27 September 1947, 30.

97. Ibid.

98. *Variety,* 16 March 1948, 27.

99. *Chicago Daily News,* 17 September 1948, 32.

100. Bogart, *The Age of Television,* 87.

101. *New York Times,* 3 June 1948, XX 6.

102. Ibid.

103. *Chicago Daily News,* 27 September 1948, 32.

104. Tavernkeeper, quoted in Macrory, "The Tavern and the Community," 628.

105. Hansen, *Babel and Babylon,* 24.

106. *Recreation* (January 1948): 484.

107. *Newsweek,* 27 October 1947, 82.

Star Trek Rerun, Reread, Rewritten

Fan Writing as Textual Poaching

HENRY JENKINS III

In late December 1986, *Newsweek* (Leerhsen, 1986, p. 66) marked the twentieth anniversary of *Star Trek* with a cover story on the program's fans, "the Trekkies, who love nothing more than to watch the same seventy-nine episodes over and over." The *Newsweek* article, with its relentless focus on conspicuous consumption and "infantile" behavior and its patronizing language and smug superiority to all fan activity, is a textbook example of the stereotyped representation of fans found in both popular writing and academic criticism, "Hang on: You are being beamed to one of those *Star Trek* conventions, where grown-ups greet each other with the Vulcan salute and offer in reverent tones to pay $100 for the autobiography of Leonard Nimoy" (p. 66). Fans are characterized as "kooks" obsessed with trivia, celebrities, and collectibles; as misfits and crazies; as "a lot of overweight women, a lot of divorced and single women" (p. 68). Borrowing heavily from pop Freud, ersatz Adorno, and pulp sociology, *Newsweek* explains the "Trekkie phenomenon" in terms of repetition compulsion, infantile regression, commodity fetishism, nostalgic complacency, and future shock. Perhaps most telling, *Newsweek* consistently treats *Trek* fans as a problem to be solved, a mystery to be understood, rather than as a type of cultural activity that many find satisfying and pleasurable.[1]

Academic writers depict fans in many of the same terms. For Robin Wood (1986, p. 164), the fantasy film fan is "reconstructed as a child, surrendering to the reactivation of a set of values and structures [the] adult self has long since repudiated." The fan is trapped within a repetition compulsion similar to that which an infant experiences through the *fort/da* game. A return to such "banal" texts could not possibly be warranted by their intellectual content but can only be motivated by a return to "the lost breast" (p. 169), by the need for reassurance provided by the passive reexperience of familiar pleasures. "The pleasure offered by the *Star Wars* films corresponds very closely to our basic conditioning; it is extremely reactionary, as all mindless and automatic pleasure tends to be. The finer pleasures are those we have to work for" (p. 164). Wood valorizes academically respectable texts and reading practices at the expense of popular works and their fans. Academic rereading produces new insights; fan rereading rehashes old experiences.[2]

As these two articles illustrate, the fan constitutes a scandalous category in contemporary American culture, one that provokes an excessive response from those committed to the interests of textual producers and institutionalized interpreters and calls into question the logic by which others order their aesthetic experiences. Fans appear to be frighteningly out of control, undisciplined and unrepentant, rogue readers. Rejecting aesthetic distance, fans passionately embrace favored texts and attempt to integrate media representations within their own social experience. Like cultural scavengers, fans reclaim works that others regard as worthless and trash, finding them a rewarding source of popular capital. Like rebellious children, fans refuse to read by the rules imposed upon them by the schoolmasters. For fans, reading becomes a type of play, responsive only to its own loosely structured rules and generating its own types of pleasure.

Michel de Certeau (1984) has characterized this type of reading as "poaching," an impertinent raid on the literary preserve that takes away only those things that seem useful or pleasurable to the reader. "Far from being writers . . . readers are travellers; they move across lands belonging to someone else, like nomads poaching their way across fields they did not write, despoiling the wealth of Egypt to enjoy it themselves" (p. 174). De Certeau perceives popular reading as a series of "advances and retreats, tactics and games played with the text" (p. 175), as a type of cultural bricolage through which readers fragment texts and reassemble the broken shards according to their own blueprint, salvaging bits and pieces of found material in making sense of their own social experience. Far from viewing consumption as imposing meanings upon the public, de Certeau suggests, consumption involves reclaiming textual material, "making it one's own, appropriating or reappropriating it" (p. 166).

Yet, such wanton conduct cannot be sanctioned; it must be contained, through ridicule if necessary, since it challenges the very notion of literature as a type of private property to be controlled by textual producers and their academic interpreters. Public attacks on media fans keep other viewers in line, making it uncomfortable for readers to adopt such inappropriate strategies. One woman recalled the negative impact popular representations of the fan had on her early cultural life:

> Journalists and photographers always went for the people furthest out of mainstream humanity . . . showing the reader the handicapped, the very obese, the strange and the childish in order to "entertain" the "average reader." Of course, a teenager very unsure of herself and already labeled "weird" would run in panic. (Ludlow, 1987, p. 17)

Such representations isolate potential fans from others who share common interests and reading practices and marginalize fan-related activities as outside the mainstream and beneath dignity. These same stereotypes reassure academic writers of the validity of their own interpretations of the program content, readings made in conformity with established critical protocols, and free them from any need to come into direct contact with the program's crazed followers.[3]

In this essay, I propose an alternative approach to fan experience, one that perceives "Trekkers" (as they prefer to be called) not as cultural dupes, social misfits, or mindless consumers but rather as, in de Certeau's term, "poachers" of textual meanings. Behind the exotic stereotypes fostered by the media lies a largely unexplored terrain of cultural activity, a subterranean network of readers and writers who remake programs in their own image. "Fandom" is a vehicle for marginalized subcultural groups (women, the young, gays, etc.) to pry open space for their cultural concerns within dominant representations; it is a way of appropriating media texts and rereading them in a fashion that serves different interests, a way of transforming mass culture into a popular culture.

I do not believe this essay represents the last word on *Star Trek* fans, a cultural community that is far too multivocal to be open to easy description. Rather, I explore some aspects of current fan activity that seem particularly relevant to cultural studies. My primary concern is with what happens when these fans produce their own texts, texts that inflect program content with their own social experience and displace commercially produced commodities for a kind of popular economy. For these fans, *Star Trek* is not simply something that can be reread; it is something that can and must be rewritten in order to make it more responsive to their needs, in order to make it a better producer of personal meanings and pleasures.

No legalistic notion of literary property can adequately constrain the rapid proliferation of meanings surrounding a popular text. Yet, there are other constraints, ethical constraints and self-imposed rules, that are enacted by the fans, either individually or as part of a larger community, in response to their felt need to legitimate their unorthodox appropriation of mass media texts. E. P. Thompson (1971) suggests that eighteenth and nineteenth century peasant leaders, the historical poachers behind de Certeau's apt metaphor, responded to a kind of "moral economy," an informal set of consensual norms that justified their uprisings against the landowners and tax collectors in order to restore a preexisting order being corrupted by its avowed protectors. Similarly, the fans often cast themselves not as poachers but as loyalists, rescuing essential elements of the primary text misused by those who maintain copyright control over the program materials. Respecting literary property even as they seek to appropriate it for their own uses, these fans become reluctant poachers, hesitant about their relationship to the program text, uneasy about the degree of manipulation they can legitimately perform on its materials, and policing each other for abuses of their interpretive license. They wander across a terrain pockmarked with confusions and contradictions. These ambiguities become transparent when fan writing is examined as a particular type of reader-text interaction. My discussion consequently has a double focus: first, I discuss how the fans force the primary text to accommodate their own interests, and then I reconsider the issue of literary property rights in light of the moral economy of the fan community.

Fans: From Reading to Writing

The popularity of *Star Trek* has motivated a wide range of cultural productions and creative reworkings of program materials: from children's backyard play to adult interaction games, from needlework to elaborate costumes, from private fantasies to computer programming. This ability to transform personal reaction into social interaction, spectator culture into participatory culture, is one of the central characteristics of fandom. One becomes a fan not by being a regular viewer of a particular program but by translating that viewing into some type of cultural activity, by sharing feelings and thoughts about the program content with friends, by joining a community of other fans who share common interests. For fans, consumption sparks production, reading generates writing, until the terms seem logically inseparable. In fan writer Jean Lorrah's words (1984, p. 1):

> Trekfandom . . . is friends and letters and crafts and fanzines and trivia and costumes and artwork and filksongs [fan parodies] and buttons and film clips and conventions—something for everybody who has in common the inspiration of a television show which grew far beyond its TV and film incarnations to become a living part of world culture.

Lorrah's description blurs all boundaries between producers and consumers, spectators and participants, the commercial and the home crafted, to construct an image of fandom as a cultural and social network that spans the globe.

Many fans characterize their entry into fandom in terms of a movement from social and cultural isolation, doubly imposed upon them as women within a patriarchal society and as seekers after alternative pleasures within dominant media representations, toward more and more active participation in a community receptive to their cultural productions, a community where they may feel a sense of belonging. One fan recalls:

> I met one girl who liked some of the TV shows I liked . . . but I was otherwise a bookworm, no friends, working in the school library. Then my

friend and I met some other girls a grade ahead of us but ga-ga over *ST*. From the beginning, we met each Friday night at one of the two homes that had a color TV to watch *Star Trek* together. . . . Silence was mandatory except during commercials, and, afterwards, we "discussed" each episode. We re-wrote each story and corrected the wrongs done to "Our Guys" by the writers. We memorized bits of dialog. We even started to write our own adventures. (Caruthers-Montgomery, 1987, p. 8).

Some fans are drawn gradually from intimate interactions with others who live near them toward participation in a broader network of fans who attend regional, national, and even international science fiction conventions. One fan writes of her first convention: "I have been to so many conventions since those days, but this one was the ultimate experience. I walked into that Lunacon and felt like I had come home without ever realizing I had been lost" (Deneroff, 1987, p. 3). Another remarks simply, "I met folks who were just as nuts as I was, I had a wonderful time" (Lay, 1987, p. 15).

For some women, trapped within low paying jobs or within the socially isolated sphere of the homemaker, participation within a national, or international, network of fans grants a degree of dignity and respect otherwise lacking. For others, fandom offers a training ground for the development of professional skills and an outlet for creative impulses constrained by their workday lives. Fan slang draws a sharp contrast between the mundane, the realm of everyday experience and those who dwell exclusively within that space, and fandom, an alternative sphere of cultural experience that restores the excitement and freedom that must be repressed to function in ordinary life. One fan writes, "Not only does 'mundane' mean 'everyday life,' it is also a term used to describe narrow-minded, pettiness, judgmental, conformity, and a shallow and silly nature. It is used by people who feel very alienated from society" (Osborne, 1987, p. 4). To enter fandom is to escape from the mundane into the marvelous.

The need to maintain contact with these new friends, often scattered over a broad geographic area, can require that speculations and fantasies about the program content take written form, first as personal letters and later as more public newsletters, "letterzines," or fan fiction magazines. Fan viewers become fan writers.

Over the twenty years since *Star Trek* was first aired, fan writing has achieved a semi-institutional status. Fan magazines, sometimes hand typed, photocopied, and stapled, other times offset printed and commercially bound, are distributed through the mails and sold at conventions, frequently reaching an international readership. *Writer's Digest* (Cooper, 1987) recently estimated that there were more than 300 amateur press publications that regularly allowed fans to explore aspects of their favorite films and television programs. Although a wide variety of different media texts have sparked some fan writing, including *Star Wars, Blake's Seven, Battlestar Galactica, Doctor Who, Miami Vice, Road Warrior, Remington Steele, The Man From U.N.C.L.E., Simon and Simon, The A-Team,* and *Hill Street Blues, Star Trek* continues to play the central role within fan writing. *Datazine*, one of several magazines that serve as central clearing houses for information about fanzines, lists some 120 different *Star Trek* centered publications in distribution. Although fanzines may take a variety of forms, fans generally divide them into two major categories: "letterzines" that publish short articles and letters from fans on issues surrounding their favorite shows and "fiction-zines" that publish short stories, poems, and novels concerning the program characters and concepts.[4] Some fan-produced novels, notably the works of Jean Lorrah (1976a, 1978) and Jacqueline Lichtenberg (1976), have achieved a canonized status in the fan community, remaining more or less in constant demand for more than a decade.[5]

It is important to be careful in distinguishing between these fan-generated materials and commercially produced works, such as the series of *Star Trek* novels released by Pocket Books under the official supervision of Paramount, the studio that owns the rights to the *Star Trek* characters. Fanzines are totally unauthorized by the program producers and face the constant threat of legal action for their open violation of the producer's copyright authority over the show's characters and concepts. Paramount has tended to treat fan magazines with benign neglect as long as they are handled on an exclusively nonprofit basis. Producer Gene Roddenberry and many of the cast members have contributed to such magazines. Bantam Books even released several anthologies showcasing the work of *Star Trek* fan writers (Marshak and Culbreath, 1978).

Other producers have not been as kind. Lucasfilm initially sought to control *Star Wars* fan publications, seeing them as a rival to its officially sponsored fan organization, and later threatened to prosecute editors who published works that violated the "family values" associated with the original films. Such a scheme has met considerable resistance from the fan community that generally regards Lucas's actions as unwarranted interference in its own creative activity. Several fanzine editors have continued to distribute adult-oriented *Star Wars* stories through an underground network of special friends, even though such works are no longer publicly advertised through *Datazine* or sold openly at conventions. A heated editorial in *Slaysu*, a fanzine that routinely published feminist-inflected erotica set in various media universes, reflects these writers' opinions:

> Lucasfilm is saying, "you must enjoy the characters of the *Star Wars* universe for male reasons. Your sexuality must be correct and proper by my (male) definition." I am not male. I do not want to be. I refuse to be a poor imitation, or worse, someone's idiotic ideal of femininity. Lucasfilm has said, in essence, "this is what we see in the *Star Wars* films and we are telling you that this is what you will see." (Siebert, 1982, p. 44)

C. A. Siebert's editorial asserts the rights of fanzine writers to consciously revise the character of the original texts, to draw elements from dominant culture in order to produce underground art that explicitly challenges patriarchal assumptions. Siebert and the other editors deny the traditional property rights of textual producers in favor of a right of free play with the program materials, a right of readers to use media texts in their own ways and of writers to reconstruct characters in their own terms. Once characters are inserted into popular discourse, regardless of their source of origin, they become the property of the fans who fantasize about them, not the copyright holders who merchandise them. Yet the relationship between fan texts and primary texts is often more complex than Siebert's defiant stance might suggest, and some fans do feel bound by a degree of fidelity to the original series' conceptions of those characters and their interactions.

Gender and Writing

Fan writing is an almost exclusively feminine response to mass media texts. Men actively participate in a wide range of fan-related activities, notably interactive games and conference planning committees, roles consistent with patriarchal norms that typically relegate combat—even combat fantasies—and organizational authority to the masculine sphere. Fan writers and fanzine readers, however, are almost always female. Camille Bacon-Smith (1986) has estimated that more than 90 percent of all fan writers are female. The greatest percentage of male participation is found in the "letterzines," like *Comlink* and *Treklink*, and in "nonfiction" magazines, like *Trek* that publish speculative essays on aspects of the program universe. Men may feel comfortable joining discussions of future technologies or military lifestyle but not in pondering Vulcan sexuality, McCoy's childhood, or Kirk's love life.

Why this predominance of women within the fan writing community? Research suggests that men and women have been socialized to read for different purposes and in different ways. David Bleich (1986) asked a mixed group of college students to comment, in a free association fashion, on a body of canonized literary works. His analysis of their responses suggests that men focused primarily on narrative organization and authorial intent while women devoted more energy to reconstructing the textual world and understanding the characters. He writes, "Women enter the world of the novel, take it as something 'there' for that purpose; men see the novel as a result of someone's action and construe its meaning or logic in those terms" (p. 239). In a related study, Bleich asked some 120 University of Indiana freshmen to "retell as fully and as accurately as you can [William] Faulkner's 'Barn Burning' " (p. 255) and, again, notes substantial differences between men and women:

> The men retold the story as if the purpose was to deliver a clear simple structure or chain of information: these are the main characters, this is the main action, this is how it turned out. . . . The women present the narrative as if it were an atmosphere or an experience. (p. 256)

Bleich finds that women were more willing to enjoy free play with the story content, making inferences about character relationships that took them well beyond the information explicitly contained within the text. Such data strongly suggest that the practice of fan writing, the compulsion to expand speculations about characters and story events beyond textual boundaries, draws heavily upon the types of interpretive strategies more common to the feminine than to the masculine.

Bleich's observations provide only a partial explanation, since they do not fully account for why many women find it necessary to go beyond the narrative information while most men do not. As Teresa de Lauretis (1982, p. 106) points out, female characters often exist only in the margins of male-centered narratives:

> Medusa and the Sphinx, like the other ancient monsters, have survived inscribed in hero narratives, in someone else's story, not their own; so they are figures or markers of positions—places and topoi—through which the hero and his story move to their destination and to accomplish meaning.

Texts written by and for men yield easy pleasures to their male readers, yet may resist feminine pleasure. To fully enjoy the text, women are often forced to perform a type of intellectual transvesticism, identifying with male characters in opposition to their own cultural experiences or to construct unwritten countertexts through their daydreams or through their oral interaction with other women that allow them to explore their own narrative concerns. This need to reclaim feminine interests from the margins of masculine texts produces endless speculation, speculation that draws the reader well beyond textual boundaries into the domain of the intertextual. Mary Ellen Brown and Linda Barwick (1987) show how women's gossip about soap opera inserts program content into an existing feminine oral culture. Fan writing represents the logical next step in this cultural process: the transformation of oral countertexts into a more tangible form, the translation of verbal speculations into written works that can be shared with a broader circle of women. In order to do so, the women's status must change; no longer simply spectators, these women become textual producers.

Just as women's gossip about soap operas assumes a place within a pre-existing feminine oral culture, fan writing adopts forms and functions traditional to women's literary culture. Cheris Kramarae (1981, pp. 3–4) traces the history of women's efforts to "find ways to express themselves outside the dominant modes of expression used by men," to circumvent the ideologically constructed interpretive strategies of masculine literary genres. Kramarae concludes that women have found the greatest room to explore their feelings and ideas within privately circulated letters and diaries and through collective writing projects. Similarly, Carroll Smith-Rosenberg (1985) discusses the ways that the exchange of letters allowed nineteenth century women to maintain close ties with other women, even when separated by great geographic distances and isolated within the narrow confines of Victorian marriage. Such letters provided a covert vehicle for women to explore common concerns and even ridicule the men in their lives. Smith-Rosenberg (p. 45) concludes:

> Nineteenth-century women were, as Nathaniel Hawthorne reminds us, "damned scribblers." They spoke endlessly to one another in private letters and journals . . . about religion, gender roles, their sexuality and men's

about prostitution, seduction, and intemperance, about unwanted preg-
nancies and desired education, about their relation to the family and the
family's to the world.

Fan writing, with its circulation conducted largely through the mails,
with its marketing mostly a matter of word of mouth, with the often collective construction of fantasy universes, and with its highly confessional
tone, clearly follows within that same tradition and serves some of the same
functions. The ready-made characters of popular culture provide these
women with a set of common references for discussing their similar experiences and feelings with others with whom they may never have enjoyed face-
to-face contact. They draw upon these shared points of reference to confront many of the same issues that concerned nineteenth century women:
religion, gender roles, sexuality, family, and professional ambition.

Why Star Trek?

While most texts within a male-dominated culture presumably have the
capacity to spark some sort of feminine countertext, only certain programs
have generated the type of extended written responses characteristic of fandom. Why, then, has the bulk of fan writing centered around science fiction, a genre that Judith Spector (1986, p. 163) argues until recently has
been hostile toward women, a genre "by, for and about men of action"?
Why has it also engaged other genres like science fiction (the cop show, the
detective drama, or the western) that have represented the traditional domain
of male readers? Why do these women struggle to reclaim such seemingly
unfertile soil when there are so many other texts that more traditionally
reflect feminine interests and that feminist media critics are now trying to
reclaim for their cause? In short, why *Star Trek?*

Obviously, no single factor can adequately account for all fanzines, a
literary form that necessarily involves the translation of homogeneous media
texts into a plurality of personal and subcultural responses. One partial explanation, however, might be that traditionally feminine texts (the soap opera,
the popular romance, the "women's picture," etc.) do not need as much
reworking as science fiction and westerns in order to accommodate the social
experience of women. The resistance of such texts to feminist reconstruction may require a greater expenditure of creative effort and therefore may
push women toward a more thorough reworking of program materials than
so-called feminine texts that can be more easily assimilated or negated.

Another explanation might be that these so-called feminine texts satisfy, at least partially, the desires of traditional women yet fail to meet the
needs of more professionally oriented women. A particular fascination of
Star Trek for these women appears to be rooted in the way that the program seems to hold out a suggestion of nontraditional feminine pleasures,
of greater and more active involvement for women within the adventure of
professional space travel, while finally reneging on those promises. Sexual
equality was an essential component of producer Roddenberry's optimistic

vision of the future; a woman, Number One (Majel Barrett), was originally slated to be the Enterprise's second in command. Network executives, however, consistently fought efforts to break with traditional feminine stereotypes, fearing the alienation of more conservative audience members (Whitfield and Roddenberry, 1968). Number One was scratched after the program pilot, but throughout the run of the series women were often cast in nontraditional jobs, everything from Romulan commanders to weapon specialists. The networks, however reluctantly, were offering women a future, a "final frontier" that included them.

Fan writers, though, frequently express dissatisfaction with these women's characterizations within the episodes. In the words of fan writer Pamela Rose (1977, p. 48), "When a woman is a guest star on *Star Trek,* nine out of ten times there is something wrong with her." Rose notes that these female characters have been granted positions of power within the program, only to demonstrate through their erratic emotion-driven conduct that women are unfit to fill such roles. Another fan writer, Toni Lay (1986, p. 15), expresses mixed feelings about *Star Trek's* social vision:

> It was ahead of its time in some ways, like showing that a Caucasian, all-American, all-male crew was not the only possibility for space travel. Still, the show was sadly deficient in other ways, in particular, its treatment of women. Most of the time, women were referred to as "girls." And women were never shown in a position of authority unless they were aliens, i.e., Deela, T'Pau, Natira, Sylvia, etc. It was like the show was saying "equal opportunity is OK for their women but not for our girls."

Lay states that she felt "devastated" over the repeated failure of the series and the later feature films to give Lieutenant Penda Uhura command duties commensurate with her rank: "When the going gets tough, the tough leave the womenfolk behind" (p. 15). She contends that Uhura and the other women characters should have been given a chance to demonstrate what they could do when confronted by the same types of problems that their male counterparts so heroically overcome. The constant availability of the original episodes through reruns and shifts in the status of women within American society throughout the past two decades have only made these unfulfilled promises more difficult to accept, requiring progressively greater efforts to restructure the program in order to allow it to produce pleasures appropriate to the current reception context.

Indeed, many fan writers characterize themselves as "repairing the damage" caused by the program's inconsistent and often demeaning treatment of its female characters. Jane Land (1986, p. 1), for instance, characterizes her fan novel, *Kista,* as "an attempt to rescue one of *Star Trek*'s female characters [Christine Chapel] from an artificially imposed case of foolishness." Promising to show "the way the future never was," *The Woman's List,* a recently established fanzine with an explicitly feminist orientation, has called for "material dealing with all range of possibilities for women, including: women of color, lesbians, women of alien cultures, and women of all ages and backgrounds." Its editors acknowledge that their publication's project necessarily involves telling the types of stories that network policy blocked from airing when the series was originally produced. A recent flier for that publication explains:

> We hope to raise and explore those questions which the network censors, the television genre, and the prevailing norms of the time made it difficult to address. We believe that both the nature of human interaction and sexual mores and the structure of both families and relationships will have changed by the 23rd century and we are interested in exploring those changes.

Telling such stories requires the stripping away of stereotypically feminine traits. The series characters must be reconceptualized in ways that suggest hidden motivations and interests heretofore unsuspected. They must be reshaped into full-blooded feminist role models. While, in the series, Chapel is defined almost exclusively in terms of her unrequited passion for Spock and her professional subservience to Dr. McCoy, Land represents her as a fiercely independent woman, capable of accepting love only on her own terms, ready to pursue her own ambitions wherever they take her, and outspoken in response to the patronizing attitudes of the command crew. Siebert (1980, p. 33) has performed a similar operation on the character of Lieutenant Uhura, as this passage from one of her stories suggests:

> There were too few men like Spock who saw her as a person. Even Captain Kirk, she smiled, especially Captain Kirk, saw her as a woman first. He let her do certain things but only because military discipline required it. Whenever there was any danger, he tried to protect her. . . . Uhura smiled sadly, she would go on as she had been, outwardly a feminine toy, inwardly a woman who was capable and human.

Here, Siebert attempts to resolve the apparent contradiction created within the series text by Uhura's official status as a command officer and her constant displays of "feminine frailty." Uhura's situation, Siebert suggests, is characteristic of the way that women must mask their actual competency behind traditionally feminine mannerisms within a world dominated by patriarchal assumptions and masculine authority. By rehabilitating Uhura's character in this fashion, Siebert has constructed a vehicle through which she can document the overt and subtle forms of sexual discrimination that an ambitious and determined woman faces as she struggles for a command post in Star Fleet (or for that matter, within a twentieth century corporate board room).

Fan writers like Siebert, Land, and Karen Bates (1982; 1983; 1984), whose novels explore the progression of a Chapel-Spock marriage through many of the problems encountered by contemporary couples trying to juggle the conflicting demands of career and family, speak directly to the concerns of professional women in a way that more traditionally feminine works fail to do.[6] These writers create situations where Chapel and Uhura must heroically overcome the same types of obstacles that challenge their male counterparts within the primary texts and often discuss directly the types of personal and professional problems particular to working women. Land's recent fan novel, *Demeter* (1987), is exemplary in its treatment of the professional life of its central character, Nurse Chapel. Land deftly melds action sequences with debates about gender relations and professional discrimination, images of command decisions with intimate glimpses of a Spock— Chapel marriage. An all-woman crew, headed by Uhura and Chapel, are dispatched on a mission to a feminist separatist space colony under siege from a pack of intergalactic drug smugglers who regard rape as a manly sport. In helping the colonists to overpower their would-be assailants, the women are at last given a chance to demonstrate their professional competence under fire and force Captain Kirk to reevaluate some of his command policies. *Demeter* raises significant questions about the possibilities of male— female interaction outside of patriarchal dominance. The meeting of a variety of different planetary cultures that represent alternative social philosophies and organizations, alternative ways of coping with the same essential debates surrounding sexual difference, allows for a far-reaching exploration of contemporary gender relations.

From Space Opera to Soap Opera

If works like *Demeter* constitute intriguing prototypes for a new breed of feminist popular literature, they frequently do so within conventions borrowed as much from more traditionally feminine forms of mass culture as from *Star Trek* itself. For one thing, the female fans perceive the individual episodes as contributing to one great program text. As a result, fan stories often follow the format of a continuous serial rather than operating as a series of self-enclosed works. Tania Modleski (1982) demonstrates the ways that the serial format of much women's fiction, particularly of soap operas, responds to the rhythms of women's social experience. The shaky financing characteristic of the fanzine mode of production, the writers' predilections to engage in endless speculations about the program content and to continually revise their understanding of the textual world, amplifies the tendency of women's fiction to postpone resolution, transforming *Star Trek* into a never ending story. Fan fiction marches forward through a series of digressions as new speculations cause the writers to halt the advance of their chronicles, to introduce events that must have occurred prior to the start of their stories, or to introduce secondary plot lines that pull them from the main movement of the event chain. This type of writing activity has been labeled a "story tree." Bacon-Smith (1986, p. 26) explains: .

> The most characteristic feature of the story tree is that the stories do not fall in a linear sequence. A root story may offer unresolved situations, secondary characters whose actions during the main events are not described or a resolution is unsatisfactory to some readers. Writers then branch out from that story, completing dropped subplots, exploring the reactions of minor characters to major events.

This approach, characteristic of women's writing in a number of cultures, stems from a sense of life as continuous rather than fragmented into a series of discrete events, from an outlook that is experience centered and not goal oriented: "Closure doesn't make sense to them. At the end of the story, characters go on living in the nebulous world of the not yet written. They develop, modify their relationships over time, age, raise families" (p. 28).

Moreover, as Bacon-Smith's comments suggest, this type of reading and writing strategy focuses greater attention on ongoing character relationships than on more temporally concentrated plot elements. Long-time fan writer Lichtenberg (personal communication, August 1987) summarizes the difference: "Men want a physical problem with physical action leading to a physical resolution. Women want a psychological problem with psychological action leading to a psychological resolution." These women express a desire for narratives that concentrate on the character relationships and explore them in a "realistic" or "mature" fashion rather than in purely formulaic terms, stories that are "true" and "believable" and not "syrupy" or "sweet." Fan writers seek to satisfy these demands through their own *Star Trek* fiction, to write the type of stories that they and other fans desire to read.

The result is a type of genre switching, the rereading and rewriting of "space opera" as an exotic type of romance (and, often, the reconceptualization of romance itself as feminist fiction). Fanzines rarely publish exclusively action-oriented stories glorifying the Enterprise's victories over the Klingon-Romulan Alliance, its conquest of alien creatures, its restructuring of planetary governments, or its repair of potential flaws in new technologies, despite the prevalence of such plots in the original episodes. When such elements do appear, they are usually evoked as a background against which the more typical romance or relationship-centered stories are played or as a test through which female protagonists can demonstrate their professional skills. In doing so, these fan writers draw inspiration from feminist science fiction writers, including Johanna Russ, Marion Zimmer Bradley, Zenna Henderson, Marge Piercy, Andre Norton, and Ursula Le Guin. These writers' entry into the genre in the late 1960s and early 70s helped to redefine reader expectations about what constituted science fiction, pushing the genre toward greater and greater interest in soft science and sociological concerns and increased attention on interpersonal relationships and gender roles.[7] *Star Trek*, produced in a period when masculine concerns still dominated science fiction, is reconsidered in light of the newer, more feminist orientation of the genre, becoming less a program about the Enterprise's struggles against the Klingon-Romulan Alliance and more an examination of a character's efforts to come to grips with conflicting emotional needs and professional responsibilities.

Women, confronting a traditionally masculine space opera, choose to read it instead as a type of women's fiction. In constructing their own stories about the series characters, they turn frequently to the more familiar and comfortable formulas of the soap, the romance, and the feminist coming-of-age novel for models of storytelling technique. While the fans themselves often dismiss such genres as too focused upon mundane concerns to be of great interest, the influence of such materials may be harder to escape. As Elizabeth Segel (1986) suggests, our initial introduction to reading, the gender-based designation of certain books as suitable for young girls and others for young boys, can be a powerful determinant of our later reading and writing strategies, determining, in part, the relative accessibility of basic genre models for use in making sense of ready-made texts and for constructing personal fantasies. As fans attempt to reconstruct the feminine counter-texts that exist on the margins of the original series episodes, they, in the process, refocus the series around traditional feminine and contemporary feminist concerns, around sexuality and gender politics, around religion, family, marriage, and romance.

Many fans' first stories take the form of romantic fantasies about the series characters and frequently involve inserting glorified versions of themselves into the world of Star Fleet. The Bethann (1976, p. 54) story, "The Measure of Love," for instance, deals with a young woman, recently transferred to the Enterprise, who has a love affair with Kirk:

> We went to dinner that evening. Till that time, I was sure he'd never really noticed me. Sitting across the table from him, I realized just what a vital alive person this man was. I had dreamed of him, but never imagined my hopes might become a reality. But, this was real—not a dream. His eyes were intense, yet they twinkled in an amused sort of way.
> "Captain . . . "
> "Call me Jim."

Her romance with Kirk comes to an abrupt end when the young woman transfers to another ship without telling the captain that she carries his child because she does not want her love to interfere with his career.

Fans are often harshly critical of these so-called "Lieutenant Mary Sue" stories, which one writer labels "groupie fantasies" (Hunter, 1977, p. 78), because of their self-indulgence, their often hackneyed writing styles, their formulaic plots, and their violations of the established characterizations. In reconstituting *Star Trek* as a popular romance, these young women reshape the series characters into traditional romantic heroes, into "someone who is intensely and exclusively interested in her and in her needs" (Radway, 1984, p. 149). Yet, many fan writers are more interested in what happens when this romantic ideal confronts a world that places professional duty over personal needs, when men and women must somehow reconcile careers and marriage in a confusing period of shifting gender relationships. Veteran fan writer Kendra Hunter (1977, p. 78) writes, "Kirk is not going to go off into the sunset with anyone because he is owned body and soul by the Enterprise." *Treklink* editor Joan Verba (1986, p. 2) comments, "No believable character is gushed over by so many normally level-headed characters such as Kirk and Spock as a typical Mary Sue." Nor are the women of tomorrow apt to place any man, even Jim Kirk, totally above all other concerns.

Some, though by no means all, of the most sophisticated fan fiction also takes the form of the romance. Both Radway (1984) and Modleski (1982) note popular romances' obsession with a semiotics of masculinity, with the need to read men's often repressed emotional states from the subtle signs of outward gesture and expression. The cold logic of Vulcan, the desire to suppress all signs of emotion, make Spock and Sarek especially rich for such interpretations as in the following passage from Lorrah's *Full Moon Rising* (1976b, pp. 9–10):

> The intense sensuality she saw in him [Sarek] in other ways suggested a hidden sexuality. She had noticed everything from the way he appreciated the beauty of a moonlit night or a finely-cut sapphire to the way his strongly-molded hands caressed the mellowed leather binding of the book she had given him. . . . That incredible control which she could not penetrate. Sometimes he deliberately let her see beyond it, as he had done earlier this evening, but if she succeeded in making him lose control he would never be able to forgive her.

In Lorrah's writings, the alienness of Vulcan culture becomes a metaphor for the many things that separate men and women, for the factors that prevent intimacy within marriage. She describes her fiction as the story of "two people who are different physically, mentally, and emotionally, but who nonetheless manage to make a pretty good marriage" (p. 2). While Vulcan restraint suggests the emotional sterility of traditional masculinity, their alien sexuality allows Lorrah to propose alternatives. Her Vulcans find sexual inequality to be illogical and allow for very little difference in the treatment of men and women. (This is an assumption shared by many fan writers.) Moreover, the Vulcan mindmeld grants a degree of sexual and emotional intimacy unknown on earth; Vulcan men even employ this power to relieve women of labor pains and to share the experience of childbirth. Her lengthy writings on the decades-long romance between Amanda and Sarek represent a painstaking effort to construct a feminist utopia, to propose how traditional marriage might be reworked to allow it to satisfy the personal and professional needs of both men and women.

Frequently, the fictional formulas of popular romance are tempered by women's common social experiences as lovers, wives, and mothers under patriarchy. In Bates's novels, Nurse Chapel must confront and overcome her feelings of abandonment and jealousy during those long periods of time when her husband, Spock, is deeply absorbed in his work. *Starweaver Two* (1982, p. 10) describes this pattern:

> The pattern had been repeated so often, it was ingrained. . . . Days would pass without a word between them because of the hours he labored and pored over his computers. Their shifts rarely matched and the few hours they could be together disappeared for one reason or another.

Far from an idyllic romance, Bates's characters struggle to make their marriage work in a world where professionalism is everything and the personal counts for relatively little. Land's version of a Chapel–Spock marriage is complicated by the existence of children who must remain at home under the care of Sarek and Amanda while their parents pursue their space adventures. In one scene, Chapel confesses her confused feelings about this situation to a young Andorian friend: "I spend my life weighing the children's needs against my needs against Spock's needs, and at any given time I know I'm shortchanging someone" (1987, p. 27).

While some male fans denigrate these types of fan fiction as "soap operas with Kirk and Spock" (Blaes, 1986a, p. 6), these women see themselves as constructing soap operas with a difference, soap operas that reflect a feminist vision. In Siebert's words (1982, pp. 44–45), "I write erotic stories for myself and for other women who will not settle for being less than human." Siebert suggests that her stories about Uhura and her struggle for recognition and romance in a male-dominated Star Fleet have helped her to resolve her own conflicting feelings within a world of changing gender relations and to explore hidden aspects of her own sexuality. Through her erotica, she hopes to increase other women's awareness of the need to struggle against entrenched patriarchal norms. Unlike their counterparts in Harlequin romances, these women refuse to accept marriage and the love of a man as their primary goal. Their stories push toward resolutions that allow Chapel or Uhura to achieve both professional advancement and personal satisfaction. Unlike almost every other form of popular fiction, fanzine stories frequently explore the maturing of relationships beyond the nuptial vows, seeing marriage as continually open to new adventures, new conflicts, and new discoveries.

The point of contact between feminism and the popular romance is largely a product of these writers' particular brand of feminism, one that, for the most part, is closer to the views of Betty Friedan than to those of Andrea Dworkin. It is a feminism that urges a sharing of feelings and lifestyles between men and women rather than radical separation or unresolvable differences. It is a literature of reform, not of revolt. The women still acknowledge their need for the companionship of men, for men who care for them and make them feel special, even as they are asking for those relationships to be conducted in different terms. Land's Nurse Chapel, who in *Demeter* is both fascinated and repelled by the feminist separatist colony, reflects these women's ambiguous and sometimes contradictory responses toward more radical forms of feminism. In the end, Chapel recognizes the potential need for such a place, for a "room of one's own," yet sees greater potential in achieving a more liberated relationship between men and women. She learns to develop self-sufficiency, yet chooses to share her life with her husband, Spock, and to achieve a deeper understanding of their differing expectations about their relationship. Each writer grapples with these concerns in her own terms, yet most achieve some compromise between the needs of women for independence and self-sufficiency on the one hand and their needs for romance and companionship on the other. If this does not constitute a radical break with the romance formula, it does represent a progressive reformulation of that formula which pushes toward a gradual redefinition of existing gender roles within marriage and the work place.

The Moral Economy of Fan Fiction

Their underground status allows fan writers the creative freedom to promote a range of different interpretations of the basic program material and a variety of reconstructions of marginalized characters and interests, to explore a diversity of different solutions to the dilemma of contemporary gender relations. Fandom's IDIC philosophy (Infinite Diversity in Infinite Combinations, a cornerstone of Vulcan thought) actively encourages its participants to explore and find pleasure within their different and often contradictory responses to the program text. It should not be forgotten, however, that fan writing involves a translation of personal response into a social expression and that fans, like any other interpretive community, generate their own norms that work to insure a reasonable degree of conformity between readings of the primary text. The economic risk of fanzine publishing and the desire for personal popularity insures some responsiveness to audience demand, discouraging totally idiosyncratic versions of the program content. Fans try to write stories to please other fans; lines of development that do not find popular support usually cannot achieve financial viability.

Moreover, the strange mixture of fascination and frustration characteristic of fan response means that fans continue to respect the creators of the original series, even as they wish to rework some program materials to better satisfy their personal interests. Their desire to revise the program material is often counterbalanced by their desire to remain faithful to those aspects of the show that first captured their interests. E. P. Thompson (1971, p. 78) has employed the term "moral economy" to describe the way that eighteenth century peasant leaders and street rioters legitimized their revolts through an appeal to "traditional rights and customs" and "the wider consensus of the community," asserting that their actions worked to protect existing property rights against those who sought to abuse them for their own gain. The peasants' conception of a moral economy allowed them to claim for themselves the right to judge the legitimacy both of their own actions and those of the landowners and property holders: "Consensus was so strong that it overrode motives of fear or deference" (pp. 78–79).

An analogous situation exists in fandom: the fans respect the original texts, yet fear that their conceptions of the characters and concepts may be jeopardized by those who wish to exploit them for easy profits, a category that typically includes Paramount and the network but excludes Roddenberry and many of the show's writers. The ideology of fandom involves both a commitment to some degree of conformity to the original program materials as well as a perceived right to evaluate the legitimacy of any use of those materials, either by textual producers or by textual consumers. The fans perceive themselves as rescuing the show from its producers who have manhandled its characters and then allowed it to die. In one fan's words, "I think we have made *ST* uniquely our own, so we do have all the right in the world (universe) to try to change it for the better when the gang at Paramount starts worshipping the almighty dollar, as they are wont to do" (Schnuelle, 1987,

p. 9). Rather than rewriting the series content, the fans claim to be keeping *Star Trek* alive in the face of network indifference and studio incompetence, of remaining true to the text that first captured their interest some twenty years before: "This relationship came into being because the fan writers loved the characters and cared about the ideas that are *Star Trek* and they refused to let it fade away into oblivion" (Hunter, 1977, p. 77).

Such a relationship obligates fans to preserve a certain degree of fidelity to program materials, even as they seek to rework them toward their own ends. *Trek* magazine contributor Kendra Hunter (1977, p. 83) writes, "*Trek* is a format for expressing rights, opinions, and ideals. Most every imaginable idea can be expressed through *Trek*. . . . But there is a right way." Gross infidelity to the series concepts constitutes what fans call "character rape" and falls outside of the community's norms. In Hunter's words (p. 75):

> A writer, either professional or amateur, must realize that she . . . is not omnipotent. She cannot force her characters to do as she pleases. . . . The writer must have respect for her characters or those created by others that she is using, and have a full working knowledge of each before committing her words to paper.

Hunter's conception of character rape, one widely shared within the fan community, rejects abuses by the original series writers as well as by the most novice fan. It implies that the fans themselves, not the program producers, are best qualified to arbitrate conflicting claims about character psychology because they care about the characters in a way that more commercially motivated parties frequently do not. In practice, the concept of character rape frees fans to reject large chunks of the aired material, including entire episodes, and even to radically restructure the concerns of the show in the name of defending the purity of the original series concept. What determines the range of permissible fan narratives is finally not fidelity to the original texts but consensus within the fan community itself. The text that they so lovingly preserve is the *Star Trek* that they created through their own speculations, not the one that Roddenberry produced for network air play.

Consequently, the fan community continually debates what constitutes a legitimate reworking of program materials and what represents a violation of the special reader-text relationship that the fans hope to foster. The earliest *Star Trek* fan writers were careful to work within the framework of the information explicitly included within the broadcast episodes and to minimize their breaks with series conventions. In fan writer Jean Lorrah's words (1976a, p. 1), "Anyone creating a *Star Trek* universe is bound by what was seen in the aired episodes; however, he is free to extrapolate from those episodes to explain what was seen in them." Leslie Thompson (1974, p. 208) explains, "If the reasoning [of fan speculations] doesn't fit into the framework of the events as given [on the program], then it cannot apply no matter how logical or detailed it may be." As *Star Trek* fan writing has come to assume an institutional status in its own right and therefore to require less legitimization through appeals to textual fidelity, a new conception of fan fiction has emerged, one that perceives the stories not as a necessary expansion of the original series text but rather as chronicles of alternate universes, similar to the program world in some ways and different in others:

> The "alternative universe" is a handy concept wherein you take the basic *Star Trek* concept and spin it off into all kinds of ideas that could never be aired. One reason Paramount may be so liberal about fanzines is that by their very nature most fanzine stories could never be sold professionally. (L. Slusher, personal communication, August 1987)

Such an approach frees the writers to engage in much broader play with the program concepts and characterizations, to produce stories that reflect more diverse visions of human interrelationships and future worlds, to rewrite elements within the primary texts that hinder fan interests. Yet, even alternate universe stories struggle to maintain some consistency with the original broadcast material and to establish some point of contact with existing fan interests, just as more faithful fan writers feel compelled to rewrite and revise the program material in order to keep it alive in a new cultural context.

Borrowed Terms: Kirk/Spock Stories

The debate in fan circles surrounding Kirk/Spock (K/S) fiction, stories that posit a homoerotic relationship between the show's two primary characters and frequently offer detailed accounts of their sexual couplings, illustrates these differing conceptions of the relationship between fan fiction and the primary series text.[8] Over the past decade, K/S stories have emerged from the margins of fandom toward numerical dominance over *Star Trek* fan fiction, a movement that has been met with considerable opposition from more traditional fans. For many, such stories constitute the worst form of character rape, a total violation of the established characterizations. Kendra Hunter (1977, p. 81) argues that "it is out of character for both men, and as such comes across in the stories as bad writing. . . . A relationship as complex and deep as Kirk/Spock does not climax with a sexual relationship." Other fans agree but for other reasons. "I do not accept the K/S homosexual precept as plausible," writes one fan. "The notion that two men that are as close as Kirk and Spock are cannot be 'just friends' is indefensible to me" (Landers, 1986, p. 10). Others struggle to reconcile the information provided on the show with their own assumptions about the nature of human sexuality: "It is just as possible for their friendship to progress into a love-affair, for that is what it is, than to remain status quo. . . . Most of us see Kirk and Spock simply as two people who love each other and just happen to be of the same gender" (Snaider, 1987, p. 10).

Some K/S fans frankly acknowledge the gap between the series characterizations and their own representations yet refuse to allow their fantasy life to be governed by the limitations of what was actually aired. One fan writes, "While I read K/S and enjoy it, when you stop to review the two main characters of *Star Trek* as extrapolated from the TV series, a sexual relationship between them is absurd" (Chandler, 1987, p. 10). Another argues somewhat differently:

> We actually saw a very small portion of the lives of the Enterprise crew through 79 episodes and some six hours of movies. . . . How can we possibly define the entire personalities of Kirk, Spock, etc., if we only go by what we've seen on screen? Surely there is more to them than that! . . . Since I doubt any two of us would agree on a definition of what is "in character," I leave it to the skill of the writer to make the reader believe in the story she is trying to tell. There isn't any limit to what could be depicted as accurate behavior for our heroes. (Moore, 1986, p. 7)

Many fans find this bold rejection of program limitations on creative activity, this open appropriation of characters, to be unacceptable since it violates the moral economy of fan writing and threatens fan fiction's privileged relationship to the primary text:

> [If] "there isn't any limit to what could be depicted as accurate behavior of our heroes," we might well have been treated to the sight of Spock shooting up heroin or Kirk raping a yeoman on the bridge (or vice-versa). . . . The writer whose characters don't have clearly defined personalities, [through] limits and idiosyncrasies and definite characteristics, is the writer who is either very inexperienced or who doesn't have any respect for his characters, not to mention his audience. (Slusher, 1986, p. 11)

Yet, I have shown, all fan writing necessarily involves an appropriation of series characters and a reworking of program concepts as the text is forced to respond to the fan's own social agenda and interpretive strategies. What K/S does openly, all fans do covertly. In constructing the feminine countertext that lurks in the margins of the primary text, these readers necessarily redefine the text in the process of rereading and rewriting it. As one fan acknowledges, "If K/S has 'created new characters and called them by old names,' then all of fandom is guilty of the same" (Moore, 1986, p. 7). Jane Land (1987, p. ii) agrees: "All writers alter and transform the basic *Trek* universe to some extent, choosing some things to emphasize and others to play down, filtering the characters and the concepts through their own perceptions."

If these fans have rewritten *Star Trek* in their own terms, however, many of them are reluctant to break all ties to the primary text that sparked their creative activity and, hence, feel the necessity to legitimate their activity through appeals to textual fidelity. The fans are uncertain how far they can push against the limitations of the original material without violating and finally destroying a relationship that has given them great pleasure. Some feel stifled by those constraints; others find comfort within them. Some claim the program as their personal property, "treating the series episodes like silly putty," as one fan put it (Blaes, 1987, p. 6). Others seek compromises with the textual producers, treating the original program as something shared between them.

What should be remembered is that whether they cast themselves as rebels or loyalists, it is the fans themselves who are determining what aspects of the original series concept are binding on their play with the program material and to what degree. The fans have embraced *Star Trek* because they found its vision somehow compatible with their own, and they have assimilated only those textual materials that feel comfortable to them. Whenever a choice must be made between fidelity to their program and fidelity to their own social norms, it is almost inevitably made in favor of lived experience. The women's conception of the *Star Trek* realm as inhabited by psychologically rounded and realistic characters insures that no characterization that violated their own social perceptions could be satisfactory. The reason some fans reject K/S fiction has, in the end, less to do with the stated reason that it violates established characterization than with unstated beliefs about the nature of human sexuality that determine what types of character conduct can be viewed as plausible. When push comes to shove, as Hodge and Tripp (1986, p. 144) recently suggested, "Nontelevisual meanings can swamp televisual meanings" and usually do.

Conclusion

The fans are reluctant poachers who steal only those things that they truly love, who seize televisual property only to protect it against abuse by those who created it and who have claimed ownership over it. In embracing popular texts, the fans claim those works as their own, remaking them in their own image, forcing them to respond to their needs and to gratify their desires. Female fans transform *Star Trek* into women's culture, shifting it from space opera into feminist romance, bringing to the surface the unwritten feminine countertext that hides in the margins of the written masculine text. Kirk's story becomes Uhura's story and Chapel's and Amanda's as well as the story of the women who weave their own personal experiences into the lives of the characters. Consumption becomes production; reading becomes writing; spectator culture becomes participatory culture.

Neither the popular stereotype of the crazed Trekkie nor academic notions of commodity fetishism or repetition compulsion are adequate to explain the complexity of fan culture. Rather, fan writers suggest the need to redefine the politics of reading, to view textual property not as the exclusive domain of textual producers but as open to repossession by textual consumers. Fans continuously debate the etiquette of this relationship, yet all take for granted the fact that they are finally free to do with the text as they please. The world of *Star Trek* is what they choose to make it: "If there were no fandom, the aired episodes would stand as they are, and yet they would be just old reruns of some old series with no more meaning than old reruns of *I Love Lucy*" (Hunter, 1977, p. 77). The one text shatters and becomes many texts as it is fit into the lives of the people who use it, each in her or his own way, each for her or his own purposes.

Modleski (1986) recently, and I believe mistakenly, criticized what she understands to be the thrust of the cultural studies tradition: the claim that somehow mass culture texts empower readers. Fans are not empowered *by* mass culture; fans are empowered *over* mass culture. Like de Certeau's poachers, the fans harvest fields that they did not cultivate and draw upon materials not of their making, materials already at hand in their cultural environment; yet, they make those raw materials work for them. They employ images and concepts drawn from mass culture texts to explore their subordinate status, to envision alternatives, to voice their frustrations and anger, and to share their new understandings with others. Resistance comes from the uses they make of these popular texts, from what they add to them and what they do with them, not from subversive meanings that are somehow embedded within them.

Ethnographic research has uncovered numerous instances where this occurs. Australian schoolchildren turn to *Prisoner* in search of insight into their own institutional experience, even translating schoolyard play into an act of open subordination against the teachers' authority (Hodge and Tripp, 1986; Palmer, 1986). American kindergartners find in the otherness of Pee-Wee Herman a clue to their own insecure status as semisocialized beings (Jenkins, in press). British gay clubs host *Dynasty* and *Dallas* drag balls, relishing the bitchiness and trashiness of nighttime soap operas as a negation of traditional middle class taste and decorum (Finch, 1986). European leftists express their hostility to Western capitalism through their love–hate relationship with *Dallas* (Ang, 1986). Nobody regards these fan activities as a magical cure for the social ills of post-industrial capitalism. They are no substitution for meaningful change, but they can be used effectively to build popular support for such change, to challenge the power of the culture industry to construct the common sense of a mass society, and to restore a much-needed excitement to the struggle against subordination.

Alert to the challenge such uses pose to their cultural hegemony, textual producers openly protest this uncontrollable proliferation of meanings from their texts, this popular rewriting of their stories, this trespass upon their literary properties. Actor William Shatner (Kirk), for instance, has said of *Star Trek* fan fiction: "People read into it things that were not intended. In *Star Trek*'s case, in many instances, things were done just for entertainment purposes" (Spelling, Lofficier, and Lofficier, 1987, p. 40). Producers insist upon their right to regulate what their texts may mean and what types of pleasure they can produce. Yet, such remarks carry little weight. Undaunted by the barking dogs, the "no trespassing" signs, and the threats of prosecution, the fans already have poached those texts from under the proprietors' noses.

Notes

1. An earlier draft of this essay was presented at the 1985 Iowa Symposium and Conference on Television Criticism: Public and Academic Responsibility. I am

indebted to Cathy Schwichtenberg, John Fiske, David Bordwell, and Janice Radway for their helpful suggestions as I was rewriting it for *CSMC*. I am particularly indebted to Signe Hovde and Cynthia Benson Jenkins for introducing me to the world of fan writing; without them my research could not have been completed. I have tried to contact all of the fans quoted in this text and to gain their permission to discuss their work. I appreciate their cooperation and helpful suggestions.

2. For representative examples of other scholarly treatments of *Star Trek* and its fans, see Blair (1983), Greenberg (1984), Jewett and Lawrence (1977), and Tyre (1977). Attitudes range from the generally sympathetic Blair to the openly hostile Jewett and Lawrence.

3. No scholarly treatment of *Star Trek* fan culture can avoid these pitfalls, if only because making such a work accessible to an academic audience requires a translation of fan discourse into other terms, terms that may never be fully adequate to the original. I come to both *Star Trek* and fan fiction as a fan first and a scholar second. My participation as a fan long precedes my academic interest in it. I have sought, where possible, to employ fan terms and to quote fans directly in discussing their goals and orientations toward the program and their own writing. I have shared drafts of this essay with fans and have incorporated their comments into the revision process. I have allowed them the dignity of being quoted from their carefully crafted, well-considered published works rather than from a spontaneous interview that would be more controlled by the researcher than by the informant. I leave it to my readers to determine whether this approach allows for a less mediated reflection of fan culture than previous academic treatments of this subject.

4. The terms "letterzine" and "fictionzine" are derived from fan discourse. The two types of fanzines relate to each other in complex ways. Although there are undoubtedly some fans who read only one type of publication, many read both. Some letterzines, *Treklink* for instance, function as consumer guides and sounding boards for debates about the fictionzines.

5. Both Lorrah and Lichtenberg have achieved some success as professional science fiction writers. For an interesting discussion of the relationship between fan writing and professional science fiction writing, see Randall (1985).

6. Although a wide range of fanzines were considered in researching this essay, I have decided, for the purposes of clarity, to draw my examples largely from the work of a limited number of fan writers. While no selection could accurately reflect the full range of fan writing, I felt that Bates, Land, Lorrah, and Siebert had all achieved some success within the fan community, suggesting that they exemplified, at least to some fans, the types of writing that were desirable and reflected basic tendencies within the form. Further, these writers have produced a large enough body of work to allow some commentary about their overall project rather than localized discussions of individual stories. I have also, wherever possible, focused my discussion around works still currently in circulation and therefore available to other researchers interested in exploring this topic. No slight is intended to the large number of other fan writers who also met these criteria and who, in some cases, are even better known within the fan community.

7. I am indebted to K. C. D'alessandro and Mary Carbine for probing questions that refined my thoughts on this particular issue.

8. The area of Kirk/Spock fiction falls beyond the project of this particular paper. My reason for discussing it here is because of the light its controversial reception sheds on the norms of fan fiction and the various ways fan writers situate themselves toward the primary text. For a more detailed discussion of this particular type of fan writing,

see Lamb and Veith (1986), who argue that K/S stories, far from representing a cultural expression of the gay community, constitute another way of feminizing the concerns of the original series text and of addressing feminist concern within the domain of a popular culture that offers little space for heroic action by women.

References

Ang, I. (1986). *Watching Dallas*. London: Methuen.

Bacon-Smith, C. (1986, November 16). Spock among the women. *The New York Times Book Review*, pp. 1, 26, 28.

Bates, K. A. (1982). *Starweaver two*. Missouri Valley, Iowa: Ankar Press.

—— (1983). *Nuages one*. Tucson, Ariz.: Checkmate Press.

—— (1984). *Nuages two*. Tucson, Ariz.: Checkmate Press.

Bethann. (1976). The measure of love. *Grup*, 5: 53–62.

Blaes, T. (1986a). Letter. *Treklink*, 5: 6.

—— (1987). Letter. *Treklink*, 9: 6–7.

Blair, K. (1983). Sex and *Star Trek*. *Science Fiction Studies*, 10: 292–97.

Bleich, D. (1986). Gender interests in reading and language. In E. A. Flynn and P. P. Schweickart (eds.), *Gender and reading: Essays on readers, texts and contexts* (pp. 234–66). Baltimore: Johns Hopkins University Press.

Brown, M. E., and Barwick, L. (1987, May). *Fables and endless generations: Soap opera and women's culture*. Paper presented at a meeting of the Society of Cinema Studies, Montreal.

Caruthers-Montgomery, P. L. (1987). Letter. *Comlink*, 28: 8.

Chandler, M. (1987). Letter. *Treklink*, 8: 10.

Cooper, C. (1987, February). Opportunities in the "media fanzine" market. *Writer's Digest*, p. 45.

de Certeau, M. (1984). *The practice of everyday life*. Berkeley: University of California Press.

de Lauretis, T. (1982). *Alice doesn't: Feminism, semiotics, cinema*. Bloomington: Indiana University Press.

Deneroff, L. (1987). A reflection on the early days of *Star Trek* fandom. *Comlink*, 28: 3–4.

Finch, M. (1986). Sex and address in *Dynasty*. *Screen*, 27: 24–42.

Greenberg, H. (1984). In search of Spock: A psychoanalytic inquiry. *Journal of Popular Film and Television*, 12: 53–65.

Hodge, R., and Tripp, D. (1986). *Children and television: A semiotic approach*. Cambridge: Polity Press.

Hunter, K. (1977). Characterization rape. In W. Irwin and G. B. Love (eds.), *The best of Trek* 2 (pp. 74–85). New York: New American Library.

Jenkins, H. (in press). "Going bonkers!" Children, play and Pee-Wee. *Camera Obscura*, 18.

Jewett, R., and Lawrence, J. S. (1977). *The American monomyth*. Garden City, N.Y.: Anchor Press.

Kramarae, C. (1981). *Women and men speaking*. Rowley, Mass.: Newburry House.

Lamb, P. F., and Veith, D. L. (1986). Romantic myth, transcendence, and *Star Trek* zines. In D. Palumbo (ed.), *Erotic universe: Sexuality and fantastic literature* (pp. 235–56). New York: Greenwood Press.

Land, J. (1986). *Kista*. Larchmont, N.Y.: Author.

———— (1987). *Demeter.* Larchmont, N.Y.: Author.

Landers, R. (1986). Letter. *Treklink,* 7: 10.

Lay, T. (1986). Letter. *Comlink,* 28: 14–16.

Leerhsen, C. (1986, December 22). *Star Trek*'s nine lives. *Newsweek,* pp. 66–73.

Lichtenberg, J. (1976). *Kraith collected.* Grosse Point Park, Mich.: Ceiling Press.

Lorrah, J. (1976a). *The night of twin moons.* Murray, Ky.: Author.

———— (1976b). *Full moon rising.* Bronx, N.Y.: Author.

———— (1978). The Vulcan character in the NTM universe. In J. Lorrah (ed.), *NTM collected* (Vol. 1, pp. 1–3). Murray, Ky.: Author.

———— (1984). *The Vulcan academy murders.* New York: Pocket Books.

Ludlow, J. (1987). Letter. *Comlink,* 28: 17–18.

Marshak, S., and Culbreath, M. (1978). *Star Trek: The new voyages.* New York: Bantam Books.

Modleski, T. (1982). *Loving with a vengeance: Mass-produced fantasies for women.* Hamden, Conn.: Archon Books.

———— (1986). *Studies in entertainment: Critical approaches to mass culture.* Bloomington: Indiana University Press.

Moore, R. (1986). Letter. *Treklink,* 4: 7–8.

Osborne, E. (1987). Letter. *Treklink,* 9: 3–4.

Palmer, P. (1986). *The lively audience.* Sidney, Australia: Unwyn & Allen.

Radway, J. (1984). *Reading the romance: Women, patriarchy and popular literature.* Chapel Hill: University of North Carolina Press.

Randall, M. (1985). Conquering the galaxy for fun and profit. In C. West (Ed.), *Words in our pockets* (pp. 233–41). Paradise, Calif.: Dustbooks.

Rose, P. (1977). Women in the federation. In W. Irwin and G. B. Love (Eds.), *The best of Trek 2* (pp. 46–52). New York: New American Library.

Schnuelle, S. (1987). Letter. *Sociotrek,* 4: 8–9.

Segel, E. (1986). Gender and childhood reading. In E. A. Flynn and P. P. Schweickart (eds.), *Gender and reading: Essays on readers, texts and contexts* (pp. 164–85). Baltimore: Johns Hopkins University Press.

Siebert, C. A. (1980). Journey's end at lover's meeting. *Slaysu,* 1: 28–34.

———— (1982). By any other name. *Slaysu,* 4: 44–45.

Smith-Rosenberg, C. (1985). *Disorderly conduct: Gender in Victorian America.* New York: Knopf.

Snaider, T. (1987). Letter. *Treklink,* 8: 10.

Spector, J. (1986). Science fiction and the sex war: A womb of one's own. In J. Spector (ed.), *Gender studies: New directions in feminist criticism* (pp. 161–83). Bowling Green, Ohio: Bowling Green State University Press.

Spelling, I., Lofficier, R., and Lofficier, J-M. (1987, May). William Shatner, captain's log: *Star Trek V. Starlog,* pp. 37–41.

Thompson, E. P. (1971). The moral economy of the English crowd in the 18th century. *Past and present,* 50: 76–136.

Thompson, L. (1974). *Star Trek* mysteries—Solved! In W. Irwin and G. B. Love (eds.), *The best of Trek* (pp. 207–14). New York: New American Library.

Tyre, W. B. (1977). *Star Trek* as myth and television as myth maker. *Journal of Popular Culture,* 10: 711–19.

Verba, J. (1986). Editor's corner, *Treklink,* 6: 1–4.

Whitfield, S. E., and Roddenberry, G. (1968). *The making of Star Trek.* New York: Ballantine Books.

Wood, R. (1986). *Hollywood from Vietnam to Reagan.* New York: Columbia University Press.

Making Distinctions in TV Audience Research

Case Study of a Troubling Interview

ELLEN SEITER

Discussions about the television audience have proliferated recently. After a period of preoccupation with textual analyses of television, audience studies have been an attempt, in part, to verify empirically the kinds of ideological readings constructed by (white and middle-class) critics.[1] The new critical interest in television audiences can be traced to 1980 when David Morley published his study of *Nationwide,* but it was in 1986 that the debate on television audiences emerged as the focus of scholarly attention at gatherings such as the International Television Studies Conference. Recently, the debate about audience studies has taken place at a high level of abstraction, as witness Martin Allor's useful essay "Relocating the site of the audience" published with four responses in a recent issue of *Critical Studies in Mass Communication.*[2] In this [essay] I wish to discuss the political issues of audience studies in the terms laid out in Pierre Bourdieu's *Distinction,* and to discuss the problem of the "self-reflexive" researcher in the context of one case study. By doing so, I hope to encourage a change within the current academic discussion of audiences. I feel we need to take up more concretely the problems of research as a practice.

I believe cultural studies must focus on the differences in class and cultural capital which typify the relationship between the academic and the subject of audience studies. Nowhere is this more vivid than in the study of television. The problem emerges most clearly when we discuss empirical research as a practice. Here I describe an interview with two white men that illustrates some of the political problems of interpretation in audience stud-

From *Cultural Studies,* vol. 4, no. 1. Reprinted with permission of the author, *Cultural Studies,* and Routledge.

ies. But in doing so I also make a gesture that scholars in television and film studies endlessly repeat in our work. I completely ignore racial difference, and thereby contribute to the racism which permeates academic discourse.

This is the story of a ninety-minute interview that I conducted with co-researcher Hans Borchers as part of a larger study on television soap operas carried out in Oregon during the summer of 1986.[3] Out of twenty-six such interviews we conducted, I have chosen this interview because of my interest in gender and class, and in the discomfort many people feel when they identify themselves as members of the television audience. This interview took place in the home of Jim Dubois, sixty-two years old, and his housemate Larry Howe, about fifty-five years old. (I have changed their names here.) Both men are retired graphic artists, who moved to Eugene from California two years ago. The interview was conducted by myself (an American film and television professor in my early thirties) and Hans Borchers (a German American studies professor in his early forties). All four of us are white. I wish to describe how our subjects reacted to us as interviewers, how the inferior television audience was persistently identified as female, and how the power differential between us as academic interviewers and Jim and Larry as subjects related to the playing out of class difference during the interview.

Throughout the interview, it was uppermost in these men's minds that we were academics. For them, it was an honor to talk to us and an opportunity to be heard by persons of authority and standing. They made a concerted effort to appear cosmopolitan and sophisticated. For them, our visit offered a chance to reveal their own personal knowledge, and their opinions about society and the media. They had no interest whatsoever in offering us interpretative, textual readings of television programs, as we wanted them to do. In fact, they exhibited a kind of "incompetence" as viewers in this regard: they were unable to reproduce critical categories common to *TV Guide* and academic television criticism.[4] All fiction shows could be labeled soap opera: situation comedies and medical shows, alike. Yet many television shows were seen by Mr. Howe to conform to a more personal, master narrative about the painful relations between generations, which stemmed from his own bitter experience as a father.

This interview made me personally uncomfortable, because of my age and my gender, and because of my status as an academic. When we talk about examining our own subjectivities as researchers, we also need to ask what it means to ask someone else about television viewing. Television watching can be a touchy subject, precisely because of its association with a lack of education, with idleness and unemployment, and its identification as an "addiction" of women and children. This interview exemplifies the defensiveness that men and women unprotected by academic credentials may feel in admitting to television viewing in part because of its connotations of feminine passivity, laziness, and vulgarity.

For me, the interview raised profound methodological questions about "unstructured" interviewing. Our goal, which we discussed as a research team at great length, was to hear whatever soap opera viewers wanted to tell us. We wanted to follow digressions, to be receptive to unanticipated areas of discussion. (The psychoanalytic scenario was clearly in the back of our minds.) But our subjects wanted to present themselves in a good light. Though we were strangers, they knew we were academics and to a large extent that dictated the kinds of things that were said to us. That is especially prominent in this interview where our "subjects" were doubly defensive as men and as members of an older generation.

I am going to describe the dynamics and the sequence of conversational events that took place when we visited Mr. Howe and Mr. Dubois's home at some length. When we extract quotes from this context, much of their significance is lost. Very often, the meaning of statements as part of an exchange (and an unequal one) between researcher and subject is obscured.

While this interview is atypical in many respects of our experiences with soap opera viewers, especially women, it vividly demonstrates something that happened in all the interviews. People often compare their own television viewing to that of the imagined mass audience, one that is more interested, more duped, more entertained, more gullible than they are. Academics as television viewers are no exception to this rule. The imagination of that other television viewer is deeply implicated in the class/gender system. For Mr. Howe and Mr. Dubois, television's contaminating effects were directly and persistently related to the feminine (a tendency they share with academic writing about the mass media, from the Frankfurt School on).[5] This interview also exemplifies the extent to which television as a "mass" form is viewed in a very different way by those without access to college educations and more authentic bourgeois culture. For working-class and petit-bourgeois viewers, television is alternately relied on as a source of education and condemned for its failure to confirm and to replicate experience.

The Interview

> Torn by all the contradictions between an objectively dominated condition and would-be participation in the dominant values, the petit bourgeois is haunted by the appearance he offers to others and the judgment they make of it. He constantly overshoots the mark for fear of falling short, betraying his uncertainty and anxiety about belonging in his anxiety to show or give the impression that he belongs. . . . He is bound to be seen as the man of appearances, haunted by the look of others and endlessly occupied with being seen in a good light.[6]

Mr. Howe and Mr. Dubois began the interview with a disclaimer about the amount of time spent viewing and the insistence that they only watch soap operas occasionally because they are usually out in the afternoons. This was an unusual start for the interview because Mr. Howe had answered a newspaper advertisement asking to interview soap opera viewers. Mr. Dubois explained that he only watched occasionally when seized by the distant hope that "maybe today we'll see something good happen rather than something tragic happening, ... I guess soap operas make you glad that you don't have more problems than you do." Mr. Dubois then offered an excuse for why they do watch: to see the houses and locations on the shows: "That home is beautiful. We'd like to own it." The vineyard on *Falcon Crest* is shot on location in Santa Barbara, where Larry used to live.

This being said in defense of their interest in that show, Mr. Howe moved on to a statement of his preferences, based in part on a critique of soap opera in general:

> I think the soap operas that I can tolerate the most are the ones that don't take place in one room for the whole episode—where they stand there and talk each other to death. And never move outside. I like to see some automobile travel, some outdoor scenery, not just two people or three people at a table sitting there yakking each other to death.

Despite our resolutions to be non-directive, we reverted to the tactic of trying to elicit a comparative critical scheme (and ended up sounding like network focus group supervisors). We asked: "which are the worst that way?" (Here we desperately try for some comparative rating, an attempt to be systematic.) The answer is an equation of this problem with women and with tragedy. Mr. Dubois explained: "I think the afternoon ones have a tendency to be too tragic . . . it is more tragic in the afternoon, because afternoons are geared to woman, and woman likes to cry and likes to see somebody else's tragedy. . . . 'Oh, I'm not doing so bad, Look at her.' And they relate to that, whereas I, as a man, can't relate to that."

Mr. Howe then broke in with a kind of mini-lecture typical of the interview, in which he described to us the origins of television before the First World War, and the Berlin Olympic telecasts. Mr. H was trying to display his knowledge about a topic he (erroneously) assumed we would be interested in and could confirm his expertise at (a mistaken assumption given our lack of knowledge or interest in the *technological* origins of television). We politely listened but did not reinforce this kind of talk. We were more receptive to Mr. D when he returned to the topic of soap opera. Still attributing the tragic sensibility to women, but now generalizing about the problems of illness, he told us this story: "I'd never been in the hospital in my life—so it's always an adventure—until recently. I had a minor heart attack. I was rushed to the hospital in emergency. So then all the *General Hospital* things that went on, that I had seen, sort of became real to me. I couldn't believe that I was in the hospital playing the part of a very, very sick man." As an older viewer, illness is the most authentic fiction television presents to Mr. D.

Mr. H broke in for five minutes with a discussion of medical students inviting Robert Young to be graduation speaker because they had confused Marcus Welby with a real doctor. We were feeling more and more uncomfortable with Mr. Howe. He sounded eccentric to us, and his story mixed up. I believed *he* must be wrong, not the educated medical students. But this story allowed him to formulate his strong objections to TV: "it just goes to show you how they can trivialize, that's the word, they can trivialize anything, and make it seem insignificant." He applied this tendency to trivialize to priests, nuns, doctors, and then—wanting to spark our interest—professors.

Mr. H proceeded to draw an opposition between professors and scriptwriters, who "misinform the public," "when they set themselves up as something to be admired or respected. I read about what high ratings they have, well I get resentful because of the fact . . . well what are they measuring themselves against . . . what is the mentality of the people that are watching?" Along with the imagined other viewers, many people we interviewed felt this enormous antagonism towards the television industry's creative personnel. Writers were constantly coming under attack for boring the audience, or patronizing them.

At this point, Mr. Dubois made a revelation: Mr. H is a self-taught man. Mr. D proudly described how much research his friend had done, and how television material instigated his research activities. "When he sees something that is definitely a mistake and wrong, he'll check on it." Mr. H explained: "I can't get into secret government archives. I can't get past security clearances on military bases. But there are ways of finding things out. Societies that I have knowledge of, the people who are members of societies. Through letter writing. Library textbooks." Mr. D continued to praise him: "He's an avid reader, so he knows his stuff. Also he has, he really has a photographic memory . . . which I rely on and he relies on."

This story about research unsanctioned by the academy, convinced me that Mr. H was a crackpot. Returning to his anger at the box, Mr. Howe told a story about Elvis Presley once firing a "45 caliber six-shooter" at his television set.

In his comprehensive empirical study of French cultural differences, Bourdieu discusses the difference between legitimate and illegitimate self-education, between the kind of autodidacticism practiced by academics, and the kind that Mr. Howe does:

> There is nothing paradoxical in the fact that in its ends and means the educational system defines the enterprise of "legitimate autodidacticism" that is ever more strongly demanded as one rises in the educational hierarchy (between sections, disciplines, and specialties and so forth, or between levels). The essentially contradictory phrase "legitimate autodidacticism" is intended to indicate the difference in kind between the highly valued "extra-curricular" culture of the holder of academic qualifications and the illegitimate extra-curricular culture of the autodidact. Illegitimate extra-curricular culture, whether it be the knowledge accumulated by the self-taught or the "experience" acquired in and through practice, outside the control of the institution specifically mandated to inculcate it and officially sanction its acquisition, like the art of cooking or herbal medicine, craftsmen's skills or the stand-in's irreplaceable knowledge, is only valorized to the strict extent of its technical efficiency, without any social added value, and is exposed to legal sanctions whenever it emerges from the domestic universe to compete with the authorized competences. (Bordieu, *Distinction*, p. 25)

Information is routinely given as one of the "uses and gratifications" of media use. But I think it is difficult for academics involved in television studies to imagine the frustration and anger provoked by a dependency on television for education and a lifelong exclusion from elite forms of higher education. Some of the flashes of rage in this interview on Mr. Howe's part, and many of the stunned silences on mine and Hans's, stemmed from our face-to-face confrontation of this difference in access to cultural capital. I emphasize this point because it is an arena where the distinction between legitimate and illegitmate autodidacticism is one we as academics have an interest in maintaining.

I had already placed Mr. Dubois and Mr. Howe in class terms by their home furnishings—carefully maintained, early American matching pieces, of which they were proud. Taste in things like clothes, food and furniture, and patterns of consumerism is one of the earliest acquired and most striking forms of class distinction, according to Bourdieu. At this point in the interview, Mr. Dubois revealed that he had a career in the fashion industry and used the television, in a specialized professional way, to learn about style:

> they show the home, they show the furniture, well this is a little bit, it's not all a loss, it's a little bit of an education for me. I know what early American furniture looks like, or Renaissance furniture looks like. I know what pseudo-modern furniture looks like . . . so it's sort of educational for me . . . even though the plot may be absolutely ridiculous.

Then the conversation turned to a brief discussion of the various things that bother them about television: too much sex; too many commercial interruptions. On guard against a perception on our part that they were too familiar with television, Mr. Howe then drew a distinction between themselves and "others who have TVs in every room . . . if we have other things to do we just go and do them . . . otherwise we'd just sit around and watch TV all day." Mr. D: "if it's raining and we can't get out to do the things that we want to do out of doors, that's when we'll watch. As I told you, most afternoon programs are geared to ladies. That's when they show all the gushy. . . ." Mr. H: "They can stand there and iron or they can stand there and prepare food or whatever and watch TV. . . . " Despite the fact that these men have lived in households without women for twenty years, domestic work is seen as the domain of women, the domain of women watching television.

Hans asked if they talk with other viewers about television, since this aspect has been conspicuously absent in this, compared to our other interviews. Mr. D talked about a friend who is a real fan, who arranges her lunch hour around them. This led to the following exchange:

> *Mr. H:* Well, you know, where the word came from . . . it's actually true . . . it's a shortening of the word fanatic.
>
> *Mr. D:* She was brought up with soaps, because her mother, Mrs. Applebaum, a lovely lady, I really love her . . . she was an avid watcher . . . she was a housewife and this was her passion.

> *Mr. H:* Is that the lady that every time she coughs or sneezes bubbles come
> out of her mouth? He said she was brought up on soaps. . . .

Hans, cutting short the joke which we obviously did not find funny, broke in to ask whether soaps have changed, commenting that most of our interviews had been with younger people. Mr. H speculated that "the young people see through soap operas and consider them to be so absurd that they don't bother with them." But Hans contradicted him: "They watch them alright." Mr. D then confirmed this, displaying his knowledge about the young and about fashion trends: "They talk today's language . . . they use the slang . . . they'll also use even in the commercials, as well as the story itself . . . hard rock sounds and stuff like that. The clothes that they wear is the updated clothes." Mr. D then mentioned that he called up his son, a lawyer, to verify the implausibility of one of the legal plots on the show. Again, the theme of "research" appears, and Mr. D lets us know that he has access to real knowledge, and is not being taken in by television.

Mr. H then asked us about the popularity of American TV in Europe, something he has read about and which horrifies him. This allowed him to share with us more of his knowledge. He has traveled in Germany, he has a keen interest in the Soviet Union and subscribes to *Soviet Life.* He told us the history of the Karl May society. We listened politely but uninterestedly to these things. But at this moment Mr. H was telling us what he wanted to talk about. For him, talking to academics and to a European professor was a rare opportunity. For our part, we had no real interest in his encyclopedic knowledge or in his generalizations about twentieth-century culture, which repeatedly took the form of the statement "instead of art imitating life, life imitates art," woven throughout his comments.

To force him back into the position of the everyday television fan, we asked what other shows they watch. Mr. H continued in his educated tone: "private detectives type adventure shows, police shows, travelogue shows, historical and archeological productions, such as Jacques Cousteau . . . the discovery that dolphins have an intelligence now thought to be as high or perhaps even higher than human beings." This list is not only entirely respectable in terms of bourgeois cultural norms, it is also (not coincidentally) composed entirely of "gender genres." And his preoccupation with education (read class distinctions), voiced throughout the interview, surfaces here again in the fascination with *intelligence,* albeit in animals. Mr. D contributed that they like to watch documentaries about animals and about castles. "They take you through every old castle . . . we're interested in all sorts of old buildings . . . and one of our goals and dreams is that we want to someday buy a Victorian old home and try to restore it."

This returned Mr. H to a recounting of his travels in Germany. But Mr. D continued to describe the show about castles: "And that's what amazes me . . . the art, the paintings, the old paintings, and where they came from."

Mr. H interrupted here to mention his favorite show, *Murder, She Wrote.* He explained that they have surmised that the show is shot in the actress's own home on the East Coast, in "a beautiful area and a beautiful home." We asked why he said it was like a soap opera, still trying, even after an hour, to draw out these critical categories. He explained that there is "a lot more talking than any action of any kind . . . that program is just very talkative." But Mr. D interrupted, "Larry, it's logical talk though. They are trying to solve a crime. At least a crime is committed." This led to a debate about whether *Hill Street Blues* and *Barney Miller* are soap operas, with Jim explaining to Larry the differences. "They label it a comedy. They don't label it a serious drama or a series."

Now Mr. H returned to his theme which sounded like something he planned to say before we arrived, "it's got to be negative and down in order to be . . ." (soap opera). Mr. D explained again "I think it was originally started for ladies that were doing their laundry and their wash and they were using this soap."

Sensing the end of the interview. Mr. H now brought up the most personal and the most passionate judgment of television. As in many interviews we conducted, feelings of real anger or despair surfaced at the end of the conversation, as more personal details from the past were brought in.

> One point I will say. If you want to call it resentment you could call it that . . . it is always the parents' fault. Never the kids that are old enough to make their own decisions. They are always made to look good. Or victims of the way their parents raised them. . . . Just as though they had no control over their own lives as all brainless boobs. All the father's fault. Father never knows anything. He's a boob, an idiot. Only mother knows how to make decisions. Or the kids are the heroes always. . . .

He continued:

> *Father Knows Best* was a satire on father knowing best. He was made to look like a ridiculous buffoon. That was another . . . you could call it a situation comedy, if you want. I think it borderline soap opera. But always the kids come out looking perfect. . . . Looking back now, I never suspected what my parents had to go through. I was one of those that was sympathizing with the kids until I became a parent and had children of my own. Now all of a sudden I'd just as soon slap the little monsters around. . . .

Mr. Dubois got in the last words before we broke up the interview: "That's my theme song. I know what it is like to be young but you don't know what it is to be old."

Conclusion

In writing up this interview, I have done extensive editing. I have attributed intentions and feelings to others. I have bolstered some generalizations I wanted to make with the authority of the real empirical subject. I have emphasized a couple of points, the role of gender and the role of cultural capital, which I would like to pursue here. Before doing so, let me also argue that audience studies might be helped at this point in time by the publication of unedited transcripts along with analyses. In a partial fashion, I hope to have demonstrated here how certain statements, if taken out of context in a discussion of something like "genres" or sitcoms might create quite a different impression than when the interview is taken in sequence. Clearly, more concern should be paid to language in audience studies, and to the social context which produces it.

What I have described here involves many "errors" in terms of the goals of unstructured, "ethnographic" interviewing. These problems were accentuated by a lack of rapport in the interview, but I do not believe that these errors are avoidable. We must pay more attention to methodology in empirical audience studies, and at the very least describe these methods more fully. But the problem will not disappear by adopting a more "correct" method of interviewing. The social identities of academic researchers and the social identities of our TV viewing subjects are not only different, they are differently valued. We cannot lose sight of the differences that exist between us and our subjects outside of our discussions about television. This interview underscores the fact that the differences that may be played out in conversation between interviewer and subject (I use the term advisedly) are antagonistic differences, based on hierarchically arranged cultural differences. Recognizing such distinctions will be difficult for academics, Marxists or not, because of our highly homogeneous work environment, and our intensive professional socialization.

Television may be particularly fascinating to us because it seems to provide access to the "other," the working-class, the female audience, the fantasized agents of revolutionary change. But it will not suffice to imagine ourselves to *be* this other audience, or to adopt the position of the enthusiastic fan, as John Fiske has recommended. "Slumming it" on our part merely obscures the fact that we are in a dominant relation in terms of access to cultural capital. Sitting down face to face, doing interviews with people different from us, *does* help raise consciousness about these issues. Empirical study *is* necessary to understand television viewing. But we must not pretend that the differences we find will be sympathetic or ideologically correct or even comprehensible from our own class and race and gender positions.

As a feminist, I did not find Mr. H to be a particularly sympathetic subject (my irritation at his sexist jokes being, of course, a marker of my own class background). The currents of hostility and aggression which ran through Mr. H's conversation, culminating in the discussion of his children, were disturbing to me. In my other work I have tended to focus on interviews in all-female groups where a certain level of rapport was established, and where the subjects were much more malleable to my direction of the interview, more forthcoming, more interesting because they related the media to their personal histories. Feminist linguists have found some evidence that women interrupt less often and rarely speak in lengthy monologues: we certainly found this true in our interviews.

But Mr. H and Mr. D remind us about an important lesson in terms of the "gendered spectator." They offer a vivid example of the denigration of women as an ego-defense. I am reminded of Bourdieu's point that

> explicit aesthetic choices are in fact often constituted in opposition to the choices of the groups closest in social space, with whom the competition is most direct and most immediate, and more precisely, no doubt, in relation to those choices most clearly marked by the intention of marking distinction vis-à-vis lower groups. (p. 60)

The two men offer two different positions from which to do so (there are many more). Mr. H occupies the more machismo tradition (and appears the most ignorant about television). Television appeals to women because it is downbeat, emotional, talky. He is for history, for research, for facts, for action. He despises or resists character identification. He would rather "prove himself" by talking about his educational exploits. He dominates the conversation repeatedly. Mr. D sets up an equally rigid dichotomy between himself and the woman as spectator. But he is more involved with television and approaches it from the position of an aesthete: he is interested in [topics] such as clothes, fashion, home design, architecture, art, forms which may challenge heterosexual male norms. What is curious here is the similarity in relationship to the construction of the audience "other as female" despite these differences. It suggests the importance of mapping out the interplay of class and gender differences on the field of cultural consumption.

The interview was full of miscommunications, and these miscommunications were often based on class differences, on the unequal possession of cultural capital. When interviewing those less educated, or with less ambitions to appear educated, than Mr. H, this has been less of a problem. It is precisely because he aspired to bridge the gap which separated him from us that he made more mistakes. His system of references—Soviet life, German castles, secret societies, the military—was very different from our own, but we could recognize it as undistinguished. Throughout the interview, our status of academics compelled Mr. H to range widely over topics, to boast, to wander, to interrogate us about our opinions and knowledge. We did not want to surrender control of this verbal "exchange," and this increased the undercurrent of hostility in the interview. The gap in class between Mr. Howe and us, with its different priorities—material artifacts over ideas, history over sociology, encyclopedic knowledge over theory—is a relationship based not just in difference but in the antagonism of competing class values.

> The struggle between the dominant fractions and the dominated fractions tends, in its ideological retranslation, to be organized by oppositions that are almost superimposible on those which the dominant vision sets up between the dominant class and the dominated classes: on the one hand, freedom, disinterestedness, the "purity" of sublimated tastes, salvation in the hereafter; on the other, necessity, self-interest, base material satisfactions, salvation in this world. (Bourdieu, *Distinction*, p. 254)

Bourdieu argues that nothing is better able to express social differences than the field of cultural goods—and here I would substitute television—because "the relationship of distinction is objectively inscribed within it, and is reactivated, intentionally or not, in each act of consumption, through the instruments of economic and cultural appropriation which it requires" (*Distinction*, p. 226). Obviously, Bourdieu's ideas would have to be reworked to suit the United States. But his work attests to the importance of relating television to other cultural fields, food, art, clothes, furniture, films, newspapers, and so on, the better to see class distinctions at work. In this broader context, it may be possible to avoid portraying television as a paragon of cultural pluralism (something for everyone, separate but equal, everybody happy). Though it is farthest from our intentions, critical scholars engaged in empirical cultural studies have borne a slight resemblance to market researchers. The challenge is to investigate popular tastes *and* explain how these tastes are distributed in relations of domination. To do so will also necessitate recognizing our own dominance and our own class interests within the system of cultural distinctions.

Notes

Thanks to Roy Metcalf for his extensive help on the project and his excellent transcription; and to Gabriele Kreutzner, Eva-Maria Warth, and Hans Borchers, my coworkers on the Soap Opera Project.

1. Charlotte Brunsdon, "Text and audience," in E. Seiter, H. Borchers, G. Kreutzner, and E. Warth (eds.) *Remote Control: Television, Audiences and Cultural Power* (London: Routledge, 1989), pp. 116–29.

2. Martin Allor, "Relocating the site of the audience," *Critical Studies in Mass Communication* 5: 3 (1988), 217–33.

3. This study has been written up in the essay "Don't treat us like we're so stupid and naive: Towards an ethnography of soap opera viewers," in Seiter, Borchers, Kreutzner, and Warth, eds., *Remote Control*, pp. 223–47.

4. In this sense they were the opposite of Umberto Eco's "model readers." See my "Eco's TV guide: The soaps," *Tabloid* 5 (1982).

5. See Andreas Huyssens, "Mass culture as woman: Modernism's other," in *After the Great Divide* (Bloomington: Indiana University Press, 1986).

6. Pierre Bourdieu, *Distinction: A Social Critique of the Judgement of Taste*, trans. Richard Nice (Cambridge, Mass.: Harvard University Press, 1984), p. 253.

The Transcript

Because so little ethnographic data is published in full, the transcript of the interview upon which this article is based is included in the hope that others will find it useful to their research.

    HB: As I told you on the phone, we're a team of four people and the whole thing is funded by a German research foundation. The reason we are doing these interviews is to find out how people watch soap opera, what people's watching experiences are?

ES: We don't have a set plan of questions that we want to ask you. We are interested in what *your* opinions are about soap opera.

Mr. H: We're being recorded right now?

HB: Yes. So which are your favorite soap operas? Which are the soap operas you watch?

Mr. D: Well since we spend most of our afternoons out we prefer to watch any of the soaps that are on in prime time. The reason why, I think both Larry and I, have a tendency to watch these things occasionally, is because we are both semi-retired and some of the programs, other than soaps, are very very bad . . . that we figured, well, maybe today we'll see something good happen rather than something tragic happening, which the soaps have a tendency to do . . . they're always fighting with each other, they're always against each other. As a matter of fact, I think that the characters are written in that way. Instead of trying to make you feel better they make you feel worse. And we enjoy some of them. *Dynasty,* we watch *Dynasty.* And some of the new ones that are coming up . . . the new one with Charlton Heston . . . we both happen to like Charlton Heston's performances, and that's why we watch. *The Colbys* is the same. Of course, it's a spin-off of all the others. And after a while, after watching a few years, you begin to realize that it's repetitive. They repeat. If they don't have a certain problem in one, they'll have it in another. And . . . another reason why I think that I usually watch serials . . . I like to see how they work out their problems. I like to see how they work it out.

Mr. H: Well, I guess, soap operas, in one way, make you glad that you don't have any more problems in life than you do. To make a comparison between your own life's ups and downs and whatever they have manufactured into each individual soap opera. Everything seems to be so terrible, you know, it's a tragedy about to happen all the time. Somebody's ill and dying or a child dies stillborn or a marriage is about to break up because of another woman or another man. It's just that, I guess, the soap operas would die on the vine if they were geared to happy events. They have to gear to bad events, because evidently the human animal is only interested in hearing and seeing the bad. You couldn't have a happy ending; you couldn't have an enjoyable program with people just normally enjoying themselves or children behaving normally—they have to behave abnormally. Adults have to act crazy and be on drugs or liquor in order for people to enjoy it. And that gives the people, not necessarily me, but most people, I think, have a vicarious sense of pleasure that. . . . Thank God that's not the way I lead my life . . . or. . . . There but for the grace of God go I. . . . That's what it's geared to—the negative, the black side, the dark side of life.

HB: May I ask which soap operas are you referring to? The nighttime soap operas?

Mr. H: Some daytime early hours and other night time. *ATWT* [As the World Turns] is one. *Dynasty* is another, like he mentioned.

Mr. D: *Falcon's Crest* is one of my favorites. It just so happens that both of us like certain scenes . . . other than old houses, like in *FC.* That home is beautiful. We'd like to own it.

Mr. H: *Dallas* is a favorite. Not necessarily, but I mean it's the least bad of most of the rest. It's the most . . . the one you can tolerate the most.

Mr. D: It doesn't, you see, *Dallas* doesn't put women in a good light. They are all lousy. They are all full of hate, envy, and jealousy. They are all out for . . . *Dallas* tends to make you feel that these women are out to power hunt. And they want to take it away from men. But *FC* has its good points and its bad points. One of the good points is that it's a vineyard . . . and Larry comes from Santa Barbara where there are an awful lot of vineyards. So those scenes are familiar to him and I've been there and I like Santa Barbara—at least I used to. Anyway, so the scenes that they show in the vineyards, and the story involved around the family struggle on the show interests me, and interests him.

ES: You mentioned the house on *Falcon Crest.* Which house is that?

Mr. D: Her home. Jane Wyman's home. The big house. The big estate.

Mr. H: Used to be a Roman Catholic . . . like a monastery, many years ago. And it was sold and then it was . . . the area around it was converted into an area of a large amount of growing of grapes for wine purposes. They had their own separate wine cellars where the . . . oh, I remember now . . . did you ever hear of a Roman Catholic order called the Christian Brothers? That's the name of the order. In fact, they even have that label on their wines. Christian Brothers. But, what I was going to say is that, I think the soap operas that I can tolerate the most are the ones that don't take place in one room for the whole episode—where they stand there and talk each other to death. And never move outside. I like to see some automobile travel, some outdoor scenery, not just two people or three people at a table sitting there yakking each other to death.

ES: Which ones are the worst that way?

Mr. D: I think the afternoon ones have a tendency to be too tragic. They pull you down, whereas the nighttime ones have some element of surprise or adventure or sometimes, occasionally, things turn out well. The girl gets the guy that she's after and she finds that divorcing her husband is not as bad as she thought it would be. That she's not going to commit suicide. Those things, I seem to think that they make it more tragic in the afternoon, because afternoons are geared to woman, and woman likes to cry and they like to see somebody else's tragedy. It makes, as Larry said, it makes their own lives more tolerable. "Oh, I'm not doing so bad. Look at her." And they relate to that, whereas I, as a man, can't relate to that. But I can relate to the . . . evening ones which show these powerful guys who are greedy and out for power and out to destroy and full of hate and everything else. It's man's inhumanity to man—and I can understand that. Not that I relate to it . . . I think it's disgusting . . . I think it's terrible. JR is hateful. I realize that most of these writers, that write soaps, try to gear it to make it more exciting that way. So they exaggerate everything. They exaggerate the want of power. And although I shouldn't say exaggerate, maybe I've led a very sheltered life, and I haven't seen it that exaggerated in my life time.

HB: When you say exaggerate do you mean exaggerate compared to actual life, business life, for example?

Mr. D: I think they make it more exciting that way. Now I've been in business for a long time and I know that there's thievery and I know that there's competition and I know that people are really pitted against each other, but I don't think they tend to think violently, as I say this is one of the exaggerations on soaps. They think violently. If a guy gets mad at this woman because she's trying to take his business away—he slaps her around. I mean, to me, I've never seen it—maybe it does happen—maybe it does happen. That's what I say, maybe I've been sheltered. Maybe I feel, because I'm nice and I wouldn't do that they should be nice. I realize that it is fiction and so I accept it as fiction. I can't really say that I would feel that this is true to life to me.

HB: What do you think of the women on these shows who don't let themselves be slapped around, who fight back?

Mr. D: They can be pretty vicious too. Joan Collins is the most vicious of them all. She don't let anything get in her way. She's a strong woman. Maybe there are women like that. Maybe there are. I haven't ever met any. So that's why I feel its sort of vicious.

Mr. H: I was just going to remark on a phrase, that I've heard a lot of times, about how art imitates life. I've seen an increasing tendency, at least in this country, cause I haven't traveled to other countries for a number of years, whereby there is a tendency to turn things completely around backwards. To the point where life is imitating art. That's not the way it should be, that's upside-down. Life should not imitate art—art should imitate life. More and more people are being . . . I call it a subtle form of brainwashing . . . where people are concluding that that is the way to behave because they saw it on television, that's accepted behavior. They're are not thinking for themselves. They're allowing that thing over there to do their thinking for them. I don't do that—I refuse to do that. That's where I say that more and more life is imitating art and I don't like that trend at all. And specially is that bad with kids—impressionable little kids who grow up. This is the first completely, 100 percent, television generation, as it has been called now. Completely, from the time of infancy on up to adulthood, complete television generation, first time. More and more, kids do some terrible things and then they tell the police later on. . . . Well, I. . . . How did you get such a bizarre idea. . . . Well, I saw it on TV. Life is imitating art, supposedly art. And another thing I don't like about these soap operas; they commercial you to death. You know what I mean. Every ten seconds they break into the story, they chop it up, and you don't know what's happening anyhow, because while the commercial is running so is the soap opera running. So that when they stop with the commercial and put you back on the soap opera you've lost track of where you were. Instead of stopping the episode of soap opera right where they cut in for the commercial . . . they don't . . . because they're in a timeslot, see. And they can only run so many minutes. So what they are doing is making a sandwich out of it. They are putting the commercial on top of the soap opera and running both of them together at the same time. And that's chopping off the soap opera, and what have you got left; when you've got a dozen commercials in the space of one soap opera.

HB: I'd like to ask you when did you first encounter TV or soap opera, for that matter?

Mr. H: Well, I guess, the first one about thirty years ago. They had 'em.

Mr. D: They also had them on radio.

Mr. H: Television has been around a number of years. Did you know television was around before World War II. In three countries—the United States, England, and in Germany all had viable working television networks. Did you know that the first Olympics . . . not the first . . . but the 1936 Berlin Olympics were televised back to Berlin. 1936! I would say that my television watching started thirty years ago, but my soap opera . . . I never looked . . . I never . . . what I'm trying to say is I never searched them out. They just happened to come along. That goes back to about 1960, I'd say.

HB: Which show was that, do you remember?

Mr. H: No, I don't. That's how important it was.

Mr. D: At that time, I believe, Larry, if you remember correctly, they came out with all these hospital and doctor. . . .

Mr. H: That's right. You're right. You broke the log jam there. *Ben Casey* was one. *Dr. Kildare* was another. Let's see, what else? *General Hospital,* that was another. That was a biggy. Now you start jogging the. . . .

Mr. D: And everybody was taking their pulses and. . . .

Mr. H: They did that to death on those hospital shows.

Mr. D: After a while, I guess, both the writers and directors and everybody else, and even the actors, were sick of them, because they had too many. Some of them are still on. *General Hospital* is still on.

HB: Do you still watch it?

Mr. D: Occasionally.

HB: Does it make sense to watch occasionally?

Mr. D: Occasionally. Not really. Sometimes . . . in *General Hospital,* I notice, what they do is they fill you in. They give you, at least, a synopsis, of part of the story that you haven't seen or may have missed. So, but occasionally also you'll all of a sudden you'll see a new character and you'll wonder where they came from. But . . . in those hospital series . . . it seems they get involved with one or two cases . . . that are new . . . and they complete them. Either the guy dies or he lives or the lady has her baby or whatever. Or she gets her disease and it is cured or it's terminal. So when they tell you it's going to be terminal already and you sob a little bit . . . you cry a little bit . . . and you feel sorry for the poor dear and these things are terrible. See now those things are more or less true to life. Those hospital things, I mean, we all have had family that have departed from chronic illnesses and stuff. I've never been in the hospital in my life—so it's always an adventure—until recently. I had a minor heart attack. I was rushed to the hospital in emergency. So then all the *GH* things that went on, that I had seen, sort of became real to me. I couldn't believe that I was in the hospital playing the part of a very, very sick man.

Mr. H: Want to hear something incredible that happened a few years ago regarding one soap opera? So incredible that you won't believe it. It happened in regard to this, uh, soap opera that starred Robert Young as a guy named Dr. Marcus Welby. Now the graduating class of Columbia University in New York . . . of the medical school department of Columbia University . . . now this has to do with life imitating art. That guy has been an actor all his adult life, he has no medical training at all, except reading cues and reading the script. The graduating class, and this was not a spoof either, they were quite serious about it . . . they had been indoctrinated, or at least several of them in positions of power in the graduating class . . . to bring whoever they chose as a speaker . . . a valedictorian speaker at their graduating class. So they actually extended an invitation to Robert Young, in Hollywood, to speak . . . to come and make a commencement address at their graduating class, in the late 1970s . . . and he was on his way to doing it until the authorities at the school, at Columbia U., found out about it. They went right through the roof. The only person authorized to speak at any graduating class at a medical school is an MD. Not a professor. Not a faculty member. Not an outsider. And certainly not an actor. An MD. A fully qualified doctor. But these kids . . . or I say kids, they're in their late twenties . . . were so indoctrinated with this idea that he was a real qualified doctor. And when they were asked later . . . they were called in on the carpet and asked if this was their idea of some kind of a practical joke or something. They looked wide-eyed. No it wasn't a practical joke, they were deadly serious. They actually called for a movie actor to come in and give a commencement address on medicine . . . on what we could expect in the future in the medical world. The guy knows nothing about that—except his cue cards and his script. This is what I mean by . . . not art imitating life but life imitating art. That's how deeply these soap operas among others affect people's thinking. And I still think that that is a classic case of how incredible these things are in influencing people's lives.

HB: Are you saying . . . would this have wider application on television or just on soap opera?

Mr. H: Wider. Not just soap operas. But in this case it was Marcus Welby, MD. Now they put MD on the tail end of that program. . . . I don't know how they got that by the medical association or medical society or AMA. Because the guy was in no way an MD. But it just goes to show you how they can trivialize, that's the word, they can trivialize anything, and make it seem insignificant. They do it with priests. They do it with nuns. They do it with doctors. With scientific people . . . professors . . . who spend all their lives studying intently and dedicating themselves to the pursuit of that single goal . . . and then they bring in some jerk-off actor, who nobody has seen before, and they put a white smock on him and call him Professor This or Professor That or Professor The Other, you know. Something so ridiculous that several times in these soap operas. . . . I'm not saying I'm so smart and they're so dumb, but I am saying that several times there have been some statements made, that were no doubt part of the script, that were so stupid that, unless you were a complete dunderhead, you would catch it. And realize that the scriptwriters don't really know what they are talking about.

HB: The way you speak about soap opera and soap opera actors you sound pretty resentful, I must say.

Mr. H: Only resentful when they misinform the public. When they set themselves up as something to be admired or respected. I read about what high ratings they have, well, I get resentful because of the fact. . . . Well what are they measuring themselves against to get those high ratings? What is the mentality of the people that are watching, if that's what they constitute high ratings. Like that Marcus Welby episode, what does it take to get high ratings like that? I mean, there are those medical students, that already invited a man on his way there. He had to cancel out at the last minute. Wouldn't you get resentful if your medical school was used for that?

HB: Do you ever have discussions among each other after having watched a soap opera?

Mr. D: You see, Larry likes to research an awful lot. He's into that. And when he sees something that is definitely a mistake and wrong, he'll check on it.

Mr. H: Whatever is necessary. What I can do. I can't get into secret government archives. I can't get past security clearances on military bases. But there are ways of finding things out. Societies that I have knowledge of, the people who are members of societies. Through letter writing. Library textbooks.

Mr. D: He's an avid reader, so he knows his stuff. Also he has, he really has a photographic memory . . . which I rely on and he relies on.

Mr. H: I'm not really resentful as much as I am . . . direct and maybe a little blunt. Because when it comes to something that is just a bunch of poppycock I don't believe . . . it's like a friend told me . . . a good simile is. . . . Some people, he said, insist on washing and perfuming the garbage before they throw it out. You know what I mean. In this blunt way, what he was saying is, that some things that are so useless and silly are made to seem important . . . and valuable. And in other ways, important things are trivialized 'til they become nothing . . . and that's what I . . . I won't go along with. You might think that that would practically say that I never watch soap operas, 'cause a lot of that is trivial. But I watch them because like I first said, a lot of times it makes you glad that you don't have any more problems in your life than you do.

HB: Do you ever get mad at a show to the point where you talk to the screen?

Mr. H: No. Nor do I get as mad as Elvis Presley once got at his television. He was watching with a couple of friends one time, in Nashville, Tenn., one time, and this is a documented fact . . . and he saw something that he didn't like . . . whether it was a commercial that broke in on his particular program . . . he, normally, went around frequently with a 45 caliber six-shooter in his waist band . . . he pulled that out and he shot his television set out . . . right in the dining room of his big mansion in Nashville, Tenn. That was a well-known story. Then he told his friends. . . . Take it out and throw it on the dump. But his two friends, then and there, decided they didn't want to work for him any more . . . they didn't know but what he might take a shot at them sometime if he got mad at them.

Mr. D: There are other times where, as I mentioned before, some of these new series, that are being on television today, are shot on location and I, in my small way, have been involved in fashion vision, which was commercialized by going to department stores and making short films, commercial films, of the fashions or the sales that they were having or whatever they were having. And it was started by a friend of mine and I went in with him, but that lasted a very, very short while . . . 'til we lost a lot of money. We lost a lot of time. So I've been behind the scene, these things. And that's when I started to notice things . . . when you're on location, and you go to a different location, you find things that you feel are for you. And on these programs that I watch, occasionally, they show the area, they show the home . . . to fit in with the character. . . . they show the furniture. So little by little I felt . . . well, this is a little bit . . . it's not all a loss. It's a little bit of an education for me. I know what early American furniture looks like, or Renaissance furniture looks like. I know what pseudo-modern furniture looks like. So it's sort of educational for me . . . even though the plot may be absolutely ridiculous.

ES: What is there about the furniture and the homes on *Dynasty,* or *Colbys?*

Mr. D: I like them. Of course, when they go into the sexual scenes and give you this business of a round bed . . . I've never had a desire for a round bed. Also, I feel that, as I said before, that evidently the writers have to do that. They over-exaggerate . . . even in the sex scenes . . . such wild passion. And then the next part of the series they're fighting and you know. Course that happens too—I guess love can turn to hate. For many reasons. One thing I do object to when it comes to families . . . when there is such violent hatred between a father and a son or a father and a daughter that she actually comes out . . . "I want to kill my own father." That bothers me. That bothers me, but I also realize that this is fiction, and maybe the writers have to do that. Another objection I have, and Larry has mentioned it already, is that when you finally get interested and you want to relate to it . . . you want to get involved with the story . . . a commercial comes on. So you go wash a dish or . . . go to the bathroom.

HB: Another topic we're interested in is how *do* you watch soap operas? do you do other things or do you concentrate . . . ?

Mr. D: It depends. It depends on how much time or where our minds are. If we have other pressing things to do and we can watch as well as accomplish something else without just sitting and watching . . . we'll do that.

Mr. H: Normally we don't do anything in here and that's where the TV set is . . . we only have one . . . some people have a TV set in every room so they can do this and that and they can stand there and watch a small set. But we would have to do everything in here in order to be able to do that. So we . . . if we have other things to do we just go and do them. If we expect to get anything done, otherwise we'd just sit around and watch TV and nothing else gets done.

Mr. D: Occasionally we do have the time and we're a little bit tired of running around all afternoon, especially in warm weather, so we'll . . . all of a sudden we'll decide we'll relax. Tonight we'll watch television and forget about all this other stuff. And then we'll do it the next day. I was advised to do that by my doctor. He said don't pile it up.

HB: So when you watch a daytime soap opera it's accidental?

Mr. D: It all depends. If it's raining and we can't get out to do the things that we want to do out of doors . . . that's when we'll watch in the afternoon. And as I told you, most afternoon programs are geared to ladies. That's when they show all the gushy. . . .

Mr. H: They can stand there and iron or they can stand there and prepare food or whatever and watch TV.

HB: Do you ever get a chance to talk to other viewers about soap opera?

Mr. D: I have a very, very good friend . . . been a friend for about forty-five years I've known her . . . she is now working in a hospital in LA. That lady has been watching soaps most of her life, and she's such an avid watcher that even at work she goes into her boss and tells him. . . . My program is on. And that's when she takes her break. They have a little TV set in the lunch room. Her boss doesn't mind. Shirley . . . she works in the Veteran's Hospital . . . her husband . . . that's why they have a TV . . . her husband sells them . . . he works for a Japanese company. He's one of their top salesman . . . so that's why they have a TV set.

Mr. H: Well, you know where the word fan came from . . . it's actually true . . . it's a shortening of the word fanatic.

Mr. D: She was brought up with soaps, because her mother, Mrs. Applebaum, a lovely lady, I really love her, . . . she was an avid watcher . . . she was a housewife and this was her passion.

Mr. H: Is that the lady that every time she coughs or sneezes bubbles come out of her mouth? . . . he said she was brought up with soaps.

Mr. D: One thing I want to tell you, while we're on the subject of soaps. They used to have a satire called *Soap*. That was on, at least when it started, it was on late at night because they used all kinds of foul language and very sexy talk and all kinds of really . . . almost porno situations . . . so they didn't want young people watching. Now they are showing it again, and it's about three o'clock in the afternoon. So, occasionally, when I see this is on, I turn it on and I wonder how they really get away with it. At three o'clock in the afternoon there are children home.

Mr. H: It shows you the passage of a few years. . . .

Mr. D: It's very funny and I know it's satirical and sometimes they go to an extreme to hook you, to grab you.

HB: You just reminded me of a question I wanted to ask before. Most of the people we have interviewed are younger, younger people of twenty, twenty-five, thirty years of age and they don't have the soap opera experience you have. Would you say that soap opera has changed?

Mr. H: I think the young people of today, whether this is good or bad I'm not necessarily prepared to say, but I think the young people see through soap operas and consider them to be so absurd that they don't bother with them. The plotting is so thin and so threadbare . . . it's like tissue paper . . . and they . . . as they put it . . . it doesn't turn them on. But if a rock and roll music show came on that would turn them on. All that banging and beating and screaming and wailing and yowling and howling and growling that would turn them on. But a soap opera . . . two people talking themselves to death . . . they'd sit there. . . .

HB: They watch them alright.

Mr. D: I'll tell you why. Because they have changed a great deal. Each . . . every ten years they gear it to a certain type of viewer, so they do have . . . you'll see . . . and even in the soaps they don't talk the same way. They talk today's language . . . they use the slang . . . they'll use also, even in the commercials, as well as the story itself, they'll use occasionally hard rock sounds and stuff like that. The clothes that they wear is the updated clothes.

That's the same way it's been even many, many years ago. The clothing of each generation, or each ten years, of course fashion changes. The whole outlook seems to change. They go . . . I have two sons . . . I went through the hippie period with them . . . the era . . . and then I went through other . . . now one of my sons is a lawyer. So occasionally, when I see a soap with some legal background in it, I discuss it with my son. Because he doesn't watch them too much—he's too busy being a lawyer. But I tell him . . . is this true . . . and he'll tell me if there is a case that they tried to tell you about on your soap . . . and I ask him . . . Ron is this factual? Could this really happen—could a guy really get off? . . . so he says. . . . In these days, he probably could get off. No matter what crime he's committed and as he says. . . . Because the prisons are overcrowded, the system . . . the criminal system is . . . we don't have enough policemen around and things like that. So things change and I think that soaps change with them . . . they have to. They have to in order to make them even a tiny bit credible.

HB: Speaking of clothes. What do you think of the clothes on *Dynasty,* Krystle's clothes, for example?

Mr. D: Nothing but the best. Those women are so gorgeous. I wish I was young again.

HB: I'm probably not telling you anything new when I tell you that *Dynasty* is also very popular in Germany.

Mr. H: Is it? That brought to mind a question I was going to ask you about how much I have noticed since I was over in that part of the world . . . I don't know what is going on now, I only know what I read. It seems like Europe has been so heavily influenced by American television, but a subtle change has come about in this country . . . many of the things that in this country are almost ridiculed or put down as being silly or stupid are taken with far greater credibility over in Europe than they are here. And that's peculiar, there is another example of instead of art following life, life following art. I find that reversing of reality . . . is what it is. A reversal of reality. What should be often isn't and what should not be is. I think to myself. . . . My God . . . I mean this may sound very unflattering, but I think to myself. . . . My God, what is going on over there? Are people losing their minds or something? Can't they discriminate between the real and the fantasy? Because some of it is so palpably absurd, not just the soaps . . . I'm talking about TV in general. That . . . you think, how could such and such a show be popular? 'Cause you talk to people, like here or where I used to live . . . a group of people . . . and all of them are against a certain show . . . well you can say. . . . Well tastes change between certain people. What you and your friends don't like somebody else would like. Yet some things are so really bad that you can't imagine how they could be popular.

HB: Not just *Dynasty. Dallas, Falcon Crest, Bonanza.*

Mr. D: Well *Bonanza* is . . . used to be my favorite, because I like westerns.

Mr. H: You also have the Karl May Society. Have you ever heard of that?
[Tape ends]

Mr. H: In Russia, no less, they have the equivalent of a Karl May Society. They actually get out and have summer encampments every year . . . they dress up in cowboy . . . in western costumes, authentic down to the last detail, also in various Indian costumes, authentic down to the last detail.

They even have connections with various Indian tribes in this country to send them eagle feathers, of a certain type, not from eagles that have been killed but from eagles that have been salvaged out of the woods or whatever—because they want the authentic thing. And in Leningrad and Kiev and Odessa and all over Russia they have this network of enthusiasts. . . . My deep interest, as he said, when I get into something, I've got to get to the bottom of it. Find out about it . . . I won't rest until I do find out about it . . . and then I got a copy of a magazine called *Soviet Life*. From a friend. . . . Have you seen this magazine? It's a color . . . a full-color publication and it looks like what used to be *Life* magazine in this country. And in that particular issue was confirmation of what I had heard. About seven pages were devoted to text and photographs of these Russian citizens, male and female, youngsters, adults, young people in their twenties, dressed up as Indians on the one hand (Kiowas, Paiutes, Apaches, Commanchees) and on the other hand as cowboys and original federal soldiers dating back to our American Civil War. Now I can't believe any of this. You know what started it, believe it or not, there's a thread of continuity between your interview, with me and Jack, and what got this society going in Russia, about twenty years ago. It was an American soap opera devoted to the wild west. It wasn't *Dynasty* or *Falcon Crest* or *Dallas* and I'm not sure it was *Big Valley,* but it was . . . it might have been *Bonanza*. Because that came out at a very crucial moment, shortly after WWII and when Russia was recovering from the effects of WWII. I don't know what triggered it off but all of a sudden . . . it's just like after a rain, all of a sudden the grass springs up. . . .

HB: What's the connection between *Bonanza* and *Karl May?*

Mr. H: Karl May is another thing entirely. Karl May pre-dates television. Karl May is a horse of a different color. But without television there is that same preoccupation with the American wild west . . . and did you know that the favorite viewing of both Adolph Hitler and Joseph Stalin, in their private movie theaters in the Reichschancellory in Berlin or the Kremlin in Russia, were American cowboy movies. And this, I think, was a take off into later versions of soap operas that dealt with the wild west. Did you know there are, and have been a number of soap operas. But not Karl May, but I mean this Russian version of it almost sprang completely from television and a television soap opera. He may be right, I can't put my finger on it, but it can all be traced back to one soap opera. After the Second World War. It started in about 1955. About ten years after the war. And it had Russian in the subtitles printed on the screen. . . . It was still in English . . . but Russian subtitles. And all of a sudden enough people got interested, so intently in this . . . again, another example of instead of art imitating life, life imitating art. So it does have a great effect, in some cases, soap operas have a great effect on people's thinking.

HB: To return for the last few minutes of our interview to American television. What other shows do you appreciate Mr. Howe? Are there other shows you *do* appreciate opposed to these others?

Mr. H: Numerous. For instance, private detectives type adventure shows, police shows, travelogue shows, historical and archaeological productions, such as Jacques Cousteau. There are a couple of others that are involved, having to do with the sea, with dolphins. The discovery that dolphins have an intelligence now thought to be as high or perhaps even higher than human beings. So they can learn a language. They have an experimental school in Florida where they're teaching dolphins to speak the English language. Really fantastic things.

Mr. D: We get a great deal of pleasure out of watching certain documentaries, specially about animals. We are both animal lovers. Not only about animals—they have a new thing that has been on television recently—about the old English castles. Which is fascinating. It's usually a series—they usually have about three or four of them. They take you through every old castle . . . we're interested in all sorts of old buildings . . . and one of our goals and dreams is that we want to some day buy a Victorian old home and try to restore it.

Mr. H: I would like to get back some day and see my favorite castle in all of Germany. The number one. By myself. But I have one favorite castle that I want to see again. One that was built by King Ludwig of Bavaria.

Mr. D: So they take you through the home and they tell you all about the artifacts. And that's what amazes me . . . the art, the paintings, the old paintings and where they came from. And I'm very surprised that in a lot of these old mansions there are a lot of the Dutch and German and French paintings from way back are on those walls. Besides the old English paintings and it's fascinating.

Mr. H: Don't forget to tell them about a program that's a favorite with you, well it is with me too, and it's almost like a soap opera and it's shot in a movie actress's . . . what Jack believes and I tend to agree with him . . . in her own home on the East Coast. It's called *Murder, She Wrote.* It's very much like a soap opera. What's her name . . . Angela Lansbury. She's the detective lady. It's taken strictly from Agatha Christie's books. And the interior of the home, the kitchen and everything . . . after seeing several episodes . . . Jack became convinced that it was shot on location . . . right in her own home. And when he's talking about paintings and all these artifacts and everything . . . it's a very beautiful area and a very beautiful home.

HB: Why do you say it's like a soap opera?

Mr. H: Because of the way the script seems to go. There is . . . it is a trademark of soap operas that there is a lot more talking than any action of any kind. Chase scenes or searches out in the woods or . . . so much of it is talking in a room between two or three people. That program is just very talkative. That's why it resembles a soap opera. Maybe it's not meant to be, but. . . .

Mr. D: Larry, it's logical talk though. They are trying to solve a crime. At least a crime is committed.

Mr. H: I'm not knocking it—I'm just saying it reminds me of a soap opera.

HB: What do you think of *Hill Street Blues?* That's a detective show I watch.

Mr. H: I saw it last night. Sometimes they have good episodes and other times they're too silly for words. I don't know what happens to the script writers . . . they must have a bad day or something.

Mr. D: Hill Street Blues with me has a tendency to be a little too violent. A little bit too much violence for me, so I wouldn't consider it among my favorite shows.

Mr. H Barney Miller, that's almost a soap opera type.

Mr. D: But that's comedy.

HB: I was going to say, isn't that a sitcom?

Mr. H: Almost. Would you say that's a separate category? Can't soap operas also be funny?

Mr. D: They label it a comedy. They don't label it a serious drama or a series. Like we're used to watching within old movies . . . we used to go and watch serials.

Mr. H: In other words, it's got to be negative and down in order to be. . . . Which leads you to wonder why it was labeled soap opera in the first place. Why that name? Unless it was being put down as a form of entertainment.

Mr. D: I think it was originally started for ladies that were doing their laundry and their wash and they were using this soap.

Mr. H: Here's another category . . . this was films now not television . . . they applied it to TV . . . but first it became known in films, cowboys movies were, at one point, back about the late 1940s or 50s all of a sudden became known as horse operas. There again is the use of the word opera, like as to ridicule the type of show. On one hand you ridicule it by putting the word soap in front of the word opera and on the other hand you ridicule the cowboy movie by putting the word horse in front of it. Because opera is serious drama as well as music. So to sort of trivialize it, I think, I suspect, I'm not positive, but I suspect, as a means of trivializing it or putting it down you call it a soap opera on the one hand and a horse opera on the other. I've long wondered about that.

HB: You think *Hill Street Blues* falls into the category of soap operas?

Mr. H: Borderline. Borderline.

HB: It does have this little love thing going on between . . . what are the names. Furillo and. . . .

Mr. H: One point I will say, if you want to call it resentment you could call it that, I do resent the point that they seem to be so intent on . . . in most soap operas dealing with juveniles and juvenile problems of any kind and that is that always, always, always the parents come out looking bad. It is always the parents' fault. Never the kids that are old enough to make their own decisions. They are always made to look good. Or victims of the way their parents raised them. Just as though they had no control over their own lives at all. Like they were brainless boobs. It's all the parents' fault. All the father's fault. Father never knows anything. He's a boob—an idiot. Only mother knows how to make decisions. Or on the other hand mother is a drunk, she runs around with other men and father has to try to hold the family together. The kids are the heroes, always.

HB: Hasn't this always been the case? In television shows of the sixties?

Mr. H: To a large degree. *Father Knows Best* was a satire on father knowing best. He was made to look like a ridiculous buffoon. *My Three Sons* was another. That was another . . . you could call it a situation comedy, if you want. I think it borderline soap opera. But always the kids come out looking perfect. No fault can be found with them. Only the parents. It's just like one guy told me . . . He was a product of that generation. . . . He said. . . . Looking back now, I never suspected what my parents had to go through. I was one of those that was sympathizing with the kids until I became a parent and had children of my own. Now all of a sudden I'd just as soon slap the little monsters around. God, what a change in him.

Mr. D: That's my theme song. I know what it's like to be young but you don't know what it is to be old.

Mr. H: Orson Welles made a very good . . . well-known song . . . a 45 r.p.m. with that title.

Mr. D: I'd like to get a tape made and send it to both my kids.

HB: Well, this has been very interesting and helpful.

"The Cultural Debate of the Ages"

History, Culture, and Media Politics in Public Reception

JOSTEIN GRIPSRUD

Who watches programs about the inside of the brain on Wednesday nights? [We want] television for those who watch it!

Freddy Andersen, chairman, "Friends of *Dynasty*"

The Importance of Geography

Transnational television productions are inserted in a very wide variety of specific cultural and political contexts all over the globe. There is, consequently, a definite need to consider the specificities of these contexts if one wants to understand the different receptions of these productions. I would like to give just one example before I present my own research. Yahia Mahamdi (1988) has, in a very interesting study, demonstrated how the reception of *Dallas* in Algeria was shaped by, first, the particularly central place of television as a source of entertainment in that country, especially for women, who had in the preceding years been, so to speak, pushed out of cinemas and into their homes. Second, *Dallas* was, to begin with, extremely popular, according to Mahamdi, because it represented a widespread dream of affluence among frustrated, poverty-stricken Algerians. But then, in the second season, its popularity dropped drastically because of the perceived severe immorality of its characters. In both phases, the serial was interpreted as a representation of real conditions in the US, and compared to the Algerian situation. According to Mahamdi, Algerians concluded that western modernity and affluence were not worth their price in moral decay.

The political and social situation in Norway when *Dynasty* was broadcast was radically different, but that country's historically produced cultural and political specificities also "framed" the viewing experience in a principally similar, yet qualitatively different, manner.

Contrary to reported popular belief in the USA, Norway is not a refrigerator, even if an American refrigerator was once named after it (Norge). It is a mountainous country, facing the North Atlantic, with just over 4 million inhabitants who have a lot of space to share, statistically speaking. Its name indicates that its coastline was early on known as the way to go north, and it does reach far north of the Arctic circle. It is still more or less habitable even in the far north, because of the Gulf Stream. Apart from the economic and sociocultural difference between its northern and its more populous southern part, a major dividing line has historically been drawn between the east and west in southern Norway. A mountain range in the interior divides the dramatic "fjord" landscapes of the west coast with its North Atlantic climate, from the more open valleys and plains of the east, with its forests, inland climate and relatively densely populated urban areas, particularly around Oslo, the capital.

These geographical observations are meant, first, to indicate that Norway is situated slightly off-center, to say the least, compared with the major metropolitan areas of continental Europe. But it has been far from isolated: due to its natural resources it was early on involved in the international economy. Second, geographical factors explain some of its social and cultural peculiarities. In order to understand the meaning(s) of the *Dynasty* event in Norway, one has to understand the country's broadcasting traditions, which are tied to the wider socio-cultural and political history. A very brief historical outline is therefore necessary if we want to grasp the relations between general and particular issues here. This chapter is, then, devoted to a descriptive analysis of the most clearly media-political dimensions of the public reception of *Dynasty*. The main point is to show how it was possible for a Hollywood television serial to become both a sign of a historical shift in broadcasting and cultural traditions and also an instrument for such change. The *Dynasty* experience may be said to have brought about change, on the one hand, in the way Norwegians relate to television and, to some extent, popular culture in general, and, on the other hand, in the way the public service broadcasting institution conceives of, and tries to fulfill, its functions in a new media environment. The introduction of regular audience measurements and new ideas about programming and scheduling are among the most obvious signs in the latter category.

This chapter is, then, the one where specifically Norwegian circumstances will have to be given some attention. To an international readership, some passages or references may seem unusually "local," uninteresting or even exotic. It is worth pointing out, however, that non-Anglo-American students in all media and cultural studies, at least in the western world, have had to familiarize themselves with "local" and "exotic" American and British phenomena for decades. The chapter could then be seen as a practical lesson in what non-American and non-British students and scholars have to go through if they want to follow scholarly writing in "international" media and cultural studies.

Norway: A Crash Course

In 1980, the Norwegian Broadcasting Corporation (Norsk Rikskringkasting, NRK) operated the single public service radio channel and the single television channel available to most inhabitants. Though 25 percent of the people (all of them living in the eastern part of the country) could receive Swedish (public service) radio and television, it is on the whole correct to say that Norway was one of the very last remaining one-channel countries in Europe at this time. The comparison with Albania was made by some participants in the public discussions on an expansion of television services.

The 1980s then brought a revolution in the field of broadcasting in general and television in particular. A second national public radio channel was followed by a multitude of local commercial stations. At present (1993/4) there are four national radio channels, one of which is commercially financed. Norway got its second terrestrial TV channel on 5 September 1991, commercially financed but with an obligation to a public service profile. It now reaches about 90 percent of the population. Two other commercial Norwegian-language channels, one of them transmitting from London, are accessible only by way of satellite and cable. About 40 percent of all households now either receive cable or have satellite dishes, and thus have up to forty foreign channels to choose from.

In order to understand just how dramatic these changes have been, they must be seen in the light of the country's particular history, sociology and culture. Single-channel broadcasting was in accordance with fundamental features of Norwegian society, which has been described as not only homogeneous (in terms of ethnicity, culture and language) but also as "singularistic" (Galtung and Gleditsch 1975). The latter term refers to the level of social institutions, where "pluralistic" has indeed been a foreign word. More than 90 percent of the population are formally members of the same official/public Lutheran church; 99.5 percent of all children go to public schools with very minor pedagogical differences between them; at high school level (16–18 year olds) 95 percent go to schools within the same public system. In other words, Norwegians are not used to institutional alternatives.

The relative ethnic and cultural homogeneity of the country (with the exception of the relatively small Sámi (Lapp) population mainly based in the far north) is of course one reason for this. Another is the fact that Norway has been too small and lacking in resources for the development of, say, a system of private schools alongside the public system. Also important, though, is an egalitarian tradition related both to the social structure and to the historically dominating cultural and ideological formations: Norway was never really feudal and has lacked both an aristocracy and later a bourgeoisie comparable to those of other, more populous countries. Conservatives have historically used this fact to reassure themselves that the danger of a revolutionary uprising was quite small, and left-wing socialists have at times complained that the only bourgeoisie in Norway worth mentioning was the *petite* part of it. This is not to say that Norway has been without class divisions and class struggles—between the world wars its labor movement was more radical than those of most other western European countries. This shows how a relatively low degree of class difference in terms of income, lifestyle, etc. has been an operative factor in the country's social, political and cultural development—not least by way of an ideological agreement that this feature is something quite unique to Norwegian society.

The impression made on foreign observers may have been like that of Elihu Katz, who once said to me that "the country was so peaceful you had to find something to fight about." He was thinking of the century-long struggles over the language issue. This has its roots in the fact that Norway was a part of Denmark for 400 years until 1814, when it was handed over to Sweden after the Napoleonic wars. In the vacuum of the transitional period, the country got its (for the time) remarkably democratic Constitution, and a parliament. Even if the Constitution stated that all laws should be written in Norwegian, the only written Norwegian at the time was pure Danish. Two strategies developed on this issue. One aimed at a gradual "Norwegianization" of written Danish by bringing it closer to the Norwegian spoken by the educated upper class. The result was the now dominant form of written Norwegian, which is close to spoken Norwegian particularly in the east and in major urban areas. The other strategy aimed at a "New Norse," developed in the mid-nineteenth century from studies of popular dialects seen as being close to the Old Norse of the Middle Ages, i.e. dialects in rural areas, predominantly in the west and in the mountain regions. The language question became a central dividing issue for more than a century primarily because it was tied to socio-cultural differences and conflicts of interest between geographical areas (east/west) and, more generally, between center and periphery (city/countryside). The fact that the "periphery's alternative," New Norse, both survived and achieved quite a strong position is in itself an indication of the relatively strong political and cultural position of regionalism and various popular movements (cf. Gripsrud 1994).

A parliamentary system of government was introduced in 1884, and in 1905 the union with Sweden was abolished. Norway thus has a relatively short history as an independent country, and this may be part of the reason why concerns with nationality have played a more important role in Norwegian cultural politics than for instance in Denmark or Sweden. The Constitution, from the beginning, granted considerable influence to farmers/peasants and other nonbourgeois groups, and the parliament early on installed a system of local democratic rule that provided further opportunities for political influence to farmers in the predominantly agrarian society of that period. In the struggle for a parliamentary system (against the power of the Swedish king), a nationalist and democratic/populist alliance between liberal representatives of the urban bourgeoisie and representatives of farmers and rural areas developed into a political party. This party/alliance was important in two ways in our context. It represented the socio-cultural periphery of the country in important issues, exemplified in support for the New Norse language. It also provided political opportunities for the growing industrial working class (universal suffrage was granted to men in 1898, to women in 1913) as well as a basis for the later development of a relatively stable social democracy, a "welfare state" supported by a high degree of cross-political consensus. Last but not least, it gave "nationalism" ties to progressive, democratic social and cultural politics. This is important to keep in mind when a "national" rhetoric is used in public debates on, say, transnational popular culture.

Parties that later emerged from the above-mentioned party/alliance also provided the political basis for the establishment of the NRK (the Norwegian Broadcasting Corporation) as a broadcasting monopoly, financed by license fee, in 1933. These parties were the social democratic labor party, the liberal party (the remains of the original alliance) and the agrarian party. This political constellation reflected a social and cultural alliance between the working class and its organizations on the one hand and various rural-based classes and cultural organizations on the other which until recently played a major role in a number of political issues and situations (such as the struggles over EC membership). Both were opposed to the powers and expressed interests of the urban bourgeoisie and the conservative party. The in many ways quite reactionary agrarian party helped the social democrats to form their first government in 1935 (two weeks in 1928 do not really count), and the social democrats remained in power until the mid-1960s. (See also Rokkan 1966, 1967 for classical accounts of the above features of Norwegian politics.)

The BBC vs. The NRK: Exclusive vs. Inclusive Official Culture

Like its British counterpart and ideal, the BBC, the NRK was expressly devoted to a programming policy intended to serve popular/public enlightenment purposes in a variety of ways. But, as the above historical sketch is supposed to indicate, the form, tone and character of the enlightenment orientations of the two corporations were from the beginning somewhat different. A key element in the British version of public service broadcasting was, according to Raymond Williams (1975: 33), that

> a dominant version of the national culture had already been established, in an unusually compact ruling-class, so that public service could be effectively understood and administered as a service according to the values of an existing public definition, with an effective paternalist definition of both service and responsibility.

Consequently, in the British context, enlightenment in the tradition associated with Lord Reith could be described as a "top-down project, based on the shared cultural assumptions of the aristocracy and the metropolitan bourgeoisie with their emphasis on art and high culture" (Syvertsen 1992: 95). In Norway, both the labor movement and a complex of rural-based socio-cultural and political organizations (particularly those tied to the New Norse language) significantly influenced the composition and overall profile of programming. Various enlightenment elements were of a practical type, and the cultural programming reflected both a rural, "national" folk culture, urban high culture and the mainly, but not only, distributional cultural policies of the labor movement.

This meant that the NRK was always quite open to certain forms of folk and popular culture, forms that were acceptable to the intellectuals who represented the major socio-cultural and political forces in the public sphere. Both the NRK and the BBC relied on the standards that were held by their respective national establishments in cultural affairs. Their differences stem from the differences between these establishments. The NRK was clearly also paternalistic in its attitude towards its audiences: "the emphasis was on *raising* rather than *reflecting* popular taste and standards" (Syvertsen 1992: 95). There was definitely the same emphasis in the cultural politics of the major mass movements (Gripsrud 1981, 1990). But the allegiance of certain intellectual elites to "folk" and "progressive" cultural forms may be said to have kept the domain of "official culture" more complex and inclusive, and less stable, than in most other European countries, particularly outside Scandinavia.

A concrete manifestation of this can be seen in the existence of two National Theatres in Oslo: one historically a cultural center for the urban elites, playing the preferred repertoire of these groups, and one tied to movement(s) for the New Norse language, supported in the capital by politicians, university professors, writers and other intellectuals with rural backgrounds and nationalist and populist inclinations. This latter theater was opened in the presence of the king and prime minister in 1913 and has existed ever since, receiving increasing public financial support like other theaters, with a repertoire mixing popular genres (folk comedy, musicals), mainstream classics and various "avant-garde" pieces. Its degree of national-popular cultural "opposition" or difference was in other words blessed by the state from the beginning.

Social-Democratic Broadcasting

In the first 30–35 years after World War II, then, Norway was a one-channel, social-democratic country (even if "bourgeois" coalitions formed governments at times after the mid-1960s), with an official culture relatively open to certain popular cultural forms. But the various factions of the cultural elite—urban-conservative, New-Norse national-populist and socialist alike—were united in their continuing rejection of the transnational, more or less industrial forms of popular culture that had been enjoyed by "ordinary people" at least since the second half of the nineteenth century. To the nationally produced "pulp" literature were added imported western, detective and romance novels. Film was installed as the major popular form of public entertainment in urban areas from about 1905, and represented a significant contribution to the "Americanization" of Norwegian popular culture. "American action films were popular in Norway in early 1914," when the capital alone had twenty cinemas (Thompson 1985: 38). In 1915, half of the films that passed through the state censor's office were American (Evensmo 1967), and in the late 1920s, US films constituted between 63 and 70 percent of the total footage screened in Norway (Thompson 1985: 129). The syncopated music known as jazz was played both on gramophone records and by Norwegian orchestras from the mid-1920s on. Apart from occasional films and very few crime novels, none of this was accepted as "quality" culture by the cultural elites until the late 1960s. It was not national, it was not progressive, it was not art. It was only popular because it appealed to all the "lowest" dispositions in people.

The resistance of the cultural elites to transnational—modern—popular culture was part of the reason why Norway was among the very last countries in Europe to introduce a regular television service, in August 1960. Intellectuals reported from abroad in the early 1950s that the new medium had devastating effects on national cultures and education, and a nationally acclaimed writer said that if television was introduced, Norway might as well forget about its written language(s): it would all be "jazz and boxing" anyway (cf. Dahl 1981: 65). But since both leading politicians and most of the people wanted television anyway, for different reasons, technical preparations and experimental transmissions took place throughout the decade up to the official opening.

As previously with radio, heavy investment in technical facilities for the distribution of signals all over the large, sparsely populated and mountainous country was given priority over the expansion of programming. Equal opportunities for all citizens to enjoy broadcasting services was a central social-democratic goal, in keeping both with regionalism and widespread egalitarian ideals. In 1967, television reached the northernmost county (Finnmark). At that time several hundred thousand people living in the shadows of various mountains still could not receive signals or had only poor reception. But it is still fair to say that in the late 1960s TV sets were to be found in most of the country's households. Color was gradually introduced from about the same time.

In its first years, NRK-TV transmitted only a couple of hours of programs per day, more at weekends. According to statistics, it was up to 3.8 hours daily in April 1967, and 6.8 hours in February ten years later (Østbye 1982: 288). Still, television almost immediately managed to position itself as the very center of the public sphere, both as mediator and as originator of public debates—and as a subject for day-to-day talk between people.

In the 1960s, two topics dominated in discussions on programming: explicit sex and "incomprehensible" modern drama (Beckett and Pinter, for instance). In fact, both subjects were in particular tied to domestic and

Nordic drama productions. Nobody questioned the amount of nighttime
educational programming (on natural sciences, religion, politics or various
forms of "high culture"), and the Friday night hour of American or British
crime series (notably *Perry Mason* and *The Saint*) was clearly both tremen-
dously popular and accepted by those who otherwise rejected transnational
popular culture. The same goes for the Saturday night episodes of *Gunsmoke*. This show might have gained some extra popularity due to James
Arness's Norwegian descent, but it was actually the comic character Festus
who was most popular—he even had a particular brand of canned meatballs
named after him. In retrospect, and with particular relevance to the *Dynasty*
phenomenon, the general acceptance of these imported shows was probably not least related to the fact that they all represented typically male-
oriented genres, even if adjusted to television's typical family audiences. Two
very long-running British serials, *The Forsyte Saga* and (in the early 1970s)
Family at War, were both extremely popular, while, for different reasons,
also legitimate for the elites. The first had an aura of British literary culture,
the second had, in addition to its focus on family problems, an aura of classic social realism and shared experiences of war and class differences.

British imports have always been important elements in NRK programming. The self-imposed limit on the proportion of imported programming was set at 50 percent, but has normally been closer to 40. Typically, UK productions in 1977 constituted about one-third of the imported
material, one-fifth came from other Nordic countries and a bit less than
one-fifth were of US origin (Østbye 1982: 277). In 1983, total imports
were down to 30 percent, the UK supplying 32 percent of this amount, the
US 20 (Bakke 1986: 137). Most of the US imports have always been feature films, followed by occasional detective series and sitcoms. Norway and
Denmark were in 1983 the only countries in Europe where most of the
imported program time came from the UK (Denmark, 27 percent) (ibid.).
British productions, both factual and fictional genres, have enjoyed both
prestige and, in most cases, widespread popularity in Norway. But a certain
popular form of British television was not imported: soap operas. In fact,
no real soap opera from anywhere had ever been seen on Norwegian screens
when *Dynasty* was bought. It is telling of the general profile of NRK programming that Norwegians encountered soap opera first through a parody
of the genre: the US hit sitcom *Soap*.

Domestic and Nordic drama was still sometimes debated along traditional lines throughout the 1970s. But the typical debates of this decade
centred on politics. The NRK was accused of being a leftist stronghold, with
a more or less systematically biased coverage of both politics and culture.
Even if these accusations were vastly exaggerated, there may have been at
least some truth in them. The relatively much rarer and weaker claims that
the opposite was the case could be seen as one indication of this. Nicholas
Garnham has said that the BBC "through the 1960's and 1970's betrayed
public service broadcasting by progressively alienating the potential supporters of the public service ideal both among the audience and among

broadcasters" (1990: 129). Apart from the corporation's London-based imposition of a political and cultural elite's "tastes and views of the world," Garnham attributes most of the BBC's failure to its lack of positive response to "the more democratic and participatory climate of the late 1960's and the early 1970's," which resulted in "a situation where political progressives have increasingly come to see the BBC [...] as the major obstacle to reform and the main target for attack" (ibid.: 130). In Norway, "political progressives" clearly perceived the NRK differently, as more complex and, in some areas, a potential ally, an institution in which there was significant support for a critical view on both international and national issues of the period. Still a relatively young and small institution, NRK-TV had many employees with generational and social ties to the socio-cultural conjuncture signified by "1968," and the strong social-democratic traditions of the NRK as a whole meant that the leftist tendencies within the social-democratic movement in general were also represented at various levels.

Liberalist Media Revolution and the Dynasty Debate

All of the above old struggles over the NRK's programming dramatically lost importance in the 1980s. A whole new set of questions was brought to the fore, concerning the role of broadcasting media and public service broadcasting in particular, involving wide-reaching issues of socio-cultural values and interests in general. The number of television channels in Europe as a whole tripled between 1983 and 1986, and things were rapidly changing in Norway too. Satellite television, an explosive growth in the home video (and video rental) market, rapid expansion of cable services, etc., all happened more or less simultaneously.

The conservative party came to power in a minority government in 1981, and its minister of cultural affairs immediately started drafting and implementing a liberalist turn in media policies. This party had never very actively supported the NRK monopoly, but had on the other hand not been able or willing really to challenge it before, not least because the party's "cultural" faction (as opposed to the "industrial" one) saw the monopoly as the best way to secure cultural quality and moral standards in programming. Towards the end of the 1970s the balance between the two factions shifted, and so did the attitude to the NRK's monopoly. Action for change was now politically possible, first of all because the signs were obvious that complete national control over broadcasting was about to be made obsolete by technological developments. But a much more general ideological turn to the "right," which the election of the conservative government (replaced by a "non-socialist" coalition after only one-and-a-half years) itself represented, was also important. The conservative ministry of culture almost immediately authorized newspapers, voluntary associations of various sorts and cable companies to start local radio and television stations, and also to retransmit satellite television via cable (from Satellite Television Ltd, later known as Sky Channel). This change in policy was interestingly legitimated

as a defense of Norwegian culture, since "greater diversity and plurality" in
the Norwegian output was necessary in the light of the "threats" from the
increasing availability of international television. Even if conservatives lost
support in the elections throughout the 1980s, and the labor party was in
(minority) government from 1986 to 1989, their offensive of the early 1980s
to liberalize broadcasting laid the basic premises of later developments. In
1987 a new "narrowcasting" Act was passed which allowed commercial local
radio, and in 1988 a new Cable Act removed the licensing system for satellite retransmissions, so that "anyone" (who had the financial resources necessary) could establish commercial television services—if only by satellite.
(All of the above summary of developments draws on Syvertsen 1992: 202ff.)

The *Dynasty* event took place in the midst of these rapid and radical
changes. It crystallized most of the wider cultural and ideological issues
involved: notions of "free choice," "cultural quality," "internationalization
of culture," "commercialization of the media," etc. The serial and the debate
over it contributed to a decisive historical shift in the media and cultural
domain.

An intricate complex of factors produced the new situation. International technological developments and telecommunications policies may
have functioned as first movers, but several other economic, social, political and cultural forces also made significant contributions. It was precisely
because the *Dynasty* phenomenon in Norway had so many determinants and
implications that it could with quite a degree of justification be called "the
cultural debate of the ages" by a contemporary observer (Dahl 1983). The
very heated public debate over the serial had many features in common with
traditional cultural debates. However, three major elements created a decisive historical shift which marked the debate as unique: (a) the rapid, technologically induced changes in the field(s) of radio, television and video;
(b) a general strengthening of "commercialism" in all media, print included;
and last but not least (c) the strong presence of "ordinary people," speaking up for their cultural tastes and programming preferences.

The importance of the last element has, in my view, been underestimated in most of the critical scholarly discourse on the political implications
of technological shifts in the distribution of audio-visual media and the con-
comitant crisis of public service broadcasting all over western Europe. This
is what I attempt to argue in the following theoretical section.

Technology, Culture, and Politics in the Broadcasting Revolution

Researchers operating from a theoretical basis labelled "political economy"
have studied the political consequences of the rapidly developing video,
satellite and cable technologies. They have pointed out how the economic-
political struggles for de- and reregulation have served to secure profits for
the transnational corporations most heavily involved in the field, and how
all of this is part of a more comprehensive restructuring of the relationships

between capital and the state and between capital, culture and the public sphere. The general, quite pessimistic perspective has been that which Philip Elliott once formulated: "what we face is a continuation of the shift away from involving people in society as political citizens of nation states towards involving them as consumption units in a corporate world" (Elliott 1986: 106).

While this in my view is certainly a correct diagnosis of a major contemporary trend, prominent representatives of the "political economy" group of scholars have tended to reduce developments to a mere expression of capital's ongoing quest for new exploits. As put by Nicholas Garnham, the proliferation of potential audio-visual channels "is not a response to consumer demand but the result both of the search of multi-national hardware manufacturers for new markets, and of the industrial and economic strategies of various governments" (Garnham 1984: 2). This argument leaves out the fact that a quest for new markets ultimately relies on an *anticipated* consumer demand. Such anticipations will necessarily, since managers of transnational corporations are not stupid, at least not in financial matters, be based on some empirically grounded understanding of what consumers would like to have if it were available.

In other words, the enormous interest in developing viable domestic video products, in developing cable systems and satellite television, has been rationally founded in some knowledge of what people would want if it were offered: more popular entertainment of various kinds, twenty-four-hour services ("never-ending flow"), a wider spectrum of program material available at any given time, etc. The sheer fascination with technological wonders which for instance enables us to see something going on at the very same moment on a different continent is also worth considering. Among my own very first memories of watching television is the direct transatlantic Telstar transmission of President Kennedy's speech in 1962. The meaning of this event, not least to a generation which was used to having Radio Luxembourg as a primary source of popular music, was that it promised an end to national parochialism, the opening up of greatly increased, exciting cultural opportunities, in short a significant new turn in the vastly expanded space for a number of wishes, demands and desires offered by modernity at least since the mid-nineteenth century.

In my view, this means it is time for another look also at Raymond Williams's now classic statement: "*It is not only that the supply of broadcasting facilities preceded the demand; it is that the means of communication preceded their content*" (Williams 1975: 25). While it is probably true that there was no strong or explicit demand for the specific forms of radio and television services that developed from 1920 on, the idea of direct transmissions of live images to people's homes preceded the actual development of the necessary technologies by several decades—just as the development of the film medium had been foreshadowed by the magic lantern and photography. It may be true that the definite contents of film or broadcasting media were not demanded or foreseen. But a series of drawings published in 1882 by the French artist Robida, in which moving pictures were transmitted on the walls of people's living rooms, casts some doubt even on this:

> One of the screens showed a teacher giving a mathematics lesson; another showed a dressmaker displaying his wares (a prediction of "shopping by television" a century before it became reality); another had a ballet being performed; and yet another showed a full-scale desert war being fought, while viewers gazed in horror from their comfortable chairs. (Wheen 1985: 11)

It seems to me that these drawings indicate the existence of not only ideas about moving images in private homes, but also quite specific anticipations of what such images would be about: education, art, commercial presentations and news/documentary. None of these forms of content were, of course, specific to television: the medium was, both in these imaginative drawings and in its actual development, mainly an apparatus for the distribution of pre-existing, external material and genres.

Robida was, importantly, not alone. In 1891, the major New Norse writer, Arne Garborg, published a novel in which a character, representing positivist optimism, envisaged a future in which people, in their own homes, had "screens" by which they could choose to watch and listen to opera, ballet, circus, religious services, parliamentary debates or concerts. In the US, in the very same year, Edison proclaimed in newspapers that "he was within a few months of achieving direct transmission of live events into the home," complete with sound and images, and similar ideas also circulated in popular books and magazines (Sklar 1976: 11). Even if a really functioning television technology still lay decades away, there is little doubt that widespread, quite specific visions of the medium indicated a vast potential market for it. It was simply in perfect keeping both with the "mobile privatization" (Williams) characteristic of modernity, and wishes and desires shaped by the same social processes.

This historical detour is also relevant to an understanding of the developments of audio-visual technologies in the 1970s and 1980s. Corporations (and governments) worked intensely in this field with strictly economic (and military) motivations. This made for very rapid and dynamic developments, and certain essential premises for the use of these technologies were certainly not established out of concerns for a (more) democratic public sphere. But the corporations could at the same time be said to have worked with the support of potential customers among "ordinary people" of various kinds. The increased imaginary mobility and real, if limited, freedom of choice that VCRs and satellite and cable television have made available to most people is in accordance with their deep-seated, historically shaped wishes, demands and desires.

It is absolutely necessary to come to terms with these wishes, demands and desires in some way, if critical intellectuals are to have any chance of establishing a dialogue with the majority of television audiences. This seems to have been realized by, for instance, Nicholas Garnham, who has talked about the need to change "the contempt and lack of sympathy for popular tastes still all too prevalent among supposedly progressive cultural workers in the film and video field" (1990: 134). But the following paragraph may in my view also reveal a lack of understanding of the challenge:

> On the other hand we have also to accept that the steadily increasing privatization of cultural consumption makes the public itself resistant to participatory models of cultural production and consumption. That the UK at a time of deep recession was the fastest growing market in the world for video-recorders should give us pause for thought. It is clear therefore that much campaigning work needs to be done within the socialist movement to change deeply ingrained attitudes to cultural production and consumption before there is any hope of achieving concrete reforms. (Garnham 1990: 134)

Since this comes after Garnham has said that "any socialist response to cable and satellite must be, so far as possible, to oppose expansion and face openly and coherently the inevitable charges of Luddism" (ibid.: 133), it seems to me that he intends to campaign against the widespread lust for a plenitude of television channels. Such an intention is reminiscent of the battles fought by socialist and communist parties before World War II against the "individualism" and "bourgeois immorality" of phenomena such as syncopated dance music and Hollywood movies. It was and is a totally futile project, because it is fundamentally at odds with the appeal of the phenomena in question to people whose desires and ideas of a better life are shaped by their situations, their actual life-worlds, in modern or late modern capitalist societies. These desires and dreams will have to be recognized as they are, as an essential part of the basis on which progressive media and cultural policies must build. The question must then be raised if they are really adequately served by the existing or planned offerings. It is probable that quite a few of those eager to get as many channels as possible will sooner or later sing along with Bruce Springsteen about "57 channels and nothin' on." That is when, if not sooner, a believable and attractive alternative, which is not simply a return to the good old days, should be ready for presentation.

My point here is, then, that if rapid, capital-driven technological developments presented entirely new premises for debates on broadcasting in the early 1980s, these premises also made for a release of popular wishes and desires for a different kind of broadcasting. These wishes and desires "went public" in the debate over *Dynasty,* and Norwegian "progressive" intellectuals had a hard time trying to deal with them. It is, finally, time to have a closer, concrete look at this debate.

Public Pressure on Public Televison: How Dynasty Got into the Schedule

The press played a leading role not only in the public debate on *Dynasty,* but also in a debate which led to the NRK's purchase of the serial. It is important here to note that a debate in the Norwegian press is something entirely different from a debate in, say, the US press. In fact, Norway is quite unique in the western world in terms of newspaper readership. In the year of the "cultural debate of the ages," 1983, so-called "lesser-educated" Norwegians (i.e. those with up to nine years' schooling) spent on average forty-two minutes per day reading newspapers. The more educated spent fifty-two minutes, according to the same survey (Høst 1983: 135). Norway has all in all about 160 papers published more or less daily for a population of 4.1 million. In 1991, 34 percent of the population over 9 years of age read at least one paper per day, 30 percent read two papers and 20 percent claimed to read three or more papers (Central Bureau of Statistics, Report no. 12, 1992). In other words, a press debate in the Norwegian context is not something concerning only a minority with the equivalent of a college education, as it might be in the USA.

The newspapers, especially the nationally distributed Oslo tabloids, initially contributed to audience expectations about *Dynasty* by writing about the international success of its rival and generic predecessor, *Dallas*—and the NRK's attitude towards that show. The NRK had refused to buy *Dallas,* and the reason given was its "low quality." The tabloids created something almost amounting to a "public outcry" about this, since Swedish public service TV started showing *Dallas* in the 1980–1 season. The chorus of course was "why can't we take it if the Swedes can?"—a loaded question, given Norway's widespread national inferiority complex. (Sweden has twice as many inhabitants and, contrary to Norway, produces cars—Volvo and Saab.) Also important here is the fact that hundreds of thousands in the eastern parts of Norway could actually watch Swedish television, so other parts of the country suffered from geographically determined injustice. The fuss over the NRK's rejection of *Dallas,* and the fact that that show was already a tremendous international success, prompted a private video import company to buy the exclusive rights to distribute *Dallas* in Norway (thus making it impossible for the NRK to change its mind), even though they had to rely on video rentals since only one channel of broadcast TV existed. The NRK's decision to buy *Dynasty* was then made, indirectly as a result of the public pressure building mainly through the two tabloids, *Verdens Gang (VG)* and *Dagbladet* in the *Dallas* case. "We *had* to buy it" (*Dynasty*), the then leader of NRK-TV's film and series department, Rigmor Hansson Rodin, told me in a telephone interview in the autumn of 1983.

The fact was that there were also internal struggles in the NRK leading up to the actual buying of the serial. The present head of the culture section, Stein Roger Bull, was at the time in charge of the entertainment department. He and associates in his department exploited the vagueness of the borders between the departments for film/series and entertainment by simply announcing that if film and series did not buy *Dynasty,* they would (taped interview, spring 1992). Bull and his colleagues also gained support from people in film and series who were more willing than their boss to listen to the "demand" publicly expressed in the tabloids. The stubborn boss, Rigmor Hansson Rodin, then gave in, and bought the first episodes of *Dynasty.* Not surprisingly, her department presented the show officially as being of much higher quality than *Dallas.*

This story of how *Dynasty* came to be presented on Norwegian TV screens indicates how intimate the relations have been between the Oslo dailies—the two tabloids in particular—and the NRK. These relations have developed in the one-channel situation. The two tabloids have a combined national circulation of well above half a million copies per day, a huge figure in a small population. They are quite different from the tabloids of certain other countries, in that they have a reputation for quite solid reporting in certain fields: *Dagbladet* has, for instance, a tradition of being a central forum for liberal and radical intellectuals. Since their circulation is so large, this made (and makes) them not only powerful agents in the politico-cultural field, but also significant simply as barometers of widespread views, sentiments and opinions. The people in the NRK who wanted to buy *Dynasty* could use these papers to confirm their own feeling: that a certain puritan public service regime in programming was over, and that the survival of public service television depended on the corporation's ability to open up to the tastes of a now more vocal, less subservient audience.

In terms of internal politics, the advocates (and activists) for *Dynasty* could count on a growing support for their views at the executive level of the NRK. The corporation was at this point marked by a growing awareness of the fact that they were, willingly or not, facing a situation of real competition. Swedish television had been, as mentioned above, an alternative to parts of its audience, but it was no longer the only one. As of April 1982, Rupert Murdoch's Sky Channel was distributed by cable in central areas, and its blatantly commercial programming had become a topic of public debate. The number of VCRs increased rapidly, from 75,000 in 1979 to about 500,000 at the end of 1986. In Norway, significantly, these machines were mainly used to play rented tapes with films and series.

The total turnover in the video rental business increased from 240 million kroner (some £24 million, more than US $30 million) in 1982 to 850 million kroner in 1986 (NRK 1987: 9). A more comprehensive adjustment to a competitive market situation was already beginning, and the buying of *Dynasty* was part of a reorientation which was further developed as the debate about the serial went on. In short, the NRK itself took on many of the features traditionally associated with commercial broadcasting. I will return to this in a slightly more detailed way towards the end of this chapter.

Public Debate, Popular Participation

The debate on *Dynasty* opened quite modestly in a small (if politically not insignificant) Christian Oslo daily and other local newspapers. The Christian paper asked a bishop and leaders of Christian organizations the key question for much later debate and research: "Why do we watch that sort of thing?"(*Vårt Land*, 19 May 1983). The journalist pointed out that *Dynasty* was obviously something "everybody" was watching while at the same time claiming that the show was "meaningless, hopeless and spineless." One of the Christian leaders did not "conceal" that he had seen one of the two episodes broadcast at that time, and claimed that the serial "glorifies a life of abundance, power and, in part, immorality." But it was still mainly a "waste of time." Other leaders interviewed said that the show appealed to escapism, and noted its focus on wealth, family problems and sex. One of them, with a professional background in NRK-TV, also mentioned the high degree of professionalism in the production. In his judgment, the most problematic aspect of the serial, in moral terms, was the way it portrayed Blake Carrington: he was given sympathetic features in a way which could make his "brutality in business" seem legitimate. The bishop basically said that he had no time for serials and that he preferred soccer and crime series on TV. In other words, after two episodes Christians had noted the strong appeal of *Dynasty*, but still had no strong negative opinion about it.

However, an interview in a local paper (*Fredrikstad Blad*, 21 May) could be seen as an indication both of what was about to come and of the degree of arrogant ignorance which marked much of the later criticism of the show: a female member of the government- and parliament-appointed Broadcasting Council, Liv Nordhaug, said that she had "certainly not" watched *Dynasty* at all, but judging from the pre-showing presentation of it, she found it "sad" that this was the kind of entertainment NRK had chosen to offer people on Saturday nights. It was obviously a purely speculative production about decadent life in the upper upper classes, and she would certainly inquire about the reasons for it being shown in the next council meeting.

Readers' letters in a social democratic paper published just outside Oslo (*Akershus Arbeiderblad*) also complained about *Dynasty* as a sign of increasing commercialization of NRK's programming (24 May 1983). But the public debate did not really get rolling until the show had been harshly attacked by a well-known marxist-leninist ("maoist") writer, Jon Michelet. He spoke in a meeting on 26 May 1983 of the Broadcasting Council, of which he was a member. According to newspaper reports the following day, Michelet said that *Dynasty* should be taken off the schedule as soon as possible, because it was "non-culture from beginning to end"; it made "*Dallas* look like a piece by Shakespeare"; it demonstrated "how decay marks current American acting." The show was called a "soap-stew"; the characters were "made not of cardboard, but of ice." All of this concerned the "cultural quality" of the show. The other major thrust of his argument was that the serial was entirely irrelevant for Norwegian viewers, since the characters had a private park the size of the huge forests north of Oslo and a swimming pool the size of one of Norway's largest inland lakes: "only one in a million of the world's population is interested in the problems dealt with in this serial."

It is important to note here that Michelet owed most of his (macho) reputation as a writer to his widely read novels, which attempt to use male-oriented popular genres (crime/detective fiction and thrillers) as vehicles for a "progressive" political "message." This indicates that he did not react in this way out of contempt for popular culture or popular genres in general. Even if he himself was not aware of it, it was quite obviously not least what *Dynasty* had in common with popular *feminine* genres that disturbed him. In Norway this at the time meant literary (in books and weeklies) and filmic family sagas and romances, often set in aristocratic or very upper-class circles, texts very far from the officially preferred "social realism" of Michelet and his political group. Michelet's attack on *Dynasty* is thus an early indication of the mostly implicit gender dimension to the struggle over the serial.

Two days later, Michelet was invited to a debate in the current affairs radio magazine *Ukeslutt* ("Weekend"), which the NRK then transmitted on both radio channels. He met with the editor of the most rapidly growing weekly, *Se og Hør* ("Look and listen"), a populist "reportage" magazine which may be seen as a Norwegian version of the US *National Enquirer*. This editor did of course defend *Dynasty* as very popular entertainment, which deserved to continue for as long as audiences wanted it, while Michelet repeated his attacks. Shortly after the (live) discussion between the two had started, the switchboard at NRK almost melted as hundreds of people called in from all over the country (at one moment, 300 incoming calls were registered simultaneously) (*Aftenposten*, 30 May). The majority opinion in these calls was not only massively in favor of the show, it was massively aggressive in its attitude to Michelet ("dictator," "worse than Hitler") and what he was seen to represent—the cultural elites who had prevented the screening of program like *Dynasty* for decades.

This spontaneous "telephone storm" was followed up by the tabloid *Dagbladet* over the weekend. The paper invited its readers to phone in and have their say on the issue. Over two full pages, then, the paper could declare (31 May) that *Dynasty* was "dividing Norway." A selection of twenty-four callers, identified by full name, address and profession, were quoted. Negative and positive opinions about the show were more or less equally represented, as were women and men in both camps.

Such newspaper-organized phone-ins became a staple element of the public discussion, which went on in waves for about a year, reaching peak levels each time the NRK was running out of episodes and had to decide whether to buy more. A stunning crescendo took place in June 1984, when the NRK had finally decided to end *Dynasty* (if only for a while, as it later turned out). The phone-ins were of course not only pseudo-polls but also staged pseudo-debates, in the sense that none of the callers ever confronted any of the others, and what was printed was of course always the journalists' rendering of the callers' views. Nevertheless, these multi-interviews with dozens of ordinary people were very effective in forming the impression that *Dynasty* was the central topic of debate in the public sphere, and that the sentiments involved were extremely strong.

A somewhat peculiar indication of the scale of engagement in the debates occurred in October 1983, when the organization "Friends of *Dynasty*" was formed in response to NRK threats to take *Dynasty* off the schedule. The man behind it was Freddy Andersen (the English first name connoting lower-class tastes), a driving instructor in an urban area on the west coast reputed for its enthusiasm for American culture. He advertised in the national populist tabloid *VG* that he was starting this organization, which soon gained hundreds of members from all over the country. In interviews on radio and in a number of papers he invited anyone supporting the demand for "television for those who watch it," not just for "those who work in the NRK" or other minorities, to join in (*Stavanger Aftenblad,* 25 October 1983). Andersen was popular with journalists (and presumably also readers) because he so bluntly stated his preferences and phrased his anger at NRK traditions so entertainingly: "Who watches programs about the inside of the brain on Wednesday nights? And who needs a whole series about psychiatry which only makes you go nutty?" (ibid.). In one interview he said that the program on the "inside of the brain" should be transmitted either before children's TV at 6 p.m. or at 3 a.m.; in another interview he suggested that it should be distributed on video cassettes to "doctors who don't remember their lessons" (*Haugesunds Avis,* 1 November.) Children's TV should consist of imported cartoons and comedies, not "a Norwegian lady reading from a book." The rest of an ideal TV night would contain news, a Norwegian soft-news magazine, *Dynasty* and a James Bond film. All of this would cost almost nothing compared to the Norwegian mini-series *Jenny* (based on a novel about a young female writer living in Italy around the turn of the century), which was getting on Andersen's nerves, not least because he estimated the production cost at 25 million Norwegian kroner (approximately US $3.5 million).

Freddy Andersen was in other words totally at odds with every "responsible" principle of broadcasting, and this is part of the reason why his initiative attracted so much attention. Such views were previously only heard in conversations among "ordinary people," in bars, among neighbors, at work. They were well known, but had hardly ever before been promoted so eagerly and openly in the public sphere. Even if "Friends of *Dynasty*" never had more than 1,000 members, it was not insignificant as a sign of the accumulated frustrations the *Dynasty* debate released in large parts of the NRK's audience. The opinions dominating in the newspaper phone-ins confirmed the impression that Mr Andersen was a true "voice of the people."

The phone-ins were supplemented by interviews with all kinds of celebrities and people in various more or less powerful positions. Only a few weeks after Michelet's first attack on the serial, it seemed as if all such people on both local and national levels had given their opinion. The more serious part of the discussion took the traditional form of relatively long, more or less polemical newspaper articles, two of which early on presented more comprehensive, model arguments.

Dynasty *as the Future of Television*

In *Dagbladet* on 4 June 1983, Rolv Wesenlund, a very popular comedy actor, pointed to the company Michelet attracted when he attacked *Dynasty:* Christians "who hate to see divorce, nude swimming, hash and alcohol consumption with ice-cubes, the extreme Right which does not approve of the serial format, plus the leftist intellectual elite which actually doesn't like TV at all. *And* popular enlighteners who are against entertainment as a phenomenon." All of these united to keep the soap opera off Norwegian TV screens—"at least until the satellites arrive, and they will do so in multitudes." Wesenlund maintained that "broadcasting diversity can today only be countered by coercive means and prohibition of antennas." He claimed to represent a "silent majority" who had to live with the total dominance of "narrow" programming for much too long, and complained that those who enjoyed these "narrow" programs now showed a total lack of democratic tolerance of majority preferences when demanding that *Dynasty* be removed. He looked forward to the near future where systematic ratings would govern TV output, and raised the thought that TV possibly "*is* an entertainment machine with news."

Wesenlund thus made *Dynasty* a (positive) symbol of the future of the medium, a technologically sustained future in which Christian moralism and left and right cultural snobbism would no longer dictate programming and hinder the dominance of the majority's preferred stuff: entertainment. His rhetorical appeal to democracy did not, however, include consideration for the rights of minorities. His idea of broadcasting "diversity" amounted only to a whole-hearted welcome to a time where "entertainment with news" would sum up the contents of television.

Jon Michelet answered a few days later (8 June). He pointed to the fact that he had received a lot of support from all political corners and all social groups for his attack on *Dynasty*. Consequently, he doubted the existence of a compact, uniform "silent majority." He stressed that he was not interested in censorship, he had only said that *Dynasty* should be taken off as soon as possible, and it was evidently not possible at that moment. He expressed his delight in the way thousands of people in the ongoing debate made use of their right to free expression of opinions. "An open debate is better than polls and ratings as a source of advice for the NRK," he said, stressing at the same time the editorial independence and responsibility of the corporation itself. The importance of the *Dynasty* debate he had started was that it provided the NRK with lots of policy advice "in an epoch where TV2 is on its way and satellites hang in the sky." He admitted that the NRK had to compete and provide an answer to the "wave of good and bad" stuff which was coming, but the question was whether the answer should be to turn "yellow" and accept all kinds of speculation, "buy the worst non-culture, cultivate all the cheapest tricks." "The big battle about to come" would be about the possibility for survival of Norwegian culture and "our Norwegian character [*egenart*]." More money for Norwegian television entertainment was necessary, according to Michelet, who also claimed to have support for this view in "popular demand." He suggested moving *Dynasty* from its spot on Saturday night prime time (the major television night in Norway), and finally declared:

> If I have contributed to an *increase* in the interest in the Denver-clan and its backstage managers, it is my comfort that we now have a *critical* interest in them. Maybe *Dynasty* should run for even more than the 14 episodes hitherto bought, as a lasting stimulus for the will among Norwegian TV-

viewers and politicians to take a stand on the future of television in this small country with only one channel but with a lot of media worms in the ground and a big sky up above?

For both Michelet and Wesenlund, then, the ongoing and anticipated internationalization and commercialization of television was a central part of the framework in which *Dynasty* was understood. *Dynasty* played the same role in Norway as *Dallas* elsewhere in Europe; it came to represent a future of television that seemed terrible to almost anyone with some sort of position or stake in official culture. As signalled by Michelet, the show itself was less important than its alleged referent: a TV universe completely dominated by TV entertainment of its kind. This is in fact a first and very important dimension of the meaning(s) of *Dynasty* (and *Dallas* elsewhere), not only in public debates, but also in households, for individual members of the audience. These two prime-time shows came at a time when they acquired enormous "metatextual" importance not least because of concurrent developments and debates over broadcasting, media and cultural policies. Had they (or something like them) hypothetically arrived in the early 1970s or in the late 1980s, they might well have been very popular, but they would hardly have drawn the same enormous attention, hardly been regarded with such extraordinary excitement, for or against.

The 1980s: Changing Cultural Values

Pressure on traditional broadcasting policies was not the only factor that made the early 1980s a suitable moment for "daring" prime-time soaps about the super-rich. The change in western political and cultural conjunctures during the second half of the 1970s also prepared the ground for them. This conjunctural shift, a widespread "right turn" after a decade where various "left" forces had been on the offensive, was no doubt tied in various ways to the international recession after the 1973 oil crisis. In Norway, this recession was experienced very differently from many other countries, because the 1970s were also the decade when the North Sea oil adventure really took off. The social-democratic government helped to postpone the effects of the recession by spending money from the North Sea in advance, so to speak. There was little unemployment, and a steady increase in wages. Norway continued its social-democratic tradition of giving priority to public spending. Hans Magnus Enzensberger in an essay on the Norwegian "offbeat" situation (first published in 1984) sums up his impressions like this:

> It is not private wealth but the wealth of society that counts. Consequently, citizens may with satisfaction observe that the number of employees in the [public] health system has doubled since 1970, and that the social security funds today spend three times as much money as they did before the oil-age began. The public sector has grown immensely. The redistribution of wealth is a demanding work that costs a lot of money. Local administration alone has increased its staff by 74 percent in less than ten years, a nice growth in the number of jobs. [. . .] It has also been expensive for Norwegians that they

wish to maintain the existing pattern of habitation in the country. [. . .] "Where there are people there should be schools and hospitals, and buses and ferries should go there." This infrastructure devours resources: 49 airports with regular departures are more expensive than two or three. [. . .] Private extravagance is regarded with suspicion, public luxury with patriotic pride. In a small place in Østfold [county] I saw an old American film with twelve other people in the audience. It was shown in a municipal cinema with 1200 exquisitely upholstered seats. The airconditioned, mosaic-decorated town halls I have visited in the most remote areas of the country were simply monumental. (Enzensberger 1987: 179)

Enzensberger lived in Norway for a few years in the 1960s, and the passage quoted was probably also influenced by what he had experienced then. What he did not see or at least emphasize in his report from 1983/4 was the change taking place at precisely that time in the views on the traditional balance between the private and the public sectors and in socio-cultural values. Oil had brought a sector with extraordinarily high wages and profits and a hectic, Klondyke-like atmosphere to both industry and financial businesses. It was a sign of the times that, in Stavanger, the country's oil capital, one of the many nouveaux riches entrepreneurs called his luxury boat *Black Money* (yes, in English).

From the mid-1970s, the leftist political orientations previously on the offensive, not least in connection with the broad popular resistance against EC membership, lost support. A generational shift gradually took place in high schools and later in universities, whereby the dominance of politically radical students, interested in theory, was replaced by a wave of much more pragmatic, apolitical or conservative students seeking careers in marketing and similar areas. Not only did Norway get its fair share of yuppies, the climate from 1980 on was, on the whole, perfectly in tune with the ideological melodies being played elsewhere in western Europe and in the US. The conservative government installed after the election in 1981 was a sign of the times, even if it may be said to have represented a form of conservatism resembling middle-of-the-road social democracy, compared with Reagan and Thatcher. It challenged the traditional strength of the public sector with arguments taken both from liberalist economics and from liberalist ideological thinking. The force of these arguments can be seen in the social-democratic party's internal discussions on the concept of "freedom" and support for a campaign for a more "open society," e.g. the liberalization of laws and regulations concerning opening hours (working hours) in the service sector. A financial boom was in a very visible way accompanied by booms in other sectors in the early and mid-1980s: spurred also by liberalized alcohol regulations, the total number of restaurant seats in the city of Bergen alone rose by 300 percent in about three years.

The *Dynasty* debate was consequently also fueled by all of these parallel shifts in cultural values. The show's focus on business, wealth, conspicuous consumption and individualized power struggles was in tune with dominant discourses on politics and culture at the time. Small houses on the prairie and British miners were definitely "out," tycoons and champagne were "in," at least in terms of their ability to kindle the imagination of large and vocal audience groups. *Dynasty* was showing what seemed to fascinate most people most deeply at the time: unlimited consumption and the lifestyles of the rich and famous.

Christian Concerns and Grassroots Fascination

The debate branched out in various ways. A Christian organization monitoring broadcasting supported Michelet's critique of the series in their own way:

> From a Christian point of view, we have serious objections to the ideas about life which are presented in *Dynasty*. Divorce, infidelity, alcohol abuse, sex and intrigue—all is presented as a sweet and good life. Many of those in our own country who have been through some of this "sweet" life know what despair and human tragedy can result from it. We read about it in the papers every day. The NRK should buy or produce series about normal people who live together in true love for each other. It is our duty as Christians to point out that life as God wants us to lead it, is the life that best protects human beings and society. (Statement printed in several papers, 30 and 31 May 1983)

This Christian, moral rejection of the serial was repeated again and again in the debate. Officially, Christian people were not supposed to watch *Dynasty* at all—it would be harmful to their moral standards, especially those of younger people. Still, the show remained popular also with the religiously active: in the spring of 1984, it was front-page news in Christian papers that since *Dynasty* was moved from Saturdays to Wednesdays in autumn 1983 it had proved destructive to organized Christian activities like Bible groups, choir practices, etc. People simply preferred watching *Dynasty* to these meetings and activities. When this story was presented in the national tabloid *Dagbladet* on 4 April 1984, the heading was "KRYSTLE BEATS CHRIST."

This split between the active Christian grassroots and their clerical and lay leaders was unique. "Ordinary Christian people" would previously have shunned programs that were declared immoral by their leaders. This time instead they adjusted the schedules of their Christian activities and flocked in front of their screens, even if the moral condemnation of the serial was reiterated by non-Christian groups. The episode transmitted immediately after the radio debate between Michelet and the *Se og Hør* editor fueled such moral objections outside Christian circles as well. A social-democratic paper published near Oslo said in its editorial on 31 May 1983:

> The most recent episode of *Dynasty* fully demonstrates just how far American companies are willing to go in order to entertain us. In this episode we witness how two of the spoiled rich kids get high on marijuana before throwing themselves naked into daddy's swimming pool. Will the next be that we are to be entertained by watching the spoiled kids—in order to

maintain the excitement—give us a lesson in how to take cocaine or possibly heroin? (*Akershus Arbeiderblad,* 31 May 1983)

Stuff like this would normally have infuriated every organized Christian if it had been Nordic TV drama. With *Dynasty,* the reaction was largely different. According to many in the audience who talked about the moral quality of the show, in newspaper phone-ins or in letters to the NRK, *Dynasty* very clearly represented a contrast to all the sex, swearing, drunkenness and general filth that marked the (stereo)typical Nordic social-realist drama productions they had seen. In other words, it seems that a number of textual characteristics were able to balance the portrayal of morally condemnable behavior, in such a way as to maintain the overall respectability of the serial in the eyes of very many "ordinary" people, active Christians or not.

Writers and (Other) Intellectuals

In another part of the cultural spectrum, literary people and other intellectuals also discussed *Dynasty.* Jon Michelet's total rejection of the serial was widely supported in these circles, but the reaction was more nuanced in some quarters. In order to understand this section of the public debate, it is necessary to know why a revolutionary maoist (hence in principle Stalinist) writer could be a member of the official Broadcasting Council. This advisory council has twenty-five members, fourteen appointed by parliament, eleven by the government, and is supposed to deal primarily with programming issues.

In the 1970s Norway's New Left was marked by the peculiar strength of its maoist faction, organized in the communist party AKP(M-L) from 1973. The party's members and sympathizers were extremely active in a number of "front" organizations in various political fields. The total commitment of the "M-L" movement's members, their strong rhetoric, uncompromising fighting spirit and roots in the 1960s student movement also brought them a surprisingly large following among artists of various kinds. They were active in the introduction of quite aggressive and successful trade-union politics in artists' organizations. A number of the most talented writers and visual artists joined the "M-L" movement around 1970, Michelet among them. Their artistic productions in various media (literature, visual arts, film) were marked by their party's official support for the classic "social realism" doctrine, even if most of them (luckily, many would say) had problems in ridding themselves of all the modernism that had formed their artistic identities and ambitions in the 1960s. Certain novelists and visual artists belonging to the movement were quite successful in terms of critical acclaim and popularity with the educated middle class. Their party never reached more than extremely minimal support in elections, but their cultural and political importance in non-parliamentary fields was considerable. They managed in the 1970s to establish the only maoist daily in Europe outside Albania, *Klassekampen* ("The class struggle"), which is now generally recognized for its reporting particularly in business/economics and politics. The appointment of Jon Michelet to the Broadcasting Council represented a recognition of the cultural strength of the maoist group and also of Michelet's success as a writer of "political" thrillers and crime novels.

Socialist writers and intellectuals who rejected Stalinism and social realism were forced to define themselves in relation to the maoist group. Many of these have been labelled "social modernists" because of their interest in further developing socially critical modernist traditions in the arts. Not least in literature, this "social modernism" was marked by an open attitude towards and an engagement with transnational popular culture in various forms: jazz, rock and pop music; detective, crime and Western genres in film and literature. This acknowledgement of significant elements in popular culture was in stark contrast to the maoist rejection in the mid-1970s of the electric guitar as an "imperialist instrument." Even if never made official policy, the rejection of this instrument and the music associated with it was indicative of a quite strong nationalist element in the cultural ideology of the maoist group.

While these two leftist groups—social realists and social modernists—were clearly on the offensive in the 1970s, the arts were certainly far from totally dominated by them. More traditional, liberal and conservative artists and critics, both in aesthetic and political terms, were of course still active and held important positions in the various institutions of art. In the public debate over *Dynasty,* people belonging to these non-socialist circles of various kinds were all very clear in their condemnation of the serial's (lack of) quality, thus maintaining the traditional resistance to transnational popular culture.

The only category of intellectuals that might have presented a different, more nuanced perspective was the one I have loosely labelled "social modernists." Some of these are/were critics with a background or basis in academia, others were professional artists. A surprising move by the then editor of the most prestigious literary journal, *Vinduet* ("The window,") Janneken Øverland, revealed an interesting split in this non-maoist, more or less radical group. In her editorial in the journal's first issue in 1984, which had Krystle Carrington's face all over the front cover, Øverland wrote:

> Whatever one may think of "ladies' novels," Krystle, or crime fiction, there is one thing the professional writers of literary series, TV scripts and crime stories know how to do: create viewer and reader involvement. They are able to force people to return to the kiosk or the screen or the paperback to get to know more. They reach their audience by creating a need they themselves then set out to satisfy.
>
> [. . .] This is not to be read as a call for Norwegian authors to write more "simple," more "understandable," "trivial" books—it is rather meant as an appeal to individual writers and a milieu which seen from the sideline now seems more dead than it has been for a long time. [. . .] Write as excitingly as Krystle is beautiful, scare us as seriously as Alexis is evil, and seduce us just as openly to read good literature as the tabloids seduce buyers with celebrity weddings and royal visits. Let yourself at least be pro-

voked and stimulated by the enormous need for fantasy, for fairy tales and adventure which the preoccupation with popular culture reveals.

The liberal tabloid *Dagbladet,* with its historical reputation as a forum for literary and intellectual debate, interviewed some authors about Øverland's challenge. The most celebrated and probably intellectually dominant of the "social modernists," Kjartan Fløgstad, said that these were not new ideas, and that Norwegian literature over the last ten years—including his own writing—had employed elements of various forms of popular culture to a much greater extent than had the literature of neighboring countries. He now rather feared that the increasing commercialization of the public sphere would turn writers and other artists into media clowns, and in that perspective it was increasingly important to "stick to the seriousness of literature." Two other authors, one female and one male, both representatives of slightly more traditionalist writing, rejected Øverland's idea. While they stressed that certain forms of popular culture could be inspiring and that writing "good entertainment" could be perfectly respectable, they saw a writing governed by a commercial orientation as being fundamentally at odds with the basic principles of serious writing.

The most interesting element in this little literary debate is that which is missing, both in Øverland's editorial and in the invited responses in *Dagbladet:* reflections on the gendered character of popular culture. Both *Vinduet* and other serious literary journals had previously, in the 1970s, had issues devoted to various forms of popular literature and popular culture. But they were all about male-oriented genres. Nobody mentioned the fact that *Dynasty,* as a form of soap opera, in its focus on "domestic" problems and by way of the prominent role of women both in the serial and in its production, must be seen in the light of feminine traditions in popular culture. This is particularly surprising in Øverland's case, since she, both as a scholar and in various other literary capacities, had been associated with feminism in general and feminist criticism in particular. The issue of *Vinduet* in which this editorial appeared was devoted to popular genres, and contained articles about contemporary hospital romances and nineteenth-century popular romances—articles which for the first time in a leading journal took these genres seriously. Nevertheless, the gender issue was not dealt with directly in the editorial at all.

This blind spot marks the public debate as a whole. One of the reasons is of course that the show also offered so many male-oriented elements that it exerted a major draw on male audiences, too. Still, many of the pejorative metaphors used by those who were against the serial obviously referred to traits it shared with traditional feminine genres (and certain constructions of feminity)—it was "sickly sweet," "sentimental," "slow," "soapy," "glossy," etc. One of the very few people to present a more sympathetic, reflective interpretation of the serial in the press was a woman (Berit Hoff, in *Dagbladet,* 12 July 1984). She pointed to *Dynasty*'s melodramatic structures and devices, but she did not mention the historical gendering of this aesthetic or attempt more specifically to criticize the gender bias in the aesthetic condemnations. Such a bias would in fact seem particularly obvious since the attitude towards male-oriented genres had for quite some time been generally positive within the "social modernist camp."

Commodified Debate in a Changing Public Sphere

The picture of the debate provided so far is of course not in any way complete. I have for instance not talked about a number of longer contributed articles in different newspapers, in which the serial was analyzed as a sign of the times, either in the US or in Norway or both places. The main point in these (often quite sensible) contributions was not to condemn the show, but rather to understand what it was saying and why it seemed so fascinating to so many. A few papers also had some of their more intelligent journalists write articles about the international market for television material, and the US dominance in that market. It is an interesting fact that the latter kind of articles never appeared in the two national tabloids; they were mainly done in the larger regional papers, such as *Stavanger Aftenblad*. The national tabloids concentrated almost exclusively on the "popular opinion about *Dynasty*" angle. Politically, this was important in that it influenced NRK's decisions concerning the prolongation or ending of *Dynasty*'s run. But this influential part of the press did not spend any resources to speak of on a more far-reaching, systematic presentation of information on what actually went on in the international TV business, the world's "information order" or other such issues.

Part of my initial interest in the total coverage of *Dynasty* in the Norwegian media was its exemplary relevance to Jürgen Habermas's theory of the "structural transformation" of the public sphere (1971). Habermas describes a historical process through which the "space" or "sphere" for "disinterested," truth-seeking debate over political, social and cultural issues tends to be crushed between state interventionism on the one hand and private interests of various kinds on the other. The latter category of interests are also represented by political parties, organizing people according to their class positions in the "private" sphere of production, so that the downfall of the classic bourgeois public sphere was actually accelerated by parties which entered the public sphere in order to represent the "private" interests of the working class, rather than seek the truth in dialogue with other disinterested participants. But this is only one element in the "invasion" of private interests; perhaps more important (and more in line with other Frankfurt School ideas) is Habermas's perspective on the increasing importance of private economic interests in the very foundations of the public sphere: the media. When the media themselves become predominantly means for making profit, the public debate is turned into a commodity which the public then consume rather than participate in (1971: 149).

The problem then is not that the public debate dies out. On the contrary, it flourishes as never before, since it is "guaranteed thoughtful care" in a plurality of organized, carefully arranged ways. The problem is that the commodification of debates alters their logic, their form and function. They become spectacle, staged entertainment: "position and counter position are, in advance, committed to certain rules of entertainment," Habermas says, and "when conflicts are brought into the public discussion, they are immediately displaced to the plane of personal friction" (ibid.: 152).

The Norwegian *Dynasty* event can clearly be used as an illustration of such developments. It really took off after the radio "duel" between Michelet and the *Se og Hør* editor, and was further developed through the printed "duel" between Michelet and Wesenlund. In both instances, the tone of the debates was quite personal. The phone-ins organized by the tabloids (predominantly) functioned first to build their corporate images as "servants of the people," second to provide quite entertaining material with hardly any substantial arguments to support the opinions expressed. All the interviews with all kinds of more or less prominent people, in all kinds of newspapers, similarly amounted to little more than a *simulation* of a debate: a collection of opinions, not sustained arguments. Along with most of the journalistic coverage of the *Dynasty* event, the duels, phone-ins and interviews altogether clearly display the characteristics of a commodified debate.

Some of the "letters to the editor," certain longer articles submitted to some of the papers and some of the journalistic coverage can on the other hand be regarded as contributions to a serious debate on both the serial itself and the wider perspectives of the whole incident. But such contributions were rarely aimed at providing concrete advice on whether *Dynasty* should continue or not, or on any other specific, politico-practical issue. In that sense they were politically impotent, since the "effect" of their argumentation on the international trade in television fiction or the symptomatic meanings of *Dynasty* can hardly be "measured" in any way at all.

It seems, then, as if the most clearly "commodified" part of the debate was the part of it that was politically most effective, in the sense that it really did influence the NRK's programming. It worked to construct an impression of *Dynasty* as immensely popular with an otherwise "silent majority." While one may with Habermas lament the lack of substantial arguments in a debate transformed into spectacle, it is still quite obvious that the spectacle (in this case, at least) was a representation of some very real desires and sentiments in large audience groups who normally would not participate in a "responsible" public debate. Various surveys confirmed this impression, both by showing how vast an audience *Dynasty* drew to the screens every week, and by indicating a solid majority for the continuation of the serial. A national survey with 1,003 respondents, reported in *Aftenposten*, 27 July 1983, showed that 22 percent had watched all the episodes so far and 48 percent had watched "some" of them; 61 percent of all respondents would watch the serial if it continued. In the following year, the audience seemed to grow rather than shrink. The NRK was again and again "forced" to continue the serial, in spite of pressures from, for example, the Broadcasting Council to do the opposite.

After the first thirteen episodes (counted as fourteen in Norway, since the first was shown in two parts), twenty-two more were bought, with explicit reference made to the "wishes of the audience." In fact, it was noted that the Director of NRK-TV, Otto Nes, in a TV interview of 20 June 1983, referred to the audience as the NRK's "customers" (*Aftenposten*, 21 June). This was the first time this term was used by NRK executives, indicating how *Dynasty* became a turning point in the way NRK-TV conceived of its relations with the audience. When the NRK ran out of episodes again, towards the end of October, they decided to go against the advice of the television sub-committee of the Broadcasting Council, and bought more episodes, again pointing to the wishes of the majority of its "customers." The show was moved from Saturdays to Wednesdays though, and in that sense it was somewhat "downgraded." Even if 25 April 1984 was then set as the absolute final date of *Dynasty* in Norway, the serial's run was again prolonged, until it finally ended in cascades of newspaper coverage on 11 July 1984.

Though it may be hard to accept in some circles, it seems one has to conclude that the "commercialization" of both television and print media actually, in this case, contributed to a form of cultural democratization. "Television for those who watch it" had been much too limited thus far, and the international commercial success shows that *Dynasty* was recognized as "our kind of entertainment" by large groups. The commodified forms of (pseudo-)debate formed a pressure which could not be neglected.

On the other hand, it also remains a fact that the larger political, cultural and social issues underlying the debate were hardly clarified in its tabloid, "spectacularized," commodified forms. Serious, enlightening contributions were almost drowned, i.e. overlooked, in the noise of sensationalist media. This fact does not engender optimism with regard to the future of the public sphere, if commercialization and commodification are to rule more or less unrestrained. The Norwegian *Dynasty* debate demonstrates, however, that commercial media may serve to remind intellectuals of the social exclusions which historically have followed the characteristic forms of serious, enlightened discourse in the "bourgeois" public sphere. The challenge consists in negotiating between the need for a democratic representation of views and interests and the need for a non-manipulative, true exchange of arguments (cf. also Gripsrud 1991).

The Role of Research—and the Researcher

My own project was immediately picked up in some media as a contribution to the *Dynasty* debate. The fact that research was going on was met with a positive curiosity in some papers where the show was celebrated, and with scorn among those who were against the serial. At a later stage someone ironically suggested, in a letter to the major newspaper of Norway's second-largest city, *Bergens Tidende,* that a whole team of researchers should immediately be put to the task of explaining the popularity and deeper meanings of *Falcon Crest*. In other words, the use of tax-payers' money for such a ridiculous project was implicitly opposed. For years after 1984 I was interviewed about my *Dynasty* research by a number of newspapers, regional and national, and by local and national radio. I gave various kinds of talks, not least to groups of teachers, primarily at high school (sixth-form) level. All of this never made me a celebrity (I was never on TV), but it was once used against me in a newspaper debate on police brutality in which I was more or less accidentally involved: I was called a "soap opera researcher" (and consequently not to be taken seriously).

It was, in other words, quite clear that research on *Dynasty* could not be politically innocent or neutral, at least not in Norway. The attention gathered by my project reveals the immediate "political" nature of any media research that addresses issues central to public and popular concerns. At a more specific level it is probably telling of the differences between the social positions and roles of researchers and other intellectuals in different national contexts. A research associate or Ph.D. student doing something along the lines of my work would probably not receive the same kind of public/media attention in most larger western countries, and particularly not in the US. The immediate involvement of research such as mine in the public debate and in various professional or further education events presents the researcher with a pressing need to reflect on the political implications of his or her work, theory, methodology, hypotheses and overarching hermeneutical perspectives. Journalists and the public expect clear answers to all sorts of value-laden and complicated questions, not cryptic remarks about theoretical problems or methodological technicalities, not strictly academic talk about the postmodern condition; and they want the answers right away, not in three years. It is not so easy, then, in a country like Norway, to achieve the kind of splendid isolation that also marks certain interesting and, in many ways, advanced academic discourses in the media and cultural studies field(s), and I have at times deplored this. But when it actually seems to *matter* what researchers say, when people in media institutions and the general public take an interest, one's work takes on a different meaning, that of social action, of some kind of practical political responsibility, beyond the often more or less inconsequential battles within academia.

In my case, I tried to convey three kinds of "messages" in my various encounters with the media and the public. First, I tried to sketch the various overarching perspectives that made the *Dynasty* phenomenon interesting to me: the historical changes in our media environment, the historical opposition between high and low culture and its gendered dimensions, the questions of cultural identity in an increasingly internationalized media culture, the role of public broadcasting. I tried to say that there were more questions than definite answers here, but also that there was less ground for pessimism than many representatives of official culture seemed to think. Second, I took the opportunities I had to relate some factual knowledge about both the American TV industry and the textual traditions in the light of which *Dynasty* should be seen, these being primarily the daytime soap opera and melodrama. I also often pointed out the particular interest shown in the serial (according to surveys) by women. Third, I tried to balance respectful support for those in the audience who were most seriously engaged in the show with a slightly more ironic or playful attitude which was definitely closer to my own personal feelings about the serial. This latter point also allowed for a certain display of irony in relation to my own work, letting me show that I did not regard myself and my work in the somewhat pompous, complacent manner of the traditional academic.

I realize, then, that my voice in the public debate was basically heard as one advocating acceptance of the show; indirectly, because I, a university person, took it seriously without joining those who condemned it; directly, because I defended the right to enjoy it and also suggested ways of coming to terms with it for those who had problems either accepting their own fascination or simply understanding why anyone would find anything of interest, at all, in the serial. I remember more or less instructing, in private circumstances, an academic friend on how to "camp" the show, i.e., focus on and appreciate its elements of irony and willful "bad taste," and thus have a good time watching it. This was also—less explicitly—part of the talks/teaching I gave about the show to audiences such as teachers. At times, members of the audience—particularly women—would thank me for confirming that they were not so silly even if they had long been watching the serial with a mixture of keen interest and self-conscious irony, the latter tied also to a feeling of being guilty of bad taste.

Not that it had much to do with my work, but the public discourse about *Dynasty* throughout the 1980s developed largely in the direction of ironic acceptance. Its first run ended in the summer of 1984, but it returned twice in the second half of the 1980s. TV critics increasingly took to a humorous, ironic but still often enthusiastic tone when writing about the show. Headings such as "Oh—these lovely bubbles," "Marvellous Krystle last night," "Bye-bye in a blood-bath" all appeared in *Dagbladet* in 1987 and 1988. This shift in tone indicates how *Dynasty* may have functioned as a training in "camp" attitudes to television, particularly in the educated middle classes. The product, in Marx's abstract terms, demanded a particular "manner of consumption," and thus also produced a certain, adequate consumer subject.

Before closing this chapter, I will first briefly sketch *Dynasty's* fate in Norway after its initial, first-year run and then finally sum up some of the event's consequences for the NRK and broadcasting policies.

Dynasty's Gradually Fading Appeal

When *Dynasty* ended on the NRK in July 1984, it was picked up by a video import and distribution company, DMD-International. They immediately advertised twenty-seven episodes for rental at a package price of 490 Norwegian kroner, i.e. about £45, less than US $70. The price was close to the total license fee then paid for a year of NRK services. The ads claimed that "80,000 Norwegian families have said 'We wish to continue following *Dynasty* on video'—and so can you!" This made it sound as if 80,000 families had already bought the video package but it seems that this figure only or at best referred to an estimate made on the basis of market research. At the beginning of August, a representative of DMD-International said more than 40,000 had bought the rental series ("The Dynasty Ticket") (*Bergens Tidende*, 3 August), while his boss claimed that 50,000 "tickets" had been sold, and that he expected a total sale of 80,000 (*Bergens Tidende*, 6 August). These figures were doubted by some observers, since the total number of VCRs in Norway at the time was about 200,000, many of which were owned by companies, schools and other institutions. Still, even if only 40,000 "tickets" were sold, at the price mentioned, it is an indication of the strength of the determination in the show's core audiences to go on watching for as long as possible.

As *Dynasty* left the NRK, it also left the public sphere almost completely for a while. Its replacement, *Falcon Crest*, did not create anything like either the public enthusiasm or the anger associated with its predecessor. The NRK still claimed to have audience figures from weekly surveys which indicated that it was "very popular" and "normally high" in its attendance. Other signs of interest among viewers were coverage in the popular weeklies and quite a few angry phone calls to the NRK when the show was skipped one Wednesday before Christmas. But the temperature was definitely lower. When asked to explain this, Janneken Øverland, the editor of the literary journal *Vinduet*, said:

> *Dynasty* managed in a relatively intelligent way to play with some fantasies which were more provoking than those in this serial. In some way or other, *Falcon Crest's* temperature is too low. It does not follow its themes far enough, sensations are more dispersed, and there's a lot of repetitions. It's as if it's not as grandiose and vulgar as *Dynasty*. There is something they have not achieved within the same format. (*Bergens Tidende*, 6 February 1985)

Even if Øverland also pointed to the fact that *Dynasty* came first, and added that "professional culture-debaters" are not really interested in such shows at all, this general characterization of the differences between the two serials indicates that the *Dynasty* debate cannot be seen as resulting almost exclusively from more or less contextual and accidental factors. The *Dynasty* text simply had particular dimensions and properties, such as those mentioned by Øverland in the above quote, which created very strong emotional engagement both for and against it. Its role as a point of crystallization for a complex set of issues could not have been played by just any never-ending American show. This is an important part of the reason why I insist on the centrality of the text in the process of communication, and, consequently, on the centrality of textual analysis in communication research of all kinds.

Dynasty continued to fascinate a very large audience when it was back on NRK-TV after DMD-International's video rights expired in the summer of 1986. Except for a few weeks' break around Christmas, it ran without interruptions in its Wednesday spot until 23 September 1987. By then the energy of its fans must have weakened, since it was replaced by *Falcon Crest* without any protest to speak of. The third and final run started on 18 May 1988, and ended on 14 December that year. I had a survey done by a local market research company in the city of Bergen in December 1988. In what was still largely a one-channel situation, total audience figures were still very high: 63% of the women interviewed and 57% of the men claimed to have seen at least part of the serial in its last run. But the interest was significantly lower than in 1984: 44% of the women and 30% of the men estimated they had watched more than 75% of the episodes in 1988; in my 1984 survey the corresponding figures were 62% for women and 37% for men. The differences between educational levels became more pronounced. In 1984, 59% of those with less than nine years of school, and 39% of those with more than fifteen years, claimed to have watched more than 75% of the episodes. In 1988, the result was practically the same (60%) for the lowest educated, while only 10% of those in the most educated group now said they had watched more than 75% of the episodes broadcast that autumn. Interestingly, the drop in viewer interest seemed to be most marked in areas of the city where cable TV had now become widespread. *Dynasty* was not alone in the category of transnational fictional entertainment any more.

After 145 episodes, an NRK executive could say he was disappointed by the serial's quality over the last six months and that the NRK would now like some variation in the menu (*VG*, 14 December 1988)—without provoking any uproar among audiences. It was not so much that the serial was no longer watched by so many: it was more that it had lost some of their strong interest, their emotional investment. Both the very strong initial fascination that *Dynasty* exerted and the gradual weakening of its hold on audiences are important heuristic pointers.

The World's Viewers Prefer Indigenous Programs

Certain Norwegian newspapers had surveys done during *Dynasty's* first run, in 1983–4, which seemed to yield contradictory results, since high audience attendance was coupled with low scores in terms of evaluation ("did you like the program"). This could of course be related to the fact that audiences knew that *Dynasty* was regarded as a "low-quality" show by the cultural elites, and that watching it was regarded as slightly "immoral" since it was just "superficial entertainment" (cf. Alasuutari 1992). But audiences were, in fact, generally not afraid to "admit" that they had watched *Dynasty*, even if some, particularly those well educated, may have understated their attendance. A better explanation is simply that Norwegian audiences, like those of just about any other country of the world, prefer domestically produced fictional programs to foreign ones, including those from the US, particularly if they are of a certain professional standard. This is convincingly documented in the UNESCO report *Import/Export: International Flow of Television Fiction* (Larsen 1990). A series of national and regional surveys (Africa, Asia, Europe, Latin America, North America) shows that indigenous productions get the highest ratings, suggesting that they provide audiences with a different, "fuller" and more satisfactory experience than even the most popular of US shows.

This finding has been further elaborated and convincingly documented in a number of empirical, qualitative reception studies in several European countries in recent years. Anne Hjorth (1984) compared Danish women's reception of *Dallas* and the Danish serial (more precisely, feuilleton—it had an ending), *Daughters of War,* using loosely structured interviews with women of different social classes. She concluded as follows:

> The fascination *Dallas* offers is stronger than that of most other programs, because it so directly appeals to the ambivalent (and unconscious) emotional and psychic conflicts in viewers, and because it provides an aesthetic bombardment of the senses. It gives primarily a "here-and-now" experience. The viewer is kept in front of the screen—and her ambivalences maintained—and this results in a feeling of frustration and emptiness. *Daughters of War* is also fascinating, but it also has a greater use-value, because it is closer to women's everyday experiences and leaves more space for the conscious co-creation of the text through relating it to viewers' own experiences. It therefore provides an experience which can be brought out of the viewing experience itself—"you can take it home with you"—into life, one's own! (Hjorth 1984: 358)

This conclusion has later been largely confirmed in similar studies by, for instance, Birgitta Höijer in Sweden (1992), who compared the reception of *Falcon Crest* to that of the Swedish serial (feuilleton) *Three Loves;* and, in Belgium, Daniel Biltereyst (1991). Biltereyst compared the reception of a US sitcom (*She's the Sheriff*) with that of an indigenous (Flemish) sitcom (*De Kollega's*), and found, even for this genre, that the domestic program was both more liked and understood in a more complex way since it required the application of local cultural codes. As a result, "[i]t is safe to say that the indigenous drama functioned as a forum for introspection to consider themes of identity and current political, cultural and social issues, while in the responses to the US program such issues hardly arose" (Biltereyst 1991: 489).

This is not, however, to say that US programs are not really wanted by audiences across the globe. They are popular for a number of reasons, particularly their high professional standards, their tempo and their glamour, their references to the US as a kind of modernity's concrete utopia. But, even if they are sometimes able strongly to engage viewers who partly recognize themselves in their fictional worlds, US shows do not deliver what viewers treasure most: strong, many-sided, meaningful experiential relations to their own lives and conditions.

Consequences for Public Service Television

"In order to create something like the *Dynasty* debate now, we would have to program soft-porn, something like *Playboy Late Night*," Stein Roger Bull, present head of NRK-TV's section for culture, told me in my interview with him in 1992. It did not sound as if the idea was too far out to be considered.

Bull was throughout the 1980s a pioneering spirit for a revision of NRK programming in view of the increasing competition from other channels, foreign at first and later also domestic. He was not only, as noted above instrumental in bringing *Dynasty* to the NRK in 1983. In early 1985, he engineered a 3.5-hour entertainment program on Saturday nights which was designed as an imitation of commercial television's "flow," including advertisements for various non-commercial organizations and generally accepted "causes" (health, road safety, etc.). When interviewed about the program, Bull referred to the audience as "customers," and mentioned a single ambition behind the program and its design: "We wish to prevent people switching to Swedish TV or Sky Channel" (*Dagbladet*, 15 January 1985). Such an openly and exclusively competitive legitimation of a program, completely empty in terms of (other) intended meanings and ideas concerning the show's qualitative dimensions, had never been heard before in Norway.

In autumn 1984, after *Dynasty* "went rental," another entertainment program in the variety format also signalled the introduction of a modernized form of TV in NRK, obviously created to imitate commercial television's typically very segmented and flashy visual style: *Lørdagssirkus* ("Saturday circus"). This program's link to commercialism was also clear at other levels—from its logo/trademark being repeated a dozen times throughout the show to its thematic preoccupation with fashion and the fashionable, and its "non-commercial" marketing of cultural products such as LPs, books, theatre performances and Oslo cafés.

Even if *Lørdagssirkus* was marked by its ties to openly commercial television and often seemed extremely superficial and yuppie-affected, it also represented a renewal of NRK-television in important ways. The show's producer, Per Selstrøm, said it was the first time he had made an entertainment program with his own generation in mind, not that of his parents. He was then about 40.

Bull and Selstrøm supported *Dynasty* and the shift it represented towards a new relation with the audience for the NRK. The tabloid-mediated pressure from the audience that resulted in the buying and repeated continuations of that serial also reminded the NRK that they simply needed to know more of what their audiences were thinking. "We must also get better at using these reports when we're making program," NRK-TV's Program Director Otto Nes said, pointing to a shelf full of reports from the corporation's audience research (*Aftenposten*, 28 December 1985). The NRK had until then only surveyed their audience once a year. A highly significant consequence of the *Dynasty* experience was that it revealed the need for much more frequent and detailed monitoring of the audience and its reactions. The NRK started buying audience surveys on a weekly basis after or during the *Dynasty* experience, and they now finance (along with the major commercial channels) a people-meter system operating according to current American principles, complete with overnight ratings and shares.

It is my conclusion, then, that *Dynasty* was both a *sign* of a historical shift in Norwegian broadcasting and, particularly by way of the public debate about it, also an *instrument* for change. It revealed that a rather rigid traditionalism and narrowness of taste in public service broadcasting had been overtaken, and it opened the eyes of NRK executives, politicians and various kinds of intellectuals to the realities of competition in the airwaves.

Program Director Otto Nes said in 1985 that "Pure entertainment will have more room as competition for viewers increases, and we have not so far been good enough at meeting the new challenge" (*Aftenposten*, 28 December 1985). But transnational entertainment has definitely not filled the NRK's prime time. Apart from finally broadcasting a British soap, *East-Enders*, in a late afternoon/early evening spot (for a while), the most striking change in the NRK's programming has been a rearrangement of the schedule to include a broadly popular program, domestic or imported, every evening in the slot immediately after the 7:30 (now 7:00) news program. Other adjustments include a solid strengthening of regional production (mostly for the national channel), emphasis on domestic entertainment (particularly for Saturday nights), extended sports coverage, maintenance and renewal of the traditionally strong production for children and teenagers. Important steps have, finally, also been taken to increase expenditure on drama, in several genres. Certain categories of cultural programming (such as classical music) have less space, but on the whole one can hardly say that the NRK has given up on its public service obligations. It has generally attempted to secure its position by maintaining broad support in the audiences. The one-channel system made such support relatively easy to obtain, and also of less importance. Increased dependency on audience support holds a number of problems, but it is hard to see that it in itself implies a weakening of democratic influence on public television. Just as Brecht once pointed out that people could "vote with their feet" when fleeing oppression, TV audiences vote directly on the quality of programs by pushing the buttons of the remote control.

References

Alasuutari, Pertti. (1992) "'I'm Ashamed to Admit It But I Have Watched Dallas': The Moral Hierarchy of Television Programs." *Media, Culture and Society* 14: 561–82.

Bakke, Marit. (1986) "Culture at Stake." In D. McQual and K. Siune (eds.), *New Media Politics: Comparative Perspectives in Western Europe.* London, Beverly Hills, New Delhi: Sage.

Biltereyst, Daniel. (1991) "Resisting American Hegemony: A Comparative Analysis of the Reception of Domestic and US Fiction." *European Journal of Communication*, 6: 469–97.

Dahl, Hans F. (1983) "Commentary," *Dagbladet*, 2 November.

———. (1981) *Fra Gutenberg til Gjerde*. Oslo: Aschehoug.

Elliott, Philip. (1986) "Intellectuals, the 'Information Society' and the Disappearance of the Public Sphere." In R. Collins et al. (eds.) *Media, Culture, and Society: A Critical Reader*. London, Beverly Hills, New Delhi: Sage.

Enzensberger, Hans Magnus. (1987) "Norwegian Off-beat." In *Oh, Europe! Impressions from Seven Countries and an Epilogue from the Year 2006*. Oslo: Universitetsforlaget.

Evensmo, Sigurd. (1967) *Det Store Tivoli*. Oslo: Gyldendal.

Galtung, Johan and Gleditsch, Nils P. (1975) "Norge I Verdenssamfunnet." In N. Rogoff Ramsey (ed.) *Det Norske Samfunn*, 2: 742–806.

Garnham, Nicholas. (1990) *Capitalism and Communication: Global Culture and the Economics of Information*. London, Newbury Park, and New Delhi: Sage.

———. (1984) "Introduction." In A. Mattelart, X. Delcourt and M. Mattelart, *International Image Markets: In Search of an Alternative Perspective*. London: Comedia.

Gripsrud, Jostein. (1994) "Intellectuals as Constructors of Cultural Identity." *Cultural Studies*, May.

———. (1991) "The Aesthetics and Politics of Melodrama." In P. Dahlgren and C. Sparks (eds.), *Journalism and Popular Culture*. London, Newbury Park, New Delhi: Sage.

———. (1990) *Folkeopplysningas dialektikk: perspektiv pa norskdomsrorsla og amaterteateret 1890–1940*. Oslo: Det Norske Samlaget.

———. (1981) *La denne var scene bli flammen . . . Pespektiv og praksis I og omkring sosialdemokratiets arbeiderteater ca 1890–1940*. Oslo: Universitetsforlaget.

Habermas, Jürgen. (1971) *Borgerlig offentlighet*. Oslo: Gyldendal Norsk Forlag.

Hjorth, Anne. (1984) *When Women Watch TV: On Media Research and Reception*. MA Dissertation, Department of Literary Studies, University of Copenhagen. Published by Media Research Department: Danish Broadcasting Corporation.

Hoijer, Birgitta. (1992) "Reception of Television Narration as a Socio-Cognitive Process: A Schema-Theoretical Outline." *Poetics* 21: 283–304.

Host, Sigurd. (1983) *Bruk av massemedier I Norge*. Oslo: Institutt for Presseforskning.

Mahamdi, Yahia. (1988) "Algerian Television and the *Dallas* Phenomenon: Cultural Imperialism or Appropriation." Paper Presented to the 16th Congress of the International Association for Mass Communication Research, Barcelona. (Reprinted in the IAMCR collection, *Mass Communication and Cultural Identity*, Vol. 1.)

NRK. (1987) *NRK mot ar 2000*. Oslo.

Rokkan, Stein. (1967) "Geography, Religion and Social Class: Crosscutting Cleavages in Norwegian Politics." In S.M. Lipset and S. Rokkan (eds.) *Party Systems and Voter Alignments*. New York: Free Press.

———. (1966) "Norway: Numerical Democracy and Corporate Pluralism." In Robert A. Dahl (ed.) *Political Oppositions in Western Democracies*. New Haven: Yale University Press.

Sklar, Robert. (1976) *Movie Made America: A Cultural History of American Movies*. New York: Vintage Books.

Syversten, Trine, (1992) *Public Television in Transition.* Ph.D. Dissertation, University of Leicester. Published as Levende Bilder no. 5/92, Oslo: KULT/ NAVE.

Thompson, Kristin. (1985) *Exporting Entertainment: America in the World Film Market 1907–1934.* London: BFI Publishing.

Wheen, Francis. (1985) *Television.* London: Century Publishing.

Williams, Raymond. (1975) *Television: Technology and Cultural Form.* New York: Schocken Books.

Part IV

OVERVIEWS

The passing of the network era, the emergence of multiple distribution channels and remote control devices, and perhaps the coming convergence of television and computer enhance, in some ways, our ability to establish overviews. Clear historical changes provide opportunities for comparison and contrast, for reconsidering older approaches, and for seeing (or creating) larger explanatory patterns. One result is that in these reconsiderations we can identify not only the explanations, but the grounds on which they were made. This, in turn, should sharpen our sense that television is always "television," characteristic of time and place, institutional arrangements of power, and particular responses fostered by these particularities. Still, we should not fall too easily into easy categorizations of "then" and "now," "there" and "here." Overlooking continuities in the search for difference can lead to false distinctions. The essays that follow provide material for these sorts of critical considerations.

The essay by Newcomb and Hirsch must be more and more identified by its links to "the network era." The notion that television serves as a site of negotiation for cultural issues, images, and ideas surely stands as one important continuity within various formations of television practices, but the processes and procedures surrounding the negotiation within television texts and by television audiences have shifted dramatically. For example, the notion of the "viewing strip" as a text was put forward as a strategy for capturing possible ideological and cultural complexity in television. But it was unwittingly premised on a limited number of options for viewers. The concept remains valid—viewer-activated selections from among institutional offerings. The difference is that it is nearly impossible to identify a "viewing strip" constructed with a remote-control device from among the "50 channel universe." The negotiation processes at work may be more complex than ever, as viewers select from what might be an ever widening set of approaches to issues and ideas. Or those processes may simply be totally absent as viewers "surf" rather than view.

One way to describe these changes is to point out that the "cultural forum" model, in its reliance on notions of "ritual," assumes that "television" is constructed on something similar to a religious base, a widely shared and deeply held set of narrow assumptions. (Indeed, it is precisely because the model did not fully acknowledge the limitations on those assumptions that it has often been critiqued for its lack of a concept of "power.") But the newer "television" seems to be constructed on something more akin to a library or newsstand model. And lest we assume that this is an acceptance of "the market" as a democratic device, we should quickly notice that the library remains highly controlled and the newsstand provides only a limited number of selections.

What is likely in either model, however, is that viewers deploy multiple viewing strategies in varying contexts, another concept missing from the original "forum" model. And this problem is merely one example of how changes in television make it clear that generalizations are almost always historically situated and that critical interventions are inevitably tied to those situations.

Todd Gitlin's essay suffers far less from changes in technologies and practices. It is still quite possible to apply his descriptions of the hegemonic strategies of prime-time television. As he suggests, the "ideological core" remains and is difficult to change. But alterations in television programming strategies, the (potentially) greater number of ideological perspectives, and new delivery systems put some strain on the model of containment he forwards. For some critics, for example, cable television offerings are merely "more of the same." For others, certain specialized channels have opened new spaces for the contestation of that ideological core. Perhaps still greater tests will come with new technologies promising more control by viewers.

David Thorburn also describes a television of an earlier era. But it is quite remarkable that much of what he has to say about television drama's narrative strategies remains so precisely descriptive of much television content. It is true that most dramatic series are more highly serialized in contemporary schedules, but that narrative device is, in some ways, merely the intensification of Thorburn's concept of the "multiplicity principle," by which TV drama draws on itself to make new stories. Nevertheless, it is also clear (and this point is also significant for the "forum" model) that television drama makes up a smaller and smaller portion of what we know as "television." This fact is reflected throughout this collection, which now focuses on a wider range of genres than was the case in earlier editions.

It is exactly this issue that stands central in Charlotte Brunsdon's "What Is the 'Television' of Television Studies?" One answer to the question is that the "television" of television studies "has been produced differently by different scholars and interest groups." We create the objects of our study with our definitions—a useful and cautionary lesson for any good critic. Moreover, Brunsdon shows how television studies has drawn on a host of more grounded disciplines such as literary study, sociology, and anthropology for its models. The result for her is that the field is best defined and made exciting by its "hybridity." This concept is most useful in considering television systems that seem themselves ever more hybridized, blended with other expressive forms, other technological devices, and used in contexts that extend far beyond the traditional viewing of the set in the living room.

David Marc asks what is perhaps a more drastic question than Brunsdon's—"What Was Broadcasting?" His concern is not that of a historian of economics or technology, however, but that of cultural critic. The deeper question that emerges in the introductory passage of his essay is this: "how can an expansion in the number of cultural options accompany a contraction of democratic values and institutions?" To answer both these questions Marc explores the cultural role of broadcasting, "the stuff of culture being 'cast broadly,'" and laments the fragmentation and isolation afforded by the newer technologies of cable television and the videocassette recorder.

For purposes of this collection his essay also suggests the break between "network" and "postnetwork" television, and indicates the fundamental reasons for the many varying approaches and topics that are now the content of the anthology. In fact, it is possible to suggest that Brunsdon's essay might be retitled "What *Was* the Television of Television Studies?" While both essays certainly imply a call for more precise historical study of the broadcasting and television that was, they are less clear on what the new questions might be.

John Thornton Caldwell's essay addresses the same shift under the subheading of "The Crisis of Network Television." The "crisis," of course, is the recognition by the U.S. television industry of Marc's observation: "The Broadcast Era is kaput." Caldwell finds new questions for critics in the industry's attempt to respond to that realization. His essay is a remarkable for the way in which it synthesizes approaches to the study of this newer "television." It surveys the economic necessity for change, the technologies that became available and pointed those changes in certain directions, and the aesthetic strategies that were developed with those technologies in response to those necessities.

His term for the new, postnetwork television is "televisuality," by which he means, as indicated in the title of his essay, "excessive style." The fundamental problem for television makers and programmers in the postnetwork era is, in Caldwell's formulation, how to achieve distinction. In other parts of the book from which this chapter is drawn, he charts various forms of stylistic excess, various forms of televisuality. His argument is compelling and he uses it not only to describe and analyze television programming, but also to pose a critique to other forms of television analysis and criticism.

The danger here, of course, is that in attempting such a comprehensive overview, Caldwell, too, will face other changes which make this generalization seem accurate only for the particular "television" he has addressed.

The two final essays in this collection return to consideration of the meaning of television in expanded contexts. James Hay's reflections on changes in Italian television are grounded in concerns for ways in which the medium reconfigures "space." But the spaces with which he is concerned are conceptual as well as literal. How does television "map" our sense of who and where we are? How does one nation define itself in its television systems (a question at the heart of David Marc's concerns)? More pointedly, how does one nation, one culture, define itself in the face of television offerings from other nations and cultures, offerings filled with their own notions of "Italianness"?

The questions posed by Eric Michaels are related to these, and are among the most profound emerging in the brief history of television studies. For his question goes not only to issues of national cultural interaction and definition, but also to issues of cultural survival. Invited to Australia to study potential Aboriginal uses of television—by which was meant the uses of nationally broadcast, satellite delivered Australian television—Michaels's decision to assist in the *making* of television by Aboriginal groups implied a host of political, cultural, economic, controversies. The "television" created in the course of his work was surely unlike the "televisions" studied in most of the essays in this collection. Yet all the questions raised by those other essays come into play. The history of Aboriginal television must be defined in relation to developing technologies and with regard to other forms of expression. The texts produced can be studied as genres, as individual expression, and again, in contrast to what we know as "conventional" television. Audience responses are hugely complicated by specific cultural detail, detail that seems visible in its unusual characteristics, but which should call up the "strangeness" of taken for granted viewing habits in other contexts.

And finally, Aboriginal television takes its place in constructing our generalized understanding of the medium. It instructs by contrasting example and emphatically declares that it is "televisions" that must be studied. In some version, some technological, economic, aesthetic configuration, it is—they are—more fully than ever a part of our experience.

Michaels's questioning of political, moral, and ethical implications of Aboriginal television, and the Aboriginal uses of conventional television, requires us to ask those same questions about any "television" that we study. This is, finally, the point of television criticism—to ensure the ongoing critical evaluation of this medium in our lived experience.

Television as
a Cultural Forum

HORACE NEWCOMB and PAUL M. HIRSCH

A cultural basis for the analysis and criticism of television is, for us, the bridge between a concern for television as a communications medium, central to contemporary society, and television as aesthetic object, the expressive medium that, through its storytelling functions, unites and examines a culture. The shortcomings of each of these approaches taken alone are manifold.

The first is based primarily in a concern for understanding specific messages that may have specific effects, and grounds its analysis in "communication" narrowly defined. Complexities of image, style, resonance, narrativity, history, metaphor, and so on are reduced in favor of that content that can be more precisely, some say more objectively, described. The content categories are not allowed to emerge from the text, as is the case in naturalistic observation and in textual analysis. Rather they are predefined in order to be measured more easily. The incidence of certain content categories may be cited as significant, or their "effects" more clearly correlated with some behavior. This concern for measuring is, of course, the result of conceiving television in one way rather than another, as "communication" rather than as "art."

The narrowest versions of this form of analysis need not concern us here. It is to the best versions that we must look, to those that do admit to a range of aesthetic expression and something of a variety of reception.

Reprinted from *Quarterly Review of Film Studies,* Summer 1983, with permission of the publisher and authors. Copyright © 1983.

Even when we examine these closely, however, we see that they often assume a monolithic "meaning" in television content. The concern is for "dominant" messages embedded in the pleasant disguise of fictional entertainment, and the concern of the researcher is often that the control of these messages is, more than anything else, a complex sort of political control. The critique that emerges, then, is consciously or unconsciously a critique of the society that is transmitting and maintaining the dominant ideology with the assistance, again conscious or unconscious, of those who control communications technologies and businesses. (Ironically, this perspective does not depend on political perspective or persuasion. It is held by groups on the "right" who see American values being subverted, as well as by those on the "left" who see American values being imposed.)

Such a position assumes that the audience shares or "gets" the same messages and their meanings as the researcher finds. At times, like the literary critic, the researcher assumes this on the basis of superior insight, technique, or sensibility. In a more "scientific" manner the researcher may seek to establish a correlation between the discovered messages and the understanding of the audience. Rarely, however, does the message analyst allow for the possibility that the audience, while sharing this one meaning, may create many others that have not been examined, asked about, or controlled for.

The television "critic" on the other hand, often basing his work on the analysis of literature or film, succeeds in calling attention to the distinctive qualities of the medium, to the special nature of television fiction. But this approach all too often ignores important questions of production and reception. Intent on correcting what it takes to be a skewed interest in such matters, it often avoids the "business" of television and its "technology." These critics, much like their counterparts in the social sciences, usually assume that viewers should understand programs in the way the critic does, or that the audience is incapable of properly evaluating the entertaining work and should accept the critic's superior judgment.

The differences between the two views of what television is and does rest, in part, on the now familiar distinction between transportation and ritual views of communication processes. The social scientific, or communication theory model outlined above (and we do not claim that it is an exhaustive description) rests most thoroughly on the transportation view. As articulated by James Carey, this model holds that communication is a "process of transmitting messages at a distance for the purpose of control. The archetypal case of communication then is persuasion, attitude change, behavior modification, socialization through the transmission of information, influence, or conditioning."[1]

The more "literary" or "aesthetically based" approach leans toward, but hardly comes to terms with, ritual models of communication. As put by Carey, the ritual view sees communication "not directed toward the extension of messages in space but the maintenance of society in time; not the act of imparting information but the representation of shared beliefs."[2]

Carey also cuts through the middle of these definitions with a more succinct one of his own: "Communication is a symbolic process whereby reality is produced, maintained, repaired, and transformed."[3] It is in the attempt to amplify this basic observation that we present a cultural basis for the analysis of television. We hardly suggest that such an approach is entirely new, or that others are unaware of or do not share many of our assumptions. On the contrary, we find a growing awareness in many disciplines of the nature of symbolic thought, communication, and action, and we see attempts to understand television emerging rapidly from this body of shared concerns.[4]

Our own model for television is grounded in an examination of the cultural role of entertainment and parallels this with a close analysis of television program content in all its various textual levels and forms. We focus on the collective, cultural view of the social construction and negotiation of reality, on the creation of what Carey refers to as "public thought."[5] It is not difficult to see television as central to this process of public thinking. As Hirsch has pointed out,[6] it is now our national medium, replacing those media— film, radio, picture magazines, newspapers—that once served a similar function. Those who create for such media are, in the words of anthropologist Marshall Sahlins, "hucksters of the symbol."[7] They are cultural *bricoleurs,* seeking and creating new meaning in the combination of cultural elements with embedded significance. They respond to real events, changes in social structure and organization, and to shifts in attitude and value. They also respond to technological shift, the coming of cable or the use of videotape recorders. We think it is clear that the television producer should be added to Sahlins's list of "hucksters." They work in precisely the manner he describes, as do television writers and, to a lesser extent, directors and actors. So too do programmers and network executives who must make decisions about the programs they purchase, develop, and air. At each step of this complicated process they function as cultural interpreters.

Similar notions have often been outlined by scholars of popular culture focusing on the formal characteristics of popular entertainment.[8] To those insights cultural theory adds the possibility of matching formal analysis with cultural and social practice. The best theoretical explanation for this link is suggested to us in the continuing work of anthropologist Victor Turner. This work focuses on cultural ritual and reminds us that ritual must be seen as process rather than as product, a notion not often applied to the study of television, yet crucial to an adequate understanding of the medium.

Specifically we make use of one aspect of Turner's analysis, his view of the *liminal* stage of the ritual process. This is the "inbetween" stage, when one is neither totally in nor out of society. It is a stage of license, when rules may be broken or bent, when roles may be reversed, when categories may be overturned. Its essence, suggests Turner,

> is to be found in its release from normal constraints, making possible the deconstruction of the "uninteresting" constructions of common sense, the "meaningfulness of ordinary life," . . . into cultural units which may then

be reconstructed in novel ways, some of them bizarre to the point of monstrosity. . . . Liminality is the domain of the "interesting" or of "uncommon sense."[9]

Turner does not limit this observation to traditional societies engaged in
the *practice* of ritual. He also applies his views to postindustrial, complex
societies. In doing so he finds the liminal domain in the arts—all of them.[10]
"The dismemberment of ritual has . . . provided the opportunity of theatre
in the high culture and carnival at the folk level. A multiplicity of desacral-
ized performative genres have assumed, prismatically, the task of plural cultural reflexivity."[11] In short, contemporary cultures examine themselves
through their arts, much as traditional societies do via the experience of ritual. Ritual and the arts offer a metalanguage, a way of understanding who
and what we are, how values and attitudes are adjusted, how meaning shifts.
    In contributing to this process, particularly in American society, where
its role is central, television fulfills what Fiske and Hartley refer to as the
"bardic function" of contemporary societies.[12] In its role as central cultural
medium it presents a multiplicity of meanings rather than a monolithic dominant point of view. It often focuses on our most prevalent concerns, our
deepest dilemmas. Our most traditional views, those that are repressive and
reactionary, as well as those that are subversive and emancipatory, are upheld,
examined, maintained, and transformed. The emphasis is on process rather
than product, on discussion rather than indoctrination, on contradiction and
confusion rather than coherence. It is with this view that we turn to an
analysis of the texts of television that demonstrates and supports the conception of television as a cultural forum.

This new perspective requires that we revise some of our notions regarding
television analysis, criticism, and research. The function of the creator as
bricoleur, taken from Sahlins, is again indicated and clarified. The focus on
"uncommon sense," on the freedom afforded by the idea of television as a
liminal realm helps us to understand the reliance on and interest in forms,
plots, and character types that are not at all familiar in our lived experience.
The skewed demography of the world of television is not quite so bizarre
and repressive once we admit that it is the realm in which we allow our
monsters to come out and play, our dreams to be wrought into pictures,
our fantasies transformed into plot structures. Cowboys, detectives, bionic
men, and great green hulks; fatherly physicians, glamorous female detectives, and tightly knit families living out the pain of the Great Depression;
all these become part of the dramatic logic of public thought.
    Shows such as *Fantasy Island* and *Love Boat,* difficult to account for
within traditional critical systems except as examples of trivia and romance,
are easily understood. Islands and boats are among the most fitting liminal
metaphors, as Homer, Bacon, Shakespeare, and Melville, among others, have
recognized. So, too, are the worlds of the Western and the detective story.
With this view we can see the "bizarre" world of situation comedy as a

means of deconstructing the world of "common sense" in which all, or most, of us live and work. It also enables us to explain such strange phenomena as game shows and late night talk fests. In short, almost any version of the television text functions as a forum in which important cultural topics may be considered. We illustrate this not with a contemporary program where problems almost always appear on the surface of the show, but with an episode of *Father Knows Best* from the early 1960s. We begin by noting that *FKB* is often cited as an innocuous series, constructed around unstinting paeans to American middle-class virtues and blissfully ignorant of social conflict. In short, it is precisely the sort of television program that reproduces dominant ideology by lulling its audience into a dream world where the status quo is the only status.

In the episode in question Betty Anderson, the older daughter in the family, breaks a great many rules by deciding that she will become an engineer. Over great protest, she is given an internship with a surveying crew as part of a high school "career education" program. But the head of the surveying crew, a young college student, drives her away with taunts and insensitivity. She walks off the job on the first day. Later in the week the young man comes to the Anderson home where Jim Anderson chides him with fatherly anger. The young man apologizes and Betty, overhearing him from the other room, runs upstairs, changes clothes, and comes down. The show ends with their flirtation underway.

Traditional ideological criticism, conducted from the communications or the textual analysis perspective, would remark on the way in which social conflict is ultimately subordinated in this dramatic structure to the personal, the emotional. Commentary would focus on the way in which the questioning of the role structure is shifted away from the world of work to the domestic arena. The emphasis would be on the conclusion of the episode in which Betty's real problem of identity and sex-role, and society's problem of sex-role discrimination, is bound by a more traditional conflict and thereby defused, contained, and redirected. Such a reading is possible, indeed accurate.

We would point out, however, that our emotional sympathy is with Betty throughout this episode. Nowhere does the text instruct the viewer that her concerns are unnatural, no matter how unnaturally they may be framed by other members of the cast. Every argument that can be made for a strong feminist perspective is condensed into the brief, half-hour presentation. The concept of the cultural forum, then, offers a different interpretation. We suggest that in popular culture generally, in television specifically, the raising of questions is as important as the answering of them. That is, it is equally important that an audience be introduced to the problems surrounding sex-role discrimination as it is to conclude the episode in a traditional manner. Indeed, it would be startling to think that mainstream texts in mass society would overtly challenge dominant ideas. But this hardly prevents the oppositional ideas from appearing. Put another way, we argue that television does not present firm ideological conclusions—despite its *formal* conclusions—so much as it *comments on* ideological problems. The conflicts we see in television drama, embedded in familiar and nonthreatening frames, are conflicts ongoing in American social experience and cultural history. In a few cases we might see strong perspectives that argue for the absolute correctness of one point of view or another. But for the most part the rhetoric of television drama is a rhetoric of discussion. Shows such as *All in the Family*, or *The Defenders*, or *Gunsmoke*, which raise the forum/discussion to an intense and obvious level, often make best use of the medium and become highly successful. We see statements *about* the issues and it should be clear that ideological positions can be balanced within the forum by others from a different perspective.

We recognize, of course, that this variety works for the most part within the limits of American monopoly-capitalism and within the range of American pluralism. It is an effective pluralistic forum only insofar as American political pluralism is or can be.[13] We also note, however, that one of the primary functions of the popular culture forum, the television forum, is to monitor the limits and the effectiveness of this pluralism, perhaps the only "public" forum in which this role is performed. As content shifts and attracts the attention of groups and individuals, criticism and reform can be initiated. We will have more to say on this topic shortly.

Our intention here is hardly to argue for the richness of *Father Knows Best* as a television text or as social commentary. Indeed, in our view, any emphasis on individual episodes, series, or even genres, misses the central point of the forum concept. While each of these units can and does present its audiences with incredibly mixed ideas, it is television as a whole system that presents a mass audience with the range and variety of ideas and ideologies inherent in American culture. In order to fully understand the role of television in that culture, we must examine a variety of analytical foci and, finally, see them as parts of a greater whole.

We can, for instance, concentrate on a single episode of television content, as we have done in our example. In our view most television shows offer something of this range of complexity. Not every one of them treats social problems of such immediacy, but submerged in any episode are assumptions about who and what we are. Conflicting viewpoints of social issues are, in fact, the elements that structure most television programs.

At the series level this complexity is heightened. In spite of notions to the contrary, most television shows do change over time. Stanley Cavell has recently suggested that this serial nature of television is perhaps its defining characteristic.[14] By contrast we see that feature only as a primary aspect of the rhetoric of television, one that shifts meaning and shades ideology as series develop. Even a series such as *The Brady Bunch* dealt with ever more complex issues merely because the children, on whom the show focused, grew older. In other cases, shows such as *The Waltons* shifted in content and meaning because they represented shifts in historical time. As the series moved out of the period of the Great Depression, through World War II, and into the postwar period, its tone and emphasis shifted too. In some cases, of course, this sort of change is structured into the show from the beginning, even when the appearance is that of static, undeveloping nature. In *All in the Family* the possibility of change and Archie's resistance to it form the central dramatic problem and offer the central opportunity for dramatic richness, a richness that has developed over many years until the character we now see bears little resemblance to the one we met in the beginning. This is also true of *M*A*S*H*, although there the structured conflicts have more to do with framing than with character development. In *M*A*S*H* we are caught in an anti-war rhetoric that cannot end a war. A truly radical alternative, a desertion or an insurrection, would end the series. But it would also end the "discussion" of this issue. We remain trapped, like American culture in its historical reality, with a dream and the rhetoric of peace and with a bitter experience that denies them.

The model of the forum extends beyond the use of the series with attention to genre. One tendency of genre studies has been to focus on similarities within forms, to indicate the ways in which all Westerns, situation comedies, detective shows, and so on are alike. Clearly, however, it is in the economic interests of producers to build on audience familiarity with generic patterns and instill novelty into those generically based presentations. Truly innovative forms that use the generic base as a foundation are likely to be among the more successful shows. This also means that the shows, despite generic similarity, will carry individual rhetorical slants. As a result, while shows like *M*A*S*H*, *The Mary Tyler Moore Show*, and *All in the Family* may all treat similar issues, those issues will have different meanings because of the variations in character, tone, history, style, and so on, despite a general "liberal" tone. Other shows, minus that tone, will clash in varying degrees. The notion that they are all, in some sense, "situation comedies" does not adequately explain the treatment of ideas within them.

This hardly diminishes the strength of generic variation as yet another version of differences within the forum. The rhetoric of the soap opera *pattern* is different from that of the situation comedy and that of the detective show. Thus, when similar topics are treated within different generic frames another level of "discussion" is at work.

It is for this reason that we find it important to examine strips of television programming, "flow" as Raymond Williams refers to it.[15] Within these flow strips we may find opposing ideas abutting one another. We may find opposing treatments of the same ideas. And we will certainly find a viewing behavior that is more akin to actual experience than that found when concentrating on the individual show, the series, or the genre. The forum model, then, has led us into a new exploration of the definition of the television text. We are now examining the "viewing strip" as a potential text and are discovering that in the range of options offered by any given evening's television, the forum is indeed a more accurate model of what goes on *within* television than any other that we know of. By taping entire weeks of television content, and tracing various potential strips in the body of that week, we can construct a huge range of potential "texts" that may have been seen by individual viewers.

Each level of text—the strip as text, the television week, the television day—is compounded yet again by the history of the medium. Our hypothesis is that we might track the history of America's social discussions of the past three decades by examining the multiple rhetorics of television during that period. Given the problematic state of television archiving, a careful study of that hypothesis presents an enormous difficulty. It is, nevertheless, an exciting prospect.

Clearly, our emphasis is on the treatment of issues, on rhetoric. We recognize the validity of analytical structures that emphasize television's skewed demographic patterns, its particular social aberrations, or other "unrealistic distortions" of the world of experience. But we also recognize that in order to make sense of those structures and patterns researchers return again and again to the "meaning" of that television world, to the processes and problems of interpretation. In our view this practice is hardly limited to those of us who study television. It is also open to audiences who view it each evening and to professionals who create for the medium.

The goal of every producer is to create the difference that makes a difference, to maintain an audience with sufficient reference to the known and recognized, but to move ahead into something that distinguishes his show for the program buyer, the scheduler, and most importantly, for the mass audience. As recent work by Newcomb and Alley shows,[16] the goal of many producers, the most successful and powerful ones, is also to include personal ideas in their work, to use television as all artists use their media, as means of personal expression. Given this goal it is possible to examine the work of individual producers as other units of analysis and to compare the work of different producers as expressions within the forum. We need only think of the work of Quinn Martin and Jack Webb, or to contrast their work with that of Norman Lear or Gary Marshall, to recognize the individuality at work within television making. Choices by producers to work in certain generic forms, to express certain political, moral, and ethical attitudes, to explore certain sociocultural topics, all affect the nature of the ultimate "flow text" of television seen by viewers and assure a range of variations within that text.

The existence of this variation is borne out by varying responses among those who view television. A degree of this variance occurs among professional television critics who like and dislike shows for different reasons. But because television critics, certainly in American journalistic situations, are more alike than different in many ways, a more important indicator of the range of responses is that found among "ordinary" viewers, or the disagreements implied by audience acceptance and enthusiasm for program material soundly disavowed by professional critics. Work by Himmleweit in England[17] and Neuman in America[18] indicates that individual viewers do function as "critics," do make important distinctions, and are able, under certain circumstances, to articulate the bases for their judgments. While this work is just beginning, it is still possible to suggest from anecdotal evidence that people agree and disagree with television for a variety of reasons. They find in television texts representations of and challenges to their own ideas, and must somehow come to terms with what is there.

If disagreements cut too deeply into the value structure of the individual, if television threatens the sense of cultural security, the individual may take steps to engage the medium at the level of personal action. Most often this occurs in the form of letters to the network or to local stations, and again, the pattern is not new to television. It has occurred with every other mass medium in modern industrial society.

Nor is it merely the formation of groups or the expression of personal points of view that indicates the working of a forum. It is the *range* of response, the directly contradictory readings of the medium, that cue us to its multiple meanings. Groups may object to the same programs, for example, for entirely opposing reasons. In *Charlie's Angels* feminists may find yet another example of sexist repression, while fundamentalist religious groups may find examples of moral decay expressed in the sexual freedom, the personal appearance, or the "unfeminine" behavior of the protagonists. Other viewers doubtless find the expression of meaningful liberation of women. At this level, the point is hardly that one group is "right" and another "wrong," much less that one is "right" while the other is "left." Individuals and groups are, for many reasons, involved in making their own meanings from the television text.

This variation in interpretive strategies can be related to suggestions made by Stuart Hall in his influential essay, "Encoding and Decoding in the Television Discourse."[19] There he suggests three basic modes of interpretation, corresponding to the interpreter's political stance within the social structure. The interpretation may be "dominant," accepting the prevailing ideological structure. It may be "oppositional," rejecting the basic aspects of the structure. Or it may be "negotiated," creating a sort of personal synthesis. As later work by some of Hall's colleagues suggests, however, it quickly becomes necessary to expand the range of possible interpretations.[20] Following these suggestions to a radical extreme it might be possible to argue that every individual interpretation of television content could, in some way, be "different." Clearly, however, communication is dependent on a greater degree of shared meanings, and expressions of popular entertainment are perhaps even more dependent on the shared level than many other forms of discourse. Our concern then is for the ways in which interpretation is negotiated in society. Special interest groups that focus, at times, on television provide us with readily available resources for the study of interpretive practices.

We see these groups as representative of metaphoric "fault lines" in American society. Television is the terrain in which the faults are expressed and worked out. In studying the groups, their rhetoric, the issues on which they focus, their tactics, their forms of organization, we hope to demonstrate that the idea of the "forum" is more than a metaphor in its own right. In forming special interest groups, or in using such groups to speak about television, citizens actually enter the forum. Television shoves them toward action, toward expression of ideas and values. At this level the model of "television as a cultural forum" enables us to examine "the sociology of interpretation."

Here much attention needs to be given to the historical aspects of this form of activity. How has the definition of issues changed over time? How has that change correlated with change in the television texts? These are important questions which, while difficult to study, are crucial to a full understanding of the role of television in culture. It is primarily through this sort of study that we will be able to define much more precisely the limits of the forum, for groups form monitoring devices that alert us to shortcomings not only in the world of television representation, but to the world of political experience as well. We know, for example, that because of heightened concern on the part of special interest groups, and responses from the creative and institutional communities of television industries, the "fictional" population of black citizens now roughly equals that of the actual population. Regardless of whether such a match is "good" or "necessary," regardless of the nature of the depiction of blacks on television, this indicates that the forum extends beyond the screen. The issue of violence, also deserving close study, is more mixed, varying from year to year. The influence of groups, of individuals, of studies, of the terrible consequences of murder and assassination, however, cannot be denied. Television does not exist in a realm of its own, cut off from the influence of citizens. Our aim is to discover, as precisely as possible, the ways in which the varied worlds interact.

Throughout this kind of analysis, then, it is necessary to cite a range of varied responses to the texts of television. Using the viewing "strip" as the appropriate text of television, and recognizing that it is filled with varied topics and approaches to those topics, we begin to think of the television viewer as a *bricoleur* who matches the creator in the making of meanings. Bringing values and attitudes, a universe of personal experiences and concerns, to the texts, the viewer selects, examines, acknowledges, and makes texts of his or her own.[21] If we conceive of special interest groups as representatives of *patterns* of cultural attitude and response, we have a potent source of study.

On the production end of this process, in addition to the work of individual producers, we must examine the role of network executives who must purchase and program television content. They, too, are cultural interpreters, intent on "reading" the culture through its relation to the "market." Executives who head and staff the internal censor agencies of each network, the offices of Broadcast Standards or Standards and Practices, are in a similar position. Perhaps as much as any individual or group they present us with a source of rich material for analysis. They are actively engaged in gauging cultural values. Their own research, the assumptions and the findings, needs to be re-analyzed for cultural implications, as does the work of the programmers. In determining who is doing what, with whom, at what times, they are interpreting social behavior in America and assigning it meaning. They are using television as a cultural litmus that can be applied in defining such problematic concepts as "childhood," "family," "maturity," and "appropriate." With the Standards and Practices offices, they interpret *and* define the permissible and the "normal." But their interpretations of behavior open to us as many questions as answers, and an appropriate overview, a new model of television is necessary in order to best understand their work and ours.

This new model of "television as a cultural forum" fits the experience of television more accurately than others we have seen applied. Our assumption is that it opens a range of new questions and calls for re-analysis of older findings from both the textual-critical approach and the mass communications research perspective. Ultimately the new model is a simple one. It recognizes the range of interpretation of television content that is now admitted even by those analysts most concerned with television's presentation and maintenance of dominant ideological messages and meanings. But it differs from those perspectives because it does not see this as surprising or unusual. For the most part, that is what central storytelling systems do in all societies. We are far more concerned with the ways in which television contributes to change than with mapping the obvious ways in which it maintains dominant viewpoints. Most research on television, most textual analysis, has assumed that the medium is thin, repetitive, similar, nearly identical in textual formation, easily defined, described, and explained. The variety of response on the part of audiences has been received, as a result of this view, as extraordinary, an astonishing "discovery."

We begin with the observation, based on careful textual analysis, that television is dense, rich, and complex rather than impoverished. Any selection, any cut, any set of questions that is extracted from that text must somehow account for that density, must account for what is *not* studied or measured, for the opposing meanings, for the answering images and symbols. Audiences appear to make meaning by selecting that which touches experience and personal history. The range of responses then should be taken as commonplace rather than as unexpected. But research and critical analysis cannot afford so personal a view. Rather, they must somehow define and describe the inventory that makes possible the multiple meanings extracted by audiences, creators, and network decision makers.

Our model is based on the assumption and observation that only so rich a text could attract a mass audience in a complex culture. The forum offers a perspective that is as complex, as contradictory and confused, as much in process as American culture is in experience. Its texture matches that of our daily experiences. If we can understand it better, then perhaps we will better understand the world we live in, the actions that we must take in order to live there.

Notes

The authors would like to express their appreciation to the John and Mary R. Markle Foundation for support in the preparation of this [essay] and their ongoing study of the role of television as a cultural forum in American society. The ideas in this [essay] were first presented, in different form, at the seminar on "The Mass Production of Mythology," New York Institute for the Humanities, New York University, February 1981. Mary Douglas, Seminar Director.

1. James Carey, "A Cultural Approach to Communications," *Communications* 2 (December 1975).

2. Ibid.

3. James Carey, "Culture and Communications," *Communications Research* (April 1975).

4. See Roger Silverstone, *The Message of Television: Myth and Narrative in Contemporary Culture* (London: Heinemann, 1981), on structural and narrative analysis; John Fiske and John Hartley, *Reading Television* (London: Methuen, 1978), on the semiotic and cultural bases for the analysis of television; David Thorburn, *The Story Machine* (Oxford University Press: forthcoming), on the aesthetics of television; Himmleweit, Hilda et al., "The Audience as Critic: An Approach to the Study of Entertainment," in *The Entertainment Functions of Television,* ed. Percy Tannenbaum (New York: Lawrence Erlbaum Associates, 1980) and W. Russel Neuman, "Television and American Culture: The Mass Medium and the Pluralist Audience," *Public Opinion Quarterly,* 46: 4 (Winter 1982), pp. 471–87, on the role of the audience as critic; Todd Gitlin, "Prime Time Ideology: The Hegemonic Process in Television Entertainment," *Social Problems* 26:3 (1979), and Douglas Kellner, "TV, Ideology, and Emancipatory Popular Culture," *Socialist Review* 45 (May–June, 1979), on hegemony and new applications of critical theory; James T. Lull, "The Social Uses of Television," *Human Communications Research* 7:3 (1980), and "Family Communication Patterns and the Social Uses of Television," *Communications Research* 7: 3 (1979), and Tim Meyer, Paul Traudt, and James Anderson, "Non-Traditional Mass Communication Research Methods: Observational Case Studies of Media Use in Natural Settings, *Communication Yearbook IV,* ed. Dan Nimmo (New Brunswick, N.J.: Transaction Books), on audience ethnography and symbolic interactionism; and, most importantly, the ongoing work of The Center for Contemporary Cultural Studies at Birmingham University, England, most recently published in *Culture, Media, Language,* ed. Stuart Hall et al. (London: Hutchinson, in association with The Center for Contemporary Cultural Studies, 1980), on the interaction of culture and textual analysis from a thoughtful political perspective.

5. Carey, 1976.

6. Paul Hirsch, "The Role of Popular Culture and Television in Contemporary Society," *Television: The Critical View,* ed. Horace Newcomb (New York: Oxford University Press, 1979, 1982).

7. Marshall Sahlins, *Culture and Practical Reason* (Chicago: University of Chicago Press, 1976), p. 217.

8. John Cawelti, *Adventure, Mystery, and Romance* (Chicago: University of Chicago Press, 1976), and David Thorburn, "Television Melodrama," *Television: The Critical View* (New York: Oxford University Press, 1979, 1982).

9. Victor Turner, "Process, System, and Symbol: A New Anthropological Synthesis," *Daedalus* (Summer 1977), p. 68.

10. In various works Turner uses both the terms "liminal" and "liminoid" to refer to works of imagination and entertainment in contemporary culture. The latter term is used to clearly mark the distinction between events that have distinct behavioral consequences and those that do not. As Turner suggests, the consequences of entertainment in contemporary culture are hardly as profound as those of the liminal stage of ritual in traditional culture. We are aware of this basic distinction but use the former term in order to avoid a fuller explanation of the neologism. See Turner, "Afterword," to *The Reversible World*, Barbara Babcock, ed. (Ithaca: Cornell University Press, 1979), and "Liminal to Liminoid, in Play, Flow, and Ritual: An Essay in Comparative Symbology," *Rice University Studies*, 60:3 (1974).

11. Turner, 1977, p. 73.

12. Fiske and Hartley, 1978, p. 85.

13. We are indebted to Prof. Mary Douglas for encouraging this observation. At the presentation of these ideas at the New York Institute for the Humanities seminar on "The Mass Production of Mythology," she checked our enthusiasm for a pluralistic model of television by stating accurately and succinctly, "there are pluralisms and pluralisms." This comment led us to consider more thoroughly the means by which the forum and responses to it function as a tool with which to monitor the quality of pluralism in American social life, including its entertainments. The observation added a much needed component to our planned historical analysis.

14. Stanley Cavell, "The Fact of Television," *Daedalus* 3: 4 (Fall 1982).

15. Raymond Williams, *Television, Technology and Cultural Form* (New York: Schocken, 1971), p. 86 ff.

16. Horace Newcomb and Robert Alley, *The Television Producer as Artist in American Commercial Television* (New York: Oxford University Press, 1983).

17. Ibid.

18. Ibid.

19. Stuart Hall, "Encoding and Decoding in the Television Discourse," *Culture, Media, Language* (London: Hutchinson, in association with The Center for Contemporary Cultural Studies, 1980).

20. See Dave Morley and Charlotte Brunsdon, *Everyday Television: "Nationwide"* (London: British Film Institute, 1978), and Morley, "Subjects, Readers, Texts," in *Culture, Media, Language*.

21. We are indebted to Louis Black and Eric Michaels of the Radio-TV-Film department of the University of Texas-Austin for calling this aspect of televiewing to Newcomb's attention. It creates a much desired balance to Sahlin's view of the creator as *bricoleur* and indicates yet another matter in which the forum model enhances our ability to account for more aspects of the television experience. See, especially, Eric Michaels, *TV Tribes*, unpublished Ph.D. dissertation, University of Texas-Austin, 1982.

Prime Time Ideology

The Hegemonic Process
in Television Entertainment

TODD GITLIN

Every society works to reproduce itself—and its internal conflicts—within
its cultural order, the structure of practices and meanings around which the
society takes shape. So much is tautology. In this [essay] I look at contemporary mass media in the United States as one cultural system promoting that reproduction. I try to show how ideology is relayed through various features of American television, and how television programs register
larger ideological structures and changes. The question here is not, What is
the impact of these programs? but rather a prior one, What do these programs mean? For only after thinking through their possible meanings as cultural objects and as signs of cultural interactions among producers and audiences may we begin intelligibly to ask about their "effects."

The attempt to understand the sources and transformations of ideology
in American society has been leading social theorists not only to social-
psychological investigations, but to a long overdue interest in Antonio
Gramsci's (1971) notion of ideological hegemony. It was Gramsci who, in
the late twenties and thirties, with the rise of fascism and the failure of the
Western European working-class movements, began to consider why the
working class was not necessarily revolutionary; why it could, in fact, yield
to fascism. Condemned to a fascist prison precisely because the insurrec-
tionary workers' movement in Northern Italy just after World War I failed,
Gramsci spent years trying to account for the defeat, resorting in large measure to the concept of hegemony: bourgeois domination of the thought,

---

© 1979 by the Society for the Study of Social Problems. Reprinted from *Social Problems,* vol. 26, no. 3, February 1979, pp. 251–66, by permission.

the common sense, the life-ways and everyday assumptions of the working class. Gramsci counterposed "hegemony" to "coercion"; these were two analytically distinct processes through which ruling classes secure the consent of the dominated. Gramsci did not always make plain where to draw the line between hegemony and coercion; or rather, as Perry Anderson shows convincingly (1976),[1] he drew the line differently at different times. Nonetheless, ambiguities aside, Gramsci's distinction was a great advance for radical thought, for it called attention to the routine structures of everyday thought—down to "common sense" itself—which worked to sustain class domination and tyranny. That is to say, paradoxically, it took the working class seriously enough as a potential agent of revolution to hold it accountable for its failures.

Because Leninism failed abysmally throughout the West, Western Marxists and non-Marxist radicals have both been drawn back to Gramsci, hoping to address the evident fact that the Western working classes are not predestined toward socialist revolution.[2] In Europe this fact could be taken as strategic rather than normative wisdom on the part of the working class; but in America the working class is not only hostile to revolutionary *strategy*, it seems to disdain the socialist *goal* as well. At the very least, although a recent Peter Hart opinion poll showed that Americans abstractly "favor" workers' control, Americans do not seem to care enough about it to organize very widely in its behalf. While there are abundant "contradictions" throughout American society, they are played out substantially in the realm of "culture" or "ideology," which orthodox Marxism had consigned to the secondary category of "superstructure." Meanwhile, critical theory—especially in the work of T. W. Adorno and Max Horkheimer—had argued with great force that the dominant forms of commercial ("mass") culture were crystallizations of authoritarian ideology; yet despite the ingenuity and brilliance of particular feats of critical exegesis (Adorno, 1954, 1974; Adorno and Horkheimer, 1972), they seemed to be arguing that the "culture industry" was not only meretricious but wholly and statically complete. In the seventies, some of their approaches along with Gramsci's have been elaborated and furthered by Alvin W. Gouldner (1976; see also Kellner, 1978) and Raymond Williams (1973), in distinctly provocative ways.

In this [essay] I wish to contribute to the process of bringing the discussion of cultural hegemony down to earth. For much of the discussion so far remains abstract, almost as if cultural hegemony were a substance with a life of its own, a sort of immutable fog that has settled over the whole public life of capitalist societies to confound the truth of the proletarian telos. Thus to the questions, "Why are radical ideas suppressed in the schools?", "Why do workers oppose socialism?" and so on, comes the single Delphic answer: hegemony. "Hegemony" becomes the magical explanation of last resort. And as such it is useful neither as explanation nor as guide to action. If "hegemony" explains everything in the sphere of culture, it explains nothing.

Concurrent with the theoretical discussion, but on a different plane, looms an entire sub-industry criticizing and explicating specific mass-cultural products and straining to find "emancipatory" if not "revolutionary" meanings in them. Thus in 1977 there was cacophony about the TV version of *Roots;* this year the trend-setter seems to be TV's handling of violence. Mass media criticism becomes mass-mediated, an auxiliary sideshow serving cultural producers as well as the wider public of the cultural spectacle. Piece by piece we see fast and furious analysis of this movie, that TV show, that book, that spectator sport. Many of these pieces have merit one by one, but as a whole they do not accumulate toward a more general theory of how the cultural forms are managed and reproduced—and how they change. Without analytic point, item-by-item analyses of the standard fare of mass culture rurr the risk of degenerating into high-toned gossip, even a kind of critical groupie-ism. Unaware of the ambiguity of their own motives and strategies, the partial critics may be yielding to a displaced envy, where criticism covertly asks to be taken into the spotlight along with the celebrity culture ostensibly under criticism. Yet another trouble is that partial critiques in the mass-culture tradition don't help us understand the *hold* and the *limits* of cultural products, the degree to which people do and do not incorporate mass-cultural forms, sing the jingles, wear the corporate T-shirts, and most important, permit their life-worlds to be demarcated by them.

My task in what follows is to propose some features of a lexicon for discussing the forms of hegemony in the concrete. Elsewhere I have described some of the operations of cultural hegemony in the sphere of television news, especially in the news's framing procedures for opposition movements (Gitlin, 1977a,b).[3] Here I wish to speak of the realm of entertainment: about television entertainment in particular—as the most pervasive and (in the living room sense) *familiar* of our cultural sites—and about movies secondarily. How do the *formal* devices of TV prime time programs encourage viewers to experience themselves as anti-political, privately accumulating individuals (also see Gitlin, 1977c)? And how do these forms express social conflict, containing and diverting the images of contrary social possibilities? I want to isolate a few of the routine devices, though of course in reality they do not operate in isolation; rather, they work in combination, where their force is often enough magnified (though they can also work in contradictory ways). And, crucially, it must be borne in mind throughout this discussion that the forms of mass-cultural production do not either spring up or operate independently of the rest of social life. Commercial culture does not *manufacture* ideology; it *relays* and *reproduces* and *processes* and *packages* and *focuses* ideology that is constantly arising both from social elites and from active social groups and movements throughout the society (as well as within media organizations and practices).

A more complete analysis of ideological process in a commercial society would look both above and below, to elites and to audiences. Above, it would take a long look at the economics and politics of broadcasting, at its relation to the FCC, the Congress, the President, the courts; in case studies and with a developing theory of ideology it would study media's peculiar combination and refraction of corporate, political, bureaucratic, and professional interests, giving the media a sort of limited independence—or what Marxists are calling "relative autonomy"—in the upper reaches of the political-economic system. Below, as Raymond Williams has insisted, cultural hegemony operates within a whole social life-pattern; the people who consume mass-mediated products are also the people who work, reside, compete, go to school, live in families. And there are a good many traditional and material interests at stake for audiences: the political inertia of the American population now, for example, certainly has something to do with the continuing productivity of the goods-producing and -distributing industries, not simply with the force of mass culture. Let me try to avoid misunderstanding at the outset by insisting that *I will not be arguing that the forms of hegemonic entertainment superimpose themselves automatically and finally onto the consciousness or behavior of all audiences at all times:* it remains for sociologists to generate what Dave Morley (1974)[4] has called "an ethnography of audiences," and to study what Ronald Abramson (1978) calls "the phenomenology of audiences" if we are to have anything like a satisfactory account of how audiences consciously and unconsciously process, transform, and are transformed by the contents of television. For many years the subject of media effects was severely narrowed by a behaviorist definition of the problem (see Gitlin, 1978a); more recently, the "agenda-setting function" of mass media has been usefully studied in news media, but not in entertainment. (On the other hand, the very pervasiveness of TV entertainment makes laboratory study of its "effects" almost inconceivable.) It remains to incorporate occasional sociological insights into the actual behavior of TV audiences[5] into a more general theory of the interaction—a theory which avoids both the mechanical assumptions of behaviorism and the trivialities of the "uses and gratifications" approach.

But alas, that more general theory of the interaction is not on the horizon. My more modest attempt in this extremely preliminary essay is to sketch an approach to the hegemonic thrust of some TV forms, not to address the deflection, resistance, and reinterpretation achieved by audiences. I will show that hegemonic ideology is systematically preferred by certain features of TV programs, and that at the same time alternative and oppositional values are brought into the cultural system, and domesticated into hegemonic forms at times, by the routine workings of the market. Hegemony is reasserted in different ways at different times, even by different logics; if this variety is analytically messy, the messiness corresponds to a disordered ideological order, a contradictory society. This said, I proceed to some of the forms in which ideological hegemony is embedded: *format and formula; genre; setting and character type; slant;* and *solution.* Then these particulars will suggest a somewhat more fully developed theory of hegemony.

Format and Formula

Until recently at least, the TV schedule has been dominated by standard lengths and cadences, standardized packages of TV entertainment appearing, as the announcers used to say, "same time, same station." This week-to-week-ness—or, in the case of soap operas, day-to-dayness—obstructed the development of characters; at least the primary characters had to be preserved intact for next week's show. Perry Mason was Perry Mason, once and for all; if you watched the reruns, you couldn't know from character or set whether you were watching the first or the last in the series. For commercial and production reasons which are in practice inseparable—and this is why ideological hegemony is not reducible to the economic interests of elites—the regular schedule prefers the repeatable formula: it is far easier for production companies to hire writers to write for standardized, static characters than for characters who develop. Assembly-line production works through regularity of time slot, of duration, and of character to convey images of social steadiness: come what may, *Gunsmoke* or *Kojak* will check in to your mind at a certain time on a certain evening. Should they lose ratings (at least at the "upscale" reaches of the "demographics," where ratings translate into disposable dollars),[6] their replacements would be—for a time, at least!—equally reliable. Moreover, the standard curve of narrative action—stock characters encounter new version of stock situation; the plot thickens, allowing stock characters to show their standard stuff; the plot resolves—over twenty-two or fifty minutes is itself a source of rigidity and forced regularity.

In these ways, the usual programs are performances that rehearse social fixity: they express and cement the obduracy of a social world impervious to substantial change. Yet at the same time there are signs of routine obsolescence, as hunks of last year's regular schedule drop from sight only to be supplanted by this season's attractions. Standardization and the threat of evanescence are curiously linked: they match the intertwined processes of commodity production, predictability, and obsolescence in a high-consumption society. I speculate that they help instruct audiences in the rightness and naturalness of a world that, in only apparent paradox, regularly requires an irregularity, an unreliability which it calls progress. In this way, the regular changes in TV programs, like the regular elections of public officials, seem to affirm the sovereignty of the audience while keeping deep alternatives off the agenda. Elite authority and consumer choice are affirmed at once—this is one of the central operations of the hegemonic liberal capitalist ideology.

Then, too, by organizing the "free time" of persons into end-to-end interchangeable units, broadcasting extends, and harmonizes with, the industrialization of time. Media time and school time, with their equivalent units and curves of action, mirror the time of clocked labor and reinforce the seeming naturalness of clock time. Anyone who reads Harry Braverman's *Labor and Monopoly Capital* can trace the steady degradation of the work process, both white and blue collar, through the twentieth century, even if Braverman has exaggerated the extent of the process by focusing on managerial *strategies* more than on actual work *processes*. Something similar has happened in other life-sectors.[7] Leisure is industrialized, duration is homogenized, even excitement is routinized, and the standard repeated TV format is an important component of the process. And typically, too, capitalism provides relief from these confines for its more favored citizens, those who can afford to buy their way out of the standardized social reality which capitalism produces. Thus Sony and RCA now sell home video recorders, enabling customers to tape programs they'd otherwise miss. The widely felt need to overcome assembly-line "leisure" time becomes the source of a new market—to sell the means for private, commoditized solutions to the time-jam.

Commercials, of course, are also major features of the regular TV format. There can be no question but that commercials have a good deal to do with shaping and maintaining markets—no advertiser dreams of cutting advertising costs as long as the competition is still on the air. But commercials also have important *indirect* consequences on the contours of consciousness overall: they get us accustomed to thinking of ourselves and behaving as a *market* rather than a *public,* as consumers rather than citizens. Public problems (like air pollution) are propounded as susceptible to private commodity solutions (like eyedrops). In the process, commercials acculturate us to interruption through the rest of our lives. Time and attention are not one's own; the established social powers have the capacity to colonize consciousness, and unconsciousness, as they see fit. By watching, the audience one by one consents. Regardless of the commercial's "effect" on our behavior, we are consenting to its domination of the public space. Yet we should note that this colonizing process does not actually require commercials, as long as it can form discrete packages of ideological content that call forth discontinuous responses in the audience. Even public broadcasting's children's shows take over the commercial forms to their own educational ends—and supplant narrative forms by herky-jerky bustle. The producers of *Sesame Street,* in likening knowledge to commercial products ("and now a message from the letter B"), may well be legitimizing the commercial form in its discontinuity and in its invasiveness. Again, regularity and discontinuity, superficially discrepant, may be linked at a deep level of meaning. And perhaps the deepest privatizing function of television, its most powerful impact on public life, may lie in the most obvious thing about it: we receive the images in the privacy of our living rooms, making public discourse and response difficult. At the same time, the paradox is that at any given time many viewers are receiving images discrepant with many of their beliefs, challenging their received opinions.

TV routines have been built into the broadcast schedule since its inception. But arguably their regularity has been waning since Norman Lear's first comedy, *All in the Family,* made its network debut in 1971. Lear's contribution to TV content was obvious: where previous shows might have made passing reference to social conflict, Lear brought wrenching social issues into the very mainspring of his series, uniting his characters, as Michael Arlen once pointed out, in a harshly funny *resentment* peculiarly appealing to audiences of the Nixon era and its cynical, disabused sequel.[8] As I'll argue below, the hegemonic ideology is maintained in the seventies by *domesticating* divisive issues where in the fifties it would have simply *ignored* them.

Lear also let his characters develop. Edith Bunker grew less sappy and more feminist and commonsensical; Gloria and Mike moved next door, and finally to California. On the threshold of this generational rupture, Mike broke through his stereotype by expressing affection for Archie, and Archie, oh-so-reluctantly but definitely for all that, hugged back and broke through his own. And of course other Lear characters, the Jeffersons and Maude, had earlier been spun off into their own shows, as *The Mary Tyler Moore Show* had spawned *Rhoda* and *Phyllis*. These changes resulted from commercial decisions; they were built on intelligent business perceptions that an audience existed for situation comedies directly addressing racism, sexism, and the decomposition of conventional families. But there is no such thing as a strictly economic "explanation" for production choice, since the success of a show—despite market research—is not foreordained. In the context of my argument, the importance of such developments lies in their partial break with the established, static formulae of prime time television.

Evidently daytime soap operas have also been sliding into character development and a direct exploitation of divisive social issues, rather than going on constructing a race-free, class-free, feminism-free world. And more conspicuously, the "mini-series" has now disrupted the taken-for-granted repetitiveness of the prime time format. Both content and form mattered to the commercial success of *Roots;* certainly the industry, speaking through trade journals, was convinced that the phenomenon was rooted in the series' break with the week-to-week format. When the programming wizards at ABC decided to put the show on for eight straight nights, they were also, inadvertently, making it possible for characters to *develop* within the bounds of a single show. And of course they were rendering the whole sequence immensely more powerful than if it had been diffused over eight weeks. The very format was testimony to the fact that history takes place as a continuing process in which people grow up, have children, die; that people experience their lives within the domain of social institutions. This is no small achievement in a country that routinely denies the rich texture of history.

In any event, the first thing that industry seems to have learned from its success with *Roots* is that they had a new hot formula, the night-after-night series with some claim to historical verisimilitude. So, according to *Broadcasting*, they began preparing a number of "docu-drama" series, of which 1977's products included NBC's three-part series *Loose Change* and *King*, and its four-part *Holocaust*, this latter evidently planned before the *Roots* broadcast. How many of those first announced as in progress will actually be broadcast is something else again—one awaits the networks' domestication and trivializing of the radicalism of *All God's Children: The Life of Nate Shaw*, announced in early 1977. *Roots'* financial success—ABC sold its commercial minutes for $120,000, compared to that season's usual $85,000 to $90,000—might not be repeatable. Perhaps the network could not expect audiences to tune in more than once every few years to a series that began one night at eight o'clock, the next night at nine, and the next at eight again. In summary it is hard to say to what extent these format changes signify an acceleration of the networks' competition for advertising dollars, and to what extent they reveal the networks' responses to the restiveness and boredom of the mass audience, or the emergence of new potential audiences. But in any case the shifts are there, and constitute a fruitful territory for any thinking about the course of popular culture.

Genre[9]

The networks try to finance and choose programs that will likely attract the largest conceivable audiences of spenders; this imperative requires that the broadcasting elites have in mind some notion of popular taste from moment to moment. Genre, in other words, is necessarily somewhat sensitive; in its rough outlines, if not in detail, it tells us something about popular moods. Indeed, since there are only three networks, there is something of an over-sensitivity to a given success; the pendulum tends to swing hard to replicate a winner. Thus *Charlie's Angels* engenders *Flying High* and *American Girls*, about stewardesses and female reporters respectively, each on a long leash under male authority.

Here I suggest only a few signs of this sensitivity to shifting moods and group identities in the audience. The adult western of the middle and late fifties, with its drama of solitary righteousness and suppressed libidinousness, for example, can be seen in retrospect to have played on the quiet malaise under the surface of the complacency of the Eisenhower years, even in contradictory ways. Some lone heroes were identified with traditionally frontier-American informal and individualistic relations to authority (Paladin in *Have Gun, Will Travel*, Bart Maverick in *Maverick*), standing for sturdy individualism struggling for hedonistic values and taking law-and-order wryly. Meanwhile, other heroes were decent officials like *Gunsmoke's* Matt Dillon, affirming the decency of paternalistic law and order against the temptations of worldly pleasure. With the rise of the Camelot mystique, and the vigorous "long twilight struggle" that John F. Kennedy personified, spy stories like *Mission: Impossible* and *The Man From U.N.C.L.E.* were well suited to capitalize on the macho CIA aura. More recently, police stories, with cops surmounting humanist illusions to draw thin blue lines against anarchocriminal barbarism, afford a variety of official ways of coping with "the social issue," ranging from *Starsky and Hutch's* muted homoeroticism to *Barney Miller's* team pluralism. The single-women shows following from *Mary Tyler Moore* acknowledge in their privatized ways that some sort of feminism is here to stay, and work to contain it with hilarious versions of "new life styles" for single career women. Such shows probably appeal to the market of "upscale" singles with relatively large disposable incomes, women who are disaffected from the traditional imagery of housewife and helpmeet. In the current wave of "jiggle" or "T&A" shows patterned on *Charlie's Angels* (the terms are widely used in the industry), the attempt is to appeal to the prurience of the male audience by keeping the "girls" free of romance, thus catering to male (and female?) backlash against feminism. The black sitcoms probably reflect the rise of a black middle class with the purchasing power to bring forth advertisers, while also appealing *as comedies*—for conflicting reasons, perhaps—to important parts of the white audience. (Serious black drama would be far more threatening to the majority audience.)

Whenever possible it is illuminating to trace the transformations in a genre over a longer period of time. For example, the shows of technological prowess have metamorphosed over four decades as hegemonic ideology has been contested by alternative cultural forms. In work not yet published, Tom Andrae of the Political Science Department at the University of California, Berkeley, shows how the Superman archetype began in 1933 as a menace to society; then became something of a New Dealing, anti-Establishmentarian individualist casting his lot with the oppressed and, at times, against the State; and only in the forties metamorphosed into the current incarnation who prosecutes criminals in the name of "the American way." Then the straight-arrow Superman of the forties and fifties was supplemented by the whimsical, self-satirical Batman and the Marvel Comics series of the sixties and seventies, symbols of power gone silly, no longer prepossessing. In playing against the conventions, their producers seem to have been exhibiting the self-consciousness of genre so popular among "high arts" too, as with Pop and minimal art. Thus shifts in genre presuppose the changing mentality of critical masses of writers and cultural producers; yet these changes would not take root commercially without corresponding changes in the dispositions (even the self-consciousness) of large audiences. In other words, changes in cultural ideals and in audience sensibilities must be harmonized to make for shifts in genre or formula.

Finally, the latest form of technological hero corresponds to an authoritarian turn in hegemonic ideology, as well as to a shift in popular (at least children's) mentality. The seventies generation of physically augmented, obedient, patriotic superheroes (*The Six Million Dollar Man* and *The Bionic Woman*) differ from the earlier waves in being organizational products through and through; these team players have no private lives from which they are recruited task by task, as in *Mission: Impossible,* but they are actually *invented* by the State, to whom they owe their lives.

Televised sports too is best understood as an entertainment genre, one of the most powerful.[10] What we know as professional sports today is inseparably intertwined with the networks' development of the sports market. TV sports is rather consistently framed to reproduce dominant American values. First, although TV is ostensibly a medium for the eyes, the sound is often decisive in taking the action off the field. The audience is not trusted to come to its own conclusions. The announcers are not simply describing events ("Reggie Jackson hits a ground ball to shortstop"), but interpreting them ("World Series 1978! It's great to be here"). One may see here a process equivalent to advertising's project of taking human qualities out of the consumer and removing them to the product: sexy perfume, zesty beer.

In televised sports, the hegemonic impositions have, if anything, probably become more intense over the last twenty years. One technique for interpreting the event is to regale the audience with bits of information in the form of "stats." "A lot of people forget they won eleven out of their last twelve games. . . ." "There was an extraordinary game in last year's World Series. . . ." "Rick Barry hasn't missed two free throws in a row for 72 games. . . ." "The last time the Warriors were in Milwaukee Clifford Ray *also* blocked two shots in the second quarter." How *about* that? The announcers can't shut up; they're constantly chattering. And the stat flashed on the screen further removes the action from the field. What is one to make of all this? Why would anyone want to know a player's free throw percentage not only during the regular season but during the playoffs?

But the trivialities have their reason: they amount to an interpretation that flatters and disdains the audience at the same time. It flatters in small ways, giving you the chance to be the one person on the block who already possessed this tidbit of fact. At the same time, symbolically, it treats you as someone who really knows what's going on in the world. Out of control of social reality, you may flatter yourself that the substitute world of sports is a corner of the world you can really grasp. Indeed, throughout modern society, the availability of statistics is often mistaken for the availability of knowledge and deep meaning. To know the number of megatons in the nuclear arsenal is not to grasp its horror; but we are tempted to bury our fear in the possession of comforting fact. To have made "body counts" in Vietnam was not to be in control of the countryside, but the U.S. Army flattered itself that the stats looked good. TV sports shows, encouraging the audience to value stats, harmonize with a stat-happy society. Not that TV operates independently of the sports event itself; in fact, the event is increasingly organized to fit the structure of the broadcast. There are extra time-outs to permit the network to sell more commercial time. Michael Real of San Diego State University used a stopwatch to calculate that during the 1974 Super Bowl, the football was actually moving for—seven minutes (Real, 1977). Meanwhile, electronic billboards transplant the stats into the stadium itself.

Another framing practice is the reduction of the sports experience to a sequence of individual achievements. In a fusion of populist and capitalist dogma, everyone is somehow the best. This one has "great hands," this one has "a great slam dunk," that one's "great on defense." This indiscriminate commendation raises the premium on personal competition, and at the same time undermines the meaning of personal achievement: everyone is excellent at something, as at a child's birthday party. I was most struck by the force of this sort of framing during the NBA basketball playoffs of 1975, when, after a season of hearing Bill King announce the games over local KTVU, I found myself watching and hearing the network version. King's Warriors were not CBS's. A fine irony: King with his weird mustache and San Francisco panache was talking about team relations and team strategy; CBS, with its organization-man team of announcers, could talk of little besides the personal records of the players. Again, at one point during the 1977 basketball playoffs, CBS's Brent Musburger gushed: "I've got one of the greatest players of all time [Rick Barry] and one of the greatest referees of all time [Mendy Rudolph] sitting next to me! . . . I'm surrounded by experts!" All in all, the network exalts statistics, personal competition, expertise. The message is: The way to understand things is by storing up statistics and tracing their trajectories. This is training in observation without comprehension.

Everything is technique and know-how; nothing is purpose. Likewise, the instant replay generates the thrill of recreating the play, even second-guessing the referee. The appeal is to the American tradition of exalting means over ends: this is the same spirit that animates popular science magazines and do-it-yourself. It's a complicated and contradictory spirit, one that lends itself to the preservation of craft values in a time of assembly-line production, and at the same time distracts interest from any desire to control the goals of the central work process.

The significance of this fetishism of means is hard to decipher. Though the network version appeals to technical thinking, the announcers are not only small-minded but incompetent to boot. No sooner have they dutifully complimented a new acquisition as "a fine addition to the club" than often enough he flubs a play. But still they function as cheerleaders, revving up the razzle-dazzle rhetoric and reminding us how uniquely favored we are by the spectacle. By staying tuned in, somehow we're "participating" in sports history—indeed, by proxy, in history itself. The pulsing theme music and electronic logo reinforce this sense of hot-shot glamor. The breathlessness never lets up, and it has its pecuniary motives: if we can be convinced that the game really is fascinating (even if it's a dog), we're more likely to stay tuned for the commercials for which Miller Lite and Goodyear have paid $100,000 a minute to rent our attention.

On the other hand, the network version does not inevitably succeed in forcing itself upon our consciousness and defining our reception of the event. TV audiences don't necessarily succumb to the announcers' hype. In semi-public situations like barrooms, audiences are more likely to see through the trivialization and ignorance and—in "para-social interaction"—to tell the announcers off. But in the privacy of living rooms, the announcers' framing probably penetrates farther into the collective definition of the event. It should not be surprising that one fairly common counter-hegemonic practice is to watch the broadcast picture without the network sound, listening to the local announcer on the radio.

Setting and Character Type

Closely related to genre and its changes are setting and character type. And here again we see shifting market tolerances making for certain changes in content, while the core of hegemonic values remains virtually impervious.

In the fifties, when the TV forms were first devised, the standard TV series presented—in Herbert Gold's phrase—happy people with happy problems. In the seventies it is more complicated: there are unhappy people with happy ways of coping. But the set itself propounds a vision of consumer happiness. Living rooms and kitchens usually display the standard package of consumer goods. Even where the set is ratty, as in *Sanford and Son,* or working-class, as in *All in the Family,* the bright color of the TV tube almost always glamorizes the surroundings so that there will be no sharp break between the glorious color of the program and the glorious color of the commercial. In the more primitive fifties, by contrast, it was still possible for a series like *The Honeymooners* or *The Phil Silvers Show* (Sergeant Bilko) to get by with one or two simple sets per show: the life of a good skit was in its accomplished *acting.* But that series, in its sympathetic treatment of working-class mores, was exceptional. Color broadcasting accomplishes the glamorous ideal willy-nilly.

Permissible character types have evolved, partly because of changes in the structure of broadcasting power. In the fifties, before the quiz show scandal, advertising agencies contracted directly with production companies to produce TV series (Barnouw, 1970). They ordered up exactly what they wanted, as if by the yard; and with some important but occasional exceptions—I'll mention some in a moment—what they wanted was glamor and fun, a showcase for commercials. In 1954, for example, one agency wrote to the playwright Elmer Rice explaining why his *Street Scene,* with its "lower class social level," would be unsuitable for telecasting:

> We know of no advertiser or advertising agency of any importance in this country who would knowingly allow the products which he is trying to advertise to the public to become associated with the squalor . . . and general "down" character . . . of *Street Scene.* . . .
>
> On the contrary it is the general policy of advertisers to glamorize their products, the people who buy them, and the whole American social and economic scene. . . . The American consuming public as presented by the advertising industry today is middle class, not lower class; happy in general, not miserable and frustrated. . . . (Barnouw, 1970:33)

Later in the fifties, comedies were able to represent discrepant settings, permitting viewers both to identify and to indulge their sense of superiority through comic distance: *The Honeymooners* and *Bilko,* which capitalized on Jackie Gleason's and Phil Silver's enormous personal popularity (a personality cult can always perform wonders and break rules), were able to extend dignity to working-class characters in anti-glamorous situations (see Czitrom, 1977).

Beginning in 1960, the networks took direct control of production away from advertisers. And since the networks are less provincial than particular advertisers, since they are more closely attuned to general tolerances in the population, and since they are firmly in charge of a buyer's market for advertising (as long as they produce shows that *some* corporation will sponsor), it now became possible—if by no means easy—for independent production companies to get somewhat distinct cultural forms, like Norman Lear's comedies, on the air. The near-universality of television set ownership, at the same time, creates the possibility of a wider range of audiences, including minority-group, working-class and age-segmented audiences, than existed in the fifties, and thus makes possible a wider range of fictional characters. Thus changes in the organization of TV production, as well as new market pressures, have helped to change the prevalent settings and character types on television.

But the power of corporate ideology over character types remains very strong, and sets limits on the permissible; the changes from the fifties through the sixties and seventies should be understood in the context of essential cultural features that have *not* changed. To show the quality of deliberate choice that is often operating, consider a book called *The Youth Market,* by two admen, published in 1970, counseling companies on ways to pick "the right character for your product":

> But in our opinion, if you want to create your own hardhitting spokesman to children, the most effective route is the superhero-miracle worker. He certainly can demonstrate food products, drug items, many kinds of toys, and innumerable household items. . . . The character should be adventurous. And he should be on the right side of the law. A child must be able to mimic his hero, whether he is James Bond, Superman or Dick Tracy; to be able to fight and shoot to kill without punishment or guilt feelings. (Helitzer and Heyel, 1970)

If this sort of thinking is resisted within the industry itself, it's not so much because of commitments to artistry in television as such, but more because there are other markets that are not "penetrated" by these hard-hitting heroes. The industry is noticing, for example, that *Roots* brought to the tube an audience who don't normally watch TV. The homes-using-television levels during the week of *Roots* were up between 6 and 12 percent over the programs of the previous year (*Broadcasting,* January 31, 1977). Untapped markets—often composed of people who have, or wish to have, somewhat alternative views of the world—can only be brought in by unusual sorts of programming. There is room in the schedule for rebellious human slaves just as there is room for hard-hitting patriotic-technological heroes. In other words—and contrary to a simplistic argument against television manipulation by network elites—the receptivity of enormous parts of the population is an important limiting factor affecting what gets on television. On the other hand, network elites do not risk investing in *regular* heroes who will challenge the core values of corporate capitalist society: who are, say, explicit socialists, or union organizers, or for that matter born-again evangelists. But like the dramatic series *Playhouse 90* in the fifties, TV movies permit a somewhat wider range of choice than weekly series. It is apparently easier for producers to sell exceptional material for one-shot showings—whether sympathetic to lesbian mothers, critical of the 1950s blacklist or of Senator Joseph McCarthy. Most likely these important exceptions have prestige value for the networks.

Slant

Within the formula of a program, a specific slant often pushes through, registering a certain position on a particular public issue. When issues are politically charged, when there is overt social conflict, programs capitalize on the currency. ("Capitalize" is an interesting word, referring both to use and to profit.) In the program's brief compass, only the most stereotyped characters are deemed to "register" on the audience, and therefore slant, embedded in character, is almost always simplistic and thin. The specific slant is sometimes mistaken for the whole of ideological tilt or "bias," as if the bias dissolves when no position is taken on a topical issue. But the week-after-week angle of the show is more basic, a hardened definition of a routine situation *within which* the specific topical slant emerges. The occasional topical slant then seems to anchor the program's general meanings. For instance, a 1977 show of *The Six Million Dollar Man* told the story of a Russian-East German plot to stop the testing of the new B-1 bomber; by implication, it linked the domestic movement against the B-1 to the foreign Red menace. Likewise, in the late sixties and seventies, police and spy dramas have commonly clucked over violent terrorists and heavily armed "anarchist" maniacs, labeled as "radicals" or "revolutionaries," giving the cops a chance to justify their heavy armament and crude machismo. But the other common variety of slant is sympathetic to forms of deviance which are either private (the lesbian mother shown to be a good mother to her children) or quietly reformist (the brief vogue for *Storefront Lawyers* and the like in the early seventies). The usual slants, then, fall into two categories: either (a) a legitimation of depoliticized forms of deviance, usually ethnic or sexual; or (b) a delegitimation of the dangerous, the violent, the out-of-bounds.

The slants that find their way into network programs, in short, are not uniform. Can we say anything systematic about them? Whereas in the fifties family dramas and sit-coms usually ignored—or indirectly sublimated—the existence of deep social problems in the world outside the set, programs of the seventies much more often domesticate them. From *Ozzie and Harriet* or *Father Knows Best* to *All in the Family* or *The Jeffersons* marks a distinct shift for formula, character, and slant: a shift, among other things, in the image of how a family copes with the world outside. Again, changes in content have in large part to be referred back to changes in social values and sensibilities, particularly the values of writers, actors, and other practitioners: there is a large audience now that prefers acknowledging and domesticating social problems directly rather than ignoring them or treating them only indirectly and in a sublimated way; there are also media practitioners who have some roots in the rebellions of the sixties. Whether hegemonic style will operate more by exclusion (fifties) than by domestication (seventies) will depend on the level of public dissensus as well as on internal factors of media organization (the fifties blacklist of TV writers probably exercised a chilling effect on subject matter and slant; so did the fact that sponsors directly developed their own shows).

Solution

Finally, cultural hegemony operates through the solutions proposed to difficult problems. However grave the problems posed, however rich the imbroglio, the episodes regularly end with the click of a solution: an arrest, a defiant smile, an I-told-you-so explanation. The characters we have been asked to care about are alive and well, ready for next week. Such a world is not so much fictional as fake. However deeply the problem is located within society, it will be solved among a few persons: the heroes must attain a solution that leaves the rest of the society untouched. The self-enclosed world of the TV drama justifies itself, and its exclusions, by "wrapping it all up." Occasional exceptions are either short-lived, like *East Side, West Side,* or independently syndicated outside the networks, like Lear's *Mary Hartman, Mary Hartman.* On the networks, *All in the Family* has been unusual in sometimes ending obliquely, softly, or ironically, refusing to pretend to solve a social problem that cannot, in fact, be solved by the actions of the Bunkers alone. The Lou Grant show is also partial to downbeat, alienating endings.

Likewise, in mid-seventies mass-market films like *Chinatown, Rollerball, Network,* and *King Kong,* we see an interesting form of closure: as befits the common cynicism and helplessness, society owns the victory. Reluctant heroes go up against vast impersonal forces, often multinational corporations like the same Gulf & Western (sent up as "Engulf & Devour" in Mel Brook's *Silent Movie*) that, through its Paramount subsidiary, produces some of these films. Driven to anger or bitterness by the evident corruption, the rebels break loose—only to bring the whole structure crashing down on them. (In the case of *King Kong,* the great ape falls of his own weight— from the World Trade Center roof, no less—after the helicopter gunships "zap" him.) These popular films appeal to a kind of populism and rebelliousness, usually of a routine and vapid sort, but then close off the possibilities of effective opposition. The rich get richer and the incoherent rebels get bought and killed.

Often the sense of frustration funneled through these films is diffuse and ambiguous enough to encourage a variety of political responses. While many left-wing cultural critics raved about *Network,* for example, right-wing politicians in Southern California campaigned for Proposition 13 using the film's slogan, "I'm mad as hell and I'm not going to take it any more." Indeed, *the fact that the same film is subject to a variety of conflicting yet plausible interpretations may suggest a crisis in hegemonic ideology.* The economic system is demonstrably troubled, but the traditional liberal recourse, the State, is no longer widely enough trusted to provide reassurance. Articulate social groups do not know whom to blame; public opinion is fluid and volatile, and people at all levels in the society withdraw from public participation.[11] In this situation, commercial culture succeeds with diverse interest groups, as well as with the baffled and ambivalent, precisely by propounding ambiguous or even self-contradictory situations and solutions.

The Hegemonic Process in Liberal Capitalism

Again it bears emphasizing that, for all these tricks of the entertainment trade, the mass-cultural system is not one-dimensional. High-consumption corporate capitalism implies a certain sensitivity to audience taste, taste which is never wholly manufactured. Shows are made by guessing at audience desires and tolerances, and finding ways to speak to them that perpetuate the going system.[12] (Addressing one set of needs entails scanting and distorting others, ordinarily the less mean, less invidious, less aggressive, less reducible to commodity forms.) The cultural hegemony system that results is not a closed system. It leaks. Its very structure leaks, at the least because it remains to some extent competitive. Networks sell the audience's attention to advertisers who want what they think will be a suitably big, suitably rich audience for their products; since the show is bait, advertisers will put up with—or rather buy into—a great many possible baits, as long as they seem likely to attract a buying audience. In the news, there are also traditions of real though limited journalistic independence, traditions whose modern extension causes businessmen, indeed, to loathe the press. In their 1976 book *Ethics and Profits,* Leonard Silk and David Vogel quote a number of big businessmen complaining about the raw deal they get from the press. A typical comment: "Even though the press is a business, it doesn't reflect business values." That is, it has a certain real interest in truth—partial, superficial, occasion- and celebrity-centered truth, but truth nevertheless.

Outside the news, the networks have no particular interest in truth as such, but they remain sensitive to currents of interest in the population, including the yank and haul and insistence of popular movements. With few ethical or strategic reasons not to absorb trends, they are adept at perpetuating them with new formats, new styles, tie-in commodities (dolls, posters, T-shirts, fan magazines) that fans love. In any case, it is in no small measure because of the economic drives themselves that *the hegemonic system itself amplifies legitimated forms of opposition.* In liberal capitalism, hegemonic ideology develops by domesticating opposition, absorbing it into forms compatible with the core ideological structure. Consent is managed by absorption as well as by exclusion. The hegemonic ideology changes in order to remain hegemonic; that is the peculiar nature of the dominant ideology of liberal capitalism.

Raymond Williams (1977) has insisted rightly on the difference between two types of non-hegemonic ideology: *alternative* forms, presenting a distinct but supplementary and containable view of the world, and *oppositional* forms, rarer and more tenuous within commercial culture, intimating an authentically different social order. Williams makes the useful distinction between *residual* forms, descending from declining social formations, and *emergent* forms, reflecting formations on the rise. Although it is easier to speak of these possibilities in the abstract than in the concrete, and although it is not clear what the emergent formations are (this is one of the major questions for social analysis now), these concepts may help organize an agenda for thought and research on popular culture. I would add to William's own carefully modulated remarks on the subject only that there is no reason a priori to expect that emergent forms will be expressed as the ideologies of rising *classes,* or as "proletarian ideology" in particular; currently in the United States the emergent forms have to do with racial minorities and other ethnic groups, with women, with singles, with homosexuals, with old-age subcultures, as well as with technocrats and with political interest groups (loosely but not inflexibly linked to corporate interests) with particular strategic goals (like the new militarists of the Committee on the Present Danger). Analysis of the hegemonic ideology and its rivals should not be allowed to lapse into some form of what C. Wright Mills (1948) called the "labor metaphysic."

One point should be clear: the hegemonic system is not cut-and-dried, not definitive. It has continually to be reproduced, continually superimposed, continually to be negotiated and managed, in order to override the alternative and, occasionally, the oppositional forms. To put it another way: major social conflicts are transported *into* the cultural system, where the hegemonic process frames them, form and content both, into compatibility with dominant systems of meaning. Alternative material is routinely *incorporated:* brought into the body of cultural production. Occasionally oppositional material may succeed in being indigestible; that material is excluded from the media discourse and returned to the cultural margins from which it came, while *elements* of it are incorporated into the dominant forms.

In these terms, *Roots* was an alternative form, representing slaves as unblinkable facts of American history, blacks as victimized humans and humans nonetheless. In the end, perhaps, the story is dominated by the chance for upward mobility; the upshot of travail is freedom. Where Alex Haley's book is subtitled "The Saga of an American Family," ABC's version carries the label—and the self-congratulation—"The *Triumph* of an American Family." It is hard to say categorically which story prevails; in any case there is a tension, a struggle, between the collective agony and the triumph of a single family. That struggle is the friction in the works of the hegemonic system.

And all the evident friction within television entertainment—as well as within the schools, the family, religion, sexuality, and the State—points back to a deeper truth about bourgeois culture. In the United States, at least, hegemonic ideology is extremely complex and absorptive; it is only by absorbing and domesticating conflicting definitions of reality and demands on it, in fact, that it remains hegemonic. In this way, the hegemonic ideology of liberal capitalism is dramatically different from the ideologies of precapitalist societies, and from the dominant ideology of authoritarian socialist or fascist regimes. What permits it to absorb and domesticate critique is not something accidental to capitalist ideology, but rather its core. *The hegemonic ideology of liberal capitalist society is deeply and essentially conflicted in a number of ways.* As Daniel Bell (1976) has argued, it urges people to work hard, but proposes that real satisfaction is to be found in leisure, which ostensibly embodies values opposed to work.[13] More profoundly, at the center of liberal capitalist ideology there is a tension between the affirmation of patriarchal authority—currently enshrined in the national security state—and the affirmation of individual worth and self-determination. Bourgeois ideology in all its incarnations has been from the first a contradiction in terms, affirming "life, liberty and the pursuit of happiness," or "liberty, equality, fraternity," as if these ideals are compatible, even mutually dependent, at all times in all places, as they were for one revolutionary group at one time in one place. But all anti-bourgeois movements wage their battles precisely in terms of liberty, equality, or fraternity (or, recently, sorority); they press on liberal capitalist ideology *in its own name*.

Thus we can understand something of the vulnerability of bourgeois ideology, as well as its persistence. In the twentieth century, the dominant ideology has shifted toward sanctifying consumer satisfaction as the premium definition of "the pursuit of happiness," in this way justifying corporate domination of the economy. What is hegemonic in consumer capitalist ideology is precisely the notion that happiness, or liberty, or equality, or fraternity can be affirmed through the existing private commodity forms, under the benign, protective eye of the national security state. This ideological core is what remains essentially unchanged and unchallenged in television entertainment, at the same time the inner tensions persist and are even magnified.

Notes

An earlier version of this paper was delivered to the 73rd Annual Meeting of the American Sociological Association, San Francisco, September 1978. Thanks to Victoria Bonnell, Bruce Dancis, Wally Goldfrank, Karen Shapiro, and several anonymous reviewers for stimulating comments on earlier drafts.

1. Anderson has read Gramsci closely to tease out this and other ambiguities in Gramsci's diffuse and at times Aesopian texts. (Gramsci was writing in a fascist prison, he was concerned about passing censorship, and he was at times gravely ill.)

2. In my reading, the most thoughtful specific approach to this question since Gramsci, using comparative structural categories to explain the emergence or absence of socialist class consciousness, is Mann (1973). Mann's analysis takes us to structural features of American society that detract from revolutionary consciousness and organization. Although my [essay] does not discuss social-structural and historical features, I do not wish their absence to be interpreted as a belief that culture is all-determining. This [essay] discusses aspects of the hegemonic culture, and makes no claims to a more sweeping theory of American society.

3. In Part III of the latter, I discuss the theory of hegemony more extensively. Published in *The Whole World Is Watching: Mass Media and the New Left, 1965–70,* Berkeley: University of California Press, 1980.

4. See also, Willis (n.d.) for an excellent discussion of the limits of both ideological analysis of cultural artifacts and the social meaning system of audiences, when each is taken by itself and isolated from the other.

5. Most strikingly, see Blum's (1964) findings on black viewers putting down TV shows while watching them. See also Willis's (n.d.) program for studying the substantive meanings of particular pop music records for distinct youth subcultures; but note that it is easier to study the active uses of music than TV, since music is more often heard publicly and because, there being so many choices, the preference for a particular set of songs or singers or beats expresses more about the mentality of the audience than is true for TV.

6. A few years ago, *Gunsmoke* was cancelled although it was still among the top ten shows in Nielsen ratings. The audience was primarily older and disproportionately rural, thus an audience less well sold to advertisers. So much for the networks' democratic rationale.

7. Borrowing "on time," over commensurable, arithmetically calculated lengths of time, is part of the same process: production, consumption, and acculturation made compatible.

8. The time of the show is important to its success or failure. Lear's *All in the Family* was rejected by ABC before CBS bought it. An earlier attempt to bring problems of class, race, and poverty into the heart of television series was *East Side, West Side* of 1964, in which George C. Scott played a caring social worker consistently unable to accomplish much for his clients. As time went on, the Scott character came to the conclusion that politics might accomplish what social work could not, and changed jobs, going to work as the assistant to a liberal Congressman. It was rumored about that the hero was going to discover there, too, the limits of reformism—but the show was cancelled, presumably for low ratings. Perhaps Lear's shows, by contrast, have lasted in part *because they are comedies:* audiences will let their defenses down for some good laughs, even on themselves, at least when the characters are, like Archie Bunker himself, ambiguous normative symbols. At the same time, the comedy form allows white racists to indulge themselves in Archie's rationalizations without seeing that the joke is on them.

9. I use the term *loosely* to refer to general categories of TV entertainment, like "adult western," "cops and robbers," "black shows." Genre is not an objective feature of the cultural universe, but a conventional name for a convention, and should not be reified—as both cultural analysis and practice often do—into a cultural essence.

10. This discussion of televised sports was published in similar form (Gitlin, 1978b).

11. In another essay I will be arguing that forms of pseudo-participation (including cult movies like *Rocky Horror Picture Show* and *Animal House,* along with religious sects) are developing simultaneously to fill the vacuum left by the declining of credible radical politics, and to provide ritual forms of expression that alienated groups cannot find within the political culture.

12. See the careful, important, and unfairly neglected discussion of the tricky needs issue in Leiss (1976). Leiss cuts through the Frankfurt premise that commodity culture addresses false needs by arguing that audience needs for happiness, diversion, self-assertion, and so on are ontologically real; what commercial culture does is not to invent needs (how could it do that?) but to insist upon the possibility of meeting them through the purchase of commodities. For Leiss, all specifically human needs are social; they develop within one social form or another. From this argument—and, less rigorously but more daringly from Ewen (1976)—flow powerful political implications I cannot develop here. On the early popularity of entertainment forms which cannot possibly be laid at the door of a modern "culture industry" and media-produced needs, see Altick (1978).

13. There is considerable truth in Bell's thesis. Then why do I say "ostensibly"? Bell exaggerates his case against "adversary culture" by emphasizing changes in avantgarde culture above all (Pop Art, happenings, John Cage, etc.); if he looked at *popular* culture, he would more likely find ways in which aspects of the culture of consumption *support* key aspects of the culture of production. I offer my discussion of sports as one instance. Morris Dickstein's (1977) affirmation of the critical

culture of the sixties commits the counterpart error of overemphasizing the importance of *other* selected domains of literary and avant-garde culture.

References

Abramson, Ronald (1978) Unpublished manuscript, notes on critical theory distributed at the West Coast Critical Communications Conference, Stanford University.

Adorno, Theodor W. (1954) "How to look at television." *Hollywood Quarterly of Film, Radio and Television.* Spring. Reprinted 1975: 474–88 in Bernard Rosenberg and David Manning White (eds.), *Mass Culture.* New York: Free Press.

———. (1974) "The stars down to earth. The Los Angeles Times Astrology Column." *Telos* 19. Spring 1974 (1957): 13–90.

Adorno, Theodor W., and Max Horkheimer (1972) "The culture industry: Enlightenment as mass deception." Pp. 120–167 in Adorno and Horkheimer, *Dialectic of Enlightenment* (1944). New York: Seabury.

Altick, Richard (1978) *The Shows of London.* Cambridge: Harvard University Press.

Anderson, Perry (1976) "The antinomies of Antonio Gramsci." *New Left Review* 100 (November 1976-January 1977): 5–78.

Barnouw, Erik (1970) *The Image Empire.* New York: Oxford University Press.

Bell, Daniel (1976) *The Cultural Contradictions of Capitalism.* New York: Basic Books.

Blum, Alan F. (1964) "Lower-class Negro television spectators: The concept of pseudo-jovial scepticism." Pp. 429–435 in Arthur B. Shostak and William Gomberg (eds.), *Blue-Collar World.* Englewood Cliffs, N.J.: Prentice-Hall.

Braverman, Harry (1974) *Labor and Monopoly Capital: The Degradation of Work in the Twentieth Century.* New York: Monthly Review Press.

Czitrom, Danny (1977) "Bilko: A sitcom for all seasons." *Cultural Correspondence* 4: 16–19.

Dickstein, Morris (1977) *Gates of Eden.* New York: Basic Books.

Ewen, Stuart (1976) *Captains of Consciousness.* New York: McGraw-Hill.

Gitlin, Todd (1977a) "Spotlights and shadows: Television and the culture of politics." *College English* April: 789–801.

———. (1977b) "'The whole world is watching': Mass media and the new left, 1965–70." Doctoral dissertation, University of California, Berkeley.

———. (1977c) "The televised professional." *Social Policy* (November/December): 94–99.

———. (1978a) "Media sociology: The dominant paradigm." *Theory and Society* 6:205–53.

———. (1978b) "Life as instant replay." *East Bay Voice* (November–December): 14.

Gouldner, Alvin W. (1976) *The Dialectic of Ideology and Technology.* New York: Seabury.

Gramsci, Antonio (1971) *Selections From the Prison Notebooks.* Quintin Hoare and Geoffrey Nowell Smith (eds.) New York: International Publishers.

Helitzer, Melvin, and Carl Heyel (1970) The Youth Market: Its Dimensions, Influence and Opportunities for You. Quoted pp. 62–63 in William Melody, *Children's Television* (1973). New Haven: Yale University Press.

Kellner, Douglas (1978) "Ideology, Marxism, and advanced capitalism." *Socialist Review* 42 (November–December): 37–66.

Leiss, William (1976) *The Limits to Satisfaction.* Toronto: University of Toronto Press.

Mann, Michael (1973) *Consciousness and Action Among the Western Working Class.* London: Macmillan.

Mills, C. Wright (1948) *The New Men of Power.* New York: Harcourt, Brace.

Morley, Dave (1974) "Reconceptualizing the media audience: Towards an ethnography of audiences." Mimeograph, Centre for Contemporary Cultural Studies, University of Birmingham.

Real, Michael R. (1977) *Mass-Mediated Culture.* Englewood Cliffs, N.J.: Prentice-Hall.

Silk, Leonard, and David Vogel (1976) *Ethics and Profits.* New York: Simon and Schuster.

Williams, Raymond (1973) "Base and superstructure in Marxist cultural theory." *New Left Review:* 82.

——. (1977) *Marxism and Literature.* New York: Oxford University Press.

Willis, Paul (n.d.) "Symbolism and practice: A theory for the social meaning of pop music." Mimeograph, Centre for Contemporary Cultural Studies, University of Birmingham.

Television Melodrama

DAVID THORBURN

*I remember with what a smile of saying something daring and
inacceptable John Erskine told an undergraduate class that some day
we would understand that plot and melodrama were good things for
a novel to have and that* Bleak House *was a very good novel indeed.*

Lionel Trilling, *A Gathering of Fugitives*

Although much of what I say will touch significantly on the medium as a
whole, I want to focus here on a single broad category of television programming—what *TV Guide* and the newspaper listings, with greater insight
than they realize, designate as "melodrama." I believe that at its increasingly frequent best, this fundamental television genre so richly exploits the
conventions of its medium as to be clearly distinguishable from its ancestors in the theater, in the novel, and in films. And I also believe, though
this more extravagant corollary judgment can only be implied in my present argument, that television melodrama has been our culture's most characteristic aesthetic form, and one of its most complex and serious forms as
well, for at least the past decade and probably longer.

Melo is the Greek and word for music. The term *melodrama* is said to
have originated as a neutral designation for a spoken dramatic text with a
musical accompaniment or background, an offshoot or spin-off of opera.
The term came into widespread use in England during the nineteenth century, when it was appropriated by theatrical entrepreneurs as a legal device
to circumvent statutes that restricted the performances of legitimate drama
to certain theaters. In current popular and (much) learned usage, *melodrama*
is a resolutely pejorative term, also originating early in the last century,
denoting a sentimental, artificially plotted drama that sacrifices characterization to extravagant incident, makes sensational appeals to the emotions
of its audience, and ends on a happy or at least a morally reassuring note.

Reprinted from *Television as a Cultural Force*, ed. Douglass Cater and Richard Adler,
by permission of Praeger Publishers, Aspen Institute Program on Communications
and Society, and the author. Copyright © 1976 by David Thorburn.

Neither the older, neutral nor the current, disparaging definitions are remotely adequate, however. The best recent writings on melodrama, drawing sustenance from a larger body of work concerned with popular culture in general, have begun to articulate a far more complex definition, one that plausibly refuses to restrict melodrama to the theater, and vigorously challenges long-cherished distinctions between high and low culture—even going so far as to question some of our primary assumptions about the nature and possibilities of art itself. In this emerging conception, melodrama must be understood to include not only popular trash composed by hack novelists and filmmakers—Conrad's forgotten rival Stanley Weyman, for example; Jacqueline Susann; the director Richard Fleischer—but also such complex, though still widely accessible, artworks as the novels of Samuel Richardson and Dickens, or the films of Hitchcock and Kurosawa. What is crucial to this new definition, though, is not the actual attributes of melodrama itself, which remain essentially unchanged; nor the extension of melodrama's claims to prose fiction and film, which many readers and viewers have long accepted in any case. What is crucial is the way in which the old dispraised attributes of melodrama are understood, the contexts to which they are returned, the respectful scrutiny they are assumed to deserve.[1]

What does it signify, for example, to acknowledge that the structure of melodrama enacts of fantasy of reassurance, and that the happy or moralistic endings so characteristic of the form are reductive and arbitrary—a denial of our "real" world where events refuse to be coherent and where (as Nabokov austerely says) harm is the norm? The desperate or cunning or spirited stratagems by which this escape from reality is accomplished must still retain a fundamental interest. They must still instruct us, with whatever obliqueness, concerning the nature of that reality from which escape or respite has been sought. Consider the episode of the Cave of Montesinos in *Don Quixote,* in which the hero, no mean melodramatist himself, descends into a cavern to dream or conjure a pure vision of love and chivalry and returns with a tale in which a knight's heart is cut from his breast and salted to keep it fresh for his lady. This is an emblem, a crystallizing enactment, of the process whereby our freest, most necessary fantasies are anchored in the harsh, prosaic actualities of life. And Sancho's suspicious but also respectful and deeply attentive interrogation of Quixote's dream instructs us as to how we might profitably interrogate melodrama.

Again, consider the reassurance-structure of melodrama in relation to two other defining features of the form: its persistent and much-contemned habit of moral simplification and its lust for topicality, its hunger to engage or represent behavior and moral attitudes that belong to its particular day and time, especially behavior shocking or threatening to prevailing moral codes. When critics or viewers describe how television panders to its audience, these qualities of simplification and topicality are frequently cited in evidence. The audience wants to be titillated but also wants to be confirmed in its moral sloth, the argument goes, and so the melodramatist sells stories in which crime and criminals are absorbed into paradigms of moral conflict, into allegories of good and evil, in which the good almost always win. The trouble with such a view is not in what it describes, which is often accurate enough, but in its rush to judgment. Perhaps, as Roland Barthes proposes in his stunning essay on wrestling, we ought to learn to see such texts from the standpoint of the audience, whose pleasures in witnessing these spectacles of excess and grandiloquence may be deeper than we know, and whose intimate familiarity with such texts may lead them to perceive as complex aesthetic conventions what the traditional high culture sees only as simple stereotypes.[2]

Suppose that the reassuring conclusions and the moral allegorizing of melodrama are regarded in this way, as *conventions,* as "rules" of the genre in the same way that the iambic pentameter and the rimed couplet at the end of a sonnet are "rules" for that form. From this angle, these recurring features of melodrama can be perceived as the *enabling conditions* for an encounter with forbidden or deeply disturbing materials: not an escape into blindness or easy reassurance, but an instrument for seeing. And from this angle, melodrama becomes a peculiarly significant public forum, complicated and immensely enriched because its discourse is aesthetic and broadly popular: a forum or arena in which traditional ways of feeling and thinking are brought into continuous, strained relation with powerful intuitions of change and contingency.

This is the spirit in which I turn to television melodrama. In this category I include most made-for-television movies, the soap operas, and all the lawyers, cowboys, cops and docs, the fugitives and adventurers, the fraternal and filial comrades who have filled the prime hours of so many American nights for the last thirty years.[3] I have no wish to deny that these entertainments are market commodities first and last, imprisoned by rigid timetables and stereotyped formulas, compelled endlessly to imagine and reimagine as story and as performance the conventional wisdom, the lies and fantasies, and the muddled ambivalent values of our bourgeois industrial culture. These qualities are, in fact, the primary source of their interest for me, and of the complicated pleasures they uniquely offer.

Confined (but also nourished) by its own foreshortened history and by formal and thematic conventions whose origins are not so much aesthetic as economic, television melodrama is a derivative art, just now emerging from its infancy. It is effective more often in parts of stories than in their wholes, and in thrall to censoring pressures that limit its range. But like all true art, television melodrama is cunning, having discovered (or, more often, stumbled upon) strategies for using the constraints within which it must live.

Its essential artistic resource is the actor's performance, and one explanation—there are many others—for the disesteem in which television melodrama is held is that we have yet to articulate an adequate aesthetics for the art of performance. Far more decisively than the movie-actor, the television-actor creates and controls the meaning of what we see on the screen. In order to understand television drama, and in order to find authentic standards for judging it as art, we must learn to recognize and to value the discipline, energy, and intelligence that must be expended by the actor who succeeds in creating what we too casually call a *truthful* or *believable* performance. What happens when an actor's performance arouses our latent faculties of imaginative sympathy and moral judgment, when he causes us to acknowledge that what he is doing is true to the tangled potency of real experience, not simply impressive or clever, but *true*—what happens then is art.

It is important to be clear about what acting, especially television-acting, is or can be: nothing less than a reverent attentiveness to the pain and beauty in the lives of others, an attentiveness made accessible to us in a wonderfully instructive process wherein the performer's own impulses to self-assertion realize themselves only by surrendering or yielding to the claims of the character he wishes to portray. Richard Poirier, our best theorist of performance, puts the case as follows: "performance . . . is an action which must go through passages that both impede the action and give it form, much as a sculptor not only is impelled to shape his material but is in turn shaped by it, his impulse to mastery always chastened, sometimes made tender and possibly witty by the recalcitrance of what he is working on."[4]

Television has always challenged the actor. The medium's reduced visual scale grants him a primacy unavailable in the theater or in the movies, where an amplitude of things and spaces offers competition for the eye's attention. Its elaborate, enforced obedience to various formulas for plot and characterization virtually require him to recover from within himself and from his broadly stereotyped assignment nuances of gesture, inflection, and movement that will at least hint at individual or idiosyncratic qualities. And despite our failure clearly to acknowledge this, the history of television as a dramatic medium is, at the very least, a history of exceptional artistic accomplishment by actors. The performances in television melodrama today are much richer than in the past, though there were many remarkable performances even in the early days. The greater freedom afforded to writers and actors is part of the reason for this, but (as I will try to indicate shortly) the far more decisive reason is the extraordinary sophistication the genre has achieved.

Lacking access to even the most elementary scholarly resources—bibliographies, systematic collections of films or tapes, even moderately reliable histories of the art—I can only appeal to our (hopefully) common memory of the highly professional and serious acting regularly displayed in series such as *Naked City, Twilight Zone, Route 66, Gunsmoke, The Defenders, Cade's County, Stoney Burke, East Side, West Side, The Name of the Game,* and others whose titles could be supplied by anyone who has watched American television over the past twenty or twenty-five years. Often the least promising dramatic formulas were transformed by vivid and highly intelligent performances. I remember with particular pleasure and respect, for example, Steve McQueen's arresting portrayal of the callow bounty hunter Josh Randall in the western series, *Wanted: Dead or Alive*—the jittery lean grace of his physical movements, the balked, dangerous tenderness registered by his voice and eyes in his encounters with women; the mingling of deference and menace that always enlivened his dealings with older men, outlaws and sheriffs mainly, between whom this memorable boy-hero seemed fixed or caught, but willingly so. McQueen's subsequent apotheosis in the movies was obviously deserved, but I have often felt his performances on the large screen were less tensely intelligent, more self-indulgent than his brilliant early work in television.

If we could free ourselves from our ingrained expectations concerning dramatic form and from our reluctance to acknowledge that art is always a commodity of some kind, constrained by the technology necessary to its production and by the needs of the audience for which it is intended, then we might begin to see how ingeniously television melodrama contrives to nourish its basic resource—the actor—even as it surrenders to those economic pressures that seem most imprisoning.

Consider, for example, the ubiquitous commercials. They are so widely deplored that even those who think themselves friendly to the medium cannot restrain their outrage over such unambiguous evidence of the huckster's contempt for art's claim to continuity. Thus, a writer in the official journal of the National Academy of Television Arts and Sciences, meditating sadly on "the total absence" of serious television drama, refers in passing to "the horrors of continuous, brutal interruption."[5]

That commercials have shaped television melodrama decisively is obvious, of course. But, as with most of the limitations to which the genre is subjected, these enforced pauses are merely formal conventions. They are no more intrinsically hostile to art than the unities observed by the French neoclassical theater or the serial installments in which so many Victorian novels had to be written. Their essential effect has been the refinement of a segmented dramatic structure peculiarly suited to a formula-story whose ending is predictable—the doctor will save the patient, the cop will catch the criminal—and whose capacity to surprise or otherwise engage its audience must therefore depend largely on the localized vividness and potency of the smaller units or episodes that comprise the whole.

Television melodrama achieves this episodic or segmented vividness in several ways, but its most dependable and recurring strategy is to require its actors to display themselves intensely and energetically from the very beginning. In its most characteristic and most interesting form, television melodrama will contrive its separate units such that they will have substantial independent weight and interest, usually enacting in miniature the larger patterns and emotional rhythms of the whole drama. Thus, each segment will show us a character, or several characters, confronting some difficulty or other; the character's behavior and (especially) his emotional responses will intensify, then achieve some sort of climactic or resolving pitch at the commercial break; and this pattern will be repeated incrementally in subsequent segments.

To describe this characteristic structure is to clarify what those who complain of the genre's improbability never acknowledge: that television melodrama is in some respects an *operatic* rather than a conventionally dra-

matic form—a fact openly indicated by the term *soap opera*. No one goes
to Italian opera expecting a realistic plot, and since applause for the important arias is an inflexible convention, no one expects such works to proceed
without interruption. The pleasures of this kind of opera are largely (though
not exclusively) the pleasures of the brilliant individual performance, and
good operas in this tradition are those in which the composer has contrived
roles which test as fully as possible the vocal capacities of the performers.

Similarly, good television melodramas are those in which an intricately
formulaic plot conspires perfectly with the commercial interruptions to
encourage a rich articulation of the separate parts of the work, and thus to
call forth from the realistic actor the full energies of his performer's gifts.
What is implausible in such works is the continual necessity for emotional
display by the characters. In real life we are rarely called upon to feel so
intensely, and never in such neatly escalating sequences. But the emotions
dramatized by these improbable plots are not in themselves unreal, or at
least they need not be—and television melodrama often becomes more
truthful as it becomes more implausible.

As an example of this recurring paradox—it will be entirely familiar to
any serious reader of Dickens—consider the following generically typical
episode from the weekly series, *Medical Center*. An active middle-aged man
falls victim to an aneurysm judged certain to kill him within a few years.
This affliction being strategically located for dramatic use, the operation that
could save his life may also leave him impotent—a fate nasty enough for
anyone, but psychologically debilitating for this unlucky fellow who has
divorced his first wife and married a much younger woman. The early scenes
establish his fear of aging and his intensely physical relationship with his
young wife with fine lucid economy. Now the plot elaborates further complications and develops new, related central centers of interest. His doctor—
the series regular who is (sometimes) an arresting derivation of his television ancestors, Doctors Kildare and Ben Casey—is discovered to be a close,
longtime friend whose involvement in the case is deeply personal. Confident of his surgeon's skills and much younger than his patient, the doctor
is angrily unsympathetic to the older man's reluctance to save his life at the
expense of his sexuality. Next, the rejected wife, brilliantly played by Barbara Rush, is introduced. She works—by a marvelous arbitrary coincidence—
in the very hospital in which her ex-husband is being treated. There follows
a complex scene in the hospital room in which the former wife acts out her
tangled, deep feelings toward the man who has rejected her and toward the
woman who has replaced her. In their tensely guarded repartee, the husband and ex-wife are shown to be bound to one another in a vulnerable
knowingness made in decades of uneasy intimacy that no divorce can erase
and that the new girl-wife must observe as an outsider. Later scenes require
emotional confrontations—some of them equally subtle—between the doctor and each wife, between doctor and patient, between old wife and new.

These nearly mathematic symmetries conspire with still further plot complications to create a story that is implausible in the extreme. Though

aneurysms are dangerous, they rarely threaten impotence. Though impotence is a real problem, few men are free to choose a short happy life of potency, and fewer still are surrounded in such crises by characters whose relations to them so fully articulate such a wide spectrum of human needs and attitudes. The test of such an arbitrary contrivance is not the plausibility of whose but the accuracy and truthfulness of its parts, the extent to which its various strategies of artificial heightening permit an open enactment of feelings and desires that are only latent or diffused in the muddled incoherence of the real world. And although my argument does not depend on the success or failure of one or of one dozen specific melodramas—the genre's manifest complexity and its enormous popularity being sufficient to justify intensive and respectful study—I should say that the program just described was for me a serious aesthetic experience. I was caught by the persuasiveness of the actors' performances, and my sympathies were tested by the meanings those fine performances released. The credibility of the young wife's reluctant, pained acknowledgment that a life without sex *would* be a crippled life; the authenticity of the husband's partly childish, partly admirable reverence for his carnal aliveness; and, especially, the complex genuineness of his ambivalent continuing bonds with his first wife—all this was there on the screen. Far from falsifying life, it quickened one's awareness of the burdens and costs of human relationships.

That the plots of nearly all current television melodramas tend, as in this episode of *Medical Center,* to be more artificially contrived than those of earlier years seems to me a measure not of the genre's unoriginality but of its maturity, its increasingly bold and self-conscious capacity to *use* formal requirements which it cannot in any case evade, and to exploit (rather than be exploited by) various formulas for characterization. Nearly all the better series melodramas of recent years, in fact, have resorted quite openly to what might be called a *multiplicity principle:* a principle of plotting or organization whereby a particular drama will draw not once or twice but many times upon the immense store of stories and situations created by the genre's brief but crowded history. The multiplicity principle allows not less but more reality to enter the genre. Where the old formulas had been developed exhaustively and singly through the whole of a story—that is how they became stereotypes—they are now treated elliptically in a plot that deploys many of them simultaneously. The familiar character-types and situations thus become more suggestive and less imprisoning. There is no pretense that a given character has been wholly "explained" by the plot, and the formula has the liberating effect of creating a premise or base on which the actor is free to build. By minimizing the need for long establishing or expository sequences, the multiplicity principle allows the story to leave aside the question of *how* these emotional entanglements were arrived at and to concentrate its energies on their credible and powerful present enactment.

These and other stratagems—which result in richer, more plausible characterizations and also permit elegant variations of tone—are possible because television melodrama can rely confidently on one resource that is always essential to the vitality of any artform: an audience impressive not simply in its numbers but also in its genuine sophistication, its deep familiarity with the history and conventions of the genre. For so literate an audience, the smallest departure from conventional expectations can become meaningful, and this creatures endless chances for surprise and nuanced variation, even for thematic subtlety.

In his instructive book on American films of the forties and fifties, Michael Wood speaks nostalgically of his membership in "the universal movie audience" of that time. This audience of tens of millions was able to see the movies as a coherent world, "a country of familiar faces, . . . a system of assumptions and beliefs and preoccupations, a fund of often interchangeable plots, characters, patches of dialog, and sets." By relying on the audience's familiarity with other movies, Wood says, the films of that era constituted "a living tradition of the kind that literary critics always used to be mourning for."[6]

This description fits contemporary television even more closely than it does those earlier movies, since most members of the TV audience have lived through the whole history of the medium. They know its habits, its formulas, its stars, and its recurring character actors with a confident, easy intimacy that may well be unique in the history of popular art. Moreover, television's capacity to make its history and evolution continuously available (even to younger members in its universal audience) is surely without precedent, for the system of reruns has now reached the point of transforming television into a continuous, living museum which displays for daily or weekly consumption texts from every stage of the medium's past.

Outsiders from the high culture who visit TV melodrama occasionally in order to issue their tedious reports about our cultural malaise are simply not seeing what the TV audience sees. They are especially blind to the complex allusiveness with which television melodrama uses its actors. For example, in a recent episode of the elegant *Columbo* series, Peter Falk's adventures occurred onboard a luxury liner and brought him into partnership with the captain of the ship, played by Patrick Macnee, the smooth British actor who starred in the popular spy series, *The Avengers.* The scenes between Falk and Macnee were continuously enlivened not simply by the different acting styles of the two performers but also by the attitudes toward heroism, moral authority, and aesthetic taste represented in the kinds of programs with which each star has been associated. The uneasy, comic partnership between these characters—Falk's grungy, American-ethnic slyness contrasting with, and finally mocking, Macnee's British public school elegance and fastidiousness—was further complicated by the presence in the show of the guest villain, played by yet another star of a successful TV series of a few years ago—Robert Vaughn of *The Man From U.N.C.L.E.* Vaughn's character had something of the sartorial, upper-class *elan* of Macnee's ship's master but, drawing on qualities established in his earlier TV role, was tougher, wholly American, more calculating, and ruthless. Macnee, of course, proved no match for Vaughn's unmannerly cunning, but Falk-

Columbo succeeded in exposing him in a climax that expressed not only the show's usual fantasy of working-class intelligence overcoming aristocratic guile, but also the victory of American versions of popular entertainment over their British counterparts.

The aesthetic and human claims of most television melodrama would surely be much weakened, if not completely obliterated, on any other medium, and I have come to believe that the species of melodrama to be found on television today is a unique dramatic form, offering an especially persuasive resolution of the contradiction or tension that has been inherent in melodrama since the time of Euripides. As Peter Brooks reminds us in his provocative essay on the centrality of the melodramatic mode in romantic and modern culture, stage melodrama represents "a popular form of the tragic, exploiting similar emotions within the context of the ordinary." Melodrama is a "popular" form, we may say, both because it is favored by audiences and because it insists (or tries to insist) on the dignity and importance of the ordinary, usually bourgeois world of the theatergoer himself. The difficulty with this enterprise, of course, is the same for Arthur Miller in our own day as it was for Thomas Middleton in Jacobean London: displacing the action and characters from a mythic or heroically stylized world to an ordinary world—from Thebes to Brooklyn—involves a commitment to a kind of realism that is innately resistant to exactly those intense passionate enactments that the melodramatist wishes to invoke. Melodrama is thus always in conflict with itself, gesturing simultaneously toward ordinary reality *and* toward a moral and emotional heightening that is rarely encountered in the "real" world.

Although it can never be made to disappear, this conflict is minimized, or is capable of being minimized, by television—and in a way that is simply impossible in the live theater and that is nearly always less effective on the enlarged movie-screen. The melodramatic mode is peculiarly congenial to television, its inherent contradictions are less glaring and damaging there, because the medium is uniquely hospitable to the spatial confinements of the theater and to the profound realistic intimacy of the film.

Few would dispute the cinema's advantages over the theater as realistic medium. As every serious film begins of reminding us, the camera's ability to record the dense multiplicity of the external world and to reveal character in all its outer nuance and idiosyncrasy grands a visually authenticating power to the medium that has no equivalent in the theater. Though the stage owns advantages peculiar to its character as a live medium, it is clearly an artform more stylized, less visually realistic than the film, and it tests its performers in a somewhat different way. Perhaps the crucial difference is also the most obvious one: the distance between the audience and the actor in even the most intimate theatrical environment requires facial and vocal gestures as well as bodily movements "broader" and more excessive than those demanded by the camera, which can achieve a lover's closeness to the performer.

The cinema's photographic realism is not, of course, an unfixed blessing. But it is incalculably valuable to melodrama because, by encouraging understatement from its actors, it can help to ratify extravagant or intense emotions that would seem far less credible in the theater. And although television is the dwarf child of the film, constrained and scaled down in a great many ways, its very smallness can become an advantage to the melodramatic imagination. This is so because if the cinema's particularizing immediacy is friendly to melodrama, certain other characteristics of the medium are hostile to it. The extended duration of most film, the camera's freedom of movement, the more-than-life-sized dimensions of the cinematic image—all these create what has been called the film's mythopoeic tendency, its inevitable effect of magnification. Since the natural domain of melodrama is indoors, in those ordinary and enclosed spaces wherein most of us act out our deepest needs and feelings—bedrooms, offices, courtrooms, hospitals— the reduced visual field of television is, or can be, far more nourishing than the larger, naturally expansive movie-screen. And for the kind of psychologically nuanced performance elicited by good melodrama, the smaller television screen would seem even more appropriate: perfectly adapted, in fact, to record those intimately minute physical and vocal gestures on which the art of the realistic actor depends, yet happily free of the cinema's malicious (if often innocent) power to transform merely robust nostrils into Brobdingnagian caverns, minor facial irregularities into craterous deformities.

Television's matchless respect for the idiosyncratic expressiveness of the ordinary human face and its unique hospitality to the confining spaces of our ordinary world are virtues exploited repeatedly in all the better melodramas. But perhaps they are given special decisiveness in *Kojak,* a classy police series whose gifted leading player has been previously consigned almost entirely to gangster parts, primarily (one supposes) because of the cinema's blindness to the uncosmetic beauty of his large bald head and generously irregular face. In its first two years particularly, before Savalas's character stiffened into the macho stereotype currently staring out upon us from magazine advertisements for razor blades and men's toiletries, *Kojak* was a genuine work of art, intricately designed to exploit its star's distinctively urban flamboyance, his gift for registering a long, modulated range of sarcastic vocal inflections and facial maneuvers, his talent for persuasive ranting. The show earned its general excellence not only because of Savalas's energetic performance, but also because its writers contrived supporting roles that complemented the central character with rare, individuating clarity, because the boldly artificial plotting in most episodes pressed toward the revelation of character rather than shoot-em-up action, and because, finally, the whole enterprise was forced into artfulness by the economic and technological environment that determined its life.

This last is at once the most decisive and most instructive fact about *Kojak,* as it is about television melodrama generally. Because *Kojak* is filmed in Hollywood on a restricted budget, the show must invoke New York elliptically, in ingenious process shots and in stock footage taken from the full-length (and much less impressive) television-movie that served as a pilot for the series. The writers for the program are thus driven to devise stories that will allow the principle characters to appear in confined locations that can be created on or near studio sound-stages—offices, interrogation rooms, dingy bars, city apartments, nondescript alleys, highway underpasses, all the neutral and enclosed spaces common to urban life generally. As a result, *Kojak* often succeeds in projecting a sense of the city that is more compelling and intelligent than that which is offered in many films and television movies filmed on location: its menacing closeness, its capacity to harbor and even to generate certain kinds of crime, its watchful, unsettling accuracy as a custodian of the lists and records and documents that open a track to the very center of our lives. *Kojak*'s clear superiority to another, ostensibly more original and exotic police series, *Hawaii Five-O*, is good partial evidence for the liberating virtues of such confinement. This latter series is filmed on location at enormous expense and is often much concerned to give a flavor of Honolulu particularly. Yet it yields too easily to an obsession with scenic vistas and furious action sequences which threaten to transform the program into a mere travelogue and which always seem unnaturally confined by the reduced scale of the television screen.

That the characters in *Kojak* frequently press beyond the usual stereotypes is also partly a result of the show's inability to indulge in all the outdoor muscle-flexing, chasing, and shooting made possible by location filming. Savalas's Kojak especially is a richly individuated creation, his policeman's cunning a natural expression of his lifelong, intimate involvement in the very ecology of the city. A flamboyant, aggressive man, Kojak is continually engaged in a kind of joyful contest for recognition and even for mastery with the environment that surrounds him. The studio sets on which most of the action occurs, and the many close-up shots in each episode, reinforce and nurture these traits perfectly, for they help Savalas to work with real subtlety— to project not simply his character's impulse to define himself against the city's enclosures but also a wary, half-loving respect for such imprisonments, a sense indeed that they are the very instrument of his self-realization.

Kojak's expensive silk-lined suits and hats and the prancing vitality of his physical movements are merely the outer expressions of what is shown repeatedly to be an enterprise of personal fulfillment that depends mostly on force of intellect. His intelligence is not bookish—the son of a Greek immigrant, he never attended college—but it is genuine and powerfully self-defining because he must depend on his knowledge of the city in order to prevent a crime or catch a criminal. Proud of his superior mental quickness and urban knowingness, Kojak frequently behaves with the egotistical flair of a bold, demanding scholar, reveling in his ability to instruct subordinates in how many clues they have overlooked and even (in one episode) performing with histrionic brilliance as a teacher before a class of students at the police academy. Objecting to this series because it ratifies the stereotype of the super-cop is as silly as objecting to Sherlock Holmes on similar grounds. Like Holmes in many ways, Kojak is a man who realizes deeply private needs and inclinations in the doing of his work. Not law-and-order simplicities, but intelligence and self-realization are what *Kojak* celebrates. The genius of the series is to have conceived a character whose portrayal calls forth from Savalas exactly what his appearance and talents most suit him to do.

The distinction of *Kojak* in its first two seasons seems to me reasonably representative of the achievements of television melodrama in recent years. During the past season, I have seen dozens of programs—episodes of *Harry-O, Police Story, Baretta, Medical Center,* the now-defunct *Medical Story,* several made-for-TV movies, and portions at least of the new mini-series melodramas being developed by ABC—whose claims to attention were fully as strong as *Kojak*'s. Their partial but genuine excellence constitutes an especially salutary reminder of the fact that art always thrives on restraints and prohibitions, indeed that it requires them if it is to survive at all. Like the Renaissance sonnet or Racine's theater, television melodrama is always most successful when it most fully embraces that which confines it, when *all* the limitations imposed upon it—including such requirements as the sixty- or ninety-minute time slot, the commercial interruptions, the small dimensions of the screen, even the consequences of low-budget filming—become instruments of use, conventions whose combined workings create unpretentious and spirited dramatic entertainments, works of popular art that are engrossing, serious, and imaginative.

That such honorific adjectives are rarely applied to television melodrama, that we have effectively refused even to consider the genre in aesthetic terms is a cultural fact and, ultimately, a political fact almost as interesting as the artworks we have been ignoring. Perhaps because television melodrama is an authentically popular art—unlike rubber hamburgers, encounter group theater or electric-kool-aid journalism—our understanding of it has been conditioned (if not thwarted entirely) by the enormous authority American high culture grants to avant-garde conceptions of the artist as an adversary figure in mortal conflict with his society. Our attitude toward the medium has been conditioned also by even more deeply ingrained assumptions about the separate high dignity of aesthetic experience—an activity we are schooled to imagine as uncontaminated by the marketplace, usually at enmity with the everyday world, and dignified by the very rituals of payment and dress and travel and isolation variously required for its enjoyment. It is hard, in an atmosphere which accords art a special if not an openly subversive status, to think of television as an aesthetic medium, for scarcely another institution in American life is at once so familiarly *un*special and so profoundly a creature of the economic and technological genius of advanced industrial capitalism.

Almost everything that is said or written about television, and especially about television drama, is tainted by such prejudices; more often it is in utter servitude to them. And although television itself would no doubt benefit significantly if its nature were perceived and described more objectively, it is the larger culture—whose signature is daily and hourly to be found there—that would benefit far more.

In the introduction to *The Idea of a Theater,* Francis Fergusson reminds us that genuinely popular dramatic art is always powerfully conservative in certain ways, offering stories that insist on "their continuity with the common sense of the community." Hamlet could enjoin the players to hold a mirror up to nature, "to show . . . the very age and body of the time his form and pressure" because, Fergusson tells us, "the Elizabethan theater was itself a mirror which had been formed at the center of the culture of its time, and at the center of the life and awareness of the community." That we have no television Shakespeare is obvious enough, I guess. But we do already have our Thomas Kyds and our Chapmans. A Marlowe, even a Ben Jonson, is not inconceivable. It is time we noticed them.[7]

Notes

1. The bibliography of serious recent work on melodrama is not overly intimidating, but some exciting and important work has been done. I list here only pieces that have directly influenced my present argument, and I refer the reader to their notes and bibliographies for a fuller survey of the scholarship. Earl F. Bargainnier summarizes recent definitions of melodrama and offers a short history of the genre as practiced by dramatists of the eighteenth and nineteenth centuries in "Melodrama as Formula," *Journal of Popular Culture* 9 (Winter, 1975). John G. Cawelti's indispensable *Adventure, Mystery, and Romance* (Chicago, 1976) focuses closely and originally on melodrama at several points. Peter Brooks's "The Melodramatic Imagination," in *Romanticism: Vistas, Instances, Continuities,* ed. David Thorburn and Geoffrey Hartman (Cornell, 1973), boldly argues that melodrama is a primary literary and visionary mode in romantic and modern culture. Much recent Dickens criticism is helpful on melodrama, but see especially Robert Garis, *The Dickens Theatre* (Oxford, 1965), and essays by Barbara Hardy, George H. Ford, and W. J. Harvey in the Dickens volume of the Twentieth-Century Views series, ed. Martin Price (Prentice-Hall, 1967). Melodrama's complex, even symbiotic linkages with the economic and social institutions of capitalist democracy are a continuing (if implicit) theme of Ian Watt's classic *The Rise of the Novel* (University of California Press, 1957), and of Leo Braudy's remarkable essay on Richardson, "Penetration and Impenetrability in Clarissa," in *New Approaches to Eighteenth-Century Literature,* ed. Phillip Harth (Columbia University Press, 1974).

2. Roland Barthes, "The World of Wrestling," in *Mythologies,* trans. Annette Lavers (Hill and Wang, 1972). I am grateful to Jo Anne Lee of the University of California, Santa Barbara, for making me see the connection between Barthes's notions and television drama.

3. I will not discuss soap opera directly, partly because its serial nature differentiates it in certain respects from the prime-time shows, and also because this interesting subgenre of TV melodrama has received some preliminary attention from others. See, for instance, Frederick L. Kaplan, "Intimacy and Conformity in American Soap Opera," *Journal of Popular Culture* 9 (Winter, 1975); Renata Adler, "Afternoon Television: Unhappiness Enough and Time," *The New Yorker* 47 (February 12, 1972); Marjorie Perloff, "Soap Bubbles." *The New Republic* (May 10, 1975);

and the useful chapter on the soaps in Horace Newcomb's pioneering (if tentative) *TV, The Most Popular Art* (Anchor, 1974). Newcomb's book also contains sections on the prime-time shows I am calling melodramas. For an intelligent fan's impressions of soap opera, see Dan Wakefield's *All Her Children* (Doubleday, 1976).

4. Richard Poirier, *The Performing Self* (Oxford, 1971), p. xiv. I am deeply indebted to this crucial book, and to Poirier's later elaborations on this theory of performance in two pieces on ballet and another on Bette Midler (*The New Republic,* January 5, 1974; March 15, 1975; August 2 and 9, 1975).

5. John Houseman, "TV Drama in the U.S.A.," *Television Quarterly* 10 (Summer, 1973), p. 12.

6. Michael Wood, *America in the Movies* (Basic Books, 1975), pp. 10–11.

7. Though they are not to be held accountable for the uses to which I have put their advice, the following friends have read earlier versions of this essay and have saved me from many errors: Sheridan Blau, Leo Braudy, John Cawelti, Peter Clecak, Howard Felperin, Richard Slotkin, Alan Stephens, and Eugene Waith.

What Is the "Television" of Television Studies?

CHARLOTTE BRUNSDON

The existence of *The Television Studies Book,* published for the first time in 1997, in the company of other recent readers and introductory texts such as Corner and Harvey's *Television Times* (1996) or Selby and Cowdery's *How to Study Television* (1995) testifies to the existence—at least in the minds of some authors, teachers and publishers—of something called television studies. Indeed, it is possible, in the 1990s, in Britain, to take degree courses in television studies in a way which was inconceivable in as recent a past as the 1970s. In this essay I want to unpick the obviousness of television studies—*question:* what is television studies? *answer:* it's the study of television, of course—to show how the television of the discipline, like the flow of talk now thought of as normal for the medium, is particular and historical. My main concern will be the tracing of the hybrid origins of television studies in answer to the question "where does television studies come from?" In this endeavor, I will sketch one outline of the ways and sites in which television has been attended to seriously. My underlying argument, however, is that there is nothing obvious about the television of television studies. This television, the television studied in television studies, is a production of the complex interplay of different histories—disciplinary, national, economic, technological, legislative—which not only did not exist until recently, but is currently, contestedly, being produced even as, simultane-

---

ously, the nationally regulated terrestrial broadcasting systems which are its primary referent move into convulsion. Where does television studies come from and what does it study?

Television studies is the relatively recent, aspirationally disciplinary name given to the academic study of television. Modelled by analogy on longer established fields of study, the name suggests that there is an object, "television," which, in courses named, for example, "Introduction to Television Studies," is the self-evident object of study using accepted methodologies. This may be increasingly the case, but historically, most of the formative academic research on television was inaugurated in other fields and contexts. The "television" of television studies is a relatively new phenomenon, just as many of the key television scholars are employed in departments of sociology, politics, communication arts, speech, theater, media and film studies. If it is now possible, in 1996, to speak of a field of study, "television studies" in the Anglophone academy, in a way in which it was not in 1970, the distinctive characteristics of this field of study include its disciplinary hybridity and continuing debate about how to conceptualize the object of study "television." These debates, which are and have been both political and methodological, are further complicated in an international frame by the historical peculiarities of national broadcasting systems. Thus, for example, the television studies that developed in Britain or Scandinavia, while often addressing US television programs, did so within the taken-for-granted dominance of public service models. This television, and this television studies, was one in which, at a deep level, there was an assumed address to a viewer as citizen. John Corner's recent book, *Television Form and Public Address* (1995), provides a fine example of this tradition. In contrast, the US system is one organized on commercial principles, textually distinguished by the normality of advertising spots and breaks. The viewer is primarily a consumer. In the first instance, then, television studies signifies the contested, nationally inflected, academic address to television as primary object of study—rather than, as I discuss below, television as part of international media economies or television as site of drama in performance.

Television Studies: A Story Told in Six Anthologies

There have been two prerequisites for development of the primarily Anglophone discipline of television studies. The first was that television as such be regarded as worthy of study. This apparently obvious point is significant in relation to a medium which has historically attracted distrust, fear and contempt. These responses, which often involve the invocation of television as both origin and symptom of social ills, have, as many scholars have pointed out, homologies with responses to earlier popular genres and forms such as the novel and the cinema. Debate about the significance and value of television persists, and much academic and popular writing about the medium is haunted by anxiety about the cultural legitimacy of watching television. The second prerequisite was that television be granted, conceptually, some autonomy and specificity as a medium. Thus television had to be regarded as more than simply a transmitter of world, civic or artistic events and as distinguishable from other of the "mass media." Indeed, much of the literature of television studies could be characterized as attempting to formulate accounts of the specificity of television, often using comparison with, on the one hand, radio (broadcast, liveness, civic address), and on the other, cinema (moving pictures, fantasy), with particular attention, as discussed below, to debate about the nature of the television text and the television audience.[1] Increasingly significant also are the emergent histories of television—whether it be the autobiographical accounts of insiders, such as Grace Wyndham Goldie's history of her years at the BBC, *Facing the Nation* (1978), or the painstaking archival research of historians such as William Boddy with his history of the Quiz scandals in 1950s US television (1990), or Lynn Spigel with her pioneering study of the way in which television was "installed" in the US living room in the 1950s (*Make Room for TV*, 1993).

Television studies emerged in the 1970s and 1980s from three major bodies of commentary on television: journalism, literary/dramatic criticism and the social sciences. These are the main bodies of work in which attention was paid to television, although the attention, and the television, of each was different, as I will show. Each, in the 1970s and 1980s, was also affected by the changing ideas about gender provoked by second wave feminism, a movement which turned out to have its own interests in television. Of the founding bodies of commentary, the first, and most familiar, was daily and weekly journalism. This has generally taken the form of guides to viewing and reviews of recent programs. Television reviewing has, historically, been strongly personally voiced, with this authorial voice rendering continuity to the diverse topics and programs addressed.[2] The repeated production of a discriminating "I who view" could also be seen as a compensatory symptom of the anxiety about viewing in the first place, most marked in the instances when the review seems insistently about critic rather than program. Nonetheless, some of this writing has offered formulations of great insight in its address to broadcast form—for example the work of James Thurber (1948), Raymond Williams (1968, 1974), Philip Purser (1992) or Nancy Banks-Smith (in the *Guardian*)—which is only now being recognized as one of the origins of the discipline of television studies. This television is a television watched and judged for a range of reasons: as entertainment, for information, as a national event, although rare is the critic who comments on the news or those elements of broadcast output thought of as unexceptional and normal, such as continuity announcing or long-running chat shows.

The second body of commentary is also organized through ideas of authorship, but here it is the writer or dramatist who forms the legitimation for the attention to television. Critical method here is extrapolated from traditional literary and dramatic criticism, and the television attracts serious critical attention as a "home theater." Indicative texts here would be the early collection edited by Howard Thomas, *Armchair Theatre* (1959), or

Contents

Contents

Figure 1 Contents pages of George Brandt (ed.) *British Television Drama* (Cambridge University Press, 1981) and George Brandt (ed.), *British Television Drama in the 1980s* (Cambridge: Cambridge University

the later, more academic volume edited by George Brandt, *British Television Drama* (1981). Television here is broadcast drama, interesting both because a new medium makes new demands on creative personae and because new technologies make available new audiences. Until the 1980s, the address of this type of work was almost exclusively to "high culture": plays and occasionally series by known playwrights, often featuring theatrical actors. This emphasis can be clearly seen by contrasting the contents pages of Brandt's 1981 collection and his 1993 collection, *British Television Drama in the 1980s* (*see* Fig. 1). The 1981 volume is organized into chapters named after writers. This points to the significance of the writer as author within this understanding of television, and to the privileging of a notion of authorial *œuvre* over individual work. Only with an understanding of this traditional approach to television drama is it possible to see how exceptional Raymond Williams's defense of television soap opera is in *Drama in Performance* (1968), or Horace Newcomb's validation of popular genres in *TV: The Most Popular Art* (1974). Brandt's 1993 volume reveals a considerable shift of emphasis. While there is still a residual, formative structure of the writer, chapters here are named by program, and lower forms, such as the soap opera and the situation comedy, make an appearance. Not all authors and artists are men. Most indicative, perhaps, of the emergence of television as an object of study on new terms is a contrast of Appendix 1 of each book. In 1981 the appendix is of "Plays published." In 1993 it is "Programs on videotape." Although his 1993 introduction expresses considerable hostility to television studies, I would argue that by 1993 Brandt's notion of television drama has been "television studied." To understand how this has come about requires a return to my sketch of the origins of the discipline.

Both of these bodies of commentary, the journalistic and the literary/dramatic, are mainly concerned to address what was shown on the screen, and thus conceive of television mainly as a text within the arts/humanities academic traditions. The privileged object is generally a self-bounded work of fiction.[3] Other early attention to television draws, in different ways, on the social sciences to address the production, circulation and function of television in contemporary society. Here, research has tended not to address the television text as such, but instead to conceptualize television either through notions of its social *function* and *effects,* or within a governing question of *cui bono?* (whose good is served?). Thus television, along with other of the mass media, is conceptualized within frameworks principally concerned with the maintenance of social order; the reproduction of the *status quo,* the relationship between the state, media ownership and citizenship; the constitution of the public sphere. With these concerns, privileged areas of inquiry have tended to be non-textual: patterns of international cross-media ownership; national and international regulation of media production and distribution; professional ideologies; public opinion; media audiences. Television, here, is more often an *instance* or *site* than a text. Methodologies here have been greatly contested, particularly in the extent to which Marxist frameworks or those associated with the critical sociology of the Frankfurt School have been employed. For scholars differ as to whether the mass media should be studied as one element in the smooth functioning of society, or as contributing to the reproduction of particular patterns of dominance—for example, the blonde "Anglo" idea of feminine beauty as a world-wide ideal for all women. *Mass Communication and Society,* a collection edited by James Curran, Michael Gurevitch and Janet Woollacott in 1977, as a course textbook for the Open University, provides an indicative text here (*see* Fig. 2).

While television is addressed in this volume—for example, Chapters 9 and 10 offer specific case studies, while Chapter 2 is primarily concerned with the establishment of the BBC—it is television conceived of within the field of mass communications. Television is conceived of as part of a web of communications media which mediate, reproduce and are reproduced by cultures structured through patterns of class dominance. What is particularly interesting about this reader is the way in which it also seeks to problematize the field of mass communication, repeatedly preferring the work of scholars working within the traditions of critical sociology and the emergent cultural studies to the US traditions of "mass comm." The editors' introduction makes this point trenchantly, with its clearly articulated project of a *theoretical* rather than "empiricist" or "instrumentalist" communication studies. How else to explain the presence of Walter Benjamin, who wrote, in the 1930s, not about television, but about how the status of art was transformed in the age of mechanical reproduction?

But the inclusion of James Carey, Stuart Hall, Dick Hebdige and Walter Benjamin in this volume points to the increasing relevance of the emerging discipline of cultural studies to the understanding of culture and communication—and television (these are terms here understood in a *public* sense). The conceptualization of the field is a conceptualization of a global economy—this *is* an international vision—and overlapping public spheres. It is the contrasting emphasis on the private, the intimate and the domestic which has distinguished feminist approaches to the media in general, and television in particular. Much early feminist research on television in the mass communications field was concerned with questions of women's employment and their lack of visibility on the television screen. But very quickly feminists also began to investigate the idea of television as a despised domestic medium with programming aimed at housewives. The key genre here was the soap opera, a genre which exists in many different forms all over the world. And although different national serials do have different types of format, they share the contempt with which they are often regarded, the way in which they are seen as feminine and much less important than the world of politics and the public sphere. An indicative collection here is *Regarding Television,* published by the American Film Institute in 1983. This book, which was edited by E. Ann Kaplan from a conference she organized at Rutgers University in 1981, begins to show the impact of feminist research on television in a more sustained way than the individual articles

Contents

Figure 2 Contents page of James Curran, Michael Gurevitch and Janet Woollacott (eds), *Mass Communication and Society* (London: Edward Arnold, 1977).

that were being published (*see* Fig. 3). Here there are four articles on soap opera, while others, such as Margaret Morse's work on sport, also address questions raised by feminist theory.

The way in which the essays on soap opera address their object is also significant. For while some of the essays, such as Sandy Flitterman's, are concerned with the television text, others, such as Tania Modleski's, are concerned with the distracted ways of watching that the genre allows. The influence of feminist scholars on television studies, then, on the one hand, directed attention to the despised genre of soap opera, and on the other, drew attention to the ways in which television was watched in the home.

The impact of this research can be seen if we compare the 1977 Curran, Gurevitch and Woollacott reader (*see* Fig. 2) with a 1991 Curran and Gurevitch reader, *Mass Media and Society* (*see* Fig. 4). While there are a range of differences between the first and second readers, with the second generally tending towards survey articles rather than case studies and reprinted material, what is noticeable in this context is what is surveyed. As with the Brandt, there is a noticeable feminization of the object of study. Lower forms appear: here, "romantic drama," there, soap opera. There are two articles which make a direct address to feminist media research, those by Ang and Hermes, and van Zoonen. While the field is still conceived in ways familiar from the 1977 collection, there have also been some shifts in the recognition of the gender agenda. Here we see that television is still conceptualized within the broader international frameworks of mass communications, but in fact the feminist essays are strongly dependent on television research to make their arguments. The definition of television has shifted between this anthology and the earlier 1977 one.

One further contents list from the "early" period (1981) is illuminating here, showing the way in which television studies also emerged from a cluster of work best understood as film and cultural studies. This contents page comes from a reader for another Open University course, *Popular Television and Film,* edited by Tony Bennett, Susan Boyd-Bowman, Colin Mercer and Janet Woollacott (*see* Fig. 5). Like the Kaplan collection, this collection has articles by film scholars writing about television, but here the book is clearly seen to be about both film and television. The television is British television, although the cinema is Hollywood.

This collection offers much more attention to television as text, and marks a significant move away from conceiving that text solely as serious drama. Thus there are articles on football and sitcoms although the last part of the book does concentrate on *Days of Hope,* a four-part series directed by Ken Loach and produced by Tony Garnett about the British General Strike in 1926. Whilst the collection does include Laura Mulvey's famous article on visual pleasure, feminist work is not much in evidence. The move away from high art is a move to football, science and crime series. However, it is also clear that approaches from film studies, particularly through notions of genre, produce yet another understanding of television, which is here also informed by work in cultural studies. This collection was published

Table of Contents

Figure 3 Contents page of E. Ann Kaplan (ed.), *Regarding Television* (Los Angeles: American Film Institute, 1983).

Contents

Figure 4 Contents page of James Curran and Michael Gurevitch (eds), *Mass Media and Society* (London: Edward Arnold, 1991)

Contents

Figure 5   Contents page of Tony Bennett, Susan Boyd-Bowman, Colin Mercer and Janet Woollacott (eds), *Popular Television and Film* (London: British Film Institute in association with the Open University, 1981).

in the same year as the first George Brandt collection, but has very different emphases. However, when we examine them together, as I have here, the 1993 Brandt collection is much easier to place. We see how *Television Drama in the 1980s* is the result of much broader definitions of what in television is worth paying attention to, just as we can see that the 1991 Curran and Gurevitch collection has responded to some of the same debates.

What Does Television Studies Study?
Text, Audience, and Representation

From these diverse origins developed the "television" of television studies. In contrast to the television of the social sciences, this television was very "textualized." The concentration was on programs and genres rather than industry and economy. This was not, in general, a television discussed in relation to issues of working practices, labor relations, exports and national and international legislation. In contrast to the emphases of literary and dramatic criticism, it was a television of low and popular culture. A television of sitcoms, soaps and crime series, rather than a television of playwrights, a television of ideology rather than aesthetics. And there have proved to be three particular areas of interest in the literature of this television studies: the definition of the television text, the textual analysis of the representations of the social world offered therein, and the investigation of the television audience. I will discuss each of these areas briefly, concentrating on debate about the television text partly because it is here that we find debate specific to the medium and partly because other chapters in *The Television Studies Book* offer extended discussion and examples of research into audiences and the textual analysis of programs and genres.

Much innovatory work in television studies has been focused on the definition of the television text and this debate could be seen as one of the constituting frameworks of the field. The common-sense view points to the individual program as a unit, and this view has firm grounding in the way television is produced. Television is, for the most part, made as programs or runs of programs: series, serials and mini-series. However, this is not necessarily how television is watched, despite the considerable currency of the view that it is somehow better for the viewer to choose to watch particular programs rather than just having the television on. Indeed, BBC television in the 1950s featured "interludes" between programs, most famously *The Potter's Wheel,* a short film showing a pair of hands making a clay pot on a wheel, to ensure that viewers did not just drift from one program to another. It is precisely this possible "drifting" through an evening's viewing that has come to seem, to many commentators, one of the unique features of television watching, and hence something that must be attended to in any account of the television text.

The inaugural formulation is Raymond Williams's argument, in his 1974 book, *Television: Technology and Cultural Form,* that "the defining feature of broadcasting" is "planned flow" (1974: 86). Williams developed these ideas through reflecting on four years of reviewing television for the weekly periodical *The Listener*, when he suggests that the separating of the television text into recognizable generic program units, which makes the reviewer's job much easier, somehow misses "the central television experience: the fact of flow" (1974: 95). Williams's own discussion of flow draws on analysis of both British and US television and he is careful to insist on the natural variation of broadcasting systems and types and management of flow, but his attempt to describe what is specific to the watching of television has been internationally generative, particularly in combination with some of the more recent empirical studies of how people do (or don't) watch television.

If Williams's idea of flow has been principally understood to focus attention on television viewing as involving more viewing and less choosing than a critical focus on individual programs would suggest, other critics have picked up the micro-narratives of which so much television is composed. Thus John Ellis approached the television text using a model ultimately derived from film studies, although he is precisely concerned, in his book *Visible Fictions* (1982), to differentiate cinema and television. Ellis suggests that the key unit of the television text is the "segment," which he defines as "small, sequential unities of images and sounds whose maximum duration seems to be about five minutes" (1982: 112). Broadcast television, Ellis argues, is composed of different types of combination of segment: sometimes sequential, as in drama series, sometimes cumulative, as in news broadcasts and commercials. As with Williams's "flow," the radical element in Ellis's "segment" is the way in which it transgresses common-sense boundaries like "program" or "documentary" and "fiction" to bring to the analyst's attention common and defining features of broadcast television as a medium.

However, it has also been argued that the television text cannot be conceptualized without attention to the structure of national broadcasting institutions and the financing of program production. In this context, Nick Browne (1984) has argued that the US television system is best approached through a notion of the "super-text." Browne is concerned to address the specificities of the US commercial television system in contrast to the public service models—particularly the British one—which have been so generative a context for formative and influential thinking on television such as that of Raymond Williams and Stuart Hall. Browne defines the "super-text" as, initially, a television program and all introductory and interstitial material in that program's place in a schedule. He is thus insisting on an "impure" idea of the text, arguing that the program as broadcast at a particular time in the working week, interrupted by ads and announcements, condenses the political economy of television. Advertising, in Browne's schema, is the central mediating institution in US television, linking program schedules to the wider world of production and consumption.

The final concept to be considered in the discussion about the television text is Newcomb and Hirsch's idea of the "viewing strip" (1983). This concept suggests a mediation between broadcast provision and individual choice, attempting to grasp the way in which individuals negotiate their way through the "flow" on offer, putting together a sequence of viewing of their own selection. Thus different individuals might produce very different "texts"—viewing strips—from the same night's viewing. Implicit within the notion of the viewing strip—although not a prerequisite—is the remote control device, allowing channel change and channel-surfing. And it is this tool of audience agency which points us to the second substantial area of innovatory scholarship in television studies, the address to the audience.

The hybrid disciplinary origins of television studies are particularly evident in the approach to the television audience. Here, particularly in the 1980s, we find the convergence of potentially antagonistic paradigms, represented most vividly in an interdisciplinary conference on the television audience held in 1990 at the University of Illinois, where scholars from a range of disciplines met to debate and contest their versions of the audience, and how it can be appropriately investigated (Schroder, 1987; Hay, Grossberg and Wartella, 1996). Very simply, on the one hand, research traditions in the social sciences focus on the empirical investigation of the already existing audience. Research design here tends to seek representative samples of particular populations and/or viewers of a particular type of programming (adolescent boys and violence; women and soap opera). Research on the television audience has historically been dominated, particularly in the USA, by large-scale quantitative surveys, often designed using a model of the "effects" of the media, of which television is not necessarily a differentiated element. Within the social sciences, this "effects" model has been challenged by what is known as the "uses and gratifications" model. In James Halloran's famous formulation, "we should ask not what the media does to people, but what people do to the media" (1970). Herta Herzog's 1944 research on the listeners to radio daytime serials was an inaugural project within this "uses and gratifications" tradition, which has recently produced the international project on the international decoding of the US prime-time serial, *Dallas* (Liebes and Katz, 1990).

This social science history of empirical audience investigation has been confronted, on the other hand, by ideas of a textually constituted "reader" with their origins in literary and film studies. This is a very different conceptualization of the audience, drawing on literary, semiotic and psychoanalytic theory to suggest—in different and disputed ways—that the text constructs a "subject position" from which it is intelligible. In this body of work, the context of consumption and the social origins of audience members are irrelevant to the making of meaning which originates in the text. However—and it is thus that we see the potential convergence with social science "uses and gratifications" models—literary theorists such as Umberto Eco (1994) have posed the extent to which the reader should be seen as active in meaning-making. It is, in this context, difficult to separate the development of television studies from that of cultural studies, for it is within cultural studies that we begin to find, in the 1980s, sophisticated theorizations and empirical investigations of the complex, contextual interplay of text and "reader" in the making of meaning, as in, for example, the work of Janice Radway (1984) on the readers of romance fiction.

The inaugural formulations on television in the field of cultural studies are those of Stuart Hall in essays such as "Encoding and decoding in television discourse" (1974) and David Morley's audience research (*The Nationwide Audience,* 1980). However, this television-specific work cannot theoretically be completely separated from other cultural studies research which stressed the often oppositional agency of individuals in response to contemporary culture. British cultural studies has proved a successful export, the theoretical paradigms there employed meeting and sometimes clashing with those used, internationally, in more generalized academic reorientation towards the study of popular culture and entertainment in the 1970s and 1980s. Examples of influential television scholars working within cultural studies paradigms would be Ien Ang and John Fiske. Ang's work on the television audience (1985, 1991, 1995) ranges from a study of *Dallas* fans in the Netherlands to the interrogation of existing ideas of audience in a postmodern, global context. John Fiske's work has been particularly successful in introducing British cultural studies to a US audience, and his 1987 book *Television Culture* was one of the first books about television to take seriously the feminist agenda that has been so important to the recent development of the field. For if television studies is understood as a barely established institutional space, carved out by scholars of television from, on the one hand, mass communications and traditional Marxist political economy, and on the other, cinema, drama and literary studies, the significance of feminist research to the establishment of this connotationally feminized field cannot be underestimated, even if it is not always recognized.

The interest of new social movements in issues of representation, which has been generative for film and literary studies as well as for television studies, has produced sustained interventions by a range of scholars, approaching texts with questions about the representation of particular social groups and the interpretation of programs such as, for example, *thirtysomething, Pee Wee's Playhouse, Cagney and Lacey* and *The Cosby Show.* Feminist scholars have, since the mid-1970s, tended to focus particularly on programs for women and those which have key female protagonists. Key work here would include Julie D'Acci's study of *Cagney and Lacey* (1994), which is unusual in its attention to the conditions of production, and the now substantial literature on soap opera. In the USA, the televised proceedings of the Anita Hill/Clarence Thomas hearings prompted much analysis, which, while almost never about television alone, did reveal the ways in which cultural studies approaches to television generated complex and sophisticated analyses of media events (Lubiano, 1993). Research by Sut Jhally and Justin Lewis (1992) has addressed the complex meanings about class and "race" produced by viewers of *The Cosby Show,* but most audience research in this "representational" paradigm has been with white audiences. Jacqueline Bobo and Ellen Seiter (1991) argue that this is partly a consequence of the "whiteness" of the academy which makes research about viewing in the domestic environment potentially a further extension of surveillance for those ethnicized by the dominant culture. Herman Gray (1993) has suggested that there is a repeated "avoidance and deferral of racial difference" in critical television analysis, a deferral achieved partly through the separation of the analysis of the formal operations of the television apparatus from attention to issues of race. This argument has resonance here, for we could suggest that the television of television studies, to a considerable degree echoing the address of Anglophone broadcast television, in the post-war period, has been constructed "whitely." This would be a matter, not so much of who is writing, but what they write about and to whom it is addressed. There is a growing body of work which suggests the beginning of change—for example, Darnell Hunt's 1997 analysis of the televising and viewing of the Rodney King beating, which analyzes what Hunt nominates as a process of "raceing" for spectators, or Lynn Spigel's work on the white flight of the space race as figured in 1950s US sci-fi sitcoms (1997). However, in the context of a discussion of the television of television studies, these are minority and relatively recent works.[4] So it becomes not only a question of what is the television of television studies, but, as indeed with the question of the address of the medium, who is assumed to be the student?

Conclusion: History

The television of television studies, then, is a relatively recent phenomenon. It has been produced in the last period in which television broadcasting will be dominated by nationally regulated terrestrial broadcasters, the last three decades of the twentieth century. Its origins lie in more established fields of study, principally literature and the social sciences, with a strong contribution from the theoretical models used in film and cultural studies. Feminist scholarship has been particularly significant in pointing to the private and domestic aspects of a medium which, in the social sciences, has been mainly conceptualized in terms of the public sphere. Generally, the television of television studies is a contemporary, politicized television analyzed because it is understood to be a powerful medium. However, these politics are generally understood at a textual, rather than an institutional level, with much research undertaken to investigate the way in which the social world and particular social groups are—or are not—represented, rather than the more traditional political economy approaches, which see patterns of ownership and regulation as politically determining.

I started this essay by posing the idea that it is not obvious what the television of television studies is. Television, as an object of study, has been produced differently by different scholars and interest groups, and I have offered only a brief sketch. I have, for example, given little attention here to the television studied by those primarily concerned with its effects on children, or to research conducted by advertisers and broadcasting institutions.[5] But I hope I have established the significant contours in the development, particularly in Britain, of the infant discipline, television studies. Throughout the essay, I have suggested the ways in which this television is different to the television studied in other contexts. I am not trying to draw lines of disciplinary purity—this study *is* television studies, that isn't— although the disciplinary provenance of particular research is always illuminating. Instead, I have tried to show the way in which books such as Williams's *Television: Technology and Cultural Form* (1974) and John Fiske and John Hartley's *Reading Television* (1978) inaugurated and represent new ways of thinking about television. What seems exciting about this hybrid discipline is its hybridity. The field of television studies is only enriched by returning to some of the questions and emphases of its originary disciplines. For example, the internationalism of studies of the political economy of the media sometimes seems lacking in television studies, as does an understanding of the production of texts, as opposed to their productivity. The significance of qualitative audience research in television studies should not prevent the recognition of the importance of working with larger samples. Deconstructing the assumption that the only television of aesthetic interest is the single play should not lead to the abandonment of the critical analysis of the role of the writer on television. If "television studies" now has some recognition, its dynamic potential is best realized not in policing its boundaries, but in providing a context in which scholars working on what is often considered a trivial medium can meet rigorous assessment by colleagues and the benefits of inter- and multidisciplinary approaches.

This can perhaps be most interestingly exemplified in relation to the different histories we can find in television studies. For if, on the one hand, the archives of the broadcasting institutions and production companies offer relatively conventional sources for the historian, the absence of much television history *as television* is rather more demanding. Similarly, the increasing tide of ephemera generated by the medium raises historiographical questions also posed by the use of sources of contested evidentiary status such as women's magazines. In the 1990s, explicitly historical projects which use this range of material, such as Janet Thumim's (1995) research on British television for women in the 1950s, meet older, contemporary production studies which trace the complex interplay of factors involved in getting programs on screen. Examples here might include Tom Burns's study of the professional culture of the BBC (1977), *Movie* magazine's study of *Upstairs, Downstairs* (Barr, Hillier and Perkins, 1975) or Philip Schlesinger's study of "The News," *Putting "Reality" Together* (1978). That is, as television studies enters the text-book stage of its existence, it is possible to look back and see a very wide range of texts as contributing to its development. This broad view, I would argue, is necessary if the television of television studies is not to be a limited and impoverished object of study. But also, this broad view begins to give us a much richer understanding of the history of television and how it has been understood historically. This history of television is a rapidly expanding field, creating a retrospective history for the discipline, but also documenting the period of nationally regulated terrestrial broadcasting which is now coming to an end. Whatever we thought the television of television studies was when it was being invented in the 1970s, what is becoming increasingly clear is that what it is now is history.

Notes

An earlier version of part of this essay has been published as the entry on "Television Studies" in Horace Newcomb (ed.), *Encyclopedia of Television* (Chicago: Fitzroy Dearborn, 1997). Thanks to Laura Mulvey's BFI MA group (1996–7), the Midlands Television Research group, Jason Jacobs and David Morley for comments.

1. Scannell and Cardiff's *Social History of British Broadcasting* (1991), while concerned with the history of radio, establishes the framework for the consideration of British television as a broadcast medium, something developed in Scannell's edited collection, *Broadcast Talk* (1991). John Ellis's *Visible Fictions* (1982) provides an interesting counter-point in its discussion of television in relation to cinema.

2. Detailed discussion of the reviewing and criticism of television can be found in McArthur (1980), Caughie (1984) and Poole (1984).

3. David Edgar (1982) makes a strong argument for the significance of drama documentary within the output of television, but this was relatively unusual at the time.

4. Other work relevant here would be George Lipsitz's (1988) account of the mobilization of immigrant identities into early US network shows; Jim Pines's edited collection of interviews with black contributors to British television (1992); John Fiske's *Media Matters* (1995); Karen Ross's history of the intertwined origins of black film-making and television (1996); and Richard Dyer's discussion of "whiteness" in the British television serial, *The Jewel in the Crown.* (1996).

5. See Buckingham (1996) and Seiter (1993).

References and Further Reading

Ang, I., 1985: *Watching Dallas.* London: Methuen.

———, 1991: *Desperately Seeking the Audience.* London: Routledge.

———, 1995: *Living Room Wars.* London: Routledge.

Barr, C., Hillier, J. and Perkins, V., 1975: "The making of a television series: *Upstairs Downstairs.*" *Movie* 21: 46–63.

Bennett, T., Boyd-Bowman, S., Mercer, C. and Woollacott, J. (eds), 1981: *Popular Television and Film.* London: British Film Institute in association with the Open University.

Bobo, J., and Seiter, E., 1991: "Black feminism and media criticism." *Screen*, 32.3, reprinted in C. Brunsdon, J. D'Acci and L. Spigel (eds), 1997, *Feminist Television Criticism: A Reader.* Oxford: Oxford University Press.

Boddy, W., 1990: *Fifties Television: The Industry and its Critics.* Urbana and Chicago: University of Illinois Press.

Brandt, G., 1981: *British Television Drama.* Cambridge: Cambridge University Press.

———, 1993: *British Television Drama in the 1980s.* Cambridge: Cambridge University Press.

Browne, N., 1984: "The political economy of the television (super) text." *Quarterly Review of Film Studies*, 9, 3, reprinted in Horace Newcomb (ed), 1994, *Television: The Critical View.* New York: Oxford University Press.

Buckingham, D., 1996: *Moving Images. Understanding Children's Emotional Responses to Television.* Manchester: Manchester University Press.

Burns, T., 1977: *The BBC: Public Institution, Private World.* London: Macmillan.

Caughie, J., 1984: "Television criticism: a discourse in search of an object." *Screen,* 25, 4–5, 109–20.

Corner, J., 1995: *Television Form and Public Address.* London: Edward Arnold.

Corner, J., and Harvey, S. (eds), 1996: *Television Times: A Reader.* London: Arnold.

Curran, J. and Gurevitch, M., 1991: *Mass Media and Society.* London: Edward Arnold.

Curran, J., Gurevitch, M. and Woollacott, J., 1977: *Mass Communication and Society.* London: Edward Arnold.

D'Acci, J., 1994: *Defining Women: Television and the Case of Cagney and Lacey.* Chapel Hill: University of North Carolina Press.

Dyer, R., 1996: "'There's nothing I can do! Nothing!': femininity, seriality and whiteness in *The Jewel in the Crown.*" *Screen,* 37, 3:225–39.

Eco, U., 1994: "Does the audience have bad effects on television?" (first published 1977). In R. Lumley (ed.), *Umberto Eco: Apocalypse Postponed.* London: British Film Institute.

Edgar, D., 1982: "On drama documentary." In F. Pike (ed) *Ah! Mischief.* London: Faber and Faber.

Ellis, J., 1982: *Visible Fictions.* London: Routledge and Kegan Paul.

Fiske, J., 1987: *Television Culture.* London: Methuen.

———, 1995: *Media Matters.* Minneapolis: University of Minnesota Press.

Fiske, J. and Hartley, J., 1978: *Reading Television.* London: Methuen.

Goldie, G. W., 1978: *Facing the Nation: Television and Politics 1936–1976.* London: The Bodley Head.

Gray, H., 1993: "The endless slide of difference: critical television studies, television and the question of race." *Critical Studies in Mass Communication,* June: 190–7.

Hall, S., 1980 "Encoding/decoding" (first published 1974). In Hall *et al.* (eds), *Culture, Media, Language.* London and Birmingham: Hutchinson and the Centre for Contemporary Cultural Studies.

Hall, S., Hobson, D., Lowe, A., and Willis, P. (eds) 1980: *Culture, Media, Language.* London and Birmingham: Hutchinson and Centre for Contemporary Cultural Studies.

Halloran, J., 1970: *The Effects of Television.* London: Panther.

Hay, J., Grossberg, L. and Wartella, E. (eds) 1996: *The Audience and its Landscape.* Boulder, CO: Westview.

Heide, M., 1995: *Television Culture and Women's Lives.* Philadelphia: University of Pennsylvania Press.

Herzog, H., 1944: "What do we really know about daytime serial listeners?" In Paul Lazarsfeld and Frank Stanton (eds), *Radio Research 1942–43.* New York: Duell, Sloan and Pearce.

Hunt, D. M., 1997: *Screening the Los Angeles "Riots": Race, Seeing and Resistance.* Cambridge: Cambridge University Press.

Jhally, S. and Lewis, J., 1992: *Enlightened Racism:* The Cosby Show, *Audiences and the Myth of the American Dream.* Boulder, CO: Westview Press.

Kaplan, E. A., 1983: *Regarding Television.* Los Angeles: American Film Institute.

Liebes, T. and Katz, E., 1990: *The Export of Meaning.* Oxford: Oxford University Press.

Lipsitz, G., 1988: "The meaning of memory: family, class and ethnicity in early network television programs." *Camera Obscura*, 16: 79–116.

Lubiano, W., 1993: "Black ladies, welfare queens and state minstrels: ideological war by narrative means." In Toni Morrison (ed.) *Race-ing Justice, En-gendering Power*. London: Chatto and Windus.

McArthur, C., 1980: "Points of review: television criticism in the press." *Screen Education*, 35: 59–61.

Morley, D., 1980: *The Nationwide Audience*. London: British Film Institute.

———, 1992: *Television, Audiences and Cultural Studies*. London: Routledge.

Newcomb, H., 1974: *TV: The Most Popular Art*. New York: Anchor.

Newcomb, H. and Hirsch, P., 1983: "Television as a cultural forum." Reprinted in Newcomb (ed.) (1994) *Television: The Critical View*. New York: Oxford University Press.

Pines, J., 1992: *Black and White in Colour*. London: British Film Institute.

Poole, M., 1984: "The cult of the generalist. British TV criticism, 1936–83." *Screen*, 25, 4–5: 41–61.

Purser, P., 1992: *Done Viewing*. London: Quartet.

Radway, J., 1984: *Reading the Romance: Women, Patriarchy and Popular Literature*. Chapel Hill: University of North Carolina Press.

Ross, K., 1996: *Black and White Media*. Cambridge: Polity.

Scannell, P. (ed.), 1991: *Broadcast Talk*. London: Sage.

Scannell, P. and Cardiff, D., 1991: *The Social History of Broadcasting, Vol. 1 1922–1939*. London: Basil Blackwell.

Schlesinger, P., 1978: *Putting "Reality" Together*. London: Constable.

Schroder, K. C., 1987: "Convergence of antagonistic traditions? The case of audience research." *European Journal of Communication*, 2, 7–31.

Selby, K. and Cowdery, R., 1995: *How to Study Television*. Houndmills: Macmillan.

Seiter, E., 1993: *Sold Separately: Parents and Children in Consumer Culture*. New Jersey: Rutgers University Press.

Spigel, L., 1993: *Make Room for TV*. Chicago: University of Chicago Press.

———, 1997: "White flight." In L. Spigel and M. Curtin (eds), *The Revolution Wasn't Televised*. New York: Routledge.

Thomas, H. (ed.), 1959: *The Armchair Theatre*. London: Weidenfeld and Nicolson.

Thumim, J., 1995: "'A live commercial for icing sugar.'" Researching the historical audience: gender and broadcast television in the 1950s." *Screen* 36, 1: 48–55.

Thurber, J., 1948: *The Beast in Me and Other Animals*. New York: Harcourt Brace.

Williams, R., 1968: *Drama in Performance* (extended edition). London: C.A. Watts.

———, 1974: *Television, Technology and Cultural Form*. London: Collins.

———, 1989: *Raymond Williams on Television*, ed. Alan O'Connor. London: Routledge.

What Was Broadcasting?

DAVID MARC

A Signal Cast Broadly

Like the national debt, the homeless population, gun ownership, and job insecurity, television grew prodigiously in the 1980s. In terms of quantity, a steadily increasing number of channels served a steadily increasing number of audiences who were putting their sets to a steadily increasing number of uses. In terms of quality, programming got simultaneously much better and much worse than it ever had been, establishing a fresh context for the mediocrity that still dominates it (and every other artistic endeavor thus far attempted). Ironically, during this period of prolific expansion in the form, function, and spectrum of television, broadcasting steadily diminished in importance.

This is neither a joke nor an academic language trick, but rather an apparently invisible fact. American culture was conquered and dominated for more than five decades by common-band broadcast transmission. Two technological innovations ended that reign: closed circuit delivery systems (e.g., cable) and self-programming options (e.g., the VCR). The diminishing importance of broadcasting in American mass communication has directly paralleled profound economic restructurings and social polarizations that have reshaped society. A perplexing question crystallizes in the face of this: how can an expansion in the number of cultural options accompany a contraction of democratic values and institutions?

"General interest" broadcasting, much like universal suffrage, retains inherently democratic potentials, even though the process is often manipulated toward anti-democratic ends. The spectacular feat of rhetoric, music, drama, and the other stuff of culture being "cast broadly" to a full complement of citizenry should have marked the crossing of an important threshold in the development of democracy. Structured for transdemographic address, broadcasting solicits rich and poor, egghead and illiterate, gang member and unaffiliated, theocrat and atheist, offering all parties abrupt

association as members of a single audience, and adding the security of physical isolation from each other in the bargain. Before the rise of the commercial broadcasting networks in the late 1920s, only the great transnational
religious networks, such as Christianity and Islam, had ever pitched a cultural tent so wide.

An entire nation-state addressed by its leader as one big audience is a
distilled image of the twentieth century, likely to share prominence in CD-
ROM textbooks with the camps, the mushroom clouds, and the automobile. The remembered figures of the century will surely be broadcast figures, including radio characters such as Hitler, Churchill, and Roosevelt as
well as TV characters such as Cronkite, Reagan, and Oprah.[1] In the case of
the radio stars, heads of state imitated a quainter state of technology: the
passionate address to the crowd in the public space. By contrast, the TV
people have tended to function as spokespersons and interlocutors, calmly
promoting the ways of life and points of view of their corporate sponsors.
Mussolini did his radio work from a balcony; Pat Robertson makes eye contact from a studio chair.

It is already a cliché to mention that what we have come to call The
News was created in print during the nineteenth century as the telegraph
allowed newspapers to gather information instantaneously from distant
points without having to transport it. The character of the daily news has
since that time been altered repeatedly by a sequence of adaptations to electronic media: broadcast radio, broadcast television, cable television, on-line
services, and so on. Less attention, however, has been paid to what cumulative effects the resulting *imago mundi* might have on the imagination of
history, which now can be thought of as the mega-news.

We have already seen how the audio-visually documented assassination
of John F. Kennedy levitated him and his presidency into an historiographical
mythosphere once occupied only by the likes of Washington, Jefferson, and
Lincoln. By contrast, William McKinley never had a chance. The O. J. Simpson trial is assured a place in the popular history of twentieth-century American jurisprudence that few if any Supreme Court rulings might hope to
occupy; Judge Ito has already eclipsed Oliver Wendell Holmes in recognition factor. Father Coughlin will have generated far more usable material
than Pope John XXIII, and Billy Graham more than both. Who is likely to
be a more dominant presence in the digital archives? Albert Einstein or Carl
Sagan? Dr. Freud or Dr. Ruth? Charles Darwin or Pat Robertson? Mother
Teresa already has a higher F-score than Albert Schweitzer. In the future
the past will belong to the audio-visually reproducible. The giants of the
arts and sciences who, for whatever reason, failed to climb the transmission
towers of the twentieth century can expect to be remaindered to the specialists' bin.

If the current thrust toward market-specific communication persists,
then the kind of transdemographic fame achieved so cheaply in the mass
broadcasting environment is less likely to occur. The ubiquity achieved in
their time by Jackie Gleason, Jack Webb, or Paul Henning's sitcom char-

acters is becoming a goal coveted primarily by national politicians who must still play by the rules of mass culture because of the legal constraints of universal suffrage, a system instituted during the same year (1920) that the first radio station went on the air.[2] Whereas the term "crossover" once referred to the launching of a personality or a work from a particular taste culture base to mass distribution, now the term is used more often to refer to the cross-fertilization of two or three taste cultures. Examples from the early 1990s include such coups as Tony Bennett's capture of youth market music share and the revival of cigar smoking among 18- to 34-year-old white-collar males. The Broadcast Era, a period roughly stretching from the establishment of network radio in the 1920s to the achievement of 50 percent cable penetration in the 1980s, becomes more historically distinct every time another half dozen channels are added to the cable mix.

It is the culture of broadcasting that made Elvis and the Beatles possible, and it is the decline of broadcasting that makes such personalities less feasible all the time. In both cases the artists began their careers as demographically particular phenomena. But their wild successes in the niche-oriented record industry, part of the newly splintered culture of broadcast radio, were viewed as indications of their readiness for the massest of all cultures: pre-cable broadcast network television. They emerged from the night spots of Memphis and Hamburg to appear on *The Ed Sullivan Show*. In the cable environment, however, *The Ed Sullivan Show* is no longer possible.

As its vulgar expressions of massness become more exotic, the Broadcast Era may become enshrined as a kind of biblical era of mass communications, a heightened past during which miracles occurred and rules were handed down to carry generations into future millennia. An archival item such as Edward R. Murrow's onsite accounts of the London blitzkrieg, broadcast over the CBS radio network, may assume etiological proportions, a prophetic foreshadowing of Peter Arnet's reports from Baghdad on CNN during the Gulf War. In terms of marketing technology, the Murrow audiotape of 1941, while technologically primitive, was produced at the critical mass of mass culture, while the Arnet videotape of 1991 functioned more as a special interest item for war fans and other parties drawn in by a knowledge of the seriousness of the situation or the involvement of relatives. MTV, HBO, The Nashville Network, and a dozen other cable channels completely ignored the war (i.e., did not carry it), inviting their viewers to do the same.

"Total war" of the old 1914/1939 variety, like the mass culture that spawned it, has splintered into a collection of special-interest conflagrations: a terrorist bombing here, an ethnic war there, a volley of retaliatory assassinations, and so on. In an age dominated by entertainment on demand, the effect of war on any given demographic tribe—whether grouped by age, income, race, religion, leisuretime pursuit, or whatever—is likely to determine the extent and character of coverage. No doubt an audience for war—war regardless of content—will identify itself. That audience may consist of such interested groups as history buffs, chauvinists, pacifists, and weapons enthusiasts. An audience in perpetual denial of such presentations is equally inevitable. It might include drug or sex addicts, certain religious zealots not concerned with the vanity of secular events, and the maniacally embittered survivors of busted romances. Others, perhaps most viewers, may dutifully integrate the war into their daily viewing habits or perhaps give it some extra minutes of pause while channel-surfing.

Now that broadcasting is slipping to the technological margins of a national communication system characterized by discriminate targeting, it is easy to forget that radio emerged from the laboratory as a wholesaler's market-specific product. First known as the wireless telegraph or radiotelegraph, it was primarily sold as a wholesale military-industrial tool that extended the capabilities of telegraphy to ocean-going vessels, providing revolutionary solutions to shipping problems that had been on record at least since the time of Homer.

For more than two decades following Marconi's celebrated demonstration of 1896, little serious attention was given to the possibilities of broadcasting as a cultural medium. First of all, the original broadcasts consisted of aural dots and dashes and not everyone found decoding a user-friendly activity. Meanwhile, the military applications of the invention were clear enough; the U.S. Navy began lobbying for control of wireless telegraphy as early as 1905, taking note of the promise it was showing in the Russo-Japanese War.

Though no previously existing entertainment company was involved in the early development of American broadcasting, some of the pioneer patents were issued to the United Fruit Company, which established a string of stations—the first radio network—for ship-to-shore broadcasting in the Caribbean basin and Eastern seaboard, the farm-to-market expanse of its tropical fruit business. The company's high-tech communication system was money well spent. Bad weather, over-stocked markets, and other problems endemic to moving around hundreds of tons of bananas were directly addressed.[3]

With the Radio Act of 1912, the U.S. government in effect claimed ownership of the airwaves, that otherwise empty space hanging over the nation and stretching up into the ionosphere or beyond. To civil libertarians and anarchists such a presumption may seem absurd, something like the claims of Virginia, Massachusetts, and other early coastal colonies to legal hegemony over every inch of the North America occupying their latitude coordinates across the continent to the Pacific. But the concept of government ownership of the air (or "ether" as it was then called) was accepted without much argument. While most of the general public had little idea of the implications of this concession, it appealed to both the laissez-faire capitalists and the progressive reformers who occupied the center of American political bureaucracy and debate.

Big business was naturally friendly to the idea of turning something that seemed virtually intangible into a material commodity that could be measured, bought, and sold. A Marxist of the period might say that the commodification of air gave the robber barons something new to rob. But there were attractions for socialists and fellow-travelers as well. If air was a natural resource, like copper for telegraph wires or forests for newsprint, it could theoretically be regulated for the good of the commonweal. Culture could be put within the reach of the common person. Market or public trust? The Wilson Administration made its position clear when it assigned radio oversight to the Department of Commerce (Bureau of Navigation) in 1913.

Any new means of communication is bound to become a means of personal expression, and even at this early juncture there were active broadcasters whose purposes were neither industrial nor civic. Approximately 8,500 licenses were issued to individuals in the U.S. between 1913 and 1917. The amateurs entertained each other with speech, music, and whatever else they could think of that might send a joyful noise hurtling out into space, and they did so with no apparent means of making money in return. Quite to the contrary, there was an irretrievable ante to be paid by the independent licensees.

Broadcasting emerged as a techno-hobby, a late-night-and-weekend pastime for upscale hardware owners, much like current-day Internet surfing. Comparing the geographical range of backyard transmission equipment became a tinkerer's sport known as DXing. In the spirit of competition, Maine and Texas found something to say to each other. Isolationists, Anglophiles, and supporters of the Kaiser made their points in the original cyber chat-room. It was even reported that the early patent-holder Dr. Lee DeForest courted his wife by installing a receiver in her home and airing his professions of love from a rooftop transmitter.[4] However, before World War I, entertainment broadcasting was an activity to spend money on, not to make money from.

As always, some were quicker than others to see the possibilities of turning a buck. In a 1916 memorandum filed to his boss at the American Marconi Company (later RCA), David Sarnoff proposed that the wireless telegraph be made into a "household utility in the same sense as the piano or phonograph."[5] Calling this adaptation of broadcasting to the domestic market a "Radio Music Box," he proposed that it "be placed on a table in the parlor or living room." Sarnoff was moved to speculate on further applications of the technology:

> The same principle can be extended to numerous other fields as, for example, receiving of lectures at home which can be made perfectly audible; also events of national importance can be simultaneously received and announced.[6]

Advertising, it must be noted, played no role in Sarnoff's diversification scheme. The economic purpose of the Radio Music Box was to turn a specialized wholesaling operation into a vast retail supermarket by creating an incentive for every consumer to buy a set. American Marconi would then meet the newly created demand by assembly-line techniques. What Henry Ford's Model T had done for personal transportation, Sarnoff's Music box would do for culture and communication: create a mass market.[7] The sell-

ing of commercial time had no recognized advocates in the radio industry
at this time. The revolutionary pivot that would put advertising executives
and tradespeople in positions of direct authority over the form and content
of drama, music, and other primary cultural activities for the balance of the
twentieth century was too distasteful for Victorian sensibilities to support,
if not too bizarre to grasp. Sarnoff's idea was to offer the music service
gratis, to pull the consumer in off the street to buy a radio; he had reimagined culture as a loss leader for the sale of a home appliance.

The Music Box Memo was not treated seriously by management when
it was filed, and even if it had been, no immediate action could have been
taken on it. Only months later, the U.S. formally entered World War I, and
President Woodrow Wilson, by executive order, had all broadcasting equipment impounded, sealed, and placed under the direct control of the Department of the Navy. By contrast, not a single printing press was put under
lock and key, ink being explicitly protected by a Constitutional Amendment—and the very first one at that. More significantly, not a single piece
of film equipment was seized, even though the movies, like radio, did not
enjoy specifically protected status. This refusal to extend free speech to
broadcasting set an unblushing precedent for government control of radio
(and eventually of television). It was the right of every American to make a
speech in a public square; reading that same speech into a radio microphone
could bring federal retribution.

After the Armistice, Wilson unlocked the box. The Navy had hoped to
retain its management of the federal government's new air supply, but the
Harding Administration kicked radio back to the Commerce Department,
which was headed by Herbert Hoover. Had the Navy successfully made its
case that radio constituted a primarily military-industrial strategic asset,
broadcasting might have remained the exclusive domain of admirals, manufacturing CEOs, and backyard inventors. Commercial entertainment
broadcasting could have been delayed for years.

Instead it moved hastily along. Westinghouse jumped in first with
KDKA, constructing the station's studio in a canvas tent on the roof of its
Pittsburgh headquarters. Other starting-line players included General Electric (WGY, Schenectady), AT&T (WEAF, New York) and RCA (WJR, New
York). Its prewar reluctance notwithstanding, when RCA did move into
home entertainment, it did so in a big way; it dominated the business until
the 1970s.[8] In 1927 the company trumped its competitors by establishing
two coast-to-coast network services that would eventually be capable of
delivering entertainment programming to every corner of the nation.

The original forms of radio broadcasting—ship-to-shore and backyard—
continued to grow. Most countries soon compelled flag vessels to carry full
interactive radio capabilities—transmitters, receivers and licensed personnel
who could operate them. Amateur broadcasting meanwhile was recognized
as a bonafide hobby and a small set-aside was made on the radio spectrum
for "hams." A few philanthropic and educational institutions took to the air

as well. But the growth area of broadcasting as an industry, art, and technology shifted decisively to the commercial distribution of mass communication. Broadcasting took on the task of developing a mass culture, an appropriate software for the functional capabilities of its hardware.

With manufacturer's offering free software to any and all consumers, personal radios sold like hotcakes during the 1920s. The NAB estimates that 60,000 American households had radios in 1922; by 1929, the number topped ten million.[9] Owen D. Young, the president of RCA, characterized the popularity of mass entertainment broadcasting as the "surprise party" of the radio industry.[10] Young had imagined a different future for the medium, personally lobbying Washington for a federal charter that would grant his company a full monopoly on radio transmission for reasons of national security[11] It is no stretch to find in all this a kind of recapitulation of the genesis of the American film industry: the country club blue-blood had underestimated the appetite of the unwashed masses for culture, while the immigrant child from the Lower East Side of Manhattan (quite arguably America's unwashed masses capital) knew from firsthand experience that such an appetite could not be overestimated.

The "surprise party" would be fun while it lasted, but market saturation was of course inevitable. The long-term challenge to the emerging mass broadcasting industry was this: once a radio in the parlor was as common as a chicken in every pot, how could a buck be made off the thing? Various plans were proposed. Sarnoff, never at a creative loss, advocated a system based on the model being developed in Britain, where set owners paid license fees which were turned over directly to a state enterprise, the British Broadcasting Company. Sarnoff's special twist for the American version, however, would be that the license fees would be turned over to a private sector corporation—his. In essence, the tax-collecting powers of the federal government would be put at the disposal of RCA. The scheme was a show biz variation on Owen Young's national security concept.[12]

While Sarnoff lobbied his plan, however, AT&T, which already had its share of highly-evolved relationships with the federal government, was putting in a creative claim of its own. Radio, Ma Bell pointed out, was part of its "natural monopoly." Broadcasting? Merely a form of telephone service that did not use wires. But, anticipating resistance to this imaginative interpretation of the new technological environment, the telephone company hedged its bets. As early as 1922, AT&T's New York station began exploring the possibilities of "toll broadcasting," or charging fees in return for airing commercial messages. Among its first customers were a co-op apartment house development in Queens and American Express.[13] Eventually the telephone company was persuaded to get out of the software end of the broadcasting business in return for a "natural monopoly" on connecting the stations to the networks.

Radio advertising, which in effect appointed retail sales-people as gate-keepers to the most potent communication system in the culture, did not appeal to everyone. In fact, it was almost as distasteful to traditionalist conservatives as it was to Marxists. Eugene V. Debs and Secretary of Commerce Hoover, to name one unlikely pair, could be counted among its opponents.

Debs and others on the Left of course saw the privatized airwaves as another public asset stolen from The People by The Capitalists. This is easy enough to grasp. Rightwing opposition to radio advertising might be a bit more difficult to fathom in the neo-conservative 1990s. However, to Old Right conservatives the very idea that the purveyors of toothpaste, floorwax, automobiles, and the like—tradespeople—should have any say at all in the nation's cultural programming was nothing less than abhorrent and far too revolutionary to be counted as conservative thinking.

Herbert Hoover's support of the free market would become the stuff of legend during the Great Depression. But his faith in laissez-faire economics did not extend to the arts. The regulation of culture was best left to academics and clerics. Hoover went so far as to tell the Radio Conference of 1922 that he found it "inconceivable that we should allow so great a possibility for service and for news and for entertainment and education . . . to be drowned in advertising chatter.[14] Seventy-five years later, acceptance of the direct hegemony of trade over culture is the fundamental distinction separating Neocons from Traditionalists.

In Britain, where class prerogative allowed traditional cultural gatekeepers greater entrée into the corridors of power, the BBC had been created precisely to avoid such a disaster for English culture (and theoretically for Scottish and Welsh culture as well). In the United States, a far less secure intellectual class made little noise on the subject. A look at scholarly reaction reveals that radio figured more prominently in the imaginations of physicists during the 1920s than in that of rhetoricians or critics. This failure of American intellectuals to take an early activist interest in the aesthetic formulation and cultural impact of radio broadcasting would be repeated thirty years later with television.

Gilbert Seldes was a notable exception to the general neglect of responsibility. He recognized radio drama as a form of national theater almost as soon as network broadcasting began. When TV arrived, Seldes would find himself at the fore-front, alone, once again. As early as 1937 he published a piece in the *Atlantic Monthly* under the sci-fi title, "The 'Errors' of Television."[15]

The Closing of the American Circuit

The period during which broadcasting thoroughly dominated mass communications and culture in the United States lasted for approximately sixty years. Historians usually divided it into its two most apparent components: radio (c. 1925–55) and television (c. 1955–85).[16] The rises, descents, and plateaus of the two broadcasting media have many parallels:

- Each technology was the product of private-sector corporate competition that was accelerated by war-time government research-and-development money.

- Each was retailed to the public as a free home entertainment system whose transmission and production costs would be borne by advertisers, leaving only the cost of the receiver to be paid directly by the user.
- Each saturated the entire nation, region by region and household by household, with centrally controlled, rigidly proscribed programming genres, rhetorical idioms, and content boundaries.
- Each established itself as a primary venue of American culture in an astonishingly short time.
- Each was displaced from its preeminent position by its own technological offspring.
- Each survived its brief golden age by reconditioning its programming to supplement, complement, and otherwise accommodate the new medium that was eclipsing it.

In short, broadcast television forced broadcast radio to define a subordinate role for itself in a new communication environment; thirty years later cable television forced broadcast television to do the same. Broadcast TV then can be seen as a transitional bridge between the primitive system of audio-only broadcasting and the currently expanding spectral frontiers of closed circuit and self-programmable video. As such, broadcast television shares conjunctive and disjunctive relationships with both. Perhaps the generational progression of the three communication technologies has provoked so little critical comment because of the almost obsessive focus of writers on the traumatic cleavage that subordinated print to audiovisual media in all areas of American life (except formal education) over the course of the twentieth century. It is perhaps only natural that writers have been more sensitive to the marginalization of literacy than to the particulars of how it was accomplished.

Marshall McLuhan was an exception to this rule. Writing at the chronological and spiritual heart of the Broadcast Era, he offered himself as an unabashed eyewitness to the technological amendments to Western epistemology that were deemphasizing the functions of print in day-to-day life. One of the very few intellectuals not suffering chronic denial over the crucial ebb of literacy during the 1950s and '60s, he was well prepared to watch the new electronic culture shepherd its audience from radio-centered to television-centered lives.

Despite the space-age mythology that grew up around him, McLuhan was essentially a literary person, a conservative of the old school who found electronic popular culture "monstrous and sickening," personally preferring the rarefied ink of Joyce, Eliot, or Hopkins.[17] But as a traditionalist, his interest in media effects was shaped by a strong concern for the future of language in general and English in particular. Whereas his critical contemporaries (Dwight Macdonald, T. W. Adorno, et al.) harped on "mass culture" and focused almost exclusively on the cultural dislocations caused by the shift away from print, McLuhan was at least as interested in finding the continuities that bind media as he was in their disjunctive relationships. A

Cambridge Ph.D. in English led him to a vision of TV as an elliptical return to the "normal" focus of human perception—which was audio-visual—after some three odd centuries of abstract literacy.

Fond of publicly testing ideas-in-progress, McLuhan rarely took the trouble to distinguish the local and ephemeral from the universal and eternal in his "probes," as he called them. For example, he linked radio and television as two "acoustic" (or sound-dominated) media. Despite the addition of visual image, McLuhan found watching TV an essentially aural experience.[18] This observation, however, may have been more topical than structurally intrinsic. McLuhan was, after all, a member of the cusp generation of TV watchers, and most early television was conceived and produced by (former) radio artists to attract (former) radio listeners. McLuhan himself often pointed out that the first content of any new medium is a previous medium.

Of more enduring interest is the distinction McLuhan found separating the two forms of broadcasting:

> There is a basic principle that distinguishes a hot medium like radio from a cool one . . . like TV. Hot media are . . . low in participation, and cool media are high in participation or completion by the audience[19]

Radio, as a hot medium, forces the listener to imagine the source of communication (i.e., to create a visual image). Among people who can both hear and see, ear data naturally stimulate a need for eye data, a sensory cueing sequence not difficult to trace to survival needs in the woods or the city. One hears a new sound; one looks to see what it is. This, in McLuhan's view, is not full involvement with the image, but rather a distraction from the sounds the listener is actually hearing. By imagining the missing visual component, the listener abandons the real sounds coming from the radio (or "the sound image") to embark on an instinctual search for sense, order, security, or whatever your religious inclination demands you call it. This turns radio images (words, music, tone, volume, inflection, signal quality, and so on) into mere cues for the construction of personally imagined faces, bodies, movements, settings, sound-making implements, and so on. The listener is not participating in radio; radio is participating in the listener, stimulating idiosyncratic memories and reconstructions. The listener is in truth abandoning the authentic sound coming out of the radio.

Radio does not embrace (or "involve"); it propels. To use radio, the listener must create a kind of cyber-image on an internal screen (or what in quainter times was called the imagination). This description of the mechanics of human perception may help account for such otherwise bizarre phenomena as the popularity of ventriloquism and dancing on network radio during the 1930s and '40s. A full range of sensory involvement with radio is impossible because of its demand for an internally-generated cerebral picture that rationally satisfies the externally-generated sound.

This need for focused mental activity at the expense of full sensory involvement (only the ear counts) makes listening somewhat like reading, which also uses only one sense to collect data (the eye) and makes even greater demands for imaginative thought because both sound *and* picture must be internally generated from the suggestions of ink. Degree of intellectual activity tends to be a measure of status in Western civilization, putting reading at the top of the list. It also explains the relatively high status of radio among TV-age intellectuals (a status it did not generally enjoy during the radio age). "The arts without intellectual context," wrote T. S. Eliot as radio was moving over for television, "are vanity."[20]

Since only aural cues are available from the radio, the sensorium (as McLuhan called the full range of sensory capacity) contracts from its multiple capabilities to concentrated focus on the ear. The internal energy expended on forcing rational context on physical sensation—the working imagination processing the data provided by a single sense—generates the "heat." This correlates well with the nostalgic folk wisdom that scolds TV with the axiom, "You still need an imagination to enjoy a radio drama."

TV, a "cool" medium, delivers images whole. This leads to greater sensory (as opposed to rational) participation. Video communication requires little or no active contribution from the viewer's cerebral capacities to satisfy the need for primary meaning. Offered no direct challenge or role in immediate comprehension, the conscious mind is invited by television to give itself freely to the image and to seek the unimpeded savor of visceral response. Man Thinking, to borrow an image from Emerson, yields to Viewer Kicking Back. Furthermore, reassured by both aural *and* visual satisfaction, other sensory capacities are free to playfully simulate visceral involvement with the televisual image.

McLuhan was especially keen on TV's extraordinary effect on involving the viewer's tactile sense. The meteoric rise of television as a primary medium of pornography almost immediately following the introduction of the VCR seems to bear him out. The relaxation of abstract cerebral activity allowed by televiewing is further augmented by the cool setting it typically allows. Pornographic cinema has pretty much been put out of business by home video. While the sleaziness of the dark public space was no doubt an attraction for some, millions more were impeded from enjoying audio-visually stimulated masturbation by those conditions. Film is simply too hot a medium for this purpose; full participation in the image is blocked by threatening social and even legal concerns. The VCR turned the trenchcoat into an antique symbol overnight.

But pornography is merely one example of the many tactile options afforded by television. The medium is commonly used to achieve numbness or even narcosis in hospitals, airports, and geriatric institutions. Some years after McLuhan's death the personal computer screen added the tactile pleasures of hand-eye coordination afforded by the joystick and the mouse button. By requiring so little collaborative imaginative energy to convey meaning, TV is extremely, perhaps overwhelmingly, user friendly. The need for control (ego) is ameliorated in favor of the pleasure of automatic response (id). The high degree of low effort participation allowed by TV viewing is its "coolness."

Ed Sullivan Is No Longer Possible

In contrast to the perceptual gulf McLuhan found separating televiewing from radio-listening, the two have a fundamental ideological similarity when specifically used as broadcast media, a bond that has been revealed in the context of closed-circuit prevalence. Broadcasting by its nature is an evangelical activity, whether it is used to preach the gospel of consumerism (commercial TV) or the gospel of ethical culture (PBS). A broadcast typically invites everyone who can receive its messages to sympathize, empathize, learn the creed, buy the products, and join the fold.

In contrast to broadcasting's intrinsic catholicism, narrowcasting is structurally biased toward sectarianism. It balkanizes the massive inclusionary twentieth-century public created by broadcasting into exclusionary tribes, castes, sects, interests, and "lifestyles." Narrowcasting is more suitable for preaching to the converted than for the kind of street-corner appeal apropos to over-the-air transmission.

A quintessentially Modern system, broadcasting presents the democracy of indiscrimination. It makes a standing offer to all. In the wired world, however, such cultural broadside seems clumsy, corrupt, naive, and vulgar (in no particular order). Narrowcasters eschew the commercial carpet bombing of broadcasting strategy in favor of surgical demographic strikes. Viewers are sorted and flattered with various suggestions of inside respect for their special identities of age, sex, race, leisure pursuit, and so on. Ironically, narrowcasting turns even religious evangelism, one of its founding interests, into sectarian cheerleading. Who watches the religious cable networks in the first place? Agnostics? Atheists? Skeptics? Unitarians? Viewers carrying such profiles have likely erased the Family Channel, the Trinity Broadcasting Network, and other religious services from their sequential tuning memories (those of them, that is, who can follow the operating manual).

It is unlikely that the severe social dislocations and polarizations that have taken place in American society since the end of the Broadcast Era are merely coincidental to this carving up of the nation-as-audience into a nation-of-audiences. Whether cable TV is cause, effect or both in the deterioration of public life that has accompanied it is by no means clear. But the subject seems ripe for probing.

A germinating example of this historical congruence can be found in the climax of the anti-segregation civil rights struggle and the rise of various forms of neo-separatism that ensued. This movement from an ideal of public citizenship to an ideal of consanguine solidarity occurred during roughly the same window of time that includes the climax of the Broadcast Era and the ensuing ascendancy of cable TV. Many integrationists who had given their energy to grand inclusionary causes such as breaking Jim Crow, insuring universal suffrage, and establishing citizenship-based rather than race-based education systems were shocked by the abrupt tide of the new separatism. The academics among them especially went into a state of active denial, re-imagining this backlash against integration as a progressive innovation: cultural pluralism. CP, it was contended, would stimulate pride and self-confidence in minorities and at the same time educate myopic majorities. Some theoreticians held that CP might bring about a re-lateralization of cultural exchange between racial and ethnic groups as a remedy to the top-down verticalism of commercial mass cultural programming.[21]

In practice, however, the new focus on the cultivation of micro-identities came at the direct expense of more inclusionary identities, such as polis, nation, and civilization. The absolutely inclusionary identity—humanity—was particularly hard hit.

The spectacle caused by isolation from macro-identity has been mostly bizarre and atrocious: anti-abortion "pro-lifers" murdering doctors; anti-racists establishing segregated lunch tables in university cafeterias; anti-vivisectionists valuing life too much to consider the interests of the sick; the administering of racial quotas by advocates of fairness. Far from empowering the citizenry, cultural pluralism has deprived society of citizens.

CP has proved its greatest effectiveness as an instrument of social control, perhaps *the* definitive framework for maintaining the status quo in an information-based, consumption-oriented society. Cultural pluralism turned out to be a Post-modern performance of a reliable old technique: divide and conquer. The 500-channel prophecy promises more of the same.

In terms of aesthetic quality, the Broadcast era of the mid-twentieth century presented the same problems, writ mass, that have plagued democratically minded art fans since the eighteenth century revolutions in America and France. Tocqueville observed that as the total number of consumers of any product (art included) increases, the percentage of what he called "fastidious consumers" decreases.[22] To increase the total number of consumers is the logical, not to say structural goal for a technology designed, quite literally, to "cast a signal broadly." When broadcasting is successful on its own terms, a decline in the influence of the fastidious can be taken for granted. There is of course evidence from the Broadcast Era that contradicts this point—I have tried to include some of it in this book—but the paucity tends to prove the rule.

Broadcasting in the United States developed as the most unadulterated form of mass culture in history. Such purity is not likely to be seen again. By the late 1920s the broadcasting industry had defined its cash product as sheer human tonnage; the goods were delivered to the customer in bales and bushels for more than half a century. Any aesthetic quality that programming might manifest—whether judged high, low, or otherwise—could be considered no more than a byproduct of the transaction. When the demand for quantity did happen to yield Hi-Q (let's say, Edward R. Murrow, *Playhouse 90, The Honeymooners, Green Acres,* or *Hill Street Blues*), that was a cause for celebration and self-congratulation: a shining case for freemarket capitalism's compatibility with a fine democratic culture. Here, ladies and gentlemen, was Madison Avenue making real the visions of Walt Whitman. When the system yielded something less, which it did prolifically, well, tough shit.

If there is a particular quality among audiences that the masters of the Broadcast Era grew to value and cultivate, it was "non-fastidiousness" precisely in Tocqueville's sense. The best audience for broadcasting emerged as an audience with as little discriminatory capability as possible in matters of taste (the programs) and rhetoric (the commercials). Sarnoff's hedge against the total mass culture of broadcasting, the Blue Network, proved unnecessary. Maestro Toscanini retired and the NBC Symphony Orchestra was disbanded. Divested of "high culture," the Blue Network became ABC.

This ordering of priorities gave rise to an institutionalized focus in broadcasting on the production of programs that could attract enormous audiences in which "fastidious" consumers shrank to statistical insignificance. If a network television program in 1961 alienated a couple of million people with the banality of its dialogue, the moral obtuseness of its plot or the decibel level of its laughtrack, what did it matter? The three-network oligarchy split the difference and the "rejection" hardly showed up in the numbers. If and when an egg-head was captured by TV's coolness (and let's face it, sooner or later most were), he or she didn't have many places to go on the dial.

PBS was established in the late 1960s as a holding pen for such viewers. Sarnoff, Paley, and other leading commercial broadcasters were enthusiastic contributors to public television. Why not let the taxpayers pick up the obligations of commercial licensees? Under the new conditions of narrowcasting, however, there is no such thing as a marginal audience for commercial television. Now that they are prepared to make a profit from its audience, commercial interests are anxious to privatize PBS and get government off their backs.

The appreciation of originality and complexity had always been the province of the few, and remained so despite the theoretical opportunities for change offered by broadcasting. Simplicity was ever the watchword in both drama and news: good was better than evil; beauty more attractive than ugliness; safety more desirable than danger. The more vulnerable the audience to oversimplified, outrageous, absurd, or non-sequitorial claims about the general uses and specific attributes of salable products—the better.

The hunger for fictional, non-fictional, and purposely confused narratives that would present life as some kind of comprehensible or less frightening experience was not new. Vertically organized religions and oral folklore traditions had addressed themselves to satisfying it for millennia. Since the Enlightenment, a canonical secular culture had emerged among the reading middle classes that served much the same purpose. But broadcasting brought with it a commercial incursion into domestic space that was unprecedented.

The parlor magazine rack, a nineteenth-century invention, had established a beachhead for advertising in the household. But broadcasting began an onslaught that finished the home as a viable refuge from commerce. The incursion of advertising into the home begun by the newspaper and magazine was turned into a full-scale invasion by radio. By the time visual image, color, stereo, remote control, big screen, cable, VCR, and online computer services had been added, the very clothing on people's backs had become flourishing advertising media. Broadcasting was instrumental in creating this revolution. It shifted the primary concern of American society from productivity to consumption.

All this may have been good for business, but partisans of the arts found it bad for culture. The bad dream of the Old Right had come true; the tradespeople were indeed in charge. As for the Left, it proved a fatal nightmare; the consciousness of the People had become the product of a privately-owned factory. The objections that were raised to such a system were mostly set in print and therefore not well known. When complaints were made by a T. S. Eliot or a Norman Thomas it was easy to dismiss them as the subjective judgments of antidemocratic snobs and social engineers who can't or won't get the jokes.

With full TV saturation in reach by the end of the 1950s, the broadcasting industry was only too glad to cultivate images of its opponents as snobs, eggheads, and patronizing dogooders. In 1957, for example, this editorial pronouncement was made by *Television Age,* a trade publication:

> Television is a mass medium—a medium for the masses, not for that minority of superior gentry with spherical crania who dwell in ivory towers of pseudo-intellectualism and drool over Strindberg.[23]

Leading industry executives, mostly graduates of exclusive and expensive colleges, did what they could to equate criticism of the quality of TV shows with attacks on democracy. Robert Sarnoff, working in Dad's shop, dismissed the naysayers as "dilettantes" enamored of "phony social philosophy in plays about beatniks and characters full of self-pity."[24] Dr. Frank Stanton of CBS went so far as to tell the FCC that for broadcasters to recognize criteria other than ratings in their programming decisions would be tantamount to "turn(ing) our back on democracy." An affiliate station owner was quoted in *Variety* as complaining of high-brow "autocrats who would set up a cultural tyranny."[25]

This model of thinking has outlived the Broadcast Era to become a template through which the "natural" order of an information society emerges. The old differentiation of "high culture" and "popular culture" is rephrased as a distinction, between "culture" and "entertainment." In matters of entertainment, business is perceived as serving the public, while the arts-and-education establishment is seen as teasing the public about culture. (Nonestablishment artists and educators are seen as just plain nuts.) As a result, opposition to television is opposition to the free market and, by easy extension, opposition to freedom itself. It may seem ironic that at the same time most people readily admit that "TV is bad for you." But examples of this kind of contradiction are everywhere: alcohol, tobacco, firearms, and so on.

Invoking the Frankfurt School or the Cambridge Anglo-Catholics in discussions of contemporary culture (i.e., TV) is like expecting baseball players on Old-Timers' Day to perform as they did during the careers that got them invited.[26] The Traditionalist Right worships individualism and promotes conformity. The Left (Old, New, or Middle-aged) promotes unpopular stances in the name of popular will. An understanding of this futility of superimposing print-based Left-Right arguments on contemporary media analysis is the foundation of what has become neo-conservatism. Neocons relate to television and entertainment much as old-fashioned conservatives related to religion. The movement has its true-believers and its cynics; the former accept the spiritual legitimacy of consumerism, the latter are willing to tolerate and even cultivate a measure of bread and a surfeit of circuses for the sake of preserving general order.

The economic viability of television is more easily proven than are the medium's capacities for cultural attainment. The businessfolk can prove their point with charts and graphs—documents that carry the force, if not exactly the mantle, of reason and even science. As for the artfolk, a paralyzing addiction to moral relativism hasn't helped make a case for aesthetic worth as the rightful concern of a democratic society. The primary justification for the arts in public life had been defined: investment opportunity.

Those who believe it is something more or other than that must be prepared to answer some questions. What do you have in mind? The advance of the human spirit? The improvement of the soul? The betterment of humankind? These concepts have been reduced by relativism to the status of voodoo. People with faith in that kind of stuff might have better luck calling the Psychic Friends Network. The balance of anarchy and order—always the meat-and-potatoes issue in getting through the day—depends on reason negotiated from material objectives, not from the pleasure of a vision. Walt Whitman could not see a difference between the two; today hardly anyone suspects similarities.

Narrowcasting, though also principally aimed at the selling of things, avoids many of the "hyper-democratic" by-products that broadcasting inevitably yields in its commitment to maximum distribution. The broadcaster makes a pitch to an entire nation, people, or culture. To the narrowcaster, this kind of sheer quantity is occasionally a virtue but rarely a paramount goal. The narrowcaster seeks not all, but a rightly constituted group: a subculture, a segregated element, a gang, or an affinity center of some sort which contains its own variations on right and wrong, which has its own interests to pursue and to protect and its own acknowledgment that its principle of organization is a fundamental asset.

The definitive footage of America's Broadcast Era is a montage of extraordinary moments of national galvanization: a JFK press conference; *The Ed Sullivan Show;* homeboy walks on the moon; *Roots;* Nixon resigning; thousands of shticks, gestures, and logos familiar across the neighborhood lines of the transdemographic village. Broadcasting was a national theater for a nation that emphatically refused to have one. This kind of thing can still be attempted in the narrowcasting environment, but only on well promoted special occasions: the final episode of *Cheers*, the Gulf War; certain championship sporting events.[27] For any single event, channels that do not carry will always outnumber channels that do carry. Is the civil defense system prepared for these new conditions?

A Martian is addressing the UN General Assembly. All the channels in the basic cable package that bother with news coverage (maybe ten of the fifty) are carrying it live. But just in case I'm not in the mood, I can exercise my freedom to change the channel. HBO's got *Close Encounters*. The Comedy Channel is showing clips of stand-up routines about aliens. On *The 700 Club*, Pat Robertson is revealing the prediction of the alien's visit in scripture. *Beavis and Butthead* invite the space dude home and make fun of dated videos such as "Major Tom" and "Rocket Man." USA is sticking with professional wrestling, though a Martian contender may soon challenge the champ. Bravo is taking no note of the event. Top management at the Sci-Fi Channel debates whether this thing will be good for business or destroy the company. Highlights of the Martian's speech are bound to replay for days on Headline News. C-SPAN will surely rerun the whole thing. Each tribe beats its own drums to spread the news. The Broadcast Era is kaput.

Appendix: Broadcast Network Prime Time Viewing Suggestions 1984–96

The Simpsons (Fox, 1989-present) brings the white noise of consumption-centered life to thundering crescendos.

Law and Order (NBC, 1990-present) is so well-written that following daily reruns may improve attention span.

NYPD Blue (ABC, 1992-present) offers better acting and writing than most live theater, and it's a lot cheaper.

There are surely other series from this period that will be worth watching in the future for all kinds of reasons, but these share the virtue of being humane.

Notes

1. By characterizing all six of these examples as "broadcast figures," I do not mean to gloss over the differences separating radio and television characters. In *Understanding Media: The Extensions of Man* (New York: Signet, 1962), for example, McLuhan writes, "Had TV come first, there would have been no Hitler at all" (p. 261).

2. The Westinghouse Corporation's Pittsburgh station, KDKA, is generally recognized as the first regularly operating commercial station offering daily radio service to the public in the United States. It is still in operation today.

3. Sterling and Kittross, 2nd ed., p. 35.

4. *Empire of the Air,* prod. Ken Burns (Radio Pioneers Film Project, 1991). It might also be noted that Dr. and Mrs. DeForest were divorced within a matter of weeks, perhaps an omen of things to come in terms of love in the information age.

5. Sterling and Kittross, *Stay Tuned,* 2nd ed., p. 43.

6. Ibid.

7. See *The American Automobile: A Brief History* (Chicago: University of Chicago Press, 1965): In 1908 Ford sold 5986 Model T automobiles at $859 a car; in 1916, with the price down to $360, the company sold 577,036.

8. Ironically, the undoing of RCA was another home entertainment project, this one at the end of the Broadcast Era: the video laser disc. Hoping to beat its competitors to the starting line in self-programmable television, the company introduced a stylus-based system. The system never caught on. Instead it was overwhelmed by the success of the Japanese VHS and Beta videotape systems. In 1985, after a $500 million loss, RCA was forced to give up on its videodisc system; General Electric swallowed the company whole in less than a year. See Erik Barnouw, *Tube of Plenty,* 2nd rev. ed., pp. 505–10.

9. Sterling and Kittross, *Stay Tuned,* 2nd ed., p. 656.

10. As cited by William Boddy, *Fifties Television: The Industry and Its Critics* (Champaign-Urbana: University of Illinois Press, 1993), p. 24.

11. Barnouw, *Tube of Plenty,* 2nd rev. ed., p. 24.

12. Various frameworks were proposed in the United States during the 1920s for rationalizing "natural monopolies" in a system that otherwise professed dedication to the "free market." See Robert A. Caro, *The Power Broker: Robert Moses and the Fall of New York* (New York: Knopf, 1974) for the most audacious and successful of these plans.

13. Barnouw, *Tube of Plenty,* 2nd rev. ed., pp. 40–50.

14. Herbert Hoover, Speech to First Washington Radio Conference, 27 February 1922, as quoted in Czitrom, *Media and the American Mind,* p. 76.

15. Gilbert Seldes, "The 'Errors' of Television," *Atlantic Monthly* (May, 1937): 531–41.

16. The parameters of these two thirty-year periods are approximate but by no means arbitrary. By 1925, there were 571 radio stations broadcasting in the United States and over a third of American households were equipped with receivers. RCA

was already planning its National Broadcasting Company for a 1927 coast-to-coast debut. As for television, the freeze on new stations that began in 1948 ended in 1952 and as a result a flurry of new transmitters followed. Between 1952 and 1955, the number of TV stations rose from 108 to 422, and almost two-thirds of American households had purchased sets. Also, 1955 was the year Dumont went dark, leaving the three-network broadcasting system that would utterly dominate television until the end of the Broadcast Era. (All figures taken from Sterling and Kittross, *Stay Tuned*, 2nd ed., Appendix C1-B, Appendix C8-A.)

17. Philip Marchand, *Marshall McLuhan: The Medium and the Messenger* (New York: Ticknor and Fields, 1989), p. 43.

18. McLuhan discusses the "acoustic" nature of television in *McLuhan: The Man and the Message*, a 1985 CBC documentary produced by Stephanie McLuhan and Tom Wolfe. It is conceivable that had McLuhan lived to see three developments he might have changed his mind on this:

- the improved home television image (color, stereo, big-screen, etc.);
- evolved visual skills and techniques used by television artists;
- a shrinking appetite for narrative by audiences preferring montage and other forms of visual stimulation to catharsis, the restoration of harmony, or other traditional dramatic climaxes and satisfactions.

19. Marshall McLuhan, *Understanding Media: The Extensions of Man*, 2nd ed., especially Introduction to the Second Edition, vii–xi, and Chapter Two, "Media Hot and Cold," 36–45.

20. T. S. Eliot, "Notes Toward the Definition of Culture," *Christianity and Culture: The Idea of a Christian Society and Notes Toward the Definition of Culture* (New York: Harcourt Brace, 1948), p. 95.

21. Born in the midst of the "cultural pluralism," the Internet creates an instant gulf between Users and Non-users and then sorts Users by their biases. It has proved an excellent communication system for rightwing extremists. Given the relatively high level of literacy—reading, writing, thinking in sentences, typing—necessary to operate the system, mass usage is not likely in the foreseeable future.

22. In commercial broadcasting the "product" is audience attendance, which is manufactured wholesale under the auspices of the broadcasters and then delivered by them to retailers. Art—drama, music, rhetoric, and so on—can be understood in this context as a byproduct of that process. Tocqueville's characterization, however, is still applicable.

23. As cited in Boddy, *Fifties Television*, p. 237.

24. Ibid.

25. Ibid., pp. 236–37. Ironically, many of these same charges of "elitism" are today leveled not *by* the entertainment moguls but *against* them, often by religious fundamentalists.

26. I have covered the characterization of "Left vs. Right" as a medium-specific print debate in some detail in "Mass Memory: The Past in the Age of Television" (Chapter Two), *Bonfire of the Humanities: Television, Subliteracy, and Long-Term Memory Loss* (Syracuse, N.Y.: Syracuse University Press, 1995).

27. In coining the term "global village," McLuhan may have had the entire globe in mind; indeed, since his death, that concept has become technologically feasible and progressively easier. However, I am using the term "global" somewhat metaphorically to refer to the transdemographic nation rather than the planet.

Excessive Style
The Crisis of Network Television

JOHN THORNTON CALDWELL

Television is to communication what the chainsaw is to logging.

Director David Lynch[1]

There isn't much out there that looks real.

Director/cameraman Ron Dexter[2]

Disruptive Practice

On the Friday September 8, 1989, edition of ABC's nightly news, erudite anchor Peter Jennings bemoaned the advent of what he termed "trash television." Prefacing his remarks by reference to a previous report by ABC on the subject, Jennings described the phenomenon with a forewarning. Norms of quality, restraint, and decorum notwithstanding, the new and ugly genre would in fact shortly premiere. Citing H. L. Mencken's adage about not overestimating the intelligence of the American people, Jennings signed off that evening with an obvious air of resignation. The class struggle, one sensed, might soon be lost.

Within two evenings, Jennings's warning was fulfilled. The highly evolved intertextuality that characterized television of the late 1980s was about to witness one of its most extreme manifestations to date. On Saturday, September 9, independent station KHJ-Channel 9 of Los Angeles uncorked the one-hour premiere of *American Gladiators* in syndication to stations throughout the country. Two nights later superstation KTLA-Channel 5 of Los Angeles aired its own nationwide trash spectacular—a two-hour premiere version of a show named *Rock-and-Rollergames*. Later that fall, pay-per-view television made available to cable viewers nationwide a special called *Thunder and Mud*. This latter trash hybrid featured various

---

low-culture luminaries, and included Jessica Hahn of the recent PTL-Jim Bakker sex scandal, female mud wrestlers, wild-man comedian Sam Kinison, and the all-woman heavy-metal rock group She-Rok. The *Los Angeles Times* labeled the spectacle "Sex, Mud, and Rock-and-Roll." The producers, however, preferred the derivative punch of *Thud* to the official program title *Thunder and Mud.* To the show's makers, *Thud* was a "combination female mud-wrestling act-heavy-metal rock concert-game show with some comedy bits thrown in."[3] If any doubts remained about mass culture's reigning aesthetic in 1989, it was certainly clear that stylistic and generic restraint were not among its properties.

   Rock-and-Rollergames was slated, interestingly, to air against the widely popular and front-running network sitcom *Roseanne.* Such competition was formidable given the vertically scheduled and heavily promoted sequence of shows that followed *Roseanne* Tuesday nights on ABC. Given trash television's excessive and low-culture pretense, such competition was significant, since *Roseanne* was being celebrated as television's premier "low-culture" hit; a status it had achieved with both viewers and tabloids during the previous season. By late fall, KHJ-TV had shifted *Rock-and-Rollergames* to Saturday mornings, and had renamed (and reduced) the spectacle to *Rollergames,* still in wide syndication in 1993. *American Gladiators* found itself shifted later in the year to the weekend schedule, and in subsequent years to late weekday afternoon strips. Together with its primetime airings, *Gladiators* found a lucrative niche by actively extending its competition out into the audience. Open trials were held throughout the country in highly publicized gladiator competitions at places like the Los Angeles Coliseum. Although trash television did not turn out to be an overwhelmingly dominant genre in primetime, *Gladiators* and other shows continued successfully in production with much success through the next four seasons. Muscle-bound, steroid-pumped women gladiators like Zap continued to grace the pages of *TV Guide* and the sets of celebrity talk shows through 1993.[4] A medieval variant of the trash spectacular, called *Knights and Warriors,* entered the trash programming fray in 1992–1993. Nickelodeon hyped and cablecast its hyperactive trash-gladiatorial clones, *Guts* and *Guts: All Stars,* for the younger set throughout the 1993–1994 season.

   Although the genre was defined from the start by its distinctive no-holds barred look, trash spectaculars were also symptomatic of a broader and more persistent stylistic tendency in contemporary television—one that was not always castigated as trash nor limited to low-culture content. That is, trash-spectaculars can be seen as a stylistic bridge between lower trash shows—like professional wrestling or *The Morton Downey, Jr.* shock-talk show (series that exploited very low production values to blankly document hyperactive onstage performances for the fan situated squarely in the stands or on the sofa)—and higher televisual forms that more extensively *choreograph* visual design, movement, and editing *specifically for the camera.* Even mid-1980s shows with higher cultural pretension or prestige, like *Max Headroom* or *Moonlighting* on ABC or MTV's manic game show *Remote Con-*

trol, frequently stoked their presentational engines with excesses not unlike those that characterized trash spectaculars. Although broadcast manifestations of the televisual tendency took many shapes, stylistic excess has continued to rear its ostensibly ugly head—even in the ethically pure confines of Peter Jennings's network news division.

Bells and Whistles and Business as (Un)Usual

We don't shy away from the aesthetic nature of the business. We have one foot on the edge, and we have to keep it there.

—Local station executive, WSVN-TV, Miami

Starting in the 1980s, American mass-market television underwent an uneven shift in the conceptual and ideological paradigms that governed its look and presentational demeanor.[5] In several important programming and institutional areas, television moved from a framework that approached broadcasting primarily as a form of word-based rhetoric and transmission, with all the issues that such terms suggest, to a visually based mythology, framework, and aesthetic based on an extreme self-consciousness of style. This is not just to say that television simply became more visual, as if improved production values allowed for increasing formal sophistication. Such a view falls prey to the problematic notion that developments in technology cause formal changes and that image and sound sophistication are merely by-products of technical evolution. Rather, in many ways television by 1990 had retheorized its aesthetic and presentational task.[6] With increasing frequency, style itself became the subject, the signified, if you will, of television. In fact, this self-consciousness of style became so great that it can more accurately be described as an activity—as a performance of style—rather than as a particular look.[7] Television has come to flaunt and display style. Programs battle for identifiable style-markers and distinct looks in order to gain audience share within the competitive broadcast flow. Because of the sheer scope of the broadcast flow, however—a context that simultaneously works to make televised material anonymous—television tends to counteract the process of stylistic individuation.[8] In short, style, long seen as a mere signifier and vessel for content, issues, and ideas, has now itself become one of television's most privileged and showcased signifieds. Why television changed in this way is, of course, a broader and important question. Any credible answer to the question is only possible after systematically and patiently analyzing representative program texts. By closely examining style and ideology in a range of shows and series that celebrate the visual, the decorative, or the extravagant a more fundamental reconsideration of the status of the image in television becomes possible.

Televisuality was a historical phenomenon with clear ideological implications. It was not simply an isolated period of formalism or escapism in American television or a new golden age. Although quality was being consciously celebrated in the industry during this period, the celebration had as much to do with business conditions as it did with the presence of sensitive or serious television artists.[9] Nor was televisuality merely an end-product of postmodernism.[10] The growing value of excessive style on primetime network and cable television during the 1980s cannot simply be explained solely by reference to an aesthetic point of view. Rather, the stylistic emphasis that emerged during this period resulted from a number of interrelated tendencies and changes: in the industry's mode of production, in programming practice, in the audience and its expectations, and in an economic crisis in network television. This confluence of material practices and institutional pressures suggests that televisual style was the symptom of a much broader period of transition in the mass media and American culture. Yet historical changes are seldom total. Six principles—ranging from formal and generic concerns to economic and programming functions—further define and delimit the extent of televisuality. These qualifications will be more fully examined through close analysis in the chapters that follow.

1. *Televisuality was a stylizing* performance—*an exhibitionism that utilized many different looks.* The presentational manner of televisuality was not singularly tied to either low- or high-culture pretense. With many variant guises—from opulent cinematic spectacles to graphics-crunching workaday visual effects—televisuality cut across generic categories and affected some narrative forms more than others. For example, the miniseries proved to be a quintessential televisual form, while the video-originated sitcom—at least with a few notable exceptions—resisted radical stylistic change. Conceived of as a *presentational attitude,* a display of knowing *exhibitionism,* any one of many specific visual looks and stylizations could be marshaled for the spectacle. The process of stylization rather than style—an activity rather than a static look—was the factor that defined televisual exhibitionism.

Consider *Entertainment Tonight,* for example, a hallmark televisual show that influenced a spate of tabloid, reality, and magazine shows during the 1980s. *Variety* hailed *ET,* a forerunner of tabloid horses *A Current Affair* and *Inside Edition,* as "the granddaddy of all magazine strips" for its "brighter look and provocative stories."[11] Having survived over three thousand individual episodes and having prospered nationally in syndication for over a decade by 1993, the show's executive producer explained the show's secret to success: "We continued to update our graphics and other elements of production, the bells and whistles. If you look at our show, let's say once a month for the last seven years, the only constants are the title, the theme, and John and Mary hosting the weekday show. Everything else continues to change. So we go through a continual process of reinventing the wheel."[12] *ET,* then, airing five days a week, year-round, defines itself not by its magazine-style discourse or host-centered happy talk, but by the fact that the viewer can always expect the show's style—its visual and graphic "bells and whistles"—to change. Televisuality, then, is about constantly reinventing the stylistic wheel.

2. *Televisuality represented a* structural inversion. Televisual practice also challenged television's existing formal and presentational hierarchies.

Many shows evidenced a structural inversion between narrative and discourse, form and content, subject and style. What had always been relegated to the background now frequently became the foreground. Stylistic flourishes had typically been contained through narrative motivation in classical Hollywood film and television. In many shows by the mid-1980s however, style was no longer a bracketed flourish, but was the text of the show. The *presentational status* of style changed—and it changed in markets and contexts far from the prestige programming produced by Hollywood's primetime producers.

Broadcasting magazine, for instance, described the dramatic financial reversal of the Fox television affiliate in Miami's highly competitive market. The ratings success of WSVN-TV was seen as a result of the station "pumping out" seven hours of news "that mirrors the music video in its unabashed appeal to younger viewers—flashy graphics, rapid-fire images, and an emphasis on style." While the trades saw the economic wisdom of stylistic overhauls like this one, television critics marveled at the station's able use of an aggressive, wall-to-wall visual style to revive a dead station.[13] Even the vice presidents at WSVN theorized the journalistic success of the station in artistic terms, as a precarious but necessary form of aesthetic risk taking.[14] By marketing cutting-edge news as constructivist plays of image and text, even affiliate station M.B.A-types now posed as the avant-garde.

3. Televisuality was an industrial product.   Frequently ignored or underestimated by scholars, television's mode of production has had a dramatic impact on the presentational guises, the narrative forms, and the politics of mainstream television. More than just blank infrastructure, television's technological and production base is smart—it theorizes, orchestrates, and interprets televisual meanings—and is partisan. The mode of production is also anything but static; it changes. The production base, then, is both a product of shifting cultural and economic needs and a factor that affects how we receive and utilize television and video. In order to talk adequately about television style or narrative, one needs at least to recognize that *television is manufactured.*

Technology, geographical issues, and labor practices were all important components in the formation of a televisual mode of production. There was, for example, a direct relationship between certain production tools—the video-assist, the Rank-Cintel, digital video effects—and popular program styles in the 1980s. Yet these tools did not cause television's penchant for style. Rather, they helped comprise an array of conditions, and a context, that allowed for exhibitionism. Digital video technology, for instance, has had an enormous effect on the look of mass-market television, yet it has not infiltrated all of television's dominant genres. Primetime workhorse Universal Television, for example, justified digital technology only in terms of specific narrative needs: "We're getting more and more into digital. There's no standard formula that's applied to every single show, and every show doesn't get the same services in the same way from the same facility. With sitcoms, we're not into the digital domain yet—not to say that it won't be happening soon."[15] Digital imaging, then, once thought to be a futurist preoccupation now shadows even conservative television genres in Hollywood. Yet far from the sitcoms and genres of Studio City and Burbank, the same effects became defining factors and prized properties. At a very different level in broadcasting during this period even local stations began to manufacture alternative identities around a technologically driven aesthetic. In "personnel upgrades" regional broadcasters like WRAL-Channel 5 in Raleigh, North Carolina expected key production personnel to have visual arts degrees and electronic imaging technologies skills. News and promotional producers as well were now expected to "be able to write and produce promos that sell and touch emotion, (and) *must be proficient in all aspects of production with an eye for visuals that cut through the clutter.*"[16] Even outside of primetime's prestige television, then, market competition was defined as clutter; and striking visuals and high-tech graphics as obligatory corporate strategies. New televisual tools had arisen to meet the dense onslaught of programming alternatives.

    4. Televisuality was a programming phenomenon: Showcase television in itself was nothing new, but the degree to which broadcasters showcased to counter-program was distinctive. Television history offers important and influential precedents for quality television: the Weaver years at NBC in the 1950s; the MTM/Tinker years at CBS in the 1970s; the Lear era at CBS in the 1970s. Programming designed around special-event status was also not entirely new, although the kind of prestige and programming spin that special events offered threatened to dominate television by the late 1980s. Everything on television now seems to be pitched at the viewer as a special event—from nondescript movies of the week to the live coverage of some local catastrophe on the eleven o'clock news—so much so in fact, that the term *special* is now almost meaningless. Showcase and event strategies that used to be limited to sweeps now pervade the entire year. No programming confesses to being commonplace.

    While event-status television offered programmers one way to schedule nightly strips, "narrowcasting"—a result of demographic and ratings changes starting in the late 1970s—allowed for a different kind of aesthetic sensitivity in primetime programming. Broadcasters began to value smaller audiences if the income-earning potential and purchasing power of those audiences were high enough to offset their limited numbers. Narrowcast shows that averaged ratings and shares in the low- and mid-teens in the late 1980s—like ABC's *thirtysomething* and CBS's *Tour of Duty*—would never have survived a decade earlier, given the higher ratings expectations in broadcasting at that time.[17] The audience numbers needed for primetime success continued to fall in the 1980s. Although the Nielsens were slow to change from their ideal of an average viewing family, advertisers, cable, and direct broadcast satellite systems (DBS) executives were obsessed with clarifying ever narrower niches tied to economic, racial, age, and regional differences.[18]

This industrial reconfiguration of the audience, in the name of cultural diversification, helped spawn the need for cultural- and ethnic-specific styles and looks. Fox, Black Entertainment Television, TNT, and Lifetime each developed distinctive and highly coded looks that reflected their narrowcast niches and network personalities. Gender- and ethnic-specific groups do not, apparently, coalesce around content-specific narration alone. Stylistic ghettos continue to be manufactured by cable and broadcast networks according to maps of their supposed niche potential.

5. *Televisuality was a* function of audience: While the audience was being redefined and retheorized from the outside by broadcast and cable programmers, the cultural abilities of audiences had also apparently changed by the 1980s. While trash spectaculars betrayed new stylistic appetites in what have traditionally been deemed lower-taste cultures, the networks during this period learned to cash in on yuppie demographics as well. Many viewers expected and watched programs that made additional aesthetic and conceptual demands not evident in earlier programming. Even if such demands came in the form of irony or pastiche, shows like *Late Night with David Letterman* on NBC and *The Gary Shandling Show* on HBO presupposed a certain minimal level of educational, financial, and cultural capital. Such a background provided viewers both with an air of distinction—as viewers in the know—and presupposed enough free time to actually watch late-night programming, terrain once written off as fringe.

The fact that television was no longer anonymous, also presupposed fundamental changes in the audience. While many British directors in Hollywood—Ridley Scott (*Thelma and Louise*), Tony Scott (*Top Gun*), and Alan Parker (*Mississippi Burning*)—had started as highly respected television commercial directors before breaking into features, American film directors before the 1980s had typically been segregated away from television agency work. There was, and to some degree still is, an ego problem and an institutional wall between the advertising and feature-film worlds. This segregation, however, began to change in the mid-1980s. Heavyweight film directors now were self-consciously hyped as producers of TV commercials.[19] David Lynch (*Blue Velvet*) designed pretentious primetime Obsession ads; Martin Scorsese (*Mean Streets*) produced an opulent Georgio Armani cologne spot for a mere $750,000; Rob Reiner (*A Few Good Men*) and Richard Donner (*Lethal Weapon*) both directed big-production-value Coca-Cola spots; Francis Ford Coppola (*Apocalypse Now*) directed a sensitive and familial thirty-second road-movie for GM that was never aired; Woody Allen (*Annie Hall*) spun out a commercial supermarket farce; Jean-Luc Godard (*Tout Va Bien*) did an avant-garde and overblown European Nike ad; and the venerable Michelangelo Antonioni (*Blow-up*)—the closest thing that serious Western cinema has to an aesthetic patriarch—choreographed a psychedelic spot for Renault.

The clients of these figures were inevitably impressed with their auteurist entourage, at least before the spots were produced and aired. Agency directors who had dominated the field outside of Hollywood, however, were less than happy with this opportunistic invasion of showcased aesthetes on television. Clio Award—winning director Joe Pytka grumbled that such auteurs underestimated the difficulty of the fifteen- and thirty-second short-forms.[20] Nevertheless, the auteur-importing mode—popularized by Ridley Scott, Spike Lee, and David Lynch in the mid-1980s—remained a viable fashion well into the 1990s with CAA's strong-armed invasion of the ad world from Hollywood in 1993.[21] The auteur-import business raises important questions about television practice: who is patronizing whom? CAA now acts more like televisual Medicis—with directors Donner and Reiner their kept artists—than traditional point-of-sale admen. Aesthetic promotion now flows both ways in commercial television—to the client and the patron—in a corporate ritual seldom kept from the audience. Audience consciousness and facility makes this commerce of authorial intent possible. Marketing aesthetic prestige presupposes and strokes audience distinction and self-consciousness.

    6. Televisuality was a product of economic crisis.   Televisuality cannot be theorized apart from the crisis that network television underwent after 1980. Stylistic excess can be seen as one way that mainstream television attempted to deal with the growing threat and eventual success of cable. Stylistic showcases, high-production value programming, and Hollywood stylishness can all be seen as tactics by which the networks and their prime-time producers tried to protect market share in the face of an increasingly competitive national market. No longer could CBS, NBC, and ABC—protected by the government as near monopolies since the late 1940s and early 1950s—assume the level of cash flow that they had enjoyed up to the late 1970s. Although the networks faced the first cable players in 1980 and 1981 with a smug and self-confident public face, this facade began to crack as each year took its toll on corporate profits. CNN and MTV were merely the first in a line of very profitable challengers to sign on to cable for the long haul. The trades gave blow-by-blow accounts of the precipitous decline in network primetime viewing. The networks had enjoyed complete dominance—an incredible 90 share—during the 1979–1980 season, but saw this figure plummet to a mere 64/65 share by 1989–1990.[22]

    Complicating things further still, the new fourth network, Fox, was profitable by 1989 and was eating directly into shares of the big three. Financial analysts reported that 40–45 percent of Fox's additional revenues in 1993 would come at the expense of ABC, directly reducing the network's yearly revenues by $50 million.[23] Fox's growing appetite was a network problem, not just because there were fewer pieces of market pie to share with Fox, but because of the demographic stratification within those pieces. Fox gained its market toehold and survived by specializing in the hip 18–34 demographic, but now was expanding into ABC's 18–49 year old range. Escalating and unrealistic production budgets were also part of the network diagnosis. The trades explained the collapse of quality network shows like *thirtysomething,*

I'll Fly Away, and *The Wonder Years* as a result of inflated budgets. Even half-hour shows could now regularly cost $1.2 million per episode—an unheard-of level even for hour-long series two decades earlier.[24] By the late 1980s front-page stories in the national press were loudly trumpeting the demise of the networks, who were "under attack"—besieged by an array of new video delivery technologies.[25] By the early 1990s, the networks were publicly wringing their hands, as victims of cable, of unfair regulatory policies, and of syndication rules. Government regulators characterized the market as driven by "ferocious competition that was unimagined ten years ago."[26]

In one decade, network viewership declined by a corporation-wrecking 25 percent. This hemorrhaging of viewership may seem ironic, given the fact that high-style *televisuality also emerged during the very same years.* I will argue in the pages that follow, however, that televisuality addressed the very same economic problem that hostile takeovers would tackle in 1986 and 1987. Stylistic exhibitionism and downsizing were obviously very different organizational tactics. One came from programming and encouraged budget-busting expenditures of capital; the other came from corporate management and brought with it widespread layoffs and fiscal austerity. Yet both, paradoxically, attempted to solve the same corporate crisis: the declining market share of the networks. In some ways, this was payback time for network television. The market incursion of network broadcasters in the 1950s had itself created an economic crisis in Hollywood that sent the film studios scrambling for excessively styled forms: cinemascope, technicolor and 3-D. Depending on how one looked at it, televisuality in the 1980s was either a self-fulfilling deathwish by extravagant producers, or a calculated business tactic that increased market share.

The Terrain

Televisuality can be mapped out along several axes: formal, authorial, generic, and historical. From a formal perspective, televisual programs gained notoriety by exploiting one of two general, and production-based, stylistic worlds: the cinematic and the videographic. The cinematic refers, obviously, to a film look in television. Exhibitionist television in the 1980s meant more than shooting on film, however, since many nondescript shows have been shot on film since the early 1950s. Rather, cinematic values brought to television spectacle, high-production values, and feature-style cinematography. Series that utilized this mode typically promised broadcasters and audiences alike television's big picture. Situated at the top of the programming hierarchy, shows like *Moonlighting, Crime Stories, Wiseguy,* and *Beauty and the Beast* fit well with the financial expectations of network primetime programming. They also inevitably drew critical attention by their very programming presence and cinematic air of distinction. It was as if the televisual producers packaged labels with their cinematic shows that read: *"Panavision Shows That We Care."*

Televisual programs that exploited the videographic guise, on the other hand, were more pervasive and perhaps more anonymous than cinematic ones, but were certainly no less extravagant in terms of stylistic permutation. In fact, for technological reasons, videographic shows made available to producers, at any given time, more stylistic options. That is, such shows had more embellishment potential given their origins in electronic manipulation. Far different from the bland and neutral look that characterized video-origination studio productions in earlier decades, videographic televisuality since the 1980s has been marked by acute hyperactivity and an obsession with effects. If MTV helped encourage the stampede to film origination in primetime, then CNN demonstrated the pervasive possibilities of videographic presentation. Starting in 1980—and without any apparent or overt aesthetic agenda—CNN created and celebrated a consciousness of the televisual apparatus: an appreciation for multiple electronic feeds, image-text combinations, videographics, and studios with banks of monitors that evoked video installations. Ted Turner had coauthored the kind of cyberspace that video-freaks and visionaries had only fantasized about in the late 1960s.

The "give 'em hell" look of MTV, on the other hand, popularized a mode of production that changed the very way television was produced beginning in 1981. By shooting on various film formats and then posting electronically on tape, indie producers were no longer rigidly locked into a single production medium. Earlier telefilm producers, by contrast, were required to produce a single conformed negative for broadcast and a positive print made from source material that was uniform in format and stock. With the MTV prototype, however, it no longer mattered where the material came from (stock, live, graphic material), what format it was shot on (super-8mm, 16mm, 35mm), or whether it was black and white or color. Once transferred in post-production to electronically recorded tape, almost any element could be combined or composited, mixed and matched, in useable configurations. Not only were labor and business structured differently in the new videographic worlds—CNN was a nonunion shop and MTV utilized an eclectic mix of production personnel (from studio technicians to independent producers to animators to video artists)—but the very technologies that gave MTV national audiences allowed for and encouraged a different kind of look and stylistic expectation.

By the time of its network airing in 1986, then, *Max Headroom* was merely a self-conscious and premeditated reference and homage to an existing industry-proven, videographic prototype. Like two other pervasive forms, primetime commercial spots and music videos, *Max Headroom* operated between the two stylistic modes by mixing and matching elements from both cinema and digital imaging. Purer forms of videographic televisuality were actually more common in cost-effective and low-end programming, like *Entertainment Tonight, Hard Copy, America's Most Wanted*, and *Rescue 911*. Live coverage—especially of crises like the Gulf War, the L.A. rebellion, and the yearly spectacle of the Super Bowl—has had an especially ravenous appetite for videographic exhibitionism. Although videographic series typically evoke less critical attention than prestige cinematic programming, they frequently undergo more tortured attempts to crank-out aesthetic embellishment. A fetish for effects rules the videographic domain. This emerging formal axis between the cinematic and the videographic can also be sketched out in historical terms (Table 1). While *Moonlighting, Crime Stories, The Equalizer,* and *thirtysomething* continued to push film-based primetime into more excessive directions, *Max Headroom, Pee-Wee's Playhouse,* and *Remote Control synthesized* the electronic and videographic lessons of MTV and CNN for new national audiences.

A second way to understand televisual programming is to consider it along an axis formed by relative degrees of authorial intent and manufactured notoriety. Commercial spots were certainly not unique in flaunting directorial auras to the mass audience. Part of the emergence of the quality myth in 1980s television was that television was no longer simply anonymous as many theorists had suggested. Names of producers and directors assumed an ever more important role in popular discourses about television. While Aaron Spelling and Norman Lear were already household names, other producer-creators like Michael Mann and Stephen Bochco began to be discussed alongside their actors and series in popular magazines and newspapers. As with American film in the 1960s, authorial intent played an important role as an indicator and guarantor of aesthetic quality in primetime programming of the 1980s.

The centrality of this process can be demonstrated by considering televisual authorship within three organizing systems: marquee/signature television, mainstream conversions, and auteurist imports. Not only do the corporate and cooperative origins of television complicate singular attributions of authorship, but the various degrees of authorial deference within the industry show that televisual authorship is also part of calculated programming strategy. While many shows merit no authorial attribution by broadcasters, some demanding shows exploit it as a lifejacket, as a prop for survival, as a device used to weather programming clutter and to find loyal audiences. When *Brooklyn Bridge* suffered threats of network cancelation in 1992 and 1993 due to poor ratings, the show's producer took stage before the press on a regular basis—proof positive that there was indeed a series of substance hidden under the very nose of the American people. Such showcase producers are manufactured by production companies and networks as banner-carriers, much in the way that Stephen Bochco and Michael Mann were showcased in 1981 and 1984. Other signature producer types, like Marshall Herskovitz, Diane English, David Letterman, and Joshua Brand, continue this showcasing tradition. As signature producers, each has functioned as a promotional marquee; a spotlit entré for programming seasons on their respective networks: ABC, CBS, NBC, and Fox (Table 2).

While these marquee producer-creators are television insiders—honed, disciplined, and groomed through the ranks of the primetime industry—a second group of televisual authors come from the outside. Auteur imports

Table 1   The Historical Field Televisual Events

1980	1981	1982	1983	1984	1985	1986

The Cinematic

1980	1981	1982	1983	1984	1985	1986
					•Moonlighting	
				•Miami Vice		•thirtysomething
	•Hill Street Blues		•St. Elsewhere			•The Equalizer
	•Dynasty		•Winds of War		•Amazing Stories	
	•MTV			•Nike spots		•Crime Story
•CNN		•Marco Polo		•Chiat/Day Macintosh spots		
	•Entertainment Tonight					•Pee-Wee's Playhou
		•Late Night with David Letterman				•SNL Opening
			•Nickelodeon		•Live Aid	
					•West 57th Street	

The Videographic

NOTE: The *general* position of the titles laid out along the vertical axis suggests the *degree* to which the s‹ utilized one of the two most privileged televisual modes plotted: the cinematic or the videographic m‹ Although many of the positions are only approximations (since some shows might emphasize one trait in ‹ episode and the other in another installment), some clear and direct lineages are evident: from CNN to ‹ *Aid* to the coverage of the L.A. rebellion and *Zoo TV* on the electronic, videographic axis; and from MT‹ *Miami Vice* to *Quantum Leap* and *Cop Rock* on the cinematic axis. Note as well that other shows, like ‹

from Hollywood and feature filmmaking typically elicit even more press than the Bochcos and Manns, but usually garner much poorer ratings. Among the great ironies of programming in the past decade has been, first, that television now attracts a wide range of film directors, and second, that most of these directors "fail" when brought on board to produce shows for networks. The list of auteur imports in primetime television since 1980 reads like a who's who list at Cannes: Spike Lee, Francis Ford Coppola, Steven Spielberg, George Lucas, David Lynch, Ridley Scott, Robert DeNiro, Barry Levinson, and Oliver Stone have all "done" TV. If the insider showcase producers are signature banner-carriers who give a network's seasonal offerings personality, then the auteur imports are aesthetic badges and trophies of distinction pure and simple. To the networks, any financial risk that comes with Lucas, Spielberg, and Stone is, apparently, worth it. What the networks

1987	1988	1989	1990	1991	1992	1993
						•Wild Palms
			•Cop Rock	•Northern Exposure		•seaQuest dsv
Max Headroom	•Quantum Leap			•Homefront		•Tribeca
Beauty and the Beast			•Twin Peaks	•I'll Fly Away	•Picket Fences	
	•China Beach			•Brooklyn Bridge		
		•Midnight Caller		•Seinfeld	•Young Indiana Jones	
War and Remembrance				•Camarena	•Hat Squad	•Homicide
	•Lonesome Dove					
T&T Spots		•Men	•Herman's Head		•Phillips' Clear Sound spots	
			•The Simpsons		•X Files	
Obsession spots			•In Living Color		•Animaniacs	
Tracy Ullman Show		•American Gladiators			•Mighty Morphin Power Rangers	
Remote Control		•The Julie Brown Show			•P.D.I. Morphing spots	
Max Headroom			•Hard Copy	•Roundhouse		
Current Affair		•Rock-and-Rollergames			•1992 Olympics	
	•Unsolved Mysteries		•America's Funniest Home Videos			
	•America's Most Wanted				•Honda VR spots	
				•I-Witness Video		
			•Gulf War		•Zoo TV/Fox	
				•L.A. rebellion		•Bradymania

...droom in 1987, was influential on both ends of the stylistic spectrum: it flaunted the postmodern, dystopic ...matic looks of Ridley Scott's feature *Blade Runner,* but collaged them with endlessly dense videographic ...cybernetic configurations, surveillance, etc. Whenever possible, the series listed correspond to the years above them in the table, although space limitations mean that these are only approximations. Many of ...hows and series laid out on this chart will be discussed in the pages and chapters that follow.

get in return is a visionary aura of artistry and aesthetic challenge—an attitude they can toy with, at least until cancelation inevitably comes. Never mind the fact that much of the rest of programming is by comparison authorially mundane. Even if for a fleeting season, this imported class and visionary flash promises to work wonders for network programming—at least when aired and hyped in the right way; as when Levinson's *Homicide* was slated after the Super Bowl telecast or when Oliver Stone's *Wild Palms* barraged the viewer on multiple May sweeps nights in 1993.

So what, you say, Lynch, Levinson, and Stone were no more than bright but very curious flashes in the programming pan. This kind of import business in itself is no proof that televisuality dominated broadcasting during the 1980s. Yet, the auteurist import business is really just the tip of an iceberg. A third category of television producer-directors shows that author-

Table 2   The Players Primetime Televisuality

I. Showcase Producers Marquee Signatures Network Banner Carriers	II. Mainstream Conversions Acquired Mannerisms Embellished Genres	III. Auteur—Imports Cinematic Spectacle Visionary Emigres

Bochco, Steven
Hill Street Blues,
  1981–1987
L.A. Law, 1986–1993
Cop Rock, 1990–1991
NYPD Blue, 1993–
	Bellasario, Donald
	Magnum P. I., 1980–1988
	Tales of the Gold Monkey,
	  1982
	Airwolf, 1984–1988
	Quantum Leap, 1989–1993
		Spielberg, Steven
		Amazing Stories, 1985–1987
		seaQuest dsv, 1993–1994

Mann, Michael
Miami Vice, 1984–1989
Crime Story, 1986–1988
Drug Wars: Camarena Story,
  1990
	Cannell, Stephen J.
	The A-Team, 1983–1987
	Riptide, 1984–1986
	Stingray, 1986–1987
	Wiseguy, 1987–1990
	Silk Stalkings, 1991–
		Coppola, Francis
		The Outsiders, 1989–1990
		Faerie Tale Theater, 1986
		The Conversation, 1995–
		
		Lynch, David
		Obsession spots, 1990
		Twin Peaks, 1990–1991
		American Chronicles,
		  1990–1991
		Hotel Room, HBO, 1993

English, Diane Murphy Brown, 1988– Double Rush, 1995–	*Spelling, Aaron* Love Boat, 1977–1986 Fantasy Island, 1978–1984 Dynasty, 1981–1989 Hotel, 1983–1988 And the Band Played On, 1994	

Letterman, David
Late Night With, NBC,
  1982–1993
David Letterman Show,
  1993–
		Scott, Ridley
		Chiat/Day Mac spots, 1984
		
		Townsend, Robert
		Townsend Television,
		  1993–1994
		Parent' Hood, 1995–
		McDonald's Spots, 1995–

Kelly, David Picket Fences, 1992– Chicago Hope, 1994–	*Brooks, James L.* Mary Tyler Moore, 1970–1977 Tracey Ullman Show, 1987–1990 The Simpsons, 1990–	
Herskovitz and Zwick thirtysomething, 1987–1992 My So-Called Life, 1994–		*Spheeris, Penelope* Thunder and Mud, 1989 Prison Stories HBO, 1991 *McBride, Jim* The Wonder Years, 1990
Brand and Falsey St. Elsewhere, 1983–1984 Northern Exposure, 1990– I'll Fly Away, 1991–1994		*Lee, Spike* MTV Spots, 1986 Saturday Night Live, 1986 Air Jordan/Nike spots, 19 *Lucas, George* The Young Indiana Jones, 1992–1994, 1994– *DeNiro, Robert* Tribeca, 1993 *Zemeckis, Robert* Tales from the Crypt, 19 *Levinson, Barry* Homicide, 1993–1995 *Stone, Oliver* Wild Palms, 1993

ship and excessive televisual style are linked in lower forms of television as well. The last fifteen years or so have also seen a marked stylistic change in successful but middle-of-the-road primetime producing figures. If stylistic exhibitionism was substantive and pervasive it should have affected these types of figures as well. Consider the marked stylistic differences between early and late works by Stephen J. Cannell, Donald Bellasario, Aaron Spelling, and James L. Brooks. In *Magnum P.I., The A-Team,* and *Love Boat,* Bellasario, Cannell, and Spelling all succeeded by exploiting flesh and chrome rather than a stylized look. Such extra-cinematic objects were typically displayed in front of a neutral camera. The production apparatus was designed to show off and allow physical action and anatomy rather than pictorial or narrative embellishment. Later series by the same producers, however, show something very different. By the end of the decade Bellasario authored the quintessential televisual show *Quantum Leap;* Cannell choreographed *Sting-Ray,* a *Miami Vice* clone; and Spelling banked on cinematic opulence in *Dynasty.* Other producers, like James L. Brooks—considered a quality producer by industry types and critics alike—actually gained their fame by making shows that were *visually uninteresting.* Brooks's early accomplishment in the rather bland-looking 1970s sitcom *Mary Tyler Moore* seems sedate by comparison to the presentational volatility and niche mentality of his *Tracey Ullman* show at Fox in the late 1980s. Even very competent, but middle-of-the-road producers, then, learned to value and exploit style for its own sake during this period. Who says television can't teach old dogs new tricks?

A third way of delineating the forms and functions of televisuality is to examine them within the framework of genre, since stylistic exhibitionism has not equally influenced all program formats. The extent of the trend can be better understood by comparing genres that favored televisual performance and those that did not. Television's bread-and-butter genres—where stylistic excess is an exception—include daytime talk shows, soap operas, video-origination sitcoms, nonprimetime public affairs shows, some public access cable shows, nonprofit public service announcement spots (PSAs), and late-night off-air test patterns. While PSAs and infomercials function as cheap but lucrative filler, the sitcom may have resisted televisuality for ideological reasons; that is, because of its inherently conservative cultural function.[27] In an ideological sense the sitcom, in almost every decade, always manages to reconfigure and update the nuclear family. In 1980s shows like *Full House* this meant awkwardly linking multiple parents of the same sex together as surrogate parental figures.[28] With the very myth, viability, and survival of the nuclear family as its chief creative task, primetime sitcoms had little need for the presentational possibilities—and the air of distinction—offered by stylistic exhibitionism. For a number of reasons, then, some genres simply do not care about style.

Many others, however, continue to share a marked penchant for stylistic exhibition. Although I have referred already to prestige film-origination genres—the miniseries, primetime soaps, and quality hour-long dramatic series—

many other film-based shows market visual excess in broadcast and cable delivery systems: hyperactive children's television, archival syndicated programs, sitcoms and their parodies on Nickelodeon, feature film presentations on pay-cable channels, and a boundless number of commercial spots shot on film and aired across the channel spectrum. While many televisual program forms survived the industry's economic crash of 1989–1992, several flagship televisual genres from the 1980s—the miniseries, primetime soaps, and primetime dramas—were prematurely, and with some self-serving eulogies, declared dead by industry executives at the start of the 1990s.

Video-origination genres, by contrast, have continued to share a penchant for exhibitionism and include: network television sports shows, cable news, music television, magazine shows, most reality programming, home shopping networks, local commercials for cars and personal injury lawyers, and a veritable ton of interstitial and nonprogram material airing around the clock on almost all non-pay channels. Supermodel Cindy Crawford's videographic showcase, *House of Style* on MTV, provides but one explicit example of the exhibitionism that pervades television outside of primetime. Fashion- or anatomy-conscious thirteen-year-old white suburban girls or boys who watch her show are enticed by a type of performance that differs little from other televisual appeals made during off-primetime programming ghettos. Super-discount, high-volume auto-malls bankroll thirty- and sixty-second spot frenzies on the weekends; while ex-Fox CEO Barry Diller's QVC network teases home-shoppers with graphics-dense consumer bait. When down-home, regionally owned, right-to-work corporations like Wal-Mart produce national ads that look like a cinematographer's showreel, the implications are clear: mass retailing has made televisuality not just a passing production fashion, but a national consumer buying trend.

Modes and Guises

Popular TV critics have been accused by academics of wrongly isolating important and deserving shows out of the continual, redundant, and monotonous broadcast flow.[29] David Marc, for example, has argued against the critical and textual isolation of episodes, because: "The salient impact of television comes not from 'special events,' . . . but from day-to-day exposure. The power of television resides in its normalcy."[30] According to this perspective, individual episodes are rarely memorable, although series and their cosmologies are. Most academic theorists have followed this lead by attempting to elaborate fundamental structural and ideological conditions that comprise television's flow, the super-text, and the audience. I am arguing something very different here: that special television is a concern not just of critics, but of the industry and the audience alike. A great deal of television in the last fifteen years is significant precisely because it self-consciously rejects the monotonous implications of the flow and the conservatism of a slowly changing series cosmology. Whether or not televisual shows actually succeed in providing alternatives to this kind of stasis is not the issue. What is important is that they promote special status and pretend to both difference and change. Apart from a few important scholarly works, the very idea of special television has been undertheorized as an industry strategy and stylistic preoccupation.[31] Special television has historically played an important role in programming, and continues to do so today.

I have already indicated that many forms of televisuality have a difficult time raising their stylistic heads above the broadcast clutter, yet the obsession with distinction and with special status pervades both high and low forms of televisuality. *Whether deserving or not,* production technologies and writer-directors alike now continually angle for attributions of distinction. Many primetime televisual shows, for example, can be viewed as "loss leaders."[32] From this merchandising perspective, it does not totally matter if distinctive televisual shows—like *Homefront, Brooklyn Bridge,* and *Wild Palms*—score low ratings, return poor advertising revenues, and face cancelation. After all, most shows have low ratings and are canceled. The cancelation rate for new series is in fact overwhelmingly high and has been for some time. That is the very nature of television. The condition of turnover, an inherent part of program development, makes the critical emphasis on lauding select survivors a shortsighted fallacy. Since the 1970s, when shows like *All in the Family, Mary Tyler Moore,* and *M.A.S.H.* were designated and artificially isolated as distinctive, critics have ignored the vast majority of shows that come and go. Many shows that disappeared, ironically, made even more earnest formal and narrative claims to distinction than those critically privileged Emmy and ratings winners. Given the fact that most of the shows on television are ultimately ratings losers, which type of series should be deemed more symptomatic of a period, the few with high ratings and prestige, or the greater number with high prestige-claims but predictably low numbers? The ratings dominance in the mid-1980s of the conservatively styled *Cosby Show,* for example, does little to conceal the fact that almost everyone else up and down the ratings ladder was struggling to keep their signature looks above water. Distinction is an obligatory and pervasive programming tactic, not just a retrospective and limited critical attribution.

This kind of perspective—the cultural logic of distinction, of televisual loss leaders and special events—cannot be explained, however, without recognizing the fundamental role that style plays in facilitating distinction. More than just case-by-case formal taxonomies of televisual modes, then, the studies that follow aim to describe the favored guises of televisuality as part of a broader aesthetic economy. Coexistent with American mall culture, stylistic designations foreground television's obsession with merchandising and consumerism. The guises—boutique, loss leader, digital franchising, tabloid, trash, and ontological strip-mall—suggest both the programming logic of televisual forms and the types of presentational appeals and relationships televisual forms establish with viewers. Couching the performance of style in economic terms does more than just remove the discussion from the airless confines of formalism, it also demonstrates the fundamental industrial and cultural import of stylistic representations in television. Although my construal of an aesthetic economy may be open to criticism, the concept does not necessarily constrain or ignore the force of economic and political realities in the world at large. Television is part of the world at large and cannot be viewed apart from business conditions. This framework enables us to see televisuality as the industrial instrument and socially motivated ritual that it is. Unlike the fine arts, television aesthetics have never been locked into an intellectual netherworld of pure discourse.[33]

Those arrays of videographic signals and codes that are used pervasively in mass market television make up what might be called, in another context, its televisual language.[34] This language, furthermore, has emerged as part of a broader ideology of stylistic excess, one that pervades contemporary American television and mass culture alike.[35] Yet it is important to note from the start that even in the mass-produced industrial West, there is surely no singular ideology at work in mass culture.[36] For this reason, any paradigms that I refer to must be seen as part of a broader bundle of privileged views, some of which contradict each other. Paradigms can *compete, contradict,* and *coexist.*[37] Also, by "emergence," I hope to suggest that ideology, here taken to include even the way we think about art and imagery, involves an *uneven development.* Mythologizing takes place over time and so is inevitably partial or irregular in its presence.[38] A gloss of Thomas Kuhn's "paradigm shifts" in the history of science might suggest that revolutions in worldviews are drastic, comprehensive, and complete.[39] Last epoch's paradigms are, as it were, cleanly banished by new worldviews to the outdated ash heap of history. But this oversimplification of Kuhn in no way describes cultural change in the late twentieth century. Because there is no cultural pope to centrally organize and determine aesthetic culture, today's mass-media Copernicus must instead ply his or her paradigmatic wares on an open market—on a multinational electronic bazaar, only loosely regulated by the Federal Communications Commission (FCC).

For these reasons competing ideologies continue to coexist in broadcast and cable television. The visually and cinematically sophisticated *thirtysomething,* for example, was merchandised in book form even after its cancelation—a unique compendium of great and "sensitive" writing—as a way of "reliving moments with our favorite family."[40] Other shows, like Rush Limbaugh's syndicated right-wing shock-talk show, still invoke and use reductive studio production modes more typical of the 1970s than the 1980s. The question of which aesthetic paradigm governs television, in fact, depends as much on who you ask as on anything else. Robert S. Alley and Horace Newcomb, for example, claim that television is a "producer's medium"—but do so only after interviewing numerous television producers.[41] Jack Kuney argues that television is a director's medium—that the director "sets both the tone of the program and determines a show's impact on its audience"—after interviewing numerous television directors.[42] Whose medium do you think television would be if, instead, one interviewed editors, lighting designers, art directors or camera people; that is, any one of the hundreds of other people involved in primetime program production?

The tension between aesthetic paradigms is not, then, limited to academic debates. Such conflict is an inevitable part of the television industry, as any one who has left a production "due to creative differences" can tell you. Given this context, then, the occasional presence of low-resolution or amorphous imagery within the present broadcast or cable spectrum does not disprove that a new aesthetic sensibility has emerged.[43] The trends and practices that I am theorizing are part of a *trajectory* of influences; notions that are bought and sold, aired and syndicated, cloned and spun-off. Even the ways that style is performed changes from season to season. Yet the widespread sensibility and urge to aestheticize and stylize suggests that televisuality is more than a passing fashion.

Nagging Theoretical Suspicions

Because so many recent trends in critical theory set themselves up in stark opposition to the aesthetic, the project outlined here may seem on shaky ground at best. John Fiske defines cultural studies, for instance, as a "political" framework in polar opposition to a study of culture's "aesthetic" products.[44] Why erase the aesthetic, in this way, as a theoretical and analytical category? What can be gained by this analytical retreat? Several important tactical assumptions, championed in high theory, work to hobble effective analyses of televisual style. Before examining how a number of fundamental and strategic intellectual commitments have worked to conspiratorialize the image, it is important to consider how several more tactical schools in contemporary theory have impacted televisual analysis. Less antagonists of the image than heuristic complications, postmodernism, "deindustrialized" cultural studies, "glance theory," and the "ideology of liveness" myth all merit reexamination in light of television's penchant for exhibitionism.

Postmodernism. Given the traits of televisuality that I've already sketched out, one might ask, "Why not simply go to the postmodern theory as a basis for interpretation?" After all, the disembodies signifiers and textual extravagance that I describe here are central components in the postmodernist paradigm as well. This may be so. But stated simply, apart from textual description, postmodernism has little to offer broader explanations of American television. This is not because postmodern theory is wrong, only because the theory cannot be used easily to distinguish between what is postmodern and what is not postmodern in American television. Any systematic look at the history of television soon shows that all of those formal and narrative traits once thought to be unique and defining properties of postmodernism—intertextuality, pastiche, multiple and collaged presentational forms—have also been defining properties of television from its inception. Television history, unlike Hollywood film history, cannot be as neatly periodized into sequential stylistic categories: primitive, classical, baroque, modern, and postmodern. The hip gratifications that result from discovering loaded intertexts in *The Simpsons,* for example, are not necessarily unique to television in the 1990s, and tend to overshadow the fact that intertextuality was a central component in television from the start. Comedy-variety shows in the late 1940s and early 1950s—and not just Ernie Kovacs—repeatedly parodied and pastiched cultural conventions. Many other shows on both the local and national level combined intertextual fragments taken from various traditions—newsfilm, vaudeville, photography, radio comedy and drama—into single thirty- and sixty-minute program blocks. From a postmodernist point-of-view, 1940s and 1950s television had it all: self-reflexivity in *Burns and Allen,* intertextuality in *Texaco Star Theater,* direct address in *The Continental,* pastiche in *Your Show of Shows;* and social topicality—modernism's nemesis—in *I Love Lucy* and *The Loretta Young Show* (both made allusions to the Korean War for example).[45] Unlike classical Hollywood cinema, television had no centered gaze from the very start, and seldom had any seamless or overarching narrative. Multiple narrational modes issued from the same works, and audiences were constantly made aware of television's artifice and embellishment. In these ways, then, television has always been postmodern. Television has always been *textually messy*—that is, textural rather than transparent.

Consider, for example, two recent cable programs that gained critical notoriety in 1993: *Mystery Science Theater 3000* on Comedy Central and *Beavis and Butt-head* on MTV. Both bear all of the celebrated hallmarks of postmodernism and both utilize the same basic structuring motif: the series' "stars" sit and watch the same thing the audience watches, but make off-handed, on-camera comments that are either ironic, banal, hip, sexually loaded, or simply gross. Although *Beavis and Butt-head* is intended for a teen and preteen crowd that can appreciate a world numbed by too much glue-sniffing and *Mystery Science Theater 3000* is intended for jaded yuppies, both make an on-screen mockery of "found footage": *Mystery Science* desconstructs old low-budget trash and horror films; *Beavis and Butt-head* deconstructs heavy metal, music videos, and phantom video artifacts. Both are hip, ironic, and somewhat smart as well. Distinctively postmodern? Well, not quite. In the late 1940s Dumont Network's *Window on the World* used the same device. Dumont's host takes a breather from the show's on-stage action to mock and free-associate about bizarre turn-of-the-century archival footage unspooling in the studio's film chain. As beauty contestants in Atlantic City parade before the viewer, the announcer ironically mocks both their bizarre bodies and their ridiculous fashions. Like *Mystery* and *Beavis,* there is no laugh track. Like *Mystery* and *Beavis, Window* ironically deconstructs the newsreel for a knowing and hip *1949* audience. Like the audience for *The Simpsons* and for *Beavis and Butt-head,* Dumont is playing its intertexts for those "in the know." Television has either always been postmodern, or its postmodern tactics are a part of a much different and less celebrated dynamic.

Apart from its descriptive capabilities however, postmodernism also speculates on the big picture behind such devices and attitudes. Fredric Jameson sees in such tactics late capitalism's logic and obsessive reenforcement of consumption. Jean Baudrillard is more fatalistic, and depoliticizes the universe even as he hallucinates about global spectacle. Jean-François Lyotard finds in postmodern practices evidence of the disappearance of distinctions between subject and object. But how do these explanations account for industrial and historical changes in American television? The descriptive tools of postmodern theory are powerful, but the theoretical grounding is frequently tautological. That is, once an account has committed itself to Jameson, Baudrillard, or Lyotard's logic, it tends to end up back at that logic even after exhaustive analysis. Postmodern theory can tell cultural analysts little more than the theory has already confessed to up front. Postmodern theory determines analysis, determines theory, determines analysis in an endless loop. I hope, in some small way not to prejudge this period in American television history by imposing tautological postmodern explanations. Such haste not only depreciates history, it also requires an analytical act of faith.

Deindustrialized cultural studies. Because of its underlying interest in popular culture and audience, this book shares in many of the tenets and objectives of cultural studies. Yet cultural studies, at least as it is sometimes marketed in academia and when it focuses on media, tends to gloss over one of the most important components of televisuality—the industry. This evasion is ironic given cultural studies current fascination with "technologies"—of gender, of cybernetics, of surveillance, of the body, of medical discourses. Even as television studies disappear into cultural studies, the field tends to ignore the extensive technological base of the subject itself: TV technology. It is perhaps easier to traverse multiple pop culture fields, than to account for workhorse technologies that comprise the dominant institution through which mainstream America consumes culture. The television industry may not be as flashy as VR and cyberpunk (tell that to Cindy Crawford, Billy Idol, and the folks over at *Liquid Television*), but it is, depending on one's perspective, surely no less problematic or ideologically complex.

As the academic turf called culture is taken on by humanities and arts colleges, media theorists now range freely and easily over the discursive and problematic turf once owned by sociologists, anthropologists, and political scientists. This recent and important intellectual overhaul, the leap to the culturally macroscopic as an antidote to disciplinary Balkanization, risks ignoring the need for more preliminary and extensive groundwork studies on questions of cultural and institutional *stylistics*. Even the development of a stylistic poetics of television is an important project.[46] It has become an academic fashion in recent years for intellectuals to go native, and so wed high critical theory with thoroughly vernacular forms from low culture. Recent anthologies suggest an institutional desire for validation at the hands of the everyday and the banal.[47] I am less interested in wielding the weapons of high theory to stake intellectual claim to the lowly than in explicating and questioning the ways that low culture itself performs and theorizes. All programming forms are complicated and mediated by style and technology even though "scientific" approaches, and many cultural studies approaches, tend to avoid or downplay this fact.[48] My call here, then, is not simply "back to the text," but back to the "televisual apparatus."[49] For after recognizing and accounting for the centrality and complexities of style, it is important to move beyond mere formal taxonomies. Describing how televisual technologies allow for, but also cut off and delimit, engagement with viewers, is surely an important concern for critical and cultural studies alike.

Glance theory: the myth of distraction. Glance theory, perhaps more than any other academic model, sidetracked television studies from a fuller understanding of the extreme stylization emergent in television in the 1980s. The myth's most cherished assumption? That television viewers are, by nature distracted and inattentive. Although its roots lie in the earlier work of Marshall McLuhan and Raymond Williams, John Ellis was the most forceful proponent of this definitive view. He argued that TV viewers not only lacked "intensity," but that they also gave up looking at all, by "delegating" their sight to the TV set.[50] This view—what I would call a "surrendered gaze theory"—while very influential, could not be a less accurate or useful description of emergent televisuality. Variations of the glance theory are however, commonplace: "We turn on the set casually; we rarely attend to it with full concentration. It is generally permissible to talk or to carry out other activities in its presence . . . (activities that) preclude absorption."[51] Ellis's position is an elaboration of Williams's earlier concept of the television "flow."[52] Within Williams's elaboration of the flow and McLuhan's rich speculations on media are keys to glance theory's flaws: "*The mode of the TV image has nothing in common with film* or photo."[53]

This extreme dualism between film and television—this mythology of "essential media differences" espoused by McLuhan—forms the categorical basis for many future speculations on television, including the glance theory. Once one assumes that there are innate experiential differences between the two media, then critical theorists are merely left to explain, post facto, the cultural and political reasons for those differences. Strangely enough however, Ellis and Williams deduced from this premise conclusions that were diametrically opposed to those of McLuhan. Whereas McLuhan argued that the low-resolution phenomenon fostered a highly active viewer response, one necessitated by the need to give conceptual closure to video's mosaiclike imagery, Ellis and Williams deduce just the opposite.[54] For them, the mosaiclike crudeness fosters inattentiveness and distraction, an inherent phenomenon that programmers try to overcome with the flow. Most contemporary critical works on television have followed the rationalizations of the later Williams-Ellis model of glance theory as an ideology, rather than the phenomenologically based and ostensibly naive futurism of McLuhan.[55] Ironically, the very same dualism—of essential media differences—gave one tradition an *active* viewer, and the other a viewer that *acquiesced.*

This distracted surrender gaze theory seems so far from an accurate portrayal of contemporary television consumption that one wonders whether glance theorists base their explanations of TV only on primitive shows produced in the early, formative years of the medium. When Ellis describes the "ignorance" and inability of TV viewers to know about the obscure and "inconsequential details" of television personalities, he seems to have mistaken TV viewers for what he describes as entranced and uniquely committed "cinephiles." Any cursory survey of the massive popular literature on television—including *Soap Opera Digest, TV Guide, People Magazine,* and others—will show a *extreme consciousness* by viewers of personality, marketing, and star promotion. Such literature also replicates on a mass scale a great amount of narrative detail in television, by summarizing a wide range of plot and character details in soaps and other genres.[56] The videophile—an impossibility according to Ellis—by the 1990s is actually a very informed and motivated viewer.[57] Contrary to glance theory, the committed TV viewer is overtly addressed and "asked to start watching" important televised events. The morasslike flow of television may be more difficult for the TV viewer to wade through than film, but television rewards discrimination, style consciousness, and viewer loyalty in ways that counteract the clutter. Whereas viewership for film is a one-shot experience that comes and goes, spectatorship in television can be quite intense and ingrained over time. Any definition of television based on the viewer's "fundamental inattentiveness" is shortsighted.[58]

The credence given glance theory in subsequent applications was due as much to television's inherent domestic context as to anything else. The notion of inattentiveness fit well the new emphasis on the home and on the "social use" and "object use" of the television set itself—an object that had to compete with other pieces of furniture "in a lighted room."[59] Again, the chief principles of glance theory are invoked: a distracted viewing context, a weak display, and a *very* unmotivated viewer.[60] Although some critics questioned the characterization of television's "regime of vision" as one where the viewer "lacks concentration," others extended the distraction model by shifting and overemphasizing the use of television sound rather than sight.[61] Even recent updates of the glance theory are based on the very problematic notion that television viewers are not actually *viewing* television but that the television is in the background while viewers are actually doing something else.[62] In an otherwise insightful analysis of video replay and video rental movies, one recent theorist attacks theory's aversion to low-culture viewing pleasures, while at the same time, continuing the orthodoxy that "there is a specific way" that television is watched. But if this particular TV viewer is *actually doing something else,* as the author says—while television is merely issuing-forth in the background—why extrapolate that this preoccupation with something else is symptomatic of the way television is *always* watched? Why not use an engaged and entranced viewer as the example upon which to build a theory of viewership?

Once the phenomenological basis for glance theory was academically sanctioned, however, more complicated ideological and psychoanalytic explanations were rushed to the fore. Since cinema spectatorship was commonly construed as psychologically regressive and hallucinatory—as a "total-izing, womblike, dream-state"—television, forever cinema's antithesis, was couched as just the opposite.[63] Following Freud, Jacques Lacan, and Chris-tian Metz, film's viewing hallucination, like the dream, was described as an "artificially psycho(tic)" state that focused on the *pleasure of the image*.[64] Television's "more casual" forms of looking, by contrast, "substituted live-ness and directness for the dream-state, immediacy and presentness for regression."[65] Because repeated television viewing presupposes *some kind* of pleasure however, psychoanalytic theorists sought the source of this pleas-ure and unity in places *other* than cinema's womblike state. From this point of view, television viewers, despite distractions and interruptions, achieve "an exhilarating sense" of power when they range across and "control" a wide variety of flow material. The ability to choose visually rather than to hallucinate visually is seen as a key to the pleasures of televisual distraction.

The fact that *some* TV viewers *are* deeply engaged in specific programs—and do find *pleasure* in entranced isolation while watching a show, star, or favorite performer—puts the validity of the psychoanalytic account into ques-tion. Since the conditions presupposed by the psychoanalytic glance theory are neither necessary or sufficient prerequisites for viewing, the applicabil-ity of the theory is severely compromised. Further problematizing psychol-ogistic extensions of the glance are attempts to solidify the gaze versus glance, film versus video dichotomies into a model that explains male ver-sus female gendering. It has become popular to see televisual distraction as a feminizing process and to extrapolate to polar conclusions that cast cine-matic spectatorship as male and televisual spectatorship as female. The cen-trality of the housewife in the early decades of television does lend credence to this theory. There are, however, many pervasive and hyperactive forms of televisuality that can in no way be construed as feminine.[66] In fact, a number of hypermasculinist televisual tendencies have been an important part of television from the start.

Four correctives then, are in order: first, the viewer is not always, nor inherently, distracted. Second, if theorists would consider the similarities between television and film—rather than base universalizing assumptions on their "inevitable" differences—glance and surrender theories would fall from their privileged theoretical pedestals. Third, psychoanalytic and feminizing extensions of glance theory tend to put critical analysis into essential and rigidly gendered straitjackets. Fourth, and finally, even if viewers are inat-tentive, television works hard visually, not just through aural appeals, to attract the attention of the audience; after all, it is still very much in televi-sion's best narrative and economic interests to engage the viewer. Theorists should not jump to theoretical conclusions just because there is an ironing board in the room.

The ideology of liveness myth. Any effective analysis of televisual style must also shake itself of one other theoretical obsession: liveness. In recent American television, liveness is frequently packaged as an artifact. As often as not, pictorialism rather than realism, rules the context in which liveness is flaunted and seen. This practice of live embellishment flies in the face of some of the most cherished mythologies of television, ones that presuppose immediacy and nowness as the basis for television. Whereas glance theory focuses specifically on the nature of reception, the liveness mythology implicates production and cultural issues as well. The notion surely has its origins in the history of television production. In the pre-tape 1950s, television *was* live and broadcasters celebrated this distinctive fact. Yet, definitions of television and liveness emerged in phenomenological studies in the 1960s, in prescriptive aesthetics and manifestos in the 1970s, and in sophisticated poststructuralist analyses of the 1980s. Never mind that the technical medium itself has changed dramatically, and that it has done so several times. In high theory, the liveness paradigm simply will not die.

Although hardly ever cited by critical theorists, McLuhan laid the foundation for the academic myth of liveness, when he defined the medium as an "all-at-onceness" created by global television's erasure of time and space.[67] Other theorists expanded on the notion of television's innate liveness and nowness by examining the medium's broader appetite for currency and presentness even in non-live genres. Peter Wood argued from psychoanalysis that television's similarity to dreams caused it to evoke a "great wealth of familiar and often current material stored in the viewer's mind."[68] Horace Newcomb proposed a television aesthetic that was based in part on a commitment to the present, although he used the designation "history" to describe this form of currency. Newcomb alluded to the power of the present in television by arguing that "the television formula requires that we use our contemporary historical concerns as subject matter."[69] That is, sitcoms and historical programs alike elaborate contemporary cultural issues and current events. Within this tradition, then, everything in programming, *fiction as well as news and live coverage,* is a cultural and psychological operation defined by the present. Presentness and the past are inextricably related.

The myth of nowness also fed back into alternative production practice starting in the late 1960s. Video artists and electronic politicos alike embraced the liveness myth as a key to radical video production. Techno apologists argued that the instantaneous electronic medium altered "habitual ways of seeing" and transformed human experience. The technology-determined revolution was at hand.[70] Artists found in the "real-time" experience of live video, a fundamental force that could alter both personal experience and social practice.[71] Temporality was construed as magic; simultaneity as shamanism; and video art as altered consciousness. Video installations, environments, and small format tapes were designed and hyped around the concept.[72] Poet and modernist aesthetician David Antin, in a prescriptive treatise for media art, pursued what he termed the "*distinctive* features of the medium." Like Harold Rosenberg's advocacy of abstract expressionism before him (arguments that reduced painting to existential action), and Clement Greenberg's rationales for minimalism (ideas that reduced visual art to flatness and reflexivity), Antin attempted to reduce the phenomenon of television to its essence and its industrial obligation. Antin described video's fundamental and defining components as time and immediacy.[73] Postformalist critics and theorists like Rosalind Krauss later used simultaneity and liveness to demonstrate the centrality of psychosexual narcissism in the work of important video artists.[74] Works by Vito Acconci, Elizabeth Holt, and others exploited the medium's liveness through feedback loops and lengthy and indulgent performances, all as ways of exposing the human subject's "unchanging condition of perpetual frustration."[75] In an art world disciplined by rituals of specificity, video's immediacy myth was the perfect weapon for critical exclusion.

Even outside the limited institutions of video art, criticism, and theory, however, the liveness myth was snowballing. Basic production texts praised television's unique ontological burden for "realism and *authenticity*."[76] Others contrasted the event-bound time of television to the innately sequential and objective time of film. Television's "most distinctive function [is] the live transmission of events. . . . The now of the television event is equal to the now of the actual event."[77] Mimicking the rhetoric of network television, then, production theorists argued that good television exploits the sense of nowness, since it is inextricably linked to an external event. Liveness, then, came to have completely different ideological effects, depending on the theorist who invoked it. For prescriptive modernist critics and video visionaries, on the one hand, liveness was a key to disruptive and *radical* artistic practice. Conventional production people like Alan Wurtzel and Herbert Zettl, on the other hand, argued that liveness was a fundamental quality of any good *mainstream* production work. The myth still held center stage, although the political implications of liveness clearly remained in the eye of the beholder.

During the 1980s television theorists who immigrated from film studies—a field that had spent nearly two decades deconstructing the ontology and ideology of realism—provided convincing explanations for the popularity of a related concept in television: the liveness ideology.[78] That is, liveness was seen to cover over the excessive heterogeneity and confusion of the broadcast flow by giving the medium a sense of abiding presentness.[79] Unlike many earlier critical theories, this view correctly noted that liveness in television is neither neutral, simple, nor unproblematic.[80] Other examinations also exposed liveness as a construction, but were even more explicit in *overstating the notion that liveness "pervades every moment of broadcast."*[81] As long as high theory continues to overestimate the centrality of liveness in television—even as it critiques liveness—it will also underestimate or ignore other modes of practice and production: the performance of the visual and stylistic exhibitionism.

More recent studies suggest that the industry has deontologized its own focus. Television now defines itself less by its inherent temporality and presentness than by pleasure, style, and commodity. Todd Gitlin's anthology of television criticism shows a renewed interest in "a common attention to the implications of form and style."[82] His own analysis is a highly visual account of the mood and tone of imagery and style in high-tech car commercials and the blank sleekness of *Miami Vice*.[83] David Marc takes as his analytical object a genre in television historically related to, and defined by, liveness. The comedy-variety show is linked to stand-up comedy and other overtly presentational forms of comedy that unfold in real-time. Presentational comedy, then, involves the traits one associates with liveness: improvisation, snafus, and spontaneity. Marc, however, describes the genre not around the notion of liveness, but as a spectacle of excess, a "framed" artform that "accepts the badge of artifice."[84] Margaret Morse's recent work analyses television within an American culture that invests heavily in rituals of distraction.[85] Television is linked to the ontology of the freeway, the shopping mall, and theme parks. These three recent approaches, Gitlin's *iconographic* view of television, Marc's explication of *artifice* in liveness, and Morse's *architectonic* analysis and critique, are all indicators of the importance *style and materiality, rather than temporality,* have come to play in contemporary television.

Yet, the ideology of liveness myth lives on, even if in modified form. A sophisticated analysis of catastrophe programming on television describes the ideology of time, and the sense of continuity that drives it on, as both a target and victim of broadcast catastrophes.[86] Liveness, at least when linked to death and disaster, is textually disruptive but ultimately pleasurable since its coverage works to assure domestic viewers that the catastrophe is not happening to them.[87] Television is again defined, even in this catastrophe theory, by its temporality and not by its image.[88] Yet, if catastrophic liveness *is* marginal and disruptive, then it is also an exception that proves the rule; it is an exception that indicates the dominance on a day-to-day basis of more conventional image and sound pleasures. If traumatic liveness induces extreme anxiety in the viewer, then hypostatized time and massive regularity comfort the viewer by providing a rich but contained televisual spectacle, an endless play of image and sound. The degree to which liveness and simultaneity still govern even recent theorizations is suggested by catastrophe theory's account of the new telecommunications technology: "The more rapid internationalization of television via the *immediacy* of satellites . . . replicates the *emphasis on transmission*.[89] Such an account suggests that liveness and immediacy will be even more important in global television than they are today.

This view ignores the fact that even satellite system broadcasts in Asia and Africa today seldom emphasize either immediacy or liveness. Star Network out of Hong Kong, for example, has become a quintessential packager of aged entertainment products—music videos, dramas, reruns—rather than a conduit for liveness, immediacy, or catastrophe. Very little, in fact, looks live or transmitted in international broadcasting. Even the domestic broadcasting of live and unscripted media events—like ABC's *Monday Night Football,* or major league baseball—are comprehensively planned, scripted, and rehearsed; are in fact highly regulated and rigidly controlled performances, fabricated to fit a restricted block of viewing time.[90] Now, as in McLuhan's

1960s, the resilience of the liveness myth still has as much to do with a vague notion (and hope?) of technological determinism as it does with anything else. As long as theorists look to the new technologies of television to prove the centrality of presence, simultaneity, nowness, or transmission, they perpetuate one of broadcasting's most self-serving and historical mythologies. Television has always boasted liveness as its claim to fame and mark of distinction, even though the programming that floods from its channels seldom supports this air of distinction and pretense of liveness.

In the spring of 1993, Mike Myers and Dana Carvey, stars of the recent hit film *Wayne's World*, hosted *Short Attention-Span Theater* on Comedy Central.[91] In the new world of cable, apparently, even *Saturday Night Live* alums could parody television's glance theory. Yet the trades discussed their appearance not as an indication of television's inherent distraction, but as just the opposite: the episode aimed to break the limitations of niche advertising by attracting a different audience. Niche economics on cable, after all, preclude the kind of inattentiveness that theorists celebrate as one of television's defining qualities.

Television and its performers have been no less conscious of the *stylistic* possibilities of liveness. David Koresh, founder of the Branch Davidian sect, proved that he understood the quintessential nature of televisual production when he forewarned: "The riots in Los Angeles would pale in comparison to what was going to happen in Waco, Texas."[92] Unlike his apocalyptic predecessor Jim Jones in Guyana—who suicidally fled to the afterlife rather than face NBC's approaching electronic news gathering (ENG) cameras—Koresh betrayed neither ontological subtlety nor televisual stage fright. The fires that raged when Los Angeles burned in 1992 provided not a sense of simultaneity or realism, but rather a powerful and codified template for stylized and horrific spectacle. The alienated televisuality of the L.A. rebellion could be appropriated and choreographed for the benefit of the mass audience, even by those in other places and with very different apocalyptic ends. Unfortunately for David Koresh and his followers, the ATF assault troops in Waco proved that the televisual spectacle, once unleashed, had an unforgiving mind of its own.

Notes

1. Quoted in Laurence Jarvik and Nancy Strickland, "Cinema Very TV," *California* (July 1989), 198.

2. Quoted in Christina Bunish, "The Search for Realism: Directors David Steinberg, Ron Dexter and Bob Eggers Face the Challenges of Capturing Reality," *Film and Video* (September 1990), 66.

3. Jeff Kaye, "Sex, Mud and Rock and Roll," *Los Angeles Times*, November 9, 1989, F1.

4. Kevin Cosgrove, "Regis' Recipe for a Healthy Life," *TV Guide*, March 6, 1993, 8–11.

5. I choose the term "mass-market" television rather than the more traditional concept of "network" television, since broadcasting had clearly been overhauled and

pluralized by 1990. "Mass-market" expresses a kind of programming and economic scale that is not limited to a few privileged broadcast corporations, but rather encompasses other institutions that work over national media markets with high-production value programming. This term, then, would include Fox (the fourth network), superstations, large-scale syndication companies, CNN, MTV, and other media corporations that produce and program on a national level.

6. Retheorization refers to how changes in practice and production discourse evidence shifts in working assumptions and orienting perspectives, not to the intentional and conscious formulation of theoretical premises and principles as ends in themselves.

7. Performative aspects of media have traditionally been associated with dramatic and theatrical elements, whereas style is typically postured as a static and fixed formal property owned by works of art. Here, with the concept "performance of style," I hope to indicate a shift away from an assumption of style as static property toward style as a hyperactive presentational process.

8. "Individuation" is a popular psychological term referring to a person's development of distinct ego boundaries and distinguishable personal behaviors. Stylistic individuation could, however, be as easily described in economic terms as a kind of product differentiation. Looking at the overt discourse of practitioners in the media industry suggests, however, the importance and degree of investment given to construing creative personas behind program looks and production accomplishments. The psychologizing of the media discourse by practitioners should not be taken as a refutation of broader economic interests, however, for the two strata are probably intricately tied to each other.

9. Still one of the most engaging and detailed accounts of the golden age of live anthology drama in the 1950s is Eric Barnouw's *Tube of Plenty: The Evolution of American Television* (New York: Oxford University Press, 1975, 1992), a book that isolates skilled and serious artists at the center of broadcasting's live and dramatic showcases during that period.

10. The extent to which this type of production practice challenges privileged academic theories—like postmodernism and cultural studies—is discussed more fully at the end of this introduction, and in the chapters that follow.

11. John Dempsey, "More Mags Will Fly in the Fall: Too Much of a Good Thing?" *Variety*, April 12, 1989, reprinted in Marilyn Matelski and David Thomas, *Variety: Broadcast-Video Sourcebook I* (Boston: Focal Press, 1990), 27. *Entertainment Tonight* is produced by Paramount Television; *A Current Affair* is a production of *20th Century Fox Television;* and *Inside Edition* is produced and syndicated by King World.

12. Jim Van Messel, executive producer, *Entertainment Tonight* as quoted in Mike Freeman, "*Entertainment Tonight* Turns 3,000," *Broadcasting and Cable,* May 8, 1993, 30.

13. Said the critics: "What they've done is close to a miracle. They were dead and found the fountain of youth." TV Critic Tom Jicha, quoted in Harry A. Jessell, "New Wave Newscasts Anchor WSVN Makeover: Ex-Affiliate Finds a New Niche," *Broadcasting,* October 12, 1992, 24.

14. Joel Cheatwood, vice-president of news, and Bob Leider, executive vice-president, WSVN-TV, quoted in ibid.

15. Bruce Sandzimier, vice-president of editorial, Universal Television. Katherine Stalter, "Working in the New Post Environment," *Film and Video* (April 1993), 100.

16. "Help Wanted, Program Production and Others," *Broadcasting,* November 30, 1992, 57. In mundane station management activities like hiring, WRAL-TV5 in North Carolina, in personnel upgrades, now expected its graphic designers to have visual arts design degrees and to be proficient in Paintbox, animation, and still-store technologies. Even verbal- and text-oriented broadcast positions, like that of the news promotion producer at WRAL, were advertised and keyed to essential visual communications skills.

17. David Poltrack, CBS's senior vice-president of planning and research. Richard Zoglin, "The Big Boy's Blues," *Time,* October 17, 1988, 59.

18. This diversification trend mirrors, of course, developments over the last century in advertising.

19. These examples are described in Jeffrey Wells, "Is It the Reel Thing: Big Name Directors Try to Bring Film Magic to Coke Ads," *Los Angeles Times,* February 17, 1993. F1, F6.

20. Ibid., F7.

21. See discussion in chapter 10 of this book, "Televisual Economy," of the changes in business structure that CAA's appearance as a major agency player in 1993 caused.

22. *Variety,* September 30, 1987. *Variety,* September 13, 1989, reprinted in Matelski and Thomas, 73.

23. By 1994 the network's growth was predicted "to cost ABC at least $75 million per year in lost revenue." Tom Wolzien, as quoted in Geoffrey Foisie, "Fox Hounds ABC-TV, *Broadcasting and Cable,* June 14, 1993, 65.

24. "The real killer" of *Wonder Years* "was economics not prudishness." Coupled with escalating cast salaries, "the budget soared to $1.2 million per half-hour episode. Many hour-long dramas are shot for less." Steve Weinstein, "Reeling in the Bittersweet 'Wonder Years'," *Los Angeles Times,* May 12, 1993, F1, F6.

25. "Zapped: The Networks Under Attack," *Time,* October 17, 1988, 56–61.

26. *Broadcasting,* July 4, 1989. Cited also in J. Fred MacDonald, *One Nation Under Television* (New York: Pantheon, 1990), 253.

27. Two recent books underscore the recurrent academic view that the sitcom works to reinforce status quo values. Ella Taylor, *Primtetime Families* (Berkeley: University of California Press, 1989), demonstrates the resilience of the myth of the nuclear family on network television up to its conservative reconstitution in 1980s sitcoms. Darrel Hamamoto, *Nervous Laughter: Television Situation Comedy and Liberal Democratic Ideology* (New York: Praeger Publishers, 1990), makes a compelling case that the sitcom—even in its liberal manifestations—has systematically worked to elide racial and ethnic issues and threats to the mainstream, white, status quo.

28. *Full House* (ABC, 1987–1993).

29. Raymond Williams, *Television, Technology, and Cultural Form* (New York: Schockes, 1975).

30. David Marc, *Demographic Vistas: Television in American Culture* (Philadelphia: University of Pennsylvania Press, 1983), 5.

31. These exceptions include, of course, Jane Feuer et al. *MTM: Quality Television* (London: British Film Institute, 1985), and Horace Newcomb and Robert S. Alley, *The Producer's Medium* (New York: Oxford University Press, 1983).

32. The mercantile analogy of the "loss leader" is applied in the analysis of epic forms of televisuality, like the miniseries, in chapter 6.

33. This criticism holds true for fine art up to and including the period of high modernism. Although the intellectual-theoretical crutch that I speak of has always

been more important to the art world than to Hollywood, various conceptual, video, and performances artists since 1968 have attempted to break through the art world's ideological props by engaging and critiquing the institution's support systems and economic industry.

34. If one were to view the research of this book within the tradition of film theory, the idea of a media-specific "language" certainly has ample precedent. Here, however—in a project that seeks to explicate the nature of *nonverbal* semiosis in television—the linguistic term creates problems of its own for analysis. Given my focus then, the analysis that follows will target: (1) visual modes of presentation distinctive to television; (2) aesthetic modes that are borrowed and redefined by television; and (3) cultural practices that impinge upon and inform these modes. The presentational modes that I refer to are generally and predominantly nonverbal and differ from orthodox film language. Media language models tend to focus on and privilege editing, narrative structure, and syntax. Televisuality, by contrast, privileges images—with *simultaneous* components typically displayed within a shared frame. In general, the televisual modes that I am theorizing represent a divergence from classical narrative cinema and television.

35. Having summarized my project in this way, a few additional words about terminology and definitions are in order. In television programming's shift toward visuality—both as a formal trait and as program content—stylistic signifiers are regularly stripped from their traditional signifieds and made open to continual redefinition and reuse. Given the centrality of what postmodernism terms disembodied signifiers, however, televisuality can also be profitably seen as an *industrial process* of assigning and bestowing value, not just as a look. But televisuality should be seen as more than just an industrial shift to, and preoccupation with, visual imagery. In a less macroscopic but no less important sense, televisuality also refers to that trait now common in television whereby programs intentionally engage the viewer with *multiple* and *simultaneous* layers of perceptual and discursive information, many times overwhelming him or her by combining visual, spatial, gestural, and iconic signals. Televisuality is, in this sense, a phenomenon of communicative and *semiotic overabundance*. Although isolated examples of the phenomenon existed in earlier periods in television history, and frequented feature film history, television popularized and cashed-in on this semiotic process and display of overabundance in the 1980s. Finally, televisuality implicates more than just industrial and aesthetic issues, and the final chapters will attempt to address the trend's historical and ideological significance.

36. I am utilizing "ideology" in the way that E. Ann Kaplan defines the Althusserian variant of the term. In *Rocking Around the Clock* (New York: Methuen, 1987), 188, she describes ideology as a "series of representations and images, reflecting conceptions of 'reality' that any society assumes. Ideology thus no longer refers to beliefs people consciously hold but to myths that a society lives by, as if these myths referred to some natural, unproblematic reality." In this sense image and style-practice can be seen as part of any ideology and cultural mythology.

37. One key to understanding the ideology of style can be found in the contradictory and competing aspects at work within an emerging paradigm or myth. Structural anthropology has taken the narrative process (by which contradictions are covered over and resolved) to be a key to a culture's mythology. See Claude Lévi-Strauss, "The Structural Study of Myth," *Structural Anthropology*, trans. Claire Jacobson and Brooke Grundfest Schoepf (New York: Basic Books, 1963), 206–231. Mimi White in her essay "Ideological Analysis and Television," *Channels of Discourse*, ed. Robert Allen (Chapel Hill: University of North Carolina Press, 1987),

134–171, has argued that it is precisely television's textual contradictions that expose the workings of ideology.

38. In describing the emergence of visuality as "uneven, partial, and irregular," I do not aim to lessen its importance as a distinct and identifiable phenomena. Rather, I hope to show its presence and power as an historical phenomenon—in the same way that Nick Browne's analysis of post-May 1968 French film theory demonstrated that "history assumes the aspect of an ensemble of unevenly developed, stratified and shifting relations enacted in a new social setting. Old connections are broken and displaced; new structures and commitments are in the process of emerging. The sense of uneven, fragmented movement of diverse but associated themes makes the ensemble of these texts an unfinished work site." Nick Browne, ed., *Cahiers du Cinéma: 1969–1972, The Politics of Representation* (Cambridge: Harvard University Press, 1990), 1. I will argue that the same scale of contentious shifting has occurred in recent television, but for very different reasons.

39. I hope when analyzing media to synthesize Kuhn's influential concept of epochal paradigm shifts, with the less cognitive perspectives of cultural-ideology studies and social mythology. Thomas Kuhn, *The Structure of Scientific Revolutions* (Chicago: University of Chicago Press, 1962).

40. The "writers of *thirtysomething,*" *thirtysomething stories* (New York: Pocket Books, 1992).

41. Newcomb and Alley, *The Producer's Medium.*

42. Jack Kuney, *Television Directors on Directing* (New York: Praeger Publishers, 1990).

43. And surely with the proliferation of infomercials and talk shows, more of these low-resolution forms of TV are on the way.

44. John Fiske states that "the term 'culture,' used in the phrase 'culture studies,' is neither aesthetic and humanist in emphasis, but political. . . . Culture is not, then, the aesthetic product . . . but rather a way of living in an industrial society." "British Cultural Studies and Television," in *Channels of Discourse,* 254. A good collection of more recent cultural studies works is Tony Bennett, Susan Boyd-Bowman, Colin Mercer, and Janet Woollacott, eds., *Popular Television and Film: A Reader* (London: British Film Institute, 1981).

45. A number of these shows will be discussed in more detail in chapter 2. Pastiche and mocking parody were a requisite part of *Your Show of Shows* ("Ten From *Your Show of Shows,*" n.d., (PVA-1906t). The textual fold-in of the military took place in *I Love Lucy,* "Lucy Gets Drafted," December 24, 1951 (PVA-81t), and the *Loretta Young Show,* "Dateline Korea," March 13, 1955, (PVA-8890t).

46. In current media theory, poetics has become a problematic concept. David Bordwell, in *Making Meaning* (Cambridge: Harvard University Press, 1989), 263ff., makes a case for poetics as a substitute for the excesses and shortcomings of most current interpretive-based film study. While the notion of poetics is caught up in this current debate, it is worth noting that its earlier usage by the Russian formalists assumed that the framework included a cultural and political dimension. More current theorists like Michael Renov, in a keynote address at the Thirteenth Annual Ohio University Film Conference on Documentary, called for a new project to develop a systematic "poetics of documentary" (Athens, Ohio, November 1990). Certainly the focus of poetics on stylistic formation, materiality, perceptibility, and function are worth addressing and applying to contemporary television practice. Such a strategy is not incompatible with ideological analysis.

47. Colin MacCabe, ed., *High Theory/Low Culture: Analyzing Popular Television and Film* (New York: St. Martin's Press, 1986).

48. Given this semiotic density and the abundance of channels involved in perception, it is likely that if one has not accurately defined the stylistically complicated object of investigation, then one is not even accounting for or controlling the constants and variables involved in the process. In short, a lot of close textual and aesthetic work needs to be done even before the broadcasting scholar can do good science. Academic broadcasting studies have tended to overlook the extreme complexity of the actual viewing situation and of the televisual text itself, in lieu of a dominant concern with master interpretive allegories, verbal content, or social meanings and effects. Much work remains to be done in terms of accurately describing the texts and intertexts that present and perform such contents and effects.

49. The history of film theory clearly demonstrates the limitations of formal taxonomies, which tend to reify description and overvalue aesthetic norms. It is worth noting in this regard that perhaps the two most influential media taxonomists, Christian Metz and Sergei Eisenstein, at least eventually changed course by correctly seeing and describing taxonomies within and as a part of an ideological and psychological dynamic. Eisenstein's writings clearly demonstrated a tension between syntactical taxonomies and constructivist inclinations on the one hand (tendencies he shared with other montage theorists like Lev Kuleshov and V. I. Pudovkin), and his overarching sense or obligation, on the other hand, to account for film's formal taxonomies as social and political weapons. *Film Form: Essays in Film Theory,* ed. and trans. by Jay Leyda (New York: Harcourt Brace, 1949) and *Film Sense,* ed. and trans. by Jay Leyda (New York: Harcourt Brace, 1942). Christian Metz first emerged in the 1960s as a theorist whose work promised scientific and endless noninterpretive cross-sections of film form and film structure in works like *Film Language,* trans. by Michael Taylor (New York: Oxford University Press, 1974). By 1976, Metz's *The Imaginary Signifier* (Bloomington: Indiana University Press, 1976) seemed to turn its back on the dead syntactical categorization of his earlier work by leaping to complicated conjectures about the spectator's social and psychological self. The scope of analysis is limited, once this impulse in theory has categorized, or promised to categorize, all of its formal options and taxonomies.

50. "It is TV that looks at the world; the TV viewer glances across TV as it looks. This delegation of the look to TV and *consequent loss of intensity in the viewer's own activity of viewing* has several consequences." John Ellis, *Visible Fictions: Cinema, Television, Video* (London: Routlege and Kegan Paul, 1982), 164.

51. Richard Adler continues: "The inevitable commercial interruptions virtually preclude prolonged absorption." "Introduction: A Context for Criticism," *Television as a Cultural Force,* ed. Richard Adler (New York: Praeger, 1976), 6.

52. Both Ellis and Williams sought to describe the fundamental components of the medium and experience of television. But glance theory also partakes of and elaborates an earlier academic schema, that is, the globalizing polar dichotomies that Marshall McLuhan described when comparing television to film. Raymond Williams, *Television, Technology and Cultural Form* (New York: Schocken, 1975).

53. "The mode of the TV image has nothing in common with film or photo, except that it offers also a nonverbal gestalt or posture of forms. With TV the viewer is the screen. . . . The TV image is visually low in data. . . . The film image offers many more millions of data per second, and the viewer does not have to make the same drastic reduction of items to form his impression. He tends instead to accept

the full image as a package deal." Marshall McLuhan, *Understanding Media: The Extensions of Man* (New York: McGraw-Hill, 1964), 272.

54. McLuhan comments that "the viewer of the TV image, with technical control over the image, unconsciously reconfigures the dots into an abstract work of art, on the pattern of Seurat or Rouault. . . . The TV image is now a mosaic mesh of white and dark spots." *Understanding Media*, 273.

55. Ellis, in fact, makes the incredible generalization that: "The broadcast TV viewer is not engaged by TV representation to any great degree: broadcast TV has not so far produced a group of telephiles to match the cinephiles who have seen everything and know the least inconsequential detail about the most obscure actor and directors. Broadcast TV does not habitually offer any great incentives to start watching TV." (*Visible Fictions*, 162.) Williams argued that since television does not exist in discrete and isolated programs, but rather is constantly interrupted and linked to other programming in the evening, analysts should study the expanded programming sequence rather than individual units. Because of this basic understanding, later theorists would conclude that such a fragmented and cluttered aesthetic object would not logically entice viewers to the kind of intense engagement that cinephiles experience at the cinema.

56. In addition to the substantial popular publishing industry that focuses on television, television programming itself encourages style and detail consciousness on the part of viewers. Shows like *Entertainment Tonight* and *Arsenio*, and many other clones on cable, constantly spotlight the content and style of television.

57. In all fairness to Ellis, and others, glance theory may have accounted more credibly for television in the 1970s or early 1980s. Regardless of its origins, however, glance theory is made suspect by current television practice. The primetime television industry especially fashions programs and nonprogram materials with increasing style- and fashion-consciousness. Even when Ellis was writing, *MTV* and *Miami Vice* and miniseries like *Shogun* had established highly *visual* arenas for narrative, music, and drama. In the decade that followed a growing concern with stylishness evolved out of these forms. Some shows mimicked *MTV* and *Vice*. Others made their own claims for unique visual style (*Crime Story, Max Headroom, Hill Street Blues, L.A. Law*). By 1989, shows like CBS's *Beauty and the Beast* were mise-en-scène-strong and narrative-weak. Writers for such shows were faced with script assignments requiring many viewer pages and having long nonverbal scenes displaying auspicious and expressionist lighting effects. Directional lighting, colored gels, smoke, and synth music permeated primetime programming. The artistic reference in look was closer to Rembrandt than it was to the "ideology of inattentiveness" that glance theorists promoted. *TV Guide* promoted the special nature of such shows: these were not shows to be glanced at. Television by 1990 was in many cases self-consciously hip and excessively styled. There was no longer a zero-degree formal syntax and style at work here. The idea of a neutral and colorless writing, in short, a de-aestheticized style in the work of Alain Robbe-Grillet was promoted by Roland Barthes in *Writing Degree Zero* (New York: Hill and Wang, 1953), xvi, 76. The zero-degree style of TV in the 1950s and early 1960s was a dominant rather than radical or modernist tendency. Glance theory simply missed the opportunity to elucidate and explain the newer and important televisual forms—a refusal that helped reinforce television theory's denigration of the image.

58. In a critique of Ellis's book, "Television at a Glance," by Brian Winston (*Quarterly Review of Film Studies* 9, no. 3 [Summer 1984], 256–261), the British theoretical tradition from which Ellis's work comes is interrogated and rejected. Win-

ston attacks almost all of Ellis's central assumptions: his ideas about television and enigma, the medium's essential temporal regularity, the importance of the nuclear family, the emphasis on the glance as a defining factor, and his underlying attitude and valuation of popular culture in general. Strangely enough, few have followed through on Winston's suggestions. Among my goals here are: (1) to show that glance theory and the related mythology of liveness predated the work of Ellis in American media studies by many years; (2) to demonstrate that glance theory continues to be widespread and popular in more contemporary critical work and cultural studies; and finally, (3) to suggest how the assumption and misperception of inattentiveness may actually be a key to television's underlying logic and appetite for embellishment, ornamentation, and stylishness.

59. In his explanation of the symbolic social use of television in the home Dennis Giles states: "But given the distractions of home viewing, given the fact that the TV image rarely dominates a room by its size alone and that it competes against other possible objects of vision in a lighted room, TV pictures are less forceful than theatrical movie images in holding the viewer's attention." Dennis Giles, "Television Reception," *Journal of Film and Video* 37, no. 3, (Summer 1985): 12–25.

60. Since Giles is concerned with the symbolic function of television set as furniture and icon, his remarks are suggestive. They tend, however, to devalue the aural-visual spectacle that television increasingly tries to heighten.

61. "[Television] emphasizes another invocatory drive: hearing; *sound dominates* [and] ensures continuity of attention," says Robert Deming, in "The Television Spectator-Subject," *Journal of Film and Video* 37, no. 3 (Summer 1985): 49.

62. A recent analysis by Valerie Walkerdine shows the extent of this TV-as-background assumption: "There is a specific way in which television is watched. This differs from the fascinated concentration of the spectator in the darkened cinema, and also from the way that television is often *used as a backdrop to domestic routines.*" Valerie Walkerdine, "Video Replay," in Manuel Alverado and John O. Thomson, eds., *The Media Reader* (London: British Film Institute, 1990), 349.

63. "The *totalizing, womblike effects of the film-viewing situation represent* [for Baudry], the activation of an unconscious desire to return to an earlier state of psychic development, one before the formation of the ego, in which the divisions between the self and other, internal and external, have not yet taken shape." Sandy Flitterman-Lewis, "Psychoanalysis, Film, and Television," in Robert Allen, ed., *Channels of Discourse,* 182.

64. This "womblike," "artificially psycho[tic]" state of the film viewer as a dreamer is for Flitterman-Lewis tied directly to the visual emphasis of cinema. What links this process to the cinema is the fact that it occurs in terms of visual images—what the child sees at this point (a unified image that is distanced and objectified) forms how he or she will interact with others at later stages in life. Ibid., 183.

65. Flitterman-Lewis contrasts television to this process in several important ways. Thus television substitutes liveness and directness for the dream state, immediacy and presentness for regression. It also modifies primary identification in ways that support its *more casual forms of looking.* The television viewer is a distracted viewer.

66. See especially the discussion of the live-remote mode in chapter 9, and the militarist guises of crisis coverage in chapter 11.

67. "It is the total involvement in all-inclusive *nowness* that occurs in young lives via TV's mosaic image." McLuhan, *Understanding Media,* 292. "Ours is a brand new world of *allatonceness.* 'Time' has ceased, 'space' has vanished. We now

live in a global village . . . a *simultaneous* happening" (italics mine). Marshall McLuhan and Quentin Fiore, *The Medium Is the Message: An Inventory of Effects* (New York: Bantam Books, 1967), 63.

68. Peter H. Wood, "Television as Dream," in *Television as a Cultural Force,* Richard Adler, ed. (New York: Praeger, 1976), 23.

69. Horace Newcomb, *Television: The Most Popular Art* (New York: Anchor Books, 1974), 258.

70. "What is video then? Video is a process of expression that is *instantaneous,* electronic, and playable on one or more screens, through images and sound *transforming time into experience* and altering the habitual way the audience has of seeing. The soul of video is change, not permanence." Jonathan Price, *Video Visions: A Medium Discovers Itself* (New York: New American Library, 1972), 4.

71. What started in part as a countercultural and social movement to appropriate the tools of television production became within this aesthetic a way to alter personal consciousness. A focus on liveness, real time, and simultaneity could be wielded, in short, for both social and political ends.

72. Since video is a medium of *real time,* that is, because it transmits the temporal quality of the process being recorded, it alters our experience of our own memory, of history, and of daily life. Frank Gillette, "Masque in Real Time," in Ira Schneider and Beryl Korot, eds., *Video Art* (New York: Harcourt, Brace, Jovanovich, 1976), 219.

73. The industry wishes, or feels obligated, to maintain the illusion of *immediacy,* which it defines rather precisely as "the *feeling* that what one sees on the TV screen is living and actual reality, *at that very moment taking place*" (italics mine). David Antin, "Video: The Distinctive Features of the Medium," in *Video Art,* 177. It followed from this aesthetic that important video art (video art worthy to be curated, collected, and funded) was videowork that exploited the property of liveness and real time.

74. "These are the two features of the everyday use of medium that are suggestive for a discussion of video: the simultaneous reception and projection of an image, and the human psyche as a conduit." Rosalind Krauss, "Video: The Aesthetics of Narcissism," in *New Artists Video,* Gregory Battcock, ed. (New York: Dutton, 1978), 45.

75. The popularity among critics of real time and narcissistic video was due in part to the fact that such work overtly illustrated Lacan's "mirror stage"—a heuristic and psychoanalytic paradigm that became increasingly fashionable in intellectual circles during the decade. Yet, such work, legitimized only by prescriptive theory in the 1970s, ultimately had little impact on television production in general. Krauss, "Video: The Aesthetics of Narcissism," 55.

76. "Television viewers have come to expect a higher degree of *realism and authenticity* in every aspect of television, from news and documentaries to entertainment and sports programming. Shooting on location is one way to enhance a production" (italics mine). Alan Wurtzel, *Television Production* (New York: McGraw-Hill, 1979), 510.

77. "You should think of television performing *its most distinctive function, the live transmission of events.* . . . Contrary to film, the basic unit of television, the television frame, consists of an ever-changing picture mosaic. . . . Each television frame is in a continual state of becoming. . . . As such, the sequence of the actual event, cannot be reversed when shown on television. . . . *The now of the television event is equal to the now of the actual event* in terms of objective time, that is, the instantaneous perception by the observer of the actual event and by the television viewer"

(italics mine). Herbert Zettl, *Sight, Sound, Motion: Applied Media Aesthetics* (Belmont, Calif.: Wadsworth, 1973), 263.

78. "In terms of mode of address, I have argued that notions of 'liveness' lend a sense of flow which overcomes extreme fragmentation of space." Jane Feuer, "The Concept of Live Television: Ontology as Ideology," in *Regarding Television*, E. Ann Kaplan, ed. (Los Angeles: The American Film Institute, 1983), 19.

79. Feuer's explanation is so good because it ties the liveness ideology to one of the most influential concepts in television critical theory, the flow. Yet, assertions about the centrality of liveness made from the analysis of one talk show raise other problems. Williams, *Television*, 86–118.

80. "Television's self-referential discourse plays upon the connotative richness of the term 'live,' confounding its simple or technical denotation with a wealth of allusiveness. Even the simplest meaning of 'live'—that the time of the event corresponds to the transmission and viewing times—reverberates with suggestions of 'being there' . . . 'bringing it to you as it really is.' The contradictory television coinage 'live on tape' captures the slippage involved." Feuer, "The Concept of Live Television," 14. This view is important in correcting earlier glosses and essentialisms of liveness *theory*, but wrong, as I hope to show later, if it implies that liveness is a dominant myth in television *practice*. Other important myths are also at work; myths that suggest neither simultaneity, presentness, or "being there." With the emergence of pictorialism and the preoccupation with individuated program looks as common objectives in recent television, there is no reason to position liveness as *the* determining ideology. Rather liveness has become one stylistic item on the larger menu of visuality. This view, then, is an inversion of Feuer's. Whereas Feuer argues that stylistic codes produce realism and liveness, I am suggesting that liveness is a visual code and component of a broader stylistic operation. It is a look that can be marshaled at will, feigned and knowingly exchanged with ontologically aware viewers.

81. Robert Vianello critiques the conflation of the live and the real by showing that liveness is a complicated and political construct in "The Power Politics of 'Live' Television" (*Journal of Film and Video* 37, 3 [Summer 1985], 39), yet overvalues liveness by claiming that its promise "pervades every moment" of broadcast: "It is on these instantaneous and spontaneous transmissions that television truly establishes itself as a social institution of the real. . . . Television becomes the perpetual possibility of making contact with the real; it is this possibility which pervades every moment of broadcast."

82. Todd Gitlin, "Introduction: Looking Through The Screen," in Todd Gitlin, ed., *Watching Television* (New York: Pantheon, 1986), 6.

83. Gitlin, "Car Commercials and Miami Vice: 'We Build Excitement,' " in *Watching*, 136–161.

84. Marc, *Demographic Vistas*, 21.

85. Margaret Morse, "The Ontology of Everyday Distraction," in *Logics of Television: Essays in Cultural Criticism*, Patricia Mellencamp, ed. (Bloomington: Indiana University Press, 1990), 193–221.

86. "Successive, simultaneous time, measured by regular, on-the-half-hour programming . . . indefinitely multiplied by cable and satellite transmission, hypostasized by familiar formats and aging stars in reruns and remakes, trivialized by scandal and gossip, is disrupted by the discontinuity of catastrophe coverage. So-called heterogeneity or diversity ceases as do commercials and TV continuity time as we focus on a single event. . . . TV time of regularity and repetition, continuity and 'normalcy,' contains the potential of interruption, the thrill of live coverage of death

events." Patricia Mellencamp, "TV Time and Catastrophe: Or Beyond the Pleasure Principle of Television," *Logics*, 243–244. Mellencamp has reversed the logic of the liveness myth, while at the same time acknowledging and presuming its centrality. Unlike earlier liveness theorists, for her "simultaneity" does not stand for liveness but for a massively and artificiality constructed temporality. That is, television is no longer seen as simultaneous with *live events*, but as simultaneous with itself and with *other programs* that happen at the same time. In Mellencamp's reversal, "liveness" stands not for the the dominant norm in television, but as the potentially disruptive agent that can attack and expose conventional programming pleasures.

87. Ibid., 261–262.

88. This view of catastrophic temporality seems to devalue the fact that even catastrophes are immediately stylized and constrained as pictures and endless loops, with encrusted graphics, in a process of almost immediate representation that can make even the Kennedy assassination or fires caused by arson in Malibu in some sense pleasurable. Certainly stylized catastrophe loops are more pleasurable to most than coverage of the same events on the radio.

89. The full quote reads: "The more rapid internationalization of television via the *immediacy* of satellites on a *global* allocation of an electromagnetic spectrum never imagined as nationally determined, replicates the *emphasis on transmission*." Patricia Mellencamp, "Prologue," in *Logics of Television*, 3. (italics mine).

90. Probably the most forceful indication of the continuing centrality of liveness in contemporary media theory is Daniel Dayan and Elihu Katz's *Media Events* (Cambridge: Harvard University Press, 1992), published after this chapter was written. A very good critique of Dayan and Katz, and a reconsideration of ontological aspects of liveness, is James Friedman, "Live Television: Ceremony, (Re)presentation, Unstructured and Unscripted Events," presented at the Screen Studies Conference, Glasgow, Scotland, June 1993.

91. Sharon D. Moshavi, "Niche Cable Networks Attract Advertisers of Same Genre," *Broadcasting and Cable* (March 8, 1993). 47.

92. Louis Sahagun and Michael Kennedy, "FBI Puts Blame on Koresh for Cultists' Death," *Los Angeles Times*, April 21, 1993, A13.

Invisible Cities/
Visible Geographies
Toward a Cultural Geography
of Italian Television in the 1990s

JAMES HAY

There is in Italo Calvino's *Invisible Cities* at least one parable upon which I would like to reflect for just a moment as a way of shaping a discussion about the "cultural geography" of Italian TV in the 1990s and as a way of beginning to address some of the general issues involved in the study of nationhood and media borders. Calvino's text is constructed as a discourse between the late-Medieval Italian explorer and trader, Marco Polo, and the Mongolian emperor, Kublai Khan—two mythic figures who converse at the historic threshold of the European Renaissance and the emergence of global trade routes for Western commercial interests. Much of the text is given to Marco's accounts or narrative reconstructions of places—generally cities—through which he has passed before meeting the Great Khan. These accounts are, however, occassionally interrupted by a somewhat amused Khan who, having never visited these cities himself, wonders whether the cities in his empire described by Marco are really all that Marco says they are, or whether they are but exotic images produced by the vagabond eye of the Italian explorer.

The Khan is particularly confused about the relations among the places Marco recounts. The cities seem too randomly selected and conjoined through Marco's wandering narrative (and narrative wandering). From his position of privilege, where he has formed an image of a "model," quintessential city, the Khan presses Marco to explain their commonality, their connectedness, their "code"—something that would guarantee his power,

Reprinted with permission from the *Quarterly Review of Film and Video,* © Harwood Academic Publishers (Summer 1993).

as emperor, to decipher them, to gauge and predict, to rule. At one point, the Khan even convinces himself that Marco's cities resemble one another, "as if the passage from one to another involved not a journey but a change of elements." The relation among these places particularly becomes an issue in their conversation when Marco carefully assembles before the Khan an array of natural objects and artifacts, each collected from a different city on his journey. Between Marco and the Khan, the objects (neither only metaphoric or metonymic any longer) *become* the cities; but across the black and white tiles of the floor where they have been arranged, they also can be moved and rearranged, in a game not unlike chess:

> Arranging the objects in a certain order on the black and white tiles, and occasionally shifting them with studied moves, the ambassador [Marco] tried to depict for the monarch's eyes the vicissitudes of his travels, the conditions of the empire, the prerogatives of the distant provincial seats.
>
> Kublai was a keen chess player; following Marco's movements, he observed that certain pieces implied or excluded the vicinity of other pieces and were shifted along certain lines. Ignoring the objects' variety of form, he could grasp the system of arranging one with respect to the others on the majolica floor. He thought: "If each city is like a game of chess, the day when I have learned the rules, I shall finally possess my empire, even if I shall never succeed in knowing all the cities it contains."

The Khan is repeatedly troubled because he has no way of refuting Marco's accounts; Marco's cities and his seemingly random, incomplete *passages* that link them are enigmas that can only be deciphered through the Khan's own *maps* of his vast empire. Thus Calvino's text offers a way of thinking about the power and politics, the enabling and constraining qualities, of Marco's narrative of places along his journey. Before hearing Marco's tales, the Khan had understood his empire and his place at the center of that empire through his own atlas—an official and totalizing dictionary of maps, each offering its own image of his cities and, perhaps more importantly for a Khan, their differences and interconnectedness. Marco's accounts of cities along his path constitute a matrix of emblems (a "logograph," to use Calvino's expression) through which the Khan must now imagine and decipher his empire, that is, the empire as *his*.

Because *Invisible Cities* offers a narrative about the interfacing of two symbolic systems or narrative practices *and* of two positions (two ways of thinking about positions) in a power system, it underscores how discursive relations result from, generate, and gradually transform relations of power and status, how discursive relations become sites for struggles to claim territory for constructing identity. The Khan's sense of discursive and political order, for instance, is predicated upon the affective power of an *essentialized* city-image that models the vast distance and circumference of an empire he can only imagine. Marco, however, explains that, as an explorer-merchant, he relies upon his own conception of a model city—one that is constituted *entirely* of "exceptions, exclusions, incongruities, contradictions" and that in this way includes all of the places he is recounting.

The Khan continually asks Marco if his cities are real or the result of Marco's narration and his own reading of them. Marco, on the other hand, repeatedly asks the Khan if his map has room for new emblems. Because the Khan's perspective and system (reinforced by his current collection of maps) is totalizing, he reproaches Marco because his descriptions of cities lack a sense of connectedness. Marco responds that he recognizes only the cities, not what lies outside them. While Marco's cities are texts (spaces that take form through the temporality of narration), the Khan's empire is an atlas-dictionary (the necessary embodiment of his desire for stability and fixity). Yet through their dialogue, one can't help but recognize that the empire, as map, is comprised only of those places for which there are words or that are imaginable through a narrative. One also comes to recognize that both Marco's travel narrative and the Khan's sense of domain are constrained and tested by each other's way of imaging and imagining spatial relations. In this sense, *Invisible Cities* calls attention to the provisional and contingent nature of maps and coordinates, while affirming the indispensability of spatial references. And while Marco's narrative does not quite produce a "map," it does offer an inventory/itinerary of places that, through an accumulation of meaning, through their position in his narratives and their relation to Venice (his starting point or "home") and his encounter with Kubla Khan, produce a narrative space within which he, the Khan, and the reader are caught.

I find this parable useful in a discussion about the current formation and transformation of "*media* borders" not necessarily because the postmodern world is prone to reimagining (as Umberto Eco might suggest) a "new" Middle Ages, but precisely because of the issues it raises about the discursive or narrative production of territory/domain, about the narrative or cultural politics of mapping and geography, about historic transformations in territoriality brought about by convergences or collisions between conflicting narrative systems and positions, about the transformation of material "places" into narrative or imagined "spaces" and about the production of space in particular places.

Many of these points have been developed more fully by other theorists of space. The discourse between Kublai Khan and Marco Polo plays out the distinction that Gilles Deleuze and Felix Guattari draw between the "rhizomatic" production of space through maps and the mimetic, permanent, and totalizing vision of place offered by "tracings," through Deleuze and Guattari emphasize what this distinction has to do with *politics* of spatial production.[1] The point above about the relation between "space" and "place" is elaborated by Michel de Certeau, who suggests that discourses/stories may traverse and circulate amidst places but they also produce and, through their circulation, performance, and practice, constitute a discursive or narrative space by establishing implicit contracts between interlocutors.[2] De Certeau thus wants to acknowledge not only the transformative capabilities of narrative, that is, that stories organize places and how one navigates a place, but also that the production of space is tied to particular places or locations. The French social theorist Henri Lefebvre is concerned with somewhat the same issue when he discusses how social relations are predicated upon complexly *coherent* yet *changing* relations among "spatial practices," "representations of space," and "representational spaces" (or among, what he also terms, "perceived," "conceived," and "lived" space)[3] Both Lefebvre and de Certeau, furthermore, share Calvino's interest in how understandings of the past and future are bound up with understandings of space. Whereas de Certeau is concerned with the dynamic relation among memories, stories, and spaces, Lefebvre directs his attention to how spatial production historically enables and constrains future spaces, ideologies, and social relations. While none of these critical treatments or dramatizations of spatial production or perception overtly concern the current media environment or current media practices, they introduce an important set of issues into a discussion of nationhood, cultural identity, and media borders that I want to address briefly here.[4]

Over the 1980s, the emergence of various media practices have significantly reorganized perceptions of place and territory through their role in the formation of *narrative networks*. Here I am thinking of how the proliferation of cable and satellite broadcasting facilitated the practice of narrowcasting and how the increasingly common integration of television broadcasting and telecommunication processes through fiber optics or the rapid expansion of domestic computer use have made way for a variety of "interactive" systems and networkings (from "1–900" shopping/dating networks to "computer-net" systems such as Bitnet and Prodigy). And while I want to recognize what these formations or media networkings have to do with the emergence of new industries and a new regime of consumption that have most frequently been discussed by theorists of neo- or post-Fordism,[5] I'm equally interested in how they have become the point of the formation of culture, identity, allegiances, and alliances in the 1990s across and within previously existing geographic and media borders. In other words, I want to consider strategies for understanding (in part through a new "media geography") how cultural identity is currently formed through the production of social space in this current media environment and, particularly, how current media networkings have produced territoriality, alliances, and allegiances that aren't quite confined to cities, nations, or geographic regions but that must still be imaged or imagined through these places (and through these places as signs). And because the production of allegiances through these narrative networks occurs within and around *already* recognized geographies, it becomes just as necessary to recognize how these formations produce understandings about relations to the past (i.e., how, in many cases, their role in the formation of social identity occurs through discourses about rupture, the "new," tradition, and "competing" identities or formations).

Considering some of the recent transformations of television broadcasting in the United States for instance, one could consider not only how networks such as Black Entertainment Television and the Christian Broadcasting (a.k.a. the Family) Network have become the historic points for imaging and producing Black and Christian culture/identity through cable networking of narrative practices and styles, but also how WGN, TBS, or TNN have transformed their broadcasting bases (Chicago, Atlanta, Nashville) into symbolic centers for the formation of television audiences and into *coordinates* for a changing media geography of the nation. Atlanta and Chicago, in particular, are cities whose "renaissance" over the 1980s had as much to do with city replanning and the erection of tourist centers as with these networks' role in conventionalizing ways of reading ("accessing") these cities. A "superstation" such as WGN places "local Chicago news" into national circulation, organizes its programming and advertising through an iconography of Chicago (recoding, for example, the forever-syndicated *Andy Griffith Show* through the iconography of contemporary Chicago for a national audience) and, expanding the circuit of Cub baseball, sustains a network of "fans" whose bond is ritualistically acknowledged through Harry Carey's greeting of visiting fans from locations outside Chicago throughout the broadcast of each game (again, for a national audience).

Examples such as these, not to mention the circulation of metaphoric, narrativized, and endlessly translated cities such as *Dallas,* make it necessary that we begin to rethink issues such as nationhood and the formation of cultural identity with greater regard to the ways that the current media technologies or practices have significantly contributed to redefining the spatial features of our environment. Most recently, the Clinton-Gore administration has suggested the possibility of a federally subsidized "electronic superhighway"—a venture they have likened to the transformation of national life resulting from the federal highway systems since the New Deal programs of the 1930s.[6] Whether as policy, metaphor, or utopian vision, such a project holds significant implications both for the broadcasting, telecommunications, and computer industries and for the flow and reception of various traditional and emerging narrative forms. It also is a vivid example of how the immediate future of national cultural politics is being played out on and over a changing grid of spatial relations.

There may well be something of interest for media and cultural analysis in the body of studies described as "postmodern geography" (work by Edward Soja, David Harvey, and Manuel Castells is perhaps the most well known), particularly in their attempt to move issues about the social production/perception of space closer to issues tied to postmodernity and in their recognition that one needs new strategies for understanding the politics of mapping in the contemporary cultural environment.[7] But while their interventions into debates about the relation between postmodernism, Marxism, and geography rightly criticize media and cultural analysis for having ignored for too long the significance of media and culture as the site where social conceptions of space are produced, these same studies have seemed particularly ill-equipped to discuss the complexity of these media and cultural processes, preferring instead to work within the generalizations of postmodernist theory, as David Harvey does when, echoing familiar eulogizing by Jean Baudrillard, he sums up television by proposing that "the whole world's cuisine is now assembled in one place in almost exactly the same way that the world's geographical complexity is nightly reduced to a series of images on a static television screen."[8]

Where issues concerning postmodernism, media practices, and the reformulation of spatial relations have all been brought to bear more directly on the question of national identity, the analyses tend to over-emphasize the political economy of media and postmodernity—such that both are understood as broadly determined by the emergence of "late" (or in Lasch and Urry's terms, "disorganized") capitalism.[9] These studies rightly acknowledge the necessity of rethinking the formation of national identity and the concept of *community* within "postmodernism" (and, in so doing, considering postmodernism "as a question of geography" or spatial relations). Morley and Robins, in particular, have called attention to the role of new media technologies in producing a new kind of relationship between space and place: "through their capacity to transgress frontiers and subvert territories, they [new media technologies] are implicated in a complex interplay of deterritorialization and reterritorialization."[10] But while their attempt to understand nationhood through the formation of "electronic communities," which they discuss primarily within a global-local nexus, acknowledges the importance of discussing media as sites for the production of culture and identity, their wedding of postmodernism and post-Fordism explains spatial relations in only the broadest sense of culture and tends to ignore the discursive and textual features of spatial relations, culture, and identity.

Without refuting the general argument of these treatments of national identity "beyond Fordism" (and by returning to issues about the discursive production of space and place raised in *Invisible Cities*), I therefore want to reconsider the strategic implications of introducing this problematic of spatial production and perception into media and cultural studies of nationhood by outlining how some of the issues might be engaged in a discussion about the relation between spatial production and changing media practices in Italy. And I particularly want to consider how one might begin to see media practices as sites for the production of these relations. Let me restate the problematic. First, how have changing media practices, technologies, and networks produced a sense of territoriality and perceptions of space in everyday life? Second, how, on the one hand, has this process of territorialization involved the production and perception of space that may not be represented within an established or institutional geography of places? Third, how, on the other hand, does this process occur through particular places that can only be imaged or imagined through an existing lexicon, symbolic order, and narrative logic for coding space, even though this symbolic order may be reorganized (the traffic of symbols redirected) as a result of these new media practices? Fourth, how is this process of territorialization, reterritorialization, and deterritorialization a form of cultural politics in which media practices play a changing role?

In order to recognize these processes in Italy, one would have to consider the complex and changing role of film and television (as industrial, narrative, ideological, and cultural systems) in the formation of spatial perceptions, particularly with respect to historically competing, emerging, and residual ways of modeling—of imaging and imagining—spatial relations.

To begin, one might consider how the emergence of film in Italy occurred within Italian Futurism's discourses on the "modern" or modernistic nature of twentieth century Italian environment and life. Over the first four decades of the twentieth century, Italian Futurists attempted increasingly to articulate their "project" through a discourse on the relation between art and the Nation (and, by the 1920s, Fascism), while their verse, prose, theatrical set design and performance, public spectacle in the form of street parades, choreography, graphic art, sculpture, architectural visions, interior designs, photography, and even films, all aggressively reformulated the neoclassical and Enlightenment perceptions of space that still dominated "institutional" Italian culture. They frequently described all of these forms as informed by and producing a new "geometric splendor"—an expression referring as much to their recasting or erasure of spatial relations through art as to their repositioning art in relation to traditional culture and contemporary Italy.

Their prolific production of manifestoes did as much to elaborate the historic significance of their artistic practice as to establish a circuit of recognition about Futurist sensibility in modern Italian life. Their celebration of Speed attempted to deflate the notion that time and space were static points and to concentrate on trajectories; they celebrated a "new" relation between linguistic and spatial simultaneity, in which elements move without relation to material geography and environmental conditions. These issues and concepts converge for Italian Futurists in their metaphor of the "Futurist city" and in neologisms such as *velo-citta'* (a play upon the Italian words for "velocity" and "city"); both were hyper-technological tropes for conceptualizing Futurist production of art as image-spaces in a Modern and Urban Italy (Enrico Prampolini's "Space Rhythms" or Giacomo Balla's Speedseries), for imagining a new urban architecture through Futurist design (Mario Chiatone, Antonio Sant'Elia, and Virgilio Marchi's City-series), for highlighting and celebrating the "modern" spatial relations and perspectives of Italian cities (Carlo Carra's treatment of the Galleria in Milan), and for producing new ways of perceiving temporal and spatial relations in Italian cities whose architectonics and organization were still bound to spatial modeling in the Renaissance, Middle Ages, and even Classical period (Giacomo Balla's early paintings that refigured Rome, the Ancient City, through Futurist "abstract dynamism").

During the 1920s and 1930s, the emergence of a film industry, policy, and culture in Italy (i.e., the emergence of film as a national-popular cultural form) became the point of a crisis over signifying the relation between the City and the Country, between established and emerging myths of a rural and urban Italy.[11] The myth of the Nation, and of the nation as a Popular Domain, was contingent upon cinema's increasing role in mediating these conflicting ways of imaging and imagining spatial relations. This mediation occurred as much through the production of film *narratives* as through the inauguration of traveling cinema caravans, which brought movies to rural Italy, and through the construction of Cinecitta' (Cinema City), which not only attempted to remap the territoriality of Hollywood—of Hollywood films in Italy—but which became the most public emblem of a city built upon the realization of a national-popular culture and the symbolic center of a "new order" and a new Empire. Clearly all of this contributed in those years to the meaning of public and everyday discourses about the *domain* of Fascism.

More than cinema, however, radio broadcasting during the 1920s and 1930s transformed Italy into a national "network" where the Futurist vision of spatial simultaneity became wedded, in part through Fascism, to the notion that the Nation was a unified place, or rather, a space without separate places. The differences among cities, between cities and towns, between the north and the south, between public and domestic life (between listening to a broadcast in a piazza versus receiving it in the home) could be imagined by listeners as having disappeared, as each place became a point of simultaneous reception.

If post-war film production rejected its pre-war legacy, it was perhaps most evident in its reimaging and imagining of the nation as cinematic space, particularly through the practice of location filming which not only "reinserted" localities onto the cinematic map of the Nation which had been produced over the 1920s and 1930s. Here I am thinking about films ranging from Rosselini's *Paisa'*, which literally remaps an Italy emerging from Allied occupation, to DeSica's narratives set in the "backstreets" of Rome and Milan, to films set in specific localities outside these famous, cinematically mythologized cities, to a "woman's film" such as *Girls of the Spanish Steps* in the mid-1950s that constructs a mythic *path* of everyday life in postwar Rome for a group of for working women.

It is also significant that Italian television emerges within, though quickly reorganizes, "neo-realist" film practices that were conventionalizing ways of perceiving the nation as a matrix of spatial relations. While the emergence of RAI television broadcasting (the first channel in the early 1950s and the second channel in 1961) may have initially operated within the practices and national networking of a national radio system, the number of Italians who owned television sets grew so slowly that the circuit of reception was much different than radio. The small number of television sets in Italy also encouraged group and public viewings, the spirit of which can be most vividly recognized in the popular late 1950s and early 1960s television gameshow, *Campanile sera*. Visually and narratively, this series articulated images of regional identity with national identity, weekly staging nationally-televised competition between two teams from different regions and crosscutting between studio participants and on-location scenes of the competing towns' inhabitants gathered in the town piazza. In a sense, these new television broadcasting practices enabled the kind of image of national cohesion that filmmaking, and particularly neo-realist styles, had avoided.

Over the 1960s and 1970s, the increasing convergence, competition, and conflict in Italy between film and television, as cultural forms of spatial modeling, contributed to several significant reformulations of urban space and of the relation of regional culture to national identity. Some of the more acclaimed Italian films from the late 1950s and early 1960s, such as Antonioni's *La notte* (1961) and *L'eclisse* (1962) or Fellini's *La dolce vita* (1959), through narratives that chart the convolution, absurdity, and repetition of characters' paths in Rome and Milan, begin to work against the notion that urban space is organized around a center (or around a town piazza, as in *Campanile sera*). And in the wake of films such as Passolini's *Accatone* (1961) and *Mama Roma* (1962), and through later films such as *Brutti, sporchi, cattivi* (1976), the city becomes an invisible force in narratives set entirely in an urban periphery.

These trends, particularly this latter one, are historically significant in that they offer a cultural framework for the emergence of the third RAI channel during the 1970s—a channel that was virtually established by and identified with the Italian Communist Party in an effort to promote regional broadcasting and culture that had become marginalized by the traditional two RAI networks. While the older RAI channels' penchant for on-location productions (e.g., *Sabato sera*—weekend variety shows broadcast live from different locations; *Linea verde*—weekend live features about local rituals in agricultural areas; soccer broadcasting) had transformed various Italian localities into stages for public spectacle, they had always maintained their linkage with *national* broadcasting based in Rome and, through RAI personalities, performers, and commentators, reproduced "national" myths about the culture of that region. Thus by the 1970s, RAI television's *nationalization* or *centralization* of regional culture and its implementation of the PAL standard (as a kind of television border that prevented the reception of "foreign" broadcasting) became the bases for "national culture," even though the RAI's role/image as arbiter of national culture precipitated a series of spatial relations between Rome and other localities and between Italy and other national cultures that came to be increasingly challenged through RAI 3 and the emerging "private" stations and networks.

Local broadcasting, which became more common by the mid-1970s after the legalization of private cable broadcasting and as a result of initiatives by the Italian Left to "decentralize" broadcasting and encourage local political reform, undercut somewhat the RAI's historic effort to construct and claim (through production values and programming) the political and cultural "center" of Italian life. While the concept of "local" broadcasting suggested regional, "non-national" discursive formations and audiences, it also became the form of broadcasting for discourses and audiences (neo-Fascists, the ultra-Left, youth, feminists, homosexuals) constructed as *marginal* under the traditional RAI practices. In a sense, the ambiguity surrounding the meaning of "local" programming (and the great variety of local programming practices) made it incongruous with a broadcasting formation such as the RAI's, modeled in terms of a center-periphery nexus. And it is no coincidence that the reformulation of the "local"–"national" distinction during the late 1970s made way for the formation of multiple national cable networks, which were not necessarily given to narrowcasting practices but were certainly prone to constructing themselves as the mediators of the taste cultures of geographically and demographically defined audiences and consumers.

In the late 1970s, the emerging private networks, formed through the proliferating number of "local" networks, did not resist their image as regional programmers in order to avoid being perceived as at odds with the RAI's image as mediator of a national culture. But by the 1980s, with the enormous success of the *Dallas*-ethos in Italy, Berlusconi's private networks resituated national television and reimaged a national audience within a television practice that was at once regional and cosmopolitan. The private networks' initial flooding of Italian television with foreign television productions and films so redirected the traffic of symbols and texts for a national audience and contributed to the image of the private networks as cosmopolitan that in 1986 the RAI (in an affair whose financial ramifications resulted in both parlimentary and court battles) spent a reported $20 million to finance a two-week long series of live, evening broadcasts from New York featuring a cast of American celebrities famous in Italy.

The U.S.-Italian axis becomes particularly significant for Italian television broadcasting between 1982 and 1987, not only because U.S. films and telefilms account for an average of 80 percent of programming on the fledgling private networks but also because narrativized cities such as *Dallas* (on the private networks) or Miami (i.e., -*Vice* on the RAI) became coordinates for a new media and cultural geography—the mythoi that structured America in Italian popular culture, but also televisual cities whose "stories" were organized around *invisible* (and quasi-legitimate) international markets. (A timely metaphor in Italy for the story and status of television itself in the age of cable and privatization!) Particularly interesting in this regard were the press releases and newspaper reviews of the premiere episode of *Miami Vice* in 1986, which directed much attention to the impact of Italian design and fashion styles (e.g., the series' use of designs by Ferrari, Versaci, and Memphis) and to the issue of reading "Italian" style (and the meaning of "made in Italy") through a popular American television series. As TV text in Italy, Miami became a complex of narrative spaces or scenes linked largely through the power of style; but in this case, style had as much to do with the sense of an affective alliance among a group of consumers (as was more the case in the United States) as with the cultural identity of a nation in the age of cable broadcasting.

The Madonna concert in Torino, sponsored by Coke and RAI 1 and broadcast by RAI 1 to a number of other European countries in 1987, is one of the most provocative examples of TV's role in resituating the nation within a new cultural geography. It is not simply another example of the RAI's traditional role as broadcaster of such national-popular spectacles as the annual San Remo music festival, but more an effort to refashion its image by making it at once both cosmopolitan (particularly as that image is signified here by tapping into the construction of youth in Italian television culture through music video and its stars) *and* Italian. Particularly significant in this latter respect were the attempts just preceding Madonna's performance to underscore Madonna's "Italian-ness"—that is, Madonna's roots in Italy, the legacy of Italy in Madonna, and the RAI's mediation of both— by visiting her relatives' town in the Abruzzi (relatives, I might add, whom she had never met before) and then staging a reunion between Madonna and these relatives.

The distinction, common throughout the 1980s, between public and private television (and between Rome and Milan as television *centers*) has already become more complex. By 1991 there were six kinds of television networks in Italy: the three RAI networks, the national private networks that transmit from inside Italy, national private networks that broadcast expressly into Italy from other countries (e.g., Capo d'Istria, a Berlusconi sports network originating in Yugoslavia), quasi-national networks of loosely connected regional stations (e.g., Odeon), strictly regional stations, and a pay-TV network received by roughly 80 percent of Italy (Tele piu' uno, which broadcasts movies without commercial interruption).[12] Each of these systems is oriented around particular programming practices and genre preferences and each attempts to maintain its own "circuit of reception" that becomes an important context for understanding the cultural geography of Italy in the 1990s.

In the age of satellite broadcasting and amidst the economic, political, and cultural transformations that have produced and will be produced by the EEC, networking and circuits of reception increasingly occur across the borders of the Italian state. In Italy, television customers can purchase satellite dishes to receive broadcasts from throughout Europe. In several regions, cultural alliances are produced and maintained across state borders through TV broadcasting: Lombardy receives Swiss programming, while Piedmont and Liguria receive French Programming. Since the late 1980s, Berlusconi has begun broadcasting ventures in France, Spain, and Germany and is a co-financier of a broadcasting company in Belgium; he has also attempted to co-produce, with other European producers, a mini-series set in Italy and other European countries that could be broadcast in different European countries. His Canale 5 has recently broadcast a quiz show, *Bellezza al bagno,* which, in the tradition of pan-European quiz shows such as *Europa Europa* and *Jeux sans fronte'res,* stages competition among contestants from different nations (though, significantly, all are nations/stations from his TV empire). Berlusconi has long sought to gain access to a satellite which would not only enable him to enter the trans-national traffic of sports culture in Europe but to link his stations across Europe into the first pan-European private network. And recently the RAI has instituted its own "RAI-Sat," a state-satellite network (there is some debate as to whether it constitutes a fourth state channel) that programs material from other European state-broadcasting while it broadcasts Italian productions, often in different languages and with subtitles, to other European countries.

There is a significant difference between the Nation realized simultaneously in various places (as was the case before the 1970s) and the Nation produced through multiple networks and amidst more localized and transnational programming and narrowcasting, each attempting to define culture and everyday life. Certainly it is tempting to claim, as Eco does, that "neo-television" in Italy operates through a discursivity that is more postmodernist than modernist. But frequently such theorizing has more to say about how these television practices all produce a kind of grand cultural logic rather than how they become the terrain for a cultural politics—for the resistances and competition—through which identities, alliances, and allegiances are produced. Likewise, the problem with many current attempts to theorize media's role in the production of cultural identity "beyond Fordism" and in the age of a "global economy" is that they end up equivocating postmodernism (as a cultural logic) with post-Fordism (as the logic of late capitalism). Indeed it is very important to recognize that identities are formed through media and cultural practices that are now as much local as they are global. But this local-global model does not get at the complexity and transitoriness of media formations and networks or the cultural geographies produced through them; the examples in Italy that I cite above are not unequivocally local or trans-national. Theories of post-Fordist media and culture fail, furthermore, to acknowledge how the very concepts of "local" and "global" are always *constructed* through media and other cultural discourses and through emerging and residual ways of imagining spatial relations. And above all, attempts to theorize postmodernism and post-Fordism as the cultural and economic terrain for the formation of identities frequently closes off the issue of nationhood by over-emphasizing merely the formation of culture across borders and capitalism's formation of new global markets. While the broader transformations explained by theories of post-modernism and post-Fordism may have a great deal to do with understanding the media's role in the formation of cultural identity and geography, the issue of national identity and the struggle over marking or defining national borders are more crucial than ever. (In this regard, the Italian examples seem just as pertinent as the Clinton-Gore proposal mentioned above.) What seems necessary for current media and cultural studies, in this regard, is a critical geography that is just as much concerned with the highly localized and global production and perception of spatial relations as it is with how particular nations can be understood as political states, as economic and cultural spaces for multiple media formations, as signs that circulate along competing networks and through specific narrative practices, and as audiences whose perceptions of the nation, their locality, and the world are bound up with their implication in changing media practices. And this critical geography needs to come to terms with the media's role in mapping the distinctions and interconnectedness of places as much as it needs to develop strategies for recognizing its "invisible cities"—for recognizing, in short, that because media studies involves geography, it has a stake in remapping and reimagining alliances.

As the Calvino text reminds us, empires may be conceived through spatial models, but models are themselves assemblages of interchangeable coordinates. The activity of charting media and cultural formations, therefore, not only involves recognizing how and where model-building occurs but how this charting itself produces "logogriphs" for future empire-building, future cartography and future explores of new passages:

> Kublai asked Marco: "You, who go about exploring and who see signs, can tell me toward which of these futures the favoring winds are driving us."
>
> [Marco responds:] "For these ports I could not draw a route on the map or set a date for the landing. At times all I need is a brief glimpse, an opening in the midst of an incongruous landscape, a glint of lights in the fog, the dialogue of two passersby meeting in the crowd, and I think that, setting out from there, I will put together, piece by piece, the perfect city, made of fragments mixed with the rest, of instants separated by intervals, of signals one sends out, not knowing who receives them. If I tell you that the city toward which my journey tends is discontinuous in space and time, now scattered, now more condensed, you must not believe the search for it can stop. Perhaps while we speak, it is rising, scattered, within the confines of your empire; you can hunt for it, *but only in the way I have said*" [italics mine].

Calvino never overtly elaborates the consequences of this historical convergence of two discursive positions and systems, though the next may be read as an outline for a cartography of "new times." And certainly the relation between Kublai Khan and Marco Polo has nothing and everything to do with the production of spatial relations in modern and postmodern Italian culture. Therefore, just as *Invisible Cities* offers a way of thinking about the cultural geography of Italian television, this outline of the changing relation of nationhood and culture in Italy may offer a way of thinking about the consequences of the convergence that Calvino narrates.

Notes

I want to express my appreciation to Franco Minganti and Waddick Doyle for their assistance in my research of Italian television.

1. See Gilles Deleuze and Felix Guattari, *On the Line*, trans. John Johnston (New York: Semiotext(e), 1983).

2. See Michel de Certeau, "Spatial Practices," *The Practice of Everyday Life*, trans. Steven Rendall (Los Angeles: University of California Press, 1984).

3. See Henri Lefebvre, *The Production of Space*, trans. Donald Nicholson-Smith (Oxford, Cambridge, Mass.: Blackwell, 1990). One could also consider Pierre Bourdieu's conceptualization of "social space" as a "habitus"—a structured and struc-

turing system for representing "place" or position. See particularly Bourdieu, "The Economy of Practices," *Distinction: A Social Critique of the Judgement of Taste,* trans. Richard Nice (Cambridge, Mass.: Harvard University Press, 1984).

4. In the original version of this essay, I elaborate reasons why recent geopolitical and geo-economic transformations, coupled with changing global, national, and local media practices that have resituated the place of film and television in everyday life, all have made it increasingly difficult to understand the complexity of spatial production surrounding media formations either through traditional Marxist and structuralist theories of film and television or through traditional political economies of mass media. I am nonetheless indebted to the recent work of two individuals: Eric Michaels's treatment of "aboriginality," Australia, and the production of culture through contemporary media and Meaghan Morris's provocative examples of how issues of spatial production can be brought into a discussion of nationhood, media, and postmodern culture. See, for instance, Eric Michaels's *For a Cultural Future* (Melbourne: Artspace, 1987) and Meaghan Morris's "At Henry Parkes Motel," *Cultural Studies* 2:1 (January 1988), pp. 1–47; "Tooth and Claw: Tales of Survival, and *Crocodile Dundee,*" *The Pirate's Fiancee: Feminism, Reading, and Postmodernism* (London, New York: Verso, 1988); "*Panorama:* The Live, the Dead and the Living," *Island in the Stream,* ed. Paul Foss (Leichhardt, New South Wales: Pluto Press, 1988).

5. Stuart Hall and Martin Jacques, eds., *New Times: The Changing Face of Politics in the 1990s* (London and New York: Verso, 1989).

6. See John Markoff, "Building the Electronic Superhighway," *New York Times,* January 24, 1993.

7. See Edward Soja, *Postmodern Geographies: The Reassertion of Space in Critical Social Theory* (London, New York: Verso, 1989); David Harvey, *The Condition of Postmodernity* (Oxford, Cambridge, Mass.: Basil Blackwell, 1989); Manuel Castells, *The Informational City* (Oxford, Cambridge, Mass.: Basil Blackwell, 1989).

8. Harvey, *Postmodernity,* p. 300. After devoting most of his book to Renaissance, Enlightenment, and Modernist conceptions of space and geography, Harvey's discussion of spatiality and postmodernism, in one of his last short chapters, is unfortunately only one more reading of *Blade Runner*—a reading that focuses largely on the film's recombinant features, has relatively little to do with spatial relations, adds little to the numerous references to this film as a quintessential example of a postmodernist aesthetic, and generally smoothes out the film's ironies and contradictions.

9. Kevin Robins, "Reimagined Communities? European Image Spaces, Beyond Fordism," *Cultural Studies* 3 (May 1989), pp. 145–61; Kevin Robins and David Morley, "Spaces of Identity: Communications Technologies and the Reconfiguration of Europe," *Screen* 30 (Autumn 1989), pp. 10–34.

10. Robins and Morley, "Reimagined Communities?" p. 22.

11. See James Hay, *Popular Film Culture in Fascist Italy: The Passing of the Rex* (Bloomington: Indiana University Press, 1987).

12. There are currently plans for two additional pay-channels, Tele piu' 2 and 3—one entirely for sports programming and the other for "educational" programming.

For a Cultural Future

ERIC MICHAELS

On 1 April 1985, daily television transmissions began from the studios of the Warlpiri Media Association at the Yuendumu community on the edge of Central Australia's Tanami desert. Television signals, when broadcast as radio waves, assure a kind of mute immortality: they radiate endlessly beyond their site of creation, so this first program might be playing right now to the rings of Saturn. But it no longer exists at its point of origin in Australia. The message, the events behind it, their circumstances and meanings have mostly been ignored, and are likely to be forgotten. This is why I recall such events here: to reassert their significance and to establish in print their remarkable history.

All content the Warlpiri Media Association transmits is locally produced. Almost all of it is in the Warlpiri Aboriginal language. Some is live: schoolchildren reading their assignments, community announcements, old men telling stories, young blokes acting cheeky. The station also draws on a videotape library of several hundred hours of material that had been produced in the community since 1982 (a description of this material and the conditions of its production is one of the main purposes of this essay). Yuendumu's four-hour schedule was, by percentage, and perhaps absolute hours, in excess of the Australian content of any other Australian television station. The transmissions were unauthorized, unfunded, uncommercial, and illegal.

From *For a Cultural Future: Francis Jupurrla Makes TV at Yuendumu* by Eric Michaels, Melbourne: Artspace, 1987 (Art and Criticism Monograph Series, Vol. 3). Reprinted by permission of Empress Publishing Ltd., PO Box 134, Rose Bay, NSW 2029, Australia.

There were no provisions within the Australian Broadcasting Laws for this kind of service.

Yuendumu television was probably Australia's first public television service, although it might be misleading to make too much of this. Open Channel sponsored experimental community access TV transmissions in Melbourne for a few days during 1982. The Ernabella Aboriginal community had been experimenting along similar lines since 1984, and began their own daily service days after Yuendumu started theirs. Even before, throughout remote Australia, small transmitters had been pirated so that mining camps and cattle stations could watch Kung Fu and Action Adventure videos instead of the approved and licensed Australian Broadcasting Corporation (ABC) "high culture" satellite feed, which became available to outback communities in 1984–85. Issues of community access and local transmission had been on the agenda certainly since the Whitlam government, but they had lain dormant in Fraser's and then Hawke's official broadcasting agendas. In the 1980s, inexpensive home video systems proved subversive of the bureaucracy's tedious intents, while satellite penetration and sustained interest in production by independents had all kept issues of public television very much alive in the public arena.

Yuendumu's accomplishment must be seen in the context of these developments. Yuendumu's need and motivation to broadcast should also be considered in evaluating any claim to the accolade of pioneer. There was, in the early 1980s, a considerable creative interest among Aborigines in the new entertainment technology becoming available to remote communities. There was equally a motivated, articulate, and general concern about the possible unwanted consequences of television, especially among senior Aborigines and local indigenous educators. In particular, the absence of local Aboriginal languages from any proposed service was a major issue. Without traditional language, how could any media service be anything but culturally subversive? Native speakers of indigenous languages understood (a good deal better than anyone else) that this was something only they could correct.

There are more than twenty-two Aboriginal languages currently spoken in the Central Australian satellite footprint. The simple logistics of providing for all these languages on a single service indicate clearly a fundamental mismatch. The bias of mass broadcasting is concentration and unification; the bias of Aboriginal culture is diversity and autonomy. Electronic media are everywhere; Aboriginal culture is local and land-based. Only local communities can express and maintain linguistic autonomy. No one elsewhere can do this for the local community—not in Canberra, Sydney, or even Alice Springs. Indeed, Warlpiri speakers at Yuendumu make much of the distinctions between their dialect and the one spoken by the Lajamanu Warlpiri, 600 kilometers away on the other side of the Tanami desert. These differences are proper, for they articulate a characteristic cultural diversity. The problem of language signals a more general problem of social diversity that introduced media pose for indigenous peoples everywhere: how to respond to the insistent pressure towards standardization, the homogenizing tendencies of contemporary world culture?

Postmodernist critique provides very little guidance here. Indeed, the temptation to promote Warlpiri media by demonstrating a privileged authenticity—the appeal to traditionalism—which legitimates these forms, would be firmly resisted. How can we even employ such terms? "Authentic" and "inauthentic" are now merely labels assigned and reassigned as manipulable moves in a recombinatory game. Postmodernism may promote an appetite for primitive provenances, but it has proven to be an ultra-consumerist appetite, using up the object to the point of exhaustion, of "sophistication," so as to risk making it disappear entirely. It would be better to shift ontologies, by problematizing the very term "originality" and denying that any appeals to this category can be legitimated. Then, we refuse degrees of difference or value that might distinguish between the expressive acts (or even the persons) of Warlpiri videomakers, urban Koorie artists in Fitzroy, Aboriginal arts bureaucrats in Canberra, a Black commercial media industry in Alice Springs—none of these could be called more truly "Aboriginal" than any other. This redirects the mode of analysis to a different if somewhat more fashionable inquiry: who asks such a question, under what circumstances, and so forth? An analysis of the history of the official constitution of Aboriginality, as well as its *mise en discourse,* its rhetorical and institutional deployment, might explain, for instance, current moves towards pana-boriginalism. At least, it can provide a much needed caveat to the banal and profoundly racist war that is being waged in this country.

Despite the importance of subjecting Aboriginal expression to these critical debates, there is a danger that they lead away from the specific pleasures to be found in an encounter with the Warlpiri and their video. And it is these pleasures I want to describe, indeed promote as something more than the product of my own research interests—even if this risks reasserting authenticity, with an almost naive empiricist's faith, and employing a positivist's notebook to amass the particulars necessary to bring these "alien" texts into focus. What I am seeking is also a way to test critical theory's application to ethnographic subjects. It is possible that such an investigation will supersede the dilemma that tradition, ethnicity, and value have variously posed for empiricism.

Of course, to understand what happened with media at Yuendumu—and what didn't—one needs to describe more than just local circumstances. It will be necessary to reference the State and its interventions again and again. Warlpiri media, no less than its history, is the product of a struggle between official and unofficial discourses that seem always stacked in the State's favor. This might suggest a discouraging future for Yuendumu Television. Given the government's present policy of promoting media centralization and homogenization, we would expect that Yuendumu will soon be overwhelmed by national media services, including "approved" regional Aboriginal broadcasters who serve the State's objectives of ethnicization, standardization, even aboriginalization, at the expense of local language, representation, autonomy. If this scenario is realized, then Yuendumu's community station seems likely to join the detritus of other development projects which litter the contemporary Aboriginal landscape, and shocked Euro-

peans will take this as one more example of Aboriginal intractability and failure of effort—if not genes. We won't know that the experience of television for remote Aborigines could have been any different: for example, a
networked cooperative of autonomous community stations resisting hegemony and homogenization. Instead, we expect Warlpiri television to disappear as no more than a footnote to Australian media history, leaving unre-
marked its singular contribution to a public media, and its capacity to
articulate alternative—unofficial—aboriginalities.

But something in Warlpiri reckoning confounds their institutionalisa-
tion and the grim prophecy this conveys. A similar logic predicted the disappearance of their people and culture generations ago, but proved false. A
miraculous autonomy, almost fierce stubbornness, delivers the Warlpiri from
these overwhelming odds and assures their survival, if not eventual victory.

How Warlpiri People Make Television

Videomaker Francis Kelly does not like to be called by name. He prefers I
call him Jupurrurla. This is a "skin" or subsection term which identifies him
as a member of one of eight divisions of the Warlpiri people, sometimes
called totemic groups by anthropologists. Better yet, I should call him *panji*,
a Kriol word for brother-in-law. The term is a relative one, in both senses.
It does not merely classify our identities, but describes our relatedness. It is
through such identities and relationships that cultural expression arises for
Warlpiri people, and the description of these must precede any discussion
of Aboriginal creativity.

Warlpiri people are born to their skins, a matter determined by parent-
age, a result of marriage and birth. But I became a Japanangka—brother-
in-law to Jupurrurla—by assignment of the Yuendumu Community Council. One result of my classification is that it enables Francis and me to use
this term to position our relationship in respect to the broader Warlpiri community. It establishes that we are not merely two independent individuals,
free to recreate ourselves and our obligations at each social occasion. Rather,
we are persons whose individuality is created and defined by a preexisting
order. In this case, being brothers-in-law means that we should maintain an
amiable, cooperative reciprocity. We can joke, but only in certain ways and
not others. We should give things to each other. My "sister" will become
wives for Jupurrurla; I might take his "sisters" for wives in return.

These distinctions refer to a symbolic divisioning of the community into
"two sides" engaged in reciprocal obligations. But it implies also a division
of expressive (e.g., ceremonial) labor, and particular relations of ritual production reaching into all Warlpiri social life and action. For certain ceremonies this division is articulated as roles the Warlpiri name *Kirda* and *Kurdungurlu*, two classes which share responsibility for ritual display: one to
perform, the other to stage-manage and witness. The roles are situational
and invertable, so identification as Kirda "Boss" and Kurdungurlu "Helper"
may alter from event to event. As "brothers-in-law," Jupurrula and I will
always find ourselves on different sides of this opposition, although the roles

WARLPIRI SUBSECTIONS

Understanding how Warlpiri people articulate their relationships, through marriage and descent is critical to explaining videomaking as a mode of cultural inscription and reproduction. A basic diagram of Warlpiri "skin names" is required to follow the argument.[1] In a simplistic (patrilineal) sense, the eight terms represent divisions of four father/son groups:

ONE SIDE	OTHER SIDE
Japangardi	*Jupurrurla*
Japanangka	*Jangala*
Japaljarri	*Jampijimpa*
Jungarrayi	*Jakamarra*

(In the case of women, "N" is substituted for "J" in the initial position)

As these names designate marriage choices and imply descent lines, one can treat this diagram as a abstracted matrix from which an entire universe of social relations can be extrapolated. Both Aborigines and anthropologists do this, but the connection between these ideological models and social practice has been questioned in recent literature. The present treatment intends to remain mostly in the domain of social practice, and so avoids any explicit position on these more scholastic questions.

themselves may reverse from setting to setting. This see-saw balancing act that shifts roles back and forth over time affected all our collaborations.

Warlpiri brothers-in-law can also trace their relationships and their obligations more circuitously through mothers and grandparents. This describes a quite complex round of kin, which eventually encompasses the entire Warlpiri "nation" of over 5,000 people. It can even go beyond this, identifying marriages and ceremonial ties which relate to corresponding skin groups among Pitjanjatjara people to the south, Pintubi to the west, and Arrente, Anmatjarra, Kaitij, Warrumungu, and others to the north and east. Thus, a potentially vast social matrix is interpolated with every greeting.

I introduce the reader to Jupurrurla to promote a consideration of his art: videotaped works of Warlpiri life transmitted at the Yuendumu television station in this desert community 300 kilometres north-west of Alice Springs. But it is not quite correct to identify Jupurrurla as the author of these tapes, to assign him personal responsibility for beginning video production at Yuendumu, or for founding the Warlpiri Media Association, although these are the functions he symbolizes for us here.

In fact, the first videomaker at the Yuendumu community was Jupurrurla's actual brother-in-law, a Japanangka. It was Japanangka who was already videotaping local sporting events when I first came to Central Australia early in 1983. It was Japanangka who responded to the prospect of satellite television by saying "We can fight fire with fire . . . ", making a reference to the traditional Warlpiri ritual, the Fire Ceremony or *Warlukurlangu*, and assigning this name to their artist's association. But Japanangka, for all his talent and rage, found the mantle of "boss" for the video too onerous—for to be a boss is to be obligated. During 1983–84, a sensitive series of negotiations transferred the authority for Yuendumu video to Jupurrurla. Part of Jupurrurla's success in this role resulted from his cleverness in distributing the resources associated with the video project. He trained and then shared the work with a Japaljarri, another Japanangka, a Japangardi, and a Jangala. Eventually, all the male subsections had video access through at least one of their members.

Obviously, the identification of an individual artist as the subject for critical attention is problematized where personhood is reckoned in this fashion. Rather than gloss over this issue, or treat it romantically within a fantasy of primitive collectivity, I want to assert more precisely its centrality for any discussion of Warlpiri expression. And I want to use this example to signal other differences between Aboriginal and European creative practices, differences which need to be admitted and understood if the distinctiveness and contribution of Warlpiri creativity is to be evaluated critically in a contemporary climate—the goal of this essay. These differences include what may be unfamiliar to readers:

- ideological sources and access to inspiration;
- cultural constraints on invention and imagination;
- epistemological bases for representation and actuality;
- indistinctiveness of boundaries between authorship and oeuvre;
- restrictions on who makes or views expressive acts.

By describing these, I hope to avert some likely consequences of European enthusiasm for Aboriginal media which results in the appropriation of such forms to construct a generic "primitive" only to illustrate modern (and, more recently, postmodern) fantasies of evolutionary sequences. In a practical sense, I also want to subvert the bureaucratization of these forms, such as may be expressed in the training programs, funding guidelines, or development projects which claim to advance Aborigines, but always impose standards alien to the art (because these will be alien to the culture producing it). Wherever Australian officialdom appropriates a population, as it has attempted to do with the Aborigines, it quickly bureaucratizes such relationships in the name of social welfare. This assuredly defeats the emergence of these sovereign forms of expression, as it would defeat Jupurrurla's own avowed objective to create *Yapa*—that is, truly Warlpiri—media.

Those European Art practices since the Renaissance and Industrial Revolution which constitute the artist as an independent inventor/producer of original products for the consumption/use of public audiences, do not apply to the Aboriginal tradition. This has been said before, in more or less accurate ways, and led to some questions (misplaced, I think) about the "authenticity" of "traditional" Aboriginal designs, such as those painted in acrylics and now made available to the international art maker.² In the case of Jupurrurla's art, the implicit question of authenticity becomes explicit: Jupurrurla, in Bob Marley T-shirt and Adidas runners, armed with his video portapak, resists identification as a savage updating some archaic technology to produce curiosities of primitive tradition for the jaded modern gaze. Jupurrurla is indisputably a sophisticated cultural broker who employs videotape and electronic technology to express and resolve political, theological, and aesthetic contradictions that arise in uniquely contemporary circumstances. This will be demonstrated in the case of two videotapes which the Warlpiri Media Association has produced: *Coniston Story* and *Warlukurlangu (Fire Ceremony)*.

The choice of these two out of a corpus of hundreds of hours of tape was a difficult one. Not even included is Jupurrurla's most cherished production, *Trip to Lapi-Lapi*, the record of a long trip into the Western Desert to re-open country people had not seen for decades, a tape that often causes its audiences to weep openly. Neither are the politically explicit tapes, those documenting confrontations with government officials which became important elements in Warlpiri negotiating strategies: these tapes cause people to shout, to address the screen, and then each other, sometimes provoking direct action. But my purpose in this monograph is not to survey the whole of the work, the various emergent genres, or the remarkable bush networks which arose to carry these tapes when official channels such as the new satellite were closed.³ My choice of tapes was made because they illustrate best some things about the Warlpiri mode of video production: how Jupurrurla and others discovered ways to fit the new technology to their particular information-based culture. The only way of beginning such an analysis is by locating the sources of Warlpiri expression in an oral tradition.

[At this point in his more extended essay Michaels offers brief discussions of "The Law" and "Restricted Expressions." For the Walpiri people of Yuendumu video had to be inserted into these traditional categories, understood as part of them. The definitions of these categories and their application are, I believe, clear from the contexts of Michaels's analysis of the Fire Ceremony.

He also preceeds his analysis of the Fire Ceremony events with a discussion of another complex tape and screening under the subheading "*Coniston Story:* Warlpiri Modes of Video Production." Inclusion of the full essay was impossible for this volume, but the reader is urged to examine the full text of Michaels's work.]

The Fire Ceremony: For a Cultural Future

In 1972, anthropologist Nicolas Peterson and filmmaker Roger Sandall arranged with the old men to film a ritual of signal importance for the Warlpiri: Warlukurlangu, the Fire Ceremony. In a subsequent journal article,⁴ Peterson described these ceremonies in terms of the functions of Aboriginal social organization. He identified such Warlpiri ceremonies as a means of resolving conflict, or of negotiating disputes, a kind of pressure valve for the community as a whole. One pair of patrilines (or "side") of the community acts as Kurdungurlu, and arranges a spectacular dancing ground, delineated by great columns of brush and featuring highly decorated poles. The Kirda side paints up, and dances. Following several days and nights of dancing, they don elaborate costumes festooned with dry brush. At night they dance towards the fire, and are then beaten about with burning torches by the Kurdungurlu. Finally, the huge towers of brush are themselves ignited and the entire dance ground seems engulfed in flame. Following some period (it may be months or even years) the ceremony is repeated, but the personnel reverse their roles. The Kurdungurlu become Kirda, and receive their punishment in turn.

Visually and thematically, this ceremony satisfies the most extreme European appetite for savage theatre, a morality play of the sort Artaud describes for Balinese ritual dance—what could be more literally signaling through the flames than this? Yet I do not think the Peterson/Sandall film does this, partly due to the technical limitations of lighting for their black-and-white film stock, and partly because of the observational distance maintained throughout the filming. The effect is less dramatic, more properly "ethnographic" (and, perhaps wisely, politically less confrontative). It was approved by the community at the time it was edited in 1972 by Kim McKenzie, and joined other such films in the somewhat obscure archives of the Australian Institute of Aboriginal Studies, used mostly for research and occasional classroom illustration.

Remarkably, the ceremony lapsed shortly after this film was made. When I arrived at Yuendumu in 1983, the Fire Ceremony seemed little more than a memory. Various reasons were offered:

- one of the owners had died, and a prohibition applied to its performance;
- it had been traded with another community;
- the church had suppressed its performance.

These are not competing explanations, but may have in combination discouraged Warlukurlangu. The interdiction by the church (and the state, in some versions) was difficult to substantiate, though it was widely believed. Some of the more dramatic forms of punishment employed in the ceremony contradict Western manners, if not morals. There seemed to be some recognition among the Warlpiri that the Fire Ceremony was essentially incompatible with the expectations of settlement life, and the impotent fantasies of dependency and development they were required to promote. The Fire Ceremony was an explicit expression of Warlpiri autonomy, and for nearly a generation it was obscured. The question arises, as it does also in accounting for the ceremony's recent revival: what role did introduced media play in this history?

Yet Warlukurlangu persisted in certain covert ways. The very first video-tape which the community itself directed in 1983 recorded an apparently casual afternoon of traditional dancing held at the women's museum. Such spontaneous public dance events are comparatively rare at Yuendumu. Dances occur in formal ceremonies, or during visits, in modern competitions and recitals, or in rehearsal for any of these. Yet this event appeared to meet none of these criteria. Equally curious was the insistence on the presence of the video camera. These were early days—Jupurrurla had not yet taken up the camera, and Japanangka and myself were having trouble arranging the shoot. A delegation of old men showed up at each of our camps and announced that we must hurry; the dancing wouldn't start till the video got there. What was taped was not only some quite spectacular dancing, but an emotional experience involving the whole community. When I afterwards asked some of the younger men the reason for all the weeping, they explained that people were so happy to see this dance again. I later discovered I had seen excerpts of the dances associated with the Fire Ceremony.

Some months later, I was invited to a meeting of the old men in the video studio. They had written to Peterson, asking for a copy of the film, and now were there to review it. I set up a camera and we videotaped this session. As it was clear that many of the on-film participants would now be dead, how the community negotiated this fact in terms of their review was very important. The question of the film's possible circulation was raised. Following a spirited discussion, the old men (as mentioned above) came to the decision that all the people who died were "in the background": the film could be shown in the camps. Outside, a group of women elders had assembled, and were occasionally peeking through the window. Some were crying. They did not agree that the deceased were sufficiently backgrounded, and it made them "too sorry to look." These women did not watch the film, but didn't dispute the right of the men to view or show it.

It became clear that the community was gearing up to perform the Fire Ceremony again for the first time in this generation. As preparations proceeded, video influenced the ritual in many ways. For example, the senior men announced that the Peterson film was "number one Law," and recommended that we shoot the videotape of exactly the same scenes in precisely the same order. (When this did not happen, no one in fact remarked on the difference.) Andrew Japaljarri Spencer, who acted as first cameraman, stood in Kurdungurlu relationship to the ceremony. This meant that he produced an intimate record of the ceremony from his "on the side" perspective.

We are at close-up range for some of the most dramatic moments, alongside the men actually administering the fiery punishments. Jupurrurla absented himself from this production. Although he was willing to do certain preproduction work, and subsequent editing and technical services, he would not act as cameraman because he would be a Kirda for this event. Quite sensibly, he pointed out that if Kirda were cameramen, the camera might catch on fire. Jupurrurla was not unaware, like many of the younger men, that he too might catch on fire, so at the climax of the ceremony they were nowhere to be found.

The tape of this major ceremony was copied the very next day and presented to a delegation from the nearby Willowra community, who were in fact in the midst of learning and acquiring the ceremony for performances themselves. This is a traditional aspect of certain classes of ceremonies. In oral societies where information is more valued than material resources, ceremonies can be commodities in which ritual information is a medium of exchange. This exchange may take years, and repeated performances, to accomplish. For instance, there was a dramatic (if not unexpected) moment when a more careful review of the tape revealed that one of the painted ceremonial poles had been rather too slowly panned, rendering its sacred design too explicit. This design had not yet been exchanged, and so the Willowra people might learn it—and reproduce it—from the tape. Runners went out to intercept the Willowra mob, and to replace their copy with one that had the offending section blanked out.

These new tapes of the Fire Ceremony circulated around the Yuendumu community, and in their raw state were highly popular. In fact, it became difficult to keep track of the copies. This was one of the motivations to proceed with broadcasting—more to assure the security of the video originals and provide adequate local circulation of tapes than to achieve any explicitly political intent. But perhaps there was a broader public statement to be made with the record of these events. I recommended, and was authorized to propose to the Australian Institute of Aboriginal Studies, that we edit together the tapes to produce an account which would describe both the ceremony and its reproductions. We had the Peterson film, the community dance, the review of the film, and the extraordinary footage of the 1984 performance. This seemed to me an excellent and visually striking way to articulate the ceremony in terms of some of the more fundamental questions concerning the place of such media in Warlpiri life. The Intitute did not support the idea, and when one of the central performers died shortly thereafter, the community dropped the matter. The tapes took their place on a shelf in the archive that Jupurrurla labeled "not to look." Later, however, the Institute did transfer the Sandall/Peterson film to videotape, and put it into general distribution without, to my knowledge, informing the community that this was being done.

There is no point in isolating any one instance of this failure to address or resolve the problems that the appropriation of Warlpiri images poses. The situation is so general that it proves how fundamental the misunderstandings must be. Alien producers do not know what they take away from the Aborigines whose images, designs, dances, songs, and stories they record. Aborigines are learning to be more careful in these matters. But the conventions of copyright are profoundly different from one context to the other. Perhaps these urgent questions will never be solved: "Who owns that dance now on film?," "Who has the authority to prevent broadcast of that picture of my father who just died?," "How can we make sure women will not see these places we showed to the male film crew?," "Will we see any of the money these people made with our pictures?" . . . Whenever "appropriate" Australian authorities are confronted with such questions, they go straight to the too-hard basket, not only because they are truly difficult questions, but also because they refer to equivocal political positions.

Underlying the problem is not only a failure to specify the processes of reproduction and their place in oral traditions; there is also a contradiction of values regarding the possibilities for Aboriginal futures, and the preferred paths towards these. Many Aborigines do wish to be identified, recognized, and acknowledged in modern media, as well as to become practitioners of their own. They recognize the prestige, the political value, the economic bargaining position that a well-placed story in the national press can provide. They attempt to evaluate the advantages—and what they are told is the necessity—of compromising certain cultural forms to achieve this. But the elements of this exchange, the discrimination between what is fundamental and what is negotiable, resists schematization. On neither side is there a clear sense of what can be given up and what must be kept if Aborigines are to avoid being reprocessed in the great sausage machine of modern mass media. For them, it is the *practices* of cultural reproduction that are essential. If by the next generation the means of representing and reproducing cultural forms are appropriated and lost, then all is destroyed. What remains will just be a few children's stories, place names for use by tourist or housing developments, some boomerangs that don't come back, a Hollywood-manufactured myth of exotica. These will only serve to mask the economic and social oppression of a people who then come into existence primarily in relation to that oppression.

The criteria for Aboriginal media must concern these consequences of recording for cultural reproduction in traditional oral societies. Warlpiri people put it more simply: "Can video make our culture strong? Or will it make us lose our Law?"

The problem about answering this sort of question as straightforwardly as it deserves, is that it usually is asked in deceptive cause/effect terms: What will TV do to Aborigines? The Warlpiri experience resists this formulation. Jupurrurla demonstrates that such questions cannot be answered outside the specific kin-based experiences of their local communities. His productions further demonstrate that television and video are not any one, self-evident thing, a singular cause which can then predict effects. Indeed, Yuendumu's videomakers demonstrate that their television is something wholly unanticipated, and unexplained, by dominant and familiar industrial forms.

Here I want to emphasise *the continuity of modes of cultural production across media,* something that might be too easily over-looked by an ethnocentric focus on content. My researches identify how Jupurrurla and other Warlpiri videomakers have learned ways of using the medium which conform to the basic premises of their tradition in its essential oral form. They demonstrate that this is possible, but also that their efforts are yet vulnerable, easily jeopardized by the invasion of alien and professional media producers.

My work has been subject to criticism for this attention to traditional forms and for encouraging their persistence into modern life. The argument is not meant to be romantic: my intent has been to specify the place of the Law in any struggle by indigenous people for cultural and political autonomy. In the case of Warlpiri television, the mechanisms for achieving this were discovered to lie wholly in the domain of cultural reproduction, in the culture's ability to construct itself, to image itself, through its own eyes as well as the world's.

In the confrontation between Dreamtime and Ourtime, what future is possible? The very terms of such an inquiry have histories that tend to delimit any assured, autonomous future. For example, if it were true that my analysis of Warlpiri TV provided no more than a protectionist agenda, then the charge of romantic indulgence in an idealized past might be justified. I would have failed to escape a "time" that anthropologists call the "ethnographic present"—a fabricated, synchronic moment that, like the Dreamtime, exists in ideological space, not material history. It is implicated in nearly all anthropology, as well as most ethnographic discourse. Certainly, the questions of time that seem essential here cannot be elucidated by constructs of timelessness.

It seems likely that grounding Aborigines in such false, atemporal histories results in projecting them instead into a particular named future whose characteristics are implied by that remarkable word, "Lifestyle." This term now substitutes everywhere for the term culture to indicate the latter's demise in a period of ultra-merchandise. Culture—a learned, inherited tradition—is superseded by a borrowed, or gratuitous model; what your parents and grandparents taught you didn't offer much choice about membership. Lifestyles are, by contrast, assemblages of commodified symbols, operating in concert as packages which can be bought, sold, traded, or lost. The word proves unnervingly durable, serving to describe housing, automobiles, restaurants, clothes, things you wear, things that wear you—most strikingly, both "lifestyle condoms" for men and, for women, sanitary napkins that "fit your lifestyle." Warlpiri people, when projected into this Lifestyle Future; cease to be Warlpiri; they are subsumed as "Aborigines," in an effort to invent them as a sort of special ethnic group able to be inserted into the fragile fantasies of contemporary Australian multiculturalism. Is there no other future for the Warlpiri than as merely another collectivity who have bartered away their history for a "lifestyle?"

I propose an alternative here, and name it the Cultural Future. By this I mean an agenda for cultural maintenance which not only assumes some privileged authority for traditional modes of cultural production, but argues also that the political survival of indigenous people is dependent upon their capacity to continue reproducing these forms.

What I read as the lesson of the Dreaming is that it has always privileged these processes of reproduction over their products, and that this has been the secret of the persistence of Aboriginal cultural identities as well as the basis for their claims to continuity. This analysis confirms Jupurrurla's and Japanangka's claims that TV is a two-edged sword, both a blessing and a curse, a "fire" that has to be fought with fire. The same medium can prove to be the instrument of salvation or destruction. This is why a simple prediction of the medium's effects is so difficult to make. Video and television intrude in the processes of social and cultural reproduction in ways that literate (missionary, bureaucratic, educational) interventions never managed to accomplish. Its potential force is greater than guns, or grog, or even the insidious paternalisms which seek to claim it.

But in a cultural future, *Coniston Story* operates over time to privilege the Japangardi/Japanangka version of that history, to insert it bit by bit into the Dreaming tracks around Crown Creek until the tape itself crumbles and its memory is distributed selectively alongs the paths of local kinship. In this future, when the mourning period for that old Japangardi is passed, his relations will take the Fire Ceremony tape from the "not to look" shelf and review it again, in regard to the presence or absence of recent performances of the ceremony. Audiences at Yuendumu will reinterpret what is on the tape, bring some fellows into the foreground and disattend to others. They might declare this "a proper law tape," and then go on to perform the ceremony exactly the same, but different. I expect, in the highly active interpretative sessions that these attendances have become, there will be much negotiation necessary to resolve apparent contradictions evoked by the recorded history. I expect that a cultural future allows the space and autonomy for this to happen.

In a lifestyle (ethnic, anti-cultural) future, it's not so certain that anyone will be there at Yuendumu to worry about all this. Why should they? After all, the place has only cultural value, lacking any commercial rationale for the lifestyle economy. But if people are to be situated in this future, we can assume that they will be faced with a very different kind of, and participation in, media. Their relation to the forces and modes of cultural reproduction will be quite passive: they will be constituted as an audience, rendered consumers, even though there's not much money to buy anything (the local store is reduced to selling tinned stew and Kung Fu video tapes). But it would be mistaken to claim that the ethnic cultural policy has ignored Aborigines. In fact, they play a major part in the construction of the national, multicultural image; in this scenario, they become niggers. Then they will be regularly on the airways, appearing as well-adjusted families in situation comedies, as models in cosmetic ads, as people who didn't get a "fair go" on *60 Minutes*. Nationally prominent, academically certified Aborigines will discuss Aboriginality on the ABC and commercial stations, filling in the legislated requirements for Australian content. In the lifestyle future, Aborigines can be big media business.

The people at Yuendumu will watch all this on their government-provided, receive-only satellite earth stations; but we can only speculate about what identifications and evaluations they will make. Perhaps the matter will not be inconsequential. Imported programs supplant, but may not so directly intrude on, cultural reproduction. Rather, it is when some archivist wandering through the ABC film library chances on an old undocumented copy of the Peterson Fire Ceremony film, one of the competing versions of the Coniston massacre, or even some old and valuable Baldwin Spencer footage, circa 1929, of Central Australian native dances, that something truly momentous happens. In pursuit of a moment of "primitivism," the tapes go to air, via satellite, to thousands of communities at once, including those of its subjects, their descendants, their relations, their partners in ritual exchange, their children, their women (or men). One more repository guarded by oral secrecy is breached, one more ceremony is rendered worthless, one more possible claim to authenticity is consumed by the voracious appetite of the simulacra for the appearance of reality. At Yuendumu, this already causes fights, verbal and physical, even threatened payback murders, in the hopeless attempt to ascribe blame in the matter, to find within the kin network the one responsible, so that by punishing him or her the tear in the fabric of social reproduction can be repaired. However, the kin links to descendants of Rupert Murdoch or David Hill or Bob Hawke may prove more difficult to trace, and the mechanisms for adjudication impossible to uncover.

A cultural future can only result from political resistance. It will not be founded on any appeal to nostalgia: not nostalgia for a past whose existence will always be obscure and unknown, nor a nostalgia we project into a future conceived only in terms of the convoluted temporalities of our own present. The tenses are difficult to follow here—but in a sense, that is precisely the critical responsibility now before us. Francis Jupurrurla Kelly makes, is making, television at Yuendumu. He intends to continue, and so assure a cultural future for Warlpiri people. His tapes and broadcasts reach forward and backwards through various temporal orders, and attempt somehow to bridge the Dreaming and the historical. This, too, is a struggle which generates Jupurrurla's art.

The only basis for non-Warlpiri interest in their video must recognize these explicitly contemporary contradictions. Channel Four at Yuendumu resists nostalgic sentiment and troubles our desire for a privileged glimpse of otherness. It is we who are rendered other, not its subject. Ultimately, it must be from this compromising position that such work is viewed.

Notes

The people at Yuendumu were not entirely happy with this text when I brought it for them to review prior to publication. We took out the few offending pictorial images—this wasn't the problem. It was said by some that the pessimism I expressed seemed unwarranted. Certainly, the evidence of continuing motivation and activity at the TV studio was startling. This was late August 1987, and my visit coincided with the installation of a satellite earthstation receiver which introduced the live ABC program schedule to Yuendumu after so many years of waiting, worrying, and preparing.

There still was no license to legitimize the service that Jupurrurla began that week, mixing local programming with the incoming signal (Warlpiri News and documentaries at 6:30 P.M.). Nor had the equipment repaired itself magically since the last visit: signal strength remained unpredictable, and edits were completely unstable. But the community was still passionately involved in making and watching Warlpiri television. This became clear when a battle ensued with the very first day's transmission. Warlpiri News replaced the *EastEnders,* and at least one European resident was incensed. Jupurrurla decided (somewhat unilaterally, it seemed to me) that the service would shut off at 10:30 P.M., so that kids could go to bed and be sure of getting off to school in the morning. No *Rock Arena.* No late movies. It seemed likely there would be a lot of hot negotiating in the coming months.

1. See J. Meggitt, *The Desert People,* Angus & Robertson, 1962, for the classic description of Warlpiri kinship and social organization.

2. P. Loveday and P. Cook, *Aboriginal Arts and Crafts and the Market,* Darwin, Australian National University North Australia Research Unit Monograph, 1983.

3. These cases are explored in detail in E. Michaels, *The Aboriginal Invention of Television, Central Australia, 1982–86,* Canberra, Australian Institute of Aboriginal Studies, 1986.

4. N. Peterson, "Bulawandi: A Central Australian Ceremony for the Resolution of Conflict", in *Australian Aboriginal Anthropology,* ed. R. M. Berndt, Perth, University of Western Australia Press for the Australian Institute of Aboriginal Studies, 1970, pp. 200–215.

About the Authors

MARK ALVEY is administrative associate at the Field Museum of Natural History in Chicago. He is the author of articles on television history with particular focus on American television in the 1960s.

CHRISTOPHER ANDERSON teaches in the Communication and Culture Department at Indiana University and has been a Fulbright fellow at Aarhus University, Denmark. He is the author of numerous articles on film and television and of *Hollywood TV: The Studio System in the Fifties*.

DAVID BARKER has taught at Texas Christian University, the University of Missouri, and Concordia University in Austin, Texas. He is currently studying at the Austin Presbyterian Theological Seminary.

IB BONDEBJERG is a research professor in film and media studies at the University of Copenhagen. He is author of numerous works on film and television and coeditor of *Television in Scandinavia*.

CHARLOTTE BRUNSDON is a lecturer in film and television studies at the University of Warwick, England. She is the author of numerous articles on film and television and of *Screen Tastes: Soap Opera to Satellite Dishes* and coeditor of *Feminist Television Criticism*.

MILLY BUONANNO teaches media studies at the University of Florence, Italy. She is the author of numerous books and articles on Italian television and popular culture and director of the EuroFiction Project.

JACKIE BYARS teaches film and television studies at Wayne State University. She is the author of articles on television and the book *All That Hollywood Allows: Re-reading Gender in 1950s Melodrama*.

JOHN THORNTON CALDWELL teaches television studies in the Department of Film and Television at the University of California, Los Angeles. He is the author of *Televisuality: Style, Crisis, and Authority in American Television*, as well as articles on television and film. His productions have been broadcast in the United States and Australia.

JOHN CORNER is a professor of politics and communication studies at the University of Liverpool in England. He is the author of numerous books and articles on film and television, most recently *Studying Media: Problems of Theory and Method*. He is an editor of the journal *Media, Culture, and Society*.

JULIE D'ACCI teaches in the Communication Arts department at the University of Wisconsin-Madison. She is the author of *Defining Women: Television and the Case of Cagney and Lacey* and coeditor of *Feminist Television Criticism*.

DANIEL DAYAN is a fellow of the Centre National de la Research Scientifique in Paris and external professor of Communication at the University of Oslo, Norway. He has also taught at the Annenberg School for Communication at the University of Southern California. He is coeditor of the French Communication Studies journal *Hermes*.

TODD GITLIN teaches sociology, communication, and journalism at New York University. He is the author of *Inside Prime Time, The Twilight of Common Dreams: Why America Is Wracked by the Culture Wars*, and the novels *The Murder of Albert Einstein* and *Sacrifice*.

HERMAN GRAY teaches sociology and media studies at the University of California at Santa Cruz. He is the author of *Watching Race: Television and the Struggle for Blackness* and numerous articles on mass media and the African-American experience.

JOSTEIN GRIPSRUD teaches in the Communications Department at the University of Bergen, Norway. He is the author of *The Dynasty Years: Hollywood Television and Critical Media Studies* and the editor of *Television and Common Knowledge*.

JAMES HAY teaches in the Speech Communication Department at the University of Illinois at Urbana-Champaign. He is the author of *Popular Film Culture in Fascist Italy: The Passing of the Rex* and articles on television and cultural spaces and on Italian media.

HAL HIMMELSTEIN is chair of the Department of Radio and Television at Brooklyn College of the City University of New York. He is the author of *Television Myth and the American Mind* and has worked extensively on media issues in Finland and Russia.

PAUL M. HIRSCH teaches in the Kellogg School of Management at Northwestern University. He is the author of many articles on management practices and on mass media organizations.

HENRY JENKINS III teaches at the Massachusetts Institute of Technology. He is the author of numerous books and articles on film, television and popular culture, most recently *From Barbie to Mortal Kombat: Gender and Computer Games,* and coauthor, with John Tulloch, of *Science Fiction Audiences: Watching Dr. Who and Star Trek.*

SUT JHALLY teaches in the Communications Department at the University of Massachusetts at Amherst. He is the author of *Dreamworlds: Desire Sex/Power in Rock Video,* coauthor of *Enlightened Racism: The Cosby Show, Audiences, and the Myth of the American Dream.* He is also a founder of the Media Education Foundation and producer of numerous videotapes on media and culture.

ELIHU KATZ teaches sociology and communications at Hebrew University in Jerusalem, where he is past scientific director of the Guttman Institute for Applied Social Research. He is also the Regents Professor of Communications at the Annenberg School of Communication at the University of Pennsylvania. He is the author of numerous books and articles dealing with mass communication.

DOUGLAS KELLNER is a professor of philosophy at the University of Texas at Austin. He is the author of numerous articles and books on American film, television, and popular culture, including *Media Culture: Cultural Studies, Identity and Politics Between the Modern and Postmodern,* and *Articulating the Global and the Local: Globalization and Cultural Studies.*

PAT KIRKHAM is a professor of design history at the Bard Graduate Center for Studies in the Decorative Arts in New York. She writes on film, television, and gender and is coeditor of *You Tarzan and Me Jane.*

JUSTIN LEWIS teaches in the Communications Department at the University of Massachusetts at Amherst. He is the author of *The Ideological Octopus: An Exploration of Television and its Audiences; Viewing, Reading, Listening: Audiences and Cultural Reception,* and coauthor of *Enlightened Racism: The Cosby Show, Audiences, and the Myth of the American Dream.*

DAVID MARC teaches in the Communications Department at Syracuse University. He is the author of several books on television, including *Bonfire of the Humanities: Television, Subliteracy, and Long-Term Memory Loss*, and coauthor of *Prime Time, Prime Movers: From I Love Lucy To L.A. Law—America's Greatest TV Shows and the People Who Created Them*.

ANNA McCARTHY teaches in the Cinema Studies Program of the Tisch School of the Arts, New York University. She is the author of numerous articles on film and television.

CHARLES McGRATH is the editor of the *New York Times Book Review*. He is coeditor of *Books of the Century: A Hundred Years of Authors, Ideas, and Literature: From the New York Times*.

ADRIENNE L. McLEAN teaches film and television studies in the School of Fine Arts and Humanities at the University of Texas at Dallas.

EILEEN R. MEEHAN teaches in the Media Arts Department at the University of Arizona. She has written widely on the political economy of popular entertainment.

JOSHUA MEYROWITZ teaches in the Communications Program at the University of New Hampshire. He is the author of *No Sense of Place: The Impact of Electronic Media on Social Behavior* and numerous articles on television, society, and culture.

ERIC MICHAELS was formerly a research associate of the Australian Institute for Aboriginal Studies and taught at Griffith University. He is the author of *For a Cultural Future* and of numerous articles on aboriginal culture and art as well as on mass media.

HORACE NEWCOMB teaches in the Radio-Television-Film Department at the University of Texas at Austin. He writes about television and cultural theory.

AMÉRICA RODRIGUEZ teaches in the Radio-Television-Film Department at the University of Texas at Austin. She has published numerous articles on Latino media industries and audiences. She is the author of *Making Latino News: Race, Language, Class*.

ELLEN SEITER teaches in the Communications Department at the University of California at San Diego. She is author of books and numerous articles on television, most recently *Television and New Media Audiences*.

BEVERLEY SKEGGS is codirector of the Institute for Women's Studies at Lancaster University. She has published *Formations of Class and Gender: Becoming Respectable* and *Feminist Cultural Theory: Production and Process*.

MICHAEL SKOVMAND is associate professor of English literature, University of Aarhus, Denmark. He is editor of and contributor to *The Angry Young Men, George Orwell and 1984* and *Media Fictions*. His recent work on mass media has focused on questions of taste and the popular.

LYNN SPIGEL teaches in the School of Cinema and Television Studies at the University of Southern California. She is the author of *Make Room for TV* and coeditor of *Private Screenings: Television and the Female Consumer; The Revolution Wasn't Televised: Sixties Television and Social Conflict;* and *Feminist Television Criticism*.

DAVID THORBURN teaches humanities and is director of the Program in Cultural Studies at the Massachusetts Institute of Technology. He writes about television and the popular arts.

BERNARD TIMBERG teaches in the Communication Department at Johnson C. Smith University. He is the author of numerous articles about television and of the forthcoming *Titans of Talk*.

PHIL WILLIAMS was a student in the American Studies program at Purdue University. He writes about American television and popular culture.